Nissan Juke

Owners Workshop Manual

John S. Mead

Models covered *(6380 - 352)*

Hatchback/SUV
Petrol: 1.2 litre (1197cc) & 1.6 litre (1598cc non-turbo)
Turbo-diesel: 1.5 litre (1461cc)

Does NOT cover models with 1.6 litre turbo petrol engine, 'Nismo' high performance versions, 'Xtronic' CVT transmission or 4WD models

ABCDE
FGHIJ
KLMNO
PQR

A book in the **Haynes Owners Workshop Manual Series**

ISBN **978 1 78521 380 9**

British Library Cataloguing in Publication Data
A catalogue record for this book is available from the British Library.

Printed in India

Haynes Group Limited
Sparkford, Yeovil, Somerset BA22 7JJ, England

Haynes North America, Inc
2801 Townsgate Road, Suite 340, Thousand Oaks, CA 91361

Disclaimer

There are risks associated with automotive repairs. The ability to make repairs depends on the individual's skill, experience and proper tools. Individuals should act with due care and acknowledge and assume the risk of performing automotive repairs.

The purpose of this manual is to provide comprehensive, useful and accessible automotive repair information, to help you get the best value from your vehicle. However, this manual is not a substitute for a professional certified technician or mechanic.

This repair manual is produced by a third party and is not associated with an individual vehicle manufacturer. If there is any doubt or discrepancy between this manual and the owner's manual or the factory service manual, please refer to the factory service manual or seek assistance from a professional certified technician or mechanic.

Even though we have prepared this manual with extreme care and every attempt is made to ensure that the information in this manual is correct, neither the publisher nor the author can accept responsibility for loss, damage or injury caused by any errors in, or omissions from, the information given.

Contents

Contents

The Nissan Juke 5-door hatchback, sports utility vehicle was introduced in the UK in September 2010. During the course of production, various trim levels were introduced and in 2014 the range was updated. This involved some small changes to the external and internal appearance of the vehicle and the addition of a 1.2 litre turbocharged petrol engine.

The Juke range is available with three sizes of petrol engines and one diesel engine. Covered in this manual are the 1.2 litre (1197 cc) and 1.6 litre (1598 cc) petrol engines, both being of double overhead camshaft (DOHC) 16-valve design. Both engines feature multi-point fuel injection and are equipped with an extensive range of emissions control systems. A 1.6 litre (1618 cc) turbocharged petrol engine is also available but is not covered in this manual. The diesel engine is a 1.5 litre unit, being of single overhead camshaft (SOHC) 8-valve design. This is a Renault diesel engine, which is a well-proven design and has been used previously in numerous Renault and Nissan vehicles.

All models covered in this manual have front-wheel drive with fully independent front suspension, and semi-independent rear suspension with a torsion beam and trailing arms.

A five or six-speed manual transmission is fitted as standard across the range, with a constantly variable automatic transmission (not covered in this manual) optionally available on certain models.

A wide range of standard and optional equipment is available within the Juke range including air conditioning, central locking, electric windows, an electric sunroof, an anti-lock braking system, electronic stability program and supplementary restraint system.

For the home mechanic, the Juke is a straightforward vehicle to maintain, and most of the items requiring frequent attention are easily accessible.

Your Nissan Juke Manual

The aim of this manual is to help you get the best value from your vehicle. It can do so in several ways. It can help you decide what work must be done (even should you choose to get it done by a garage), provide information on routine maintenance and servicing, and give a logical course of action and diagnosis when random faults occur. However, it is hoped that you will use the manual by tackling the work yourself. On simpler jobs, it may even be quicker than booking the car into a garage and going there twice, to leave and collect it. Perhaps most important, a lot of money can be saved by avoiding the costs a garage must charge to cover its labour and overheads.

The manual has drawings and descriptions to show the function of the various components, so that their layout can be understood. Then the tasks are described and photographed in a clear step-by-step sequence.

References to the 'left' or 'right' are in the sense of a person in the driver's seat, facing forward.

Acknowledgements

Thanks are due to Draper Tools Limited, who provided some of the workshop tools, and to all those people at Sparkford who helped in the production of this Manual.

We take great pride in the accuracy of information given in this manual, but vehicle manufacturers make alterations and design changes during the production run of a particular vehicle of which they do not inform us. No liability can be accepted by the authors or publishers for loss, damage or injury caused by any errors in, or omissions from, the information given.

Working on your car can be dangerous. This page shows just some of the potential risks and hazards, with the aim of creating a safety-conscious attitude.

General hazards

Scalding

- Don't remove the radiator or expansion tank cap while the engine is hot.
- Engine oil, transmission fluid or power steering fluid may also be dangerously hot if the engine has recently been running.

Burning

- Beware of burns from the exhaust system and from any part of the engine. Brake discs and drums can also be extremely hot immediately after use.

Crushing

- When working under or near a raised vehicle, always supplement the jack with axle stands, or use drive-on ramps. ***Never venture under a car which is only supported by a jack.***

- Take care if loosening or tightening high-torque nuts when the vehicle is on stands. Initial loosening and final tightening should be done with the wheels on the ground.

Fire

- Fuel is highly flammable; fuel vapour is explosive.
- Don't let fuel spill onto a hot engine.
- Do not smoke or allow naked lights (including pilot lights) anywhere near a vehicle being worked on. Also beware of creating sparks (electrically or by use of tools).
- Fuel vapour is heavier than air, so don't work on the fuel system with the vehicle over an inspection pit.
- Another cause of fire is an electrical overload or short-circuit. Take care when repairing or modifying the vehicle wiring.
- Keep a fire extinguisher handy, of a type suitable for use on fuel and electrical fires.

Electric shock

- Ignition HT and Xenon headlight voltages can be dangerous, especially to people with heart problems or a pacemaker. Don't work on or near these systems with the engine running or the ignition switched on.

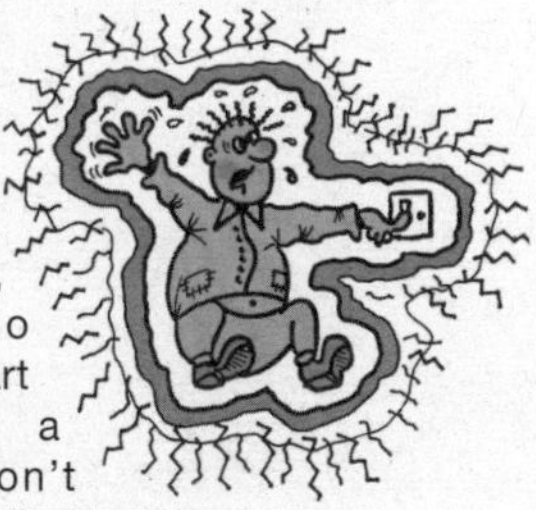

- Mains voltage is also dangerous. Make sure that any mains-operated equipment is correctly earthed. Mains power points should be protected by a residual current device (RCD) circuit breaker.

Fume or gas intoxication

- Exhaust fumes are poisonous; they can contain carbon monoxide, which is rapidly fatal if inhaled. Never run the engine in a confined space such as a garage with the doors shut.
- Fuel vapour is also poisonous, as are the vapours from some cleaning solvents and paint thinners.

Poisonous or irritant substances

- Avoid skin contact with battery acid and with any fuel, fluid or lubricant, especially antifreeze, brake hydraulic fluid and Diesel fuel. Don't syphon them by mouth. If such a substance is swallowed or gets into the eyes, seek medical advice.
- Prolonged contact with used engine oil can cause skin cancer. Wear gloves or use a barrier cream if necessary. Change out of oil-soaked clothes and do not keep oily rags in your pocket.
- Air conditioning refrigerant forms a poisonous gas if exposed to a naked flame (including a cigarette). It can also cause skin burns on contact.

Asbestos

- Asbestos dust can cause cancer if inhaled or swallowed. Asbestos may be found in gaskets and in brake and clutch linings. When dealing with such components it is safest to assume that they contain asbestos.

Special hazards

Hydrofluoric acid

- This extremely corrosive acid is formed when certain types of synthetic rubber, found in some O-rings, oil seals, fuel hoses etc, are exposed to temperatures above 4000C. The rubber changes into a charred or sticky substance containing the acid. *Once formed, the acid remains dangerous for years. If it gets onto the skin, it may be necessary to amputate the limb concerned.*
- When dealing with a vehicle which has suffered a fire, or with components salvaged from such a vehicle, wear protective gloves and discard them after use.

The battery

- Batteries contain sulphuric acid, which attacks clothing, eyes and skin. Take care when topping-up or carrying the battery.
- The hydrogen gas given off by the battery is highly explosive. Never cause a spark or allow a naked light nearby. Be careful when connecting and disconnecting battery chargers or jump leads.

Air bags

- Air bags can cause injury if they go off accidentally. Take care when removing the steering wheel and trim panels. Special storage instructions may apply.

Diesel injection equipment

- Diesel injection pumps supply fuel at very high pressure. Take care when working on the fuel injectors and fuel pipes.

Warning: Never expose the hands, face or any other part of the body to injector spray; the fuel can penetrate the skin with potentially fatal results.

Remember...

DO

- Do use eye protection when using power tools, and when working under the vehicle.
- Do wear gloves or use barrier cream to protect your hands when necessary.
- Do get someone to check periodically that all is well when working alone on the vehicle.
- Do keep loose clothing and long hair well out of the way of moving mechanical parts.
- Do remove rings, wristwatch etc, before working on the vehicle – especially the electrical system.
- Do ensure that any lifting or jacking equipment has a safe working load rating adequate for the job.

DON'T

- Don't attempt to lift a heavy component which may be beyond your capability – get assistance.
- Don't rush to finish a job, or take unverified short cuts.
- Don't use ill-fitting tools which may slip and cause injury.
- Don't leave tools or parts lying around where someone can trip over them. Mop up oil and fuel spills at once.
- Don't allow children or pets to play in or near a vehicle being worked on.

The following pages are intended to help in dealing with common roadside emergencies and breakdowns. You will find more detailed fault finding information in the Reference chapter, and repair information in the main chapters.

If your car won't start and the starter motor doesn't turn

- ☐ Open the bonnet and make sure that the battery terminals are clean and tight.
- ☐ Switch on the headlights and try to start the engine. If the headlights go very dim when you're trying to start, the battery is probably flat. Try jump starting using another car.

If your car won't start even though the starter motor turns as normal

- ☐ Is there fuel in the tank?
- ☐ Is there moisture on electrical components under the bonnet? Switch off the ignition, and then wipe off any obvious dampness with a dry cloth. Spray a water-repellent aerosol product (WD-40 or equivalent) on ignition and fuel system electrical connectors like those shown in the photos.

A Remove the plastic cover and check the condition and security of the battery connections.

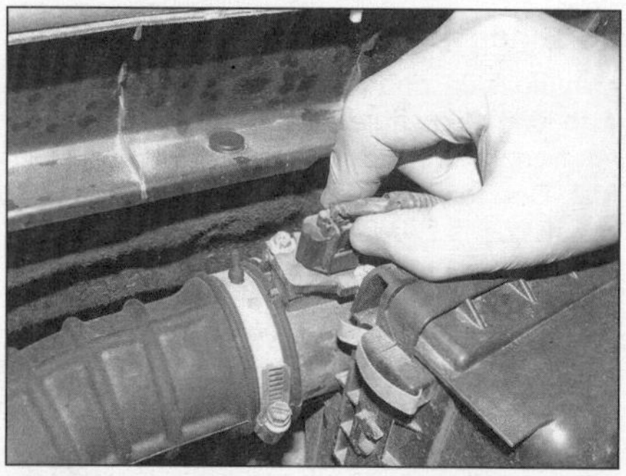

B Check that the mass airflow sensor wiring connector is secure (where fitted).

C Check the camshaft sensor wiring connectors are securely connected.

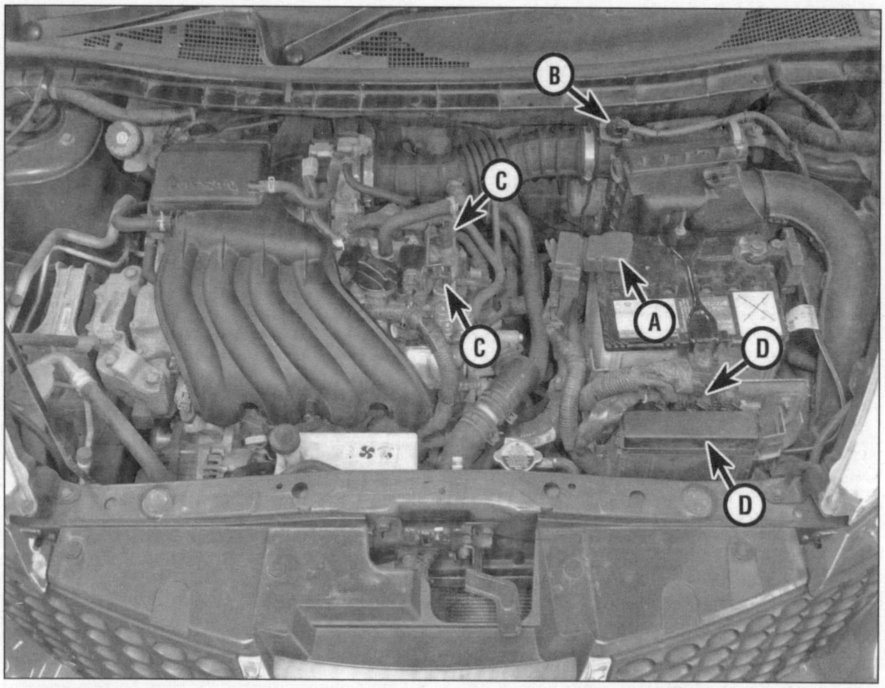

Check that electrical connections are secure (with the ignition switched off) and spray them with a water dispersant spray like WD-40 if you suspect a problem due to damp.

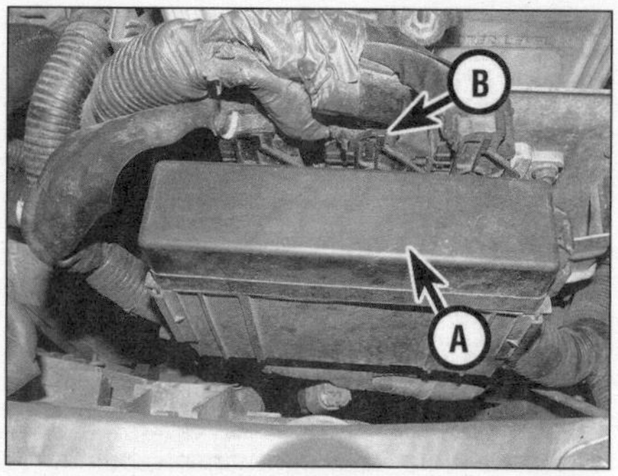

D Check the condition of the fuses in the engine compartment fusebox (A) and ensure that all principle wiring connectors are secure (B).

Jump starting

HAYNES HiNT ***Jump starting will get you out of trouble, but you must correct whatever made the battery go flat in the first place. There are three possibilities:***

1 The battery has been drained by repeated attempts to start, or by leaving the lights on.

2 The charging system is not working properly (alternator drivebelt slack or broken, alternator wiring fault or alternator itself faulty).

3 The battery itself is at fault (electrolyte low, or battery worn out).

When jump-starting a car, observe the following precautions:

Caution: Remove the key in case the central locking engages when the jump leads are connected

✓ Before connecting the booster battery, make sure that the ignition is switched off.
✓ Ensure that all electrical equipment (lights, heater, wipers, etc) is switched off.
✓ Take note of any special precautions printed on the battery case.
✓ Make sure that the booster battery is the same voltage as the discharged one in the vehicle.
✓ If the battery is being jump-started from the battery in another vehicle, the two vehicles MUST NOT TOUCH each other.
✓ Make sure that the transmission is in neutral.

HAYNES HiNT ***Budget jump leads can be a false economy, as they often do not pass enough current to start large capacity or diesel engines. They can also get hot.***

1 Connect one end of the red jump lead to the positive (+) terminal of the flat battery.

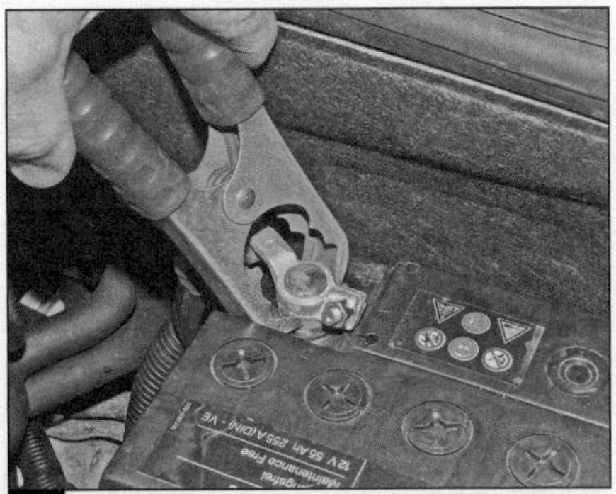

2 Connect the other end of the red lead to the positive (+) terminal of the booster battery.

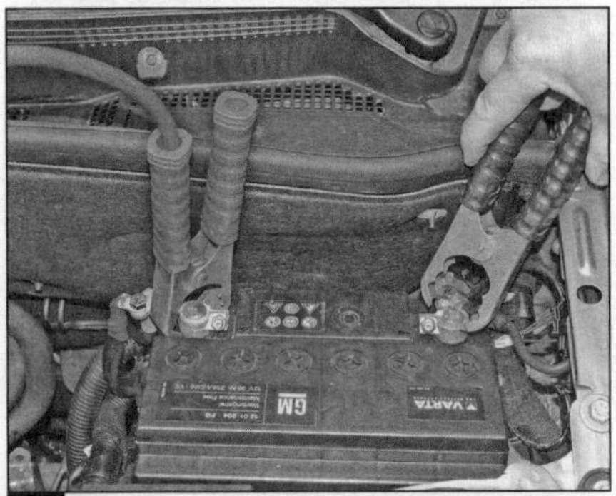

3 Connect one end of the black jump lead to the negative (-) terminal of the booster battery.

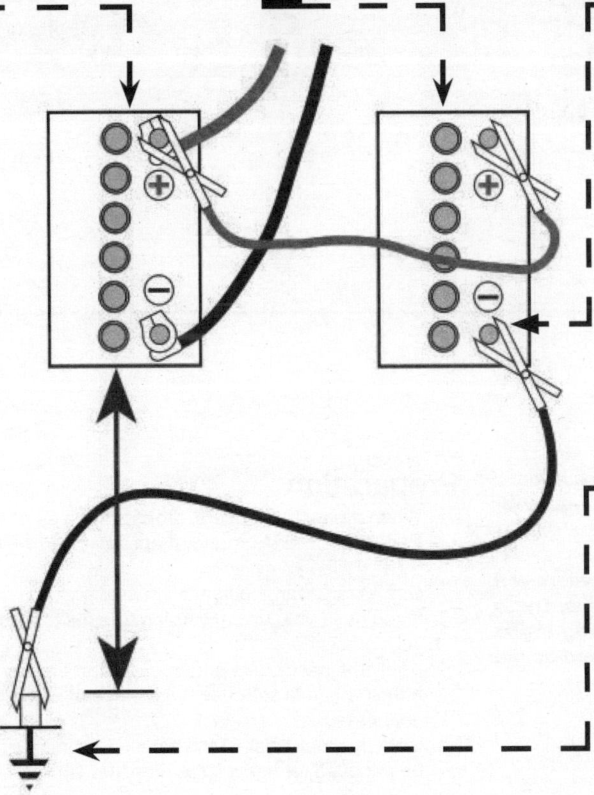

4 Connect the other end of the black jump lead to a bolt or bracket on the engine block, well away from the battery, on the vehicle to be started.

5 Make sure that the jump leads will not come into contact with the fan, drive-belts or other moving parts of the engine.

6 Start the engine using the booster battery and run it at idle speed. Switch on the lights, rear window demister and heater blower motor, then disconnect the jump leads in the reverse order of connection. Turn off the lights etc.

Identifying leaks

Puddles on the garage floor or drive, or obvious wetness under the bonnet or underneath the car, suggest a leak that needs investigating. It can sometimes be difficult to decide where the leak is coming from, especially if an engine undershield is fitted. Leaking oil or fluid can also be blown rearwards by the passage of air under the car, giving a false impression of where the problem lies.

HAYNES HiNT ***The smell of a fluid leaking from the car may provide a clue to what's leaking. Some fluids are distinctively coloured. It may help to remove the engine undershield, clean the car carefully and to park it over some clean paper overnight as an aid to locating the source of the leak. Remember that some leaks may only occur while the engine is running.***

Warning: Most automotive oils and fluids are poisonous. Wash them off skin, and change out of contaminated clothing, without delay.

Sump oil

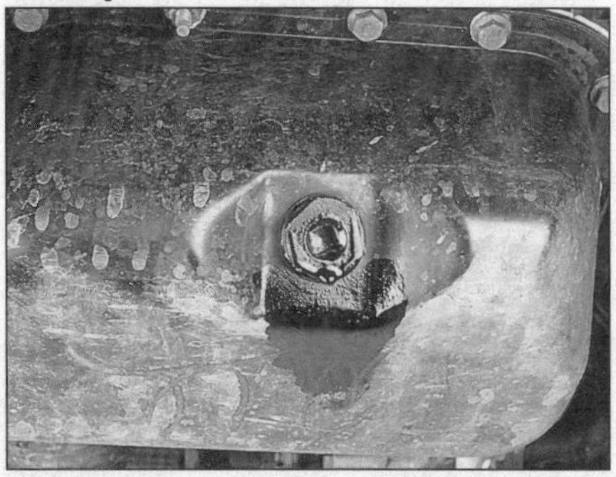

Engine oil may leak from the drain plug...

Oil from filter

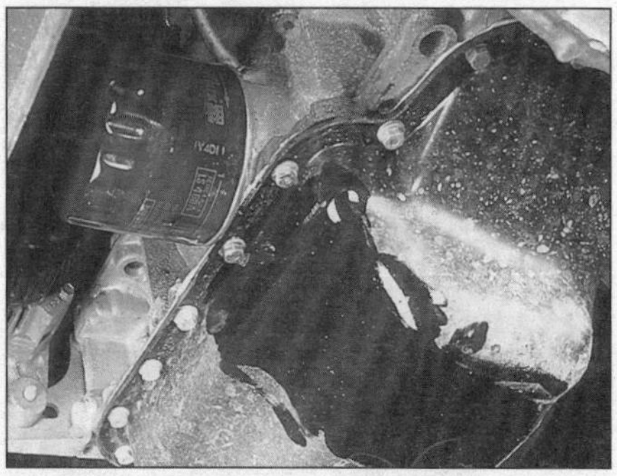

...or from the base of the oil filter.

Gearbox oil

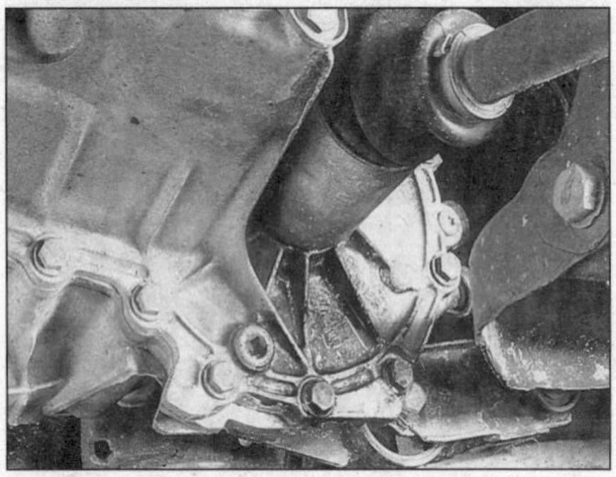

Gearbox oil can leak from the seals at the inboard ends of the driveshafts.

Antifreeze

Leaking antifreeze often leaves a crystalline deposit like this.

Brake fluid

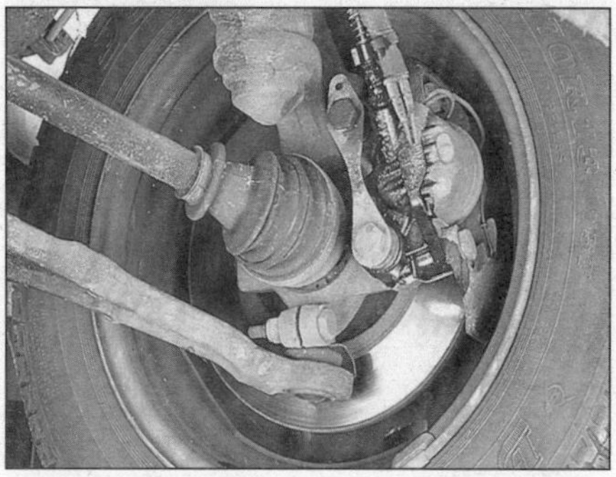

A leak occurring at a wheel is almost certainly brake fluid.

Wheel changing

Note: *Certain Juke models are equipped with a puncture repair kit and do not have a spare wheel and jack. If your car has a puncture repair kit, refer to the information contained on the next page.*

Warning: Do not change a wheel in a situation where you risk being hit by another vehicle. On busy roads, try to stop in a lay-by or a gateway. Be wary of passing traffic while changing the wheel – it is easy to become distracted by the job in hand.

Preparation

- ☐ When a puncture occurs, stop as soon as it is safe to do so.
- ☐ Park on firm level ground, if possible, and well out of the way of other traffic.
- ☐ Use hazard warning lights if necessary.
- ☐ If you have one, use a warning triangle to alert other drivers of your presence.
- ☐ Apply the handbrake and engage first or reverse gear.
- ☐ If the ground is soft, use a flat piece of wood to spread the load under the foot of the jack.
- ☐ Place a chock against the wheel diagonally opposite the wheel to be removed, or use a large stone (or similar) to stop the car rolling.

Changing the wheel

1 The spare wheel and tools are stored in the luggage compartment, lift up the floor panel/carpet.

2 The jack and tools are located in a storage box under the floor panel. Note that on some models, the jack is located behind a panel on the right-hand side of the luggage compartment.

3 Lift out the tool storage box for access to the spare wheel.

4 Unscrew the centre fastener and remove the spare wheel from the luggage compartment.

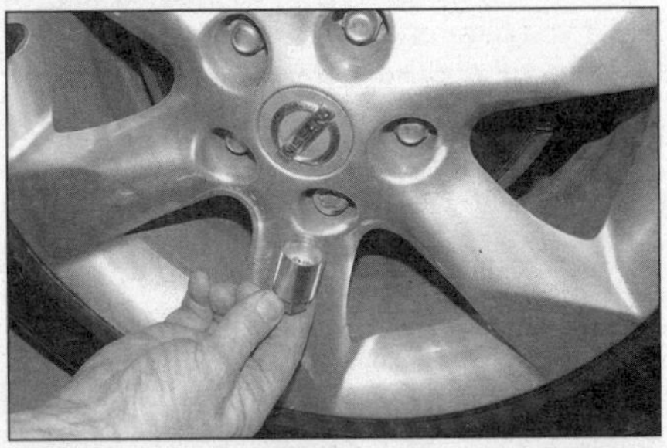

5 Where anti-theft wheel nuts are fitted, unscrew the anti-theft nut using the special tool provided – normally stored in the passenger glovebox or toolkit.

6 With the vehicle still on the ground, use the tool provided to slacken each wheel nut by half a turn.

7 Make sure the jack is located on firm ground, and engage the jack head correctly with the sill. Then raise the jack until the wheel is raised clear of the ground.

8 Unscrew the wheel nuts and remove the wheel. Place the wheel under the vehicle sill in case the jack fails.

9 Fit the spare wheel and screw in the bolts. Lightly tighten the nuts with the wheel brace then lower the car to the ground.

10 Securely tighten the wheel nuts in a diagonal sequence then refit the wheel trim/hub cap/wheel nut covers (as applicable). Stow the punctured wheel and tools back in the boot, and secure them in position.

Finally . . .

- ☐ Remove the wheel chock.
- ☐ Check the tyre pressure on the wheel just fitted. If it is low, or if you don't have a pressure gauge with you, drive slowly to the next garage and inflate the tyre to the correct pressure.
- ☐ The wheel nuts should be slackened and retightened to the specified torque at the earliest possible opportunity (see Chapter 1A or 1B).
- ☐ Have the damaged tyre or wheel repaired as soon as possible, or another puncture will leave you stranded. If a compact spare wheel is fitted (as pictured), speed and distance restrictions apply. Drive with caution and refit the repaired tyre as soon as possible.

Using the puncture repair kit

Warning: Do not attempt to repair a punctured tyre in a situation where you risk being hit by other traffic. On busy roads, try to stop in a lay-by or a gateway. Be wary of passing traffic while using the kit – it is easy to become distracted by the job in hand.

Preparation

- ☐ When a puncture occurs, stop as soon as it is safe to do so.
- ☐ Park on firm level ground, if possible, and well out of the way of other traffic.
- ☐ Use hazard warning lights if necessary.
- ☐ If you have one, use a warning triangle to alert other drivers of your presence.
- ☐ Apply the handbrake and engage first or reverse gear.

Repairing the puncture

To connect and operate the puncture repair kit, proceed as follows.

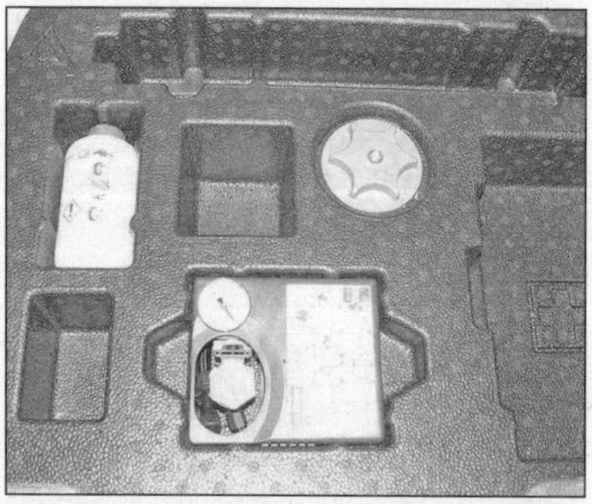

1 Lift up the luggage compartment floor panel/carpet and take out the sealant bottle and the air compressor.

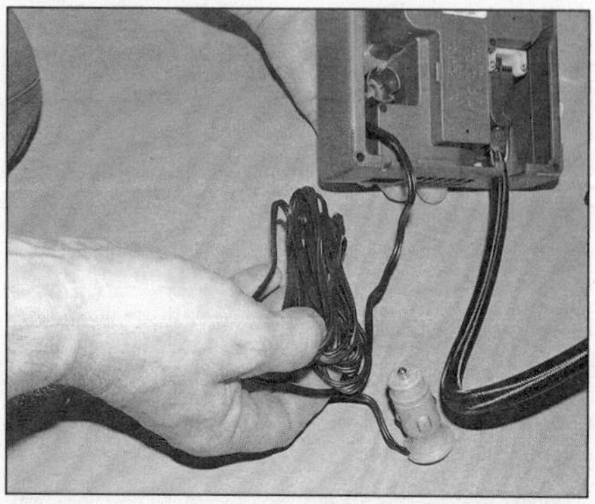

2 Take the air hose and electrical cable out of the air compressor.

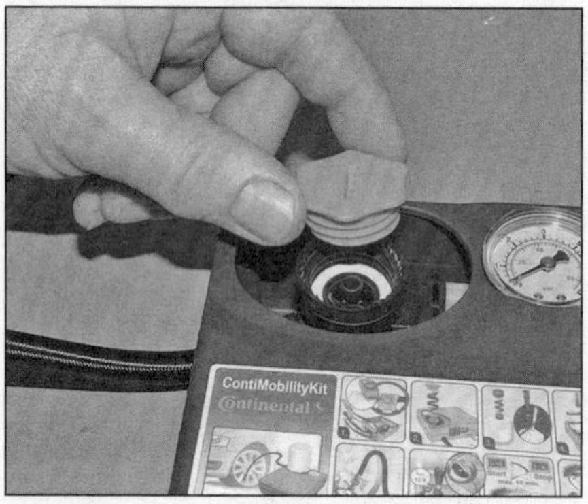

3 Remove the orange cap of the sealant bottle holder from the air compressor.

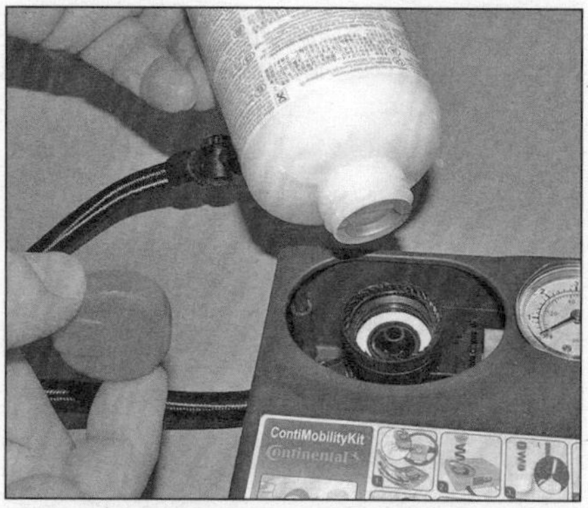

4 Remove the cap from the sealant bottle, then shake the bottle and position it on the air compressor.

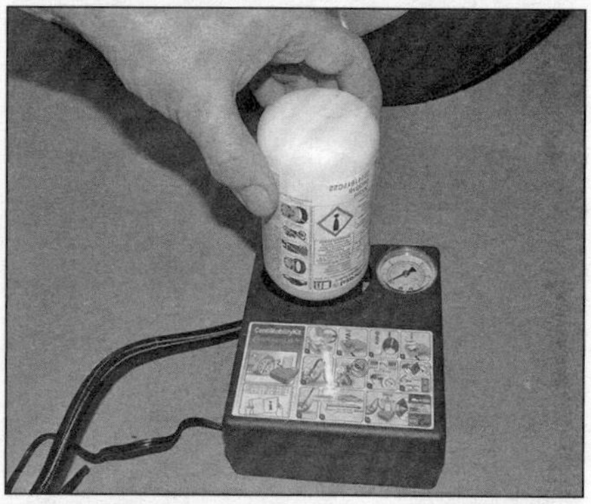

5 Screw the sealant bottle clockwise onto the bottle holder on the air compressor.

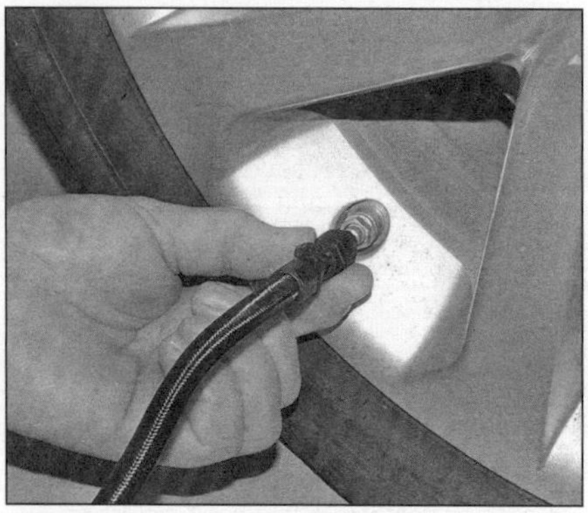

6 Unscrew the dust cap from the punctured tyre, and screw the air hose onto the tyre valve.

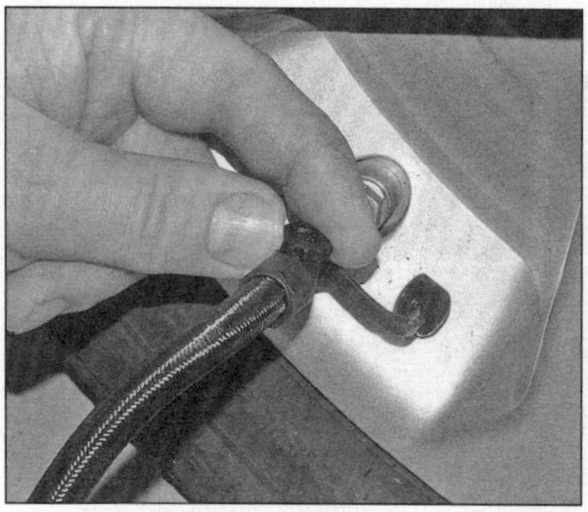

7 Make sure that the air compressor switch is in the off (O) position and that the pressure relief valve on the end of the air hose is securely closed.

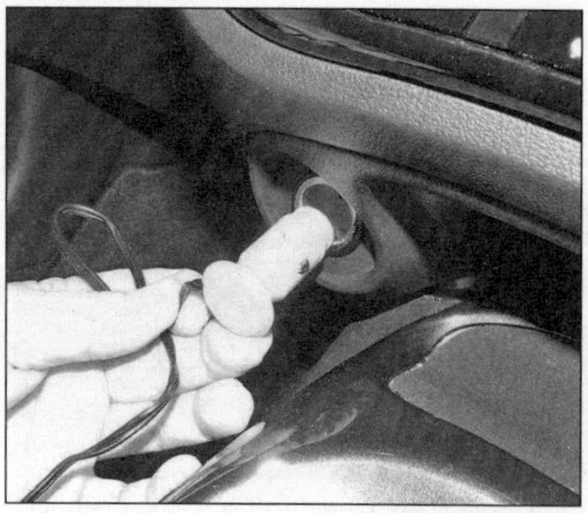

8 Plug the electrical cable into the accessory socket or cigarette lighter

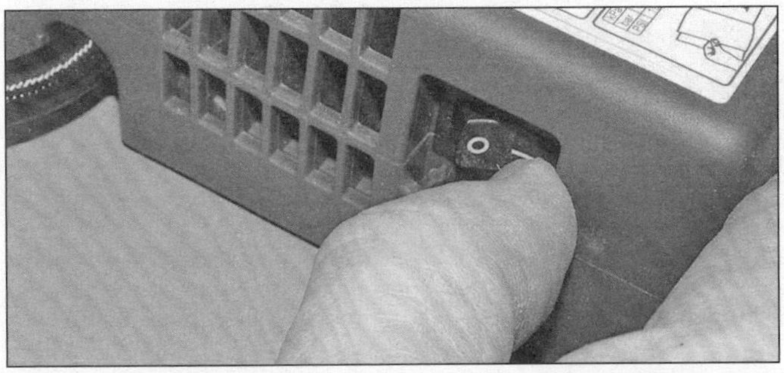

9 Place the ignition switch in the ACC position then move the switch on the air compressor to the (1) position to start the compressor. Open the pressure relief valve on the end of the air hose to inflate the tyre. The correct tyre pressure (see Lubricants, fluids and tyre pressures) should be obtained within 10 minutes. The pressure relief valve can then be closed and the air compressor switched off. Do not operate the compressor for more than 10 minutes.

Important notes

- ☐ If the correct tyre pressure is not obtained within 10 minutes, it is likely that the tyre is too badly damaged to be repaired with the kit.
- ☐ The maximum speed sticker attached to the air compressor should be placed in the driver's field of view. Do not exceed the permitted maximum speed until an undamaged wheel and tyre have been fitted.
- ☐ On completion, disconnect the air hose and continue driving immediately so that the sealant is evenly distributed around the inside of the tyre.
- ☐ After driving approximately 6 miles (but no more than 10 minutes) stop and check the tyre pressure by connecting the air hose to the tyre valve and opening the pressure relief valve. As long as the pressure indicated on the gauge is more than 1.3 bar (19 psi) it may be adjusted to the correct value using the air compressor. If the pressure has fallen below 1.3 bar (19 psi) the repair has not been successful and the car should not be driven. It will therefore be necessary to seek roadside assistance.

Towing

When all else fails, you may find yourself having to get a tow home. Long-distance recovery should only be done by a garage or breakdown service. For shorter distances, DIY towing using another car is easy enough, but observe the following points:

- ☐ Use a proper tow-rope – they are not expensive. The vehicle being towed must display an ON TOW sign in its rear window.
- ☐ Always turn the ignition key to the 'on' position when the vehicle is being towed, so that the steering lock is released, and that the direction indicator and brake lights work.
- ☐ The towing eye is located under the floor panel in the luggage compartment. To fit the eye, unclip the access cover from the front bumper and screw the eye firmly into position **(see illustrations)**.
- ☐ Before being towed, release the handbrake and select neutral on the transmission.
- ☐ Note that greater-than-usual pedal pressure will be required to operate the brakes, since the vacuum servo unit is only operational with the engine running.
- ☐ The driver of the car being towed must keep the tow-rope taut at all times to avoid snatching.
- ☐ Make sure that both drivers know the route before setting off.
- ☐ Only drive at moderate speeds and keep the distance towed to a minimum. Drive smoothly and allow plenty of time for slowing down at junctions.

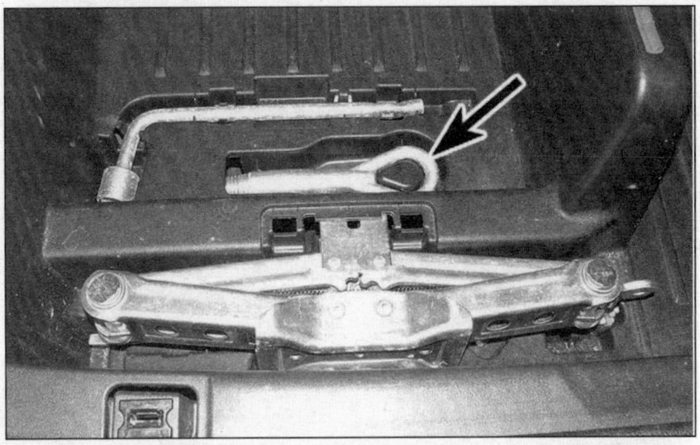

The towing eye is located with the tools in the luggage compartment

Unclip the access cover from the bumper...

...and then screw the towing eye in securely...

...using the wheel brace through the eye to tighten

Introduction

There are some very simple checks which need only take a few minutes to carry out, but which could save you a lot of inconvenience and expense.

These checks require no great skill or special tools, and the small amount of time they take to perform could prove to be very well spent, for example;

☐ Keeping an eye on tyre condition and pressures, will not only help to stop them wearing out prematurely, but could also save your life.

☐ Many breakdowns are caused by electrical problems. Battery-related faults are particularly common, and a quick check on a regular basis will often prevent the majority of these.

☐ If your car develops a brake fluid leak, the first time you might know about it is when your brakes don't work properly. Checking the level regularly will give advance warning of this kind of problem.

☐ If the oil or coolant levels run low, the cost of repairing any engine damage will be far greater than fixing the leak, for example.

Underbonnet check points

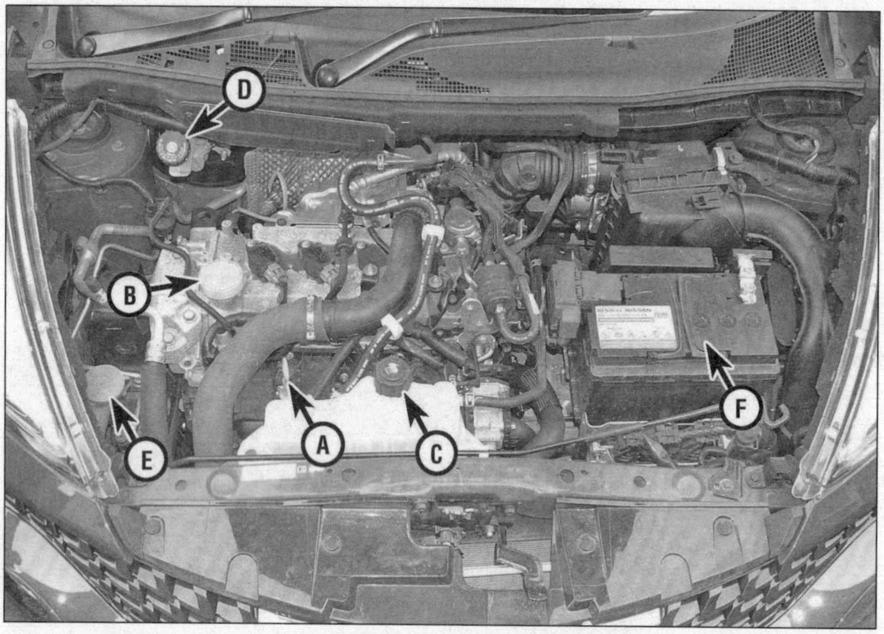

◀ **1.2 litre petrol engine**

A *Engine oil level dipstick*
B *Engine oil filler cap*
C *Coolant expansion tank*
D *Brake (and clutch) fluid reservoir*
E *Screen washer fluid reservoir*
F *Battery*

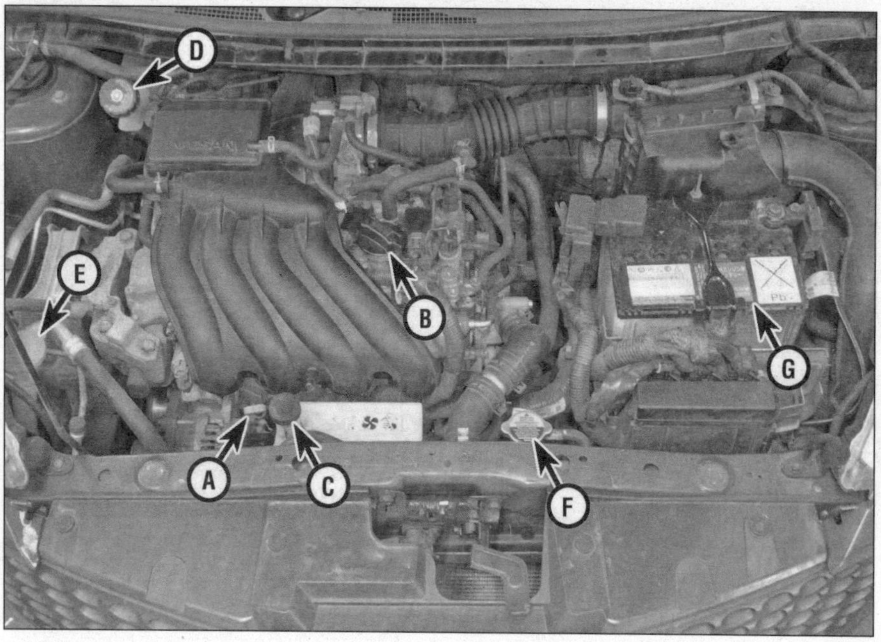

◀ **1.6 litre petrol engine**

A *Engine oil level dipstick*
B *Engine oil filler cap*
C *Coolant expansion tank*
D *Brake (and clutch) fluid reservoir*
E *Screen washer fluid reservoir*
F *Radiator pressure cap*
G *Battery*

▶ Diesel engine (Type 1)

A *Combined engine oil level dipstick and filler cap*
B *Coolant expansion tank*
C *Brake (and clutch) fluid reservoir*
D *Screen washer fluid reservoir*
E *Battery*

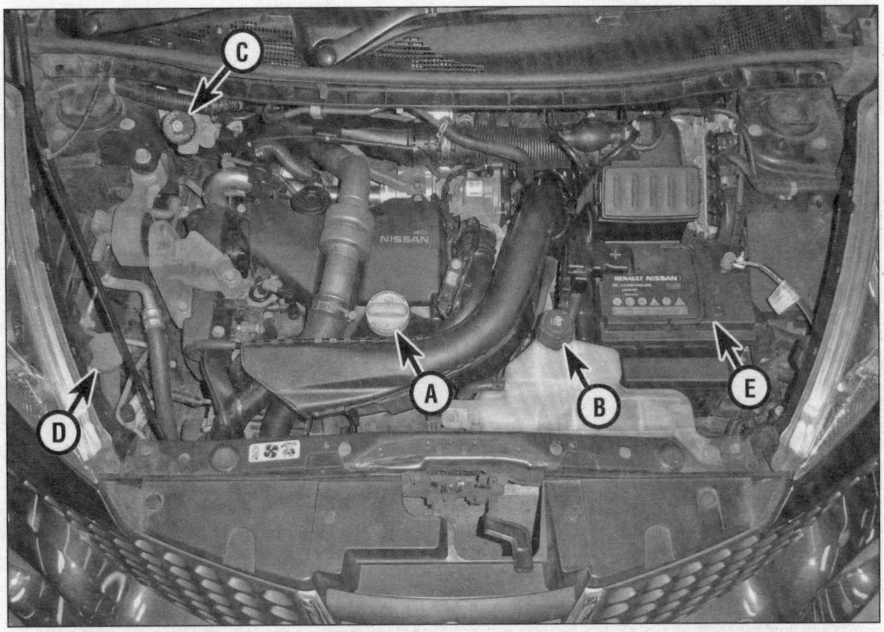

▶ Diesel engine (Type 2)

A *Combined engine oil level dipstick and filler cap*
B *Coolant expansion tank*
C *Brake (and clutch) fluid reservoir*
D *Screen washer fluid reservoir*
E *Battery*

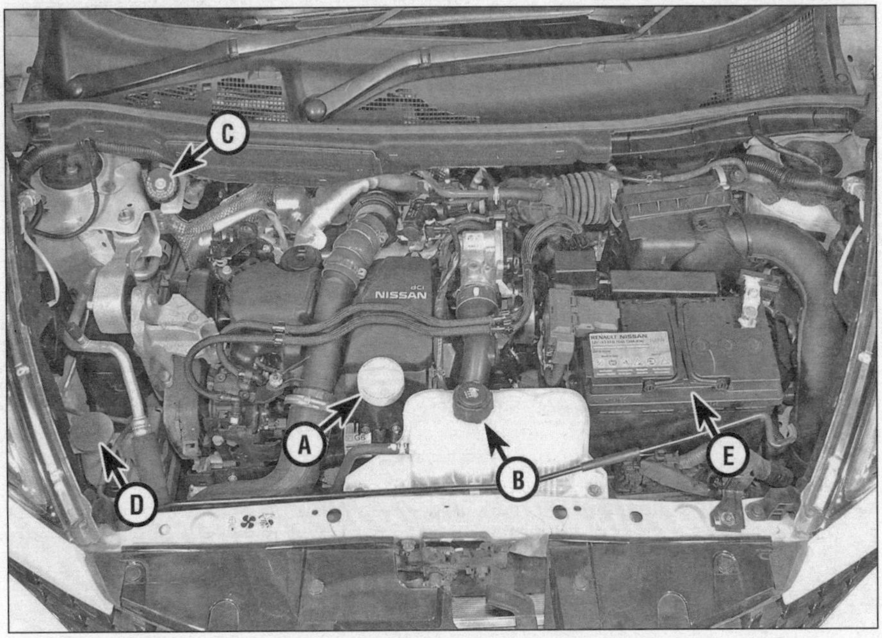

Engine oil level

Before you start

✔ Make sure that your car is on level ground.

✔ Check the oil level before the car is driven, or at least 5 minutes after the engine has been switched off.

> **HAYNES HiNT** ***If the oil is checked immediately after driving the vehicle, some of the oil will remain in the upper engine components, resulting in an inaccurate reading on the dipstick.***

The correct oil

Modern engines place great demands on their oil. It is very important that the correct oil for your car is used (see *Lubricants and fluids*).

Car care

● If you have to add oil frequently, you should check whether you have any oil leaks. Place some clean paper under the car overnight, and check for stains in the morning. If there are no leaks, the engine may be burning oil.

● Always maintain the level between the upper and lower dipstick marks **(see photo 3)**. If the level is too low severe engine damage may occur. Oil seal failure may result if the engine is overfilled by adding too much oil.

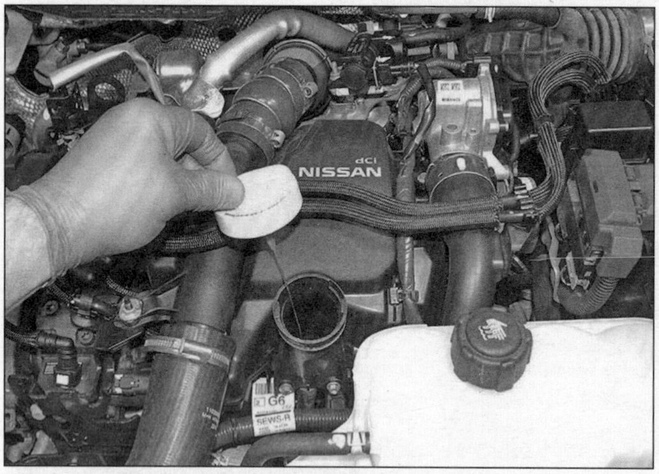

1 The dipstick is located at the front of the engine (see Underbonnet check points); the dipstick is brightly coloured (yellow or orange) or has a picture of an oil-can on the top for identification. Withdraw the dipstick. Note that on diesel engines the dipstick is part of the oil filler cap.

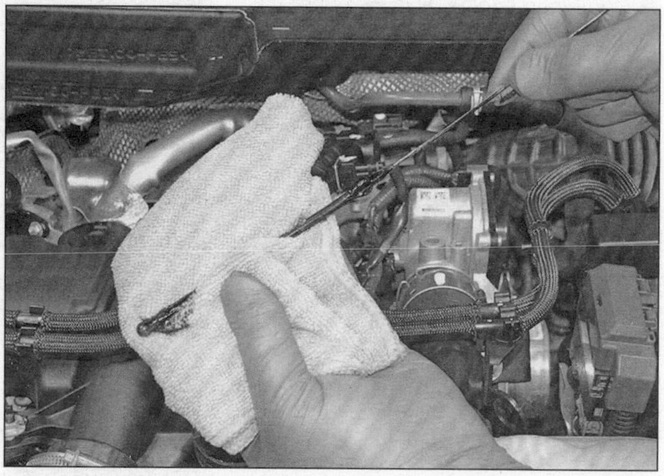

2 Using a clean rag or paper towel remove all oil from the dipstick. Insert the clean dipstick into the tube as far as it will go, then withdraw it again.

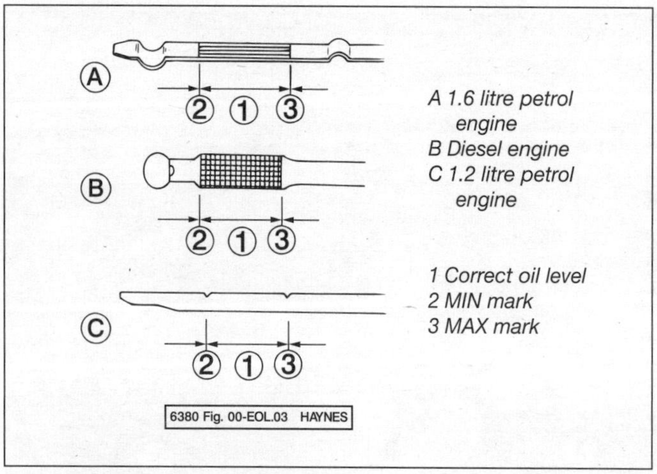

3 Note the oil level on the end of the dipstick, which should be between the upper (MAX) mark and lower (MIN) mark. Approximately 1.0 litre of oil will raise the level from the lower mark to the upper mark.

4 Oil is added through the filler cap. Unscrew the cap and top-up the level; a funnel may help to reduce spillage. Add the oil slowly, checking the level on the dipstick often. Don't overfill (see *Car care*).

Brake and clutch fluid level

Warning: Brake fluid can harm your eyes and damage painted surfaces, so use extreme caution when handling and pouring it.

Warning: Do not use fluid that has been standing open for some time, as it absorbs moisture from the air, which can cause a dangerous loss of braking effectiveness.

Before you start

✔ Make sure that your car is on level ground.

Safety first!

● If the reservoir requires repeated topping-up this is an indication of a fluid leak somewhere in the system, which should be investigated immediately.

● If a leak is suspected, the car should not be driven until the braking system has been checked. Never take any risks where brakes are concerned.

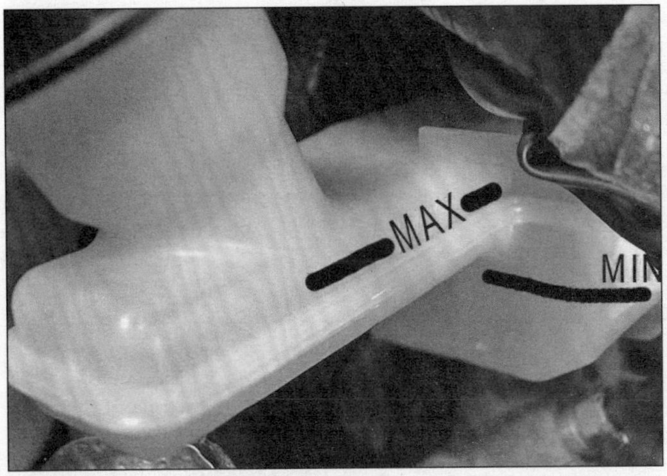

1 The upper (MAX) and lower (MIN) fluid level markings are on the side of the reservoir, which is located at the rear of the engine compartment.

2 If topping-up is necessary, first wipe clean the area around the filler cap with a clean cloth.

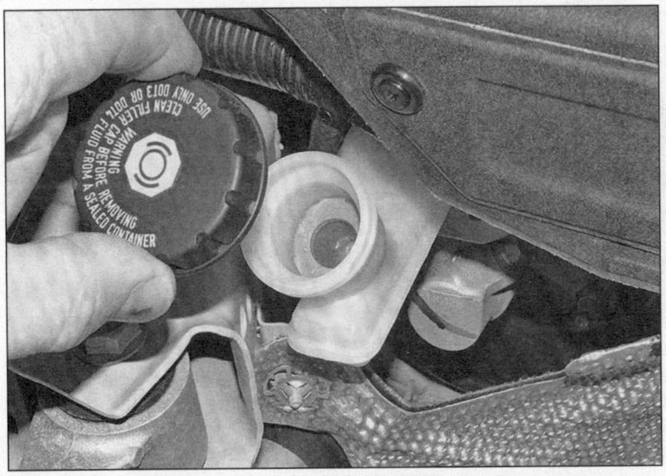

3 Unscrew the cap and remove it from the top of the reservoir.

4 Carefully add fluid, avoiding spilling it on the surrounding paintwork. Use only the specified type of hydraulic fluid. After filling to the correct level, refit the cap and tighten it securely. Wipe off any spilt fluid.

Coolant level

Warning: DO NOT attempt to remove the expansion tank pressure cap when the engine is hot, as there is a very great risk of scalding.

Warning: Do not leave open containers of coolant about, as it is poisonous.

Car care

● Adding coolant should not be necessary on a regular basis. If frequent topping-up is required, it is likely there is a leak. Check the radiator, all hoses and joint faces for signs of staining or wetness, and rectify as necessary.

● It is important that antifreeze is used in the cooling system all year round, not just during the winter months. Don't top-up with water alone, as the antifreeze will become too diluted.

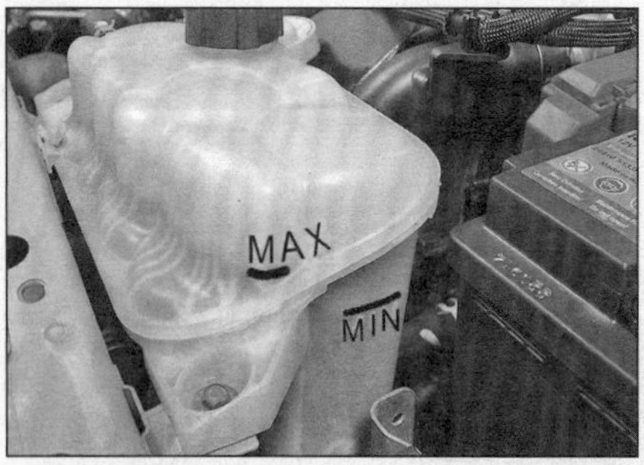

1 The coolant level must be checked with the engine cold; the coolant level should be between the MAX and MIN marks on the expansion tank.

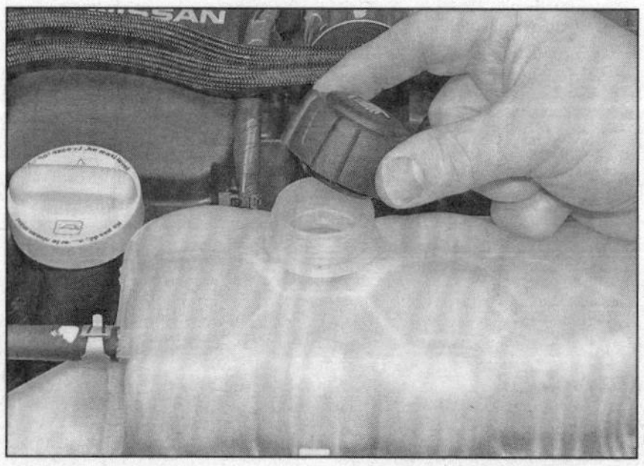

2 If topping-up is necessary, remove the pressure cap (see **Warning**) from the expansion tank, which is located at the front of the engine compartment.

3 Add a mixture of water and antifreeze to the expansion tank until the coolant level is between the level marks. Once the level is correct, securely refit the cap.

Bulbs and fuses

✔ Check all external lights and the horn. Refer to Chapter 12, Section 2 for details if any of the circuits are found to be inoperative.

✔ Visually check all accessible wiring connectors, harnesses and retaining clips for security, and for signs of chafing or damage.

HAYNES HiNT ***If you need to check your brake lights and indicators unaided, back up to a wall or garage door and operate the lights. The reflected light should show if they are working properly.***

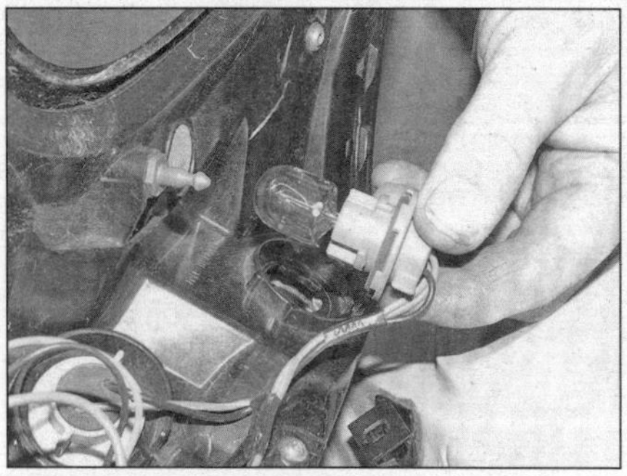

1 If a single indicator light, brake light, sidelight or headlight has failed, it is likely that a bulb has blown, and will need to be renewed. Refer to Chapter 12, Section 5 for details. If both brake lights have failed, it is possible that the switch has failed (see Chapter 9, Section 18).

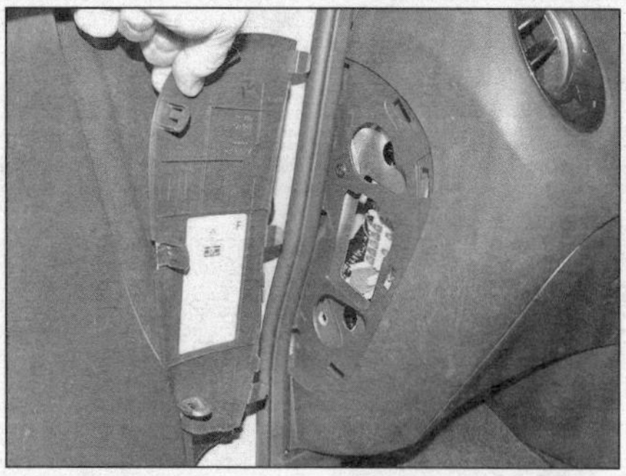

2 If more than one indicator or tail light has failed, it is likely that either a fuse has blown or that there is a fault in the circuit. Fuses are located behind a cover at the left-hand end of the facia.

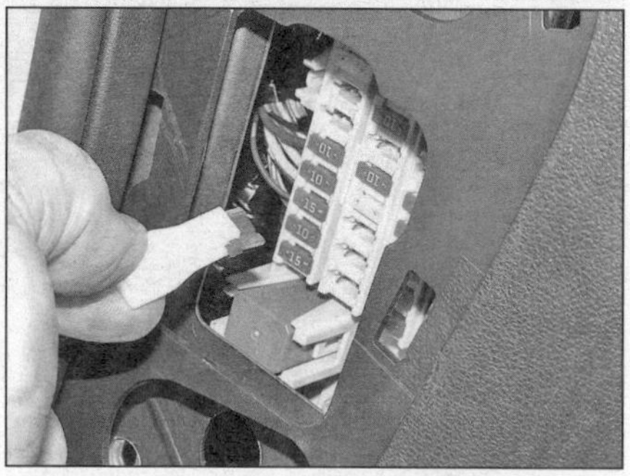

3 Additional fuses are usually located in the engine compartment fusebox. To renew a blown fuse, simply pull it out and fit a new fuse of the correct rating (see *Wiring diagrams*). If the fuse blows again, it is important that you find out why – a complete checking procedure is given in Chapter 12, Section 2.

Battery

Caution: Before carrying out any work on the vehicle battery, read the precautions given in Safety first! in Section 3.

✔ Make sure that the battery tray is in good condition, and that the clamp is tight. Corrosion on the tray, retaining clamp and the battery itself can be removed with a solution of water and baking soda. Thoroughly rinse all cleaned areas with water. Any metal parts damaged by corrosion should be covered with a zinc-based primer, and then painted.

✔ Periodically (approximately every three months), check the charge condition of the battery, as described in Chapter 5A, Section 2.

✔ If the battery is flat, and you need to jump start your vehicle, see *Roadside repairs*.

HAYNES HiNT

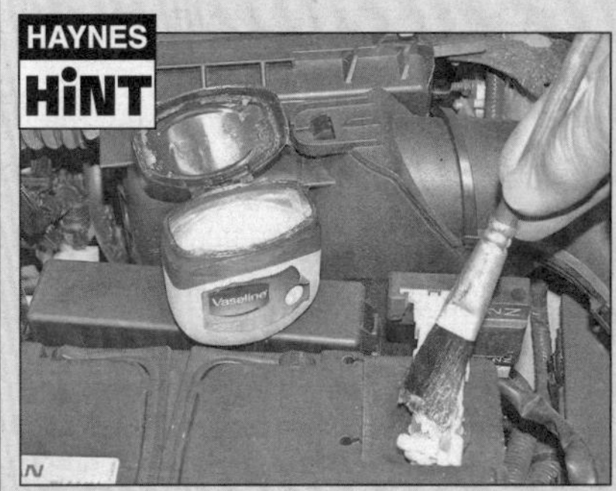

Battery corrosion can be kept to a minimum by applying a layer of petroleum jelly to the clamps and terminals after they are reconnected.

1 Lift the plastic cover to gain access to the battery positive terminal, which is located on the left-hand side of the engine compartment. The exterior of the battery should be inspected periodically for damage such as a cracked case or cover.

2 Check the battery lead clamps for tightness to ensure good electrical connections, and check the leads for signs of damage.

3 If corrosion (white, fluffy deposits) is evident, remove the cables from the battery terminals, clean them with a small wire brush, then refit them. Automotive stores sell a tool for cleaning the battery post…

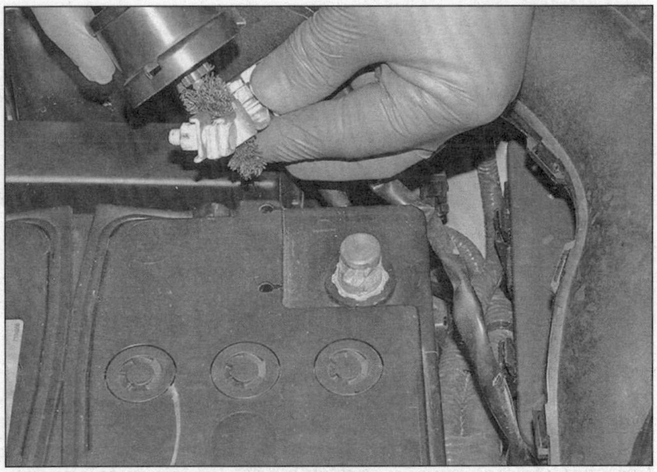

4 …as well as the battery cable clamps.

Tyre condition and pressure

It is very important that tyres are in good condition, and at the correct pressure – having a tyre failure at any speed is highly dangerous.

Tyre wear is influenced by driving style – harsh braking and acceleration, or fast cornering, will all produce more rapid tyre wear. As a general rule, the front tyres wear out faster than the rears. Interchanging the tyres from front to rear ("rotating" the tyres) may result in more even wear. However, if this is completely effective, you may have the expense of replacing all four tyres at once!

Remove any nails or stones embedded in the tread before they penetrate the tyre to cause deflation. If removal of a nail does reveal that the tyre has been punctured, refit the nail so that its point of penetration is marked. Then immediately change the wheel, and have the tyre repaired by a tyre dealer.

Regularly check the tyres for damage in the form of cuts or bulges, especially in the sidewalls. Periodically remove the wheels, and clean any dirt or mud from the inside and outside surfaces. Examine the wheel rims for signs of rusting, corrosion or other damage. Light alloy wheels are easily damaged by "kerbing" whilst parking; steel wheels may also become dented or buckled. A new wheel is very often the only way to overcome severe damage.

New tyres should be balanced when they are fitted, but it may become necessary to re-balance them as they wear, or if the balance weights fitted to the wheel rim should fall off. Unbalanced tyres will wear more quickly, as will the steering and suspension components. Wheel imbalance is normally signified by vibration, particularly at a certain speed (typically around 50 mph). If this vibration is felt only through the steering, then it is likely that just the front wheels need balancing. If, however, the vibration is felt through the whole car, the rear wheels could be out of balance. Wheel balancing should be carried out by a tyre dealer or garage.

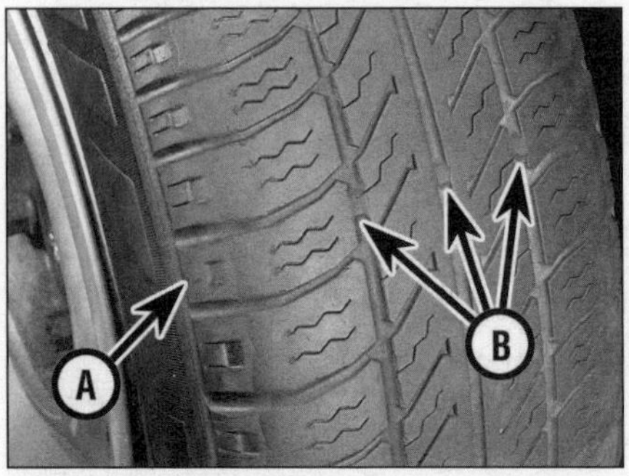

1 *Tread Depth - visual check*
The original tyres have tread wear safety bands (B), which will appear when the tread depth reaches approximately 1.6 mm. The band positions are indicated by a triangular mark on the tyre sidewall (A).

2 *Tread Depth - manual check*
Alternatively, tread wear can be monitored with a simple, inexpensive device known as a tread depth indicator gauge.

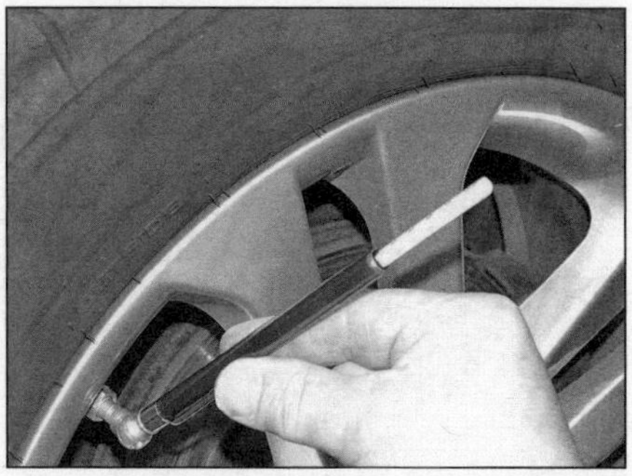

3 *Tyre Pressure Check*
Check the tyre pressures regularly with the tyres cold. Do not adjust the tyre pressures immediately after the vehicle has been used, or an inaccurate setting will result.

Tyre tread wear patterns

Shoulder Wear

Underinflation (wear on both sides)
Under-inflation will cause overheating of the tyre, because the tyre will flex too much, and the tread will not sit correctly on the road surface. This will cause a loss of grip and excessive wear, not to mention the danger of sudden tyre failure due to heat build-up.
Check and adjust pressures
Incorrect wheel camber (wear on one side)
Repair or renew suspension parts
Hard cornering
Reduce speed!

Centre Wear

Overinflation
Over-inflation will cause rapid wear of the centre part of the tyre tread, coupled with reduced grip, harsher ride, and the danger of shock damage occurring in the tyre casing.
Check and adjust pressures

If you sometimes have to inflate your car's tyres to the higher pressures specified for maximum load or sustained high speed, don't forget to reduce the pressures to normal afterwards.

Uneven Wear

Front tyres may wear unevenly as a result of wheel misalignment. Most tyre dealers and garages can check and adjust the wheel alignment (or "tracking") for a modest charge.
Incorrect camber or castor
Repair or renew suspension parts
Malfunctioning suspension
Repair or renew suspension parts
Unbalanced wheel
Balance tyres
Incorrect toe setting
Adjust front wheel alignment
Note: *The feathered edge of the tread which typifies toe wear is best checked by feel.*

Washer fluid level

● Screenwash additives not only keep the windscreen clean during foul weather, they also prevent the washer system freezing in cold weather – which is when you are likely to need it most. Don't top-up using plain water as the screenwash will become too diluted, and will freeze during cold weather.

Warning: On no account use coolant antifreeze in the washer system, as this may damage the paintwork.

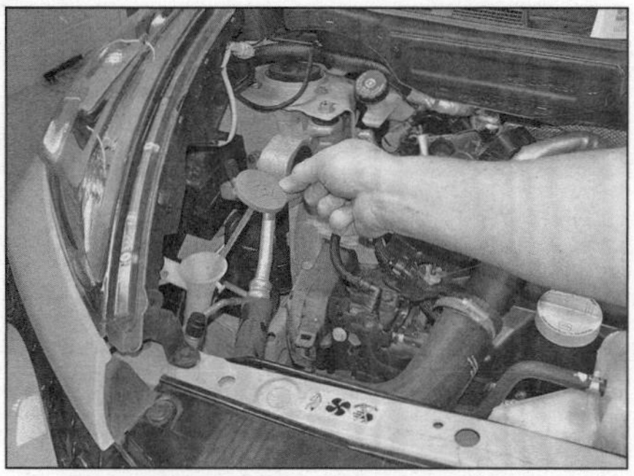

1 The washer fluid reservoir is located in the right-hand front corner of the engine compartment. To check the fluid level, open the cap, place your thumb over the vent hole in the centre of the cap, and withdraw the cap and tube. The fluid level can then be seen in the transparent tube.

2 If topping-up is necessary, add water and a screenwash additive in the quantities recommended on the bottle.

Wiper blades

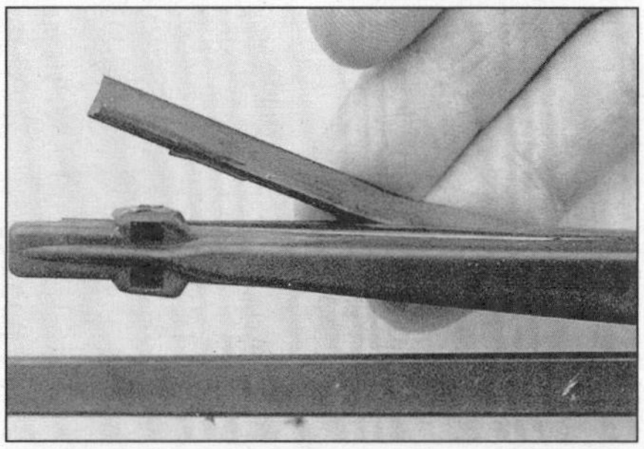

1 Check the condition of the wiper blades: if they are cracked or show signs of deterioration, or if the glass swept area is smeared, renew them. For maximum clarity of vision, wiper blades should be renewed annually.

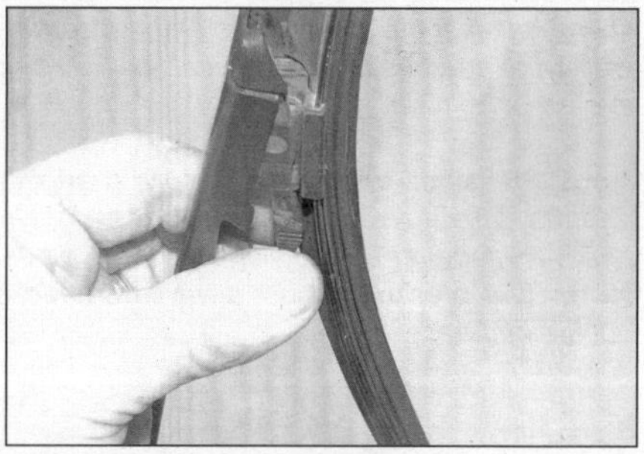

2 To remove a windscreen wiper blade, turn the ignition on and push the wiper switch stalk upwards, twice in quick succession. This places the arms in the 'service' position. Lift the wiper from the screen and squeeze the lower ends of the retaining clip together...

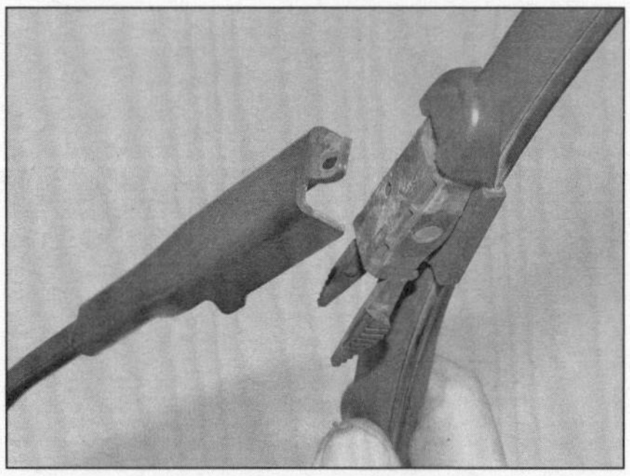

3 ...and disengage the blade by unhooking it from the end of the wiper arm, taking care not to allow the wiper arm to spring back and damage the windscreen. When completed, return the blades to the park position by pushing the wiper switch stalk upwards once with the ignition on.

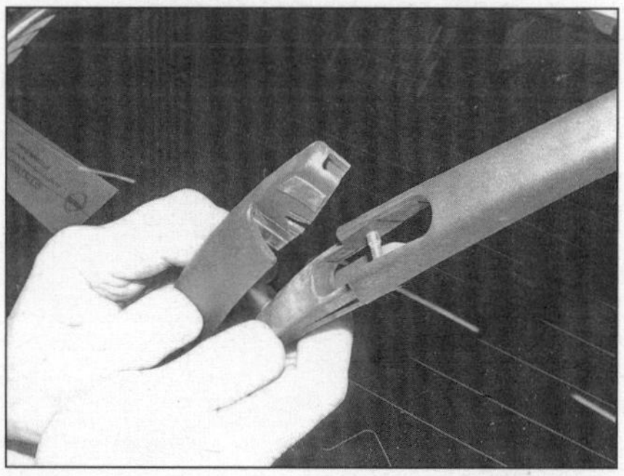

4 To remove the rear wiper blade, lift the wiper arm and then unclip it from the arm, taking care not to allow the armto spring back and damage the rear screen.

Lubricants and fluids

Engine

Petrol engines:	Genuine Nissan engine oil - SAE 5W30, API SL/SM specification
Diesel engines:	Genuine Nissan engine oil - SAE 5W30 DPF or SAE 5W30, low SAPS ACEA C4 specification

Cooling system

All models	Genuine Nissan long life coolant or equivalant

Transmission

RS5F92R (5-speed) and RS6F94R (6-speed)	Genuine Nissan MT-XZ gear oil TL/JR type or API GL-4, viscosity SAE 75W-80

Braking and clutch system

All models	Genuine Nissan brake fluid or equivalent hydraulic fluid to DOT 4

Tyre pressures

Note: *The make of tyres, the sizes and the pressures for each vehicle are given on a label attached to the driver's door A-pillar* ***(see illustration).****On models with a space-saver spare wheel, a separate pressure is given for the spare tyre, and care must be taken not to misread the sticker; the space-saver wheel is inflated to a lot higher pressure than the standard tyres (typically 60 psi). On models with a space-saver spare wheel, note that the spare is for temporary use only; whilst the spare is fitted, the vehicle should not be driven at speeds in excess of 50 mph.*

Note: *Pressures on the label apply to original-equipment tyres listed, and may vary if any other makes or type of tyre is fitted; check with the tyre manufacturer or supplier for correct pressures if necessary.*
Note: *Tyre pressures must always be checked with the tyres cold to ensure accuracy.*

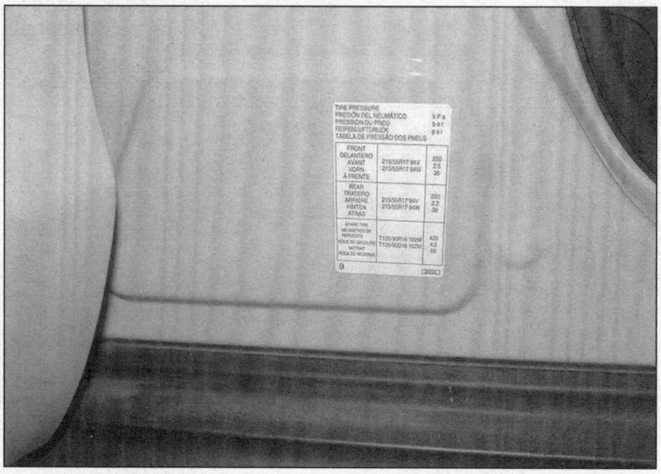

Chapter 1A
Routine maintenance and servicing – petrol models

Contents

Degrees of difficulty

Easy, suitable for novice with little experience	**Fairly easy,** suitable for beginner with some experience	**Fairly difficult,** suitable for competent DIY mechanic	**Difficult,** suitable for experienced DIY mechanic	**Very difficult,** suitable for expert DIY or professional

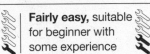

Servicing specifications

Lubricants and fluids

Refer to *Lubricants, fluids and tyre pressures*

Capacities

	1.2 litre engines	1.6 litre engines
Engine oil (with filter):	4.6 litres	4.3 litres
Difference between MAX and MIN dipstick marks	Approx. 1.0 litre	Approx. 1.0 litre
Cooling system:	7.6 litres	6.7 litres
Transmission:		
5-speed models	2.3 litres	
6-speed models	2.0 litres	
Fuel tank	46.0 litres	

Cooling system

	Antifreeze	Water
Antifreeze mixture (ethylene glycol antifreeze):		
Protection down to –15°C	30%	70%
Protection down to –35°C	50%	50%

Note: *Refer to antifreeze manufacturer for latest recommendations.*

Fuel system

	1.2 litre engine	1.6 litre engine
Idle speed (not adjustable – controlled by ECU):	750 ± 50 rpm	650 ± 50 rpm

Ignition system

	1.2 litre engines	1.6 litre engines
Spark plug type:	NGK ILKAR7F7G	NGK DILZKAR6A11
Electrode gap:	0.65 mm	1.1 mm

Auxiliary drivebelts

Drivebelt deflection:		
1.2 litre engines	Self-adjusting by automatic tensioner	
1.6 litre engines (used belt):	**Setting**	**Limit**
With air conditioning	4.9 to 5.2 mm	10.0 mm
Without air conditioning	4.3 to 4.7 mm	9.1 mm
1.6 litre engines (new belt):	**Setting**	
With air conditioning	4.1 to 4.4 mm	
Without air conditioning	3.7 to 3.9 mm	

Note: *In all cases, the drivebelt deflection is measured by applying a force of 98 Nm (10 kg, 22 lb) as described in the text.*

Brakes

Minimum front and rear brake pad friction material thickness	2.0 mm
Minimum handbrake shoe lining thickness	1.5 mm
Number of clicks required to fully apply handbrake	9 to 10 clicks
Number of clicks required operating handbrake 'on' warning light	1 click
Disc runout limit (attached to vehicle)	0.1 mm

Suspension and steering

Front wheel toe setting	2.0 mm ± 1.0 mm toe-in

Torque wrench settings

	Nm	lbf ft
Auxilliary drivebelt tensioning pulley nut (1.6 litre engines):		
Stage 1 (adjustment position)	5	4
Stage 2	35	26
Cylinder block coolant drain plug	10	7
Engine sump drain plug:		
1.2 litre engines	50	37
1.6 litre engines	34	25
Manual transmission:		
5-speed:		
Filler/level plug (plastic plug)	3	2
Drain plug	22	16
6-speed:		
Filler/level plug (plastic plug)	3	2
Drain plug	24	18
Roadwheel nuts	112	83
Spark plugs:		
1.2 litre engines	24	18
1.6 litre engines	20	15

1 Maintenance schedule

The maintenance intervals in this manual are provided with the assumption that you, not the dealer, will be carrying out the work. These are the minimum maintenance intervals based on the schedule recommended by us for vehicles driven daily. If you wish to keep your vehicle in peak condition at all times, you may wish to perform some of these procedures more often. We encourage frequent maintenance because it enhances the efficiency, performance and resale value of your vehicle. If the vehicle is driven in dusty areas, used to tow a trailer, or driven frequently at slow speeds (idling in traffic) or on short journeys, more frequent maintenance intervals are recommended. Nissan recommend that many of their service intervals are halved for vehicles which are used under these conditions.

When the vehicle is new, it should be serviced by a dealer service department (or other workshop recognised by the vehicle manufacturer as providing the same standard of service) in order to preserve the warranty. The vehicle manufacturer may reject warranty claims if you are unable to prove that servicing has been carried out as and when specified, using only original equipment parts or parts certified to be of equivalent quality.

Every 250 miles or weekly

- ☐ Refer to *Weekly checks*

Every 12 500 miles or 12 months – whichever comes first

- ☐ Renew the engine oil and filter (Section 5)
- ☐ Check all underbonnet components and hoses for fluid leaks (Section 6)
- ☐ Check the brake pads and renew if necessary (Section 7)
- ☐ Check the operation of the handbrake (Section 8)
- ☐ Check the operation of the clutch (Section 9)
- ☐ Check the condition of the air conditioning system components (Section 10)
- ☐ Check the condition of the emissions control system hoses and components (Section 11)
- ☐ Check the condition of the auxiliary drivebelts, and renew if necessary (Section 12)

Every 12 500 miles or 12 months – whichever comes first (continued)

- ☐ Check the steering and suspension components for condition and security (Section 13)
- ☐ Check the condition of the driveshaft rubber gaiters (Section 14)
- ☐ Check the wheel alignment (Section 15)
- ☐ Check the condition of the exhaust system and mountings (Section 16)
- ☐ Check the operation and security of all seat belts (Section 17)
- ☐ Check the operation of all electrical systems (Section 18)
- ☐ Lubricate all hinges and locks (Section 19)
- ☐ Check the manual transmission oil level (Section 20)
- ☐ Carry out a road test (Section 21)

Every 25 000 miles or 2 years – whichever comes first

- ☐ Renew the pollen filter (Section 22)
- ☐ Renew the brake fluid (Section 23)

Every 37 500 miles or 3 years – whichever comes first

- ☐ Renew the air filter element (Section 24)
- ☐ Renew the coolant (Section 25)

Every 50 000 miles or 4 years – whichever comes first

- ☐ Renew the spark plugs (Section 26)

2 Component locations

Front underbody view

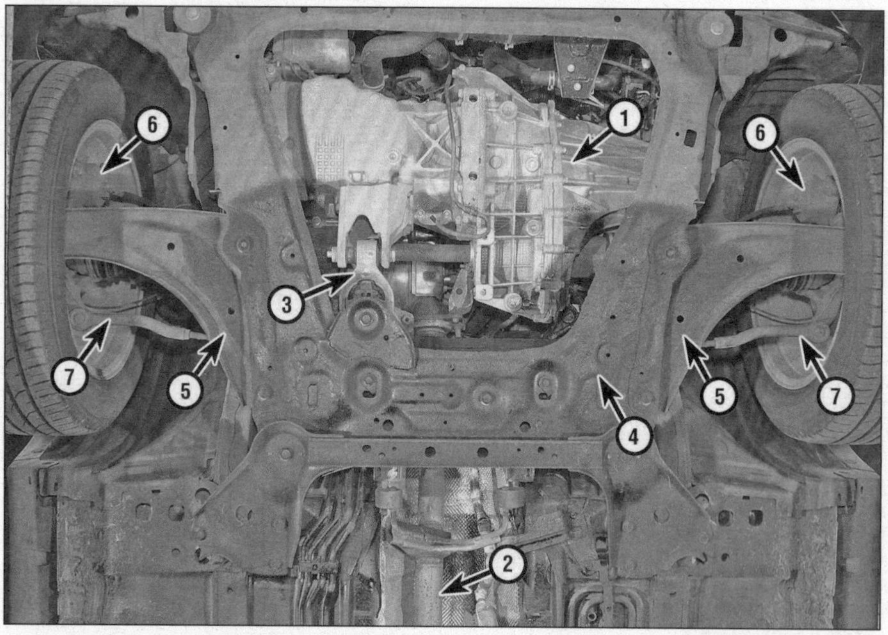

1 Transmission
2 Exhaust front pipe
3 Rear engine/transmission mounting
4 Subframe
5 Front suspension lower arm
6 Brake calipers
7 Steering track rod end

Rear underbody view

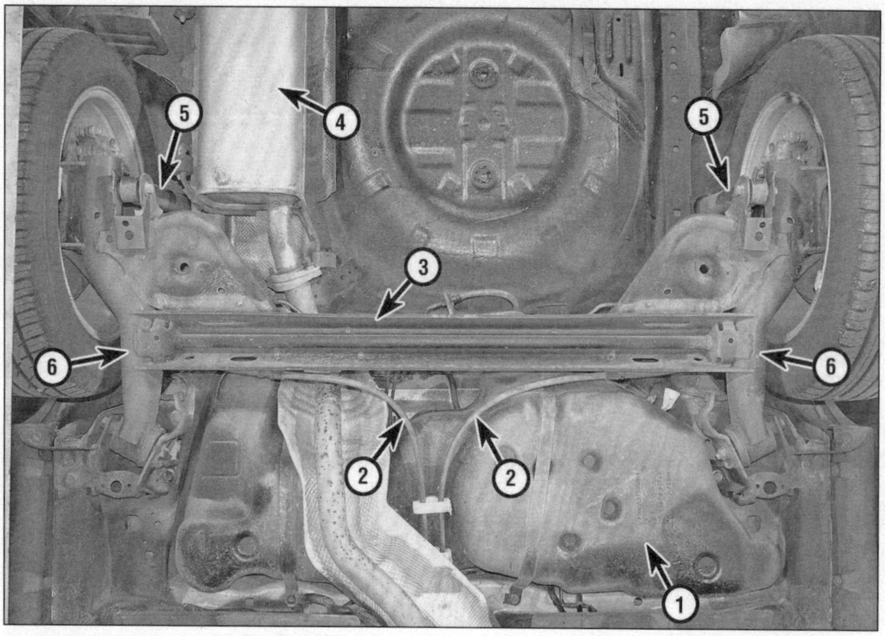

1 Fuel tank
2 Handbrake cables
3 Rear axle torsion beam
4 Exhaust rear silencer and tailpipe
5 Shock absorbers
6 Rear trailing arms

Underbonnet view – 1.2 litre engine

1 Engine oil filler cap
2 Engine oil level dipstick
3 Windscreen washer bottle
4 Ignition coils
5 Brake fluid reservoir
6 Air cleaner assembly
7 Coolant expansion tank
8 Engine management electronic control unit (ECU)
9 Battery
10 Fuse/relay box

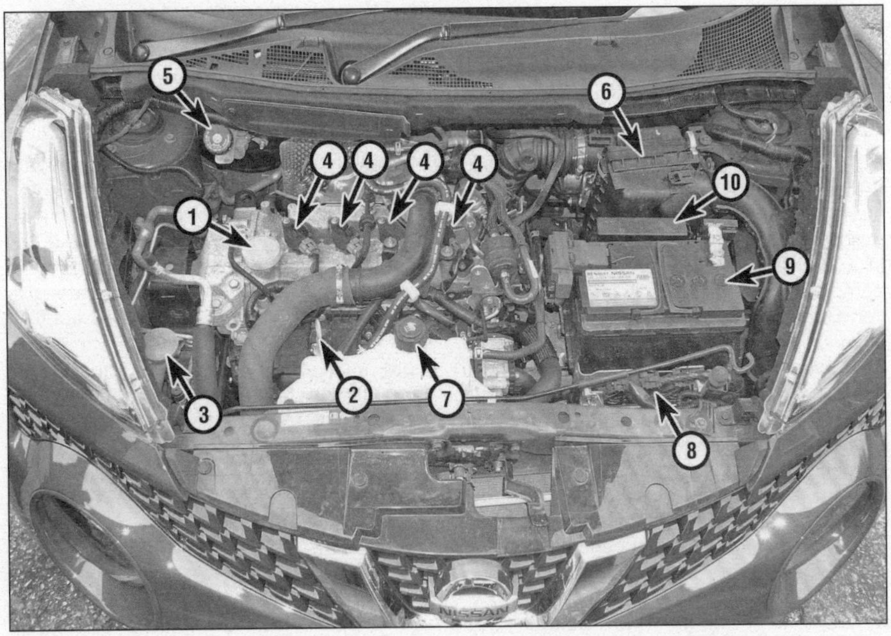

Underbonnet view – 1.6 litre engine

1 Engine oil filler cap
2 Engine oil level dipstick
3 Windscreen washer bottle
4 Radiator pressure cap
5 Brake fluid reservoir
6 Air cleaner assembly
7 Coolant expansion tank
8 Engine management electronic control unit (ECU)
9 Battery
10 Fuse/relay box

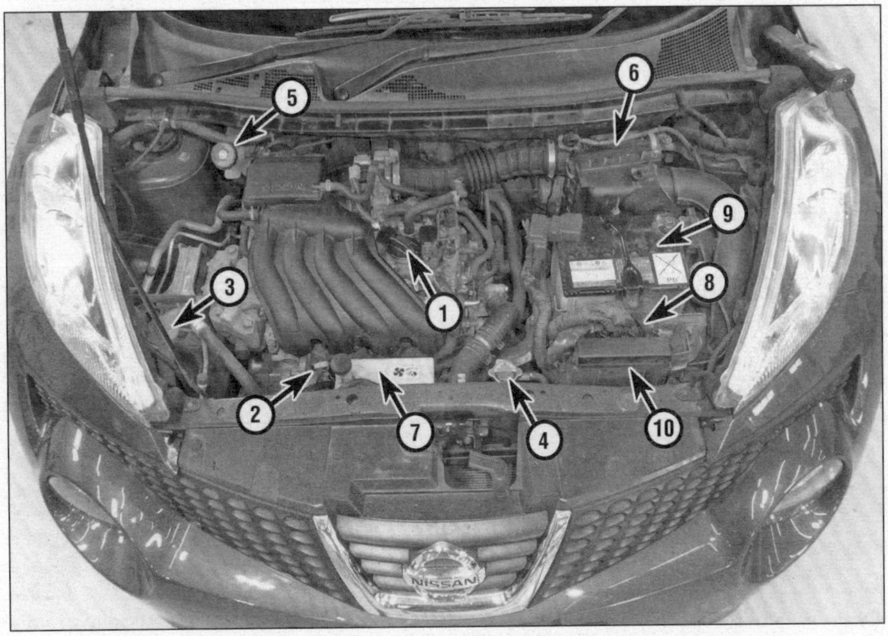

3 General Information

1 This Chapter is designed to help the home mechanic maintain his/her vehicle for safety, economy, long life and peak performance.
2 The Chapter contains a master maintenance schedule, followed by sections dealing specifically with each task on the schedule. Visual checks, adjustments, component renewal and other helpful items are included. Refer to the accompanying illustrations of the engine compartment and the underside of the vehicle for the locations of the various components.
3 Servicing of your vehicle in accordance with the mileage/time maintenance schedule and the following sections will provide a planned maintenance programme, which should result in a long and reliable service life. This is a comprehensive plan, so maintaining some items but not others at the specified service intervals, will not produce the same results.
4 As you service your vehicle, you will discover that many of the procedures can – and should – be grouped together, because of the particular procedure being performed, or because of the close proximity of two otherwise-unrelated components to one another. For example, if the vehicle is raised for any reason, the exhaust can be inspected at the same time as the suspension and steering components.
5 The first step in this maintenance programme is to prepare you before the actual work begins. Read through all the sections relevant to the work to be carried out, then make a list and gather all the parts and tools required. If a problem is encountered, seek advice from a parts specialist, or a dealer service department.

4 Regular maintenance

1 If, from the time the vehicle is new, the routine maintenance schedule is followed closely, and frequent checks are made of fluid levels and high-wear items, as suggested throughout this manual, the engine will be kept in relatively good running condition, and the need for additional work will be minimised.
2 It is possible that there will be times when the engine is running poorly, due to lack of regular maintenance. This is even more likely if a used vehicle, which has not received regular and frequent maintenance checks, is purchased. In such cases, additional work may need to be carried out, outside of the regular maintenance intervals.
3 If engine wear is suspected, a compression test will provide valuable information regarding the overall performance of the main internal components. Such a test can be used as a basis to decide on the extent of the work to be carried out. If for example a compression test indicates serious internal engine wear, conventional maintenance as described in this Chapter will not greatly improve the performance of the engine, and may prove a waste of time and money, unless extensive overhaul work (Chapter 2D) is carried out first.
4 The following series of operations are those most often required to improve the performance of a generally poor-running engine:

Primary operations

a) Check all the engine-related fluids (See Weekly checks in Chapter 0, Section 5).
b) Check the condition of all hoses, and check for fluid leaks (Section 6).
c) Clean, inspect and test the battery (See Weekly checks in Chapter 0, Section 5 and Chapter 5A, Section 2).
d) Renew the spark plugs (Section 26).
e) Check the condition and tension of the auxiliary drivebelts (Section 12).
f) Check the condition of the air filter, and renew if necessary (Section 24).

5 If the above operations do not prove fully effective, carry out the following secondary operations:

Secondary operations

6 All items listed under Primary operations, plus the following:
a) Check the charging system (Chapter 5A).
b) Check the ignition system (Chapter 5B).
c) Check the fuel, exhaust and emission control systems (Chapter 4A or Chapter 4C).

5 Engine oil and filter renewal

1 Frequent oil and filter changes are the most important preventative maintenance procedures that can be undertaken by the DIY owner. As engine oil ages, it becomes diluted and contaminated, which leads to premature engine wear.
2 Before starting this procedure, gather together all the necessary tools and materials. Also make sure that you have plenty of clean rags and newspapers handy, to mop-up any spills. Ideally, the engine oil should be warm, as it will drain more easily, and more built-up sludge will be removed with it.
3 Take care not to touch the exhaust or any other hot parts of the engine when working under the vehicle. To avoid any possibility of scalding, and to protect yourself from possible skin irritants and other harmful contaminants in used engine oils, it is advisable to wear gloves when carrying out this work.
4 Access to the underside of the vehicle will be greatly improved if it can be raised on a lift, driven onto ramps, or jacked up and supported on axle stands (see *Jacking and vehicle support*). Whichever method is chosen, make sure that the vehicle remains level, or if it is at an angle, that the drain plug is at the lowest point. The drain plug is located at the rear of the sump **(see illustration)**.
5 Remove the oil filler cap from the cylinder head cover (twist it anti-clockwise and withdraw it).
6 Using a spanner, or a suitable socket and bar, slacken the drain plug about half a turn. Position the draining container under the drain plug, and then remove the plug completely **(see illustrations)**. If possible, try to keep the plug pressed into the sump while unscrewing it by hand the last couple of turns.
7 Allow some time for the oil to drain, noting that it may be necessary to reposition the container as the oil flow slows to a trickle.
8 After all the oil has drained; wipe the drain plug with a clean rag. Remove the old sealing washer from the drain plug and fit a new one. Clean the area around the drain plug

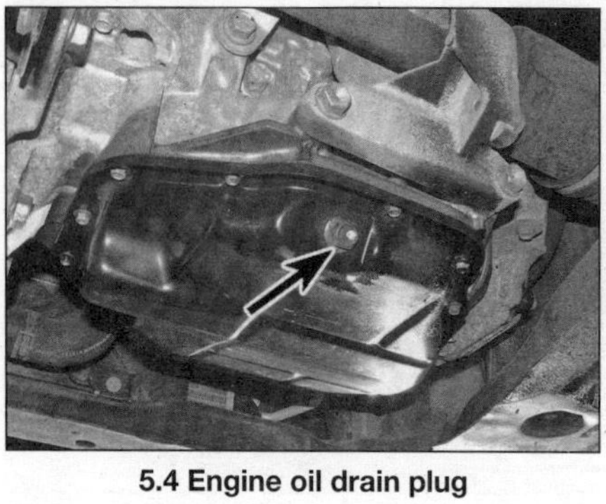

5.4 Engine oil drain plug

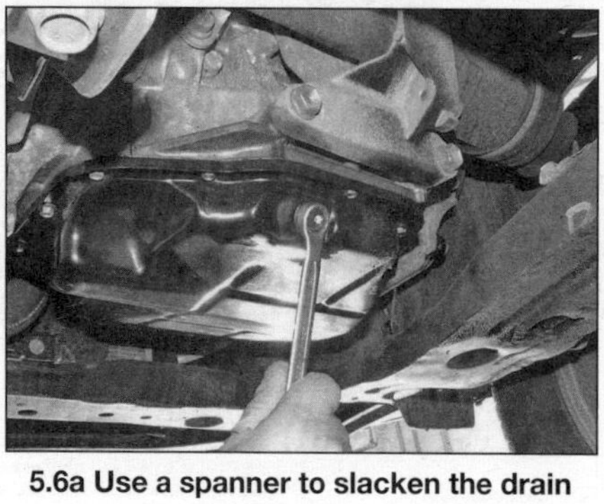

5.6a Use a spanner to slacken the drain plug...

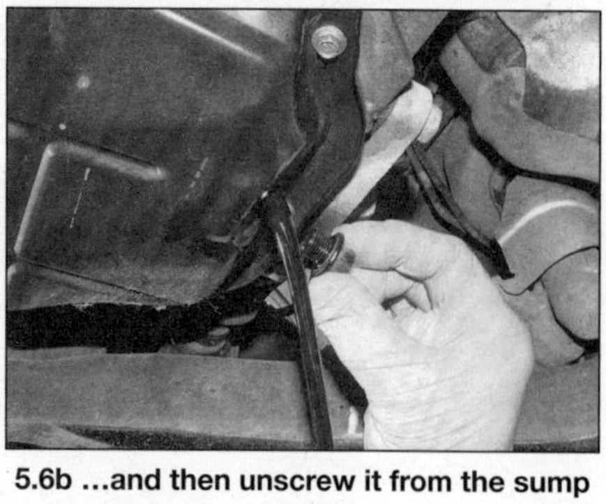

5.6b ...and then unscrew it from the sump

5.8 Fit a new sealing washer to the drain plug

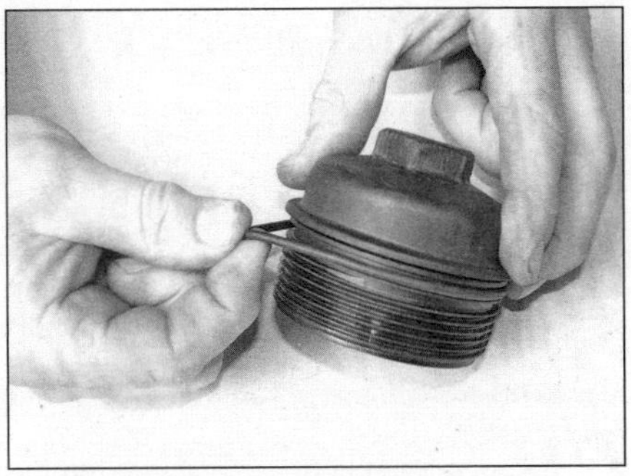

5.10 Renew the filter cap O-ring seal

5.12 Oil filter location on the front of the engine

opening, and refit the plug complete with the new sealing washer **(see illustration)**. Tighten the drain plug securely – preferably to the specified torque, using a torque wrench.

1.2 litre engines

9 On 1.2 litre engines, the oil filter is located in the upper alloy sump housing underneath the engine. Move the container into position under the oil filter to catch the oil spillage, then using a suitable socket, unscrew the oil filter cap and remove it from the engine. Pull out the old filter and wipe clean the inside of the housing and cap.

10 Remove the O-ring from the oil filter cap and locate the new O-ring in position **(see illustration)**. Lubricate the O-ring and the threads of the cap with a little clean engine oil.

11 Fit the new filter element to the housing/cap then screw the cap back into position. Tighten the cap to the specified torque.

1.6 litre engines

12 On 1.6 litre engines, the oil filter is located at the front of the cylinder block – access is most easily obtained from underneath the vehicle **(see illustration)**.

13 Move the container into position under the oil filter to catch the oil spillage.

14 Use an oil filter removal tool (if required) to slacken the filter initially, then unscrew it by hand the rest of the way **(see illustration)**. Be prepared for some oil spillage as the filter is removed. Empty the oil from the old filter into the container, before disposal.

15 Use a clean rag to remove all oil, dirt and sludge from the filter sealing area on the engine cylinder block. Check the old filter to make sure that the rubber sealing ring has not stuck to the engine. If it has, carefully remove it.

16 Apply a light coating of clean engine oil to the sealing ring on the new filter, and then screw the filter into position on the engine **(see illustrations)**. Lightly tighten the filter until its sealing ring contacts the block, and then tighten it through a further two-thirds of a turn. Tighten the filter firmly by hand only – do not use any tools.

All engines

17 Remove the old oil and all tools from under the vehicle then lower the vehicle to the ground.

18 Fill the engine through the oil filler hole in the cylinder head cover, using the correct grade and type of oil (see *Weekly checks*). Pour in half the specified quantity of oil first, and then wait a few minutes for the oil to drain into the sump. Continue to add oil, a small quantity at a time, until the level is up to the lower mark on the dipstick. Adding a further 1.0 litre will bring the level up to the upper mark on the dipstick. Refit the oil filler cap when correct level is achieved.

19 Start the engine and run it for a few minutes, while checking for leaks around the oil filter seal and the sump drain plug. Note that there may be a delay of a few seconds before the low oil pressure warning light goes out when the engine is first started, as the oil circulates through the new oil filter and the engine oil galleries before the pressure builds-up. Do not run the engine above idle speed while the warning light is on.

20 Stop the engine, and wait a few minutes for the oil to settle in the sump once more. With the new oil circulated and the filter now completely full, recheck the level on the dipstick, and add more oil as necessary.

21 Dispose of the used engine oil and filter safely, referring to *General repair procedures* on page REF•8. Do not discard the old filter with domestic household waste. The provision for waste oil disposal provided by many local council recycling facilities generally has a filter receptacle alongside.

6 Hose and fluid leak check

1 Visually inspect the engine joint faces, gaskets and seals for any signs of water or oil leaks. Pay particular attention to the areas around the cylinder head cover, cylinder head, oil filter and sump joint faces. Over a period of time, some very slight seepage from these areas is to be expected – what you are really looking for is any indication of a serious leak. Should a leak be found, renew the offending gasket or oil seal by referring to the appropriate Chapters in this manual.

2 Also check the security and condition of all the engine-related pipes and hoses. Ensure

5.14 Slackening the oil filter with a removal tool

5.16a Apply clean oil to the seal...

5.16b ...and then fit the new oil filter

that all cable ties or securing clips are in place and in good condition. Clips, which are broken or missing, can lead to chafing of the hoses pipes or wiring which could cause more serious problems in the future.

3 Carefully check the radiator hoses and heater hoses along their entire length. Renew any hose, which is cracked, swollen or deteriorated. Cracks will show up better if the hose is squeezed. Pay close attention to the hose clips that secures the hoses to the cooling system components. Hose clips can pinch and puncture hoses, resulting in cooling system leaks. If the crimped-type hose clips are used, it may be a good idea to fit standard worm-drive clips.

4 Inspect all the cooling system components (hoses, joint faces, etc) for leaks. Where any problems of this nature are found on system components, renew the component or gasket with reference to Chapter 3.

5 With the vehicle raised, inspect the petrol tank and filler neck for punctures, cracks and other damage. The connection between the filler neck and tank is especially critical. Sometimes a rubber filler neck or connecting hose will leak due to loose retaining clamps or deteriorated rubber.

6 Carefully check all rubber hoses and metal fuel lines leading away from the petrol tank. Check for loose connections, deteriorated hoses, crimped lines and other damage. Pay particular attention to the vent pipes and hoses, which often loop up around the filler neck and can become blocked or crimped. Follow the lines to the front of the vehicle, carefully inspecting them all the way. Renew damaged sections as necessary.

7 Check the condition of all brake fluid hoses.

8 From within the engine compartment, check the security of all fuel hose attachments and pipe unions, and inspect the fuel hoses and vacuum hoses for kinks, chafing and deterioration.

7 Brake pad condition check – front and rear

Front brake pads

1 Firmly apply the handbrake, and then jack up the front of the vehicle and support it securely on axle stands (see *Jacking and vehicle support*). Remove the front roadwheels.

2 If any pad's friction material is worn to the specified thickness or less; all four pads must be renewed as a set(see Haynes Hint).

Note: *If any pad is approaching the minimum thickness, consider renewal as a precautionary measure in case the pads wear out before the next service.*

HINT:

3 For a comprehensive check, the brake pads should be removed and cleaned. This will permit the operation of the caliper to be checked, and the condition of the brake disc itself to be fully examined on both sides. Refer to Chapter 9, Section 4 for further information.

Rear brake pads

4 Chock the front wheels then jack up the rear of the vehicle and support it securely on axle stands (see *Jacking and vehicle support*). Remove the rear roadwheels.

5 Proceed as described for the front brake pads in paragraphs 2 and 3.

8 Handbrake check and adjustment

Check

1 The handbrake should be capable of holding the parked vehicle stationary, even on steep slopes, when applied with moderate force. The mechanism should be firm and positive in feel, with no trace of stiffness or sponginess from the cables, and the mechanism should release immediately the handbrake lever is released. If the mechanism does not operate satisfactorily, it should be checked immediately.

2 To check the operation of the handbrake, chock the front wheels then jack up the rear of the vehicle and support it securely on axle stands (see *Jacking and vehicle support*).

3 Fully release the handbrake, and check that the rear road wheels can be rotated by hand – slight dragging is acceptable, but it should be possible to turn each wheel easily without undue force.

4 Operate the handbrake lever up and down approximately 10 times, to establish the correct shoe-to-drum clearance.

5 With the handbrake lever released, again, check that the rear road wheels can still be rotated.

6 Apply normal moderate pressure to operate the handbrake lever, and count the number of clicks necessary to bring the lever to the fully applied position, (this should be approx. 9 to 10 clicks). Check that the road wheels are locked with the lever fully applied.

Adjustment

7 If the number of clicks required to fully apply the handbrake is not as specified, proceed as follows.

8 Working inside the vehicle, unclip the plastic trim surrounding the handbrake lever, from the top of the centre console.

9 The handbrake cable adjustment nut can now be accessed through the top of the centre console. Measure the length of thread, protruding through the nut, as a guide for refitting **(see illustration)**. Slacken the adjustment nut until it is at the end of the threaded part of the cable.

10 If not already done, chock the front wheels then jack up the rear of the vehicle

HAYNES HiNT

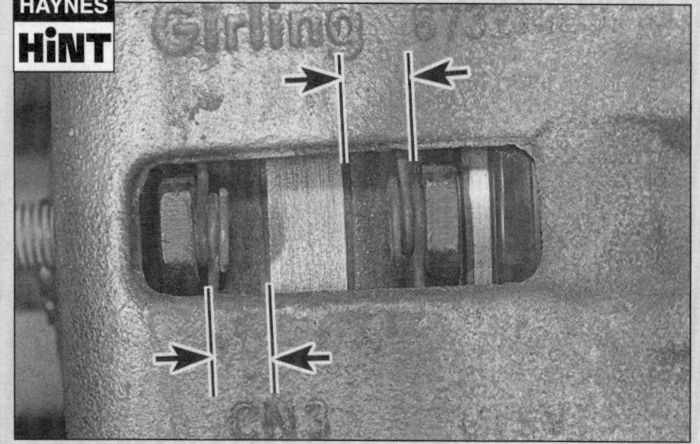

For a quick check, the thickness of friction material remaining on each brake pad can be measured through the aperture in the caliper body.

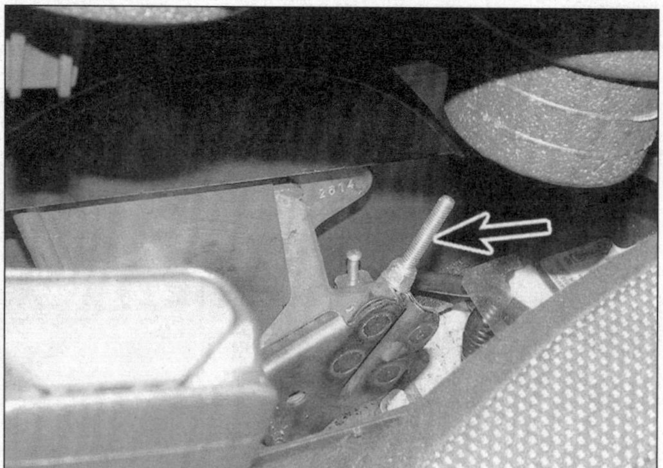

8.9 Measure the length of thread, before slackening the adjusting nut

8.11a Remove the rubber grommet...

8.11b ...and turn the adjuster...

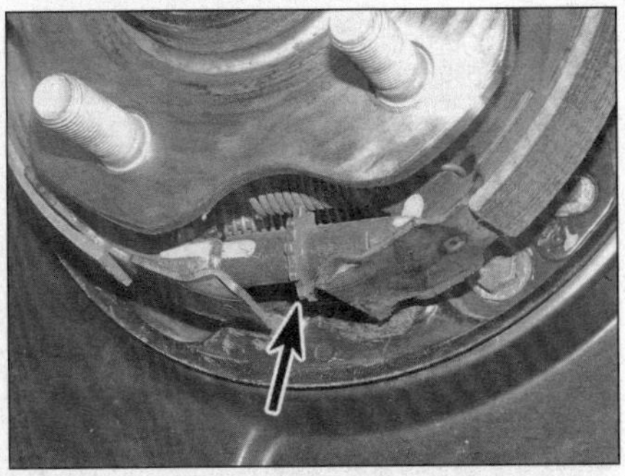

8.11c ...between the lower part of the brake shoes

and support it securely on axle stands (see *Jacking and vehicle support*). Remove the rear road wheels.

11 Working on each side at a time, adjust the shoe positions as follows. Turn the rear disc until the access hole is positioned over the adjuster serrations. Using a screwdriver through the hole in the brake disc, tighten the adjuster until the brake disc cannot be rotated, then back the adjuster off, so that the brake disc is free to turn without any drag **(see illustrations)**. Repeat the adjustment on the other side of the vehicle, and then refit the plug to the access holes in the brake disc.

12 Working inside the vehicle, tighten the adjuster nut on the end of the front handbrake cable, until the handbrake operates correctly at approximately 9 to 10 clicks.

13 When tightening the adjuster nut on the end of the front cable, make sure the two rear cables are still located in the equalizer bar, under the rear end of the centre console.

14 Check that the handbrake 'on' warning light illuminates after the first click.

15 Refit the plastic trim to the centre console and check the handbrake operation as described previously in this Section.

16 If this adjustment cannot be achieved, check the condition of the handbrake shoes as described in Chapter 9, Section 6.

17 On completion, refit the road wheels, and then lower the vehicle to the ground.

9 Clutch operation check

1 Check that the clutch pedal moves smoothly and easily through its full travel. Check the hydraulic system for leaks; check also that the clutch itself functions correctly, with no trace of slip or drag. If excessive effort is required to operate the clutch, check the pedal assembly to ensure that its pivot is properly greased. Refer to Chapter 6 for further information.

10 Air conditioning system check

Note: *Before proceeding, refer to the precautions given in Chapter 3, Section 10, regarding work on the air conditioning system.*

1 Check the tension and condition of the auxiliary drivebelt, which drives the air conditioning compressor, as described in Section 12.

2 Check the condition of the condenser fins, and clean them out if necessary (remove the front bumper/grille panel for access). Clean any dirt and insects from the fins using compressed air, or a soft brush. Be careful not to damage the condenser.

3 Operate the air conditioning system for at least 10 minutes each month, even during cold weather, to keep the seals, etc, in good condition.

4 Regularly inspect the refrigerant pipes, hoses and unions for security and condition.

5 The most common cause of poor cooling is simply a low system refrigerant charge. If a noticeable drop in cool air output occurs, one of the following checks will help to determine if the refrigerant level is low.

6 Warm up the engine to normal operating temperature.

7 Move the temperature control knob to the coldest setting, and move the blower motor control knob to the highest setting. Open the doors (to ensure that the air conditioning system does not shut off as soon as it cools the passenger compartment).

8 With the compressor engaged – the compressor clutch will make an audible click, and the centre of the clutch will rotate – On some models, there is a sight glass in the top of the receiver/drier bottle, if air bubbles are present in the sight glass, or the refrigerant looks foamy, the charge is low.

9 If no sight glass is fitted, feel the inlet and outlet pipes at the compressor. One side should be cold, and the other hot. If there is no perceptible difference in temperature between the two pipes, this indicates a fault with the compressor, a low refrigerant charge, or some other system fault – consult a Nissan dealer or air conditioning specialist for advice.

10 The air conditioning system will lose a proportion of its charge through normal seepage – so it is as well to regard periodic recharging as a maintenance operation. Recharging must be done by a Nissan dealer or an air conditioning specialist.

11 Do Not under any circumstances attempt to open any of the refrigerant lines, or renew any of the components, until the system has been evacuated of its refrigerant, as it is potentially dangerous (see Chapter 3, Section 10).

11 Emissions control systems check

1 Details of the emissions control system components and testing are given in Chapter 4C, Section 2.

2 Checking consists simply of a visual check for obvious signs of damaged or leaking hoses and joints.

12 Auxiliary drivebelt checking and renewal

Checking drivebelt condition

1 Firmly apply the handbrake, and then jack up the front of the vehicle and support it securely on axle stands (see *Jacking and vehicle support*). Remove the right-hand front roadwheel.

2 Remove the wheel arch liner on the right-hand side as described in Chapter 11, Section 21.

3 Using a suitable socket and extension bar fitted to the crankshaft pulley bolt, rotate the crankshaft so that the entire length of the drivebelts can be examined. Examine the drivebelts for cracks, splitting, fraying or damage. Check also for signs of glazing (shiny patches) and for separation of the belt plies

12.3 Check for drivebelt wear

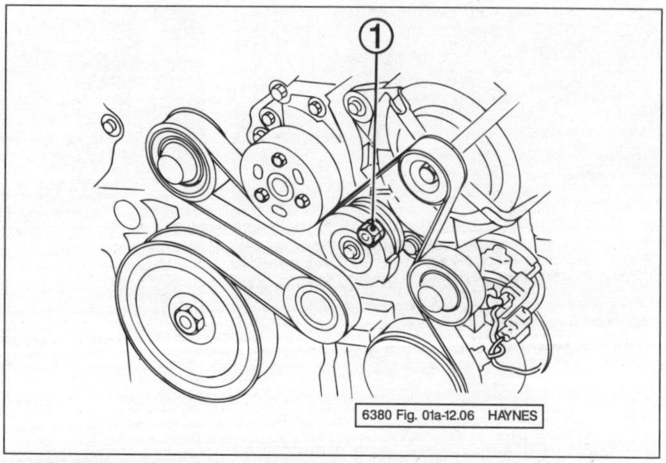

12.6 Turn the drivebelt tensioner (1) clockwise to release the tension on the belt

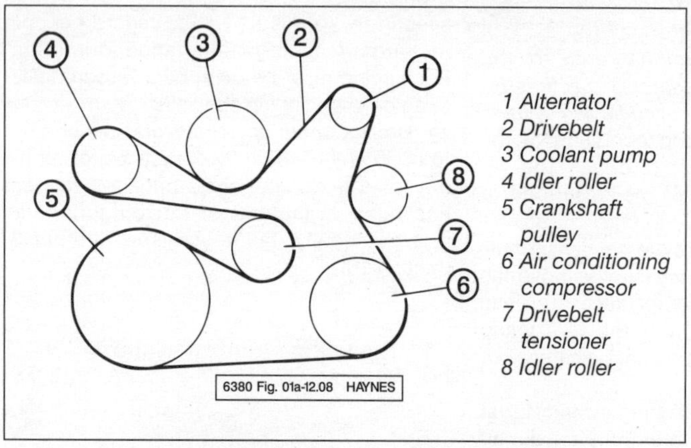

12.8 Auxilliary drivebelt routing (1.2 litre engines)

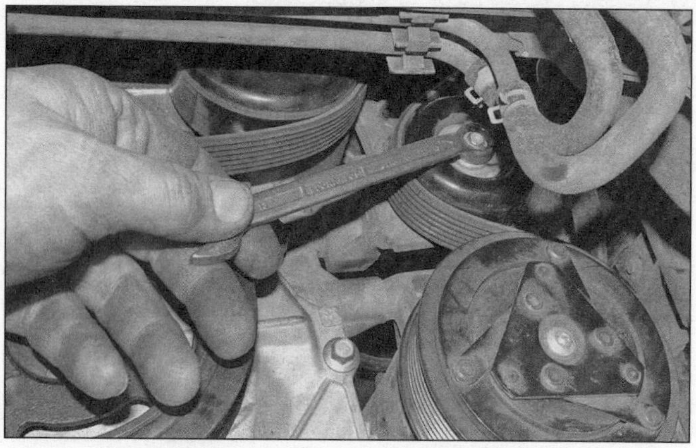

12.11 Slacken the tensioner pulley securing nut

(see illustration). Renew the belt if worn or damaged.

4 If the condition of the belt is satisfactory, check the drivebelt tension as described below under the relevant sub-heading.

1.2 litre engines

Removal

5 If not already done, proceed as described in paragraphs 1 and 2.

6 Working under the right-hand front wheel arch, release the tension on the belt by turning the tensioner clockwise (as viewed from the right-hand side of the car) using a 16 mm spanner or socket **(see illustration)**.

7 Hold the tensioner in the released position, slip the belt off the pulleys, then release the tensioner. If the belt is to be re-used mark the direction of rotation on the belt.

Refitting

8 Fit the belt around the pulleys, then turn the tensioner clockwise again and slip the belt over the tensioner roller **(see illustration)**. Carefully release the pressure and the spring loaded tensioner will move anti-clockwise so the belt will automatically become tensioned.

9 Refit the wheel arch liner as described in Chapter 11, Section 21, then refit the roadwheel and lower the vehicle to the ground. Tighten the road wheels to the specified torque setting.

1.6 litre engines

Removal

10 If not already done, proceed as described in paragraphs 1 and 2.

11 Working under the right-hand front wheel arch, slacken the nut securing the tensioner pulley to the mounting bracket, by a quarter of a turn **(see illustration)**. This nut does not require slackening too much, or it will cause the tensioner pulley to twist, and then it will prevent the belt from being adjusted correctly on refitting.

12 Rotate the adjuster bolt to slacken the tensioner pulley, until there is sufficient slack for the drivebelt to be removed from the pulleys **(see illustrations)**. If the belt is to be

12.12a Slacken the tensioner pulley adjusting bolt...

12.12b ...and remove the auxiliary drivebelt

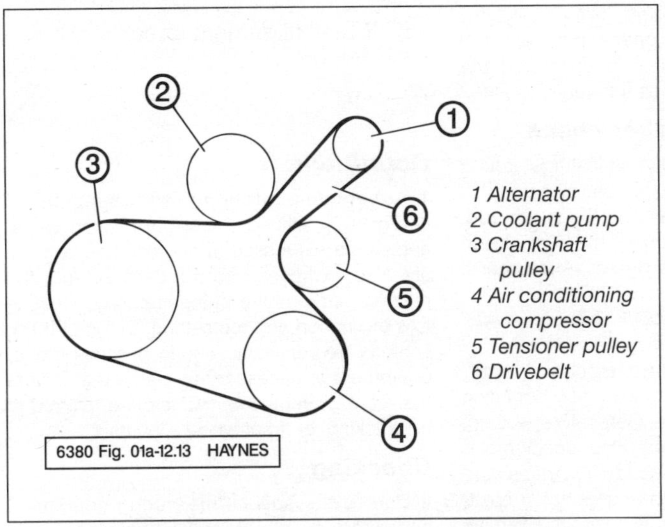

12.13 Auxiliary drivebelt routing (1.6 litre engines)

12.16 Check the deflection of the drive belt

re-used mark the direction of rotation on the belt.

Refitting

13 Fit the belt around the pulleys **(see illustration)**, then take up the slack in the belt by tightening the adjuster bolt. If the belt is new, ensure that the belt is of the correct type and length.

14 Correct tensioning of the drivebelt will ensure that it has a long life. Beware, however, of over tightening, as this can cause wear in the bearings.

15 The belt tension is checked at the mid-point between the pulleys on the lower belt run. Referring to the Specifications given at the start of this Chapter, apply the specified force and check that the belt deflection is within the specified range.

16 To adjust the tension, rotate the adjuster bolt until the correct tension is achieved **(see illustration)**, see specifications at the beginning of this Chapter. Make sure the nut securing the tensioner pulley is tightened to the Stage 1 (adjustment position), as described in the torque settings at the beginning of this Chapter. If this is not done, then the tensioner pulley could twist and prevent the belt from being adjusted correctly.

17 Once the belt is correctly tensioned, rotate the crankshaft a couple of times and recheck the tension.

18 When all is correct, tighten the tensioner pulley retaining nut to its Stage 2, specified torque setting.

19 Refit the wheel arch liner and roadwheel then lower the vehicle to the ground. Tighten the roadwheel nuts to the specified torque setting.

13 Steering and suspension check

Front suspension and steering

1 Firmly apply the handbrake, and then jack up the front of the vehicle and support it securely on axle stands (see *Jacking and vehicle support*).

2 Visually inspect the balljoint dust covers and the steering rack and pinion gaiters for splits, chafing or deterioration **(see illustrations)**. Any wear of these components will cause loss of lubricant, together with dirt and water entry, resulting in rapid deterioration of the balljoints or steering gear.

3 Grasp the roadwheel at the 12 o'clock and 6 o'clock positions, and try to rock it **(see illustration)**. Very slight free play may be felt, but if the movement is appreciable, further investigation is necessary to determine the source. Continue rocking the wheel while an assistant depresses the footbrake. If the movement is now eliminated or significantly

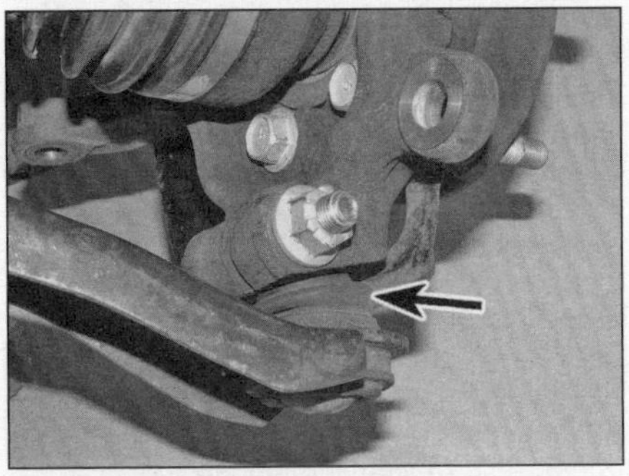

13.2a Check the ball joint dust covers...

13.2b ...the steering rack gaiters...

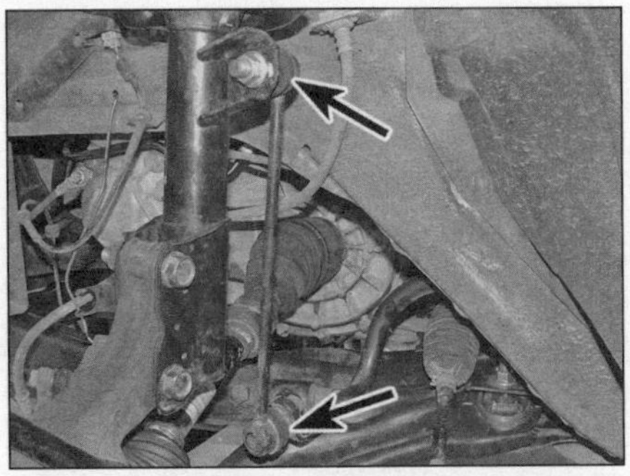

13.2c ...and the anti-roll bar drop link ball joint dust covers

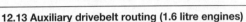

13.3 Check for wear in the hub bearings by grasping the wheel and trying to rock it

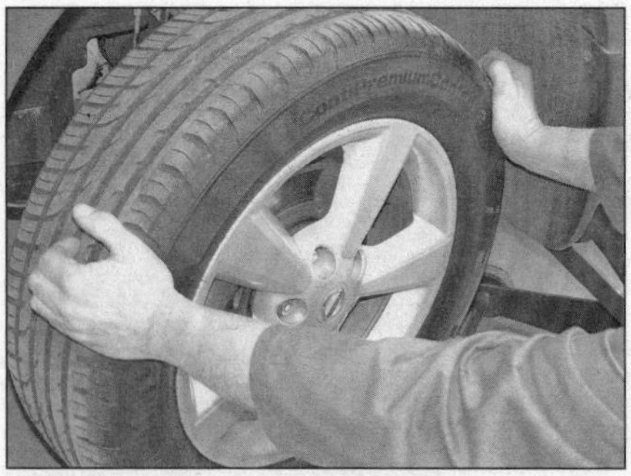

13.4 Check for wear in the steering rack or ball joints by grasping the wheel and trying to rock it

reduced, it is likely that the hub bearings are at fault. If the free play is still evident with the footbrake depressed, then there is wear in the suspension joints or mountings.

4 Now grasp the wheel at the 9 o'clock and 3 o'clock positions, and try to rock it as before **(see illustration)**. Any movement felt now may again be caused by wear in the hub bearings or the steering track rod balljoints. If the inner or outer balljoint is worn, the visual movement will be obvious.

5 Using a large screwdriver or flat bar, check for wear in the suspension mounting bushes by levering between the relevant suspension component and its attachment point. Some movement is to be expected as the mountings are made of rubber, but excessive wear should be obvious. Also check the condition of any visible rubber bushes, looking for splits, cracks or contamination of the rubber.

6 With the car standing on its wheels, have an assistant turn the steering wheel back-and-forth about an eighth of a turn each way. There should be very little, if any, lost movement between the steering wheel and roadwheels. If this is not the case, closely observe the joints and mountings previously described, but in addition check the steering column universal joints for wear, and also check the rack-and-pinion steering gear itself.

Rear suspension

7 Chock the front wheels, then jack up the rear of the vehicle and support securely on axle stands (see *Jacking and vehicle support*).

8 Working as described previously for the front suspension, check the rear hub bearings, the suspension bushes and the shock absorber mountings for wear.

Strut/shock absorber check

9 Check for any signs of fluid leakage around the suspension strut/shock absorber body, or from the rubber gaiter around the piston rod. Should any fluid be noticed, the suspension strut/shock absorber is defective internally, and should be renewed.

Note: *Suspension struts/shock absorbers should always be renewed in pairs on the same axle.*

10 The efficiency of the suspension strut/shock absorber may be checked by bouncing the vehicle at each corner. Generally speaking, the body will return to its normal position and stop after being depressed. If it rises and returns on a rebound, the suspension strut/shock absorber is probably suspect. Examine the suspension strut/shock absorber upper and lower mountings for any signs of wear.

14 Driveshaft gaiter check

1 With the vehicle raised and securely supported on stands (see *Jacking and vehicle support*), turn the steering onto full lock, then slowly rotate the roadwheel. Inspect the condition of the outer constant velocity (CV) joint rubber gaiters, squeezing the gaiters to open out the folds **(see illustration)**. Check for signs of cracking, splits or deterioration of the rubber, which may allow the grease to escape, and lead to water and grit entry into the joint. Also check the security and condition of the retaining clips. Repeat these checks on the inner CV joints. If any damage or deterioration is found, the gaiters should be renewed as described in Chapter 8, Section 3.

2 At the same time, check the general condition of the CV joints themselves by first holding the driveshaft and attempting to rotate the wheel. Repeat this check by holding the inner joint and attempting to rotate the driveshaft. Any appreciable movement indicates wear in the joints, wear in the driveshaft splines, or a loose driveshaft retaining nut.

15 Wheel alignment check

Definitions

1 A vehicle's steering and suspension geometry is defined in four basic settings – all angles are expressed in degrees (toe settings are also expressed as a measurement); the relevant settings are camber, castor, steering axis inclination and toe setting. Some of these settings are adjustable, and in all cases special equipment is necessary to check them. Note that front wheel toe setting is often referred to as 'tracking' or 'front wheel alignment'.

Checking

2 Due to the special measuring equipment necessary to check the wheel alignment, and the skill required to use it properly, the checking and adjustment of these settings is best left to a Nissan dealer or similar expert. Note that most tyre-fitting shops now possess sophisticated checking equipment.

16 Exhaust system check

1 With the engine cold (at least an hour after the vehicle has been driven), check the complete exhaust system from the engine to the end of the tailpipe. The exhaust system is most easily checked with the vehicle raised on a hoist, or suitably supported on axle stands, so that the exhaust components are readily visible and accessible.

2 Check the exhaust pipes and connections for evidence of leaks, severe corrosion and damage. Make sure that all brackets and mountings are in good condition, and that all relevant nuts and bolts are tight **(see illustration)**. Leakage at any of the joints or in other parts of the system will usually show up as a black sooty stain in the vicinity of the leak.

3 Rattles and other noises can often be traced to the exhaust system, especially the brackets and mountings **(see illustration)**. Try to move

14.1 Check the driveshaft rubber gaiters

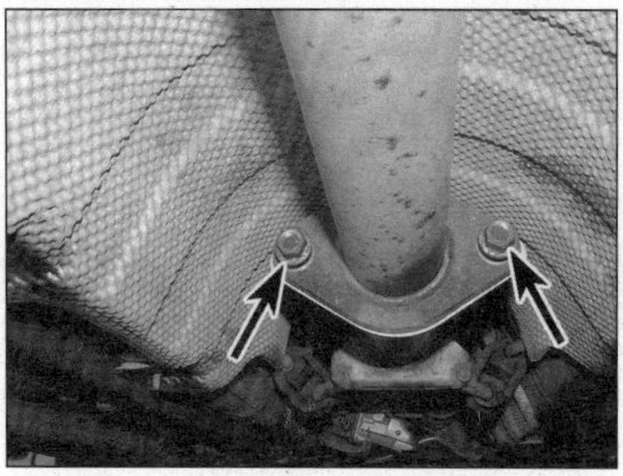

16.2 Check the exhaust system securing bolts

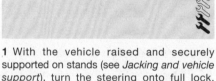

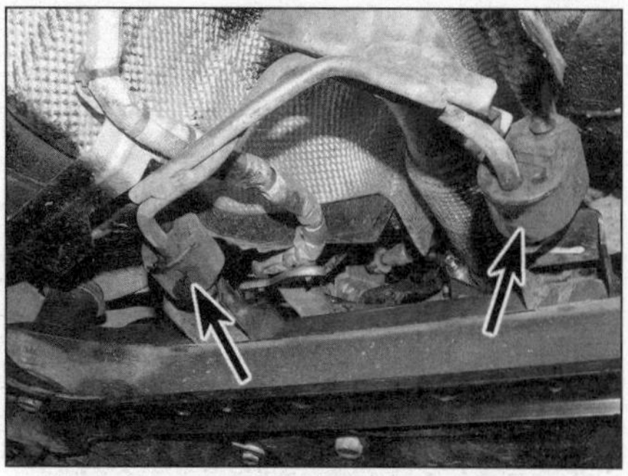

16.3 Check the exhaust system rubber mountings

the pipes and silencers. If the components are able to come into contact with the body or suspension parts, secure the system with new mountings. Otherwise separate the joints (if possible) and twist the pipes as necessary to provide additional clearance.

17 Seat belt check

1 All models are fitted with three-point diagonal inertia reel seat belts for all seats.
2 Inspect the belts for signs of fraying or other damage. Also check the operation of the buckles and retractor mechanisms, and ensure that all mounting bolts are securely tightened. Note that the bolts are shouldered so that the belt anchor points are free to rotate.
3 If there is any sign of damage, or any doubt about the condition of a belt, it must be renewed. If the vehicle has been involved in a collision, any belts in use at the time should be renewed as a matter of course, and all other belts should be checked carefully.
4 Use only warm water and non-detergent soap to clean the belts. Never use any chemical cleaners, strong detergents, dyes or bleaches. Keep the belts fully extended until they have dried naturally – do not apply heat to dry them.

18 Electrical systems check

1 Check the operation of all electrical equipment, i.e. lights, direction indicators, horn, etc. Refer to the appropriate Sections of Chapter 12 for details if any of the circuits are found to be inoperative.
2 Note that stop-light switch adjustment is described in Chapter 9, Section 18.
3 Visually check all accessible wiring connectors, harnesses and retaining clips for security, and for signs of chafing or damage. Rectify any faults found.

19 Hinge and lock lubrication

1 Work around the vehicle, and lubricate the hinges of the bonnet, doors and tailgate or boot lid with a light machine oil.
2 Lightly lubricate the bonnet release mechanism and the exposed sections of the inner cable with a smear of grease. Similarly, lubricate the tailgate/fuel filler flap release mechanisms, where accessible.
3 Check carefully the security and operation of all hinges, latches and locks, adjusting them where required (see Chapter 11). Check the operation of the central locking system.
4 Check the condition and operation of the tailgate struts, renewing them if either is leaking or no longer able to support the tailgate securely when raised.

20 Manual transmission oil level check

1 Park the car on a level surface. The oil level must be checked before the car is driven, or at least 5 minutes after the engine has been switched off. If the oil is checked immediately after driving the car, some of the oil will remain distributed around the transmission components, resulting in an inaccurate level reading. To improve access, position the car over an inspection pit, or raise the car off the ground and position it on axle stands, (see *Jacking and vehicle support*) making sure the vehicle remains level to the ground.
2 Wipe clean the area around the filler/level plug, and unscrew it from the casing. On 5-speed transmissions the filler/level plug is situated on the front of the transmission and on 6-speed transmissions it is situated on the left-hand rear of the transmission unit, behind the driveshaft **(see illustrations)**.
3 The oil level should reach the lower edge of the filler/level hole. A certain amount of oil will have gathered behind the filler/level plug and will trickle out when it is removed; this does not necessarily indicate that the level is correct. To ensure that a true level is established, wait until the initial trickle has stopped, then add oil as necessary until a trickle of new oil can be seen emerging. The level will be correct when the flow ceases; use only good-quality oil of the specified type.
4 On 6-speed transmissions, remove the left-hand front road wheel for better access to the filler/level plug. Use a length of hose and a funnel to make topping up easier **(see illustrations)**.
5 Refilling the transmission is an extremely awkward operation; above all, allow plenty of time for the oil level to settle properly before checking it. If a large amount had to be added to the transmission and a large amount flows out on checking the level, refit the filler/level plug, and take the vehicle on a short journey. This will allow the new oil to be distributed fully around the transmission components. On returning, recheck the level when the oil has settled again.
6 If the transmission has been overfilled so that oil flows out as soon as the filler/level plug is removed, check that the car is completely level (front-to-rear and side-to-side). If necessary, allow the surplus to drain off into a suitable container.
7 When the level is correct, refit the filler/level plug, tightening it to the specified torque wrench setting. Wash off any spilt oil.

21 Road test

Instruments and electrical equipment

1 Check the operation of all instruments and electrical equipment.
2 Make sure that all instruments read correctly, and switch on all electrical equipment in turn to check that it functions properly.

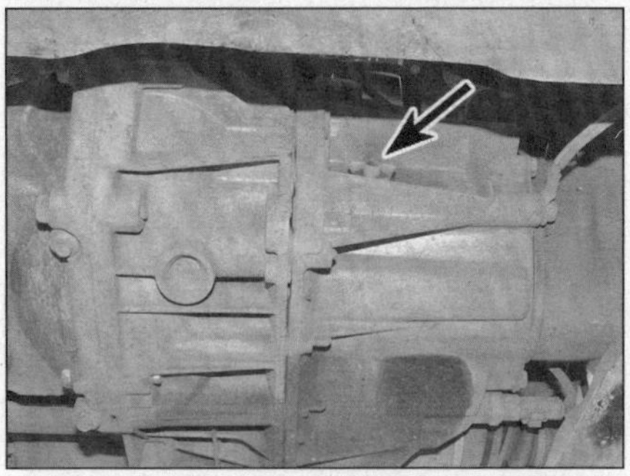

20.2a Transmission oil filler/level plug – 5-speed transmissions

20.2b Transmission oil filler/level plug – 6-speed transmissions

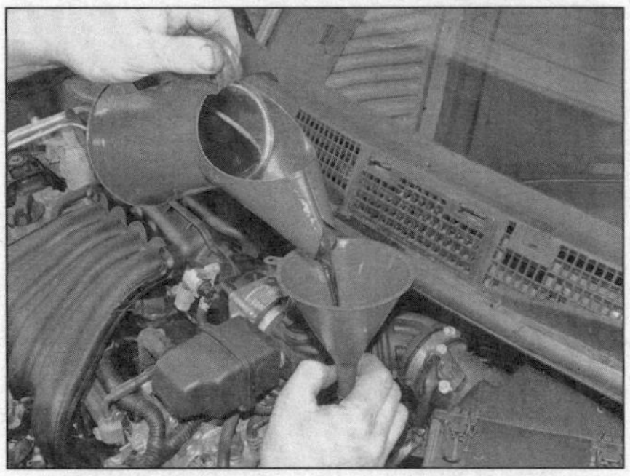

20.4a Using a funnel and hose...

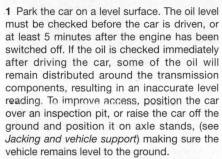

20.4b ...to fill up the transmission

Steering and suspension

3 Check for any abnormalities in the steering, suspension, handling or road feel.
4 Drive the vehicle, and check that there are no unusual vibrations or noises.
5 Check that the steering feels positive, with no excessive 'sloppiness', or roughness, and check for any suspension noises when cornering and driving over bumps.

Drivetrain

6 Check the performance of the engine, clutch, transmission and driveshafts.
7 Listen for any unusual noises from the engine, clutch and transmission.
8 Make sure that the engine runs smoothly when idling, and that there is no hesitation when accelerating.
9 Check that the clutch action is smooth and progressive, that the drive is taken up smoothly, and that the pedal travel is not excessive. Also listen for any noises when the clutch pedal is depressed.
10 Check that all gears can be engaged smoothly without noise, and that the gear lever action is smooth and not abnormally vague or 'notchy'.
11 Listen for a metallic clicking sound from the front of the vehicle as the vehicle is driven slowly in a circle with the steering on full lock. Carry out this check in both directions. If a clicking noise is heard, this indicates wear in a driveshaft joint; in which case the joint (or complete driveshaft) must be renewed see Chapter 8, Section 2.

Braking system

12 Make sure that the vehicle does not pull to one side when braking, and that the wheels do not lock when braking hard.
13 Check that there is no vibration through the steering when braking.
14 Check that the handbrake operates correctly without excessive movement of the lever, and that it holds the vehicle stationary on a slope.
15 Test the operation of the brake servo unit as follows. Depress the footbrake four or five times to exhaust the vacuum, and then start the engine. As the engine starts, there should be a noticeable 'give' in the brake pedal as vacuum builds-up. Allow the engine to run for at least two minutes and then switch it off. If the brake pedal is depressed again, it should be possible to detect a hiss from the servo as the pedal is depressed. After about four or five applications, no further hissing should be heard, and the pedal should feel considerably harder.

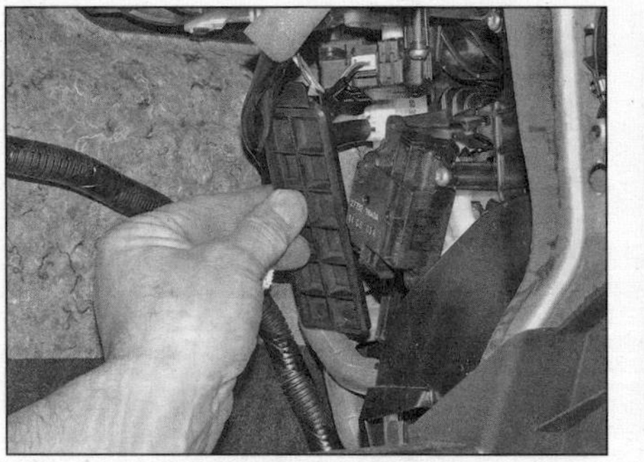

22.2 Unclip the filter cover

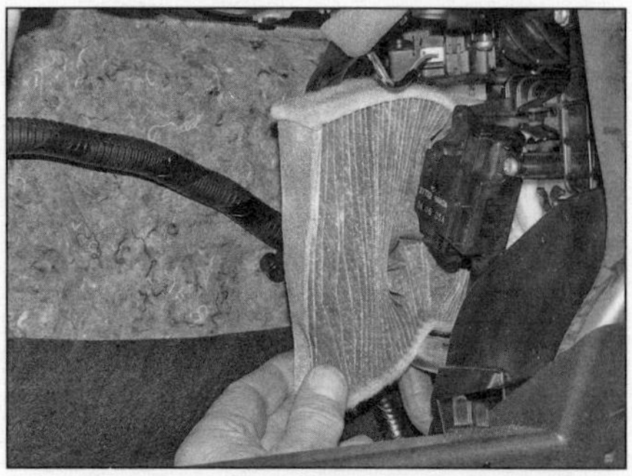

22.3 Withdraw the pollen filter from the housing

22 Pollen filter renewal

1 Remove the glovebox as described in Chapter 11, Section 26.
2 Working through the glovebox aperture, unclip the filter cover and remove it from the rear of the heater housing unit **(see illustration)**.
3 Withdraw the filter from the housing, then wipe clean the area around the filter location **(see illustration)**.
4 Fit the new filter to the housing, in the same way as it was removed, making sure it is fitted in the correct position, with the arrows facing towards the inside of the vehicle.
5 Refit the filter cover to the housing, then refit the glovebox.

23 Brake fluid renewal

Warning: Brake hydraulic fluid can harm your eyes and damage painted surfaces, so use extreme caution when handling and pouring it. Do not use fluid that has been standing open for some time, as it absorbs moisture from the air. Excess moisture content can cause a dangerous loss of braking effectiveness.
Caution: Switch off the ignition and disconnect the battery negative terminal (refer to battery disconnection and reconnection in Chapter 5A, Section 3), before carrying out the bleeding procedure.
1 The procedure is similar to that for the bleeding of the hydraulic system as described in Chapter 9, Section 2. The brake fluid reservoir should be emptied by syphoning, using a clean poultry baster or similar before starting, then refilled with fresh fluid. Allowance should be made for the old fluid to be expelled when bleeding a section of the circuit.
2 Working as described in Chapter 9, Section 2, open the first bleed screw in the sequence and pump the brake pedal gently until nearly all the fluid has been emptied from the master cylinder reservoir.
3 Top-up to the MAX level with more fresh fluid, and continue pumping until new fluid can be seen emerging from the bleed screw. Tighten the screw and top the reservoir level up to the MAX level line **(see illustration)**.
4 Work through all the remaining bleed screws in the sequence until new fluid can be seen at all of them **(see illustration)**. Be careful to keep the master cylinder reservoir topped-up to above the MIN level at all times, or air may enter the system and greatly increase the length of the task.
5 When the operation is complete, check that all bleed screws are securely tightened, and that their dust caps are refitted **(see illustration)**. Wash off all traces of spilt fluid,

23.3 Topping-up the brake fluid

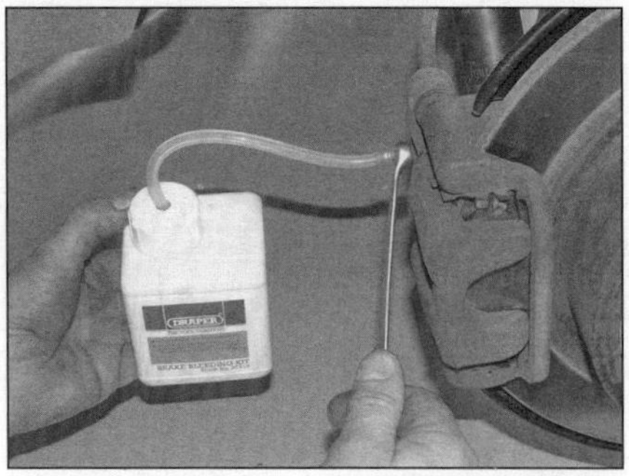

23.4 Using a brake bleeding bottle

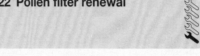

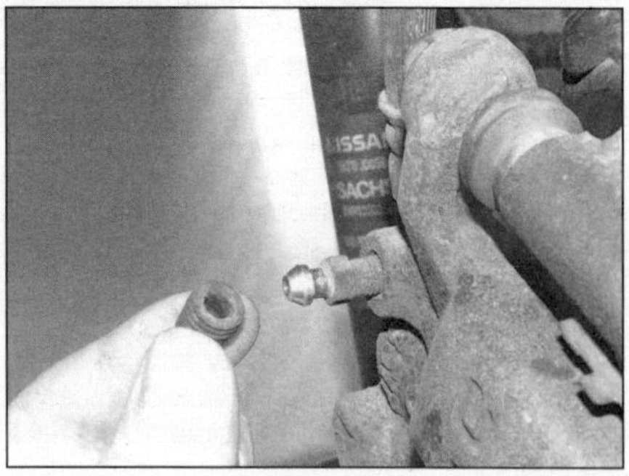

23.5 Make sure all bleed screws are fitted with dust caps

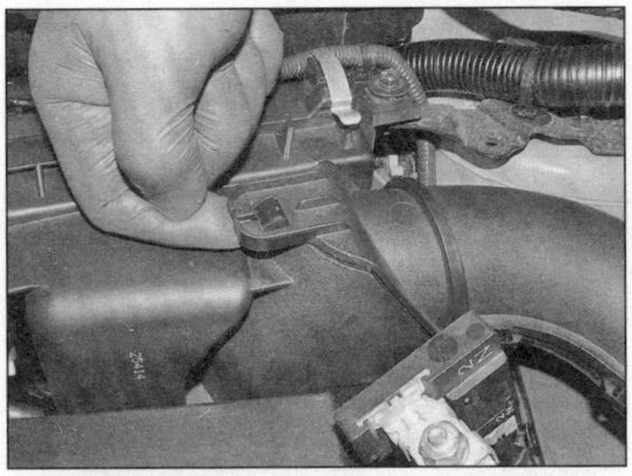

24.2 Disengage the upper inlet air duct from the air cleaner filter housing

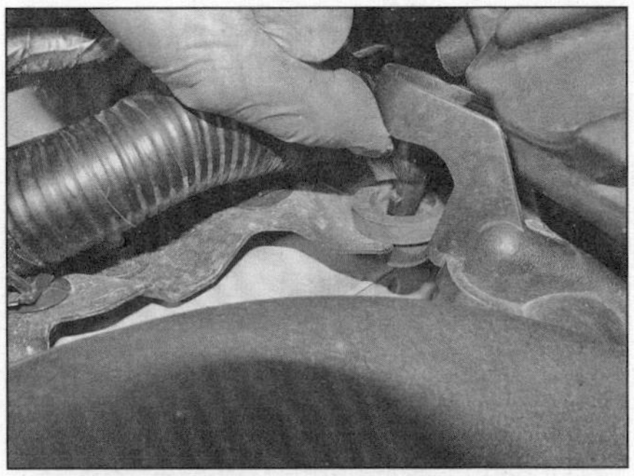

24.3a Disengage the lower mounting peg from the grommet...

24.3b ...and remove the inlet air duct

and recheck the master cylinder reservoir fluid level.

6 Check the operation of the brakes before taking the car on the road.

7 Dispose safely of the used brake fluid with reference to *General repair procedures* on page REF•8.

24 Air filter element renewal

1 The air filter is situated in the air cleaner housing at the left-hand rear of the engine compartment.

2 Lift up the tab and disengage the upper inlet air duct from the air cleaner filter housing **(see illustration)**.

3 Lift the inlet air duct upward to disengage the lower mounting peg from the grommet, and remove the duct from the engine compartment **(see illustrations)**.

4 Release the two retaining clips and separate the air cleaner filter housing from the air cleaner case **(see illustrations)**.

5 Lift the old air filter element out of the filter housing, noting which way round it is fitted **(see illustration)**.

6 Wipe the inside of the air cleaner filter housing and air cleaner case with a clean cloth to remove all traces of dirt and debris.

7 Install the new filter element in the housing, then refit the housing and secure it in position with the two retaining clips.

8 Refit the upper air inlet duct.

25 Coolant renewal

Warning: Wait until the engine is cold before starting this procedure. Do not allow antifreeze to come in contact with your skin, or with the painted surfaces of the vehicle. Rinse off spills immediately with plenty of water. Never leave antifreeze lying around in an open container, or in a puddle in the driveway or garage floor. Children and pets are attracted by its sweet smell, but antifreeze can be fatal if ingested.

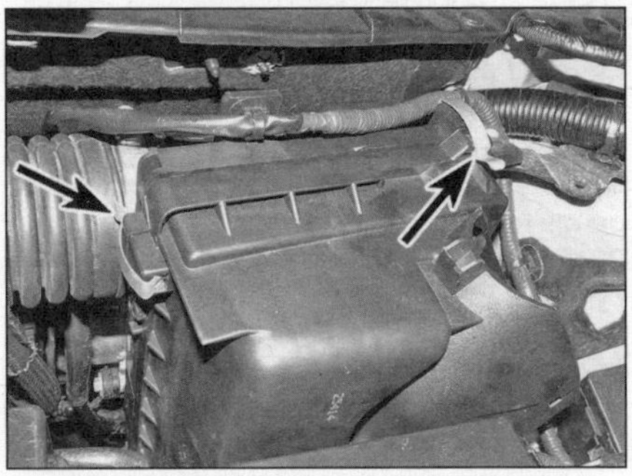

24.4a Release the two retaining clips...

Cooling system draining

1 To drain the cooling system, first cover the coolant expansion tank cap (1.2 litre engines) or radiator cap (1.6 litre engines) with a wad of rag, and slowly turn the cap anti-clockwise to relieve the pressure in the cooling system (a hissing sound will normally be heard). Wait until any pressure remaining in the system is released, then continue to turn the cap until it can be removed. On 1.6 litre engines, also remove the coolant expansion tank cap.

2 Position a suitable container beneath the drain plug at the base of the radiator. Unscrew the drain plug and allow the coolant to drain into the container.

3 If necessary, remove the coolant expansion tank, drain out the coolant, and then refit the tank, ensuring that the hoses are securely reconnected. Take care not to spill coolant on the surrounding components.

24.5 Remove the filter element from the housing

24.4b ...and separate the air cleaner filter housing from the air cleaner case

4 On 1.6 litre engines, reposition the container under the cylinder block drain plug, which is located at the rear of the cylinder block, at the timing chain end **(see illustration)**. Note that a cylinder block drain plug is not fitted to 1.2 litre engines.

5 Remove the cylinder block drain plug, and drain the coolant from the cylinder block.

6 If the coolant has been drained for a reason other than renewal, then provided it is clean and less than three years old, it can be re-used.

Cooling system flushing

7 If coolant renewal has been neglected, or if the antifreeze mixture has become diluted, then in time, the cooling system may gradually lose efficiency, as the coolant passages become restricted due to rust, scale deposits, and other sediment. The cooling system efficiency can be restored by flushing the system clean.

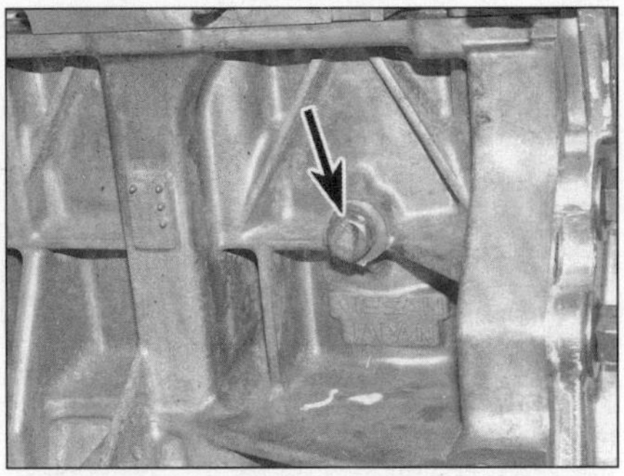

25.4 Cylinder block coolant drain plug

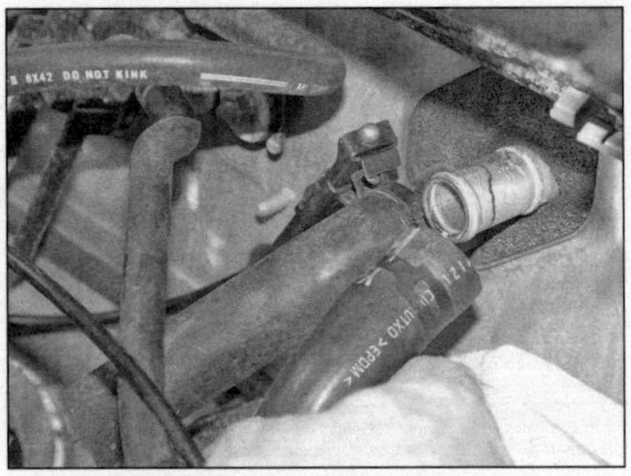

25.15 Disconnect the heater upper hose

8 The radiator should be flushed independently of the engine, to avoid unnecessary contamination.

9 To flush the radiator, fit and tighten the radiator pressure cap (1.6 litre engines), and if the radiator is fitted to the vehicle, clamp the hose running from the top of the radiator to the coolant expansion tank.

10 Disconnect the top and bottom hoses at the radiator, and then insert a garden hose into the radiator top inlet. Direct a flow of clean water through the radiator, and continue flushing until clean water emerges from the radiator bottom outlet. If after a reasonable period the water still does not run clear, the radiator can be flushed with a good proprietary cleaning agent. It is important that the cleaning agent manufacturer's instructions are followed carefully. If the contamination is particularly bad, insert the hose in the radiator bottom outlet, and flush the radiator in reverse ('reverse-flushing').

11 Remove the thermostat as described in Chapter 3, Section 4.

12 With the radiator top and bottom hoses disconnected from the radiator, insert a hose into the radiator bottom hose. Direct a clean flow of water through the engine, and continue flushing until clean water emerges from the radiator top hose and/or thermostat opening. Now insert the hose into the radiator top hose and repeat the procedure.

13 On completion of flushing, refit the thermostat with reference to Chapter 3, Section 4, and reconnect the hoses.

Cooling system filling

1.2 litre engines

14 Before attempting to fill the cooling system, make sure that all hoses and clips are in good condition, and that the clips are tight. Note that an antifreeze mixture must be used all year round, to prevent corrosion of the alloy engine components.

15 If not already done reconnect the radiator hoses, then disconnect the upper heater matrix hose from the rear of the bulkhead **(see illustration)**. Raise the hose until it is above the 'MAX' line on the coolant expansion tank.

16 Unscrew the air bleed screw from the upper left-hand side of the radiator.

17 Position containers under the radiator and under the disconnected heater matrix hose. Very slowly refill the cooling system through the expansion tank, until coolant runs from the radiator air bleed screw, then refit and tighten the screw.

18 Continue to fill the system through the expansion tank until the coolant, free from air bubbles, emerges from the heater hose. Refit the heater hose back to the bulkhead heater connection, once the coolant escaping is free from air bubbles.

19 Continue to fill the expansion tank until the coolant level reaches the MAX mark.

20 Start the engine, and increase the engine speed to approx 1500 rpm for two to three minutes, keeping the coolant level at 'MAX', then refit the expansion tank cap.

21 Run the engine for approximately 10 minutes at 2500 rpm (until the thermostat operates). Check the coolant temperature gauge for signs of overheating.

22 Stop the engine; allow it to cool completely, and then check for leaks, particularly around the disturbed components. With the system cold (the system must be cold for an accurate coolant level indication), check the level in the expansion tank.

23 If necessary, top-up the coolant level in the expansion tank to the MAX level mark. Repeat the procedures contained in paragraphs 21 to 23 until the coolant level in the expansion tank no longer drops.

1.6 litre engines

24 Before attempting to fill the cooling system, reconnect the radiator hoses if not already done. Make sure that all hoses and clips are in good condition, and that the clips are tight. Note that an antifreeze mixture must be used all year round, to prevent corrosion of the alloy engine components.

25 Disconnect the upper heater matrix hose from the rear of the bulkhead **(see illus= tration 25.15)**, and raise it until it is above the 'MAX' line on the coolant expansion tank. Remove the inlet air hose between the air cleaner and the throttle housing for access to the heater hose.

26 Position the container under the cylinder block drain plug, then very slowly refill the cooling system through the radiator, until coolant runs from the cylinder block drain plug aperture. Coat the threads of the drain plug with suitable sealant, then refit and tighten the plug to the specified torque.

27 Continue to slowly fill the system until coolant, free from air bubbles, emerges from the heater hose. Refit the heater hose back to the bulkhead heater connection, once the coolant escaping is free from air bubbles. Reconnect the inlet air hose between the air cleaner and the throttle housing.

28 Continue to fill the radiator until the coolant level is up to the filler neck, then refit the radiator cap. Add coolant to the expansion tank until the coolant level reaches the MAX mark.

29 Start the engine, and increase the engine speed to approx 1500 rpm for two to three minutes, keeping the coolant level at 'MAX', then refit the expansion tank cap.

30 Run the engine for approximately 10 minutes at 2500 rpm (until the thermostat operates). Check the coolant temperature gauge for signs of overheating.

31 Stop the engine; allow it to cool completely, and then check for leaks, particularly around the disturbed components. With the system cold (the system must be cold for an accurate coolant level indication), check the level in the radiator and expansion tank.

32 If necessary, top-up the coolant level in the radiator, then top-up the expansion tank to the MAX level mark. Repeat the procedures contained in paragraphs 30 to 32 until the coolant level in the expansion tank no longer drops.

Antifreeze mixture

33 Always use an ethylene glycol based antifreeze, which is suitable for use in mixed-metal cooling systems. The quantity of antifreeze and levels of protection are indicated in the Specifications.

34 Before adding antifreeze, the cooling system should be completely drained, preferably flushed, and all hoses and clips checked for condition and security.

35 After filling with antifreeze, a label should be attached to the radiator or expansion tank stating the type and concentration of antifreeze used, and the date installed. Any subsequent topping-up should be made with the same type and concentration of antifreeze.

Caution: Do not use engine antifreeze in the windscreen/tailgate/headlight washer system, as it will cause damage to the vehicle paintwork.

26 Spark plug renewal

1 The correct functioning of the spark plugs is vital for the correct running and efficiency of the engine. It is essential that the plugs fitted are appropriate for the engine (the suitable type is given in the Specifications in Section. If this type is used and the engine is in good condition, the spark plugs should not need attention between scheduled renewal intervals. Spark plug cleaning is rarely necessary, and should not be attempted unless specialised equipment is available, as damage can easily be caused to the firing ends.

2 On 1.2 litre engines remove the air inlet hose as described in Chapter 4A, Section 2. On 1.6 litre engines, remove the inlet manifold as described in Chapter 4A, Section 14.

26.3 Disconnect the coil wiring connectors

26.4a Remove the retaining bolts...

26.4b ...and withdraw the ignition coils

26.5 Clean out the spark plug recesses in the top of the cover

26.6 Using a spark plug deep socket to remove the spark plugs

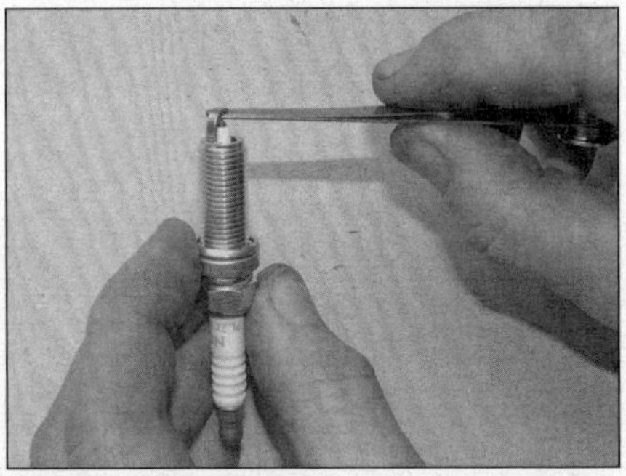

26.11 Measuring the spark plug gap with feeler blades

3 Disconnect the wiring connectors from the four ignition coils **(see illustration)**.

4 Undo the retaining bolts and withdraw the ignition coils from the top of the spark plugs **(see illustrations)**.

5 It is advisable to remove the dirt from the spark plug recesses using a clean brush, vacuum cleaner or compressed air before removing the plugs, to prevent dirt dropping into the cylinders **(see illustration)**.

6 Unscrew the plugs using a spark plug spanner, suitable box spanner or a deep socket and extension bar. Keep the socket aligned with the spark plug; otherwise if it is forcibly moved to one side, the ceramic insulator may be broken off. As each plug is removed **(see illustration)**, examine it as follows.

7 Examination of the spark plugs will give a good indication of the condition of the engine. If the insulator nose of the spark plug is clean and white, with no deposits, this is indicative of too hot a plug (a hot plug transfers heat away from the electrode slowly, a cold plug transfers heat away quickly) or a possible engine management system fault.

8 If the tip and insulator nose are covered with hard black-looking deposits, then this is also indicative of a possible problem in the engine management system. Should the plug be black and oily, and then it is likely that the engine is fairly worn.

9 It is normal for the insulator nose to be covered with light tan to greyish-brown deposits, indicating that both the spark plug and the engine are in good condition.

10 The spark plug electrode gap is of considerable importance as, if it is too large or too small, the size of the spark and its efficiency will be seriously impaired. The gap should be set to the value given in the Specifications in Section.

11 To set it, measure the gap with a feeler blade and then bend open, or closed, the outer plug electrode until the correct gap is achieved **(see illustration)**. The centre electrode should never be bent, as this may crack the insulator and cause plug failure, if nothing worse.

12 Special spark plug electrode gap adjusting tools are available from most motor accessory shops, or from some spark plug manufacturers.

13 Before fitting the spark plugs, check that the threaded connector sleeves (where fitted) are tight, and that the plug exterior surfaces and threads are clean. Insert each spark plug by hand, taking care to enter the plug threads correctly (see **Haynes Hint**).

14 Tighten the plug to the specified torque using the spark plug socket and a torque wrench. Refit the remaining spark plugs in the same manner.

15 Refit the ignition coils to the top of the spark plugs and tighten the retaining bolts, ensuring the wiring connectors are fitted securely to the ignition coils.

16 On 1.2 litre engines refit the air inlet hose as described in Chapter 4A, Section 2. On 1.6 litre engines, refit the inlet manifold as described in Chapter 4A, Section 14.

HAYNES HiNT

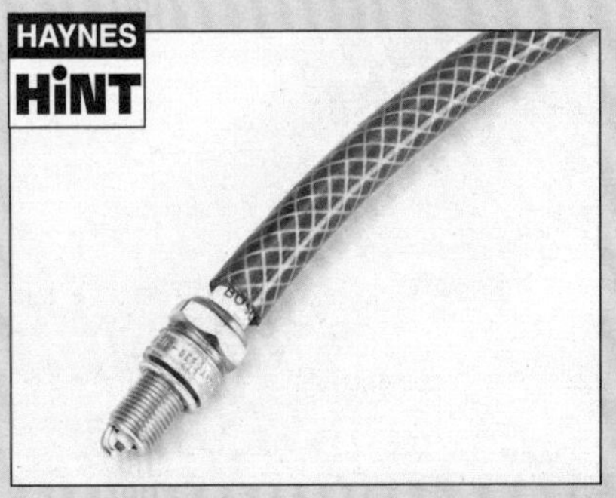

It is very often difficult to insert spark plugs into their holes without cross-threading them. To avoid this possibility, fit a short length of 8 mm internal diameter rubber hose over the end of the spark plug. The flexible hose acts as a universal joint to help align the plug with the plug hole. Should the plug begin to cross-thread, the hose will slip on the spark plug, preventing thread damage to the cylinder head.

Chapter 1B
Routine maintenance and servicing – diesel models

Contents

Degrees of difficulty

Easy, suitable for novice with little experience	**Fairly easy,** suitable for beginner with some experience	**Fairly difficult,** suitable for competent DIY mechanic	**Difficult,** suitable for experienced DIY mechanic	**Very difficult,** suitable for expert DIY or professional

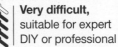

Servicing specifications

Lubricants and fluids

Refer to *Lubricants, fluids and tyre pressures*

Capacities

Engine oil (with filter)	4.5 litres
Difference between MAX and MIN dipstick marks	Approx. 1.0 litre
Cooling system:	
Type 1 engines	7.6 litres
Type 2 engines	7.4 litres
Transmission	2.0 litres
Fuel tank	46.0 litres

Cooling system

	Antifreeze	Water
Antifreeze mixture (ethylene glycol antifreeze):		
Protection down to –15°C	30%	70%
Protection down to –35°C	50%	50%

Note: *Refer to antifreeze manufacturer for latest recommendations.*

Fuel system

Idle speed (not adjustable – controlled by ECU)	850 ± 50 rpm

Brakes

Minimum front and rear brake pad friction material thickness	2.0 mm
Minimum handbrake shoe lining thickness	1.5 mm
Number of clicks required to fully apply handbrake	9 to 10 clicks
Number of clicks required operating handbrake 'on' warning light	1 click
Disc runout limit (attached to vehicle)	0.1 mm

Suspension and steering

Front wheel toe setting	2.0 mm ± 1.0 mm toe-in

Torque wrench settings

	Nm	lbf ft
Auxiliary drivebelt tensioner mounting bolt	40	30
Manual transmission:		
Filler/level plug (plastic plug)	3	2
Drain plug	24	18
Roadwheel nuts	112	83
Sump oil drain plug	20	15

1 Maintenance schedule

1 The maintenance intervals in this manual are provided with the assumption that you, not the dealer, will be carrying out the work. These are the minimum maintenance intervals based on the schedule recommended by us for vehicles driven daily. If you wish to keep your vehicle in peak condition at all times, you may wish to perform some of these procedures more often. We encourage frequent maintenance because it enhances the efficiency, performance and resale value of your vehicle. If the vehicle is driven in dusty areas, used to tow a trailer, or driven frequently at slow speeds (idling in traffic) or on short journeys, more frequent maintenance intervals are recommended. Nissan recommend that many of their service intervals are halved for vehicles which are used under these conditions.

2 When the vehicle is new, it should be serviced by a dealer service department (or other workshop recognised by the vehicle manufacturer as providing the same standard of service) in order to preserve the warranty. The vehicle manufacturer may reject warranty claims if you are unable to prove that servicing has been carried out as and when specified, using only original equipment parts or parts certified to be of equivalent quality.

Every 250 miles or weekly

- ☐ Refer to *Weekly checks*

Every 12 500 miles or 12 months – whichever comes first

- ☐ Renew the engine oil and filter (Section 5)
- ☐ Drain any water from the fuel filter (Section 6)
- ☐ Check all underbonnet components and hoses for fluid leaks (Section 7)
- ☐ Check the brake pads and renew if necessary (Section 8)
- ☐ Check the operation of the handbrake (Section 9)
- ☐ Check the operation of the clutch (Section 10)
- ☐ Check the condition of the air conditioning system components (Section 11)
- ☐ Check the condition of the auxiliary drivebelts, and renew if necessary (Section 12)
- ☐ Check the steering and suspension components for condition and security (Section 13)
- ☐ Check the condition of the driveshaft rubber gaiters (Section 14)

Every 12 500 miles or 12 months – whichever comes first (continued)

- ☐ Check the wheel alignment (Section 15)
- ☐ Check the condition of the exhaust system and mountings (Section 16)
- ☐ Check the operation and security of all seat belts (Section 17)
- ☐ Check the operation of all electrical systems (Section 18)
- ☐ Lubricate all hinges and locks (Section 19)
- ☐ Check the manual transmission oil level (Section 20)
- ☐ Carry out a road test (Section 21)

Every 25 000 miles or 2 years – whichever comes first

- ☐ Renew the pollen filter (Section 22)
- ☐ Renew the brake fluid (Section 23)
- ☐ Renew the fuel filter (Section 24)

Every 37 500 miles or 3 years – whichever comes first

- ☐ Renew the air filter element (Section 25)
- ☐ Renew the coolant (Section 26)

Every 50 000 miles or 4 years – whichever comes first

- ☐ Renew the timing belt (Section 27)*

Note: **Although the specified interval for timing belt renewal is 90 000 miles or 5 years, it is strongly recommended that the interval is reduced to 50 000 miles or 4 years on vehicles which are subjected to intensive use, i.e. mainly short journeys or a lot of stop-start driving. The actual belt renewal interval is therefore very much up to the individual owner, but bear in mind that severe engine damage may result if the belt breaks.*

2 Component locations

Front underbody view

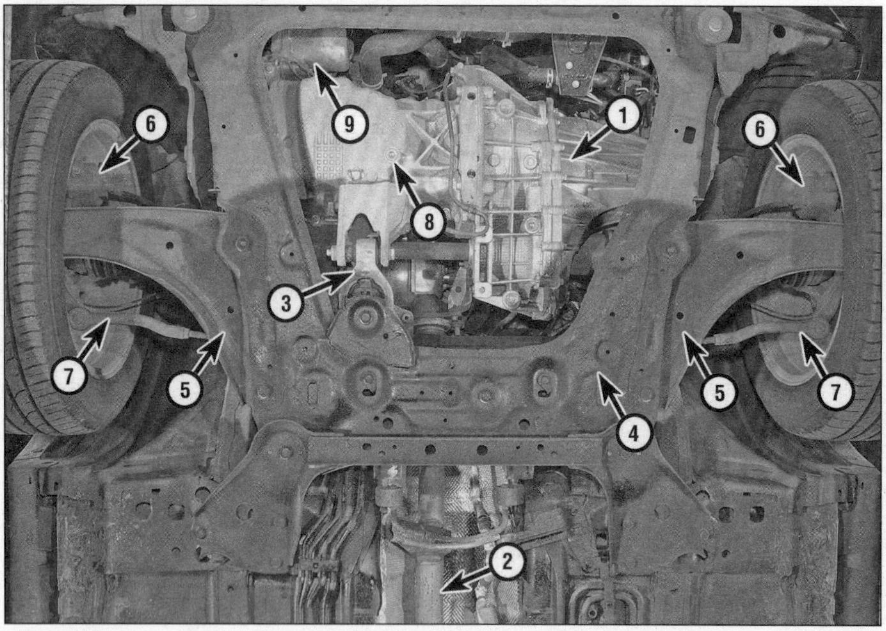

1 Transmission
2 Exhaust front pipe
3 Rear engine/transmission mounting
4 Subframe
5 Front suspension lower arm
6 Brake calipers
7 Steering track rod end
8 Engine oil drain plug
9 Air conditioning compressor

Rear underbody view

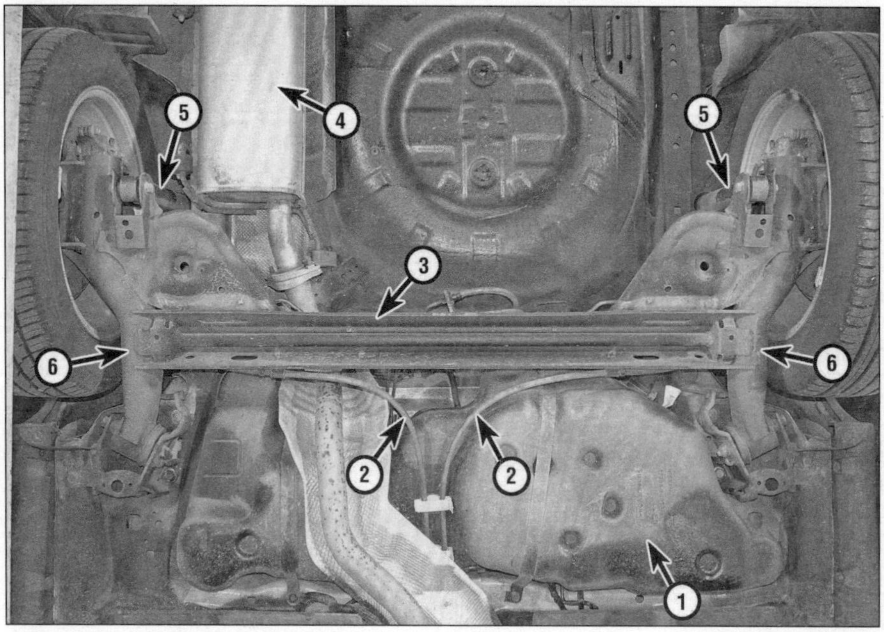

1 Fuel tank
2 Handbrake cables
3 Rear axle torsion beam
4 Exhaust rear silencer and tailpipe
5 Shock absorbers
6 Rear trailing arms

Underbonnet view – Type 1 engine

1 Engine oil filler cap/dipstick
2 Windscreen washer bottle
3 Fuel system priming pump
4 Brake fluid reservoir
5 Air cleaner assembly
6 Coolant expansion tank
7 Engine management electronic control unit (ECU)
8 Battery
9 Fuse/relay box

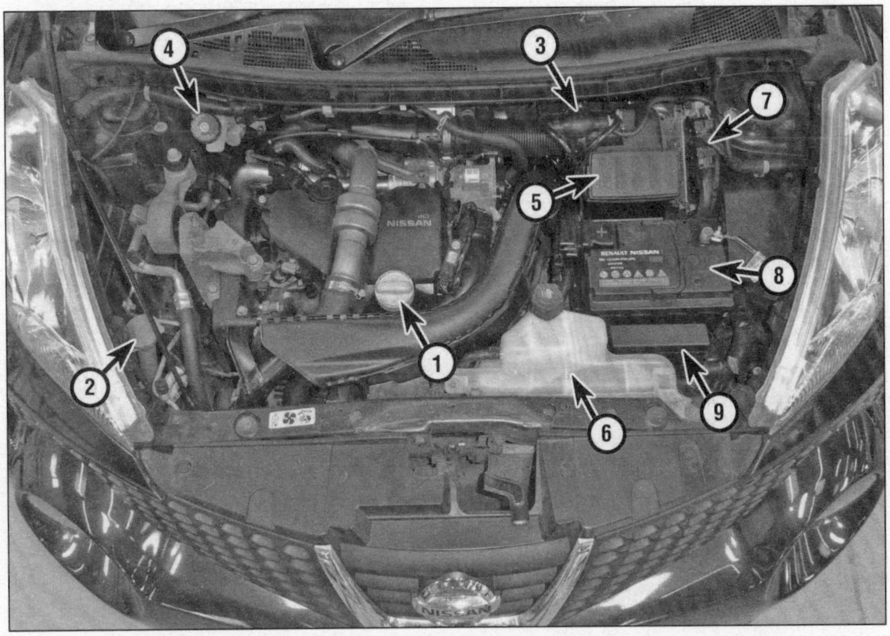

Underbonnet view – Type 2 engine

1 Engine oil filler cap/dipstick
2 Windscreen washer bottle
3 Brake fluid reservoir
4 Air cleaner assembly
5 Coolant expansion tank
6 Engine management electronic control unit (ECU)
7 Battery
8 Fuse/relay box

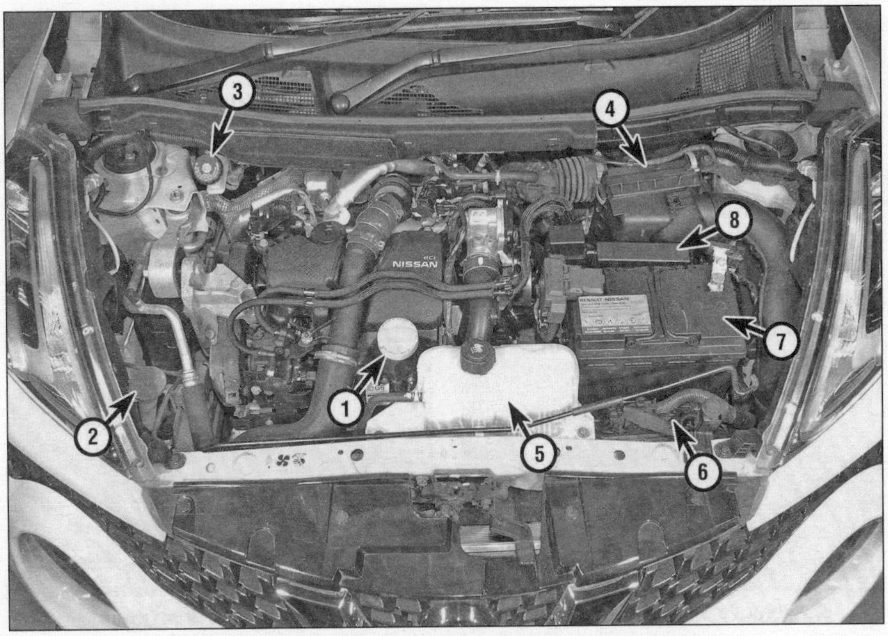

3 General Information

1 This Chapter is designed to help the home mechanic maintain his/her vehicle for safety, economy, long life and peak performance.
2 The Chapter contains a master maintenance schedule, followed by Sections dealing specifically with each task in the schedule. Visual checks, adjustments, component renewal and other helpful items are included. Refer to the accompanying illustrations of the engine compartment and the underside of the vehicle for the locations of the various components.
3 Servicing your vehicle in accordance with the mileage/time maintenance schedule and the following Sections will provide a planned maintenance programme, which should result in a long and reliable service life. This is a comprehensive plan, so maintaining some items but not others at the specified service intervals will not produce the same results.
4 As you service your vehicle, you will discover that many of the procedures can – and should – be grouped together, because of the particular procedure being performed, or because of the close proximity of two otherwise-unrelated components to one another. For example, if the vehicle is raised for any reason, the exhaust can be inspected at the same time as the suspension and steering components.
5 The first step in this maintenance programme is to prepare yourself before the actual work begins. Read through all the Sections relevant to the work to be carried out, then make a list and gather together all the parts and tools required. If a problem is encountered, seek advice from a parts specialist, or a dealer service department.

4 Regular maintenance

1 If, from the time the vehicle is new, the routine maintenance schedule is followed closely, and frequent checks are made of fluid levels and high-wear items, as suggested throughout this manual, the engine will be kept in relatively good running condition, and the need for additional work will be minimised.
2 It is possible that there will be times when the engine is running poorly due to the lack of regular maintenance. This is even more likely if a used vehicle, which has not received regular and frequent maintenance checks, is purchased. In such cases, additional work may need to be carried out, outside of the regular maintenance intervals.
3 If engine wear is suspected, a compression test or leakdown test will provide valuable information regarding the overall performance of the main internal components. Such a test can be used as a basis to decide on the extent of the work to be carried out. If, for example, a compression test indicates serious internal engine wear, conventional maintenance as described in this Chapter will not greatly improve the performance of the engine, and may prove a waste of time and money, unless extensive overhaul work is carried out first.
4 The following series of operations are those most often required to improve the performance of a generally poor-running engine:

Primary operations

a) Clean, inspect and test the battery (see Weekly checks in Chapter 0 Section 5).
b) Check all the engine-related fluids (see Weekly checks in Chapter 0, Section 5).
c) Check the condition and tension of the auxiliary drivebelt (Section 12).
d) Check the condition of the air filter element, and renew if necessary (Section 25).
e) Check the fuel filter – drain off any water and renew the filter if necessary (Section 6 and Section 24).
f) Check the condition of all hoses, and check for fluid leaks (Section 7).

5 If the above operations do not prove fully effective, carry out the following secondary operations:

Secondary operations

6 All items listed under Primary operations, plus the following:
a) Check the charging system (Chapter 5A).
b) Check the preheating system (Chapter 5A).
c) Check the fuel system (Chapter 4B).

5 Engine oil and filter renewal

1 Frequent oil and filter changes are the most important preventative maintenance procedures that can be undertaken by the DIY owner. As engine oil ages, it becomes diluted and contaminated, which leads to premature engine wear.
2 Before starting this procedure, gather together all the necessary tools and materials. Also make sure that you have plenty of clean rags and newspapers handy, to mop-up any spills. Ideally, the engine oil should be warm, as it will drain more easily, and more built-up sludge will be removed with it.
3 Take care not to touch the exhaust or any other hot parts of the engine when working under the vehicle. To avoid any possibility of scalding, and to protect yourself from possible skin irritants and other harmful contaminants in used engine oils, it is advisable to wear gloves when carrying out this work.
4 Access to the underside of the vehicle will be greatly improved if it can be raised on a lift, driven onto ramps, or jacked up and supported on axle stands (see *Jacking and vehicle support*). Whichever method is chosen, make sure that the vehicle remains level, or if it is at an angle, that the drain plug is at the lowest point. The drain plug is located at the rear of the sump.
5 Remove the oil filler cap from the oil filler tube at the front of the engine. Note that the the dipstick is part of the oil filler cap **(see illustration)**.
6 Slacken the drain plug about half a turn, position the draining container under the drain plug, and then remove the plug completely **(see illustration)**. If possible, try to keep the plug pressed into the sump while unscrewing it by hand the last couple of turns.
7 Allow some time for the oil to drain, noting that it may be necessary to reposition the container as the oil flow slows to a trickle.
8 After all the oil has drained; wipe the drain plug with a clean rag. Remove the old sealing washer from the drain plug and fit a new one. Clean the area around the drain plug opening, and refit the plug complete with the new sealing washer **(see illustration)**. Tighten

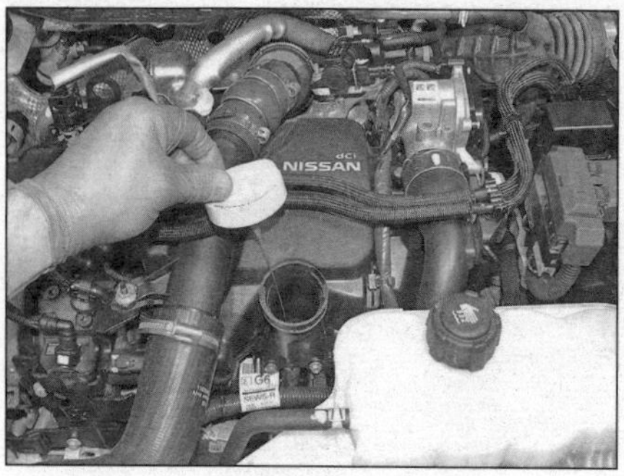

5.5 Remove oil filler cap/dipstick

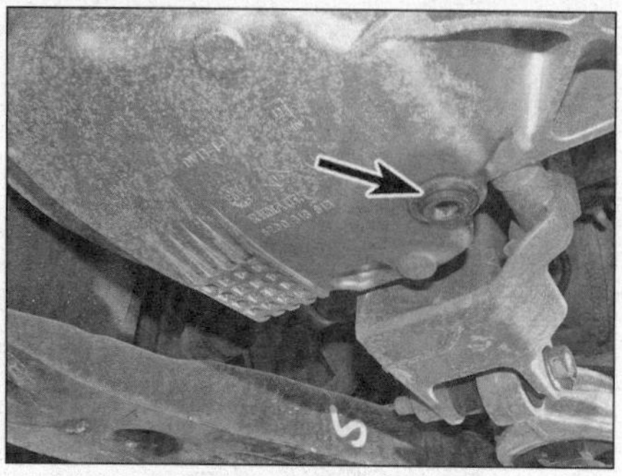
5.6 Engine oil drain plug

5.8 Fit a new sealing washer to the drain plug

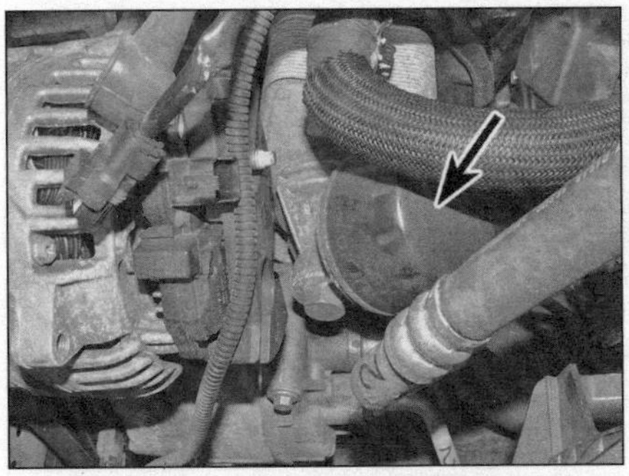

5.9 Oil filter location on the front of the engine

5.11 Slacken the oil filter with a removal tool

5.13 Apply clean oil to the seal on the oil filter

the drain plug securely – preferably to the specified torque, using a torque wrench.

9 The oil filter is located at the front of the cylinder block – access is most easily obtained from above **(see illustration)**.

10 Move the container into position under the oil filter, to catch any oil spillage.

11 Use an oil filter removal tool to slacken the filter initially, then unscrew it by hand the rest of the way **(see illustration)**. Position it with its open end uppermost to prevent further spillage of oil, then empty the oil from the old filter into the container.

12 Use a clean rag to remove any oil, dirt and sludge from the filter sealing area on the engine. Check the old filter to make sure that the rubber sealing ring has not stuck to the engine. If it has, carefully remove it.

13 Apply a light coating of clean engine oil to the sealing ring on the new filter **(see illustration)**, then screw the filter into position on the engine. Lightly tighten the filter until its sealing ring contacts the block, and then tighten it through a further two-thirds of a turn. Tighten the filter firmly by hand only – do not use any tools.

14 Remove the old oil and all tools from under the vehicle then lower the vehicle to the ground.

15 Fill the engine through the oil filler tube on the front of the engine, using the correct grade and type of oil (refer to *Weekly checks* for details of topping-up). Pour in half the specified quantity of oil first, and then wait a few minutes for the oil to drain into the sump. Continue to add oil, a small quantity at a time, until the level is up to the lower mark on the dipstick. Adding approximately a further 1.0 litre will bring the level up to the upper mark on the dipstick. Refit the oil filler cap when correct level is achieved.

16 Start the engine and run it for a few minutes, while checking for leaks around the oil filter seal and the sump drain plug. Note that there may be a delay of a few seconds before the low oil pressure warning light goes out when the engine is first started, as the oil circulates through the new oil filter and the engine oil galleries before the pressure builds-up. Do not run the engine above idle speed while the warning light is on.

17 Stop the engine, and wait a few minutes for the oil to settle in the sump once more. With the new oil circulated and the filter now completely full, recheck the level on the dipstick, and add more oil as necessary.

18 Dispose of the used engine oil safely with reference to *General repair procedures* on page REF•8. Do not discard the old filter with domestic household waste. The provision for waste oil disposal provided by many local council recycling facilities generally has a filter receptacle alongside.

6 Fuel filter water draining

Type 1 engines

1 The fuel filter is located on the engine compartment bulkhead, slightly to the left of centre. A water drain screw is provided on the base of the fuel filter **(see illustration)**.

2 Remove the air cleaner assembly as described in Chapter 4B, Section 2, for access to the fuel filter.

3 Place a suitable container beneath the drain screw. To make draining easier, a suitable length of tubing can be attached to the outlet pipe at the centre of the screw to direct the fuel flow. If desired, access can be improved by lifting the filter out of its mounting bracket and raising the filter assembly to a more convenient position – if this is done, take care not to strain the fuel hoses.

4 Open the drain screw by turning it anti-clockwise, then operate the hand priming pump a couple of times to allow the fuel to flow through the filter **(see illustration)**.

5 Allow the entire contents of the filter to drain into the container, and then securely tighten the drain screw. Remove the length of tubing from the filter outlet.

6 If removed, refit the filter to its mounting bracket, then refit the air cleaner assembly as described in Chapter 4B, Section 2.

7 Prime and bleed the fuel system as described in Chapter 4B, Section 5.

8 Dispose of the used fuel safely with reference to *General repair procedures* on page REF•8. Do not discard the fuel with domestic household waste. Most local council recycling facilities have a provision for waste oil/fuel disposal.

Type 2 engines

9 The fuel filter is located on the engine compartment bulkhead, slightly to the left of centre. A water drain screw is provided on the top of the fuel filter.

10 Remove the air cleaner assembly as described in Chapter 4B, Section 2. Access to the filter is still very limited even with the air cleaner removed and it may also be necessary to remove the windscreen cowl panel and cowl panel extension as described in Chapter 11, Section 21.

11 Extract the retaining clip securing the

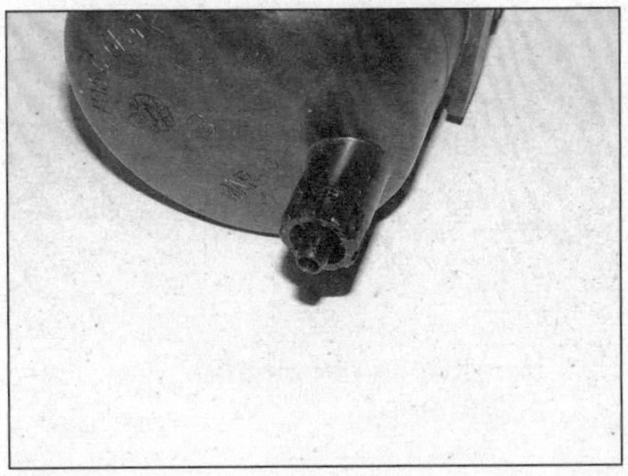

6.1 Water drain screw fitted to base of filter

6.4 Operate the hand priming pump to allow fuel to flow through the filter

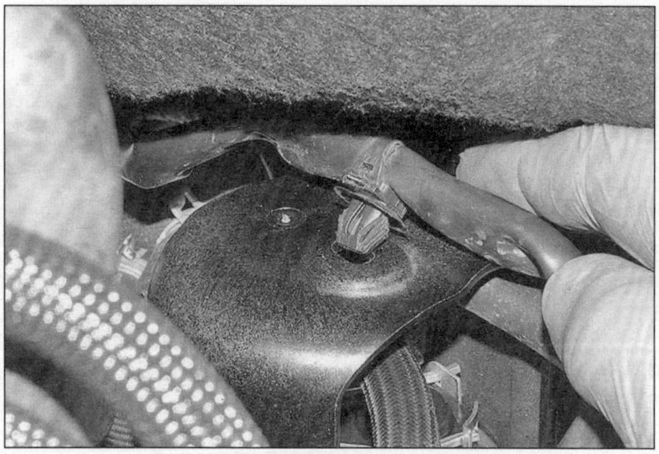

6.11 Extract the wiring harness retaining clip

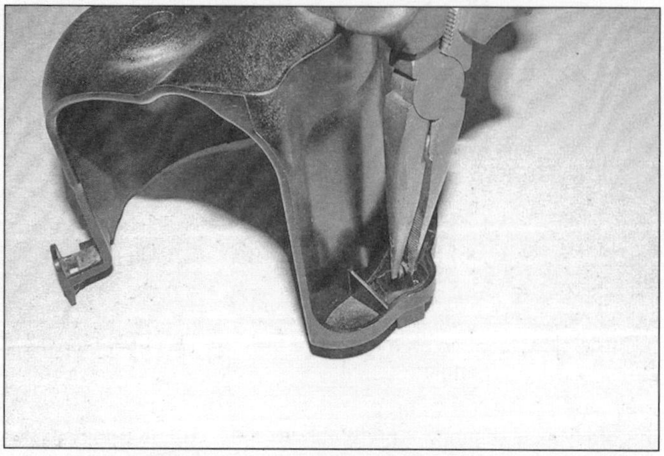

6.12a Squeeze together the plastic cover retaining tabs (shown with cover removed)...

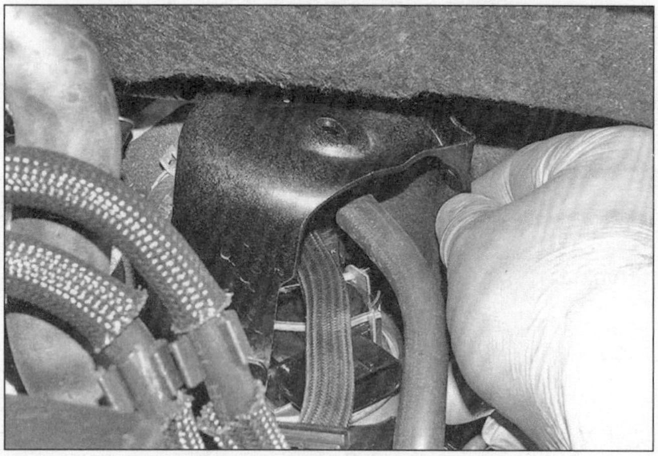

6.12b ...and lift the cover off the filter

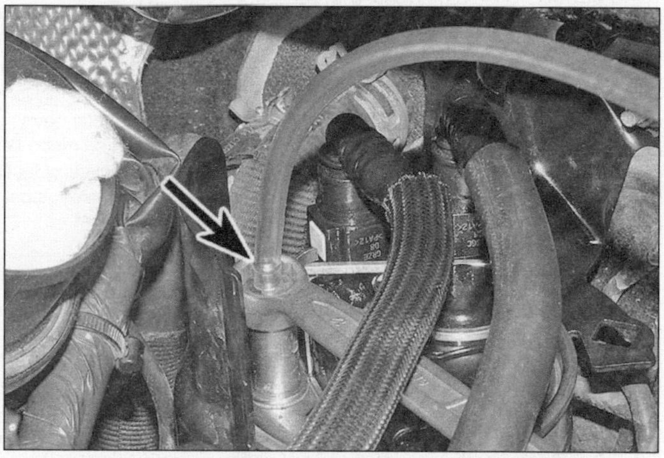

6.13 Attach a suitable length of tubing to the drain screw

wiring harness to the fuel filter plastic cover **(see illustration)**.

12 Squeeze together the retaining tabs and remove the plastic cover from the top of the filter **(see illustrations)**.

13 Attach a suitable length of tubing and a spanner to the drain screw located on the top of the filter **(see illustration)**. Place the other end of the tubing in a suitable container.

14 Open the drain screw by turning it anti-clockwise, then switch on the ignition without starting the engine. The in-tank fuel pump will operate and pump fresh fuel to the filter. This in turn will force any water, together with fuel out of the drain screw.

15 When only fresh fuel and no further water flows from the drain screw, switch off the ignition. Tighten the drain screw securely and remove the tubing.

16 Refit the plastic cover to the top of the filter and clip the wiring harness back into the cover.

17 Refit the air cleaner assembly as described in Chapter 4B, Section 2.

18 Refit the windscreen cowl panel extension and cowl panel as described in Chapter 11, Section 21.

19 Dispose of the used fuel safely with reference to *General repair procedures* on page REF•8. Do not discard the fuel with domestic household waste. Most local council recycling facilities have a provision for waste oil/fuel disposal.

7 Hose and fluid leak check

1 See Chapter 1A, Section 6.

8 Brake pad condition check – front and rear

1 See Chapter 1A, Section 7.

9 Handbrake check and adjustment

1 See Chapter 1A, Section 8.

10 Clutch operation check

1 See Chapter 1A, Section 9.

11 Air conditioning system check

1 See Chapter 1A, Section 10.

12 Auxiliary drivebelt check and renewal

Note: *Nissan recommend that the belt be always renewed if it is removed, along with the automatic tensioner. The belt and tensioner should be renewed every 90 000 miles or 6 years regardless of condition.*

Checking

1 The auxiliary drivebelt is located on the right-hand side of the engine.

12.6 Check for drivebelt wear

12.7a Turning the spanner clockwise from under the vehicle...

2 Due to their function and material makeup, drivebelts are prone to failure after a period of time and should therefore be inspected, and if necessary adjusted periodically.
3 A basic check for obvious faults can be made from the engine compartment. However, because the belt runs very close to the right hand inner wing a through inspection can only be made from below.
4 Jack up the front of the car, and support it on axle stands (see *Jacking and vehicle support*). Remove the right-hand roadwheel.
5 Remove the wheel arch liner on the right-hand side as described in Chapter 11, Section 21.
6 With the engine stopped, inspect the full length of the drivebelt for cracks and separation of the belt plies **(see illustration)**. It will be necessary to turn the engine (using a spanner or socket and bar on the crankshaft pulley bolt) in order to move the belt from the pulleys so that the belt can be inspected thoroughly. Twist the belt between the pulleys so that both sides can be viewed. Also, check for fraying and glazing which gives the belt a shiny appearance. Check the pulleys for nicks, cracks, distortion and corrosion.

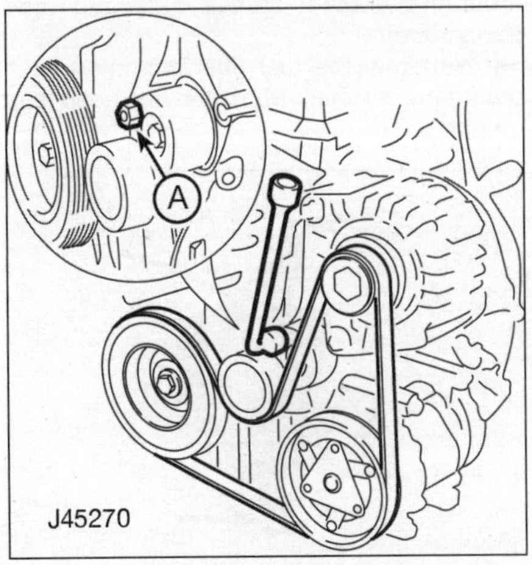

12.7b ... or from above, using hexagon (A) on the tensioner pulley

Renewal

7 Using a spanner on the outer nut on the tensioner, turn the tensioner clockwise to release the tension on the belt **(see illustrations)**, then lift the drivebelt from the pulleys, noting its fitted position on the pulleys.
8 If the belt is removed, it is recommended by Nissan that it must be renewed.
9 Unbolt the tensioner unit and fit a new one, tightening the retaining bolt to the specified torque.
10 Using the spanner on the outer nut on the tensioner, hold the tensioner clockwise, to allow the new belt to be fitted around the pulleys, making sure that it is correctly located in the grooves.
11 Fit a socket to the crankshaft pulley and rotate the engine several times to check the belt alignment.
12 Refit the wheel arch liner and roadwheel, then lower the vehicle to the ground. Tighten the roadwheel nuts to the specified torque.

13 Steering and suspension check

1 See Chapter 1A, Section 13.

14 Driveshaft gaiter check

1 See Chapter 1A, Section 14.

15 Wheel alignment check

1 See Chapter 1A, Section 15.

16 Exhaust system check

1 See Chapter 1A, Section 16.

17 Seat belt check

1 See Chapter 1A, Section 17.

18 Electrical systems check

1 See Chapter 1A, Section 18.

19 Hinge and lock lubrication

1 See Chapter 1A, Section 19.

20 Manual transmission oil level check

1 See Chapter 1A, Section 20.

21 Road test

1 See Chapter 1A, Section 21.

22 Pollen filter renewal

1 See Chapter 1A, Section 22.

23 Brake fluid renewal

1 See Chapter 1A, Section 23.

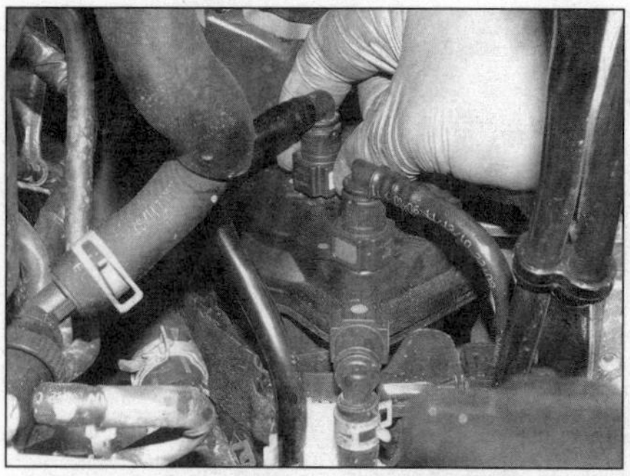

24.3 Disconnect the fuel hose quick-release connectors from the filter

24.4 Lift the filter up and out of the mounting bracket

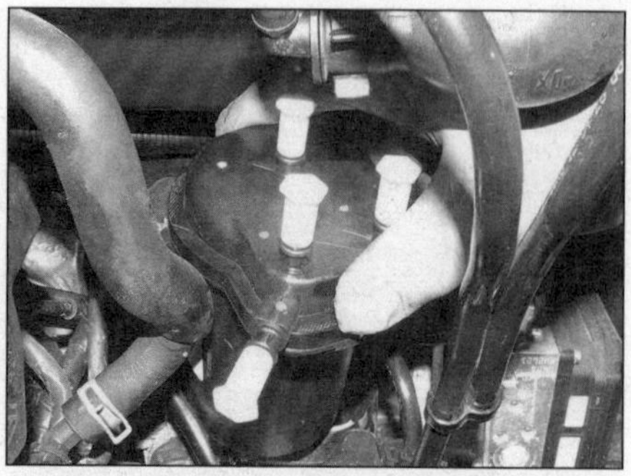

24.5 Fit the new filter to the mounting bracket

24 Fuel filter renewal

Caution: Do not allow dirt to enter the fuel system during this procedure.

Type 1 engines

1 The fuel filter is located on the engine compartment bulkhead, slightly to the left of centre.

2 Remove the air cleaner assembly as described in Chapter 4B, Section 2, for access to the fuel filter.

3 Depress the coloured square section of the fuel hose quick-release connector and disconnect the fuel hoses from the filter **(see illustration)**. Note that the four fuel hose connectors are colour coded red, green, white and blue with corresponding coloured dots adjacent to each outlet on the filter. Suitably cap or plug the hoses as they are disconnected.

4 Lift the filter up and out of its mounting bracket and remove it from the engine compartment **(see illustration)**.

5 Fit the new filter to the mounting bracket and reconnect the fuel lines to the top of the filter, matching the coloured connectors with the corresponding coloured dots on the filter **(see illustration)**.

6 Refit the air cleaner assembly as described in Chapter 4B, Section 2.

7 Prime and bleed the fuel system as described in Chapter 4B, Section 5.

Type 2 engines

8 The fuel filter is located on the engine compartment bulkhead, slightly to the left of centre.

9 Remove the air cleaner assembly as described in Chapter 4B, Section 2. Access to the filter is still very limited even with the air cleaner removed and it may also be necessary to remove the windscreen cowl panel and cowl panel extension as described in Chapter 11, Section 21.

10 Disconnect the water level sensor wiring connector from the top of the filter **(see illustration)**.

11 Extract the retaining clip securing the wiring harness to the fuel filter plastic cover **(see illustration 6.11)**.

12 Squeeze together the retaining tabs and remove the plastic cover from the top of the filter **(see illustrations 6.12a and 6.12b)**.

13 Note the fitted position of the fuel hoses, then depress the coloured square section of the fuel hose quick-release connector and disconnect the fuel hoses from the filter **(see illustration)**. Suitably cap or plug the hoses and filter outlets.

14 Release the wiring and hoses from the fuel filter crash protector as necessary, then undo the two nuts and remove the crash protector from the filter bracket **(see illustrations)**.

15 Undo the three nuts securing the filter mounting bracket to the bulkhead **(see illustration)**.

16 Withdraw the fuel filter, complete with mounting bracket, from the bulkhead and

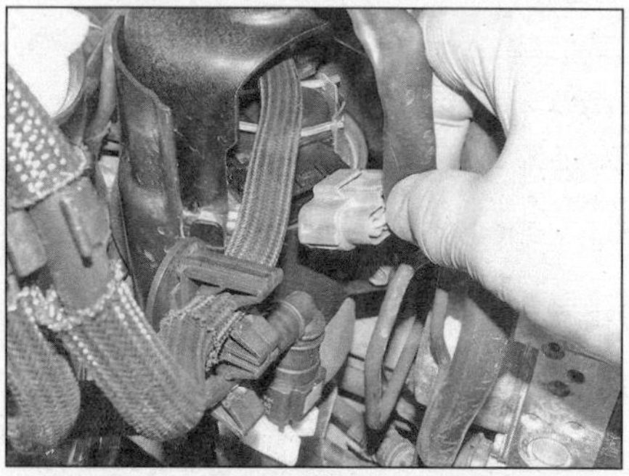

24.10 Disconnect the water level sensor wiring connector

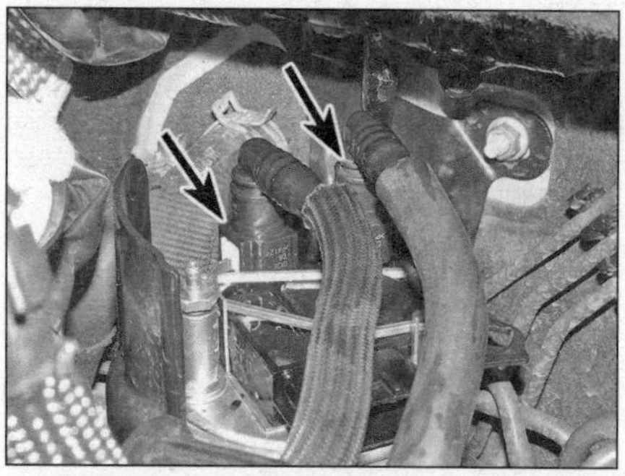

24.13 Disconnect the fuel hoses from the filter

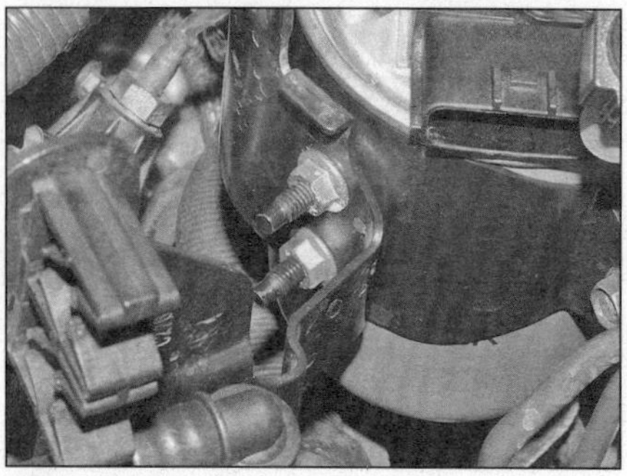

24.14a Undo the crash protector retaining nuts...

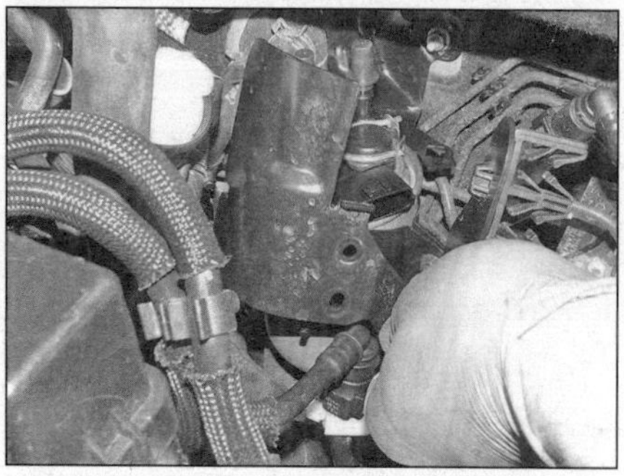

24.14b ...and remove the crash protector from the filter mounging bracket

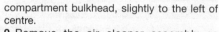

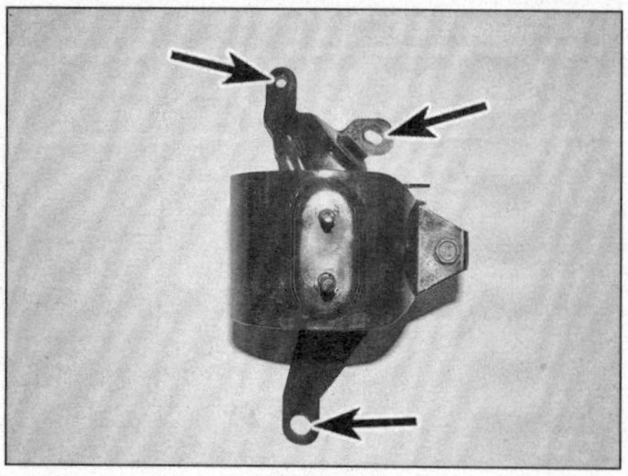

24.15 Fuel filter mounting bracket retaining nut locations (shown with bracket removed)

24.16 Withdraw the filter and mounting bracket from the bulkhead

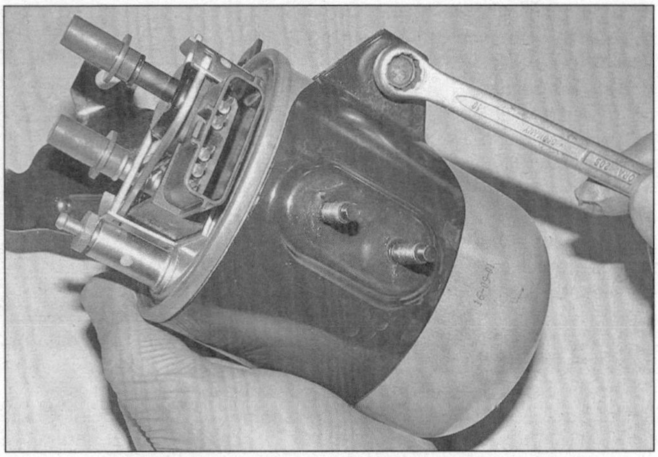

24.17a Slacken the filter mounting bracket clamp bolt...

24.17b ...and remove the filter from the bracket

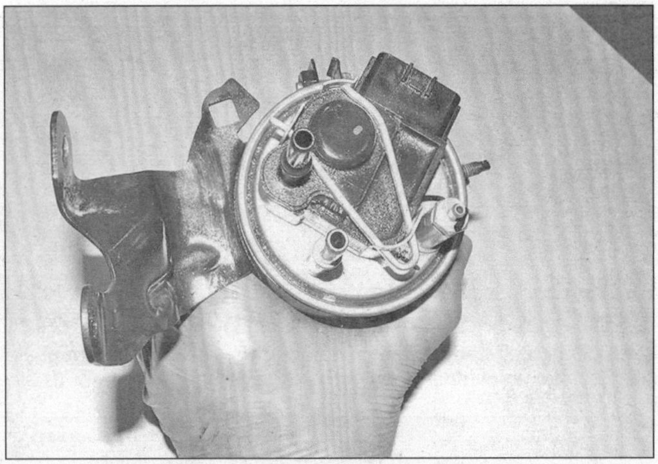

24.18 Correct orientation of the fuel filter in the mounting bracket

remove it from the engine compartment **(see illustration)**.

17 Slacken the mounting bracket clamp bolt and remove the filter from the bracket **(see illustrations)**.

18 Fit the new filter to the mounting bracket and position it as shown **(see illustration)**. Tighten the clamp bolt to secure the filter.

19 Locate the fuel filter and mounting bracket back in position on the engine compartment bulkhead. Refit the three retaining nuts and tighten them securely.

20 Refit the crach protector to the filter mounting bracket and secure with the two nuts. Reatach the hoses and wiring as necessary.

21 Reconnect the fuel hoses to the filter outlets in the positions noted during removal,

22 Refit the plastic cover to the top of the filter and clip the wiring harness back into the cover.

23 Reconnect the water level sensor wiring connector to the top of the filter.

24 Prime and bleed the fuel system as described in Chapter 4B, Section 5.

25 Refit the air cleaner assembly as described in Chapter 4B, Section 2.

26 Refit the windscreen cowl panel extension and cowl panel as described in Chapter 11, Section 21.

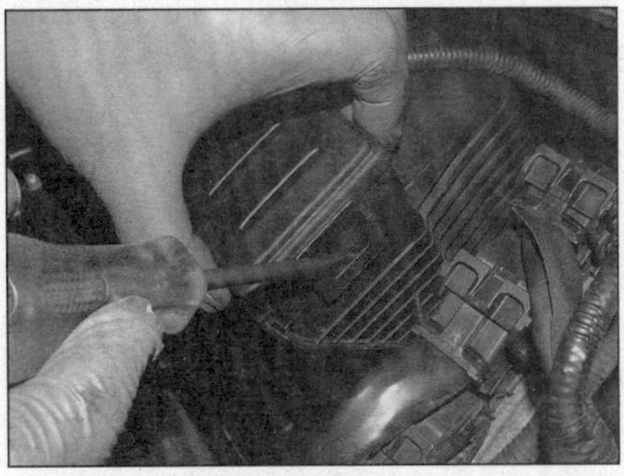

25.2a Depress the tab at each end of the air cleaner cover...

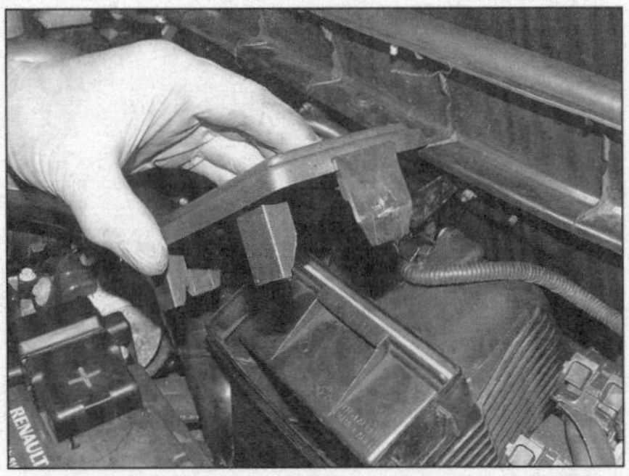

25.2b ...and lift the cover off the air cleaner housing

25 Air filter element renewal

Type 1 engines

1 The air filter is situated in the air cleaner housing at the left-hand rear of the engine compartment.

2 Using a screwdriver, depress the two retaining tabs (one at each end of the cover), and lift the cover off the air cleaner housing **(see illustrations)**.

3 Withdraw the air filter holder out of the

housing, then withdraw the filter element from the holder, noting which way round it is fitted **(see illustrations)**.

4 Wipe the inside of the air filter housing and cover with a clean cloth to remove all traces of dirt and debris.

5 Install the new filter element in the holder, then refit the holder to the housing. Push the holder toward the rear of the car to engage it with the housing **(see illustrations)**.

6 Refit the air cleaner cover to the housing **(see illustration)**.

25.3a Withdraw the filter holder from the housing...

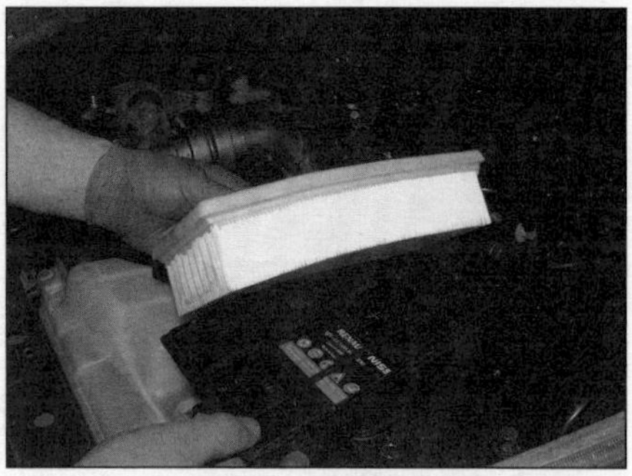

25.3b ...then withdraw the element from the holder

Type 2 engines

7 The air filter is situated in the air cleaner housing at the left-hand rear of the engine compartment.

8 Lift up the tab and disengage the upper inlet air duct from the air cleaner filter housing **(see illustration)**.

9 Lift the inlet air duct upward to disengage the lower mounting peg from the grommet, and remove the duct from the engine compartment **(see illustrations)**.

10 Release the two retaining clips and separate the air cleaner filter housing from the air cleaner case **(see illustrations)**.

11 Lift the old air filter element out of the filter housing, noting which way round it is fitted **(see illustration)**.

25.5a Refit the filter element and holder to the air cleaner housing...

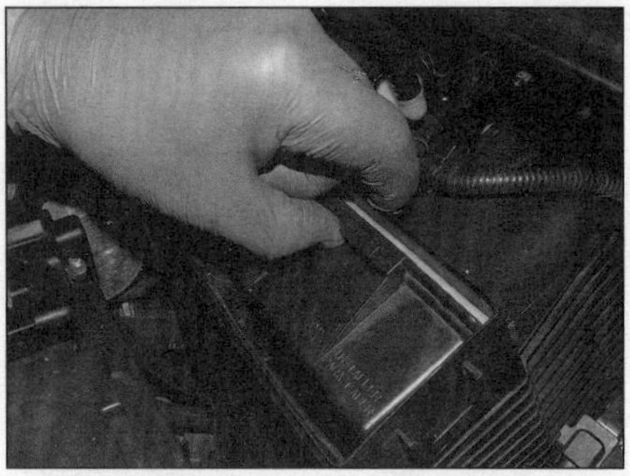

25.5b ...then push the holder toward the rear of the car to secure

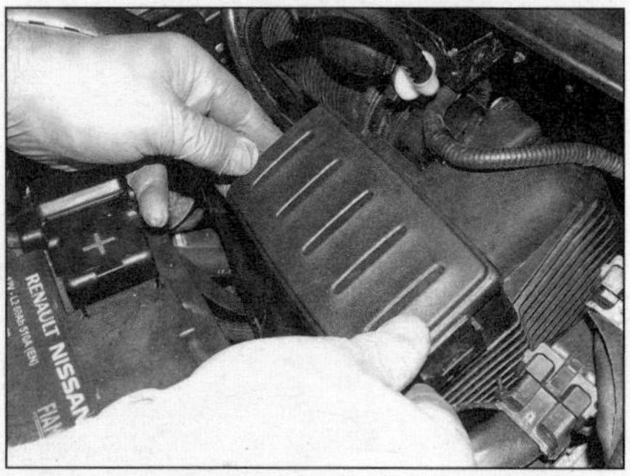

25.6 Refit the air cleaner cover to the housing

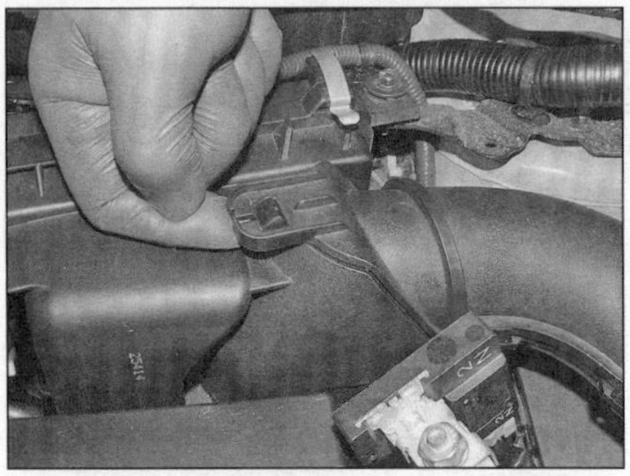

25.8 Disengage the upper inlet air duct from the air cleaner filter housing

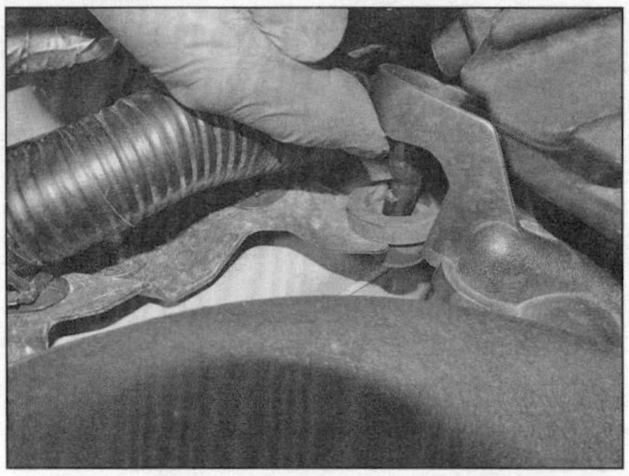

25.9a Disengage the lower mounting peg from the grommet...

25.9b ...and remove the inlet air duct

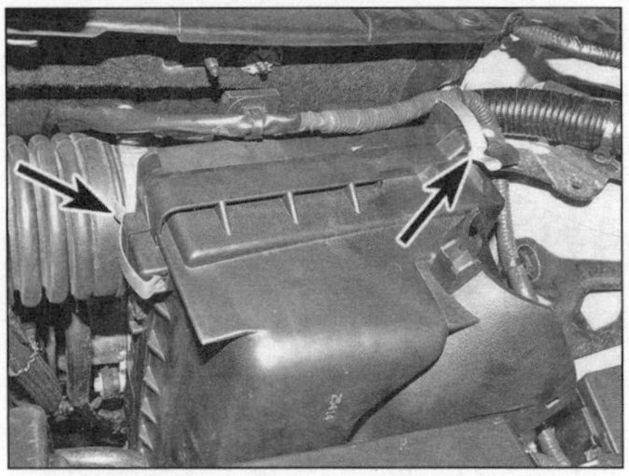

25.10a Release the two retaining clips...

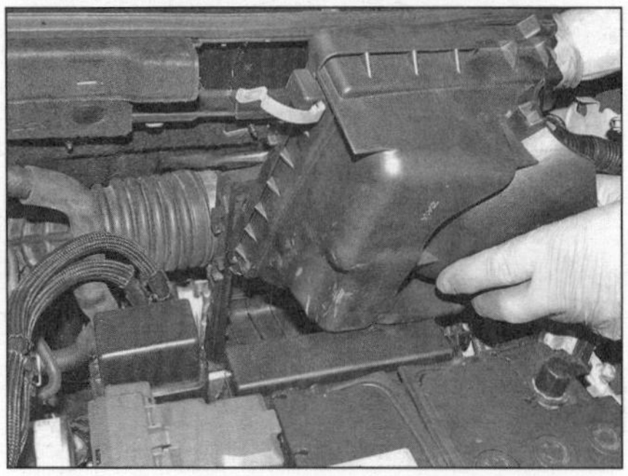

25.10b ...and separate the air cleaner filter housing from the air cleaner case

25.11 Remove the filter element from the housing

12 Wipe the inside of the air cleaner filter housing and air cleaner case with a clean cloth to remove all traces of dirt and debris.

13 Install the new filter element in the housing, then refit the housing and secure it in position with the two retaining clips.

14 Refit the upper air inlet duct.

26 Coolant renewal

Warning: Wait until the engine is cold before starting this procedure. Do not allow antifreeze to come in contact with your skin, or with the painted surfaces of the vehicle. Rinse off spills immediately with plenty of water. Never leave antifreeze lying around in an open container, or in a puddle in the driveway or garage floor. Children and pets are attracted by its sweet smell, but antifreeze can be fatal if ingested.

Cooling system draining

1 To drain the cooling system, first cover the coolant expansion tank cap with a wad of rag, and slowly turn the cap anti-clockwise to relieve the pressure in the cooling system (a hissing sound will normally be heard). Wait until any pressure remaining in the system is released, then continue to turn the cap until it can be removed.

2 Position a suitable container beneath the drain plug at the base of the radiator. Unscrew the drain plug and allow the coolant to drain into the container.

3 If necessary, remove the coolant expansion tank, drain out the coolant, and then refit the tank, ensuring that the hoses are securely reconnected. Take care not to spill coolant on the surrounding components.

4 If the coolant has been drained for a reason other than renewal, then provided it is clean and less than three years old, it can be re-used.

Cooling system flushing

5 If coolant renewal has been neglected, or if the antifreeze mixture has become diluted, then in time, the cooling system may gradually lose efficiency, as the coolant passages become restricted due to rust, scale deposits, and other sediment. The cooling system efficiency can be restored by flushing the system clean.

6 The radiator should be flushed independently of the engine, to avoid unnecessary contamination.

7 If the radiator is fitted to the vehicle, clamp the hose running from the top of the radiator to the coolant expansion tank.

8 Disconnect the top and bottom hoses at the radiator, and then insert a garden hose into the radiator top inlet. Direct a flow of clean water through the radiator, and continue flushing until clean water emerges from the radiator bottom outlet. If after a reasonable period the water still does not run clear, the radiator can be flushed with a good proprietary cleaning agent. It is important that the cleaning agent manufacturer's instructions are followed carefully. If the contamination is particularly bad, insert the hose in the radiator bottom outlet, and flush the radiator in reverse ('reverse-flushing').

9 To flush the remainder of the system, remove the thermostat as described in Chapter 3, Section 4.

10 With the radiator top and bottom hoses disconnected from the radiator, insert a hose into the radiator bottom hose. Direct a clean flow of water through the engine, and continue flushing until clean water emerges from the radiator top hose and/or thermostat opening. Now insert the hose into the radiator top hose and repeat the procedure.

11 On completion of flushing, refit the thermostat with reference to Chapter 3, Section 4, and reconnect the hoses.

Cooling system filling

12 Before attempting to fill the cooling system, reconnect the radiator hoses if not already done. Make sure that all hoses and clips are in good condition, and that the clips are tight. Note that an antifreeze mixture must be used all year round, to prevent corrosion of the alloy engine components.

13 Disconnect the upper heater matrix hose from the rear of the bulkhead **(see illustration)**, and raise it until it is above the 'MAX' line on the coolant expansion tank. Remove the inlet air hose between the air cleaner and the turbocharger for access to the heater hose.

14 Position the container under the disconnected heater hose and very slowly fill the system until coolant, free from air bubbles, emerges from the heater hose. Refit the heater hose back to the bulkhead heater connection, once the coolant escaping is free from air bubbles. Reconnect the inlet air hose between the air cleaner and the turbocharger.

15 Continue to fill the the expansion tank until the coolant level reaches the MAX mark.

16 Start the engine, and increase the engine speed to approx 1500 rpm for two to three minutes, keeping the coolant level at 'MAX', then refit the expansion tank cap.

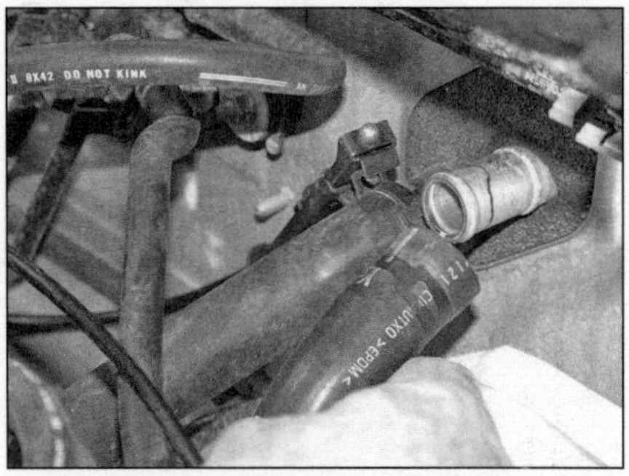

26.13 Disconnect the heater upper hose

17 Run the engine for approximately 10 minutes at 2500 rpm (until the thermostat operates). Check the coolant temperature gauge for signs of overheating.

18 Stop the engine; allow it to cool completely, and then check for leaks, particularly around the disturbed components. With the system cold (the system must be cold for an accurate coolant level indication), check the level in the expansion tank.

19 If necessary, top-up the coolant level in the expansion tank to the MAX level mark. Repeat the procedures contained in paragraphs 17 to 19 until the coolant level in the expansion tank no longer drops.

Antifreeze mixture

20 Always use an ethylene glycol based antifreeze, which is suitable for use in mixed-metal cooling systems. The quantity of antifreeze and levels of protection are indicated in the Specifications.

21 Before adding antifreeze, the cooling system should be completely drained, preferably flushed, and all hoses and clips checked for condition and security.

22 After filling with antifreeze, a label should be attached to the radiator or expansion tank stating the type and concentration of antifreeze used, and the date installed. Any subsequent topping-up should be made with the same type and concentration of antifreeze.

Caution: Do not use engine antifreeze in the windscreen/tailgate/headlight washer system, as it will cause damage to the vehicle paintwork.

27 Timing belt renewal

1 See Chapter 2C, Section 6.

Chapter 2 Part A
1.2 litre petrol engine in-car repair procedures

Contents

Degrees of difficulty

Easy, suitable for novice with little experience	**Fairly easy,** suitable for beginner with some experience	**Fairly difficult,** suitable for competent DIY mechanic	**Difficult,** suitable for experienced DIY mechanic	**Very difficult,** suitable for expert DIY or professional

Specifications

Engine (general)

Engine code	HRA2DDT
Capacity	1197 cc
Bore	72.2 mm
Stroke	73.1 mm
Direction of crankshaft rotation	Clockwise (viewed from right-hand side of vehicle)
No. 1 cylinder location	At timing chain end of engine
Firing order	1-3-4-2
Compression ratio	10 : 1

Valve clearances

Cold engine:	
Inlet	0.25 to 0.35 mm
Exhaust	0.46 to 0.54 mm

Lubrication system

Oil pump type	Rotor-type, driven off crankshaft right-hand end
Minimum oil pressure at normal operating temperature (approx. 80°C):	
At Idle speed	1.7 bars (minimum)
At 4000 rpm	3.5 bars (minimum)

Torque wrench settings

	Nm	lbf ft
Big-end bearing cap bolts: *		
Stage 1	25	18
Stage 2	Angle tighten a further 110°	
Camshaft bearing cap bolts:		
Stage 1	4	3
Stage 2	11	8
Camshaft sprocket retaining bolts	75	55
Crankshaft pulley bolt: *		
Stage 1	50	37
Stage 2	Angle-tighten a further 200°	
Cylinder head bolts: *		
Stage 1	25	18
Stage 2	Angle-tighten a further 270°	
Cylinder head closing plate bolts	25	18
Cylinder head cover bolts	10	8
Engine-to-transmission fixing bolts	62	46
Flywheel: *		
Stage 1	40	30
Stage 2	Angle-tighten a further 50°	
Left-hand transmission mounting:		
Through-bolt/stud nut	60	44
Through-bolt/stud-to-bracket	65	48
Mounting-to-bracket nuts	105	77
Mounting bracket-to-inner wing panel bolts	50	37
Mounting-to-transmission bolts	60	44
Main bearing cap bolts: *		
Stage 1	33	24
Stage 2	Angle-tighten a further 60°	
Main bearing cap support beam	25	18
Oil pump sprocket retaining nut	25	18
Rear engine/transmission torque/link arm mounting:		
Mounting-to-front subframe bolt	80	59
Mounting bracket-to-transmission bolt	80	59
Right-hand engine mounting:		
Bracket bolts to engine	60	44
Mounting bolts to inner wing	60	44
Sump oil drain plug	50	37
Lower sump oil pan bolts	10	7
Upper sump casing bolts to cylinder block	25	18
Timing chain cover bolts:		
Lower bolts x 8 (6mm)	25	18
Upper bolts x 6 (8mm)	55	41
Centre bolts x 3	10	7
Timing chain guide bolts	25	18
Timing chain tensioner bolts	10	7

**Use new nuts/bolts*

1 General Information

Using this Chapter

1 This part of Chapter 2 is devoted to in-car repair procedures for the 1.2 litre petrol engine. Similar information covering the other engine types can be found in Parts B and C. All procedures concerning engine removal and refitting, and engine block/cylinder head overhaul can be found in Part D of this Chapter.

2 Note that many operations that would normally be classed as in-car repair procedures and be covered in this Chapter, are actually covered in Part D. This is due to the design of the engine and the limited clearance in the engine compartment making it physically impossible to remove and refit many components and assemblies with the engine in the car.

3 In Parts A, B and C, the assumption is made that the engine is installed in the car, with all ancillaries connected. If the engine has been removed for overhaul, the preliminary dismantling information, which precedes each operation, may be ignored.

Engine description

4 The engine is of the sixteen-valve, in-line four-cylinder, double overhead camshaft (DOHC) type, mounted transversely at the front of the car with the transmission attached to the left-hand end.

5 The crankshaft runs in five main bearings. Thrustwashers are fitted to No 3 main bearing (upper half) to control crankshaft endfloat.

6 The connecting rods rotate on horizontally split bearing shells at their big ends. The pistons are attached to the connecting rods by gudgeon pins, which are a sliding fit in the small end of the connecting rod and retained in the pistons by circlips. The aluminium-alloy pistons are fitted with three piston rings – two compression rings and an oil control ring.

7 The cylinder block is made of aluminium alloy and the cylinder bores are an integral part of the block. On this type of engine the cylinder bores are sometimes referred to as having dry liners.

8 The inlet and exhaust valves are each closed by coil springs, and operate in guides pressed into the cylinder head; the valve seat inserts are also pressed into the cylinder head, and can be renewed separately if worn. Both camshafts have a variable valve timing sprocket at their right-hand end which is oil fed through a control solenoid valve.

9 The camshaft is driven by a timing chain, and operates the sixteen valves via bucket-type followers. The followers are situated directly below the camshafts. Valve clearances are adjusted by replacing the relevant follower with a different thickness. The camshafts rotate directly in the cylinder head.

10 Lubrication is by means of an oil pump, which is driven off the right-hand end of the crankshaft. It draws oil through a strainer located in the sump, and then forces it through an externally mounted filter into galleries in the cylinder block/crankcase. From there, the oil is distributed to the crankshaft (main bearings) and camshaft. The big-end bearings are supplied with oil via internal drillings in the crankshaft, while the camshaft bearings also receive a pressurised supply. The camshaft lobes and valves are lubricated by splash, as are all other engine components.

Repairs with engine in car

11 The design of the engine and the limited working clearance within the engine compartment dictate that the engine/transmission assembly must be removed from the car to carry out many of the more involved repair operations. Refer to Chapter 2D for procedures not contained in the following list.

12 The following work can be carried out with the engine in the car:

a) Compression pressure – testing.
b) Cylinder head cover – removal and refitting.
c) Valve clearances – checking.
d) Sump oil pan – removal and refitting.
e) Crankshaft oil seals – renewal.
f) Engine/transmission mountings – inspection and renewal.
g) Flywheel – removal, inspection and refitting.

2 Compression test – description and interpretation

1 When engine performance is down, or if misfiring occurs which cannot be attributed to the ignition or fuel systems, a compression test can provide diagnostic clues as to the engine's condition. If the test is performed regularly, it can give warning of trouble before any other symptoms become apparent.

2 The engine must be fully warmed-up to normal operating temperature, the battery must be fully charged, and the aid of an assistant will also be required.

3 Depressurise the fuel system by removing the fuel pump fuse from the fusebox – the fuses can usually be identified from the label inside the fusebox cover, or from the wiring diagrams at the end of this manual. With the fuse removed, start the engine, and allow it to run until it stalls. Try to start the engine at least twice more, to ensure that all residual pressure has been relieved.

4 Remove the spark plugs as described in Chapter 1A, Section 26.

5 Fit a compression tester to the No 1 cylinder spark plug hole – the type of tester which screws into the plug thread is to be preferred.

6 Have the assistant hold the throttle wide open, and crank the engine on the starter motor; after two or three revolutions, the compression pressure should build-up to a maximum figure, and then stabilise. Record the highest reading obtained.

7 Repeat the test on the remaining cylinders, recording the pressure in each.

8 All cylinders should produce very similar pressures in the order of 10 to 15 bars. Any one cylinder reading below 7 bars, or a difference of more than 3 bars between cylinders suggests a fault. Note that the compression should build-up quickly in a healthy engine; low compression on the first stroke, followed by gradually increasing pressure on successive strokes, indicates worn piston rings. A low compression reading on the first stroke, which does not build-up during successive strokes, indicates leaking valves or a blown head gasket (a cracked head could also be the cause). Deposits on the undersides of the valve heads can also cause low compression.

9 If the pressure in any cylinder is reduced to 10 bars or less, carry out the following test to isolate the cause. Introduce a teaspoonful of clean oil into that cylinder through its spark plug hole and repeat the test.

10 If the addition of oil temporarily improves the compression pressure, this indicates that bore or piston wear is responsible for the pressure loss. No improvement suggests that leaking or burnt valves, or a blown head gasket, may be to blame.

11 A low reading from two adjacent cylinders is almost certainly due to the head gasket having blown between them; the presence of coolant in the engine oil will confirm this.

12 If one cylinder is about 20 percent lower than the others and the engine has a slightly rough idle; a worn camshaft lobe could be the cause.

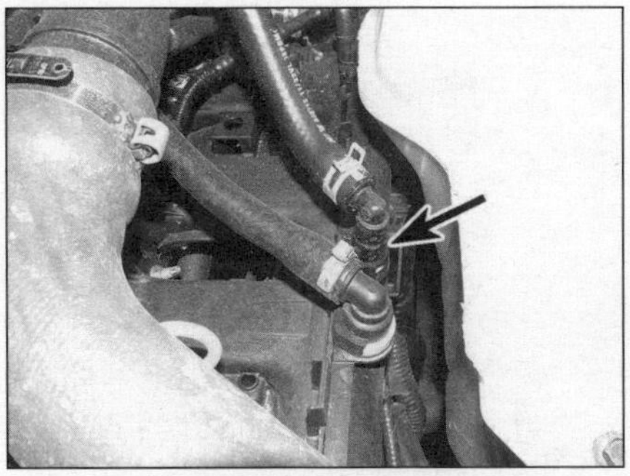

3.2 Disconnect the vacuum hose at the quick-release connector

13 If the compression reading is unusually high, the combustion chambers are probably coated with carbon deposits. If this is the case, the cylinder head should be removed and decarbonised.

14 On completion of the test, refit the spark plugs and fuel pump fuse.

3 Cylinder head cover – removal and refitting

Removal

1 Disconnect the battery negative terminal (refer to battery disconnection and reconnection in Chapter 5A, Section 3).

2 Disconnect the brake servo vacuum hose at the quick-release connector on the inlet manifold **(see illustration)**. Release the vacuum hose from the clips on the air inlet hose and move the vacuum hose to one side.

3 Remove the spark plugs as described in Chapter 1A, Section 26.

4 Remove the inlet and exhaust camshaft position sensors as described in Chapter 4A, Section 10.

5 Disconnect the crankcase ventilation hose from the front of the cylinder head cover.

6 Disconnect the evaporative emission control hose from the rear of the cylinder head cover **(see illustration)**.

7 Remove the high-pressure fuel pump as described in Chapter 4A, Section 10.

8 Undo the retaining bolts and remove the turbocharger heat shield.

9 Disconnect any remaining wiring connectors and move the wiring harness clear of the cylinder head cover.

10 Working in the reverse of the tightening sequence **(see illustration 3.17)**, slacken and remove the cylinder head cover retaining bolts. Note that bolts 1, 2 and 3 are longer than the rest.

11 Lift off the cylinder head cover, and recover the rubber seal, which goes around the outer edge of the cover, and also around each of the spark plug holes.

12 Inspect the cover seals for signs of damage and deterioration, and renew as necessary. Nissan recommends that the

3.6 Disconnect the evaporative emission control hose

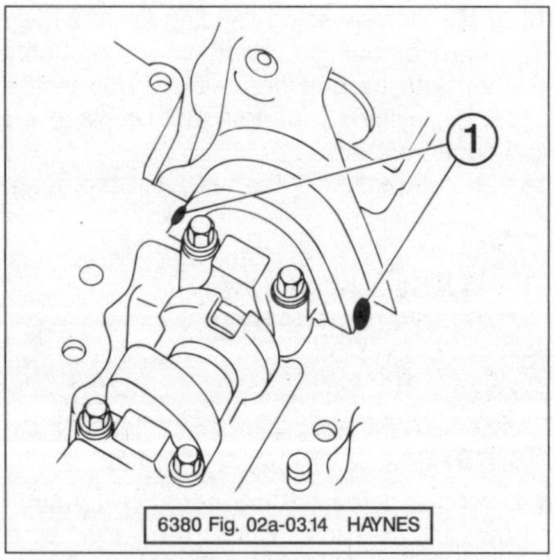

3.14 Apply sealant to the position (1) on the camshaft bearing cap

cylinder head cover seal should always be renewed, if the cover is removed.

Refitting

13 Carefully clean the cylinder head and cover mating surfaces, and remove all traces of oil.

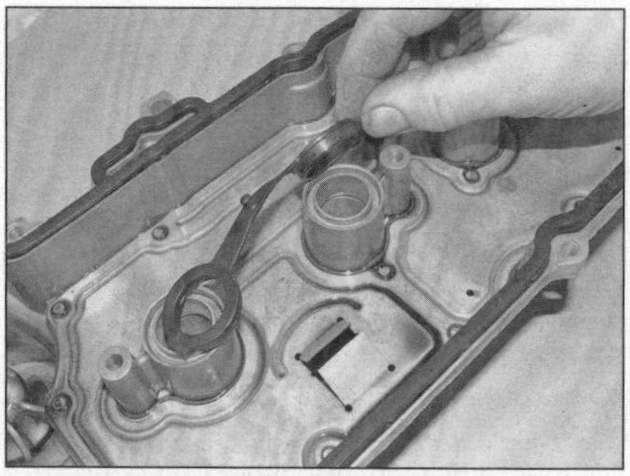

3.15 Fit the new rubber gasket to the cylinder head cover

14 Apply a small amount of sealant to each side of the exhaust camshaft bearing cap at the transmission end **(see illustration)**.

15 Fit the rubber seal to the cylinder head cover groove, ensuring that it is correctly located along its entire length, and around the four spark plug holes in the centre of the cover **(see illustration)**.

16 Carefully lower the cylinder head cover onto the cylinder head, taking great care not to displace any of the rubber seal.

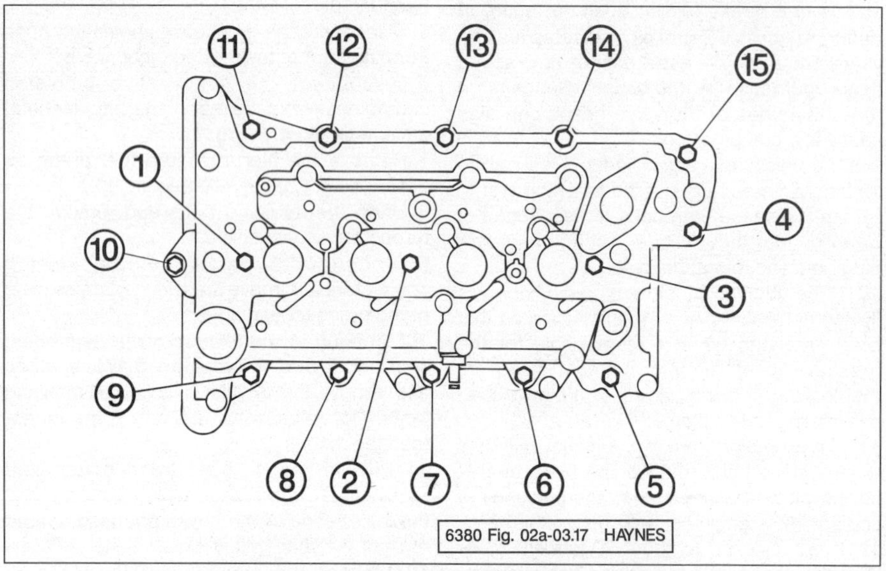

3.17 Cylinder head cover bolt tightening sequence

17 Make sure the cover is correctly seated, and then install the retaining bolts. Working in sequence, tighten all the cover screws to the specified torque **(see illustration)**.

18 The remainder of refitting is a reversal of removal.

4 Crankshaft pulley – removal and refitting

Removal

1 Remove the auxiliary drivebelt as described in Chapter 1A, Section 12.

2 To prevent crankshaft rotation while the pulley bolt is unscrewed, the pulley should be held by a suitable tool which locates in the slots in the pulley to prevent it from turning **(see illustration)**. If this is not available, select top gear and have an assistant apply the brakes firmly.

3 Unscrew the pulley bolt, along with its washer (where applicable), and remove the pulley from the crankshaft **(see illustration)**.

4 If the pulley is a tight fit on the end of the crankshaft, use a puller to withdraw the pulley from the end of the shaft. Refit the pulley bolt and screw it back into the end of the crankshaft, leaving it approx. 5 mm out from the pulley face. Fit the puller (this can be a homemade puller, using a piece of flat bar and three bols/nuts) to the pulley and tighten the centre bolt to withdraw the pulley from the end of the crankshaft **(see illustrations)**.

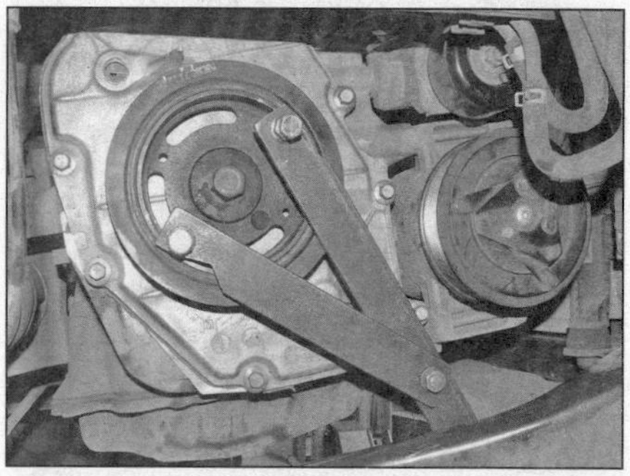

4.2 Using a homemade tool to hold the pulley

4.3 Remove the crankshaft pulley bolt

4.4a Remove the pulley using a puller…

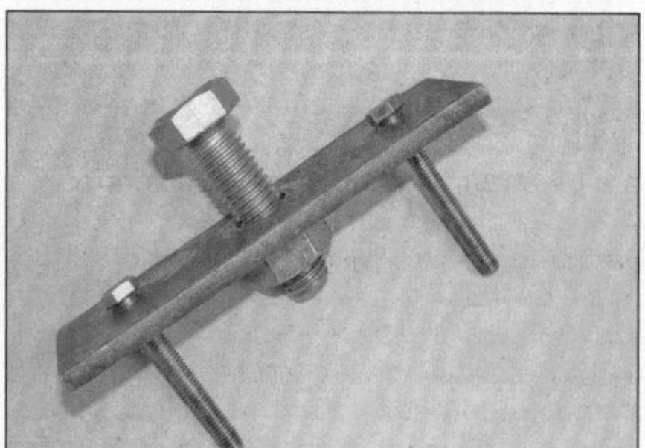

4.4b …which can be made out of a piece of flat metal bar

4.5 Align the slot in the pulley centre hub with the woodruff key

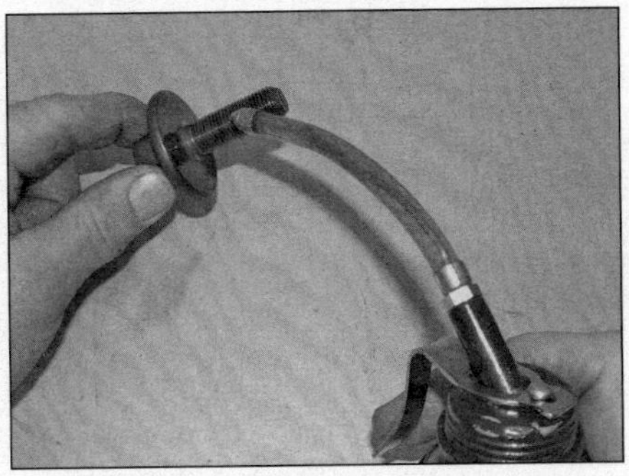

4.6 Apply a small amount of oil to the threads

5.11 Markings inside the follower for thickness

Refitting

5 Align the crankshaft pulley groove with the key **(see illustration)**, then slide the sprocket onto the crankshaft.
6 Lubricate under the head of the bolt, also the bolt threads with clean engine oil **(see illustration)**, and then refit the retaining bolt/washer.
7 Lock the crankshaft by the method used on removal, and tighten the pulley retaining bolt to the specified Stage 1 torque setting. Using an angle tightening gauge, tighten the bolt through the specified Stage 2 angle.
8 Refit the auxiliary drivebelt and adjust it as described in Chapter 1A, Section 12.

5 Valve clearances – checking and adjustment

Note: *This is not a routine operation. It should only be necessary at high mileage, after overhaul, or when investigating noise or power loss which may be attributable to the valve gear. Adjustment involves removing the camshaft and changing the cam followers (valve lifters) that are available in 31 different thicknesses (ranging from 2.96 mm to 3.56 mm, in steps of 0.02 mm).*
Note: *Checking of the valve clearances can be done with the engine in the car. If adjustment is necessary, the engine must be removed from the car to allow for camshaft removal.*

Checking

1 The importance of having the valve clearances correctly adjusted cannot be overstressed, as they vitally affect the performance of the engine. The clearances are checked as follows.
2 Draw the outline of the engine on a piece of paper, numbering the cylinders 1 to 4, with No 1 cylinder at the timing chain end of the engine. Show the position of each valve, together with the specified valve clearance. Above each valve, draw two lines for noting the actual clearance and the amount of adjustment required.
3 Remove the cylinder head cover as described in Section 3.
4 Apply the handbrake then jack up the front of the car and securely support it on axle stands (see *Jacking and vehicle support*). Remove the right-hand roadwheel.
5 Remove the front right-hand wheel arch liner as described in Chapter 11, Section 21.
6 Turn the crankshaft, using a spanner on the crankshaft pulley bolt, until the camshaft lobes for No. 1 cylinder (timing chain end) are pointing upwards.
7 Using feeler gauges, measure the clearance between the base of the cam lobe and the follower of each of the valves of No.1 cylinder, recording each clearance on the paper.
8 Rotate the crankshaft until the next set of cam lobes are pointing upwards and measure the clearance between the base of the cam lobes and the associated follower. Record each clearance on the paper.
9 Repeat this procedure until the clearances for all the valves have been recorded.
10 Calculate the difference between each measured clearance and the desired value, and record it on the piece of paper.

Adjustment

Note: *A micrometer or dial gauge and probe will be required for this operation.*
11 Where a valve clearance differs from the specified value, then the cam follower (valve lifter) for that valve must be substituted with a thinner or thicker one accordingly. The cam followers have the thickness stamped on the bottom face of the follower; e.g. 302 indicates the follower is 3.02 mm thick at the top centre of the follower **(see illustration)**.
12 If required use a micrometer or dial gauge to measure the true thickness of any follower removed, as it may have been reduced by wear.
Note: *Followers are available in thicknesses between 2.96 mm and 3.56 mm, in steps of 0.02 mm.*
13 To access the cam followers (valve lifters), first remove the camshafts as described in Chapter 2D, Section 7. Note that it will be necessary to remove the camshaft to facilitate engine removal (see Chapter 2D, Section 3).
14 The size of follower required is calculated as follows. If the measured clearance is less than specified, subtract the measured clearance from the specified clearance, and deduct the result from the thickness of the existing follower. For example:

Sample calculation – clearance too small
Clearance measured (A) = 0.16 mm
Desired clearance (B) = 0.30 mm
Difference (B – A) = 0.14 mm
Cam follower thickness fitted = 3.50 mm
Cam follower thickness required =
3.50 – 0.14 = 3.36 mm

15 If the measured clearance is greater than specified, subtract the specified clearance from the measured clearance, and add the result to the thickness of the existing follower. For example:

Sample calculation – clearance too big
Clearance measured (A) = 0.40 mm
Desired clearance (B) = 0.30 mm
Difference (A – B) = 0.10 mm
Cam follower thickness fitted = 3.26 mm
Cam follower thickness required =
3.26 + 0.10 = 3.36 mm

16 Working on each separately, lift out the follower to be renewed, then oil the new one and carefully locate it in the cylinder head, on top of the valve.
17 Refit the camshafts with reference to Chapter 2D, Section 7.
18 It will be helpful for future adjustment if a record is kept of the thickness of cam followers (valve lifters) fitted at each position. The cam followers required could be purchased in advance once the clearances and the existing follower thicknesses are known.
19 Once all valve clearances have been adjusted, rotate the crankshaft through at least four complete turns in the correct direction of rotation, to settle all disturbed followers, then recheck the clearances as described above.
20 With all valve clearances correctly adjusted, refit the cylinder head cover as described in Section 3, Then refit the engine to the car (Chapter 2D, Section 3).

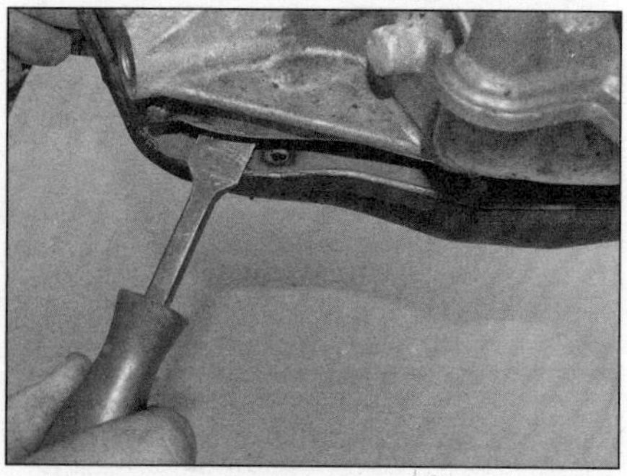

6.4 Using a flat ended scraper to prise the sump away

6 Sump – removal and refitting

Note: *The oil sump is made up of two parts; it has an upper alloy part and a lower steel oil pan. The following procedure is for the lower oil pan part. To remove the upper alloy part, the engine will need to be removed and the upper alloy sump then split from the cylinder block.*

Removal

1 Firmly apply the handbrake, and then jack up the front of the vehicle and support it securely on axle stands (see *Jacking and vehicle support*).

2 Drain the engine oil, then clean and refit the engine oil drain plug, fit a new sealing

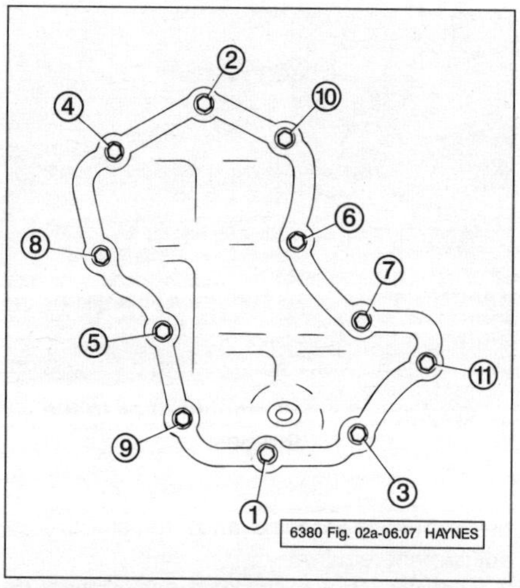

6.7 Tighten the bolts in the sequence shown

washer on refitting. And then tighten it to the specified torque. If the engine is nearing its service interval when the oil and filter are due for renewal, it is recommended that the filter is also removed, and a new one fitted. Refer to Chapter 1A, Section 5 for further information.

3 Progressively slacken and remove all of the steel oil pan retaining bolts.

4 The lower steel oil pan is sealed to the upper alloy sump casing with strong liquid gasket sealer, which is very difficult to remove, however methodical use of a spatula or thin knife will release the sump **(see illustration)**. Take care not to distort or damage the mating surfaces of the lower oil pan and upper alloy sump. Take adequate precautions to catch any oil remaining inside the sump housing, as the oil pan is removed.

Refitting

5 Clean all traces of sealant from the mating surfaces of the upper alloy part of the sump and steel oil pan, then use a clean rag to wipe out the oil pan and the sump interior.

6 Ensure that the lower oil pan and upper alloy casing mating surfaces are clean and dry. Apply a continuous bead of suitable sealant to the mating surface of the oil pan. Apply a 4 mm to 5 mm diameter bead of sealant to the oil pan, going around the inner edge of each bolt hole.

7 Offer up the sump, locating it in the correct position, and refit its retaining bolts. Tighten the bolts evenly and progressively to the specified torque and in the correct sequence **(see illustration)**.

8 After reassembly, the engine can then be refilled with fresh engine oil. Refer to Chapter 1A, Section 5, for further information.

9 Start the engine and warm it up to normal operating temperature, check for any leaks from the sump area.

7 Crankshaft oil seals – renewal

Timing chain cover oil seal

1 Remove the crankshaft pulley as described in Section 4.

2 Carefully lever the oil seal out of position, using a large flat-bladed screwdriver, taking care not to damage the end of the crankshaft or timing cover **(see illustration)**.

3 Clean the seal housing, and polish off any burrs or raised edges, which may have caused the seal to fail in the first place.

4 Lubricate the lips of the new seal with a smear of clean oil and offer up the seal ensuring its sealing lip is facing inwards. Carefully ease the seal into position, taking care not to damage its sealing lip. Drive the seal into position until it seats flush with the face of the timing chain cover **(see illustrations)**. Take care not to damage the seal lips during fitting.

5 Wash off any traces of oil, then refit the crankshaft pulley as described in Section 4.

Flywheel oil seal

6 Remove the flywheel, as described in Section 8.

7 Note the fitted position of the old seal, then prise it out of the right-hand cover/housing using a screwdriver or suitable hooked instrument, taking care not to damage the surface of the crankshaft. Alternatively, the oil seal can be removed by drilling a hole in the seal, and then inserting a self-tapping screw.

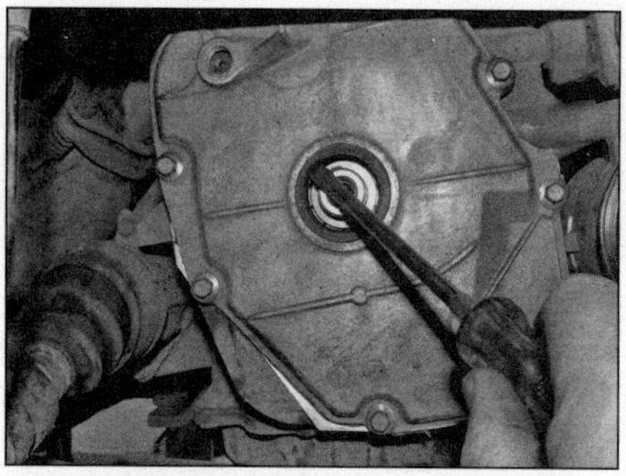

7.2 Carefully prise out the oil seal

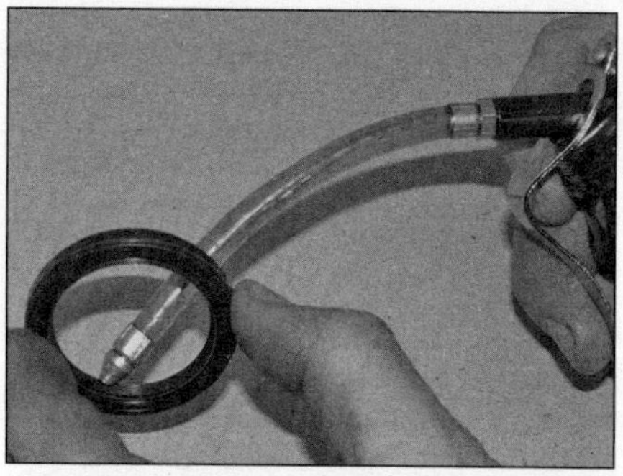

7.4a Lubricate the inner lip of the seal...

7.4b ...press the seal into position...

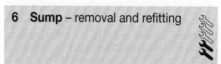

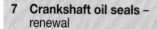

7.4c ...carefully fit the seal into the cover

7.7a Carefully drill a hole in the seal...

7.7b ...insert a self tapping screw...

7.7c ...and lever the seal out from the casing

7.8 Clean around the seal fitting surface area

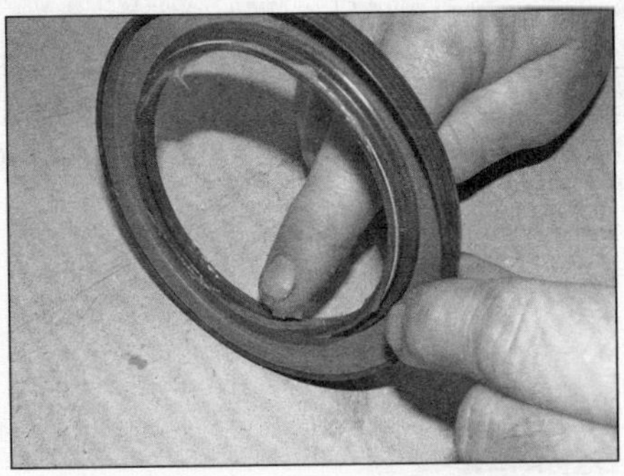

7.9a Using clean oil to lubricate the inner lip of the seal...

7.9b ...place the seal into position...

A pair of grips/pliers can then be used to pull out the oil seal **(see illustrations)**. Take care when drilling the hole, to not drill into anything other than the seal.

8 Clean the seal housing, and polish off any burrs or raised edges, which may have caused the seal to fail in the first place **(see illustration)**.

9 Lubricate with clean oil the lips of the new seal and the crankshaft shoulder, then offer up the seal to the cylinder block/crankcase. Ease the sealing lip of the seal over the crankshaft shoulder by hand only, and press the seal evenly into its recess to make it square in the casing **(see illustrations)**.

10 With the seal still protruding out from the cylinder block, apply a coat of liquid gasket/sealant all the way around the outer edge of the seal. Carefully drive the seal into position until it seats flush with the face of the cylinder block, and then wipe off the excess liquid gasket/sealant from the casing **(see illustrations)**. Make sure the outer edge of the seal is sitting flush with the cylinder block casing.

11 Wash off any traces of oil or sealant, then refit the flywheel as described in Section 8.

7.10a Apply some sealant around the outer edge of the seal...

7.10b ...press the seal fully into position...

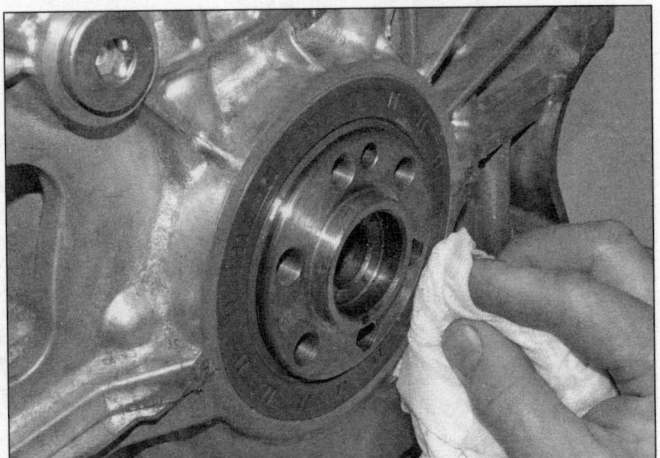

7.10c ...then clean off the excess sealant from around the casing

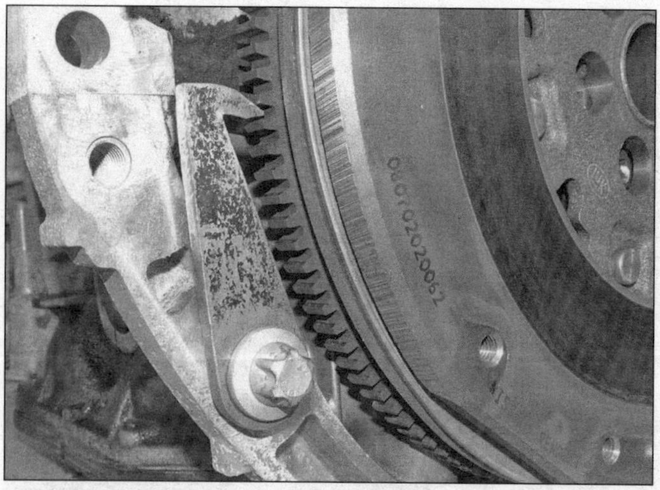

8.3 Using a tool to prevent the flywheel from turning...

8.4 ...when slackening the flywheel bolts

8 Flywheel – removal, inspection and refitting

Removal

Note: *New flywheel retaining bolts will be required for refitting.*

1 Remove the transmission as described in Chapter 7, Section 6.

2 Remove the clutch assembly as described in Chapter 6, Section 7.

3 Prevent the flywheel from turning by locking the ring gear teeth **(see illustration)**. Alternatively, bolt a strap between the flywheel and the cylinder block.

4 Slacken and remove the retaining bolts **(see illustration)**, then remove the flywheel from the end of the crankshaft. Do not drop it, as it is very heavy.

Inspection

5 If the flywheel's clutch mating surface is deeply scored, cracked or otherwise damaged, the flywheel must be renewed. Seek the advice of a Nissan dealer or engine reconditioning specialist.

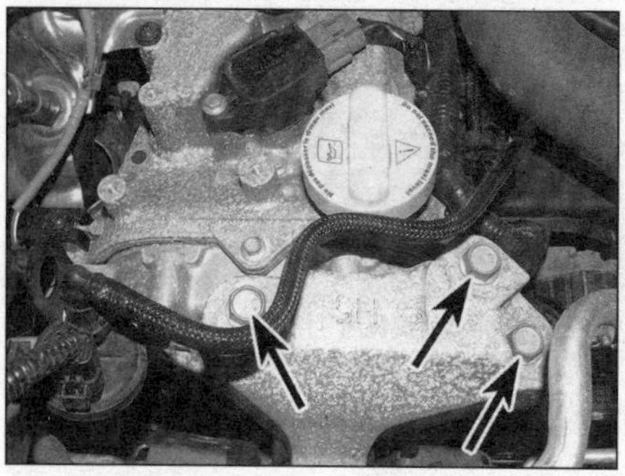

9.7 Remove the mounting bracket retaining bolts

6 If the ring gear is badly worn or has missing teeth, it must be renewed. Check with your Nissan dealer or engine reconditioning specialist, to see if the flywheel can be repaired.

Refitting

7 Clean the mating surfaces of the flywheel and crankshaft.

8 Offer up the flywheel, and fit the new retaining bolts.

9 Lock the ring gear using the method employed on dismantling, and tighten the retaining bolts to the specified Stage 1 torque, then through the Stage 2 angle, using an angle tightening gauge.

10 Refit the clutch as described in Chapter 6, Section 7.

11 Remove the locking tool, and refit the transmission as described in Chapter 7, Section 6.

9 Engine/transmission mountings – inspection and renewal

Inspection

1 If improved access is required, firmly apply the handbrake, and then jack up the front of the vehicle and support it securely on axle stands (see *Jacking and vehicle support*).

2 Check the mounting rubber to see if it is cracked, hardened or separated from the metal at any point; renew the mounting if any such damage or deterioration is evident.

3 Check that all the mounting's fasteners are securely tightened; use a torque wrench to check if possible.

4 Using a large screwdriver or a crowbar, check for wear in the mounting by carefully levering against it to check for free play. Where this is not possible, enlist the aid of an assistant to move the engine/transmission back-and-forth, or from side-to-side, while you watch the mounting. While some free play is to be expected even from new components, excessive wear should be obvious. If excessive free play is found, check first that the fasteners are correctly secured, and then renew any worn components as described below.

Renewal

Right-hand mounting

5 Disconnect the battery negative terminal (refer to battery disconnection and reconnection in Chapter 5A, Section 3).

6 Place a jack beneath the engine, with a block of wood on the jack head. Raise the jack until it is supporting the weight of the engine.

7 Slacken and remove the three retaining bolts from the inner wing panel, remove the three retaining bolts from the engine mounting bracket, and then withdraw the complete mounting from the engine compartment **(see illustration)**.

8 Check carefully for signs of wear or damage on all components, and renew them where necessary.

9 On refitting, fit the engine mounting and bracket to the inner wing panel and engine, and then securely tighten its retaining bolts to the specified torque setting.

10 With the engine mounting back in position, lower the jack and remove it from underneath the engine.

11 Reconnect the battery negative terminal.

Left-hand mounting

12 Remove the battery and tray, as described in Chapter 5A, Section 3.

13 Place a jack and block of wood beneath the transmission, and raise the jack to take the weight of the transmission.

14 Slacken and remove the through-bolt/stud

retaining nut from the centre of the mounting **(see illustration)**.

15 Slacken and remove the two outer retaining nuts, and withdraw the mounting from the mounting bracket.

16 If required, undo the retaining bolts from the inner wing panel to remove the upper mounting bracket.

17 Also, if required, undo the retaining bolts from the transmission to remove the lower mounting bracket.

18 Check carefully for signs of wear or damage on all components, and renew them where necessary.

19 On refitting, fit the upper and lower mounting brackets (where removed) and securely tighten the retaining bolts.

20 Align the left-hand rubber mounting with the bolt/stud on the lower mounting bracket and tighten its nut to the specified torque setting.

21 Refit the two outer retaining nuts, and tighten to the specified torque setting.

22 With the transmission mounting back in position, lower the jack and remove it from underneath the transmission.

23 Refit the battery and battery tray, with reference to Chapter 5A, Section 3.

Rear lower mounting

24 If not already done, firmly apply the handbrake, and then jack up the front of the vehicle and support it securely on axle stands (see *Jacking and vehicle support*).

25 Slacken and remove the bolts securing the rear mounting bracket to the transmission, and then withdraw the bracket from transmission **(see illustration)**.

26 Slacken and remove the bolt securing the rear mounting link to the subframe, and then withdraw the mounting link from subframe **(see illustration)**.

27 Check carefully for signs of wear or damage on all components, and renew them where necessary.

28 On reassembly, fit the rear mounting to the subframe, and tighten the retaining bolt to the specified torque.

9.14 Undo the centre retaining nut

29 Refit the mounting bracket to the lower part of the transmission and tighten its retaining bolts to the specified torque.

30 With the transmission rear mounting link arm back in position, lower the vehicle to the ground.

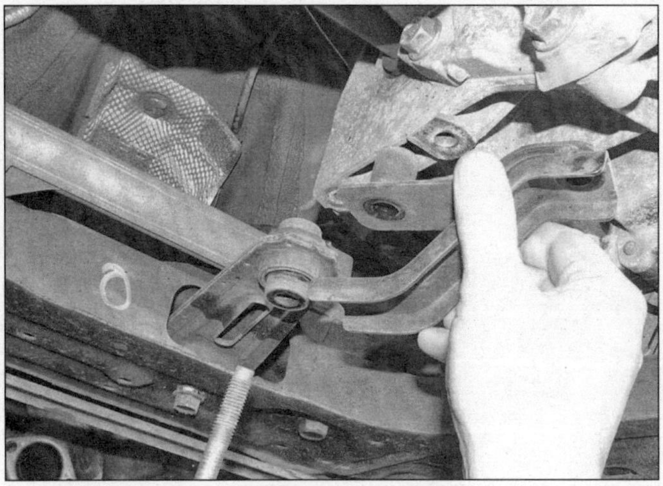

9.25 Remove the mounting bracket from the transmission

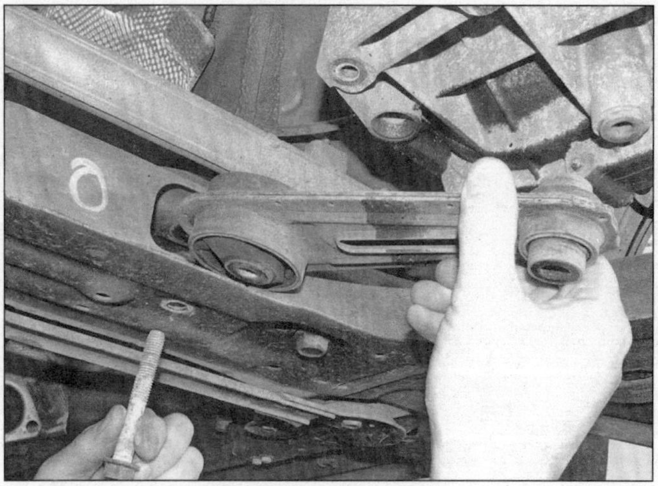

9.26 Remove the link arm from the subframe

Chapter 2 Part B
1.6 litre petrol engine in-car repair procedures

Contents

Degrees of difficulty

Easy, suitable for novice with little experience	**Fairly easy,** suitable for beginner with some experience	**Fairly difficult,** suitable for competent DIY mechanic	**Difficult,** suitable for experienced DIY mechanic	**Very difficult,** suitable for expert DIY or professional

Specifications

Engine (general)

Engine code	HR16DE
Capacity	1598 cc
Bore	78.0 mm
Stroke	83.6 mm
Direction of crankshaft rotation	Clockwise (viewed from right-hand side of vehicle)
No. 1 cylinder location	At timing chain end of block
Firing order	1-3-4-2
Compression ratio	10.7: 1
Cylinder compression pressures:	
Standard	15.1 bars
Minimum	12.7 bars
Maximum difference between cylinders	1.0 bar

Valve clearances

Cold engine:	
Inlet	0.26 to 0.34 mm
Exhaust	0.29 to 0.37 mm

Camshaft and followers

Drive	Chain
Number of bearings	5
Endfloat	0.075 to 0.153 mm
Camshaft lobe height:	
Inlet	41.705 to 41.895 mm
Exhaust	40.915 to 41.105 mm
Camshaft bearing journal outer diameter:	
No 1 bearing	27.935 to 27.955 mm
Nos 2 to 5 bearings	24.950 to 24.970 mm
Camshaft cylinder head bearing journal internal diameter:	
No 1 bearing	28.000 to 28.021 mm
Nos 2 to 5 bearings	25.000 to 25.021 mm
Camshaft journal-to-bearing clearance:	
No 1 bearing	0.045 to 0.086 mm
Nos 2 to 5 bearings	0.030 to 0.071 mm
Camshaft run-out:	
Standard	0.075 to 0.153 mm
Limit	0.02 mm
Camshaft sprocket run-out	Less than 0.15 mm
Camshaft follower outer diameter	29.977 to 29.987 mm
Cylinder head hole diameter for follower	30.000 to 30.021 mm
Camshaft follower to cylinder head clearance	0.013 to 0.044 mm

Lubrication system

Oil pump type	Rotor-type, driven off crankshaft right-hand end
Minimum oil pressure at normal operating temperature (approx. 80°C):	
At Idle speed	0.65 bars (minimum)
At 2000 rpm	2.00 bars (minimum)

Torque wrench settings

Torque wrench settings	Nm	lbf ft
Big-end bearing cap bolts:		
Stage 1	27	20
Stage 2	Completely slacken	
Stage 3	20	14
Stage 4	Angle-tighten 60°	
Camshaft bearing cap bolts (see text):		
Stage 1 – bolts 9 to 11	2	1.5
Stage 2 – bolts 1 to 8	2	1.5
Stage 3 – bolts 1 to 11	6	4.5
Stage 4 – bolts 1 to 11	11	8
Camshaft sprocket retaining bolts	79	58
Crankshaft pulley bolt:		
Stage 1	35	26
Stage 2	Angle-tighten 60°	
Cylinder head bolts:		
Stage 1	40	30
Stage 2	Angle-tighten 60°	
Stage 3	Fully slacken all the bolts	
Stage 4	40	30
Stage 5	Angle-tighten 75°	
Stage 6	Angle-tighten a further 75°	
Cylinder head cover bolts	10	8
Engine-to-transmission fixing bolts	48	35
Flywheel	108	80
Fuel rail protector shield bolts:		
Upper bolts	25	18
Lower bolts	10	7
Left-hand transmission mounting:		
Through-bolt/stud nut	60	44
Through-bolt/stud-to-bracket	65	48
Mounting-to-bracket nuts	105	77
Mounting bracket-to-inner wing panel bolts	48	36
Mounting bracket-to-transmission bolts	60	44
Main bearing cap bolts:		
Stage 1	33	24
Stage 2	Angle-tighten 60°	

Torque wrench settings (continued)	Nm	lbf ft
Oil level sensor retaining bolt	8	6
Oil pump sprocket retaining nut	25	18
Rear engine/transmission torque/link arm mounting:		
Mounting-to-front subframe bolt	80	59
Mounting bracket-to-transmission bolt	80	59
Right-hand engine mounting:		
Bracket bolts to engine	55	41
Mounting bolts to inner wing	65	48
Sump oil drain plug	34	25
Sump (lower) oil pan bolts	10	7
Sump upper casing bolts to transmission	48	35
Sump upper casing bolts to cylinder block	25	18
Timing chain cover bolts (see text):		
Lower bolts x 9 (6mm)	25	18
Upper bolts x 5 (8mm)	55	41
Timing chain guide bolts	25	18
Timing chain tensioner access plug in cover	20	15
Timing chain tensioner bolts	10	8

1 General Information

Using this Chapter

1 This Part of Chapter 2 is devoted to in-car repair procedures for the 1.6 litre petrol engine. Similar information covering the other engine types can be found in Parts A and C. All procedures concerning engine removal and refitting, and engine block/cylinder head overhaul can be found in Part D of this Chapter.

2 Note that, while it may be possible physically to overhaul items such as the piston/connecting rod assemblies while the engine is in the car, such tasks are not normally carried out as separate operations. Usually, several additional procedures (not to mention the cleaning of components and of oilways) have to be carried out. For this reason, all such tasks are classed as major overhaul procedures, and are described in Part D of this Chapter.

3 In Parts A, B and C, the assumption is made that the engine is installed in the car, with all ancillaries connected. If the engine has been removed for overhaul, the preliminary dismantling information, which precedes each operation, may be ignored.

Engine description

4 The engine is of the sixteen-valve, in-line four-cylinder, double overhead camshaft (DOHC) type, mounted transversely at the front of the car with the transmission attached to the left-hand end.

5 The crankshaft runs in five main bearings. Thrustwashers are fitted to No 3 main bearing (upper half) to control crankshaft endfloat.

6 The connecting rods rotate on horizontally split bearing shells at their big ends. The pistons are attached to the connecting rods by gudgeon pins, which are a press fit in the small end of the connecting rod. The aluminium-alloy pistons are fitted with three piston rings – two compression rings and an oil control ring.

7 The cylinder block is made of aluminium alloy and the cylinder bores are an integral part of the block. On this type of engine the cylinder bores are sometimes referred to as having dry liners.

8 The inlet and exhaust valves are each closed by coil springs, and operate in guides pressed into the cylinder head; the valve seat inserts are also pressed into the cylinder head, and can be renewed separately if worn. Both camshafts have variable valve timing sprockets which are oil fed through control solenoid valves.

9 The camshaft is driven by a timing chain, and operates the sixteen valves via bucket-type followers. The followers are situated directly below the camshafts. Valve clearances are adjusted by replacing the relevant follower with a different thickness. The camshafts rotate directly in the cylinder head.

10 Lubrication is by means of an oil pump, which is driven off the right-hand end of the crankshaft. It draws oil through a strainer located in the sump, and then forces it through an externally mounted filter into galleries in the cylinder block/crankcase. From there, the oil is distributed to the crankshaft (main bearings) and camshaft. The big-end bearings are supplied with oil via internal drillings in the crankshaft, while the camshaft bearings also receive a pressurised supply. The camshaft lobes and valves are lubricated by splash, as are all other engine components.

Repairs with engine in car

11 The following work can be carried out with the engine in the car:

a) Compression pressure – testing.
b) Cylinder head cover – removal and refitting.
c) Timing chain cover – removal and refitting.
d) Timing chain – removal, inspection and refitting.
e) Timing chain tensioner, guides and sprockets – removal, inspection and refitting.
f) Camshaft and followers – removal, inspection and refitting.
g) Valve clearances – adjustment.
h) Cylinder head – removal and refitting.
i) Cylinder head and pistons – decarbonising.
j) Sump oil pan – removal and refitting.
k) Oil pump – removal, inspection and refitting.
l) Crankshaft oil seals – renewal.
m) Engine/transmission mountings – inspection and renewal.
n) Flywheel – removal, inspection and refitting.

2 Compression test – description and interpretation

1 When engine performance is down, or if misfiring occurs which cannot be attributed to the ignition or fuel systems, a compression test can provide diagnostic clues as to the engine's condition. If the test is performed regularly, it can give warning of trouble before any other symptoms become apparent.

2 The engine must be fully warmed-up to normal operating temperature, the battery must be fully charged, and the aid of an assistant will also be required.

3 Depressurise the fuel system by removing the fuel pump fuse from the fusebox – the fuses can usually be identified from the label inside the fusebox cover, or from the wiring diagrams at the end of this manual (see Chapter 12). With the fuse removed, start the engine, and allow it to run until it stalls. Try to

3.5 Align the TDC markings

start the engine at least twice more, to ensure that all residual pressure has been relieved.

4 Remove the spark plugs as described in Chapter 1A, Section 26.

5 Fit a compression tester to the No 1 cylinder spark plug hole – the type of tester which screws into the plug thread is to be preferred.

6 Have the assistant hold the throttle wide open, and crank the engine on the starter motor; after two or three revolutions, the compression pressure should build-up to a maximum figure, and then stabilise. Record the highest reading obtained.

7 Repeat the test on the remaining cylinders, recording the pressure in each.

8 All cylinders should produce very similar pressures; any difference greater than that specified indicates the existence of a fault. Note that the compression should build-up quickly in a healthy engine; low compression on the first stroke, followed by gradually increasing pressure on successive strokes, indicates worn piston rings. A low compression reading on the first stroke, which does not build-up during successive strokes, indicates leaking valves or a blown head gasket (a cracked head could also be the cause). Deposits on the undersides of the valve heads can also cause low compression.

9 If the pressure in any cylinder is reduced to the specified minimum or less, carry out the following test to isolate the cause. Introduce a teaspoonful of clean oil into that cylinder

4.3 Cover the inlet ports using duct tape

through its spark plug hole and repeat the test.

10 If the addition of oil temporarily improves the compression pressure, this indicates that bore or piston wear is responsible for the pressure loss. No improvement suggests that leaking or burnt valves, or a blown head gasket, may be to blame.

11 A low reading from two adjacent cylinders is almost certainly due to the head gasket having blown between them; the presence of coolant in the engine oil will confirm this.

12 If one cylinder is about 20 percent lower than the others and the engine has a slightly rough idle; a worn camshaft lobe could be the cause.

13 If the compression reading is unusually high, the combustion chambers are probably coated with carbon deposits. If this is the case, the cylinder head should be removed and decarbonised.

14 On completion of the test, refit the spark plugs, inlet manifold and fuel pump fuse.

3 Top dead centre (TDC) – locating

1 Disconnect the battery negative terminal (refer to battery disconnection and reconnection in Chapter 5A, Section 3), then remove all the spark plugs as described in Chapter 1A, Section 26.

2 Apply the handbrake and ensure that the transmission is in neutral, then jack up the front of the car and support it on axle stands (see *Jacking and vehicle support*). Remove the right-hand front roadwheel.

3 Remove the right-hand front wheel arch liner as described in Chapter 11, Section 21.

4 The timing marks are in the form of notches on the crankshaft pulley rim, which align with a pointer on the timing chain cover. The TDC mark is the notch on its own to the left of the two other notches in the pulley, as viewed from under the right-hand front wheel arch.

5 Using a spanner (or socket and extension bar) applied to the crankshaft pulley bolt, rotate the crankshaft clockwise until the TDC notch on the crankshaft pulley rim is aligned with the pointer on the timing chain cover **(see illustration)**.

6 With the crankshaft in this position, Nos 1 and 4 cylinders are now at TDC, one of them on the compression stroke.

4 Cylinder head cover – removal and refitting

Removal

1 Disconnect the battery negative terminal (refer to battery disconnection and reconnection in Chapter 5A, Section 3).

2 Remove the inlet manifold as described in Chapter 4A, Section 14.

3 To prevent anything dropping down into the inlet ports in the cylinder head, use duct tape or similar to cover up the ports **(see illustration)**.

4 Disconnect the wiring connectors from the ignition coils, undo the retaining bolts and withdraw the ignition coils from the cylinder head cover.

5 Release the securing clips and disconnect the wiring connectors from the inlet and exhaust valve timing control solenoids and the fuel injectors **(see illustrations)**.

6 Disconnect the wiring connectors from the camshaft position sensors **(see illustration)**.

7 Undo the retaining bolts and remove the injector rail protector shield from the

4.5a Disconnect the wiring connector from the timing control solenoids (inlet solenoid shown)...

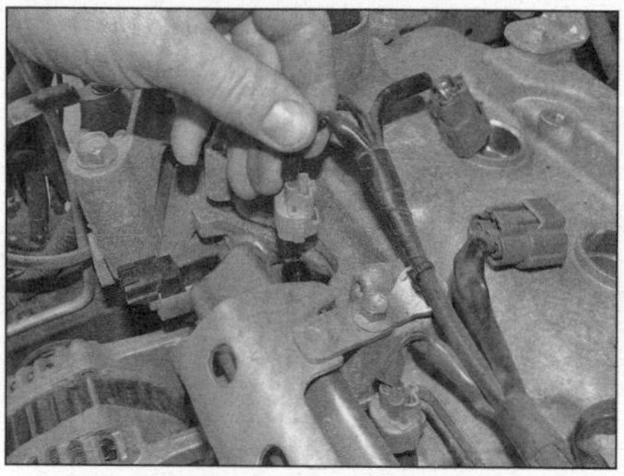

4.5b ...and the fuel injectors

4.6 Disconnect the camshaft position sensor wiring

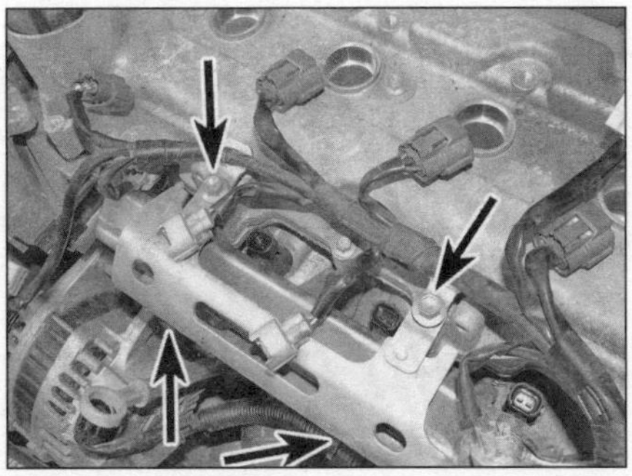

4.7 Undo the injector rail protector shield retaining bolts

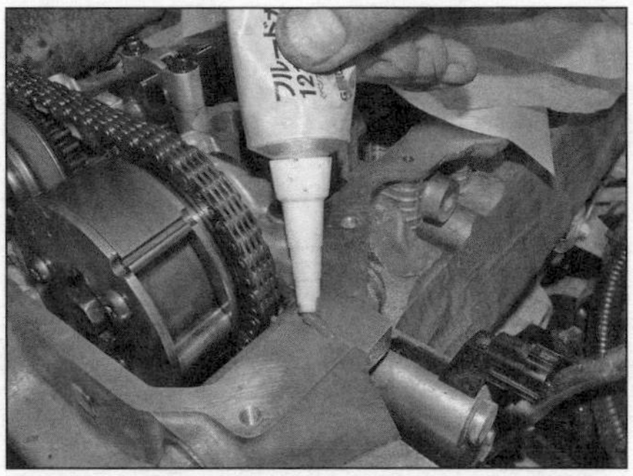

4.13 Apply sealant to the joint at both sides of the camshaft sprockets

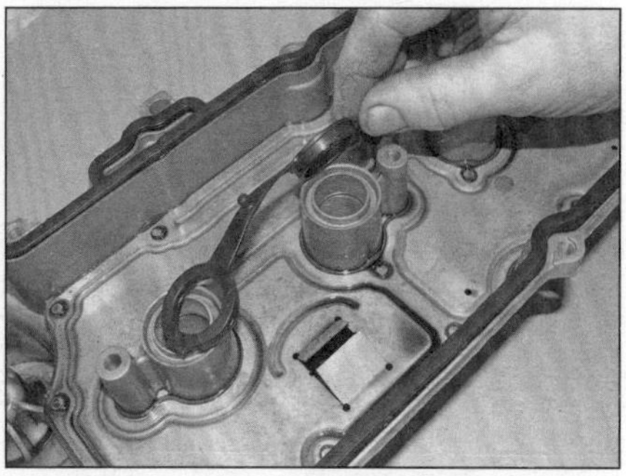

4.14 Fit the new rubber gasket to the cylinder head cover

cylinder head cover and move it to one side. If required, release the retaining clips and disconnect the wiring loom from the protector shield **(see illustration)**.

8 Release the retaining clips and disconnect the crankcase breather hose from the cylinder head cover.

9 Working in the reverse of the tightening sequence **(see illustration 4.16)**, slacken and remove the cylinder head cover retaining bolts.

10 Lift off the cylinder head cover, and recover the rubber seal, which goes around the outer edge of the cover, and also around each of the spark plug holes.

11 Inspect the cover seals for signs of damage and deterioration, and renew as necessary. Nissan recommends that the cylinder head cover seal should always be renewed, if the cover is removed.

Refitting

12 Carefully clean the cylinder head and cover mating surfaces, and remove all traces of oil.

13 Apply a small amount of sealant to where the timing chain cover joins the cylinder head **(see illustration)**.

14 Fit the rubber seal to the cylinder head cover groove, ensuring that it is correctly located along its entire length, and around the four spark plug holes in the centre of the cover **(see illustration)**.

15 Carefully lower the cylinder head cover onto the cylinder head, taking great care not to displace any of the rubber seal.

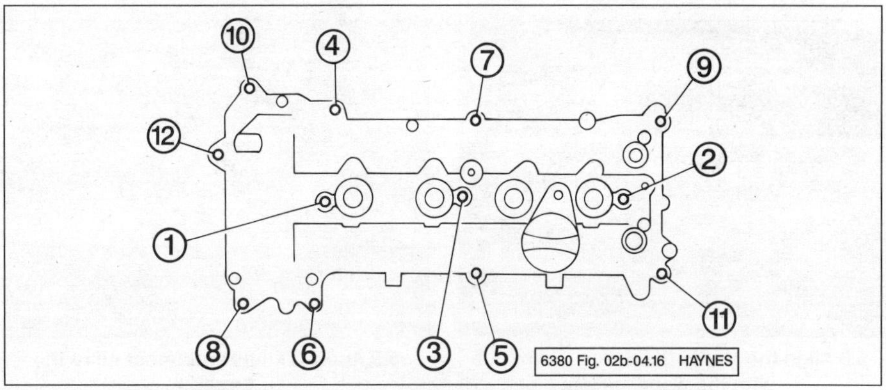

4.16 Tighten the retaining bolts in the sequence shown

16 Make sure the cover is correctly seated, and then install the retaining bolts. Working in sequence, tighten all the cover screws to the specified torque **(see illustration)**.

17 Refit the injector rail protector shield to the cylinder head cover and tighten the bolts to the specified torque. If removed, clip the wiring loom back into position on the protector shield.

18 Reconnect the wiring connectors to the valve timing control solenoids and the four fuel injectors.

19 Refit the breather hose to the cylinder head cover and secure in position with the retaining clip.

20 Refit the ignition coils and reconnect their wiring connectors.

5.3 Using a homemade tool to hold the pulley

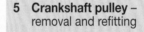

5.4 Remove the crankshaft pulley bolt

21 Reconnect the wiring connectors to the camshaft position sensors.

22 Remove the duct tape (where used) from the inlet ports in the cylinder head, and clean the inlet manifold mating surface. Refit the inlet manifold as described in Chapter 4A, Section 14.

23 Reconnect the battery negative terminal. Run the engine and check for any oil leaks around the engine cylinder head cover.

5 Crankshaft pulley – removal and refitting

Removal

1 Remove the auxiliary drivebelt as described in Chapter 1A, Section 12.

2 If necessary, position No 1 cylinder at TDC on its compression stroke as described in Section 3.

3 To prevent crankshaft rotation while the pulley bolt is unscrewed, the pulley should be held by a suitable tool which locates in the slots in the pulley to prevent it from turning **(see illustration)**. If this is not available, select top gear and have an assistant apply the brakes firmly.

4 Unscrew the pulley bolt, along with its washer (where applicable), and remove the pulley from the crankshaft **(see illustration)**.

5 If the pulley is a tight fit on the end of the

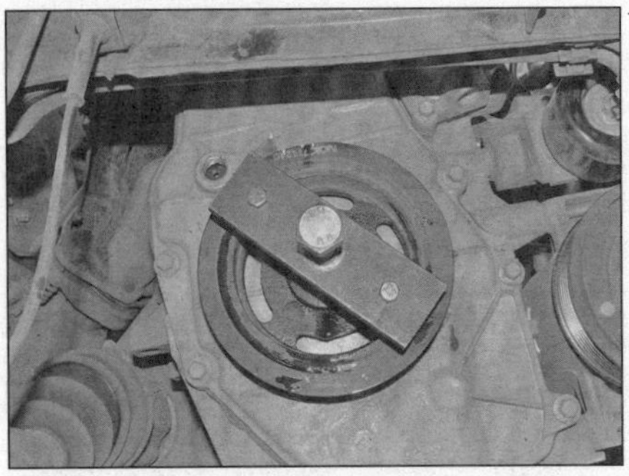

5.5a Remove the pulley using a puller...

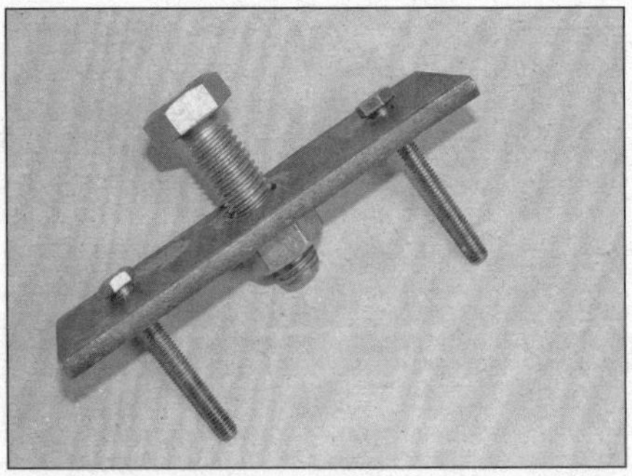

5.5b ...which can be made out of a piece of flat metal bar

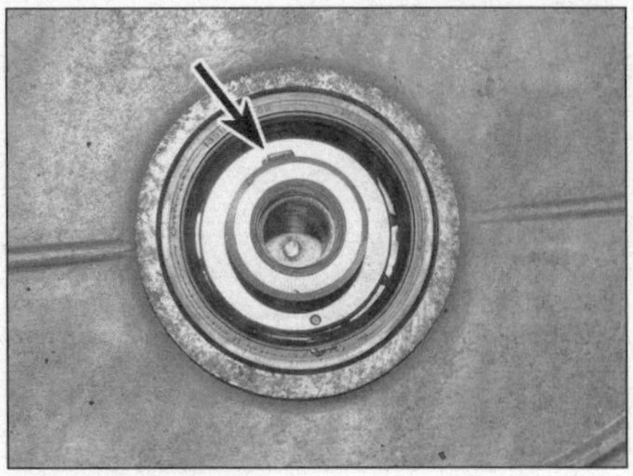

5.6 Make sure the woodruff key is located securely

5.8 Align the slot in the pulley centre hub with the woodruff key

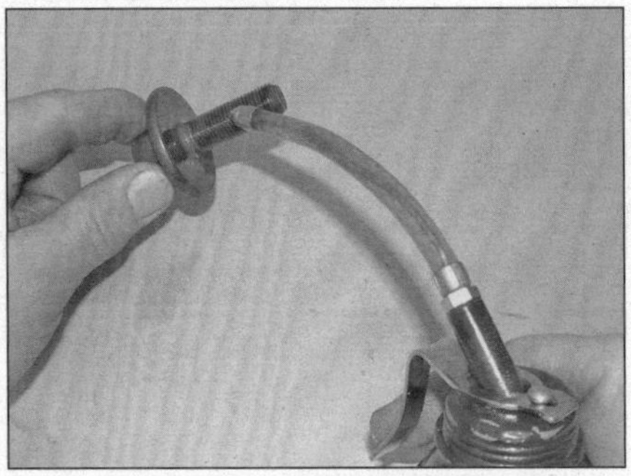

5.9 Apply a small amount of oil to the threads

crankshaft, use a puller to withdraw the pulley from the end of the shaft. Refit the pulley bolt and screw it back into the end of the crankshaft, leaving it approx. 5mm out from the pulley face. Fit the puller (this can be a homemade puller, using a piece of flat bar and three bols/nuts) to the pulley and tighten the centre bolt to withdraw the pulley from the end of the crankshaft **(see illustrations)**.

6 If the pulley Woodruff key is a loose fit in the end of the crankshaft **(see illustration)**, remove it and store it with the pulley for safekeeping.

Refitting

7 Refit the Woodruff key (where removed).

8 Align the crankshaft pulley groove with the key **(see illustration)**, then slide the sprocket onto the crankshaft.

9 Lubricate under the head of the bolt, also the bolt threads with new engine oil **(see illustration)**, and then refit the retaining bolt/washer.

10 Lock the crankshaft by the method used on removal, and tighten the pulley retaining bolt to the specified torque settings. The head of the bolt/washer has markings around its edge, dividing it into 60° segments. To carry out the final stage of the tightening procedure (angle tighten 60°), paint one of the marks on the bolt head, and also paint a mark on the pulley alongside the following 60° mark to the right of the first mark. As the bolt is tightened, when the two paint marks are aligned, the bolt has then been tightened through 60° **(see illustrations)**.

11 Refit the auxiliary drivebelt and adjust it as described in Chapter 1A, Section 12.

6 Timing chain cover – removal and refitting

Removal

1 Disconnect the battery negative terminal (refer to battery disconnection and reconnection in Chapter 5A, Section 3).

2 Firmly apply the handbrake, and then jack up the front of the vehicle and support it securely on axle stands (see *Jacking and vehicle support*). Remove right-hand front roadwheel.

3 Remove the right-hand front wheel arch liner as described in Chapter 11, Section 21.

4 Drain the engine oil, then clean and refit the engine oil drain plug using a new sealing washer, tightening it to the specified torque. If the engine is nearing its service interval when the oil and filter are due for renewal, it is recommended that the filter is also removed, and a new one fitted. After reassembly, the engine can then be refilled with fresh oil. Refer to Chapter 1A, Section 5 for further information.

5 Remove the cylinder head cover as described in Section 4.

6 Remove the crankshaft pulley as described in Section 5.

7 Remove the alternator as described in Chapter 5A, Section 5.

8 Undo the three retaining bolts and remove the coolant pump pulley **(see illustration)**.

5.10a Make alignment marks at 60° on the pulley and bolt...

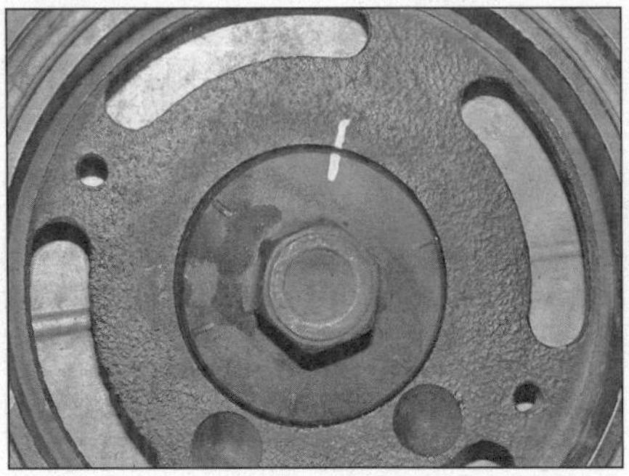

5.10b ...and turn the bolt until the marks are aligned

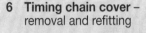

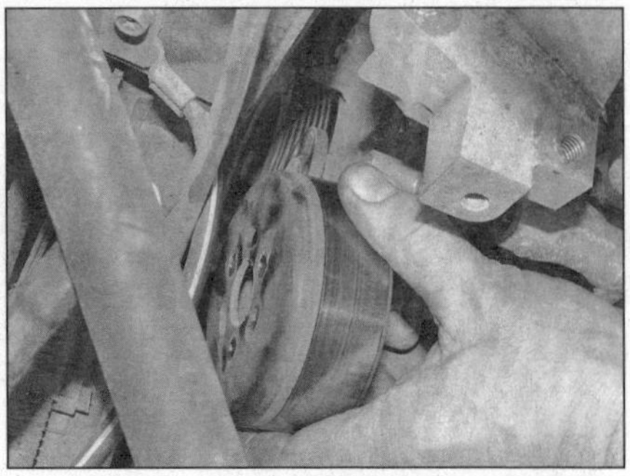

6.8 Remove the coolant pump pulley

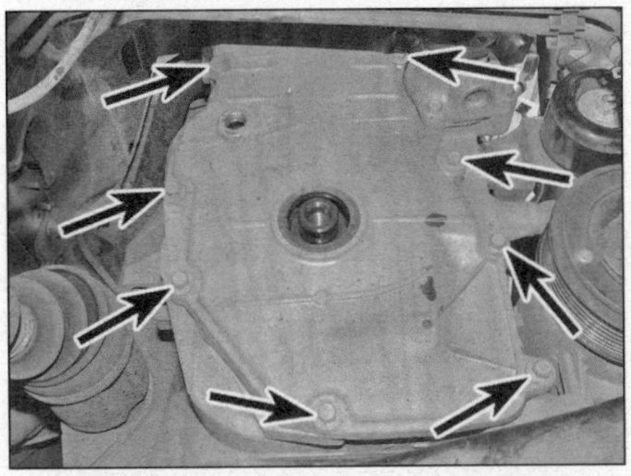

6.10 Timing chain cover lower retaining bolts

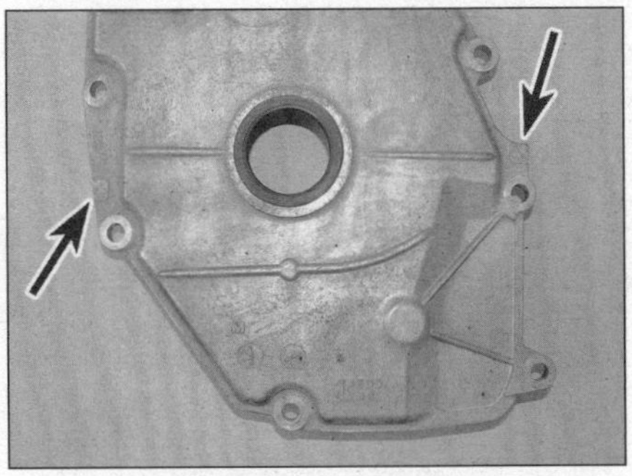

6.12a Nissan show the starting point to start prying the cover

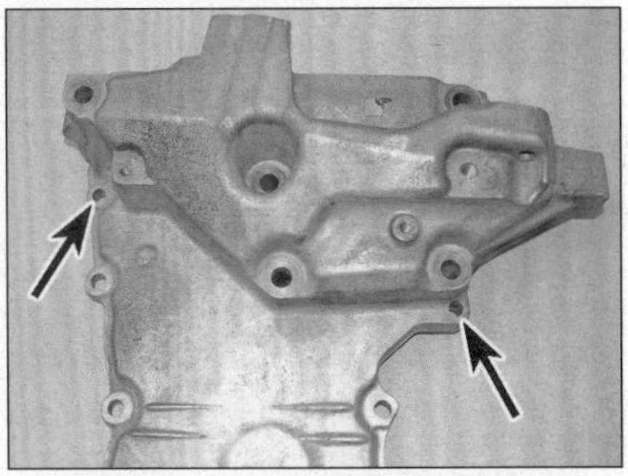

6.12b Two steel dowels are located in holes at the top of the cover

6.15a Apply a bead of sealant around the outside of the cover...

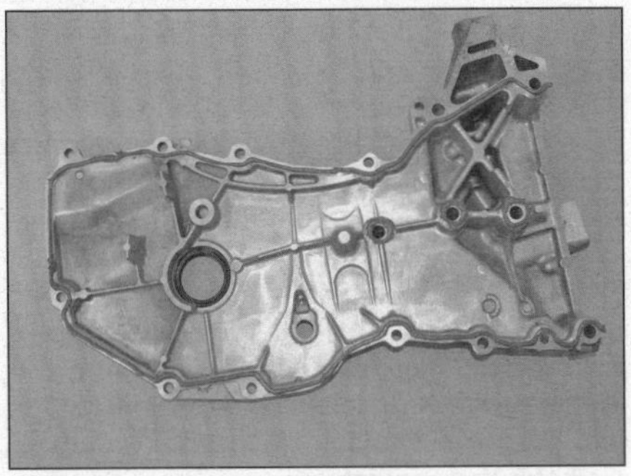

6.15b ...and around the centre locations as shown

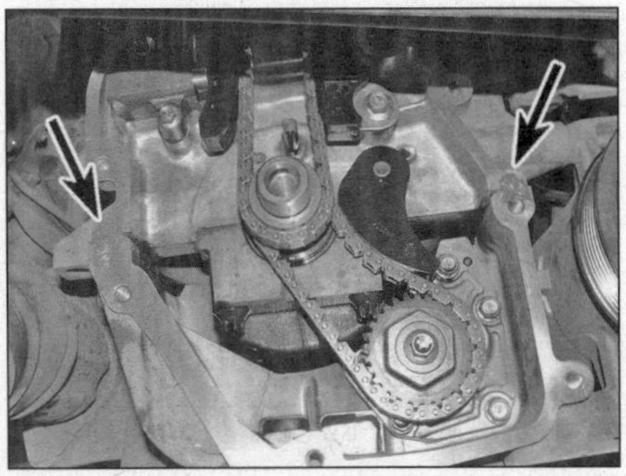

6.16 Apply sealant to the joints at both sides of the cylinder block

9 Using a jack and interposed block of wood, suitably support the engine under the sump, then undo the retaining bolts and remove the right-hand engine mounting as described in Section 15.

10 Working in the reverse of the tightening sequence **(see illustration 6.18)**, slacken and remove the timing chain cover retaining bolts. Note the correct fitted location of each bolt, as some of the bolts are different lengths. Also the five upper bolts are a larger diameter than the ten lower bolts **(see illustration)**.

11 Some of the bolts in the tightening sequence can be accessed easier from under the front wheel arch. Note it may be necessary to raise or lower the jack supporting the engine, to align the bolts with the access holes in the inner wing panel.

12 The timing chain cover has been fitted using a liquid gasket, and is bonded to the engine block/cylinder head. Taking care not to damage the timing chain cover, work your way around the outside of the cover to release it from the engine. Nissan show the starting point at each side of the lower part of the casing, where there is an area to start prying. Also note that at the top of the timing chain cover there are two steel dowels, which can become very tight in the alloy cover **(see illustrations)**.

Refitting

13 Prior to refitting the cover, it is recommended that the crankshaft oil seal should be renewed. Note the seals fitted position and the carefully lever the old seal out of the cover using a large flat-bladed screwdriver. Fit the new seal to the cover, making sure its sealing lip is facing inwards. Drive the seal into position until it seats squarely in the position noted on removal, for further information see Section 13, of this Chapter.

14 Ensure that the timing chain cover and engine cylinder block/cylinder head mating surfaces are clean/dry and free from any silicone sealer. Clean the steel dowels on the cylinder block, and apply a small amount of oil to aid fitting.

15 Apply a thin bead of suitable sealant (3 mm to 4 mm diameter) to the timing chain cover surface, not forgetting to apply sealant to the area around the three bolt passages in the upper centre of the cover **(see illustrations)**.

16 Also apply a small amount of sealant to where the cylinder block joins the cylinder head, and where the cylinder block joins the upper sump housing **(see illustration)**.

17 For this procedure the help of an assistant would be advisable; lower the timing chain cover into position taking care not to wipe the sealer off the face of the cover. With the assistant under the right-hand front wheel arch manoeuvre the cover into position over the end of the crankshaft, taking great care not to damage the oil seal lip.

18 Make sure the cover is correctly seated, and then install the retaining bolts. Working in sequence, tighten all the cover bolts to the specified torque **(see illustration)**.

19 Refit the right-hand engine mounting as described in Section 15.

20 Refit the coolant pump pulley and tighten the three retaining bolts.

21 Refit the alternator with reference to Chapter 5A, Section 5.

22 Refit the crankshaft pulley as described in Section 5.

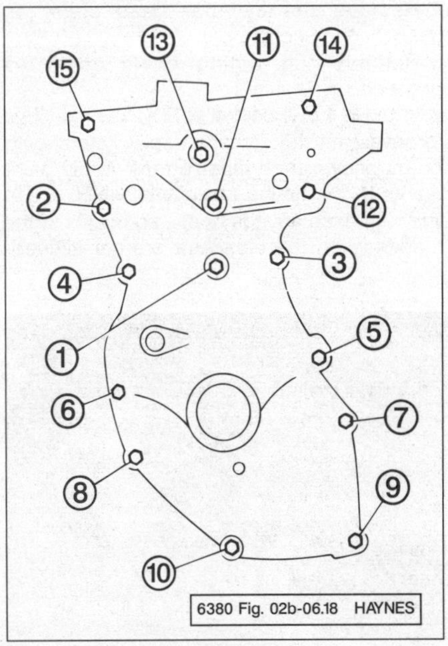

6.18 Tightening sequence for timing chain cover bolts

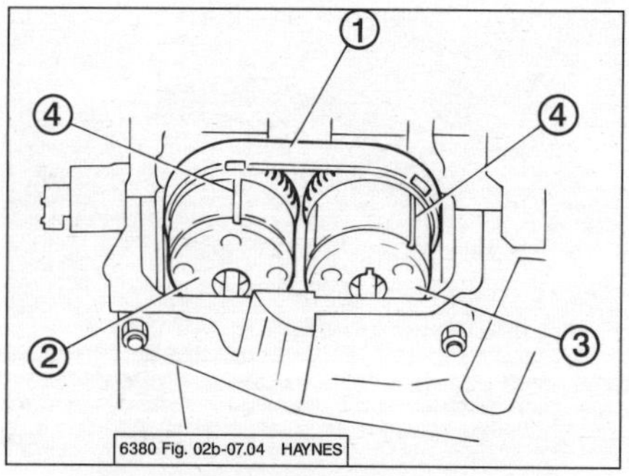

7.4 Camshaft sprocket timing mark positions with No 1 cylinder at TDC

1 Timing chain
2 Inlet camshaft sprocket
3 Exhaust camshaft sprocket
4 Timing marks (peripheral grooves)

7.5a Push the tensioner lever down...

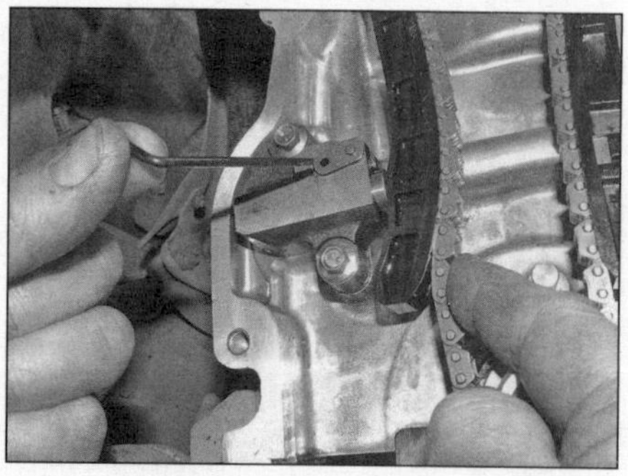

7.5b ...and insert a locking pin through the tensioner

23 Refit the cylinder head cover as described in Section 4.
24 After reassembly, the engine can then be refilled with fresh oil. Refer to Chapter 1A, Section 5 for further information.
25 Refit the inner wheel arch liner with reference to Chapter 11, Section 21.
26 Refit the front roadwheel and lower the vehicle to the ground. Tighten the roadwheel nuts to the specified torque setting.

7 Timing chain, tensioner, guides and sprockets – removal, inspection and refitting

Removal

1 Position No 1 cylinder at TDC on its compression stroke, as described in Section 3.
2 Remove the cylinder head cover as described in Section 4.
3 Remove the timing chain cover as described in Section 6.
4 With No 1 cylinder set at TDC, the markings (grooves) on the camshaft sprockets should be as shown **(see illustration)**. Apply paint marks to the timing chain links which are in line with the markings on the sprockets. If the markings on the camshaft are not aligned, it may be that it is set to be firing on No. 4 cylinder. Turn the crankshaft one complete turn clockwise to get it firing on number 1 cylinder. Note that the cam lobes on number 1 cylinder, should be pointing upwards and towards each other when firing on this cylinder.
5 Whilst holding down the tensioner lever, push the tensioner plunger back into its body. With the plunger retracted, align the hole in the lever with the hole in the tensioner body and hold it in position by inserting a small-diameter rod through the plate hole and into the body of the tensioner **(see illustrations)**.
6 Undo the two retaining bolts, and remove the tensioner from the end of the cylinder block. Keep the rod inserted into the tensioner to prevent the plunger from springing out **(see illustrations)**.
7 Release the upper pivot point of the chain tensioner guide, and remove it from the rear of the crankcase.
8 Unscrew the two mounting bolts, and remove the chain front guide from the crankcase **(see illustration)**.
9 Disengage the timing chain from the crankshaft sprocket, and manoeuvre it out from the engine.
Warning: Do not turn the crankshaft or camshafts while the timing chain is removed, otherwise piston and valve contact may occur causing damage.
10 Slacken the exhaust camshaft sprocket retaining bolt, whilst retaining the camshafts with a large open-ended spanner fitted to the hexagonal section of the shaft. Remove the bolt along with its washer (where applicable), disengage the sprocket from the end of its camshaft.
11 To remove the sprocket from the inlet camshaft, requires the inlet camshaft to be removed. See Section 9 for further information.
12 To remove the crankshaft sprocket from the end of the crankshaft, requires removing the oil pump chain and sprocket as a complete unit. See Section 12 for further information.

Inspection

13 Examine the teeth on the camshaft and crankshaft sprockets for any sign of wear or damage such as chipped, hooked or missing teeth. If there is any sign of wear or damage on either sprockets or timing chain then they should be renewed as a set.
14 Inspect the links of the timing chain for signs of wear or damage on the rollers. The extent of wear can be judged by checking the amount by which the chain can be bent sideways; a new chain will have very little sideways movement. If there is an excessive amount of side play in the chain, it must be renewed.
15 Note that it is a sensible precaution to renew the timing chain, regardless of apparent condition, if the engine has covered a high mileage, or if it has been noted that the chain has sounded noisy when the engine running.

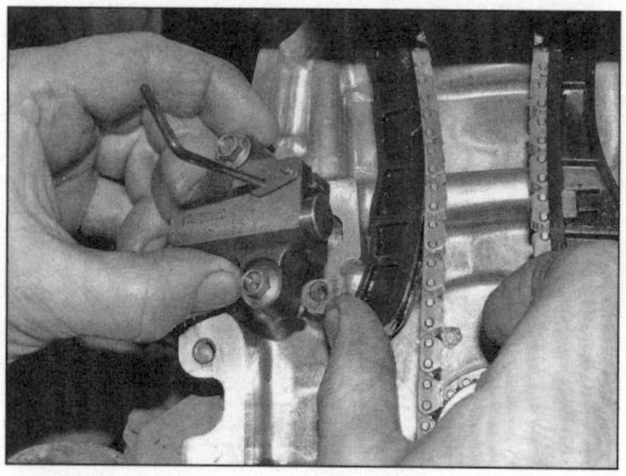

7.6a Undo the retaining bolts and remove the tensioner...

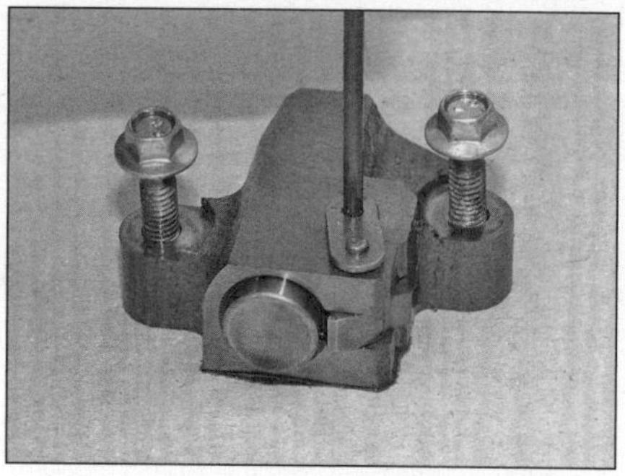

7.6b ...keeping the locking pin in place

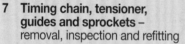

7.8 Removing the fixed chain guide

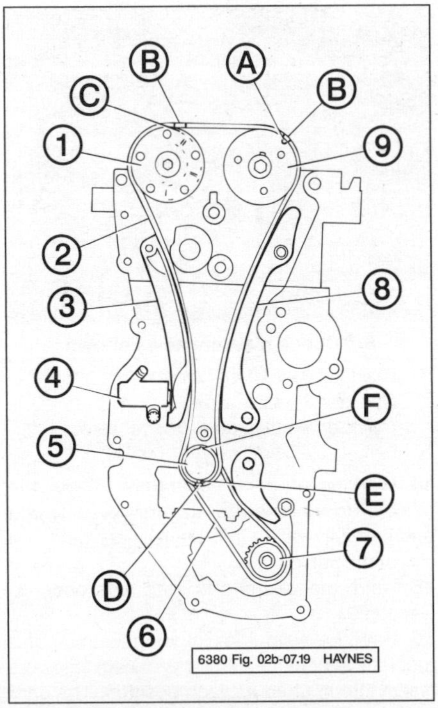

7.19 Camshaft sprocket and timing chain timing mark relationship

1 Exhaust camshaft sprocket
2 Timing chain
3 Chain tensioner guide
4 Chain tensioner
5 Crankshaft sprocket
6 Oil pump drive chain
7 Oil pump sprocket
8 Timing chain front guide
9 Inlet camshaft sprocket
A Timing mark (peripheral grove)
B Pink link on chain
C Timing mark (peripheral groove)
D Orange link on chain
E Timing mark (stamp)
F Crankshaft sprocket keyway

Although not strictly necessary, it is always worth renewing the chain and sprockets as a matched set, since it is false economy to run a new chain on worn sprockets and viceversa. If there is any doubt about the condition of the timing chain and sprockets, seek the advice of a Nissan dealer service department, who will be able to advise you as to the best course of action.

16 Examine the chain guides for signs of wear or damage to their chain contact faces, renewing any which are badly marked.

17 Check the chain tensioner for signs of wear, and check that the plunger is free to slide freely in the tensioner body. The condition of the tensioner spring can only be judged in comparison to a new component. Renew the tensioner if it is worn or there is any doubt about the condition of its tensioning spring.

Refitting

18 Check the crankshaft is still positioned at TDC (the keyway will be in the 12 o'clock position, seen from the right-hand end of the engine).

19 Manoeuvre the exhaust camshaft sprocket into position, ensuring that the timing marks are facing the position noted on removal. Engage the sprocket with the chain and align the two pink chain links with the alignment marks (grooves) on the camshaft sprockets **(see illustration)**.

20 Tighten the exhaust camshaft bolt to the specified torque setting, whilst retaining the camshaft with a large open-ended spanner fitted to the hexagonal section of the shaft.

21 Manoeuvre the chain into position, engaging it with the crankshaft sprocket so that its coloured link is aligned with the timing mark on the crankshaft sprocket **(see illustration)**. Check that all the timing marks are correctly aligned with the chain links.

7.21 Align the coloured link with the dot on the crankshaft sprocket

22 Fit the chain front fixed guide to the cylinder block, and tighten its retaining bolts to the specified torque.

23 Fit the chain rear tensioner guide to the upper pivot point and locate it in position **(see illustration)**.

24 Fit the chain tensioner to the cylinder block, and tighten its retaining bolts to the specified torque. Whilst holding the guide against the tensioner plunger, withdraw the rod, and check that the tensioner plunger is forced out against the guide to take up the slack in the chain **(see illustration)**.

25 Check that all the timing marks are still correctly aligned with the chain links. If all timing marks are aligned, fit the crankshaft pulley and turn the engine two complete turns, and check the timing marks on the sprockets are all re-aligned.

Note: *The coloured links on the chain will not be re-aligned with the marks on the sprockets. The coloured links are just for the initial set up, and will take many turns before they will line up again, with the marks on the sprockets.*

26 Remove the crankshaft pulley and refit the timing chain cover as described in Section 6.

27 Refit the crankshaft pulley as described in Section 5.

28 Refit the cylinder head cover as described in Section 4.

7.23 Locate the tensioner guide into place

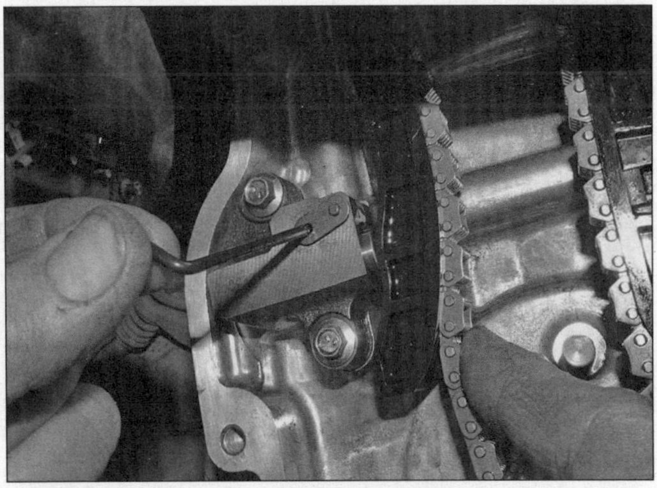

7.24 Hold pressure against the tensioner and remove the locking pin

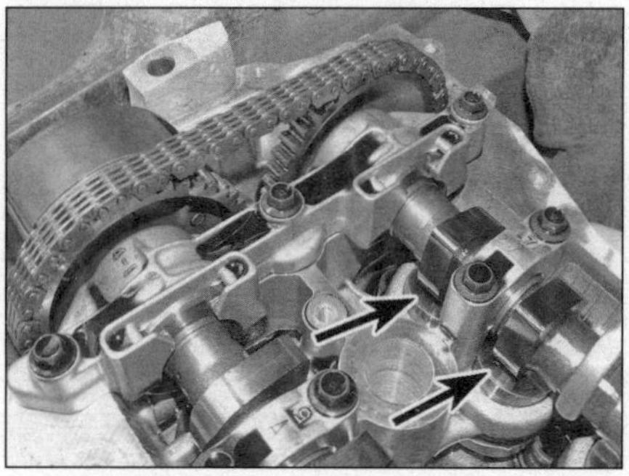

8.5a Check the clearances between the camshafts and the followers

8 Valve clearances – checking and adjustment

Note: *This is not a routine operation. It should only be necessary at high mileage, after overhaul, or when investigating noise or power loss which may be attributable to the valve gear. Adjustment involves removing the camshaft and changing the cam followers (valve lifters) that are available in 26 different thicknesses (ranging from 3.00 mm to 3.50 mm, in steps of 0.02 mm).*

Checking

1 The importance of having the valve clearances correctly adjusted cannot be overstressed, as they vitally affect the performance of the engine. The clearances are checked as follows.

2 Draw the outline of the engine on a piece of paper, numbering the cylinders 1 to 4, with No 1 cylinder at the timing chain end of the engine. Show the position of each valve, together with the specified valve clearance. Above each valve, draw two lines for noting the actual clearance and the amount of adjustment required.

3 Remove the cylinder head cover as described in Section 4.

4 Position No 1 cylinder at TDC on its compression stroke, as described in Section 3.

5 Using feeler gauges, measure the clearance between the base of the cam and the follower of the following valves, recording each clearance on the paper **(see illustrations)**.

a) No 1 cylinder inlet and exhaust valves
b) No 2 cylinder inlet valves
c) No 3 cylinder exhaust valves

6 Rotate the crankshaft through one complete turn (360°) clockwise until the TDC notch on the crankshaft pulley is realigned with the pointer. No 4 cylinder is now at TDC on its compression stroke.

7 Check the clearances of the following valves, and record them on the paper **(see illustration)**.

a) No 2 cylinder exhaust valves
b) No 3 cylinder inlet valves
c) No 4 cylinder inlet and exhaust valves

8 Calculate the difference between each

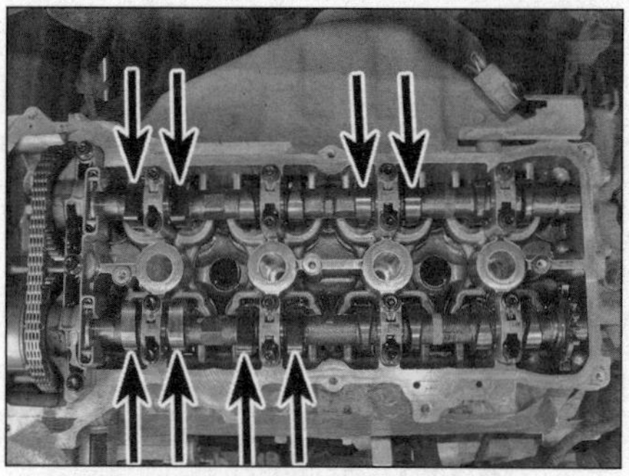

8.5b Check clearances as shown

Cylinder 1 – Inlet and Exhaust valves
Cylinder 2 – Inlet valves
Cylinder 3 – Exhaust valves

measured clearance and the desired value, and record it on the piece of paper.

Adjustment

Note: *A micrometer or dial gauge and probe will be required for this operation.*

9 Where a valve clearance differs from the specified value, then the cam follower (valve lifter) for that valve must be substituted with a thinner or thicker one accordingly. The cam followers have the thickness stamped on the bottom face of the follower; e.g. 324 indicates the follower is 3.24 mm thick at the top centre of the follower **(see illustration)**.

10 If required use a micrometer or dial gauge to measure the true thickness of any follower removed, as it may have been reduced by wear. **Note:** *Followers are available in thicknesses between 3.00 mm and 3.50 mm, in steps of 0.02 mm.*

11 To access the cam followers (valve lifters), first remove the camshafts as described in Section 9. Remove and refit each follower separately, to avoid any confusion.

12 The size of follower required is calculated as follows. If the measured clearance is less than specified, subtract the measured clearance from the specified clearance, and deduct the result from the thickness of the existing follower. For example:

Sample calculation – clearance too small
Clearance measured (A) = 0.16 mm
Desired clearance (B) = 0.30 mm
Difference (B – A) = 0.14 mm
Cam follower thickness fitted = 3.50 mm
Cam follower thickness required = 3.50 – 0.14 = 3.36 mm

13 If the measured clearance is greater than specified, subtract the specified clearance from the measured clearance, and add the result to the thickness of the existing follower. For example:

Sample calculation – clearance too big
Clearance measured (A) = 0.40 mm
Desired clearance (B) = 0.30 mm
Difference (A – B) = 0.10 mm
Cam follower thickness fitted = 3.26 mm
Cam follower thickness required = 3.26 + 0.10 = 3.36 mm

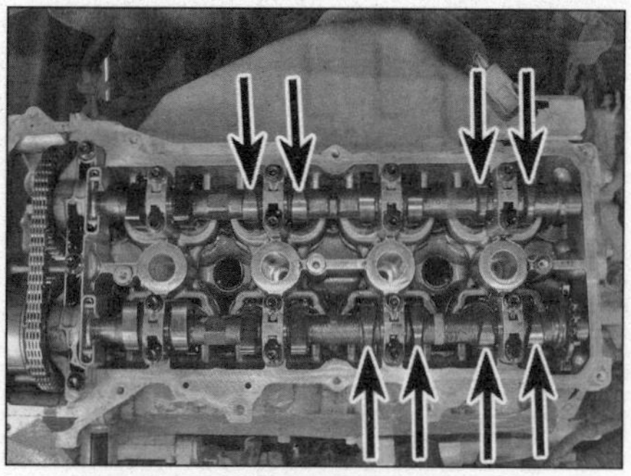

8.7 Check clearances as shown

Cylinder 2 – Exhaust valves
Cylinder 3 – Inlet valves
Cylinder 4 – Inlet and Exhaust valves

14 Working on each separately, lift out the follower to be renewed, then oil the new one and carefully locate it in the cylinder head, on top of the valve.

15 Refit the camshafts with reference to Section 9.

16 It will be helpful for future adjustment if a record is kept of the thickness of cam followers (valve lifters) fitted at each position. The cam followers required could be purchased in advance once the clearances and the existing follower thicknesses are known.

17 Once all valve clearances have been adjusted, rotate the crankshaft through at least four complete turns in the correct direction of rotation, to settle all disturbed followers, then recheck the clearances as described above.

18 With all valve clearances correctly adjusted, refit the cylinder head cover as described in Section 4, and refit all components removed to gain access to the crankshaft pulley.

9 Camshafts and followers – removal, inspection and refitting

Note: *Before the inlet camshaft variable valve timing sprocket can be removed from the camshaft, a minimum of 3.0 bars air pressure will need to be applied to the sprocket, and a 3 mm diameter locking pin will be needed to hold the sprocket in position.*

8.9 Markings inside the follower for thickness

9.4 Remove the blanking plug

9.5 Push the tensioner lever down...

9.6 ...and insert a locking pin (Allen key) through the tensioner

Removal

1 Position No 1 cylinder at TDC on its compression stroke, as described in Section 3.

2 Remove the cylinder head cover as described in Section 4.

3 With No 1 cylinder set at TDC, the markings on the camshaft sprockets should be in line. Apply paint marks to the timing chain link, which are in line with the markings on the sprockets **(see illustration 7.4)**. If the markings on the camshaft are not aligned, turn the crankshaft one turn clockwise to get it firing on number 1 cylinder. Note the cam lobes on number 1 cylinder, should be pointing upwards and towards each other when firing on this cylinder.

4 Working inside the right-hand front wheel arch, remove the blanking plug from the timing chain cover **(see illustration)**.

5 Use a thin screwdriver to hold the tensioner lever downwards, which will allow the tensioner plunger to be pushed back into its body **(see illustration)**.

6 With the aid of an assistant, turn the crankshaft sprocket anti-clockwise slightly, whilst turning the exhaust camshaft sprocket clockwise slightly. This will pull the timing chain taut, causing the tensioner plunger to be pushed back. With the plunger retracted, align the hole in the lever with the hole in the tensioner body and hold it in position by inserting a small-diameter rod through the plate hole and into the body of the tensioner **(see illustration)**. For further information on the removal and refitting of the timing chain tensioner, with the cover removed, see Section 7 of this Chapter.

9.8 Using an open ended spanner to counter hold the camshaft

7 With the tensioner locked, turn the crankshaft sprocket clockwise slightly to let the chain become slack around the camshaft sprockets.

8 Slacken the exhaust camshaft sprocket retaining bolt, whilst retaining the camshaft with a large open-ended spanner fitted to the hexagonal section on the shaft **(see illustration)**.

9 Remove the bolt along with its washer (where applicable), disengage the sprocket from the end of its camshaft, and then release it from the timing chain.

Warning: Do not turn the crankshaft or camshafts while the timing chain is removed, otherwise piston and valve contact may occur causing damage.

9.10 Remove the bearing cap housing

10 At the timing chain end of the camshafts the bearing cap housing covers both of the camshafts, undo the three retaining bolts and remove it from the cylinder head **(see illustration)**.

11 Using an air gun apply a minimum of 3 bars air pressure to the oil passage leading to the inlet camshaft variable valve timing sprocket **(see illustrations)**.

12 While keeping the air pressure applied, slowly turn the camshaft sprocket from anti-clockwise to clockwise. During this procedure a click (locking pin disengaging) is heard from the inlet sprocket. If a click has not been heard, then waggle the camshaft sprocket very slightly and gently tap the variable valve inlet sprocket with a plastic mallet **(see illustration)**.

13 Still keeping the air pressure applied, after the click (locking pin disengaging) has

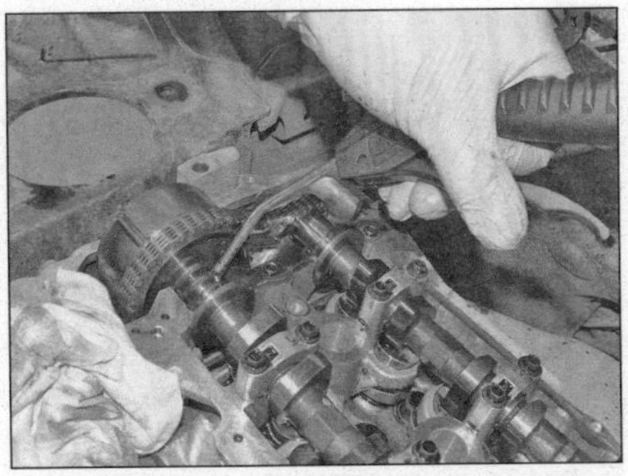
9.11a Using an air gun to apply pressure...

9.11b ...through the oil gallery hole in the camshaft

9.12 Turn the camshaft sprocket while air pressure is applied

9.14a Insert a 2.5 mm Allen key to lock the sprocket...

9.14b ...and secure it in place to prevent it falling out

9.15 Camshaft bearing cap markings

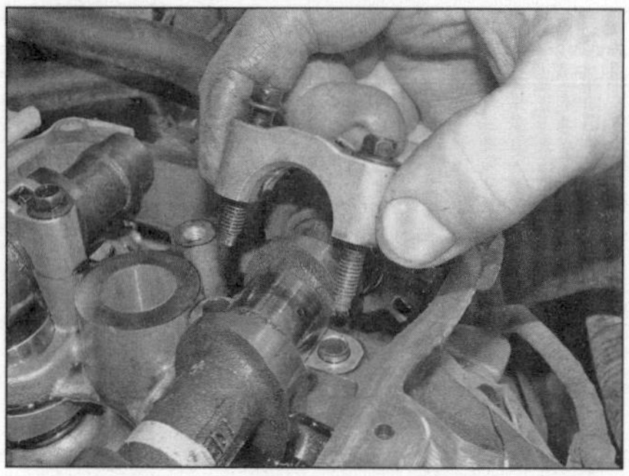

9.16 Remove the bearing caps

9.18 Using an open ended spanner to counter hold the camshaft

been heard, slowly turn the inlet camshaft in the anti-clockwise direction (to the rear of the vehicle) setting it to the most advanced position. In this position the groove and the pinhole should be in line.

14 Insert a 2.5 mm Allen key into the hole in the inlet sprocket to hold it in position **(see illustrations)**. Use the short end of the Allen key to insert into the sprocket, as the inserted part should be approximately 15 mm; tape the Allen key into position. Air pressure can now be released.

Warning: Do not remove the Allen key from the inlet sprocket until it has been refitted to the vehicle. If the Allen key is removed while the sprocket is off the engine, the locking pin inside the sprocket will be damaged by lateral load and could shear. If this happens a new sprocket will be required.

15 All remaining camshaft bearing caps have identification markings stamped into their top surface; the exhaust camshaft caps being marked 2 to 5 and the inlet camshaft caps being marked A to D; the No 2 and A caps are fitted nearest the timing chain end of the engine **(see illustration)**. Note the markings on the caps for refitting. If the caps are not marked, suitable identification marks should be made prior to removal. Using white paint or suitable marker pen, mark each cap in some way to indicate its correct fitted orientation and position. This will avoid the possibility of installing the caps in the wrong positions and/or the wrong way around on refitting.

16 Working in the reverse of the tightening sequence **(see illustration 9.34)**, evenly and progressively slacken the sixteen remaining camshaft bearing cap retaining bolts by one turn at a time, to relieve the pressure of the valve springs on the bearing caps gradually and evenly. Once the valve spring pressure has been relieved, the bolts can be fully unscrewed and the caps removed **(see illustration)**.

17 With the bearing caps removed the exhaust camshaft can be simply lifted off the top of the cylinder head, noting its fitted position. Note the position of the dowel on the sprocket end of the camshaft, and the position of the cam lobes, so that it can be refitted in the correct position for TDC on no.1 cylinder.

18 To remove the inlet camshaft, the variable valve timing sprocket will need to be removed from the end of the camshaft. To do this, the camshaft will require lifting slightly to access the retaining bolt. With the camshaft raised slightly and supported on a clean piece of cloth, slacken the camshaft sprocket securing bolt, whilst retaining the camshaft with a large open-ended spanner fitted to the hexagonal section on the shaft **(see illustration)**.

19 Remove the securing bolt, disengage the sprocket from the end of its camshaft, and then release it from the timing chain **(see illustrations)**. The timing chain cannot drop down into the timing chain cover, or drop off the bottom of the crankshaft sprocket, so it can be left in position ready for refitting.

20 Obtain sixteen small, clean plastic containers, and number them 1 to 16. Alternatively, divide a larger container into sixteen compartments. Using a rubber sucker, withdraw each follower (valve lifter) in turn, and place it in its respective container **(see**

9.19a Remove the camshaft sprocket retaining bolt...

9.19b ...remove the camshaft...

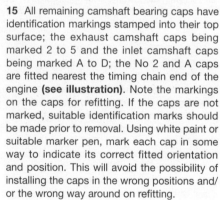

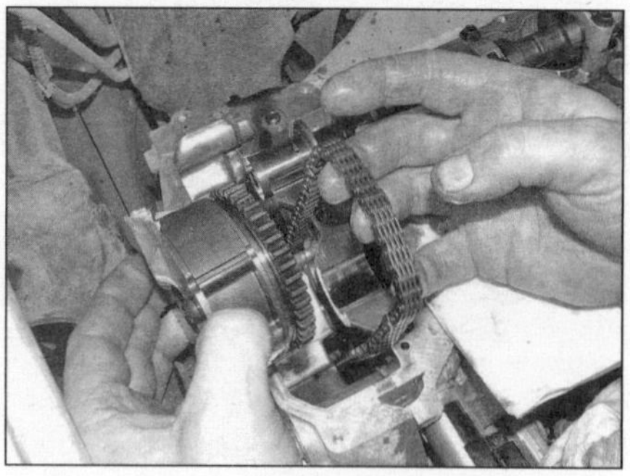

9.19c ...and unhook the timing chain from the sprocket

9.20 Remove the cam followers

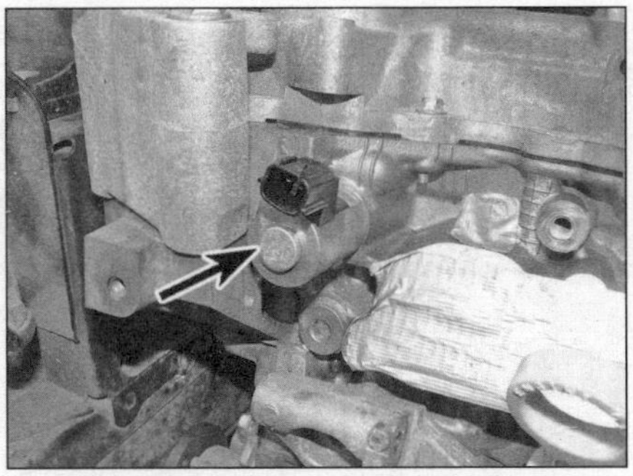

9.21 Inlet camshaft variable valve timing control solenoid

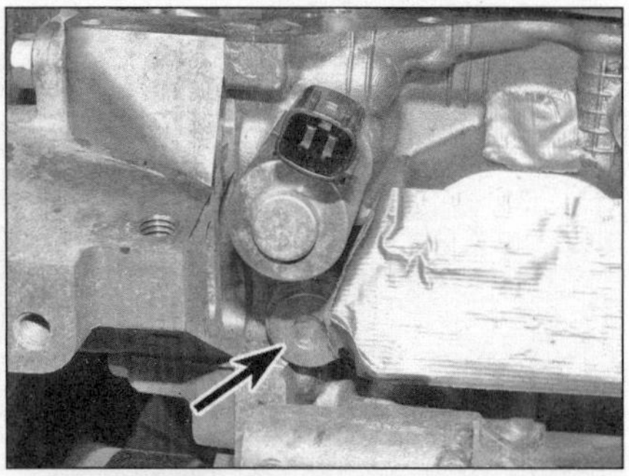

9.22 Remove plug to renew the timing control solenoid filter

illustration). Do not interchange the cam followers, or the rate of wear will be increased.

21 If required, undo the retaining bolt and remove the inlet and exhaust camshaft variable valve timing control solenoids from the front of the cylinder head **(see illustration)**.

Inspection

22 Remove the plug from below the inlet camshaft timing control solenoid and clean-out or renew the oil filter for the variable valve timing system **(see illustration)**. Do the same for the exhaust camshaft timing control solenoid.

23 Inspect the cam bearing surfaces of the head and the bearing caps. Look for score marks and deep scratches. Check the camshaft lobes for heat discoloration (blue appearance), score marks, chipped areas or flat spots.

24 Camshaft run-out can be checked by supporting each end of the camshaft on V-blocks, and measuring any run-out at the centre of the shaft using a dial gauge. If the run-out exceeds the specified limit, a new camshaft will be required.

25 Measure the height of each lobe with a micrometer **(see illustration)**, and compare the results to the figures given in the Specifications. If damage is noted or wear is excessive, new camshaft(s) must be fitted.

26 The camshaft bearing oil clearance should now be checked.

27 Fit the bearing caps to the cylinder head, using the identification markings or the marks made on removal to ensure that they are correctly positioned. Tighten the retaining bolts to the specified torque in sequence **(see illustration 9.34)**. Measure the diameter of each bearing cap journal, and compare the measurements obtained with the results given in the Specifications at the start of this Chapter. If any journal is worn beyond the service limit, the cylinder head must be renewed. The camshaft bearing oil clearance can then calculated by subtracting the camshaft bearing journal diameter from the bearing cap journal diameter.

28 Check the cam follower and cylinder head bearing surfaces for signs of wear or damage.

Refitting

29 Liberally oil the cylinder head cam follower bores and the followers. Carefully refit the followers to the cylinder head; ensuring that each follower is refitted to its original bore. Some care will be required to enter the followers squarely into their bores. Liberally oil the camshaft bearing and lobe contact surfaces **(see illustration)**.

30 Refit the exhaust camshaft to its correct

9.25 Checking the cam lobe height with a micrometer

location in the cylinder head, in the position noted on removal.

31 Locate the variable valve timing sprocket onto the inlet camshaft as the camshaft is being placed on the cylinder head **(see illustration)**. This will need to be tightened to the camshaft, before the camshaft is secured into place, so as to access the securing bolt. With the camshaft raised slightly and supported on a clean piece of cloth, tighten the camshaft sprocket securing bolt, whilst retaining the camshaft with a large open-ended spanner fitted to the hexagonal section on the shaft **(see illustration 9.18)**.

9.29 Lubricate the camshaft bearing surfaces

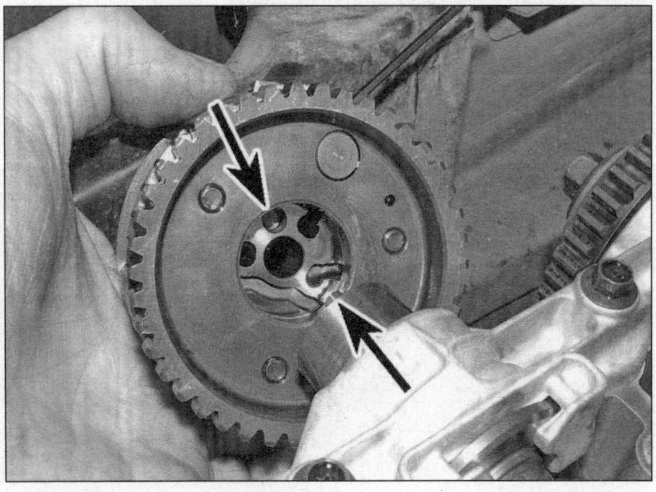

9.31 Align the locating peg on the end of the camshaft with the sprocket

9.34 Tighten the bearing caps in the sequence shown

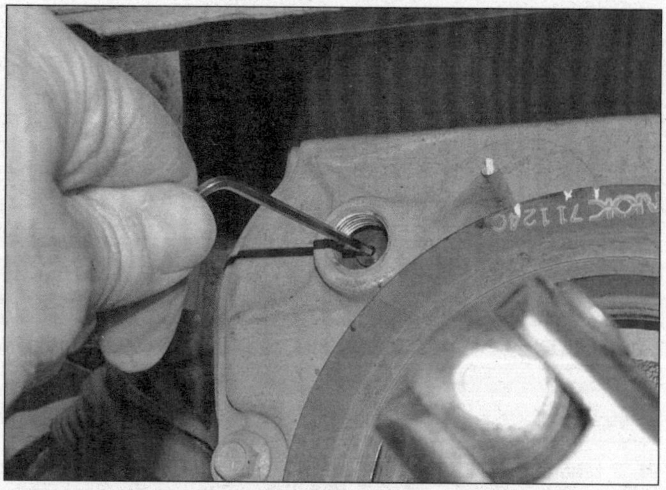

9.36 Remove the locking pin

Make sure the timing chain is located around the sprocket before the camshaft is secured into place.

32 Ensure that the bearing cap and head mating surfaces are completely clean, unmarked and free from oil.

33 Refit the bearing caps, using the identification markings or the marks made on removal to ensure that each is installed the correct way round and in its original location.

34 Working in sequence, evenly and progressively tighten the camshaft bearing cap bolts by one turn at a time until the caps touch the cylinder head **(see illustration)**. Then go round again and tighten all the bolts to the specified torque setting (see Torque wrench settings for sequence). Work only as described, to impose the pressure of the valve springs gradually and evenly on the bearing caps.

35 Refit the exhaust camshaft sprocket, making sure it is located correctly on the dowel on the end of the camshaft. Tighten the camshaft sprocket securing bolt, whilst retaining the camshaft with a large open-ended spanner fitted to the hexagonal section on the shaft, as done on removal. Make sure the chain is correctly located around the sprocket and the timing marks are aligned, as noted on removal.

36 With the crankshaft pulley and camshaft sprockets timing marks all aligned for TDC (see Section 7, for further information), remove the locking pin from the timing chain tensioner **(see illustration)**. With the pin removed turn the crankshaft clockwise slightly, so that the tension on the chain releases the tensioner to take up the slack in the chain.

37 Apply sealant to the blanking plug and refit it to the timing chain cover **(see illustrations)**.

38 Remove the tape and withdraw the locking pin from the inlet camshaft variable valve timing sprocket **(see illustration)**, slowly turn the crankshaft clockwise, to allow the sprocket to reach its most retarded position.

39 Check that the camshaft timing marks are still correctly aligned with the painted chain links and the crankshaft pulley is still set to TDC. If all timing marks are aligned, then turn the engine two complete turns, and check the timing marks on the sprockets are all re-aligned.

Note: *The painted links on the chain will not be re-aligned with the marks on the sprockets. If required, see Section 7 for further information on setting the timing.*

40 If the cylinder head/camshafts have been overhauled, check and adjust the valve clearances as described in Section 8.

41 Refit the cylinder head cover as described in Section 4.

10 Cylinder head – removal and refitting

Removal

1 Depressurise the fuel system as described in Chapter 4A, Section 6.

2 Drain the cooling system as described in Chapter 1A, Section 25.

3 Remove the timing chain as described in Section 7.

4 Remove the camshafts as described in Section 9.

5 Carry out the following operations as described in Chapter 4A.

a) Disconnect the exhaust system front pipe from the manifold.

b) Disconnect the fuel feed and return hoses from the fuel rail (plug all openings, to prevent loss of fuel and entry of dirt into the fuel system).

c) Disconnect the vacuum servo unit hose, coolant hose(s) and all the other relevant/ breather hoses from the manifold and associated valves.

6 Slacken the retaining clip(s) and disconnect the coolant hose(s) from the cylinder head.

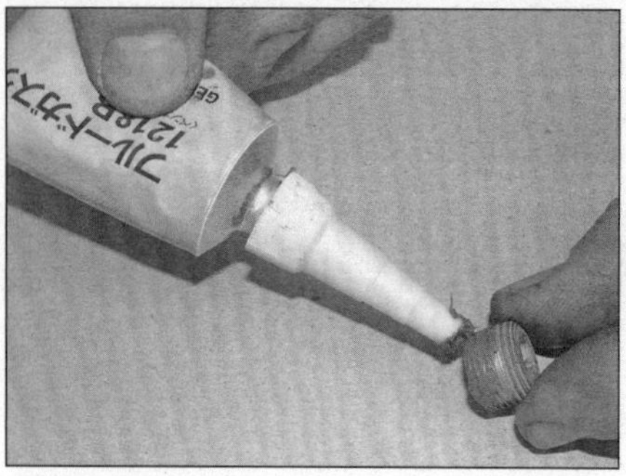

9.37a Apply some sealant to the threads...

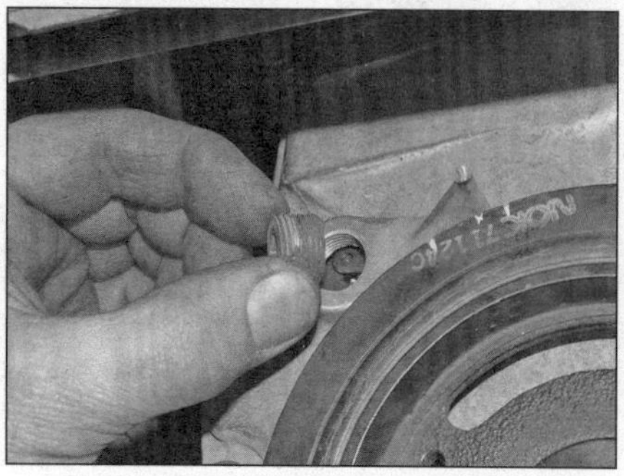

9.37b ...and refit the blanking plug

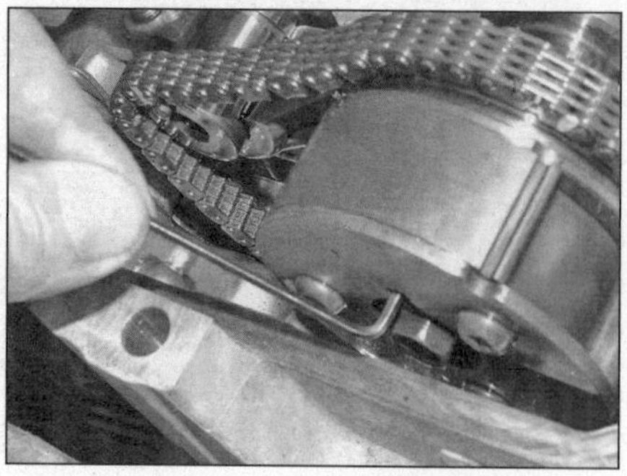

9.38 Remove the locking pin

7 Working in the reverse of the tightening sequence **(see illustration 10.22)**, progressively slacken the ten main cylinder head bolts by half a turn at a time, until all bolts can be unscrewed by hand.
8 Lift out the cylinder head bolts and recover the washers (where applicable), noting which way around they are fitted.
9 Lift the cylinder head away with the aid of an assistant, as it is a heavy assembly. Remove the gasket from the top of the block, noting the locating dowels fitted to the top of the cylinder block. If they are a loose fit in the block, remove the locating dowels, noting which way round they are fitted, and store them with the head for safekeeping.
10 If the cylinder head is to be dismantled for overhaul, then refer to Chapter 2D, Section 11.

Preparation for refitting

11 Check the condition of the cylinder head bolts, and particularly their threads, whenever they are removed. Wash the bolts and wipe dry, then check each for any sign of visible wear or damage, renewing any bolt if necessary.
12 Checking the cylinder head bolts**(see illustration)**: –
a) *Measure 10 mm up from the threaded end of the bolt and note the reading = D1.*
b) *Measure 40 mm up from the threaded end of the bolt and note the reading = D2.*
c) *Take the second reading away from the first reading (D1 – D2), and it should be no more than 0.15 mm.*

Note: *Although Nissan do not specify that the bolts must be renewed, it is strongly recommended, that the bolts should be renewed as a complete set whenever they are disturbed.*
13 The mating faces of the cylinder head and cylinder block/crankcase must be perfectly clean before refitting the head. Use a hard plastic or wood scraper to remove all traces of gasket and carbon; also clean the piston crowns. Take particular care, as the surfaces are damaged easily. Also, make sure that the carbon is not allowed to enter the oil and water passages – this is particularly important for the lubrication system, as carbon could block the oil supply to any of the engine's components. Using adhesive tape and paper, seal the water, oil and bolt holes in the cylinder block/crankcase. To prevent carbon entering the gap between the pistons and bores, smear a little grease in the gap. After cleaning each piston, use a small brush to remove all traces of grease and carbon from the gap, and then wipe away the remainder with a clean rag. Clean all the pistons in the same way.
14 Check the mating surfaces of the cylinder block/crankcase and the cylinder head for nicks, deep scratches and other damage. If slight, they may be removed carefully with a file, but if excessive, machining may be the only alternative to renewal.

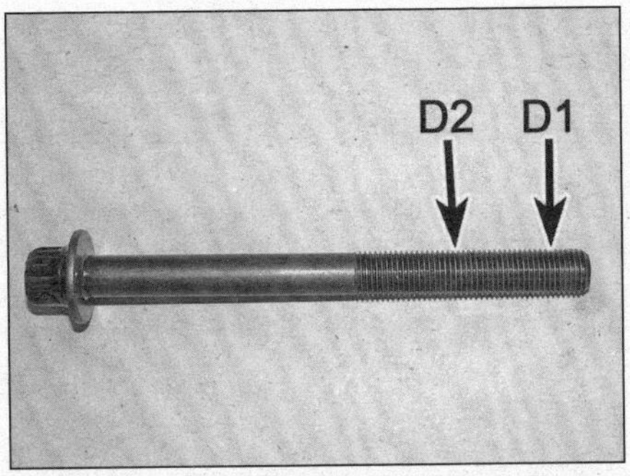

10.12 Check the cylinder head bolts for wear

15 If warpage of the cylinder head gasket surface is suspected, use a straight-edge to check it for distortion. If necessary, refer to Chapter 2D, Section 12.

Refitting

16 Wipe clean the mating surfaces of the cylinder head and cylinder block/crankcase. Check the locating dowels are in position at each end of the cylinder block/crankcase surface.
17 Fit a new gasket to the cylinder block/crankcase surface, aligning it with the locating dowels.
18 With the aid of an assistant, carefully refit the cylinder head assembly to the block, aligning it with the locating dowels.
19 Apply a smear of clean oil to the threads, and to the underside of the heads, of the cylinder head bolts.
20 Fit the washer to each head bolt, making sure it is fitted with its tapered edge uppermost.
21 Carefully enter each bolt into its relevant hole (do not drop them in) and screw in, by hand only, until finger-tight.
22 Working progressively and in sequence, tighten the cylinder head bolts to their Stage 1 torque setting, using a torque wrench and suitable socket **(see illustration)**. See Specifications at the beginning of this Chapter.
23 For Stage 2, leave the bolts a minute then, working in the reverse of the specified sequence, progressively slacken the head bolts by half a turn at a time, until all bolts can be unscrewed by hand.
24 Tighten the head bolts again by hand, then go around again in the specified sequence and tighten the ten bolts to the specified Stage 3 torque setting.
25 Go around in the specified sequence and tighten the ten cylinder head bolts through the specified Stage 4 angle setting.
26 Finally, go around again in the specified sequence and tighten the ten cylinder head bolts through the specified Stage 5 angle setting.
27 Reconnect the coolant hoses to the cylinder head and securely tighten the retaining clips.

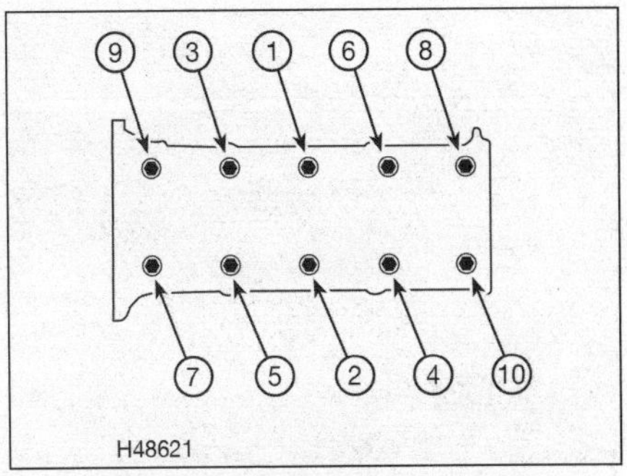

10.22 Cylinder head bolt tightening sequence

28 Working as described in Chapter 4A, carry out the following operations:
a) *Refit all disturbed wiring, hoses and control cable(s) to the inlet manifold and fuel system components.*
b) *Reconnect the exhaust system front pipe to the manifold, and reconnect the exhaust gas sensor wiring connector.*
c) *Refit the inlet manifold.*

29 Refit the camshafts to the cylinder head as described in Section 9.
30 Fit the timing chains and sprockets as described in Section 7.
31 If the cylinder head has been overhauled, check the valve clearances 'cold' prior to refitting the cylinder head cover (see Section 8).
32 Refill the cooling system as described in Chapter 1A, Section 25.
33 Start the engine and warm it up to normal operating temperature, check for any leaks from the engine, cooling circuit and fuel system.

11 Sump – removal and refitting

Note: *The oil sump is made up of two parts; it has an upper alloy part and a lower steel oil pan. The following procedure is for the lower oil pan part. To remove the upper alloy part, the engine will need to be removed and the upper alloy sump then split from the cylinder block.*

Removal

1 Firmly apply the handbrake, and then jack up the front of the vehicle and support it securely on axle stands (see *Jacking and vehicle support*).
2 Drain the engine oil, then clean and refit the engine oil drain plug, fit a new sealing washer on refitting. And then tighten it to the specified torque. If the engine is nearing its service interval when the oil and filter are due for renewal, it is recommended that the filter is also removed, and a new one fitted. Refer to Chapter 1A, Section 5 for further information.
3 Progressively slacken and remove all of the steel oil pan retaining bolts.

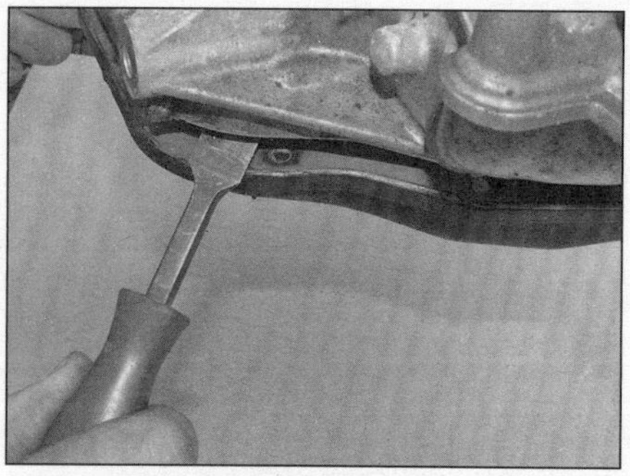

11.4 Using a flat ended scraper to prise the sump away

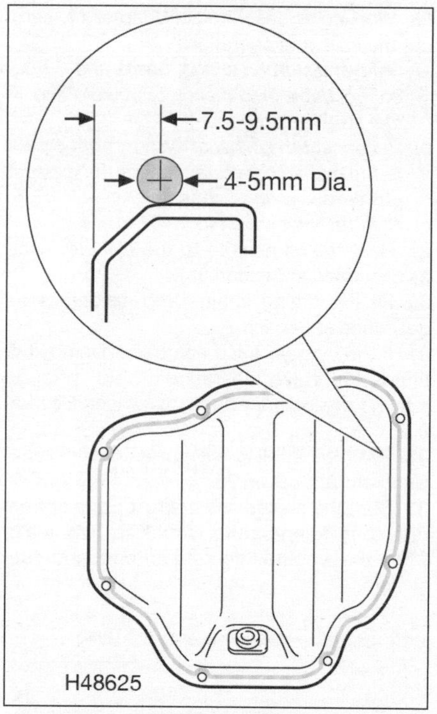

11.6 Apply a bead of sealant around the sump as shown

4 The lower steel oil pan is sealed to the upper alloy sump casing with strong liquid gasket sealer, which is very difficult to remove, however methodical use of a spatula or thin knife will release the sump **(see illustration)**. Take care not to distort or damage the mating surfaces of the lower oil pan and upper alloy sump. Take adequate precautions to catch any oil remaining inside the sump housing, as the oil pan is removed.

Refitting

5 Clean all traces of sealant from the mating surfaces of the upper alloy part of the sump and steel oil pan, then use a clean rag to wipe out the oil pan and the sump interior.

6 Ensure that the lower oil pan and upper alloy casing mating surfaces are clean and dry. Apply a continuous bead of suitable sealant to the mating surface of the oil pan. Apply a 4 mm to 5 mm diameter bead of sealant to the oil pan, going around the inner edge of each bolt hole **(see illustration)**.

7 Offer up the sump, locating it in the correct position, and refit its retaining bolts. Tighten the bolts evenly and progressively to the specified torque and in the correct sequence **(see illustration)**.

8 After reassembly, the engine can then be refilled with fresh engine oil. Refer to Chapter 1A, Section 5, for further information.

9 Start the engine and warm it up to normal operating temperature, check for any leaks from the sump area.

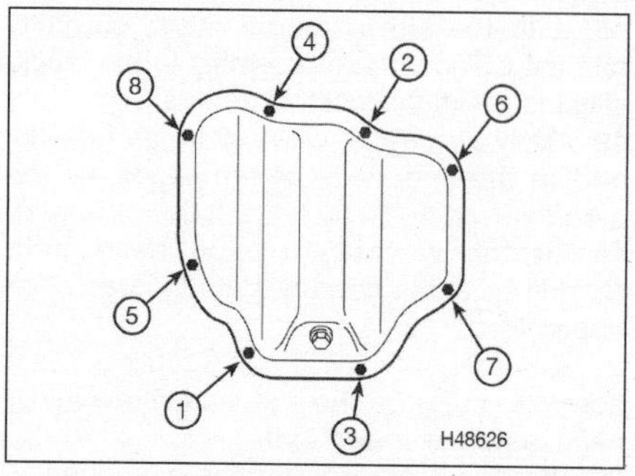

11.7 Tighten the bolts in the sequence shown

12 Oil pump, drive chain and sprockets – removal, inspection and refitting

Removal

1 Remove the timing chain as described in Section 7.

2 Remove the sump oil pan as described in Section 11.

3 Release the spring from the hole in the cylinder block and withdraw the chain tensioner from the pivot on the cylinder block **(see illustration)**.

4 Unscrew the oil pump drive sprocket retaining nut, use a socket on the end of the oil pump drive shaft to slacken the retaining nut **(see illustration)**.

5 Remove the oil pump drive chain complete with sprockets from the oil pump drive shaft and crankshaft **(see illustration)**.

6 Undo the retaining bolts and remove the

12.3 Remove the tensioner from the cylinder block

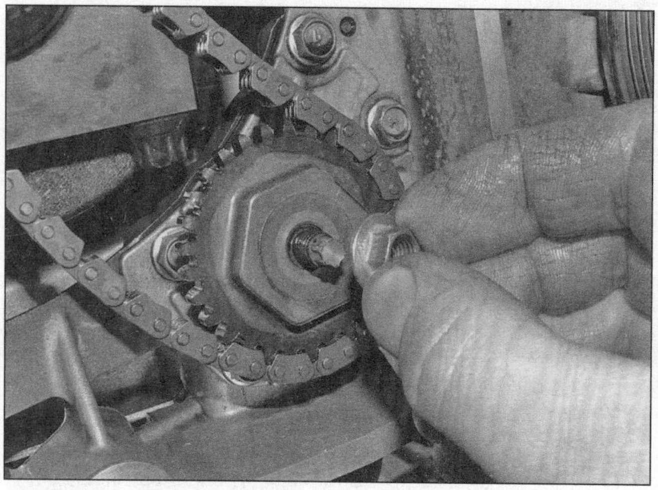

12.4 Remove the sprocket securing nut

12.5 Remove the drive chain complete with sprockets

12.6 Oil pump retaining bolts

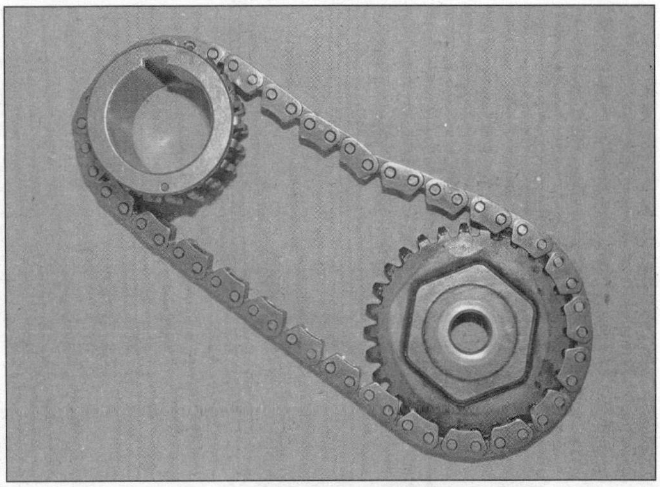
12.7 Check the condition of all components

oil pump from the upper sump housing **(see illustration)**.

Inspection

7 Clean the components and carefully examine the chain, sprockets and pump for any signs of excessive wear. If evident, it is recommended that all the components are renewed as a set **(see illustration)**.

8 Before refitting the oil pump, prime it by filling with clean engine oil whilst rotating the pump clockwise.

Refitting

9 Fit the oil pump back in place in the sump upper housing and tighten the retaining bolts.

10 Make sure the chain is located around the two sprocket correctly, and then refit them as a complete assembly to the oil pump drive shaft and crankshaft **(see illustration)**.

11 Refit the oil pump sprocket retaining nut and tighten to the specified torque setting.

12 Refit the chain tensioner to the pivot on the cylinder block, making sure the tensioner spring is located correctly in the cylinder block **(see illustration)**.

13 Refit the sump oil pan as described in Section 11.

14 Refit the timing chain cover as described in Section 7.

13 Crankshaft oil seals – renewal

Timing chain cover oil seal

1 Remove the crankshaft pulley as described in Section 5.

2 Carefully lever the oil seal out of position, using a large flat-bladed screwdriver, taking care not to damage the end of the crankshaft or timing cover **(see illustration)**.

3 Clean the seal housing, and polish off any burrs or raised edges, which may have caused the seal to fail in the first place.

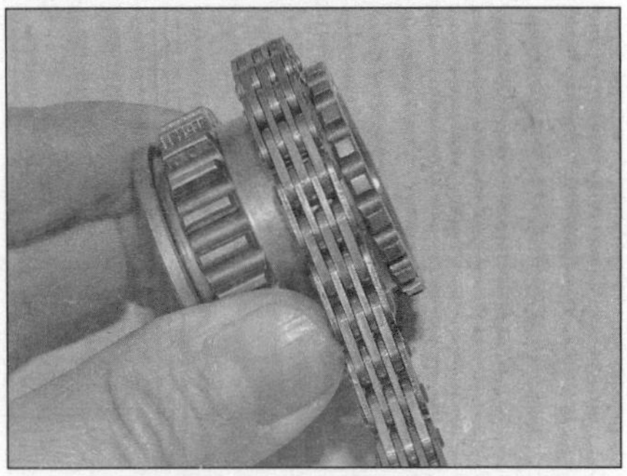
12.10 Make sure the chain is located around the sprocket correctly

4 Lubricate the lips of the new seal with a smear of clean oil and offer up the seal ensuring its sealing lip is facing inwards. Carefully ease the seal into position, taking care not to damage its sealing lip. Drive

12.12 Make sure the tensioner spring is located correctly

13.2 Carefully prise out the oil seal

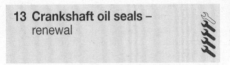

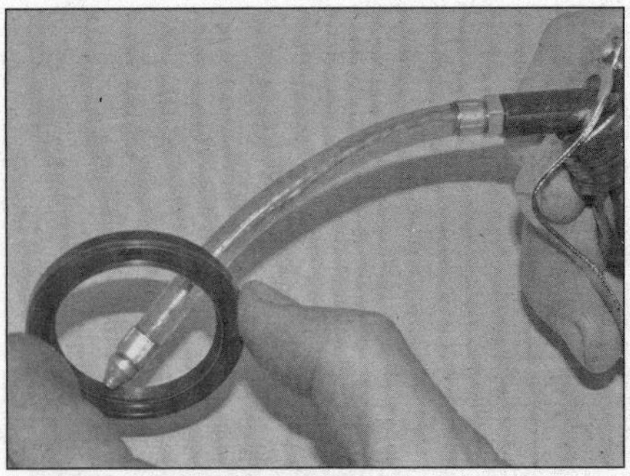
13.4a Lubricate the inner lip of the seal...

13.4b ...press the seal into position...

13.4c ...carefully fit the seal into the cover

13.7a Carefully drill a hole in the seal...

13.7b ...insert a self tapping screw...

13.7c ...and lever the seal out from the casing

13.8 Clean around the seal fitting surface area

the seal into position until it seats flush with the face of the timing chain cover **(see illustrations)**. Take care not to damage the seal lips during fitting.

5 Wash off any traces of oil, then refit the crankshaft pulley as described in Section 5.

Flywheel oil seal

6 Remove the flywheel, as described in Section 14.

7 Note the fitted position of the old seal, then prise it out of the right-hand cover/housing using a screwdriver or suitable hooked instrument, taking care not to damage the surface of the crankshaft. Alternatively, the oil seal can be removed by drilling a hole in the seal, and then inserting a self-tapping screw. A pair of grips/pliers can then be used to pull out the oil seal **(see illustrations)**. Take care when drilling the hole, to not drill into anything other than the seal.

8 Clean the seal housing, and polish off any burrs or raised edges, which may have caused the seal to fail in the first place **(see illustration)**.

9 Lubricate with clean oil the lips of the new seal and the crankshaft shoulder, then offer up the seal to the cylinder block/crankcase. Ease the sealing lip of the seal over the crankshaft shoulder by hand only, and press the seal evenly into its recess to make it square in the casing **(see illustrations)**.

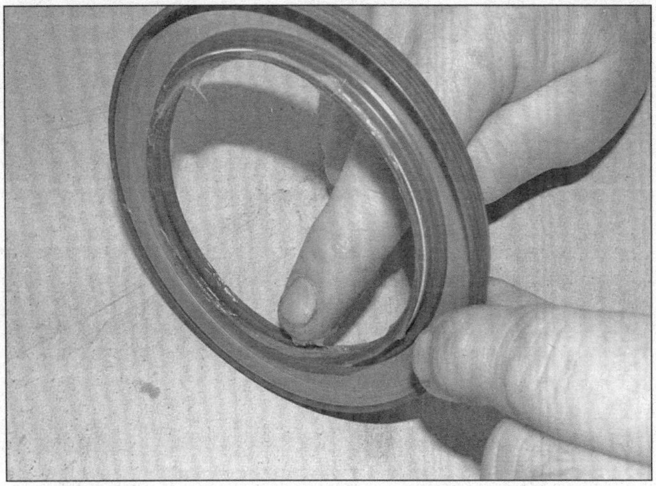
13.9a Using clean oil to lubricate the inner lip of the seal...

13.9b ...place the seal in position

13.10a Apply some sealant around the outer edge of the seal...

13.10b ... press the seal fully into position...

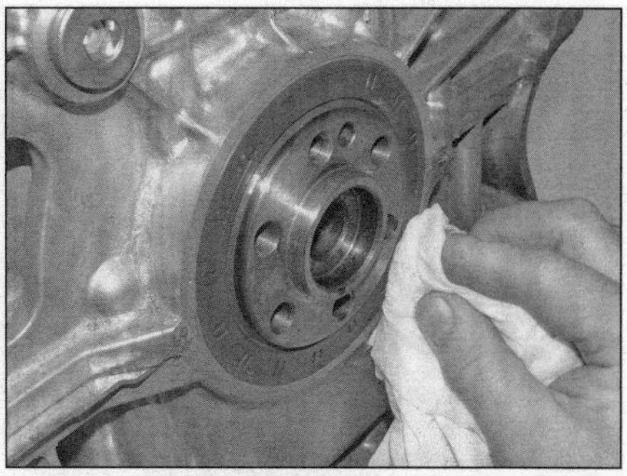

13.10c ...then clean off the excess sealant from around the casing

10 With the seal still protruding out from the cylinder block, apply a coat of liquid gasket/sealant all the way around the outer edge of the seal. Carefully drive the seal into position until it seats flush with the face of the cylinder block, and then wipe off the excess liquid gasket/sealant from the casing **(see illustrations)**. Make sure the outer edge of the seal is sitting flush with the cylinder block casing.

11 Wash off any traces of oil or sealant, then refit the flywheel as described in Section 14.

14 Flywheel – removal, inspection and refitting

Removal

1 Remove the transmission as described in Chapter 7, Section 6.

2 Remove the clutch assembly as described in Chapter 6, Section 7.

3 Prevent the flywheel from turning by locking the ring gear teeth **(see illustration)**. Alternatively, bolt a strap between the flywheel and the cylinder block.

4 Slacken and remove the retaining bolts **(see illustration)**, then remove the flywheel from the end of the crankshaft. Do not drop it, as it is very heavy.

Inspection

5 If the flywheel's clutch mating surface is deeply scored, cracked or otherwise damaged, the flywheel must be renewed. Seek the advice of a Nissan dealer or engine reconditioning specialist.

6 If the ring gear is badly worn or has missing teeth, it must be renewed. Check with your Nissan dealer or engine reconditioning specialist, to see if the flywheel can be repaired.

Refitting

7 Install the locating dowels (where removed) and refit the cover plate to the cylinder block.

8 Clean the mating surfaces of the flywheel and crankshaft.

9 Offer up the flywheel, and refit the retaining bolts.

10 Lock the ring gear using the method employed on dismantling, and tighten the retaining bolts to the specified torque.

11 Refit the clutch as described in Chapter 6, Section 7.

12 Remove the locking tool, and refit the transmission as described in Chapter 7, Section 6.

15 Engine/transmission mountings – inspection and renewal

Inspection

1 If improved access is required, firmly apply the handbrake, and then jack up the front of the vehicle and support it securely on axle stands (see *Jacking and vehicle support*).

2 Check the mounting rubber to see if it is cracked, hardened or separated from the metal at any point; renew the mounting if any such damage or deterioration is evident.

3 Check that all the mounting's fasteners are securely tightened; use a torque wrench to check if possible.

4 Using a large screwdriver or a crowbar, check for wear in the mounting by carefully levering against it to check for free play. Where this is not possible, enlist the aid of an assistant to move the engine/transmission back-and-forth, or from side-to-side, while you watch the mounting. While some free play is to be expected even from new components, excessive wear should be obvious. If excessive free play is found, check first that the fasteners are correctly secured, and then renew any worn components as described below.

Renewal

Right-hand mounting

5 Disconnect the battery negative terminal (refer to battery disconnection and reconnection in Chapter 5A Section 3).

6 Place a jack beneath the engine, with a block of wood on the jack head. Raise the jack until it is supporting the weight of the engine.

7 Slacken the securing bolt and disconnect the earth wire from the top of the mounting bracket **(see illustration)**.

8 Slacken and remove the three retaining bolts from the inner wing panel, remove the three

14.3 Using a tool to prevent the flywheel from turning...

14.4 ...when slackening the flywheel bolts

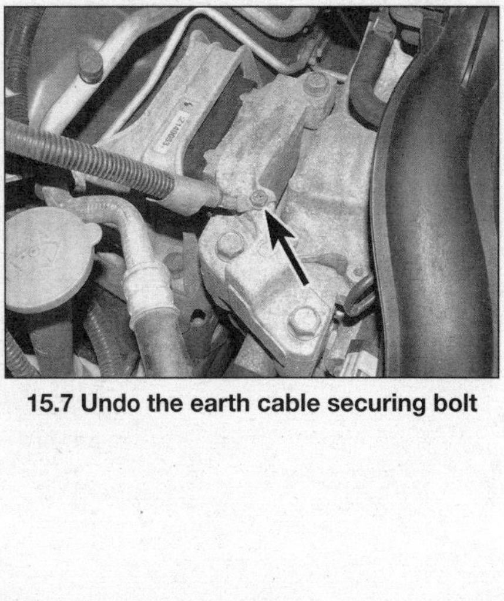

15.7 Undo the earth cable securing bolt

15.8 Remove the mounting retaining bolts and remove the mounting from the engine compartment

15.15 Undo the centre retaining nut

retaining bolts from the engine mounting bracket, and then withdraw the complete mounting from the engine compartment **(see illustrations)**.

9 Check carefully for signs of wear or damage on all components, and renew them where necessary.

10 On refitting, fit the engine mounting and bracket to the inner wing panel and engine, and then securely tighten its retaining bolts to the specified torque setting.

11 With the engine mounting back in position, lower the jack and remove it from underneath the engine.

12 Reconnect the earth cable to the top of the engine mounting and then reconnect the battery negative terminal.

Left-hand mounting

13 Remove the battery and tray, as described in Chapter 5A, Section 3.

14 Place a jack and block of wood beneath the transmission, and raise the jack to take the weight of the transmission.

15 Slacken and remove the through-bolt/stud retaining nut from the centre of the mounting **(see illustration)**.

16 Slacken and remove the two outer retaining nuts, and withdraw the mounting from the upper mounting bracket.

17 If required, undo the retaining bolts from the inner wing panel to remove the upper mounting bracket.

18 Also, if required, undo the retaining bolts from the transmission to remove the lower mounting bracket **(see illustration)**.

19 Check carefully for signs of wear or damage on all components, and renew them where necessary.

20 On refitting, fit the upper and lower mounting brackets (where removed) and securely tighten the retaining bolts.

21 Align the left-hand rubber mounting with the bolt/stud on the lower mounting bracket and tighten its nut to the specified torque setting.

22 Refit the two outer retaining nuts, and tighten to the specified torque setting.

23 With the transmission mounting back in position, lower the jack and remove it from underneath the transmission.

24 Refit the battery and battery tray, with reference to Chapter 5A, Section 3.

Rear lower mounting

25 If not already done, firmly apply the handbrake, and then jack up the front of the vehicle and support it securely on axle stands (see *Jacking and vehicle support*).

26 Slacken and remove the bolts securing the rear mounting bracket to the transmission, and then withdraw the bracket from transmission **(see illustration)**.

27 Slacken and remove the bolt securing the rear mounting link to the subframe, and then withdraw the mounting link from subframe **(see illustration)**.

28 Check carefully for signs of wear or damage on all components, and renew them where necessary.

29 On reassembly, fit the rear mounting to the subframe, and tighten the retaining bolt to the specified torque.

30 Refit the mounting bracket to the lower part of the transmission and tighten its retaining bolts to the specified torque.

31 With the transmission rear mounting link arm back in position, lower the vehicle to the ground.

15.18 Mounting bracket securing bolts

15.26 Remove the mounting bracket from the transmission

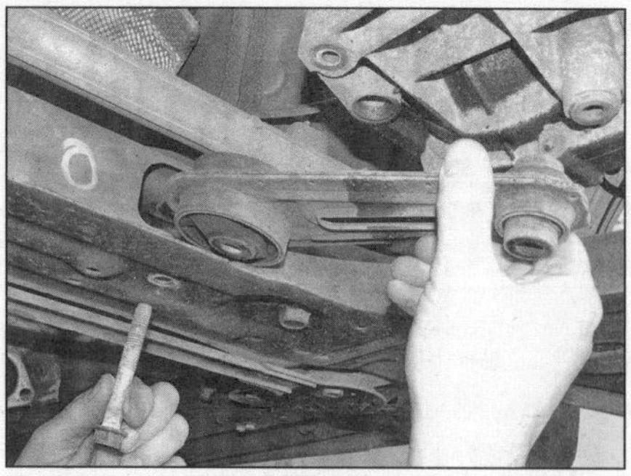

15.27 Remove the link arm from the subframe

Chapter 2 Part C
1.5 litre diesel engine in-car repair procedures

Contents

Degrees of difficulty

Easy, suitable for novice with little experience	**Fairly easy,** suitable for beginner with some experience	**Fairly difficult,** suitable for competent DIY mechanic	**Difficult,** suitable for experienced DIY mechanic	**Very difficult,** suitable for expert DIY or professional

Specifications

General

Type	Four cylinder, in-line, single overhead camshaft
Designation	K9K
Version:	
To emission standard Euro 5	K9K (Type 1)
To emission standard Euro 6	K9K (Type 2)
Capacity	1461 cc
Bore	76.0 mm
Stroke	80.5 mm
Firing order	1-3-4-2 (No 1 cylinder at flywheel end)
Direction of crankshaft rotation	Clockwise viewed from timing belt end
Compression ratio	15.2 : 1

Compression pressures

Engine warm – approximately 80°C:	
Minimum pressure	18 bars
Maximum difference between cylinders	4 bars

Camshaft and followers

Drive	Toothed belt
Number of bearings	6
Camshaft endfloat	0.080 o 0.178 mm
Camshaft lobe height:	
Inlet	44.012 to 44.018 mm
Exhaust	44.592 to 44.598 mm
Camshaft bearing journal outer diameter:	
Nos 1 to 5 bearings	24.98 to 25.00 mm
No 6 bearing	27.97 to 28.00 mm
Camshaft cylinder head bearing journal internal diameter:	
Nos 1 to 5 bearings	25.04 to 25.06 mm
No 6 bearing	28.04 to 28.06 mm
Camshaft run-out	Less than 0.05 mm
Camshaft follower outer diameter	34.965 to 34.985 mm
Cylinder head hole diameter for follower	35.000 to 35.040 mm
Camshaft follower to cylinder head clearance	0.015 to 0,075 mm

Valve clearances

Inlet	0.13 to 0.20 mm
Exhaust	0.30 to 0.375 mm

Lubrication system

System pressure (at 80°C):	
At idle	0.8 bar minimum
At 4000 rpm	3.4 bars minimum
Oil pump type	Gear-type, chain-driven off the crankshaft right-hand end
Oil level sensor resistance	6.0 to 20 ohms

Torque wrench settings

Torque wrench settings	Nm	lbf ft
Auxiliary drivebelt tensioner	40	30
Big-end bearing caps:		
Stage 1	25	18
Stage 2	Angle-tighten a further 110°	
Camshaft bearing caps	11	8
Camshaft sprocket outer retaining bolts	14	10
Camshaft sprocket centre nut:		
Stage 1	30	22
Stage 2	Angle-tighten a further 86°	
Crankshaft main bearing caps:		
Stage 1	25	18
Stage 2	Angle-tighten a further 47°	
Crankshaft pulley bolt:		
Stage 1	120	89
Stage 2	Angle-tighten a further 95°	
Crankshaft seal end cover	14	10
Cylinder block TDC blanking plug	20	15
Cylinder head bolts: *		
Stage 1	25	18
Stage 2	Angle-tighten a further 270°	
Cylinder head coolant outlet	11	8
Cylinder head cover bolts	12	9
Flywheel: *		
Stage 1	20	15
Stage 2	Angle-tighten a further 36°	
High-pressure fuel pump bolts	23	17
High-pressure fuel pump sprocket	70	52
High-pressure fuel pipe union nuts	28	21
Left-hand transmission mounting:		
Through-bolt/stud nut	60	44
Through-bolt/stud-to-bracket	75	55
Mounting-to-bracket nuts	105	77
Mounting bracket-to-inner wing panel bolts	50	37
Mounting bracket-to-transmission bolts	55	41
Oil cooler – through bolt	45	33
Oil filter body – through bolt	45	33
Oil level sensor	22	16
Oil pressure switch	25	18
Oil pump	25	18
Rear lower engine torque/link arm mounting:		
Torque link arm-to-front subframe bolt	80	59
Torque link arm-to-mounting bracket bolt	155	114
Mounting bracket-to-sump bolts	80	59
Right-hand driveshaft support bearing bolts	44	32
Right-hand engine mounting:		
Mounting bracket-to-cylinder head	20	15
Alloy mounting bracket-to-cylinder head mounting bracket	45	33
Mounting bracket bolts-to-inner wing	65	48
Torque arm mounting bolts	120	89
Sump-to-cylinder block bolts	14	10
Sump-to-transmission bolts	44	32
Timing belt tensioner	27	20

**Use new nuts/bolts*

1 General Information

How to use this Chapter

1 This Part of Chapter 2 is devoted to in-car repair procedures for the diesel engine. Similar information covering the other engine types can be found in Parts A and C. All procedures concerning engine removal and refitting, and engine block/cylinder head overhaul can be found in Part D of this Chapter.

2 Note that, while it may be possible physically to overhaul items such as the piston/connecting rod assemblies while the engine is in the car, such tasks are not normally carried out as separate operations. Usually, several additional procedures (not to mention the cleaning of components and of oilways) have to be carried out. For this reason, all such tasks are classed as major overhaul procedures, and are described in Part D of this Chapter.

3 In Parts A and B, the assumption is made that the engine is installed in the car, with all ancillaries connected. If the engine has been removed for overhaul, the preliminary dismantling information, which precedes each operation, may be ignored.

Engine description

4 The engine is of four cylinder, in-line, single overhead camshaft type, mounted transversely at the front of the vehicle.

5 The cylinder block is of cast iron with conventional dry liners bored directly into the cylinder block. The crankshaft is supported in five shell-type main bearings. Thrustwashers are fitted to No 3 main bearing to control crankshaft endfloat.

6 The connecting rods are attached to the crankshaft by 'cracked' horizontally split shell-type big-end bearings and to the pistons by gudgeon pins. The gudgeon pins are fully-floating and are retained by circlips. The aluminium alloy pistons are fitted with three piston rings, comprising two compression rings and a scraper-type oil control ring.

7 The single overhead camshaft is mounted directly in the cylinder head, and is driven by the crankshaft via a toothed timing belt.

8 The camshaft operates the valves via inverted bucket type tappets (cam followers), which operate in bores machined directly in the cylinder head. The valve clearances are adjusted by changing the cam followers, which are available in 25 different thicknesses. The inlet and exhaust valves are mounted vertically in the cylinder head and are each closed by a single valve spring.

9 The high-pressure fuel injection pump is driven by the timing belt and is described in further detail in Chapter 4B, Section 9.

10 A semi-closed crankcase ventilation system is employed, and crankcase fumes are drawn from the cylinder block and passed via a hose to the inlet tract (see Chapter 4C, Section 3 for further details).

11 Engine lubrication is by pressure feed from a gear type oil pump located beneath the crankshaft. Engine oil is fed through an externally mounted oil filter to the main oil gallery feeding the crankshaft and camshaft. Oil spray jets are fitted to the cylinder block to supply oil to the underside of the pistons. An oil cooler is mounted between the oil filter and the cylinder block.

Operations with engine in place

12 The following operations can be carried out without having to remove the engine from the vehicle:

a) Compression pressure – testing.
b) Removal and refitting of the cylinder head cover.
c) Removal and refitting of the timing belt and sprockets.
d) Renewal of the camshaft oil seals.
e) Removal and refitting of the camshaft and followers.
*f) Removal and refitting of the cylinder head.**
g) Removal and refitting of the sump.
h) Removal and refitting of the oil pump.
i) Renewal of the crankshaft oil seals.
j) Renewal of the engine mountings.
k) Removal and refitting of the flywheel.

*On all Type 2 engines, and Type 1 engines with a diesel particulate filter mounted behind the cylinder head in the engine compartment, the engine/transmission assembly must be removed for this operation. There is insufficient clearance in the engine compartment to allow for cylinder head removal and refitting with the engine/transmission assembly in the car. For this readon the procedure is contained in Chapter 2D.

2 Compression and leakdown tests – description and interpretation

Compression test

Note: *A compression tester specifically designed for diesel engines must be used for this test.*

1 When engine performance is down, or if misfiring occurs which cannot be attributed to a fault in the fuel system, a compression test can provide diagnostic clues as to the engine's condition. If the test is performed regularly it can give warning of trouble before any other symptoms become apparent.

2 A compression tester is connected to an adaptor that screws into the glow plug hole. It is unlikely to be worthwhile buying such a tester for occasional use, but it may be possible to borrow or hire one – if not, have the test performed by a garage.

3 Unless specific instructions to the contrary are supplied with the tester, observe the following points:

a) The battery must be in a good state of charge, the air filter must be clean and the engine should be at normal operating temperature.
b) All the glow plugs must be removed before starting the test and the wiring disconnected from the injectors.

4 There is no need to hold the accelerator pedal down during the test because the diesel engine air inlet is not throttled.

5 The actual compression pressures measured are not so important as the balance between cylinders. Values are given in the Specifications.

6 The cause of poor compression is less easy to establish on a diesel engine than on a petrol one. The effect of introducing oil into the cylinders ('wet' testing) is not conclusive, because there is a risk that the oil will sit in the swirl chamber or in the recess on the piston crown instead of passing to the rings. However, the following can be used as a rough guide to diagnosis.

7 All cylinders should produce very similar pressures; any difference greater than that specified indicates the existence of a fault. Note that the compression should build-up quickly in a healthy engine; low compression on the first stroke, followed by gradually increasing pressure on successive strokes, indicates worn piston rings. A low compression reading on the first stroke, which does not build-up during successive strokes, indicates leaking valves or a blown head gasket (a cracked head could also be the cause).

8 A low reading from two adjacent cylinders is almost certainly due to the head gasket having blown between them.

Leakdown test

9 A leakdown test measures the rate at which compressed air fed into the cylinder is lost. It is an alternative to a compression test and in many ways it is better, since the escaping air provides easy identification of where pressure loss is occurring (piston rings, valves or head gasket).

10 The equipment needed for leakdown testing is unlikely to be available to the home mechanic. If poor compression is suspected, have the test performed by a suitably equipped garage.

3 Top Dead Centre (TDC) for No 1 piston – locating

Note: *Special Nissan/Renault timing tools are required for this work, or tools obtained from an automotive accessory shop.*

1 Top Dead Centre (TDC) is the highest point in the cylinder that each piston reaches as the crankshaft turns. Each piston reaches TDC at the end of the compression stroke and again at the end of the exhaust stroke; however, for the purpose of timing the engine, TDC refers to the position of No 1 piston at the end of its compression stroke. No 1 piston is at the flywheel end of the engine.

2 When No 1 piston is at TDC, the timing hole in the camshaft sprocket will be aligned with the hole in the cylinder head so that the timing pin can be inserted. Additionally, if the crankshaft timing pin is fully screwed into the cylinder block, it will just contact the timing flat on the crankshaft web.

3 Setting the TDC timing is necessary to ensure that the valve timing is maintained during operations that require removal and refitting of the timing belt.

4 To set the engine at TDC, the right-hand engine mounting support and upper timing belt cover must be removed for access to the camshaft sprocket. First jack up the front of the car and securely support it on axle stands (see *Jacking and vehicle support*). Remove the front right-hand roadwheel, then refer to Chapter 11, Section 21 and remove the wheel arch liner.

5 Support the right-hand end of the engine with a support bar across the engine compartment, with a hoist, or alternatively with a jack and block of wood beneath the sump. Remove the right-hand engine mounting and torque link as described in Section 15.

6 Release the retaining clips and remove the timing belt upper cover **(see illustrations)**.

7 Undo the retaining bolts and remove the engine mounting support bracket from the end of the cylinder head **(see illustrations)**.

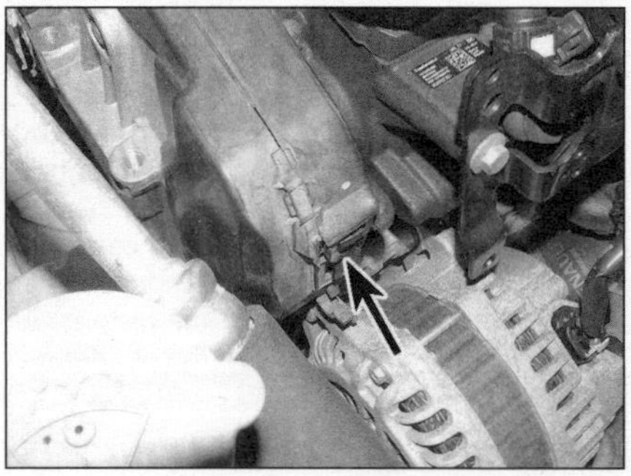

3.6a Release the retaining clips...

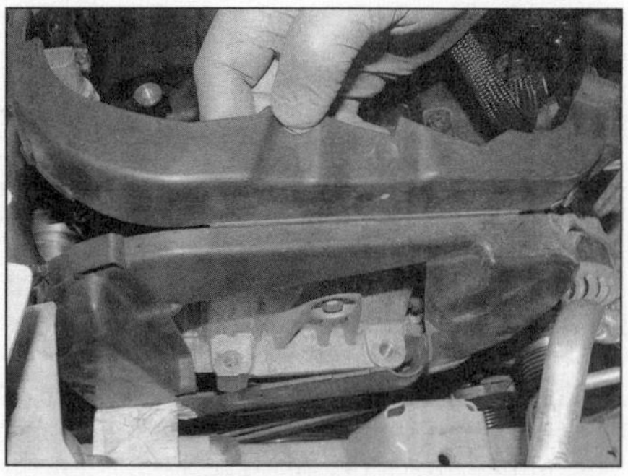

3.6b ...and remove the timing belt upper cover

8 Unscrew and remove the plug from the TDC hole on the front (transmission end) of the cylinder block **(see illustration)**. If required, remove the starter motor as described in Chapter 5A, Section 8, to make access to the TDC plug easier.

9 Using a spanner or socket on the crankshaft pulley bolt, turn the crankshaft clockwise until the timing hole in the camshaft sprocket is approaching the hole in the cylinder head.

10 Insert and tighten the special TDC pin into the cylinder block timing hole **(see illustration)**.

11 Slowly turn the crankshaft clockwise until its web contacts the timing pin. Now insert the remaining timing pin through the hole in the camshaft sprocket and into the cylinder head **(see illustration)**. The engine is now positioned with No 1 piston at TDC on its compression stroke.

Caution: Do not attempt to rotate the engine whilst the crankshaft and camshaft timing pins are in position. If the engine is to be left in this state for a long period of time, it is a good idea to place suitable warning notices inside the vehicle, and in the engine compartment. This will reduce the possibility of the engine being accidentally cranked on the starter motor, which would cause considerable damage.

12 On completion, remove the timing pins and refit all removed components.

3.7a Undo the four retaining bolts...

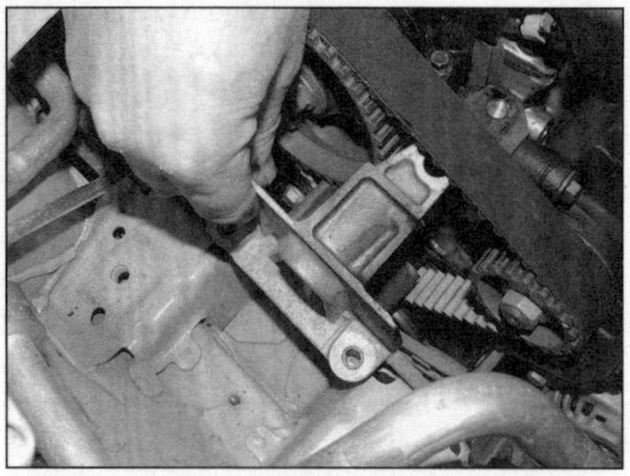

3.7b ...and remove the engine mounting support bracket

4 Cylinder head cover – removal and refitting

Removal

1 Disconnect the battery negative terminal (refer to battery disconnection and reconnection in Chapter 5A, Section 3).

2 Remove the air cleaner assembly as described in Chapter 4B, Section 2.

3 Remove the intercooler inlet pipe from the turbocharger to the intercooler as described in Chapter 4B, Section 2.

4 On Type 2 engines, undo the nut and two

3.8 Unscrew and remove the plug from the TDC hole below the starter motor

3.10 Fitting the crankshaft TDC pin

3.11 Camshaft TDC pin engaged with the sprocket and cylinder head

4.4a Undo the retaining nut...

4.4b ...the bolt at the front...

4.4c ...and the bolt at the rear, then remove the sensor bracket

bolts and remove the sensor bracket from the rear of the cylinder head **(see illustrations)**.

5 Unclip the wiring loom cable ties from the plastic engine shield/cover **(see illustration)**.

6 Undo the two retaining bolts, release the two securing clips and lift off the plastic engine shield/cover **(see illustrations)**.

7 Remove the throttle valve housing as described in Chapter 4B, Section 8.

8 Remove the fuel injectors as described in Chapter 4B, Section 10.

9 Disconnect the wiring connector from the camshaft position sensor, then undo the retaining bolt and remove it from the cylinder head cover **(see illustration)**.

10 Release the quick-release fitting and disconnect the breather hose from the rear of the cylinder head cover.

11 Support the right-hand end of the engine with a support bar across the engine compartment, with a hoist, or alternatively with a jack and block of wood beneath the sump. Remove the right-hand engine mounting and torque link as described in Section 15.

12 Release the retaining clips and remove the timing belt upper cover **(see illustrations 3.6a and 3.6b)**.

13 Working from the outer ends of the cover, spiraling inwards to the centre, slacken and remove the cylinder head cover retaining bolts.

14 Lift off the cylinder head cover, and recover the rubber seal, which goes around the outer edge of the cover **(see illustrations)**.

4.5 Unclip the wiring loom cable ties from the cover

4.6a Undo the two retaining bolts...

4.6b ...release the securing clips...

4.6c ...and remove the plastic engine shield/cover

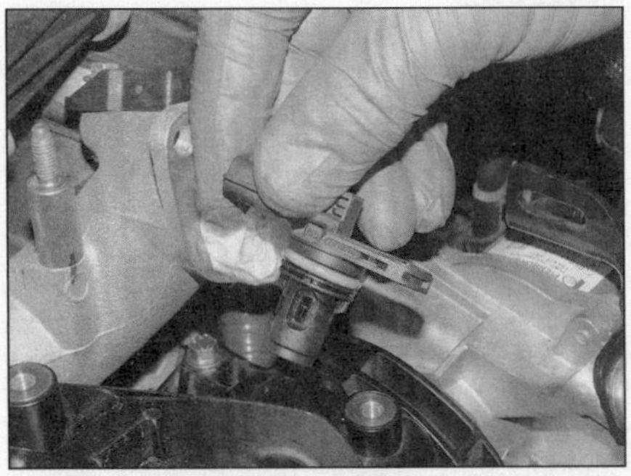

4.9 Undo the retaining bolt and remove the camshaft position sensor.

4.14a Lift off the cylinder head cover...

4.14b ...and recover the rubber seal

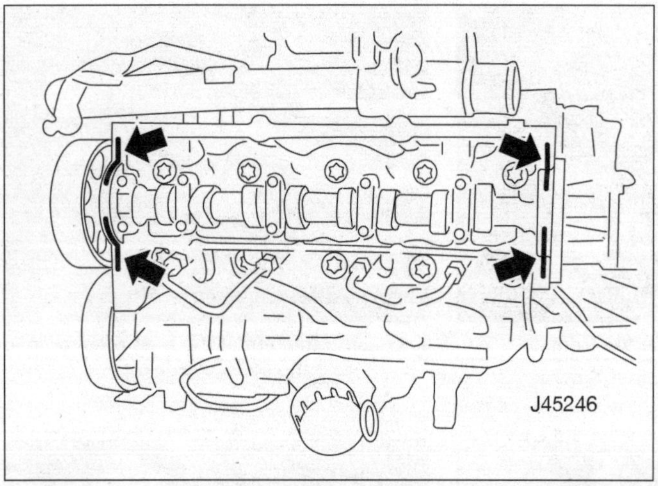

4.16 Apply 2.0 mm wide beads of sealant to the camshaft end bearing caps as shown

5.6 Using a feeler blade to check the valve clearances

15 Inspect the cover seal for signs of damage and deterioration, and renew as necessary. Nissan recommends that the cylinder head cover seal should always be renewed, if the cover is removed.

Refitting

16 Carefully clean the cylinder head and cover mating surfaces, and remove all traces of oil. Then apply four beads of sealant, 2.0 mm wide, to the camshaft end bearing caps (No's 1 and 6) **(see illustration)**.

17 Fit the rubber seal to the cylinder head cover groove, ensuring that it is correctly located along its entire length. Carefully lower the cylinder head cover onto the cylinder head, taking great care not to displace any of the rubber seal

18 Make sure the cover is correctly seated, and then install the retaining bolts. Working from the centre of the cover and spiraling outwards, tighten all the cover bolts to the specified torque.

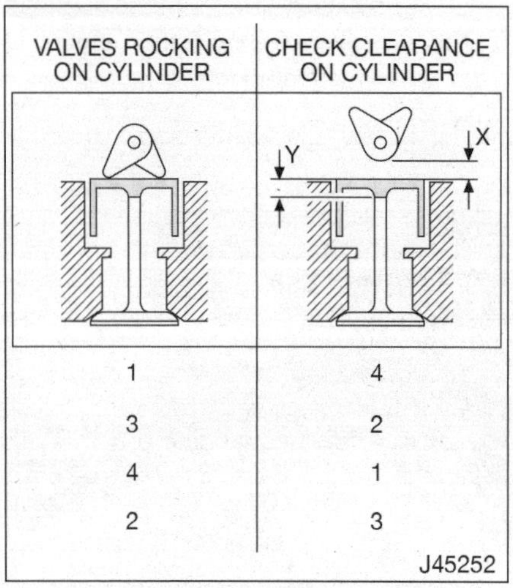

VALVES ROCKING ON CYLINDER
CHECK CLEARANCE ON CYLINDER
Y
X
1
4
3
2
4
1
2
3
J45252

5.7 Valve clearance measurement

X = Clearance Y = Cam follower thickness

19 The remainder of the refitting procedure is the reversal of removal, bearing in mind the following points:

a) Make sure the two securing clips on the front of the plastic shield/cover are secure.

b) Check all wiring connectors and retaining clips are correctly fitted and routed.

c) Tighten all the hose clips securely

5 Valve clearances – checking and adjustment

Note: *This operation is not part of the maintenance schedule. It should be undertaken if noise from the valve gear becomes evident, or if loss of performance gives cause to suspect that the clearances may be incorrect. Adjustment involves removing the camshaft and changing the cam followers (valve lifters) that are available in 25 different thicknesses.*

Checking

1 Apply the handbrake then jack up the front of the car and securely support it on axle stands (see *Jacking and vehicle support*). Remove the right-hand roadwheel.

2 Remove the front right-hand wheel arch liner as described in Chapter 11, Section 21.

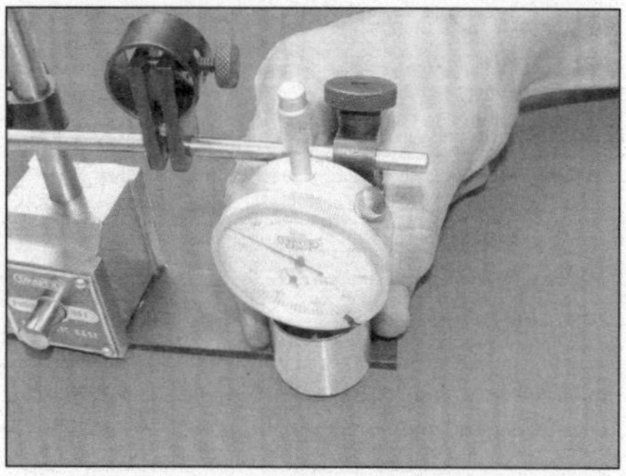

5.8 Using a dial gauge to measure the thickness of the removed cam follower

3 Remove the cylinder head cover as described in Section 4.

4 Draw the valve positions on a piece of paper, numbering them 1 to 8 from the flywheel end of the engine. Identify them as inlet or exhaust (i.e. 1E, 2I, 3E, 4I, 5E, 6I, 7E, 8I).

5 Turn the crankshaft until the valves of No 1 cylinder (flywheel end) are 'rocking'. The exhaust valve will be closing and the inlet valve will be opening. The piston of No 4 cylinder will be at the top of its compression stroke, with both valves fully closed. The clearances for both valves of No 4 cylinder may be checked at the same time.

6 Insert a feeler blade of the correct thickness (see Specifications) between the cam lobe and the top of the cam follower (valve lifter), and check that it is a firm sliding fit **(see illustration)**. If it is not, use the feeler blades to ascertain the exact clearance, and record this for use when calculating the thickness of the new cam follower required. Note that the inlet and exhaust valve clearances are different (see Specifications).

7 With No 4 cylinder valve clearances checked, turn the engine through half a turn so that No 3 valves are 'rocking', then check the valve clearances of No 2 cylinder in the same way. Similarly check the remaining valve clearances in the sequence shown **(see illustration)**.

Adjustment

Note: *A micrometer or dial gauge and probe will be required for this operation.*

8 Where a valve clearance differs from the specified value, the cam follower for that valve must be changed with a thinner or thicker one accordingly. On new followers, the thickness is stamped on the bottom face of the tappet; however, the original followers may not have any thickness stamped on them. It is therefore prudent to use a micrometer or dial gauge to measure the true thickness of any follower removed, as it may have been reduced by wear **(see illustration)**.

5.9 Removing a cam follower

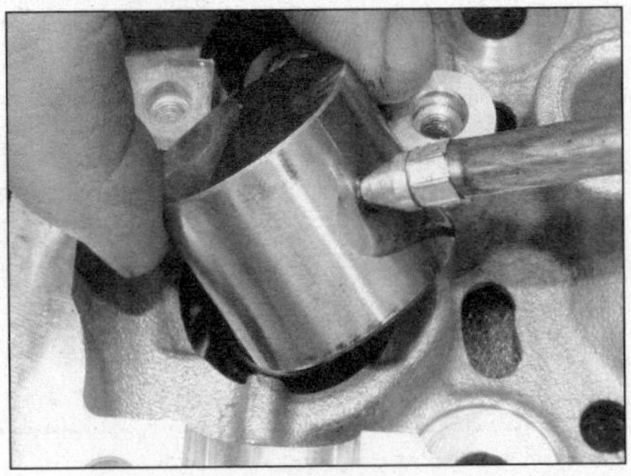

5.12 Lubricate the cam follower before refitting it

6.2 Remove the auxiliary drivebelt, then unbolt and remove the drivebelt tensioner

9 To access the cam followers, first remove the camshaft as described in Section 9. Remove and refit each follower separately, to avoid confusion **(see illustration)**.

10 The size of follower required is calculated as follows. If the measured clearance is less than specified, subtract the measured clearance from the specified clearance, and deduct the result from the thickness of the existing follower. For example:

Sample calculation – clearance too small
Clearance measured (A) = 0.15 mm
Desired clearance (B) = 0.20 mm
Difference (B – A) = 0.05 mm
Cam follower thickness fitted = 7.70 mm
Cam follower thickness required =
7.70 – 0.05 = 7.65 mm

11 If the measured clearance is greater than specified, subtract the specified clearance from the measured clearance, and add the result to the thickness of the existing follower. For example:

Sample calculation – clearance too big
Clearance measured (A) = 0.50 mm
Desired clearance (B) = 0.40 mm
Difference (A – B) = 0.10 mm
Cam follower thickness fitted = 7.55 mm
Cam follower thickness required =
7.55 + 0.10 = 7.65 mm

12 Working on each separately, lift out the follower to be renewed, then oil the new one and carefully locate it in the cylinder head **(see illustration)**.

13 Refit the camshaft with reference to Section 9.

14 Refit the cylinder head cover as described in Section 4.

15 Refit the wheel arch liner and roadwheel, then lower the car to the ground

6 Timing belt – removal, inspection and refitting

Caution: If the timing belt breaks in service, extensive engine damage will result. Renew the belt at the intervals specified in Chapter 1B, or earlier if its condition is at all doubtful.

Removal

1 Disconnect the battery negative terminal (refer to battery disconnection and reconnection in Chapter 5A, Section 3).

2 Remove the auxiliary drivebelt with reference to Chapter 1B, Section 12, and then unbolt and remove the drivebelt tensioner **(see illustration)**.

3 Position the engine with No 1 piston at Top Dead Centre (TDC) as described in Section 3.

4 Temporarily remove the timing pins while the crankshaft pulley bolt is being loosened.

Caution: Do not use the timing pins to lock the engine when removing the crankshaft pulley bolt, as the timing pins may break and cause damage to the engine.

5 Before loosening the crankshaft pulley bolt, note that the crankshaft sprocket is not keyed to the crankshaft as is the normal arrangement, therefore if the crankshaft pulley is removed it is important to have an accurate method of determining the TDC position of No 1 piston. Although the sprocket is not keyed to the crankshaft, there is still a groove in the crankshaft nose, which is at the 12 o'clock position when piston No 1 is at TDC. Unscrew the crankshaft pulley bolt while holding the crankshaft stationary. Have an assistant engage 4th gear and firmly depress the brake pedal. Alternatively, remove the starter motor and have an assistant insert a screwdriver or similar tool in the starter ring gear teeth. With the bolt removed, ease the pulley from the crankshaft **(see illustrations)**.

6 To allow the crankshaft to be turned during subsequent operations, obtain a suitable spacer, or a series of flat washers to allow the crankshaft pulley bolt to be refitted and tightened **(see illustration)**. The spacers or washers should be of a small enough diameter so that the keyway in the sprocket and crankshaft can still be observed.

7 Release the retaining tabs on both sides of

6.5a Unscrew and remove the crankshaft pulley bolt...

6.5b ...and remove the pulley

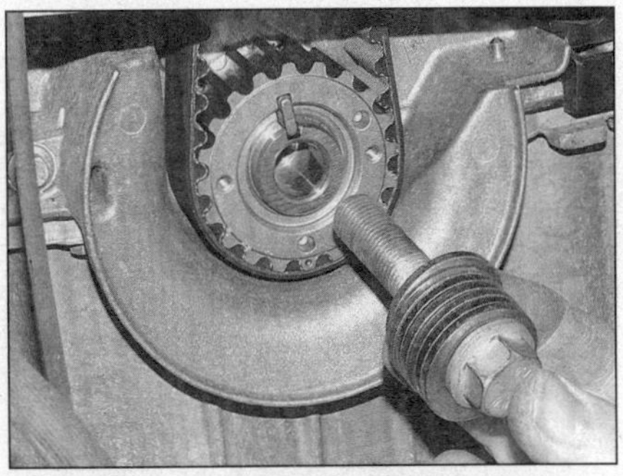

6.6 Place suitable spacers on the crankshaft pulley bolt, then refit and tighten the bolt

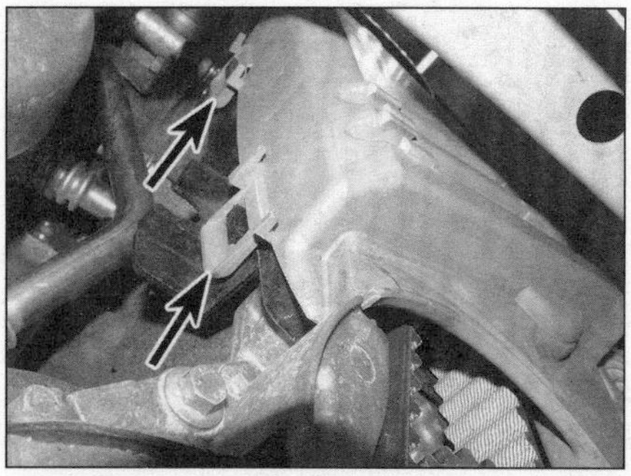

6.7a Release the retaining tabs at the rear...

6.7b ...and front of the timing belt lower cover...

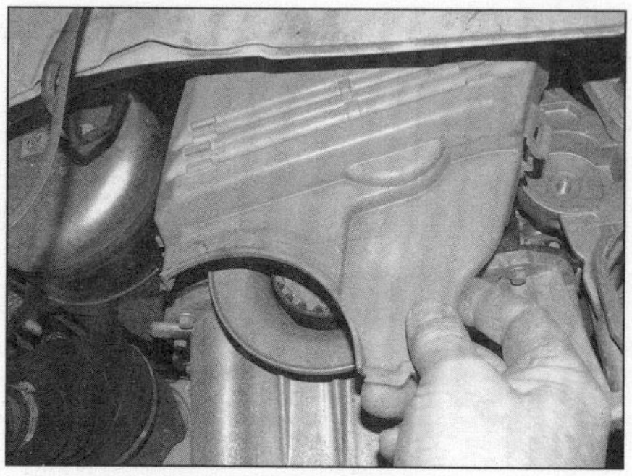

6.7c ...then remove the lower cover

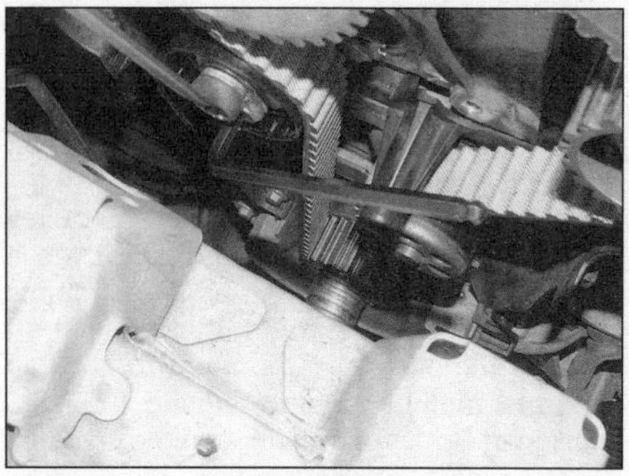

6.9 Loosen the tensioner locknut and turn the tensioner...

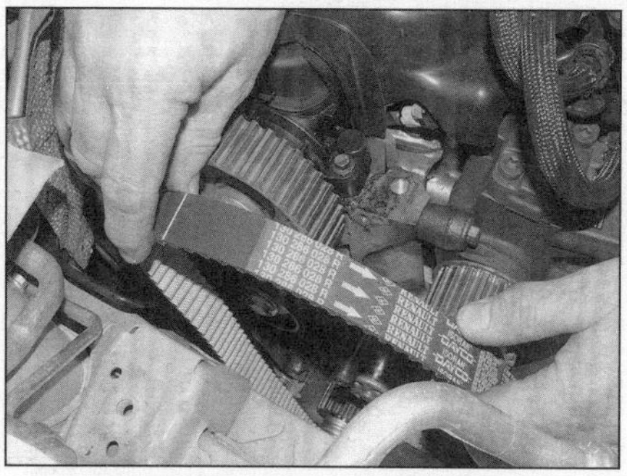

6.10 ...then release the timing belt

the timing belt lower cover and remove the cover **(see illustration)**.

8 Reposition the crankshaft at TDC and insert both timing pins again, as described in Section 3.

9 Loosen the tensioner locknut, then turn the tensioner clockwise to release the tension. If necessary, use a 6.0 mm Allen key in the eccentric hub plate to move the tensioner **(see illustration)**.

10 If the original belt is to be re-used (contrary to Nissan's recommendation), check if the belt is marked with arrows to indicate its running direction, and if necessary mark it. Similarly, make accurate alignment marks on the belt, corresponding to the timing marks on the camshaft, high-pressure fuel injection pump and crankshaft sprockets. Check that there are 18 inclusive teeth between the timing marks on the camshaft and injection pump sprockets, then release the timing belt from the camshaft sprocket, high-pressure injection pump, coolant pump pulley, crankshaft sprocket and tensioner **(see illustration)**.

11 Do not turn the camshaft or the crankshaft whilst the timing belt is removed, as there is a risk of piston-to-valve contact. If it is necessary to turn the camshaft for any reason, before doing so, turn the crankshaft anti-clockwise (viewed from the timing belt end of the engine) by a quarter turn to position all four pistons half-way down their bores. Leave the TDC pin tightened into the cylinder block.

12 Clean the sprockets, coolant pump pulley and tensioner and wipe them dry, although do not apply excessive amounts of solvent to the coolant pump and tensioner pulleys otherwise the bearing lubricant may be contaminated. Also clean the rear timing belt cover, and the cylinder head and block.

Inspection

13 Examine the timing belt carefully for any signs of cracking, fraying or general wear, particularly at the roots of the teeth. Renew the belt if there is any sign of deterioration of this nature, or if there is any oil or grease contamination. The belt must, of course, be renewed if it has completed the maximum mileage given in Chapter 1B.

14 It is recommended, that the timing belt should be renewed whenever it is disturbed. Due to the extent of damage that can be caused to the engine by belt failure, it is always best to renew the belt if it has been removed.

15 Thoroughly clean the nose of the crankshaft and the bore of the crankshaft sprocket, and also the contact surfaces of the sprocket and pulley **(see illustrations)**. This is necessary to prevent the possibility of the sprocket slipping in use.

Refitting

16 Check that the crankshaft, camshaft and high-pressure fuel injection pump sprockets are still positioned at TDC, and that the groove in the crankshaft nose is pointing upwards. If the pistons have been positioned halfway down their bores, turn the crankshaft clockwise until the web contacts the TDC tool.

17 Check that the tensioner peg is correctly located in the groove in the cylinder head.

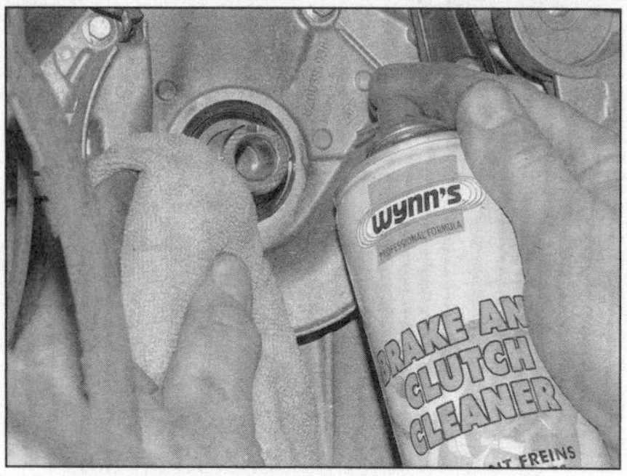

6.15a Using a suitable degreaser, thoroughly clean the crankshaft...

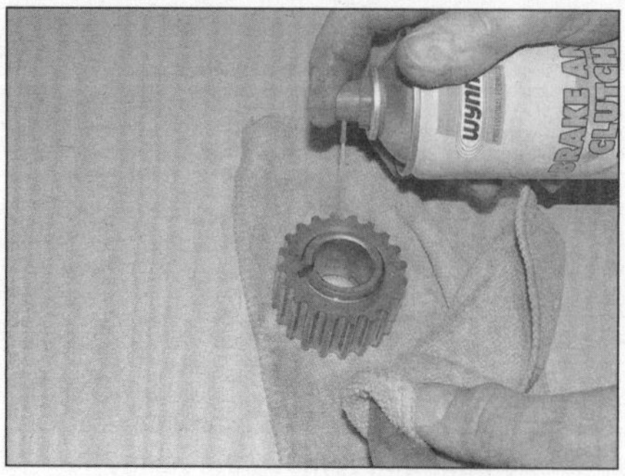

6.15b ...crankshaft sprocket...

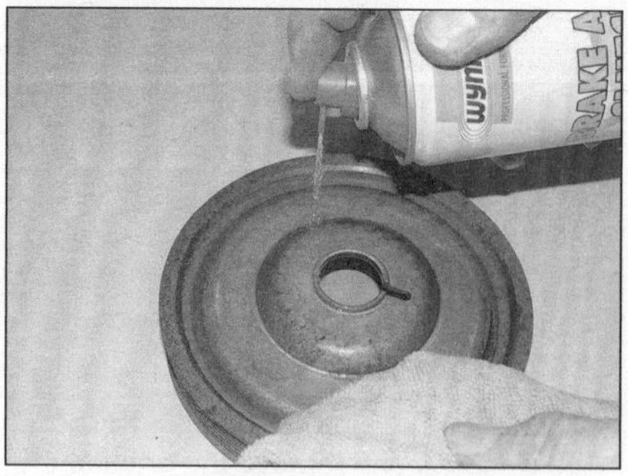

6.15c ...and crankshaft pulley

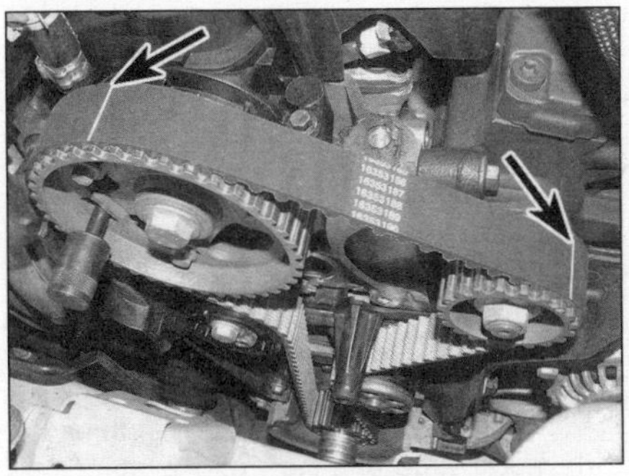

6.19a Align the timing marks on the belt...

6.19b ...with those on the camshaft sprocket...

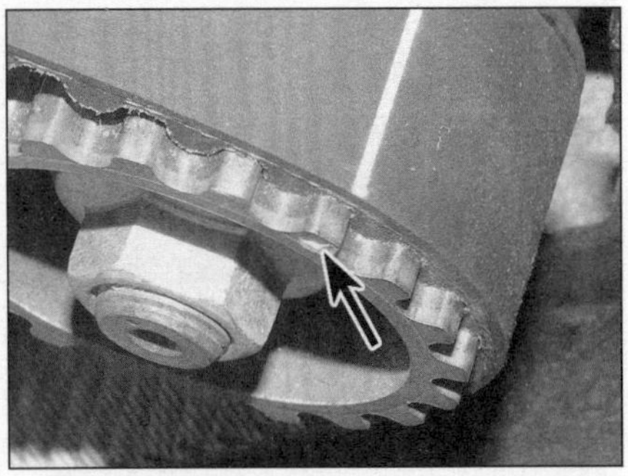

6.19c ...and fuel injection pump sprocket

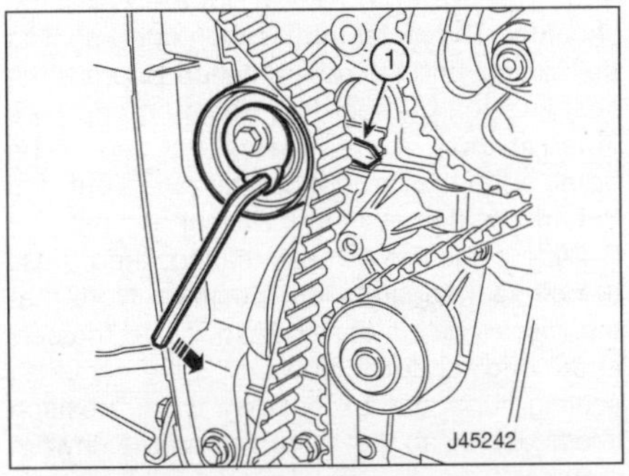

6.20a Pretension the timing belt by positioning the tensioner pointer (1)...

6.20b ...below the timing window

6.24 Position the pointer to its final setting in the middle of the timing window

18 Unscrew and remove one of the camshaft sprocket retaining bolts and slacken the other two.

19 Align the timing marks on the belt with those on the camshaft and fuel injection pump sprockets **(see illustrations)**, ensuring that the running direction arrows on the belt are pointing clockwise (viewed from the timing belt end of the engine). Note that the belt should be marked with lines across its width to act as timing marks. Fit the timing belt over the crankshaft sprocket first, followed by the coolant pump pulley, fuel injection pump sprocket, camshaft sprocket, and tensioner. There are 18 inclusive teeth between the timing marks on the camshaft and injection pump sprockets.

20 With the timing marks still aligned, use the 6.0 mm Allen key to pretension the belt by turning the tensioner anti-clockwise until the index pointer is positioned below the timing window **(see illustrations)**. Hold the tensioner stationary and tighten the locknut to the specified torque. This torque is critical, since if the nut were to come loose, considerable engine damage would result.

21 Refit the camshaft sprocket retaining bolt, then tighten all three bolts to the specified torque.

22 Remove the timing pins from the cylinder block and camshaft sprocket.

23 Turn the crankshaft two complete turns in the normal direction of rotation, but just before the camshaft sprocket timing holes are aligned, refit and tighten the crankshaft timing pin. Slowly turn the crankshaft clockwise until its web is contacting the timing pin, and then check that it is possible to insert the remaining timing pin through the hole in the camshaft sprocket and into the cylinder head. If all is aligned, then the timing pins can be removed again.

24 Hold the tensioner with the Allen key, then loosen the locknut a maximum of one turn, and turn the tensioner clockwise until the index pointer is positioned in the middle of the timing window **(see illustration)**. Tighten the locknut to the specified torque.

25 Apply sealant to the threads, then refit the blanking plug to the cylinder block and tighten it to the specified torque.

26 Refit the timing belt lower cover, then unscrew and remove the crankshaft pulley bolt and spacer/washers. Refit the crankshaft pulley and retaining bolt, then tighten the bolt to the specified torque and through the specified angle.

27 Refit the engine mounting support bracket and tighten the bolts to the specified torque.

28 Clip the upper timing cover onto the lower cover, then refit the right-hand engine mounting to the engine and body and tighten the bolts to the specified torque (see Section 15).

29 Refit the auxiliary drivebelt tensioner, then refit the auxiliary drivebelt with reference to Chapter 1B, Section 12.

30 Refit the wheel arch liner and roadwheel, then lower the car to the ground. Tighten the roadwheel nuts to the specified torque.

31 On completion, reconnect the battery negative terminal.

7 Timing belt sprockets, idler pulley and tensioner – removal and refitting

Crankshaft sprocket

Removal

1 Remove the timing belt as described in Section 6.

2 Slide the sprocket from the crankshaft; noting which way around it is fitted **(see illustration)**.

Refitting

3 Thoroughly clean the nose of the crankshaft and the bore of the crankshaft sprocket, and also the contact surfaces of the sprocket and pulley. This is necessary to prevent the possibility of the sprocket slipping in use.

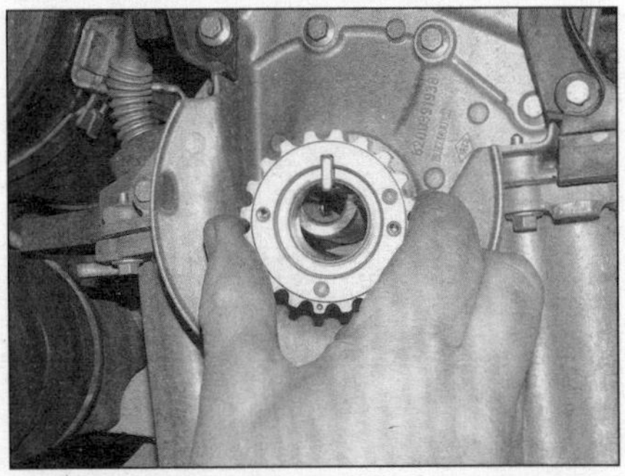

7.2 Removing the crankshaft sprocket

7.17 Removing the timing belt tensioner

4 Slide the sprocket onto the crankshaft the correct way around.

5 Refit the timing belt as described in Section 6.

High-pressure pump sprocket

Note: *A suitable puller will be required for this operation.*

Removal

6 The sprocket may be removed as follows, however, note that if it is being removed for pump renewal, a special Nissan tool is available to enable the pump to be removed without removing the timing belt. Check with your Nissan dealer for the availability of a sprocket support tool.

7 Remove the timing belt as described in Section 6.

8 Hold the sprocket stationary using a suitable gear holding tool. Alternatively, an old timing belt can be wrapped around the sprocket and held firmly with a pair of grips. Unscrew and remove the central securing nut.

9 Use a puller to release the sprocket from the taper on the pump shaft. Recover the Woodruff key from the groove in the pump shaft.

Refitting

10 Refitting is a reversal of removal, bearing in mind the following points.

a) Ensure that the Woodruff key is correctly engaged with the pump shaft and sprocket.

b) Tighten the sprocket securing nut to the specified torque.

c) Refit and tension the timing belt as described in Section 6.

Camshaft sprocket

Removal

11 Remove the timing belt as described in Section 6.

12 Hold the sprocket stationary using a suitable gear holding tool. Alternatively, an old timing belt can be wrapped around the sprocket and held firmly with a pair of grips. Unscrew and remove the central securing nut.

13 Release the sprocket from the camshaft, noting the integral spline on the sprocket and the corresponding cut-out in the end of the camshaft.

Refitting

14 Refit the camshaft sprocket, making sure that the integral spline locates in the camshaft cut-out. Insert the bolt and tighten it to the specified torque and angle, holding the sprocket stationary as during removal.

15 Refit and tension the timing belt as described in Section 6.

Tensioner

Removal

16 Remove the timing belt as described in Section 6.

17 Unscrew the securing nut and remove the washer and pivot bolt, then withdraw the tensioner assembly from the engine **(see illustration)**.

Refitting

18 Refitting is a reversal of removal. Refit and tension the timing belt as described in Section 6.

8 Camshaft oil seals – renewal

Timing belt end oil seal

1 Remove the camshaft sprocket as described in Section 7.

2 Note the fitted depth of the old oil seal. Using a small screwdriver, prise out the oil seal from the cylinder head taking care not to damage the sealing surface on the camshaft. Alternatively, the oil seal can be removed by drilling two small holes diagonally opposite each other and inserting self tapping screws in them. A pair of grips can then be used to pull out the oil seals, by pulling on each side in turn.

3 Inspect the seal rubbing surface on the camshaft. If it is grooved or rough in the area where the old seal was fitted, the new seal should be fitted slightly less deeply, so that it rubs on an unworn part of the surface.

4 Nissan technicians use a tool (Mot. 1632) to fit the oil seal. The tool consists of a threaded rod, metal tube and nut, and a machined shoulder to locate the protector/guide on. The rod is screwed into the end of the camshaft, and the protector/guide located on the shoulder. The metal tube is then fitted against the oil seal and the nut tightened to press the seal into the cylinder head/bearing cap **(see illustrations)**. If the Nissan tool cannot be obtained, a similar tool can be made out of a threaded rod, metal tube, washer and nut.

5 Wipe clean the oil seal seating, then press the oil seal squarely into position. Note that the Nissan tool is designed to locate the seal at the original depth, however, if the camshaft sealing surface is excessively worn, position it less deeply so that it locates on the unworn surface.

6 After fitting the oil seal, remove the protector/guide and tool.

7 Wipe away any excess oil, then refit the camshaft sprocket as described in Section 7.

Flywheel end sealing

8 No oil seal is fitted to the flywheel end of the camshaft. The sealing is provided by a gasket between the cylinder head and the brake vacuum pump housing. The gasket can be renewed after unbolting the vacuum pump from the cylinder head (see Chapter 9, Section 13).

9 Camshaft and followers – removal, inspection and refitting

Note: *A new camshaft oil seal will be required, and suitable sealant will be required for the camshaft bearing caps and cylinder head cover.*

8.4a Screw the rod into the end of the camshaft...

8.4b ...locate the new oil seal and protector onto the camshaft...

8.4c ...then tighten the tool to press the seal into position

9.7 The camshaft bearing caps are numbered from the flywheel end of the engine

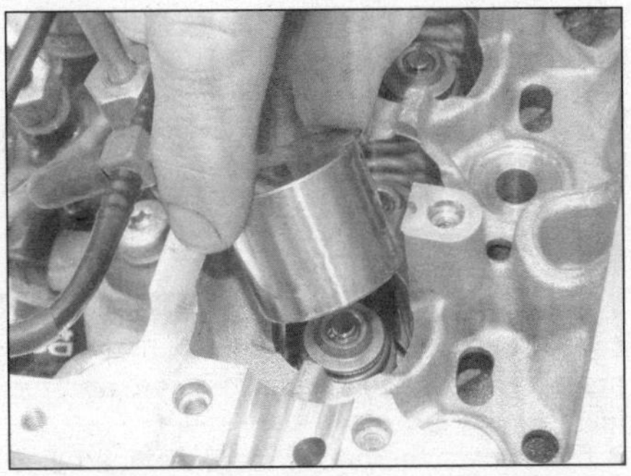

9.10 Removing the cam followers

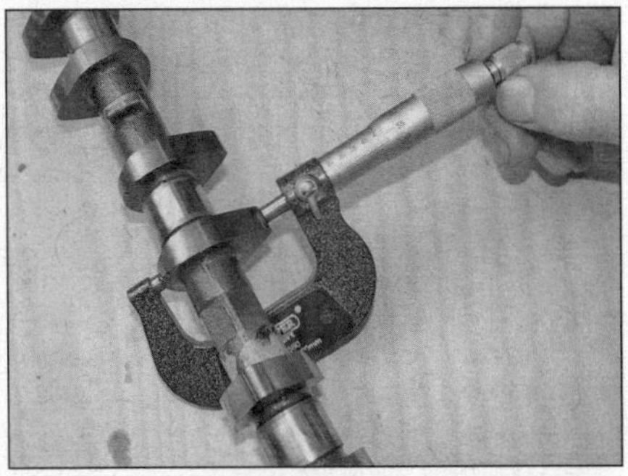

9.13 Checking the cam lobe height with a micrometer

Removal

1 Removal of the camshaft will normally only be required for access to the cam followers (e.g. for valve clearance adjustment) or during cylinder head overhaul. For cylinder head overhaul, remove the head as described in Section 10.

2 Remove the cylinder head cover as described in Section 4.

3 Remove the camshaft sprocket as described in Section 7.

4 Remove the brake vacuum pump with reference to Chapter 9, Section 13.

5 Using a dial gauge, measure the camshaft endfloat, and compare with the value given in the Specifications. This will give an indication of the amount of wear present on the thrust surfaces.

6 If the original camshaft is to be refitted, it is advisable to measure the valve clearances at this stage as described in Section 5, so that any different thickness followers required can be obtained before the camshaft is refitted.

7 Check the camshaft bearing caps for identification marks, and if none are present, make identifying marks so that they can be refitted in their original positions and the same way round. Number the caps from the flywheel end of the engine **(see illustration)**.

8 Progressively slacken the bearing cap bolts until the valve spring pressure is relieved. Remove the bolts and the bearing caps themselves.

9 Lift out the camshaft out from the top of the cylinder head, together with the oil seal, then remove the oil seal from the camshaft.

10 Remove the cam followers, keeping each identified for position **(see illustration)**. Place them in a compartmented box, or on a sheet of card marked into eight sections, so that they may be refitted to their original locations. If any of the valve clearances measured in paragraph 6 is incorrect, use a micrometer to measure the thickness of the old follower from its upper surface to the inner surface, at the centre, which contacts the valve stem. Refer to Section 5 and obtain new followers of the correct thickness.

Inspection

11 Inspect the cam bearing surfaces of the head and the bearing caps. Look for score marks and deep scratches. Check the camshaft lobes for heat discoloration (blue appearance), score marks, chipped areas or flat spots.

12 Camshaft run-out can be checked by supporting each end of the camshaft on V-blocks, and measuring any run-out at the centre of the shaft using a dial gauge. If the run-out exceeds the specified limit, a new camshaft will be required.

13 Measure the height of each lobe with a micrometer **(see illustration)**, and compare the results to the figures given in the Specifications. If damage is noted or wear is excessive, new camshaft(s) must be fitted.

14 The camshaft bearing oil clearance should now be checked.

15 Fit the bearing caps to the cylinder head, using the identification markings or the marks made on removal to ensure that they are correctly positioned. Tighten the retaining bolts to the specified torque. Measure the diameter of each bearing cap journal, and compare the measurements obtained with the results given in the Specifications. If any journal is worn beyond the service limit, the cylinder head must be renewed. The camshaft bearing oil clearance can then calculated by subtracting the camshaft bearing journal diameter from the bearing cap journal diameter.

16 Check the cam follower and cylinder head bearing surfaces for signs of wear or damage.

Refitting

17 Oil the cam followers (inside and out) and fit them to the bores from which they were removed; where applicable, fit the new followers to their correct bores.

18 Oil the camshaft bearings and place the camshaft onto the cylinder head.

19 Wipe clean the upper sealing edge of the cylinder head, then apply four beads of sealant, 1.0 mm wide, to the camshaft end bearing cap (Nos 1 and 6) contact areas as shown **(see illustrations)**.

20 Refit the camshaft bearing caps to their original locations, then insert the bearing cap bolts and progressively tighten them to the specified torque **(see illustration)**.

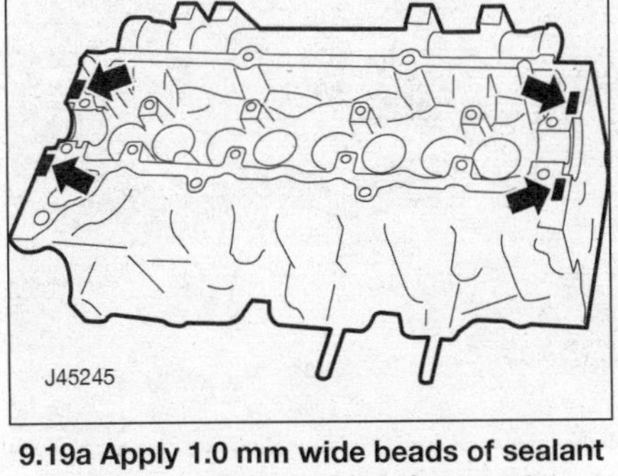

9.19a Apply 1.0 mm wide beads of sealant to the camshaft end bearing cap-to-cylinder head contact areas as shown

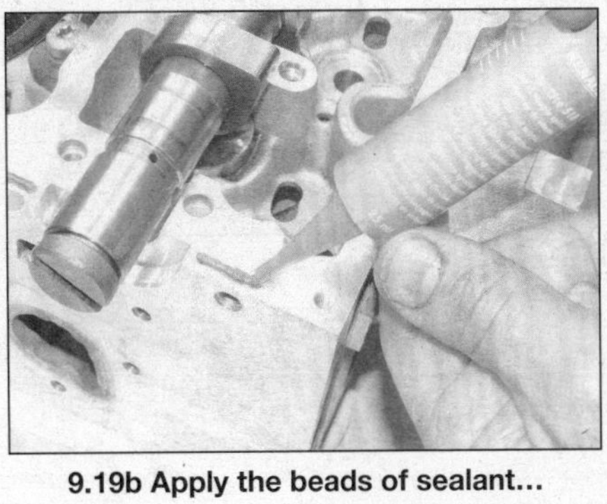

9.19b Apply the beads of sealant...

9.20 ...then refit the camshaft bearing caps

21 If a new camshaft has been fitted, measure the endfloat using a dial gauge, and check that it is within the specified limits.

22 Fit the new camshaft oil seal with reference to Section 8.

23 Refit the brake vacuum pump with reference to Chapter 9, Section 13.

24 Refit the camshaft sprocket as described in Section 7.

25 Refit the cylinder head cover as described in Section 4.

10 Cylinder head – removal and refitting

Note: *On all Type 2 engines, and Type 1 engines with a diesel particulate filter mounted behind the cylinder head in the engine compartment, the engine/transmission assembly must be removed for this operation. There is insufficient clearance in the engine compartment to allow for cylinder head removal and refitting with the engine/transmission assembly in the car. For this reason the procedure is contained in Chapter 2D, Section 9. The following procedure is therefore only applicable to Type 1 engines with a diesel particulate filter incorporated in the exhaust system front pipe.*

Note: *A new cylinder head gasket must be fitted and all cylinder head bolts must be renewed. Sealant for the cylinder head cover will also be required.*

Removal

1 Before starting work, allow the engine to cool for as long as possible, to ensure the fuel pressure in the high-pressure lines, and the fuel temperature, are at a minimum.

2 Disconnect the battery negative lead (see battery disconnection and reconnection in Chapter 5A, Section 3).

3 Drain the cooling system with reference to Chapter 1B, Section 26. Refit and tighten the drain plug after draining.

4 Remove the cylinder head cover as described in Section 4.

5 Disconnect the quick-release vacuum pipe from the brake vacuum pump on the left-hand end of the cylinder head **(see illustration)**.

6 Remove the hoses and coolant temperature sensor wiring connector, from the left-hand end of the cylinder head **(see illustrations)**.

7 Remove the timing belt, as described in Section 6, and if necessary, the camshaft sprocket (in Section 7).

10.5 Disconnect the vacuum hose

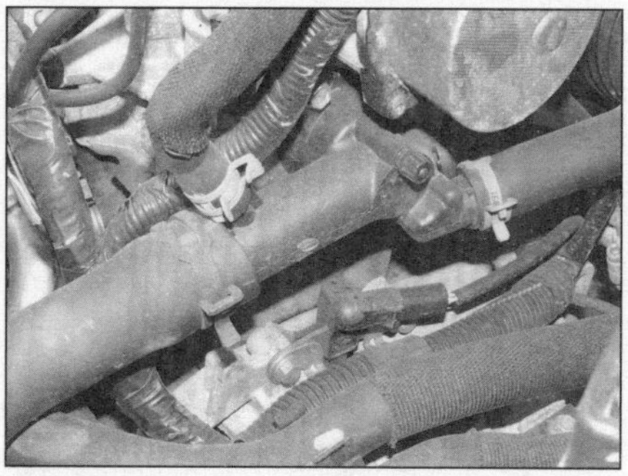

10.6a Note the position of the coolant hoses on the left-hand end of the cylinder head

8 Unbolt and remove the timing belt tensioner roller from the cylinder head.

9 Unbolt and remove the inner timing cover from the cylinder block and head **(see illustration)**.

10 Remove the high-pressure fuel pump, as described in Chapter 4B, Section 9.

11 If required, remove the fuel rail as described in Chapter 4B, Section 11.

12 Remove the turbocharger as described in Chapter 4B, Section 15.

13 Disconnect any remaining wiring from the cylinder head and associated components.

14 The cylinder head assembly complete with ancillaries is very heavy. If required, seek the aid of an assistant to help lift the cylinder head from the vehicle.

15 Before removing the cylinder head, turn the crankshaft anti-clockwise (viewed from the timing belt end of the engine) by a quarter turn to position all four pistons halfway down their bores. The TDC pin can remain in the cylinder block if necessary, however, remember that it is in position and do not turn the crankshaft further anti-clockwise.

16 Progressively slacken the cylinder head bolts in the reverse sequence to that shown **(see illustration 10.26).** With all the bolts loose, remove them.

17 Lift the cylinder head upwards off the cylinder block. If it is stuck, tap it with a hammer and block of wood to release it. Do not try to turn the cylinder head (it is located by two dowels), nor attempt to prise it free using a screwdriver inserted between the block and head faces.

18 If necessary, remove the camshaft and followers, as described in Section 9.

Preparation for refitting

19 The mating faces of the cylinder head and block must be perfectly clean before refitting the head. Use a scraper to remove all traces of gasket and carbon, and also clean the tops of the pistons. Take particular care with the aluminium cylinder head, as the soft

10.6b Disconnecting the wiring from the coolant temperature sensor

10.9 Removing the inner timing cover

10.24 Locate the new gasket on the cylinder block

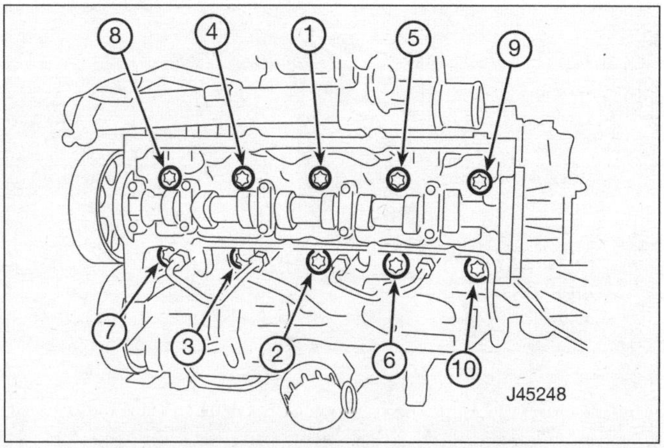

10.26 Cylinder head bolt tightening sequence

metal is damaged easily. Also, make sure that debris is not allowed to enter the oil and water channels – this is particularly important for the oil circuit, as carbon could block the oil supply to the camshaft or crankshaft bearings. Using adhesive tape and paper, seal the water, oil and bolt holes in the cylinder block. Clean the piston crowns in the same way.

20 Check the block and head for nicks, deep scratches and other damage. If slight, they may be removed carefully with a file. Machining of the cylinder head or cylinder block is not recommended by the manufacturers.

21 If warpage of the cylinder head is suspected, use a straight-edge to check it for distortion. Refer to Chapter 2D if necessary; if the warpage is more than the maximum, the cylinder head must be renewed, as regrinding is not allowed.

22 Clean out the cylinder head bolt holes in the block using a pipe cleaner, or a rag and screwdriver. Make sure that all oil is removed, otherwise there is a possibility of the block being cracked by hydraulic pressure when the bolts are tightened. Examine the bolt threads in the cylinder block for damage, and if necessary, use the correct size tap to chase out the threads. The cylinder head bolts must be renewed each time they are removed, and must not be oiled before being fitted.

Refitting

23 Where removed, refit the cam followers, camshaft and camshaft sprocket with reference to Section 9 and Section 7. Turn the camshaft so that the sprocket is at its TDC position.

24 Ensure that the cylinder head locating dowels are fitted to the cylinder block, then fit the new gasket the right way round on the cylinder block **(see illustration)**.

25 Carefully lower the cylinder head onto the dowels and gasket, then insert the new bolts and hand-tighten. Do not oil the threads or heads of the new bolts.

26 Tighten the bolts in sequence, and in the stages given in the Specifications **(see illustration)**.

27 Turn the crankshaft clockwise by a quarter turn until the internal web contacts the TDC timing pin.

28 Refit the inner timing cover back to the cylinder block and head.

29 If removed, refit the auxiliary drivebelt tensioner to the cylinder block.

30 Refit the timing belt tensioner roller to the cylinder head.

31 Refit the timing belt, as described in Section 6.

32 Refit the turbocharger, as described in Chapter 4B, Section 15.

33 If removed, refit the fuel rail as described in Chapter 4B, Section 11.

34 Refit the high-pressure fuel pump, as described in Chapter 4B, Section 9.

35 Refit the hoses and coolant temperature sensor wiring connector, to the housing on the left-hand end of the cylinder head.

36 Reconnect the quick-release vacuum pipe to the brake vacuum pump on the left-hand end of the cylinder head.

37 Refit the cylinder head cover as described in Section 4.

38 Reconnect the battery negative lead.

39 Prime and bleed the fuel system as described in Chapter 4B, Section 5.

40 Refill and bleed the cooling system as described in.

11 Sump – removal and refitting

Removal

1 Disconnect the battery negative lead (refer to battery disconnection and reconnection in Chapter 5A, Section 3).

2 Jack up the front of the vehicle and securely support it on axle stands (see *Jacking and vehicle support*). Remove the right-hand front roadwheel.

3 Drain the engine oil referring to Chapter 1B, Section 5, and then refit and tighten the drain plug, using a new washer.

4 Remove the right-hand front wheel arch liner as described in Chapter 11, Section 21.

5 Remove the rear lower engine mounting (torque link), and mounting bracket from the rear of the sump, as described in Section 15.

6 Unbolt the right-hand driveshaft support bearing from the cylinder block and sump.

7 Undo the air conditioning compressor bracket lower mounting bolt.

8 Disconnect the wiring connector and unscrew the oil level sensor from the front of the alloy sump housing **(see illustration)**. Also, if not already done, withdraw the oil level dipstick.

9 Unclip the fuel rail drain/overflow tube from the side and the lower part of the sump and move it to one side **(see illustration)**.

11.8 Oil level sensor

11.9 Unclip the fuel overflow pipe from below the sump

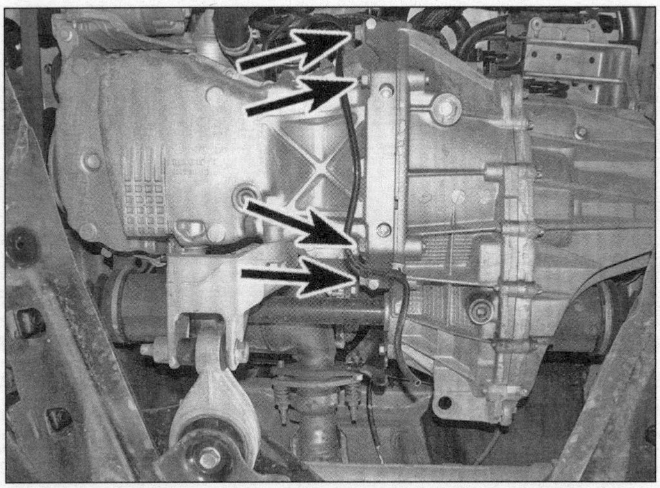

11.10 Remove the bolts through the transmission bell housing.

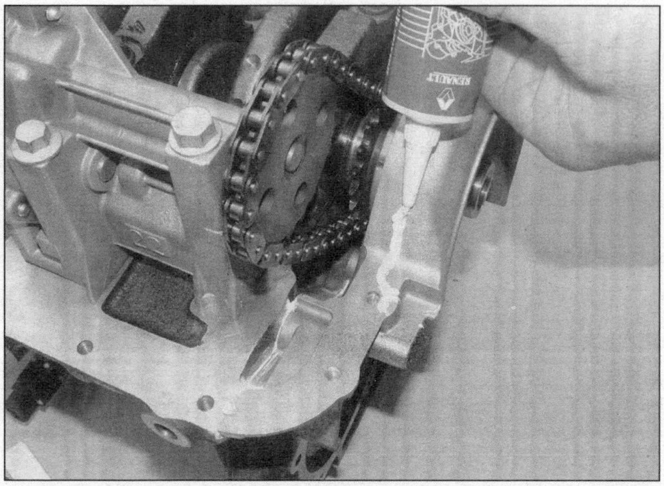

11.14 Apply sealant where the right-hand cover meets the cylinder block...

10 Slacken and remove the four bolts securing the sump to the lower part of the transmission housing **(see illustration)**.

11 Progressively slacken the bolts working in the reverse of the tightening sequence **(see illustration 11.16)** remove all the sump retaining bolts.

12 Tap the sump with a hide or plastic mallet to break the joint, and then remove the sump. Recover the gasket and discard it, as a new one must be used on refitting. There may be sealant at each end of the sump, use a spatula or thin knife to release the ends of the sump. Take care not to distort or damage the mating surfaces of the alloy sump or cylinder block. Take adequate precautions to catch any oil remaining inside the sump housing, as it is removed.

Refitting

13 Thoroughly clean the mating surfaces of the sump and cylinder block.

14 With the cylinder block lower surface clean and no traces of oil, apply four beads of sealant, 5.0 mm wide, to the crankshaft end bearing caps (No's 1 and 5), where they meet the cylinder block. Also apply a bead of sealant at the right-hand end of the cylinder block where the crankshaft oil seal housing is bolted **(see illustration)**.

15 Locate a new gasket on the sump, and then lift the sump into position on the cylinder block and use a straight-edge to align the flywheel end of the sump with the corresponding end face of the cylinder block **(see illustration)**.

16 Insert the bolts and working in the sequence shown **(see illustration)**, tighten sump retaining bolts, to the specified torque.

17 Refit the four remaining bolts from the sump to the lower part of the transmission and tighten them to the specified torque setting.

18 Refit the oil level sensor and clip the fuel drain/overflow pipe back in position under the sump.

19 Refit the engine rear lower mounting (torque link) and tighten the bolts to the specified torque.

20 Refit the right-hand driveshaft support bearing to the cylinder block and sump, tightening the retaining bolts to the specified torque.

21 Refit and securely tighten the air conditioning compressor bracket lower mounting bolt.

22 Refit the right-hand front wheel arch liner.

23 Refit the right-hand front roadwheel, then lower the car to the ground. Tighten the wheel nuts to the specified torque.

24 Reconnect the battery negative lead.

25 Fill the engine with fresh engine oil, with reference to Chapter 1B, Section 5.

Note: *Wait at least 30 minutes after the sump has been fitted, before refilling with engine oil.*

26 Start the engine and warm it up to normal operating temperature, check for any leaks from the sump area.

11.15 ...then locate a new gasket on the sump

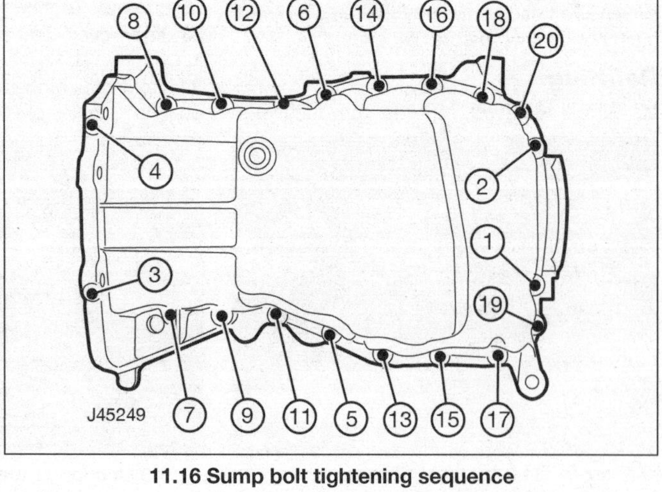

11.16 Sump bolt tightening sequence

12.2a Oil pump and mounting bolts

12.2b Removing the oil pump and drive chain

12 Oil pump and sprockets – removal, inspection and refitting

Removal

1 Remove the sump as described in Section 11.

2 Unscrew the two mounting bolts and withdraw the oil pump, tilting it to disengage its sprocket from the drive chain **(see illustrations)**. If the two locating dowels are displaced, refit them in their locations.

3 To remove the drive chain, first remove the crankshaft sprocket as described in Section 7, then unbolt the crankshaft seal end cover from the cylinder block. Where applicable, recover the gasket and discard, as a new one will be required on refitting.

4 Prise out the oil seal with a screwdriver, and discard it as a new one must be fitted on reassembly. If necessary, the new oil seal may be fitted with the right-hand cover on the bench **(see illustration)**.

5 Slide the oil pump drive sprocket and drive chain from the nose of the crankshaft. Note that the drive sprocket is not keyed to the crankshaft, but relies on the pulley bolt being tightened correctly to clamp the sprocket. It is most important that the pulley bolt is correctly tightened otherwise there is the possibility of the oil pump not functioning properly.

6 Unhook the drive chain from the drive sprocket.

Inspection

7 Clean the components and carefully examine the chain, sprockets and pump for any signs of excessive wear. If evident, it is recommended that all the components be renewed as a set.

8 Before refitting the oil pump, prime it by filling with clean engine oil whilst rotating the pump clockwise.

Refitting

9 Wipe clean the oil pump and cylinder block mating surfaces and check that the two locating dowels are fitted in the cylinder block.

10 Engage the drive chain with the drive sprocket, then slide the sprocket onto the nose of the crankshaft.

11 Fit a new gasket to the end of the cylinder block and refit the crankshaft seal end cover, insert the bolts and tighten them to the specified torque setting. If a new oil seal has already been fitted to the cover, wrap tape

12.4 Fitting a new oil seal to the right-hand cover

around the nose of the crankshaft to protect the oil seal, and then remove it on completion. If there was no gasket fitted to the cover, apply a 2.0 mm wide bead of silicone sealant to the cover sealing face, making sure that the bead runs below the bolt holes **(see illustrations)**

12 Tilt the oil pump and engage the sprocket with the drive chain, then position it on the dowels and insert the two mounting bolts. Tighten the bolts to the specified torque.

13 Refit the sump with reference to Section 11.

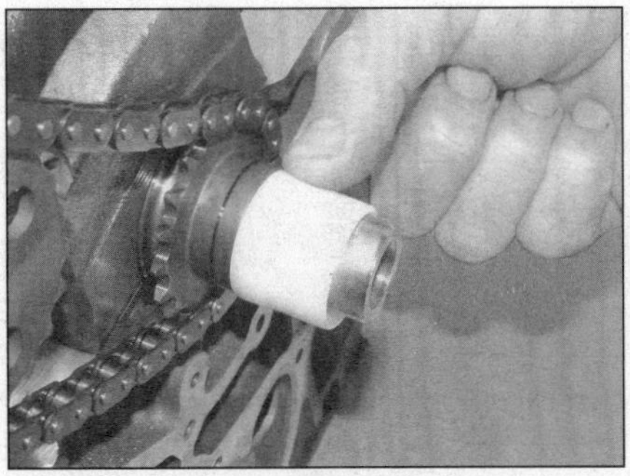

12.11a Wrap some tape around the nose of the crankshaft...

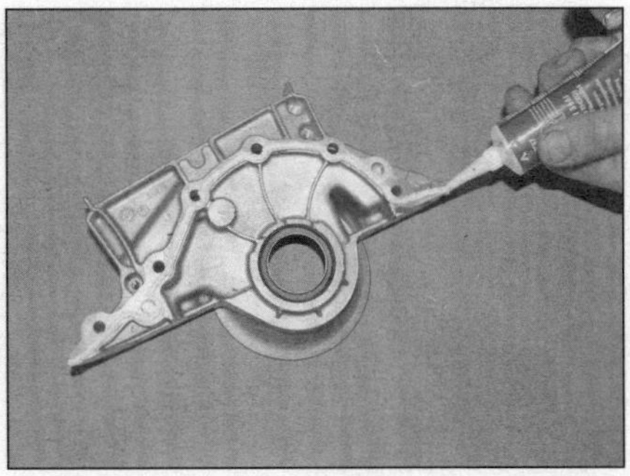

12.11b ...apply sealant to the mating faces...

12.11c ...and fit the right-hand cover

13 Crankshaft oil seals – renewal

Timing end cover oil seal

Note: *The new oil seal is extremely fragile and must only be handled by the protector. Do not touch the surface of the oil seal.*

1 Remove the crankshaft sprocket, as described in Section 7.

2 Note the fitted position of the old seal, then prise it out of the right-hand cover/housing using a screwdriver or suitable hooked instrument, taking care not to damage the surface of the crankshaft. Alternatively, the oil seal can be removed by drilling two small holes diagonally opposite each other and inserting self tapping screws in them. A pair of grips can then be used to pull out the oil seal, by pulling on each side in turn (see **Haynes Hint**).

3 Inspect the seal rubbing surface on the crankshaft. If it is grooved or rough in the area where the old seal was fitted, the new seal should be fitted slightly less deeply, so that it rubs on an unworn part of the crankshaft surface.

4 Nissan technicians use a tool (drift set SST: KV113B0220 – Mot. 1586) to fit this oil seal. The tool consists of a threaded rod, metal tube and nut, and a machined shoulder to locate the protector/guide on. The rod is screwed into the end of the crankshaft, and the protector/guide located on the shoulder. The metal tube is then fitted against the oil seal and the nut tightened to press the seal into the right-hand cover. If the Nissan tool cannot be obtained, a similar tool can be made out of a threaded rod, metal tube, washer and nut.

5 Wipe clean the oil seal seating, then press the oil seal squarely into position. Note that the Nissan tool is designed to locate the seal at the original depth, however, if the crankshaft sealing surface is excessively worn, position it less deeply so that it locates on the unworn surface.

6 After fitting the oil seal, remove the protector/guide and tool.

HAYNES HiNT

Oil seals can be removed by drilling a small hole and inserting a self-tapping screw. A pair of grips can then be used to pull out the oil seal by pulling on the screw. If difficulty is experienced, insert two screws diagonally opposite each other.

7 Refit the crankshaft sprocket as described in Section 7.

Flywheel end oil seal

8 Remove the flywheel as described in Section 14.

9 Renew the oil seal as described in paragraphs 2 to 6 inclusive **(see illustration)**. Nissan technicians use a tool (drift set SST: KV113B0210 – Mot. 1585) to fit the flywheel end oil seal.

10 Refit the flywheel with reference to Section 14.

14 Flywheel – removal, inspection and refitting

Note: *New flywheel bolts must be used on refitting.*

Removal

1 Remove the manual transmission as described in Chapter 7, Section 6.

2 Remove the clutch assembly as described in Chapter 6, Section 7.

3 Prevent the flywheel from turning by locking the ring gear teeth with a special tool.

13.9 Fitting a new oil seal to the flywheel end of the crankshaft

Alternatively, locate a long bolt in one of the engine-to-gearbox mounting bolt holes and insert a wide-bladed screwdriver or similar into the starter ring gear **(see illustrations)**.

4 Unscrew the securing bolts and withdraw the flywheel from the crankshaft. Note that the flywheel bolt holes are offset so that the flywheel can only be fitted in one position. Discard the old bolts as new ones must be used on refitting.

Inspection

5 If the flywheel's clutch mating surface is deeply scored, cracked or otherwise damaged, the flywheel must be renewed. Seek the advice of a Nissan dealer or engine reconditioning specialist.

6 If the ring gear is badly worn or has missing teeth, it must be renewed. Check with your Nissan dealer or engine reconditioning specialist, to see if the flywheel can be repaired.

Refitting

7 Locate the flywheel on the crankshaft and insert the new securing bolts, then tighten them in a diagonal sequence to the specified torque. Hold the flywheel stationary as during removal **(see illustration)**. Do not oil the new bolt threads as they are supplied with locking compound.

8 Refit the clutch as described in Chapter 6, Section 7.

9 Remove the locking tool (where used), and refit the transmission as described in Chapter 7, Section 6.

14.3a Using a home made tool to prevent the flywheel from turning...

14.3b ...or hold the flywheel stationary using a screwdriver in the starter ring gear

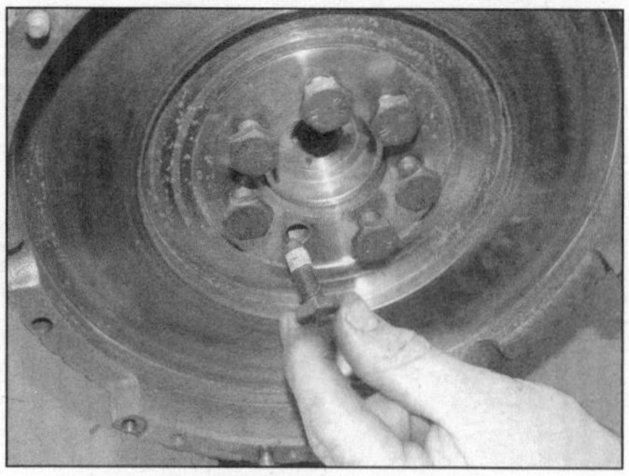

14.7 Fit new flywheel bolts

15 Engine/transmission mountings – inspection and renewal

Inspection

1 If improved access is required, firmly apply the handbrake, and then jack up the front of the vehicle and support it securely on axle stands (see *Jacking and vehicle support*).

2 Check the mounting rubber to see if it is cracked, hardened or separated from the metal at any point; renew the mounting if any such damage or deterioration is evident.

3 Check that all the mounting's fasteners are securely tightened; use a torque wrench to check if possible.

4 Using a large screwdriver or a crowbar, check for wear in the mounting by carefully levering against it to check for free play. Where this is not possible, enlist the aid of an assistant to move the engine/transmission back-and-forth, or from side-to-side, while you watch the mounting. While some free play is to be expected even from new components, excessive wear should be obvious. If excessive free play is found, check first that the fasteners are correctly secured, and then renew any worn components as described below.

Renewal

Right-hand mounting

5 Disconnect the battery negative terminal (refer to battery disconnection and reconnection in Chapter 5A, Section 3).

6 Place a jack beneath the engine, with a block of wood on the jack head. Raise the jack until it is supporting the weight of the engine **(see illustration)**.

7 Slacken the retaining bolts and remove the torque link from the engine mounting and bulkhead **(see illustrations)**.

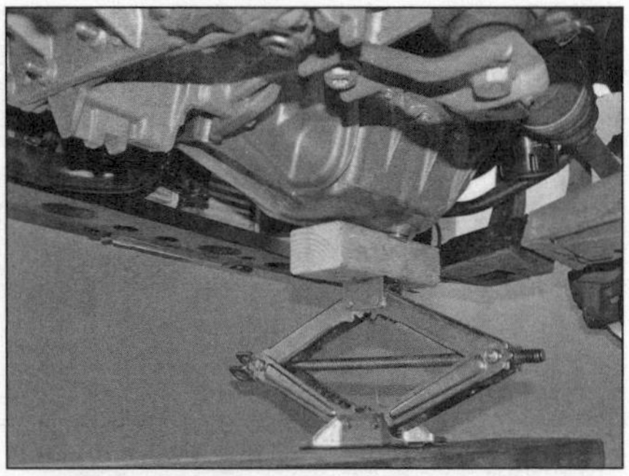

15.6 Support the engine with a suitable jack

8 Slacken and remove the three retaining bolts from the inner wing panel, remove the three retaining bolts from the engine mounting bracket, and then withdraw the complete mounting from the engine compartment **(see illustrations)**.

9 Check carefully for signs of wear or damage

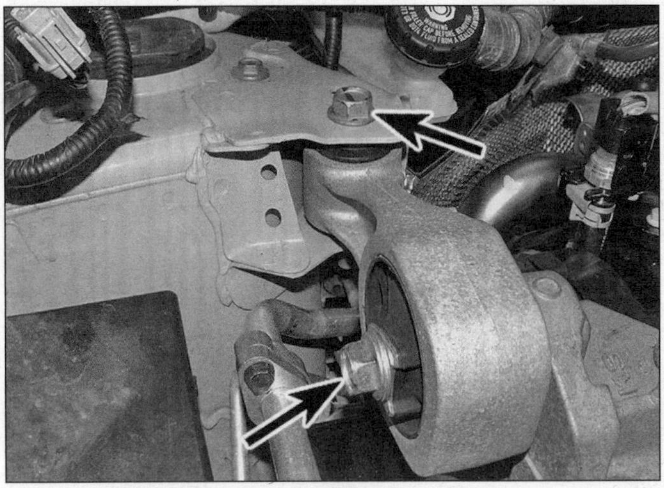

15.7a Undo the torque link retaining bolts...

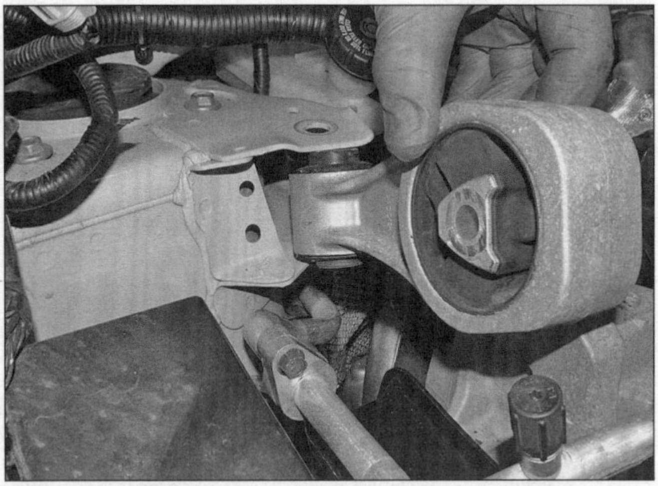

15.7b ...and remove the torque link from the engine mounting and bulkhead

15.8a Unbolt the inner wing panel bolts...

15.8b ...and the engine mounting bolts

15.16 Undo the centre retaining nut

15.27 Remove the torque link arm bolts

on all components, and renew them where necessary.

10 On refitting, fit the engine mounting and bracket to the inner wing panel and engine, and then securely tighten its retaining bolts to the specified torque setting.

11 Refit the torque link to the rear of the engine mounting and tighten the retaining bolts to the specified torque setting.

12 Lower the jack and remove it from underneath the engine.

13 On completion, reconnect the battery negative terminal.

Left-hand mounting

14 Remove the battery and tray, as described in Chapter 5A, Section 3.

15 Place a jack and block of wood beneath the transmission, and raise the jack to take the weight of the transmission.

16 Slacken and remove the through-bolt/stud retaining nut from the centre of the mounting **(see illustration)**.

17 Slacken and remove the two outer retaining nuts, and withdraw the mounting from the upper mounting bracket.

18 If required, undo the retaining bolts from the inner wing panel to remove the upper mounting bracket.

19 Also, if required, undo the retaining bolts from the transmission to remove the lower mounting bracket.

20 Check carefully for signs of wear or damage on all components, and renew them where necessary.

21 On refitting, fit the upper and lower mounting brackets (where removed) and securely tighten the retaining bolts.

22 Align the left-hand rubber mounting with the bolt/stud on the lower mounting bracket and tighten its nut to the specified torque setting.

23 Refit the two outer retaining nuts, and tighten to the specified torque setting.

24 With the transmission mounting back in position, lower the jack and remove it from underneath the transmission.

25 Refit the battery and battery tray, with reference to Chapter 5A, Section 3.

Rear lower mounting

26 If not already done, firmly apply the handbrake, and then jack up the front of the vehicle and support it securely on axle stands (see *Jacking and vehicle support*). Remove engine undertray.

27 Slacken and remove the bolts securing the rear mounting link to the subframe and the mounting bracket, and then withdraw the mounting link from under the vehicle **(see illustration)**.

28 If required, slacken and remove the bolts securing the rear mounting bracket to the sump, and then withdraw the bracket from under the vehicle.

29 Check carefully for signs of wear or damage on all components, and renew them where necessary.

30 Refit the mounting bracket to the rear of the sump housing and tighten its retaining bolts to the specified torque.

31 Fit the rear mounting link to the mounting bracket and subframe, and then tighten the retaining bolts to the specified torque.

32 With the transmission rear mounting link arm back in position, lower the vehicle to the ground.

Chapter 2 Part D
Engine removal and overhaul procedures

Contents

Degrees of difficulty

Easy, suitable for novice with little experience	**Fairly easy,** suitable for beginner with some experience	**Fairly difficult,** suitable for competent DIY mechanic	**Difficult,** suitable for experienced DIY mechanic	**Very difficult,** suitable for expert DIY or professional

Specifications

General

Engine codes:	
1.2 litre petrol engine	HRA2DDT
1.6 litre petrol engine	HR16DE
1.5 litre diesel engine	K9K

Cylinder head

Maximum gasket face distortion:	
Petrol engines	0.10 mm
Diesel engines	0.05 mm
Cylinder head height:	
1.2 litre petrol engines	124.8 mm
1.6 litre petrol engines	N/A
Diesel engines	127.0 mm

Camshaft and followers (1.2 litre petrol engines)

Drive	Chain
Number of bearings	6
Endfloat	0.203 to 0.239 mm
Camshaft lobe height:	
Inlet	44.322 to 44.522 mm
Exhaust	43.664 to 43.864 mm
Camshaft bearing journal outer diameter:	
No 1 bearing	27.934 to 28.0 mm
Nos 2 to 5 bearings	24.969 to 25.0 mm
Camshaft cylinder head bearing journal internal diameter:	
No 1 bearing	28.044 to 28.076 mm
Nos 2 to 6 bearings	25.040 to 25.060 mm
Camshaft journal-to-bearing clearance:	
No 1 bearing	0.044 to 0.142 mm
Nos 2 to 6 bearings	0.040 to 0.091 mm
Camshaft run-out	0.01 mm
Camshaft follower outer diameter	29.964 to 29.987 mm
Cylinder head hole diameter for follower	30.000 to 30.021 mm
Camshaft follower to cylinder head clearance	0.013 to 0.057 mm

Cylinder block

Maximum gasket face distortion:	
Petrol engines	0.10 mm
Diesel engines	0.03 mm

Valve springs

Spring free height:	
1.2 litre petrol engines:	
Inlet	45.0 to 47.0 mm
Exhaust	58.5 to 60.5 mm
1.6 litre petrol engines	46.73 mm
Diesel engines	43.31 mm
Spring squareness:	
1.2 litre petrol engines:	
Inlet	less than 1.4 mm
Exhaust	less than 1.8 mm
1.6 litre petrol engines	N/A
Diesel engines	less than 1.2 mm

Valves

	Inlet	Exhaust
Valve head diameter:		
1.2 litre petrol engines	26.48 to 26.72 mm	23.38 to 23.62 mm
1.6 litre petrol engines	31.60 to 31.90 mm	25.30 to 25.60 mm
Diesel engines	33.38 to 33.62 mm	28.88 to 29.12 mm
Valve stem diameter:		
1.2 litre petrol engines	5.470 to 5.485 mm	5.455 to 5.470 mm
1.6 litre petrol engines	4.965 to 4.980 mm	4.955 to 4.970 mm
Diesel engines	5.969 to 5.985 mm	5.955 to 5.971 mm
Overall length:		
1.2 litre petrol engines	100.84 mm	101.69 mm
1.6 litre petrol engines	101.73 mm	102.49 mm
Diesel engines	100.74 to 101.16 mm	100.54 to 100.96 mm

Pistons

Piston skirt diameter:	
1.2 litre petrol engines	72.15 to 72.17 mm
1.6 litre petrol engines	77.96 to 77.98 mm
Diesel engines	75.938 to 75.952 mm
Piston-to-bore clearance (petrol engines):	
1.2 litre engines	0.030 to 0.050 mm
1.6 litre engines	0.020 to 0.050 mm
Piston protrusion (diesel engines)	0.023 to 0.281 mm

Piston rings

Ring-to-groove clearance:	
1.2 litre petrol engines:	
Top compression ring	0.030 to 0.070 mm
Second compression ring	0.030 to 0.050 mm
Oil control ring	0.030 mm
1.6 litre petrol engines:	
Top compression ring	0.040 to 0.080 mm
Second compression ring	0.030 to 0.070 mm
Oil control ring	0.20 to 0.45 mm
Diesel engines:	
Top compression ring	0.10 to 0.12 mm
Second compression ring	0.08 to 0.10 mm
Oil control ring	0.03 to 0.07 mm
Ring end gaps (measured in cylinder):	
1.2 litre petrol engines:	
Top compression ring	0.15 to 0.30 mm
Second compression ring	0.40 to 0.60 mm
Oil control ring	0.20 to 0.90 mm
1.6 litre petrol engines:	
Top compression ring	0.20 to 0.30 mm
Second compression ring	0.35 to 0.50 mm
Oil control ring	0.20 to 0.45 mm
Diesel engines:	
Top compression ring	0.20 to 0.35 mm
Second compression ring	0.70 to 0.90 mm
Oil control ring	0.25 to 0.50 mm

Crankshaft

Endfloat:	
1.2 and 1.6 litre petrol engines	0.098 to 0.260 mm
Diesel engines	0.45 to 0.252 mm
Main bearing running clearance:	
1.2 and 1.6 litre petrol engines	0.024 to 0.034 mm
Diesel engines	0.010 to 0.054 mm
Big-end bearing running clearance:	
1.2 and 1.6 litre petrol engines	0.020 to 0.030 mm
Diesel engines	0.010 to 0.064 mm

Torque wrench settings

Refer to the Specifications in Chapter 2A, Chapter 2B or Chapter 2C for the relevant engine.

1 General Information

1 Included in this Part of Chapter 2B are details of removing the engine/transmission from the vehicle, and general overhaul procedures for the cylinder head, cylinder block/crankcase and all other engine internal components.

2 The information given ranges from advice concerning preparation for an overhaul and the purchase of new parts, to detailed step-by-step procedures covering removal, inspection, renovation and refitting of engine internal components.

3 Note that many operations that would normally be classed as in-car repair procedures and be covered in previous Parts of this Chapter, are actually covered in this Part. This is due to the design of the engine and the limited clearance in the engine compartment making it physically impossible to remove and refit many components and assemblies with the engine in the car.

4 After Section 4, all instructions are based on the assumption that the engine has been removed from the vehicle. For information concerning in-car engine repair, as well as the removal and refitting of those external components necessary for full overhaul, refer to Part A, B or C of this Chapter and to Section 4. Ignore any preliminary dismantling operations described in Part A, B or C, that are no longer relevant once the engine has been removed.

5 Apart from torque wrench settings, which are given at the beginning of Part A, B or C, all specifications relating to engine overhaul are at the beginning of this Part of Chapter 2.

Engine overhaul

6 It is not always easy to determine when, or if, an engine should be completely overhauled, as a number of factors must be considered.

7 High mileage is not necessarily an indication that an overhaul is needed, while low mileage does not preclude the need for an overhaul. Frequency of servicing is probably the most important consideration. An engine, which has had regular and frequent oil and filter changes, as well as other required maintenance, should give many thousands of miles of reliable service. Conversely, a neglected engine may require an overhaul very early in its life.

8 Excessive oil consumption is an indication that piston rings, valve seals and/or valve guides are in need of attention. Make sure that oil leaks are not responsible before deciding that the rings and/or guides are worn. Perform a compression test to determine the likely cause of the problem.

9 Check the oil pressure with a gauge fitted in place of the oil pressure switch, and compare it with that specified in Part A, B or C of this Chapter. If it is extremely low, the main and big-end bearings, and/or the oil pump, are probably worn out.

10 Loss of power, rough running, knocking or metallic engine noises, excessive valve gear noise, and high fuel consumption may also point to the need for an overhaul, especially if they are all present at the same time. If a complete service does not remedy the situation, major mechanical work is the only solution.

11 An engine overhaul involves restoring all internal parts to the specification of a new engine. During an overhaul, the cylinder bores are rebored (where possible) and the pistons and piston rings are renewed. New main and big-end bearings are generally fitted; if necessary, the crankshaft may be reground, to restore the journals. The valves are also serviced as well, since they are usually in less-than-perfect condition at this point. The end result should be an as-new engine that will give many trouble-free miles.

Note: *Critical cooling system components such as the hoses, thermostat and coolant pump should be renewed when an engine is overhauled. The radiator should be checked carefully, to ensure that it is not clogged or leaking. Also, it is a good idea to renew the oil pump whenever the engine is overhauled.*

12 Before beginning the engine overhaul, read through the entire procedure, to familiarise yourself with the scope and requirements of the job. Check on the availability of parts, and make sure that any necessary special tools and equipment are obtained in advance. Most work can be done with typical hand tools, although a number of precision measuring tools are required for inspecting parts to determine if they must be renewed.

13 The services provided by an engineering machine shop or engine reconditioning specialist will almost certainly be required, particularly if major repairs such as crankshaft regrinding or cylinder reboring are necessary. Apart from carrying out machining operations, these establishments will normally handle the inspection of parts; offer advice concerning reconditioning or renewal and supply new components such as pistons, piston rings and bearing shells. It is recommended that the establishment used is a member of the Federation of Engine Re-Manufacturers, or a similar society.

14 Always wait until the engine has been completely dismantled, and until all components (especially the cylinder block and the crankshaft) have been inspected, before deciding what service and repair operations must be performed by an automotive engineering works. The condition of these components will be the major factor to consider when determining whether to overhaul the original engine, or to buy a reconditioned unit. Do not, therefore, purchase parts or have overhaul work done on other components until they have been thoroughly inspected.

15 As a final note, to ensure maximum life and minimum trouble from a reconditioned engine, everything must be assembled with care, in a spotlessly-clean environment.

2 Engine removal – methods and precautions

1 If you have decided that the engine must be removed for overhaul or major repair work, several preliminary steps should be taken.

2 Locating a suitable place to work is extremely important. Adequate workspace, along with storage space for the vehicle, will be needed. If a workshop or garage is not available, at the very least, a flat, level, clean work surface is required.

3 Cleaning the engine compartment and engine/transmission before beginning the removal procedure will help keep tools clean and organised.

4 An engine hoist will also be necessary. Make sure the equipment is rated in excess of the combined weight of the engine and transmission. Safety is of primary importance, considering the potential hazards involved in removing the engine/transmission from the vehicle.

5 The help of an assistant is essential. Apart from the safety aspects involved, there are many instances when one person cannot simultaneously perform all of the operations required during engine/transmission removal.

6 Plan the operation ahead of time. Before starting work, arrange for the hire of, or obtain, all of the tools and equipment you will need. Some of the equipment necessary to perform engine/transmission removal and installation safely (in addition to an engine hoist) is as follows: a heavy-duty trolley jack, complete sets of spanners and sockets as described at the rear of this manual, wooden blocks, and plenty of rags and cleaning solvent for mopping-up spilled oil, coolant and fuel. If the hoist must be hired, make sure that you arrange for it in advance, and perform all of the operations possible without it beforehand. This will save you money and time.

7 Plan for the vehicle to be out of use for quite a while. An engineering machine shop or engine reconditioning specialist will be required to perform some of the work, which cannot be accomplished without special equipment. These places often have a busy schedule, so it would be a good idea to consult them before removing the engine, in order to accurately estimate the amount of time required to rebuild or repair components that may need work.

8 During the engine/transmission removal procedure, it is advisable to make notes of the locations of all brackets, cable ties, earthing points, etc, as well as how the wiring harnesses, hoses and electrical connections are attached and routed around the engine and engine compartment. An effective way of doing this is to take a series of photographs of the various components before they are disconnected or removed. The resulting photographs will prove invaluable when the engine is refitted.

9 Always be extremely careful when removing and refitting the engine/transmission. Serious injury can result from careless actions. Plan ahead and take your time, and a job of this nature, although major, can be accomplished successfully.

3 Engine and manual transmission – removal, separation, reconnection and refitting

Note: *The engine can be removed from the car only as a complete unit with the transmission; the two are then separated for overhaul. The engine/transmission unit is lowered out of position, and withdrawn from under the vehicle. Allow adequate clearance for the removal of the engine, between the front bumper and the ground when the vehicle is raised and supported. However, if preferred, the transmission can be removed from the engine first (as described in Chapter 7, Section 6) – this leaves the engine free to be either lifted out from above or lowered to the ground.*

Removal

1 On petrol engine models, release the pressure in the fuel system as described in Chapter 4A, Section 6. On diesel engine models, release the fuel system residual pressure by unscrewing the fuel filler cap.

2 With reference to Chapter 5A, Section 3 disconnect the battery negative terminal, then remove the battery and battery tray.

3 Firmly apply the handbrake, then jack up the front of the vehicle and support it securely on axle stands (see *Jacking and vehicle support*), bearing in mind the note at the start of this Section, about the height required. Remove both front roadwheels.

4 Remove the front wheel arch liner on the left-hand and right-hand side as described in Chapter 11, Section 21.

5 Drain the cooling system as described in Chapter 1A, Section 25 for petrol engines, or Chapter 1B, Section 26 for diesel engines. Save the coolant in a clean container, if it is fit for re-use.

6 Drain the transmission oil as described in Chapter 7, Section 2. Refit the drain and filler plugs using new sealing washers where required.

7 If the engine is to be dismantled, working as described in Chapter 1A, Section 5, for petrol engines, or Chapter 1B, Section 5 for diesel engines, drain the oil and if required remove the oil filter. Clean and refit the drain plug, tightening it to the specified torque, fit new sealing washers where required.

8 Remove both driveshafts as described in Chapter 8, Section 2.

9 Working around the engine, disconnect the wiring connectors from the alternator, starter motor, oil pressure switch, oil level switch, knock sensor, crankshaft sensor etc... depending on model. If necessary label the connectors as they are unplugged.

10 Similarly, working around the engine and engine compartment, disconnect all vacuum hoses likely to impede engine/transmission removal.

a) Remove the air cleaner assembly and air inlet ducts.
b) Disconnect the fuel feed and return hoses from the fuel rail (plug all openings, to prevent loss of fuel and entry of dirt into the fuel system).
c) Disconnect the relevant electrical connectors from the throttle housing, inlet manifold and associated components. Free the wiring from the manifold, and position it clear of the cylinder head so that it does not hinder removal.
d) Disconnect the vacuum servo unit hose, coolant hose(s), and all the other relevant/breather hoses from the manifold and associated valves.
e) On petrol engine models, remove the inlet manifold.
f) Disconnect or remove the exhaust front pipe.

11 Slacken the retaining clips, and disconnect the heater hoses and all other relevant cooling system hoses from the engine, noting each hose's correct fitted location.

12 Remove the radiator electric cooling fan and shroud assembly as described in Chapter 3, Section 5.

13 Unbolt the air conditioning compressor and position it clear of the engine. Support the weight of the compressor by tying it to the vehicle body, to prevent any excess strain being placed on the compressor lines whilst the engine is removed. Do not disconnect the refrigerant lines from the compressor.

14 Be prepared for some fluid loss as the pipe is disconnected, place some cloth around the fitting. Depress the retaining spring clip and disconnect the clutch fluid hose from the slave cylinder connector pipe. Plug the ends of the slave cylinder pipe and clutch fluid hose to prevent fluid leakage and dirt ingress.

15 Working as described in Chapter 7, Section 3, disconnect the gear linkage cables from the operating levers on the transmission.

16 Note their fitted positions and harness routing, then disconnect all wiring plugs from the transmission. If necessary label the connectors as they are unplugged.

17 Secure the radiator to the upper crossmember, making sure that the cooling fins do not get damaged.

18 Remove the front subframe from under the front of the vehicle as described in Chapter 10, Section 7.

19 Manoeuvre the engine hoist into position, and attach it to the engine/transmission using suitable lifting brackets. Raise the hoist until it is supporting the weight of the engine/transmission.

20 Mark the outline of the front engine/transmission mounting bracket bolts to use as a guide on refitting. Slacken and remove the bolts/nut and remove both right- and left-hand side mountings from the inner wing panels, as described in Chapter 2A, 2B or 2C as applicable.

21 Make a final check that any components, which would prevent the removal of the engine/transmission from the car, have been removed or disconnected. Ensure that components such as the gearchange cables are secured so that they cannot be damaged on removal.

22 If available, a low trolley should be placed under the engine/transmission assembly, to facilitate its easy removal from under the vehicle. Lower the engine/transmission assembly, making sure that nothing is trapped or damaged. Note that it may be necessary to tilt the assembly slightly to clear the body panels. Great care must be taken to ensure that no components are trapped and damaged during the removal procedure.

23 Withdraw the assembly from under the vehicle.

Separation

24 Unscrew the retaining bolts, and remove the starter motor from the transmission.

25 Ensure that both engine and transmission are adequately supported, then slacken and remove the bolts securing the transmission housing to the engine. Note the correct fitted positions of each bolt (and, where fitted, the relevant brackets) as they are removed, to use as a reference on refitting.

26 Carefully withdraw the transmission from the engine, ensuring that the weight of the transmission is not allowed to hang on the input shaft while it is engaged with the clutch friction disc.

27 If they are loose, remove the locating dowels from the engine or transmission, and keep them in a safe place.

Reconnection

28 Apply a smear of high melting-point grease to the splines of the transmission input shaft. Do not apply too much; otherwise there is a possibility of the grease contaminating the clutch friction disc.

29 Carefully offer the transmission to the engine, until the locating dowels are engaged. Ensure that the weight of the transmission is not allowed to hang on the input shaft as it is engaged with the clutch friction disc.

30 Refit the transmission housing-to-engine bolts, ensuring that all the necessary brackets are correctly positioned, and tighten them to the specified torque setting.

31 Refit the starter motor and tighten the retaining bolts.

Refitting

32 Position the engine/transmission assembly under the vehicle, then reconnect the hoist and lifting tackle to the engine lifting brackets.

33 Lift the assembly up into the engine compartment; making sure that it clears the surrounding components.

34 Refit the left-hand engine/transmission mounting bracket, ensuring that it is correctly seated in position. Manoeuvre the mounting into position, then fit the bolts securing it to the transmission and tighten them to the specified torque setting. Insert the through-bolt and nut, tightening it by hand only at this stage.

35 Fit the right-hand body mounting bracket, ensuring that it is correctly seated in position. Refit the mounting to the top of its bracket, and tighten its retaining bolts to the specified torque setting.

36 Refit the front subframe to the underside of the vehicle, as described in Chapter 10, Section 7.

37 The remainder of the refitting procedure is a direct reversal of the removal sequence, noting the following points:

a) Ensuring that the wiring harness is correctly routed and retained by all the relevant retaining clips, and all connectors are correctly and securely reconnected.
b) Prior to refitting the driveshafts to the transmission, renew the driveshaft oil seals as described in Chapter 7.
c) Ensure that all coolant hoses are correctly reconnected and securely retained by their retaining clips.
d) Refill the engine and transmission unit with correct quantity and type of lubricant, as described in the relevant Sections of Chapter 1A or Chapter 1B.
e) Refill the cooling system as described in Chapter 1A or Chapter 1B.
f) On diesel engine models, prime and bleed the fuel system as described in Chapter 4B, Section 5.
g) On completion, start the engine and check for leaks.

4 Engine overhaul – dismantling sequence

1 It is preferable to dismantle and work on the engine with it mounted on a portable engine stand. These stands can often be hired from a tool hire shop. Before the engine is mounted on a stand, the flywheel should be removed, so that the stand bolts can be tightened into the end of the cylinder block/crankcase.

2 If a stand is not available, it is possible to dismantle the engine with it blocked up on a sturdy workbench, or on the floor. Be extra careful not to tip or drop the engine when working without a stand.

3 If a reconditioned engine is to be obtained, or if the original engine is to be overhauled, the external components in the following list must be removed first. These components can then be transferred to the reconditioned engine, or refitted to the existing engine after overhaul.

a) Alternator and air conditioning compressor mounting brackets (as applicable).
b) Coolant pump and thermostat/coolant outlet housing(s) (Chapter 3).
c) Fuel system components (Chapter 4A or 4B).

d) All electrical switches and sensors, and the engine wiring harness.
e) Inlet and exhaust manifolds (Chapter 4A or 4B).
f) Engine mountings (Chapter 2A, 2B or 2C).
g) Flywheel (Chapter 2A, 2B or 2C).

Note: *When removing the external components from the engine, pay close attention to details that may be helpful or important during refitting. Note the fitted position of gaskets, seals, spacers, pins, washers, bolts, and other small items.*

4 If a 'short' engine is to be obtained (cylinder block, crankshaft, pistons and connecting rods all assembled), then the cylinder head, sump, oil pump, and timing chain/belt will have to be removed also.

5 If a complete overhaul of the existing engine is being undertaken, the engine can be dismantled, in the order given below, referring to Chapter 2A, 2B or 2C unless otherwise stated.

a) Inlet and exhaust manifolds (Chapter 4A or 4B).
b) Timing chain/belt and sprockets (on 1.2 litre petrol engines, see Section 6 of this Chapter).
c) Cylinder head (on 1.2 litre petrol engines and diesel engines, see Section 8 and Section 9 of this Chapter respectively).
d) Sump.
e) Oil pump (on 1.2 litre petrol engines, see Section 10 of this Chapter).
f) Flywheel.
g) Piston/connecting rod assemblies (see Section 14 of this Chapter).
h) Crankshaft (see Section 15 of this Chapter).

6 Before beginning the dismantling and overhaul procedures, make sure that you have all of the correct tools necessary. Refer to Tools and working facilities in, Section for further information.

5 Timing chain cover (1.2 litre petrol engines) – removal and refitting

Removal

1 With the engine removed from the car, drain the engine oil, then clean and refit the engine oil drain plug using a new sealing washer, tightening it to the specified torque. If the engine is nearing its service interval when the oil and filter are due for renewal, it is recommended that the filter is also removed, and a new one fitted. After reassembly, the engine can then be refilled with fresh oil. Refer to Chapter 1A, Section 5 for further information.

2 Remove the cylinder head cover as described in Chapter 2A, Section 3.

3 Remove the crankshaft pulley as described in Chapter 2A, Section 4.

4 Remove the alternator as described in Chapter 5A, Section 5.

5 Undo the three retaining bolts and remove the coolant pump pulley.

6 Undo the retaining bolt and remove the auxiliary drivebelt automatic tensioner from the timing chain cover.

7 Remove the cap then undo the retaining bolt and remove the auxiliary drivebelt idler roller.

8 Disconnect the wiring connector, then undo the retaining bolt and remove the inlet valve timing control solenoid from the front facing side of the timing cover. Remove the exhaust timing control solenoid from the rear facing side of the timing cover in the same way.

9 Undo the three bolts and remove the inlet camshaft end cover from the timing chain cover. Recover the O-ring seals from the cover. Remove the exhaust camshaft end cover in the same way.

10 Working in the reverse of the tightening sequence **(see illustration 5.17)**, slacken and remove the timing chain cover retaining bolts. Note the correct fitted location of each bolt, as some of the bolts are different lengths and different diameters.

11 The timing chain cover has been fitted using a liquid gasket, and is bonded to the engine block/cylinder head. Taking care not to damage the timing chain cover work your way around the outside of the cover to release it from the engine.

Refitting

12 Prior to refitting the cover, it is recommended that the crankshaft oil seal should be renewed. Note the seals fitted position and the carefully lever the old seal out of the cover using a large flat-bladed screwdriver. Fit the new seal to the cover, making sure its sealing lip is facing inwards. Drive the seal into position until it seats squarely in the position noted on removal, for further information see Chapter 2A, Section 7.

13 Ensure that the timing chain cover and engine cylinder block/cylinder head mating surfaces are clean/dry and free from any silicone sealer. Clean the steel dowels on the cylinder block, and apply a small amount of oil to aid fitting.

14 Apply a thin bead of suitable sealant (3 mm to 4 mm diameter) to the timing chain cover surface, not forgetting to apply sealant to the area around the passages in the upper centre of the cover **(see illustration)**.

15 Also apply a small amount of sealant to where the cylinder block joins the cylinder head, and where the cylinder block joins the upper sump housing **(see illustration)**.

16 Manoeuvre the cover into position over the end of the crankshaft, taking great care not to damage the oil seal lip.

17 Make sure the cover is correctly seated, and then install the retaining bolts. Working in sequence, tighten all the cover bolts to the specified torque **(see illustration)**.

18 Refit the coolant pump pulley and tighten the three retaining bolts.

19 Refit the alternator with reference to Chapter 5A, Section 5.

20 Refit the crankshaft pulley as described in Chapter 2A, Section 4.

21 Refit the cylinder head cover as described in Chapter 2A,Section 3.

5.14 Apply a bead of sealant around the outside of the cover

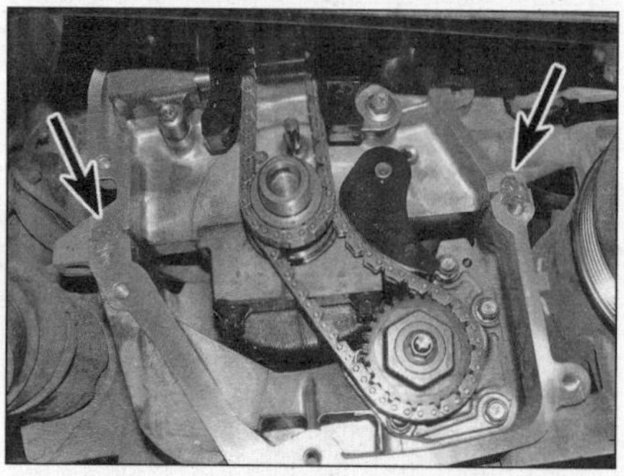

5.15 Apply sealant to the joints at both sides of the cylinder block

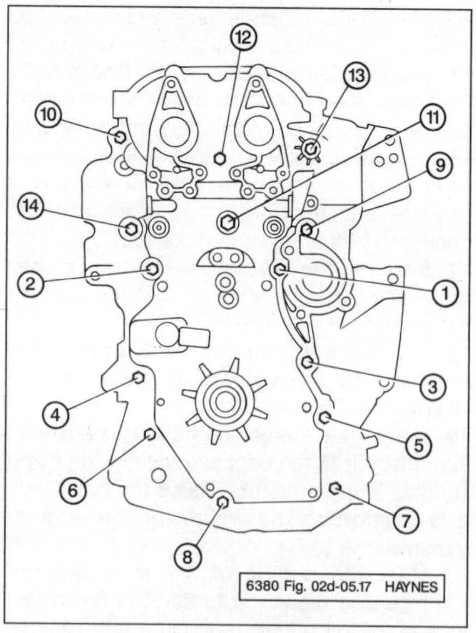

5.17 Tightening sequence for timing chain cover bolts

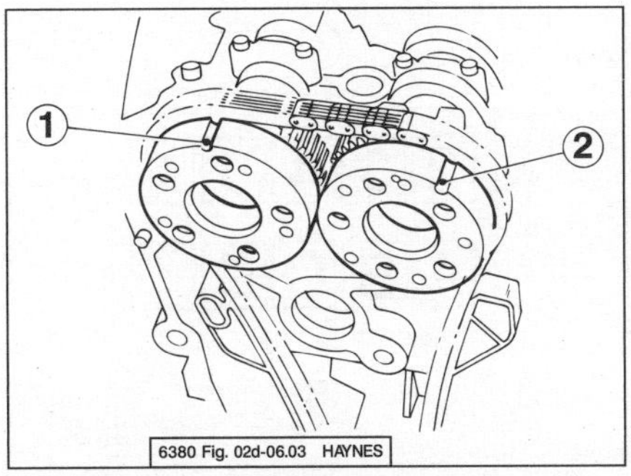

6.3 Position the timing marks (1 and 2) as shown

6.4a Push the tensioner lever down...

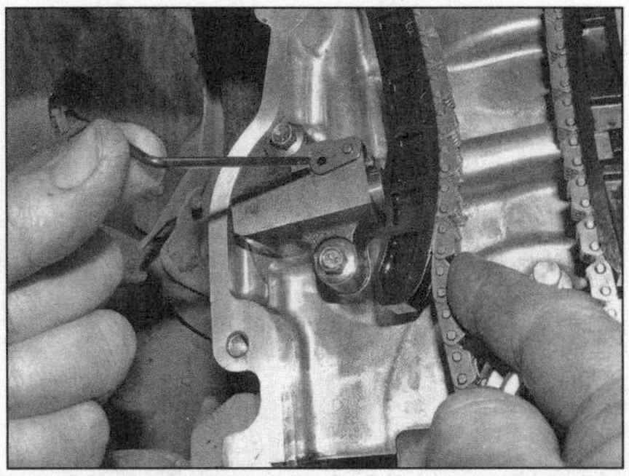

6.4b ...and insert a locking pin through the tensioner

6 Timing chain, tensioner, guides and sprockets (1.2 litre petrol engines) – removal, inspection and refitting

Removal

1 Remove the cylinder head cover as described in Chapter 2A, Section 3.

2 Remove the timing chain cover as described in Section 5 of this Chapter.

3 Set the engine at the TDC (Top Dead Centre) position for Nos 1 and 4 pistons as follows. Temporarily refit the crankshaft pulley to enable the engine to be turned. Using a socket or spanner on the crankshaft pulley bolt, turn the crankshaft until the timing marks (peripheral grooves) on the camshaft sprockets are positioned at 12 o'clock (exhaust camshaft) and 1 o'clock (inlet camshaft) **(see illustration)**. With the camshafts correctly positioned, remove the crankshaft pulley once more.

4 Whilst holding down the tensioner lever, push the tensioner plunger back into its body. With the plunger retracted, align the hole in the lever with the hole in the tensioner body and hold it in position by inserting a small-diameter rod through the plate hole and into the body of the tensioner **(see illustrations)**.

5 Undo the two retaining bolts, and remove the tensioner from the end of the cylinder block. Keep the rod inserted into the tensioner to prevent the plunger from springing out **(see illustrations)**.

6 Release the upper pivot point of the chain tensioner guide, and remove it from the rear of the crankcase **(see illustration)**.

7 Unscrew the two mounting bolts, and remove the chain front guide from the crankcase.

8 Disengage the timing chain from the crankshaft sprocket, and manoeuvre it out from the engine **(see illustration)**.

Warning: Do not turn the crankshaft or camshafts while the timing chain is removed, otherwise piston and valve contact may occur causing damage.

9 Slacken the camshaft sprocket retaining bolts, whilst retaining the camshaft with a large open-ended spanner fitted to the hexagonal section of each shaft. Remove the bolt along with its washer (where applicable), then disengage the sprocket from the end of its camshaft.

10 To remove the crankshaft sprocket from the end of the crankshaft, requires removing the oil pump chain and sprocket as a complete unit. See Section 10 for further information.

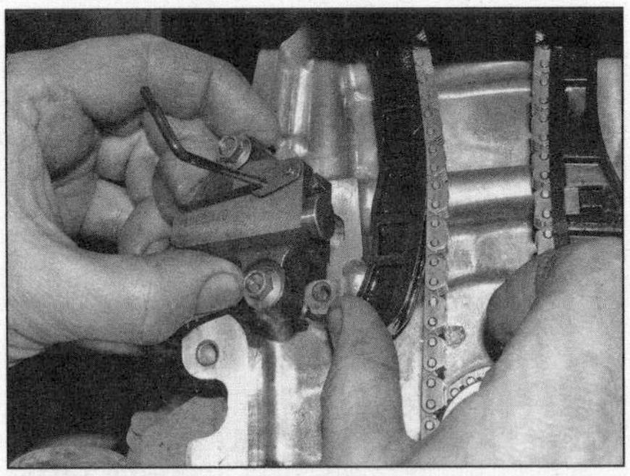

6.5a Undo the retaining bolts and remove the tensioner...

6.5b ...keeping the locking pin in place

Inspection

11 Examine the teeth on the camshaft and crankshaft sprockets for any sign of wear or damage such as chipped, hooked or missing teeth. If there is any sign of wear or damage on either sprockets or timing chain then they should be renewed as a set.

12 Inspect the links of the timing chain for signs of wear or damage on the rollers. The extent of wear can be judged by checking the amount by which the chain can be bent sideways; a new chain will have very little sideways movement. If there is an excessive amount of side play in either timing chain, it must be renewed.

13 Note that it is a sensible precaution to renew the timing chain, regardless of apparent condition, if the engine has covered a high mileage, or if it has been noted that the chain has sounded noisy when the engine running. Although not strictly necessary, it is always worth renewing the chain and sprockets as a matched set, since it is false economy to run a new chain on worn sprockets and viceversa. If there is any doubt about the condition of the timing chain and sprockets, seek the advice of a Nissan dealer service department, who will be able to advise you as to the best course of action.

14 Examine the chain guides for signs of wear or damage to their chain contact faces, renewing any which are badly marked.

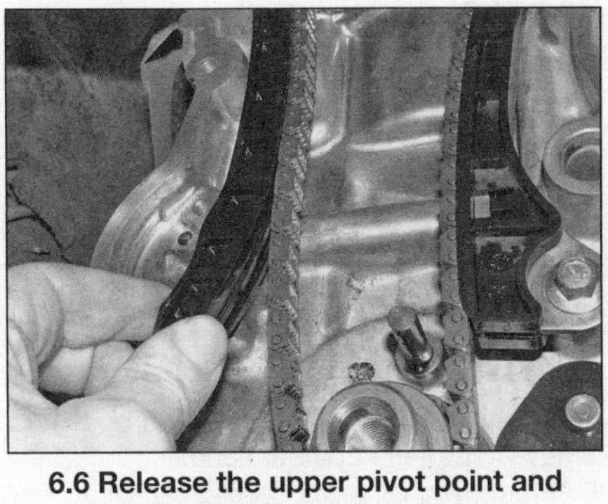

6.6 Release the upper pivot point and remove the tensioner guide

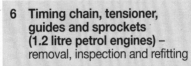

6.8 Disengage the timing chain from the crankshaft sprocket

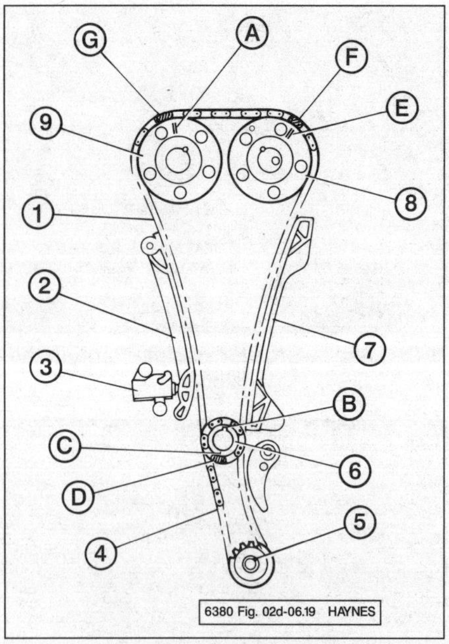

6.19 Camshaft sprocket and timing chain timing mark relationship

1 Timing chain
2 Chain tensioner guide
3 Chain tensioner
4 Oil pump drive chain
5 Oil pump sprocket
6 Crankshaft sprocket
7 Timing chain front guide
8 Inlet camshaft sprocket
9 Exhaust camshaft sprocket
A Timing mark (peripheral groove)
B Crankshaft sprocket keyway
C Crankshaft sprocket timing mark
D Coloured link
E Timing mark (peripheral groove)
F Coloured link
G Coloured link

15 Check the chain tensioner for signs of wear, and check that the plunger is free to slide freely in the tensioner body. The condition of the tensioner spring can only be judged in comparison to a new component. Renew the tensioner if it is worn or there is any doubt about the condition of its tensioning spring.

Refitting

16 Check the crankshaft is still positioned at TDC (the keyway will be in the 12 o'clock position, seen from the right-hand end of the engine).

17 Refit the sprockets to the camshafts engaging the lug on each sprocket with the slot on the camshaft. Refit the sprocket retaining bolts and tighten them to the specified torque. Retain the camshafts whilst tightening the bolts with a large open-ended spanner as used on removal.

18 Check that the camshafts are still in the TDC position **(see illustration 6.3)**.

19 Manoeuvre the chain into position, engaging it with the crankshaft sprocket so that its coloured link is aligned with the timing mark on the crankshaft sprocket. Engage the chain with the camshaft sprockets, aligning the two dark chain links with the timing marks on the sprockets **(see illustration)**.

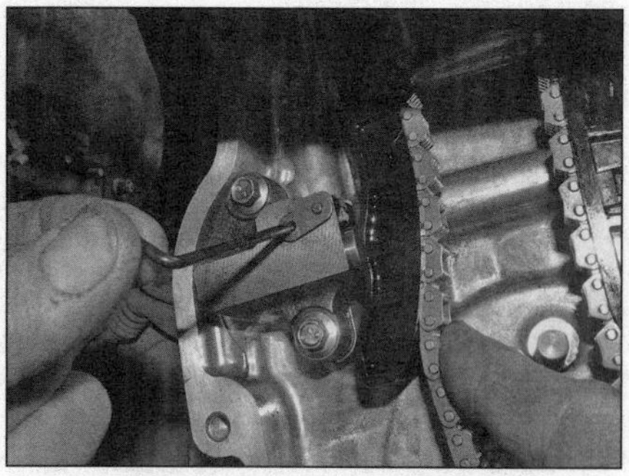

6.22 Hold pressure against the tensioner and remove the locking pin

20 Fit the chain front fixed guide to the cylinder block, and tighten its retaining bolts to the specified torque.

21 Fit the chain rear tensioner guide to the upper pivot point and locate it in position.

22 Fit the chain tensioner to the cylinder block, and tighten its retaining bolts to the specified torque. Whilst holding the guide against the tensioner plunger, withdraw the rod, and check that the tensioner plunger is forced out against the guide to take up the slack in the chain **(see illustration)**.

23 Check that all the timing marks are still correctly aligned with the chain links. If all timing marks are aligned, fit the crankshaft pulley and turn the engine two complete turns, and check the timing marks on the sprockets are all re-aligned.

Note: *The coloured links on the chain will not be re-aligned with the marks on the sprockets. The coloured links are just for the initial set up, and will take many turns before they will line up again, with the marks on the sprockets.*

24 Refit the timing chain cover as described in Section 5.

7 Camshafts and followers (1.2 litre petrol engines) – removal, inspection and refitting

Removal

1 Remove the timing chain, tensioner, guides and sprockets as described in Section 6.

2 Undo the three retaining bolts and remove the closing plate from the left-hand end of the cylinder head on the inlet camshaft side. Use a screwdriver to carefully prise free the closing plate, taking great care not to damage the mating surfaces.

3 At the timing chain end of the camshafts, the bearing cap housing covers both of the camshafts. Undo the three retaining bolts and remove it from the cylinder head.

4 All remaining camshaft bearing caps, bar one, have identification markings stamped into their

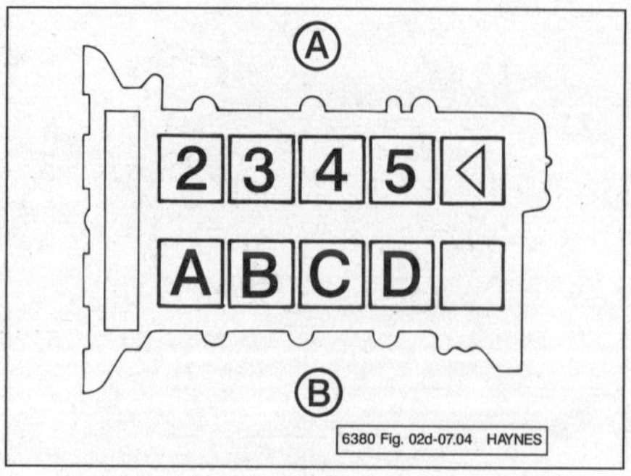

7.4 Camshaft bearing cap markings

A = Exhaust camshaft side
B = Inlet camshaft side

top surface; the exhaust camshaft caps being marked 2 to 5 (with the cap at the left-hand end just having a triangular symbol) and the inlet camshaft caps being marked A to D (with the cap at the left-hand end having no marking). The No 2 and A caps are fitted nearest the timing chain end of the engine **(see illustration)**. Note the markings on the caps for refitting. If the caps are not marked, suitable identification marks should be made prior to removal. Using white paint or suitable marker pen, mark each cap in some way to indicate its correct fitted orientation and position. This will avoid the possibility of installing the caps in the wrong positions and/or the wrong way around on refitting.

5 Working in the reverse of the tightening sequence **(see illustration 7.20)**, evenly and progressively slacken the twenty remaining camshaft bearing cap retaining bolts by one turn at a time, to relieve the pressure of the valve springs on the bearing caps gradually and evenly. Once the valve spring pressure has been relieved, the bolts can be fully unscrewed and the caps removed.

6 With the bearing caps removed the inlet and exhaust camshafts can be simply lifted off the top of the cylinder head, noting their fitted position. Note that the exhaust camshaft is the longer of the two.

7 Obtain sixteen small, clean plastic containers, and number them 1 to 16. Alternatively, divide a larger container into sixteen compartments. Using a rubber sucker, withdraw each follower (valve lifter) in turn, and place it in its respective container **(see illustration)**. Do not interchange the cam followers, or the rate of wear will be increased.

7.7 Remove the cam followers

7.12 Checking the cam lobe height with a micrometer

8 If required, undo the retaining bolt and remove the inlet and exhaust camshaft variable valve timing control solenoids from the front of the cylinder head.

Inspection

9 Remove the plug from below each timing control solenoid and clean-out or renew the oil filter for the variable valve system.

10 Inspect the cam bearing surfaces of the head and the bearing caps. Look for score marks and deep scratches. Check the camshaft lobes for heat discoloration (blue appearance), score marks, chipped areas or flat spots.

11 Camshaft run-out can be checked by supporting each end of the camshaft on V-blocks, and measuring any run-out at the centre of the shaft using a dial gauge. If the run-out exceeds the specified limit, a new camshaft will be required.

12 Measure the height of each lobe with a micrometer **(see illustration)**, and compare the results to the figures given in the Specifications. If damage is noted or wear is excessive, new camshaft(s) must be fitted.

13 The camshaft bearing oil clearance should now be checked.

14 Fit the bearing caps to the cylinder head, using the identification markings or the marks made on removal to ensure that they are correctly positioned. Tighten the retaining bolts to the specified torque in sequence **(see illustration 7.20)**. Measure the diameter of each bearing cap journal, and compare the measurements obtained with the results given in the Specifications at the start of this Chapter. If any journal is worn beyond the service limit, the cylinder head must be renewed. The camshaft bearing oil clearance can then calculated by subtracting the camshaft bearing journal diameter from the bearing cap journal diameter.

15 Check the cam follower and cylinder head bearing surfaces for signs of wear or damage.

Refitting

16 Liberally oil the cylinder head cam follower bores and the followers. Carefully refit the followers to the cylinder head; ensuring that each follower is refitted to its original bore. Some care will be required to enter the followers squarely into their bores. Liberally oil the camshaft bearing and lobe contact surfaces.

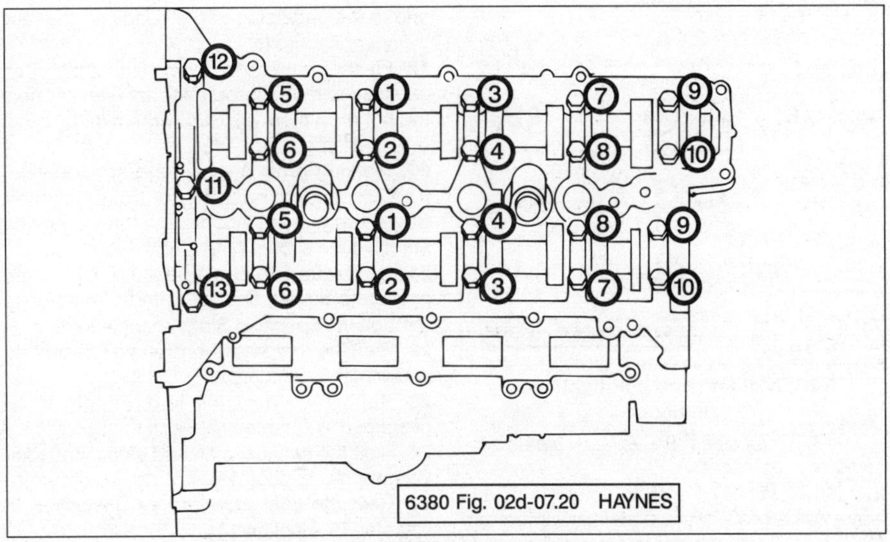

7.20 Tighten the bearing caps in the sequence shown
A = Exhaust side B = Inlet side

17 Refit the inlet and exhaust camshaft to their correct locations in the cylinder head and position them so that the sprocket locating slot is at 12 o'clock for the exhaust camshaft and 1 o'clock for the inlet camshaft.

18 Ensure that the bearing cap and head mating surfaces are completely clean, unmarked and free from oil.

19 Refit the bearing caps, using the identification markings or the marks made on removal to ensure that each is installed the correct way round and in its original location.

20 Working in sequence, evenly and progressively tighten the camshaft bearing cap bolts by one turn at a time until the caps touch the cylinder head **(see illustration)**. Then go round again and tighten all the bolts to the specified torque setting. Work only as described, to impose the pressure of the valve springs gradually and evenly on the bearing caps.

21 Thoroughly clean the cylinder head closing plate and the mating surface on the cylinder head ensuring that all traces of old sealant are removed. Apply a 3 mm bead of sealant to the mating surface of the closing plate, then refit the plate to the cylinder head. Refit the retaining bolts and tighten them to the specified torque.

22 Refit the timing chain, tensioner, guides and sprockets as described in Section 6.

23 If the cylinder head/camshafts have been overhauled, check and adjust the valve clearances as described in Chapter 2A, Section 5 before refitting the cylinder head cover.

8 Cylinder head (1.2 litre petrol engines) – removal and refitting

Removal

1 Remove the camshafts and followers as described in Section 7.

2 Remove the inlet manifold as described in Chapter 4A, Section 14.

3 Remove the exhaust manifold as described in Chapter 4A, Section 15.

4 Remove the fuel rail and injectors as described in Chapter 4A, Section 10.

5 Remove the thermostat housing as described in Chapter 3, Section 4.

6 Working in the reverse of the tightening sequence **(see illustration 8.20)**, progressively slacken the ten main cylinder head bolts by half a turn at a time, until all bolts can be unscrewed by hand.

7 Lift out the cylinder head bolts and recover the washers, noting which way around they are fitted.

8 Lift the cylinder head off the top of the block. Remove the gasket, noting the locating dowels fitted to the top of the cylinder block. If they are a loose fit in the block, remove the locating dowels, noting which way round they are fitted, and store them with the head for safekeeping.

9 If the cylinder head is to be dismantled for overhaul, refer to Section 11.

Preparation for refitting

10 The mating faces of the cylinder head and cylinder block/crankcase must be perfectly clean before refitting the head. Use a hard plastic or wood scraper to remove all traces of gasket and carbon; also clean the piston crowns. Take particular care, as the surfaces are damaged easily. Also, make sure that

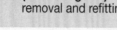

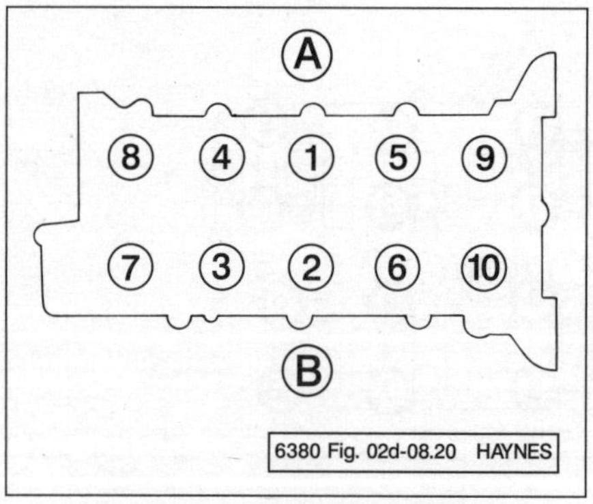

8.20 Cylinder head bolt tightening sequence

A = Inlet side B = Exhaust side

the carbon is not allowed to enter the oil and water passages – this is particularly important for the lubrication system, as carbon could block the oil supply to any of the engine's components. Using adhesive tape and paper, seal the water, oil and bolt holes in the cylinder block/crankcase. To prevent carbon entering the gap between the pistons and bores, smear a little grease in the gap. After cleaning each piston, use a small brush to remove all traces of grease and carbon from the gap, and then wipe away the remainder with a clean rag. Clean all the pistons in the same way.

11 Check the mating surfaces of the cylinder block/crankcase and the cylinder head for nicks, deep scratches and other damage. If slight, they may be removed carefully with a file, but if excessive, machining may be the only alternative to renewal.

12 Ensure that the cylinder head bolt holes in the crankcase are clean and free of oil. Syringe or soak up any oil left in the bolt holes. This is most important in order that the correct bolt tightening torque can be applied and to prevent the possibility of the block being cracked by hydraulic pressure when the bolts are tightened.

13 The cylinder head bolts must be discarded and renewed, regardless of their apparent condition.

14 If warpage of the cylinder head gasket surface is suspected, use a straight-edge to check it for distortion. If necessary, refer to Section 12.

Refitting

15 Wipe clean the mating surfaces of the cylinder head and cylinder block/crankcase. Check the locating dowels are in position at each end of the cylinder block/crankcase surface.

16 Fit a new gasket to the cylinder block/ crankcase surface, aligning it with the locating dowels.

17 With the aid of an assistant, carefully refit the cylinder head assembly to the block, aligning it with the locating dowels.

18 Apply a smear of clean oil to the threads, and to the underside of the heads, of the new cylinder head bolts.

19 Fit the washer to each head bolt, then carefully enter each bolt into its relevant hole (do not drop them in). Screw them in, by hand only, until finger-tight.

20 Working progressively and in sequence, tighten the cylinder head bolts to their Stage 1 torque setting, using a torque wrench and suitable socket **(see illustration)**.

21 Go around in the specified sequence again and tighten the ten cylinder head bolts through the specified Stage 2 angle setting.

22 Refit the thermostat housing as described in Chapter 3, Section 4.

23 Refit the fuel rail and injectors as described in Chapter 4A, Section 10.

24 Refit the exhaust manifold as described in Chapter 4A, Section 15.

25 Refit the inlet manifold as described in Chapter 4A, Section 14.

26 Refit the camshafts and followers as described in Section 7.

9 Cylinder head (diesel engines) – removal and refitting

Removal

1 With the engine removed from the car, drain the engine oil, then clean and refit the engine oil drain plug using a new sealing washer, tightening it to the specified torque. If the engine is nearing its service interval when the oil and filter are due for renewal, it is recommended that the filter is also removed, and a new one fitted. After reassembly, the engine can then be refilled with fresh oil. Refer to Chapter 1B, Section 5 for further information.

2 Remove the cylinder head cover as described in Chapter 2C, Section 4.

3 Remove the fuel injectors as described in Chapter 4B, Section 10.

4 Remove the fuel rail as described in Chapter 4B, Section 11.

5 Remove the high-pressure fuel pump as described in Chapter 4B, Section 9.

6 Remove the exhaust manifold as described in Chapter 4B, Section 13.

7 Remove the timing belt as described in Chapter 2C, Section 6.

8 Remove the camshaft and followers as described in Chapter 2C, Section 9.

9 Unbolt and remove the timing belt tensioner roller from the cylinder head.

10 Unbolt and remove the inner timing cover from the cylinder block and head.

11 Progressively slacken the cylinder head bolts in the reverse sequence to that shown **(see illustration 9.23)**. With all the bolts loose, remove them.

12 Lift the cylinder head upwards off the cylinder block. If it is stuck, tap it with a hammer and block of wood to release it. Do not try to turn the cylinder head (it is located by two dowels), nor attempt to prise it free using a screwdriver inserted between the block and head faces.

13 Remove the gasket, noting the locating dowels fitted to the top of the cylinder block. If they are a loose fit in the block, remove the locating dowels, noting which way round they are fitted, and store them with the head for safekeeping.

14 If the cylinder head is to be dismantled for overhaul, refer to Section 11.

Preparation for refitting

15 The mating faces of the cylinder head and block must be perfectly clean before refitting the head. Use a scraper to remove all traces of gasket and carbon, and also clean the tops of the pistons. Take particular care with the aluminium cylinder head, as the soft metal is damaged easily. Also, make sure that debris is not allowed to enter the oil and water channels – this is particularly important for the oil circuit, as carbon could block the oil supply to the camshaft or crankshaft bearings. Using adhesive tape and paper, seal the water, oil and bolt holes in the cylinder block. Clean the piston crowns in the same way.

16 Check the block and head for nicks, deep scratches and other damage. If slight, they may be removed carefully with a file. Machining of the cylinder head or cylinder block is not recommended by the manufacturers.

17 If warpage of the cylinder head is suspected, use a straight-edge to check it for distortion. Refer to Section 12 if necessary; if the warpage is more than the maximum, the cylinder head must be renewed, as regrinding is not allowed.

18 Clean out the cylinder head bolt holes in the block using a pipe cleaner, or a rag and screwdriver. Make sure that all oil is removed, otherwise there is a possibility of the block being cracked by hydraulic pressure when the bolts are tightened. Examine the bolt threads in the cylinder block for damage, and if necessary, use the correct size tap to chase out the threads. The cylinder head bolts must be renewed each time they are removed, and must not be oiled before being fitted.

Refitting

19 Wipe clean the mating surfaces of the cylinder head and cylinder block/crankcase. Check the locating dowels are in position at each end of the cylinder block/crankcase surface.

20 Fit a new gasket to the cylinder block/ crankcase surface, aligning it with the locating dowels.

21 With the aid of an assistant, carefully refit the cylinder head assembly to the block, aligning it with the locating dowels.

22 Fit the washer to each new head bolt, then carefully enter each bolt into its relevant hole (do not drop them in). Screw them in, by hand only, until finger-tight.

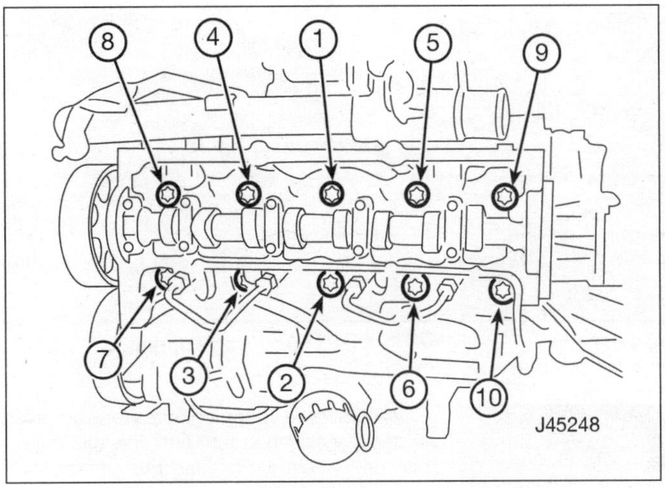

9.23 Cylinder head bolt tightening sequence

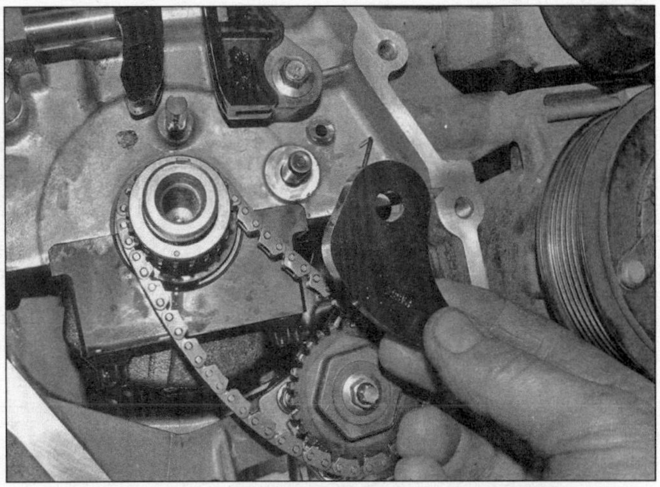

10.4 Remove the tensioner from the cylinder block

23 Working progressively and in sequence, tighten the cylinder head bolts to their Stage 1 torque setting, using a torque wrench and suitable socket **(see illustration)**.

24 Go around in the specified sequence again and tighten the ten cylinder head bolts through the specified Stage 2 angle setting.

25 Refit the inner timing cover to the cylinder block and head.

26 Refit the timing belt tensioner roller to the cylinder head and tighten the retaining bolt to the specified torque.

27 Refit the camshafts and followers as described in Chapter 2C, Section 9.

28 Refit the timing belt as described in Chapter 2C, Section 6.

29 Refit the exhaust manifold as described in Chapter 4B, Section 13.

30 Refit the high-pressure fuel pump as described in Chapter 4B, Section 9.

31 Refit the fuel rail as described in Chapter 4B, Section 11.

32 Refit the fuel injectors as described in Chapter 4B, Section 10.

33 Refit the cylinder head cover as described in Chapter 2C, Section 4.

10 Oil pump, drive chain and sprockets (1.2 litre petrol engines) – removal, inspection and refitting

Removal

1 Remove the timing chain as described in Section 6.

2 Remove the sump oil pan as described in Chapter 2A, Section 6.

3 Disconnect the wiring plug from the oil pump solenoid valve, then extract the wire retaining clip and release the solenoid valve wiring connector from the upper sump housing.

4 Release the spring from the hole in the cylinder block and withdraw the chain tensioner from the pivot on the cylinder block **(see illustration)**.

5 Unscrew the oil pump drive sprocket retaining nut, use a socket on the end of the oil pump drive shaft to slacken the retaining nut.

6 Remove the oil pump drive chain complete with sprockets from the oil pump drive shaft and crankshaft **(see illustration)**.

7 Undo the retaining bolts and remove the oil pump strainer, oil pump bracket and oil pump from the upper sump housing.

Inspection

8 Clean the components and carefully examine the chain, sprockets and pump for any signs of excessive wear. If evident, it is recommended that all the components are renewed as a set. Renew all disturbed O-ring seals as a matter of course.

9 Before refitting the oil pump, prime it by filling with clean engine oil whilst rotating the pump clockwise.

Refitting

10 Fit the oil pump components back in place in the sump upper housing and tighten the retaining bolts securely.

11 Make sure the chain is located around the two sprockets correctly, and then refit them as a complete assembly to the oil pump drive shaft and crankshaft **(see illustration)**.

12 Refit the oil pump sprocket retaining nut and tighten to the specified torque setting.

13 Refit the chain tensioner to the pivot on the cylinder block, making sure the tensioner spring is located correctly in the cylinder block **(see illustration)**.

10.6 Remove the drive chain complete with sprockets

10.11 Make sure the chain is located around the sprocket correctly

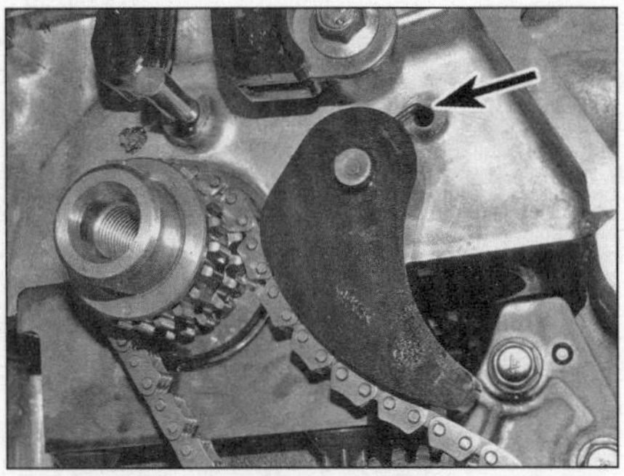

10.13 Make sure the tensioner spring is located correctly

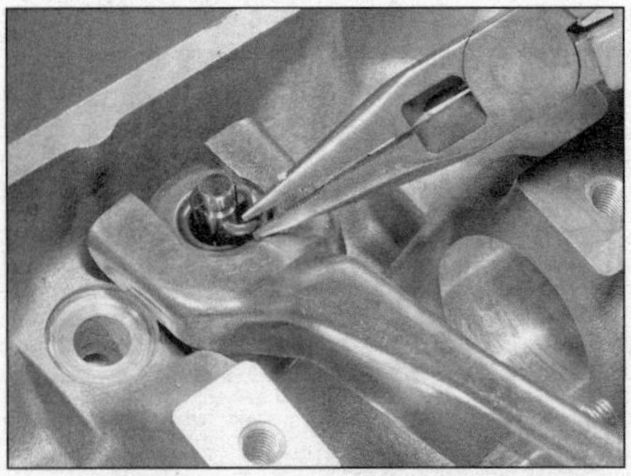

11.3a Remove the split collets...

11.3b ...then lift off the cap...

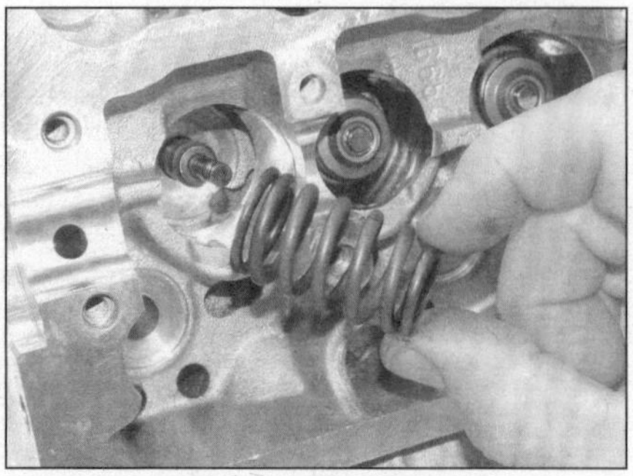

11.3c ...valve spring...

11.3d ...and the spring seat (where fitted)

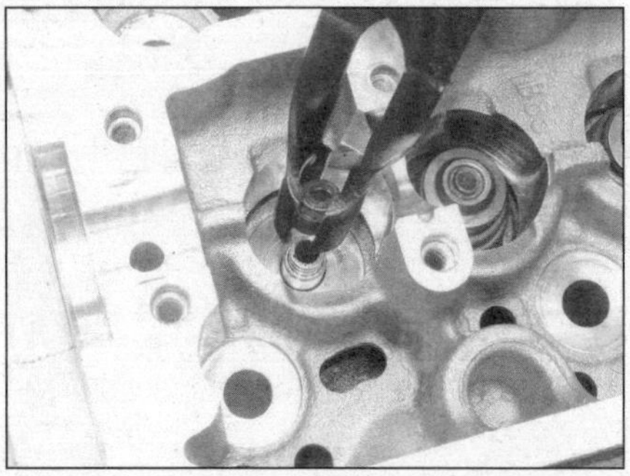

11.3e Removing the oil seal from the top of the valve guide

14 Disconnect the wiring plug from the oil pump solenoid valve, then extract the wire retaining clip and Refit the solenoid valve wiring connector to the upper sump housing and secure with the wire retaining clip. Reconnect the wiring plug.

15 Refit the sump oil pan as described in Chapter 2A, Section 6.

16 Refit the timing chain as described in Section 6.

11 Cylinder head – dismantling

Note: *New and reconditioned cylinder heads are available from the manufacturer, and from engine reconditioning specialists. Some specialist tools are required for dismantling and inspection, and new components may not be readily available.It may therefore be more practical and economical for the home mechanic to purchase a reconditioned head, rather than dismantle, inspect and recondition the original head.*

1 Remove the cylinder head with reference to the following Chapters and Sections of this manual:

- 1.2 litre petrol engines – Section 8 of this Chapter
- 1.6 litre petrol engines – Chapter 2B, Section 10
- Diesel engines – Section 9 of this Chapter

2 Remove any remaining ancillary components from the cylinder head, as necessary, referring to the relevant Chapters and Sections of this manual.

3 Using a valve spring compressor, compress each valve spring in turn until the split collets can be removed. Release the compressor, and lift off the spring retainer, spring and spring seat. Using a pair of pliers, carefully extract the valve stem seal from the top of the guide **(see illustrations)**.

4 If, when the valve spring compressor is screwed down, the spring retainer refuses to free and expose the split collets, gently tap the top of the tool, directly over the retainer, with a light hammer. This will free the retainer.

5 Withdraw the valve through the combustion chamber **(see illustration)**.

6 It is essential that each valve is stored together with its collets, retainer, spring, and spring seat. The valves should also be kept in their correct sequence, unless they are so badly worn that they are to be renewed. If they are going to be kept and used again, place each valve assembly in a labelled polythene bag or similar small container **(see illustrations)**. Note that No 1 cylinder is nearest to the timing chain end of the engine on petrol engines and nearest to the flywheel end of the engine on diesel engines.

12 Cylinder head and valves – cleaning and inspection

Cleaning

1 Scrape away all traces of old gasket material from the cylinder head.

11.5 Withdrawing a valve from the cylinder head

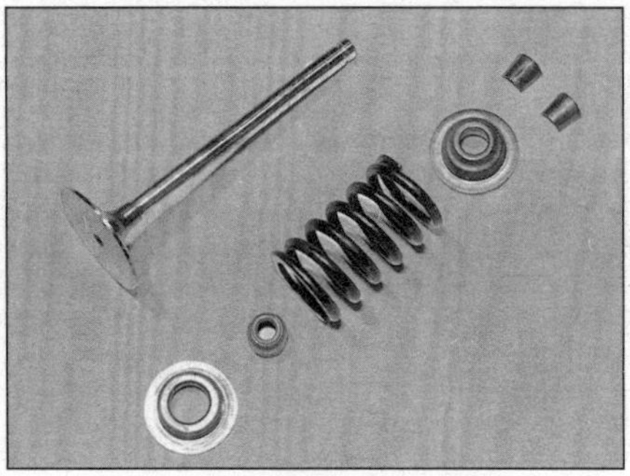

11.6a The valve components

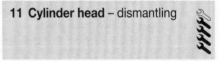

11.6b Store the components in a labelled plastic bag

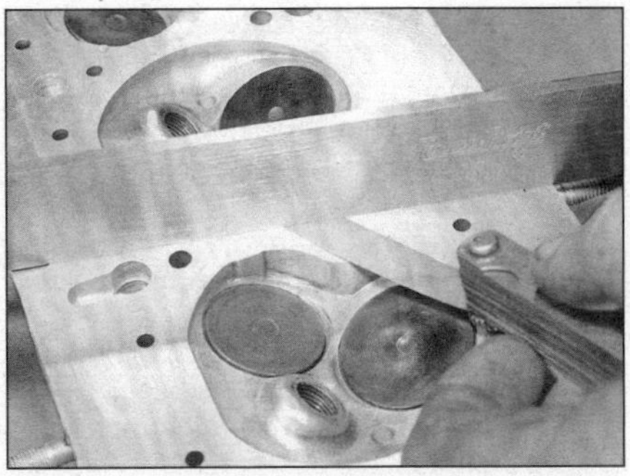

12.5 Check the cylinder head for distortion with feeler blades

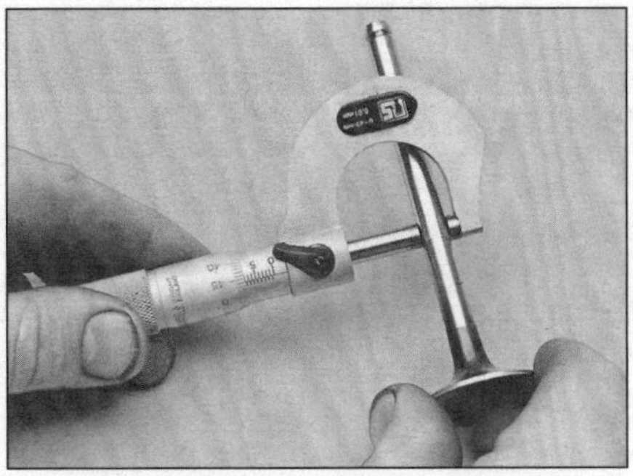

12.10 Measuring a valve stem using a micrometer

12.13 Grinding in a valve – lift the valve to distribute the paste evenly

2 Scrape away the carbon from the combustion chambers and ports, then wash the cylinder head thoroughly with paraffin or a suitable solvent.

3 Scrape off any heavy carbon deposits that may have formed on the valves, then use a power-operated wire brush to remove deposits from the valve heads and stems.

Inspection

Cylinder head

4 Inspect the head very carefully for cracks, evidence of coolant leakage, and other damage. If significant defects are found, a new cylinder head should be obtained.

5 Use a straight-edge and feeler blade to check for distortion of the cylinder head gasket surface **(see illustration)**. If the head is distorted beyond the limit given in the Specifications, seek the advice of an engine reconditioning specialist as to whether machining is possible.

6 Examine the valve seats in each of the combustion chambers. If they are severely pitted, cracked, or burned, they will need to be renewed or recut by an engine reconditioning specialist. If they are only slightly pitted, this can be removed by grinding-in the valve heads and seats with fine valve-grinding compound, as described below.

7 Check the valve guides for wear by inserting the relevant valve, and checking for side-to-side motion of the valve. A very small amount of movement is acceptable. If the movement seems excessive, remove the valve. Measure the valve stem diameter (see below), and renew the valve if it is worn. If the valve stem is not worn, the wear must be in the valve guide, and the guide must be renewed. The renewal of valve guides should be carried out by an engine reconditioning specialist, who will have the necessary tools available.

8 If renewing the valve guides, the valve seats are to be recut or reground only after the guides have been fitted.

Valves

9 Examine the head of each valve for pitting, burning, cracks, and general wear. Check the valve stem for scoring and wear ridges. Rotate the valve, and check for any obvious indication that it is bent. Look for pits and excessive wear on the tip of each valve stem. Renew any valve that shows any such signs of wear or damage.

10 If the valve appears satisfactory at this stage, measure the valve stem diameter at several points using a micrometer **(see illustration)**. Any significant difference in the readings obtained indicates wear of the valve stem. Should any of these conditions be apparent, the valve(s) must be renewed.

11 If the valves are in satisfactory condition, they should be ground (lapped) into their respective seats, to ensure a smooth, gas-tight seal. If the seat is only lightly pitted, or if it has been recut, fine grinding compound only should be used to produce the required finish. Coarse valve-grinding compound should not be used, unless a seat is badly burned or deeply pitted. If this is the case, the cylinder head and valves should be inspected by a specialist, to decide whether seat recutting, or even the renewal of the valve or seat insert (where possible) is required.

12 Valve grinding is carried out as follows, with the head supported upside-down on blocks.

13 Smear a trace of (the appropriate grade of) valve-grinding compound on the seat face, and press a suction grinding tool onto the valve head. With a semi-rotary action, grind the valve head to its seat, lifting the valve occasionally to redistribute the grinding compound **(see illustration)**. A light spring placed under the valve head will greatly ease this operation.

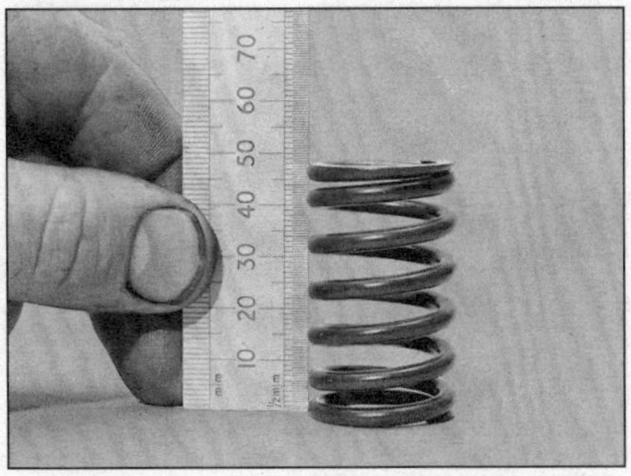

12.16 Checking the height of a valve spring

14 If coarse grinding compound is being used, work only until a dull, matt even surface is produced on both the valve seat and the valve, then wipe off the used compound, and repeat the process with fine compound. When a smooth unbroken ring of light grey matt finish is produced on both the valve and seat, the grinding operation is complete. Do not grind-in the valves any further than absolutely necessary, or the seat will be prematurely sunk into the cylinder head.

15 When all the valves have been ground-in, carefully wash off all traces of grinding compound using paraffin or a suitable solvent, before reassembling the cylinder head.

Valve components

16 Examine the valve springs for signs of damage and discoloration. The specified Nissan procedure for checking the condition of valve springs involves measuring the force necessary to compress each spring to a specified height. This is not possible without the use of the Nissan special test equipment, and therefore spring checking must be entrusted to a Nissan dealer. A rough idea of the condition of the spring can be gained by measuring the spring free length, and comparing it with a new one **(see illustration)**.

17 Stand each spring on a flat surface, and position a square alongside the edge of the spring.

18 If any of the springs are damaged, distorted or have lost their tension, obtain a complete new set of springs. It is normal to renew the valve springs as a matter of course if a major overhaul is being carried out.

19 Renew the valve stem oil seals regardless of their apparent condition.

13 Cylinder head – reassembly

1 Refit the spring seat then, working on the first valve, dip the new valve stem seal in fresh engine oil. Place it on the valve guide

13.1a Fit the valve stem oil seal...

13.1b ...and press it into the previously-noted position on the guide

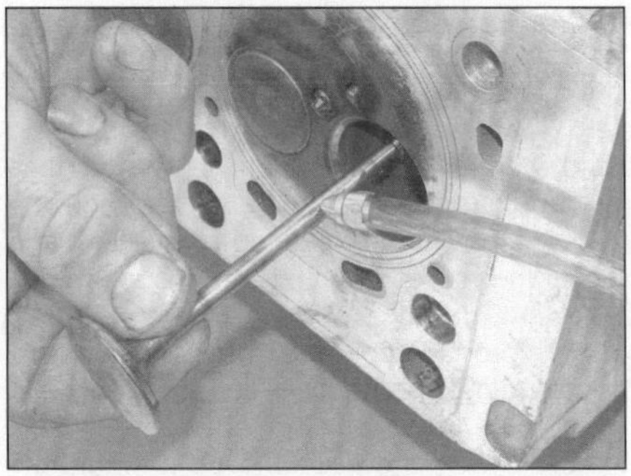

13.2 Lubricate the valve stems before fitting the valves

13.4 Use a little grease to hold the collets in place

and use a suitable socket or metal tube to press the seal firmly onto the guide **(see illustrations)**.

2 Lubricate the stems of the valves, and insert the valves into their original locations **(see illustration)**. If new valves are being fitted, insert them into the locations to which they have been ground.

3 Locate the valve spring on top of its seat; ensuring that the spring is fitted with its closer-pitched coils at the bottom, and then refit the spring retainer.

4 Compress the valve spring, and locate the split collets in the recess in the valve stem **(see illustration)**. Release the compressor, then repeat the procedure on the remaining valves.

5 With all the valves installed, place the cylinder head on blocks on the bench and, using a hammer and interposed block of wood, tap the end of each valve stem to settle the components.

6 Refit the previously removed ancillary components, then refit the cylinder head with reference to the following Chapters and Sections of this manual:

- 1.2 litre petrol engines – Section 8 of this Chapter
- 1.6 litre petrol engines – Chapter 2B, Section 10
- Diesel engines – Section 9 of this Chapter

14 Piston/connecting rod assembly – removal

1 Remove the sump, timing chain/belt, oil pump and cylinder head as described in the relevant Sections of this Chapter or in Chapter 2A, 2B or 2C as applicable.

2 On petrol engines, remove the flywheel, then undo the retaining bolts and remove the upper alloy part of the sump from the bottom of the cylinder block.

3 On 1.2 litre petrol engines, undo the retaining bolts and remove the main bearing cap support beam.

4 If there is a pronounced wear ridge at the top of any bore, it may be necessary to remove it with a scraper or ridge reamer, to avoid piston damage during removal. Such a ridge indicates excessive wear of the cylinder bore.

5 Each connecting rod and bearing cap should be stamped with its respective cylinder number, No 1 cylinder being at the timing chain end of the engine **(see illustration)**. If no markings are visible, using quick-drying paint or similar, mark each connecting rod and big-end bearing cap with its respective cylinder number on the flat machined surface provided.

6 Turn the crankshaft to bring pistons 1 and 4 to BDC (bottom dead centre).

7 Unscrew the bolts from No 1 piston big-end bearing cap. Take off the cap **(see illustration)**, and recover the bottom half bearing shell. If the bearing shells are to be re-used, tape the cap and the shell together.

8 Using a hammer handle, push the piston up through the bore, and remove it from the top of the cylinder block. Recover the bearing shell, and tape it to the connecting rod for safekeeping.

9 Loosely refit the big-end cap to the connecting rod, and secure with the bolts – this will help to keep the components in their correct order.

10 Remove No 4 piston assembly in the same way.

11 Turn the crankshaft through 180° to bring pistons 2 and 3 to BDC (bottom dead centre), and remove them in the same way.

14.5 Big-end caps marked with a centre punch

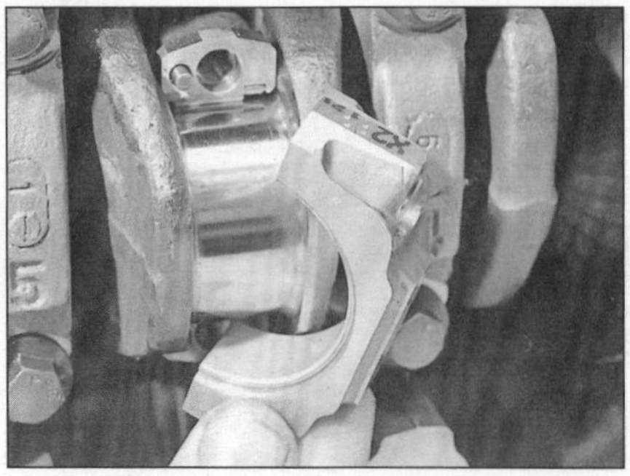

14.7 Removing a big-end bearing cap

15 Crankshaft – removal

1 Remove the pistons and connecting rods, as described in Section 14. If no work is to be done on the pistons and connecting rods, there is no need to remove the cylinder head, or to push the pistons out of the cylinder bores. The pistons should just be pushed far enough up the bores that they are positioned clear of the crankshaft journals.

2 Check the crankshaft endfloat as described in Section 18, then proceed as follows.

3 The main bearing caps should be numbered 1 to 5 from the timing chain end of the engine (petrol engines) or from the flywheel end of the engine (diesel engines) **(see**

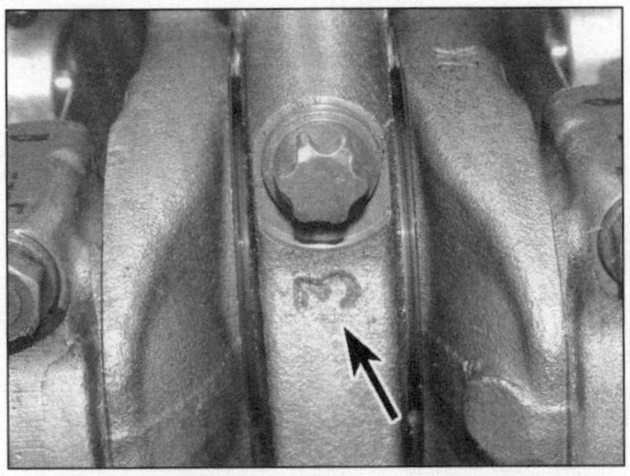

15.3 The main bearing caps are numbered for position

15.4 Removing a main bearing cap bolt

15.6 Lifting the crankshaft from the crankcase

illustration). If not, using quick-drying paint or similar, mark each cap so as to indicate its correct fitted orientation and position.

4 Working from the outer ends to the centre; progressively slacken the main bearing cap retaining bolts by a turn at a time. Once all bolts are loose, unscrew and remove them from the cylinder block **(see illustration)**.

5 Withdraw the bearing caps, and recover the lower main bearing shells. Tape each shell to its respective cap for safekeeping.

6 Carefully lift out the crankshaft, taking care not to displace the upper main bearing shells **(see illustration)**.

7 Recover the upper bearing shells from the cylinder block, and tape them to their respective caps for safekeeping.

8 Remove the thrustwasher halves from the side of No 3 main bearing **(see illustration)**, and store them with the bearing cap.

16 Cylinder block/crankcase – cleaning and inspection

Cleaning

1 Remove all external components and electrical switches/sensors from the block.

2 Scrape all traces of sealant from the cylinder block/crankcase, taking care not to damage the gasket sealing surfaces.

3 Where piston oil jet spray tubes are fitted, to the lower part of the cylinder, these should only be removed by a specialist, as damage may occur on removal

4 Remove all oil gallery plugs (where fitted). The plugs are usually very tight – they may have to be drilled out, and the holes retapped. Use new plugs when the engine is reassembled.

5 If any of the castings are extremely dirty, all should be steam-cleaned, or cleaned with a suitable degreasing agent.

6 After cleaning, clean all oil holes and oil galleries one more time. Flush all internal passages with warm water until the water runs clear. Dry thoroughly, and apply a light film of oil to the cylinder bores to prevent rusting. If possible, use compressed air to speed up the drying process, and to blow out all the oil holes and galleries.

Warning: Wear eye protection when using compressed air.

7 If the castings are not very dirty, you can do an adequate cleaning job with very hot, soapy water and a stiff brush. Take plenty of time, and do a thorough job. Regardless of the cleaning method used, be sure to clean all oil holes and galleries very thoroughly, and to dry all components well. Protect the cylinder bores as described above, to prevent rusting.

8 All threaded holes must be clean, to ensure accurate torque readings during reassembly. To clean the threads, run the correct-size tap into each of the holes to remove rust, corrosion, thread sealant or sludge, and to restore damaged threads. If possible, use compressed air to clear the holes of debris produced by this operation.

9 Apply suitable sealant to the new oil gallery plugs, and insert them into the holes in the block. Tighten them securely.

10 If the engine is not going to be reassembled right away, cover it with a large plastic bag to keep it clean; protect all mating surfaces and the cylinder bores as described above, to prevent rusting.

Inspection

11 Visually check the casting for cracks and corrosion. Look for stripped threads in the threaded holes. If there has been any history of internal water leakage, it may be worthwhile having an engine reconditioning specialist check the cylinder block/crankcase with special equipment. If defects are found, have them repaired if possible, or obtain a new block.

12 Check each cylinder bore for scuffing and scoring. Check for signs of a wear ridge at the top of the cylinder, indicating that the bore is excessively worn.

13 Accurate measuring of the cylinder bores requires specialised equipment and experience. We recommend having the bores measured by an automotive engineering workshop, which will also be able to supply appropriate pistons should a rebore be necessary.

14 If the cylinder bores and pistons are in reasonably good condition, and not worn to the specified limits, and if the piston-to-bore clearances can be maintained properly, then it will only be necessary to renew the piston rings. If this is the case, the bores should be honed, to allow the new rings to bed in correctly and provide the best possible seal. An engine reconditioning specialist will carry out this work at moderate cost.

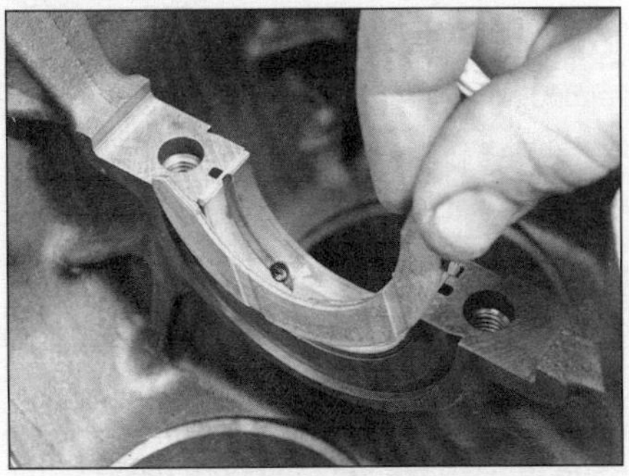

15.8 Removing the crankshaft thrustwashers

17.2 Removing a piston ring with the aid of a feeler gauge

17 Piston/connecting rod assembly – inspection

1 Before the inspection process can begin, the piston/connecting rod assemblies must be cleaned, and the original piston rings removed from the pistons.

Note: *Always use new piston rings when the engine is reassembled.*

2 Carefully expand the old rings over the top of the pistons. The use of two or three old feeler blades will be helpful in preventing the rings dropping into empty grooves **(see illustration)**. Be careful not to scratch the

18.2 Checking the crankshaft endfloat with a dial gauge

piston with the ends of the ring. The rings are brittle, and will snap if they are spread too far. They're also very sharp – protect your hands and fingers.

3 Scrape away all traces of carbon from the top of the piston. A hand-held wire brush (or a piece of fine emery cloth) can be used, once the majority of the deposits have been scraped away.

4 Remove the carbon from the ring grooves in the piston, using an old ring. Break the ring in half to do this. Be careful to remove only the carbon deposits – do not remove any metal, and do not nick or scratch the sides of the ring grooves.

5 Once the deposits have been removed, clean the piston/connecting rod assembly with paraffin or a suitable solvent, and dry thoroughly. Make sure that the oil return holes in the ring grooves are clear.

6 If the pistons and cylinder bores are not damaged or worn excessively, and if the cylinder block does not need to be rebored, the original pistons can be refitted. Normal piston wear shows up as even vertical wear on the piston thrust surfaces, and slight looseness of the top ring in its groove. New piston rings, however, should always be used when the engine is reassembled.

7 Carefully inspect each piston for cracks around the skirt, around the gudgeon pin holes, and at the piston ring 'lands' (between the ring grooves).

8 Look for scoring and scuffing on the piston skirt, holes in the piston crown, and burned areas at the edge of the crown. If the skirt is scored or scuffed, the engine may have been suffering from overheating, and/or abnormal combustion, which caused excessively high operating temperatures. The cooling and lubrication systems should be checked thoroughly. Scorch marks on the sides of the pistons show that blow-by has occurred. A hole in the piston crown, or burned areas at the edge of the piston crown, indicates that abnormal combustion (pre-ignition, knocking, or detonation) has been occurring. If any of the above problems exist, the causes must be investigated and corrected, or the damage will occur again.

9 Corrosion of the piston, in the form of pitting, indicates that coolant has been leaking into the combustion chamber and/ or the crankcase. Again, the cause must be corrected, or the problem may persist in the rebuilt engine.

10 Measure the piston ring-to-groove clearance by placing a new piston ring in each ring groove and measuring the clearance with a feeler blade. Check the clearance at three or four places around each groove. If the measured clearance is greater than specified, new pistons will be required.

11 Accurate measurement of the pistons requires specialised equipment and experience. We recommend having the piston measured by an automotive engineering workshop, which will also be able to supply appropriate pistons should a rebore be necessary.

12 Check the fit of the gudgeon pin by twisting the piston and connecting rod in opposite directions. Any noticeable play indicates excessive wear of the gudgeon pin, piston, or connecting rod small-end bearing.

13 If necessary, on models with circlips securing the gudgeon pin in place, the pistons and connecting rods can be separated and reassembled as follows. Before removing the piston from the connecting rod, mark both components to make sure they are fitted in the same position on reassembly.

Note: *On models with no circlips fitted, the gudgeon pin is a press fit in the top of the connecting rod. On these types, we recommend having the pistons removed by an automotive engineering workshop.*

14 Using a small screwdriver, prise out the circlips, and push out the gudgeon pin. If necessary, support the piston, and tap the pin out using a suitable hammer and punch, taking great care not to mark the piston/ connecting rod bores. Identify the piston, gudgeon pin and rod to ensure correct reassembly. Discard the circlips – new ones must be used on refitting.

15 Examine each connecting rod carefully for signs of damage, such as cracks around the big-end and small-end bearings. Check that the rod is not bent or distorted. Damage is highly unlikely, unless the engine has been seized or badly overheated. Detailed checking of the connecting rod assembly and any remedial action necessary can only be carried out by an engine reconditioning specialist with the necessary equipment.

16 To refit the pistons, position the piston on the connecting rod so that the markings noted on removal are positioned correctly in relation to both components.

17 Where applicable, apply a smear of clean engine oil to the gudgeon pin. Slide it into the piston and through the connecting rod small-end. If necessary, tap the pin into position using a hammer and suitable punch, whilst ensuring that the piston is securely supported. Check that the piston pivots freely on the rod, then secure the gudgeon pin in position with two new circlips. Ensure that each circlip is correctly located in its groove in the piston.

Note: *Gudgeon pin installation will be greatly eased if the piston is first warmed.*

18 Crankshaft – inspection

Checking endfloat

1 If the crankshaft endfloat is to be checked, this must be done when the crankshaft is still installed in the cylinder block/crankcase, but is free to move (see Section 15).

2 Check the endfloat using a dial gauge in contact with the end of the crankshaft. Push the crankshaft fully one way, and then zero the gauge. Push the crankshaft fully the other way, and check the endfloat **(see illustration)**. The result can be compared with the specified amount, and will give an indication as to whether new thrustwashers are required.

3 If a dial gauge is not available, feeler blades can be used. First push the crankshaft fully towards the flywheel/driveplate end of the engine, then use feeler blades to measure the gap between the No 4 crankpin web and No 3 main bearing thrustwasher.

Inspection

4 Clean the crankshaft using paraffin or a suitable solvent, and dry it, preferably with compressed air if available. Be sure to clean the oil holes with a pipe cleaner or similar probe, to ensure that they are not obstructed.

Warning: Wear eye protection when using compressed air.

5 Check the main and big-end bearing journals for uneven wear, scoring, pitting and cracking.

6 Big-end bearing wear is accompanied by distinct metallic knocking when the engine is running (particularly noticeable when the engine is pulling from low speed) and some loss of oil pressure.

7 Main bearing wear is accompanied by severe engine vibration and rumble – getting progressively worse as engine speed increases – and again by loss of oil pressure.

8 Check the bearing journal for roughness by running a finger lightly over the bearing surface. Any roughness (which will be accompanied by obvious bearing wear) indicates that the crankshaft requires regrinding (where possible) or renewal.

9 Check the oil seal contact surfaces at each end of the crankshaft for wear and damage. If the seal has worn a deep groove in the surface of the crankshaft, consult an engine overhaul specialist; repair may be possible, but otherwise a new crankshaft will be required.

10 Accurate measurement of the crankshaft requires specialised equipment and experience. We recommend having the crankshaft measured by an automotive engineering workshop, which will also be able to supply appropriate journal bearings should a regrind be necessary.

11 If the crankshaft has been reground, check for burrs around the crankshaft oil holes (the holes are usually chamfered, so burrs should not be a problem unless regrinding has been carried out carelessly). Remove any burrs with a fine file or scraper, and thoroughly clean the oil holes as described previously.

12 At the time of writing, it was not clear whether Nissan produce undersize bearing shells for all of these engines. On some engines, if the crankshaft journals have not already been reground, it may be possible to have the crankshaft reconditioned, and to fit undersize shells. If no undersize shells are available and the crankshaft has worn beyond the specified limits, it will have to be renewed. Consult your Nissan dealer or engine specialist for further information on parts availability.

19 Main and big-end bearings – inspection

1 Even though the main and big-end bearings should be renewed during the engine overhaul, the old bearings should be retained for close examination, as they may reveal valuable information about the condition of the engine. The bearing shells are graded by thickness, the grade of each shell being indicated by the colour code marked on it.

2 Bearing failure can occur due to lack of lubrication, the presence of dirt or other foreign particles, overloading the engine, or corrosion. Regardless of the cause of bearing failure, the cause must be corrected (where applicable) before the engine is reassembled, to prevent it from happening again **(see illustration)**.

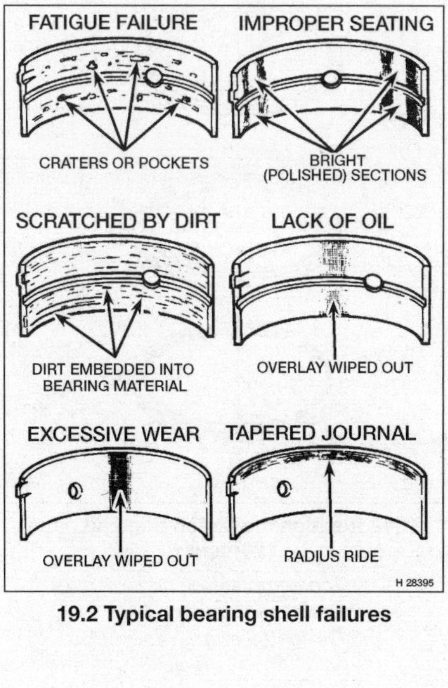

19.2 Typical bearing shell failures

3 When examining the bearing shells, remove them from the cylinder block/crankcase, the main bearing caps, the connecting rods and the connecting rod big-end bearing caps. Lay them out on a clean surface in the same general position as their location in the engine. This will enable you to match any bearing problems with the corresponding crankshaft journal. Do not touch any shell's bearing surface with your fingers while checking it, or the delicate surface may be scratched.

4 Dirt and other foreign matter get into the engine in a variety of ways. It may be left in the engine during assembly, or it may pass through filters or the crankcase ventilation system. It may get into the oil, and from there into the bearings. Metal chips from machining operations and normal engine wear are often present. Abrasives are sometimes left in engine components after reconditioning, especially when parts are not thoroughly cleaned using the proper cleaning methods. Whatever the source, these foreign objects often end up embedded in the soft bearing material, and are easily recognised. Large particles will not embed in the bearing, and will score or gouge the bearing and journal. The best prevention for this cause of bearing failure is to clean all parts thoroughly, and keep everything spotlessly clean during engine assembly. Frequent and regular engine oil and filter changes are also recommended.

5 Lack of lubrication (or lubrication breakdown) has a number of interrelated causes. Excessive heat (which thins the oil), overloading (which squeezes the oil from the bearing face) and oil leakage (from excessive bearing clearances, worn oil pump or high engine speeds) all contribute to lubrication breakdown. Blocked oil passages, which usually are the result of misaligned oil holes in a bearing shell, will also oil-starve a bearing, and destroy it. When lack of lubrication is the cause of bearing failure, the bearing material is wiped or extruded from the steel backing of the bearing. Temperatures may increase to the point where the steel backing turns blue from overheating.

6 Driving habits can have a definite effect on bearing life. Full-throttle, low-speed operation (labouring the engine) puts very high loads on bearings, tending to squeeze out the oil film. These loads cause the bearings to flex, which produces fine cracks in the bearing face (fatigue failure). Eventually, the bearing material will loosen in pieces, and tear away from the steel backing.

7 Short-distance driving leads to corrosion of bearings, because insufficient engine heat is produced to drive off the condensed water and corrosive gases. These products collect in the engine oil, forming acid and sludge. As the oil is carried to the engine bearings, the acid attacks and corrodes the bearing material.

8 Incorrect bearing installation during engine assembly will lead to bearing failure as well. Tight-fitting bearings leave insufficient bearing running clearance, and will result in oil starvation. Dirt or foreign particles trapped behind a bearing shell result in high spots on the bearing, which lead to failure.

9Do not touch any shell's bearing surface with your fingers during reassembly; there is a risk of scratching the delicate surface, or of depositing particles of dirt on it.

10 As mentioned at the beginning of this Section, the bearing shells should be renewed as a matter of course during engine overhaul; to do otherwise is false economy. Refer to Section 22 and Section 23 for details of bearing shell selection.

20 Engine overhaul – reassembly sequence

1 Before reassembly begins, ensure that all new parts have been obtained, and that all necessary tools are available. Read through the entire procedure, to familiarise yourself with the work involved, and to ensure that all items necessary for reassembly of the engine are at hand. In addition to all normal tools and materials, thread–locking compound will be needed. A suitable tube of liquid sealant will also be required for the joint faces that are fitted without gaskets; it is recommended that Nissan's Genuine Liquid Gasket (available from your Nissan dealer) is used.

2 In order to save time and avoid problems, engine reassembly can be carried out in the following order:

a) *Crankshaft (see Section 22 of this Chapter).*
b) *Piston/connecting rod assemblies (see Section 23 of this Chapter).*
c) *Flywheel (see Chapter 2A, 2B or 2C).*
d) *Oil pump (see Chapter 2B or 2C. On 1.2 litre petrol engines, see Section 10 of this Chapter).*
e) *Sump (see Chapter 2A, 2B or 2C).*
f) *Cylinder head (see Chapter 2B. On 1.2 litre petrol engines and diesel engines, see Section 8 and Section 9 of this Chapter respectively).*
g) *Timing chain/belt and sprockets (see Chapter 2B or 2C. On 1.2 litre petrol engines, see Section 6 of this Chapter).*
h) *Inlet and exhaust manifolds (see Chapter 4A or 4B).*

3 At this stage, all engine components should be absolutely clean and dry, with all faults repaired. The components should be laid out (or in individual containers) on a completely clean work surface.

21 Piston rings – refitting

1 Before fitting new piston rings, the ring end gaps must be checked as follows.

2 Lay out the piston/connecting rod assemblies and the new piston ring sets, so

21.3 Use the piston to push the rings into the cylinder bores...

that the ring sets will be matched with the same piston and cylinder during the end gap measurement and subsequent engine reassembly.

3 Insert the top ring into the first cylinder, and push it down the bore using the top of the piston **(see illustration)**. This will ensure that the ring remains square with the cylinder walls. Push the ring down into the bore until the piston skirt is level with the block mating surface, then withdraw the piston.

4 Measure the end gap using feeler gauges, and compare the measurements with the figures given in the Specifications **(see illustration)**.

5 If the gap is too small (unlikely if reputable parts are used), it must be enlarged, or the ring ends may contact each other during engine operation, causing serious damage. Ideally, new piston rings providing the correct end gap should be fitted. As a last resort, the end gap can be increased by carefully filing the ring ends with a fine file. Mount the file in a vice with soft jaws, slip the ring over the file with the ends contacting the file face, and slowly move the ring to remove material from the ends. Take care, as piston rings are sharp, and are easily broken.

6 With new piston rings, it is unlikely that the end gap will be too large. If the gaps are too large, check that you have the correct rings for the engine and for the particular cylinder bore size.

7 Repeat the checking procedure for each ring in the first cylinder, and then for the rings in the remaining cylinders. Remember to keep rings, pistons and cylinders matched up.

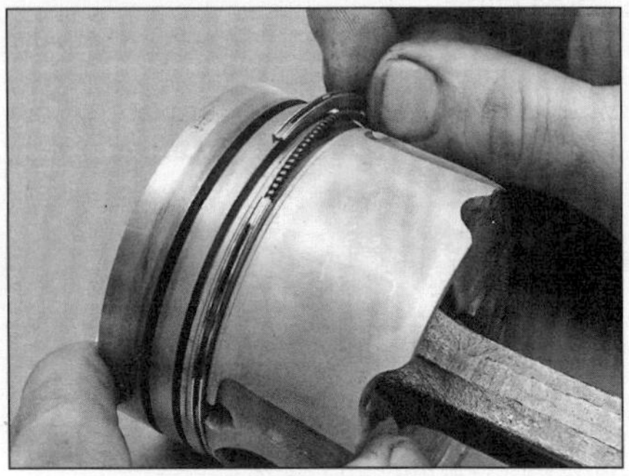

21.9b ...followed by the ring

21.4 ...then measure the ring end gaps

8 Once the ring end gaps have been checked and if necessary corrected, the rings can be fitted to the pistons.

Note: *Always follow any instructions supplied with the new piston ring sets – different manufacturers may specify different procedures. Do not mix up the top and second compression rings, as they have different cross-sections.*

9 The oil control ring (lowest on the piston) is installed first. It is composed of three separate components. Slip the expander into the groove, then install the upper side rail into the groove between the expander and the ring land, and then install the lower side rail in the same manner **(see illustrations)**.

10 Install the second ring next. Note that the second ring and top ring are different, and can be identified by their cross-sections. Making sure the ring is the correct way up, fit the ring into the middle groove on the piston, taking care not to expand the ring any more than is necessary **(see illustration)**.

11 Install the top ring in the same way; making sure the ring is the correct way up. Where the ring is symmetrical, fit it with its identification marking facing upwards.

12 With all the rings in position on the piston, space the ring end gaps correctly **(see illustration)**.

13 Repeat the above procedure for the remaining pistons and rings.

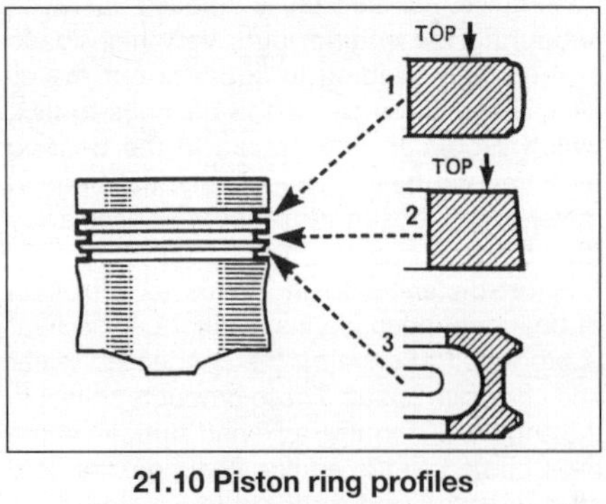

21.10 Piston ring profiles

1 Top compression ring
2 Lower compression ring
3 Oil control ring
Position the TOP markings as shown

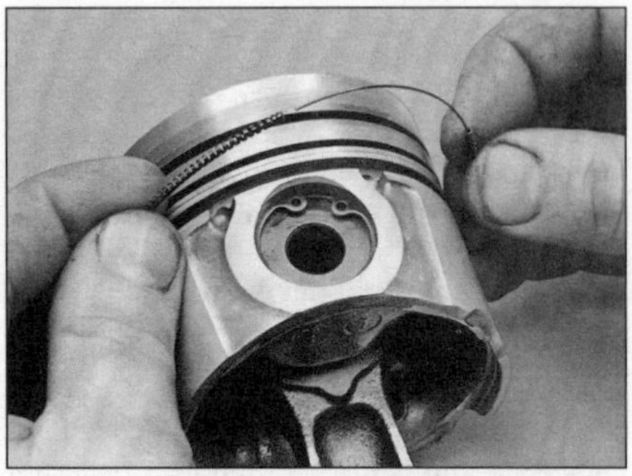

21.9a Fit the oil control ring expander...

22 Crankshaft – bearing selection and refitting

Bearing selection

1 Main bearings for the engines described in this Chapter are available in standard sizes and a range of undersizes to suit reground crankshafts. Refer to your Nissan dealer or automotive engineering workshop for details.

Refitting

2 Clean the backs of the bearing shells, and the bearing locations in both the cylinder block and the main bearing caps.

3 Press the bearing shells into their locations in the cylinder block and main bearing caps. As there are no locating tabs on the bearing shells, visually centralise each shell in its location. Take care not to touch any shell's bearing surface with your fingers. Note that all the upper bearing shells have oil holes in them; and are sometimes grooved, the lower shells are plain.

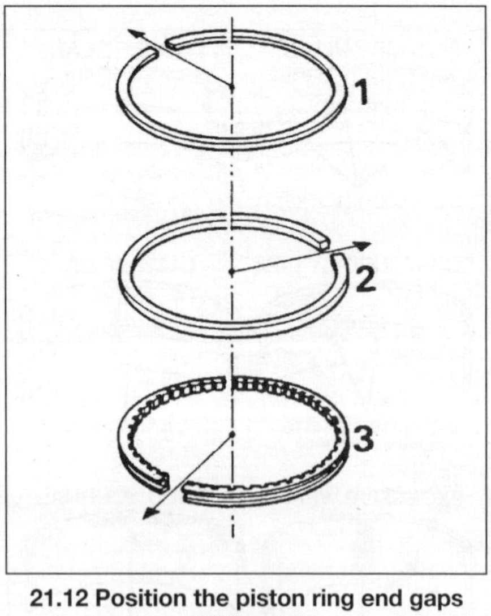

21.12 Position the piston ring end gaps 120° apart

1 Top compression ring
2 Lower compression ring
3 Oil control ring

22.5a Smear a little grease on the crankshaft thrustwashers...

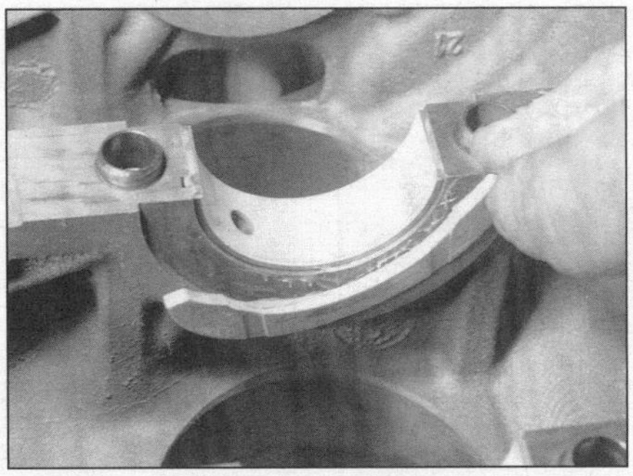

22.5b ...and stick them to the centre main bearing

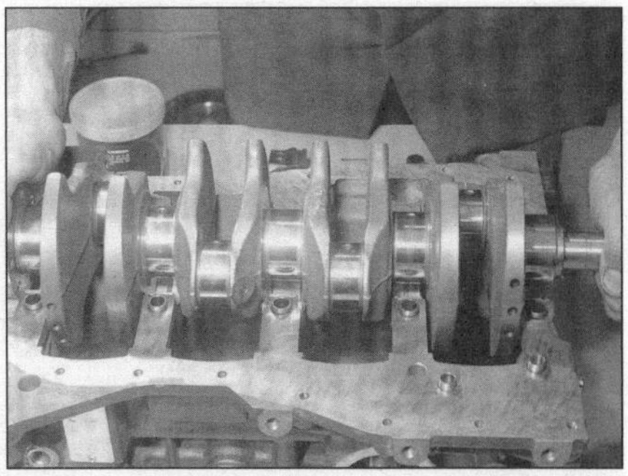

22.6 Lay the crankshaft in position in the crankcase

22.9 Fitting No 5 main bearing cap – diesel engine

22.10a Tighten the main bearing cap bolts to the specified torque...

22.10b ...then through the specified angle

4 Wipe dry the shells with a lint-free cloth. Liberally lubricate each bearing shell in the cylinder block/crankcase with clean engine oil.

5 Using a little grease, stick the upper thrustwashers to each side of the No 3 main bearing upper location; ensure that the oilway grooves on each thrustwasher face outwards (away from the cylinder block) **(see illustrations)**.

6 Lower the crankshaft into position **(see illustration)**, and check the crankshaft endfloat as described in Section 18.

7 Thoroughly degrease the mating surfaces of the cylinder block and the main bearing caps.

8 Lubricate the lower bearing shells in the main bearing caps with clean engine oil. Make sure that the bearing shell is still centralised in the cap.

9 Fit the main bearing caps **(see illustration)**, using the identification marks to ensure that they are installed in the correct locations and are fitted the correct way round. Insert the retaining bolts, tightening them by hand only.

10 Working in sequence, starting from the centre and working outwards, tighten the bearing cap retaining bolts to the specified Stage 1 torque setting. Go around in the same sequence and tighten the bolts through the specified Stage 2 angle, using an angle tightening gauge **(see illustrations)**. Check that the crankshaft rotates freely before proceeding any further.

11 Fit the piston/connecting rod assemblies as described in Section 23.

12 On diesel engines, fit a new crankshaft left-hand oil seal as described in Chapter 2C, Section 13.

23 Piston/connecting rod assembly – bearing selection and refitting

Bearing selection

1 Big-end bearings for the engines described in this Chapter are available in standard sizes and a range of undersizes to suit reground crankshafts. Refer to your Nissan dealer or automotive engineering workshop for details.

Refitting

2 Clean the backs of the bearing shells, and the bearing locations in both the connecting rod and bearing cap.

3 Press the bearing shells into their locations in the connecting rods and caps. As there are no locating tabs on the bearing shells, visually centralise each shell in its location. Take care not to touch any shell's bearing surface with your fingers, and ensure that the shells are correctly installed so that the upper shell oil hole is correctly aligned with the connecting rod oil hole.

4 Note that the following procedure assumes that the crankshaft and main bearing caps are in place (see Section 22).

5 Wipe dry the shells and connecting rods with a lint-free cloth.

6 Lubricate the cylinder bores, the pistons, and piston rings **(see illustration)**, then lay out each piston/connecting rod assembly in its respective position.

7 Start with assembly No 1. Make sure that the piston rings are still spaced as described in Section 21, and then clamp them in position with a piston ring compressor.

8 Insert the piston/connecting rod assembly into the top of cylinder No 1. Ensure that the piston marking (in the form of either an arrow, letter or a dot) on the piston crown is on the correct side of the bore, as noted on removal. Using a block of wood or hammer handle

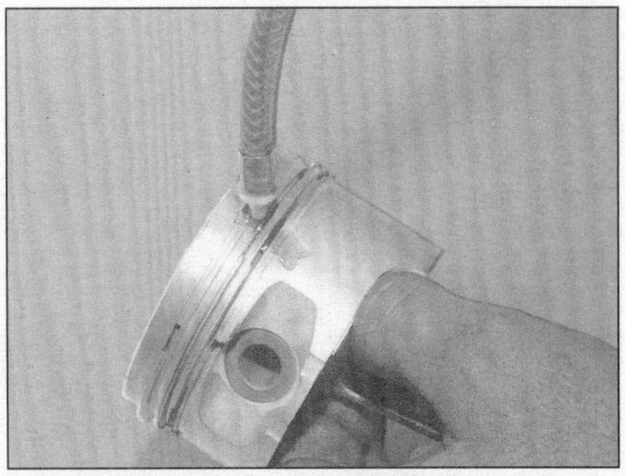

23.6 Lubricating the piston rings

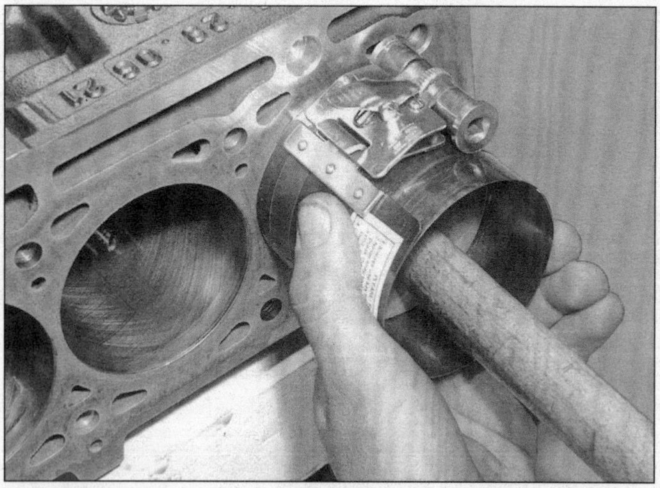

23.8 Using the wooden handle of a hammer to drive the piston into the bore

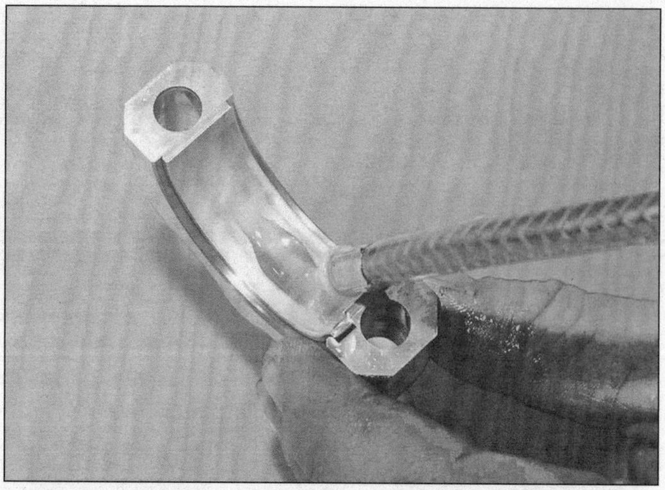

23.9 Lubricate the big-end cap bearing shell then refit the cap

against the piston crown, tap the assembly into the cylinder until the piston crown is flush with the top of the cylinder **(see illustration)**.

9 Ensure that the bearing shell is still correctly installed. Liberally lubricate the crankpin and both bearing shells. Taking care not to mark the cylinder bores, tap the piston/connecting rod assembly down the bore and onto the crankpin. Refit the big-end bearing cap **(see illustration)**, tightening its retaining bolts finger-tight at first. Note that the faces with the identification marks must match.

10 Tighten the bearing cap retaining bolts to the specified torque, then through the specified angle in the Stages given in the Specifications.

11 Rotate the crankshaft. Check that it turns freely; some stiffness is to be expected if new components have been fitted, but there should be no signs of binding or tight spots.

12 Refit the three remaining piston/connecting rod assemblies in the same way.

13 On 1.2 litre petrol engines, refit the main bearing cap support beam and progressively tighten the retaining bolts to the specified torque.

14 On all petrol engines, apply a bead of sealant to the mating face and refit the upper alloy part of the sump to the bottom of the cylinder block. Tighten all retaining bolts to the specified torque. With the upper alloy part of the sump in place, fit a new crankshaft left-hand oil seal, then refit the flywheel, referring to Chapter 2A or 2B as applicable.

15 Refit the cylinder head, oil pump, timing chain/belt and sump as described in the relevant Sections of this Chapter or in Chapter 2A, 2B or 2C as applicable.

24 Engine – initial start-up after overhaul

1 With the engine refitted in the vehicle, double-check the engine oil and coolant levels. Make a final check that everything has been reconnected, and that there are no tools or rags left in the engine compartment.

2 On diesel engine models, prime and bleed the fuel system as described in Chapter 4B, Section 5. Turn the ignition on and wait for the preheating warning light to go out.

3 Start the engine, noting that this may take a little longer than usual, due to the fuel system components having been disturbed.

4 Once started, keep the engine running at a fast tickover. Check that the oil pressure warning light goes out, then check that there are no leaks of oil, fuel and coolant. Don't be alarmed if there are some odd smells and smoke from parts getting hot and burning off oil deposits.

5 Assuming all is well; keep the engine idling until hot water is felt circulating through the top hose, then switch off the engine.

6 After a few minutes recheck the oil and coolant levels as described in *Weekly checks*, and top-up as necessary.

7 Note that there is no need to retighten the cylinder head bolts once the engine has first run after reassembly.

8 If new pistons, rings or crankshaft bearings have been fitted, the engine must be treated as new, and run-in for the first 500 miles. Do not operate the engine at full-throttle, or allow it to labour at low engine speeds in any gear. It is recommended that the oil and filter be changed at the end of this period.

Chapter 3
Cooling, heating and ventilation systems

Contents

Degrees of difficulty

Easy, suitable for novice with little experience	**Fairly easy,** suitable for beginner with some experience	**Fairly difficult,** suitable for competent DIY mechanic	**Difficult,** suitable for experienced DIY mechanic	**Very difficult,** suitable for expert DIY or professional

Specifications

General

Cooling system type	Pressurised sealed system, with front mounted radiator and electric cooling fan
Cooling system pressure:	
1.2 litre petrol engines	1.4 bar
1.6 litre petrol engines	0.8 to 1.0 bar
Diesel engines	1.3 to 1.5 bar
Reservoir capacity	0.6 litres

Thermostat

Opening temperature:	
1.2 litre petrol engines	77 to 80°C
1.6 litre petrol engines	80.5 to 83.5°C
Diesel engines	83°C

Air conditioning

Compressor model:	
1.2 litre petrol engines	Calsonic Kansei CR-12Sb
1.6 litre petrol engines	Calsonic Kansei CR-08b
Diesel engines	Calsonic Kansei CR-12Sb
Compressor type	Vane rotary
Compressor oil:	
Quantity	150 ml
Type	R (DH–PR)
Refrigerant	
Quantity	450 g
Type	R134a

Torque wrench settings

	Nm	lbf ft
Petrol engines:		
Air conditioning compressor mounting bolts	25	18
Coolant outlet housing (end of cylinder head) bolts	25	18
Coolant pump pulley securing bolts	8	6
Coolant pump securing bolts	25	18
Coolant temperature sensor	25	18
Thermostat cover securing bolts:		
1.2 litre engines	21	15
1.6 litre engines	17	13
Diesel engines:		
Air conditioning compressor mounting bolts	21	15
Coolant outlet housing (end of cylinder head) bolts	11	8
Coolant pump securing bolts	11	8

1 General information and precautions

General information

1 The cooling system is of the pressurised type, comprising a coolant pump, crossflow radiator, coolant expansion tank, electric cooling fan, thermostat, heater matrix, and all associated hoses and switches. On petrol engines, the coolant pump is driven by the auxiliary drivebelt from the crankshaft pulley. On diesel engines, the coolant pump is driven by the timing belt.

2 The system functions as follows. The coolant pump pumps cold coolant around the cylinder block and head passages, and through the heater, throttle housing, oil cooler and certain emission control components, to the thermostat.

3 When the engine is cold, the coolant is returned from the closed thermostat to the coolant pump. When the coolant reaches a predetermined temperature, the thermostat opens, and the coolant passes to the radiator. As the coolant circulates through the radiator, it is cooled by the inrush of air when the car is in forward motion. The airflow is supplemented by the action of the electric cooling fan when necessary. Upon reaching the bottom of the radiator, the coolant has now cooled, and the cycle is repeated.

4 When the engine is at normal operating temperature, the coolant expands, and some of it is released through the valve in the radiator pressure cap into the expansion tank. Coolant collects in the tank, and is returned to the radiator when the system cools.

5 The electric cooling fan assembly is mounted behind the radiator and controlled by the engine management electronic control unit in conjunction with the engine coolant temperature sensor.

Precautions

⚠ ***Warning: Do not attempt to remove the radiator/expansion tank pressure cap, or to disturb any part of the cooling system, while the engine is hot, as there is a high risk of scalding. If the pressure cap must be removed before the engine and radiator have fully cooled (even though this is not recommended), the pressure in the cooling system must first be relieved. Cover the cap with a thick layer of cloth, to avoid scalding, and slowly unscrew the pressure cap until a hissing sound is heard. When the hissing has stopped, indicating that the pressure has reduced, slowly unscrew the pressure cap until it can be removed; if more hissing sounds are heard, wait until they have stopped before unscrewing the cap completely. At all times, keep your face well away from the pressure cap opening, and protect your hands.***

⚠ ***Warning: Do not allow antifreeze to come into contact with your skin, or with the painted surfaces of the vehicle. Rinse off spills immediately, with plenty of water. Never leave antifreeze lying around in an open container, or in a puddle in the driveway or on the garage floor. Children and pets are attracted by its sweet smell, but antifreeze can be fatal if ingested.***

⚠ ***Warning: If the engine is hot, the electric cooling fan may start rotating even if the engine is not running. Be careful to keep your hands, hair, and any loose clothing well clear when working in the engine compartment.***

⚠ ***Warning: Refer to Section 10 for precautions to be observed when working on models equipped with air conditioning.***

2 Cooling system hoses – disconnection and renewal

1 The number, routing and pattern of hoses will vary according to model, but the same basic procedure applies. Before commencing work, make sure that the new hoses are to hand, along with new hose clips if needed. It is good practice to renew the hose clips at the same time as the hoses.

2 Drain the cooling system, as described in Chapter 1A, Section 25 (petrol engines) or Chapter 1B, Section 26 (diesel engines) saving the coolant if it is fit for re-use. Squirt a little penetrating oil onto the hose clips if they are corroded.

3 Release the hose clips from the hose concerned. Three types of clip are used; worm-drive, spring and 'sardine-can'. The worm-drive clip is released by turning its screw anti-clockwise. The spring clip is released by squeezing its tangs together with pliers, at the same time working the clip away from the hose stub. The 'sardine-can' clip is not re-usable, and is best cut off with snips or side-cutters.

4 Unclip any wires, cables or other hoses, which may be attached to the hose being removed. Make notes for reference when reassembling if necessary.

5 Release the hose from its stubs with a twisting motion. Be careful not to damage the stubs on delicate components such as the radiator. If the hose is stuck fast, the best course is often to cut it off using a sharp knife, but again be careful not to damage the stubs.

6 Before fitting the new hose, smear the stubs with washing-up liquid or a suitable rubber lubricant to aid fitting. Do not use oil or grease, which may attack the rubber.

7 Fit the hose clips over the ends of the hose, and then fit the hose over its stubs. Work the hose into position. When satisfied, locate and tighten the hose clips.

8 Refill the cooling system as described in Chapter 1A, Section 25 or Chapter 1B, Section 26. Run the engine, and check that there are no leaks.

9 Recheck the tightness of the hose clips on any new hoses after a few hundred miles.

10 Top-up the coolant level if necessary.

3 Radiator – removal, inspection and refitting

Note: *If leakage is the reason for removing the radiator, bear in mind that minor leaks can often be cured using a radiator sealant with the radiator left in position.*

Removal

1.2 litre petrol engines

1 Drain the cooling system as described in Chapter 1A, Section 25.

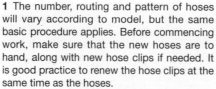

3.4 Undo the bolts securing the condenser to the radiator

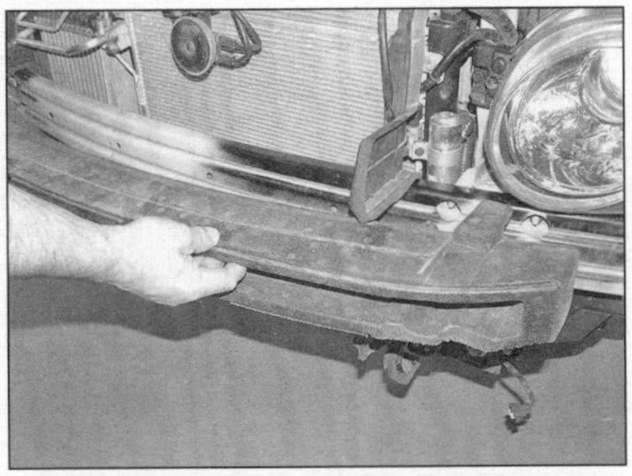

3.10a Remove the energy absorber from the front bumper brace

3.10b Undo the bumper brace retaining nuts each side and remove the brace

2 Disconnect the coolant hoses at the expansion tank, then undo the retaining bolts and remove the tank.

3 Remove the front bumper as described in Chapter 11, Section 6.

4 Undo the upper bolt each side securing the air conditioning condenser to the radiator **(see illustration)**.

5 Using cable ties or similar, suitably attach the condenser to the bonnet lock platform to prevent it dropping down during subsequent operations.

6 Remove the air inlet hose from the intercooler to the turbocharger as described in Chapter 4A, Section 2.

7 Disconnect the remaining coolant hoses from the radiator.

8 Disconnect the wiring harness connectors from the electric cooling fan and move the harness clear.

9 Using cable ties or similar, suitably attach the intercooler and the radiator and cooling fan assembly to the bonnet lock platform to prevent them dropping down during subsequent operations.

10 Remove the front bumper energy absorber, then undo the three nuts each side and remove the bumper brace **(see illustrations)**.

11 Undo the two bolts each side and remove the radiator lower support member **(see illustrations)**.

12 Cut the cable ties or similar used to retain the radiator, then carefully lower the radiator and cooling fan assembly. Withdraw the radiator and cooling fan out from under the car.

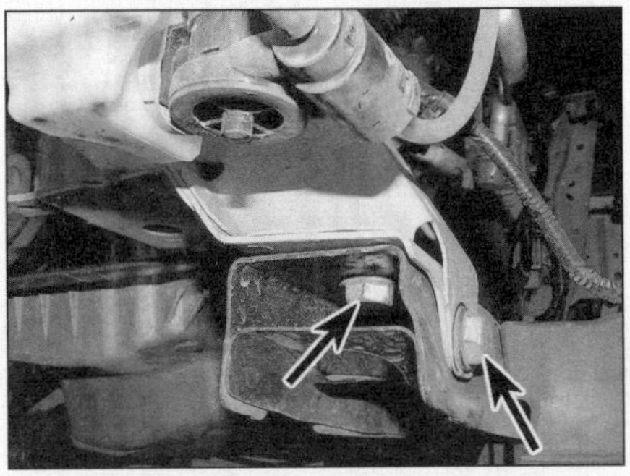

3.11a Undo the two bolts each side...

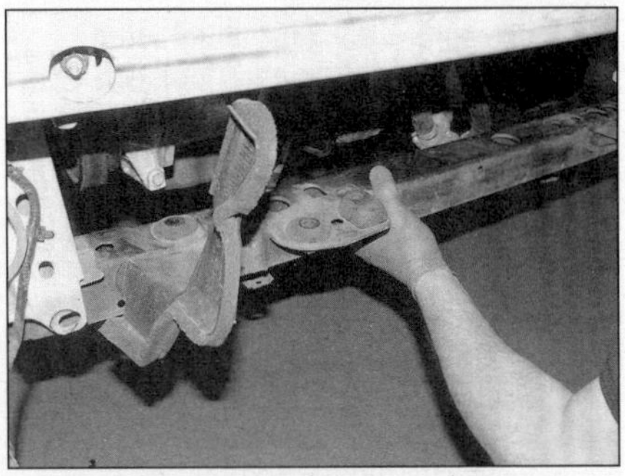

3.11b ...and remove the radiator lower support member

1.6 litre petrol engines

13 Disconnect the battery negative terminal (refer to battery disconnection and reconnection in Chapter 5A, Section 3).

14 Drain the cooling system as described in Chapter 1A, Section 25.

15 Remove the upper and lower radiator hoses.

16 Remove the front bumper as described in Chapter 11, Section 6.

17 Depress the retaining tab at the front of the coolant expansion tank and lift the tank upwards from its location **(see illustration)**. Disconnect the coolant hose and remove the expansion tank. Be prepared for coolant spillage.

18 Remove the combination lights as described in Chapter 12, Section 5.

19 Undo the two bolts and remove the horn bracket from the bonnet lock platform **(see illustration)**.

20 Remove the bonnet lock as described in Chapter 11, Section 10. Disengage the release cable from the retaining clip on the bonnet lock platform.

21 Extract the upper plastic expanding rivet securing the air guides to the bonnet lock platform on each side **(see illustration)**.

22 Suitably support the bonnet in the open position, then disengage and remove the bonnet support rod.

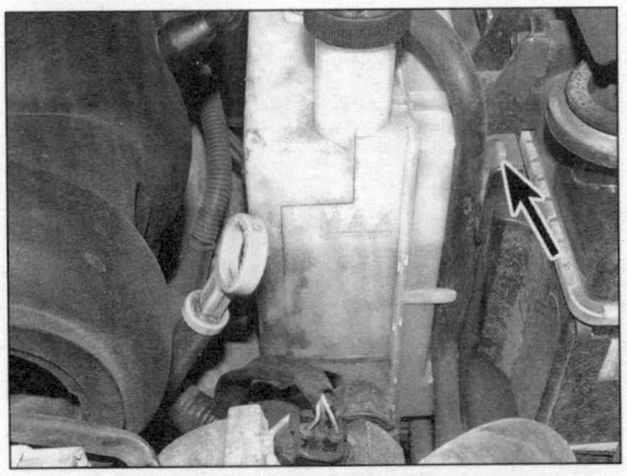

3.17 Depress the retaining tab and lift out the expansion tank

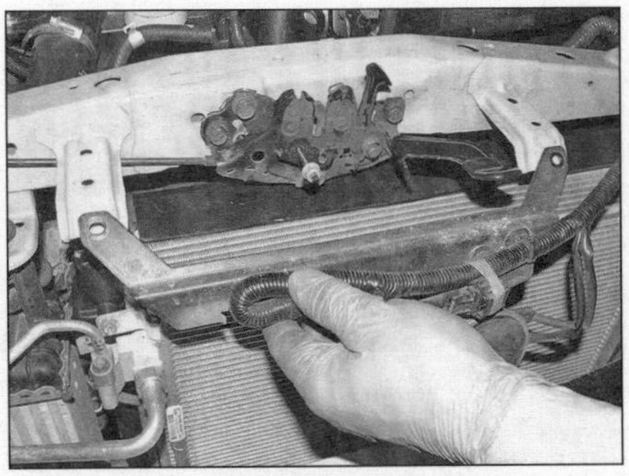

3.19 Remove the horn bracket from the bonnet lock platform

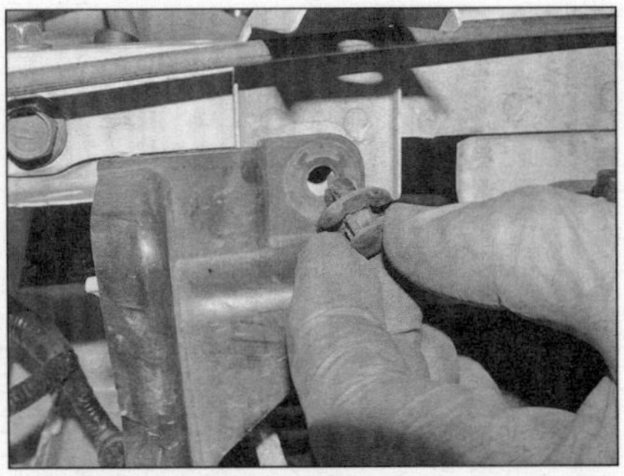

3.21 Extract the expanding rivets securing the air guides

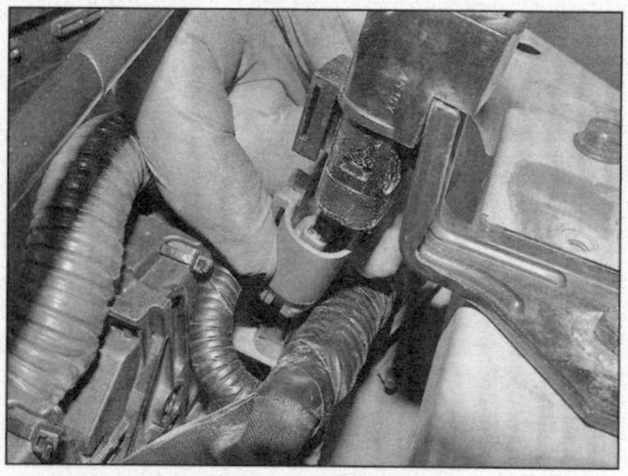

3.23 Disconnect the bonnet closure switch wiring connector

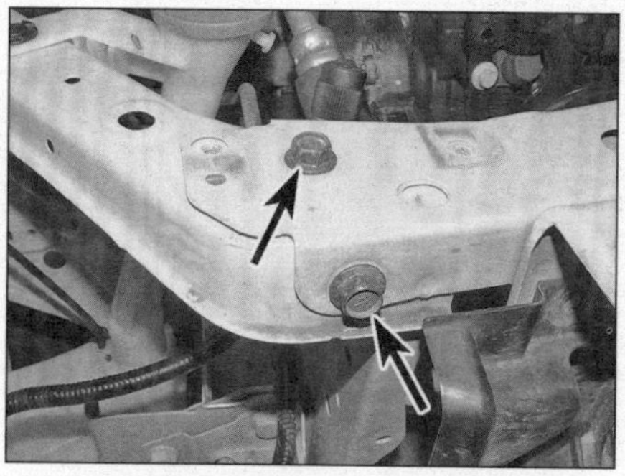

3.24 Undo the bonnet lock platform retaining bolts on each side

3.39 Remove the bonnet lock platform

23 Disconnect the wiring connector from the bonnet closure switch **(see illustration)**.

24 Undo the two bolts each side and lift off the bonnet lock platform **(see illustration)**.

25 Disconnect the wiring harness connectors from the electric cooling fan and move the harness clear.

26 Lift the radiator and cooling fan assembly upward and out of the engine compartment.

Diesel engines

27 Disconnect the battery negative terminal (refer to battery disconnection and reconnection in Chapter 5A, Section 3).

28 Drain the cooling system as described in Chapter 1B, Section 26.

29 Disconnect the coolant hoses at the expansion tank, then undo the retaining bolts and remove the tank.

30 Remove the front bumper as described in Chapter 11, Section 6.

31 Remove the air inlet hose from the intercooler to the turbocharger as described in Chapter 4B, Section 2.

32 Remove the upper and lower radiator hoses.

33 Remove the combination lights as described in Chapter 12, Section 7.

34 Undo the two bolts and remove the horn bracket from the bonnet lock platform **(see illustration 3.19)**.

35 Remove the bonnet lock as described in Chapter 11, Section 10. Disengage the release cable from the retaining clip on the bonnet lock platform.

36 Extract the upper plastic expanding rivet securing the air guides to the bonnet lock platform on each side **(see illustration 3.21)**.

37 Suitably support the bonnet in the open position, then disengage and remove the bonnet support rod.

38 Disconnect the wiring connector from the bonnet closure switch **(see illustration 3.23)**.

39 Undo the two bolts each side and lift off the bonnet lock platform **(see illustration)**.

40 Disconnect the wiring harness connectors from the electric cooling fan and move the harness clear **(see illustration)**.

41 Undo the upper bolt each side securing the air conditioning condenser to the radiator **(see illustration)**. Lift the condenser slightly to disengage the lower mountings from the radiator.

42 Lift the radiator and cooling fan assembly upward and out of the engine compartment **(see illustration)**.

Inspection

43 If the radiator has been removed due to suspected blockage, reverse-flush it as described in Chapter 1A, Section 25 or Chapter 1B, Section 26. Clean dirt and debris from the radiator fins, using an airline (in which case, wear eye protection) or a soft brush. Be careful, as the fins are sharp, and easily damaged.

44 If necessary, a radiator specialist can perform a 'flow test' on the radiator, to establish whether an internal blockage exists.

45 A leaking radiator must be referred to a specialist for permanent repair. Do not attempt to weld or solder a leaking radiator, as damage to the plastic components may result.

46 Inspect the condition of the radiator mounting rubbers and renew them if necessary.

Refitting

47 Refitting is a reversal of removal. On completion, refill the cooling system as described in Chapter 1A, Section 25 or Chapter 1B, Section 26.

4 Thermostat – removal, testing and refitting

Removal

1.2 litre petrol engines

1 The thermostat is located in a housing bolted to the front facing side of the cylinder block..

2 Drain the cooling system as described in Chapter 1A, Section 25.

3 Remove the inlet manifold as described in Chapter 4A, Section 14.

4 Noting their fitted position slacken the retaining clips and disconnect the cooling system hoses from the thermostat housing.

5 Where applicable, disconnect the housing wiring connector.

6 Place a suitable container beneath the

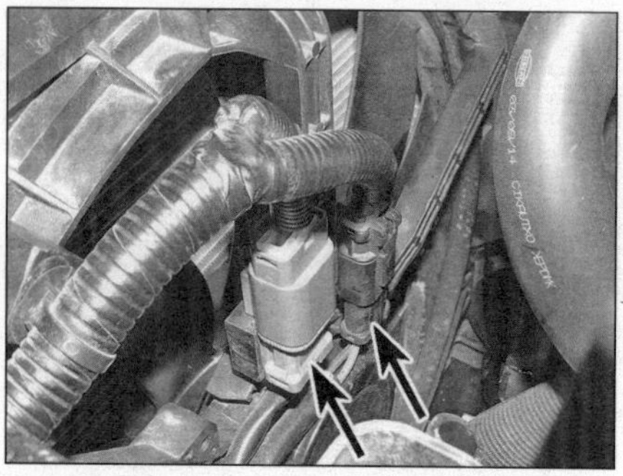

3.40 Disconnect the wiring connectors at the electric cooling fan

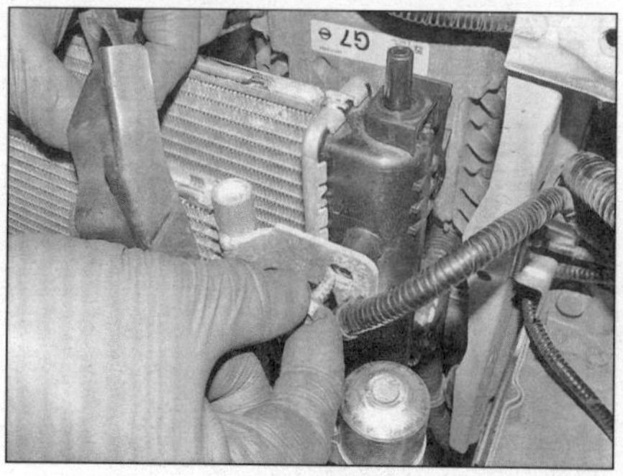

3.41 Undo the condenser securing bolts each side

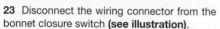

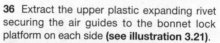

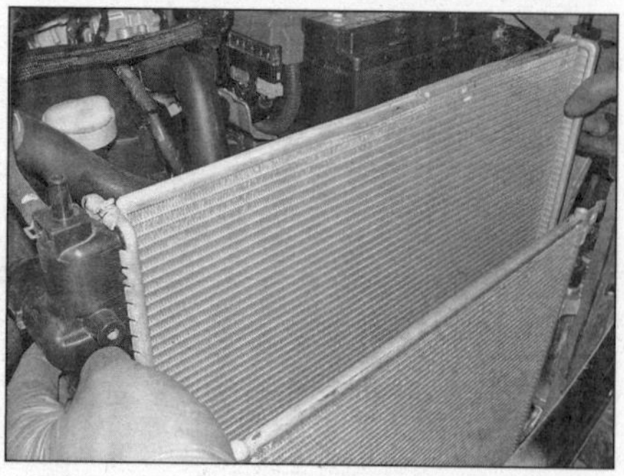

3.42 Lift out the radiator and cooling fan assembly

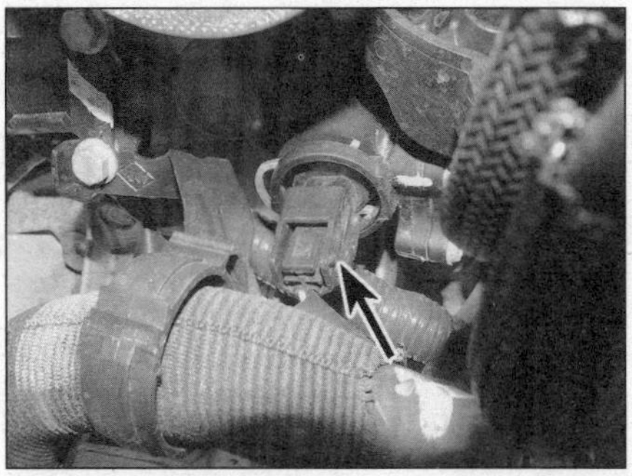

4.17 Disconnect the wiring connector from the temperature sensor

4.19a Undo the coolant housing upper bolts...

4.19b ...and lower bolt

thermostat housing and be prepared for coolant spillage.

7 Undo the two bolts and remove the thermostat housing from the cylinder block. Recover the sealing ring. Note that the thermostat is integral with the housing and cannot be separated.

1.6 litre petrol engines

8 The thermostat is located in a housing bolted to the front facing side of the cylinder block.

9 Drain the cooling system as described in Chapter 1A, Section 25.

10 Slacken the retaining clip and disconnect the radiator hose from the thermostat housing.

11 Place a suitable container beneath the thermostat housing and be prepared for coolant spillage.

12 Undo the two bolts and remove the thermostat housing from the cylinder block. Withdraw the thermostat from the housing and recover the sealing ring on the thermostat.

Diesel engines

13 The thermostat is located in a housing bolted to the left-hand side of the cylinder head, at the transmission end of the engine.

14 Remove the air cleaner assembly as described in Chapter 4B, Section 2.

15 Remove the vacuum pump as described in Chapter 9, Section 13.

16 Drain the cooling system as described in Chapter 1B, Section 26.

17 Disconnect the wiring connector from the temperature sensor in the coolant housing **(see illustration)**.

18 Noting their fitted position slacken the retaining clips and disconnect the cooling system hoses from the coolant housing.

19 Unscrew the securing bolts, and remove the coolant housing from the cylinder head **(see illustrations)**. Note the fitted position of the support bracket also secured by the housing bolts.

20 Lift the thermostat, O-ring and seal from the housing, noting the fitted position of the thermostat.

Testing

Note: *If there is any question about the operation of the thermostat, it's best to renew it – they are not usually expensive items. Testing involves heating in, or over, an open pan of boiling water, which carries with it the risk of scalding. A thermostat that has seen more than five years' service may well be past its best already.*

21 A rough test of the thermostat may be made by suspending it with a piece of string in a container full of water. Heat the water to bring it to the boil – the thermostat must open by the time the water boils. If not, renew it.

22 If a thermometer is available, the precise opening temperature of the thermostat may be determined; compare with the figures given in the Specifications. The opening temperature is also marked on the thermostat **(see illustration)**.

23 A thermostat, which fails to close as the water cools down, must also be renewed.

Refitting

24 Refitting is a reversal of removal, bearing in mind the following points:

a) *Renew all disturbed O-rings, seals and gaskets.*
b) *On 1.6 litre petrol engines, fit the thermostat with the small jiggle pin uppermost.*
c) *Refill the cooling system as described in Chapter 1A, Section 25 or Chapter 1B, Section 26.*

5 Electric cooling fan – removal and refitting

Removal

1 Remove the radiator and cooling fan assembly as described in Section 3.

2 On 1.6 litre petrol engine models, undo the retaining bolts securing the fan shroud to the radiator.

3 Depress the tabs of the fan shroud upper attachments and slide the shroud up and out of the radiator mountings **(see illustration)**.

4 Detach the fan motor wiring plugs from the fan shroud then release the wiring loom from the shroud clip **(see illustration)**.

5 Undo the retaining nut and remove the

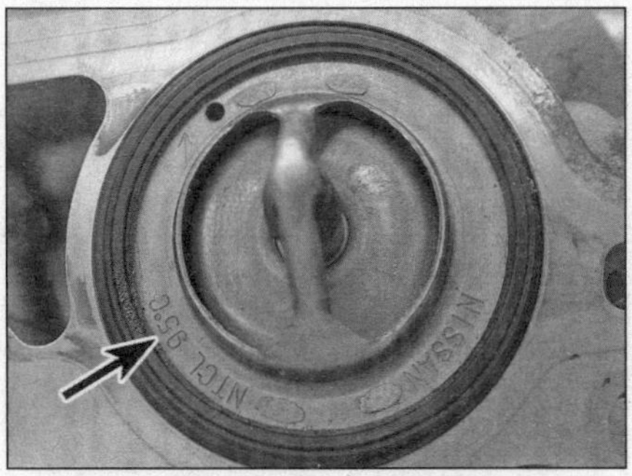

4.22 The temperature opening figure is stamped on the thermostat

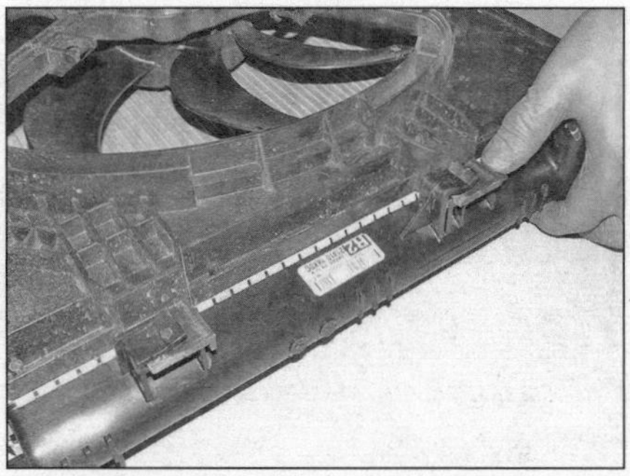

5.3 Depress the tabs and slide the shroud out of the radiator mountings

5.4 Detach the wiring plugs and loom from the fan shroud

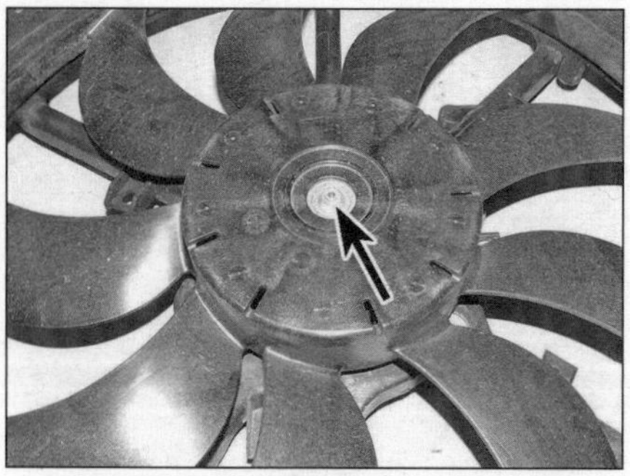

5.5 Undo the retaining nut and remove the fan blades

6.6 Disconnect the wiring connector (1.6 litre petrol engine shown)

6.8a Withdraw the retaining clip...

6.8b ...and remove the sensor and seal

fan blades from the motor spindle **(see illustration)**. Note that on diesel engine models the retaining nut has a left-hand thread and is removed by turning it clockwise.

6 Undo the three retaining bolts and remove the fan motor from the shroud.

Refitting

7 Refitting is a reversal of removal.

6 Coolant temperature sensor – testing, removal and refitting

Testing

1 The sensor is a thermistor. A thermistor is an electronic component whose electrical resistance changes at a predetermined rate as the temperature changes. The engine management electronic control unit (ECU) supplies the sensor with a set voltage and then, by measuring the current flowing in the sensor circuit, determines the engine's temperature. This information is then used, in conjunction with other inputs, to control the engine management system and associated components.

2 If the sensor circuit should fail to provide adequate information, the ECU's back-up facility will override the sensor signal. In this event, the ECU assumes a predetermined setting which will allow the engine management system to run, albeit at reduced efficiency. When this occurs, the warning light on the instrument panel will come on, and a fault code will be stored by the systems self-diagnosis facility – the advice of a Nissan dealer or specialist should be sought. The sensor itself can only be tested using special diagnostic equipment. Do not attempt to test the circuit using any other equipment, as there is a high risk of damaging the ECU.

Removal

3 The sensor is located in the coolant housing bolted to the left-hand side of the cylinder head, at the transmission end of the engine.

4 Disconnect the battery negative terminal (refer to battery disconnection and reconnection in Chapter 5A, Section 3).

5 Partially drain the cooling system to just below the level of the sensor (see Chapter 1A, Section 25 or Chapter 1B, Section 26). Alternatively, have ready a suitable bung to plug the aperture in the housing when the sensor is removed.

6 Disconnect the wiring connector from the sensor **(see illustration)**.

7 On engines where the sensor is screwed into the housing, carefully unscrew the sensor and recover the sealing ring. If the system has not been drained, plug the sensor aperture to prevent further coolant loss.

8 On engines where the sensor is clipped in place, prise out the sensor retaining circlip then remove the sensor and sealing ring from the housing **(see illustrations)**. If the system has not been drained, plug the sensor aperture to prevent further coolant loss.

Refitting

9 Check the condition of the sealing ring and renew it if necessary.

10 Refitting is a reversal of removal, but refill (or top-up) the cooling system as described in Chapter 1A, Section 25 or Chapter 1B, Section 26, and *Weekly checks*.

11 On completion, start the engine and run it until it reaches normal operating temperature. Continue to run the engine until the cooling fan cuts in and out correctly.

7 Coolant pump – removal, inspection and refitting

Removal

1 Disconnect the battery negative terminal (refer to battery disconnection and reconnection in Chapter 5A, Section 3).

2 Drain the cooling system as described in Chapter 1A, Section 25 or Chapter 1B, Section 26.

Petrol engines

3 Remove the auxiliary drivebelt as described in Chapter 1A, Section 12.

4 To make access easier remove the alternator as described in Chapter 5A, Section 5.

5 Unscrew the three retaining bolts, and remove the pulley from the coolant pump **(see illustration)**. If required, counterhold the pulley in order to unscrew the bolts. This is most easily achieved by wrapping an old drivebelt tightly around the pulley to act in a similar manner to a strap wrench.

6 Unscrew the retaining bolts, and withdraw the coolant pump from the cylinder block **(see illustration)**. Remove the gasket and discard, as a new one will be required for refitting.

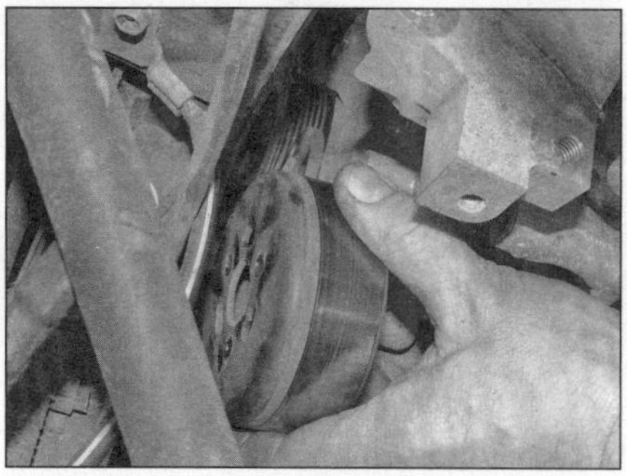

7.5 Remove the coolant pump pulley

7.6 Undo the coolant pump bolts (1.6 litre engine shown)

Diesel engines

7 Remove the timing belt as described in Chapter 2C, Section 6.

8 Undo the retaining bolts and remove the rear timing belt cover from the cylinder block **(see illustration)**.

9 Unscrew the retaining bolts, and remove the coolant pump from the cylinder block **(see illustrations)**. Remove the gasket and discard, as a new one will be required for refitting.

Inspection

10 Check the pump body and impeller for signs of excessive corrosion. Turn the impeller, and check for stiffness due to corrosion, or roughness due to excessive endplay.

11 No spare parts are available for the pump, and if faulty, worn or corroded, a new pump should be fitted.

Refitting

12 Commence refitting by thoroughly cleaning all traces of gasket from the mating faces of the pump and cylinder block.

13 Fit a new gasket to the coolant pump.

14 Place the pump in position in the cylinder block, refit the bolts to their correct locations and tighten to the specified torque.

15 On petrol engines, refit the pump pulley and tighten the retaining bolts to the specified torque. Counterhold the pulley using an old drivebelt as during removal.

16 On diesel engines, refit the timing belt as described in Chapter 2C, Section 6.

17 Refit and tension the auxiliary drivebelts as described in Chapter 1A, Section 12 or Chapter 1B, Section 12.

18 Refill the cooling system as described in Chapter 1A, Section 25 or Chapter 1B, Section 26.

19 Reconnect the battery negative terminal (refer to battery disconnection and reconnection in Chapter 5A, Section 3).

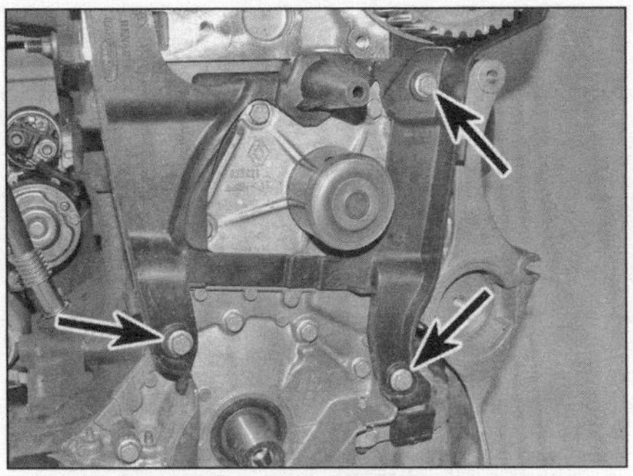

7.8 Undo the retaining bolts and remove the rear timing belt cover

7.9 Undo the pump retaining bolts

8 Heater/ventilation system – general information

Note: *Refer to Section 10 for information on the air conditioning side of the system.*

Manually-controlled system

1 The heating/ventilation system consists of a multi-speed blower motor (housed behind the facia), face level vents in the centre and at each end of the facia, and air ducts to the front footwells.

2 The control unit is located in the facia, and the controls operate flap valves to deflect and mix the air flowing through the various parts of the heating/ventilation system. The flap valves are contained in the air distribution housing, which acts as a central distribution unit, passing air to the various ducts and vents.

3 Cold air enters the system through the grille in the scuttle. If required, the airflow is boosted by the blower, and then flows through the various ducts, according to the settings of the controls. Stale air is expelled through ducts at the rear of the vehicle. If warm air is required, the cold air is passed over the heater matrix, which is heated by the engine coolant.

4 A recirculation control enables the outside air supply to be closed off, while the air inside the vehicle is recirculated. This can be useful to prevent unpleasant odours entering from outside the vehicle, but should only be used briefly, as the recirculated air inside the vehicle will soon become stale.

5 On some diesel engine models an electric heater is fitted into the heater housing. When the coolant temperature is cold, the heater warms the air before it enters the heater matrix. This quickly increases the temperature of the heater matrix on cold starts, resulting in warm air being available to heat the vehicle interior soon after start-up.

Automatic climate control

6 A fully automatic electronic climate control system is fitted to some models. The main components of the system are exactly the same as those described for the manual system, the only major difference being that the temperature, distribution and recirculation flaps in the heating/ventilation housing are operated by electric motors rather than cables.

7 The operation of the system is controlled by the electronic control module (which is incorporated in the blower motor assembly) along with the following sensors.

a) The passenger compartment sensor – informs the control module of the temperature of the air inside the passenger compartment.

b) Evaporator temperature sensor – informs the control module of the evaporator temperature.

c) Heater matrix temperature sensor – informs the control module of the heater matrix temperature.

8 Using the information from the above sensors, the control module determines the appropriate settings for the heating/ventilation system housing flaps to maintain the passenger compartment at the desired setting on the control panel.

9 If the system develops a fault, the vehicle should be taken to a Nissan dealer. A complete test of the system can then be carried out, using a special electronic diagnostic test unit, which is simply plugged into the system's diagnostic connector.

9 Heater/ventilation components – removal and refitting

Heater blower motor

1 Disconnect the battery negative terminal (refer to battery disconnection and reconnection in Chapter 5A, Section 3).

2 Remove the facia lower trim panel on the driver's side as described in Chapter 11, Section 26.

3 Remove the steering column as described in Chapter 10, Section 14.

4 Reaching up around the side of the heater housing, disconnect the wiring connector from the top of the blower motor **(see illustration)**.

5 Undo the two screws and lift off the blower motor cover **(see illustration)**.

9.4 Disconnect the wiring connector

9.5 Lift off the blower motor cover

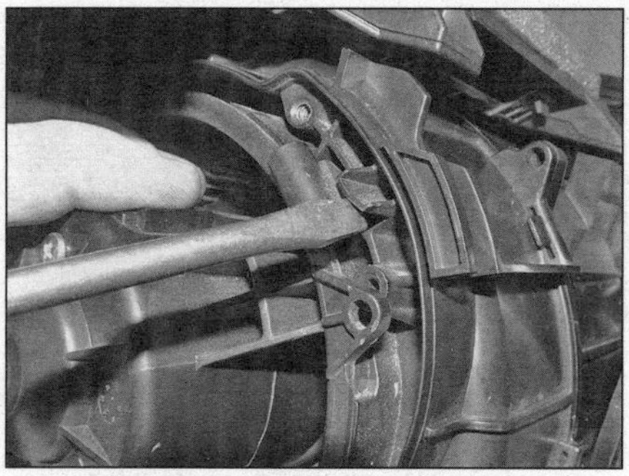

9.6a Depress the locking tab...

6 Where fitted, undo the motor retaining screw. Using a screwdriver, depress the flange locking tab, then turn the blower motor clockwise and withdraw it from the side of the heater housing **(see illustrations)**.
7 Refitting is a reversal of removal.

Heater blower motor resistor

8 Disconnect the battery negative terminal (refer to battery disconnection and reconnection in Chapter 5A, Section 3).
9 Remove the glovebox as described in Chapter 11, Section 26.
10 The resistor is located in the left-hand side of the heater housing in front of the pollen filter.
11 Disconnect the wiring connector from the blower motor resistor.
12 Undo the retaining screws and withdraw the resistor from the heater housing **(see illustrations)**.

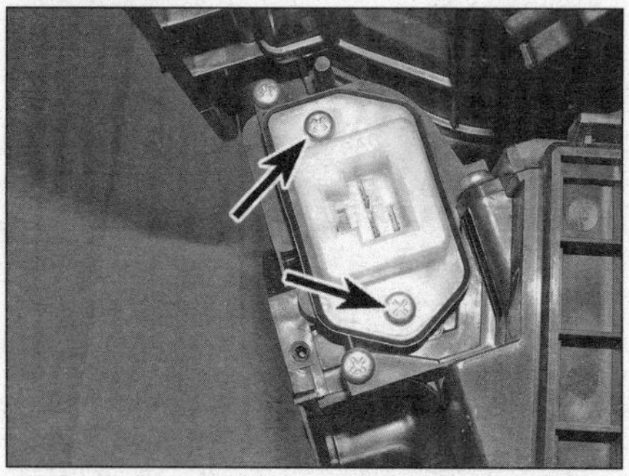

9.12a Remove the two retaining screws...

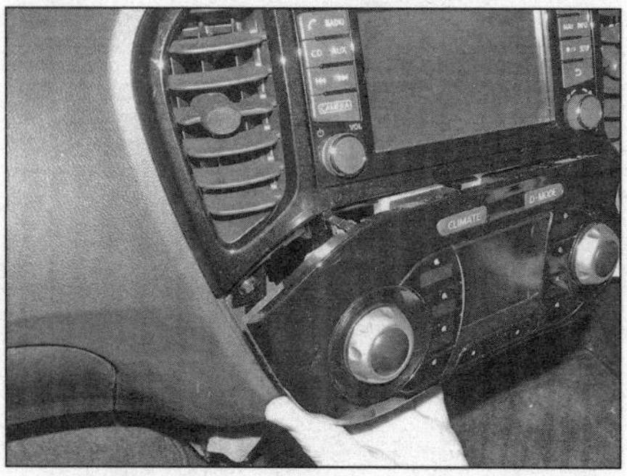

9.18a Pull the control panel away...

9.6b ...then turn the motor clockwise and remove it from the heater housing

13 Refitting is a reversal of removal.

Heater control panel

Manually operated system

14 Remove the air recirculation lever knob by holding it at the top and bottom, tilting it to the right, then the left, then disengage it from the lever. Pull the knob up and remove it from the lever.
15 Insert a screwdriver into the cut-outs at the base of the control panel trim surround on each side. Taking care not to damage the facia, pull the trim surround away to release the internal clips then remove the surround.
16 Undo the four screws securing the heater control panel to the facia. Ease the panel from its location and disconnect the control cables from the rear of the panel, noting their routing. Disconnect the wiring connector and remove the panel.

9.12b ...and withdraw the resistor from the heater housing

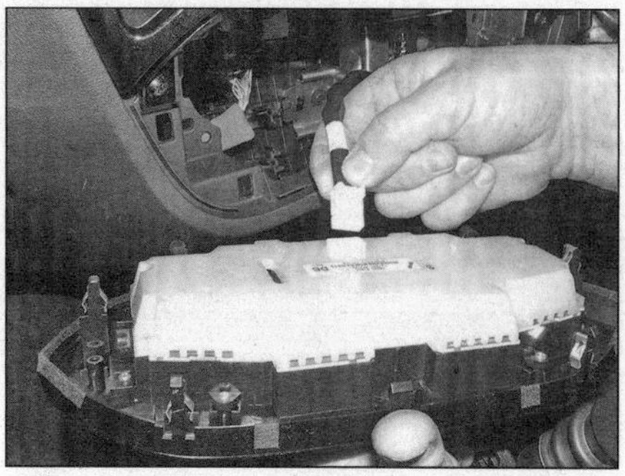

9.18b ...and disconnect the wiring connector

17 Refitting is the reverse of removal. Ensure the control cables are correctly reconnected and securely held by the retaining clips; check the operation of the control knobs before refitting the trim surround.

Automatic climate system

18 Insert a screwdriver into the cut-outs at the base of the control panel on each side. Taking care not to damage the facia, pull the control panel away to release the internal clips. Disconnect the wiring connector and remove the panel **(see illustrations)**.
19 Refitting is the reverse of removal.

Control cables

20 Remove the manually operated system control panel as described previously in this Section.
21 To remove the air recirculation flap cable or the temperature control cable, remove the glovebox as described in Chapter 11, Section 26. To remove the air flow control cable, remove the facia lower trim panel on the driver's side as described in Chapter 11, Section 26.
22 Release the retaining clip and then detach the relevant cable from the lever on the heater housing, then withdraw the cable from under the facia.
23 Refitting is the reverse of removal, ensuring the cable is secured in place by its retaining clips. Check the operation of the control panel and cables.

Heater air flap motors

24 To gain access to the air recirculation flap motor or the temperature control flap motor, remove the glovebox as described in Chapter 11, Section 26. To gain access to the air flow control flap motor, remove the facia lower trim panel on the driver's side as described in Chapter 11, Section 26.
25 Disconnect the motor wiring connector, then unscrew the retaining bolts and withdraw the relevant motor **(see illustration)**. Note, as the motor is withdrawn from the flap spindle, depending on the position of the flap, it may rotate in the heater housing.
26 Refitting is a reversal of removal, making sure the motors are located correctly on the housing. Before refitting the trim panels,

9.25 Temperature control flap motor retaining bolts

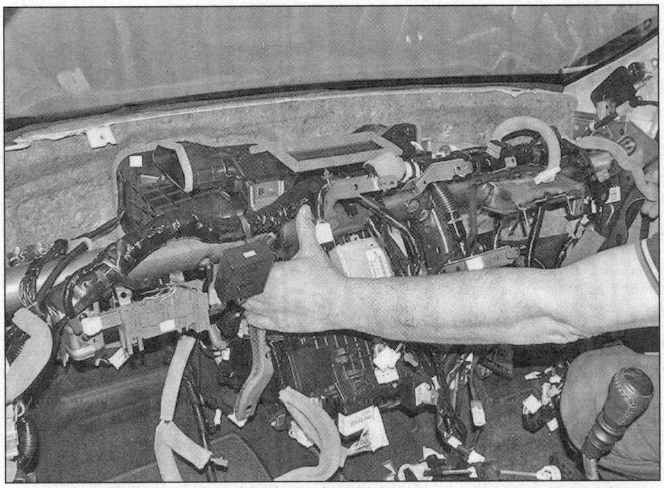

9.28 Removing the facia crossmember from over the heater housing

9.29 Remove the sealing foam from around the heater matrix pipes

check the operation of the motors, as they may need to be turned on the spindles to operate correctly.

Pollen filter

27 Remove and refit the pollen filter, as described in Chapter 1A, Section 22 or Chapter 1B, Section 22.

Heater matrix

28 This work entails removal of the centre console, complete facia assembly, wiring loom and facia crossmember **(see illustration)**, as described in Chapter 11, Section 26.

29 With the heater assembly removed from the vehicle, remove the sealing foam from around the coolant pipes **(see illustration)**.

30 Undo the retaining screw and unclip the plastic support bracket from around the coolant pipes **(see illustrations)**.

31 Undo the retaining screws and remove the heater matrix cover panel **(see illustration)**.

32 Slide the matrix out from the heater housing, keeping the coolant pipes uppermost to prevent any coolant spillage **(see illustration)**.

33 Refitting is a reversal of removal, making sure the foam seal around the heater matrix is located correctly, before sliding it back into the housing.

Additional heater (diesel models)

34 Depending on model, there may be an additional heater fitted to the right-hand side of the heater housing.

35 Remove the footwell trim panel in front of the centre console on the driver's side as described in Chapter 11, Section 25.

36 Undo the retaining screws and remove the footwell air duct.

37 Undo the retaining screws and remove the cover panel from the side of the heater housing **(see illustration)**.

38 Open the locking bar and disconnect the wiring plug for the heater element **(see illustration)**.

9.30a Undo the retaining screw...

9.30b ...and unclip the pipe support bracket

9.31 Remove the matrix cover panel

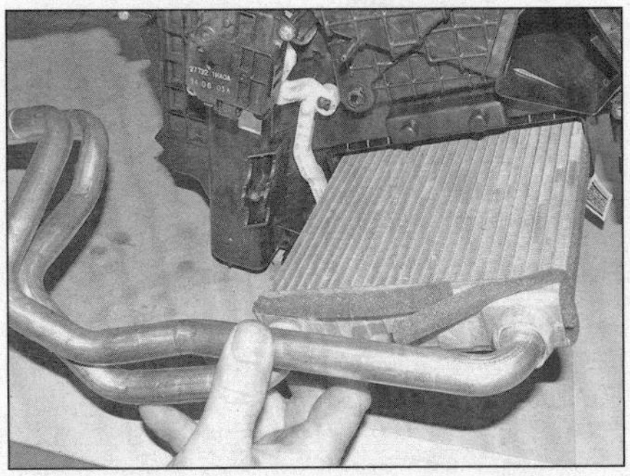

9.32 Slide the heater matrix out from the side of the housing

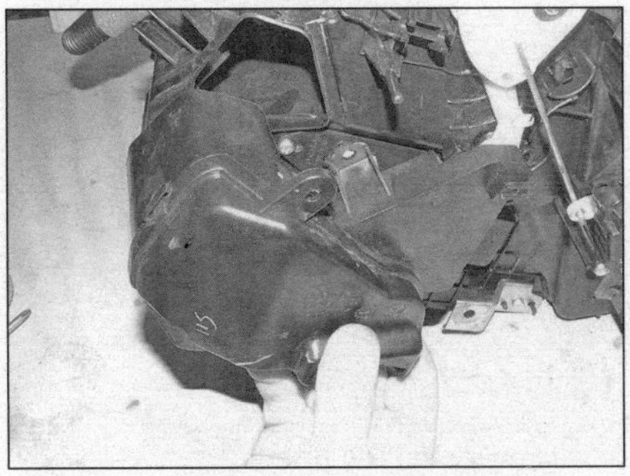

9.37 Remove the cover panel from the side of the heater housing

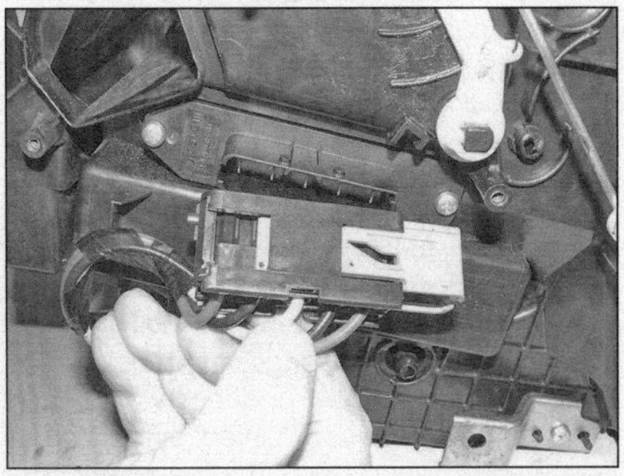

9.38 Disconnect the heater element wiring plug

9.39 Undo the retaining screws and remove the heater element

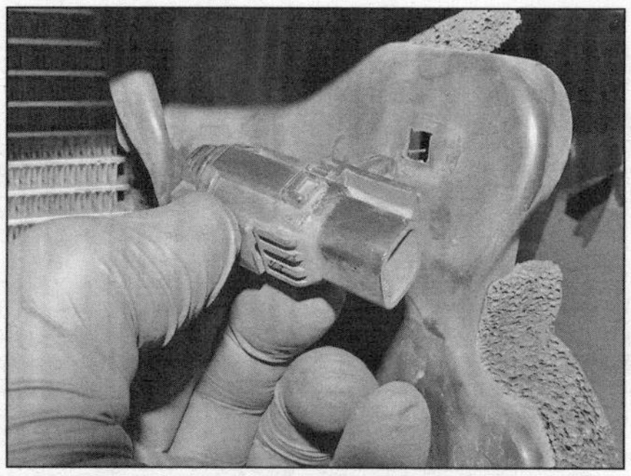

9.43 Unclip the ambient temperature sensor from the air guide

9.46 Unclip the sunlight sensor panel and disconnect the wiring connector

39 Undo the two retaining screws, and slide the heater element out from the housing **(see illustration)**.

40 Refitting is the reverse of removal.

Ambient temperature sensor

41 The ambient temperature sensor is located, at the front of the vehicle, behind the front bumper clipped to the air guide on the left-hand side.

42 To remove the sensor, remove the front bumper as described in Chapter 11, Section 6.

43 Unclip the sensor from the air guide, then disconnect the wiring connector and remove the sensor **(see illustration)**.

44 Refitting is the reverse of removal.

Sunlight sensor

45 The sunlight sensor is located on the top of the facia on the left-hand side, nearest to the windscreen.

46 Carefully unclip the sensor trim panel from the facia, then disconnect the wiring connector **(see illustration)**.

47 Refitting is the reverse of removal.

10 Air conditioning system – general information and precautions

General information

1 An air conditioning system is available on all models. It enables the temperature of incoming air to be lowered, and also dehumidifies the air, which makes for rapid demisting and increased comfort.

2 The cooling side of the system works in the same way as a domestic refrigerator. Refrigerant gas is drawn into a belt-driven compressor, and passes into a condenser mounted on the front of the radiator, where it loses heat and becomes liquid. The liquid passes through an expansion valve to an evaporator, where it changes from liquid under high pressure to gas under low pressure. This change is accompanied by a drop in temperature, which cools the evaporator. The refrigerant returns to the compressor, and the cycle begins again.

3 Air blown through the evaporator passes to the heating/ventilation housing, where it is mixed with hot air blown through the heater matrix to achieve the desired temperature in the passenger compartment.

4 The operation of the system is controlled electronically by the ECU integral with the control panel. Any problems with the system should be referred to a Nissan dealer, or suitably-equipped specialist.

Air conditioning service ports

5 The air conditioning service ports are located in the refrigerant pipes on the right-hand side of the engine compartment **(see illustration)**.

Precautions

6 When an air conditioning system is fitted, it is necessary to observe special precautions whenever dealing with any part of the system, or its associated components. The refrigerant is potentially dangerous, and should only be handled by qualified persons. Uncontrolled discharging of the refrigerant is dangerous and damaging to the environment for the following reasons.

a) *If it is splashed onto the skin, it can cause frostbite.*

b) *The refrigerant is heavier then air and so displaces oxygen. In a confined space, which is not adequately ventilated, this could lead to a risk of suffocation. The gas is odourless and colourless so there is no warning of its presence in the atmosphere.*

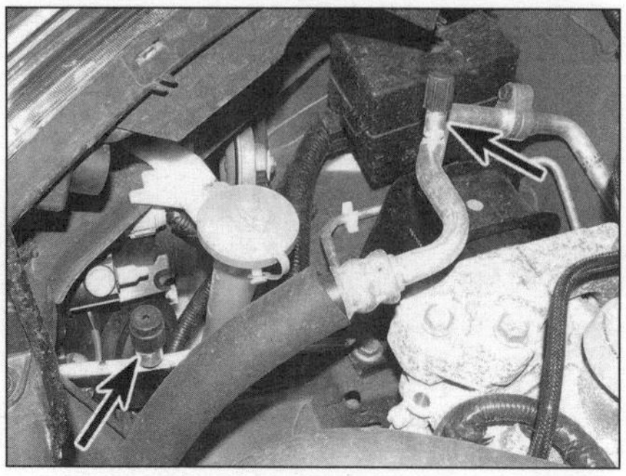

10.5 Air conditioning service ports

c) *Although not poisonous, in the presence of a naked flame (including a cigarette) it forms a noxious gas that causes headaches, nausea, etc.*

Warning: Never attempt to open any air conditioning system refrigerant pipe/hose union without first having the system fully discharged by an air conditioning specialist. On completion of work, have the system recharged with the correct type and amount of fresh refrigerant.

Warning: Always seal disconnected refrigerant pipe/hose unions as soon as they are disconnected. Failure to form an airtight seal on any union will result in the dehydrator reservoir become saturated, necessitating its renewal. Also renew all sealing rings disturbed.

Caution: Do not operate the air conditioning system if it is known to be short of refrigerant as this could damage the compressor.

11 Air conditioning system components– removal and refitting

Warning: Refer to the precautions given in Section 10 and have the system discharged by an air conditioning specialist before carrying out any work on the air conditioning system.

Compressor

Note: *If necessary for access to other components, the compressor can be unbolted and moved aside, without disconnecting its flexible hoses, after removing the auxiliary drivebelt.*

Removal

1 Have the air conditioning system fully discharged and evacuated by an air conditioning specialist.

2 Remove the auxiliary drivebelt as described in Chapter 1A, Section 12 or Chapter 1B, Section 12 (as applicable).

3 Unscrew the nut and bolt securing the

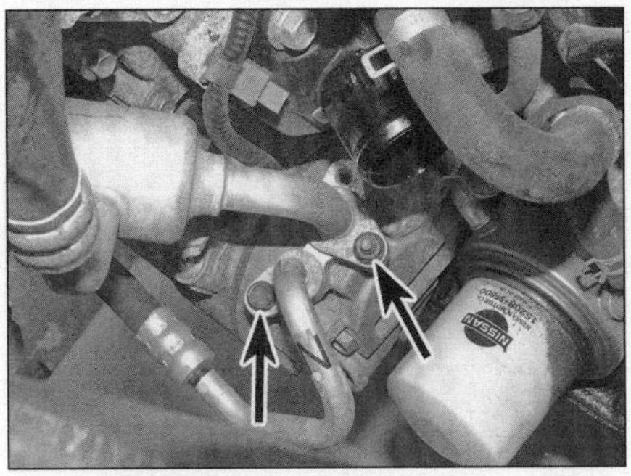
11.3a Undo the nut/bolt securing the refrigerant pipes to the compressor

11.3b Plug the compressor and pipes to prevent contamination

11.4 Disconnect the compressor wiring connector

refrigerant pipe retaining plates to the compressor **(see illustrations)**. Separate the pipes from the compressor and quickly seal the pipe and compressor unions to prevent the entry of moisture into the refrigerant circuit. Discard the sealing rings, new ones must be used on refitting.

Warning: Failure to seal the refrigerant pipe unions will result in the dehydrator reservoir become saturated, necessitating its renewal.

4 Disconnect the compressor wiring connector(s), and unclip the wiring harness from the retaining clips **(see illustration)**.

5 Unscrew the compressor mounting bolts, then free the compressor from its mounting bracket and remove it from the engine **(see illustrations)**. Where applicable, take care not to lose any spacers from the compressor mountings.

6 If the compressor is to be renewed, drain the refrigerant oil from the old compressor. The specialist who recharges the refrigerant system will need to add this amount of oil to the system.

Refitting

7 If a new compressor is being fitted, drain the refrigerant oil.

8 Where fitted, ensure any spacers are correctly fitted to the mounting bolts, then manoeuvre the compressor into position and fit the bolts. Tighten the compressor front (drivebelt pulley end) mounting bolts to the specified torque first then tighten the rear bolts.

9 Lubricate the new refrigerant pipe sealing rings with compressor oil. Remove the plugs and install the sealing rings then quickly fit the refrigerant pipes to the compressor. Ensure the refrigerant pipes are correctly joined then refit the retaining bolt, tighten it securely.

10 Reconnect the wiring connector then refit the auxiliary drivebelt (see Chapter 1A, Section 12 or Chapter 1B, Section 12).

11 Have the air conditioning system recharged with the correct type and amount of refrigerant by a specialist before using the system. Remember to inform the specialist which components have been renewed, so they can add the correct amount of oil.

11.5a Remove the compressor mounting bolts...

11.5b ...and remove the compressor

Condenser

Removal

12 Have the air conditioning system fully discharged by an air conditioning specialist.

1.2 litre petrol engine models

13 Remove the front bumper as described in Chapter 11, Section 6.

14 Remove the front bumper energy absorber, then undo the three nuts each side and remove the bumper brace **(see illustrations 3.10a and 3.10b)**.

15 Extract the upper plastic expanding rivet securing the air guides to the bonnet lock platform on each side **(see illustration 3.21)**.

16 Remove the intercooler as described in Chapter 4A, Section 13.

17 Disconnect the wiring connector from the refrigerant pressure sensor located above the receiver/dryer **(see illustration)**.

18 Undo the retaining bolts and disconnect the refrigerant pipes from the right-hand side of the condenser. Recover the O-ring seals. Separate the pipes from the condenser and quickly seal the pipe and condenser unions to prevent the entry of moisture into the refrigerant circuit. Discard the sealing rings, new ones must be used on refitting.

Warning: Failure to seal the refrigerant pipe unions will result in the dehydrator reservoir become saturated, necessitating its renewal.

19 Undo the upper mounting bolt each side, then lift the condenser up and out of the engine compartment **(see illustration)**.

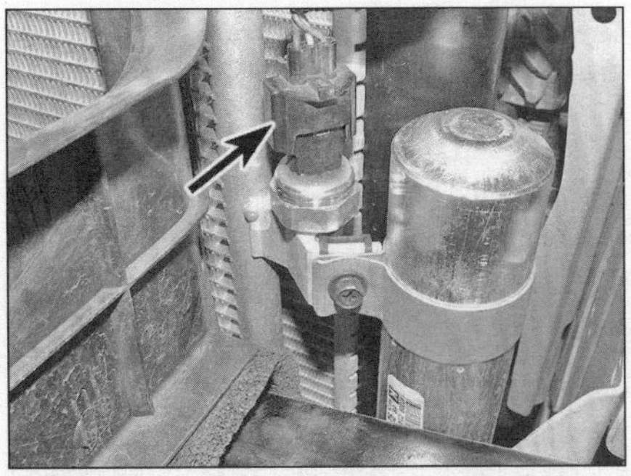
11.17 Disconnect the wiring connector from the pressure sensor

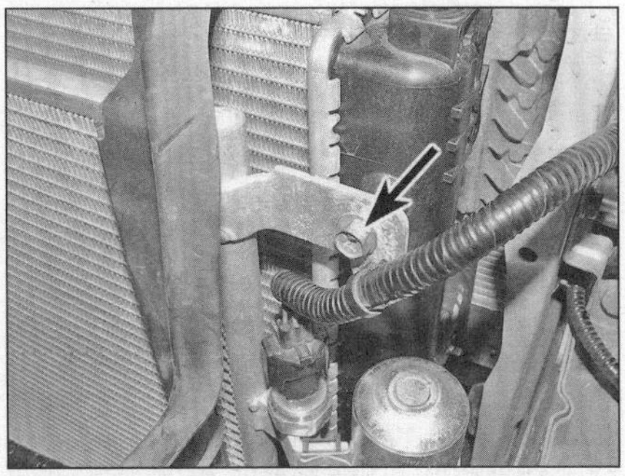
11.19 Undo the condenser mounting bolt each side

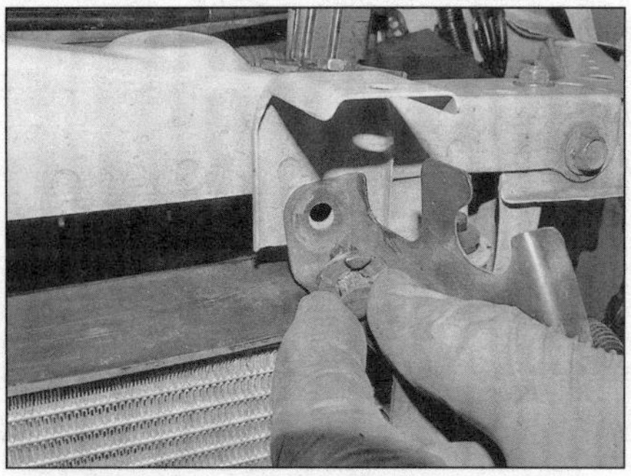

11.42 Extract the expanding rivet and remove the left-hand air guide

11.43 Undo the bolt securing the receiver/ dryer to the condenser mounting bracket

11.44 Undo the clamp bolt and lift off the receiver dryer

1.6 litre petrol engine models

20 Remove the front bumper as described in Chapter 11, Section 6.

21 Remove the combination lights as described in Chapter 12, Section 5.

22 Undo the two bolts and remove the horn bracket from the bonnet lock platform **(see illustration 3.19)**.

23 Remove the bonnet lock as described in Chapter 11, Section 10. Disengage the release cable from the retaining clip on the bonnet lock platform.

24 Extract the upper plastic expanding rivet securing the air guides to the bonnet lock platform on each side **(see illustration 3.21)**.

25 Suitably support the bonnet in the open position, then disengage and remove the bonnet support rod.

26 Disconnect the wiring connector from the bonnet closure switch **(see illustration 3.23)**.

27 Undo the two bolts each side and lift off the bonnet lock platform **(see illustration 3.24)**.

28 Disconnect the wiring connector from the refrigerant pressure sensor on the right-hand side of the condenser.

29 Undo the retaining bolts and disconnect the refrigerant pipes from the right-hand side of the condenser. Recover the O-ring seals. Separate the pipes from the condenser and quickly seal the pipe and condenser unions to prevent the entry of moisture into the refrigerant circuit. Discard the sealing rings, new ones must be used on refitting.

Warning: Failure to seal the refrigerant pipe unions will result in the dehydrator reservoir become saturated, necessitating its renewal.

30 Release the condenser from its mountings and lift it up and out from its location.

Diesel engine models

31 Remove the front bumper as described in Chapter 11, Section 6.

32 Remove the front bumper energy absorber, then undo the three nuts each side and remove the bumper brace **(see illustrations 3.10a and 3.10b)**.

33 Extract the upper plastic expanding rivet securing the air guides to the bonnet lock platform on each side **(see illustration 3.21)**.

34 Undo the two bolts and remove the horn bracket from the bonnet lock platform **(see illustration 3.19)**.

35 On Type A engines, remove the intercooler as described in Chapter 4B, Section 16.

36 Disconnect the wiring connector from the refrigerant pressure sensor located above the receiver/dryer **(see illustration 11.17)**.

37 Undo the retaining bolts and disconnect the refrigerant pipes from the right-hand side of the condenser. Recover the O-ring seals. Separate the pipes from the condenser and quickly seal the pipe and condenser unions to prevent the entry of moisture into the refrigerant circuit. Discard the sealing rings, new ones must be used on refitting.

Warning: Failure to seal the refrigerant pipe unions will result in the dehydrator reservoir become saturated, necessitating its renewal.

38 Undo the upper mounting bolt each side, then lift the condenser up and out of the engine compartment **(see illustration 11.19)**.

Refitting

39 Refitting is a reversal of removal noting the following points:

a) Ensure the condenser is seated in its mountings securely.

b) Lubricate the sealing rings with compressor oil. Remove the plugs and install the sealing rings then quickly fit the refrigerant pipes to the condenser.

c) Have the air conditioning system recharged with the correct type and amount of refrigerant by a specialist before using the system.

Receiver/dryer

Removal

1.2 litre petrol engine models and diesel engine models

40 Have the air conditioning system fully discharged by an air conditioning specialist.

41 Remove the front bumper as described in Chapter 11, Section 6.

42 Extract the upper plastic expanding rivet securing the left-hand air guide to the bonnet lock platform, then remove the air guide **(see illustration)**.

43 Undo the lower bolt securing the receiver/ dryer to the condenser mounting bracket **(see illustration)**.

44 Undo the receiver/dryer clamp bolt and lift the unit up and off the two refrigerant pipes **(see illustration)**.

45 Recover the O-ring seals from the condenser pipes, then quickly seal the pipe unions and receiver/dryer to prevent the entry of moisture into the refrigerant circuit. Discard the sealing rings, new ones must be used on refitting.

Warning: Failure to seal the refrigerant pipe unions will result in the dehydrator reservoir become saturated, necessitating its renewal.

1.6 litre petrol engine models

46 Remove the condenser as described previously in this Section.

47 Undo the lower bolt securing the receiver/ dryer to the condenser mounting bracket **(see illustration 11.43)**.

48 Undo the receiver/dryer clamp bolt and lift the unit up and off the two refrigerant pipes **(see illustration 11.44)**.

49 Recover the O-ring seals from the condenser pipes, then quickly seal the pipe unions and receiver/dryer to prevent the entry of moisture into the refrigerant circuit. Discard the sealing rings, new ones must be used on refitting.

Warning: Failure to seal the refrigerant pipe unions will result in the dehydrator reservoir become saturated, necessitating its renewal.

Refitting

50 Refitting is a reversal of removal, noting the following points:

a) Lubricate the new sealing rings with compressor oil. Remove the plugs and install the sealing rings then quickly fit the receiver/dryer.

b) Ensure the receiver/dryer is correctly seated on the refrigerant pipes, then tighten the mounting bolt and clamp bolt securely.

c) On 1.6 litre petrol engine models, refit the condenser as described previously in this Section.

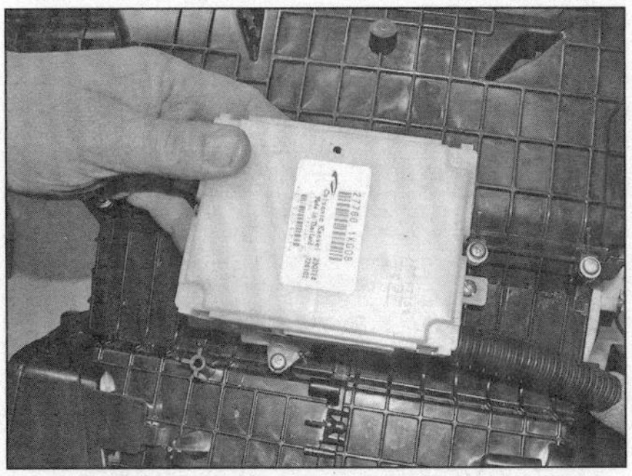

11.60 Remove the control unit from the rear of the housing

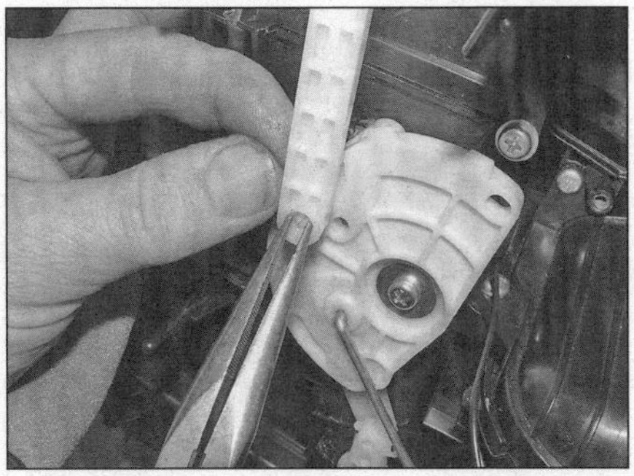

11.61 Disconnect the flap motor control linkages

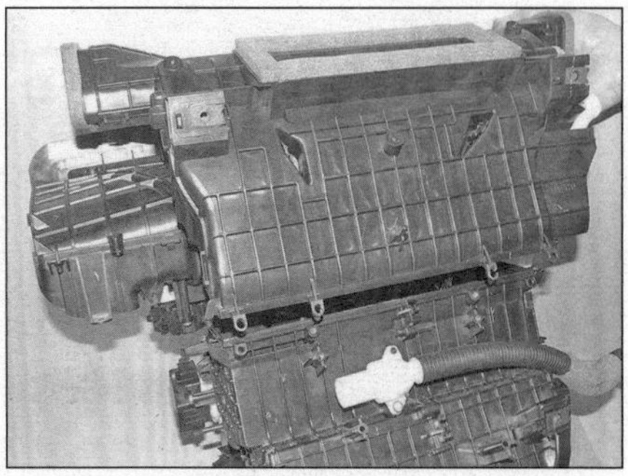

11.62 Lift off the housing upper attachment

d) Have the air conditioning system recharged with the correct type and amount of refrigerant by a specialist before using the system.

Pressure switch

Removal

51 The switch is located on the left-hand side of the condenser on 1.2 litre petrol engine models and diesel engine models. On 1.6 litre petrol engine models, the switch is located on the right-hand side of the condenser.

52 Have the air conditioning system fully discharged by an air conditioning specialist.

53 Remove the front bumper as described in Chapter 11, Section 6.

54 Disconnect the switch wiring connector **(see illustration 11.17)**.

55 Hold the switch mounting block with an adjustable spanner, then unscrew the switch from the mounting block. Recover the O-ring seal from the mounting block, then quickly seal the union to prevent the entry of moisture into the refrigerant circuit. Discard the sealing ring, a new one must be used on refitting.

Warning: Failure to seal the refrigerant union will result in the dehydrator reservoir become saturated, necessitating its renewal.

Refitting

56 Refitting is a reversal of removal noting the following points:

a) Lubricate the new switch seal with compressor oil.

b) Have the air conditioning system recharged with the correct type and amount of refrigerant by a specialist prior to using the system.

Evaporator

Removal

57 Have the air conditioning system fully discharged and evacuated by an air conditioning specialist.

58 Remove the heating/ventilation housing as described in Section 9, for the removal of the heater matrix.

59 With the heater/ventilation housing removed from the vehicle, remove the following components with reference to Section 9 :

a) Heater blower motor and resistor.

b) Control cables (where applicable).

c) Heater flap motors.

d) Pollen filter.

e) Heater matrix.

f) Additional heater (where fitted).

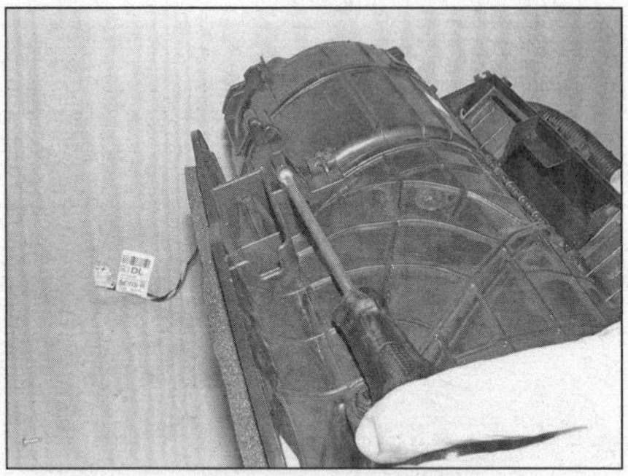

11.63a Undo the retaining screws...

60 Undo the retaining screws and remove the control unit from the rear of the housing **(see illustration)**.

61 Disconnect the flap motor control linkages as necessary to enable the two halves of the heater/ventilation housing to be separated **(see illustration)**.

62 Undo the retaining screws and lift off the housing upper attachment **(see illustration)**.

63 Undo the retaining screws and separate the air intake housing from the blower housing **(see illustrations)**.

64 Release the retaining tabs and lift off the blower housing **(see illustration)**.

11.63b ...and separate the intake housing from the blower housing

11.64 Lift off the blower housing

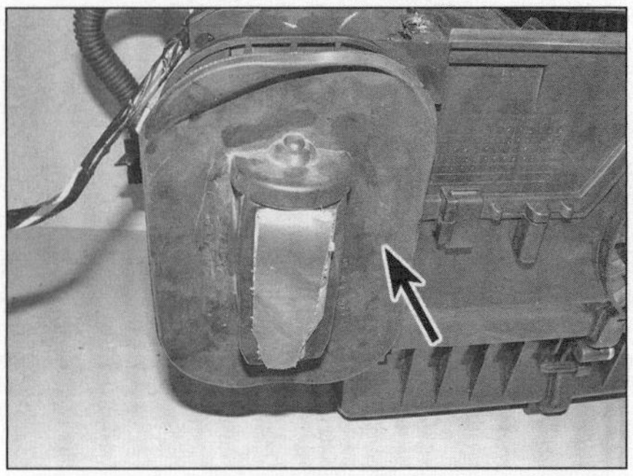

11.65 Remove the sealing foam from the expansion valve

11.66a Remove the retaining clips...

11.66b ...undo the retaining screws...

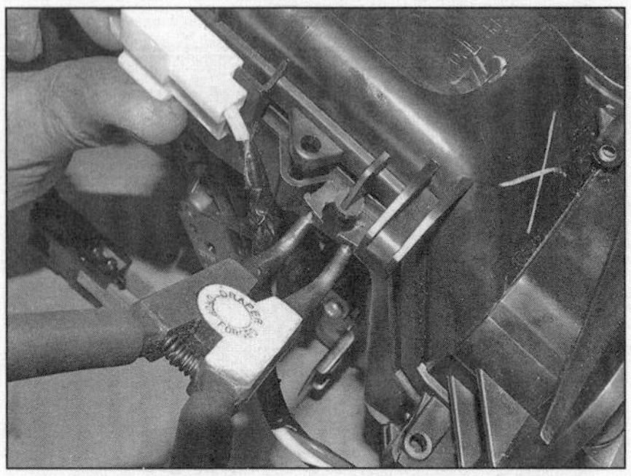

11.66c ...and spread the retaining peg slots...

11.66d ...then lift off the evaporator cover

65 Remove the sealing foam from around the refrigerant expansion valve connection **(see illustration)**.

66 Working around the casing, remove the retaining clips, undo the retaining screws and spread the retaining peg slots, then lift off the evaporator cover **(see illustrations)**.

67 Lift the evaporator from the housing, withdrawing the temperature sensor with it. If required unclip the sensor from the evaporator **(see illustrations)**.

68 If required undo the retaining screws and remove the expansion valve from the evaporator.

Refitting

69 Refitting is a reversal of removal but have the air conditioning system recharged with the correct type and amount of refrigerant by a specialist prior to using the system.

Expansion valve

Removal

70 Have the air conditioning system fully discharged and evacuated by an air conditioning specialist.

71 Remove the windscreen cowl panel and cowl panel extension as described in Chapter 11, Section 21.

72 Undo the retaining bolt and withdraw the refrigerant pipes from the expansion valve connection at the engine compartment bulkhead **(see illustration)**.

73 Plug/cover the openings in the refrigerant pipes and the expansion valve to prevent contamination/saturation.

⚠ ***Warning: Failure to seal the refrigerant pipe unions will result in the receiver/dryer becoming saturated, necessitating its renewal***

74 Pull the rubber seal from around the pipes connection at the bulkhead, and then undo the two bolts from the centre of the expansion valve, and remove it from the bulkhead.

75 Recover and discard the O-ring seals from the refrigerant pipes and expansion valve – new ones must be fitted.

Refitting

76 Refitting is a reversal of removal but have the air conditioning system recharged with the correct type and amount of refrigerant by a specialist prior to using the system.

11.67a Lift the evaporator from the housing

11.67b Temperature sensor clipped to the evaporator

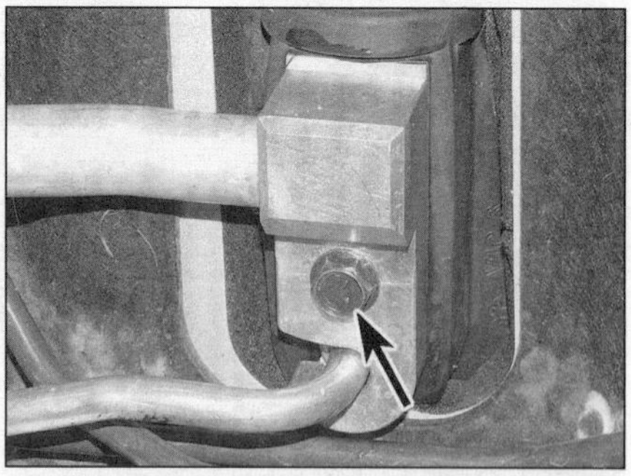

11.72 Undo the bolt and withdraw the refrigerant pipes from the expansion valve

Chapter 4 Part A
Petrol engine fuel and exhaust systems

Contents

Degrees of difficulty

Easy, suitable for novice with little experience	**Fairly easy,** suitable for beginner with some experience	**Fairly difficult,** suitable for competent DIY mechanic	**Difficult,** suitable for experienced DIY mechanic	**Very difficult,** suitable for expert DIY or professional

Specifications

General

System type:

1.2 litre engines	Hitachi Electronic Concentrated Control System (ECCS) 2 high-pressure direct injection with turbocharger
1.6 litre engines	Nissan Electronic Concentrated Control System (ECCS) multipoint injection

Fuel system data

Idle speed (not adjustable – controlled by ECU):	
1.2 litre engines	750 ± 50 rpm
1.6 litre engines	650 ± 50 rpm
Idle mixture CO content	Less than 1.0 % (not adjustable – controlled by ECU)
Fuel supply pump type	Electric, immersed in tank
High-pressure pump (1.2 litre engines)	Mechanical, driven by exhaust camshaft

Recommended fuel

Minimum octane rating	95 RON unleaded
Fuel tank capacity	46 litres

Torque wrench settings

	Nm	lbf ft
1.2 litre engines		
Camshaft position sensor	7	6
Catalytic converter support bracket bolts	20	15
Catalytic converter-to-turbocharger nuts	20	15
Crankshaft position sensor	7	6
Exhaust front pipe-to-catalytic converter nuts	21	15
Exhaust front pipe-to-intermediate pipe nuts	58	43
Exhaust intermediate pipe-to-tailpipe nuts	35	26
Exhaust manifold heat shield bolts	14	10
Exhaust manifold nuts*	30	22
Fuel pipe union nuts:		
To high pressure fuel pump	35	26
To fuel rail	25	18
Fuel rail bolts	12	9
Fuel sender/pump unit securing ring	70	52
Fuel tank mounting bolts	25	18
High-pressure fuel pump bolts	25	18
Inlet manifold nuts	10	7
Knock sensor	23	17
Throttle housing retaining bolts	8	6
Turbocharger oil return pipe flange bolts	10	7
Turbocharger oil supply pipe union:		
To turbocharger	14	10
To engine	40	30
Valve timing control solenoid bolts	10	7
1.6 litre engines		
Camshaft position sensor	10	7
Crankshaft position sensor	7	6
Exhaust front pipe-to-intermediate pipe bolts	49	36
Exhaust front pipe-to-manifold nuts	49	36
Exhaust intermediate pipe-to-tailpipe nuts	35	26
Exhaust manifold nuts*	33	25
Fuel rail nuts	25	18
Fuel rail protector shield bolts:		
Upper bolts	25	18
Lower bolts	10	7
Fuel sender/pump unit securing ring	70	52
Fuel tank mounting bolts	25	18
Inlet manifold bolts	25	18
Knock sensor	23	17
Throttle housing retaining bolts	10	7
Valve timing control solenoid bolts	10	7

**Use new nuts/bolts*

1 General information and precautions

General information

1 The fuel supply system consists of a fuel tank (which is mounted under the rear of the car, with an electric fuel pump immersed in it) and fuel feed lines. On 1.6 litre engines, the fuel pump supplies fuel to the fuel rail, which acts as a reservoir for the fuel injectors which inject fuel into the inlet tracts. On 1.2 litre engines, the tank-mounted fuel supply pump supplies fuel to the high-pressure pump mounted on the engine. The high-pressure pump supplies fuel to the fuel rail which acts as a reservoir for the four fuel injectors which inject fuel directly into the combustion chambers in the cylinder head.

2 The electronic control unit controls both the fuel injection system and the ignition system, integrating the two into a complete engine management system. Refer to Section 5 for further information on the operation of the fuel system and to Chapter 5B for details of the ignition side of the system.

Precautions

3 Refer to Chapter 4C for general information and precautions relating to the catalytic converter.

- Before disconnecting any fuel lines, or working on any part of the fuel system, the system must be depressurised as described in Section 6.
- Care must be taken when disconnecting the fuel lines. When disconnecting a fuel union or hose, loosen the union or clamp screw slowly, to avoid sudden uncontrolled fuel spillage. Take adequate fire precautions.
- When working on fuel system components, scrupulous cleanliness must be observed, and care must be taken not to introduce any foreign matter into fuel lines or components.
- After carrying out any work involving disconnection of fuel lines, it is advisable to check the connections for leaks; pressurise the system by switching the ignition on and off several times.
- Electronic control units are very sensitive components, and certain precautions must be taken to avoid damage to these units as follows.
  - a) *When carrying out welding operations on the vehicle using electric welding equipment, the battery and alternator should be disconnected.*
  - b) *Although the underbonnet-mounted control units will tolerate normal underbonnet conditions, they can be adversely affected by excess heat or*

moisture. If using welding equipment or pressure-washing equipment in the vicinity of an electronic control unit, take care not to direct heat, or jets of water or steam, at the unit. If this cannot be avoided, remove the control unit from the vehicle, and protect its wiring plug with a plastic bag.

c) Before disconnecting any wiring, or removing components, always ensure that the ignition is switched off.

d) Do not attempt to improvise fault diagnosis procedures using a test light or multimeter, as irreparable damage could be caused to the control unit.

e) After working on fuel injection/engine management system components, ensure that all wiring is correctly reconnected before reconnecting the battery or switching on the ignition.

Warning: Many of the procedures in this Chapter require the disconnection of fuel line connections, and the removal of components, which may result in some fuel spillage. Before carrying out any operation on the fuel system, refer to the precautions given in Safety first! in Chapter 0, Section 3, and follow them implicitly. Petrol is a highly-dangerous and volatile liquid, and the precautions necessary when handling it cannot be overstressed.

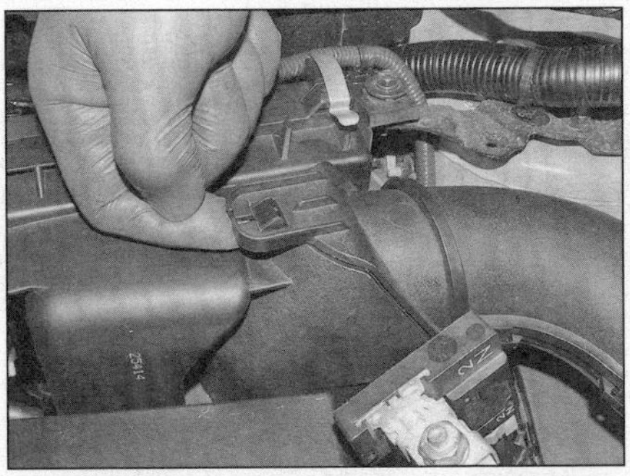

2.1 Disengage the upper inlet air duct from the air cleaner filter housing

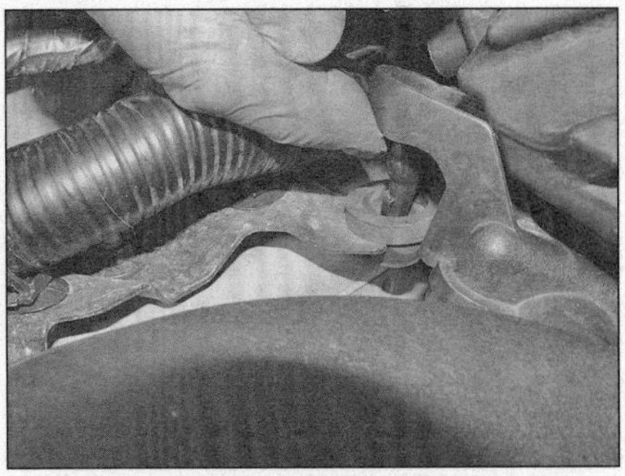

2.2a Disengage the lower mounting peg from the grommet...

2.2b ...and remove the inlet air duct

2.3 Disconnect the mass airflow sensor wiring connector

2 Air cleaner assembly and air ducts – removal and refitting

Air cleaner assembly

Removal

1 Lift up the tab and disengage the upper inlet air duct from the air cleaner filter housing **(see illustration)**.

2 Lift the inlet air duct upward to disengage the lower mounting peg from the grommet, and remove the duct from the engine compartment **(see illustrations)**.

3 On 1.6 litre engines, disconnect the wiring connector from the mass airflow sensor and release the wiring loom retaining clip from the air cleaner case **(see illustration)**.

4 Slacken the retaining clip and detach the outlet air duct from the air cleaner case **(see illustrations)**.

5 Undo the air cleaner retaining bolt **(see illustration)**. Pull the air cleaner upwards, disengaging the two lower locating pegs on the bottom of the case from the rubber mountings, then remove it from the engine compartment.

Refitting

6 Refitting is a reversal of removal, ensuring that all hoses are properly reconnected and that all ducts are correctly seated and securely held by their retaining clips.

Air ducts

Removal

Lower inlet air duct

7 To remove the lower inlet air duct from the left-hand inner wing first remove the upper air duct as described in paragraphs 1 and 2.

8 On 1.6 litre engines remove the front bumper as described in Chapter 11, Section 6, then partially remove the front wheel arch liner on the left-hand side as described in Chapter 11, Section 21.

9 Undo the air duct retaining bolt(s) and remove the air duct from the engine compartment.

Outlet air duct

10 To remove the outlet air duct from the air

2.4a Slacken the retaining clip...

2.4b ...and detach the air duct

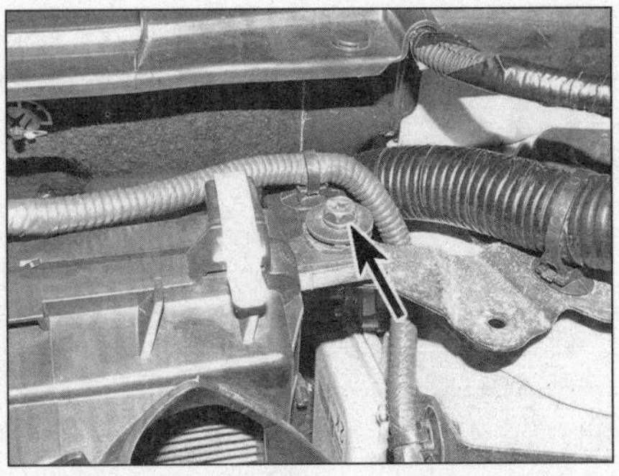

2.5 Undo the air cleaner retaining bolt

2.11 Release the clip and disconnect the crankcase ventilation hose

2.12 Remove the duct from the engine compartment

2.14 Undo the support bracket retaining nuts

cleaner to the throttle housing/turbocharger, slacken the retaining clip and detach the outlet air duct from the air cleaner case **(see illustration 2.4a and 2.4b)**.

11 Where applicable, release the clip and disconnect the crankcase ventilation hose **(see illustration)**.

12 Slacken the clip securing the other end of the duct to the throttle housing or turbocharger and remove the duct from the engine compartment **(see illustration)**.

Air inlet hose (1.2 litre engines)

13 To remove the air inlet hose from the intercooler to the turbocharger on 1.2 litre engines, first undo the retaining bolts and move the coolant expansion tank aside.

14 Release the vacuum hose from the two clips on the hose support bracket, then undo the two nuts securing the support bracket to the cylinder head cover **(see illustration)**.

15 Release the wire clips securing the air inlet hose to the intercooler and turbocharger and remove the hose from the engine compartment.

Air inlet tube (1.2 litre engines)

16 To remove the air inlet tube between the intercooler and throttle housing on 1.2 litre engines, first undo the retaining bolts and move the coolant expansion tank aside.

17 Undo the bolt securing the air inlet tube to the electric cooling fan shroud.

18 Where applicable, release the retaining clip and disconnect the breather hose from the air inlet tube upper elbow.

19 Disconnect the wiring connector from the turbocharger boost pressure sensor

20 Release the wire clip securing the air inlet tube to the intercooler.

21 Undo the two bolts securing the air inlet tube elbow to the throttle housing and remove the hose from the engine compartment **(see illustration)**.

Refitting

22 Refitting is a reversal of removal, ensuring that all hoses are properly reconnected and that all ducts are correctly seated and securely held by their retaining clips.

3 Accelerator pedal – removal and refitting

Removal

1 Remove the facia lower trim panel on the driver's side as described in Chapter 11, Section 26.

2 Reach up behind the facia, and detach the wiring connector from the top of the accelerator pedal **(see illustration)**.

3 Undo the two mounting bolts securing the pedal assembly to the bracket on the bulkhead, and remove it from underneath the facia **(see illustration)**.

4 Examine the mounting bracket and pedal pivot points for signs of wear, and renew as necessary.

Refitting

5 Refitting is a reversal of the removal procedure, applying a little multipurpose grease to the pedal pivot shaft.

4 Unleaded petrol – general information and usage

Note: *The information given in this Chapter is correct at the time of writing. If updated information is thought to be required, check with a Nissan dealer. If travelling abroad, consult one of the motoring organisations (or a similar authority) for advice on the petrol's available, and their suitability for your vehicle.*

1 All Nissan petrol engine models are designed to run on fuel with a minimum octane rating of 95 (RON). All models have a catalytic converter must be run on unleaded fuel only. Under no circumstances should leaded fuel or lead replacement petrol be used, as this may damage the catalyst.

5 Fuel Injection system – general information

1 All models are fitted with a combined fuel injection/ignition (engine management) system, controlled by an Electronic Control

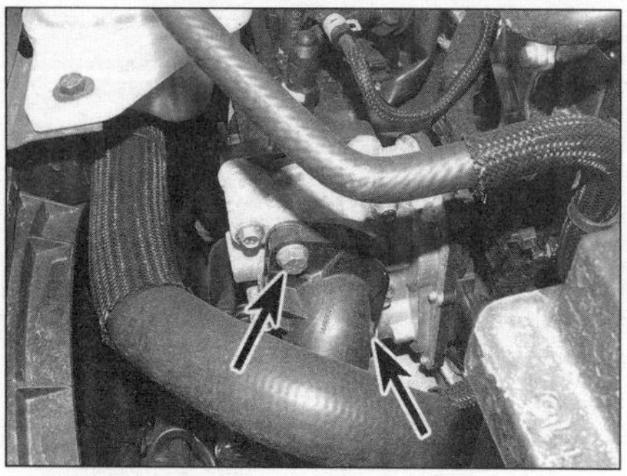
2.21 Air inlet tube elbow retaining bolts

3.2 Disconnect the wiring connector

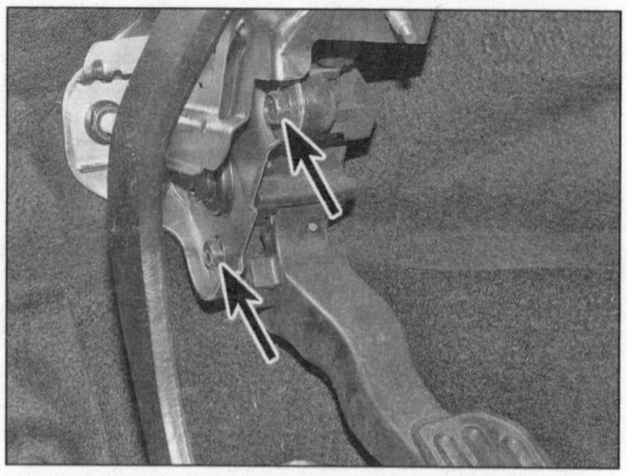
3.3 Undo the pedal mounting bolts

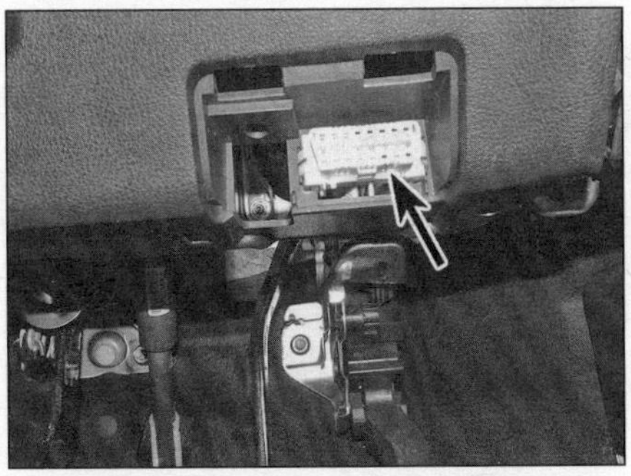
5.5 Diagnostic plug connector

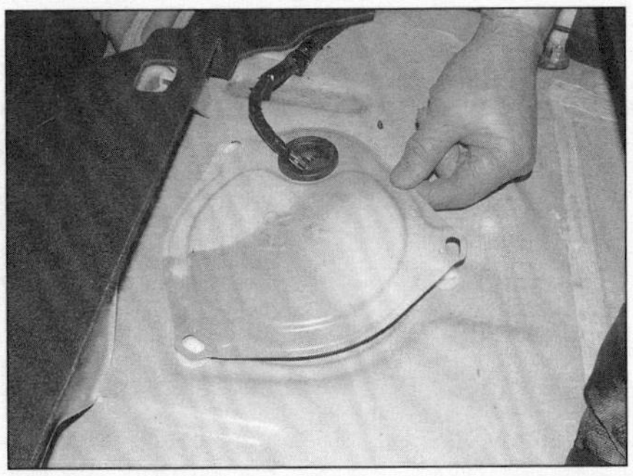
7.4 Lift off the access cover

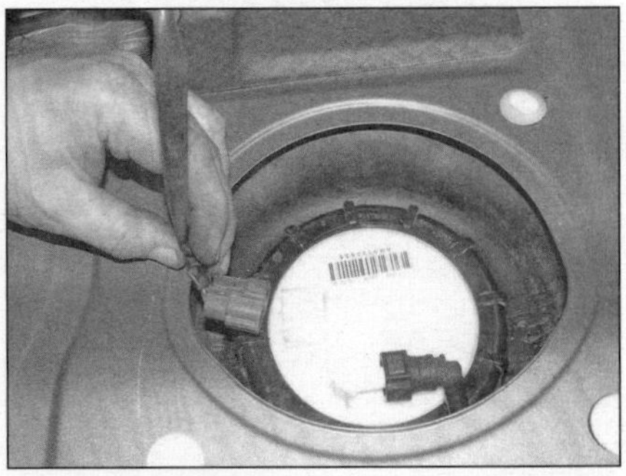
7.6 Disconnect the pump wiring connector

Unit (ECU), otherwise known as the Electronic Concentrated Control System (ECCS).

2 The electrical control system consists of the electronic control unit, along with a number of sensors, including the following:

a) *Throttle potentiometer – informs the ECU of the throttle valve position, and the rate of throttle opening/closing.*
b) *Coolant temperature sensor – informs the ECU of engine temperature.*
c) *Inlet manifold pressure sensor (1.2 litre engines) – informs the ECU of the pressure and temperature of the air in the inlet manifold.*
d) *Mass airflow sensor (1.6 litre engines) – informs the ECU of the mass and temperature of the air passing through the inlet duct.*
e) *Camshaft position sensor(s) – housed in the transmission end of the cylinder head, the sensor(s) informs the ECU of the engine speed and crankshaft position.*
f) *Crankshaft position sensor – housed in the transmission end of the cylinder block at the rear of the engine, the sensor informs the ECU of the engine speed.*
g) *Air conditioning system switch – informs the ECU if the system is in operation, to allow it to adjust the idle speed to compensate for the extra load on the engine.*
h) *Exhaust gas/oxygen sensor – informs the ECU of the oxygen content of the exhaust gases (see Chapter 4C for further information).*
i) *Knock sensor – informs the ECU when pre-ignition ('pinking') is occurring.*

3 All the above signals are analysed by the ECU. Based on this information, the ECU selects the response appropriate to those values, and controls the fuel injectors (varying their pulse width – the length of time each injector is held open – to provide a richer or weaker mixture, as appropriate). The mixture and idle speed are constantly varied by the ECU to provide the best settings for cranking, starting (with either a hot or cold engine) and engine warm-up, idle, cruising, and acceleration.

4 If there is an abnormality in any of the readings obtained from the sensors, the ECU switches to its back-up mode. If this happens, it ignores the abnormal sensor signal, and assumes a pre-programmed value, which will allow the engine to continue running, albeit at reduced efficiency. If the ECU enters its back-up mode, the warning light on the instrument panel will come on, and the relevant fault code will be stored in the ECU memory.

5 If the warning light comes on, the vehicle should be taken to a Nissan dealer or engine diagnostic specialist at the earliest opportunity. Once there, a complete test of the engine management system can be carried out, using a special electronic diagnostic test unit, which is simply plugged into the system's diagnostic connector **(see illustration)**.

6 Fuel system – depressurisation

Note: *Refer to the warning note in Section 1 before proceeding.*

Warning: The following procedure will merely relieve the pressure in the fuel system – remember that fuel will still be present in the system components, and take precautions accordingly before disconnecting any of them. Use clean rags wrapped around the connections to catch escaping fuel, and dispose of any fuel-soaked rags with care. Plug or tape over any open fuel lines, to prevent further loss of fuel or ingress of dirt.

1 The fuel system referred to in this Section is defined as the tank-mounted fuel pump, the high-pressure fuel pump (1.2 litre engines), the fuel rail and injectors, the pressure regulator, and the metal pipes and flexible hoses of the fuel lines between these components. All these contain fuel, which will be under pressure while the engine is running and/or while the ignition is switched on. The pressure will remain for some time after the ignition has been switched off, and must be relieved before any of these components are disturbed for servicing work.

2 Identify and remove the fuel pump fuse (see wiring diagram in Chapter 12) from the fusebox – the fuses can also be identified from the label inside the fusebox cover.

3 Start the engine, and allow it to run until it stalls.

4 Try to start the engine at least twice more, to ensure that all residual pressure has been relieved.

5 Disconnect the battery negative terminal (refer to battery disconnection and reconnection in Chapter 5A, Section 3).

6 For safety, the fuel pump fuse should not be refitted until all work on the fuel system has been completed. If you refit the fuse now, do not switch on the ignition until completion of work.

7 Fuel pump and fuel gauge sender unit – removal and refitting

Note: *Refer to the warning note in Section 1 before proceeding.*

Removal

1 Depressurise the fuel system as described in Section 6.

2 Disconnect the battery negative terminal (refer to battery disconnection and reconnection in Chapter 5A, Section 3).

3 To gain access to the sender unit, lift out the rear seat cushion, as described in Chapter 11, Section 22.

4 Turn the three retaining tabs through 90 degrees and lift off the access cover to expose the fuel pump and gauge sender unit **(see illustration)**.

5 Brush away any accumulated dust or dirt around the top of the sender unit so it does not drop into the fuel tank when the unit is removed.

6 Disconnect the wiring connector from the top of the sender unit **(see illustration)**.

7 Depress the coloured tabs of the quick-release fitting and disconnect the fuel

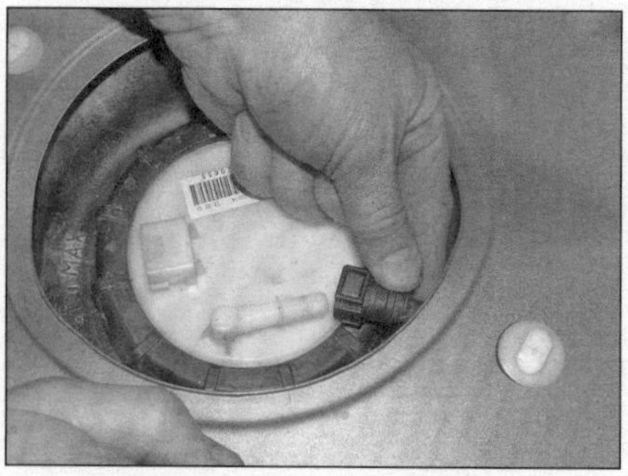

7.7 Depress the release tabs and disconnect the fuel hose

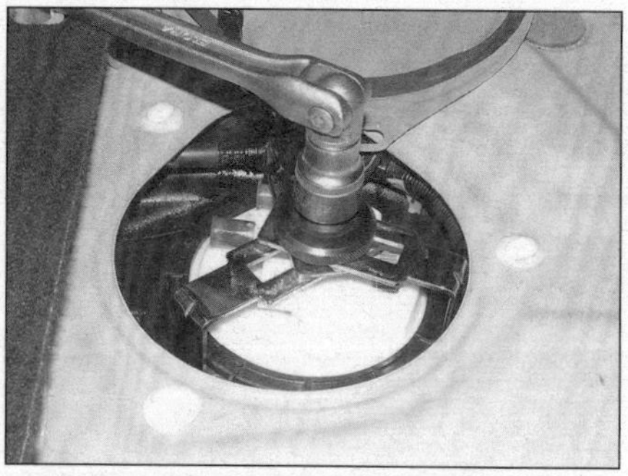

7.8a Using a locking ring removal tool to slacken the locking ring...

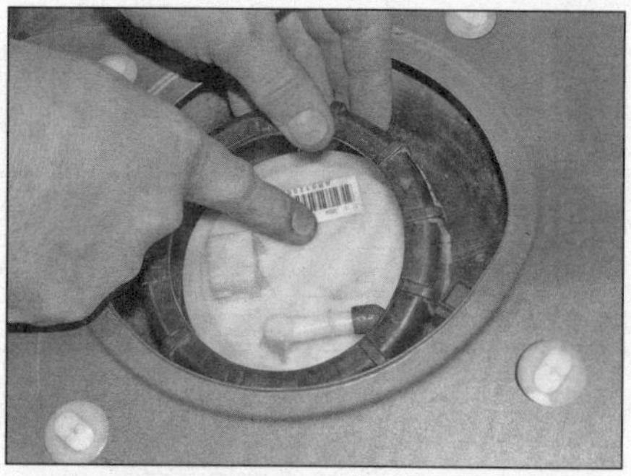

7.8b ...and remove it from the fuel tank...

hose from the top of the unit **(see illustration)**. Suitably cover the hose union and the fitting on the pump to prevent dirt ingress.

8 Twist the locking ring from the top of the fuel tank and carefully lift the sender unit out, taking care not to damage the sender unit or spill fuel onto the interior of the vehicle **(see illustrations)**.

9 Remove the sealing ring from the top of the fuel tank and discard; as a new one will be required for refitting.

10 Position the locking ring with the arrow mark pointing toward the rear of the vehicle, then temporarily screw the ring back into position on the tank. Tighten the locking ring securely.

11 Depress the legs of the gauge sender unit locking tabs with your fingers, and slide the sender unit from its location in the fuel pump body **(see illustrations)**.

12 Release the sender unit wiring from the guide at the top of the pump **(see illustration)**.

13 Using a screwdriver ease the sender unit wiring end fittings off the connectors at the top of the pump **(see illustration)**, then remove the sender unit.

Refitting

14 Refitting is a reversal of the removal procedure, noting the following points:

a) *Unscrew the temporarily refitted locking ring and fit a new sealing ring to the top of the fuel tank* **(see illustration)**.
b) *Insert the fuel pump into the tank and engage the tab on the pump with the cut-out in the tank* **(see illustration)**.
c) *Keep the fuel pump pressed down onto the sealing ring until the locking ring has been fitted and tightened. This will prevent the sealing ring from being dislodged.*
d) *Position the locking ring with the arrow mark pointing toward the rear of the vehicle, then screw the ring back into position on the tank. Securely tighten the locking ring using the removal tool.*

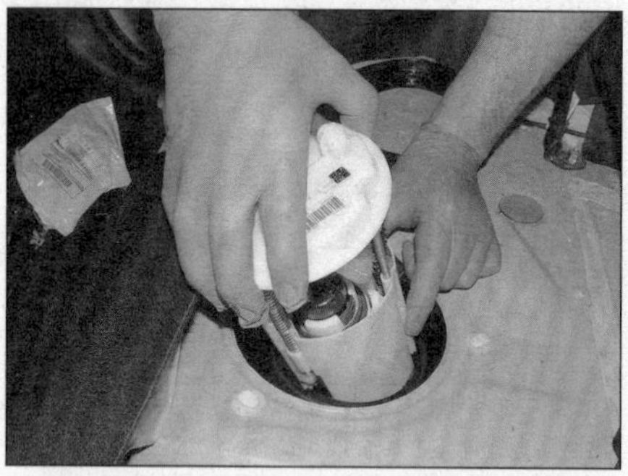

7.8c ...then withdraw the fuel pump, taking care not to damage the float arm

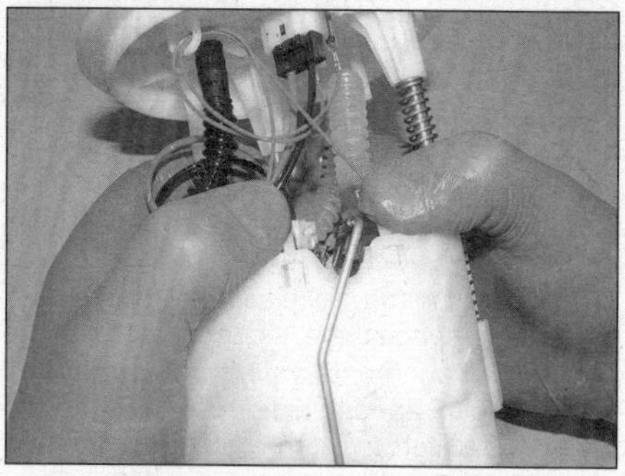

7.11a Depress the legs of the gauge sender unit locking tabs...

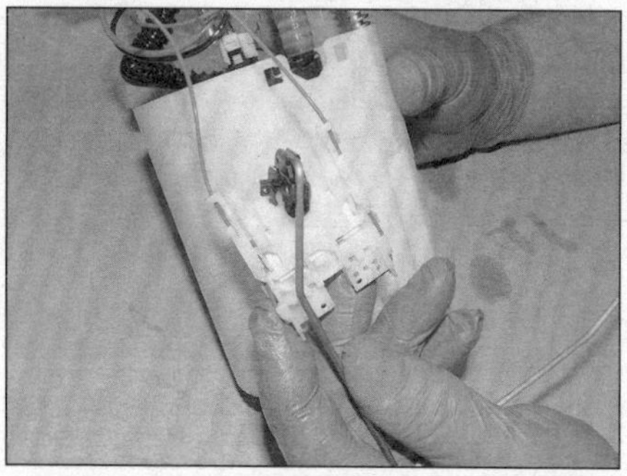

7.11b ...and slide the unit out of the fuel pump

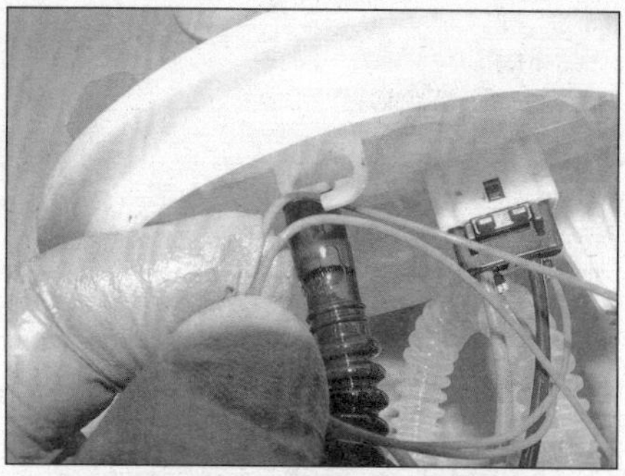

7.12 Release the wiring from the guide

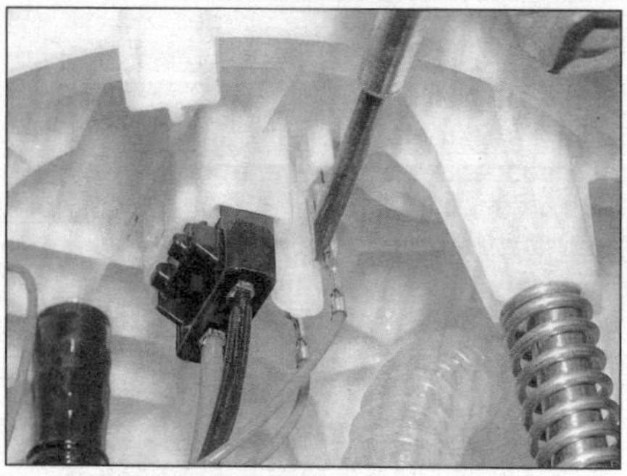

7.13 Ease the sender unit wiring end fittings off the pump connectors

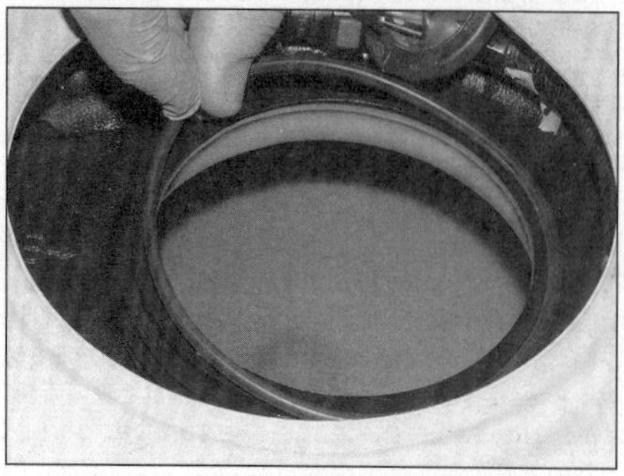

7.14a Fit a new sealing ring to the top of the tank

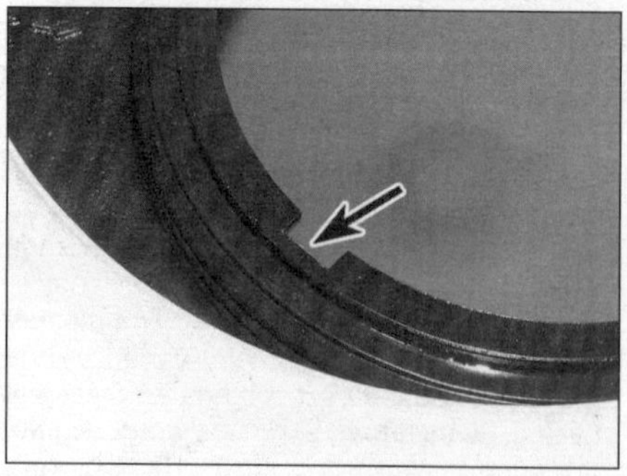

7.14b Engage the tab on the pump with the cut-out in the tank

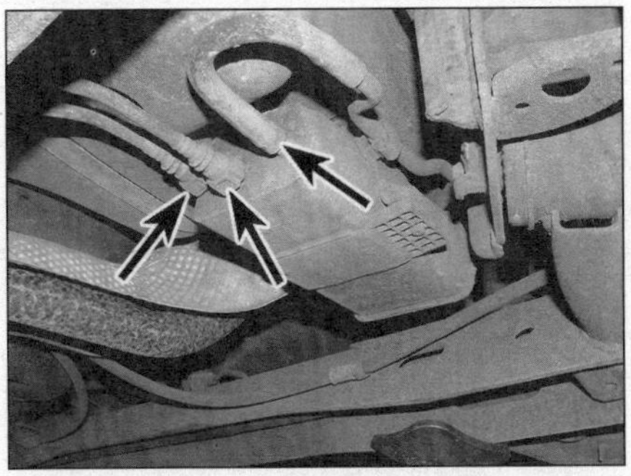

8.11 Disconnect the fuel and vent hoses at the charcoal canister

e) Ensure that the fuel hose and the wiring connector are securely reconnected to the sender unit.
f) Prior to refitting the access cover, reconnect the battery, then start the engine and check the fuel hose(s) for signs of leaks.

8 Fuel tank – removal and refitting

Note: *Refer to the warning note in Section 1 before proceeding.*

Removal

1 Before removing the fuel tank, all fuel must be drained from the tank. Since a fuel tank drain plug is not provided, it is therefore preferable to carry out the removal operation when the tank is nearly empty.
2 Depressurise the fuel system as described in Section 6.
3 Disconnect the battery negative terminal (refer to battery disconnection and reconnection in Chapter 5A, Section 3), then syphon or hand-pump the remaining fuel from the tank.
4 Disconnect the wiring connector(s) and fuel hose(s) from the fuel pump/gauge sender unit, as described in Section 7.
5 Jack up the rear of the car and securely support it on axle stands. See *Jacking and vehicle support*. Remove the right-hand rear roadwheel.
6 Remove the exhaust system intermediate pipe from below the fuel tank as described in Section 16. Release the fasteners and remove the heatshield from below the fuel tank.
7 Release the retaining clips securing the handbrake cables to the fuel tank and rear axle.
8 Working at the right-hand side rear of the fuel tank, release the retaining clip and disconnect the filler neck hose from the fuel tank.
9 Working under the right-hand wheel arch, release the retaining clip and disconnect the fuel vent pipe hose.
10 Disconnect the EVAP hose at the quick-release connector in front of the fuel tank.

8.13 Undo the fuel tank retaining strap bolts

11 Disconnect the fuel and vent hoses at the connectors on the charcoal canister located on the left-hand side of the fuel tank **(see illustration)**.
12 Place a trolley jack with an interposed block of wood beneath the tank, then raise the jack until it is supporting the weight of the tank.
13 Slacken and remove the bolts securing the two fuel tank retaining straps to the vehicle underbody **(see illustration)**.
14 Slowly lower the fuel tank out of position and remove the tank from underneath the vehicle.
15 If the tank is contaminated with sediment or water, remove the sender unit/fuel pump (Section 7) and swill the tank out with clean fuel. If any damage is evident, the tank should be renewed.

Refitting

16 Refitting is the reverse of the removal procedure, noting the following points:
a) When lifting the tank back into position, reconnect all the relevant breather hoses, and take great care to ensure that none of the hoses become trapped between the tank and vehicle body. Tighten the fuel tank mounting bolts to the specified torque setting.
b) Ensure that all pipes and hoses are correctly routed, and securely held in position with their retaining clips.
c) On completion, refill the tank with fuel, and check for signs of leakage prior to taking the vehicle on the road.

9 Throttle housing – removal and refitting

Removal

1 Disconnect the battery negative terminal (refer to battery disconnection and reconnection in Chapter 5A, Section 3).

1.2 litre engines

2 Undo the retaining bolts and move the coolant expansion tank aside.
3 Remove the air inlet tube as described in Section 2.
4 Disconnect the wiring connector from the throttle housing.

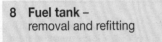

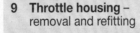

9.8 Disconnect the coolant hoses from the throttle housing

5 Slacken and remove the bolts securing the throttle housing assembly to the inlet manifold (working diagonally), and remove it from the engine compartment. Remove the O-ring seal/gasket and discard it; a new one must be used on refitting. Plug the inlet manifold port with a wad of clean cloth, to prevent the possible entry of foreign matter.

1.6 litre engines

6 Drain the cooling system as described in Chapter 1A, Section 25.
7 Remove the outlet air duct as described in Section 2.
8 Release the retaining clips and disconnect the two coolant hoses from the throttle housing **(see illustration)**.
9 Disconnect the wiring connector from the throttle housing.
10 Slacken and remove the bolts securing the throttle housing assembly to the inlet manifold (working diagonally), and remove it from the engine compartment. Remove the O-ring seal/gasket and discard it; a new one must be used on refitting. Plug the inlet manifold port with a wad of clean cloth, to prevent the possible entry of foreign matter.

Refitting

11 Refitting is a reverse of the removal procedure, bearing in mind the following points:
a) Ensure that the mating surfaces of the manifold and throttle housing are clean and dry, and fit a new O-ring seal/gasket to the manifold. Fit the throttle housing then, working in a diagonal sequence, tighten the retaining bolts to the specified torque setting.
b) On 1.6 litre engines, refill the cooling system as described in Chapter 1A, Section 25.

10 Fuel injection system components – removal and refitting

Fuel rail and injectors

Note: *Refer to the warning note in Section 1 before proceeding.*
Note: *If a faulty injector is suspected, before condemning the injector it is worth trying the effect of one of the proprietary injector-cleaning treatments.*

1.2 litre engines

Note: *Renewal of the Teflon sealing ring at the base of each injector entails the use of Nissan special tools. Have this work carried out by a Nissan dealer or fuel injection specialist. Note also that Nissan state that the fuel rail and fuel pipe must always be renewed after removal.*

1 Depressurise the fuel system as described in Section 6.

2 Disconnect the battery negative terminal (refer to battery disconnection and reconnection in Chapter 5A, Section 3).

3 Remove the inlet manifold as described in Section 14. Using duct tape (or similar), cover the intake ducts in the cylinder head to prevent anything being dropped down into the cylinders.

4 Thoroughly clean the high-pressure fuel pipe unions on the fuel rail and high-pressure fuel pump. Unscrew the union nuts, undo the support clip retaining bolt and withdraw the pipe. Plug or cover the open unions to prevent dirt entry.

5 Disconnect the wiring connector from the fuel pressure sensor on the fuel rail.

6 Disconnect the wiring connectors from the four fuel injectors, then unclip the wiring harness from the fuel rail.

7 Undo the four retaining bolts and carefully ease the fuel rail and injectors from their location in the cylinder head.

8 Using duct tape (or similar), cover the injector recesses in the cylinder head to prevent anything being dropped down inside them.

9 Release the retaining clip from the relevant injector and remove the injector out of position, and recover the sealing rings. Repeat the procedure as required to remove any other injectors.

10 Discard the seals, sealing rings, fuel pipe and fuel rail; new components must be used on refitting.

11 Refitting is a reversal of the removal procedure, noting the following points:

a) Fit new O-rings to all disturbed injectors and have new Teflon seals fitted by a Nissan dealer or specialist.

b) Apply a smear of engine oil to the O-rings to aid installation, and then ease the injectors into the new fuel rail.

c) Make sure the injector retaining clips on the fuel rail are fitted correctly.

d) On completion, start the engine and check for fuel leaks.

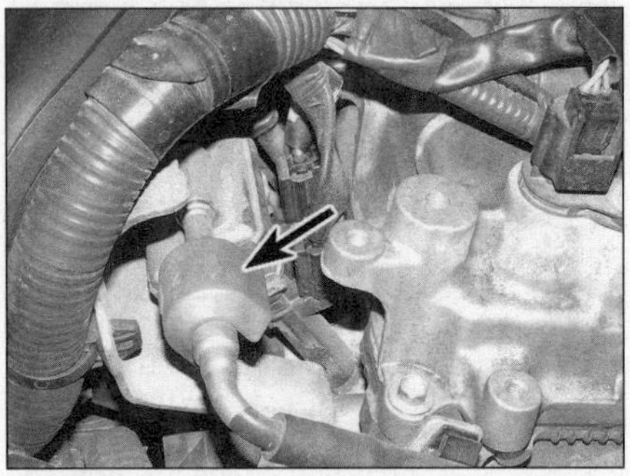

10.15 Unclip the plastic cover from the fuel rail connector

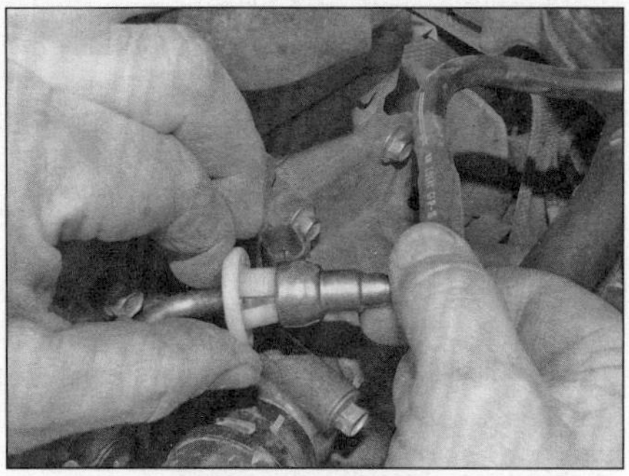

10.16a Using a plastic special tool to release the fuel pipe

10.16b The four securing tangs need to be released...

10.16c ...to disconnect the fuel pipe

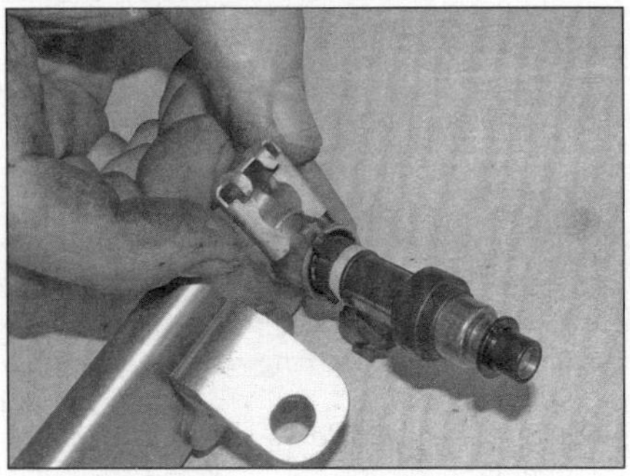

10.21a Remove the securing clip...

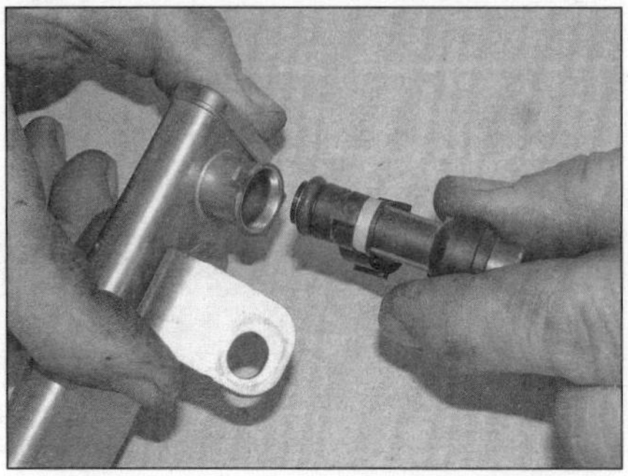

10.21b ...and withdraw the fuel injector

1.6 litre engines

12 Depressurise the fuel system as described in Section 6.

13 Disconnect the battery negative terminal (refer to battery disconnection and reconnection in Chapter 5A, Section 3).

14 Remove the inlet manifold as described in Section 14. Using duct tape (or similar), cover the intake ducts in the cylinder head to prevent anything being dropped down into the cylinders.

15 Unclip the plastic cover from the fuel rail connector at the left-hand side of the cylinder head **(see illustration)**. Note its fitted position and the direction of the arrow on the side of the cover.

16 Using a commercially available special tool, release the securing clips and disconnect the fuel pipe from the end of the fuel rail **(see illustrations)**. Plug the fuel pipe and fuel rail end to prevent dirt ingress.

17 Disconnect the wiring harness from across the top of the cylinder head cover. Disconnect it from the coils, injectors and valve timing solenoid valves, and then move it to one side.

18 Undo the four retaining bolts and remove the fuel rail protector shield from the cylinder head.

19 Slacken and remove the two fuel rail retaining nuts, and then carefully ease the fuel rail and injectors out from the cylinder head, and remove them from the vehicle.

20 Using duct tape (or similar), cover the injector recesses in the cylinder head to prevent anything being dropped down inside them.

21 Release the retaining clip from the relevant injector and remove the injector out of position, and recover the sealing rings **(see illustrations)**. Repeat the procedure as required to remove any other injectors.

22 Discard the seals and sealing rings;

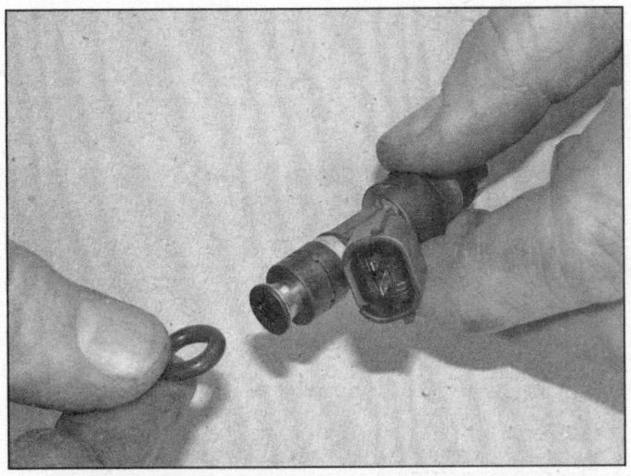

10.22 Remove the seal from the top of each injector

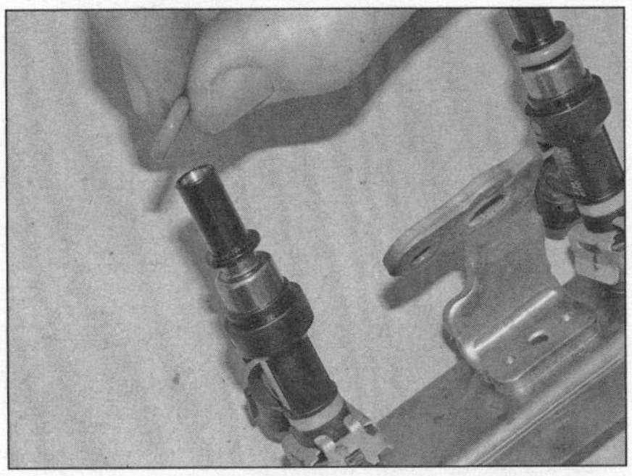

10.23a Renew all injector seals

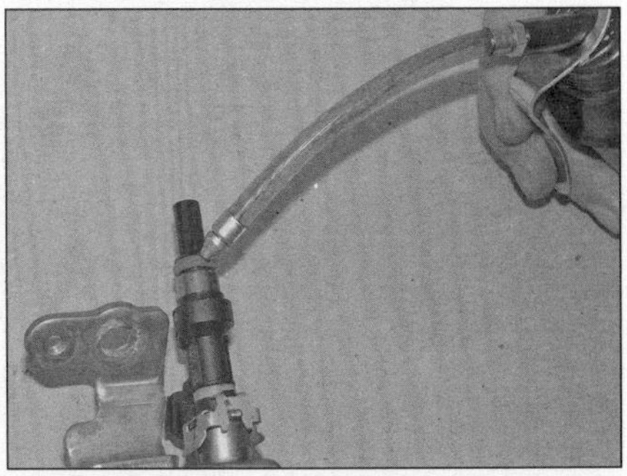

10.23b Apply a small amount of oil to the seals

new ones must be used on refitting **(see illustration)**.

23 Refitting is a reversal of the removal procedure, noting the following points:

a) *Fit new O-rings to all disturbed injectors - Green O-ring seals cylinder head end of the injector and Black O-ring seals fuel rail side of the injector* **(see illustration)**

b) *Apply a smear of engine oil to the O-rings to aid installation* **(see illustration)**, *and then ease the injectors into the fuel rail.*

c) *Make sure the injector retaining clips on the fuel rail are fitted correctly* **(see illustration)**.

d) *When fitting the plastic cover to the fuel pipe connection, make sure it is fitted securely.*

e) *On completion, start the engine and check for fuel leaks.*

Throttle potentiometer

24 The throttle potentiometer is mounted on the rear of the throttle housing and can only be renewed as a complete unit. See Section 9, for the removal and refitting procedure. Check with your local Nissan dealer for the availability of parts.

Mass airflow (MAF) sensor

25 The airflow sensor is mounted in the air cleaner housing on 1.6 litre engines.

26 Disconnect the wiring connector from the airflow sensor **(see illustration 2.3)**.

27 Undo the retaining bolts, and then remove the sensor from the air cleaner housing **(see illustration)**. Recover its sealing ring and renew.

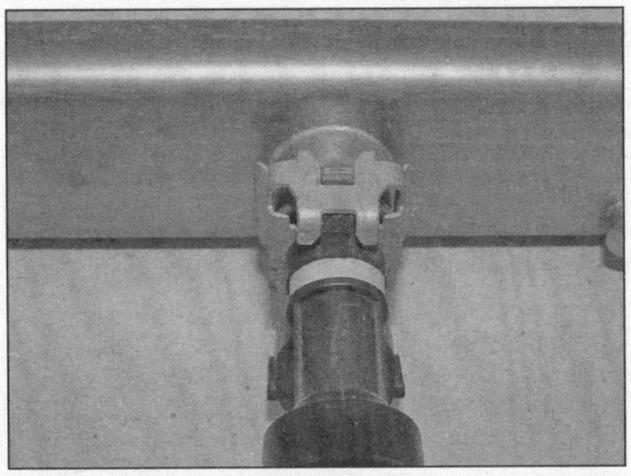

10.23c Make sure the securing clip is fitted correctly

10.27 Undo the airflow sensor retaining bolts

28 Refitting is the reverse of removal, using a new sealing ring (where applicable) and tightening its retaining screws securely.

Valve timing control solenoids

29 The valve timing control solenoids are fitted to each side of the timing chain cover on 1.2 litre engines and to each side of the right-hand end of the cylinder head on 1.6 litre engines. One solenoid serves the inlet camshaft and one serves the exhaust camshaft **(see illustration)**.

30 Disconnect the wiring connector from the relevant solenoid.

31 Undo the retaining bolt and withdraw the relevant solenoid from the timing chain cover or cylinder head **(see illustration)**. Be prepared for some oil spillage, and have some cloth ready to catch it.

32 Refitting is the reverse of removal.

Inlet air temperature (IAT) sensor

33 The inlet air temperature sensor is integral with the inlet manifold pressure sensor (1.2 litre engines) or mass airflow sensor (1.6 litre engines).

Camshaft position sensors

34 The camshaft position sensors are fitted to the transmission end of the cylinder head cover. Two sensors are used, one for each camshaft **(see illustration)**.

35 Disconnect the wiring connector from the relevant camshaft position sensor.

10.29 Inlet camshaft valve timing solenoid on 1.6 litre engines

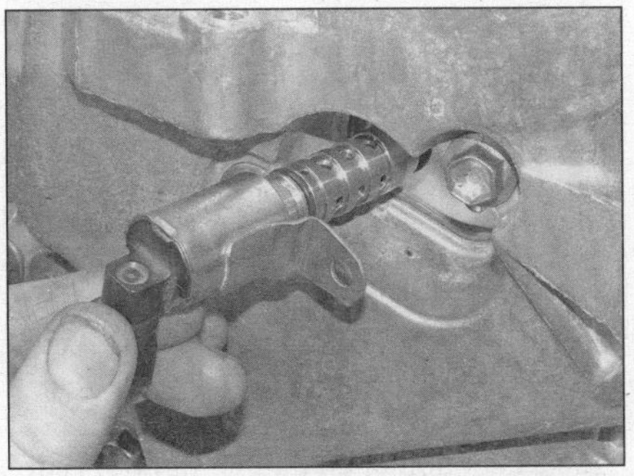

10.31 Undo the retaining bolt and withdraw the solenoid

10.34 Camshaft position sensors on 1.6 litre engines

10.40a Undo the retaining bolts...

10.40b ...and remove the sensor heatshield

36 Undo the retaining bolt and withdraw the sensor from the cover.

37 Discard the O-ring seal; a new one must be used on refitting.

38 Refitting is a reversal of the removal procedure, noting the following points:

a) Fit a new O-ring seal to the sensor.

b) Apply a smear of engine oil to the O-ring to aid installation, and then ease the sensor into position.

Crankshaft position sensor

39 The crankshaft position sensor is fitted to the rear of the cylinder block at the transmission end.

40 Undo the retaining bolts and remove the heatshield from around the sensor **(see illustrations)**.

41 Disconnect the wiring connector from the position sensor **(see illustration)**.

42 Undo the retaining bolt and withdraw the sensor from the cylinder block **(see illustration)**.

43 Refitting is a reversal of the removal procedure, noting the following points:

a) Fit a new O-ring seal to the sensor **(see illustration)**.

b) Apply a smear of engine oil to the O-ring to aid installation **(see illustration)**, *and then ease the sensor into position.*

Coolant temperature sensor

44 Refer to Chapter 3, Section 6.

Electronic Control Unit (ECU)

Note: *The engine management electronic control unit is electronically coded for the vehicle to which it is fitted; therefore new units are supplied without a code. If the ECU is being removed to enable a new unit to be fitted, a Nissan dealer must program the new unit with the information from the old ECU.*

45 The ECU is located on the left-hand side of the engine compartment, in front of the battery **(see illustration)**.

46 Disconnect the battery negative terminal (refer to battery disconnection and reconnection in Chapter 5A, Section 3).

1.2 litre engines

47 Release the locking levers, and then withdraw the three electrical connectors from the top of the ECU.

48 Undo the four retaining nuts and remove the ECU from the mounting bracket.

49 Refitting is a reverse of the removal procedure ensuring that the wiring is securely reconnected.

1.6 litre engines

50 Disconnect the two wiring connectors from the fusible link on the battery positive terminal **(see illustration)**. Release the two retaining clips and free the wiring harness from the fuse holder bracket.

51 Release the two retaining clips and free the engine management ECU wiring harness from the fuse holder bracket. Release the locking levers and disconnect the three wiring connectors from the ECU.

52 Using a flat-bladed screwdriver,

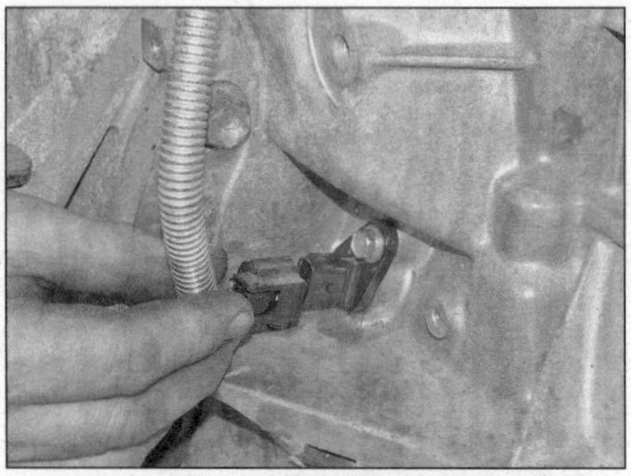

10.41 Disconnect the sensor wiring connector

10.42 Undo the bolt and withdraw the sensor

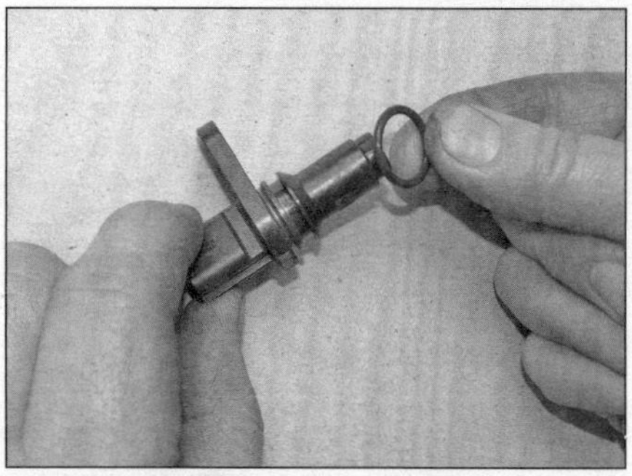

10.43a Renew the O-ring seal...

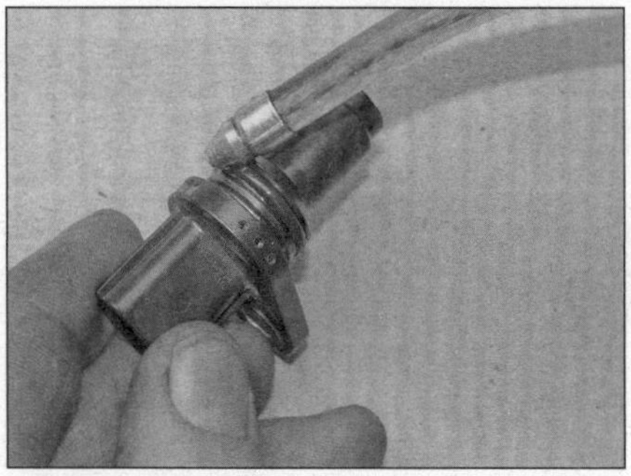

10.43b ...and lubricate with a smear of oil

10.45 Location of Electronic Control Unit (ECU)

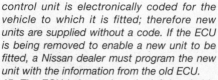

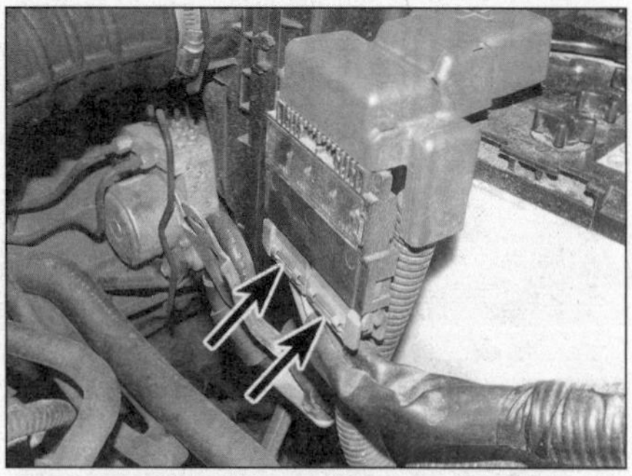

10.50 Disconnect the two wiring harness connectors from the fusible link in the battery positive terminal

10.52 Release the retaining pawls and lift the fusebox out of the mounting bracket

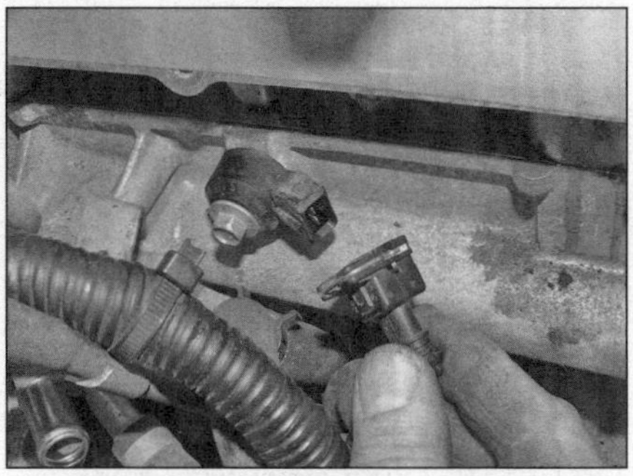

10.58 Disconnect the sensor wiring connector

10.59 Undo the sensor retaining bolt

release the two retaining tabs and withdraw the fuse holder from the mounting bracket **(see illustration)**. Move the fuse holder to one side.

53 Release the wiring harness retaining clip(s) from the front of the fuse holder bracket.

54 Undo the retaining nut and retaining bolt and remove the fuse holder bracket.

55 Undo the retaining nuts and remove the ECU from the mounting bracket.

56 Refitting is a reverse of the removal procedure ensuring that the wiring is securely reconnected.

Knock sensor

57 The knock sensor is fitted to the front of the cylinder block.

58 Disconnect the wiring connector from the sensor **(see illustration)**.

59 Undo the retaining bolt and withdraw the sensor from the cylinder block **(see illustration)**.

60 Refitting is a reversal of the removal procedure, making sure the mating face of the sensor and cylinder block are clean. Also make sure that the electrical connection on the sensor is facing towards the transmission when refitted.

Air conditioning pressure sensor

61 The air conditioning pressure sensor is screwed into the top of the receiver drier in the air conditioning circuit. Removal and refitting of the switch requires the air conditioning system to be discharged and recharged, and the home mechanic should not attempt this, (see Chapter 3, Section 11).

Manifold pressure sensor

62 The sensor is located on the top of the inlet manifold on 1.2 litre engines **(see illustration)**.

63 Disconnect the wiring connector from the sensor.

64 Undo the retaining bolt and remove the sensor from the manifold.

65 Discard the O-ring seal; a new one must be used on refitting.

66 Refitting is a reversal of the removal procedure, noting the following points:

a) Fit a new O-ring seal to the sensor.

b) Apply a smear of engine oil to the O-ring to aid installation, and then ease the sensor into position.

High-pressure fuel pump

Note: *Refer to the warning note in Section 1 before proceeding.*

67 The high-pressure fuel pump used on 1.2 litre engines is mounted on the cylinder head cover and is operated by the exhaust camshaft, via a lifter **(see illustration)**.

68 Depressurise the fuel system as described in Section 6.

69 Disconnect the battery negative terminal (refer to battery disconnection and reconnection in Chapter 5A, Section 3).

70 Remove the inlet manifold as described in Section 14. Using duct tape (or similar), cover the intake ducts in the cylinder head to prevent anything being dropped down into the cylinders.

71 Depress the coloured tabs of the quick-release fitting and disconnect the fuel supply hose from thefuel pump. Suitably cover the hose union and the fitting on the pump to prevent dirt ingress.

72 Thoroughly clean the high-pressure fuel pipe unions on the fuel rail and high-pressure fuel pump. Unscrew the union nuts, undo the support clip retaining bolt and withdraw the pipe. Plug or cover the open unions to prevent dirt entry. Note that a new fuel pipe will be required for refitting.

73 Disconnect the wiring connector from the fuel pump.

74 Undo the fuel pump retaining bolts and remove the fuel pump from the cylinder head cover. Recover the O-ring and remove the pump lifter the pump lifter.

75 Commence refitting by placing a new O-ring on the pump body. Apply a smear of engine oil to the O-ring to aid installation.

76 Place the pump lifter in position in the cylinder head cover. If the lifter is not in its lowest position, turn the crankshaft by means of the crankshaft pulley bolt until the lifter camshaft lobe points downward.

77 Refit the pump, screw in the retaining bolts and progressively tighten them to the specified torque.

78 Fit the new fuel pipe to the pump and fuel rail and tighten the pipe unions securely. Refit and tighten the support clip retaining bolt.

79 Reconnect the pump wiring connector and the fuel supply hose.

80 Refit the inlet manifold as described in Section 14.

81 On completion, start the engine and check for fuel leaks.

11 Turbocharger – description and precautions

Note: *A turbocharger is only fitted to 1.2 litre engines and is integral with the exhaust manifold.*

1 A turbocharger increases engine efficiency by raising the pressure in the inlet manifold above atmospheric pressure. Instead of the air simply being sucked into the cylinders,

10.62 Manifold pressure sensor location

10.67 High-pressure fuel pump location

it is forced in. Additional fuel is supplied in proportion to the increased air intake.

2 Energy for the operation of the turbocharger comes from the exhaust gas. The gas flows through a specially shaped housing (the turbine housing) and in so doing, spins the turbine wheel. The turbine wheel is attached to a shaft, at the end of which is another vaned wheel known as the compressor wheel. The compressor wheel spins in its own housing and compresses the inducted air on the way to the inlet manifold.

3 Between the turbocharger and the inlet manifold, the compressed air passes through an intercooler. This is an air-to-air heat exchanger, mounted behind the front bumper, in front of the air conditioning condenser and the coolant radiator. The purpose of the intercooler is to remove some of the heat gained in being compressed from the inducted air. Because cooler air is denser, removal of this heat further increases engine efficiency.

4 Boost pressure (the pressure in the inlet manifold) is limited by a wastegate, which diverts the exhaust gas away from the turbine wheel in response to a pressure-sensitive actuator. Turbocharging pressure is controlled by a boost pressure sensor located in the air inlet tube between the intercooler and the throttle housing.

5 The turbo shaft is pressure-lubricated by an oil feed pipe from the main oil gallery. The shaft 'floats' on a cushion of oil. A drain pipe returns the oil to the sump.

Precautions

- ***The turbocharger operates at extremely high speeds and temperatures. Certain precautions must be observed to avoid premature failure of the turbo or injury to the operator.***
- ***Do not race the engine immediately after start-up, especially if it is cold. Give the oil a few seconds to circulate.***
- ***Always allow the engine to return to idle speed before switching it off – do not blip the throttle and switch off, as this will leave the turbo spinning without lubrication.***
- ***Allow the engine to idle for several minutes before switching off after a high speed run.***
- ***Observe the recommended intervals for oil and filter changing, and use a reputable oil of the specified quality. Neglect of oil changing, or use of inferior oil, can cause carbon formation on the turbo shaft and subsequent failure.***

Warning: Do not operate the turbo with any parts exposed. Foreign objects falling onto the rotating vanes could cause damage and (if ejected) personal injury.

12 Turbocharger – removal and refitting

Note: *This Section describes removal and refitting of the turbocharger, together with the exhaust manifold. The turbocharger cannot be separately removed from the exhaust manifold.*

Removal

1 Apply the handbrake, then jack up the front of the vehicle, and securely support it on axle stands (see *Jacking and vehicle support*).

2 Disconnect the battery negative terminal (refer to *battery disconnection and reconnection* in Chapter 5A, Section 3).

3 Drain the cooling system as described in Chapter 1A, Section 25.

4 Remove the air cleaner assembly, outlet air duct and air inlet hose as described in Section 2.

5 Release the retaining clips and remove the exhaust gas pressure take-off hose and wastegate control hose from the turbocharger.

6 Remove the windscreen cowl panel and cowl panel extension as described in Chapter 11, Section 21.

7 Remove the catalytic converter as described in Section 16.

8 Unscrew the union and disconnect the oil supply pipe from the turbocharger, collect the copper sealing rings, then unscrew the union nut and disconnect the pipe from the engine.

9 Unscrew the bolts and detach the oil return pipe from the bottom of the turbocharger – if necessary, remove the pipe from the cylinder block.

10 Release the retaining clips and disconnect the two turbocharger coolant hoses.

11 Unscrew the turbocharger upper and lower mounting nuts, then remove the turbocharger from the exhaust manifold. Do not attempt to separate the inlet and exhaust sections of the turbocharger.

12 Remove the gasket noting that its end tab is facing the flywheel end of the engine.

Refitting

13 Refitting is a reversal of removal, using a new manifold gasket. Renew any damaged hose clamps, and use new turbocharger-to-exhaust manifold nuts which should be tightened to the specified torque. Fit new oil supply pipe O-rings and copper seals, then apply Loctite Frenetanch (or similar sealant) to the union threads before refitting the pipe and tightening the union nuts to the specified torque. Fit a new gasket to the top of the oil return pipe, and new O-ring seals to the grooves in the bottom of the pipe.

14 On completion refill the cooling system as described in Chapter 1A, Section 25.

13 Intercooler – removal and refitting

Note: *An intercooler is only fitted to 1.2 litre engines.*

Removal

1 Remove the air inlet hose and air inlet tube as described in Section 2.

2 Remove the front bumper as described in Chapter 11, Section 6.

3 Extract the upper plastic expanding rivet securing the air guides to the bonnet lock platform on each side **(see illustration)**.

4 Using cable ties or similar, suitably attach the condenser, radiator and intercooler to the bonnet lock platform to prevent them dropping down during subsequent operations.

5 Remove the front bumper energy absorber, then undo the three nuts each side and remove the bumper brace **(see illustrations)**.

13.3 Extract the expanding rivets securing the air guides

13.5a Remove the energy absorber from the front bumper brace

13.5b Undo the bumper brace retaining nuts each side and remove the brace

6 Undo the two bolts each side and remove the radiator lower support member **(see illustrations)**.

7 Cut the cable ties or similar used to retain the intercooler, then carefully lower the intercooler and withdraw it from under the car.

Refitting

8 Refitting is a reverse of the removal procedure

14 Inlet manifold – removal and refitting

Removal

1 Disconnect the battery negative terminal (refer to battery disconnection and reconnection in Chapter 5A, Section 3).

1.2 litre engines

2 Remove the air inlet hose and air inlet tube as described in Section 2.

3 Undo the retaining bolts and move the coolant expansion tank aside.

4 Disconnect the following hoses from the inlet manifold **(see illustrations)**:

a) Crankcase ventilation hose.
b) Brake servo vacuum hose.
c) Charcoal canister purge hose.
d) Water outlet vacuum hose.

5 Disconnect the wiring connectors at the inlet manifold pressure sensor and throttle housing.

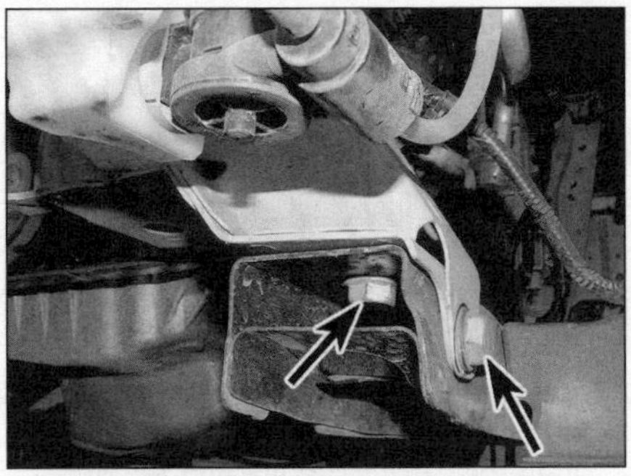

13.6a Undo the two bolts each side...

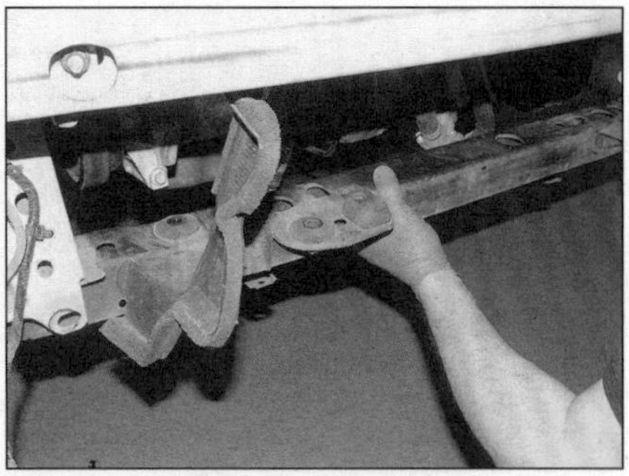

13.6b ...and remove the radiator lower support member

6 Withdraw the oil level dipstick to make access to the manifold centre bolts easier.

7 Make a final check that all the necessary vacuum/breather hoses and wiring have been disconnected from the manifold then, working from the outside to the centre, slacken and remove the manifold retaining bolts.

8 Manoeuvre the manifold away from the cylinder head, and out of the engine compartment. Remove the manifold rubber gasket and discard it, a new one will be required for refitting.

1.6 litre engines

9 Drain the cooling system as described in Chapter 1A, Section 25.

10 Remove the outlet air duct as described in Section 2.

11 Disconnect the hoses at the coolant expansion tank, then undo the retaining bolts and remove the tank.

12 Remove the oil level dipstick.

13 Release the retaining clips and disconnect the two coolant hoses from the throttle housing **(see illustration 9.8)**.

14 Disconnect the throttle housing wiring connector.

15 Disconnect the vacuum hoses and wiring connector from the charcoal canister purge control solenoid valve **(see illustration)**.

16 Undo the two bolts securing the manifold to the left-hand and right-hand sides of the cylinder head cover **(see illustrations)**.

17 Disconnect the brake servo vacuum hose from the manifold.

18 Make a final check that all the necessary vacuum/breather hoses and wiring have been disconnected from the manifold then, working from the outside to the centre, slacken and remove the manifold retaining bolts **(see illustration)**.

19 Manoeuvre the manifold away from

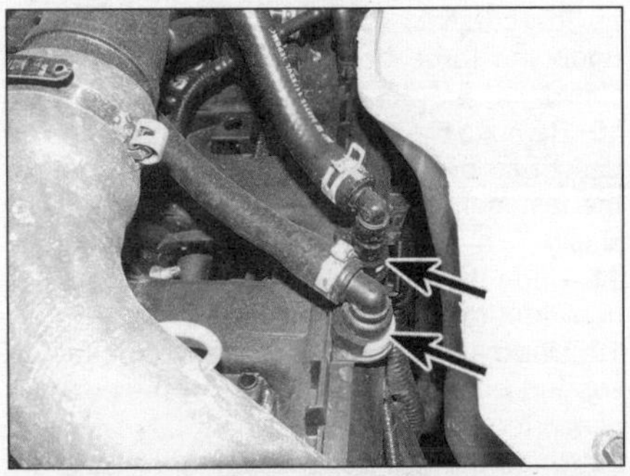

14.4a Disconnect the crankcase ventilation hose and brake servo vacuum hose...

14.4b ...and the canister purge hose and water outlet vacuum hose

14.15 Disconnect the hoses and wiring connector at the purge control solenoid valve

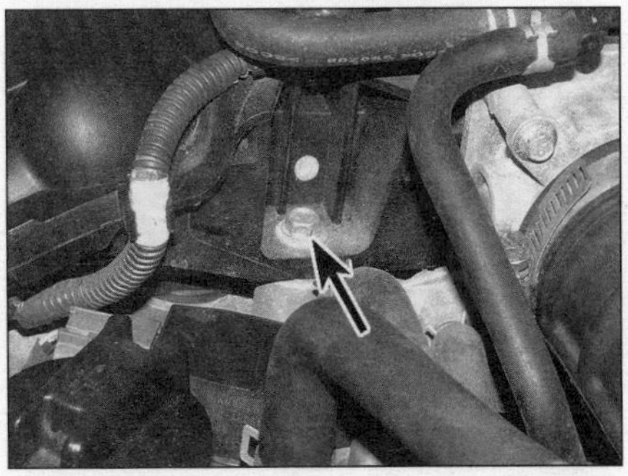

14.16a Undo the bolt securing the manifold to the cylinder head cover on the left-hand...

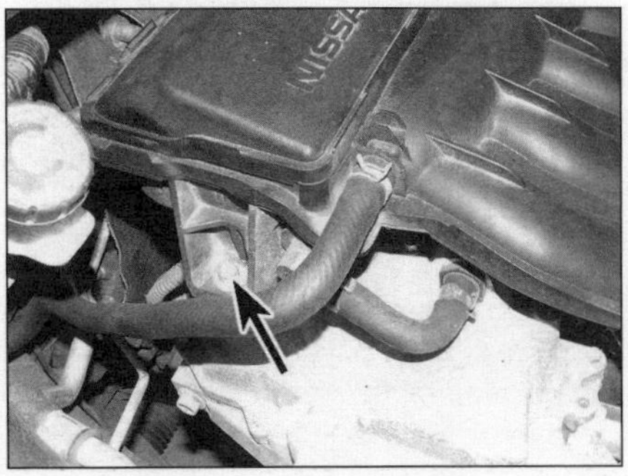

14.16b ...and right-hand side

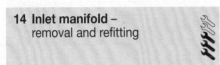

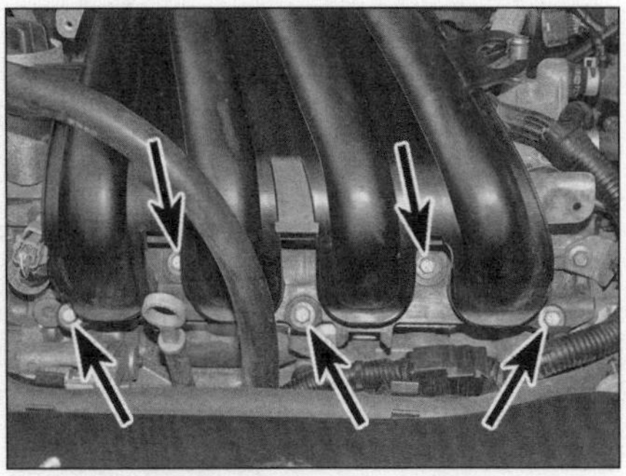

14.18 Undo the manifold retaining bolts

14.20 Ensure new manifold seals are fitted

the cylinder head, and out of the engine compartment. Remove the manifold rubber gasket and discard it, a new one will be required for refitting.

Refitting

20 Refitting is the reverse of the removal procedure, noting the following points:

a) *Ensure that the manifold and cylinder head mating surfaces are clean and dry, and fit the new rubber gasket to the manifold* **(see illustration)**.
b) *Install the manifold, and tighten its retaining bolts to the specified torque, starting at the centre and working outwards.*
c) *Ensure that all relevant hoses are reconnected to their original positions, and are securely held (where necessary) by their retaining clips.*
d) *On 1.6 litre engines, refill the cooling system as described in Chapter 1A, Section 25.*

15 Exhaust manifold – removal and refitting

Note: *On 1.2 litre engines, the exhaust manifold also incorporates the turbocharger as one assembly (see Section 12). The following procedures are only applicable to 1.6 litre engines.*

Removal

1 Disconnect the battery negative terminal (refer to battery disconnection and reconnection in Chapter 5A, Section 3).

2 Remove the exhaust system front pipe as described in Section 16.

3 Remove the outlet air duct as described in Section 2.

4 Disconnect the wiring connector, then undo the retaining bolt securing the oxygen sensor wiring harness bracket to the cylinder head on the right-hand side.

5 Undo the retaining bolts and remove the exhaust manifold upper heat shield.

6 Undo the side mounting bolt from the exhaust manifold support bracket.

7 Undo the retaining bolts and remove the exhaust manifold lower heat shield.

8 Make sure there is nothing still attached to the manifold, then working from the outside to the centre, slacken and remove the manifold retaining nuts **(see illustration)**.

9 Manoeuvre the manifold out of the engine compartment, and discard the manifold gasket.

Refitting

10 Refitting is the reverse of the removal procedure, noting the following points:

a) *Examine all the exhaust manifold studs and nuts for signs of damage and corrosion, and repair or renew any damaged studs. Note that Nissan recommends that the nuts and studs should always be renewed if removed.*
b) *Ensure that the manifold and cylinder head sealing faces are clean and flat, and fit the new manifold gasket* **(see illustration)**.
c) *Install the manifold and tighten its retaining nuts to the specified torque, starting at the centre and working outwards.*
d) *Refit the front pipe as described in Section 16.*

16 Exhaust system – general information, component removal and refitting

General information

1 On 1.2 litre engines, the exhaust system consists of four sections; the catalytic converter, the front pipe, the intermediate pipe incorporating the centre silencer and the tailpipe incorporating the rear silencer.

2 On 1.6 litre engines, the exhaust system consists of three sections; the front pipe incorporating the catalytic converter, the intermediate pipe incorporating the centre silencer and the tailpipe incorporating the rear silencer.

3 The system is suspended throughout its entire length by rubber mountings **(see illustration)**, and all exhaust sections are joined by flanged joints, which are then secured together by nuts and/or bolts. On 1.6 litre engines tension springs are also used at the front pipe flanged joints.

4 To remove the system or part of the system, firmly apply the handbrake, and then jack up the vehicle and support it securely on axle stands (see *Jacking and vehicle support*). Alternatively, position the car over an inspection pit, or on car ramps.

Front pipe (1.2 litre engines)

5 Undo the nuts securing the front pipe to the catalytic converter.

6 Undo the nuts and remove the bolts securing the front pipe to the intermediate pipe. Separate the front pipe-to-intermediate pipe joint and recover the gasket.

7 Spray a little penetrating oil on the mounting rubbers, then slide the front pipe to the rear and disengage it from the mountings. Collect the front pipe to catalytic converter gasket and remove the front pipe from under the car.

Catalytic converter (1.2 litre engines)

8 Remove the two oxygen sensors from the catalytic converter as described in Chapter 4C, Section 2.

9 Release the wiring harness from the clips on the catalytic converter heat shield, then undo the three bolts and remove the heat shield.

10 Remove the exhaust system front pipe as described previously in this Section. Release the fasteners and remove the front pipe heat shield.

11 Undo the three nuts securing the catalytic converter to the turbocharger.

12 Undo the three bolts and remove the support bracket from the side of the catalytic converter.

13 Undo the two bolts securing the catalytic converter to the engine support bracket. Withdraw the converter from the turbocharger

15.8 Undo the manifold retaining nuts

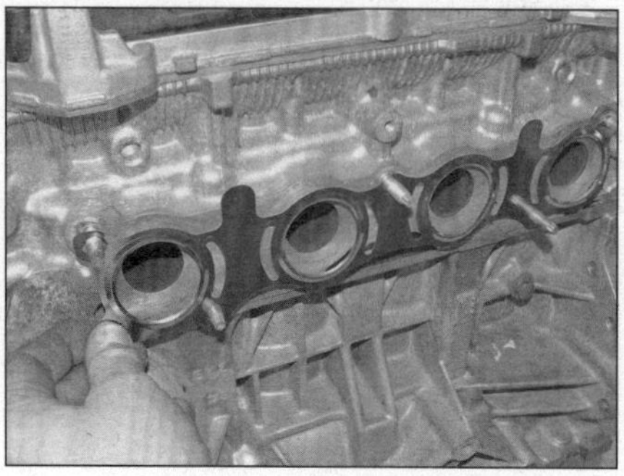

15.10 Fit a new manifold gasket

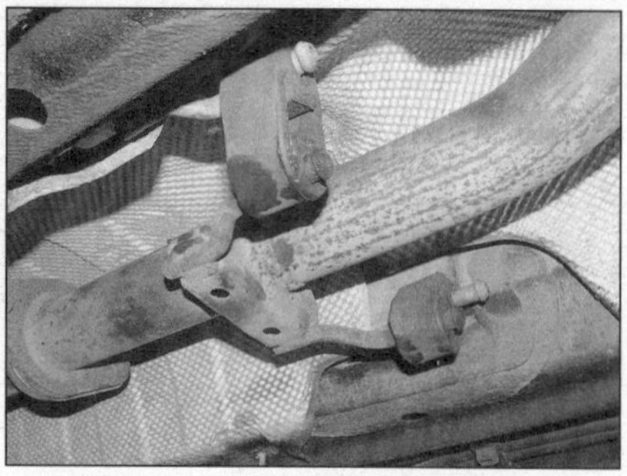

16.3 Exhaust rubber mountings

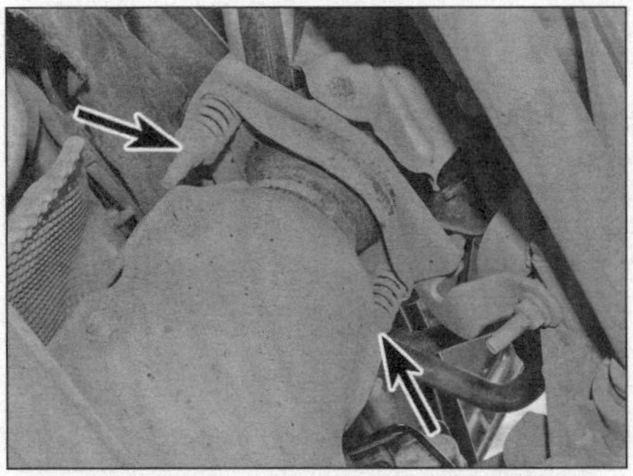

16.14 Undo the front pipe/catalytic converter to manifold nuts

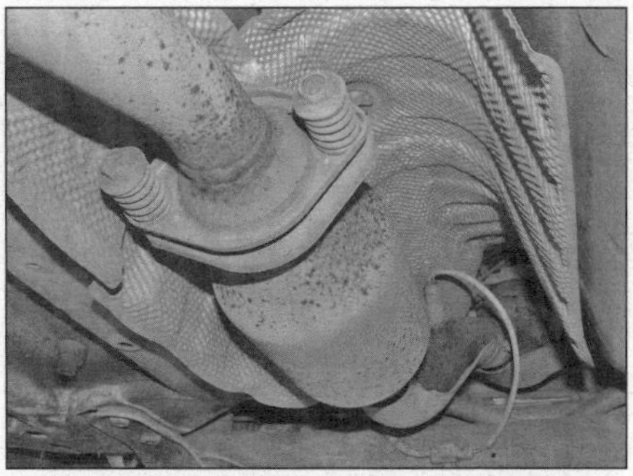

16.16 Undo the front pipe/catalytic converter to intermediate pipe bolts

16.22a Heatshield to protect fuel tank

16.22b Heatshield around silencer/catalytic converter

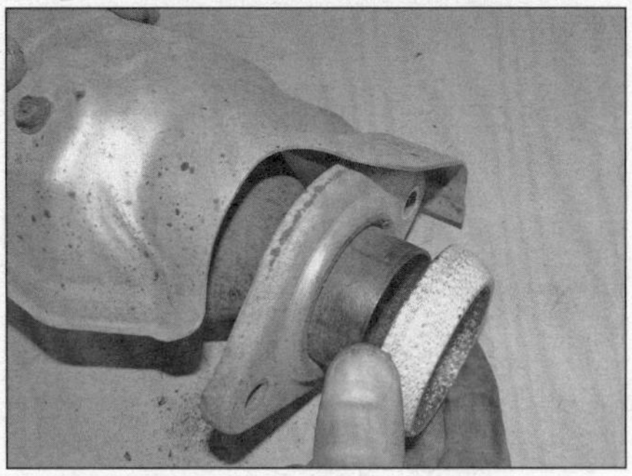

16.23a Fit new sealing rings to the silencer...

16.23b ...and the exhaust front pipe

and remove it from the engine compartment. Recover the gasket.

Front pipe/catalytic converter (1.6 litre engines)

14 Undo the nuts securing the front pipe/catalytic converter to the exhaust manifold **(see illustration)**. With the nuts removed retrieve the springs, and then separate the front pipe/catalytic converter from the exhaust manifold.

15 Trace the wiring back from the oxygen sensor to its wiring connector, and then disconnect it from the main wiring harness.

16 Slacken and remove the two bolts securing the front pipe/catalytic converter flange joint to the intermediate pipe **(see illustration)**. Spray a little penetrating oil on the mounting rubbers, then disengage the pipe from the mountings. Collect the gasket and remove the front pipe from under the car.

Intermediate pipe

17 Undo the two nuts securing the intermediate pipe to the tailpipe.

18 On 1.2 litre engines, undo the two nuts and remove the bolts securing the front pipe flange joint to the intermediate pipe, then separate the flange joint. On 1.6 litre engines, undo the two bolts, retrieve the springs, then separate the flange joint.

19 Spray a little penetrating oil on the mounting rubbers, then disengage the pipe from the mountings. Collect the gasket and remove the intermediate pipe from under the car.

Tailpipe

20 Undo the two nuts securing the intermediate pipe to the tailpipe.

21 Spray a little penetrating oil on the mounting rubbers, then disengage the pipe from the mountings. Collect the gasket and remove the tailpipe from under the car.

Heat shield(s)

22 The heat shields are secured in position by a mixture of fasteners. Some heat shields are fitted to the underside of the vehicle and some are fitted to parts of the exhaust system. When an exhaust section is renewed, transfer any relevant heat shields from the original over to the new section before installing the exhaust section on the vehicle **(see illustrations)**.

Refitting

23 Each section is refitted by a reverse of the removal sequence, noting the following points:

a) *Ensure that all traces of corrosion have been removed from the flanges, and renew all necessary gaskets* **(see illustrations)**.
b) *Inspect the rubber mountings for signs of damage or deterioration, and renew as necessary.*
c) *Prior to tightening the exhaust system fasteners, ensure that all rubber mountings are correctly located, and that there is adequate clearance between the exhaust system and vehicle underbody/suspension components, etc.*

Notes

Chapter 4 Part B
Diesel engine fuel and exhaust systems

Contents

Degrees of difficulty

Easy, suitable for novice with little experience	**Fairly easy,** suitable for beginner with some experience	**Fairly difficult,** suitable for competent DIY mechanic	**Difficult,** suitable for experienced DIY mechanic	**Very difficult,** suitable for expert DIY or professional

Specifications

General

System type	Siemens VDO electronic common-rail direct injection, with turbocharger
Firing order	1-3-4-2 (number 1 cylinder at flywheel end)
Idle speed (not adjustable – controlled by ECU)	750 ± 900 rpm (depending on engine type)
Engine designation	K9K
Version:	
To emission standard Euro 5	K9K (Type 1)
To emission standard Euro 6	K9K (Type 2)

Torque wrench settings

Torque wrench settings	Nm	lbf ft
Diesel particulate filter (Type 2 engines):		
Filter-to-support bracket bolt	25	18
Retaining strap mounting bolts	25	18
Upper clamp bolt/nut	25	18
Exhaust manifold	26	19
Exhaust system components:		
Exhaust gas pressure sensor:		
Type 1 engines	32	24
Type 2 engines	14	10
Exhaust gas temperature sensor	32	24
Front pipe-to-particulate filter or turbocharger	21	15
Intermediate pipe-to-front pipe	58	43
Particulate filter temperature sensor	32	24
Silencer-to-intermediate pipe	35	26
Fuel gauge sender unit	70	52
Fuel injectors-to-cylinder head	30	22
Fuel tank	25	18
High-pressure fuel rail	28	21
High-pressure pipe union nuts	24	18
High-pressure pump	21	15
High-pressure pump sprocket nut	70	52

Torque wrench settings (continued)

	Nm	lbf ft
Turbocharger oil return pipe flange nuts	12	9
Turbocharger oil supply pipe:		
To cylinder head	35	26
To turbocharger:		
Type 1 engines	23	17
Type 2 engines	11	8
Turbocharger-to-exhaust manifold:		
Type 1 engines	26	19
Type 2 engines	29	21

1 General information and precautions

General information

1 The fuel system consists of a rear-mounted fuel tank containing a fuel supply pump, a fuel filter, a high-pressure pump with common rail injection system, electronic injectors and associated components.

2 The main components of the system are as follows:

a) Priming bulb on the low-pressure circuit (Type 1 engines only).
b) Fuel filter.
c) High-pressure fuel pump.
d) Injector rail.
e) Pressure sensor located on the injector rail.
f) Four electronic solenoid injectors.
g) Fuel temperature sensor.
h) Coolant temperature sensor.
i) Mass airflow sensor.
j) Cylinder reference sensor.
k) Engine speed sensor.
l) Turbocharging pressure sensor.
m) EGR solenoid valve.
n) Accelerator pedal potentiometer.
o) Atmospheric pressure sensor.
p) Electronic Control Unit (ECU).

3 The common rail injection system operates as follows. On Type 1 engines, fuel is drawn from the fuel tank to the high-pressure pump by a low-pressure transfer pump integrated in the high-pressure pump. On Type 2 engines, fuel is supplied from the fuel tank to the high-pressure pump by a tank mounted fuel supply pump. On all engines, before reaching the high-pressure pump, the fuel passes through a fuel filter, where foreign matter and water are removed. As the fuel passes through the filter, it is heated by an electric heater. On reaching the high-pressure pump, the fuel is pressurised according to demand, and accumulates in the injection common-rail. The pressure in the rail is accurately maintained using a pressure sensor in the rail and a pressure regulator under the control of the engine management ECU. This arrangement keeps heat generation to a minimum, and improves engine output. The rail pressure is also maintained by the injectors themselves; short electrical pulses which are not long enough to open the injector allow fuel into the return (leak-off) circuit, and also the normal pulses which open the injectors cause a reduction in pressure. The ECU determines the exact timing and duration of the injection period according to engine operating conditions.

4 The four fuel injectors inject a homogeneous spray of fuel into the combustion chambers located in the cylinder head. The injectors operate sequentially according to the firing order of the cylinders, and each injector needle is lubricated by fuel, which accumulates in the spring chamber. Each injector has its own unique flow characteristics, which are used by the system ECU to calculate the exact quantity of fuel to inject.

5 In terms of the sensors used by the ECU to control a modern common-rail diesel system, these engines are very similar to their petrol equivalents. The ECU determines engine speed and position from a crankshaft position sensor fitted to the transmission bellhousing, which detects a reference tooth on the flywheel ring gear, and signals the ECU. A similar sensor is fitted to monitor the camshaft, to give a reference for No 1 cylinder. Further sensors are used to monitor airflow into the engine, air temperature, and turbocharging pressure. On the fuel side, fuel pressure, temperature and flow rate are all monitored via sensors on the high-pressure pump and/or the fuel rail. As with the petrol-engine models, an 'electronic' throttle is fitted, with an accelerator position sensor instead of the mechanical cable previously used.

6 Provided that the specified maintenance is carried out, the fuel injection equipment will give long and trouble-free service. The main potential cause of damage to the high-pressure pump and injectors is dirt or water in the fuel. It is highly recommended that a set of fuel line plugs is obtained – these are available from motor accessory shops and better motor factors.

7 Servicing of the high-pressure pump, injectors, and electronic equipment and sensors is very limited for the home mechanic, and any dismantling or adjustment other than that described in this Chapter must be entrusted to a Nissan dealer or a diesel fuel injection specialist.

8 If a fault appears in the injection system, first ensure that all the system wiring connectors are securely connected and free of corrosion. Should the fault persist, the vehicle should be taken to a Nissan dealer or specialist who can test the system on a diagnostic tester **(see illustration)**. The tester will locate the fault quickly and simply, alleviating the need to test all the system components individually, which is a time-consuming operation that carries a risk of damaging the ECU. It is advisable to have any faulty components renewed by the dealer as in many instances the tester is required to reprogramme the ECU in the event of component or sensor renewal.

Precautions

Warning: It is necessary to take certain precautions when working on the fuel system components, particularly the fuel injectors and high-pressure pump. Before carrying out any operations on the fuel system, refer to the precautions given in Safety first!, and to any additional warning notes at the start of the relevant Sections. Allow the engine to cool for 5 to 10 minutes to ensure the fuel pressure and temperatures are at a minimum.

Warning: Exercise extreme caution when working on the high-pressure fuel system. Do not attempt to test the fuel injectors or disconnect the high-pressure lines with the engine running. Never expose the hands or any part of the body to injector spray, as the high working pressure can cause the fuel to penetrate the skin, with possibly fatal results. You are strongly advised to have any work that involves testing the injectors under pressure carried out by a dealer or fuel injection specialist.

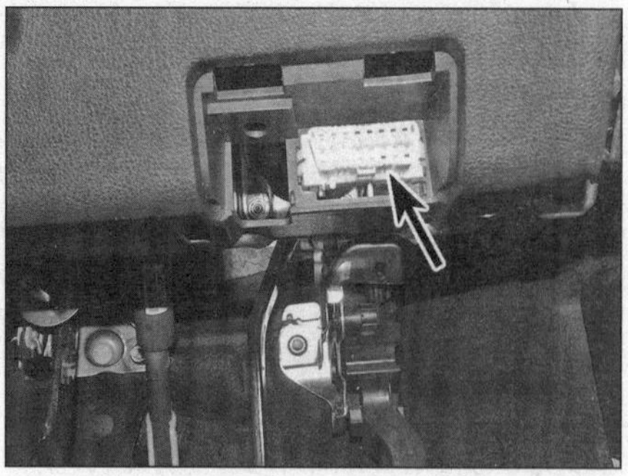

1.8 Vehicle diagnostic connector

2.3 Disconnect the wiring connector from the mass airflow sensor

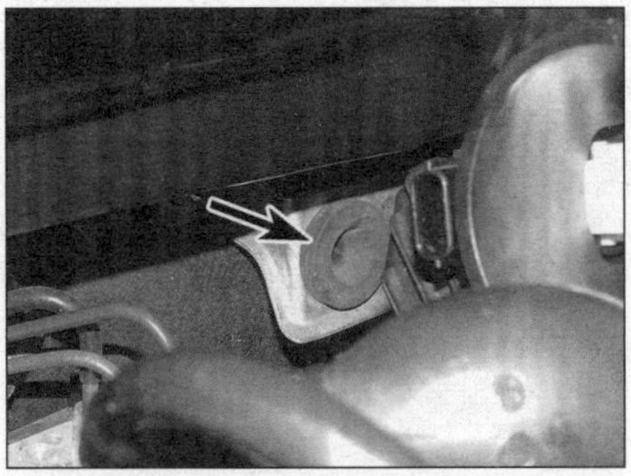

2.4a Slide the air cleaner forward to disengage the upper mounting rubber...

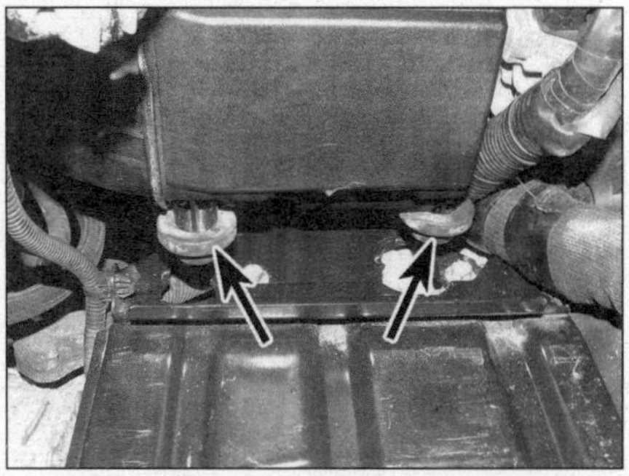

2.4b ...and lower mounting rubbers...

2.4c ...then lift it out of the engine compartment

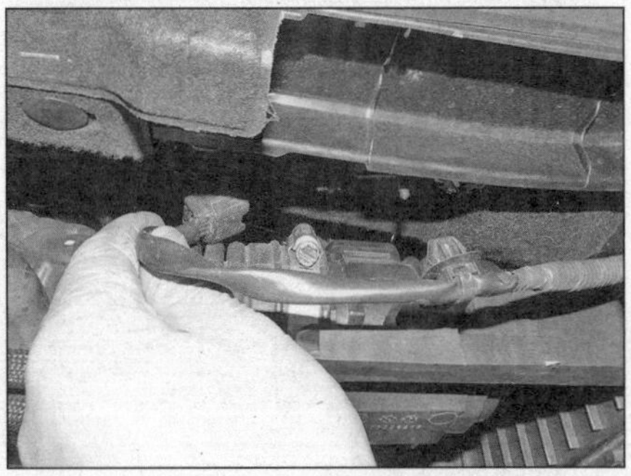

2.6a Disconnect the mass airflow sensor wiring connector...

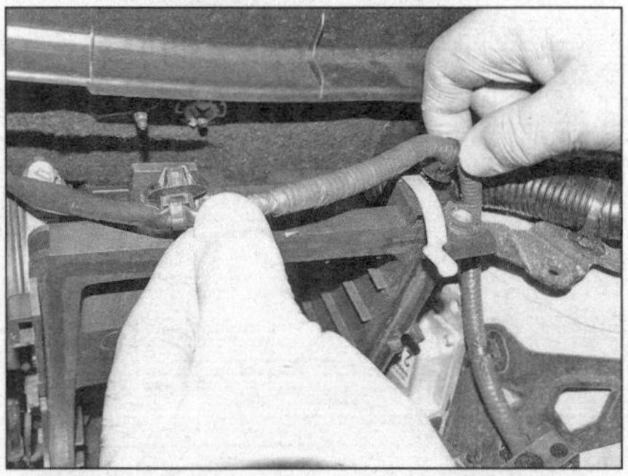

2.6b ...and release the wiring loom retaining clips from the air cleaner case

2 Air cleaner assembly and air ducts – removal and refitting

Air cleaner assembly

Removal – Type 1 engines

1 Remove the battery as described in Chapter 5A, Section 3.

2 Remove the inlet air duct and outlet air duct as described later in this Section.

3 Disconnect the wiring connector from the mass airflow sensor and release the wiring loom retaining clip from the air cleaner case **(see illustration)**.

4 Slide the air cleaner forward to disengage the mounting rubbers, then lift it out of the engine compartment **(see illustrations)**.

Removal – Type 2 engines

5 Remove the air cleaner filter element as described in Chapter 1B, Section 25.

6 Disconnect the wiring connector from the mass airflow sensor and release the wiring loom retaining clips from the air cleaner case **(see illustrations)**.

7 Slacken the retaining clip and detach the outlet air duct from the air cleaner case **(see illustrations)**.

8 Undo the air cleaner retaining bolt **(see illustration)**. Pull the air cleaner upwards, disengaging the two lower locating pegs on the bottom of the case from the rubber mountings, then remove it from the engine compartment.

Refitting – all engines

9 Refitting is a reversal of removal, ensuring that all hoses are properly reconnected and that all ducts are correctly seated and securely held by their retaining clips.

Air ducts

Removal – Type 1 engines

Inlet air duct

10 Release the hose support cable tie

2.7a Slacken the retaining clip...

2.7b ...and detach the air duct

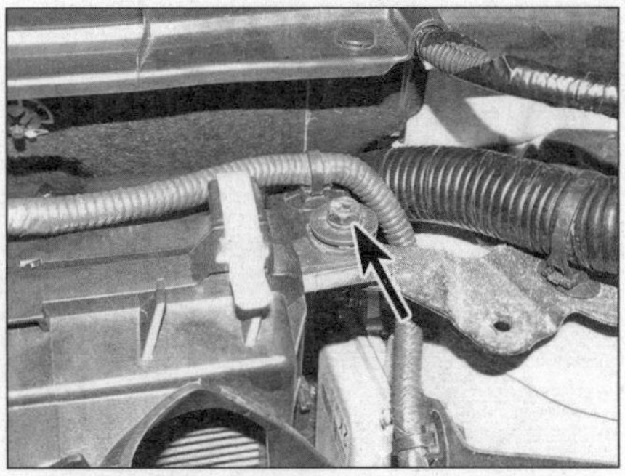

2.8 Undo the air cleaner retaining bolt

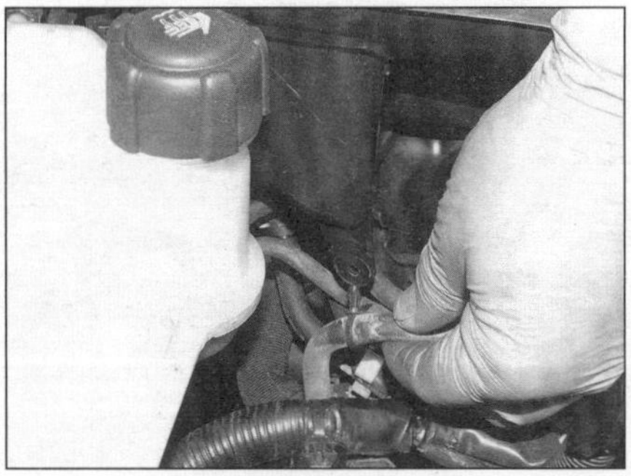
2.10 Release the cable tie from the inlet air duct

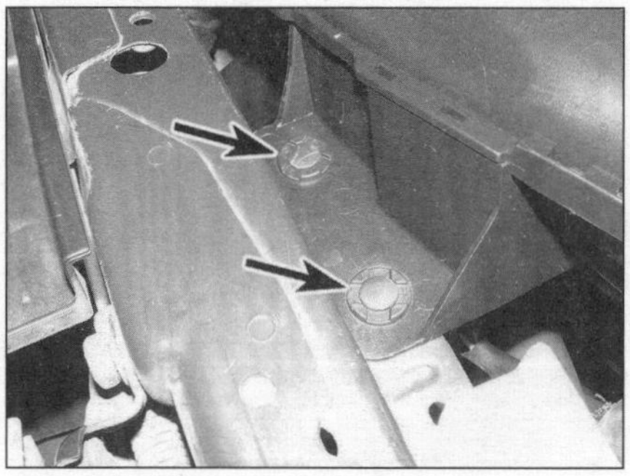
2.11 Extract the expanding rivets

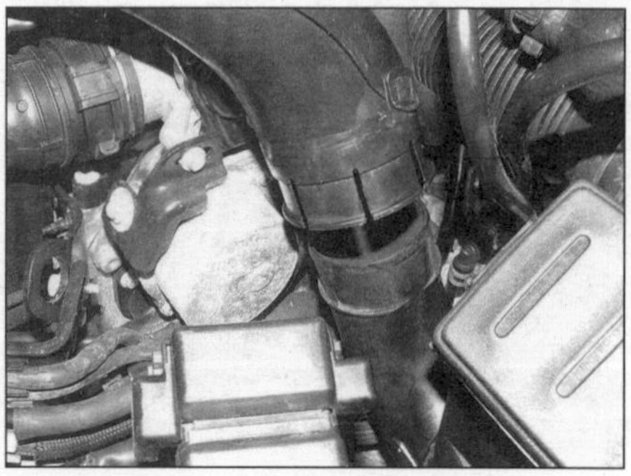
2.12 Disconnect the inlet air duct from the air cleaner assembly

2.13 Remove the priming bulb bracket from the bulkhead

2.14a Slacken the clip securing the outlet air duct to the airflow sensor...

2.14b ...and turbocharger inlet pipe...

2.14c ...then remove the duct from the engine compartment

from the base of the inlet air duct **(see illustration)**.

11 Extract the two plastic expanding rivets securing the inlet air duct to the bonnet lock platform **(see illustration)**.

12 Disconnect the inlet air duct from the air cleaner assembly and remove the duct from the engine compartment **(see illustration)**.

Outlet air duct

13 To remove the outlet air duct from the air cleaner to the turbocharger, begin by slipping the fuel system priming bulb out of its bracket on the engine compartment bulkhead. Undo the two nuts and remove the bracket from the bulkhead **(see illustration)**.

14 Slacken the clips securing the outlet air duct to the mass airflow sensor and to the turbocharger inlet pipe and remove the duct from the engine compartment **(see illustrations)**.

Turbocharger inlet pipe

15 Remove the outlet air duct as described previously in this Section.

16 Release the quick release fitting and disconnect the crankcase ventilation hose from the cylinder head cover **(see illustration)**.

17 Release the vacuum hose from the clips on the turbocharger inlet pipe **(see illustration)**.

18 Jack up the front of the car and securely support it on axle stands (see *Jacking and vehicle support*).

19 Undo the two bolts securing the lower end of the inlet pipe to the turbocharger **(see illustration)**.

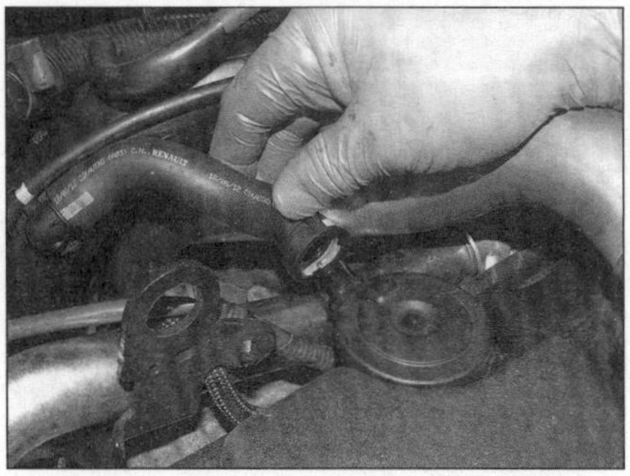
2.16 Disconnect the crankcase ventilation hose from the cylinder head cover

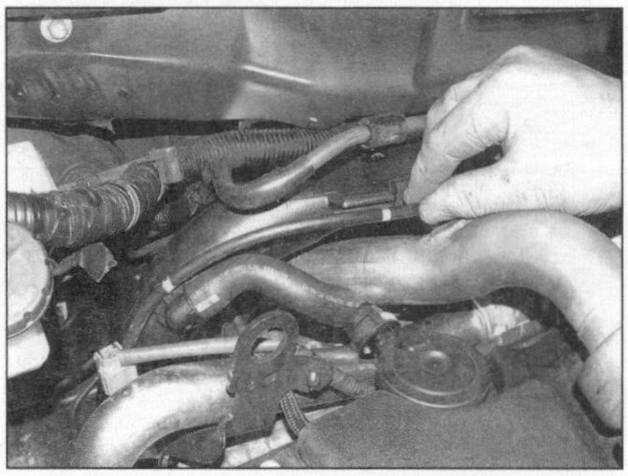
2.17 Release the vacuum hose from the turbocharger inlet pipe

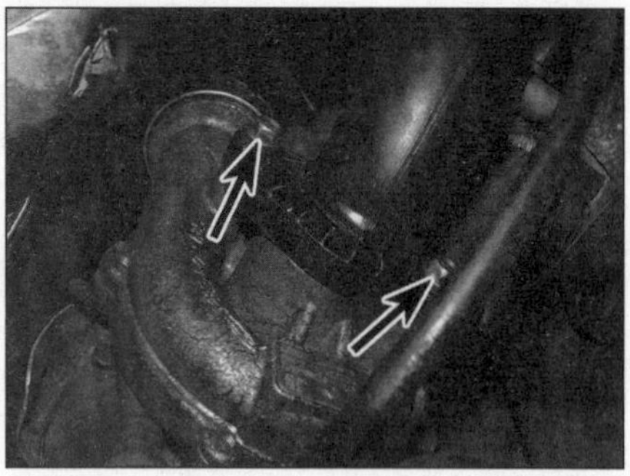
2.19 Undo the bolts securing the inlet pipe to the turbocharger

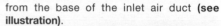

2.20a Undo the upper retaining nut...

2.20b ...and lift off the inlet pipe

2.22 Slacken the hose retaining clip and undo the support bracket bolt

20 Undo the upper retaining nut and lift the inlet pipe up and off the engine **(see illustrations)**.

Intercooler inlet pipe

21 To remove the inlet pipe from the turbocharger to the intercooler, start by removing the inlet air duct and turbocharger inlet pipe as described previously in this Section.

22 Slacken the retaining clip securing the inlet pipe to the intercooler hose, then undo the inlet pipe lower support bracket bolt **(see illustration)**.

23 Undo the inlet pipe upper support bracket bolt **(see illustration)**.

24 Extract the wire spring clip securing the intercooler inlet pipe to the turbocharger, then lift the pipe up and off the engine **(see illustration)**.

2.23 Undo the pipe upper support bracket bolt

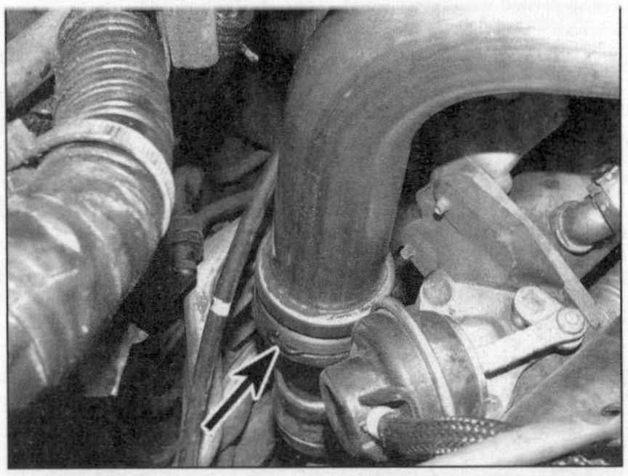

2.24 Extract the wire spring clip securing the intercooler inlet pipe to the turbocharger

Intercooler outlet pipe

25 To remove the outlet pipe from the intercooler to the throttle housing, start by removing the inlet air duct as described previously in this Section.

26 Disconnect the wiring connector from the charge air pressure sensor, then unclip the wiring harness from the outlet pipe **(see illustrations)**.

27 Extract the wire spring clip securing the intercooler outlet pipe to the throttle housing **(see illustration)**.

28 Slacken the retaining clip securing the outlet pipe to the intercooler hose, then undo the outlet pipe lower support bracket bolt **(see illustration)**.

29 Disengage the outlet pipe from the throttle housing and intercooler hose, then lift the pipe up and off the engine.

Removal – Type 2 engines

Upper inlet air duct

30 Lift up the tab and disengage the upper inlet air duct from the air cleaner filter housing **(see illustration)**.

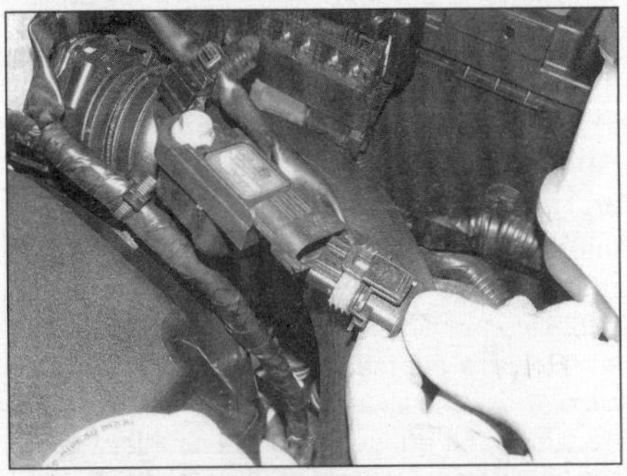

2.26a Disconnect the wiring connector from the charge air pressure sensor...

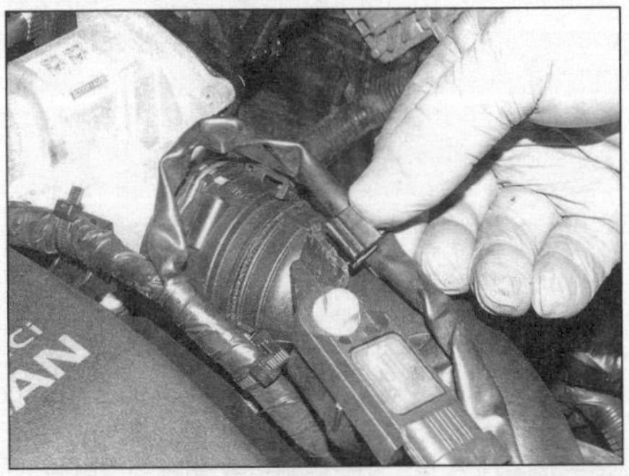

2.26b ...then unclip the wiring harness from the outlet pipe

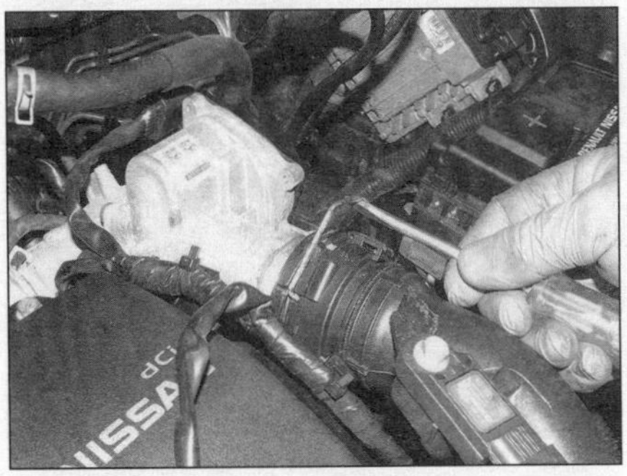

2.27 Extract the wire spring clip securing the outlet pipe to the throttle housing

2.28 Slacken the hose retaining clip

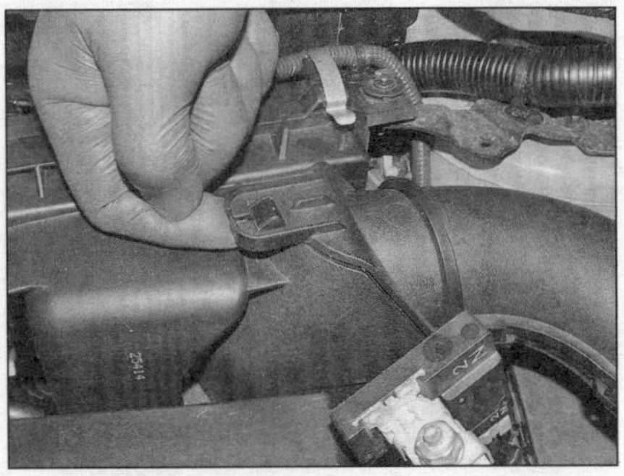

2.30 Disengage the upper inlet air duct from the air cleaner filter housing

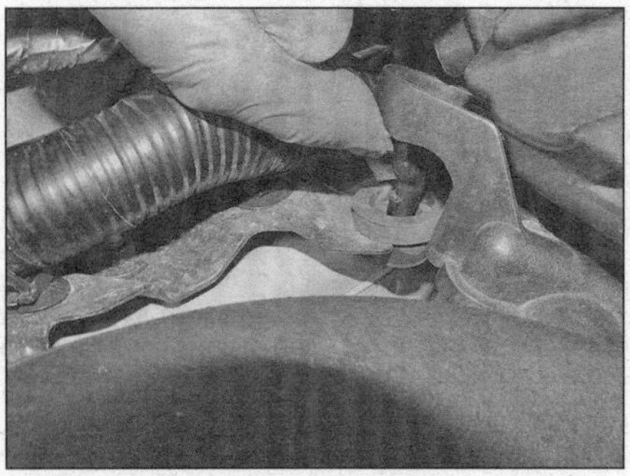

2.31a Disengage the lower mounting peg from the grommet...

2.31b ...and remove the inlet air duct

2.34a Undo the inlet air duct upper retaining bolt...

2.34b ...and lower retaining bolt

2.36 Remove the duct from the engine compartment

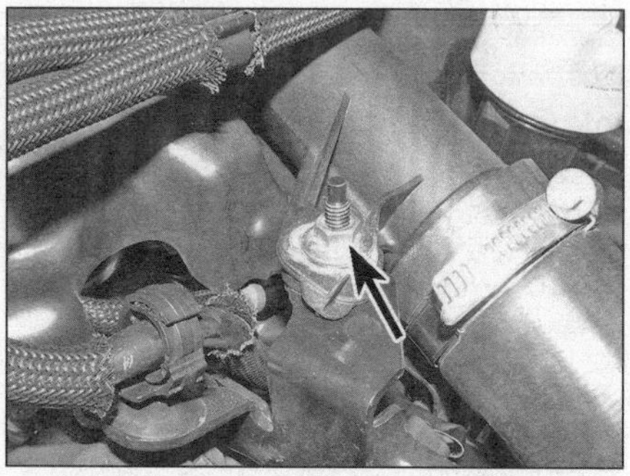

2.38 Undo the nut securing the air inlet hose to the support bracket

31 Lift the inlet air duct upward to disengage the lower mounting peg from the grommet, and remove the duct from the engine compartment **(see illustrations)**.

Lower inlet air duct

32 To remove the lower inlet air duct from the left-hand inner wing first remove the upper inlet air duct as described in paragraphs 30 and 31.

33 Remove the front wheel arch liner on the left-hand side as described in Chapter 11, Section 21.

34 Undo the air duct retaining bolts and remove the air duct from the engine compartment **(see illustrations)**.

Outlet air duct

35 To remove the outlet air duct from the air cleaner to the turbocharger, slacken the retaining clip and detach the outlet air duct from the air cleaner case **(see illustration 2.7a and 2.7b)**.

36 Slacken the clip securing the other end of the duct to the turbocharger and remove the duct from the engine compartment **(see illustration)**.

Air inlet hose

37 To remove the air inlet hose between the intercooler and turbocharger, first release the fuel hoses from the retaining clips above the air inlet hose.

38 Undo the nut securing the air inlet hose to the support bracket above the high-pressure fuel pump **(see illustration)**.

39 Release the wire clips securing the air inlet hose to the intercooler and turbocharger and remove the hose from the engine compartment **(see illustration)**.

Air inlet tube

40 To remove the air inlet tube between the intercooler and throttle housing, first undo the retaining bolts and move the coolant expansion tank aside.

41 Release the fuel hoses from the retaining clips above the air inlet tube **(see illustration)**.

42 Undo the nut securing the air inlet tube to the lower support bracket **(see illustration)**.

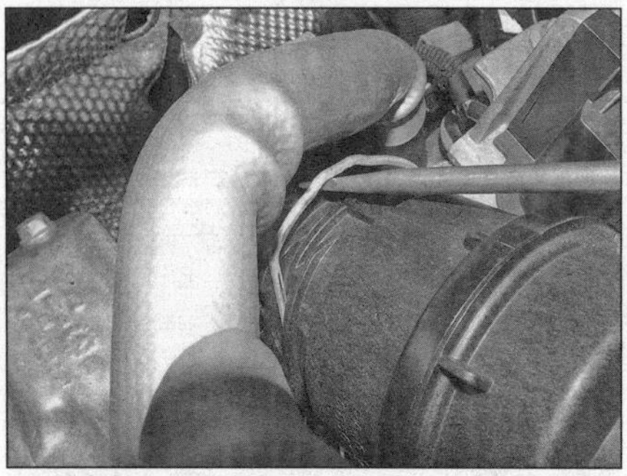

2.39 Release the wire clips securing the air inlet hose to the intercooler and turbocharger

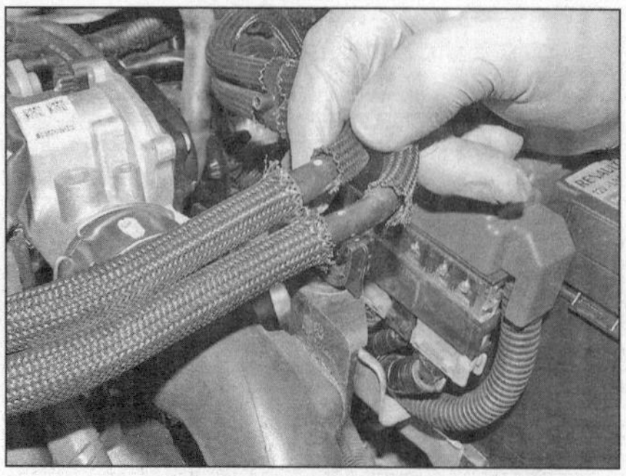

2.41 Release the fuel hoses from the retaining clips

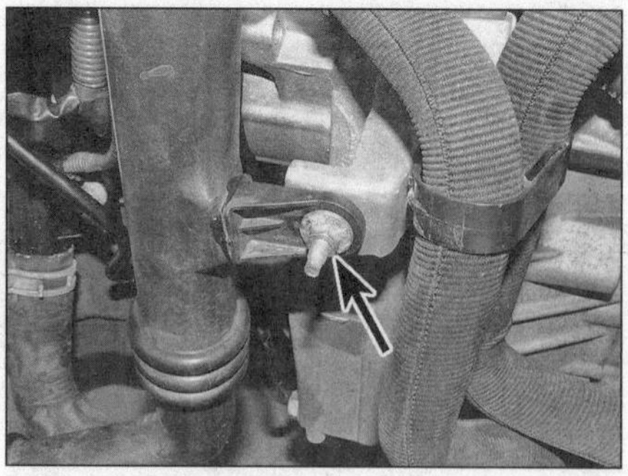

2.42 Undo the nut securing the air inlet tube to the support bracket

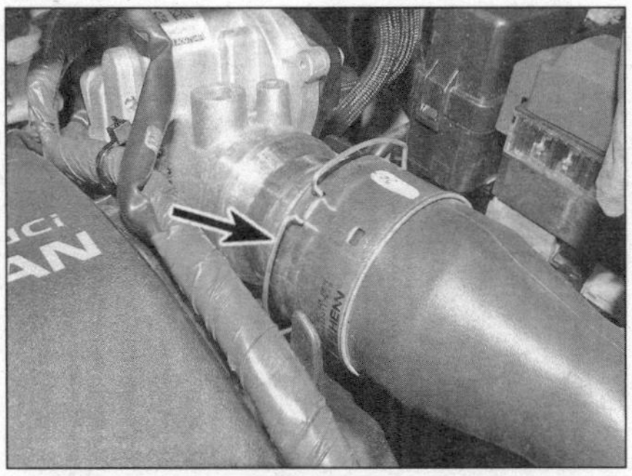
2.43 Release the wire clips securing the air inlet hose to the intercooler and throttle housing

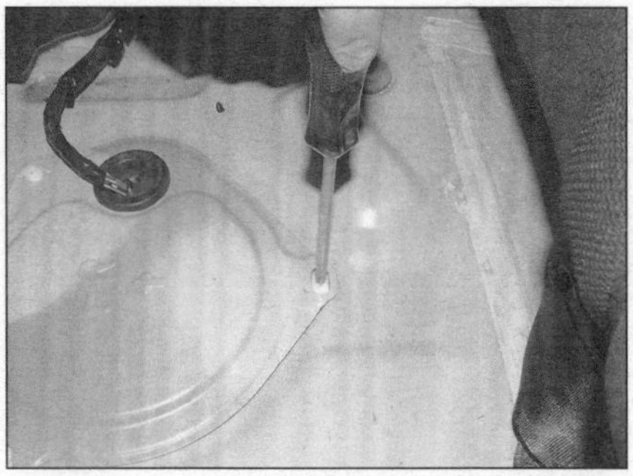
3.4a Turn the three retaining tabs through 90 degrees...

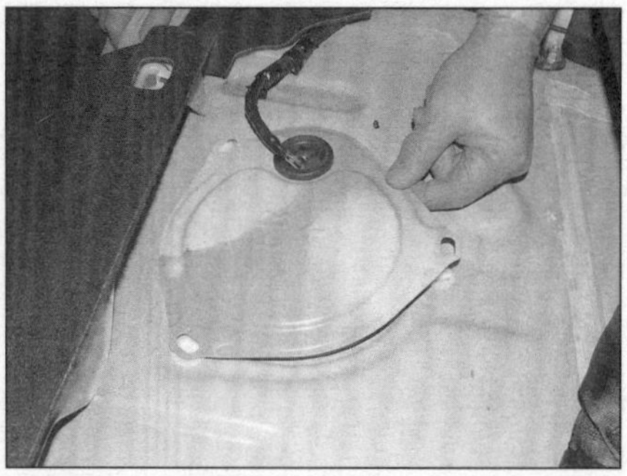
3.4b ...and lift off the access cover

43 Release the wire clips securing the air inlet tube to the intercooler and throttle housing and remove the tube from the engine compartment **(see illustration)**.

Refitting

44 Refitting is a reversal of removal, ensuring that all hoses are properly reconnected and that all ducts are correctly seated and securely held by their retaining clips.

3 Fuel pump and fuel gauge sender unit – removal and refitting

Note: *The following procedure depicts the fuel pump and gauge sender unit used on a Type 2 engine. The unit used on a Type 1 engine is similar, but only contains the gauge sender unit.*

Removal

1 Unscrew the fuel tank filler cap to relieve any residual fuel pressure still present in the system..

2 Disconnect the battery negative terminal (refer to battery disconnection and reconnection in Chapter 5A, Section 3).

3 To gain access to the sender unit, lift out the rear seat cushion, as described in Chapter 11, Section 22.

4 Turn the three retaining tabs through 90 degrees and lift off the access cover to expose the fuel pump and gauge sender unit **(see illustrations)**.

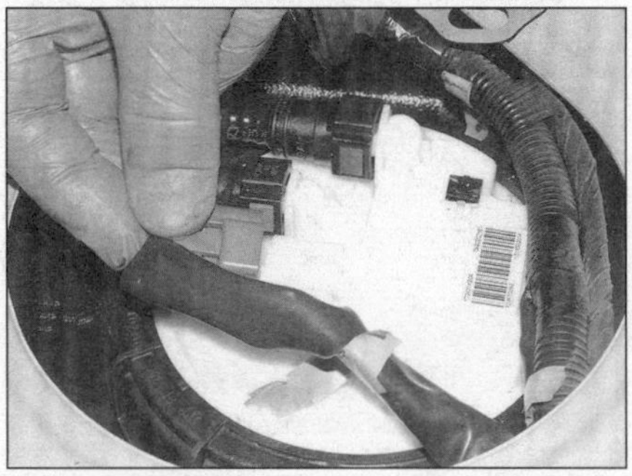
3.6 Disconnect the pump wiring connector

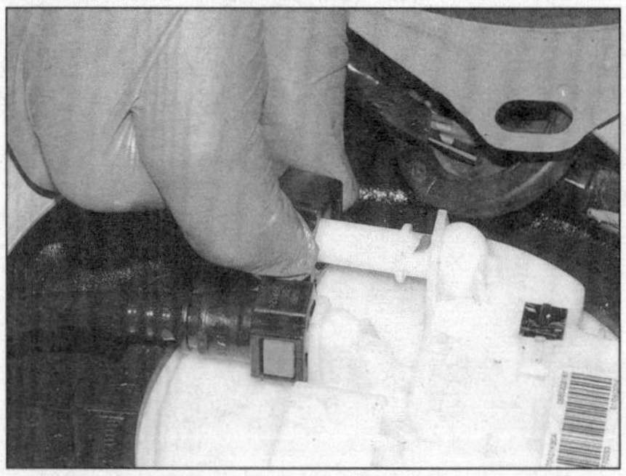
3.7 Depress the release tabs and disconnect the fuel hoses

5 Brush away any accumulated dust or dirt around the top of the sender unit so it does not drop into the fuel tank when the unit is removed.

6 Disconnect the wiring connector from the top of the sender unit **(see illustration)**.

7 Depress the coloured tabs of the quick-release fittings and disconnect the fuel hoses from the top of the unit **(see illustration)**. Suitably cover the hose unions and the fittings on the pump to prevent dirt ingress.

8 Twist the locking ring from the top of the fuel tank and carefully lift the pump/sender unit out, taking care not to damage the sender unit or spill fuel onto the interior of the vehicle **(see illustrations)**.

9 Remove the sealing ring from the top of the fuel tank and discard; as a new one will be required for refitting.

10 Position the locking ring with the arrow mark pointing toward the rear of the vehicle, then temporarily screw the ring back into position on the tank. Tighten the locking ring securely.

11 To remove the gauge sender unit from the pump on Type 2 models, depress the legs of the gauge sender unit locking tabs with your fingers, and slide the sender unit

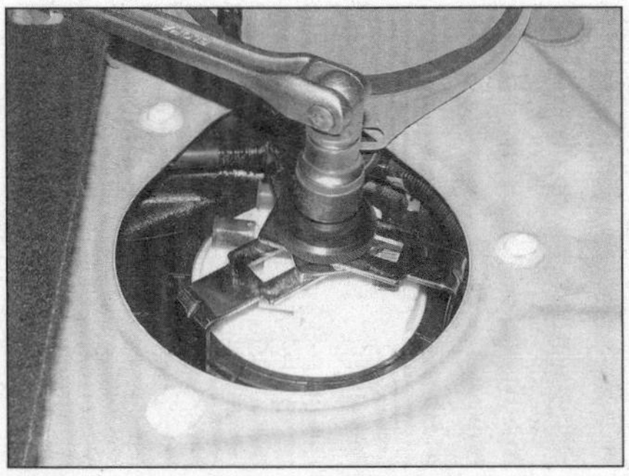
3.8a Using a locking ring removal tool to slacken the locking ring...

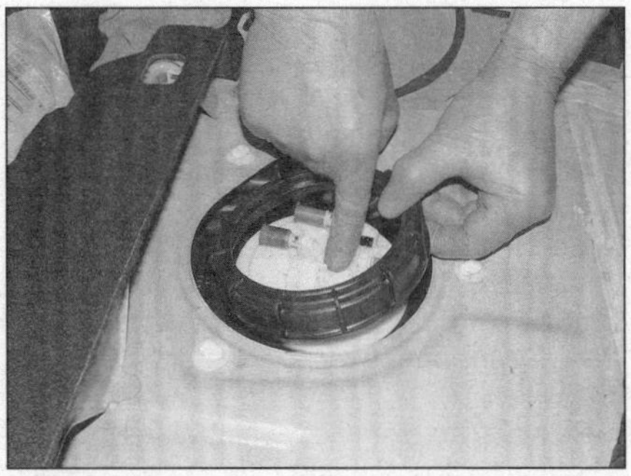
3.8b ...and remove it from the fuel tank...

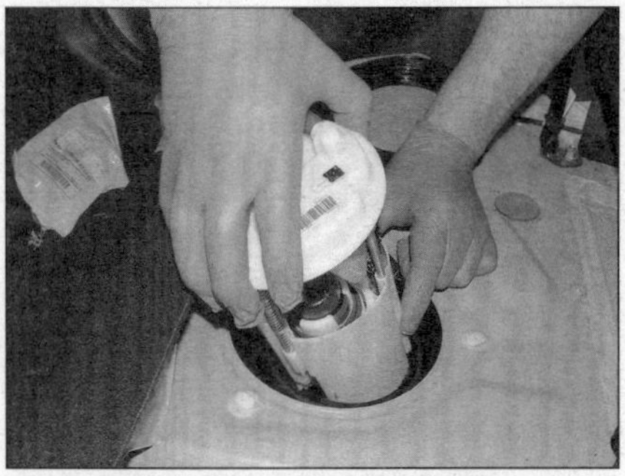
3.8c ...then withdraw the fuel pump, taking care not to damage the float arm

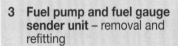

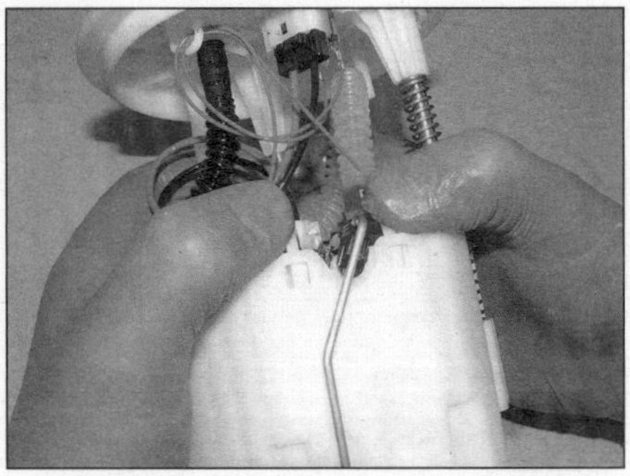
3.11a Depress the legs of the gauge sender unit locking tabs...

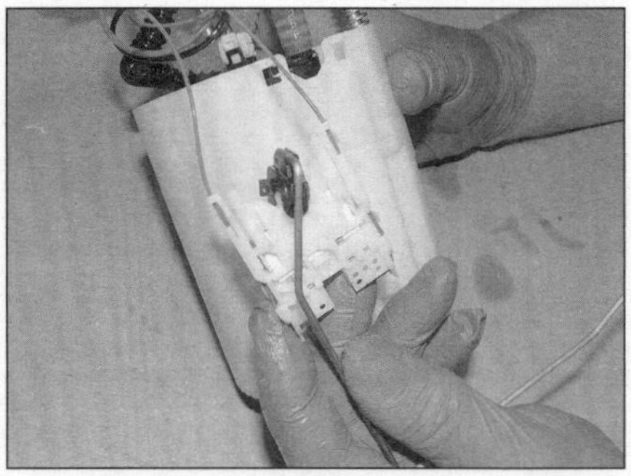
3.11b ...and slide the unit out of the fuel pump

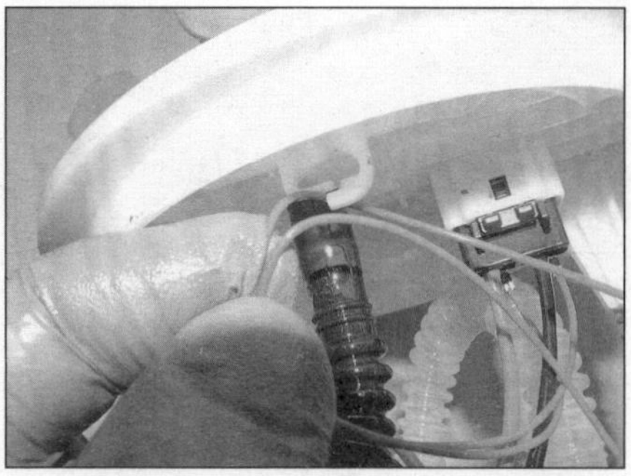
3.12 Release the wiring from the guide

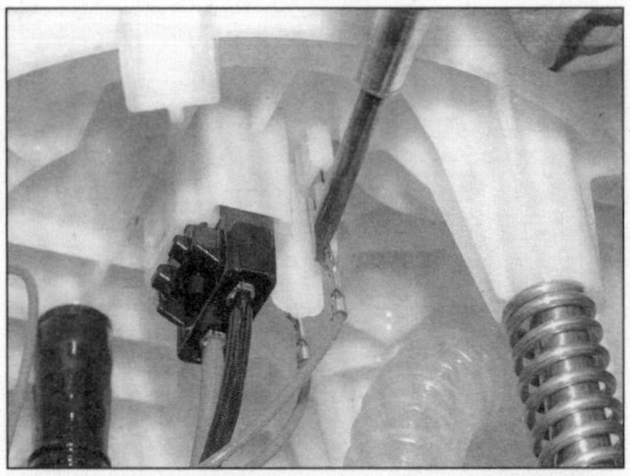
3.13 Ease the sender unit wiring end fittings off the pump connectors

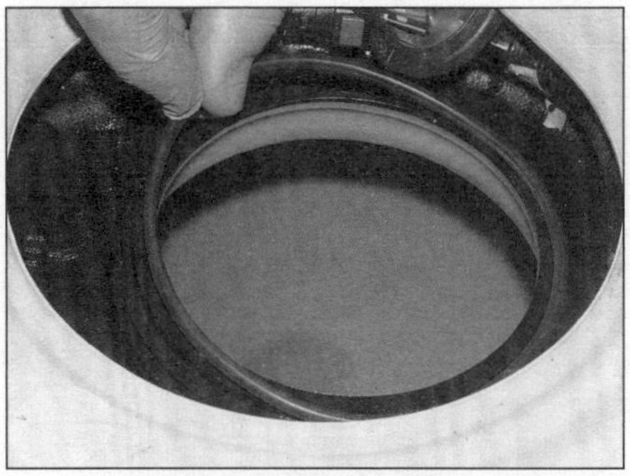
3.14a Fit a new sealing ring to the top of the tank

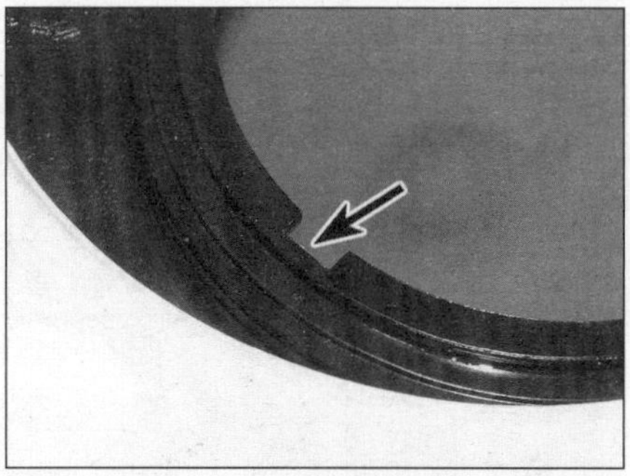
3.14b Engage the tab on the pump with the cut-out in the tank

from its location in the fuel pump body **(see illustrations)**.

12 Release the sender unit wiring from the guide at the top of the pump **(see illustration)**.

13 Using a screwdriver ease the sender unit wiring end fittings off the connectors at the top of the pump **(see illustration)**, then remove the sender unit.

Refitting

14 Refitting is a reversal of the removal procedure, noting the following points:

a) *Unscrew the temporarily refitted locking ring and fit a new sealing ring to the top of the fuel tank* **(see illustration)**.

b) *Insert the fuel pump into the tank and engage the tab on the pump with the cut-out in the tank* **(see illustration)**. *Alternatively, if no tab is present, align the three inscribed lines with the alignment mark.*

c) *Keep the fuel pump pressed down onto the sealing ring until the locking ring has been fitted and tightened. This will prevent the sealing ring from being dislodged.*

d) *Position the locking ring with the arrow mark pointing toward the rear of the vehicle, then screw the ring back into position on the tank. Securely tighten the locking ring using the removal tool.*

e) *Ensure that the fuel hose and the wiring connector are securely reconnected to the sender unit.*

f) *Prior to refitting the access cover, reconnect the battery, then start the engine and check the fuel hose(s) for signs of leaks.*

4 Fuel tank – removal and refitting

Removal

1 Before removing the fuel tank, all fuel must be drained from the tank. Since a fuel tank drain plug is not provided, it is therefore preferable to carry out the removal operation when the tank is nearly empty.

2 Unscrew the fuel tank filler cap to relieve any residual fuel pressure still present in the system.

3 Disconnect the battery negative terminal (refer to battery disconnection and reconnection in Chapter 5A, Section 3), then syphon or hand-pump the remaining fuel from the tank.

4 Disconnect the wiring connector and fuel hoses from the fuel pump/gauge sender unit, as described in Section 3.

5 Jack up the rear of the car and securely support it on axle stands. See *Jacking and vehicle support*. Remove the right-hand rear roadwheel.

6 Remove the exhaust system intermediate pipe from below the fuel tank as described in Section 17. Release the fasteners and remove the heatshield from below the fuel tank.

7 Release the retaining clips securing the handbrake cables to the fuel tank and rear axle.

8 Working at the right-hand side rear of the fuel tank, release the retaining clip and disconnect the filler neck hose from the fuel tank.

9 Working under the right-hand wheel arch, release the retaining clip and disconnect the fuel vent pipe hose.

10 Place a trolley jack with an interposed block of wood beneath the tank, then raise the jack until it is supporting the weight of the tank.

11 Slacken and remove the bolts securing the two fuel tank retaining straps to the vehicle underbody **(see illustration)**.

12 Slowly lower the fuel tank out of position and remove the tank from underneath the vehicle.

4.11 Undo the fuel tank retaining strap bolts

5.2 Diesel hand-operated priming bulb location

5.3 Squeeze the priming bulb to purge the circuit

5.6 Remove the cap from the return pipe connection on the fuel pump

13 If the tank is contaminated with sediment or water, remove the sender unit/fuel pump (Section 3) and swill the tank out with clean fuel. If any damage is evident, the tank should be renewed.

Refitting

14 Refitting is the reverse of the removal procedure, noting the following points:

a) *When lifting the tank back into position, reconnect all the relevant breather hoses, and take great care to ensure that none of the hoses become trapped between the tank and vehicle body. Tighten the fuel tank mounting bolts to the specified torque setting.*
b) *Ensure that all pipes and hoses are correctly routed, and securely held in position with their retaining clips.*
c) *On completion, refill the tank with fuel, and check for signs of leakage prior to taking the vehicle on the road.*

5 Fuel system – priming and bleeding

Warning: Refer to the precautions in Section 1 before proceeding. Do not attempt to bleed the system by loosening any of the unions on the high-pressure circuit.

Note: *Priming of the fuel system after filter renewal will be improved if the filter is filled with clean diesel fuel before securing it to the filter head. To avoid spillages of fuel, keep the filter upright during refitting.*

1 After disconnecting part of the fuel supply system or running out of fuel, it is necessary to prime the system and bleed off any air that may have entered the system components.

Type 1 engines

2 There is a priming pump to enable the system to be bled; this consists of a hand-operated priming bulb located next to the air cleaner assembly on the left-hand side of the engine compartment **(see illustration)**.

3 Lift the priming bulb out of its support bracket and squeeze it several times to purge the low-pressure circuit of air **(see illustration)**.

4 Attempt to start the engine normally, however, do not operate the starter motor for more than 5 seconds at a time. If necessary, operate the starter motor in 4 to 5 second bursts followed by pauses of 8 to 10 seconds. As soon as the engine starts, let it run at fast idle speed until a regular idle speed is reached.

5 If difficulty in purging the air from the system is experienced (engine may hunt or may not start at all), it is possible to bleed the system through the fuel return pipe connection on the high-pressure fuel pump.

6 Depress the tabs and lift off the cap on the fuel return pipe connection on the pump **(see illustration)**.

7 Connect a suitable length of clear plastic tubing to the return pipe connection and place the other end of the tubing in a container **(see illustration)**.

8 Squeeze the priming bulb repeatedly while watching the fuel emerging from the return pipe connection. When fuel free from air bubbles emerges from the return pipe connection, remove the tubing and refit the cap **(see illustration)**.

9 Start the engine, let it run at fast idle speed until a regular idle speed is reached, and then check for any fuel leaks.

10 Refit the priming bulb to its support bracket on completion.

Type 2 engines

11 Attempt to start the engine normally, however, do not operate the starter motor for more than 5 seconds at a time. If necessary, operate the starter motor in 4 to 5 second bursts followed by pauses of 8 to 10 seconds. As soon as the engine starts, let it run at fast idle speed until a regular idle speed is reached.

6 Idle speed – general

1 The engine management ECU uses the following inputs to calculate the recommended idle speed according to the varying load on the engine by peripheral electrical or mechanical components.

a) *Engine coolant temperature.*
b) *Battery voltage.*
c) *The gear selected.*
d) *Electrical consumers (heater fan, climate control system, etc).*

2 At normal engine temperature with no electrical consumers switched on and neutral selected, the engine idle speed will be 750 to 900 rpm, depending on engine type.

3 If the accelerator pedal potentiometer internal tracks are faulty, the ECU will override the idle speed to approx. 1200 rpm, and the engine management warning light will be illuminated on the instrument panel. If the brake pedal is depressed, the idle speed will revert to its normal level.

4 If there is an injector fault, the idle speed will be set to 1200 rpm and the warning light will be illuminated.

5.7 Connect a length of tubing to the return pipe connection and place the other end in a container

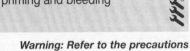

5.8 Squeeze the priming bulb until fuel free from air bubbles emerges

5 Should the idle speed be repeatedly incorrect, the car should be taken to a Nissan dealer who will have the necessary diagnostic equipment to pinpoint the faulty component responsible.

7 Accelerator pedal – removal and refitting

1 The diesel accelerator pedal has the same removal and refitting procedure as the unit fitted to petrol engines. Remove and refit the accelerator pedal, as described in Chapter 4A, Section 3.

8 Fuel system components – removal and refitting

Electronic Control Unit (ECU)

Note: *The engine management electronic control unit is electronically coded for the vehicle to which it is fitted; therefore new units are supplied without a code. If the ECU is being removed to enable a new unit to be fitted, a Nissan dealer must program the new unit with the information from the old ECU.*

1 The ECU is located on the left-hand side of the engine compartment. On Type 1 engine models it is situated on the left-hand side of the air cleaner assembly and on Type 2 engine models it is in front of the battery.

2 First disconnect the battery negative terminal (refer to battery disconnection and reconnection in Chapter 5A, Section 3).

3 On Type 1 engine models, remove the air cleaner assembly as described in Section 2.

4 Release the locking levers, and then withdraw the three electrical connectors from the top of the ECU.

5 Undo the four retaining nuts and remove the ECU from the mounting bracket **(see illustration)**.

6 Refitting is a reverse of the removal procedure ensuring that the wiring is securely reconnected.

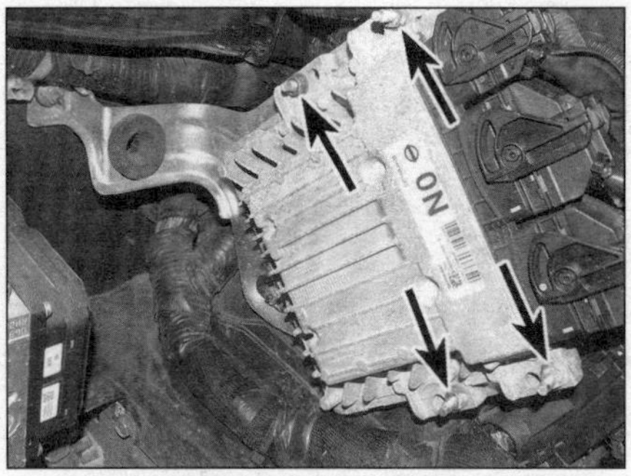

8.5 ECU retaining nuts – Type 1 engine model shown

Crankshaft position sensor

7 The crankshaft position sensor is fitted at the rear of the transmission bellhousing **(see illustration)**.

8 Disconnect the wiring connector from the position sensor.

9 Undo the retaining bolt and withdraw the sensor from the cylinder block/bellhousing.

10 Refitting is a reversal of the removal procedure, noting the following points:

a) Fit a new O-ring seal to the sensor.

b) Apply a smear of engine oil to the O-ring to aid installation **(see illustration)**, *and then ease the sensor into position.*

Camshaft position sensor

11 The camshaft position sensor is fitted to the transmission end of the cylinder head cover.

12 To gain access to the sensor, remove the plastic engine shield/cover as described in paragraphs 1 to 6 in Chapter 2C, Section 4.

13 Disconnect the wiring connector from the camshaft position sensor.

14 Undo the retaining bolt and withdraw the sensor from the cylinder head cover **(see illustration)**.

15 Discard the O-ring seal; a new one must be used on refitting.

16 Refitting is a reversal of the removal procedure, noting the following points:

a) Fit a new O-ring seal to the sensor.

b) Apply a smear of engine oil to the O-ring to aid installation, and then ease the sensor into position.

8.7 Location of crankshaft position sensor

Coolant temperature sensor

17 Refer to Chapter 3, Section 6.

Mass airflow (MAF) sensor

18 The airflow sensor (which also incorporates the inlet air temperature sensor) is mounted in the air cleaner housing.

19 Remove the air cleaner assembly as described in Section 2.

20 Undo the retaining screws, and then remove the airflow sensor from the air cleaner housing **(see illustration)**. Recover its sealing ring and renew.

21 Refitting is the reverse of removal, using a new sealing ring (where applicable) and tightening its retaining screws securely.

Inlet air temperature (IAT) sensor

22 The inlet air temperature sensor is combined with the mass airflow sensor. Remove the mass airflow sensor as described in paragraphs 18 to 20.

Throttle valve housing

23 Remove the inlet air duct (Type 1 engines only) and intercooler outlet pipe as described in Section 2.

24 Disconnect the wiring connector from the throttle valve housing.

25 Unscrew the bolts from the mounting bracket, and also the nuts/bolts from the

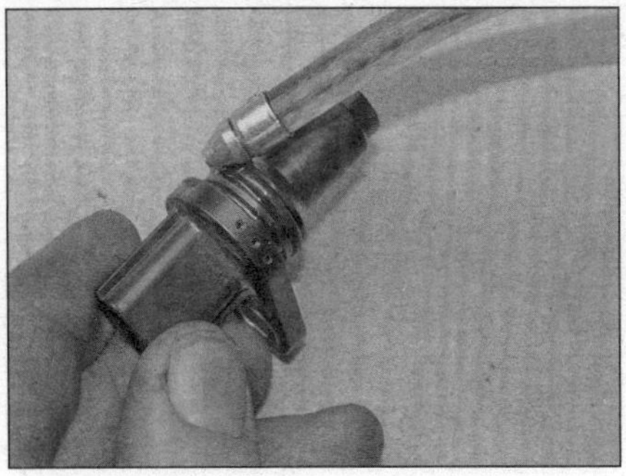

8.10 Lubricate seal with a smear of oil

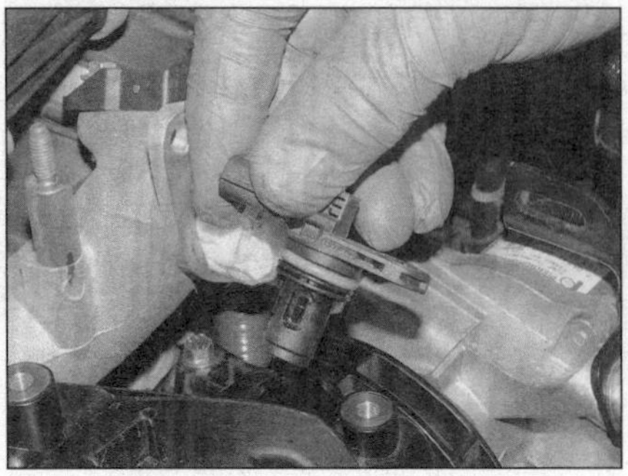

8.14 Undo the bolt and remove the camshaft position sensor

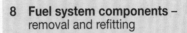

8.20 Undo the air flow sensor retaining screws

EGR valve housing, and remove the unit from the engine **(see illustrations)**. Remove and discard the gasket/seal.

26 Refitting is a reversal of removal, using a new gasket/seal.

9 High-pressure fuel pump – removal and refitting

Warning: Refer to the warning note in Section 1 before proceeding.

Caution: Before starting work, allow the engine to cool for 5 to 10 minutes, to ensure the fuel pressure and temperature are at a minimum.

Note: *The high-pressure fuel pump is removed after first removing the timing belt as described in Chapter 2C, Section 6. All high-pressure pipes removed must be renewed as a matter of course.*

Note: *Cleanliness is of critical importance when working on the fuel system of any modern diesel engine. The smallest speck of grit or dirt can cause extensive damage to the pump and injectors. Always clean thoroughly the pump and injector unions before dismantling. Immediately plug and seal all pipes and components. Components that are removed from the engine should immediately be placed in clean plastic bags.*

Removal

1 Disconnect the battery negative terminal (refer to battery disconnection and reconnection in Chapter 5A, Section 3).

2 Unscrew the fuel tank filler cap to relieve any residual fuel pressure still present in the system.

3 Refer to Section 2 and remove the inlet and outlet air ducts and hoses as necessary for access to the high-pressure fuel pump.

4 On Type 2 engines, undo the nut and two bolts and remove the sensor bracket from the rear of the cylinder head **(see illustrations)**.

5 Unclip the wiring loom cable ties from the upper plastic engine shield/cover **(see illustration)**.

6 Undo the two retaining bolts, release the two securing clips and lift off the upper plastic engine shield/cover **(see illustrations)**.

8.25a Unscrew the mounting bracket retaining bolts

8.25b Remove the throttle valve housing from the EGR valve housing

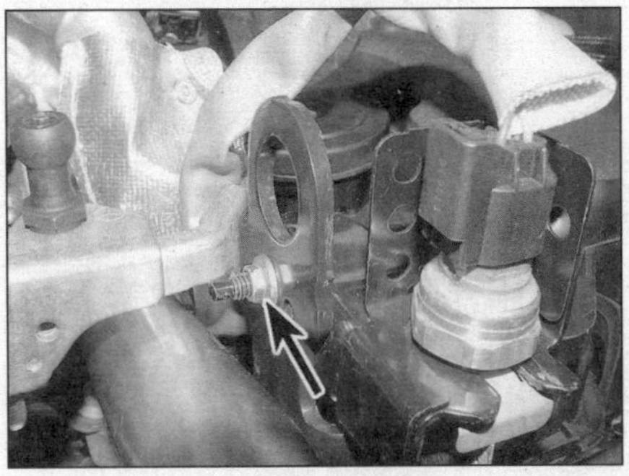

9.4a Undo the retaining nut...

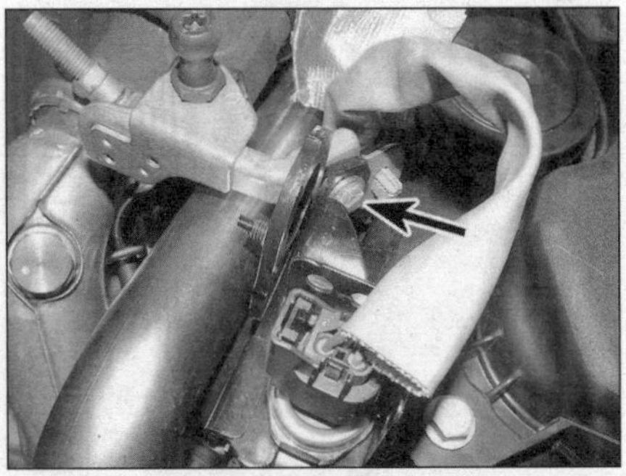

9.4b ...the bolt at the front...

9.4c ...and the bolt at the rear, then remove the sensor bracket

9.5 Unclip the wiring loom cable ties from the cover

9.6a Undo the two retaining bolts...

9.6b ...release the securing clips...

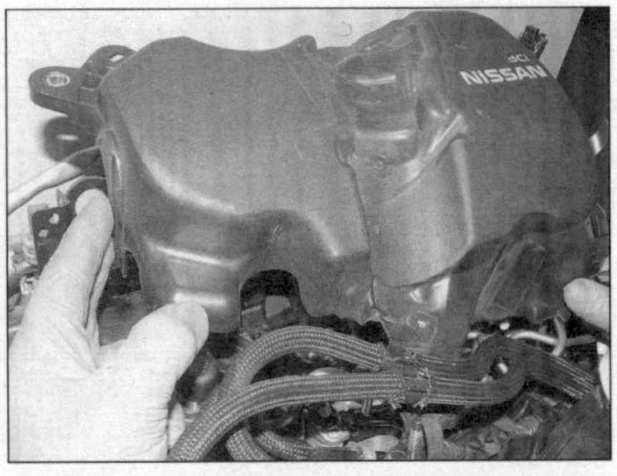

9.6c ...and remove the plastic engine shield/cover

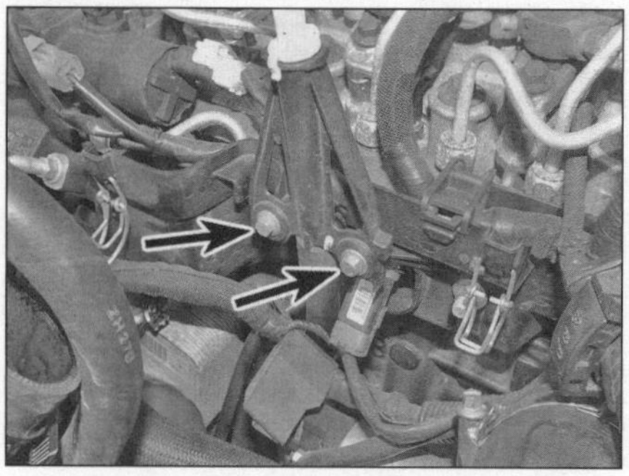

9.7a Undo the two bolts...

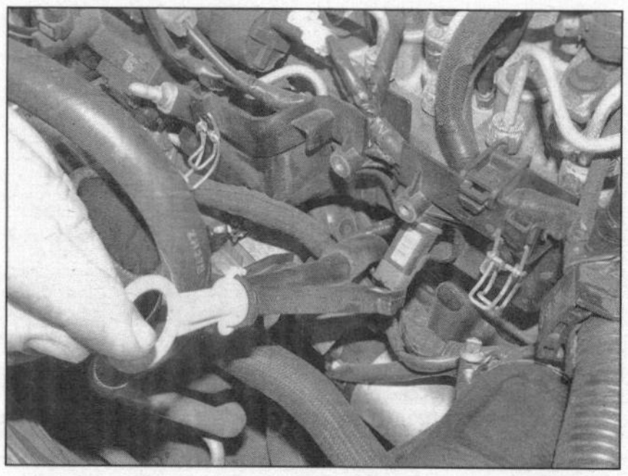

9.7b ...and pull back the dipstick bracket

9.8 Disconnect the pressure sensor wiring connector

9.9 Unclip the wiring loom from the plastic engine shield/cover

7 Undo the two retaining bolts and pull back the dipstick bracket from the front of the cylinder head **(see illustrations)**.

8 Disconnect the wiring connector from the pressure sensor on the bottom of the fuel rail **(see illustration)**.

9 Release the securing clip and remove the wiring loom from the top of the lower plastic engine shield/cover **(see illustration)**.

10 Where fitted, release the drain tube from the lower plastic engine shield/cover **(see illustration)**.

11 Undo the bolt and two nuts and remove the lower plastic engine shield/cover **(see illustrations)**.

12 Undo the two bolts and remove the bracket from the front of the high-pressure fuel pump.

13 Disconnect the three wiring connectors from the fuel pump **(see illustrations)**.

14 Place a clean rag over the alternator and then remove the fuel pipe/hoses from the pump **(see illustrations)**. As a precaution against remaining pressure in the pipes, first wrap them loosely in cloth/rag. The high-pressure pipe will need to be renewed. Seal the pump and pipe/hoses immediately. Do not allow fuel to contaminate the alternator.

15 Remove the timing belt as described in Chapter 2C, Section 6. Note it would be a sensible precaution to renew the timing belt anyway.

9.10 Unclip the drain tube from the plastic engine shield/cover

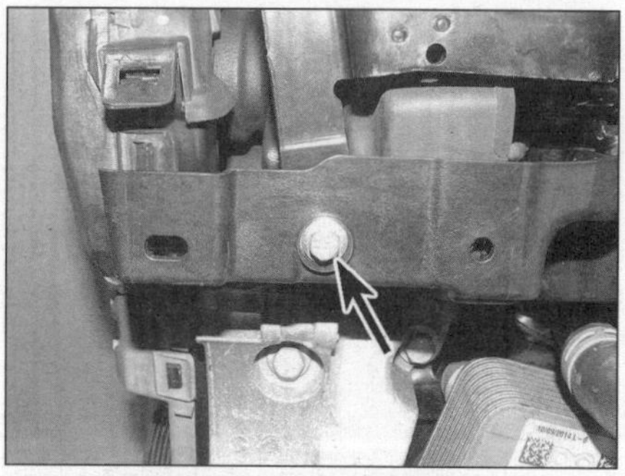

9.11a Undo the bolt...

9.11b ...and two nuts...

9.11c ...and remove the lower plastic engine shield/cover

9.13a Disconnect the wiring connectors...

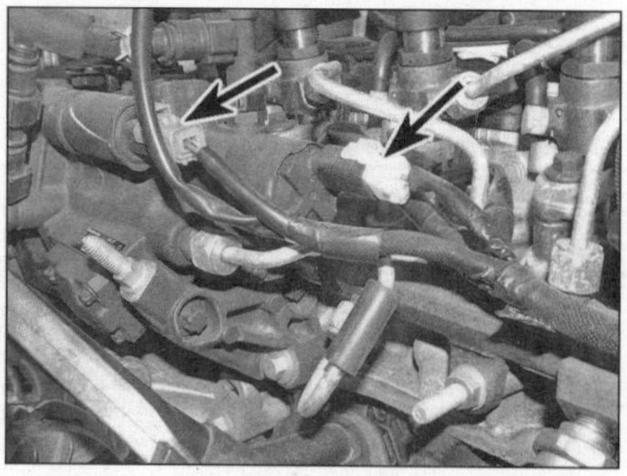

9.13b ...from the fuel pump sensors

9.14a Remove the high-pressure fuel pipe...

9.14b ...return hose...

9.14c ...return hose fitting...

9.14d ...and supply hose from the pump

16 Unbolt and remove the fuel pump, and then place the pump in a vice to remove the sprocket. Use a strap wrench and a ring spanner to do this. A puller will then be required to remove the sprocket from the pump.

Refitting

Note: *The manufacturers stipulate that the high-pressure pipe is renewed whenever it is removed.*

17 Refitting is a reversal of removal, but take care not to place the new high-pressure pipe under any stress. If fitting a new pump, it is highly recommended that the pump is primed with diesel on the bench before fitting.

18 New high-pressure pipes are supplied with a lubricant for the threads on the pipe. If no lubricant is supplied the pipes are self-lubricating and lubricant should not be applied.

19 Tighten all nuts and bolts to the specified torque and angle as applicable.

20 Prime and bleed the fuel system as described in Section 5.

21 Before restarting the engine, it may be necessary to use a diagnostic tool to clear any faults that may be stored in the engine electronic control unit (ECU).

10 Fuel injectors – testing, removal and refitting

Warning: Exercise extreme caution when working on the high-pressure fuel system. Do not attempt to test the fuel injectors or disconnect the high-pressure lines with the engine running. Never expose the hands or any part of the body to injector spray, as the high working pressure can cause the fuel to penetrate the skin, with possibly fatal results. You are strongly advised to have any work that involves testing the injectors under pressure carried out by a dealer or fuel injection specialist. Refer to the precautions given in Section 1 of this Chapter before proceeding. After switching off the engine, allow the engine to cool for 5 to 10 minutes to allow the fuel pressure to drop before disconnecting any of the high-pressure fuel pipes.

Note: *Each new injector is supplied with a unique code, which specifies its flow characteristics. This code must be programmed into the engine management ECU with a special diagnostic tool; therefore this work should be entrusted to a Nissan dealer or suitably equipped garage.*

Testing

1 It is not possible to test the fuel injectors without specialist equipment, therefore, if they are thought to be faulty, consult a Nissan dealer or diesel specialist.

Removal

Note: *Take care not to allow dirt into the injectors or fuel pipes during this procedure; clean around the area before commencing work. Note that all high-pressure pipes removed must be renewed as a matter of course. The injector flame shield washers must also be renewed.*

2 Carry out the operations described in paragraphs 1 to 11 in Section 9.

3 Before removal thoroughly clean the area around the fuel injectors.

4 Disconnect the wiring connector from the top of the fuel injector **(see illustration)**.

5 Lift up the catch on the fuel leak-off pipe connection on each injector and carefully pull the connection off the injector stub **(see illustrations)**.

6 Once all the leak-off connections are released, disconnect the return pipe union from the high-pressure fuel pump and remove the return pipe assembly from the engine

10.4 Disconnect the injector wiring connectors

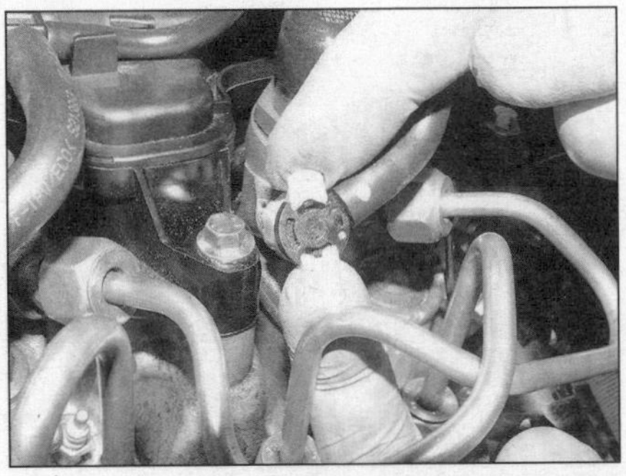

10.5a Lift up the catch on the fuel leak-off pipe connection...

10.5b ...and pull the connection off the injector stub

10.6 Disconnect the return pipe union from the high-pressure fuel pump and remove the return pipe assembly from the engine

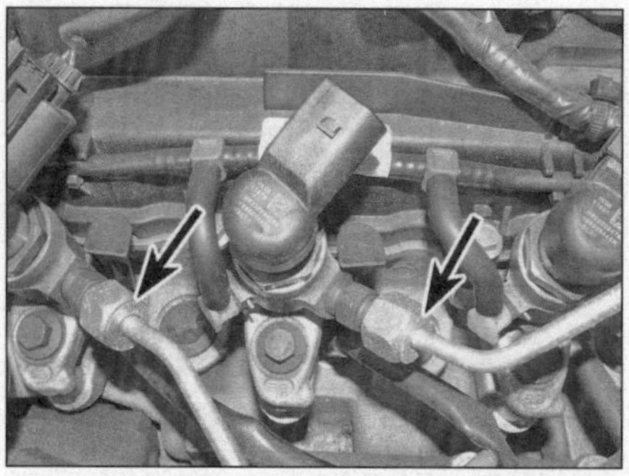

10.7a Unscrew the fuel injector pipe union nuts...

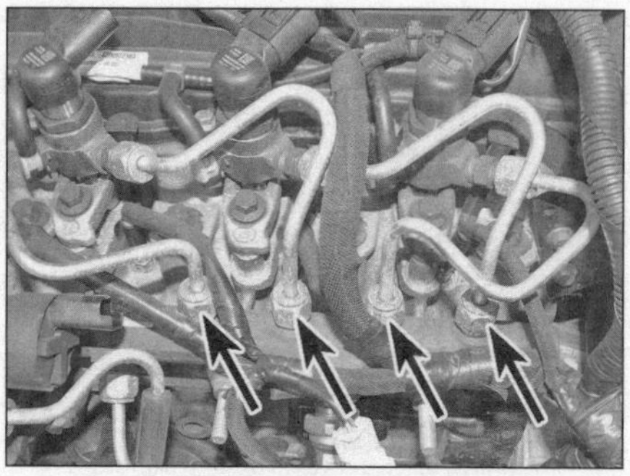

10.7b ...and also at the fuel rail

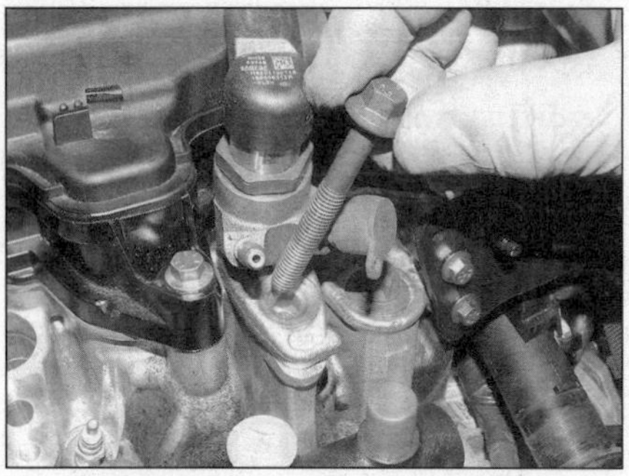

10.8a Unscrew the retaining bolt...

10.8b ...lift off the clamp plate...

10.8c ...and remove the injector

(see illustration). Tape over or plug all fuel apertures to prevent entry of dust and dirt.

7 While holding the injector central unions with one spanner, unscrew the high-pressure pipe union nuts with a further spanner. Use some cloth around the pipe unions to soak up the spilt fuel, and then loosen them. Similarly, unscrew the union nuts from the fuel rail, and then remove the pipes **(see illustrations)**. As a precaution against remaining pressure in the pipes, first wrap them loosely in cloth/rag. Discard the fuel pipe, as a new one will be required for refitting. Plug all fuel apertures to prevent entry of dust and dirt.

8 Unscrew the bolt securing each injector clamp plate to the cylinder head. Lift off the clamp plates and remove the injectors **(see illustrations)**. Suitably identify each injector as to its cylinder location.

9 Recover the copper washers between the injectors and the cylinder head and remove the leak-off pipe O-rings **(see illustrations)**.

Refitting

10 Take care not to drop the injectors or allow the needles at their tips to become damaged. The injectors are precision-made to fine limits and must not be handled roughly. In particular, do not mount them in a bench vice. It is recommended that the injectors are stored vertically at all times.

11 Clean the cylinder head, taking care to prevent foreign matter entering the fuel apertures. The injectors can be cleaned with a lint-free cloth soaked in brake cleaning fluid or fresh diesel. Do not clean them with a wire brush or emery cloth.

12 Obtain new injector sealing copper washers, new leak-off pipe O-rings and new fuel pipes for refitting.

13 Fit new copper washers between the injectors and the cylinder head and fit new leak-off pipe O-rings to the injector stubs. Insert the injectors then fit the clamp plates. Tighten the clamp plate bolts to the specified torque.

14 Fit new injector pipes, and tighten the union nuts on the injectors and the fuel rail by hand at first. With all the pipes in place tighten them to the specified torque setting, using a crow foot adaptor **(see illustration)**.

15 Refit the injector leak-off pipes to the injectors and connect the fuel return pipe to the fuel pump.

16 Reconnect the fuel injector wiring.

17 Refit the upper and lower plastic engine shield/cover with reference to Section 9.

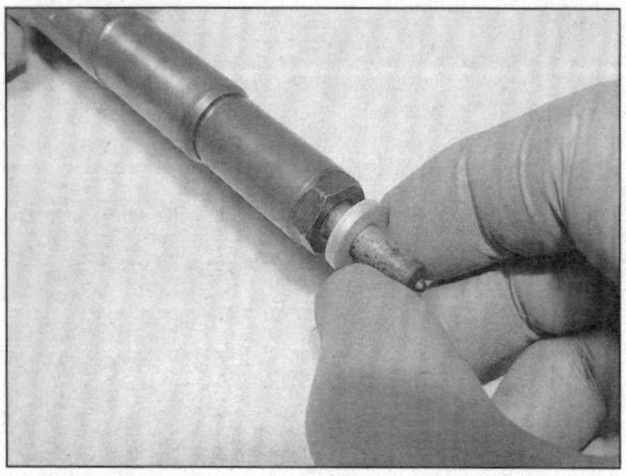

10.9a Recover the copper washers...

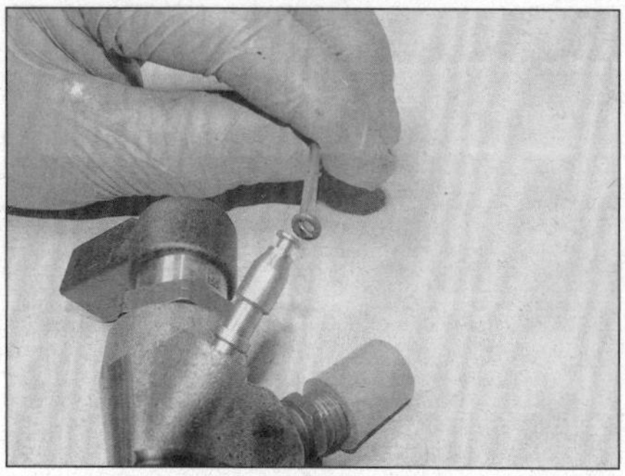

10.9b ...and leak-off pipe O-rings from the injectors

10.14 Tighten the fuel pipe unions to the specified torque using a crow foot adaptor

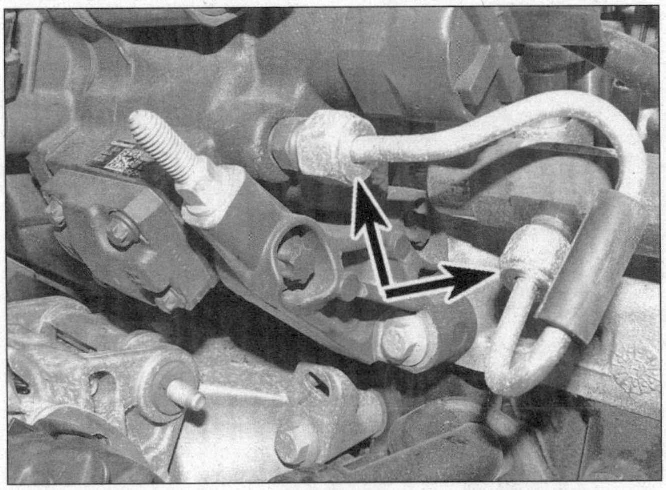

11.3 Remove the high pressure fuel pipe

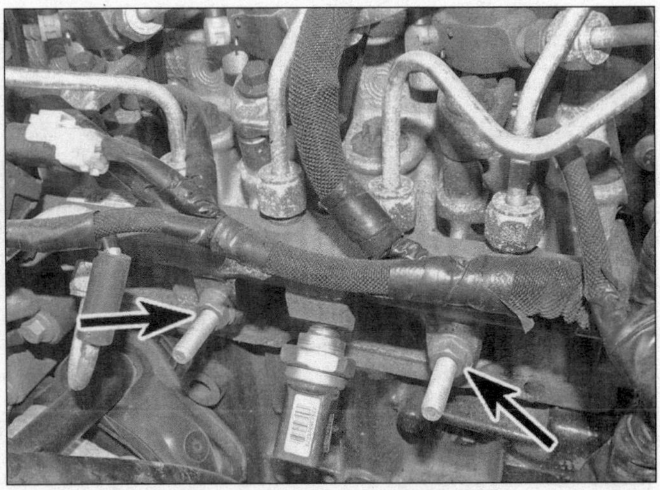

11.5 Undo the fuel rail retaining nuts

18 Reconnect the battery negative terminal (refer to battery disconnection and reconnection in Chapter 5A, Section 3).
19 If new injectors have been fitted, have the code programmed into the engine management ECU by a Nissan dealer.
20 Prime and bleed the fuel system as described in Section 5.

11 Fuel rail (common rail) – removal and refitting

Warning: Refer to the warning in Section 10 before proceeding.

Note: *Take care not to allow dirt into the fuel pipes during this procedure, clean around the area before commencing work. Note that all high-pressure pipes removed must be renewed as a matter of course.*

Removal

1 Carry out the operations described in paragraphs 1 to 11 in Section 9.
2 Disconnect the wiring connectors from the heater (glow) plugs and move the wiring loom to one side.
3 Undo the union nuts and remove the high-pressure fuel pipe from the fuel pump to the fuel rail **(see illustration)**. As a precaution against remaining pressure in the pipes, first wrap them loosely in cloth/rag. Discard the fuel pipe, as a new one will be required for refitting. Plug all fuel apertures to prevent entry of dust and dirt.
4 While holding the injector central unions with one spanner, unscrew the high-pressure pipe union nuts with a further spanner. As a precaution against remaining pressure in the pipes, first wrap them loosely in cloth/rag. Similarly, unscrew the union nuts from the fuel rail, and then remove the pipes. Discard the fuel pipes, as new ones will be required for refitting. Plug all fuel apertures to prevent entry of dust and dirt.
5 Undo the retaining nuts and remove the fuel rail from the front of the cylinder head **(see illustration)**.

Refitting

6 Refitting is a reversal of removal, but take care not to place the new high-pressure pipe under any stress. Before fitting the new pipe, lubricate the threads of the union nuts with oil from the sachet provided, and finger-tighten the nuts before tightening them to the specified torque using a crow foot adaptor. When tightening the pipe union nuts onto the injectors, counter-hold the injectors with a further spanner.
7 On completion, prime and bleed the fuel system as described in Section 5. Run the engine, and check for fuel leaks.

12 Inlet manifold – removal and refitting

1 The inlet manifold is incorporated into the cylinder head and therefore cannot be removed separately.

13 Exhaust manifold – removal and refitting

Removal

Early Type 1 engines

Note: *The following procedure is applicable to early Type 1 engines with a diesel particulate filter incorporated in the exhaust system front pipe. The procedure for later engines, with a diesel particulate filter mounted behind the cylinder head in the engine compartment, is contained in the next sub-Section.*

1 Disconnect the battery negative terminal (refer to battery disconnection and reconnection in Chapter 5A, Section 3.
2 Remove the turbocharger as described in Section 15.
3 Trace the exhaust gas temperature sensor wiring back to the harness connector and disconnect the connector. Unclip the harness to enable it to be removed with the manifold. Alternatively, unscrew the union nut and remove the exhaust gas temperature sensor probe from the exhaust manifold.
4 Unbolt the exhaust gas pressure sensor from the exhaust manifold.
5 Release the two clamps, then remove the EGR metal tube between the exhaust manifold and EGR valve. The manufacturers recommend that the two clamps are renewed as a matter of course.
6 Progressively unscrew the mounting nuts and remove the exhaust manifold from the studs on the cylinder head. Recover the metal gasket.
7 Clean the surfaces of the cylinder head and exhaust manifold, then locate a new gasket on the cylinder head studs.

Later Type 1 engines and all Type 2 engines

Note: *The following procedure is applicable to later Type 1 engines and all Type 2 engines, with a diesel particulate filter mounted behind the cylinder head in the engine compartment.*

8 Disconnect the battery negative terminal (refer to battery disconnection and reconnection in Chapter 5A, Section 3.
9 Remove the turbocharger as described in Section 15.
10 Trace the exhaust gas temperature sensor wiring back to the harness connector and disconnect the connector. Unclip the harness to enable it to be removed with the manifold. Alternatively, unscrew the union nut and remove the exhaust gas temperature sensor probe from the manifold.
11 Unscrew the union nut and remove

13.11 Unscrew the exhaust gas pressure sensor union nut

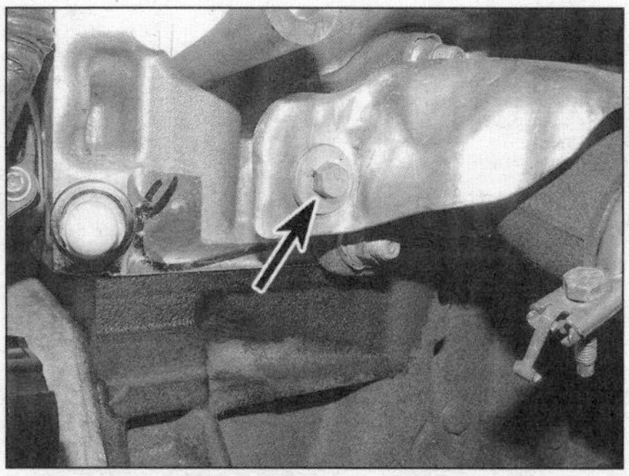
13.12a Undo the bolt on the left-hand side...

13.12b ...and right-hand side...

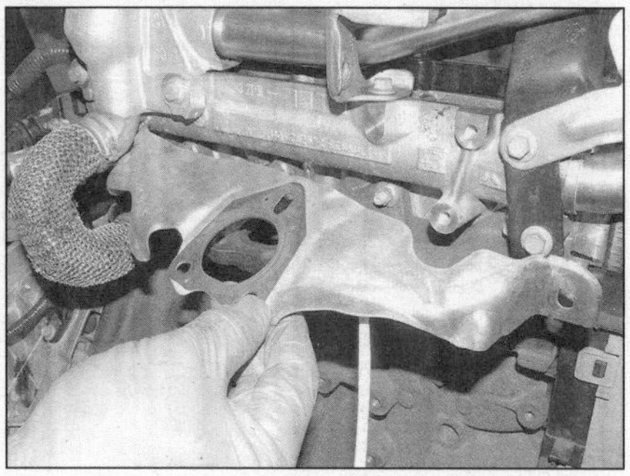
13.12c ...and lift off the manifold heat shield

the exhaust gas pressure sensor from the manifold **(see illustration)**.

12 Unscrew the two bolts and lift off the exhaust manifold heat shield **(see illustrations)**.

13 Release the two clamps, then remove the EGR metal tube between the exhaust manifold and high-pressure EGR valve **(see illustration)**. The manufacturers recommend that the two clamps are renewed as a matter of course.

14 Progressively unscrew the mounting nuts and remove the exhaust manifold from the studs on the cylinder head. Recover the metal gasket **(see illustrations)**.

Refitting

15 Refitting is the reversal of removal using a new gasket and seals, and tightening the manifold retaining nuts to the specified torque.

14 Turbocharger – description and precautions

1 A turbocharger increases engine efficiency by raising the pressure in the inlet manifold above atmospheric pressure. Instead of the air simply being sucked into the cylinders, it is forced in. Additional fuel is supplied in proportion to the increased air intake.

2 Energy for the operation of the turbocharger comes from the exhaust gas. The gas flows through a specially shaped housing (the turbine housing) and in so doing, spins the turbine wheel. The turbine wheel is attached to a shaft, at the end of which is another vaned wheel known as the compressor wheel. The compressor wheel spins in its own housing and compresses the inducted air on the way to the inlet manifold.

3 Between the turbocharger and the inlet manifold, the compressed air passes through an intercooler. This is an air-to-air heat exchanger, mounted behind the front bumper, in front of the air conditioning condenser and the coolant radiator. The purpose of the intercooler is to remove some of the heat gained in being compressed from the inducted air. Because cooler air is denser, removal of this heat further increases engine efficiency.

4 Boost pressure (the pressure in the inlet manifold) is limited by a wastegate, which diverts the exhaust gas away from the turbine wheel in response to a pressure-sensitive actuator. Turbocharging pressure is controlled by a boost pressure sensor located on the air intake.

5 The turbo shaft is pressure-lubricated by an oil feed pipe from the main oil gallery. The shaft 'floats' on a cushion of oil. A drain pipe returns the oil to the sump.

Precautions

- ***The turbocharger operates at extremely high speeds and temperatures. Certain precautions must be observed to avoid premature failure of the turbo or injury to the operator.***
- ***Do not race the engine immediately after start-up, especially if it is cold. Give the oil a few seconds to circulate.***
- ***Always allow the engine to return to idle speed before switching it off – do not blip the throttle and switch off, as this will leave the turbo spinning without lubrication.***
- ***Allow the engine to idle for several minutes before switching off after a high speed run.***
- ***Observe the recommended intervals for oil and filter changing, and use a reputable oil of the specified quality. Neglect of oil changing, or use of inferior oil, can cause carbon formation on the turbo shaft and subsequent failure.***

Warning: Do not operate the turbo with any parts exposed. Foreign objects falling onto the rotating vanes could cause damage and (if ejected) personal injury.

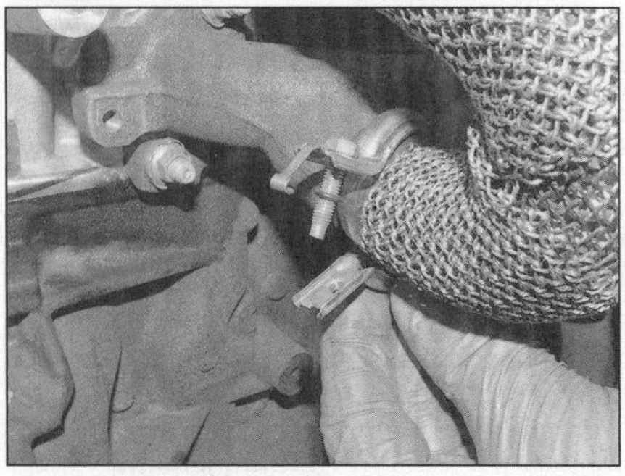
13.13 Release the clamps and remove the EGR metal tube

13.14a Remove the exhaust manifold...

13.14b ...and recover the gasket

15.8a Removing the oil supply pipe and copper sealing rings from the turbocharger

15.8b Removing the oil supply pipe from the cylinder head

15.9 Oil return pipe flange bolts on the bottom of the turbocharger

15 Turbocharger – removal and refitting

Note: *New turbocharger-to-exhaust manifold nuts must be used on refitting.*

Note: *New oil supply pipe O-rings and copper washers must be used on refitting.*

Removal

Early Type 1 engines

Note: *The following procedure is applicable to early Type 1 engines with a diesel particulate filter incorporated in the exhaust system front pipe. The procedure for later engines, with a diesel particulate filter mounted behind the cylinder head in the engine compartment, is contained in the next sub-Section.*

1 Disconnect the battery negative terminal (refer to battery disconnection and reconnection in Chapter 5A, Section 3.

2 Remove the air cleaner assembly and air ducts as described in Section 2.

3 Drain the cooling system as described in Chapter 1B, Section 26.

4 Remove the exhaust system front pipe/ particulate filter as described in Section 17.

5 Remove the EGR volume control valve housing as described in Chapter 4CSection 3.

6 Remove the EGR cooler as described in Chapter 4C, Section 3.

7 Disconnect the exhaust fuel injector quick-release connector and wiring harness connector.

8 Unscrew the union and disconnect the oil supply pipe from the turbocharger, collect the copper sealing rings, then unscrew the union nut and disconnect the pipe from the cylinder head **(see illustrations)**.

9 Unscrew the bolts and detach the oil return pipe from the bottom of the turbocharger – if necessary, remove the pipe from the cylinder block **(see illustration)**.

10 Unscrew the three nuts and remove the turbocharger outlet duct. Recover the gasket.

11 Unscrew the turbocharger upper and lower mounting nuts, then remove the turbocharger from the exhaust manifold.

Later Type 1 engines and all Type 2 engines

Note: *The following procedure is applicable to later Type 1 engines and all Type 2 engines, with a diesel particulate filter mounted behind the cylinder head in the engine compartment.*

12 Disconnect the battery negative terminal (refer to battery disconnection and reconnection in Chapter 5A, Section 3.

13 Remove the diesel particulate filter as described in Section 17.

14 Disconnect the vacuum hose from the actuator at the base of the turbocharger and release the hose from its retaining clips **(see illustrations)**.

15 Disconnect the exhaust gas temperature sensor wiring harness connector, then release the connector from the support bracket **(see illustrations)**.

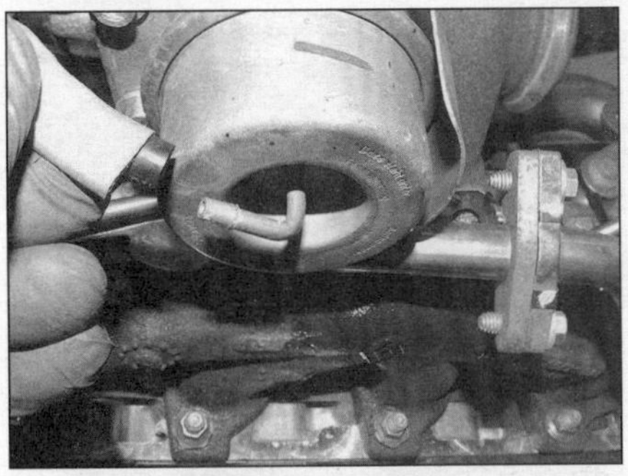

15.14a Disconnect the turbocharger vacuum hose...

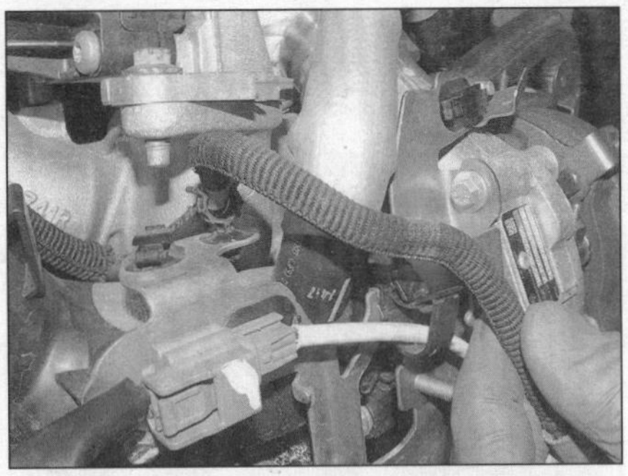

15.14b ...and release it from the retaining clips

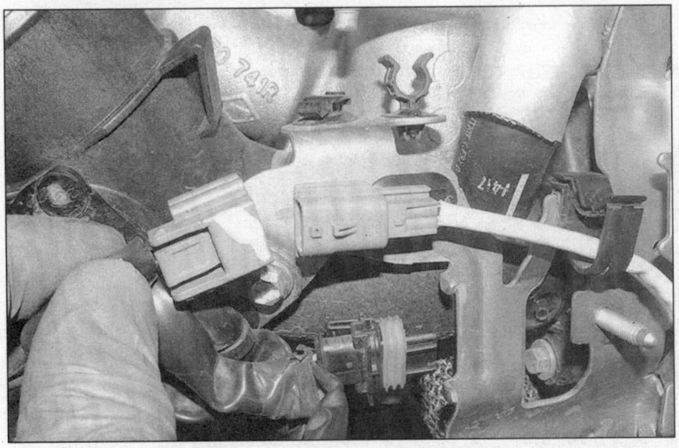

15.15a Disconnect the temperature sensor wiring connector...

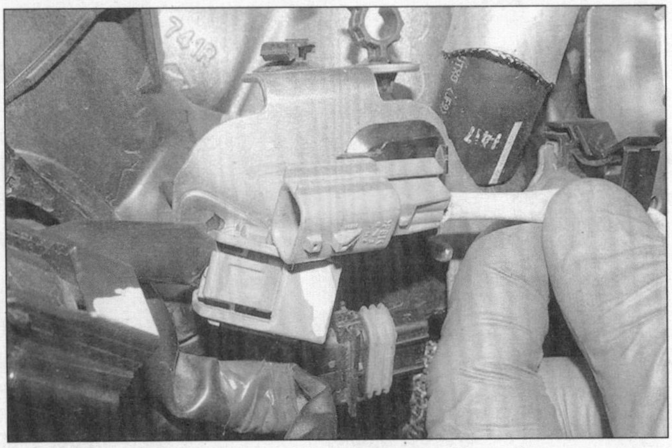

15.15b ...and release the connector from the support bracket

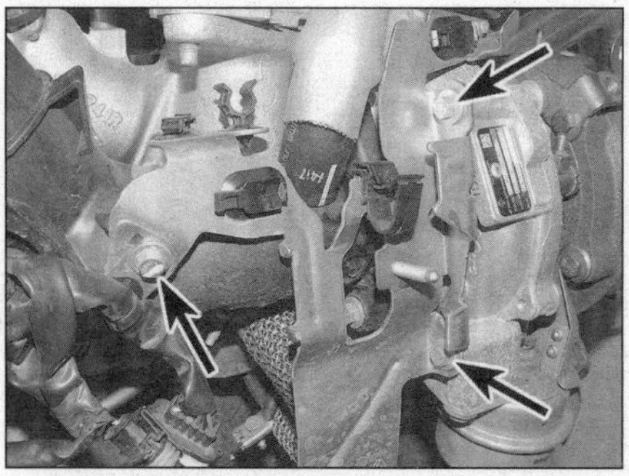

15.16a Undo the support bracket retaining bolts...

15.16b ...lift off the support bracket...

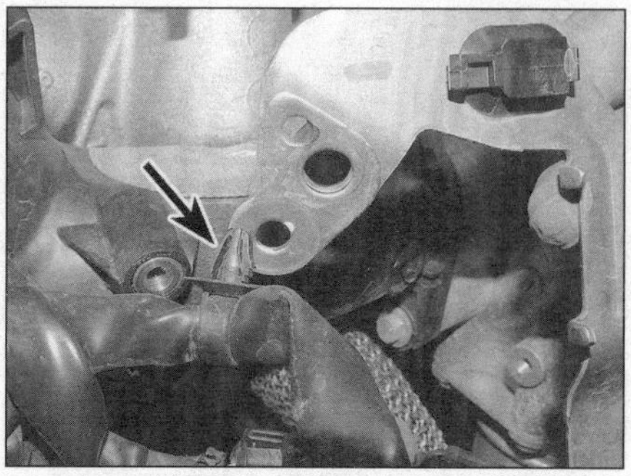

15.16c ...and unclip the wiring harness

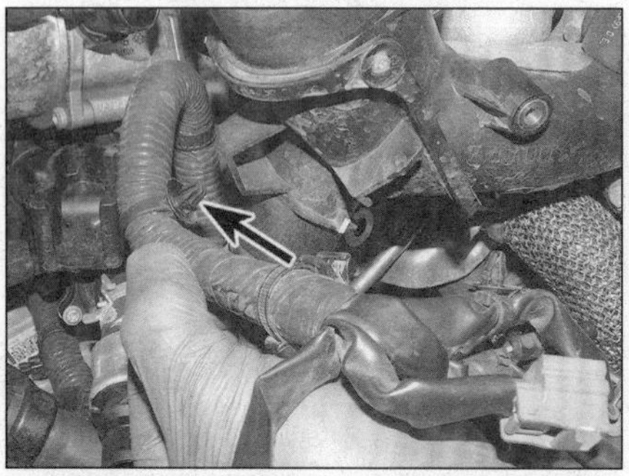

15.17 Unclip the wiring harness from the air inlet pipe

16 Undo the three bolts securing the support bracket to the turbocharger and air inlet pipe. Lift off the support bracket, unclip the wiring harness and remove the bracket **(see illustrations)**.

17 Release the clip securing the wiring harness to the air inlet pipe **(see illustration)**.

18 Undo the two retaining bolts and remove the air inlet pipe from the turbocharger **(see illustrations)**. Recover the seal.

19 Undo the bolts securing the two sections of the turbocharger oil return pipe at the connecting flange. Separate the flange and pull the lower section of the pipe out of the cylinder block **(see illustrations)**.

20 Unscrew the union and disconnect the oil supply pipe from the turbocharger, collect the copper sealing rings, then unscrew the union nut and disconnect the pipe from the cylinder head **(see illustrations)**.

21 Undo the upper retaining nut and the two lower retaining nuts securing the turbocharger to the exhaust manifold **(see illustrations)**.

22 Undo the two bolts and remove the support bracket, then lift the turbocharger off the manifold **(see illustrations)**.

23 Unscrew the two bolts and lift off the exhaust manifold heat shield/gasket **(see illustrations 13.12a, 13.12b and 13.12c)**.

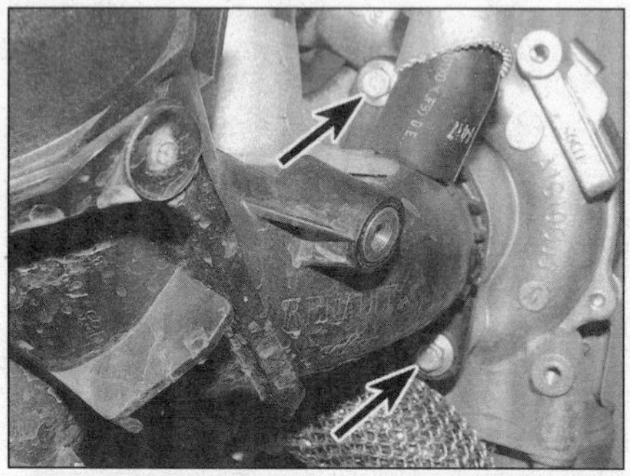

15.18a Undo the two retaining bolts...

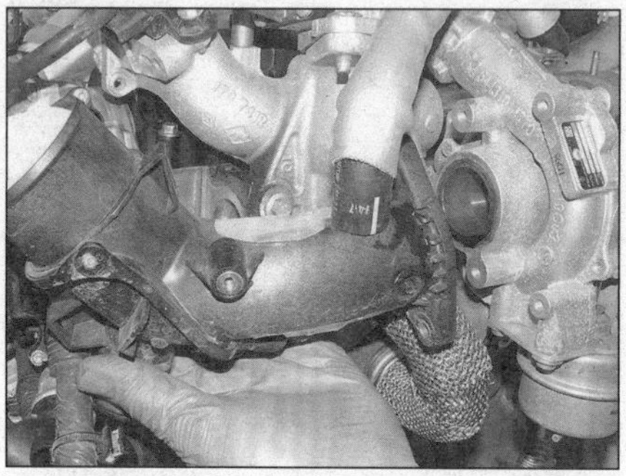

15.18b ...and remove the air inlet pipe

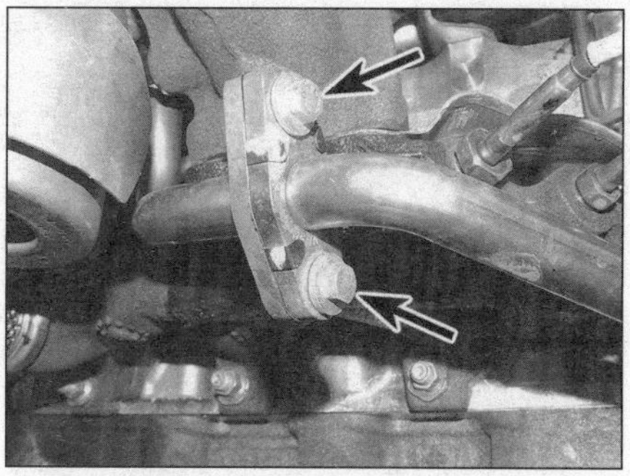

15.19a Undo the bolts securing the two sections of the oil return pipe...

15.19b ...then remove the lower section from the cylinder block

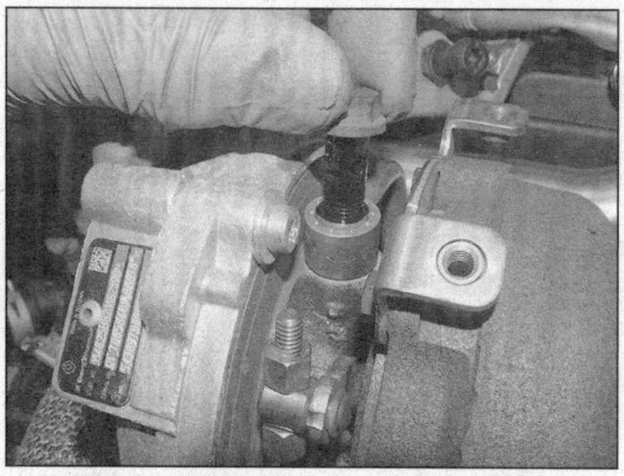

15.20a Remove the oil supply pipe and copper sealing rings from the turbocharger...

15.20b ...then unscrew the union and remove the oil supply pipe from the cylinder head

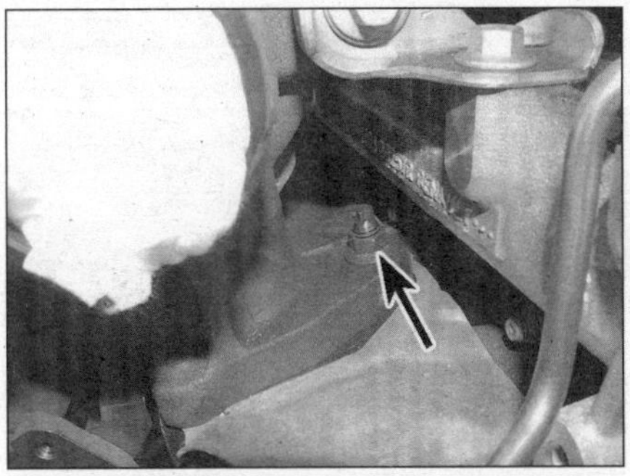
15.21a Undo the upper retaining nut...

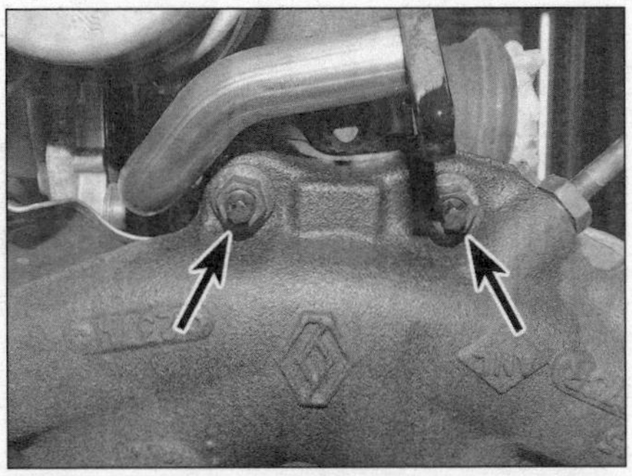
15.21b ...and two lower nuts securing the turbocharger to the manifold

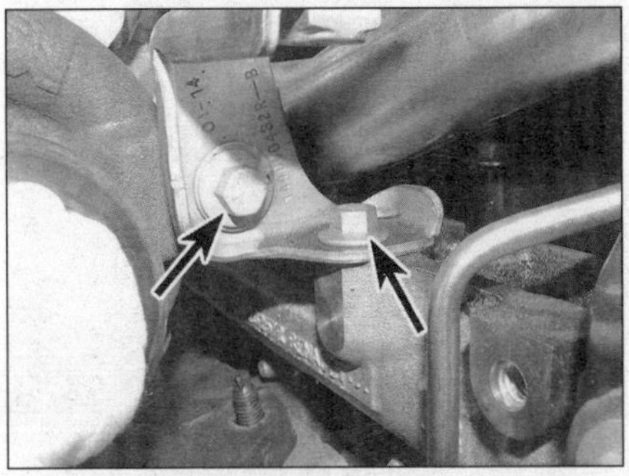
15.22a Undo the two bolts and remove the support bracket...

15.22b ...then lift the turbocharger off the manifold

Refitting

24 Refitting is a reversal of removal, but renew any damaged hose clamps, and use new turbocharger-to-exhaust manifold nuts which should be tightened to the specified torque. Fit new oil supply pipe O-rings and copper seals, then apply Loctite Frenetanch (or similar sealant) to the union threads before refitting the pipe and tightening the union to the specified torque. Fit a new gasket to the oil return pipe, and a new O-ring seal to the groove in the bottom of the pipe.

16 Intercooler – removal and refitting

Removal

1 The intercooler is located behind the front bumper, in front of the air conditioning condenser.

Type 1 engines

2 Remove the front bumper as described in Chapter 11, Section 6.

3 Remove the front bumper energy absorber, then undo the three nuts each side and remove the bumper brace **(see illustration)**.

4 Extract the two plastic expanding rivets and remove the air guide on the right-hand side **(see illustrations)**.

5 Slacken the retaining clips and disconnect the air inlet and outlet hoses from each end of the intercooler **(see illustrations)**.

16.3 Undo the retaining nuts and remove the bumper brace

16.4a Extract the upper plactic rivet...

16.4b ...and lower plastic rivet...

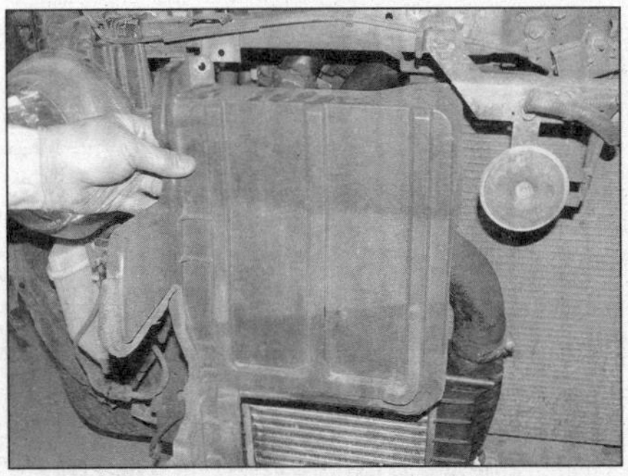
16.4c ...then remove the right-hand air guide

16.5a Slacken the retaining clips...

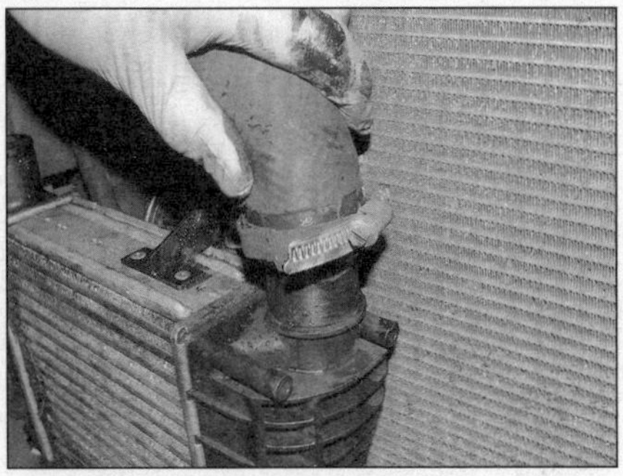
16.5b ...and disconnect the air hoses

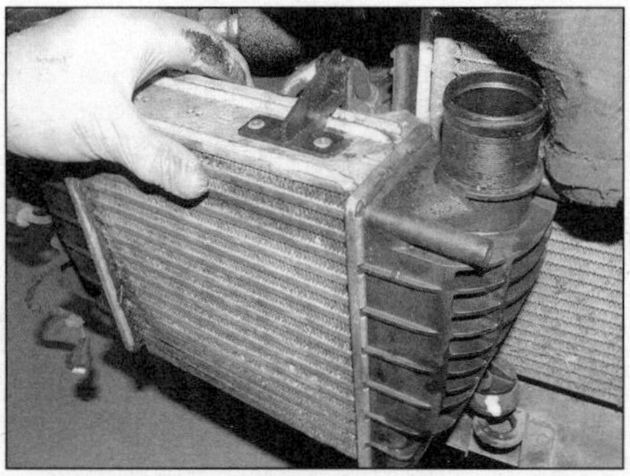
16.6 Lift the intercooler upwards to release it from the mountings

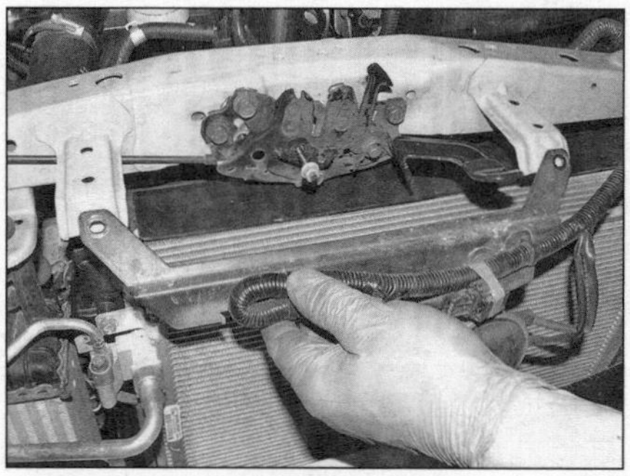
16.10 Remove the horn bracket from the bonnet lock platform

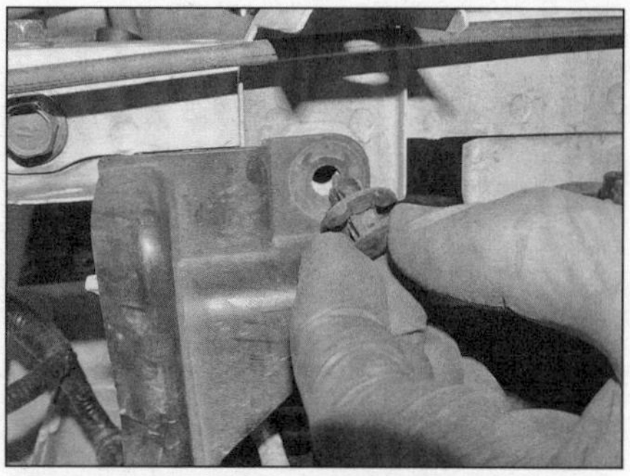
16.12 Extract the expanding rivets securing the air guides

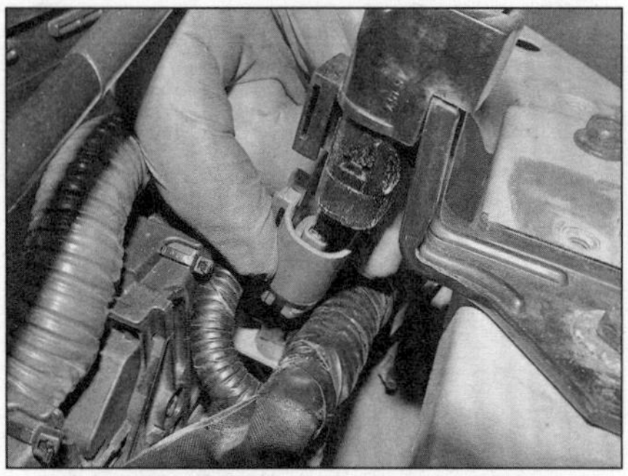
16.14 Disconnect the bonnet closure switch wiring connector

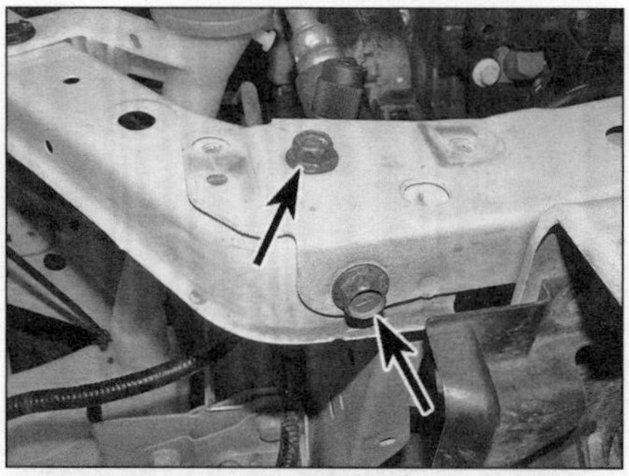
16.15a Undo the retaining bolts on each side...

16.15b ...and lift off the bonnet lock platform

6 Pull the intercooler upwards to release it from the condenser bracket and lower mountings, and remove it from the front of the vehicle **(see illustration)**.

Type 2 engines

7 Remove the front bumper as described in Chapter 11, Section 6.
8 Undo the bolts securing the coolant expansion tank to the bonnet lock platform.
9 Remove the combination lights as described in Chapter 12, Section 5.
10 Undo the two bolts and remove the horn bracket from the bonnet lock platform **(see illustration)**.
11 Remove the bonnet lock as described in Chapter 11, Section 10. Disengage the release cable from the retaining clip on the bonnet lock platform.
12 Extract the upper plastic expanding rivet securing the air guides to the bonnet lock platform on each side **(see illustration)**.
13 Suitably support the bonnet in the open position, then disengage and remove the bonnet support rod.
14 Disconnect the wiring connector from the bonnet closure switch **(see illustration)**.
15 Undo the two bolts each side and lift off the bonnet lock platform **(see illustrations)**.
16 Remove the air inlet hose and air inlet duct as described in Section 2.
17 Lift the intercooler upward and out from its location.

Refitting

18 Refitting is a reversal of removal, making sure all the connections are securely fitted.

17 Exhaust system – general information and component renewal

General information

1 The exhaust system consists of the exhaust manifold (see Section 13), the turbocharger (see Section 14), the particulate filter, the front pipe, intermediate pipe and silencer. On early Type 1 engines, the particulate filter is integral with the front pipe.
2 The system is suspended throughout its entire length by rubber mountings **(see illustration)**, and all exhaust sections are joined by flanged joints, which are then secured together by nuts.

Removal

3 To remove the system or part of the system, firmly apply the handbrake, and then jack up the vehicle and support it securely on axle stands (see *Jacking and vehicle support*). Alternatively, position the car over an inspection pit, or on car ramps.

Front pipe without particulate filter

4 Remove the intermediate pipe and silencer as described later in this Section.
5 Disconnect the exhaust throttle valve wiring connector, then unclip and move aside the wiring harness **(see illustration)**.

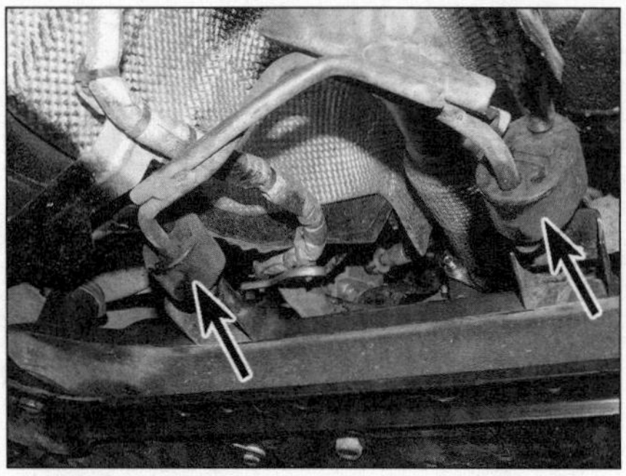
17.2 Exhaust front rubber mountings

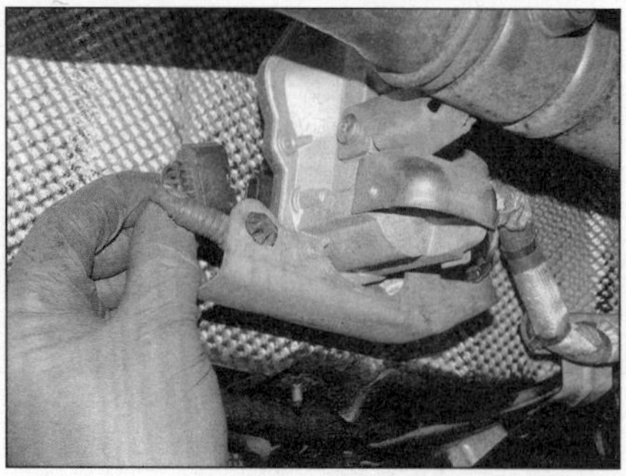
17.5 Disconnect the exhaust throttle valve wiring connector

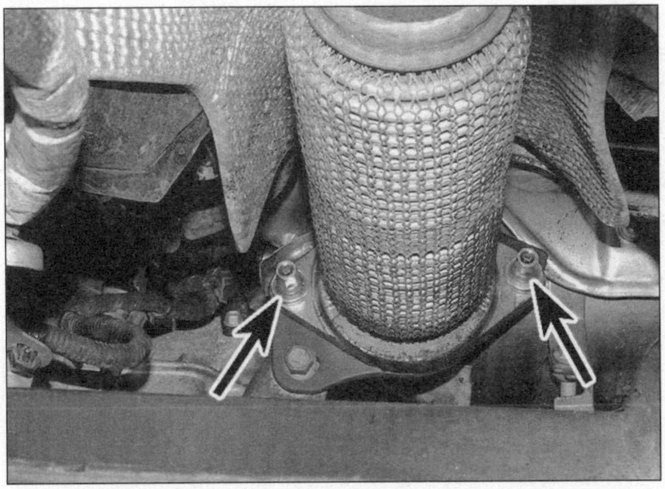

17.6 Undo the front pipe flange retaining nuts

17.7 Remove the front pipe and collect the gasket

6 Undo the nuts securing the front pipe flange to the particulate filter **(see illustration)**.

7 Spray a little penetrating oil on the mounting rubbers, then slide the front pipe to the rear and disengage it from the mountings. Remove the front pipe from under the car and collect the gasket **(see illustration)**.

Front pipe incorporating particulate filter

8 Remove the intermediate pipe and silencer as described later in this Section.

9 Undo the bolt securing the exhaust gas pressure sensor pipe bracket to the particulate filter, then unscrew the union nut and remove the pipe **(see illustration)**.

10 Unscrew the retaining nut and remove the exhaust gas temperature sensor from the particulate filter **(see illustration)**.

11 Undo the nuts securing the front pipe flange to the turbocharger **(see illustration)**.

12 Spray a little penetrating oil on the mounting rubbers, then slide the front pipe to the rear and disengage it from the mountings. Remove the front pipe from under the car and collect the gasket.

Particulate filter

13 Remove the engine/transmission assembly from the car as described in Chapter 2D, Section 3.

14 Disconnect the particulate filter temperature sensor wiring connector, then unclip the wiring harness from the support bracket **(see illustrations)**.

15 Release the exhaust gas temperature sensor wiring from the clips on the particulate filter heat shield **(see illustration)**.

16 Disconnect the pressure sensor wiring

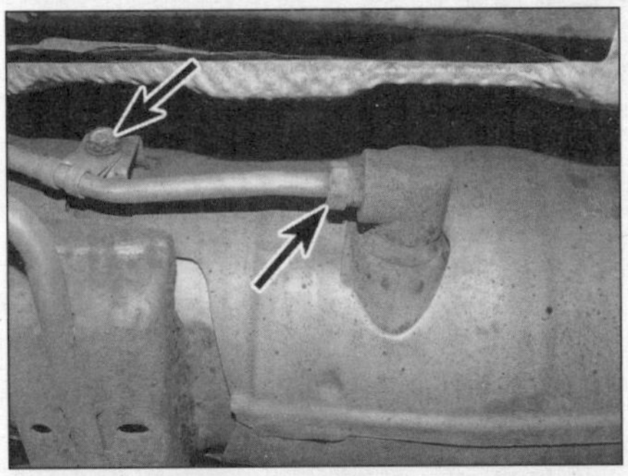

17.9 Undo the support bracket bolt, then unscrew the pressure sensor pipe union nut

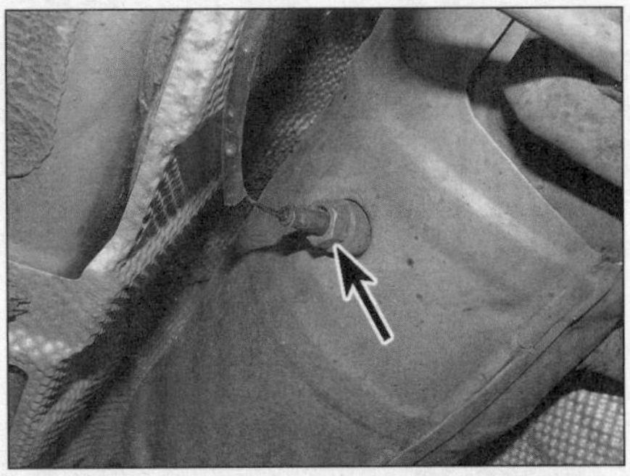

17.10 Unscrew the nut and remove the temperature sensor

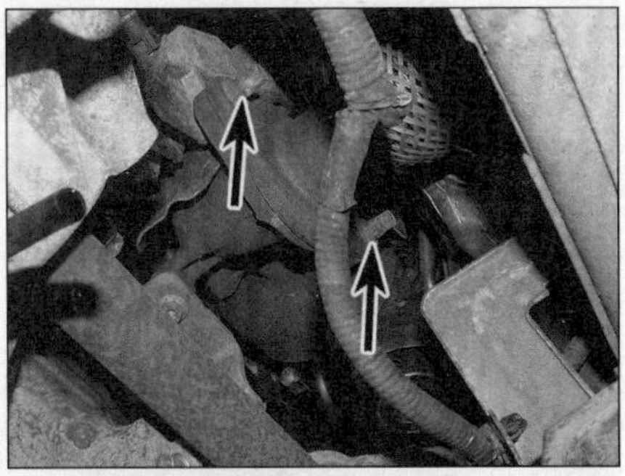

17.11 Undo the front pipe flange retaining nuts

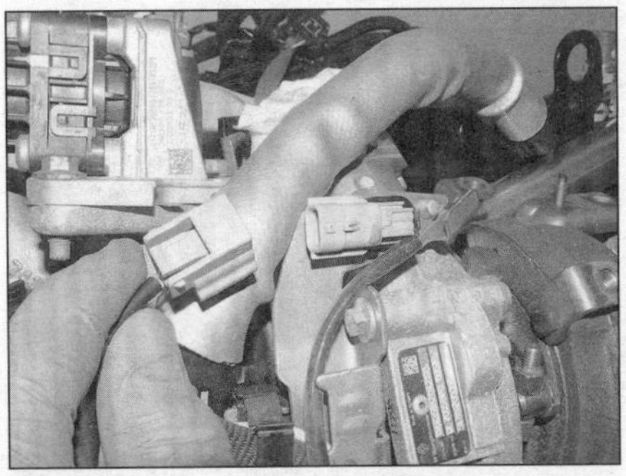

17.14a Disconnect the temperature sensor wiring connector...

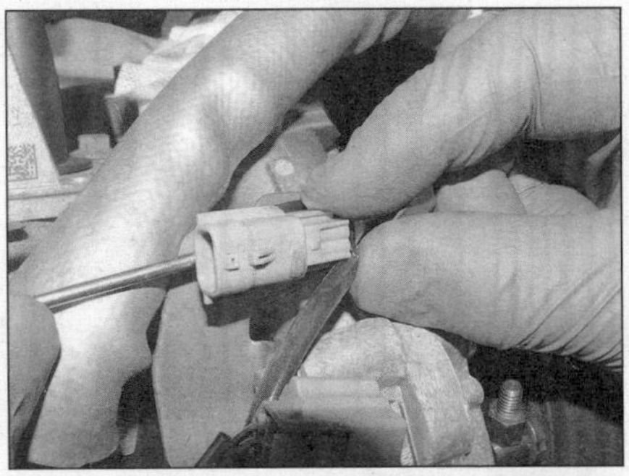

17.14b ...then unclip the harness from the support bracket

17.15 Release the temperature sensor wiring from the heat shield clips

17.16a Disconnect the pressure sensor wiring connector...

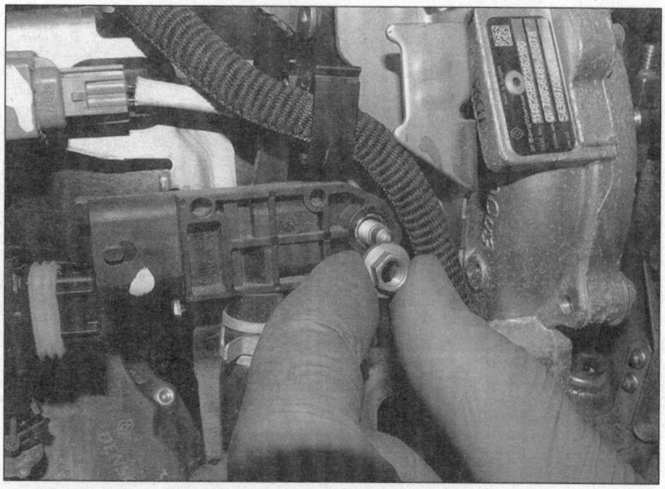

17.16b ...undo the retaining nut...

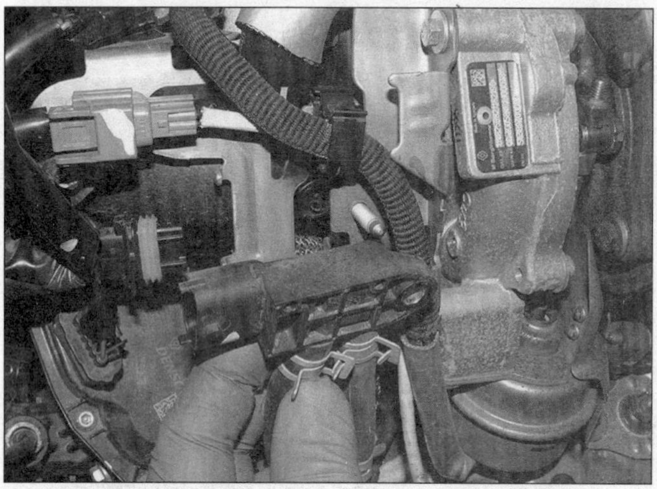

17.16c ...and slide the sensor off the mounting stud

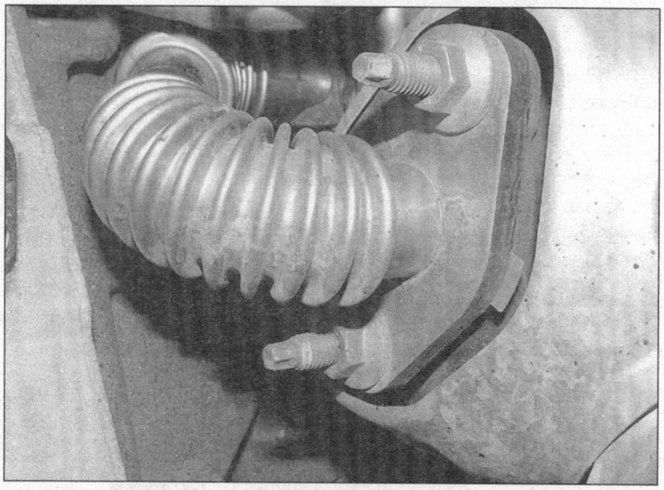

17.17 Undo the EGR cooler pipe flange nuts

connector, undo the retaining nut and slide the sensor off the mounting bracket stud **(see illustrations)**.

17 Undo the two nuts securing the EGR cooler pipe flange to the particulate filter **(see illustration)**.

18 Unscrew the particulate filter temperature sensor and remove the sensor **(see illustration)**.

19 Unscrew the retaining nut and remove the gasket plate from the filter heat shield **(see illustration)**.

20 Undo the three bolts and remove the

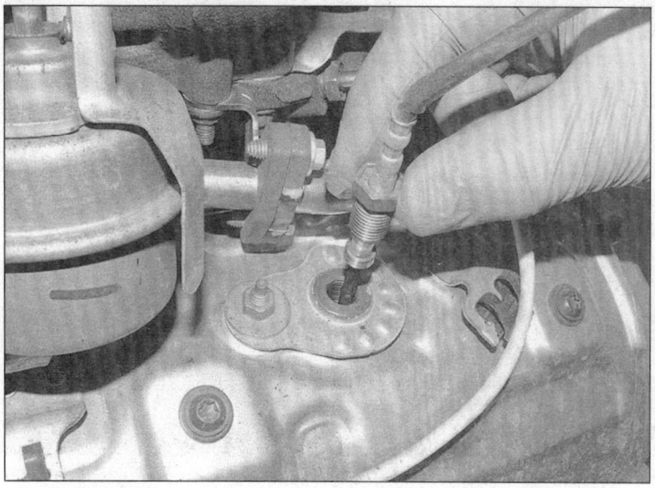

17.18 Unscrew and remove the temperature sensor

17.19 Unscrew the nut and remove the gasket plate

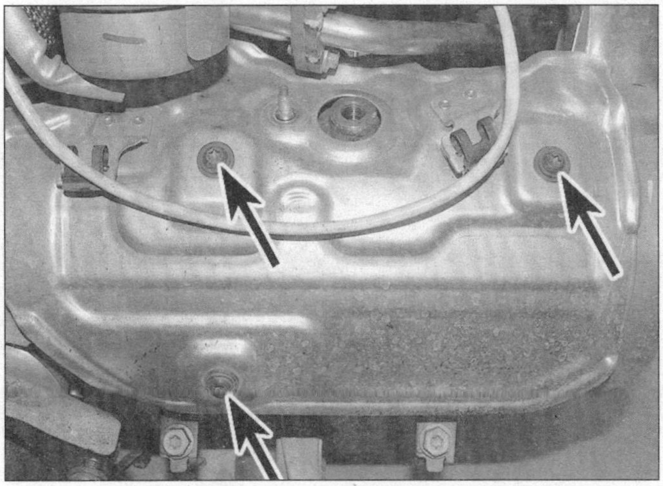
17.20a Undo the three bolts...

17.20b ...and remove the heat shield

particulate filter heat shield **(see illustrations)**.

21 Undo the bolt securing the base of the particulate filter to the support bracket **(see illustration)**.

22 Undo the nut and remove the bolt from the particular filter upper clamp **(see illustration)**.

23 Undo the two bolts securing the particulate filter retaining straps to the mounting bracket. Lift up the straps, disengage them at the rear and remove them from the filter **(see illustrations)**.

24 Using circlip pliers or similar, spread and remove the upper retaining clamp **(see illustration)**.

17.21 Undo the lower support bracket bolt

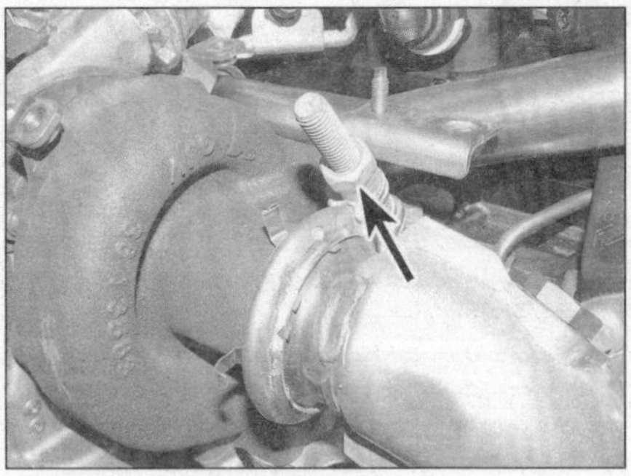
17.22 Undo the nut and remove the upper clamp bolt

17.23a Undo the filter retaining strap mounting bolts...

17.23b ...then lift up and disengage the straps

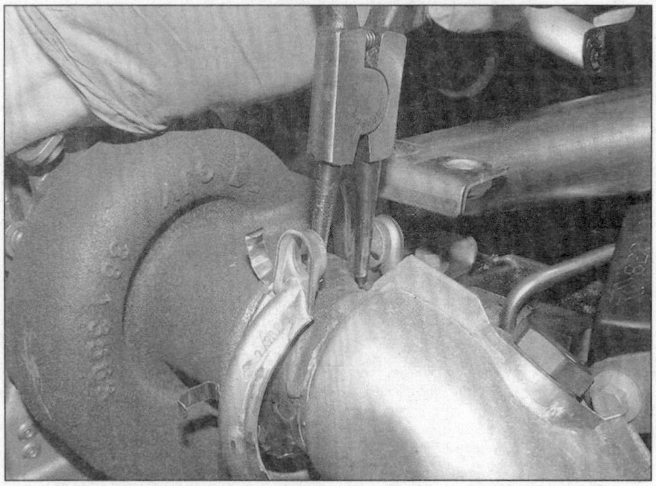
17.24 Spread and remove the filter upper retaining clamp

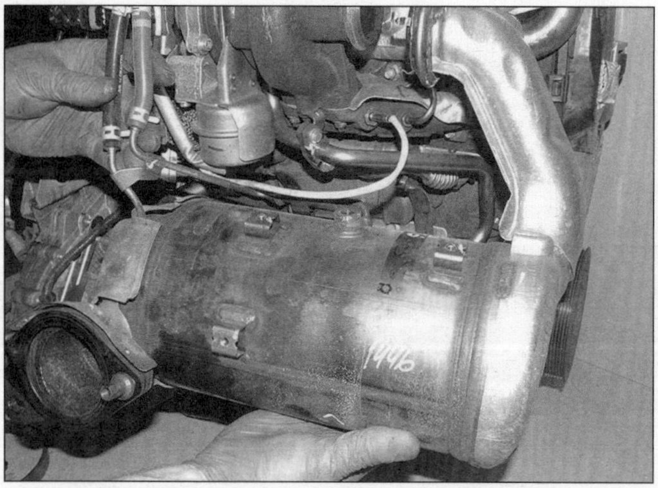

17.25 Remove the particulate filter together with the pressure sensor components

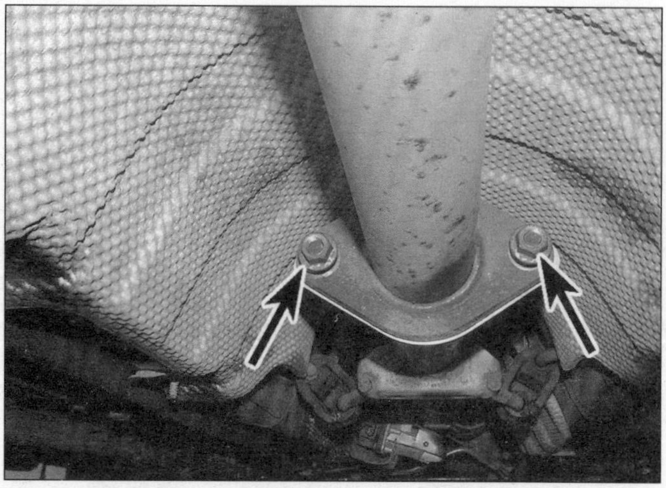

17.27 Intermediate pipe-to-front pipe retaining nuts

25 Disengage the particulate filter from its location and remove it, together with the pressure sensor, pipes and hoses **(see illustration)**. Collect the relevant gaskets and seals.

Intermediate pipe

26 Remove the silencer as described later in this Section.
27 Undo the nuts securing the intermediate pipe flange to the front pipe **(see illustration)**.
28 Spray a little penetrating oil on the mounting rubbers, then slide the intermediate pipe to the rear and disengage it from the mountings. Remove the intermediate pipe from under the car and collect the gasket.

Silencer

29 Undo the nuts securing the silencer flange to the intermediate pipe **(see illustration)**.
30 Spray a little penetrating oil on the mounting rubbers, then slide the silencer to the rear and disengage it from the mountings. Remove the silencer from under the car and collect the gasket.

Heat shield(s)

31 The heat shields are secured in position by a mixture of fasteners. Some heatshields are fitted to the underside of the vehicle. And also some are fitted to parts of the exhaust system. When an exhaust section is renewed, transfer any relevant heat shields from the original over to the new section before installing the exhaust section on the vehicle.

Refitting

32 Each section is refitted by a reverse of the removal sequence, noting the following points:

a) Ensure that all traces of corrosion have been removed from the flanges, and renew all necessary gaskets and seals.
b) Inspect the rubber mountings for signs of damage or deterioration, and renew as necessary.

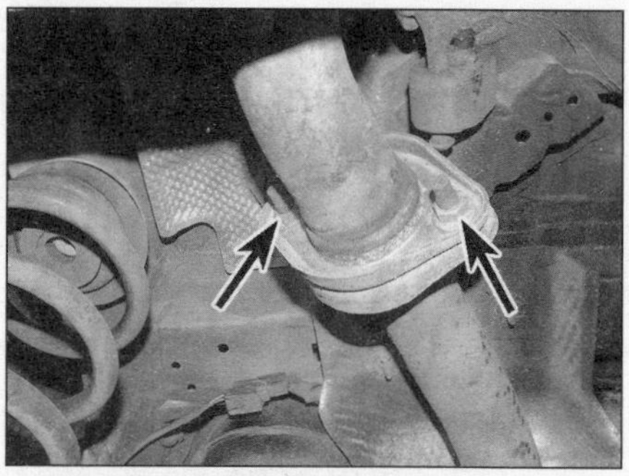

17.29 Silencer-to-intermediate pipe flange retaining nuts

c) Prior to tightening the exhaust system fasteners, ensure that all rubber mountings are correctly located, and that there is adequate clearance between the exhaust system and vehicle underbody/suspension components, etc.

Chapter 4 Part C
Emission control systems

Contents

Degrees of difficulty

Easy, suitable for novice with little experience	**Fairly easy,** suitable for beginner with some experience	**Fairly difficult,** suitable for competent DIY mechanic	**Difficult,** suitable for experienced DIY mechanic	**Very difficult,** suitable for expert DIY or professional

Specifications

Torque wrench settings	Nm	lbf ft
Petrol engines		
Oxygen (lambda) sensor:		
1.2 litre models	44	32
1.6 litre models	50	37
Early Type 1 diesel engines		
EGR cooler-to-EGR valve bolts	12	9
EGR volume control valve-to-housing mounting bolts	10	7
EGR volume control valve housing mounting bolts	25	18
EGR volume control valve housing-to-EGR cooler	12	9
Later Type 1 and all Type 2 diesel engines		
EGR cooler mounting bolts	25	18
High-pressure EGR housing-to-cylinder head	25	18
High-pressure EGR volume control valve-to-housing	25	18
Inlet duct-to-low pressure EGR volume control valve	10	7
Low pressure EGR volume control valve-to-EGR cooler	25	18
Particulate filter mounting bracket-to-cylinder block	25	18

1 General information and precautions

1 All petrol engine models use unleaded petrol and also have various other features built into the fuel/exhaust system to help minimise harmful emissions. All models are equipped with a crankcase emission control system, a catalytic converter and an evaporative emission control system to keep fuel vapour/exhaust gas emissions down to a minimum.

2 Diesel engine models are also designed to meet strict emission requirements. A crankcase emission control system, and a diesel particulate filter are fitted to keep exhaust emissions down to a minimum. An exhaust gas recirculation (EGR) system is also used to further decrease exhaust emissions.

3 The emission control systems function as follows.

Petrol engines

Crankcase emissions control

4 To reduce the emission of unburned hydrocarbons from the crankcase into the atmosphere, the engine is sealed and the blow-by gases and oil vapour are drawn from the cylinder head cover into the inlet manifold to be burned by the engine during normal combustion.

5 The gases are forced out of the crankcase by the relatively higher crankcase pressure; if the engine is worn, the raised crankcase pressure (due to increased blow-by) will cause some of the flow to return under all manifold conditions.

Exhaust emission control

6 To minimise the amount of pollutants which escape into the atmosphere, all models are fitted with a catalytic converter. The system is of the closed-loop type, in which oxygen sensors in the exhaust system provide the fuel injection/ignition system ECU with constant feedback, enabling the ECU to adjust the mixture to provide the best possible conditions for the converter to operate.

7 On all petrol engines covered by this manual, there are two heated oxygen sensors fitted to the exhaust system. The sensor upstream of thecatalytic converter determines the residual oxygen content of the exhaust gases for mixture correction. The sensor downstream of the catalytic converter monitors the function of the catalytic converter to give the driver a warning signal if there is a fault.

8 The oxygen sensor's tip is sensitive to oxygen and sends the ECU a varying voltage depending on the amount of oxygen in the exhaust gases. Peak conversion efficiency of all major pollutants occurs if the inlet air/fuel mixture is maintained at the chemically-correct ratio for the complete combustion of petrol of 14.7 parts (by weight) of air to 1 part of fuel (the 'stoichiometric' ratio). The sensor output voltage alters in a large step at this point, the ECU using the signal change as a reference point and correcting the inlet air/fuel mixture accordingly by altering the fuel injector pulse width.

Fuel evaporation emission control

9 To minimise the escape into the atmosphere of unburned hydrocarbons, a fuel evaporation emission control system is fitted. The fuel tank filler cap is sealed and a charcoal canister is mounted on the side of the fuel tank. The canister collects the petrol vapours generated in the tank when the car is parked and stores them until they can be cleared from the canister (under the control of the fuel injection/ignition system ECU) via the purge valve into the inlet manifold to be burned by the engine during normal combustion.

10 To ensure that the engine runs correctly when it is cold and/or idling and to protect the catalytic converter from the effects of an over-rich mixture, the purge control valve is not opened by the ECU until the engine has warmed-up, and the engine is under load; the valve solenoid is then modulated on and off to allow the stored vapour to pass into the inlet manifold.

Diesel engines

Crankcase emission control

11 Refer to paragraphs 4 and 5.

Exhaust emission control

12 To minimise the level of exhaust pollutants released into the atmosphere, a diesel particulate filter is fitted in the exhaust system.

13 The diesel particulate filter is either integral with the exhaust system front pipe or fitted between the front pipe and the turbocharger. The filter contains a silicon carbide honeycomb block containing microscopic channels in which the exhaust gases flow. As the gases flow through the honeycomb channels, soot particles are deposited on the channel walls. To prevent clogging of the honeycomb channels, the soot particles are burned off at regular intervals during what is known as a 'regeneration phase'. Under the control of the injection system ECU, the injection characteristics are altered to raise the temperature of the exhaust gases to approximately 600°C. At this temperature, the soot particles are effectively burned off the honeycomb walls as the exhaust gases pass through. A differential pressure sensor and temperature sensor are used to inform the ECU of the condition of the particulate filter, and the temperature of the exhaust gases during the regeneration phase. When the ECU detects that soot build-up is reducing the efficiency of the particulate filter, it will instigate the regeneration process. This occurs at regular intervals under certain driving conditions and will normally not be detected by the driver.

Exhaust gas recirculation system

14 This system is designed to recirculate small quantities of exhaust gas into the inlet tract, and therefore into the combustion process. This reduces the level of unburnt hydrocarbons present in the exhaust gas before it reaches the particulate filter. The system is controlled by the injection system ECU, using the information from its various sensors, via the electrically-operated EGR valves.

2 Petrol engine emission control systems – testing and component renewal

Crankcase emission control

1 The components of this system require no attention other than to check that the hose(s) are clear and undamaged at regular intervals.

Note: *When removing hoses to check for condition or blockage, make sure their fitted positions are noted for reassembly.*

Evaporative emission control

Testing

2 If the system is thought to be faulty, disconnect the hoses from the charcoal canister and purge control valve and check that they are clear by blowing through them. If the purge control valve(s) or charcoal canister is thought to be faulty, they must be renewed.

Charcoal (fuel vapour) canister renewal

3 The charcoal canister is located under the car attached to the left-hand side of the fuel tank **(see illustration)**.

4 Chock the front wheels then jack-up the rear of the car and securely support it on axle stands (see *Jacking and vehicle support*.

5 Note the fitted position and disconnect the hoses from the canister.

6 Undo the clamp retaining bolt and remove the canister from under the car.

7 Refitting is a reverse of the removal procedure, ensuring that the hoses are correctly reconnected.

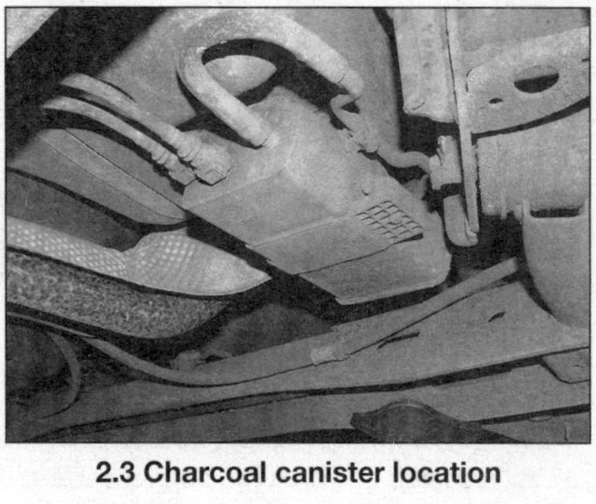

2.3 Charcoal canister location

Purge control solenoid valve renewal

8 The purge valve is mounted in the rear right-hand side of the engine compartment on 1.2 litre models, and on the inlet manifold, next to the throttle housing on 1.6 litre models **(see illustrations)**.

9 To renew the purge valve, first disconnect the wiring connector from the valve.

10 Disconnect the hoses from the valve, then lift the valve from its mounting bracket (1.2 litre models) or undo the retaining nut and remove it from the inlet manifold (1.6 litre models).

11 Refitting is a reverse of the removal procedure, ensuring that the hoses are correctly reconnected.

Exhaust emission control

Testing

12 The performance of the catalytic converter can be checked by measuring the exhaust gases using an exhaust gas analyser.

13 If the CO level at the tailpipe is too high, the vehicle should be taken to a Nissan dealer so that the complete fuel injection and ignition systems, including the oxygen sensor, can be thoroughly checked using the special diagnostic equipment. Once these have been checked and are known to be free from faults, the fault must be in the catalytic converter, which must be renewed.

Catalytic converter renewal

14 Refer to Chapter 4A, Section 16.

Oxygen (lambda) sensor renewal

Note: *The oxygen sensor is delicate and will not work if it is dropped or knocked, if its power supply is disrupted, or if any cleaning materials are used on it.*

Note: *There are two oxygen sensors – one 'upstream' and one 'downstream' of the catalytic converter.*

15 Where necessaey, firmly apply the handbrake then jack up the front of the vehicle and support it on axle stands (see *Jacking and vehicle support*).

16 Trace the wiring back from the oxygen sensor and disconnect its wiring connector, freeing the wiring from any relevant retaining clips or ties.

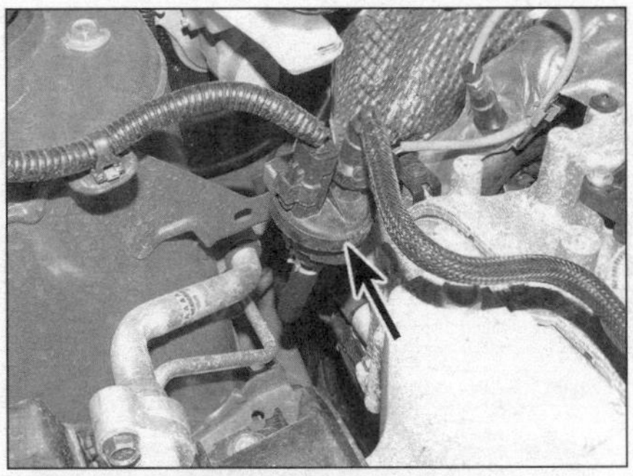

2.8a Location of the purge valve on 1.2 litre models...

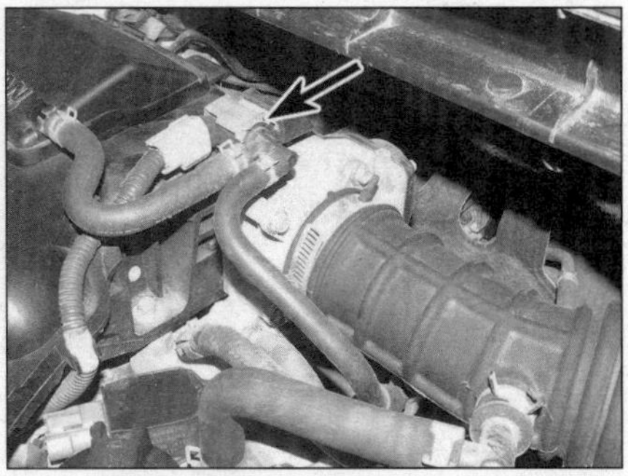

2.8b ...and on 1.6 litre models

17 Unscrew the sensor and remove it from the exhaust pipe or catalytic converter **(see illustrations)**.

18 Refitting is a reverse of the removal procedure. Prior to installing the sensor apply a smear of high-temperature grease to the sensor threads. Tighten the sensor to the specified torque and ensure that the wiring is correctly routed and in no danger of contacting either the exhaust system or engine.

3 Diesel engine emission control systems – testing and component renewal

Crankcase emission control

1 The components of this system require no attention other than to check that the hose(s) are clear and undamaged at regular intervals.

2 If the system is thought to be faulty, first check that the hoses are unobstructed and not damaged.

3 On high-mileage cars, particularly when regularly used for short journeys, a sludge-like deposit may be evident inside the system hoses and oil separators. If excessive deposits are present, the relevant component(s) should be removed and cleaned.

4 Periodically inspect the system components for security and damage, and renew them as necessary.

Exhaust emission control

Testing

5 The performance of the diesel particulate filter can be checked by measuring the exhaust gases using an exhaust gas analyser, which is suitable for diesel engines.

Particulate filter renewal

6 Refer to Chapter 4B, Section 17.

Exhaust gas recirculation system

Testing

7 Testing of the system should be entrusted to a Nissan dealer, who will have the specialist diagnostic equipment to carry out any tests.

EGR system component renewal – Early Type 1 engines

8 Drain the cooling system as described in Chapter 1B, Section 26.

9 Remove the air cleaner assembly as described in Chapter 4B, Section 2.

10 Remove the turbocharger inlet pipe and the intercooler inlet pipe as described in Chapter 4B, Section 2.

11 Remove the throttle housing as described in Chapter 4B, Section 8.

12 Disconnect the wiring connector from

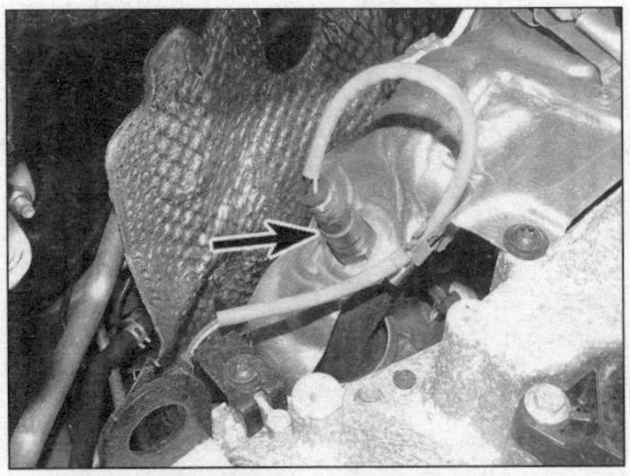

2.17a Upstream oxygen sensor – 1.2 litre models

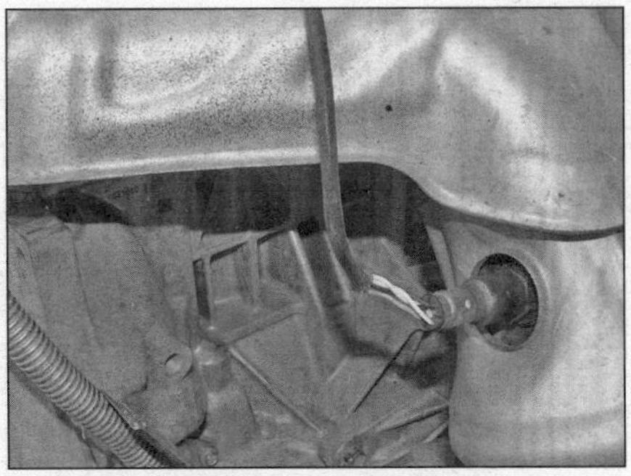

2.17b Upstream oxygen sensor – 1.6 litre models

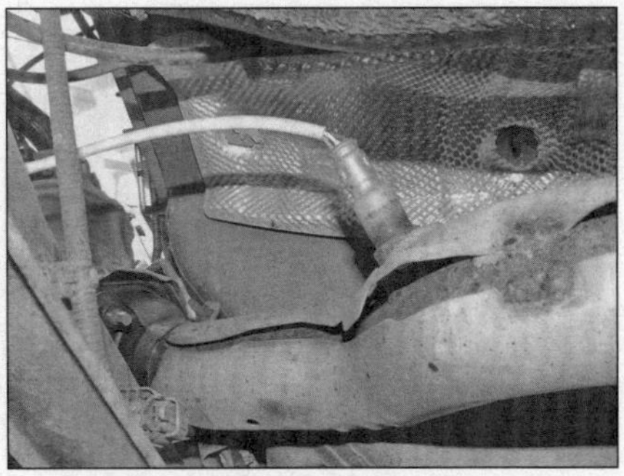

2.17c Downstream oxygen sensor – 1.6 litre models

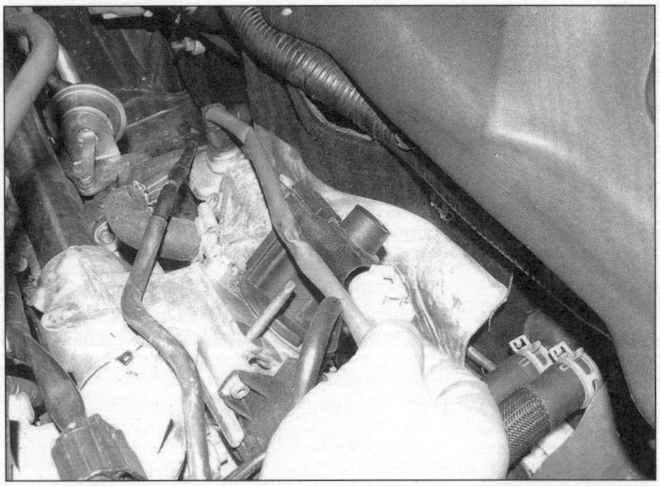

3.12 Disconnect the volume control valve wiring connector

3.14 Remove the inlet pipe

the EGR volume control valve **(see illustration)**.

13 Release the retaining clips and disconnect the coolant hose from the EGR volume control valve.

14 Unscrew the bolt and remove the air inlet metallic tube **(see illustration)**.

15 Loosen both clamps and remove the EGR convoluted metal tube from the EGR valve and exhaust manifold **(see illustration)**.

16 Where applicable unbolt and move aside any additional solenoid valves from the EGR volume control valve housing, according to model.

17 Unscrew the EGR volume control valve housing mounting bolts and remove the assembly from its location.

18 If necessary, unscrew the mounting bolts and separate the component parts of the volume control valve housing.

19 Refitting is a reversal of removal, but renew all disturbed O-rings and gaskets. Check the condition of the convoluted metal tube retaining clamps and if necessary, renew them – if the special tool is not available, use a pair of pincers to tighten the clamps until the clip is engaged.

20 On completion, refill the cooling system as described in Chapter 1B, Section 26.

3.15 Release the clamps and remove the convoluted metal tube

3.23 Disconnect the EGR temperature sensor wiring connector and unclip the harness

EGR system component renewal – Later Type 1 engines and all Type 2 engines

21 Remove the diesel particulate filter as described in Chapter 4B, Section 17.

22 Remove the turbocharger as described in Chapter 4B, Section 15.

23 Disconnect the low pressure EGR temperature sensor wiring connector, then unclip the sensor wiring harness **(see illustration)**.

24 Undo the two bolts securing the inlet duct to the low pressure EGR volume control valve. Withdraw the duct, disconnect the air hose and remove the duct **(see illustrations)**.

25 Disconnect the wiring connector at the low pressure EGR volume control valve **(see illustration)**.

26 Undo the retaining bolt and two nuts securing the low pressure EGR volume control

3.24a Undo the inlet duct retaining bolts...

3.24b ...then withdraw the duct and disconnect the air hose

3.25 Disconnect the volume control valve wiring connector

3.26a Undo the retaining bolt and two nuts...

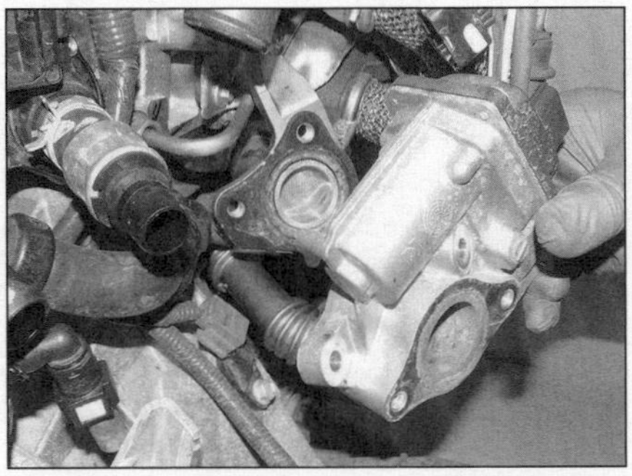

3.26b ...withdraw the volume control valve from the EGR cooler...

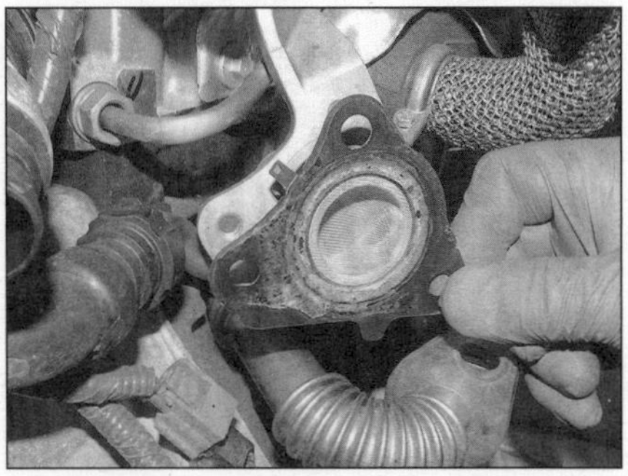

3.26c ...and collect the gasket

3.27a Remove the two particulate filter mounting straps...

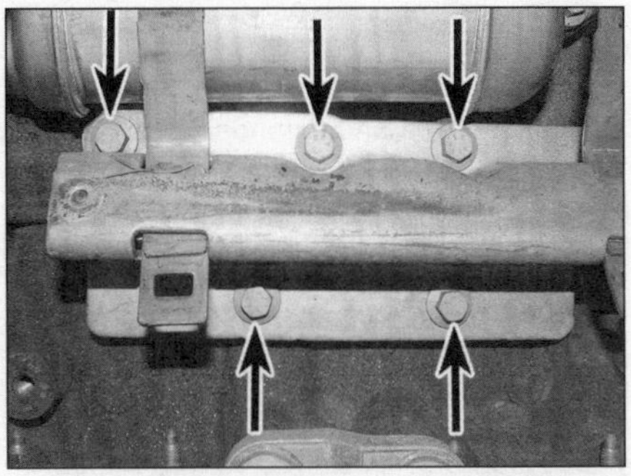

3.27b ...then undo the five bolts and remove the mounting bracket

3.28 Disconnect the coolant hose from the EGR cooler

valve to the EGR cooler. Withdraw the valve from the cooler and collect the gasket **(see illustrations)**.

27 Remove the two particulate filter mounting straps from the mounting bracket, then undo the five retaining bolts and remove the mounting bracket from the cylinder block **(see illustrations)**.

28 Release the end fitting and disconnect the coolant hose from the EGR cooler **(see illustration)**.

29 Undo the two retaining bolts at the right-hand end, and the retaining bolt at the left-hand end, then remove the EGR cooler from the cylinder block **(see illustrations)**. Collect the gasket from the cooler flange.

30 Undo the clamp bolts, open the two retaining clamps and remove the high-pressure EGR pipe from the exhaust manifold and high-pressure EGR valve housing **(see illustrations)**. Collect the sealing ring from each end of the pipe.

31 Undo the retaining bolt and remove

3.29a Undo the two bolts at the right-hand end...

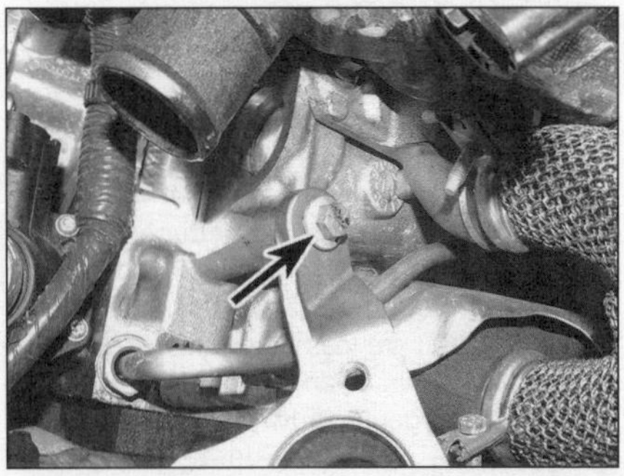

3.29b ...and the bolt at the left-hand end...

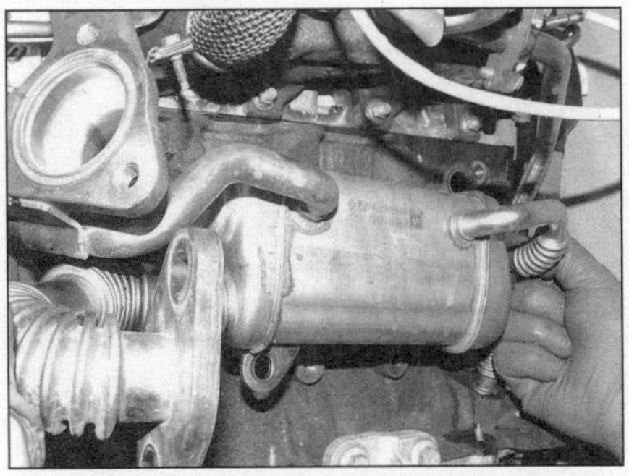

3.29c ...then remove the EGR cooler from the cylinder block

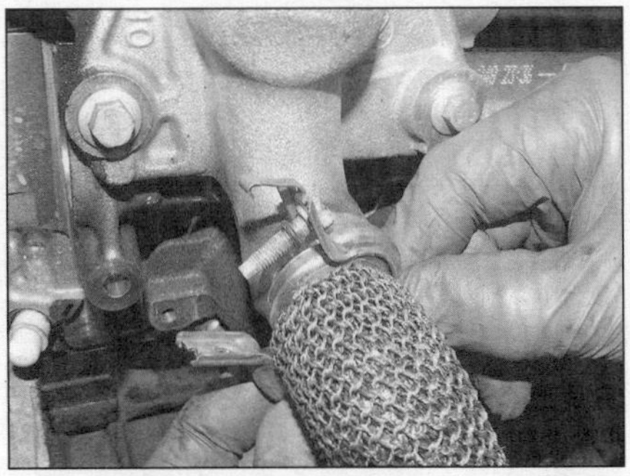

3.30a Undo the clamp bolt and remove the upper retaining clamp...

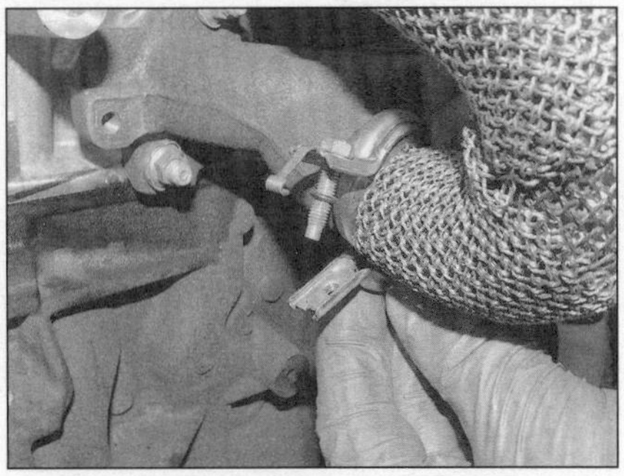

3.30b ...and lower retaining clamp, then remove the EGR pipe

3.31a Undo the retaining bolt...

3.31b ...and remove the EGR tube

3.32 Undo the two bolts and remove the high-pressure EGR valve housing

the EGR tube from the cylinder head and high-pressure ERG valve housing **(see illustrations)**. Recover the O-rings from each end of the pipe.

32 Undo the two bolts and remove the high-pressure EGR valve housing from the cylinder head **(see illustration)**.

33 If required, undo the retaining bolts and remove the high-pressure EGR volume control valve from the housing. Recover the gasket.

34 Refitting is a reversal of removal, but renew all disturbed O-rings, seals and gaskets. Ensure that all mating surfaces are clean and dry, and tighten all retaining nuts and bolts to the specified torque (where given).

4 Catalytic converter – general information and precautions

General information

Note: *The information contained in this Section is, in the main, equally applicable to the particulate filter fitted to diesel engines.*

1 The catalytic converter reduces harmful exhaust emissions by chemically converting the more poisonous gases to ones that (in theory at least) are less harmful. The chemical reaction is known as an 'oxidising' reaction, or one where oxygen is 'added'.

2 Inside the converter is a honeycomb structure, made of ceramic material and coated with the precious metals palladium, platinum and rhodium (the 'catalyst' which promotes the chemical reaction). The chemical reaction generates heat, which itself promotes the reaction – therefore, once the car has been driven several miles, the body of the converter will be very hot.

3 The ceramic structure contained within the converter is understandably fragile, and will not withstand rough treatment. Since the converter runs at a high temperature, driving through deep standing water (in flood conditions, for example) is to be avoided, since the thermal stresses imposed when plunging the hot converter into cold water may well cause the ceramic internals to fracture, resulting in a 'blocked' converter – a common cause of failure. A catalytic converter that has been damaged in this way can be checked by shaking it, do not strike it – if a rattling noise is heard, this indicates probable failure.

Precautions

4 The catalytic converter is a reliable and simple device which needs no maintenance in itself, but there are some facts of which an owner should be aware if the converter is to function properly for its full service life.

a) *DO NOT use leaded petrol (or lead-replacement petrol, LRP) in a car equipped with a catalytic converter – the lead (or other additives) will coat the precious metals, reducing their converting efficiency and will eventually destroy the converter.*
b) *Always keep the ignition and fuel systems well maintained in accordance with the manufacturer's schedule.*
c) *If the engine develops a misfire, do not drive the car at all (or at least as little as possible) until the fault is cured.*
d) *DO NOT push- or tow-start the car – this will soak the catalytic converter in unburned fuel, causing it to overheat when the engine does start.*
e) *DO NOT switch off the ignition at high engine speeds.*
f) *DO NOT use fuel or engine oil additives – these may contain substances harmful to the catalytic converter.*
g) *DO NOT continue to use the car if the engine burns oil to the extent of leaving a visible trail of blue smoke.*
h) *Remember that the catalytic converter operates at very high temperatures. DO NOT, therefore, park the car in dry undergrowth, over long grass or piles of dead leaves after a long run.*
i) *Remember that the catalytic converter is FRAGILE – do not strike it with tools during servicing work.*
j) *In some cases a sulphurous smell (like that of rotten eggs) may be noticed from the exhaust. This is common to many catalytic converter-equipped cars and once the car has covered a few thousand miles the problem should disappear.*
k) *The catalytic converter, used on a well-maintained and well-driven car, should last at least 100>000 miles – if the converter is no longer effective it must be renewed.*
l) *If a substantial loss of power is experienced, remember that this could be due to the converter being blocked. This can occur simply as a result of high mileage, but may be due to the ceramic element having fractured and collapsed internally (see paragraph 3). A new converter is the only cure in this instance.*
m) *As mentioned above, driving through deep water should be avoided if possible. The sudden cooling effect may fracture the ceramic honeycomb, damaging it beyond repair.*

Chapter 5 Part A
Starting and charging systems

Contents

Degrees of difficulty

Easy, suitable for novice with little experience	**Fairly easy,** suitable for beginner with some experience	**Fairly difficult,** suitable for competent DIY mechanic	**Difficult,** suitable for experienced DIY mechanic	**Very difficult,** suitable for expert DIY or professional

Specifications

System type — 12 volt, negative earth

Battery

Type	Low-maintenance or maintenance-free, depending on model
Charge condition:	
Poor	12.5 volts
Normal	12.6 volts
Good	12.7 volts

Alternator

Make	Mitsubishi or Bosch
Type:	
1.2 litre petrol engines	Mitsubishi A003TJ4181
1.6 litre petrol engines	Mitsubishi A002TX2191 or A002TJ1291
Diesel engines:	
Without stop/start system	Bosch LIE8
With stop/start system	Mitsubishi A003TJ4081
Output rating:	
1.2 litre petrol engines	150 amp
1.6 litre petrol engines	110 or 150 amp
Diesel engines	150 amp
Regulated output voltage	14.1 to 14.7 Volts
Minimum brush length	5.0 mm
Slip ring minimum outer diameter	22.1 mm
Rotor (field coil) resistance:	
1.2 litre petrol engines	1.7 to 2.0 ohms
1.6 litre petrol engines	1.8 to 2.2 ohms
Diesel engines	1.7 to 2.0 ohms

Starter motor

Make	Mitsubishi, Hitachi or Bosch
Type:	
1.2 litre petrol engines	Mitsubishi M000TD0375
1.6 litre petrol engines	Hitachi S114-968, S114-954, S114-901 or Mitsubishi M000T32173, M000T32178 or M000T37971
Diesel engines	Mitsubishi M000T87881, Bosch 0 001 136 008 or 0 001 170 605

Torque wrench settings

Torque wrench settings	Nm	lbf ft
Alternator mounting bolts	25	18
Glow plugs	15	11
Starter motor mounting bolts	44	32

1 General information and precautions

General information

1 The engine electrical system consists mainly of the charging and starting systems. Because of their engine-related functions, these components are covered separately from the body electrical devices such as the lights, instruments, etc (which are covered in Chapter 12). On petrol engine models, refer to Part B for information on the ignition system.

2 The electrical system is of the 12-volt negative earth type.

3 The battery is of the low-maintenance or 'maintenance-free' (sealed for life) type, and is charged by the alternator, which is belt-driven from the crankshaft pulley.

4 The starter motor is of the pre-engaged type, incorporating an integral solenoid. On starting, the solenoid moves the drive pinion into engagement with the flywheel ring gear before the starter motor is energised. Once the engine has started, a one-way clutch prevents the motor armature being driven by the engine until the pinion disengages from the flywheel.

5 Further details of the various systems are given in the relevant Sections of this Chapter. While some repair procedures are given, the usual course of action is to renew the component concerned.

Precautions

6 It is necessary to take extra care when working on the electrical system, to avoid damage to semi-conductor devices (diodes and transistors), and to avoid the risk of personal injury. In addition to the precautions given in *Safety first!*, observe the following when working on the system:

- Always remove rings, watches, etc, before working on the electrical system. Even with the battery disconnected, capacitive discharge could occur if a component's live terminal is earthed through a metal object. This could cause a shock or nasty burn.
- Do not reverse the battery connections. Components such as the alternator, electronic control units, or any other components having semi-conductor circuitry could be irreparably damaged.
- If the engine is being started using jump leads and a slave battery, connect the batteries positive-to-positive and negative-to-negative (see *Jump starting*). This also applies when connecting a battery charger.
- Never disconnect the battery terminals, the alternator, any electrical wiring, or any test instruments, when the engine is running.
- Do not allow the engine to turn the alternator when the alternator is not connected.
- Never 'test' for alternator output by 'flashing' the output lead to earth.
- Never use an ohmmeter of the type incorporating a hand-cranked generator for circuit or continuity testing.
- Always ensure that the battery negative terminal is disconnected when working on the electrical system.
- Before using electric-arc welding equipment on the car, disconnect the battery, alternator and components such as electronic control units, to protect them from the risk of damage.

2 Battery – checking, testing and charging

Checking

Standard and low-maintenance battery

1 In addition to the checks described in *Weekly checks*, the battery electrolyte level should also be periodically checked as follows.

Batteries with a translucent casing

2 On this type of battery, the electrolyte level is visible through the casing. Make sure that the level in each cell is between the UPPER and LOWER level marks on the side of the battery casing.

3 If topping-up is necessary, remove the cell cap(s) and top-up the relevant cell to the UPPER level marking using only distilled water. **Note:** *Do not use ordinary tap water, as this will damage the battery.*

4 Refit the cell cap(s), ensuring each one is securely fitted, and mop-up any spilt water.

Batteries with a solid (non-translucent) casing

5 On batteries where it is not possible to see the electrolyte level through the casing, the level is checked via the cell filler cap apertures. Remove the cap from each battery cell and, looking down through cap apertures, check that the electrolyte level is up to the base of the aperture neck.

6 If topping-up is necessary, top-up the relevant cell to the base of the neck using only distilled water.

Note: *Do not use ordinary tap water, as this will damage the battery.*

7 Refit the cell cap(s), ensuring each one is securely fitted, and mop-up any spilt water.

Testing

Standard and low-maintenance battery

8 If the vehicle covers a small annual mileage, it is worthwhile checking the specific gravity of the electrolyte every three months, to determine the state of charge of the battery. Use a hydrometer to make the check, and compare the results with the following table. Note that the specific gravity readings assume an electrolyte temperature of 15°C; for every 10°C below 15°C, subtract 0.007. For every 10°C above 15°C, add 0.007. However, for convenience, the temperatures quoted in the following table are ambient (outdoor air) temperatures, above or below 25°C:

	Above 25°C	Below 25°C
Fully-charged	1.210 to 1.230	1.270 to 1.290
70% charged	1.170 to 1.190	1.230 to 1.250
Discharged	1.050 to 1.070	1.110 to 1.130

9 If the battery condition is suspect, first check the specific gravity of electrolyte in each cell. A variation of 0.040 or more between any cells indicates loss of electrolyte, or deterioration of the internal plates.

10 If the specific gravity variation is 0.040 or more, a new battery should be fitted. If the cell variation is satisfactory but the battery is discharged, it should be charged as described later in this Section.

Maintenance-free battery

11 In cases where a 'sealed for life' maintenance-free battery is fitted, topping-up and testing of the electrolyte in each cell is not possible. The condition of the battery can therefore only be tested using a battery condition indicator or a voltmeter.

12 One type of maintenance-free battery, which may be fitted, is the 'Delco' type maintenance-free battery, with a built-in charge condition indicator **(see illustration)**. The indicator is located in the top of the battery casing, and indicates the condition of the battery from its colour. If the indicator shows green, then the battery is in a good state of charge. If the indicator turns darker, eventually to black, then the battery requires charging, as described later in this Section. If the indicator shows clear/yellow, then the electrolyte level in the battery is too low to allow further use, and the battery should be renewed. Do not attempt to charge, load or jump-start a battery when the indicator shows clear/yellow.

13 If testing the battery using a voltmeter, connect the voltmeter across the battery, and compare the result with those given in the Specifications under 'charge condition'. The test is only accurate if the battery has not been subjected to any kind of charge for the previous six hours. If this is not the case, switch on the headlights for 30 seconds, and then wait four to five minutes before testing

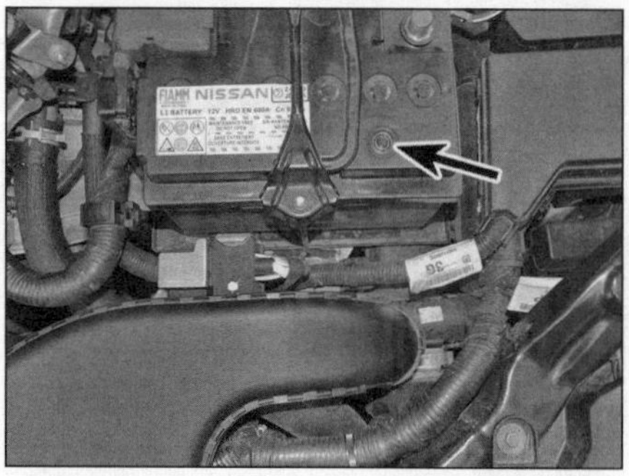

2.12 Battery charge condition indicator

the battery after switching off the headlights. All other electrical circuits must be switched off, so check that the doors and tailgate are fully shut when making the test.

14 If the voltage reading is less than 12.2 volts, then the battery is discharged, whilst a reading of 12.2 to 12.4 volts indicates a partially discharged condition.

15 If the battery is to be charged, remove it from the vehicle (Section 3) and charge it as described later in this Section.

Charging

Note: *The following is intended as a guide only. Always refer to the manufacturer's recommendations (often printed on a label attached to the battery) before charging a battery.*

Standard and low-maintenance battery

16 Charge the battery at a rate of 3.5 to 4 amps, and continue to charge the battery at this rate until no further rise in specific gravity is noted over a four-hour period.

17 Alternatively, a trickle charger charging at the rate of 1.5 amps can safely be used overnight.

18 Specially rapid 'boost' charges, which are claimed to restore the power of the battery in 1 to 2 hours, are not recommended, as they can cause serious damage to the battery plates through overheating.

19 While charging the battery, note that the temperature of the electrolyte should never exceed 38°C.

Maintenance-free battery

20 This battery type takes considerably longer to fully recharge than the standard type, the time taken being dependent on the extent of discharge, but it can take anything up to three days.

21 A constant-voltage type charger is required, to be set, when connected, to 13.9 to 14.9 volts, with a charger current below 25 amps. Using this method, the battery should be usable within three hours, giving a voltage reading of 12.5 volts, but this is for a partially discharged battery and, as mentioned, full charging can take considerably longer.

22 If the battery is to be charged from a fully discharged state (condition reading less than 12.2 volts), have it recharged by your Nissan dealer or local automotive electrician, as the charge rate is higher, and constant supervision during charging is necessary.

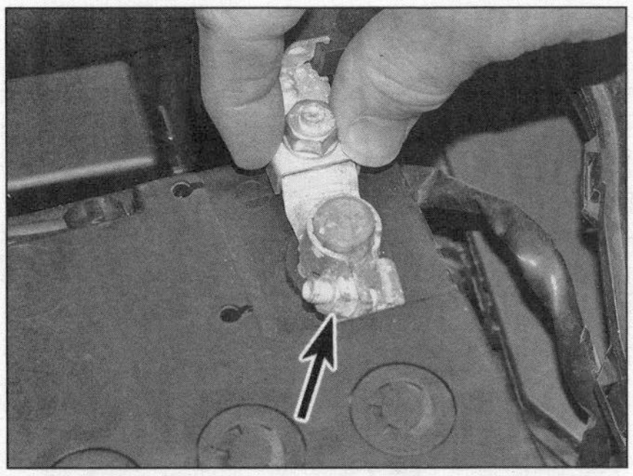

3.3 Slacken the clamp nut and disconnect the lead at the battery negative (–) terminal

3.4 Slacken the clamp nut and disconnect the lead at the battery positive (+) terminal

3 Battery – disconnection, reconnection, removal and refitting

Battery

Disconnection and reconnection

1 Numerous systems fitted to the vehicle require battery power to be available at all times, either to ensure their continued operation (such as the clock) or to maintain control unit memories which would be erased if the battery were to be disconnected. Whenever the battery is to be disconnected therefore, first note the following, to ensure that there are no unforeseen consequences of this action:

a) *First, on any vehicle with central locking, it is a wise precaution to remove the key from the ignition, and to keep it with you, so that it does not get locked in, if the central locking should engage accidentally when the battery is reconnected.*

b) *The engine management electronic control unit is of the 'self-learning' type, meaning that as it operates, it also monitors and stores the settings which give optimum engine performance under all operating conditions. When the battery is disconnected, these settings are lost and the ECU reverts to the base settings programmed into its memory at the factory. On restarting, this may lead to the engine running/idling roughly for a short while, until the ECU has re-learned the optimum settings. This process is best accomplished by taking the vehicle on a road test (for approximately 15 minutes), covering all engine speeds and loads, concentrating mainly in the 2500 to 3500 rpm region.*

c) *It will be necessary to reprogramme the electric window motors to restore the one-touch function of the buttons, after reconnection of the battery. To do this, open then fully close both front windows. With the windows closed, depress the up button of the driver's side window for approximately 5 seconds, then release it and depress the passenger side window up button for approximately 5 seconds. Repeat this procedure for the rear windows.*

d) *On all models, when reconnecting the battery after disconnection, switch on the ignition and wait 10 seconds to allow the electronic vehicle systems to stabilise and re-initialise.*

2 The battery is located at the front, left-hand side of the engine compartment.

3 Disconnect the lead at the negative (–) terminal by slackening the retaining nut and removing the terminal clamp **(see illustration)**. Note that the battery negative (–) and positive (+) terminal connections are stamped on the battery case.

4 Disconnect the lead at the battery positive (+) terminal by lifting up the terminal cover, then slackening the retaining nut and removing the terminal clamp **(see illustration)**.

5 Reconnection is a reversal of disconnection, ensuring that the battery positive (+) lead is reconnected first.

Removal

6 Disconnect the battery terminals as described previously in this Section.

7 If the battery is retained by a bracket over the top of the battery, undo the two nuts and lift off the bracket. If the battery is retained by a clamping wedge at the front of the battery, undo the retaining bolt and remove the clamping wedge **(see illustrations)**.

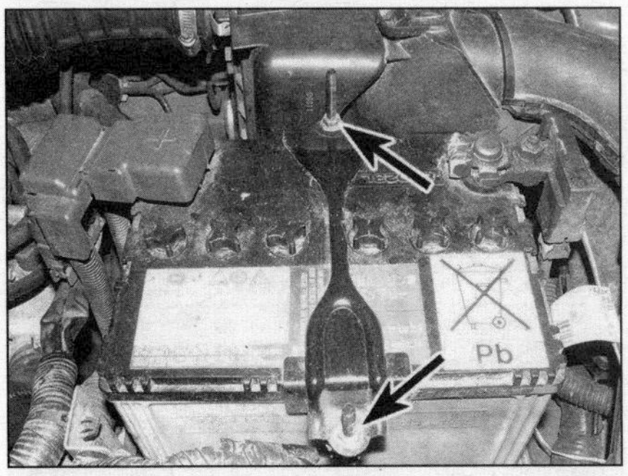

3.7a If the battery is retained by a bracket over the top, undo the two nuts and remove the bracket

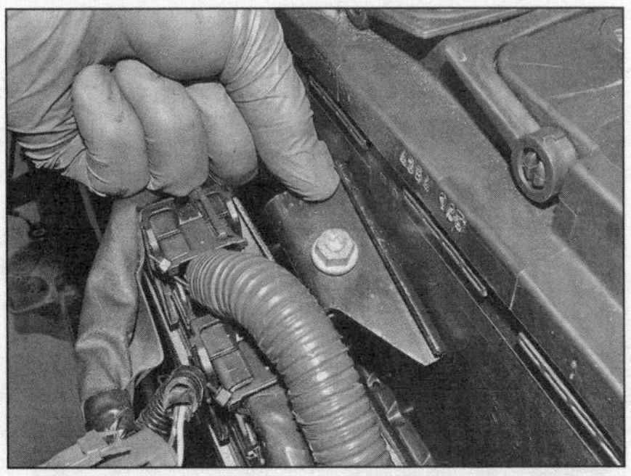

3.7b If the battery is retained by a clamping wedge, undo the retaining bolt and remove the wedge

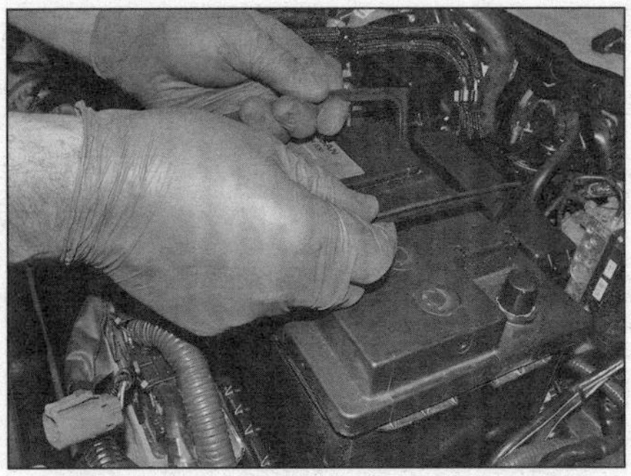

3.8 Carefully lift the battery from its location

3.13 Release the retaining pawls and lift the fusebox out of the mounting bracket

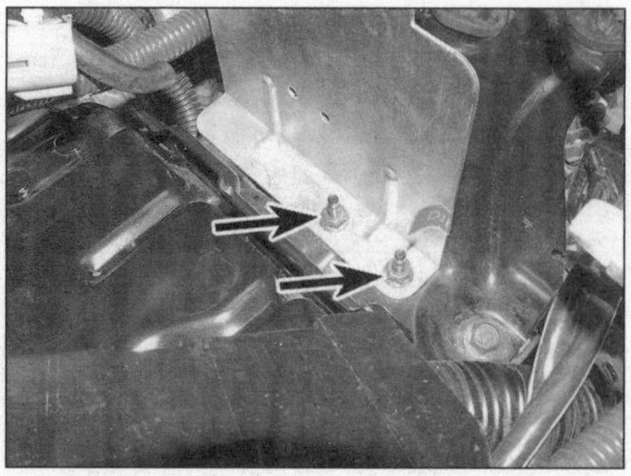

3.14a Undo the two retaining nuts...

8 Carefully lift the battery from its location and remove it from the car **(see illustration)**. Make sure the battery is kept upright at all times.

Refitting

9 Refitting is a reversal of removal. Reconnect the battery terminals as described previously in this Section.

Battery tray

Removal

1.2 litre petrol engine models and Type 2 diesel engine models

10 Remove the battery as described previously in this Section.

11 Remove the air cleaner assembly as described in Chapter 4A, Section 2 or Chapter 4B, Section 2.

12 For improved working clearance, undo the retaining bolts and move the cooling system expansion tank to one side.

13 Using a flat-blade screwdriver, release the retaining pawls at the front and side and lift the fusebox out of the mounting bracket **(see illustration)**. If necessary, disconnect the wiring connectors and remove the fusebox.

14 Undo the two retaining nuts and remove the fusebox mounting bracket from the battery tray **(see illustrations)**.

15 Undo the retaining bolt and release the wiring harness support bracket from the battery tray **(see illustration)**.

16 Undo the two nuts at the front and the two bolts at the rear and lift out the battery tray **(see illustrations)**.

17 To remove the engine management ECU mounting bracket, disconnect the three ECU wiring harness connectors, then undo the retaining nuts and bolts. Lift out the mounting bracket together with the ECU **(see illustration)**.

1.6 litre petrol engine models

18 Remove the battery as described previously in this Section.

19 Remove the air cleaner assembly as described in Chapter 4A, Section 2.

20 Disconnect the two wiring harness connectors from the fusible link in the battery

3.14b ...and remove the fusebox mounting bracket

3.15 Undo the bolt and release the wiring harness support bracket

3.16a Undo the two nuts at the front...

3.16b ...and the two bolts at the rear...

3.16c ...then lift out the battery tray

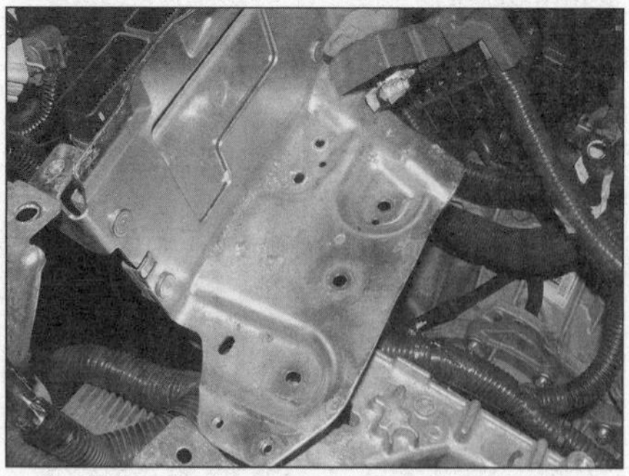

3.17 Where necessary, remove the ECU and mounting bracket

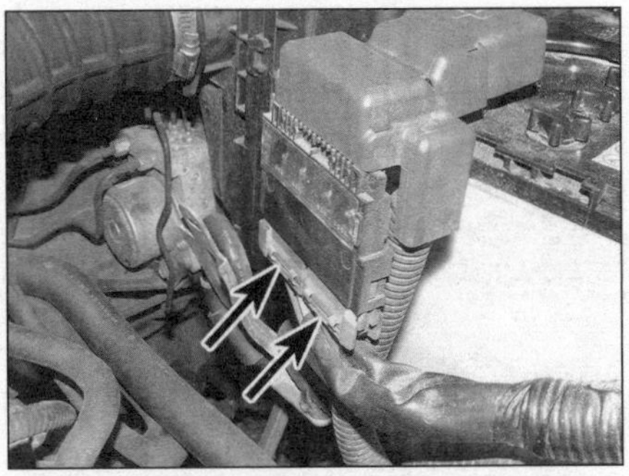

3.20 Disconnect the two wiring harness connectors from the fusible link in the battery positive terminal

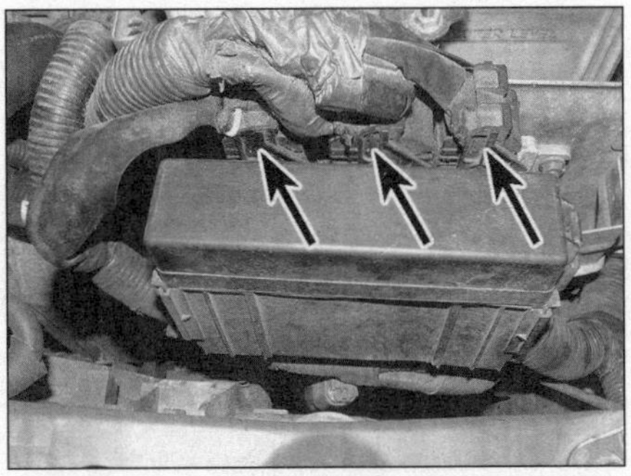

3.21a Disconnect the ECU wiring harness connectors...

3.21b ...then release the cable tie and move the wiring harness to one side

positive terminal **(see illustration)**. Release the cable ties at the front support bracket and move the wiring harness to one side.

21 Disconnect the three engine management ECU wiring harness connectors, then release the cable ties and move the wiring harness to one side **(see illustrations)**.

22 Using a flat-blade screwdriver, release the two retaining pawls and lift the fusebox out of the mounting bracket. Move the fusebox and wiring harness to one side.

23 Release the retaining clip securing the wiring harness to the fusebox mounting bracket. Undo the retaining bolt and the nut and remove the fusebox mounting bracket.

24 Undo the retaining bolts and remove the battery tray from its location.

25 If required, undo the retaining bolts and remove the engine management ECU mounting bracket complete with ECU.

Type 1 diesel engine models

26 Remove the battery as described previously in this Section.

27 Remove the air cleaner assembly as described in Chapter 4B, Section 2.

28 Undo the retaining bolts and lift the battery tray out of the engine compartment **(see illustrations)**.

29 To remove the fusebox mounting bracket, undo the two mounting bolts, release the fusebox from the mounting bracket, then remove the bracket **(see illustrations)**.

Refitting

30 Refitting is a reversal of removal.

3.28a Undo the retaining bolts...

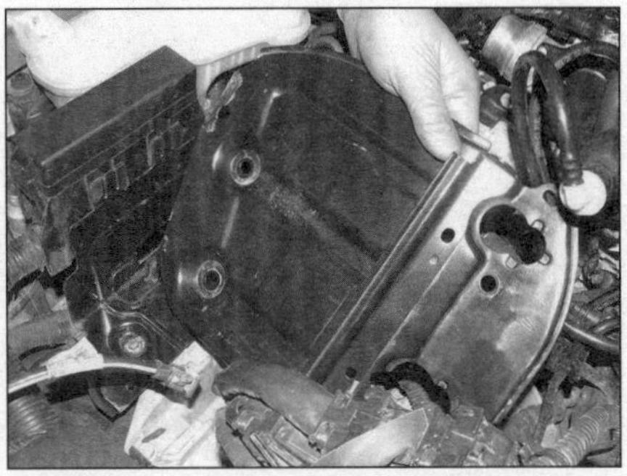

3.28b ...and lift out the battery tray

4 Charging system – testing

Note: *Refer to the precautions given in 'Safety first!' in Chapter 0, Section 3 and in Section 1 of this Chapter before starting work.*

1 If the ignition/no-charge warning light fails to come on when the ignition is switched on, first check the alternator wiring connections for security. If satisfactory, check that the warning light bulb has not blown, and that the bulbholder is secure in its location in the instrument panel. If the light still fails to come on, check the continuity of the warning light feed wire from the alternator to the bulbholder. If all is satisfactory, the alternator is at fault, and should be taken to an auto-electrician for testing and repair.

2 If the ignition warning light comes on when the engine is running, stop the engine as soon as possible. Check that the drivebelt is correctly tensioned (see Chapter 1A, Section 12 or Chapter 1B, Section 12), that the drivebelt is not contaminated (with oil or water, for example), and that the alternator connections are secure. If all is so far satisfactory, the alternator should be renewed or taken to an auto-electrician for testing and repair.

3 If the alternator output is suspect, even though the warning light functions correctly, the regulated voltage may be checked as follows.

4 Connect a voltmeter across the battery terminals, and start the engine.

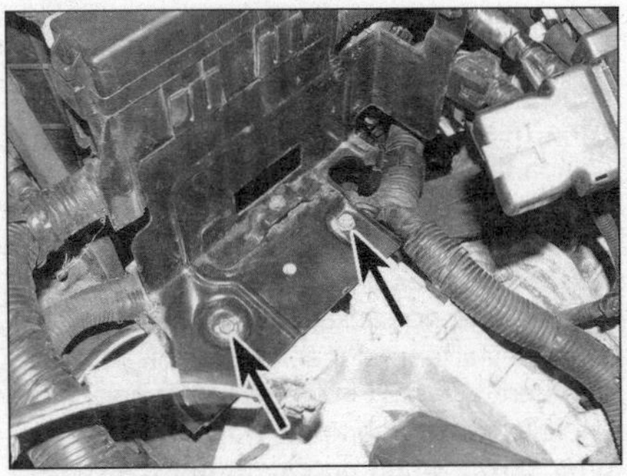

3.29a Undo the two mounting bolts...

3.29b ...release the fusebox from the mounting bracket...

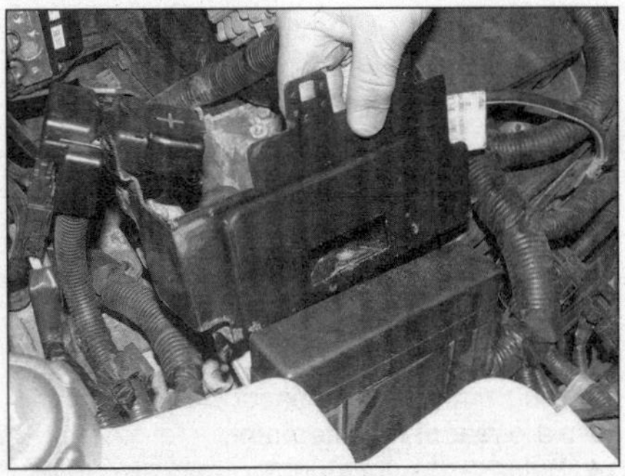

3.29c ...and remove the mounting bracket

5 Increase the engine speed until the voltmeter reading remains steady; the reading should be approximately 12 to 13 volts, and no more than 14 volts.

6 Switch on as many electrical accessories (e.g. the headlights, heated rear window and heater blower) as possible, and check that the alternator maintains the regulated voltage at around 13 to 14 volts.

7 If the regulated voltage is not as stated, the fault may be due to worn brushes, weak brush springs, a faulty voltage regulator, a faulty diode, a severed phase winding, or worn or damaged slip-rings. The alternator should be taken to an auto-electrician for testing and repair.

5 Alternator – removal and refitting

Removal

1.2 litre petrol engines

1 Disconnect the battery negative terminal (refer to battery disconnection and reconnection in Section 3).

2 Drain the cooling system as described in Chapter 1A, Section 25.

3 Remove the auxiliary drivebelt as described in Chapter 1A, Section 12.

4 Undo the cooling system expansion tank retaining bolts and move the tank to one side.

5 Remove the intercooler as described in Chapter 4A, Section 13.

6 Release the retaining clips and remove the radiator top hose.

7 Remove the rubber cover (where fitted) from the alternator terminal, then unscrew the retaining nut and disconnect the wiring cable from the rear of the alternator.

8 Release the locking clip and disconnect the wiring plug connector from the rear of the alternator.

9 Unscrew the alternator upper and lower mounting bolts and washers, and then manoeuvre the alternator away from its mounting bracket and lift it from the engine compartment **(see illustrations)**.

1.6 litre petrol engines

10 Disconnect the battery negative terminal (refer to battery disconnection and reconnection in Section 3).

11 Remove the auxiliary drivebelt as described in Chapter 1A, Section 12.

12 Undo the cooling system expansion tank retaining bolts and move the tank to one side.

13 Remove the rubber cover (where fitted) from the alternator terminal, then unscrew the retaining nut and disconnect the wiring cable from the rear of the alternator.

14 Release the locking clip and disconnect the wiring plug connector from the rear of the alternator.

5.9a Undo the two alternator mounting bolts...

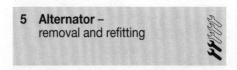

5.9b ...and withdraw the alternator

15 Unscrew the alternator upper and lower mounting bolts and washers, and then manoeuvre the alternator away from its mounting bracket and lift it from the engine compartment.

Diesel engines

16 Disconnect the battery negative terminal (refer to battery disconnection and reconnection in Section 3).

17 Remove the auxiliary drivebelt as described in Chapter 1B, Section 12.

18 Remove the inlet air ducting and hoses as necessary to gain access to the alternator as described in, Section.

19 Undo the two bolts and remove the bracket from the front of the high-pressure fuel pump.

20 Remove the rubber cover (where fitted) from the alternator terminal, then unscrew the retaining nut and disconnect the wiring cable from the rear of the alternator.

21 Release the locking clip and disconnect the wiring plug connector from the rear of the alternator.

22 Unscrew the alternator upper and lower mounting bolts and washers, and then manoeuvre the alternator away from its mounting bracket and lift it from the engine compartment. Note that the lower mounting bolt cannot be removed completely as it contacts the body side member. The mounting bracket has a cut out to allow the alternator to be withdrawn with the bolt still in place.

Refitting

23 Refitting is a reversal of removal, bearing in mind the following points:

a) *Tighten the alternator mounting bolts to the specified torque.*
b) *Refit the auxiliary drivebelt as described in Chapter 1A, Section 12 (petrol engines) or Chapter 1B, Section 12 (diesel engines).*
c) *Where applicable, refill the cooling system as described in Chapter 1A, Section 25.*
d) *Where applicable, refit the intercooler as described in Chapter 4A, Section 13.*
e) *Where applicable, refit the inlet air ducting and hoses as described in, Section.*
f) *On completion, reconnect the battery negative terminal with reference to Section 3.*

6 Alternator – testing and overhaul

1 If the alternator is thought to be suspect, it should be removed from the vehicle and taken to an auto-electrician for testing. Most auto-electricians will be able to supply and fit new parts at reasonable cost. However, check on the cost of repairs before proceeding, as it may prove more economical to obtain a new or exchange alternator.

7 Starting system – testing

Note: *Refer to the precautions given in 'Safety first!' in Chapter 0, Section 3 and in Section 1 of this Chapter before starting work.*

1 If the starter motor fails to operate when the ignition key is turned to the appropriate position, the following may be to blame:

a) *The battery is faulty.*
b) *The electrical connections between the switch, solenoid, battery and starter motor are somewhere failing to pass the necessary current from the battery through the starter to earth.*
c) *The solenoid is faulty.*
d) *The starter motor is mechanically or electrically defective.*

2 To check the battery, switch on the headlights. If they dim after a few seconds, this indicates that the battery is discharged – recharge (see Section 2) or renew the battery. If the headlights glow brightly, operate the ignition switch and observe the lights. If they dim, then this indicates that current is reaching the starter motor; therefore the fault must lie in the starter motor. If the lights continue to glow brightly (and no clicking sound can be heard from the starter motor solenoid), this indicates that there is a fault in the circuit or solenoid – see following paragraphs. If the starter motor turns slowly when operated, but the battery is in good condition, then this indicates that either the starter motor is faulty, or there is

considerable resistance somewhere in the circuit.

3 If a fault in the circuit is suspected, disconnect the battery leads (including the earth connection to the body), the starter/solenoid wiring and the engine/transmission earth strap (refer to battery disconnection and reconnection in Section 3). Thoroughly clean the connections, reconnect the leads and wiring, then use a voltmeter or test light to check that full battery voltage is available at the battery positive lead connection to the solenoid, and that the earth is sound. Smear petroleum jelly around the battery terminals to prevent corrosion – corroded connections are amongst the most frequent causes of electrical system faults.

4 If the battery and all connections are in good condition, check the circuit by disconnecting the wire from the solenoid blade terminal. Connect a voltmeter or test light between the wire end and a good earth (such as the battery negative terminal), and check that the wire is live when the ignition switch is turned to the 'start' position. If it is, then the circuit is sound – if not, the circuit wiring can be checked as described in Chapter 12.

5 The solenoid contacts can be checked by connecting a voltmeter or test light between the battery positive feed connection on the starter side of the solenoid, and earth. When the ignition switch is turned to the 'start' position, there should be a reading or lighted bulb, as applicable. If there is no reading or lighted bulb, the solenoid is faulty and should be renewed.

6 If the circuit and solenoid are proved sound, the fault must lie in the starter motor. In this event, it may be possible to have the starter motor overhauled by a specialist, but check on the availability and cost of spares before proceeding, as it may prove more economical to obtain a new or exchange motor.

8 Starter motor – removal and refitting

Removal

1.2 litre petrol engines

1 Disconnect the battery negative terminal (refer to battery disconnection and reconnection in Section 3).

2 Undo the cooling system expansion tank retaining bolts and move the tank to one side.

3 Drain the cooling system as described in Chapter 1A, Section 25.

4 Remove the inlet manifold as described in Chapter 4A, Section 14.

5 Release the retaining clips and remove the radiator bottom hose from the thermostat housing.

6 Working down the front of the engine compartment, move the wiring loom and hoses to one side to access the starter motor, which is located at the front of the cylinder block, bolted to the transmission bell housing.

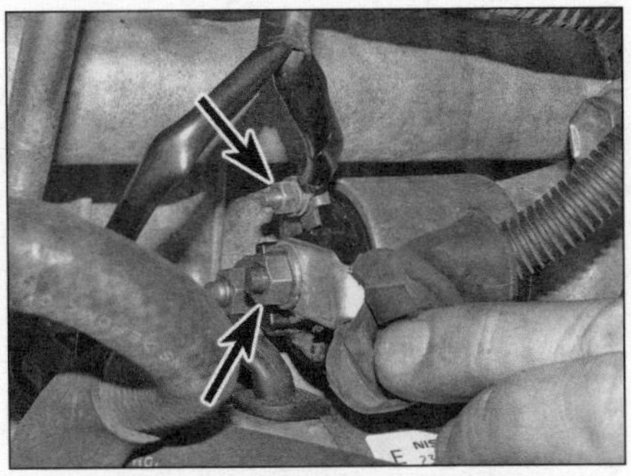

8.7a Undo the retaining nuts...

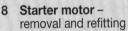

8.7b ...and disconnect the starter wiring cables

7 Pull back the rubber cover, and then slacken and remove the two retaining nuts. Disconnect the main battery cable, and the small solenoid wiring from the starter motor solenoid **(see illustrations)**.

8 Unscrew the starter motor mounting bolts, supporting the motor as the bolts are withdrawn, and manoeuvre the starter motor out from its location.

1.6 litre petrol engines

9 Disconnect the battery negative terminal (refer to battery disconnection and reconnection in Section 3).

10 Undo the cooling system expansion tank retaining bolts and move the tank to one side.

11 Disconnect the two wiring connectors from the fusible link on the battery positive terminal **(see illustration 3.21)**. Release the two retaining clips and free the wiring harness from the fuse holder bracket.

12 Release the two retaining clips and free the engine management ECU wiring harness from the fuse holder bracket. Release the locking levers and disconnect the three wiring connectors from the ECU.

13 Using a flat-bladed screwdriver, release the two retaining tabs and withdraw the fuse holder from the mounting bracket. Move the fuse holder to one side.

14 Release the wiring harness retaining clip(s) from the front of the fuse holder bracket.

15 Undo the retaining nut and retaining bolt and remove the fuse holder bracket.

16 Undo the support bracket retaining bolt and move the coolant hose and heater thermostat assembly to one side.

17 Pull back the rubber cover, and then slacken and remove the two retaining nuts. Disconnect the main battery cable, and the small solenoid wiring from the starter motor solenoid.

18 Unscrew the starter motor mounting bolts, supporting the motor as the bolts are withdrawn, and manoeuvre the starter motor out from its location.

Diesel engines

19 Disconnect the battery negative terminal (refer to battery disconnection and reconnection in Section 3).

20 Drain the cooling system as described in Chapter 1B, Section 26.

21 Release the retaining clip and disconnect the radiator bottom hose from the oil cooler/filter housing.

22 Disconnect the oil level sensor wiring connector.

23 From underneath the car, undo the retaining bolt securing the wiring harness bracket to the transmission housing. Move the bracket and harness to one side.

24 Pull back the rubber cover, and then slacken and remove the two retaining nuts. Disconnect the main battery cable, and the small solenoid wiring from the starter motor solenoid.

25 Unscrew the starter motor mounting bolts, supporting the motor as the bolts are withdrawn, and manoeuvre the starter motor out from its location.

Refitting

26 Refitting is a reversal of removal, bearing in mind the following points:

a) *Where applicable, refit the inlet manifold as described in Chapter 4A, Section 14.*
b) *On completion, refill the cooling system as described in Chapter 1A, Section 25 (petrol engines) or Chapter 1B, Section 26 (diesel engines).*

9 Starter motor – testing and overhaul

1 If the starter motor is thought to be suspect, it should be removed from the vehicle and taken to an auto-electrician for testing. Most auto-electricians will be able to supply fit new parts at reasonable cost. However, check on the cost of repairs before proceeding, as it may prove more economical to obtain a new or exchange motor.

10 Ignition switch – removal and refitting

1 The ignition switch is integral with the steering column lock, and can be removed as described in Chapter 10, Section 13.

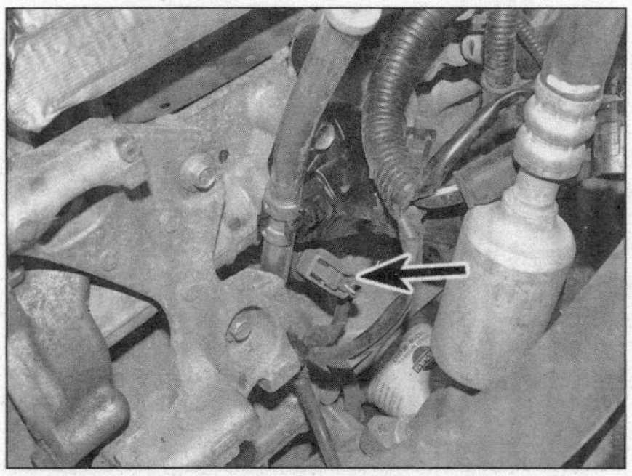
11.2 Location of oil pressure switch (1.6 litre petrol engines)

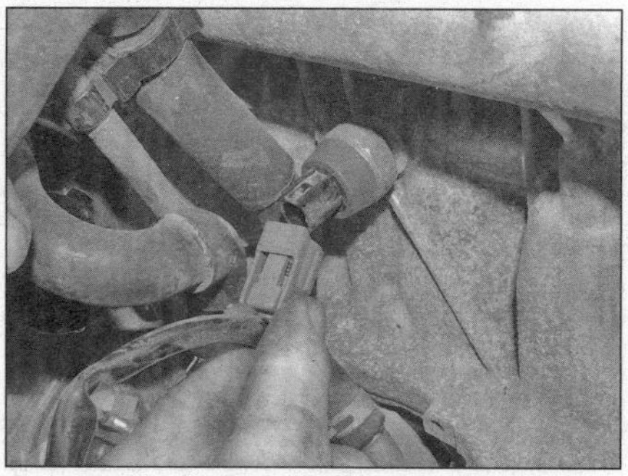
11.4 Disconnect the pressure switch wiring connector

11 Oil pressure warning light switch – removal and refitting

Removal

1 On some models, access to the switch is improved if the vehicle is jacked up and supported on axle stands (see *Jacking and vehicle support*),so that the switch can be reached from underneath.

2 On petrol engines, the switch is located at the front of the cylinder block, above the oil filter **(see illustration)**. On diesel engines, the switch is located at the front of the cylinder block, either screwed into the oil filter housing or screwed directly into the cylinder block at the transmission end.

3 Disconnect the battery negative terminal (refer to battery disconnection and reconnection in Section 3).

4 Disconnect the wiring connector from the oil pressure switch **(see illustration)**.

5 Unscrew the switch and recover the sealing washer (where fitted). Be prepared for oil spillage. If the switch is to be left removed from the engine for any length of time, plug the hole to prevent excessive oil loss.

Warning: Do not start the engine with the oil pressure switch removed.

Refitting

6 Where the switch was fitted with a sealing washer, examine the sealing washer for signs of damage or deterioration, and if necessary renew it. Where no sealing washer was fitted, clean the switch and apply a smear of sealant to its threads.

7 Refit the switch, tightening it securely, and reconnect the wiring connector.

8 Where applicable lower the vehicle to the ground.

9 Check and if necessary, top-up the engine oil as described in *Weekly checks*.

12 Oil level sensor – removal and refitting

Removal

1 Access to the sensor is improved if the vehicle is jacked up and supported on axle stands (see *Jacking and vehicle support*).

2 On petrol engines, the sensor is located at the front of the engine **(see illustration)** in the upper alloy sump housing and held in place by a securing bolt. On diesel engines, the sensor is located at the front of the engine screwed into the top of the alloy sump housing at the transmission end.

3 Disconnect the battery negative terminal (refer to battery disconnection and reconnection in Section 3).

4 Disconnect the wiring connector from the oil level sensor **(see illustration)**.

5 On petrol engines, undo the retaining bolt and withdraw the oil level sensor from the engine. Be prepared for oil spillage. If the switch is to be left removed from the engine for any length of time, plug the hole to prevent excessive oil loss.

Warning: Do not start the engine with the oil level sensor removed.

6 On diesel engines, unscrew the switch and recover the sealing washer (where fitted). Be prepared for oil spillage. If the switch is to be left removed from the engine for any length of time, plug the hole to prevent excessive oil loss.

Refitting

7 Where the sensor was fitted with a sealing washer, examine the sealing washer for signs of damage or deterioration, and if necessary renew it. Where no sealing washer was fitted, clean the sensor and apply a smear of sealant to its threads.

8 Refit the sensor, tightening tightening it securely, and reconnect the wiring connector.

9 Lower the vehicle to the ground, then check and if necessary, top-up the engine oil as described in *Weekly checks*.

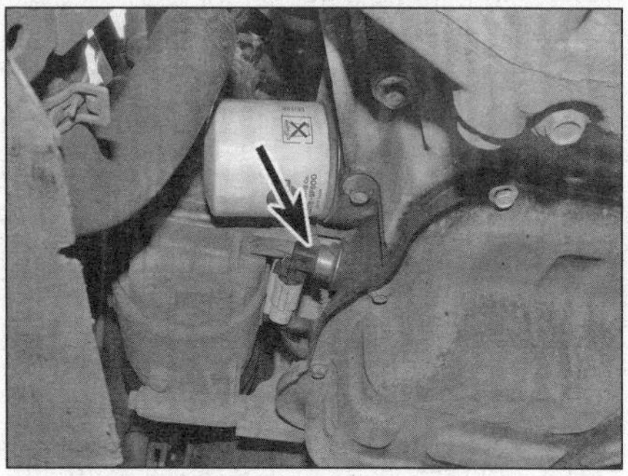
12.2 Location of oil level sensor (1.6 litre petrol engines)

12.4 Disconnect the level sensor wiring connector

13 Pre/post-heating system (diesel engines) – description and testing

Description

1 The preheating/post-heating system consists of glow plugs screwed into the combustion chambers, a control unit (relay) mounted on the left-hand side of the engine compartment, and a coolant temperature sensor located on the thermostat housing. The control unit is itself activated by the engine management ECU.

2 The glow plugs are supplied with current from the control unit in several phases, namely variable preheating, fixed preheating, starting heating, and variable post-heating.

3 The variable preheating phase occurs when the ignition is switched on, and during this phase the preheating warning light is illuminated on the instrument panel. The period of preheating depends on the temperature of the coolant and battery voltage. The maximum period of 15 seconds occurs if the coolant temperature is low and the battery voltage is less than 9.3 volts. The period varies from 15 seconds to zero seconds according to the temperature of the coolant, and when the temperature reaches 80°C, no preheating occurs. With normal battery voltage the maximum period is 10 seconds.

4 The fixed preheating phase occurs straight after the variable phase finishes, after the warning light has extinguished, and lasts for up to 5 seconds. Normally, the driver will start the engine at some point during this phase.

5 During the period when the starter motor is in operation, the glow plugs are continuously supplied with current.

6 The variable post-heating phase occurs

immediately after the engine has been started, and the period of post-heating depends on the temperature of the coolant. The maximum period of variable post-heating is 60 seconds, at which point the system is switched off. Variable post-heating will cease if the coolant temperature exceeds 80°C.

Testing

7 If the system malfunctions, testing is best carried out by a Nissan dealer or suitably equipped garage using dedicated test equipment, however, some preliminary checks may be made as follows.

8 Connect a voltmeter or 12 volt test lamp between the glow plug supply cable and earth (engine or vehicle metal). Make sure that the live connection is kept clear of the engine and bodywork.

9 Have an assistant switch on the ignition and check that voltage is applied to the glow plugs. Note the time for which the warning light is lit and the total time for which voltage is applied before the system cuts out. Switch off the ignition and compare to the times given in the previous Section.

10 If there is no supply at all, the relay, control unit or associated wiring is at fault.

11 To locate a defective glow plug, disconnect the main supply cable and the interconnecting wire from the top of the glow plugs.

12 Use a continuity tester, or 12-volt test lamp connected to the battery positive terminal, to check for continuity between each glow plug terminal and earth. The resistance of a glow plug in good condition is very low (less than 1 ohm), so if the test lamp does not light or the continuity tester shows a high resistance, the glow plug is defective.

13 If an ammeter is available, the current draw of each glow plug can be checked. After an initial surge of around 15 to 20 amps, each plug should draw around 10 amps. Any plug that draws much more or less than 10 amps is probably defective.

14 As a final check, the glow plugs can be removed and inspected as described in Section 14.

15 If the pre/post-heating system is faulty, first check the wiring to each individual component. If this does not locate the fault, ideally each component should be substituted with known good units until the fault is located. If this is not possible, take the vehicle to a Nissan dealer or diesel specialist who will have the diagnostic equipment necessary to pin point the fault quickly.

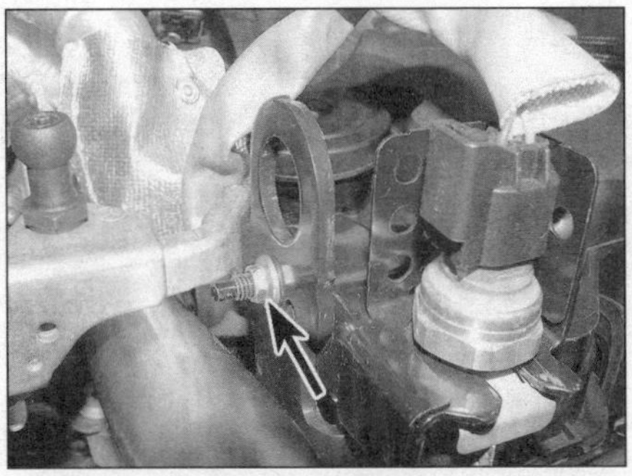

14.4a Undo the retaining nut...

14.4b ...the bolt at the front...

14.4c ...and the bolt at the rear, then remove the sensor bracket

14.5 Unclip the wiring loom cable ties from the cover

14 Glow plugs – removal, inspection and refitting

Caution: If the preheating system has just been energised, or if the engine has been running, the glow plugs may be very hot.

Removal

1 Disconnect the battery negative terminal (refer to battery disconnection and reconnection in Section 3.

2 Remove the air cleaner assembly as described in Chapter 4B, Section 2.

3 Remove the intercooler inlet pipe from the turbocharger to the intercooler as described in Chapter 4B, Section 2.

4 On Type 2 engines, undo the nut and two bolts and remove the sensor bracket from the rear of the cylinder head **(see illustrations)**.

5 Unclip the wiring loom cable ties from the plastic engine shield/cover **(see illustration)**.

6 Undo the two retaining bolts, release the two securing clips and lift off the plastic engine shield/cover **(see illustrations)**.

7 Pull the plastic leg to disconnect the

14.6a Undo the two retaining bolts...

14.6b ...release the securing clips...

14.6c ...and remove the plastic engine shield/cover

14.7 Disconnect the wiring connector

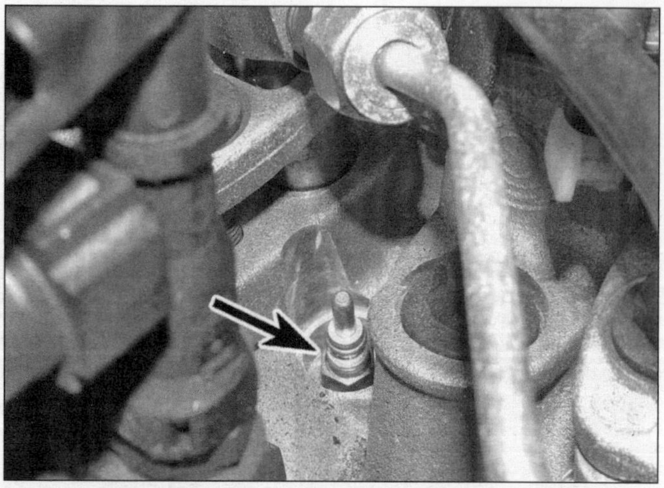

14.8 Unscrew the glow plug from the cylinder head

wiring conectors from the glow plugs **(see illustration)**.

8 Clean the surrounding area, then unscrew and remove the glow plugs from the cylinder head **(see illustration)**.

Inspection

9 Inspect the glow plugs for physical damage. Burnt or eroded glow plug tips can be caused by a bad injector spray pattern. Have the injectors checked if this sort of damage is found.

10 If the glow plugs are in good physical condition, check them electrically using a 12-volt test lamp or continuity tester with reference to the previous Section.

11 The glow plugs can be energised by applying 12-volts to them, this will verify that they heat up evenly and in the required time. Observe the following precautions:

a) Support the glow plug by clamping it carefully in a vice or self-locking pliers. Remember it will become red-hot.

b) Make sure that the power supply or test lead incorporates a fuse or overload trip to protect against damage from a short-circuit.

c) After testing, allow the glow plug to cool for several minutes before attempting to handle it.

12 A glow plug in good condition will start to glow red at the tip after drawing current for 5 seconds or so. Any plug that takes much longer to start glowing, or which starts glowing in the middle instead of at the tip, is defective.

Refitting

13 Refit by reversing the removal operations. Apply a smear of copper based anti-seize compound to the plug threads and tighten the glow plugs to the specified torque. Do not overtighten, as this can damage the glow plug element.

Chapter 5 Part B
Ignition system - petrol engines

Contents

Degrees of difficulty

Easy, suitable for novice with little experience	**Fairly easy,** suitable for beginner with some experience	**Fairly difficult,** suitable for competent DIY mechanic	**Difficult,** suitable for experienced DIY mechanic	**Very difficult,** suitable for expert DIY or professional

Specifications

General

System type	Distributorless electronic ignition, controlled by engine management electronic control unit
Firing order	1-3-4-2 (No 1 cylinder at timing chain end)
Ignition timing	Not adjustable – controlled by ECU

Torque wrench settings

	Nm	lbf ft
Ignition coil mounting bolts:		
1.2 litre engines	10	7
1.6 litre engines	7	6
Spark plugs:		
1.2 litre engines	24	18
1.6 litre engines	20	15

1 General Information

1 The system is a self-contained engine management system, which controls both the fuel injection and ignition. This Chapter deals with the ignition system components only – refer to Chapter 4A for details of the fuel system components.

2 The ignition system fitted to all models is of the increasingly popular 'distributorless' (DIS – Distributorless Ignition System) or 'static' type (there are no moving parts). The ignition system fitted to the Nissan Juke has four separate coils, one fitted to each spark plug **(see illustration)**. Each spark plug has its own dedicated 'plug-top' HT coil that fits directly onto the spark plug (no HT leads are therefore needed); on these models a spark is only generated at each plug once every engine cycle. Therefore, these systems have no distributor cap, rotor arm, or even HT leads, resulting in a simpler, more reliable system requiring even less maintenance.

3 Because there is no distributor to adjust, the ignition timing cannot be adjusted by conventional means, and the advance and retard functions are carried out by the Electronic Control Unit (ECU).

4 The ignition system consists of the spark plugs, four separate coils, and the ECU together with its associated sensors and wiring. The ECU supplies a voltage to the input stage of the ignition coil, which causes the primary windings in the coils to be energised. The supply voltage is periodically interrupted by the ECU and this results in the collapse of primary magnetic field, which then induces a much larger voltage in the secondary coil, called the HT voltage. The spark plug electrodes form a gap small enough for the HT voltage to arc across, and the resulting spark ignites the fuel/air mixture in the cylinder. The timing of this sequence of events is critical, and is regulated solely by the ECU.

5 The ECU calculates and controls the ignition timing primarily according to engine speed, crankshaft position, camshaft position, and inlet airflow rate information, received from sensors mounted on and around the engine. Other parameters that affect ignition timing are throttle position and rate of opening, inlet air temperature and coolant temperature, monitored via sensors mounted on the engine. Note that most of these sensors have a dual role, in that the information they provide is equally useful in determining the fuelling requirements as in deciding the optimum ignition or firing point – therefore, removal of some of the sensors mentioned below is described in Chapter 4A.

6 The ECU computes engine speed and crankshaft position from toothed impulse rotor attached to the engine flywheel, with an engine speed sensor whose inductive head runs just above rotor. As the crankshaft (and flywheel) rotate, the rotor 'teeth' pass the engine speed sensor, which transmits a pulse to the ECU every time a tooth passes it. At the top dead centre (TDC) position, there is one

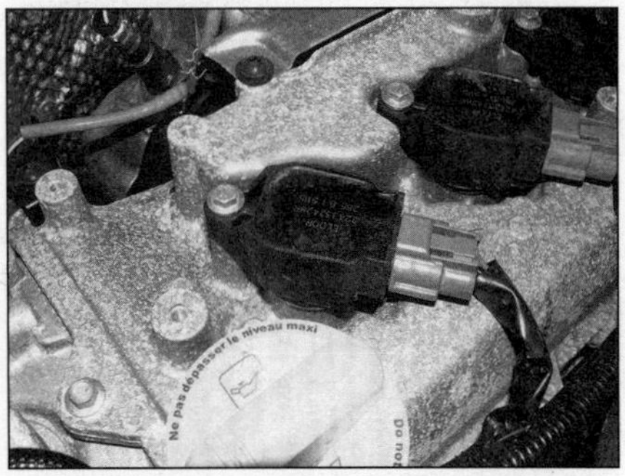

1.2 Individual ignition coils are fitted to each spark plug

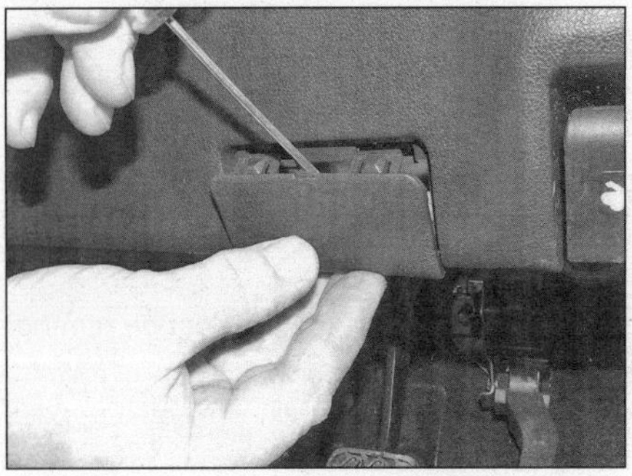

1.11a Carefully remove the facia trim panel...

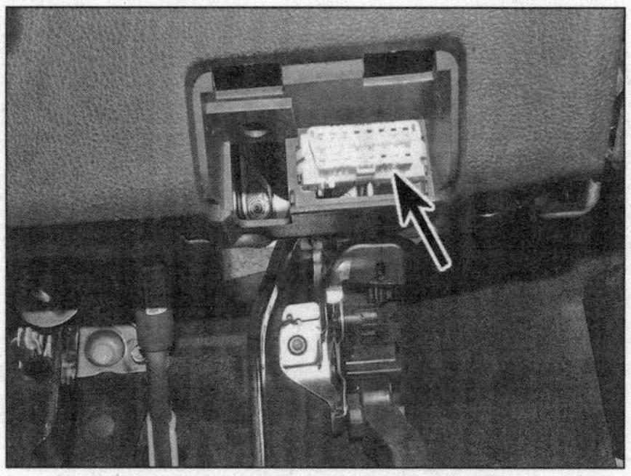

1.11b ...for access to the vehicle diagnostic plug connector

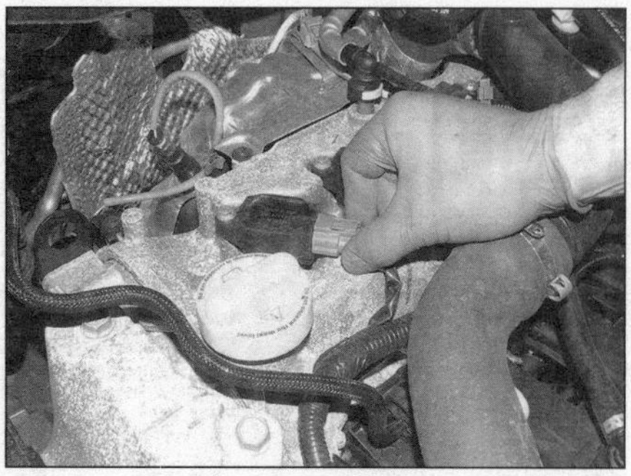

3.5 Disconnect the ignition coil wiring connector

missing tooth in the rotor periphery, which results in a longer pause between signals from the sensor. The ECU recognises the absence of a pulse from the engine speed sensor at this point, and uses it to establish the TDC position for No 1 piston. The time interval between pulses, and the location of the missing pulse, allow the ECU to accurately determine the position of the crankshaft and its speed. The camshaft position sensor enhances this information by detecting whether a particular piston is on an inlet or an exhaust cycle.

7 Information on engine load is supplied to the ECU via the mass airflow sensor (or via the inlet manifold pressure sensor, as applicable), and from the throttle position sensor. The engine load is determined by computation based on the quantity of air being drawn into the engine.

8 Sensors monitoring coolant temperature, throttle position, roadspeed, and air conditioning system operation, provide additional input signals to the ECU on vehicle operating conditions. From all this constantly changing data, the ECU selects, and if necessary modifies, a particular ignition advance setting from a map of ignition characteristics stored in its memory.

9 The ECU also uses the ignition timing to finely adjust the engine idle speed, in response to signals from the air conditioning switch (to prevent stalling), or if the alternator output voltage falls too low.

10 In the event of a fault in the system due to loss of a signal from one of the sensors, the ECU reverts to an emergency ('limp-home') program. This will allow the car to be driven, although engine operation and performance will be limited. A warning light on the instrument panel will illuminate if the fault is likely to cause an increase in harmful exhaust emissions.

11 It should be noted that comprehensive fault diagnosis of all the engine management systems described in this Chapter is only possible with dedicated electronic test equipment. In the event of a sensor failing or other fault occurring, a fault code will be stored in the ECU's fault log, which can only be extracted from the ECU using a dedicated fault code reader. The on-board diagnostic (OBD) plug is located in the passenger compartment at the lower right-hand side of the facia panel **(see illustrations)**. A Nissan dealer or specialist will obviously have such a reader, but they are also available from other suppliers. It is unlikely to be cost-effective for the private owner to purchase a fault code reader, but a well-equipped local garage or auto-electrical specialist will have one. Once the fault has been identified, the removal/refitting sequences detailed in the following Sections will then allow the appropriate component(s) to be renewed as required.

2 Ignition system – testing

Warning: Due to the high voltages produced by the electronic ignition system, extreme care must be taken when working on the system with the ignition switched on. Persons with surgically implanted cardiac pacemaker devices should keep well clear of the ignition circuits, components and test equipment.

1 If a fault appears in the ignition system, first ensure that the fault is not due to a poor electrical connection or poor maintenance; i.e. check that the air cleaner filter element is clean, that the spark plugs are in good condition and correctly gapped, that the engine breather hoses are clear and undamaged, referring to Chapter 1A for further information. If the engine is running very roughly, check the compression pressures and the valve clearances are correct. Refer to Chapter 2A for 1.2 litre engines and Chapter 2B for 1.6 litre engines.

2 The only specific ignition system checks that can be carried out by the home mechanic are those described in Chapter 1A, Section 26, relating to the spark plugs. If necessary, the system wiring and wiring connectors can be checked as described in Chapter 12, ensuring that the control unit wiring connectors have first been disconnected.

3 If the above checks fail to reveal the cause of the problem, the vehicle should be taken to a suitably equipped Nissan dealer for testing.

3 HT coil(s) – removal and refitting

Removal

1 The ignition coil units are mounted on top of each spark plug.

2 Make sure the ignition is switched off and disconnect the battery negative terminal (refer to battery disconnection and reconnection in Chapter 5A, Section 3).

3 On 1.2 litre engines, remove the inlet air duct over the top of the engine as described in Chapter 4A, Section 2.

4 On 1.6 litre engines, remove the inlet manifold as described in Chapter 4A, Section 14.

5 Disconnect the wiring connector from the ignition coil **(see illustration)**.

6 Undo the retaining bolt and withdraw the ignition coil from the cylinder head.

Refitting

7 Refitting is a reversal of the removal procedure, noting the following points:

a) Securely tighten the coil mounting bolts.

b) Make sure the wiring connectors are fitted correctly.

c) On 1.6 litre engines, refit the inlet manifold as described in Chapter 4A, Section 14.

4 Ignition timing – checking and adjustment

1 The ignition timing is under the control of the engine management system ECU and is not manually adjustable without access to dedicated electronic test equipment. A basic setting cannot be quoted because the ignition timing is constantly being altered.

2 The vehicle must be taken to a Nissan dealer if the timing requires checking or adjustment.

Chapter 6
Clutch

Contents

Degrees of difficulty

Easy, suitable for novice with little experience	**Fairly easy,** suitable for beginner with some experience	**Fairly difficult,** suitable for competent DIY mechanic	**Difficult,** suitable for experienced DIY mechanic	**Very difficult,** suitable for expert DIY or professional

Specifications

Type	Single dry plate with diaphragm spring, hydraulically operated

Friction disc

Outer diameter:	
1.2 litre petrol engines	225 mm
1.6 litre petrol engines	215 mm
Diesel engines	225 mm
Inner diameter (of friction materiel):	
1.2 litre petrol engines	150 mm
1.6 litre petrol engines	140 mm
Diesel engines	150 mm
Friction material thickness (new):	
1.2 litre petrol engines	3.1 mm
1.6 litre petrol engines	3.2 mm
Diesel engines	3.1 mm
Minimum friction material-to-rivet head depth:	
Petrol engines	0.3 mm
Diesel engines	1.0 mm
Maximum friction disc run-out	1.0 mm

Clutch pedal switches

Clearance between threaded end of switch and clutch pedal	0.74 to 1.96 mm

Torque wrench settings

Torque wrench settings	Nm	lbf ft
Clutch pedal bracket nuts	14	10
Concentric slave cylinder (CSC) retaining bolts	21	15
Pressure plate (clutch cover) retaining bolts:		
1.2 litre petrol engines	15	11
1.6 litre petrol engines	25	18
Diesel engines	15	11

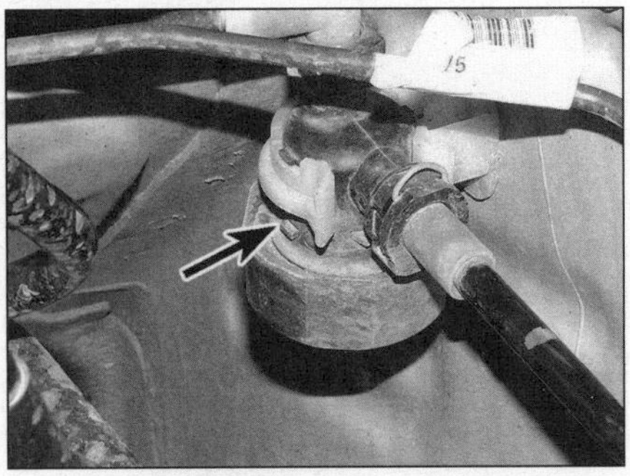

1.6 Pulsation damper location

1 General Information

1 The clutch consists of a friction disc, a pressure plate assembly, a release bearing and the release mechanism. All of these components are contained in the large cast-aluminium alloy bellhousing, and sandwiched between the engine and the transmission. The release mechanism is hydraulic, operated by a master cylinder and a slave cylinder, which is part of the release bearing. The hydraulic master cylinder is located in the pedal bracket on the bulkhead, and the clutch fluid reservoir is shared with the brake fluid reservoir on the top of the brake master cylinder. Inside the reservoir each circuit has its own compartment, so that in the event of fluid loss in the clutch circuit, the brake circuit remains fully operational.

2 The friction disc is fitted between the engine flywheel and the clutch pressure plate, and is allowed to slide on the transmission input shaft splines. It consists of two circular facings of friction material to provide the clutch bearing surface, and a spring-cushioned hub to damp out transmission shocks.

3 The pressure plate assembly is bolted to the engine flywheel, and is located by dowel pins. When the engine is running, drive is transmitted from the crankshaft via the flywheel to the friction disc (these components being clamped securely together by the pressure plate assembly), and from the friction disc to the transmission input shaft.

4 To interrupt the drive, the spring pressure must be relaxed. This is achieved by a sealed release bearing fitted concentrically around the transmission input shaft; when the driver depresses the clutch pedal, the release bearing is pressed against the fingers at the centre of the diaphragm spring. The pressure at its centre causes the springs to deform, so that it flattens and thus releases the clamping force it exerts at its periphery on the pressure plate.

5 When the pedal is released, the diaphragm spring forces the pressure plate into contact with the friction linings on the friction disc. The disc is now firmly sandwiched between the pressure plate and the flywheel, thus transmitting engine power to the transmission.

6 Wear of the friction material on the friction disc is automatically compensated for by the operation of the hydraulic system. As the friction material on the friction disc wears, the pressure plate moves towards the flywheel causing the clutch diaphragm spring inner fingers to move outwards. When the clutch pedal is released, excess fluid is expelled through the master cylinder into the fluid reservoir. There is a pulsation damper fitted in the hydraulic hose from the master cylinder to the (concentric) slave cylinder. It is located in the left-hand rear corner of the engine compartment below the air cleaner assembly **(see illustration)**.

Warning: Hydraulic fluid is poisonous, thoroughly wash off spills from bare skin without delay. Seek immediate medical advice if any fluid is swallowed or gets into the eyes. Certain types of hydraulic fluid are inflammable and may ignite when brought into contact with hot components. Hydraulic fluid is also an effective paint stripper. If spillage occurs onto painted bodywork or fittings, it should be washed off immediately, using copious quantities of cold water. It is also hygroscopic (i.e. it can absorb moisture from the air) which then renders it useless. Old fluid may have suffered contamination, and should never be re-used.

2 Hydraulic system – bleeding

Note: *Refer to the warning at the beginning of Section 1, regarding the hazards of working with hydraulic fluid.*

1 If any part of the hydraulic system is dismantled, or if air has accidentally entered the system, the system will need to be bled. The presence of air is characterised by the pedal having a spongy feel and it results in difficulty in changing gear.

2 Obtain a clean container, a suitable length of rubber or clear plastic tubing that is a tight fit over the bleed screw on the clutch slave cylinder, and a container of the specified hydraulic fluid. The help of an assistant will also be required. (If a one-man do-it-yourself bleeding kit for bleeding the brake hydraulic system is available, this can be used quite satisfactorily for the clutch also. Full information on the use of these kits may be found in Chapter 9, Section 2).

3 Remove the <span class="color0">air cleaner</span> inlet ducting from the front left-hand side of the engine compartment (see Chapter 4A, Section 2 or Chapter 4B, Section 2), to access the clutch bleed screw.

4 Remove the filler cap from the brake master cylinder reservoir, and if necessary top-up the fluid. Keep the reservoir topped-up during subsequent operations.

5 Remove the dust cap from the bleed screw at the hydraulic fluid hose connection, located on the lower front facing side of the transmission **(see illustration)**.

6 Connect one end of the bleed tube to the bleed screw, and insert the other end of the tube in the container with sufficient clean hydraulic fluid to keep the end of the tube submerged **(see illustration)**.

7 With the tube on the bleed screw, press down on the hose retaining clip **(see illustration)**, and then carefully pull the clutch fluid hose outwards from the bell housing, by 5 mm on 5-speed transmissions, and 10 mm on 6-speed transmissions. Be careful not to pull the clutch fluid hose completely out from the connection.

2.5 Remove the dust cap from the bleed screw

2.6 Air bleed bottle connected to bleed screw

2.7 Release the retaining clip

8 Have your assistant depress the clutch pedal and then slowly release it. Continue this procedure until clean hydraulic fluid, free from air bubbles, emerges from the tube. At the end of a downstroke, push the clutch fluid hose back into position, making sure the retaining clip secures the hose in place.
9 Make sure that the brake master cylinder reservoir is checked frequently to ensure that the level does not drop too far, allowing air into the system.
10 Check the operation of the clutch pedal. After a few strokes it should feel normal. Any sponginess would indicate air still present in the system. If so, carry out the procedure once again.
11 On completion remove the bleed tube and refit the dust cover. Top-up the master cylinder reservoir if necessary and refit the cap. Fluid expelled from the hydraulic system should now be discarded, as it will be contaminated with moisture, air and dirt, making it unsuitable for further use.

3 Clutch pedal – removal and refitting

Removal

1 Disconnect the battery negative terminal (refer to battery disconnection and reconnection in Chapter 5A, Section 3).
2 Remove the facia lower trim panel on the driver's side as described in Chapter 11, Section 26.
3 Disconnect the wiring connector from the clutch pedal position switch and, where fitted, from the clutch interlock switch, then unclip the wiring loom securing clip from the pedal mounting bracket **(see illustration)**.
4 Using a flat bladed screwdriver, prise the master cylinder pushrod end from the pedal pin **(see illustration)**.
5 Slacken and remove the clutch pedal mounting bracket retaining nuts, then withdraw the pedal and mounting bracket out from under the facia **(see illustrations)**.
6 Check the condition of the pedal, pivot bush and return spring assembly and renew any components as necessary.

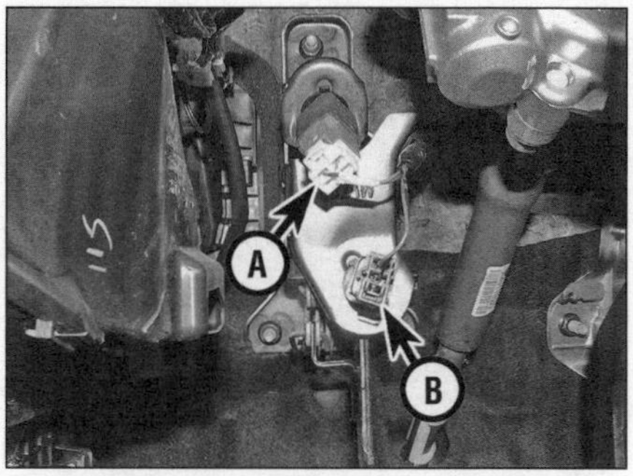

3.3 Disconnect the wiring connectors at the clutch pedal switches
A Clutch interlock switch
B Clutch pedal position switch

Refitting

7 Lubricate the pedal pivot with multipurpose grease, then manoeuvre and locate the pedal and mounting bracket on the bulkhead. Refit the retaining nuts and tighten securely.
8 Reconnect the clutch master cylinder pushrod to the clutch pedal.
9 Depress the pedal two or three times and check the operation of the clutch release mechanism.
10 Reconnect the wiring connector to the clutch pedal switch (and interlock switch, if fitted), and then secure the wiring loom back into position with the retaining clip on the pedal mounting bracket.
11 Refit the the facia lower trim panel with reference to Chapter 11, Section 26.
12 Reconnect the battery negative terminal (refer to battery disconnection and reconnection in Chapter 5A, Section 3).

4 Clutch pedal switches – removal and refitting

Removal

1 One or two clutch pedal switches may be fitted to the Juke depending on model year and equipment fitted. The switches are located on the pedal mounting bracket and where two switches are fitted the upper switch

3.4 Release the end of the pushrod from the pedal

is the clutch interlock switch and the lower switch is the clutch pedal position switch **(see illustration 3.3)**.
2 Disconnect the battery negative terminal (refer to battery disconnection and reconnection in Chapter 5A, Section 3).
3 Remove the facia lower trim panel on the driver's side as described in Chapter 11, Section 26.
4 Disconnect the wiring connector from the clutch pedal switch and, where fitted, from the clutch interlock switch.
5 Turn the relevant switch through a quarter-turn anti-clockwise and remove it from the pedal mounting bracket.

Refitting

6 Refitting is a reversal of removal, noting the following points:
a) When refitting the clutch interlock switch, fully depress the clutch pedal. Fit the switch to the pedal mounting bracket and position it so that the distance from the threaded end of the switch to the pedal is as given in the specifications. Turn the switch clockwise to secure **(see illustration)**.
b) When refitting the clutch pedal position switch, hold the clutch pedal in the released position. Fit the switch to the pedal mounting bracket and position it so that the distance from the threaded end of the switch to the pedal is as given in the specifications. Turn the switch clockwise to secure.

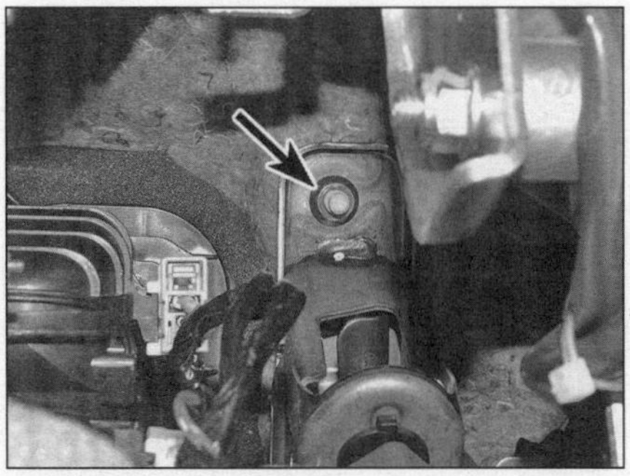

3.5a Clutch pedal upper mounting bracket nut...

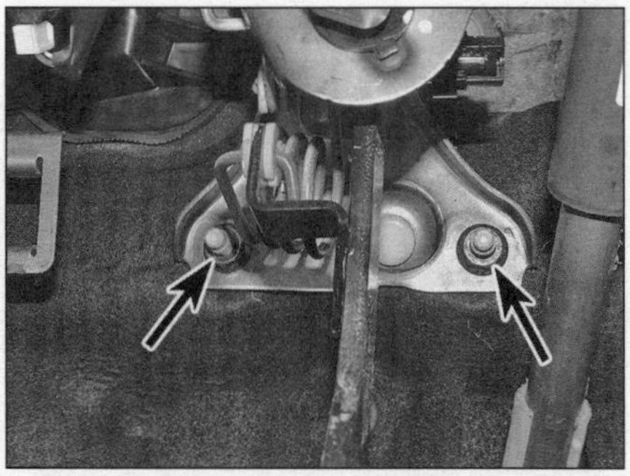

3.5b ...and lower mounting bracket nuts

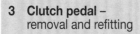

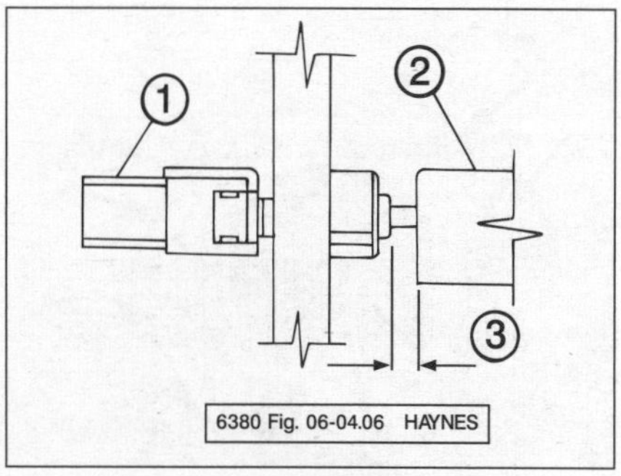

4.6 Clutch pedal switch clearance
1 Switch 2 Clutch pedal 3 Clearance

5 Master cylinder – removal and refitting

Note: *Refer to the warning at the beginning of Section 1 regarding the hazards of working with hydraulic fluid.*

Removal

1 Disconnect the battery negative terminal (refer to battery disconnection and reconnection in Chapter 5A, Section 3).

2 Using a flat bladed screwdriver, prise the master cylinder pushrod end from the clutch pedal pin **(see illustration 3.4)**.

3 To minimise hydraulic fluid loss, remove the brake master cylinder reservoir filler cap then tighten it down onto a piece of polythene to obtain an airtight seal.

4 Remove the windscreen cowl panel and cowl panel extension as described in Chapter 11, Section 21.

5 On diesel engine models, move the fuel supply and return hoses to one side to provide greater access.

6 Place absorbent rags under the clutch master cylinder pipe connections in the engine compartment and be prepared for some hydraulic fluid loss.

7 Clamp the upper hydraulic fluid supply hose leading from the brake fluid reservoir to the clutch master cylinder using a brake hose clamp.

8 Release the master cylinder hydraulic pressure pipe from the retaining clip on the engine compartment bulkhead. Be prepared for some hydraulic fluid loss, then prise out the retaining wire clip and disconnect the pipe from the master cylinder **(see illustration)**. Suitably plug or cap the pipe end to prevent further fluid loss and dirt entry.

9 Be prepared for some hydraulic fluid loss and disconnect the fluid supply hose from the top of the master cylinder. Suitably plug or cap the pipe end to prevent further fluid loss and dirt entry.

10 Rotate the master cylinder 45 degrees clockwise, and remove it from the bulkhead.

Refitting

11 Refitting the master cylinder is the reverse sequence to removal, bearing in mind the following points.

a) *Ensure that the pedal-to-master cylinder pushrod is correctly fitted.*
b) *Ensure all retaining clips are correctly refitted.*
c) *Refit the windscreen cowl panel and cowl panel extension as described in Chapter 11, Section 21.*
d) *Remove the piece of polythene from the top of the reservoir.*
e) *On completion, bleed the clutch hydraulic system as described in Section 2.*

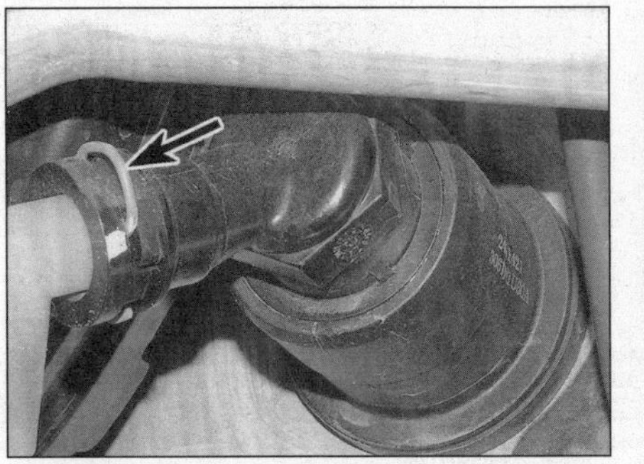

5.8 Prise out the wire clip and disconnect the pressure pipe from the master cylinder

6 Concentric slave cylinder (CSC) – removal and refitting

1 The clutch slave cylinder (Concentric Slave Cylinder) is part of the release bearing assembly; refer to Section 8, for the removal and refitting procedure.

7 Clutch assembly – removal, inspection and refitting

Warning: Dust created by clutch wear and deposited on the clutch components may contain asbestos, which is a health hazard. DO NOT blow it out with compressed air, or inhale any of it. DO NOT use petrol or petroleum-based solvents to clean off the dust. Brake system cleaner or methylated spirit should be used to flush the dust into a suitable receptacle. After the clutch components are wiped clean with rags, dispose of the contaminated rags and cleaner in a sealed, marked container.

Note: *Although some friction materials may no longer contain asbestos, it is safest to assume that they DO, and to take precautions accordingly*

7.2 Mark the position of the pressure plate on the flywheel

Removal

1 Unless the complete engine/transmission is to be removed from the car, and separated for major overhaul (see Chapter 2D, Section 3), the clutch can be reached by removing the transmission as described in Chapter 7, Section 6.

2 Before disturbing the clutch, use a dab of quick-drying paint or a marker pen to mark the relationship of the pressure plate assembly to the flywheel **(see illustration)**.

3 Working in a diagonal sequence, slacken the pressure plate bolts by half a turn at a time, until the spring pressure is released and the bolts can be unscrewed by hand **(see illustrations)**. If required lock the flywheel to prevent it from turning, by locking the ring gear teeth.

4 Prise the pressure plate assembly off its locating dowels, and collect the friction disc, noting which way round the friction disc is fitted **(see illustration)**.

Inspection

Note: *Due to the amount of work necessary*

7.3a Undo the pressure plate bolts (diesel engine shown)...

7.3b ...using a homemade tool to prevent the flywheel from turning

7.4 Remove the pressure plate complete with friction disc

7.13 Markings on friction disc – P.P.SIDE (pressure plate side)

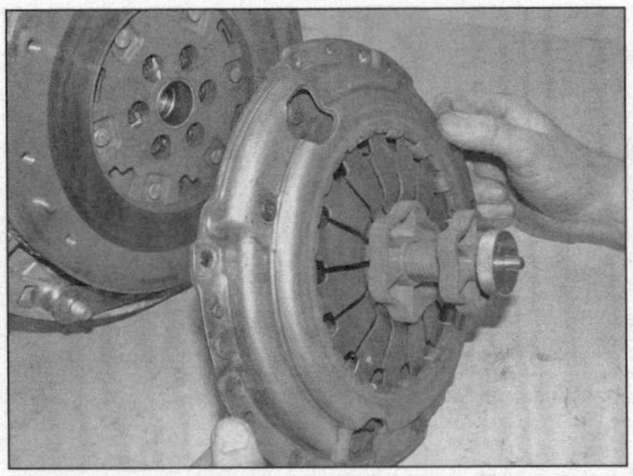

7.16a Using a special tool to centralise the friction disc...

7.16b ...on the pressure plate

to remove and refit clutch components, it is usually considered good practice to renew the clutch friction disc, pressure plate assembly and release bearing as a matched set, even if only one of these is actually worn enough to require renewal. It is worth considering the renewal of the clutch components on a preventative basis if the engine and/or transmission have been removed for some other reason.

5 When cleaning clutch components, first read the warning at the beginning of this Section. Remove the dust only as described – working with dampened cloths will help to keep dust levels to a minimum. Wherever possible, work in a well-ventilated atmosphere.

6 Check the friction disc facings for signs of wear, damage or oil contamination. If the friction material is cracked, burnt, scored or damaged, or if it is contaminated with oil or grease (shown by shiny black patches), the friction disc must be renewed.

7 If the friction material is still serviceable, check that the centre boss splines are unworn, that the torsion springs are in good condition and securely fastened, and that all the rivets are tightly fastened. If excessive wear or damage is found, the friction disc must be renewed.

8 If the friction material is fouled with oil, this must be due to an oil leak from the crankshaft left-hand oil seal, from the sump-to-cylinder block joint, or from the transmission input shaft. Renew the seal or repair the joint, as appropriate, as described in Chapter 2A, 2B, 2C or Chapter 7, before installing the new friction disc, or the new disc will quickly go the same way.

9 Check the pressure plate assembly for obvious signs of wear or damage; shake it to check for loose rivets, or worn or damaged fulcrum rings. Check that the drive straps securing the pressure plate to the cover do not show signs (such as a deep yellow or blue discoloration) of overheating. If the diaphragm spring is worn or damaged, or if its pressure is in any way suspect, the pressure plate assembly should be renewed.

10 Examine the machined bearing surfaces of the pressure plate and of the flywheel; they should be clean, completely flat, and free from scratches or scoring. If either is discoloured from excessive heat, or shows signs of cracks, it should be renewed; however, minor damage of this nature can sometimes be polished away using emery paper.

11 Check that the release bearing contact surface rotates smoothly and easily, with no sign of noise or roughness, and that the surface itself is smooth and unworn, with no signs of cracks, pitting or scoring. If there is any doubt about its condition, the bearing must be renewed

Refitting

12 On reassembly, ensure that the bearing surfaces of the flywheel and pressure plate are completely clean, smooth, and free from oil or grease. Use solvent to remove any protective grease from new components.

13 Fit the friction disc/plate so that its spring hub assembly faces away from the flywheel; there may also be a marking showing which way round the plate is to be refitted **(see illustration)**.

7.17a Align the pressure plate on the dowels on the flywheel

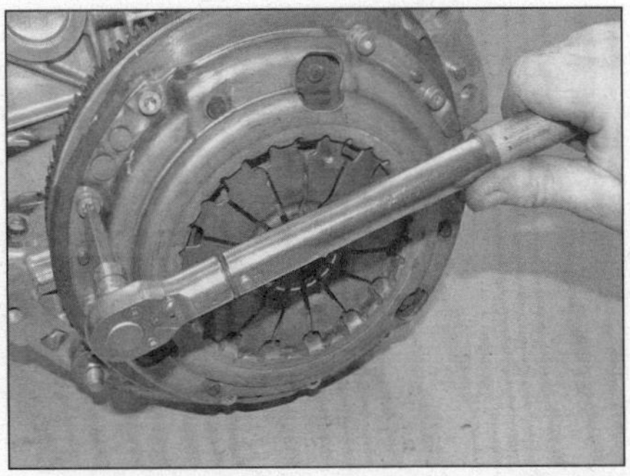

7.17b Tighten the bolts to the correct torque setting

14 Refit the pressure plate assembly, aligning the marks made on dismantling (if the original pressure plate is re-used), and locating the pressure plate on its locating dowels. Fit the pressure plate bolts, but tighten them only finger-tight so that the friction disc can still be moved.

15 The friction disc must now be centralised, so that when the transmission is refitted, its input shaft will pass through the splines at the centre of the friction disc.

16 Centralisation can be achieved by passing a screwdriver or other long bar through the friction disc, and into the hole in the crankshaft. The friction disc can then be moved around until it is centred on the crankshaft hole. Alternatively, a clutch-aligning tool can be used to eliminate the guesswork; these can be obtained from most accessory shops **(see illustrations)**.

17 When the friction disc is centralised, tighten the pressure plate bolts evenly and in a diagonal sequence to the specified torque setting **(see illustrations)**. Lock the ring gear to prevent the flywheel from turning, using the method employed when dismantling.

18 Apply a thin smear of high melting-point grease to the splines of the friction disc and the transmission input shaft.

19 Refit the transmission as described in Chapter 7, Section 6.

8 Clutch release mechanism – removal, inspection and refitting

Note: *Refer to the warning concerning the dangers of asbestos dust at the beginning of Section 7.*

Removal

1 Unless the complete engine/transmission is to be removed from the car, and separated for major overhaul (see Chapter 2D, Section 3), the clutch release mechanism can be reached by removing the transmission as described in Chapter 7, Section 6.

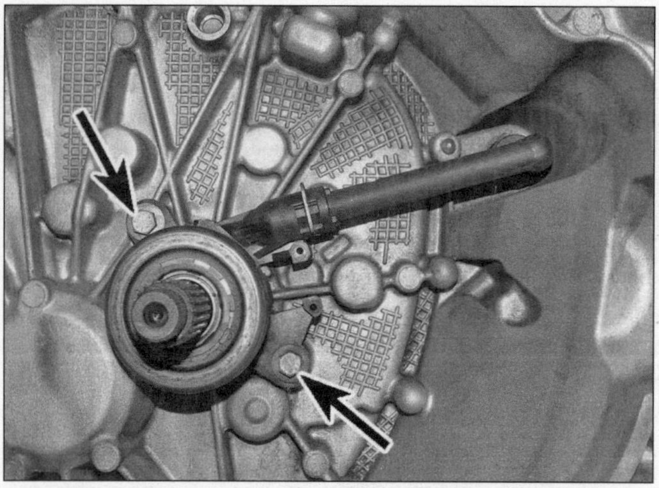

8.2 Undo the concentric slave cylinder (CSC) mounting bolts

8.4 Retaining clip securing plastic pipe to the slave cylinder

2 With the transmission removed, undo the two mounting bolts from inside the bellhousing **(see illustration)**.

3 Withdraw the concentric slave cylinder/release bearing by sliding it over the transmission input shaft. Withdraw it complete with plastic fluid pipe out from the bellhousing.

4 If required, withdraw the securing clip from the plastic fluid pipe **(see illustration)**, to disconnect it from the clutch slave cylinder/release bearing.

Inspection

5 Check the release mechanism, renewing any component, which is worn or damaged. Carefully check all bearing surfaces and points of contact.

6 When checking the release bearing itself, note that it is often considered worthwhile to renew it as a matter of course, given that a significant amount of work is required to gain access to it (note that this is the manufacturer's recommended course of action). Check that the contact surface rotates smoothly and easily, with no sign of noise or roughness. Also check that the surface itself is smooth and unworn, with no signs of cracks, pitting or scoring. If there is any doubt about its condition, the bearing must be renewed.

Refitting

7 Slide the concentric slave cylinder/release bearing over the transmission input shaft and tighten the retaining bolts to the specified torque setting.

8 Refit the transmission as described in Chapter 7, Section 6.

Chapter 7
Manual transmission

Contents

Degrees of difficulty

Easy, suitable for novice with little experience	**Fairly easy,** suitable for beginner with some experience	**Fairly difficult,** suitable for competent DIY mechanic	**Difficult,** suitable for experienced DIY mechanic	**Very difficult,** suitable for expert DIY or professional

Specifications

General

Type	Manual, five or six forward speeds and reverse. Synchromesh on all forward speeds
Designation:	
1.2 litre petrol engines	RS6F94R – (6-speed)
1.6 litre petrol engines	RS5F92R – (5 speed)
Diesel engines	RS6F94R – (6-speed)
Models code:	
1.2 litre petrol engines RS6F94R)	BV80A
1.6 litre petrol engines (RS5F92R)	1KAOA, 1KAOC, 1KAOB, 1KA1C or 1KA1B
Diesel engines (RS6F94R)	1KGOC, 1KG1B or 1KBOA

Lubrication

Oil capacities:	
5-speed transmissions	2.3 litres
6-speed transmissions	2.0 litres

Torque wrench settings

Torque wrench settings	Nm	lbf ft
Engine-to-transmission fixing bolts:		
1.2 litre petrol engines	62	46
1.6 litre petrol engines	48	35
Diesel engines	62	46
Oil drain plug	22	16
Oil filler/level plug (plastic plug)	3	2
Reversing light switch	25	18

1 General Information

1 The transmission is contained in a cast-aluminium alloy casing bolted to the left-hand end of the engine, and consists of the gearbox and final drive differential, often called a transaxle.

2 Drive is transmitted from the crankshaft via the clutch to the input shaft, which has a splined extension to accept the clutch friction disc, and rotates in sealed ball-bearings. From the input shaft, drive is transmitted to the output shaft, which rotates in a roller bearing at its right-hand end, and a sealed ball-bearing at its left-hand end. From the output shaft, the drive is transmitted to the differential crownwheel, which rotates with the differential case and planetary gears, thus driving the sun gears and driveshafts. The rotation of the planetary gears on their shaft allows the inner roadwheel to rotate at a slower speed than the outer roadwheel when the car is cornering.

3 The input and output shafts are arranged side-by-side, parallel to the crankshaft and driveshafts, so that their gear pinion teeth are in constant mesh. In the neutral position, the output shaft gear pinions rotate freely, so that drive cannot be transmitted to the crownwheel.

4 Gear selection is via a floor-mounted lever and dual cable arrangement. The selector cables cause the appropriate selector fork to move its respective synchro-sleeve along the shaft, to lock the gear pinion to the synchro-hub. Since the synchro-hubs are splined to the output shaft, this locks the pinion to the shaft so that drive can be transmitted. To ensure that gearchanging can be made quickly and quietly, a synchromesh system is fitted to all forward gears, consisting of baulk rings and spring-loaded fingers, as well as the gear pinions and synchro-hubs; the synchromesh cones are formed on the mating faces of the baulk rings and gear pinions.

2 Transmission – draining and refilling

1 This operation is much quicker and more efficient if the car is first taken on a journey of sufficient length to warm the engine/transmission up to normal operating temperature.

2 Park the car on level ground, switch off the ignition and apply the handbrake firmly. For improved access, jack up the front of the car and support it securely on axle stands (see *Jacking and vehicle support*). Note that the car must be lowered to the ground and be level to ensure accuracy when refilling and checking the oil level.

3 Wipe clean the area around the filler/level plug, which is:

a) *Screwed into the front of the transmission housing on 5-speed transmissions* **(see illustration)**.

b) *Screwed into the left-hand side of the transmission, to the rear of the driveshaft, on 6-speed transmissions* **(see illustration)**.

4 Remove the oil filler/level plug, be prepared for some oil spillage as the plug is removed.

5 Position a suitable container under the drain plug, which is situated at the lower rear of the transmission differential housing **(see illustrations)**.

6 Remove the drain plug and allow the oil to drain completely into the container **(see illustration)**. If the oil is hot, take precautions against scalding. Clean both the filler/level and the drain plug, discard the sealing washers, as new ones will be required on refitting.

7 When the oil has finished draining, clean the drain plug threads and those of the transmission casing, then fit the new sealing washer and refit the drain plug **(see illustration)**, tightening it to the specified torque wrench setting. If the car was raised for the draining operation, lower it to the ground, to make sure it is level.

8 Refilling the transmission is an awkward operation. Above all, allow plenty of time for the oil level to settle properly before checking it. Note that the car must be parked on flat level ground when checking the oil level.

9 Refill the transmission with the exact amount of the specified type of oil, then check the oil level as described in Chapter 1A, Section 20; if the correct amount was poured into the transmission, and a large amount flows out on checking the level, refit the filler/level plug and take the car on a short journey

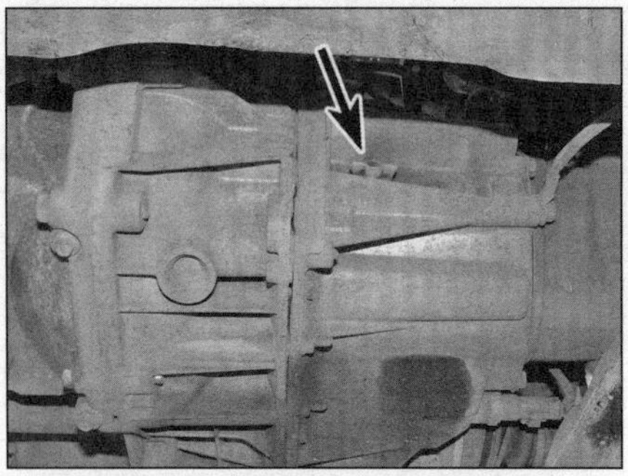

2.3a Oil filler/level plug (5-speed transmissions)

2.3b Oil filler/level plug (6-speed transmissions)

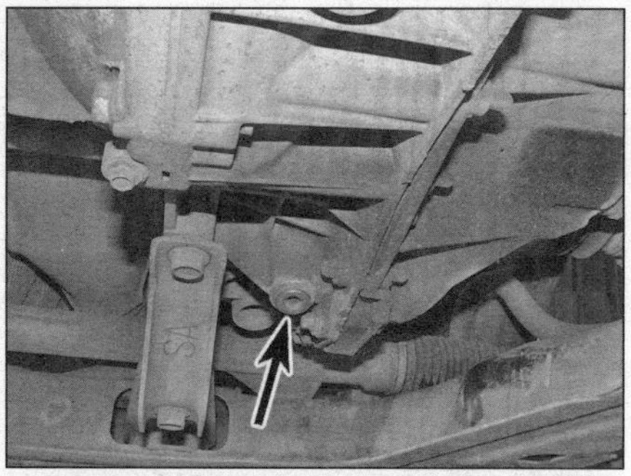

2.5a Oil drain plug (5-speed transmissions)

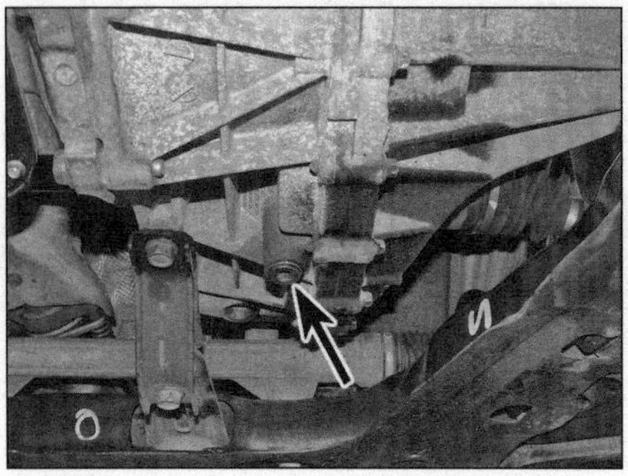

2.5b Oil drain plug (6-speed transmissions)

2.6 Drain the transmission oil

2.7 Use a new sealing washer when refitting the drain plug

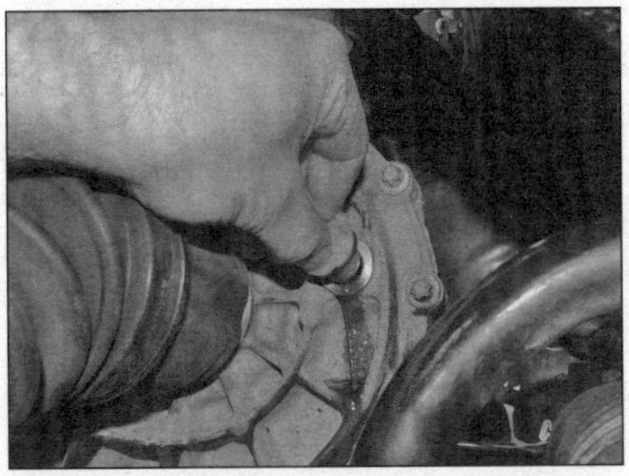

2.10 Refit the filler/level plug when fluid is correct

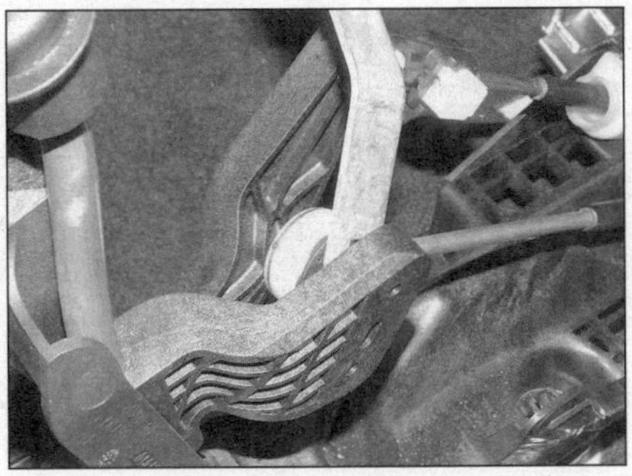

3.2a Using a suitable tool, prise free the cable end pieces...

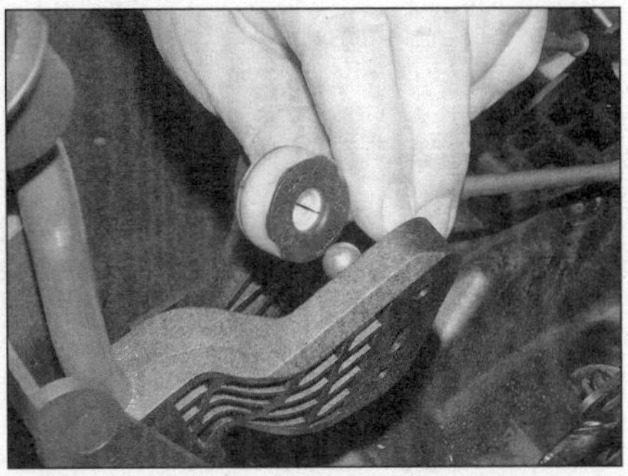

3.2b ...and disconnect the cables from the gear change levers

so that the new oil is distributed fully around the transmission components, then check the level again on your return.

10 When the level is correct, refit the filler/level plug and tighten it securely **(see illustration)**. Wash off any spilt oil.

3 Gearchange linkage – removal and refitting

Removal

Gear lever housing

1 Remove the centre console as described in Chapter 11, Section 25.

2 Pull out and disconnect the two cable ends from the ball joints on the gear change selector levers **(see illustrations)**.

3 Depress the two upper tabs and withdraw the two outer cables upwards from the gear lever housing **(see illustrations)**.

4 With the cables disconnected, undo the four mounting bolts from the bottom of the gear lever housing **(see illustrations)**, and manoeuvre the housing assembly out of position.

Gear change cables

5 Release the cables from the gear lever housing assembly, as described in paragraphs 1 to 3.

6 Remove the battery and battery tray as described in Chapter 5A, Section 3.

7 If not already done, to make access to the cables on top of the transmission housing easier, remove the air cleaner assembly, as described in Chapter 4A, Section 2 or Chapter 4B, Section 2.

8 Pull out and disconnect the two cable ends from the ball joints on the transmission selector levers.

9 Depress the two upper tabs and withdraw the two outer cables upwards from the transmission mounting bracket.

10 Firmly apply the handbrake, and then jack up the front of the vehicle and support it securely on axle stands (see *Jacking and vehicle support*).

11 From underneath the vehicle, release the fasteners and remove the heat shield from under the centre tunnel of the vehicle **(see illustrations)**. Note that depending on model, it may be necessary to remove the exhaust front pipe to give better access to the heat shield.

12 Unclip the outer cables from the support bracket on the underside of the vehicle, then release the rubber grommet from the floor

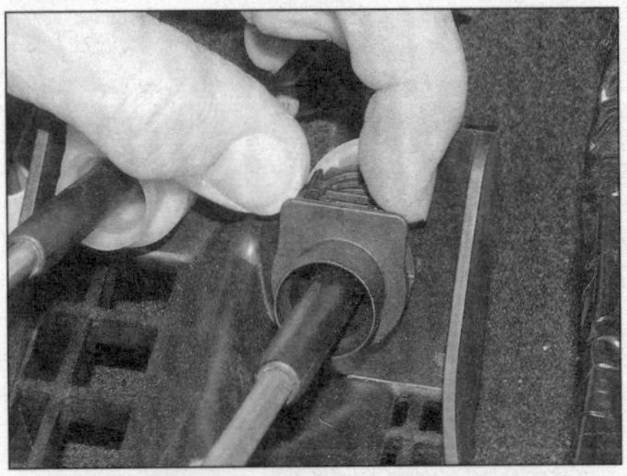

3.3a Depress the two upper tabs...

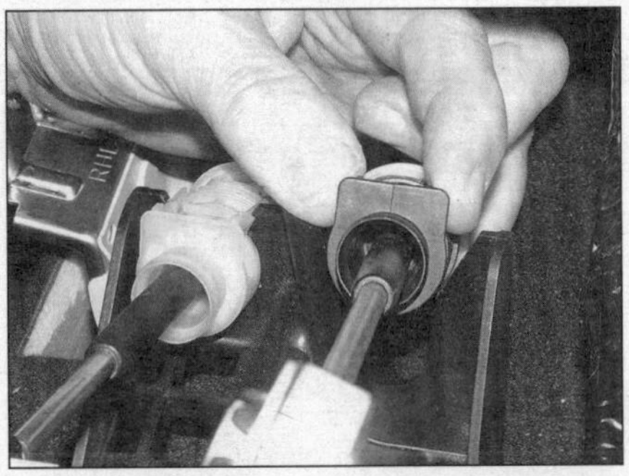

3.3b ...and pull the outer cables upward and out of the gear lever housing

3.4a Undo the gear lever housing front mounting bolts...

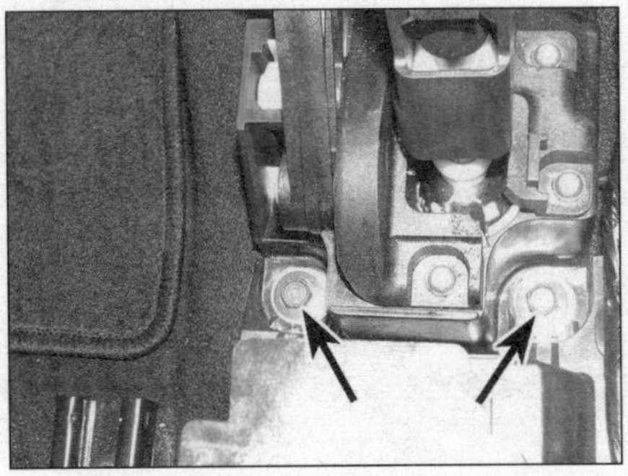

3.4b ...and rear mounting bolts

3.11a Undo the retaining clips...

3.11b ...and remove the heat shield

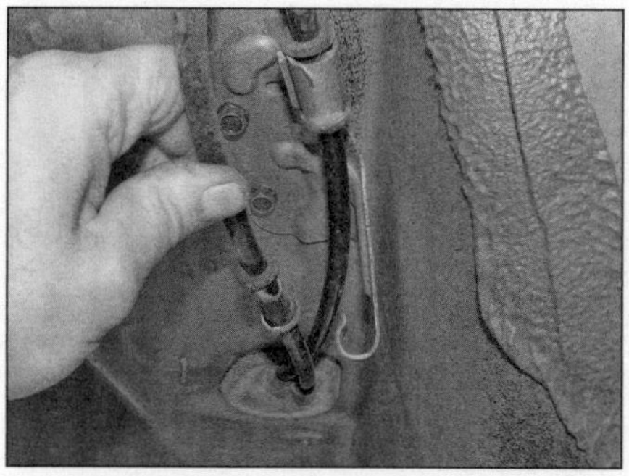

3.12a Release the cables from the support bracket...

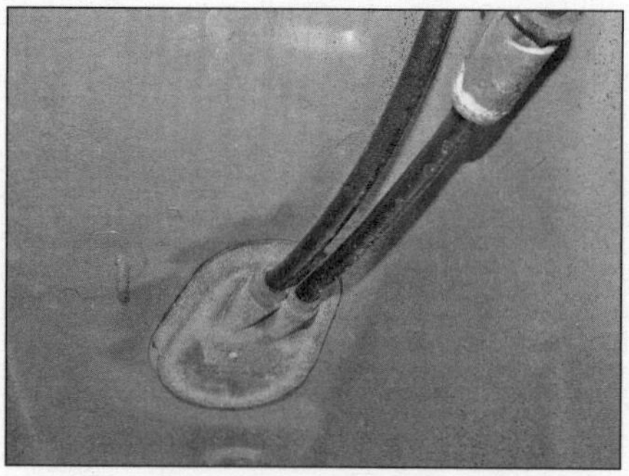

3.12b ...and remove the rubber grommet from the floor panel

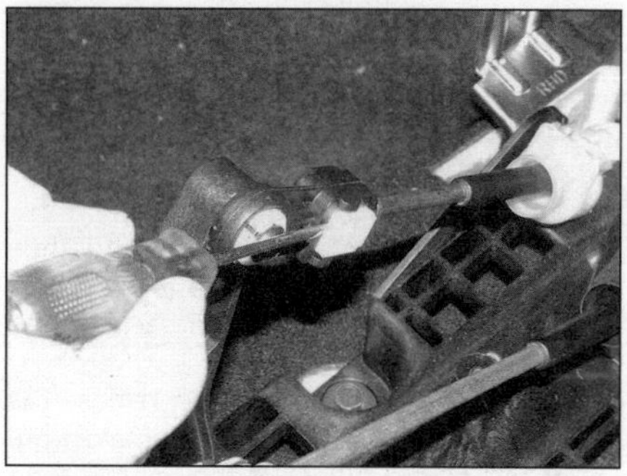

3.19 Pull out the locking clip from the selector cable end fitting

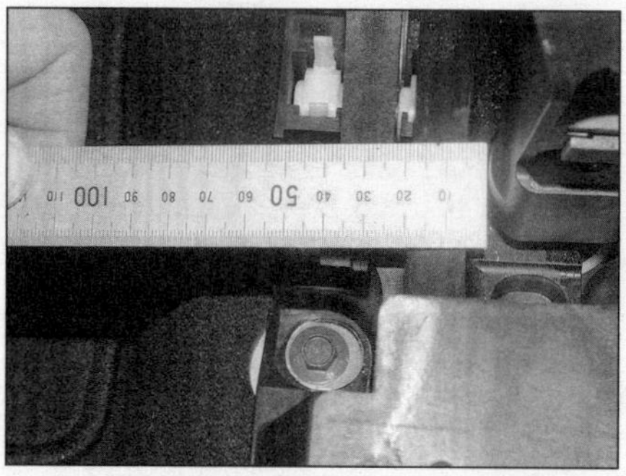

3.20 Position the gear lever base approximately 5 mm away from the edge of the housing

panel and withdraw the cables from under the vehicle **(see illustrations)**.

13 Inspect all the gear linkage components for signs of wear or damage, paying particular attention to the cables, renew worn components as necessary.

Refitting

14 Refitting is a reversal of the removal procedure, applying a smear of multipurpose grease to the gear lever pivot ball and bushes. On 6-speed transmissions check, and if necessary adjust, the selector cable before refitting the centre console.

Adjustment

Note: *Cable adjustment is only possible on 6-speed transmissions.*

15 Move the gear lever through all gear positions and check that each gear engages smoothly without binding. Check that the gear lever moves smoothly to the left and right when in the neutral position. If any abnormalities are experienced, adjust the cable as follows.

16 Adjustment is made from inside the vehicle, on the gear lever end of the left-hand selector cable.

17 Remove the centre console as described in Chapter 11, Section 25.

18 Move the gear lever to the 4th gear position.

19 Using a small screwdriver, pull out the locking clip from the selector cable end fitting; this will disengage the inner cable **(see illustration)**.

20 Take up the free play in the gear lever by positioning it so that the lever base is approximately 5 mm away from the edge of the gear lever housing **(see illustration)**. Hold the lever in this position and push the end fitting locking clip back in to lock the inner cable.

21 When completed, move the gear lever through all gears to check for smooth operation.

22 Refit the centre console as described in Chapter 11, Section 25.

4 Oil seals – renewal

Driveshaft oil seal

1 Firmly apply the handbrake, and then jack up the front of the vehicle and support it securely on axle stands (see *Jacking and vehicle support*). Remove the appropriate front roadwheel.

2 Drain the transmission oil as described in Section 2.

3 Working as described in Chapter 8, Section 2, free the inner end of the driveshaft from the transmission, and place it clear of the seal, noting that there is no need to completely remove the driveshaft; the driveshaft can be left secured to the hub. Support the driveshaft, to avoid placing any strain on the driveshaft joints or gaiters.

4 Before removing the seal, use a vernier gauge to check the seal depth in the transmission casing **(see illustration)**. This will give you the position of the seal in the transmission casing for refitting, see following measurements:

a) On 5-speed (RS5F92R) transmissions:
b) Left-hand side seal should be 5.7 to 6.3 mm
c) Right-hand side seal should be 2.4 to 3.0 mm
d) On 6-speed (RS6F94R) transmissions:
e) Left-hand side seal should be 1.2 to 1.8 mm
f) Right-hand side seal should be 2.7 to 3.3 mm

5 Carefully prise the oil seal out of the transmission using a large flat-bladed screwdriver **(see illustration)**. Take care not to damage the transmission casing as the seal is removed.

6 Remove all traces of dirt from the area around the oil seal aperture, then apply a smear of oil to the lip of the new oil seal, and locate it in its aperture **(see illustration)**.

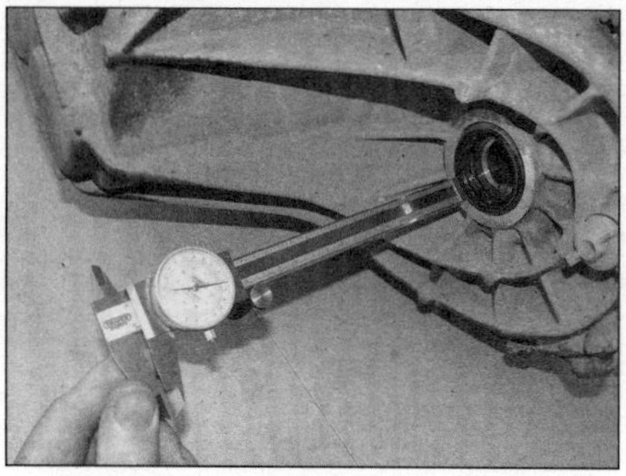

4.4 Using a vernier gauge to measure the seal depth

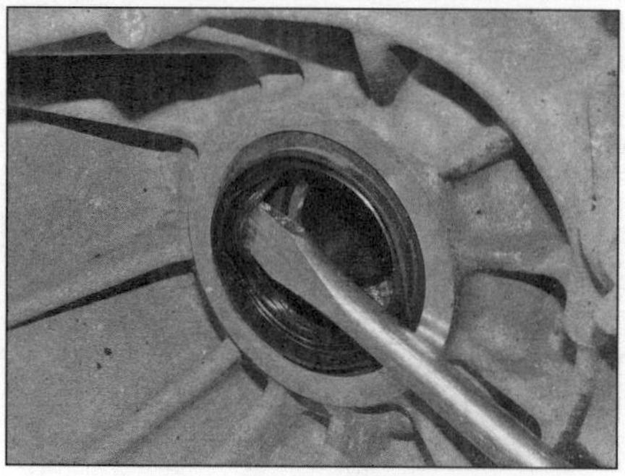

4.5 Use a large flat-bladed screwdriver to prise out the driveshaft oil seals

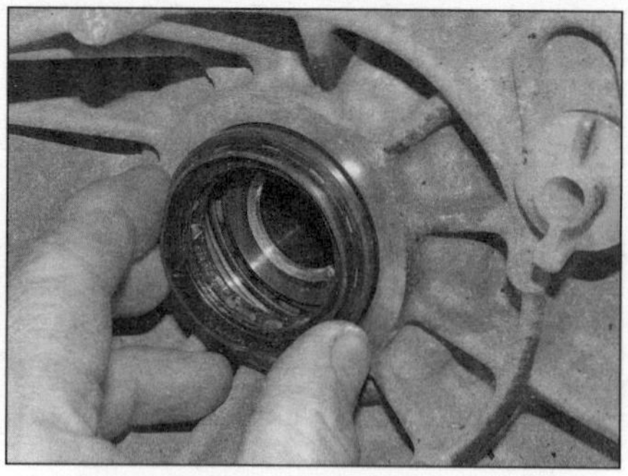

4.6 Fit the new seal squarely to the transmission...

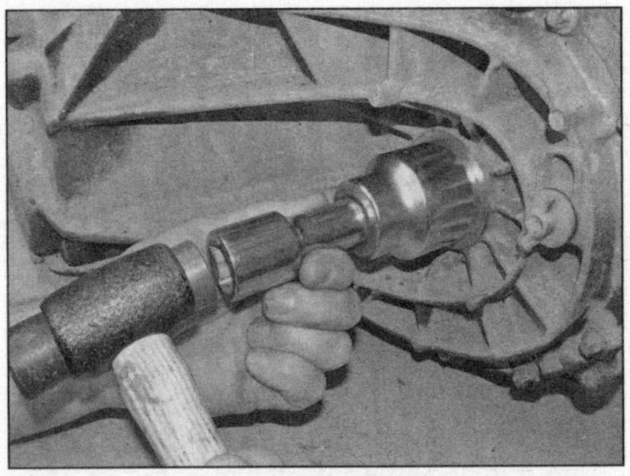

4.7 …and tap it into position using a tubular drift/socket

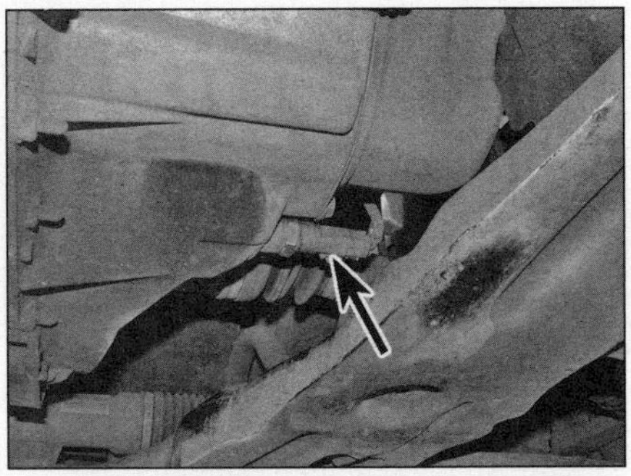

5.1a Location of reversing light switch (5-speed transmissions)

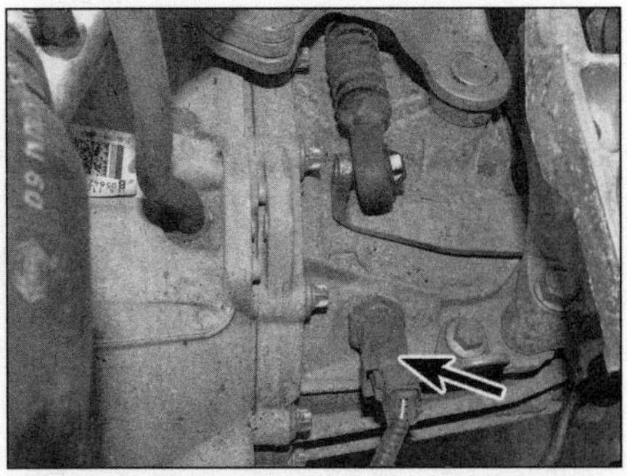

5.1b Location of reversing light switch (6-speed transmissions)

7 Drive the seal squarely into position, using a suitable tubular drift (such as a socket), which bears only on the hard outer edge of the seal **(see illustration)**. Drive the seal into position until it is at the depth specified in paragraph 4.

8 Refit the driveshaft as described in Chapter 8, Section 2.

9 Refill the transmission with the specified quantity of oil, as described in Section 2. Refer to *Lubricants, fluids and tyre pressures* for the specified type of oil to be used.

Input shaft oil seal

10 To renew the input shaft seal, the transmission must be dismantled. This task should therefore be entrusted to a Nissan dealer or transmission specialist.

5 Reversing light switch – testing, removal and refitting

Testing

1 The reversing light circuit is controlled by a plunger-type switch that is:

a) Screwed into the base of the transmission housing on its left-hand side on 5-speed transmissions **(see illustration)**.

b) Screwed into the front of the transmission housing on 6-speed transmissions **(see illustration)**.

2 If a fault develops in the circuit, first ensure that the circuit fuse has not blown (see Chapter 12, Section 3).

3 To test the switch, disconnect the wiring connector, and use a multi-meter (set to the resistance function) or a battery-and-bulb test circuit to check that there is continuity between the switch terminals only when reverse gear is selected. If this is not the case, and there are no obvious breaks or other damage to the wires, the switch is faulty and must be renewed.

5.6 Disconnect the switch wiring connector

Removal

5-speed transmissions

4 Firmly apply the handbrake, and then jack up the front of the vehicle and support it securely on axle stands (see *Jacking and vehicle support*).

5 Drain the transmission oil as described in Section 2.

6 Disconnect the wiring connector from the reversing light switch **(see illustration)**.

7 Unscrew the switch from the transmission, and remove it.

6-speed transmissions

8 Remove the air cleaner assembly as described in Chapter 4A, Section 2 or Chapter 4B, Section 2.

9 Remove the battery and battery tray as described in Chapter 5A, Section 3.

10 Disconnect the wiring connector from the reversing light switch **(see illustration 5.6)**.

11 Unscrew the switch from the transmission, and remove it.

Refitting

12 Apply suitable sealant to the switch threads, and then screw it back into the transmission housing.

6.0 Label with transmission model code

13 Tighten the switch to the specified torque, then reconnect the wiring connector and check the operation of the circuit.

14 Where applicable lower the vehicle to the ground, and top-up/refill the transmission oil (as applicable) as described in Section 2.

6 Manual transmission – removal and refitting

Note: *This Section describes the removal of the transmission leaving the engine in position in the car. Alternatively the engine and transmission can be removed together, as described in Chapter 2D, Section 3, and then separated on the bench.*

Note: *The manufacturer recommends that the clutch slave cylinder (concentric slave cylinder) is renewed whenever the transmission is removed because dust on the transmission input shaft may damage the fluid seal causing fluid leakage.*

Note: *Transmission model code number is on a label on the top of the transmission housing* ***(see illustration)****; see specifications at the beginning of this Chapter.*

Removal

1 Firmly apply the handbrake, and then jack up the front of the vehicle and support it securely on axle stands (see *Jacking and vehicle support*). Remove both front roadwheels. Remove the front wheel arch liner on the left-hand side as described in Chapter 11, Section 21.

2 Drain the transmission oil as described in Section 2, then refit the drain and filler/level plugs and tighten them to their specified torque settings.

3 Remove the battery and battery tray as described in Chapter 5A, Section 3.

4 Remove the air cleaner assembly as described in Chapter 4A, Section 2 or Chapter 4B, Section 2.

5 Remove the starter motor as described in Chapter 5A, Section 8.

6 Remove the exhaust system front pipe as described in Chapter 4A, Section 16 or Chapter 4B, Section 17.

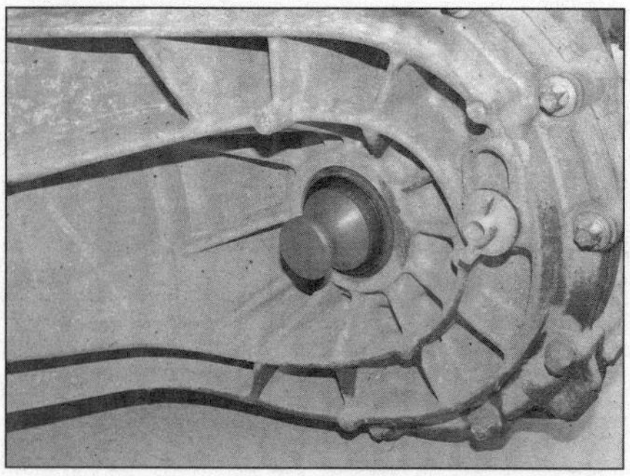
6.9 Using a dummy shaft in the differential

6.10 Undo the earth cable retaining bolt

7 Release the gearchange cables from the transmission as described in Section 3.

8 Remove the front suspension subframe as described in Chapter 10, Section 7.

9 Working as described in Chapter 8, Section 2, remove the two front driveshafts from the transmission. Note that there is no need to unscrew the driveshaft retaining nuts – each driveshaft can be left secured to the hub. But take care and support the driveshafts, to avoid placing any strain on the driveshaft joints or gaiters. With the driveshafts out of the transmission, insert a dummy shaft into differential recess **(see illustration)**.

10 Undo the retaining bolt and disconnect the earth cable from the left-hand end of the transmission **(see illustration)**.

11 Disconnect the wiring connector from the reversing light switch, see Section 5 for reversing light switch location.

12 Remove the crankshaft position sensor as described in Chapter 4A, Section 10 or Chapter 4B, Section 8.

13 Be prepared for some fluid loss as the pipe is disconnected, place some cloth around the fitting. Depress the retaining spring clip and disconnect the clutch fluid hose from the slave cylinder connector pipe **(see illustrations)**. Plug the ends of the slave cylinder pipe and clutch fluid hose to prevent fluid leakage and dirt ingress.

14 Work around the transmission and free the wiring loom from any relevant retaining clips **(see illustrations)**, and position the wiring clear of the transmission.

15 Make sure the breather pipe on top of the transmission housing is not secured to any other components. This does not have to be completely removed and left across the top of the transmission.

16 Remove the rear engine mounting bracket and torque link arm as described in Chapter 2A, 2B or 2C.

17 Place a jack with interposed block of wood beneath the engine, to take the weight of the engine. Alternatively, attach a hoist or support bar to the engine and take the weight of the engine.

18 Also place a jack and block of wood beneath the transmission, and raise the jack to take the weight of the transmission.

19 Slacken and remove the nut from the centre stud on the left-hand engine/transmission mounting. Undo the two bolts securing the mounting to the bracket, and remove the rubber mounting **(see illustration)**. For further information on engine/transmission mounting removal, see Chapter 2A, 2B or 2C.

20 Unclip the clutch fluid pipe from the clip on the mounting bracket, and then undo the retaining bolts and remove the mounting bracket from the top of the transmission **(see illustration)**.

21 With the jack positioned beneath the transmission taking the weight, slacken and remove the remaining bolts securing

6.13a Release the locking clip...

6.13b ...and disconnect the clutch fluid hose

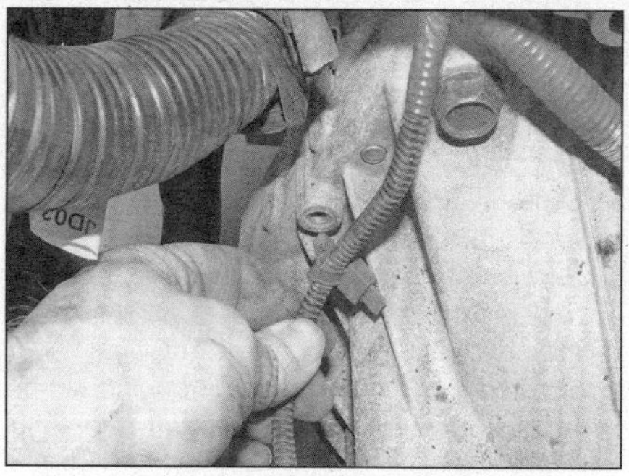
6.14a Release the wiring loom...

6.14b ...retaining clips from the transmission

6.19 Remove the transmission mounting

6.20 Undo the mounting bracket retaining bolts

the transmission housing to the engine **(see illustrations)**. Note the correct fitted positions of each bolt (and the relevant brackets) as they are removed, to use as a reference on refitting – the bolts are of different lengths. Note that it may be necessary to raise the transmission slightly to gain access to the lower bolts.

22 Make a final check that all necessary components have been disconnected, and are positioned clear of the transmission so that they will not hinder the removal procedure.

23 Move the trolley jack and transmission to the left to free it from its locating dowels. Keep the transmission fully supported until the input shaft is free of the engine.

24 Once the transmission is free, lower the jack and manoeuvre the unit out from under the car. If they are loose, remove the locating dowels from the transmission or engine, and keep them in a safe place.

Refitting

25 The transmission is refitted by a reversal of the removal procedure, bearing in mind the following points:

a) Renew the clutch concentric slave cylinder as described in Chapter 6, Section 6.
b) Apply a little high melting-point grease to the splines of the transmission input shaft. Do not apply too much; otherwise there is a possibility of the grease contaminating the clutch friction disc.
c) Ensure that the locating dowels are correctly positioned prior to installation.
d) Insert the transmission-to-engine bolts into their original locations, as noted on removal. Tighten all nuts and bolts to the specified torque (where given).
e) Refit the driveshafts as described in Chapter 8, Section 2. If required renew the driveshaft oil seals using the information given in Section 4.
f) Refit the front suspension subframe as described in Chapter 10, Section 7.
g) Bleed the clutch system as described in Chapter 6, Section 2.
h) Refit the gearchange cables as described in Section 3, and check operation.
i) On completion, refill the transmission with the specified type and quantity of lubricant as described in Section 2.

6.21a Remove the upper mounting bolts...

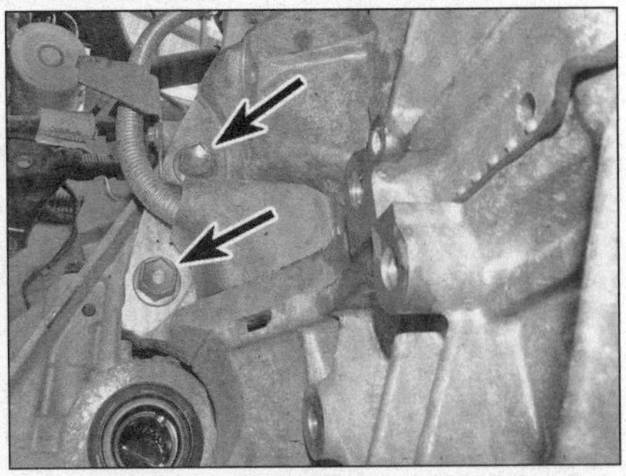

6.21b ...rear mounting bolts...

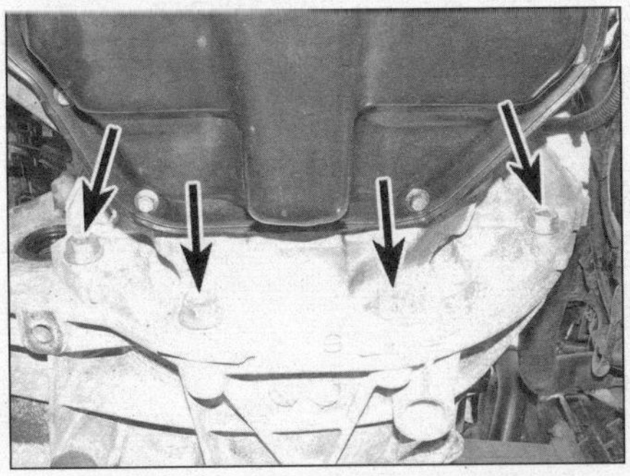

6.21c ...lower mounting bolts...

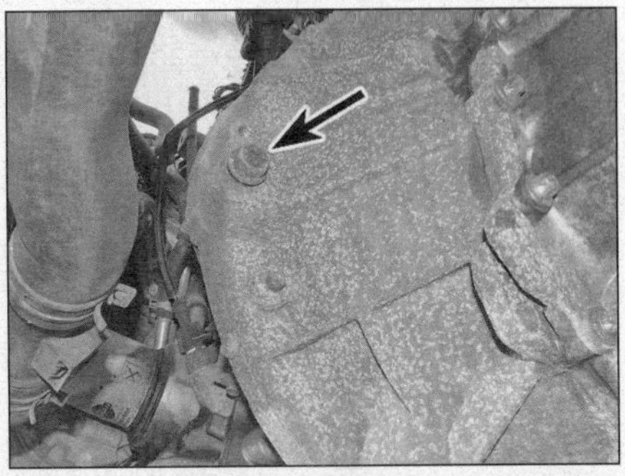

6.21d ...and front mounting bolt (6-speed transmission shown)

7 Manual transmission overhaul – general information

1 Overhauling a manual transmission is a difficult and involved job for the DIY home mechanic. In addition to dismantling and reassembling many small parts, clearances must be precisely measured and, if necessary, changed by selecting shims and spacers. Internal transmission components are also often difficult to obtain, and in many instances, extremely expensive. Because of this, if the transmission develops a fault or becomes noisy, the best course of action is to have the unit overhauled by a specialist repairer, or to obtain an exchange reconditioned unit.

2 Nevertheless, it is not impossible for the more experienced mechanic to overhaul the transmission, if the special tools are available, and the job is done in a deliberate step-by-step manner so that nothing is overlooked.

3 The tools necessary for an overhaul include internal and external circlip pliers, bearing pullers, a slide hammer, a set of pin punches, a dial test indicator, and possibly a hydraulic press. In addition, a large, sturdy workbench and a vice will be required.

4 During dismantling of the transmission, make careful notes of how each component is fitted, to make reassembly easier and accurate.

5 Before dismantling the transmission, it will help if you have some idea which area is malfunctioning. Certain problems can be closely related to specific areas in the transmission, which can make component examination and renewal easier. Refer to Fault finding in Chapter 13, Section 9 for more information.

Chapter 8
Driveshafts

Contents

Degrees of difficulty

Easy, suitable for novice with little experience	**Fairly easy,** suitable for beginner with some experience	**Fairly difficult,** suitable for competent DIY mechanic	**Difficult,** suitable for experienced DIY mechanic	**Very difficult,** suitable for expert DIY or professional

Specifications

General

Driveshaft type	Unequal length, solid steel shafts, splined to inner and outer constant velocity joints

Overhaul

Lubricant type	Nissan grease supplied with gaiter repair kit
Lubricant quantity:	
1.2 litre petrol models:	
Wheel end	110 to 130g
Transmission end	126 to 136g
1.6 litre petrol models:	
Wheel end	115 to 135g
Transmission end	114 to 124g
Diesel models:	
Wheel end	110 to 130g
Transmission end	123 to 139g

Torque wrench settings	Nm	lbf ft
Anti-roll bar drop link nut	81	60
Driveshaft retaining nut*	185	137
Lower balljoint clamp bolt nut*	55	41
Right-hand driveshaft retaining plate bolts	25	18
Right-hand driveshaft support bearing bolts	44	32
Roadwheel nuts	112	83
Track rod end-to-hub carrier nut*	34	25

**Use a new nut*

1 General Information

1 Drive is transmitted from the differential to the front wheels by means of two solid steel driveshafts of unequal length.

2 Both driveshafts are splined at their outer ends, to accept the wheel hubs, and are threaded so that each hub can be fastened to the driveshaft by a large nut and locked in position with a split pin. The inner end of each driveshaft is splined, to accept the differential sun gear.

3 Constant velocity (CV) joints are fitted to each end of the driveshafts, to ensure the smooth and efficient transmission of power at all suspension and steering angles. The outer constant velocity joints are of the ball-and-cage type, and the inner joints are of the tripod type.

2 Driveshafts – removal and refitting

Removal

1 Firmly apply the handbrake, and then jack up the front of the vehicle and support it securely on axle stands (see *Jacking and vehicle support*). Remove the appropriate roadwheel(s).

2.3 Remove the split pin

2.4 Using a fabricated tool to hold the hub stationary whilst the driveshaft nut is slackened

2.6 Undo the track rod end retaining nut

2.7 Disconnect the anti-roll bar drop link

2 To reduce spillage when the inner end of the driveshaft is withdrawn from the transmission, drain the transmission oil as described in Chapter 7, Section 2.

3 Remove the split-pin and nut retainer from the outer end of the driveshaft, discard the split-pin - a new one must be used on refitting **(see illustration)**.

4 The front hub must now be held stationary in order to loosen the driveshaft nut. Ideally, the hub should be held by a suitable tool bolted into place using two of the roadwheel nuts **(see illustration)**. Alternatively, have an assistant firmly apply the brake pedal to prevent the hub from rotating.

5 Using a socket and extension bar, slacken and remove the driveshaft retaining nut. Note that a new nut will be required for refitting.

6 Undo the retaining nut and disconnect the track rod end from the hub carrier **(see illustration)**. Refer to Chapter 10, Section 17 for further information.

7 Undo the retaining nut and disconnect the anti-roll bar drop link from the suspension strut **(see illustration)**. Refer to Chapter 10, Section 6, for further information.

8 Undo the retaining nut and withdraw the clamp bolt from the lower arm balljoint. Note that a new nut will be required for refitting **(see illustrations)**.

9 If necessary, use a chisel or screwdriver as a wedge to expand the lower portion of the swivel hub.

10 Push down on the lower arm to free the balljoint from the hub carrier **(see illustration)**, then move the hub carrier to one side and release the balljoint, taking care not to damage the balljoint rubber boot.

11 If the shaft is a tight fit in the splines in the hub, temporarily refit the driveshaft nut to the end of the driveshaft, to prevent damage to the driveshaft threads. Using a soft-faced mallet, carefully tap the driveshaft to free it from the hub carrier. If required, a suitable puller can be used to force the end of the shaft from the hub.

12 Once the driveshaft is free, remove the driveshaft nut, pull the hub carrier outwards, and fully withdraw the outer end of the

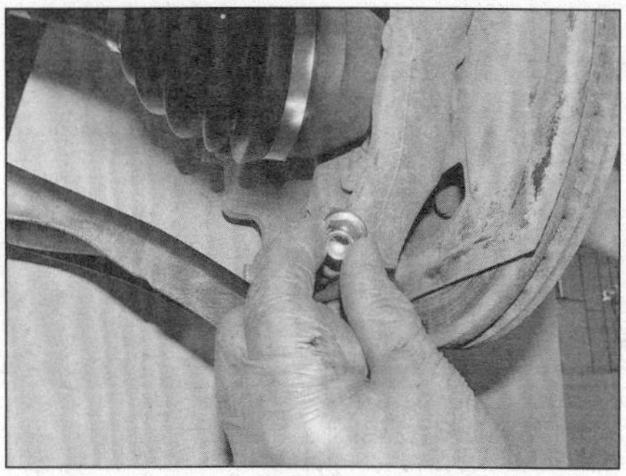

2.8a Undo the lower arm balljoint clamp bolt nut...

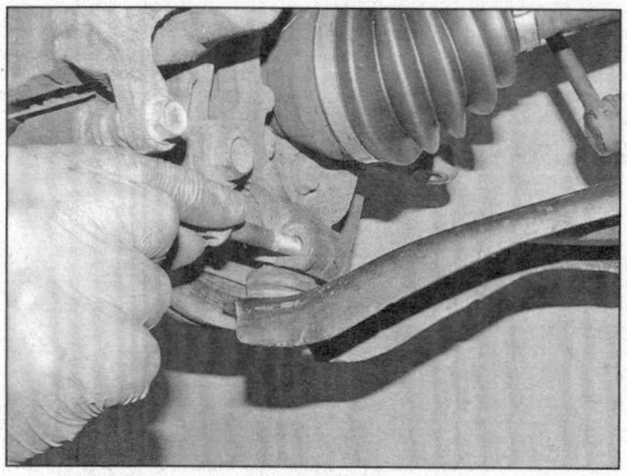

2.8b ...and remove the clamp bolt

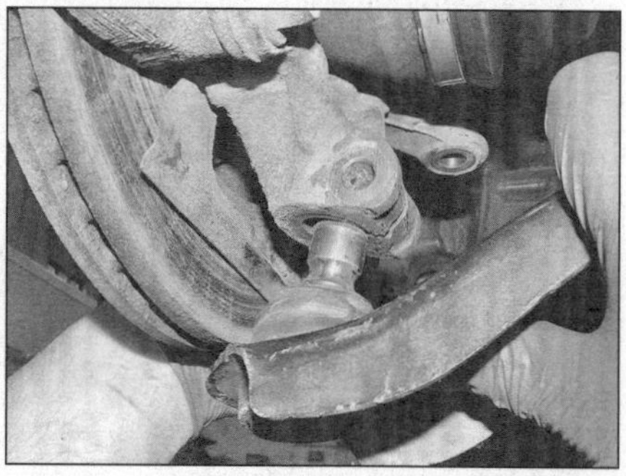

2.10 Push down on the lower arm to free the balljoint from the hub carrier

2.12 Withdraw the driveshaft from the hub

2.15a Lever the driveshaft to release the circlip...

2.15b ...and remove the driveshaft from the transmission

driveshaft from the hub **(see illustration)**. Take care not to strain the ABS wheel speed sensor wiring during this operation – if necessary, unscrew the bolt securing the sensor to the hub carrier, withdraw the sensor and position it clear of the work area.

13 Proceed as follows, according to the side being worked on.

Left-hand driveshaft

14 If the transmission oil has not been drained (see paragraph 2), have a clean container ready to catch the transmission oil/fluid as the driveshaft is withdrawn.

15 The driveshaft is held into the transmission by a spring circlip, which can take some effort to release. Using a suitable lever, on the shoulder of the driveshaft inner joint, prise it out from the transmission, and then remove the driveshaft **(see illustrations)**.

16 When the shaft is removed, insert a dummy shaft into the transmission **(see illustration)**.

Right-hand driveshaft

Note: *The following procedure is applicable to 1.2 litre petrol models and diesel models which have a driveshaft support bearing bolted to the rear of the cylinder block. On 1.6 litre petrol models, the procedure for the right-hand driveshaft is the same as the left-hand driveshaft.*

17 If the transmission oil has not been drained (see paragraph 2), have a clean container ready to catch the transmission oil/fluid as the driveshaft is withdrawn.

18 There is a support bearing, which is bolted to the rear of the sump. Undo the two bolts and remove the retaining plate from the bearing housing **(see illustrations)**. Note its fitted position for refitting, as there is a cut away in the retaining plate. Nissan recommends that this retaining plate be renewed each time it is removed.

19 Using a suitable drift, on the shoulder of the driveshaft inner joint, carefully tap it out from the transmission, and then remove the driveshaft.

20 If the bearing is a tight fit in the housing, undo the retaining bolts and remove the bearing housing from the rear of the sump, and remove the driveshaft complete with bearing housing from under the vehicle.

21 When the shaft is removed, insert a dummy shaft into the transmission **(see illustration 2.16)**.

Refitting

22 Where fitted, remove the dummy shaft from the transmission.

23 Before installing a driveshaft, examine the driveshaft oil seal in the transmission for signs of damage or deterioration and, if necessary, renew it, referring to Chapter 7, Section 4 for further information (it is advisable to renew the seal as a matter of course).

24 Thoroughly clean the driveshaft splines, and the apertures in the transmission and hub assembly. Apply a thin film of grease to

2.16 Using a dummy shaft inside the differential

the oil seal lips, and to the driveshaft splines and shoulders. Check that all driveshaft gaiter clips are securely fastened.

25 Note that the circlip at the inner end of the driveshaft must be renewed on refitting.

26 When refitting a driveshaft, great care must be taken to prevent damage to the driveshaft oil seals. Nissan specify the use of special tools, which guide the shafts through the seal lips on refitting. Provided that the seal lips and the shaft ends are lightly greased/oiled **(see illustration)**, and that care is taken on refitting, these tools should not be necessary.

27 Insert the inner end of the driveshaft into the transmission, taking care not to damage the oil seal.

28 If working on the left-hand driveshaft (and right-hand driveshaft on 1.6 litre petrol models), push the inner joint body firmly into

2.18a Undo the two retaining bolts...

2.18b ...and remove the retaining plate

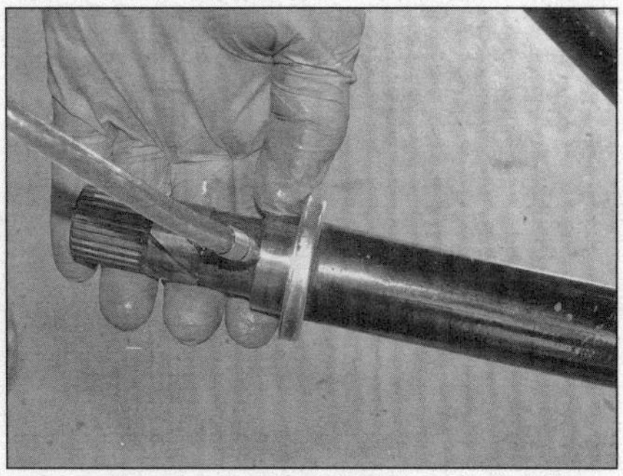

2.26 Apply a small amount of oil to the end of the driveshaft

2.37a Fit a new split-pin to the end of the driveshaft...

the transmission until the retaining circlip engages positively. Check that the circlip is correctly engaged by attempting to pull the inner joint from the transmission.

29 Apply a thin film of grease to the outer driveshaft joint splines, then engage the outer end of the driveshaft with the hub, ensuring that the splines engage correctly.

30 Fit the new driveshaft nut, but do not tighten the nut fully at this stage.

31 Lever the lower arm downward and reconnect the lower ball joint to the bottom of the hub carrier. Fit the clamp bolt and a new nut to the hub carrier and tighten to the specified torque setting.

32 On right-hand driveshafts secure the support bearing back into position, on the rear of the sump (if removed) and tighten the bolts to the specified torque setting. Make sure the retaining plate is positioned back into place on the housing, as noted on removal.

2.37b ...and bend over the split-pin legs

33 Reconnect the anti-roll bar drop link ball joint to the suspension strut and tighten the retaining nut. Refer to Chapter 10, Section 6 for further information.

34 Reconnect the track rod end to the hub carrier and tighten the new retaining nut. Refer to Chapter 10, Section 17 for further information.

35 If removed, refit the ABS wheel speed sensor and tighten its retaining bolt securely.

36 Hold the front hub stationary as during removal, then tighten the driveshaft nut to the specified torque. Locate the nut retainer over the nut, aligning one of the slots with the split pin hole in the driveshaft.

37 Fit a new split-pin and bend over the split-pin legs **(see illustrations)**.

38 Refit the roadwheel(s), and lower the vehicle to the ground.

39 Refill the transmission with oil as described in Chapter 7, Section 2.

3 Driveshaft rubber gaiters – renewal

Outer joint

1 Remove the driveshaft as described in Section 2.

2 Release the rubber gaiter retaining clips **(see illustrations)**. If required, cut through them using a junior hacksaw. Spread the clips and remove them from the gaiter.

3 Pull the gaiter back to expose the outer constant velocity joint then scoop out the excess grease **(see illustration)**.

4 If the original joint is to be re-used, make alignment marks between the joint and the driveshaft, so that it is refitted in the same position.

5 Using a brass drift and hammer, sharply strike the centre part of the outer joint to drive it off the end of the shaft **(see illustration)**. The joint is retained on the driveshaft by a circlip, and striking the joint in this manner forces the circlip into its groove, so allowing the joint to slide off.

6 Remove the circlip from the groove in the driveshaft splines, and discard it, then slide the old gaiter from the end of the shaft **(see illustrations)**. A new circlip must be fitted on reassembly.

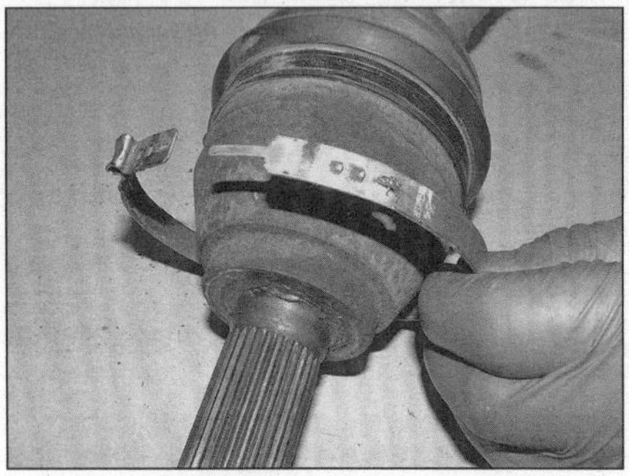

3.2a Remove the outer...

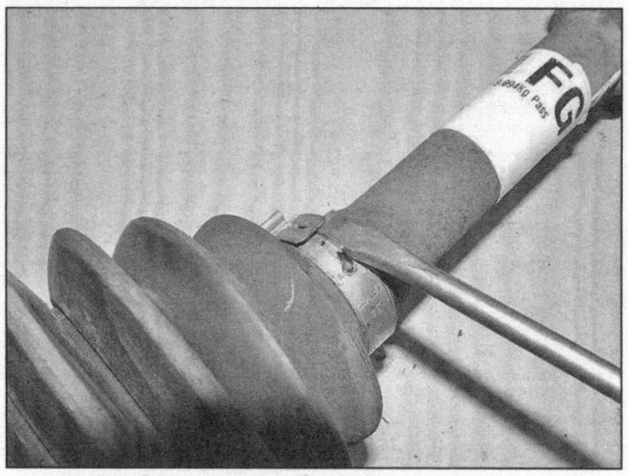

3.2b ...and inner retaining clips

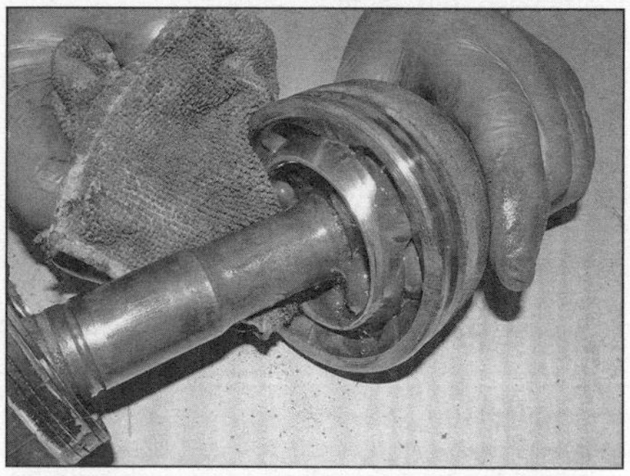

3.3 Pull back the gaiter and clean out the old grease

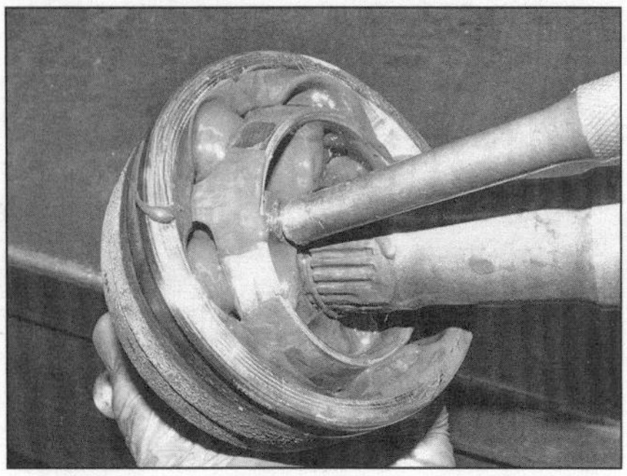

3.5 Using a soft metal drift to release the outer joint

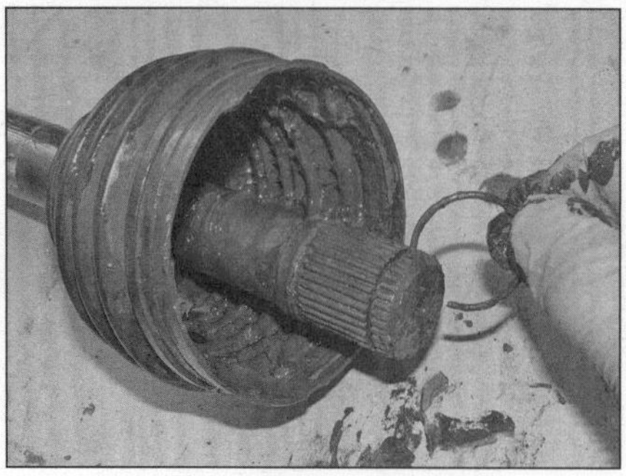

3.6a Remove the old circlip...

3.6b ...and slide the old gaiter off the shaft

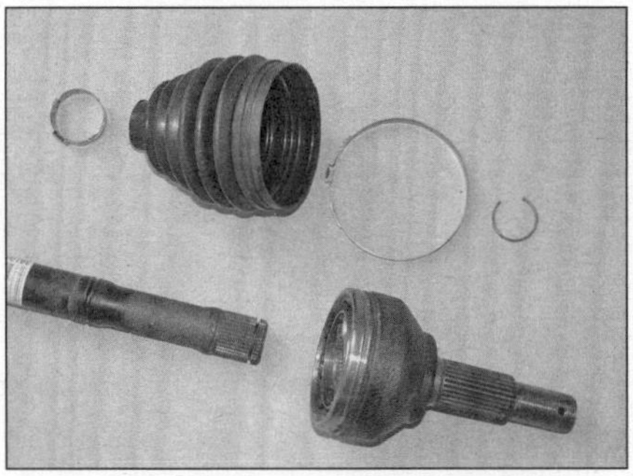

3.10 Driveshaft joint and gaiter kit

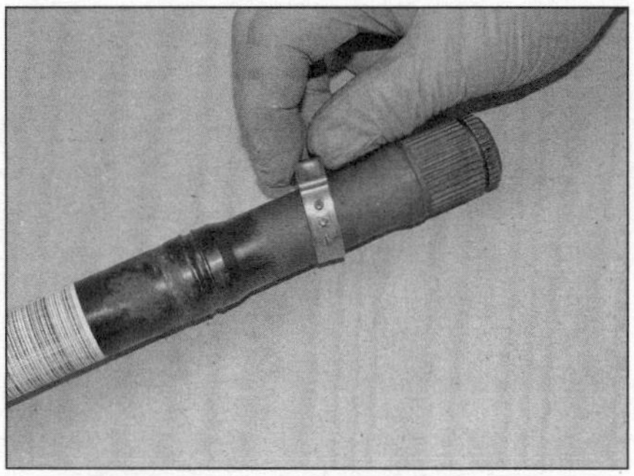

3.11a Fit the new inner retaining clip on the shaft...

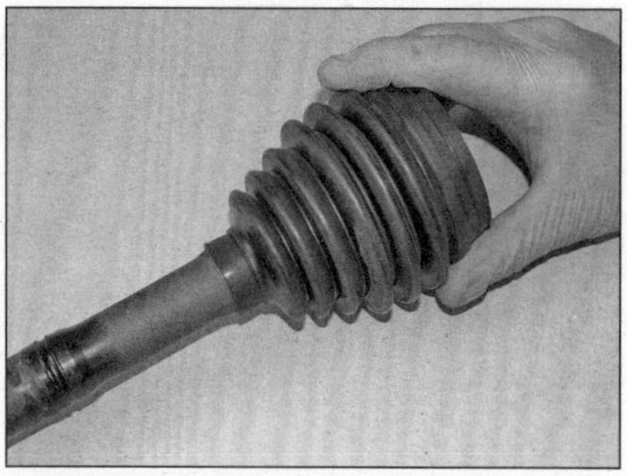

3.11b ...then slide the new gaiter onto the shaft

7 With the constant velocity joint removed from the driveshaft, thoroughly clean the joint using paraffin, or a suitable solvent, and dry it thoroughly. Carry out a visual inspection of the joint.

8 Move the inner splined driving member from side-to-side, to expose each ball in turn at the top of its track. Examine the balls for cracks, flat spots, or signs of surface pitting.

9 Inspect the ball tracks on the inner and outer members. If the tracks have widened, the balls will no longer be a tight fit. At the same time, check the ball cage windows for wear or cracking between the windows.

10 If any of the constant velocity joint components are found to be worn or damaged, it will be necessary to renew the complete joint assembly, as the internal parts are not available separately. If the joint is in satisfactory condition, obtain a repair kit consisting of a new gaiter, circlips, retaining clips **(see illustration)**, and use the correct type of grease.

11 Commence reassembly by sliding the smaller gaiter securing clip onto the driveshaft, followed by the gaiter **(see illustrations)**.

12 Fit a new joint retaining circlip to the groove in the end of the shaft **(see illustration)**.

13 Before fitting the outer joint, squeeze half of the grease supplied with the kit into the outer joint **(see illustration)**.

14 Fit the outer joint to the shaft, and engage it with the shaft splines **(see illustrations)**. If the original joint is re-used, align the previously made marks on the joint and the end of the driveshaft.

15 Take care not to damage the joint threaded end, and use a copper mallet to tap the joint onto the shaft until the circlip engages correctly behind the joint cage **(see illustration)**.

16 Use the remainder of the grease to pack the joint with the correct amount of the specified grease (supplied with the gaiter kit), then twist the joint to ensure that all the recesses are filled **(see illustration)**.

3.12 Fit the new circlip to its groove in the driveshaft splines

3.13 Squeeze half the grease supplied with the kit into the joint

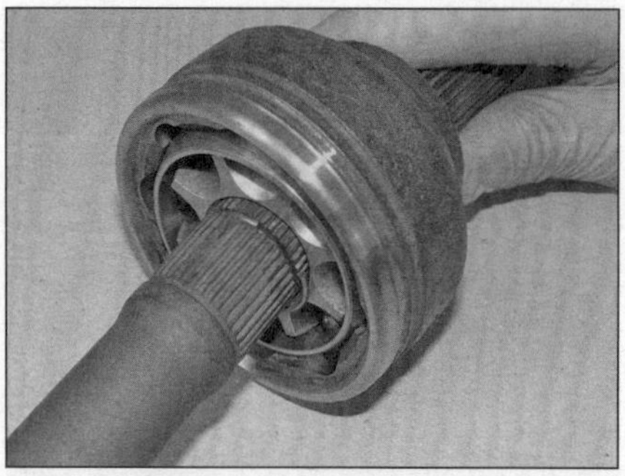

3.14a Locate the outer joint on the splines, and slide it into position...

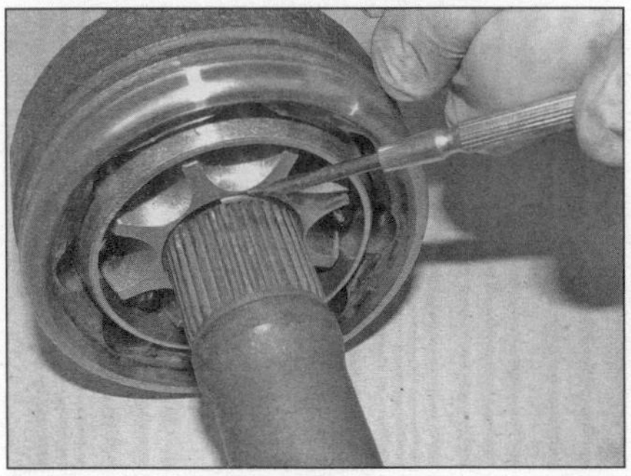

3.14b ...making sure the circlip is located correctly

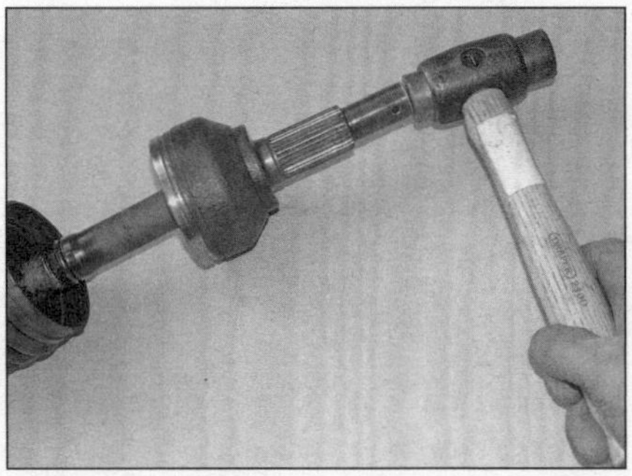

3.15 Tap the joint into place, check that the joint is secured by the circlip

3.16 Pack the joint with the remaining grease, working it into the ball tracks while twisting the joint

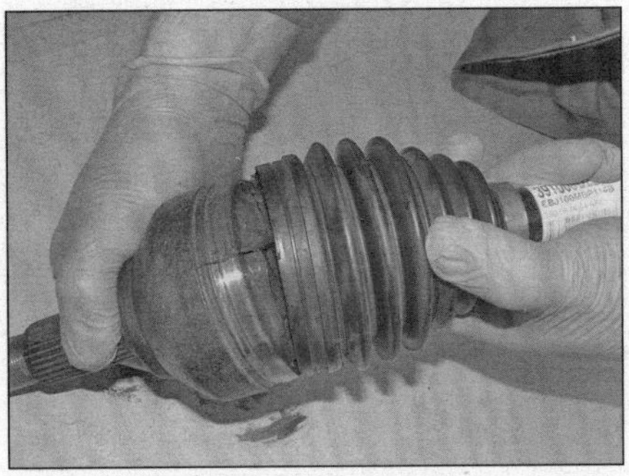

3.17 Slide the gaiter into position over the outer joint

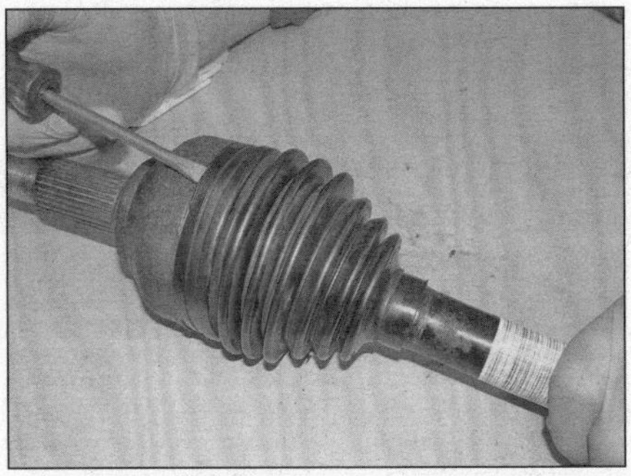

3.18 Using a screwdriver to displace the air inside the gaiter

3.19a Slide the inner retaining clip into position...

17 Check that the smaller end of the gaiter is located in the driveshaft groove, and then slide the gaiter onto the outer joint **(see illustration)**.

18 Check that the gaiter does not swell or deform when fitted. Use a screwdriver to get rid of the air inside the gaiter, and then position the gaiter in the groove in the outer joint **(see illustration)**.

19 Slide the smaller retaining clip over the gaiter, and secure it in place **(see illustrations)**.

20 Fit the new outer gaiter large retaining clip, and secure it in place **(see illustration)**.

21 Refit the driveshaft as described in Section 2.

Inner joint

22 Remove the driveshaft as described in Section 2.

23 Remove the outer CV joint and gaiter as described previously in this Section.

24 On driveshafts equipped with one or two harmonic dampers, accurately mark their installed position on the driveshaft as an aid to reassembly. Release the damper retaining clips and slide the damper(s) off the end of the driveshaft **(see illustrations)**. Note that new damper retaining clips will be required for reassembly.

25 Release the rubber gaiter retaining clips. If required, cut through them using a junior hacksaw. Slide the gaiter off the inner joint towards the outer joint end of the driveshaft **(see illustration)**.

26 Thoroughly clean the constant velocity joint components using paraffin, or a suitable solvent, and dry thoroughly. Carry out a visual inspection of the joint. If any of the joint components are worn, a new driveshaft will be required. The tripod joint assembly, driveshaft and the joint body cannot be separated and are not individually available. If the joint is in satisfactory condition, obtain a repair kit consisting of a new gaiter, retaining clips, and the correct type of grease. Where applicable, new harmonic damper retaining clips will also be required.

27 Commence reassembly by sliding the new gaiter onto the driveshaft **(see illustration)**.

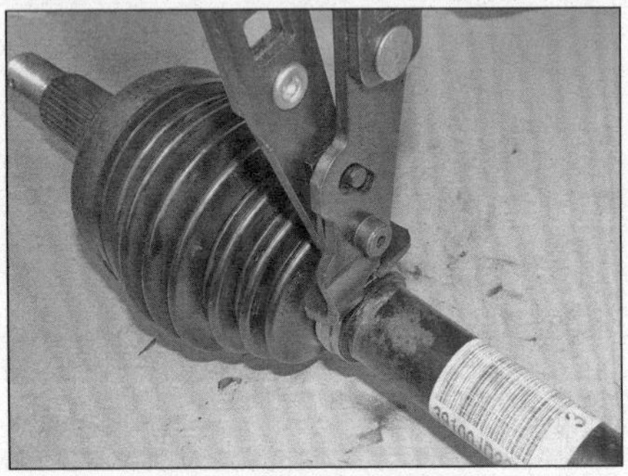

3.19b ...and secure the clip with crimping pliers

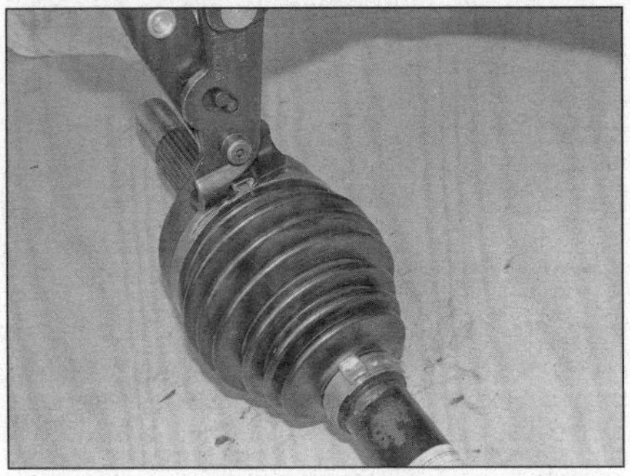

3.20 Secure the outer retaining clip with crimping pliers

3.24a Release the harmonic damper retaining clips...

3.24b ...and slide the damper off the end of the driveshaft

3.25 Release the retaining clips and slide the gaiter off the driveshaft

3.27 Slide the new gaiter onto the driveshaft

3.28 Pack the joint with grease, working it into the joint while twisting the shaft

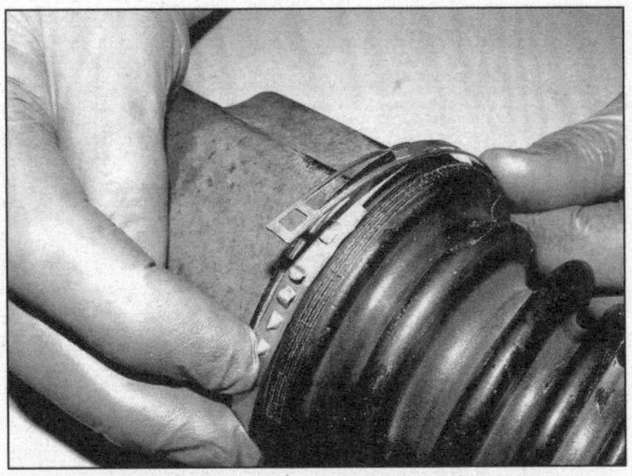

3.31a Slide the retaining clips into position...

3.31b ...and secure them into position

28 Pack the joint with the correct amount of the specified grease (supplied with the gaiter kit), and then twist the joint to ensure that all the recesses are filled **(see illustration)**.

29 Check that the smaller end of the gaiter is located in the driveshaft groove, and then slide the gaiter onto the outer body.

30 Check that the gaiter does not swell or deform when fitted. Use a screwdriver to get rid of the air inside the gaiter, then locate the larger end of the gaiter in the groove in the outer body.

31 Fit the new gaiter large securing clip, and tighten it in place **(see illustrations)**.

32 Locate the smaller gaiter securing clip on the end of the gaiter, and secure it as described previously **(see illustration)**.

33 Where applicable, slide the harmonic damper(s) and new retaining clips back onto the driveshaft and into the position noted during removal. Secure the retaining clips with crimping pliers.

34 Refit the outer CV joint and gaiter as described previously in this Section.

35 Refit the driveshaft as described in Section 2.

4 Driveshaft – inspection and overhaul

1 If any of the checks described in Chapter 1A, Section 14 or Chapter 1B, Section 14 reveal wear in any driveshaft joint, first remove the roadwheel trim or centre cap (as appropriate).

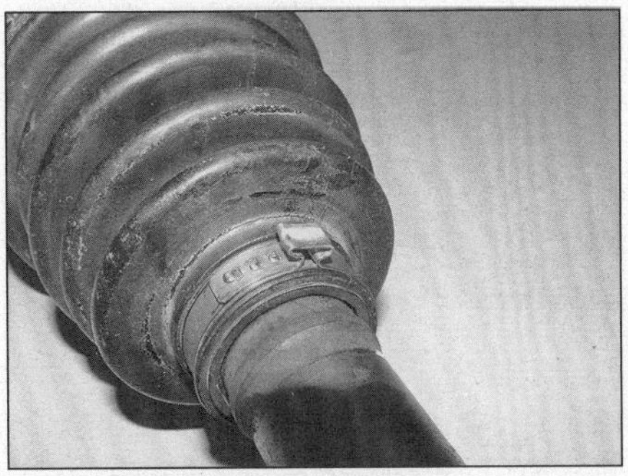

3.32 Make sure the gaiter clips are secure

4.7 Using a press to remove the bearing housing

2 Check that the driveshaft nut is correctly tightened; if in doubt, remove the split-pin. Check that the nut is tightened to the specified torque, and then refit a new split-pin. Refit the roadwheel trim or centre cap (as applicable), and repeat the check on the remaining driveshaft nut.

3 Road test the vehicle, and listen for a metallic clicking from the front as the vehicle is driven slowly in a circle on full-lock. If a clicking noise is heard, this indicates wear in the outer constant velocity joint.

4 If vibration, consistent with roadspeed, is felt through the car when accelerating, there is a possibility of wear in the inner constant velocity joints.

5 To check the joints for wear, remove the driveshafts, then dismantle them as described in Section 3. If any wear or free play is found, the relevant joint, or joint components must be renewed. Note that the inner constant velocity joints are not available separately and if worn, a new driveshaft(s) will be required.

Right-hand front driveshaft bearing

6 Remove the right-hand front driveshaft as described in Section 2.

7 If the bearing housing was removed with the driveshaft, the shaft will need to be carefully pressed from the housing **(see illustration)**.

8 Note the fitted position of the metal dust cap, and then remove it from the inner end of the driveshaft **(see illustration)**.

9 Remove the metal shield from the bearing, and then using circlip pliers, remove the circlip from the driveshaft **(see illustrations)**.

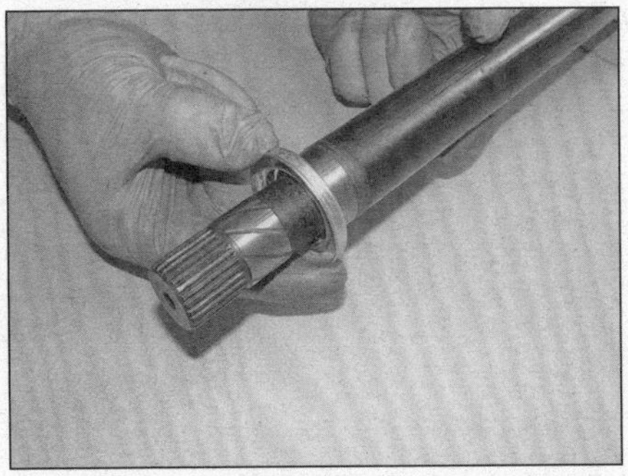

4.8 Remove the dust cap, noting its fitted position

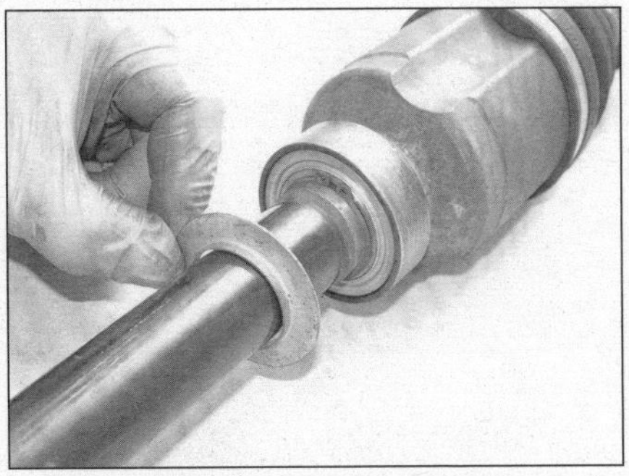

4.9a Remove the metal shield...

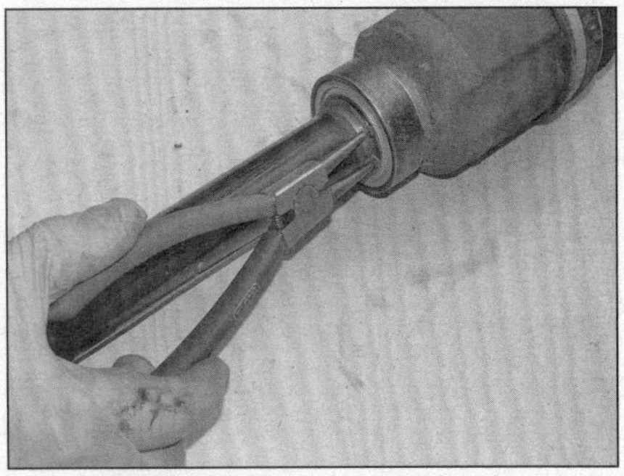

4.9b ...then remove the circlip

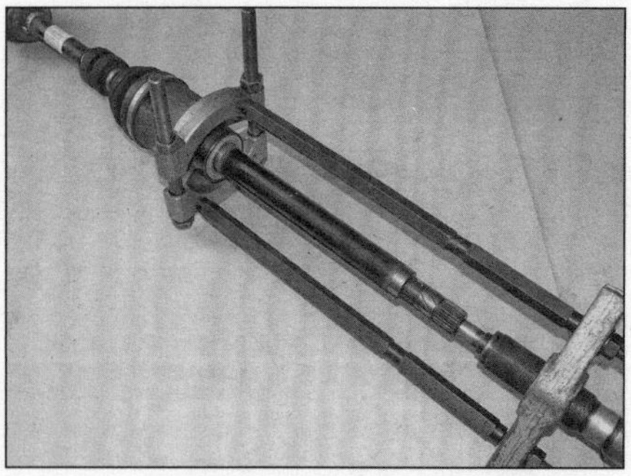

4.10 Using a long puller to remove the bearing from the shaft

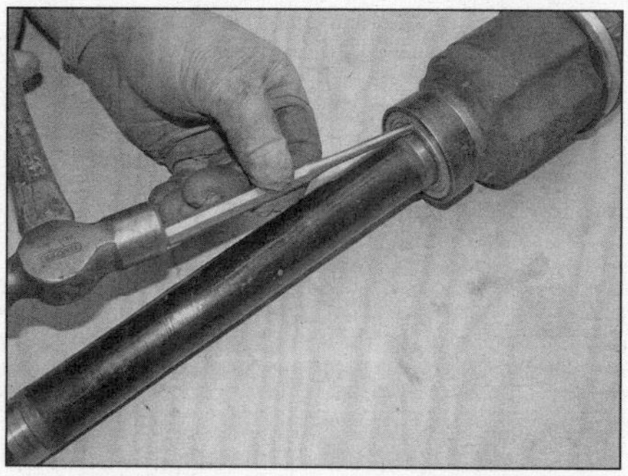

4.11 Carefully tap the new bearing back on the shaft

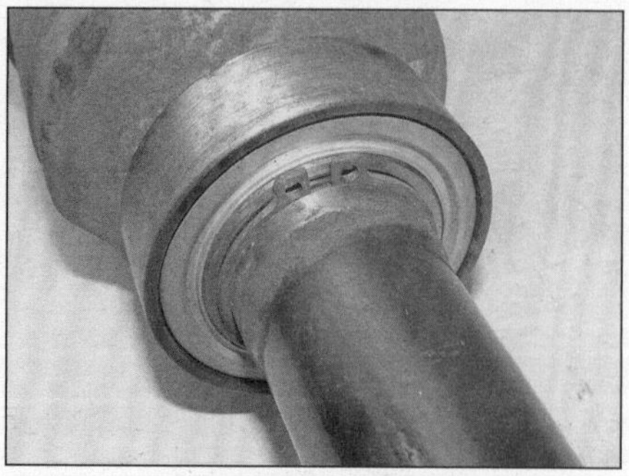

4.12 Fit a new circlip to secure the bearing

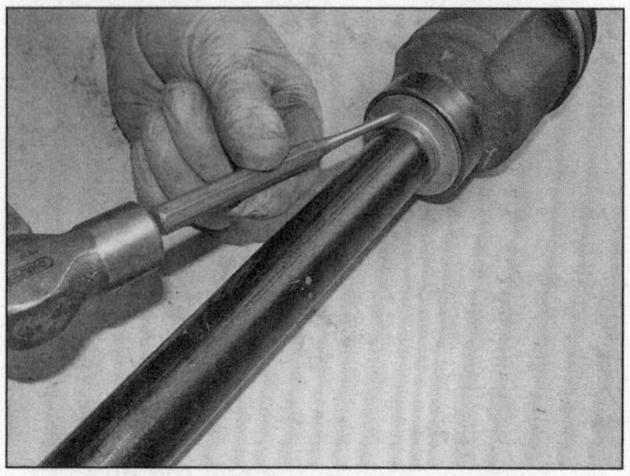

4.13 Refit the bearing shield

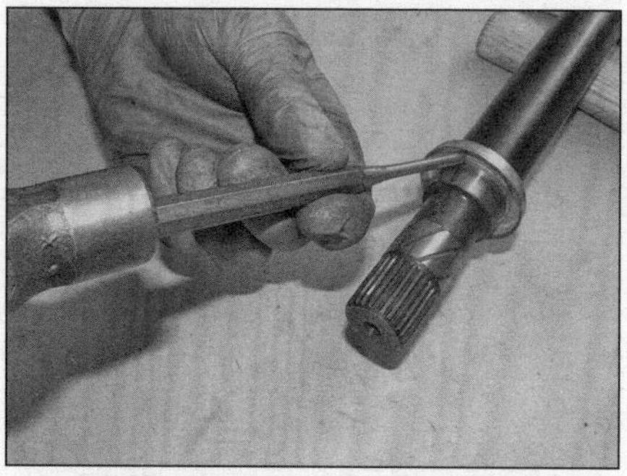

4.14 Refit the dust cap to the position noted on removal

10 Using a long puller withdraw the bearing from the driveshaft **(see illustration).**

11 Fit the new bearing onto the driveshaft and carefully tap it into position on the shaft **(see illustration).**

12 Fit the new circlip making sure it is located in the groove in the shaft **(see illustration).**

13 Fit the new metal shield onto the driveshaft and carefully tap it into position on the shaft **(see illustration).**

14 Fit the new metal dust cap onto the driveshaft and carefully tap it into the position noted on removal **(see illustration).**

15 Where applicable bolt the bearing housing to the rear of the cylinder block, then refit the driveshaft as described in Section 2.

Chapter 9
Braking system

Contents

Degrees of difficulty

Easy, suitable for novice with little experience	**Fairly easy,** suitable for beginner with some experience	**Fairly difficult,** suitable for competent DIY mechanic	**Difficult,** suitable for experienced DIY mechanic	**Very difficult,** suitable for expert DIY or professional

Specifications

General

System type	Dual hydraulic circuit with anti-lock braking system (ABS) fitted. Front ventilated disc brakes on all models. Solid rear disc brakes, with handbrake shoes in the centre of the disc/drum. Vacuum servo-assistance on all models. Cable-operated handbrake acting on rear wheels

Front brakes

Type	Ventilated disc, with single-piston sliding caliper
Disc diameter	280 mm
Standard thickness of brake disc	24.00 mm
Wear limit thickness of brake disc	22.00 mm
Maximum disc run-out	0.035 mm
Minimum pad friction material thickness	2.0 mm

Rear brakes

Type	Solid disc with single-piston sliding caliper
Disc diameter	292 mm
Rear brake disc:	
Standard thickness of brake disc	9.00 mm
Wear limit thickness of brake disc	8.00 mm
Maximum disc run-out	0.1 mm
Minimum pad friction material thickness	2.0 mm

Handbrake

Type	Drum (inside centre of disc), with leading and trailing shoes operated by cables
Drum/disc inner diameter:	
New	172 mm
Maximum inner diameter	173 mm
Maximum out-of-round	0.02 mm
Minimum shoe lining thickness	1.5 mm
Number of clicks (when handbrake fully applied)	9 to 10 clicks
Number of clicks (for warning light to be ON)	1 click

Brake pedal

Free height	160.4 to 170.4 mm	

Pedal switches

Clearance (between brake pedal and threaded end of switch)	0.74 to 1.96 mm	

Brake master cylinder

Cylinder bore diameter	23.8 mm	

Vacuum servo

Servo diameter	257.0 mm	
Input pushrod length	156.2 to 157.7 mm	

Torque wrench settings

Torque wrench settings	Nm	lbf ft
ABS wheel speed sensor securing bolts	10	7
Brake bleed screw	8	6
Brake fluid hose union banjo bolts	18	13
Brake servo/pedal bracket securing nuts	15	11
Front brake caliper guide pin bolts	26	19
Front brake caliper mounting bracket bolts	165	122
Handbrake lever mounting nuts	30	22
Master cylinder securing nuts	23	17
Rear brake caliper guide pin bolts	43	32
Rear brake caliper mounting bracket bolts	84	62
Vacuum pump bolts	20	15

1 General Information

1 The braking system is of the servo-assisted, dual-circuit hydraulic type. The arrangement of the hydraulic system is such that each circuit operates one front and one rear brake from a tandem master cylinder. Under normal circumstances, both circuits operate in unison. However, in the event of hydraulic failure in one circuit, full braking force will still be available at two diagonally opposite wheels.

2 All models are fitted with front and rear disc brakes. The front disc brakes are actuated by single-piston sliding type calipers, which ensure that equal pressure is applied to each disc pad. The rear disc brakes are also actuated by single-piston sliding type caliper, but have a separate drum brake arrangement in the centre of the brake disc to provide a separate means of handbrake application.

3 An Anti-lock Braking System (ABS) is fitted as standard equipment to all vehicles covered in this manual. On higher specification models, the ABS may also incorporate an electronic stability program and traction control. Refer to Section 20 for further information on ABS operation.

Warning: When servicing any part of the system, work carefully and methodically; also observe scrupulous cleanliness when overhauling any part of the hydraulic system. Always renew components (in axle sets, where applicable) if in doubt about their condition, and use only genuine Nissan parts, or at least those of known good quality. Note the warnings given in 'Safety first!' in Chapter 0, Section 3 and at relevant points in this Chapter concerning the dangers of asbestos dust and hydraulic fluid.

2 Hydraulic system – bleeding

Warning: Brake hydraulic fluid is poisonous; wash off immediately and thoroughly in the case of skin contact, and seek immediate medical advice if any fluid is swallowed, or gets into the eyes. Certain types of hydraulic fluid are inflammable, and may ignite when allowed into contact with hot components. When servicing any hydraulic system, it is safest to assume that the fluid IS inflammable, and to take precautions against the risk of fire as though it is petrol that is being handled. Hydraulic fluid is also an effective paint stripper, and will attack plastics; if any is spilt, it should be washed off immediately, using copious quantities of fresh water. Finally, it is hygroscopic (it absorbs moisture from the air) – old fluid may be contaminated and unfit for further use. When topping-up or renewing the fluid, always use the recommended type, and ensure that it comes from a freshly opened sealed container.

General

1 The correct operation of any hydraulic system is only possible after removing all air from the components and circuit; and this is achieved by bleeding the system.

2 During the bleeding procedure, add only clean, unused brake hydraulic fluid of the recommended type; never re-use fluid that has already been bled from the system. Ensure that sufficient fluid is available before starting work.

3 If there is any possibility of incorrect fluid being already in the system, the brake components and circuit must be flushed completely with uncontaminated, correct fluid, and new seals should be fitted throughout the system.

4 If hydraulic fluid has been lost from the system, or air has entered because of a leak, ensure that the fault is cured before proceeding further.

5 Park the vehicle on level ground, switch off the engine and select first or reverse gear, then chock the wheels and release the handbrake.

6 Check that all pipes and hoses are secure, unions tight and bleed screws closed. Remove the dust caps (where applicable), and clean any dirt from around the bleed screws.

7 Unscrew the master cylinder reservoir cap, and top the master cylinder reservoir up to the MAX level line; refit the cap loosely. Remember to maintain the fluid level at least above the MIN level line throughout the procedure; otherwise there is a risk of further air entering the system.

8 There are a number of one-man, do-it-yourself brake bleeding kits currently available from motor accessory shops. It is recommended that one of these kits is used whenever possible, as they greatly simplify the bleeding operation, and also reduce the risk of expelled air and fluid being drawn back into the system. If such a kit is not available, the basic (two-man) method must be used, which is described in detail below.

9 If a kit is to be used, prepare the vehicle as described previously, and follow the kit manufacturer's instructions, as the procedure may vary slightly according to the type being used; generally, they are as outlined below in the relevant sub-section.

10 Whichever method is used, the same sequence must be followed (paragraphs 11 and 12) to ensure that the removal of all air from the system.

Bleeding sequence

11 If the system has been only partially disconnected, and suitable precautions were taken to minimise fluid loss, it should be necessary to bleed only that part of the system (i.e. the primary or secondary circuit).

12 If the complete system is to be bled, then it should be done working in the following sequence:

a) Left-hand rear wheel.
b) Right-hand front wheel.
c) Right-hand rear wheel.
d) Left-hand front wheel.

Bleeding

Caution: Switch off the ignition and disconnect the battery negative terminal (refer to battery disconnection and reconnection in Chapter 5A, Section 3), before carrying out the bleeding procedure.

Basic (two-man) method

13 Collect a clean glass jar, a suitable length of plastic or rubber tubing which is a tight fit over the bleed screw, and a ring spanner to fit the screw. The help of an assistant will also be required.

14 Remove the dust cap from the first screw in the sequence. Fit a suitable spanner and tube to the screw, place the other end of the tube in the jar, and pour in sufficient fluid to cover the end of the tube **(see illustrations)**.

15 Ensure that the master cylinder reservoir fluid level is maintained at least above the MIN level line throughout the procedure.

16 Have the assistant fully depress the brake pedal several times to build-up pressure, and then maintain it on the final down stroke.

17 While pedal pressure is maintained, unscrew the bleed screw (approximately one turn) and allow the compressed fluid and air to flow into the jar. The assistant should maintain pedal pressure, following the pedal down to the floor if necessary, and should not release the pedal until instructed to do so. When the flow stops, tighten the bleed screw again, have the assistant release the pedal slowly, and recheck the reservoir fluid level.

18 Repeat the steps given in paragraphs 16 and 17 until the fluid emerging from the bleed screw is free from air bubbles. If the master cylinder has been drained and refilled, and air is being bled from the first screw in the sequence, allow approximately five seconds between cycles for the master cylinder passages to refill.

19 When no more air bubbles appear, tighten the bleed screw securely, remove the tube and spanner, and refit the dust cap. Do not over tighten the bleed screw.

20 Repeat the procedure on the remaining screws in the sequence, until all air is removed from the system, and the brake pedal feels firm again.

Using a one-way valve kit

21 As their name implies, these kits consist of a length of tubing with a one-way valve fitted, to prevent expelled air and fluid being drawn back into the system; some kits include a translucent container, which can be positioned so that the air bubbles can be more easily seen flowing from the end of the tube.

22 The kit is connected to the bleed screw, which is then opened. The user returns to the driver's seat, depresses the brake pedal with a smooth, steady stroke, and slowly releases it; this is repeated until the expelled fluid is clear of air bubbles.

23 Note that these kits simplify work so much that it is easy to forget the master cylinder reservoir fluid level; ensure that this is maintained at least above the MIN level line at all times.

Using a pressure-bleeding kit

24 These kits are usually operated by the reservoir of pressurised air contained in the spare tyre. However, note that it will probably be necessary to reduce the pressure to a lower level than normal; refer to the instructions supplied with the kit.

25 By connecting a pressurised, fluid-filled container to the master cylinder reservoir, bleeding can be carried out simply by opening each screw in turn (in the specified sequence), and allowing the fluid to flow out until no more air bubbles can be seen in the expelled fluid.

26 This method has the advantage that the large reservoir of fluid provides an additional safeguard against air being drawn into the system during bleeding.

27 Pressure-bleeding is particularly effective when bleeding 'difficult' systems, or when bleeding the complete system at the time of routine fluid renewal.

All methods

28 When bleeding is complete, and firm pedal feel is restored, wash off any spilt fluid, tighten the bleed screws securely, and refit their dust caps.

29 Check the hydraulic fluid level in the master cylinder reservoir, and top up if necessary.

30 Discard any hydraulic fluid that has been bled from the system; it will not be fit for re-use.

31 Check the feel of the brake pedal. If it feels at all spongy, air must still be present in the system, and further bleeding is required. Failure to bleed satisfactorily after a reasonable repetition of the bleeding procedure may be due to worn master cylinder seals.

3 Hydraulic pipes and hoses – renewal

Note: *Before starting work, refer to the note at the beginning of Section 2 concerning the dangers of hydraulic fluid.*

1 If any pipe or hose is to be renewed, minimise fluid loss by first removing the master cylinder reservoir cap, then tighten the cap down onto a piece of polythene to obtain an airtight seal. Alternatively, flexible hoses can be sealed, if required, using a proprietary brake hose clamp **(see illustration)** ; metal brake pipe unions can be plugged (if care is taken not to allow dirt into the system) or capped immediately they are disconnected. Place a wad of rag under any union that is to be disconnected, to catch any spilt fluid.

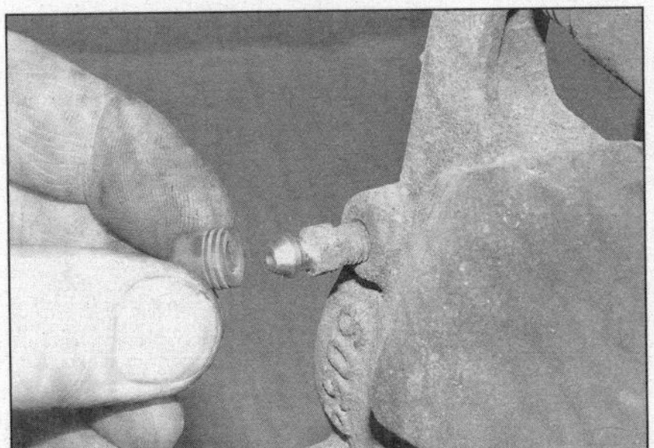

2.14a Remove the dust cap

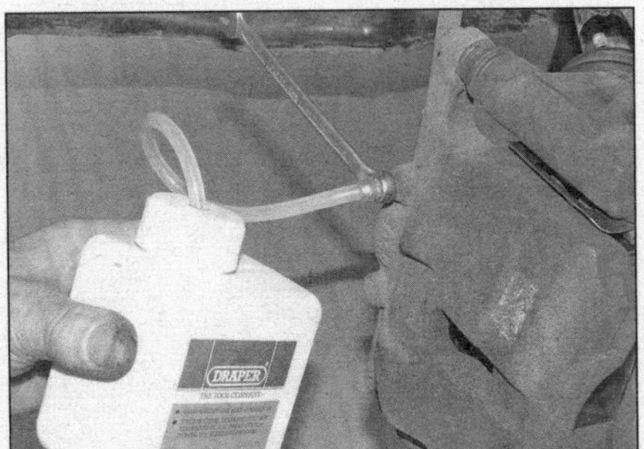

2.14b Connect the bleed kit to the bleed screw

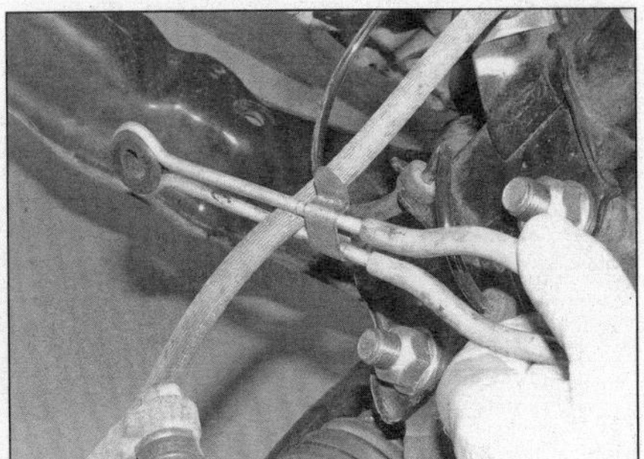

3.1 Using a brake hose clamp

3.2 Slacken the union nut and then remove the spring clip

3.6 Make sure the spring clips are secure

2 If a flexible hose is to be disconnected, unscrew the brake pipe union nut before removing the spring clip, which secures the hose to its mounting bracket **(see illustration)**.

3 To unscrew the union nuts, it is preferable to obtain a brake pipe spanner of the correct size; these are available from most large motor accessory shops. Failing this, a close-fitting open-ended spanner will be required, though if the nuts are tight or corroded their flats may be rounded-off if the spanner slips. In such a case, a self-locking wrench is often the only way to unscrew a stubborn union, but it follows that the pipe and the damaged nuts must be renewed on reassembly. Always clean a union and surrounding area before disconnecting it. If disconnecting a component with more than one union, make a careful note of the connections before disturbing any of them.

4 If a brake pipe is to be renewed, it can be obtained, cut to length and with the union nuts and end flares in place, from Nissan dealers. All that is then necessary is to bend it to shape, following the line of the original, before fitting it to the vehicle. Alternatively, most motor accessory shops can make up brake pipes from kits, but this requires very careful measurement of the original, to ensure that the new one is of the correct length. The safest answer is usually to take the original to the shop as a pattern.

5 On refitting, do not over tighten the union nuts. It is not necessary to exercise brute force to obtain a sound joint.

6 Ensure that the pipes and hoses are correctly routed, with no kinks, and that they are secured in the clips or brackets provided **(see illustration)**. After fitting, remove the polythene from the reservoir, and bleed the hydraulic system as described in Section 2. When completed, wash off any spilt fluid, and then check carefully for any fluid leaks.

4 Front brake pads – renewal

Warning: Renew BOTH sets of front brake pads at the same time – NEVER renew the pads on only one wheel, as uneven braking may result.

Warning: Note that the dust created by wear of the pads may contain asbestos, which is a health hazard. Never blow it out with compressed air, and don't inhale any of it. An approved filtering mask should be worn when working on the brakes. DO NOT use petrol or petroleum-based solvents to clean brake parts; use brake cleaner or methylated spirit only.

1 Firmly apply the handbrake, and then jack up the front of the vehicle and support it securely on axle stands (see *Jacking and vehicle support*). Remove the front roadwheels.

2 Working on one side of the vehicle, push the caliper piston into its bore by pulling the caliper outwards.

3 Unscrew the caliper lower guide pin bolt (if necessary, use a slim open-ended spanner to counterhold the head of the guide pin), then remove the bolt **(see illustration)**.

4 Pivot the caliper body upwards to expose the brake pads and secure the caliper in place **(see illustrations)**. Do not depress the brake pedal until the caliper is refitted. Take care not to strain the brake fluid hose.

5 Note the locations and orientation of the shims fitted to the rear of each pad, and the anti-rattle clips fitted to the top and bottom of the pads.

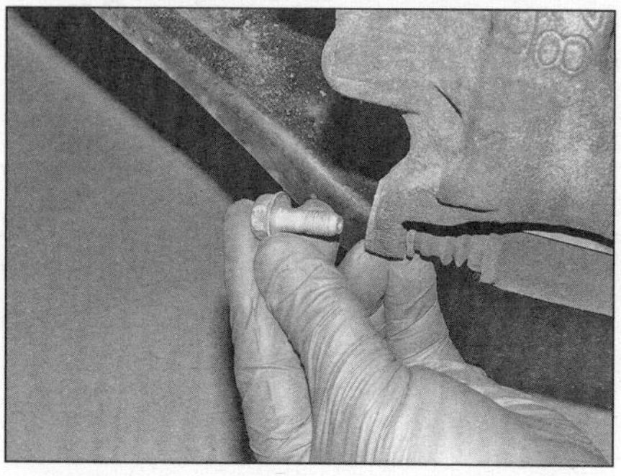

4.3 Remove the caliper lower guide pin bolt...

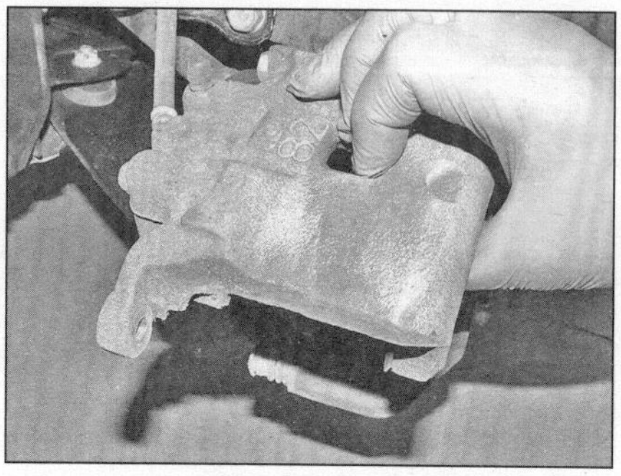

4.4a ...then pivot the caliper upwards and away from the brake pads...

4.4b ...and tie it to the suspension strut

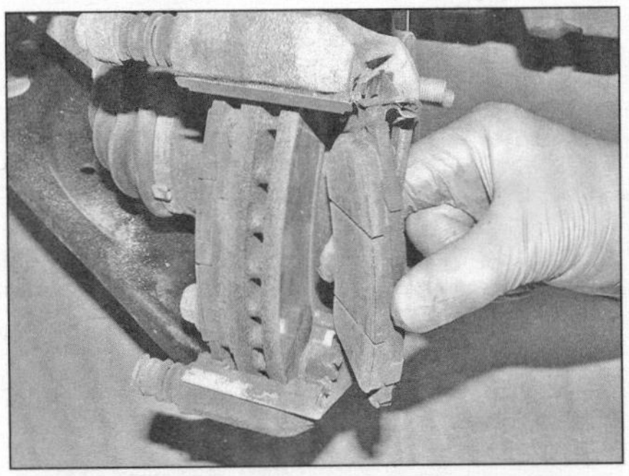
4.6a Withdraw the outer brake pad...

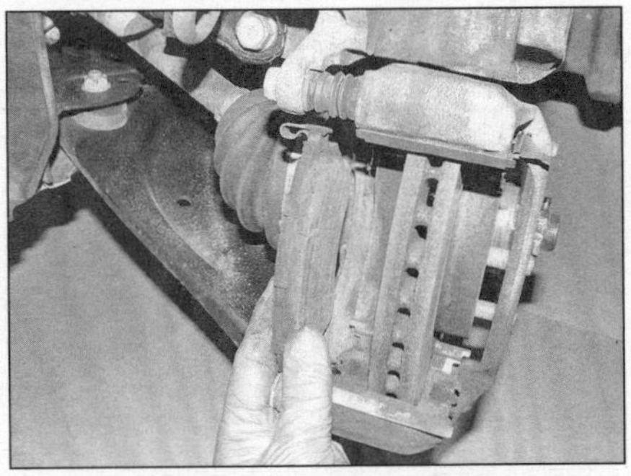
4.6b ...and inner brake pad from the caliper mounting bracket

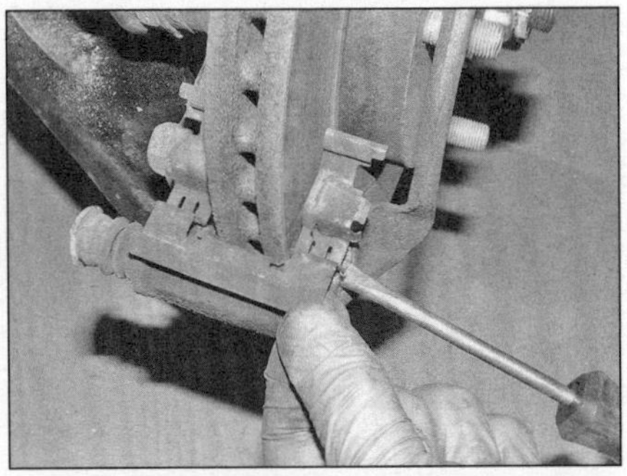
4.6c Remove the lower...

4.6d ...and upper anti-rattle clips, if required

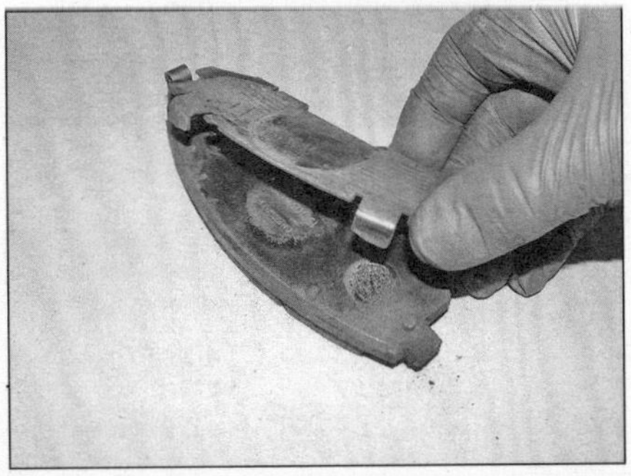
4.7 Remove the shims from the brake pads

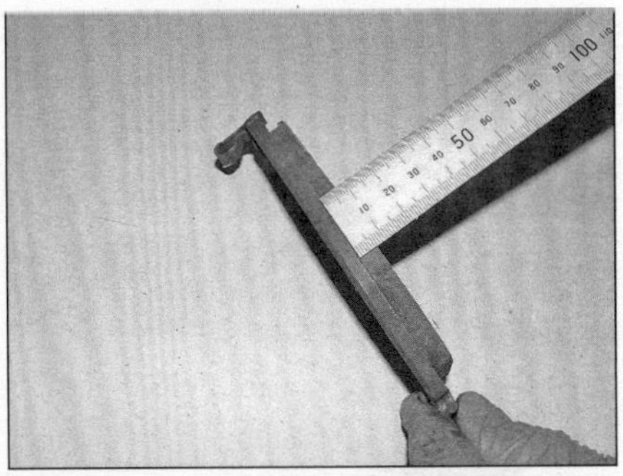
4.8 Measure the thickness of the pads friction material

6 Lift out the brake pads and shims, followed by the anti-rattle clips **(see illustrations)**.
7 Separate the shims from the brake pads, noting that there are two shims fitted to the inner pad on certain models **(see illustration)**.
8 First measure the thickness of each brake pad's friction material **(see illustration)**. If either pad is worn at any point to the specified minimum thickness or less, all four pads must be renewed. Also, the pads should be renewed if any are fouled with oil or grease; there is no satisfactory way of degreasing friction material, once contaminated. If any of the brake pads are worn unevenly, or are fouled with oil or grease, trace and rectify the cause before reassembly. New brake pads and shim/clip kits are available from Nissan dealers. Do not be tempted to swap brake pads over to compensate for uneven wear.
9 If the brake pads are still serviceable, carefully clean them using a clean, fine wire brush or similar, paying particular attention to the sides and back of the metal backing. Where applicable, clean out the grooves in the friction material, and pick out any large embedded particles of dirt or debris.
10 Clean the anti-rattle clips, shims, and the brake pad locations in the caliper body/mounting bracket.
11 Prior to fitting the pads, check that the guide pins are free to slide easily in the caliper body/mounting bracket, and check that the rubber guide pin gaiters are undamaged.
12 Brush the dust and dirt from the caliper and piston, but do not inhale it, as it is a health hazard. Inspect the dust seal around the piston for damage, and the piston for evidence of fluid leaks, corrosion or damage. If attention to any of these components is necessary, refer to Section 9.
13 If new brake pads are to be fitted, the caliper piston must be pushed back into the cylinder, to make room for them. Either use a G-clamp or similar tool **(see illustration)**, or use suitable pieces of wood as levers. Provided that the master cylinder reservoir has not been overfilled with hydraulic fluid, there should be no spillage, but keep a careful watch on the fluid level while retracting the piston. If the fluid level rises above the MAX level line at any time, the surplus fluid should be syphoned off.

Warning: Do not syphon the fluid by mouth, as it is poisonous; use a syringe or an old poultry baster.

14 Refit the upper and lower anti-rattle clips to the caliper mounting bracket **(see illustrations)**.
15 Apply a little anti-squeal brake grease to the contact surfaces of the pad backing plates

4.13 Using a piston retraction tool to push back the caliper piston

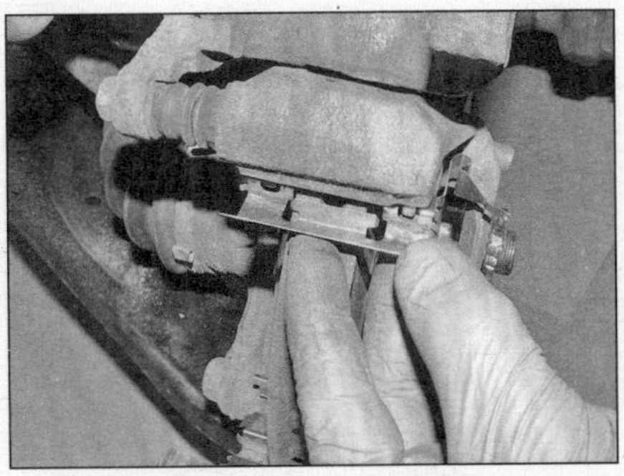
4.14a Refit the upper anti-rattle clip...

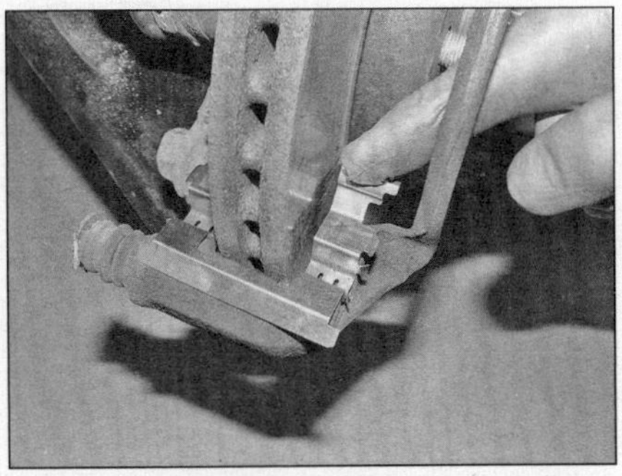
4.14b ...and lower anti-rattle clip to the caliper mounting bracket

4.15a Use the special grease to lubricate the rear of the inner brake pad...

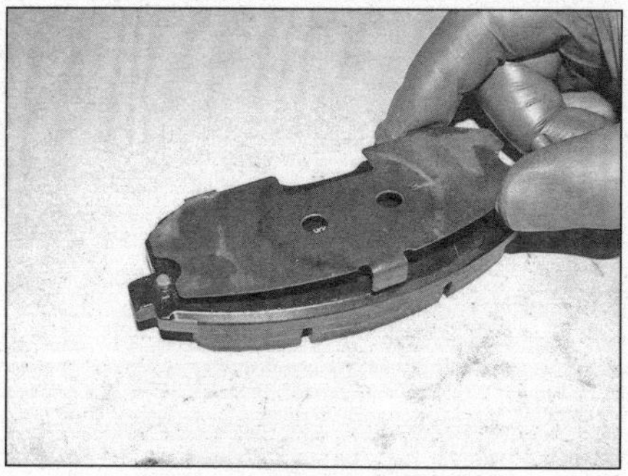

4.15b ...then locate the shim on the pad...

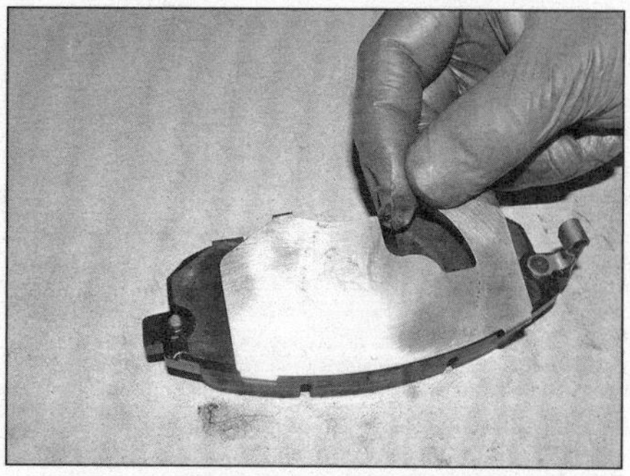

4.15c ...and where applicable, fit the second shim

4.15d Similarly, apply the special grease to the rear of the outer brake pad...

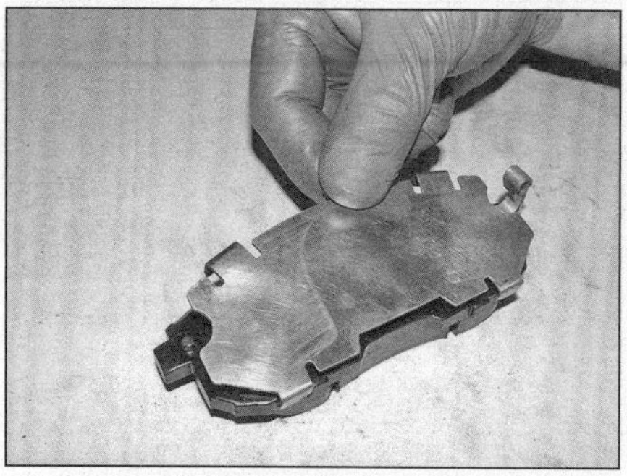

4.15e ...and place the shim in position

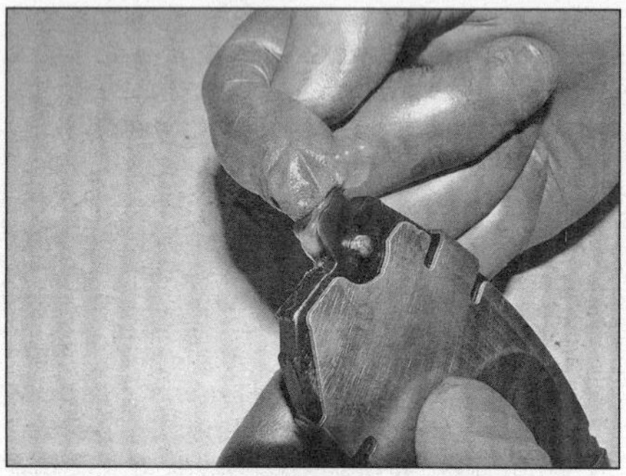

4.16a Use the special grease to lubricate the ends of the pad backing plates...

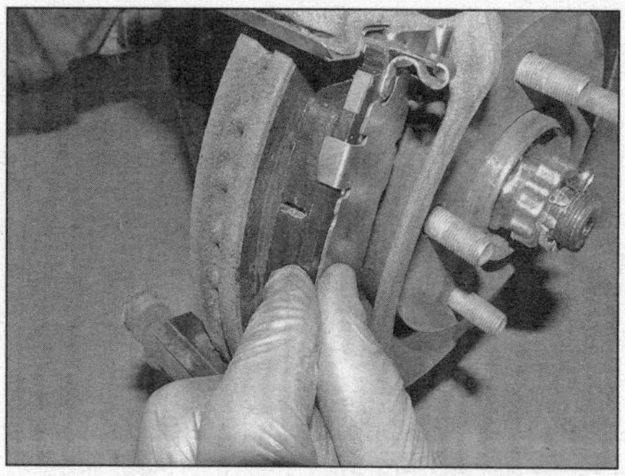

4.16b ...then refit the outer...

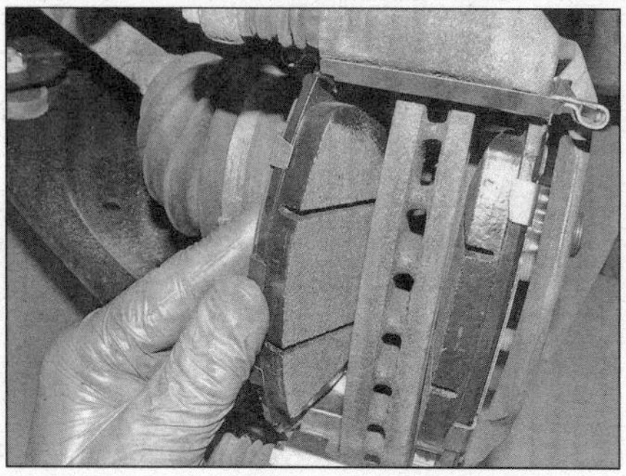

4.16c ...and inner brake pads

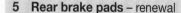

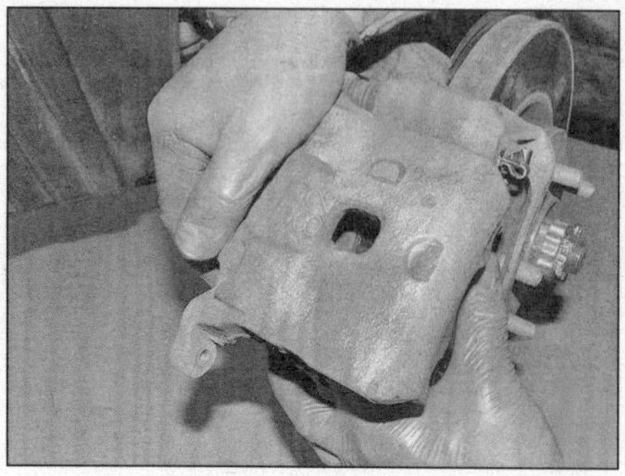

4.17 Pivot the caliper down and over the pads

and the shims, but take great care not to allow any grease onto the pad friction linings **(see illustrations)**.

16 Apply a little anti-squeal brake grease to the contact surface at each end of the pad backing plates, then refit the pads and shims in the positions noted before removal, ensuring that the pad friction material is against the disc **(see illustrations)**.

17 Pivot the caliper back into position, over the pads and mounting bracket **(see illustration)**.

18 Refit the caliper lower guide pin bolt, and then tighten it to the specified torque.

19 Check that the caliper body slides smoothly on the guide pins.

20 Repeat the procedure on the remaining front caliper.

21 With both sets of front brake pads refitted, depress the brake pedal repeatedly until the pads are pressed into firm contact with the brake disc, and normal pedal pressure is restored.

22 Refit the roadwheels, and lower the vehicle to the ground.

23 Finally, check the brake hydraulic fluid level as described in *Weekly checks*.

Caution: New pads will not give full braking efficiency until they have bedded-in. Be prepared for this, and avoid hard braking as far as possible for the first hundred miles or so after pad renewal.

5 Rear brake pads – renewal

Warning: Renew BOTH sets of rear brake pads at the same time – NEVER renew the pads on only one wheel, as uneven braking may result.

Warning: Before starting work, refer to the warning given at the beginning of Section 4, concerning the dangers of asbestos dust.

1 Chock the front wheels, then jack up the rear of the car and support it on axle stands (see *Jacking and vehicle support*). Remove the rear roadwheels, and release the handbrake fully.

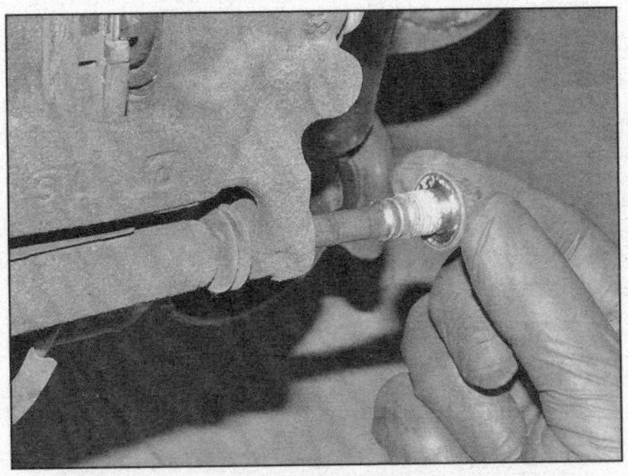
5.3 Remove the caliper lower guide pin bolt

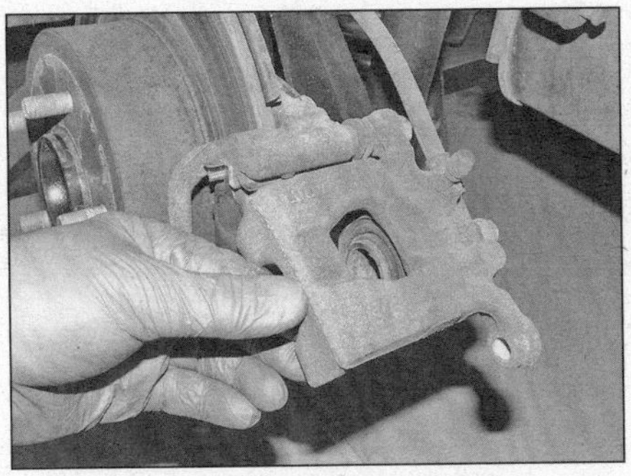
5.4a Pivot the caliper upwards...

5.4b ...and secure it to the coil spring

2 Working on one side of the vehicle, push the caliper piston into its bore by pulling the caliper outwards.
3 Unscrew the caliper lower guide pin bolt (noting that it is also the guide pin), and remove it from the caliper **(see illustration)**.
4 Pivot the caliper body upwards to expose the brake pads and secure the caliper in place **(see illustrations)**. Do not depress the brake pedal until the caliper is refitted. Take care not to strain the brake fluid hose.
5 Note the locations and orientation of the shims fitted to the rear of each pad, and the anti-rattle clips fitted to the top and bottom of the pads.
6 Lift out the brake pads and shims, followed by the anti-rattle clips **(see illustrations)**.
7 Separate the shims from the brake pads, noting their fitted position **(see illustration)**.
8 First measure the thickness of each brake pad's friction material **(see illustration)**. If either pad is worn at any point to the specified minimum thickness or less, all four pads must be renewed. Also, the pads should be renewed if any are fouled with oil or grease; there is no satisfactory way of degreasing friction material, once contaminated. If any of the brake pads are worn unevenly, or are fouled with oil or grease, trace and rectify the cause before reassembly. New brake pads and shim/clip kits are available from Nissan dealers. Do not be tempted to swap brake pads over to compensate for uneven wear.
9 If the brake pads are still serviceable, carefully clean them using a clean, fine wire brush or similar, paying particular attention to the sides and back of the metal backing. Where applicable, clean out the grooves in the friction material, and pick out any large embedded particles of dirt or debris.
10 Clean the anti-rattle clips, shims, and the brake pad locations in the caliper body/mounting bracket.
11 Prior to fitting the pads, check that the rubber guide pin gaiters are undamaged.
12 Brush the dust and dirt from the caliper and piston, but do not inhale it, as it is a health hazard. Inspect the dust seal around the piston for damage, and the piston for evidence of fluid leaks, corrosion or damage. If attention to any of these components is necessary, refer to Section 9.

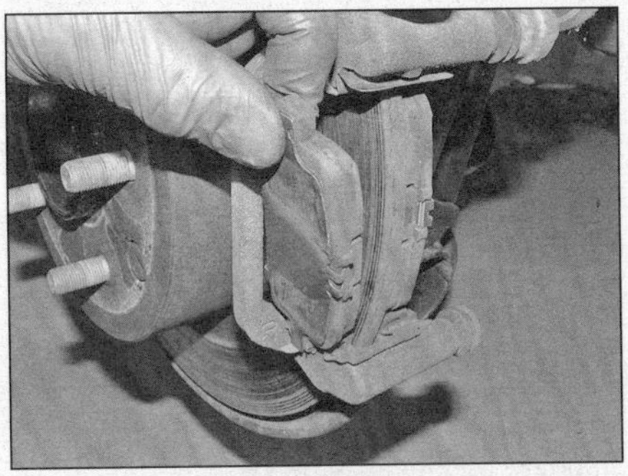
5.6a Withdraw the outer...

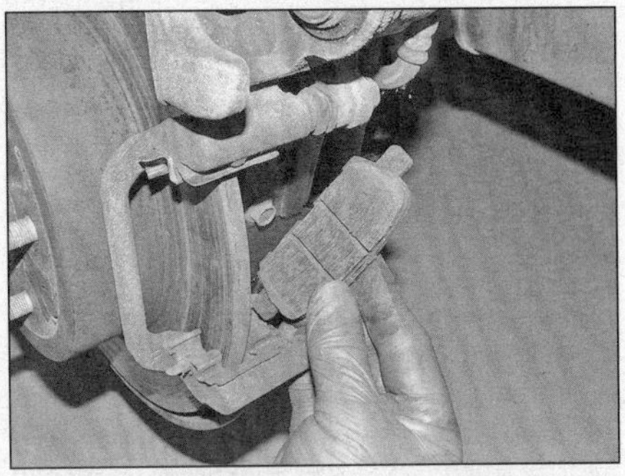
5.6b ...and inner brake pad from the caliper mounting bracket

5.6c Remove the lower...

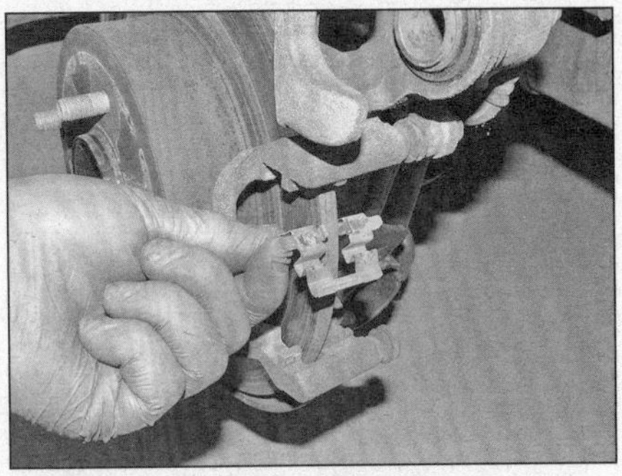
5.6d ...and upper anti-rattle clips, if required

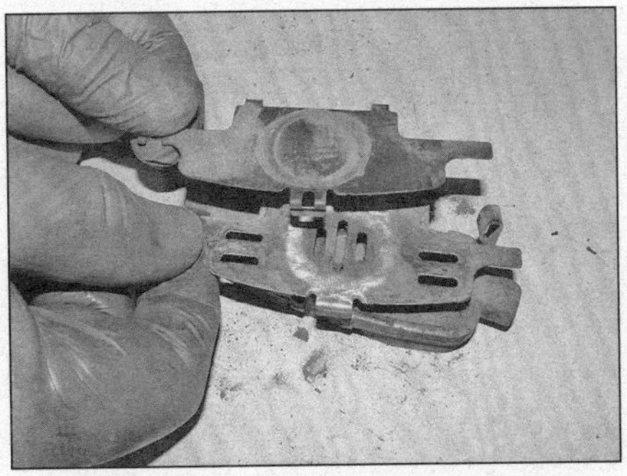
5.7 Remove the shims, noting their fitted position

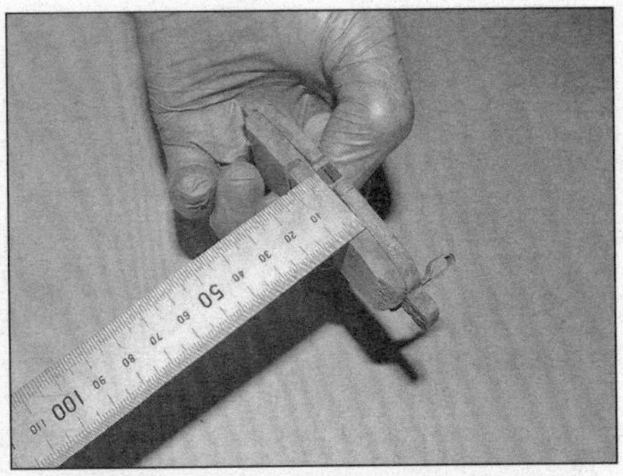
5.8 Measure the thickness of the pad friction material

5.13 Using a piston retraction tool to push back the caliper piston

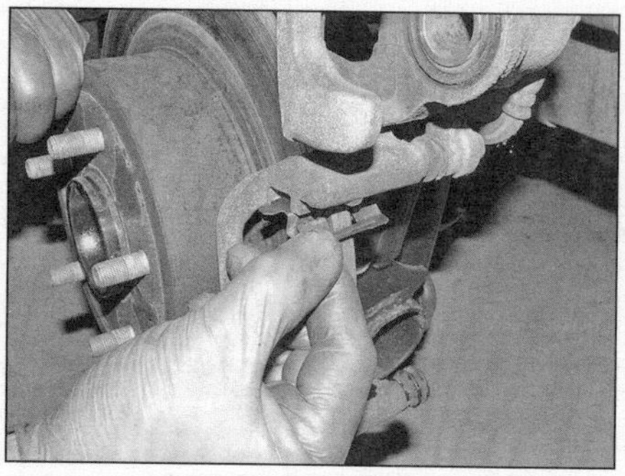

5.14a Refit the upper...

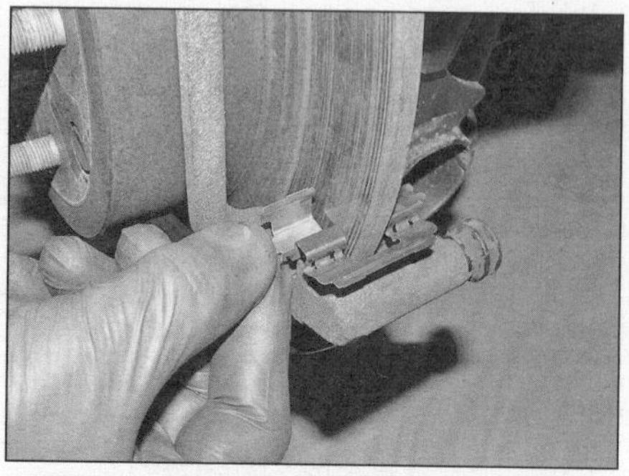

5.14b ...and lower anti-rattle clips to the caliper mounting bracket

13 If new brake pads are to be fitted, the caliper piston must be pushed back into the cylinder, to make room for them. Either use a G-clamp or similar tool **(see illustration)**, or use suitable pieces of wood as levers. Provided that the master cylinder reservoir has not been overfilled with hydraulic fluid, there should be no spillage, but keep a careful watch on the fluid level while retracting the piston. If the fluid level rises above the MAX level line at any time, the surplus should be syphoned off.

Warning: Do not syphon the fluid by mouth, as it is poisonous; use a syringe or an old poultry baster.

14 Refit the upper and lower anti-rattle clips to the caliper mounting bracket **(see illustrations)**.

15 Apply a little anti-squeal brake grease to the contact surfaces of the pad backing plates, then refit the shims. Take great care not to allow any grease onto the pad friction linings **(see illustrations)**.

16 Refit the pads and shims in the positions noted before removal, ensuring that the pad friction material is against the disc **(see illustrations)**.

17 Pivot the caliper back into position, over the pads and mounting bracket **(see illustration)**.

18 Refit the caliper lower guide pin bolt, and then tighten it to the specified torque.

19 Check that the caliper body slides smoothly on the guide pins.

20 Repeat the procedure on the remaining rear caliper.

21 With both sets of front brake pads refitted, depress the brake pedal repeatedly until the pads are pressed into firm contact with the brake disc, and normal pedal pressure is restored.

22 Refit the roadwheels, and lower the vehicle to the ground.

23 Finally, check the brake hydraulic fluid level as described in *Weekly checks*.

Caution: New pads will not give full braking efficiency until they have bedded-in. Be prepared for this, and avoid hard braking as far as possible for the first hundred miles or so after pad renewal.

6 Handbrake shoes – renewal

Warning: Renew BOTH sets of handbrake shoes at the same time – NEVER renew the shoes on only one wheel, as uneven braking may result.

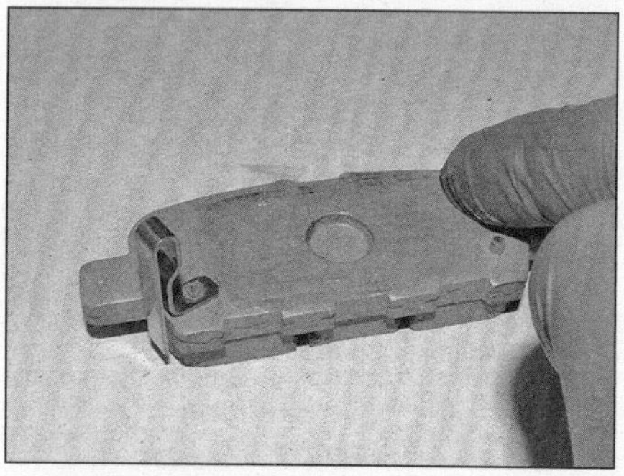

5.15a Use the special grease to lubricate the rear of the brake pad backing plates...

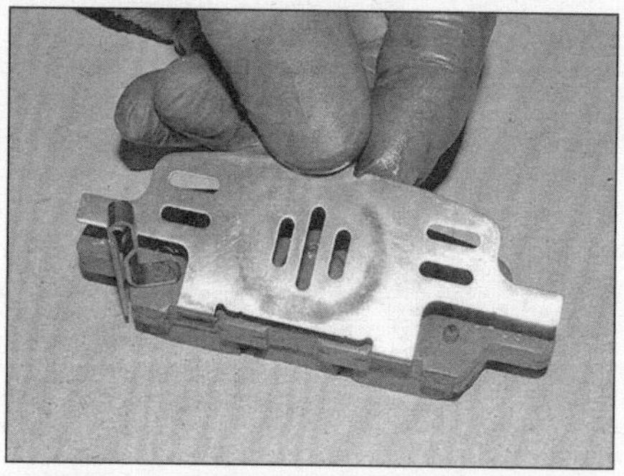

5.15b ...then locate the first shim on the pad...

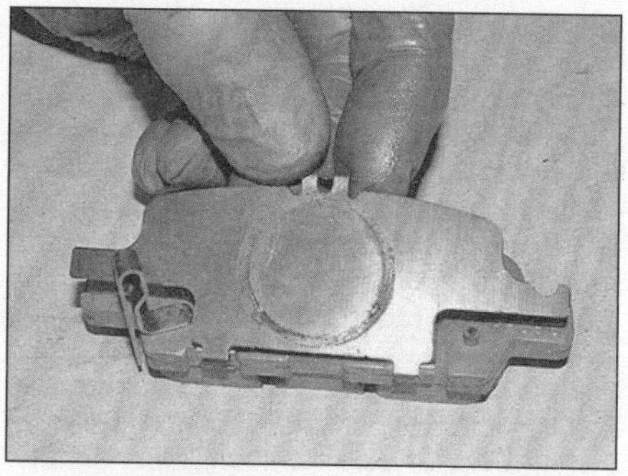

5.15c ...followed by the second shim

5.16a Refit the outer brake pad...

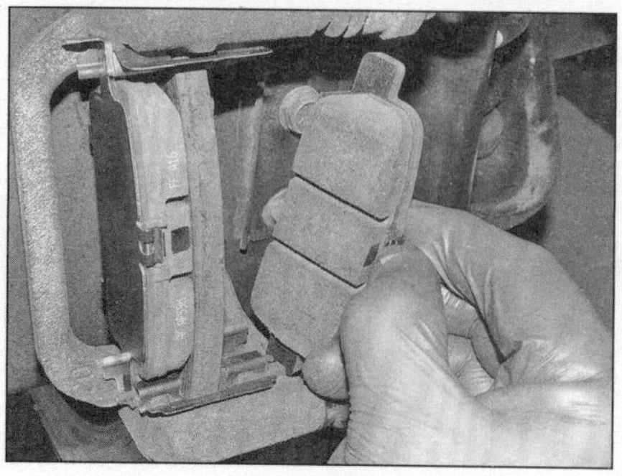

5.16b ...and inner brake pad

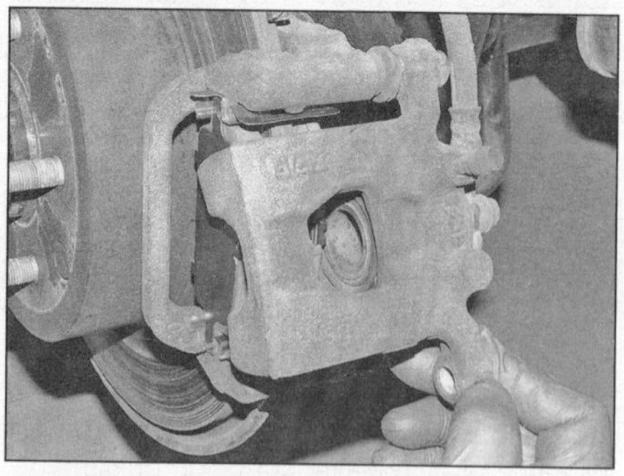

5.17 Pivot the caliper down and over the pads

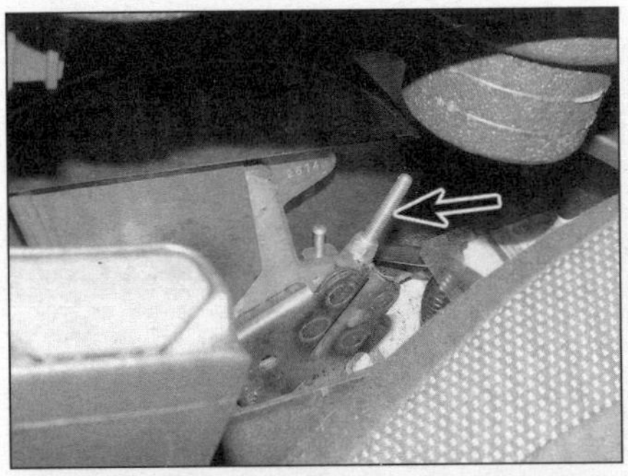

6.3 Measure the amount of thread on the handbrake adjuster

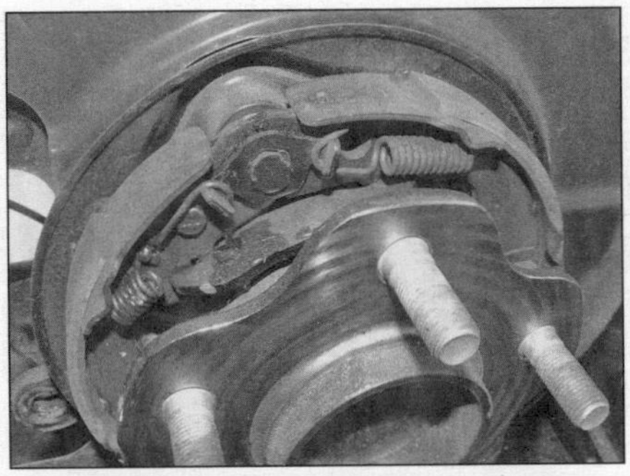

6.9a Make a note of the brake shoes, springs...

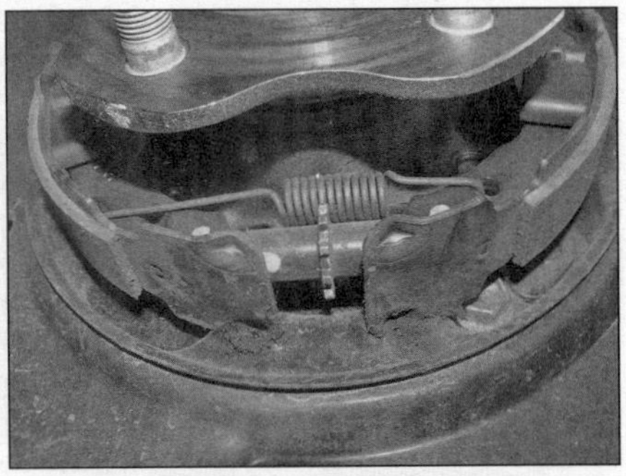

6.9b ...and adjusters fitted position

6.10a Turn the retaining pin...

6.10b ...and remove the spring clip

6.11 Open up the brake shoes and remove the adjuster

Warning: Before starting work, refer to the warning given at the beginning of Section 4, concerning the dangers of asbestos dust.

1 Chock the front wheels, then jack up the rear of the car and support it on axle stands (see *Jacking and vehicle support*). Remove the rear roadwheels, and release the handbrake fully.

2 Working inside the vehicle, unclip the plastic trim surrounding the handbrake lever, from the top of the centre console.

3 The handbrake cable adjustment nut can now be accessed through the top of the centre console. Measure the length of thread, protruding through the nut, as a guide for refitting **(see illustration)**.

4 Slacken the handbrake cable adjusting nut, until it gets to the end of the thread. Note the nut does not have to be completely removed.

5 Remove the rear brake disc, as described in Section 8.

6 Working carefully, and taking the necessary precautions, remove all traces of brake dust from the brake drum, backplate and shoes.

7 Measure the thickness of the friction material of each brake shoe at several points; if either shoe is worn at any point to the specified minimum thickness or less, all four shoes must be renewed as a set. The shoes should also be renewed if any are fouled with oil or grease; there is no satisfactory way of degreasing friction material, once contaminated.

8 If any of the brake shoes are worn unevenly, or fouled with oil or grease, trace and rectify the cause before reassembly.

9 Before removing the brake shoes, note the position of each shoe, and the location of the return and adjuster springs. Also make a note of the adjuster component locations, to aid refitting later **(see illustrations)**.

10 Using pliers, depress the shoe hold-down spring and turn the retaining pin through 90°, then lift off the shoe hold down spring **(see illustrations)**. Carry out the same procedure on the remaining brake shoe.

11 Using a pair of long nose pliers, open up the lower ends of the brake shoes and remove the adjuster strut, noting its fitted position **(see illustration)**.

12 Release the upper return spring, then withdraw the front brake shoe from the back plate and unhook the lower adjuster spring **(see illustrations)**. The one end of the return springs can be left fitted to the brake shoe, to aid refitting.

6.12a Release the upper spring...

6.12b ...and remove the front brake shoe

6.13a Release the upper spring...

6.13b ...and remove the strut plate

6.14 Release the handbrake lever from the rear brake shoe

6.15 Release the handbrake cable from the lever, if required

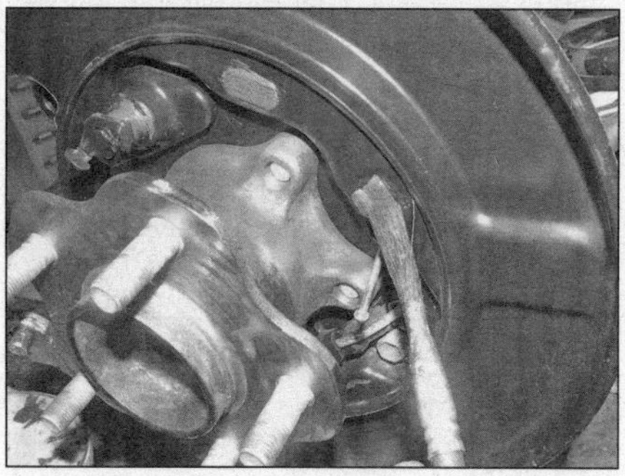

6.18 Use the special grease to lubricate the back plate

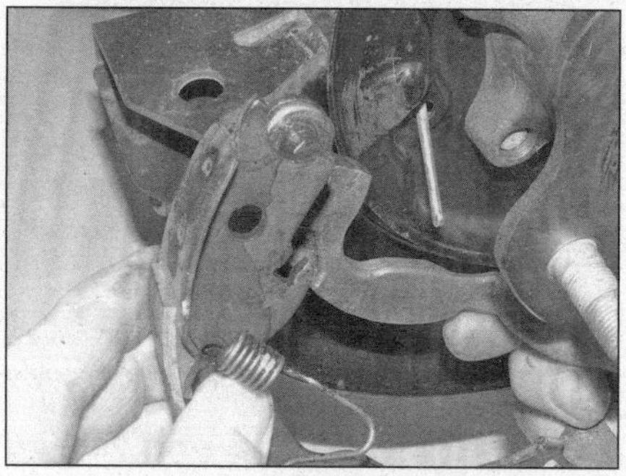

6.20a Refit the handbrake lever to the rear brake shoe...

13 Release the upper return spring, and then withdraw the strut plate from the rear brake shoe and handbrake lever **(see illustrations)**.

14 When the rear shoe is withdrawn from the back plate, release the handbrake lever from the brake shoe **(see illustration)**.

15 If required, the other end of the handbrake lever can be released from the cable by pulling back the return spring **(see illustration)**.

16 Check the condition of the forked end from the adjuster strut, and carefully examine the assembly for signs of wear or damage. Pay particular attention to the threads and the toothed adjuster wheel, and renew if necessary.

17 Check the condition of all return springs and renew any that show signs of distortion or other damage.

18 Prior to installation, clean the backplate, and apply a thin smear of high-temperature brake grease or anti-seize compound to all those surfaces of the backplate which bear on the shoes **(see illustration)**. Do not allow the lubricant to foul the friction material.

19 If removed, refit the end of the handbrake lever to the cable by pulling back the return spring.

20 Refit the handbrake lever back to the rear brake shoe, and then refit the upper return spring **(see illustrations)**.

21 Slide the strut plate back into position, in the slot in the rear brake shoe and handbrake

6.20b ...and hook the spring over the upper bracket

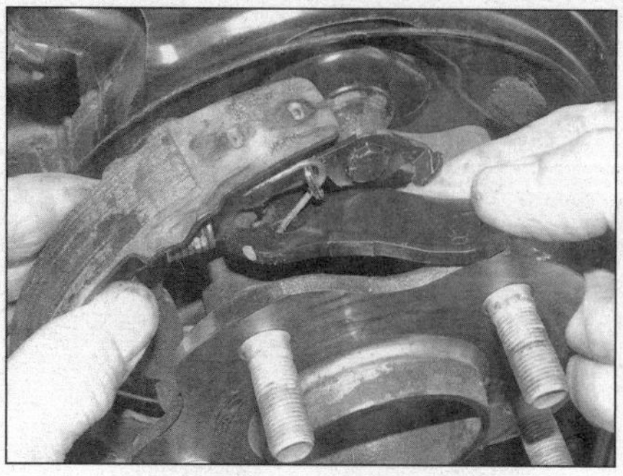

6.21a Insert the strut plate...

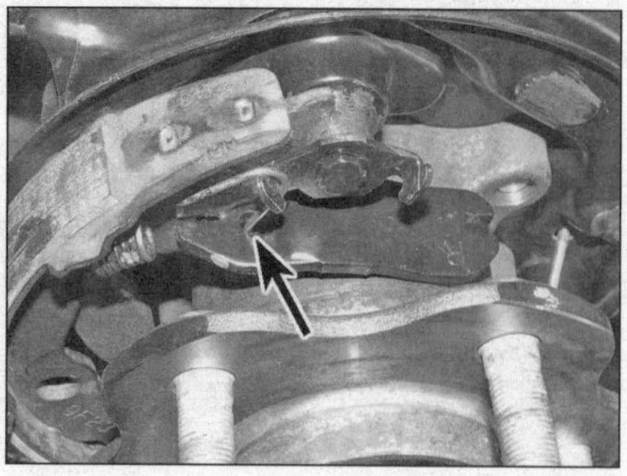

6.21b ...making sure the end of the spring locates in the hole

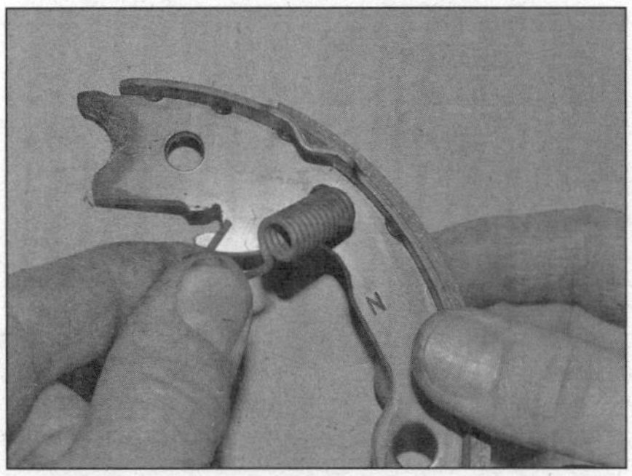

6.22a Insert the upper spring in the brake shoe...

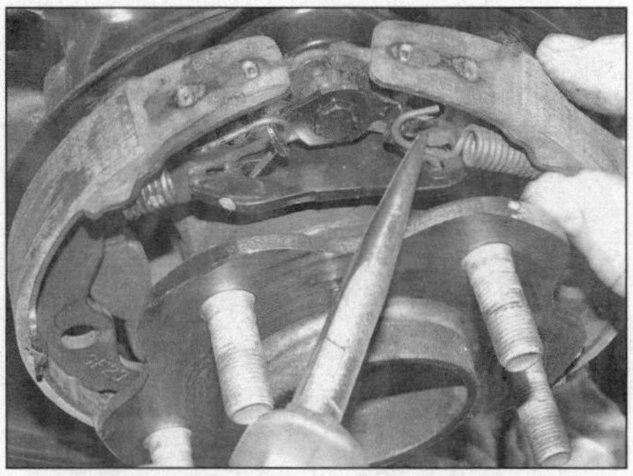

6.22b ...and hook the other end of the spring over the upper bracket

6.23 Make sure the springs and strut plate are fitted correctly

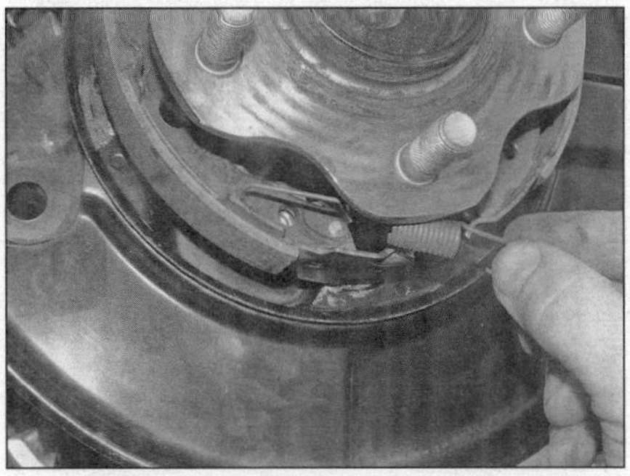

6.24 Fit the lower spring to the brake shoes

6.26a Open up the brake shoes and fit the adjuster...

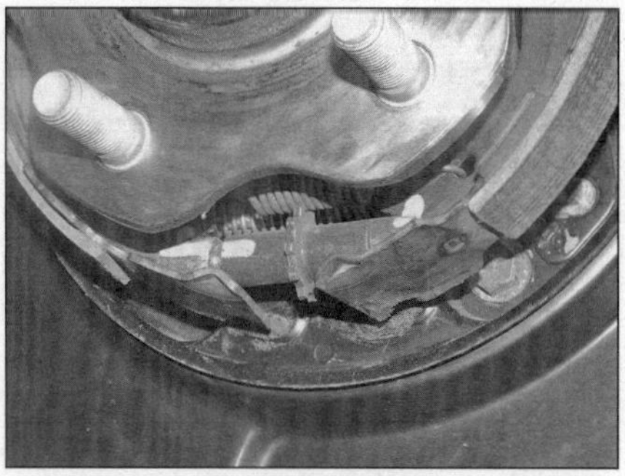

6.26b ...making sure it is fitted the correct way around

lever, locating the end of the spring in the hole in the strut plate **(see illustrations)**.

22 Refit the upper return spring to the front brake shoe, and then reconnect it to the upper mounting bracket **(see illustrations)**.

23 Make sure the upper strut plate is fitted into the slot in the front brake shoe **(see illustration)**.

24 Refit the lower return spring to the lower part of the brake shoes **(see illustration)**.

25 Shorten the adjuster strut to its minimum length by turning the toothed wheel, and apply a smear of brake grease to the contact faces at each end of the adjuster strut.

26 With the spring in place, use a pair of long nose pliers to open up the lower part of the brake shoes, and then slide the adjuster strut back into position **(see illustrations)**. Make sure the adjuster strut is fitted the correct way around (as noted on removal), and that the ends are fitted to the slots in the brake shoes.

27 Use a flat bladed screwdriver to hold the retaining pins in position, and then fit the two hold-down springs to both of the brake shoes, turning the retaining pins through 90° to secure the hold-down springs in position **(see illustrations)**.

28 Check that all components have been correctly refitted, and check that the adjuster mechanism operates correctly.

29 Using a screwdriver, turn the adjuster strut toothed wheel to expand the shoes until the brake disc/drum just slides over the shoes.

30 Refit the rear brake disc, as described in Section 8.

31 Repeat the above procedure on the remaining rear brake.

32 Check and adjust the handbrake cable as described in Chapter 1A, Section 8 or Chapter 1B, Section 9.

33 Refit the handbrake lever trim to the top of the centre console.

34 Refit the roadwheels, and then lower the vehicle to the ground.

7 Front brake disc – inspection, removal and refitting

Warning: Before starting work, refer to the warning at the beginning of Section 4 concerning the dangers of asbestos dust.

Note: *If either disc requires renewal, BOTH should be renewed at the same time, to ensure even and consistent braking. New brake pads should also be fitted.*

6.27a Hold the retaining pin in place and fit the spring clip

6.27b Turn the retaining pin...

6.27c ...and lock the spring clip in place

7.3 Checking the thickness of the brake disc with a micrometer

7.4a Secure the disc with washer and wheel nuts...

7.4b ...then check the run out of the disc with a DTI gauge

Inspection

1 Firmly apply the handbrake, and then jack up the front of the vehicle and support it securely on axle stands (see *Jacking and vehicle support*). Remove the appropriate front roadwheel.

2 Slowly rotate the brake disc so that the full area of both sides can be checked; remove the brake pads (see Section 4) if better access is required to the inboard surface. Light scoring is normal in the area swept by the brake pads, but if heavy scoring or cracks are found, the disc must be renewed.

3 It is normal to find a lip of rust and brake dust around the disc's perimeter; this can be scraped off if required. If, however, a lip has formed due to excessive wear of the brake pad swept area, then the disc's thickness must be measured using a micrometer **(see illustration)**. Take measurements at several places around the disc, at the inside and outside of the pad swept area; if the disc has worn at any point to the specified minimum thickness or less, the disc must be renewed.

4 If the disc is thought to be warped, it can be checked for run-out. Either use a dial gauge mounted on any convenient fixed point, while the disc is slowly rotated **(see illustrations)**, or use feeler blades to measure (at several points all around the disc) the clearance between the disc and a fixed point, such as the caliper mounting bracket. If the measurements obtained are at the specified maximum or beyond, the disc is excessively warped, and must be renewed; however, it is worth checking first that the hub bearing is in good condition. Also try the effect of removing the disc and turning it through 180°, to reposition it on the hub; if the run-out is still excessive, the disc must be renewed.

5 Check the disc for cracks, especially around the wheel stud holes, and any other wear or damage, and renew if necessary.

Removal

6 If not already done, firmly apply the handbrake, and then jack up the front of the vehicle and support it securely on axle stands (see *Jacking and vehicle support*). Remove the appropriate front roadwheel.

7 Unscrew the two bolts securing the caliper mounting bracket to the hub carrier **(see illustrations)**. Withdraw the caliper assembly, and suspend it using wire or string. Take care not to strain the brake fluid hose – if necessary release the hose from the securing clip(s).

8 If the original disc is to be refitted, mark the relationship between the disc and the hub, then pull the disc from the roadwheel studs **(see illustration)**.

Refitting

9 Ensure that the mating faces of the disc and the hub are clean and flat. If necessary, wipe the mating surfaces clean.

10 If the original disc is being refitted, align the marks made on the disc and hub before removal, then refit the disc.

11 If a new disc has been fitted, use a suitable solvent to wipe any preservative coating from the disc.

12 Refit the caliper, ensuring that the pads locate correctly over the disc. Then tighten the caliper mounting bracket securing bolts to the specified torque. Where applicable, refit the brake fluid hose to the clip(s).

13 Depress the brake pedal repeatedly until the pads are pressed into firm contact with the brake disc, and normal pedal pressure is restored.

14 Repeat the above procedure on the remaining brake, if a new disc was fitted.

15 Refit the roadwheel, and lower the vehicle to the ground.

8 Rear brake disc – inspection, removal and refitting

Warning: Before starting work, refer to the warning at the beginning of Section 4 concerning the dangers of asbestos dust.

Note: *If either disc requires renewal, BOTH should be renewed at the same time, to ensure even and consistent braking. New brake pads should also be fitted.*

Inspection

1 Chock the front wheels then jack up the rear of the vehicle and support it securely on axle stands (see *Jacking and vehicle support*). Remove the appropriate rear roadwheel.

2 Fully release the handbrake.

3 Proceed as described for the front disc in Section 7, but refer to Section 5 if the brake pads are to be removed.

7.7a Slacken the two caliper mounting bracket bolts...

7.7b ...and withdraw the assembly from over the brake disc

7.8 Remove the brake disc from the hub

Removal

4 If not already done, chock the front wheels then jack up the rear of the vehicle and support it securely on axle stands (see *Jacking and vehicle support*). Remove the appropriate rear roadwheel and release the handbrake.

5 Unscrew the two bolts securing the caliper mounting bracket to the trailing arm **(see illustration)**. Withdraw the caliper assembly, and suspend it using wire or string. Take care not to strain the brake fluid hose – if necessary release the hose from the securing clip(s).

6 If the original disc is to be refitted, mark the relationship between the disc and the hub, then pull the disc from the roadwheel studs **(see illustration)**.

7 If the disc cannot be withdrawn easily, it may be necessary to slacken the adjuster on the handbrake shoes inside the centre of the brake disc. Remove the grommet in the centre of the brake disc, and then slacken the handbrake shoe adjuster **(see illustrations)**. Remove brake disc from over the handbrake shoes.

Refitting

8 Ensure that the mating faces of the disc and the hub are clean and flat. If necessary, wipe the mating surfaces clean.

9 If the original disc is being refitted, align the marks made on the disc and hub before removal, then refit the disc.

10 If a new disc has been fitted, use a suitable solvent to wipe any preservative coating from the disc.

11 Refit the caliper, ensuring that the pads locate correctly over the disc. Then tighten the caliper mounting bracket securing bolts to the specified torque. Where applicable, refit the brake fluid hose to the clip(s).

12 Depress the brake pedal repeatedly until the pads are pressed into firm contact with the brake disc, and normal pedal pressure is restored.

13 Repeat the above procedure on the remaining brake, if a new disc was fitted.

14 Check and adjust the handbrake cable as described in Chapter 1A, Section 8 or Chapter 1B, Section 9.

15 Refit the roadwheel, and lower the vehicle to the ground.

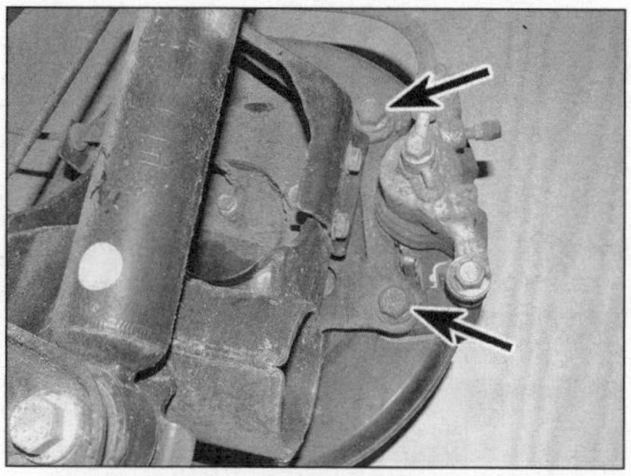

8.5 Unscrew the two caliper mounting bracket bolts

8.6 Remove the brake disc from the hub

8.7a Remove the rubber grommet...

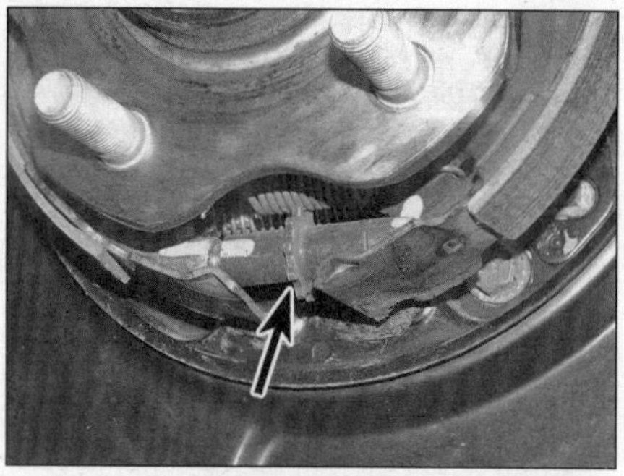

8.7b ...and slacken the adjuster wheel

9 Front brake caliper – removal, overhaul and refitting

Warning: Before starting work, refer to the note at the beginning of Section 2 concerning the dangers of hydraulic fluid, and to the warning at the beginning of Section 4 concerning the dangers of asbestos dust.

Removal

1 Firmly apply the handbrake, and then jack up the front of the vehicle and support it securely on axle stands (see *Jacking and vehicle support*). Remove the appropriate front roadwheel.

2 To minimise fluid loss during the following operations, remove the master cylinder reservoir cap, then tighten it down onto a piece of polythene to obtain an airtight seal. Alternatively, use a brake hose clamp, a G-clamp or a similar tool to clamp the flexible hose running to the caliper **(see illustration 3.1)**.

3 Clean the area around the fluid hose union on the caliper, and then unscrew the hose union banjo bolt **(see illustration)**. Recover the two sealing washers noting that new washers will be required for refitting. Cover the open ends of the banjo and the caliper, to prevent dirt ingress.

4 Remove the brake pads as described in Section 4.

5 Unscrew the caliper upper guide pin bolt. If necessary, use a slim open-ended spanner to counterhold the head of the guide pin.

6 Withdraw the caliper from the mounting bracket **(see illustration)**.

7 If desired, the caliper mounting bracket can be unbolted from the hub carrier **(see illustration)**.

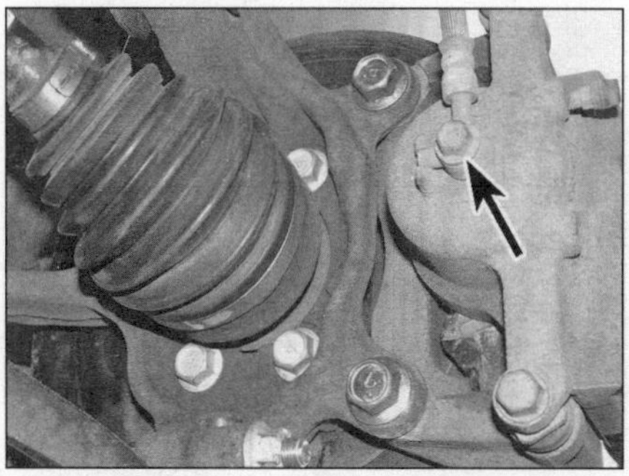

9.3 Unscrew the brake hose union bolt

9.6 Undo the upper bolt and withdraw the brake caliper

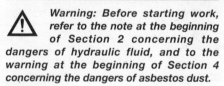

9.7 Caliper mounting bracket bolts

Overhaul

Note: *Before commencing work, check with your local dealer for the availability of parts, and ensure that the appropriate caliper overhaul kit is obtained.*

8 With the caliper on the bench, wipe away all traces of dust and dirt, but avoid inhaling the dust, as it is a health hazard.

9 Extract the caliper guide pins, if necessary by screwing the bolts into the pins, and pulling on the bolts to withdraw the pins. Peel off the rubber dust cover from each guide pin.

10 Place a small block of wood between the caliper body and the piston. Remove the piston, including the dust seal, by applying a jet of low-pressure compressed air, such as that from a tyre pump, to the fluid inlet port.

Caution: The piston may be ejected with some force. Only low pressure should be required, such as is generated by a foot pump.

11 Peel the dust seal off the piston, and use a blunt instrument, such as a knitting needle, to extract the piston seal from the caliper cylinder bore.

12 Thoroughly clean all components, using only methylated spirit or clean hydraulic fluid. Never use mineral-based solvents such as petrol or paraffin, which will attack the hydraulic system rubber components.

13 The caliper piston seal and the dust seal, the guide pin dust covers, and the bleed nipple dust cap, are only available as part of a seal kit. Since the manufacturers recommend that the piston seal and dust seal are renewed whenever they are disturbed, all of these components should be discarded, and new ones fitted on reassembly as a matter of course.

14 Carefully examine all parts of the caliper assembly, looking for signs of wear or damage. In particular, the cylinder bore and piston must be free from any signs of scratches, corrosion or wear. If there is any doubt about the condition of any part of the caliper, the relevant part should be renewed; note that if the caliper body or the mounting bracket are to be renewed, they are available only as part of the complete assembly.

15 The manufacturers recommend that minor scratches, rust, etc, may be polished away from the cylinder bore using fine emery paper, but the piston must be renewed to cure such defects. The piston surface is plated, and must not be polished with emery or similar abrasives.

16 Check that the threads in the caliper body and the mounting bracket are in good condition. Check that both guide pins are undamaged, and (when cleaned) a reasonably tight sliding fit in the mounting bracket bores.

17 Use compressed air to blow clear the fluid passages.

Warning: Wear eye protection when using compressed air.

18 Before commencing reassembly, ensure that all components are spotlessly clean and dry.

19 Soak the new piston seal in clean hydraulic fluid, and fit it to the groove in the cylinder bore, using your fingers only (no tools) to manipulate it into place.

20 Fit the new dust seal inner lip to the cylinder groove, smear clean hydraulic fluid over the piston and caliper cylinder bore, and twist the piston into the dust seal. Press the piston squarely into the cylinder, then slide the dust seal outer lip into the groove in the piston.

21 Fit a new rubber dust cover to each guide pin, and apply a smear of brake grease to the guide pins before refitting them to their bores.

Refitting

22 Where applicable, refit the caliper mounting bracket to the hub carrier, and tighten the mounting bolts to the specified torque.

23 Place the caliper in position, refit the upper guide pin bolt, and tighten it to the specified torque.

24 Refit the brake pads as described in Section 4.

25 Check that the caliper slides smoothly on the mounting bracket.

26 Check that the hydraulic fluid hose is correctly routed, without being twisted, and then reconnect the union to the caliper, using two new sealing washers. Refit the union banjo bolt, and tighten to the specified torque.

27 Remove the polythene from the master cylinder reservoir cap, or remove the clamp from the fluid hose, as applicable.

28 Bleed the hydraulic fluid circuit as described in Section 2. Note that if no other part of the system has been disturbed, it should only be necessary to bleed the relevant front circuit.

29 Depress the brake pedal repeatedly to bring the pads into contact with the brake disc, and ensure that normal pedal pressure is restored.

30 Refit the roadwheel, and lower the vehicle to the ground.

10 Rear brake caliper – removal and refitting

Warning: Before starting work, refer to the note at the beginning of Section 2 concerning the dangers of hydraulic fluid, and to the warning at the beginning of Section 4 concerning the dangers of asbestos dust.

Removal

1 Chock the front wheels then jack up the rear of the vehicle and support it securely on axle stands (see *Jacking and vehicle support*). Remove the appropriate rear roadwheel.

2 To minimise fluid loss during the following operations, remove the master cylinder reservoir cap, then tighten it down onto a piece of polythene to obtain an airtight seal. Alternatively, use a brake hose clamp, a G-clamp or a similar tool to clamp the flexible hose running to the caliper.

3 Clean the area around the fluid hose union on the caliper, and then unscrew the hose union banjo bolt **(see illustration)**. Recover the two sealing washers noting that new washers will be required for refitting. Cover the open ends of the banjo and the caliper, to prevent dirt ingress.

4 Remove the brake pads as described in Section 5.

5 Lift the caliper and then slide the upper guide pin bolt from the mounting bracket. If necessary unscrew the upper guide pin bolt from the caliper **(see illustration)**.

6 Withdraw the caliper from the mounting bracket.

7 If desired, the caliper mounting bracket can be unbolted from the trailing arm **(see illustration)**.

10.3 Unscrew the brake hose union bolt

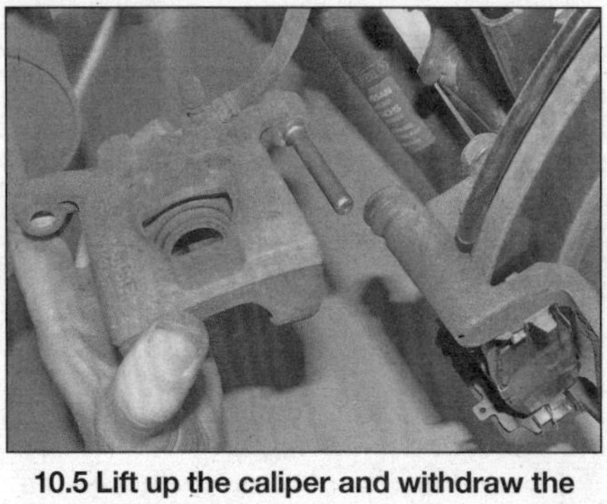

10.5 Lift up the caliper and withdraw the upper guide bolt from the mounting bracket

10.7 Undo the mounting bracket bolts and withdraw it from the brake disc

Refitting

8 Where applicable, refit the caliper mounting bracket to the hub carrier, and tighten the mounting bolts to the specified torque.
9 Place the caliper in position, refit the caliper upper guide pin bolt and tighten it to the specified torque.
10 Refit the brake pads as described in Section 5.
11 Check that the caliper slides smoothly on the mounting bracket.
12 Check that the brake fluid hose is correctly routed, without being twisted, and then reconnect the union to the caliper. Refit the union banjo bolt, using two new sealing washers, and then tighten to the specified torque.
13 Remove the polythene from the master cylinder reservoir cap, or remove the clamp from the fluid hose, as applicable.
14 Bleed the hydraulic fluid circuit as described in Section 2. Note that if no other part of the system has been disturbed, it should only be necessary to bleed the relevant rear circuit.
15 Depress the brake pedal repeatedly to bring the pads into contact with the brake disc, and ensure that normal pedal pressure is restored.
16 Refit the roadwheel, and lower the vehicle to the ground.

11 Master cylinder – removal and refitting

Warning: Before starting work, refer to the warning at the beginning of Section 2 concerning the dangers of hydraulic fluid.

Removal

1 Disconnect the battery negative terminal (refer to battery disconnection and reconnection in Chapter 5A, Section 3).
2 Remove the master cylinder fluid reservoir cap, and syphon the hydraulic fluid from the reservoir. Alternatively, open two bleed screws in the system (one in each of the dual circuit), and gently pump the brake pedal to expel the fluid through a tube connected to the bleed screws (see Section 2).

Warning: Do not syphon the fluid by mouth, as it is poisonous; use a syringe or an old poultry baster.

3 Disconnect the wiring connector from the brake fluid level sender unit on the side of the reservoir.
4 Use a brake hose clamp, a G-clamp or a similar tool, to clamp the supply hose to the clutch master cylinder, and then disconnect the hose from the reservoir.
5 Wipe clean the area around the brake pipe unions on the side of the master cylinder, and place absorbent rags beneath the pipe unions to catch any surplus fluid. Make a note of the correct fitted positions of the unions, then unscrew the union nuts and carefully withdraw the pipes. Plug or tape over the pipe ends and master cylinder orifices, to minimise the loss of brake fluid, and to prevent the entry of dirt into the system. Wash off any spilt fluid immediately with cold water.
6 Slacken and remove the two nuts securing the master cylinder to the vacuum servo unit **(see illustration)**, and then withdraw the master cylinder complete with reservoir from the engine compartment.
7 If required, tap out the retaining pin using a small punch, then pull the reservoir upwards to release it from the master cylinder.

Refitting

8 Remove all traces of dirt from the master cylinder and servo unit mating surfaces.
9 If removed, refit the reservoir to the top of the master cylinder making sure the rubber seals are fitted correctly, and tap in the retaining pin to secure.
10 Fit the master cylinder to the servo unit, ensuring that the servo unit pushrod enters the master cylinder bore centrally. Refit the master cylinder mounting nuts, and tighten them to the specified torque.
11 Place absorbent rags around and beneath the master cylinder, and then fill the reservoir with fresh hydraulic fluid.
12 Have an assistant slowly depress the brake pedal fully, and then hold it in the fully depressed position. Cover the outlet ports on the master cylinder body with your fingers then have the assistant slowly release the brake pedal. Continue this procedure until the fluid emerging from the master cylinder is free from air bubbles. Take care to collect the expelled fluid in the rags and wash off any spilt fluid immediately with cold water.
13 When all air has been bled from the master cylinder, wipe clean the brake pipe unions, then refit them to the correct master cylinder ports, as noted before removal, and tighten the union nuts securely.
14 Refit the clutch supply hose to the reservoir and remove the hose clamp. There should be no need to bleed the clutch system, but if required the clutch can be bled, as described in Chapter 6, Section 2.
15 Reconnect the wiring connector to the brake fluid level sender unit on the side of the reservoir.
16 On completion, bleed the complete hydraulic system as described in Section 2.

12 Brake pedal – removal, refitting and adjustment

Removal

1 Remove the facia lower trim panel on the driver's side as described in Chapter 11, Section 26.
2 Working in the driver's foot well, remove the R clip from the end of the servo pushrod clevis pin **(see illustration)**. Squeeze the ends of the clevis pin retainer together and remove the pin.
3 Disconnect the wiring connectors from the stop-light switch, brake pedal position switch and accelerator pedal position switch **(see illustration)**. Release the wiring harness from the clips on the brake pedal mounting bracket.
4 Unscrew the nuts securing the pedal bracket to the bulkhead (note that these nuts also secure the vacuum servo).
5 Withdraw the pedal/bracket assembly from the bulkhead and out through the footwell.
6 The brake pedal is integral with the bracket assembly, and cannot be renewed individually.

Refitting

7 Refitting is a reversal of removal (on completion, check the pedal height as described later in this Section).

11.6 Master cylinder securing nuts

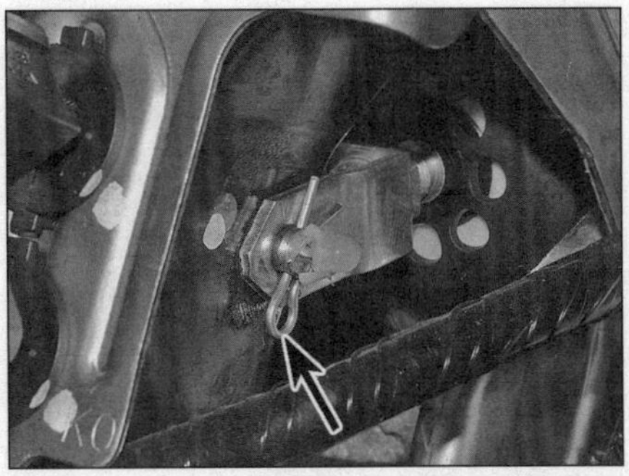

12.2 Remove the R-clip from the pushrod clevis pin

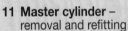

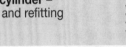

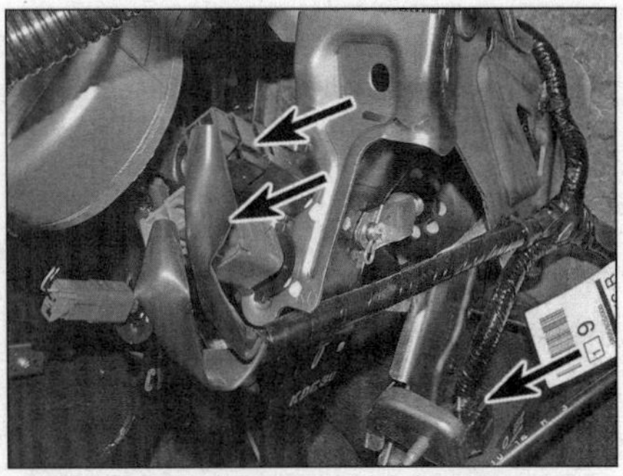

12.3 Disconnect the switch wiring connectors

Adjustment

8 The pedal free height should be measured from the top face of the pedal to the floor.

9 To improve access, remove the facia lower trim panel on the driver's side as described in Chapter 11, Section 26. Lift the carpet to give the correct measurement.

10 Measure the pedal free height. Check the measured height against the value given in the Specifications.

11 If the height of the pedal requires adjustment, proceed as follows.

12 Loosen the locknut on the servo pushrod, and turn the pushrod as required until the specified height is achieved. Retighten the locknut on completion.

13 Check that the stop-lights go out when the pedal is released. If not, adjust the switch as described in Section 18.

14 On completion, refit the trim panel.

13 Vacuum pump (diesel engines) – removal, refitting and testing

Note: *The vacuum pump is bolted to the transmission end of the cylinder head; a new gasket will be required before refitting.*

Removal

1 Remove the air cleaner assembly as described in Chapter 4B, Section 2.

2 Undo the two bolts and remove the support bracket from the side of the pump **(see illustration)**.

3 Release the retaining clip and disconnect the vacuum hoses from the pump **(see illustration)**.

4 Slacken and remove the mounting bolts securing the pump to the end of the cylinder head, then remove the pump **(see illustrations)**. Recover the gasket and discard, as a new one will be required for refitting.

Refitting

5 Ensure that the pump and cylinder head mating surfaces are clean and dry, and then fit the new gasket **(see illustration)**.

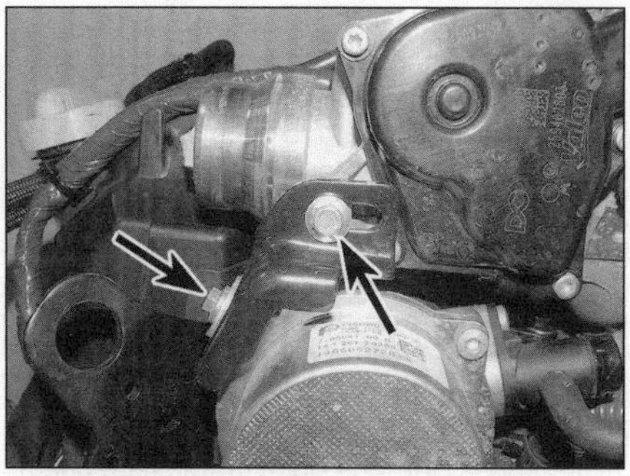

13.2 Undo the bolts and remove the support bracket

6 Manoeuvre the pump into position, aligning the drive gear with the slot in the end of the camshaft. Refit the pump mounting bolts and tighten securely.

7 Reconnect the vacuum hoses to the pump, making sure that the hoses are clipped into their relevant retaining clips.

8 Refit the support bracket to the side of the pump.

9 Refit the air cleaner assembly.

10 On completion, test the operation of the brakes as follows.

Testing

11 The operation of the braking system can be checked using a vacuum gauge.

12 Disconnect the vacuum hoes from the pump and connect the gauge to the pump using a length of hose.

13 Start the engine and allow it to idle, and then measure the vacuum created by the pump. As a guide after one minute, a minimum of approx. 700 mm Hg should be recorded.

14 If the vacuum registered is significantly less than this, it is likely that the pump is faulty. However seek the advice of a specialist, before condemning the pump.

15 Overhaul of the vacuum pump may not be possible; check the availability of spares.

13.3 Disconnect the vacuum hoses

14 Vacuum servo unit – removal and refitting

Removal

1 Disconnect the battery negative terminal (refer to battery disconnection and reconnection in Chapter 5A, Section 3).

2 Remove the windscreen cowl panel and cowl panel extension as described in Chapter 11, Section 21.

3 Where fitted, remove the clips and nuts and move the bulkhead heat shield material to one side.

4 Remove the brake master cylinder, with reference to Section 11.

5 Disconnect the vacuum hose from the servo.

6 Remove the facia lower trim panel on the driver's side as described in Chapter 11, Section 26.

7 Working in the driver's foot well, remove the R clip from the end of the servo pushrod clevis pin **(see illustration 12.2)**. Squeeze the ends of the clevis pin retainer together and remove the pin.

8 Again working in the driver's footwell, unscrew the four nuts securing the brake pedal mounting bracket to the servo studs.

9 Working in the engine compartment, withdraw the servo.

13.4a Undo the two retaining bolts (one out of view)

13.4b Removing the vacuum pump

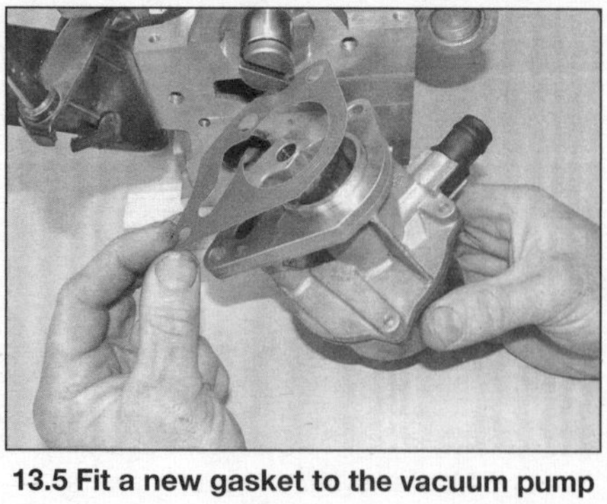

13.5 Fit a new gasket to the vacuum pump

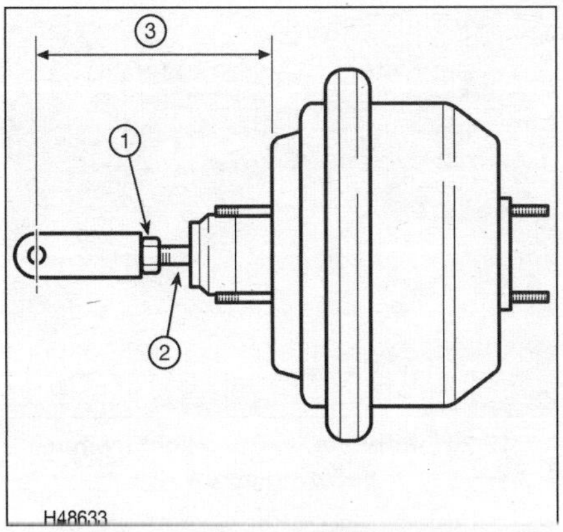

14.10 Servo input pushrod adjustment

1 Lock nut 2 Input pushrod
3 Length of input pushrod

Refitting

10 Refitting is a reversal of removal, bearing in mind the following points:

a) Before refitting the servo, check that the length of the pushrod is as specified (see Specifications), and adjust if necessary by loosening the locknut and turning the pushrod **(see illustration)***.*
b) Where applicable, tighten all fixings to the specified torque.
c) Refit the master cylinder as described in Section 11.
d) Refit the windscreen cowl panel and cowl panel extension as described in Chapter 11, Section 21.
e) On completion, check the brake pedal height as described in Section 12.

15 Vacuum servo unit check valve – removal, testing and refitting

Removal

1 The valve is integral with the vacuum hose and piping leading to the servo unit.

2 Release the retaining clips and disconnect the vacuum hose from the vacuum pipes. Take note of the direction of the arrow on the hose, which should point in the direction of the engine.

3 Release the retaining clips (where fitted), and disconnect the vacuum hoses from the valve, then withdraw the valve.

Testing

4 Examine the hose for signs of damage, and renew if necessary. The valve may be tested by blowing through it in both directions. Air should flow through the valve in one direction only – when blown through from the servo unit end of the valve. Renew the hose/valve if this is not the case.

Refitting

5 Refitting is a reversal of removal, ensuring that the arrow on the hose body points towards the engine.

6 On completion, start the engine and check the hose connections for air leaks.

16 Handbrake lever – removal and refitting

Removal

1 Disconnect the battery negative terminal (refer to battery disconnection and reconnection in Chapter 5A, Section 3).

2 Remove the centre console as described in Chapter 11, Section 25.

3 Chock the wheels, and fully release the handbrake.

4 Disconnect the wiring plug from the handbrake 'on' warning light switch **(see illustration)**.

5 Measure the number of exposed threads on the front cable adjuster (for reference when refitting), then unscrew the adjuster nut to the end of the threads **(see illustration 6.3)**.

6 Disconnect the two rear handbrake cables from the equalizer bracket at the rear of the handbrake lever **(see illustration)**.

7 Remove the three securing nuts, and withdraw the handbrake lever assembly from the floor panel **(see illustration)**.

Refitting

8 Refitting is a reversal of removal, bearing in mind the following point:

a) Screw the adjuster nut onto the front cable to give the measurement noted before removal, then check the handbrake operation, and adjust if necessary, as described in Chapter 1A, Section 8 or Chapter 1B, Section 9.
b) Before refitting the centre console, check the operation of the handbrake 'on' warning light.

17 Handbrake cables – removal and refitting

Rear cables

Removal

1 There are two rear handbrake cables, one on each side of the vehicle. To renew either rear cable, proceed as follows.

2 Remove the centre console as described in Chapter 11, Section 25.

3 Chock the front wheels then jack up the rear of the vehicle and support it securely on axle stands (see *Jacking and vehicle support*). Release the handbrake fully.

4 Remove the handbrake shoes, as described in Section 6.

5 Refer to Chapter 4A, Section 16 or Chapter 4B, Section 17 and remove the exhaust system intermediate section and heat shields as necessary for access to the handbrake cable(s).

6 Unclip the handbrake cable spring, undo the retaining bolt and withdraw the handbrake cable from the brake backplate.

7 Undo the retaining bolts and disconnect the handbrake cable retaining clips from the rear axle. Release the cable from the clips on the fuel tank.

8 Disconnect the relevant handbrake cable

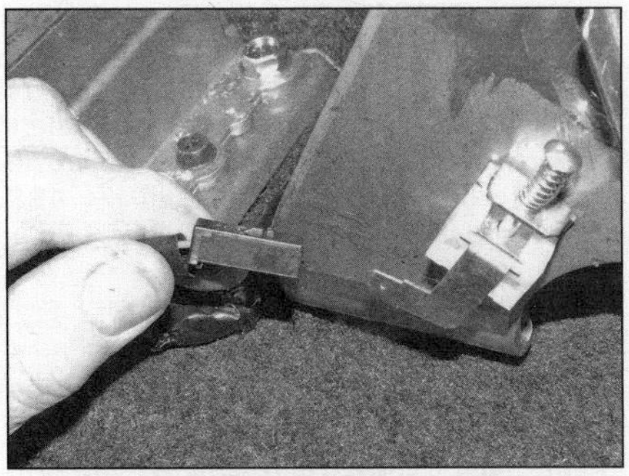

16.4 Disconnect the switch wiring connector

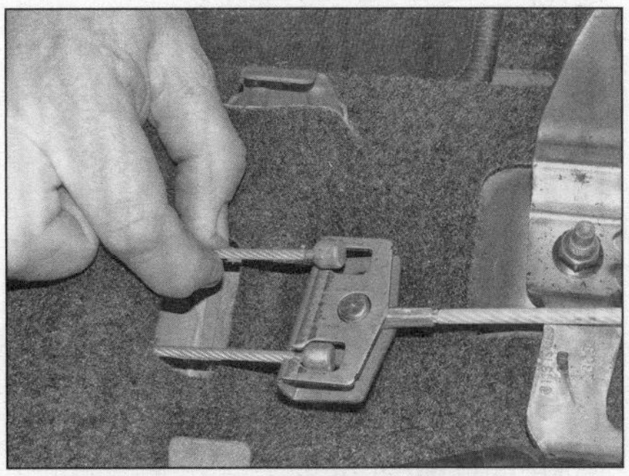

16.6 Disengage the cable end fittings from the equaliser bracket

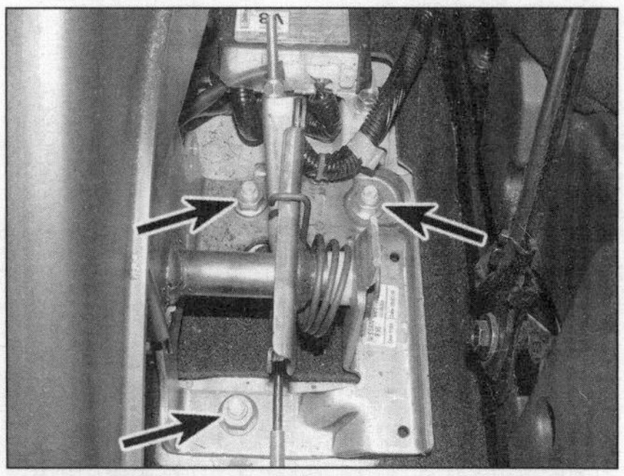

16.7 Undo the handbrake lever mounting nuts

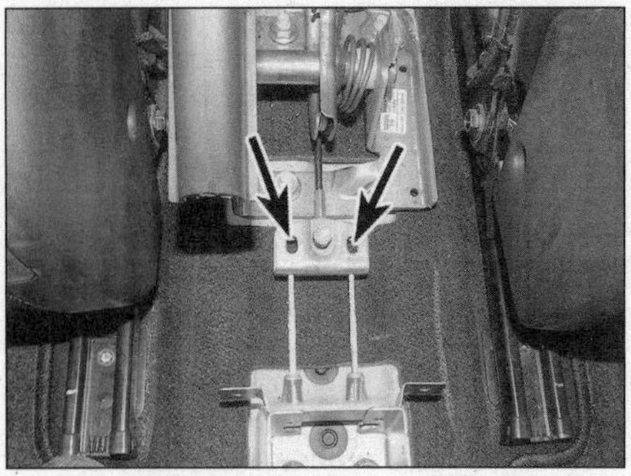

17.8 Disconnect the cables from the equalizer plate

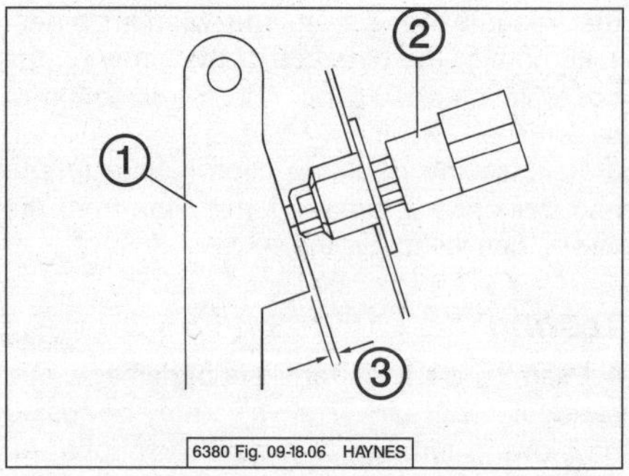

18.6 Check the pedal to switch clearance
1 Brake pedal 2 Switch 3 Clearance

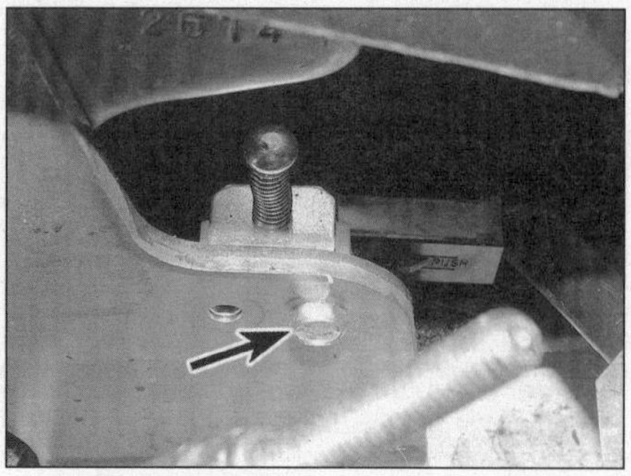

19.2 Handbrake warning light switch securing screw

from the equalizer plate at the rear of the handbrake lever **(see illustration)**.
9 With the cables disconnected from the equalizer, depress the legs of the outer cable end fitting and withdraw the relevant cable from the floor panel.

Refitting

10 Refitting is a reversal of removal, bearing in mind the following points:
a) *Refit the handbrake shoes, as described in Section 6.*
b) *On completion, check the handbrake adjustment, as described in Chapter 1A, Section 8 or Chapter 1B, Section 9.*

Front cable

Removal

11 Remove the centre console as described in Chapter 11, Section 25.
12 Measure the number of exposed threads on the front cable adjuster (for reference when refitting), then unscrew the adjuster nut from the end of the threads **(see illustration 6.3)**.
13 Disconnect the two rear handbrake cables from the equalizer plate at the rear of the handbrake lever **(see illustration 17.8)**.
14 Withdraw the front cable complete with equalizer plate out from inside the car.

Refitting

15 Refitting is a reversal of removal, bearing in mind the following points:
a) *Screw the adjuster nut onto the front cable to give the measurement noted before removal.*
b) *Check the handbrake operation, and adjust if necessary, as described in Chapter 1A, Section 8 or Chapter 1B, Section 9.*

18 Stop-light switch – removal, refitting and adjustment

Removal

1 Disconnect the battery negative terminal (refer to battery disconnection and reconnection in Chapter 5A, Section 3).
2 Remove the facia lower trim panel on the driver's side as described in Chapter 11, Section 26.
3 Disconnect the switch wiring connector from the switch **(see illustration 12.3)**. Note that there are two switches fitted to the brake pedal mounting bracket. The upper switch is the stop-light switch and the lower switch is the brake pedal position switch (used by the engine management ECU).
4 Turn the relevant switch through a quarter-turn anticlockwise and remove it from the pedal mounting bracket.

Refitting and adjustment

5 When refitting the switch, hold the pedal upwards, and then push the switch back into the mounting bracket until the plunger on the end of the switch is fully pressed back into the switch. Once in place, turn the switch clockwise to lock it back in position in the mounting bracket.
6 Measure the pedal to switch clearance **(see illustration)**. Check the measurement against the value given in the Specifications.
7 Re-connect the wiring connector(s), and then check that the stop-lights are extinguished when the brake pedal is released, and illuminated within the first few millimeters of brake pedal travel.
8 If adjustment is required, remove the switch as described previously, and then when refitting the switch, fit it further inwards or outwards on the mounting bracket, until the pedal to switch clearance is correct and the lights operate correctly.
9 When completed, refit the driver's side lower facia panel, as described in Chapter 11, Section 26.

19 Handbrake 'on' warning light switch – removal and refitting

Removal

1 Remove the centre console as described in Chapter 11, Section 25.
2 Undo the securing screw, securing the switch to the handbrake lever mounting bracket **(see illustration)**.
3 As the switch is withdrawn, disconnect the wiring connector.

Refitting

4 Refitting is a reversal of removal, check that the warning light comes on after the specified number of handbrake clicks (see Specifications).

20 Anti-lock braking system (ABS) – general information and component renewal

General information

1 Anti-lock braking is available as standard equipment on the models covered by this manual. The system is fail-safe, and is fitted in addition to the conventional braking system, meaning that the vehicle retains conventional braking in the event of an ABS failure.
2 To prevent wheel locking, the system provides a means of modulating (varying) the hydraulic pressure in the braking circuits, to control the amount of braking effort at each wheel. To achieve this, sensors mounted at all four wheels monitor the rotational speeds of the wheels, and are thus able to detect when there is a risk of wheel locking (low rotational speed, relative to vehicle speed). Solenoid valves are positioned in the brake circuits to each wheel, and the solenoid valves are incorporated in a modulator assembly, which is controlled by an electronic control unit. The electronic control unit controls the braking effort applied to each wheel, according to the information supplied by the wheel speed sensors.
3 Should an ABS fault develop, the system can only be satisfactorily tested using specialist diagnostic equipment available to a Nissan dealer. For safety reasons, owners are strongly advised against attempting to diagnose complex problems with the ABS using standard workshop equipment.

Component renewal

Wheel speed sensors

4 Jack up the front or rear of the vehicle (as applicable), and support it securely using axle stands (see *Jacking and vehicle support*). Remove the relevant roadwheel.
5 The front wheel speed sensors are located

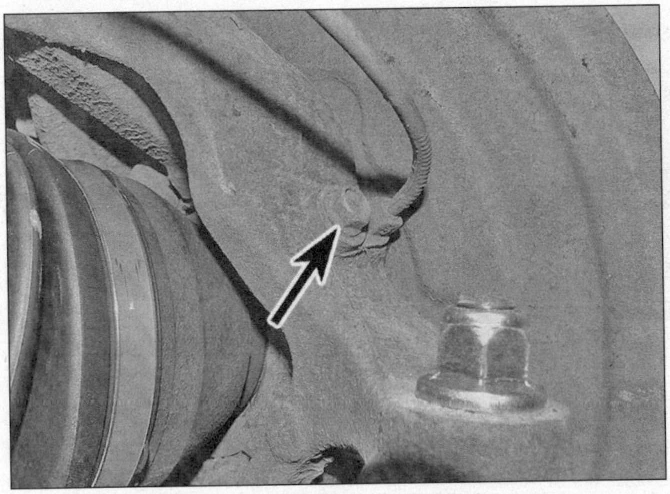
20.5a Location of front wheel speed sensor

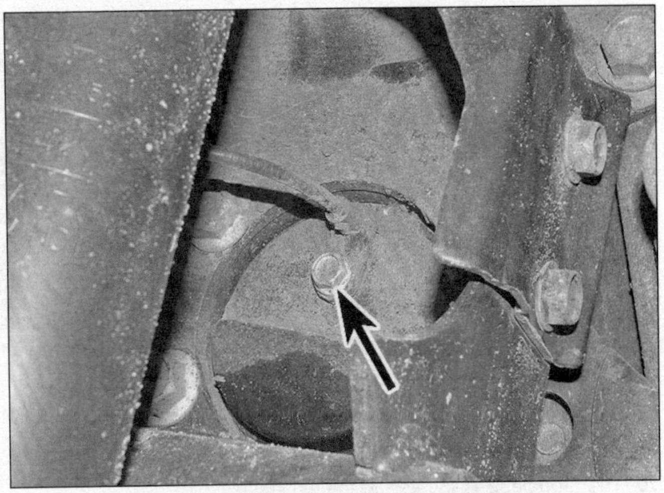
20.5b Location of rear wheel speed sensor

on the rear facing side of each wheel hub carrier, whilst the rear sensors are located on the inner face of the hub/stub axle assembly **(see illustrations)**.

6 For access to the front wheel speed sensor connector, remove the wheel arch liner as described in Chapter 11, Section 21.

7 Trace the sensor wiring back to the connector, and separate the two halves of the wiring plug. Release the wiring from the support brackets under the wheel arch, on the front suspension strut or on the rear axle assembly **(see illustrations)**.

8 Undo the retaining bolt and pull the sensor from the hub carrier/stub axle assembly **(see illustration)**. If the sensor is reluctant to move, apply releasing/penetrating fluid to the assembly, and leave it to soak for a few minutes before trying again. If the sensor still will not move, the hub carrier or rear brake disc must be removed, and the sensor driven from place.

9 Refitting is the reversal of removal, noting the following points:

a) *Ensure the mating faces of the hub carrier/stub axle assembly and sensor are clean and free from corrosion.*

b) *Apply a thin smear of anti-seize compound to mounting surfaces of the sensor and hub carrier/stub axle assembly.*

c) *Tighten the sensor retaining bolt to the specified torque.*

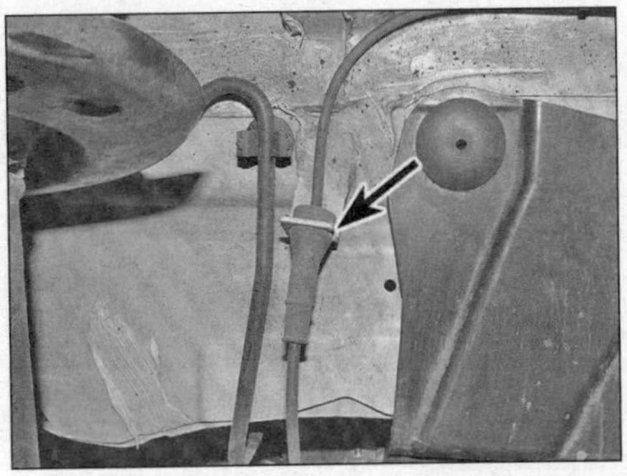
20.7a Release the front sensor wiring from the support bracket under the wheel arch...

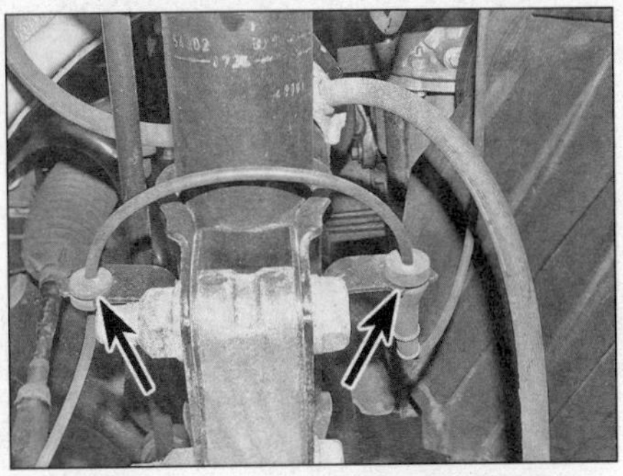
20.7b ...and on the suspension strut

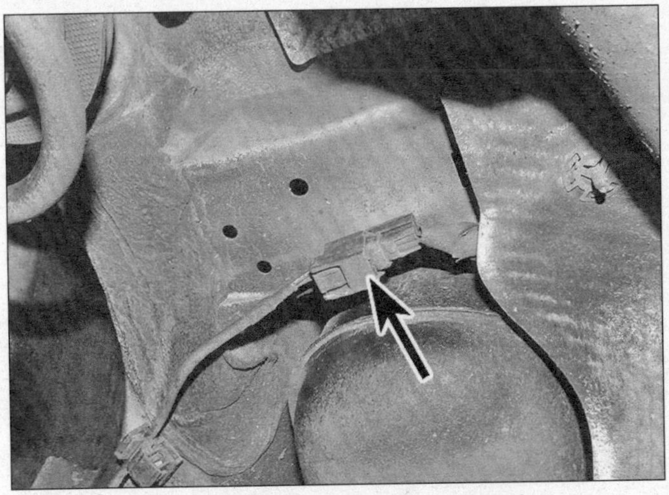
20.7c Rear wheel speed sensor wiring plug

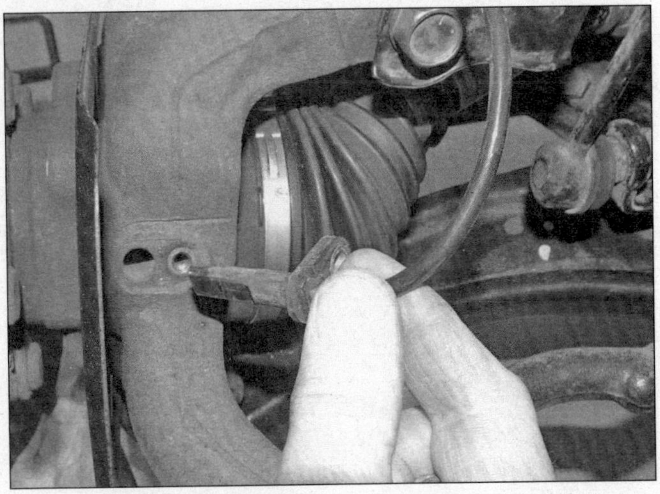
20.8 Removing the front wheel speed sensor

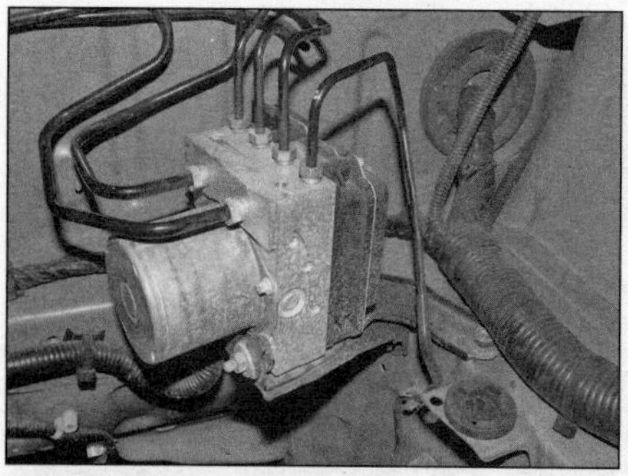

20.10 Location of ABS hydraulic modulator

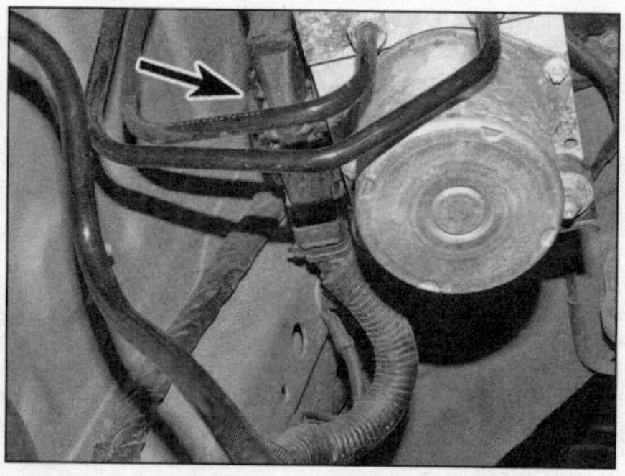

20.13 Release the wiring plug locking lever

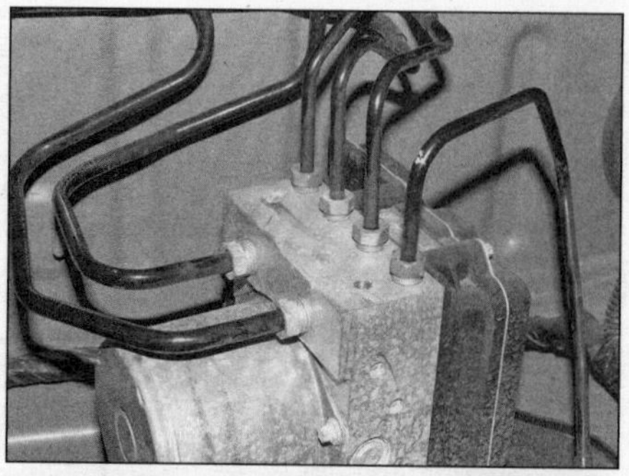

20.14 Mark the location of the various brake pipes before disconnecting them from the modulator

Hydraulic modulator

10 The modulator is located in the left-hand rear corner of the engine compartment **(see illustration)**. Disconnect the battery negative terminal (refer to battery disconnection and reconnection in Chapter 5A, Section 3).

11 Open two bleed screws in the system (one in each of the dual circuit), and gently pump the brake pedal to expel the fluid through a tube connected to the bleed screws (see Section 2). Alternatively, have some caps handy to plug the open ends of the brake pipes once they are disconnected from the actuator.

12 Remove the air cleaner assembly as described in Chapter 4A, Section 2 or Chapter 4B, Section 2.

13 Release the locking clip, and then disconnect the wiring plug from the side of the modulator **(see illustration)**.

14 Note their fitted locations, then undo the union nuts and disconnect the brake pipes from the ABS modulator **(see illustration)**. If the system has not been drained, be prepared for fluid spillage. Plug the end of the pipes to prevent dirt ingress.

15 Undo the two modulator mounting bracket retaining bolts, and lift out the modulator and mounting bracket.

16 Undo the two bolts and separate the modulator from the mounting bracket.

17 To refit the modulator, align the locating lug at the bottom of the unit with the corresponding hole in the mounting bracket, then refit and tighten the mounting bolts securely.

18 The remainder of refitting is a reversal of removal, bleeding the brake system as described in Section 2.

Chapter 10
Suspension and steering

Contents

Degrees of difficulty

Easy, suitable for novice with little experience	**Fairly easy,** suitable for beginner with some experience	**Fairly difficult,** suitable for competent DIY mechanic	**Difficult,** suitable for experienced DIY mechanic	**Very difficult,** suitable for expert DIY or professional

Specifications

Front suspension

Type	Independent with MacPherson struts and anti-roll bar

Rear suspension

Type	Semi-independent with a torsion beam and trailing arms, coil springs and telescopic shock absorbers

Steering

Type	Rack-and-pinion, electrically power-assisted

Wheel bearings

Maximum endfloat at hub (front and rear)	0.05 mm

Roadwheels and tyres

See *Weekly checks*

Front wheel alignment

Front wheel toe setting	2.0 mm ± 1.0 mm toe-in

Torque wrench settings

	Nm	lbf ft
Front suspension		
Anti-roll bar drop link nuts	81	60
Anti-roll bar mounting bracket bolts	28	21
Driveshaft retaining nut*	185	137
Front wheel bearing/hub assembly bolts	88	65
Hub carrier-to-suspension strut retaining bolt nuts*	150	111
Lower arm balljoint clamp bolt nut*	55	41
Lower arm front mounting-to-subframe bolt/nut*	155	114
Lower arm rear mounting-to-subframe bolt/nut*	142	105
Subframe mounting bolts	110	81
Subframe rear support brace retaining bolts:		
Large bolts	110	81
Small bolts	32	24
Suspension strut piston rod top nut*	68	50
Suspension strut upper mounting bolts	17	13
Rear suspension		
Rear axle front mounting bracket bolts:		
Front outer bolt	53	39
All other bolts	90	66
Rear axle pivot through-bolt nut*	150	111
Rear wheel bearing/hub assembly bolts	88	65
Shock absorber upper mounting nut*	20	15
Shock absorber lower mounting bolt/nut	93	69
Steering		
Steering column securing nuts	17	13
Steering column intermediate shaft upper universal joint clamp bolt*	35	26
Steering column intermediate shaft lower universal joint clamp bolt	50	37
Steering gear mounting bolt nuts*	97	72
Steering wheel securing nut*	34	25
Track rod end-to-steering arm/hub carrier nut*	34	25
Roadwheels		
Roadwheel nuts	112	83

*Use new nuts/bolts

1 General Information

Front suspension

1 The independent front suspension is of the MacPherson strut type, incorporating coil springs and integral telescopic shock absorbers. The upper ends of the MacPherson struts are connected to the bodyshell front suspension turrets; the lower ends are bolted to the hub carriers, which carry the wheel bearings, brake calipers and hub/disc assemblies. The hub carriers are located at their lower ends by transverse lower arms. A front anti-roll bar is fitted to all models.

Rear suspension

2 The rear suspension is of the semi-independent type, consisting of a torsion beam axle and trailing arms with coil springs and telescopic shock absorbers. The rear coil springs sit on top of the trailing arms and the shock absorbers are connected to the rear of the trailing arms.

Steering

3 The steering column has an intermediate shaft incorporating an upper and lower universal joint. The universal joints are attached to both the steering column shaft and the steering gear pinion by means of clamp bolts.

4 The steering gear is mounted on the rear of the engine/transmission subframe, and is connected to the steering arms projecting rearwards from the hub carriers. The track rods are fitted with balljoints at their inner and outer ends, to allow for suspension movement, and are threaded to facilitate adjustment.

5 Electric power steering is fitted as standard on all models. The electric motor is part of the steering column assembly inside the passenger compartment.

2 Front hub bearings – renewal

Note: *The bearing is part of the centre hub assembly and can only be replaced as a complete assembly.*

Removal

1 Firmly apply the handbrake, and then jack up the front of the vehicle and support it securely on axle stands (see *Jacking and vehicle support*). Remove the appropriate roadwheel.

2 Remove the brake disc, as described in Chapter 9, Section 7.

3 If not already done, unbolt the ABS wheel speed sensor, as described in Chapter 9, Section 20. Suspend the sensor away from the working area, to avoid the possibility of damage.

4 Disconnect the outboard end of the driveshaft from the hub carrier **(see illustration)**, as described in Chapter 8, Section 2. Note that there is no need to drain the transmission oil/fluid, or disconnect

2.4 Disconnect the driveshaft from the hub

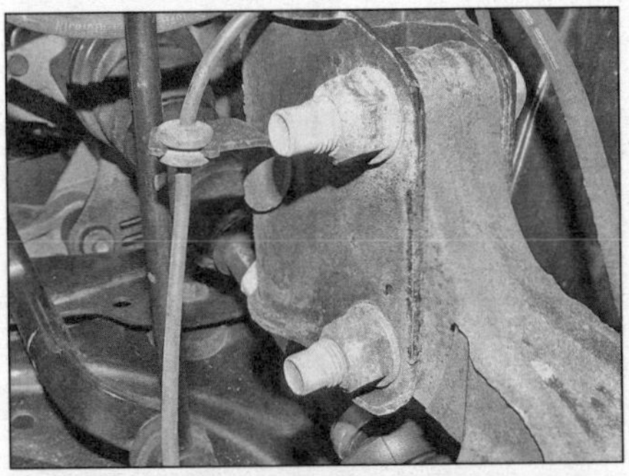

2.5 Remove the two strut-to-hub carrier retaining nuts and bolts

2.6 Hub/bearing assembly mounting bolts

2.7a Using a copper hammer to free the bearing assembly...

2.7b ...then withdraw it from the hub carrier

2.8 Remove the brake disc back plate

2.9 The centre hub may need to be pressed out of the old bearing and fitted to the new bearing

the inboard end of the driveshaft from the transmission. Do not allow the end of the driveshaft to hang down under its own weight – support the end of the driveshaft using wire or string.

5 Undo the two upper hub carrier-to-strut retaining bolt/nuts, and then remove the hub carrier from the strut **(see illustration)**. Note the fitted position of the retaining bolts for refitting; discard the nuts, as new ones will be required for refitting.

6 Slacken the four hub/bearing retaining bolts **(see illustration)**. Remove two of the bolts completely, and then leave the other two bolts screwed most of the way into the rear of the hub/bearing.

7 Using a copper hammer, hit the heads of the two bolts that remain in the rear of the hub/bearing, whilst holding the assembly on the bench **(see illustrations)**. If the hub/bearing is reluctant to move, apply releasing/penetrating fluid to the assembly, and leave it to soak for a few minutes before trying again.

8 With the hub/bearing removed from the carrier, remove the brake disc back plate, noting its fitted position **(see illustration)**.

9 Seek the advice of a Nissan dealer as to whether the new bearing is supplied complete with the centre wheel flange part of the hub or whether it is supplied separately. If it is supplied separately the wheel flange will have to be removed from the old bearing and fitted to the new bearing. Using a press (or similar), press the centre wheel flange part of the hub out from the bearing **(see illustration)**.

10 Note that one half of the bearing inner race may remain on the centre wheel flange. If so, support the wheel hub in a vice then draw off the bearing inner race, using a suitable puller.

Refitting

11 Before installing the new bearing, thoroughly clean the wheel flange, hub and the bearing location in the hub carrier.

12 Press the new bearing onto the centre wheel flange until it contacts the shoulder on the flange. This can be achieved using metal tubing, or large sockets of suitable diameter, together with threaded bar, spacers and nuts to pull the components together.

13 With the bearing fully home, fit the brake disc back plate into position (as noted on removal), and then fit the hub/bearing unit to the carrier and tighten the retaining bolts.

14 Refit the hub/bearing carrier back to the lower part of the strut and fit the retaining bolts and new nuts, in the position noted on removal. Tighten the retaining bolts to the specified torque setting.

15 Refit the outer end of the driveshaft back into the hub, as described in Chapter 8, Section 2.

16 Refit the wheel speed sensor back into the rear of the hub carrier, as described in Chapter 9, Section 20.

17 Refit the front brake disc, as described in Chapter 9, Section 7.

18 On completion, refit the roadwheel and lower the vehicle to the ground.

3 Front suspension strut – removal, overhaul and refitting

Note: *New hub carrier-to-suspension strut retaining nuts must be used on refitting.*

Removal

1 Firmly apply the handbrake, and then jack up the front of the vehicle and support it securely on axle stands (see *Jacking and vehicle support*). Remove the appropriate roadwheel.

2 Undo the retaining nut and disconnect the anti-roll bar drop link upper ball joint retaining nut from the suspension strut **(see illustration)**.

3.2 Undo the drop link upper retaining nut

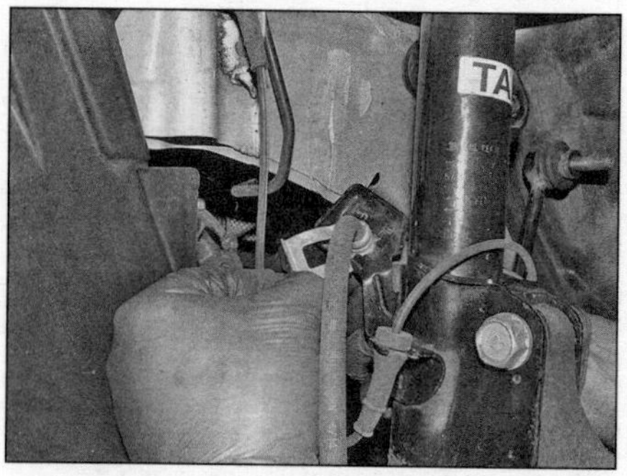

3.3 Release the brake pipe securing clip

3.4 Unclip the wheel speed sensor wiring from the support bracket

3.5 Remove the two strut-to-hub retaining nuts and bolts

3 Extract the retaining clip and release the brake hydraulic hose from the support bracket on the suspension strut **(see illustration)**.

4 Unclip the ABS wiring loom from the support bracket on the lower part of the suspension strut **(see illustration)**.

5 Undo the two nuts and withdraw the bolts securing the suspension strut to the hub carrier **(see illustration)**. Discard the nuts, as new ones must be used on refitting.

6 Open the bonnet and remove the grommet from the access hole in the windscreen cowl panel **(see illustration)**.

7 Have an assistant support the strut from underneath the wheel arch then, working in the engine compartment, unscrew the three bolts securing the top of the strut to the suspension turret **(see illustrations)**.

8 Release the lower end of the strut from the hub carrier, and then withdraw the assembly from under the wheel arch **(see illustrations)**.

Warning: Do not unscrew the centre piston rod nut at this stage.

Overhaul

Note: *Coil spring compressor tools will be required for this operation, and a new piston rod top nut must be used on reassembly.*

9 Using an Allen key to hold the piston rod, slacken the strut upper mounting nut. Do not remove the nut; only slacken to the top of the threads, so the nut is still fully on the threads.

10 Fit spring compressors to the spring, and compress the spring sufficiently to enable the upper spring seat to be turned by hand **(see illustration)**.

Warning: Do not use makeshift or improvised tools to compress the spring, as there is a danger of serious injury if the spring is not retained properly and released slowly.

11 Fully unscrew and remove the piston rod top nut. Note that it may be necessary to counterhold the piston rod, using an Allen key, as the nut is

3.6 Remove the windscreen cowl panel grommet for access to one of the strut upper mounting bolts

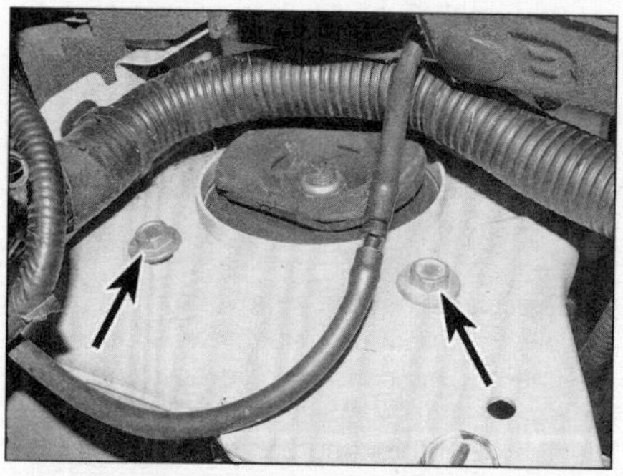

3.7a Two of the three strut upper mounting bolts are readily accessible...

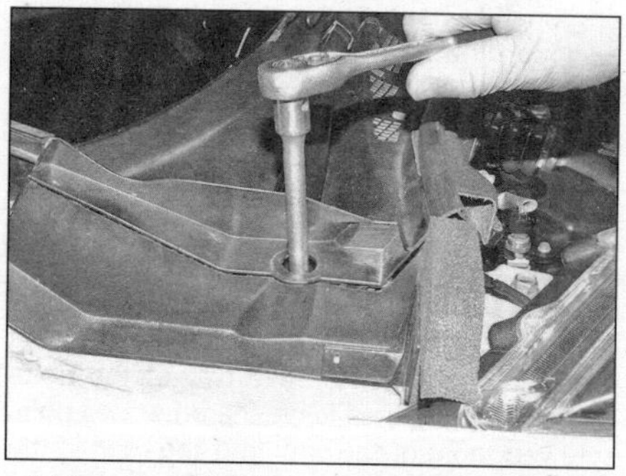

3.7b ...the third is accessed through the hole in the windscreen cowl panel

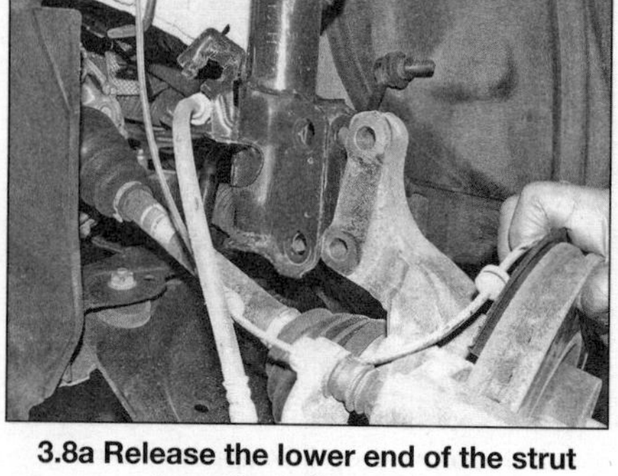

3.8a Release the lower end of the strut from the hub carrier...

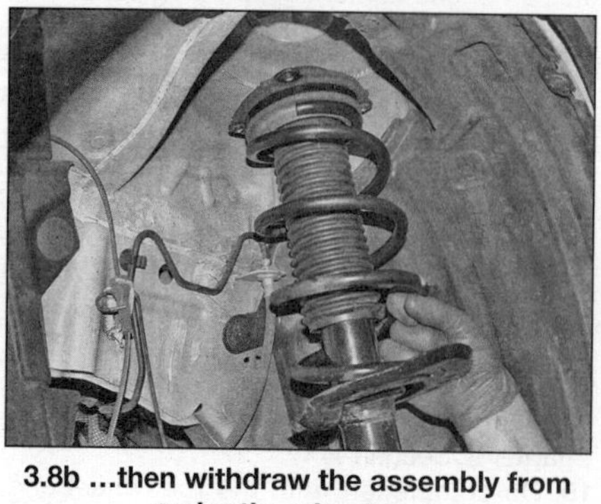

3.8b ...then withdraw the assembly from under the wheel arch

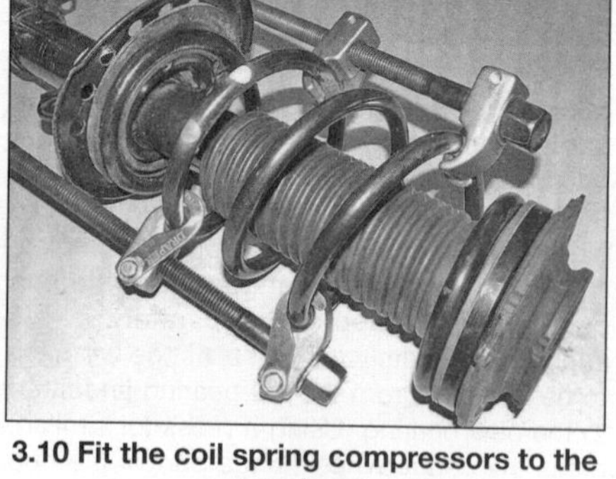

3.10 Fit the coil spring compressors to the springs

3.11a Hold the piston rod with an Allen key if necessary and unscrew the top nut

3.11b The piston rod nut can now be completely removed

3.12a Remove the upper mounting insulator and bearing...

unscrewed **(see illustrations)**. Discard the nut – a new one must be used on reassembly.

12 Withdraw the upper mounting insulator and the bearing then, if necessary, remove the bearing from the mounting insulator **(see illustrations)**.

13 Withdraw the spring, complete with the compressors, and then withdraw the dust cover and lower spring seat rubber, noting its fitted position **(see illustrations)**.

14 With the strut assembly now dismantled, examine all the components for wear, damage or deformation. Check the rubber components for deterioration. Renew any of the components as necessary.

15 Examine the strut for signs of fluid leakage. Check the piston rod for signs of pitting along its entire length, and check the strut body for signs of damage. While holding it in an upright position, test the operation of the strut by moving the piston rod through a full stroke, and then through short strokes of 50 to 100 mm. In both cases, the resistance felt should be smooth and continuous. If the resistance is jerky, or uneven, or if there is any visible sign of wear or damage to the strut, renewal is necessary.

16 If any doubt exists about the condition of the coil spring, carefully remove the spring compressors, and check the spring for distortion and signs of cracking. Renew the spring if it is damaged or distorted, or if there is any doubt as to its condition.

17 Commence reassembly by refitting the lower spring seat rubber, ensuring that it is correctly located in the recess in the lower spring seat, as noted on removal.

18 Ensure that the coil spring is compressed sufficiently to enable the upper mounting components to be fitted, and then locate the spring on the strut, ensuring that the lower end of the spring is correctly located on the lower spring seat rubber **(see illustration)**.

19 Refit the dust cover then, if removed, refit the bearing to the upper mounting insulator.

20 Refit the upper mounting insulator and position it so that the arrow on the upper flange points toward the outside of the car **(see illustration)**.

21 Fit a new piston rod top nut, and then tighten the top nut to the specified torque,

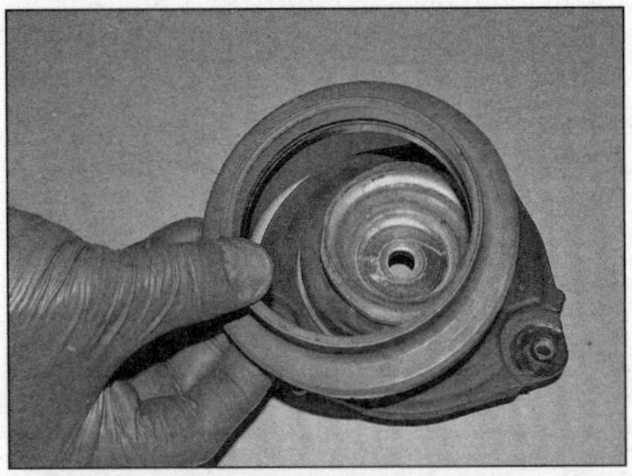
3.12b ...then remove the bearing from the mounting insulator

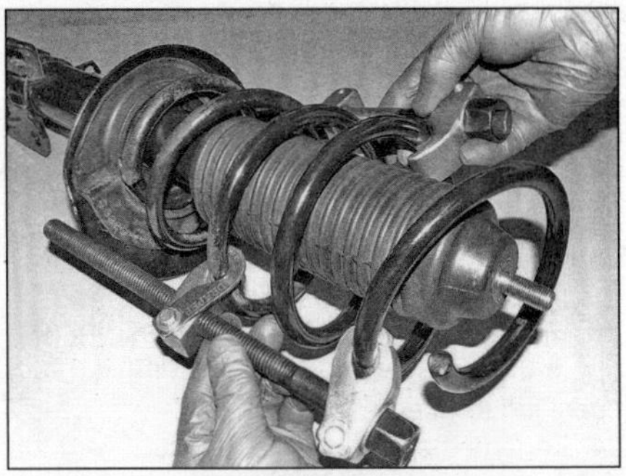
3.13a Carefully withdraw the spring and compressors...

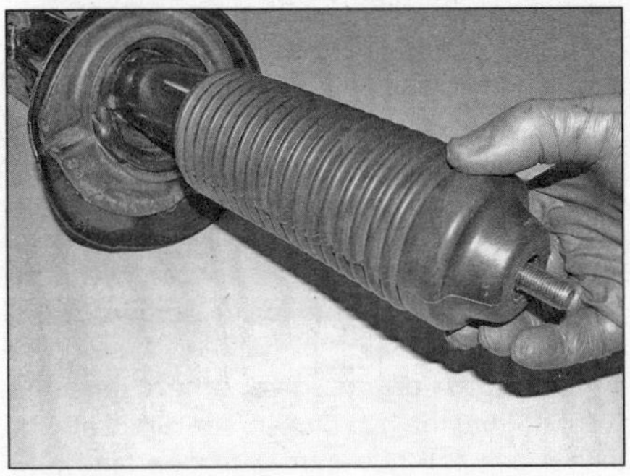
3.13b ...followed by the dust cover...

3.13c ...and lower spring seat rubber

3.18 Ensure that the lower end of the spring is against the raised stop on the spring seat rubber

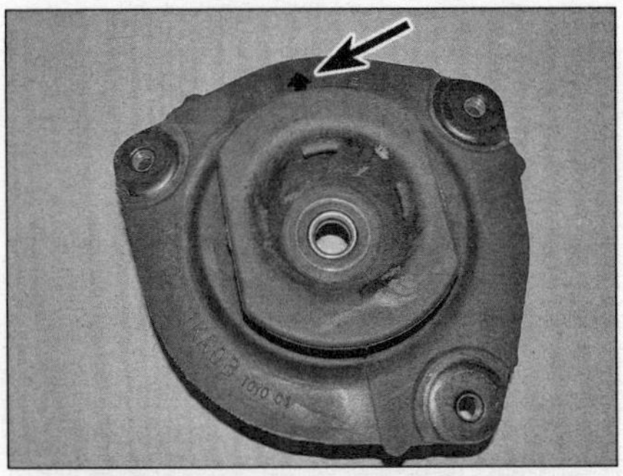
3.20 Position the upper mounting insulator with the arrow on the upper flange pointing towards the outside of the car

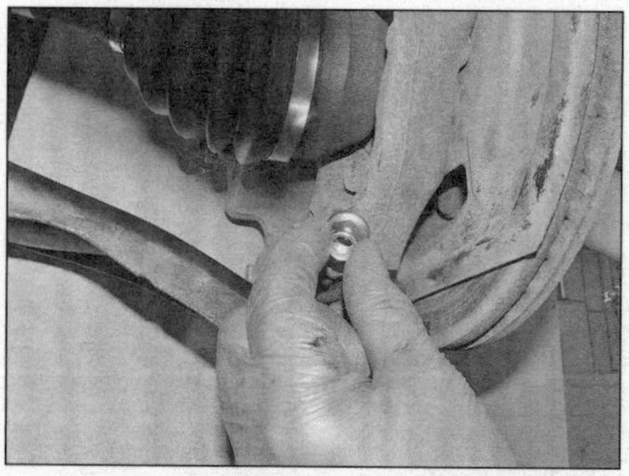

4.2a Undo the lower arm balljoint clamp bolt nut...

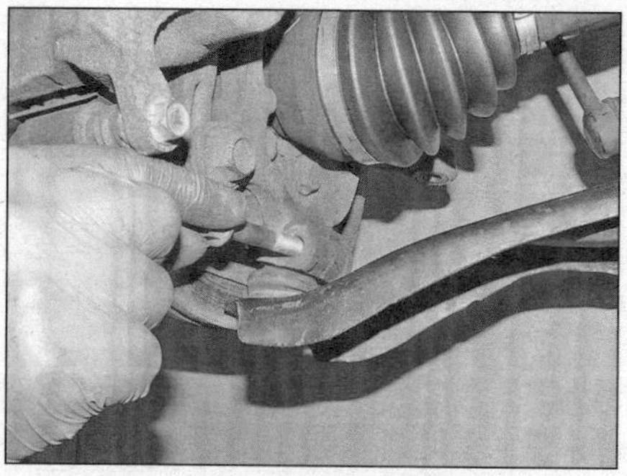

4.2b ...and remove the clamp bolt

counterholding the piston rod as during dismantling.

22 Check that the spring ends are correctly located then remove the spring compressors.

Refitting

23 Manoeuvre the strut assembly into position under the wheel arch and up into the suspension turret. Make sure the upper mounting is in the correct position, as it is fitted inside the inner wheel arch. Fit the upper mounting bolts, and tighten them to the specified torque.

24 Engage the lower end of the strut with the hub carrier and refit the securing bolts with the bolt heads toward the front of the vehicle. Fit the new nuts to the bolts, and tighten to the specified torque.

25 Refit the drop link upper ball joint to the suspension strut, and then tighten the retaining nut to the specified torque.

4.4 Push down on the lower arm to free the balljoint from the hub carrier

26 Locate the brake hydraulic hose and ABS wiring loom back in the support brackets on the suspension strut. Secure the brake hose with the retaining clip.

27 Refit the grommet to the windscreen cowl panel.

28 On completion, refit the roadwheel and lower the vehicle to the ground.

4 Front suspension lower arm – removal, inspection and refitting

Note: *The lower arm balljoint retaining nut must be renewed on refitting.*

Removal

1 Firmly apply the handbrake, and then jack up the front of the vehicle and support it securely on axle stands (see *Jacking and vehicle support*). Remove the appropriate roadwheel.

2 Undo the retaining nut and withdraw the clamp bolt from the lower arm balljoint. Note that a new nut will be required for refitting **(see illustrations)**.

3 If necessary, use a chisel or screwdriver as a wedge to expand the lower portion of the swivel hub.

4 Push down on the lower arm to free the balljoint from the hub carrier **(see illustration)**, then move the hub carrier to one side and release the balljoint, taking care not to damage the balljoint rubber boot.

5 Undo the bolt and nut securing the lower arm rear mounting to the subframe **(see illustration)**. Discard the nut – a new one must be used on refitting.

6 Unscrew the lower arm front mounting bolt and nut, and then withdraw the lower arm from the subframe **(see illustration)**. Discard the nut – a new one must be used on refitting.

Inspection

7 With the lower arm removed; examine the lower arm itself, and the mounting bushes for wear, cracks or damage. Check the balljoint for wear, excessive play, or stiffness. Also check the balljoint dust boot for cracks or damage. If the lower arm, mounting bushes or balljoint show any signs of wear or damage, the lower arm must be renewed complete as none of the components are available individually.

Refitting

8 Refitting is a reversal of removal, bearing in mind the following points:

a) *Use new nuts when refitting the lower arm mountings and the lower arm balljoint clamp bolt.*

b) *Tighten all nuts and bolts to the specified torque.*

c) *On completion the front wheel alignment should be checked, with reference to Chapter 1A, Section 15 or Chapter 1B, Section 15.*

5 Front suspension lower arm balljoint – renewal

1 At the time of writing the lower arm balljoint was not available separately and is integral with the suspension lower arm. If the balljoint is worn or damaged, the complete lower arm must be renewed as described in Section 4.

6 Front suspension anti-roll bar – removal and refitting

Removal

1 Remove the front suspension subframe as described in Section 7.

2 Unscrew the bolts, and withdraw the clamps securing the anti-roll bar to the top of the subframe **(see illustration)**.

4.5 Remove the lower arm rear mounting bolt and nut

4.6 Remove the lower arm front mounting bolt and nut

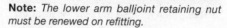

6.2 Undo the anti-roll bar clamp bolts (one side shown)

3 Lift the anti-roll bar up and off the subframe. If necessary, unscrew the retaining nuts and remove the drop links from each end of the anti-roll bar.
4 Inspect the mounting clamp rubbers for cracks or deterioration. If renewal is necessary, slide the old rubbers from the bar, and fit the new rubbers. Note that the rubbers should be positioned with the slit facing the front of the vehicle.

Refitting

5 Refitting is a reversal of removal, bearing in mind the following points:

a) Fit the mounting clamps with the open elongated bolt hole facing the front of the vehicle.
b) Tighten all nuts and bolts to the specified torque.
c) Refit the front suspension subframe as described in Section 7.

7 Front suspension subframe – removal and refitting

Note: *The steering rack, anti-roll bar and lower suspension arms will be still bolted to the subframe, as it is removed.Always renew any self-locking nuts when working on the suspension/steering components.*

Removal

1 Firmly apply the handbrake, and then jack up the front of the vehicle and support it securely on axle stands (see *Jacking and vehicle support*). Remove both front roadwheels.
2 Remove the facia lower trim panel on the driver's side as described in Chapter 11, Section 26.
3 Release the two fasteners and remove the carpet segment from around the base of the steering column **(see illustration)**.
4 Set the front roadwheels to the straight-ahead position.
5 Place a matching mark on the steering column intermediate shaft universal joint and the steering gear pinion shaft.
6 Undo the retaining bolt and disconnect the steering column intermediate shaft universal joint from the steering gear pinion shaft **(see illustration)**. Do not turn the steering wheel with the intermediate shaft disconnected.
7 Working under the vehicle, slacken and remove the through bolt securing engine/transmission rear lower mounting to the mounting bracket **(see illustration)**.
8 Working as described in Section 4 slacken and remove both front suspension lower arm balljoint clamp bolt nuts and free the balljoint shanks from the hub carriers. Discard the nuts, as new ones will be required for refitting.
9 Undo the retaining nut and disconnect the anti-roll bar drop link upper balljoint retaining nut from the suspension strut on each side **(see illustration 3.2)**.
10 Undo the retaining nut and disconnect the track rod end from the hub carrier **(see illustration)**. Refer to Section 17, for further information.
11 On diesel models, undo the retaining bolts and release the thermo plunger mounting bracket from the front of the subframe **(see illustration)**.
12 Where applicable, release the exhaust system front pipe rubber mountings from the subframe brackets **(see illustration)**.
13 Make a final check that all cables/hoses that are attached to the subframe have been released and positioned clear so that they will not hinder the removal procedure.
14 Place a jack and a suitable block of wood under the subframe to support the subframe as it is lowered.
15 Undo the subframe rear mounting bolt on each side noting that these bolts also secure the subframe rear support brace **(see illustration)**.
16 Suitably support the subframe rear support brace and undo the three retaining

7.3 Release the fasteners and remove the carpet segment from the base of the steering column

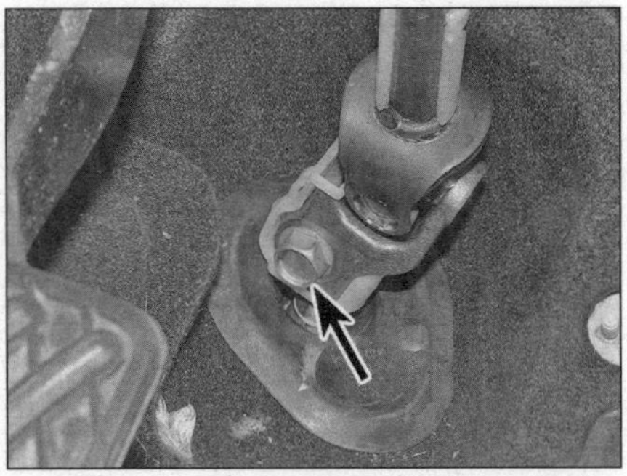

7.6 Undo the retaining bolt and disconnect the universal joint from the steering gear pinion shaft

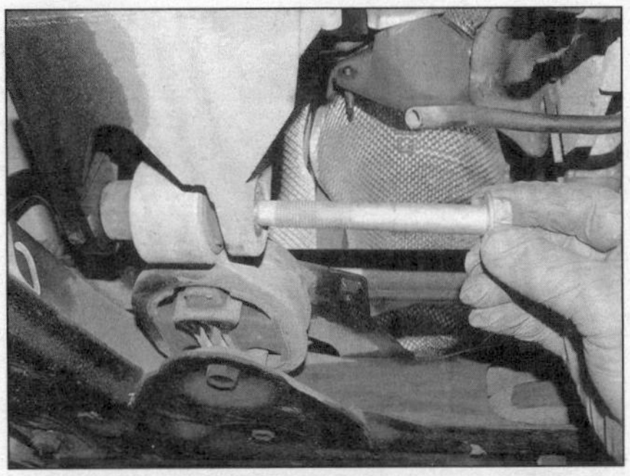

7.7 Remove the rear lower mounting through bolt

7.10 Disconnect the track rod ends

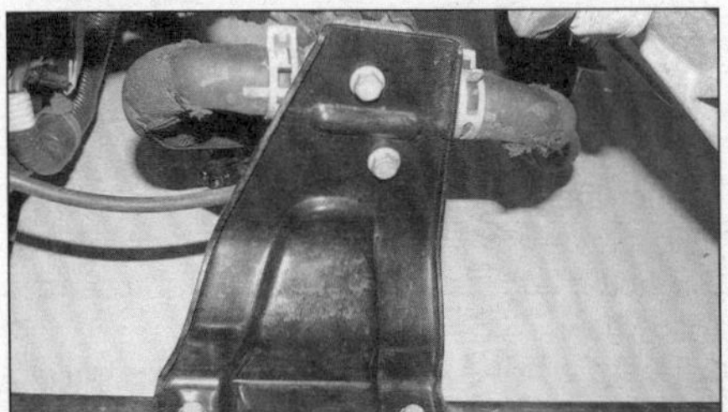

7.11 Thermo plunger mounting bracket retaining bolts – diesel models

7.12 Release the exhaust front pipe rubber mountings from the subframe

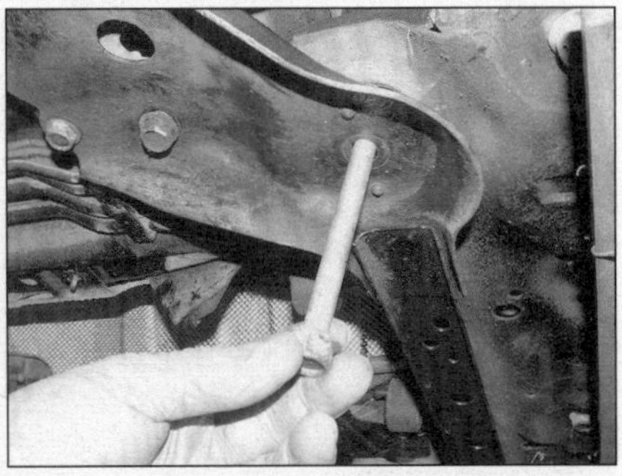

7.15 Undo the subframe rear mounting bolt on each side

7.16 Undo the three bolts each side and remove the rear support brace

7.17a Undo the subframe front mounting bolts...

7.17b ...and lower the subframe

bolts each side **(see illustration)**. Remove the support brace from the subframe.

17 Slacken and remove the subframe front mounting bolts then carefully lower the subframe assembly out of position and remove it from underneath the vehicle, taking great care to ensure that the subframe assembly does not catch anything as it is lowered out of position **(see illustrations)**.

Refitting

18 Refitting is a reversal of the removal procedure, noting the following points:

a) *Use new lower balljoint, and steering track rod end retaining nuts.*
b) *Fit and lightly tighten the subframe and rear support brace retaining bolts then, working progressively in a diagonal sequence, tighten all the bolts to the specified torque.*
c) *On completion check and, if necessary, adjust the front wheel alignment as described in Chapter 1A, Section 15or Chapter 1B, Section 15.*

8 Rear hub bearings – renewal

1 The rear hub bearings are integral with the rear hubs, and cannot be renewed independently. If the bearings require renewal, the complete hub assembly must be renewed as follows.

2 Chock the front wheels then jack up the rear of the vehicle and support it securely on axle stands (see *Jacking and vehicle support*). Remove the appropriate rear roadwheel and release the handbrake fully.

3 Remove the handbrake shoes from inside the rear brake disc, as described in Chapter 9, Section 6.

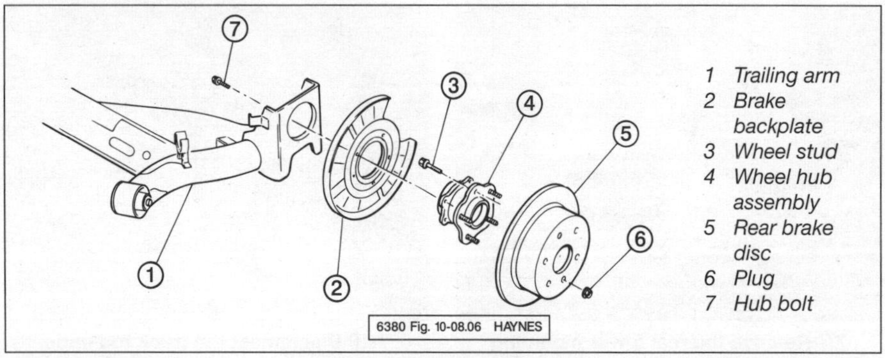

8.6 Rear wheel hub arrangement

4 Unbolt the handbrake cable and withdraw it from the lower part of the brake backplate.

5 Remove the wheel speed sensor from the rear of the hub, as described in Chapter 9, Section 20.

6 Working at the rear of the hub assembly undo the four mounting bolts, and then withdraw the hub complete with backplate from the trailing arm **(see illustration)**.

7 Remove the backplate from the rear of the old hub/bearing and fit to the new one.

8 Thoroughly clean the backplate and trailing arm, and then slide the new hub assembly and backplate into position. Make sure the two handbrake shoe retaining pins are in place in the backplate before refitting.

9 Fit the hub assembly to the trailing arm and then tighten the four retaining bolts to the specified torque.

10 Check that the hub spins freely, and then refit the handbrake shoes and brake disc, as described in Chapter 9, Section 6.

11 Refit the ABS wheel speed sensor and tighten its retaining bolt to the specified torque (see Chapter 9, Section 20).

12 Refit the roadwheel(s), lower the vehicle to the ground and tighten to the specified torque setting.

9 Rear shock absorber – removal, testing and refitting

Note: *A new shock absorber upper mounting nut must be used on refitting. Also it is advisable to always renew shock absorbers in pairs on the same axle.*

Removal

1 Chock the front wheels then jack up the rear of the vehicle and support it securely on axle stands (see *Jacking and vehicle support*). For better access remove the appropriate rear roadwheel.

2 Using a trolley jack, raise the rear trailing arm, until the shock absorber is slightly compressed.

3 From inside the luggage compartment, remove the cover in the side trim panel for access to the shock absorber upper mounting **(see illustrations)**.

9.3a Remove the cover in the side trim panel...

9.3b ...for access to the shock absorber upper mounting

4 Where fitted, remove the cap over the upper mounting nut then unscrew the nut. Use a second spanner to hold the shock absorber piston rod as the mounting nut is unscrewed.
5 Remove the dished washer and upper mounting rubber bush from the top of the shock absorber.
6 Slacken the shock absorber lower mounting bolt retaining nut, and then withdraw the bolt, disengaging the lower part of the shock absorber from the trailing arm **(see illustration)**.
7 Withdraw the shock absorber from under the rear of the vehicle. Collect the distance tube, mounting rubber bush and dished washer from the shock absorber upper mounting, followed by the rebound rubber and cover.

Testing

8 Examine the shock absorber for signs of fluid leakage. Check the piston rod for signs of pitting along its entire length, and check the body for signs of damage. While holding it in an upright position, test the operation by moving the piston rod through a full stroke, and then through short strokes of 50 to 100 mm. In both cases, the resistance felt should be smooth and continuous. If the resistance is jerky, or uneven, or if there is any visible sign of wear or damage, renewal is necessary. Also check the rubber mounting bushes for damage or deterioration, and inspect the mounting bolt for signs of wear or damage; renew if necessary.

Refitting

9 Fit the rebound rubber and cover over the piston rod followed by the dished washer, mounting rubber bush and distance tube. The dished washer should be fitted with its concave side towards the mounting rubber bush.
10 Offer up the top of the shock absorber into its upper mounting location, then refit the mounting rubber bush and dished washer. Again, the dished washer should be fitted with its concave side towards the mounting rubber bush. Fit the new retaining nut and tighten by hand at this stage.
11 Align the damper lower mounting with the trailing arm and refit the lower mounting bolt. Fit the nut, also tightening it by hand at this stage.
12 Refit the rear roadwheel then lower the vehicle to the ground and tighten the wheel bolts to the specified torque.
13 With the vehicle down on its wheels, in the normal ride height position; tighten the upper and lower shock absorber mounting bolts/nuts to the specified torque.
14 On completion refit the cover in the interior side trim panel.

10 Rear coil spring – removal and refitting

Note: *It is advisable to always renew coil springs in pairs on the same axle. New suspension securing nuts must be used on refitting*

Removal

1 Chock the front wheels then jack up the rear of the vehicle and support it securely on axle stands (see *Jacking and vehicle support*). Remove the appropriate rear roadwheel.
2 Using a trolley jack, raise the rear trailing arm, until the shock absorber is slightly compressed.
3 Slacken the shock absorber lower mounting bolt retaining nut, and then withdraw the bolt, disengaging the lower part of the shock absorber from the trailing arm **(see illustration 9.6)**.
4 Carefully lower the trailing arm on the trolley jack, taking care not to put any strain on the brake hose or wheel speed sensor wiring.
5 Withdraw the coil spring complete with upper rubber mounting from under the rear of the vehicle.
6 If required, unclip the spring lower rubber mounting from the trailing arm.

Refitting

7 Refit the coil spring back into position between the underbody and the trailing arm, making sure the upper and lower rubber mountings are in place.
8 Carefully raise the trolley jack, align the shock absorber lower mounting with the trailing arm and refit the lower mounting bolt. Fit the retaining nut and tighten it by hand at this stage.
9 Refit the rear roadwheel then lower the vehicle to the ground and tighten the wheel nuts to the specified torque.
10 With the vehicle on its wheels, in the normal ride height position; tighten the lower shock absorber mounting bolt nut to the specified torque.

11 Rear axle – removal and refitting

Removal

1 Chock the front wheels then jack up the rear of the car and support it on axle stands (see *Jacking and vehicle support*). Remove both rear roadwheels.
2 Unscrew the brake master cylinder fluid reservoir cap and screw it down onto a piece of polythene to minimise fluid loss during the following procedure.
3 Undo the bolt securing the ABS wheel speed sensor to the hub/stub axle assembly on each side **(see illustration)**. Withdraw the sensors from the stub axles and unclip the sensor wiring from the rear axle.
4 Remove the handbrake shoes from inside the rear brake discs as described in Chapter 9, Section 6.
5 Unbolt the handbrake cables and withdraw them from the lower part of the brake backplate.
6 Undo the support bracket retaining bolts and release the handbrake cables from their attachments on the rear axle.
7 Slacken the union nuts, and disconnect the brake pipes from the flexible hose unions on the rear axle **(see illustration)**. Plug the pipe and hose ends to minimise fluid loss and prevent the entry of dirt into the hydraulic system. Remove the retaining clips, and release the two flexible hoses from their mounting brackets.
8 Remove the rear coil springs as described in Section 10.
9 Support the weight of the axle assembly using two trolley jacks. Alternatively, one trolley jack and a length of wood may be used,

9.6 Shock absorber lower mounting bolt

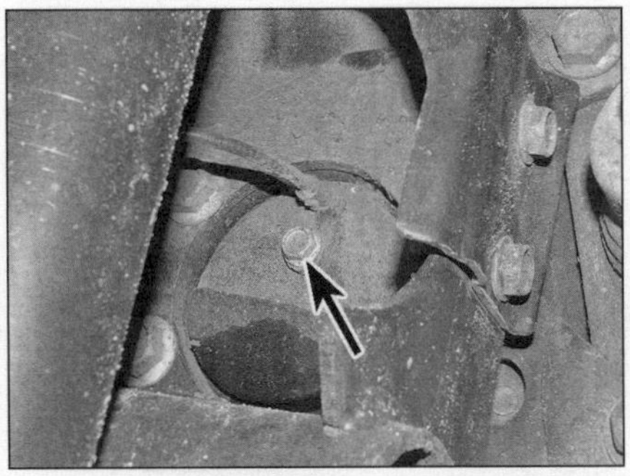

11.3 Rear wheel speed sensor retaining bolt

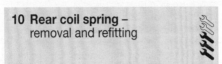

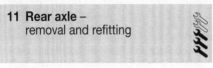

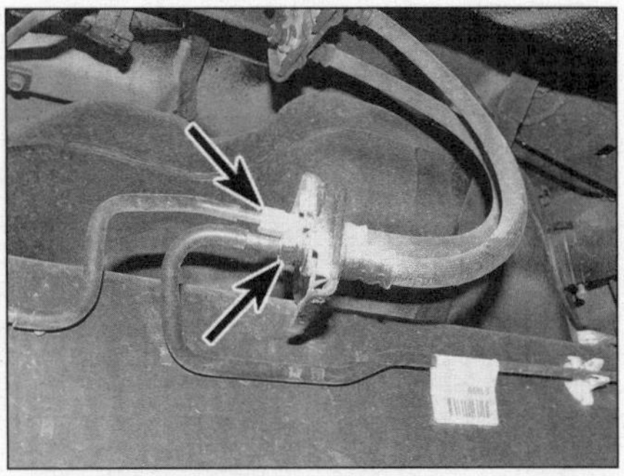

11.7 Disconnect the brake pipes from the flexible hose unions

11.10 Rear axle front mounting bracket retaining bolt (one of four left-hand side bolts shown)

but the help of an assistant will be required.

10 Undo the four bolts each side securing the axle front mounting brackets to the underbody **(see illustration)**.

11 Make a final check that all necessary components have been disconnected and positioned so that they will not hinder the removal procedure. Carefully lower the axle assembly out of position, and remove it from underneath the vehicle.

12 The brake components can be removed from the axle, referring to the relevant Sections of Chapter 9. The hub bearing units can be removed with reference to Section 8.

13 If necessary, the front mounting brackets can be removed after unscrewing the retaining nut and withdrawing the centre through-bolt. Note that new through-bolt retaining nuts will be required for reassembly.

Refitting

14 Refit any components that were removed from the axle, referring to the relevant Sections of this Chapter and Chapter 9, as applicable. If the front mounting brackets were removed, refit the brackets, but only tighten the new through-bolt nuts lightly at this stage.

15 Support the axle on the trolley jacks, and position the assembly under the rear of the vehicle.

16 Raise the jacks, then refit and lightly tighten the front mounting bracket retaining bolts. With all the bolts in place, work progressively in a diagonal sequence, and tighten all the bolts to the specified torque.

17 Refit the rear coil springs as described in Section 10.

18 Refit the brake hydraulic pipes and flexible hoses together with the retaining clips and tighten the union nuts securely.

19 Reconnect the handbrake cables to the brake backplates and underbody supports.

20 Refit the handbrake shoes and rear brake discs as described in Chapter 9, Section 6.

21 Refit the ABS wheel speed sensors, tightening the retaining bolts to the specified torque (see Chapter 9).

22 Bleed the complete brake hydraulic system, as described in Chapter 9, Section 2.

23 Adjust the handbrake as described in Chapter 1A, Section 8 or Chapter 1B, Section 9.

24 Refit the roadwheels and lower the vehicle to the ground.

25 With the vehicle on its wheels, in the normal ride height position; where applicable, tighten the new front mounting bracket through-bolt nuts to the specified torque.

12 Steering wheel – removal and refitting

Warning: The airbag is mounted in the steering wheel centre pad. Make sure that the safety recommendations given in Chapter 12, Section 20, are followed to prevent personal injury.

Removal

1 Ensure that the ignition is switched off, and then disconnect the battery negative terminal (refer to battery disconnection and reconnection in Chapter 5A, Section 3). Wait for at least ten minutes before carrying out any further work.

2 Remove the airbag unit from the centre of the steering wheel, as described in Chapter 12, Section 21.

3 Release the steering lock by inserting the ignition key and set the front wheels in the straight-ahead position.

4 Undo and remove the steering wheel retaining nut **(see illustration)**. Note that a new nut will be required for refitting.

5 Check for alignment marks between the steering wheel and the end of the steering column shaft for refitting **(see illustration)**. Make your own alignment marks, if required.

6 Withdraw the wheel from the column shaft and feed the wiring connectors through the steering wheel as the wheel is withdrawn **(see illustration)**.

7 With the steering wheel removed, check the position of the airbag rotary connector. Tape it in position to prevent it from moving, if required.

Refitting

8 Refitting is a reversal of removal, bearing in mind the following points:

a) *Ensure that the front wheels are in the straight-ahead position.*
b) *Remove the tape (where fitted) from the rotary connector, making sure it is in the correct position. Refer to Chapter 12, Section 21 for further information.*
c) *Ensure that the direction indicator switch is in the central (cancelled/off) position, otherwise the switch may be damaged as the wheel is refitted.*
d) *Make sure all the wiring connectors are secure and clipped into position.*
e) *Align the marks on the wheel and the steering column shaft before removal, and align the steering wheel with the rotary connector.*
f) *Tighten the new steering wheel securing nut to the specified torque.*
g) *Refit the airbag unit to the steering wheel as described in Chapter 12, Section 21.*

13 Ignition switch/steering column lock – removal and refitting

Note: *New shear-bolts must be used when refitting the lock assembly.*

Removal

1 Disconnect the battery negative terminal (refer to battery disconnection and reconnection in Chapter 5A, Section 3).

2 Lower the steering column to its lowest point, and then remove the steering column shrouds as described in Chapter 11, Section 26.

12.4 Undo the steering wheel retaining nut

12.5 Note the alignment marks for refitting

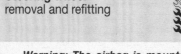

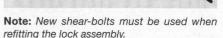

12.6 Remove the steering wheel from the column

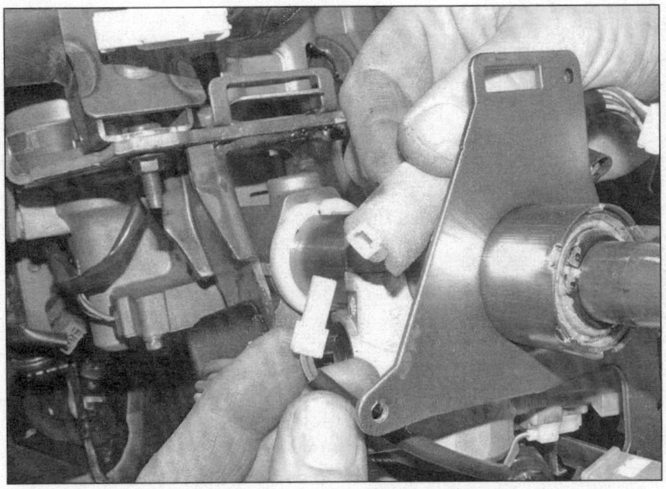

13.3a Disconnect the wiring connectors...

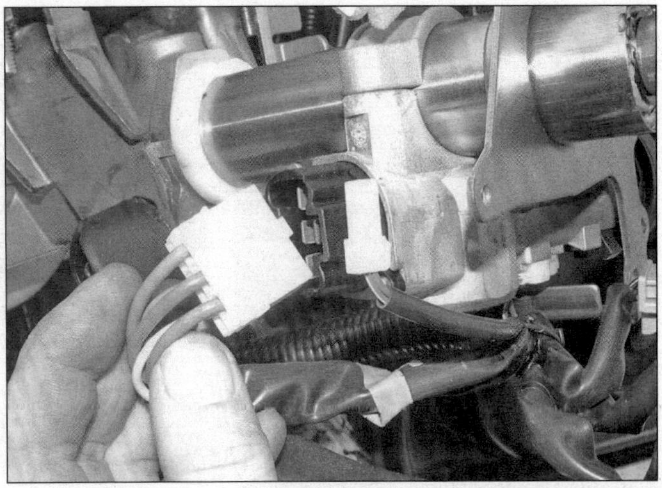

13.3b ...from the left-hand side of the column

13.4 Disconnect the wiring connector

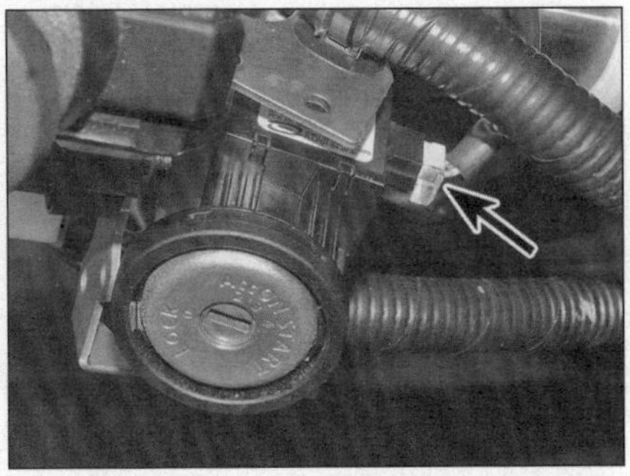

13.5a Disconnect the wiring connector...

13.5b ...undo the retaining screw...

3 Disconnect the two wiring connectors from the left-hand side of the steering column **(see illustrations)**.

4 On models with intelligent key system, disconnect the wiring connector from the top of the ignition switch **(see illustration)**.

5 Disconnect the wiring connector to the transponder ring around the ignition switch, undo the retaining screw and then withdraw the transponder ring from around the switch **(see illustrations)**.

6 To remove the lock assembly, drill out and remove the two shear-bolts from the top of the steering column **(see illustration)**, then withdraw the two sections of the lock casting from the steering column. Note that the lock assembly cannot be removed from the casting.

Refitting

7 Refitting is a reversal of removal, but when refitting the lock assembly, use two new shear-bolts, and tighten the bolts until the heads break off.

13.5c ...and withdraw the transponder ring

13.6 Drill out the lock assembly shear bolts

14 Steering column/motor – removal and refitting

Warning: All models are equipped with an airbag system. Ensure that the safety recommendations given in Chapter 12, Section 20, are followed to prevent personal injury.

Note: *The steering column comprises the electric power steering (EPS) motor, the electronic control unit and the steering column itself. All these components form one assembly and cannot be individually separated or dismantled.*

Removal

1 Disconnect the battery negative terminal (refer to battery disconnection and reconnection in Chapter 5A, Section 3).

2 Remove the steering wheel as described in Section 12.

3 Remove the steering column switches as described in Chapter 12, Section 4.

4 Remove the airbag rotary connector as described in Chapter 12, Section 21.

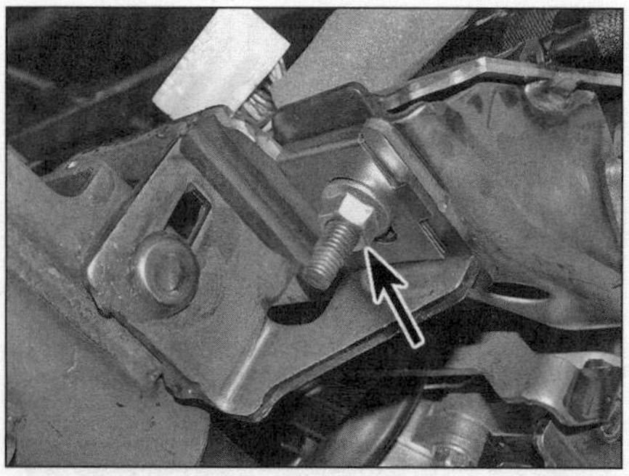

14.12a Undo the column upper mounting nuts...

14.12b ...and lower mounting nuts

5 Disconnect the wiring connectors from the ignition switch, refer to Section 13.
6 To improve access remove the driver's side lower facia panel as described in Chapter 11, Section 26.
7 Release the two fasteners and remove the carpet segment from around the base of the steering column **(see illustration 7.3)**.
8 Place a matching mark on the steering column intermediate shaft universal joint and the steering gear pinion shaft.
9 Undo the retaining bolt and disconnect the steering column intermediate shaft universal joint from the steering gear pinion shaft **(see illustration 7.6)**. Do not turn the steering wheel with the intermediate shaft disconnected.
10 Check along the steering column and free the wiring loom from the retaining clips along the column. Note its fitted position, and position it clear so that it does not hinder column removal.
11 The steering column/motor assembly is very heavy, it will be necessary to have the aid of an assistant or have something inside the footwell of the vehicle, to support the steering column/motor as it is removed.
12 Slacken and remove the four mounting nuts from the top of the column **(see illustrations)**. Carefully lower the steering column and support it while disconnecting the wiring connectors from the top of the steering column motor.
13 When the steering column/motor is free from any remaining wiring, withdraw it from inside the vehicle.

Refitting

14 Refitting is a reversal of removal, bearing in mind the following points:
a) Tighten all fastenings to their specified torque setting, where given.
b) Refit the airbag rotary connector as described in Chapter 12, Section 21.
c) Refit the steering column switches, as described in Chapter 12, Section 4.
d) Refit the steering wheel, as described in Section 12.
e) Refit the steering column shrouds and lower facia panel as described in Chapter 11, Section 26.

15 Steering gear assembly – removal, inspection and refitting

Removal

1 Firmly apply the handbrake, and then jack up the front of the vehicle and support it securely on axle stands (see *Jacking and vehicle support*). Remove the front roadwheels.
2 Remove the front suspension subframe as described in Section 7.
3 Undo the nuts, remove the mounting bolts and lift the steering gear off the subframe **(see illustration)**. Note that new mounting bolt retaining nuts will be required for refitting.

15.3 Steering gear assembly mounting bolts

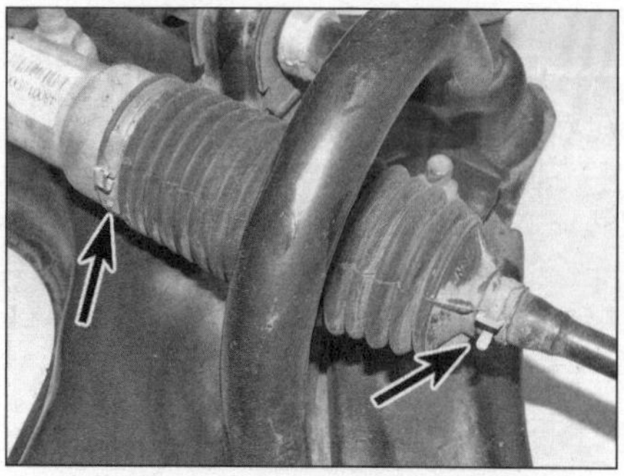

16.3 Steering rack gaiter securing clips

Inspection

4 Examine the assembly for obvious signs of wear or damage.
5 Check the rack for smooth operation through its full stroke of movement, and check that there is no binding or free play.
6 Check the track rods for deformation and cracks.
7 Check the condition of the steering gear rubber gaiters, and renew if necessary with reference to Section 16.
8 Examine the track rod ends for wear or damage, and renew if necessary with reference to Section 17.
9 Apart from renewal of the track rod ends and steering gear rubber gaiters, any further overhaul necessary should be entrusted to a Nissan dealer or specialist.

Refitting

10 Refitting is a reversal of removal, bearing in mind the following points:
a) Use new nuts on the steering gear mounting bolts.
b) Refit the front suspension subframe as described in Section 7.
c) Tighten all nuts and bolts to the specified torque settings (where given).

16 Steering gear rubber gaiters – renewal

Note: *New gaiter retaining clips should be used on refitting.*
1 Remove the relevant track rod end as described in Section 17.
2 If not already done, unscrew the track rod end locknut from the end of the track rod.
3 Mark the correct fitted position of the gaiter on the track rod, then release the gaiter securing clips **(see illustration)**. Slide the gaiter from the steering gear, and off the end of the track rod.
4 Thoroughly clean the track rod and the steering gear housing, using fine abrasive paper to polish off any corrosion, burrs or sharp edges that might damage the new gaiter sealing lips on installation. Scrape off all the grease from the old gaiter, and apply it to the track rod inner balljoint. (This assumes that grease has not been lost or contaminated as a result of damage to the old gaiter. Use fresh grease if in doubt).
5 Carefully slide the new gaiter onto the track rod, and locate it on the steering gear housing. Align the outer edge of the gaiter with the mark made on the track rod prior to removal, and then secure it in position with new retaining clips.
6 Screw the track rod end locknut onto the end of the track rod.
7 Refit the track rod end as described in Section 17.

17 Track rod end – removal and refitting

Note: *A balljoint separator tool will be required for this operation. A new track rod end retaining nut must be used on refitting.*

Removal

1 Firmly apply the handbrake, and then jack up the front of the vehicle and support it securely on axle stands (see *Jacking and vehicle support*). Remove the relevant front roadwheel.

2 Using a Torx key to prevent the ball joint from turning, slacken the nut securing the track rod end to the steering arm **(see illustration)**.

3 Using a balljoint separator tool, separate the track rod end from the steering arm **(see illustrations)**. Remove the nut and discard, as a new one must be used on refitting.

4 Clean the threads on the track rod arm with a wire brush and lubricate. Counterhold the track rod arm using the flats provided, and then slacken the track rod end locknut **(see illustration)**.

5 Counting the exact number of turns required to remove the track rod end, unscrew it from the track rod.

Refitting

6 Carefully clean the track rod end and the track rod threads.

7 Renew the track rod end if the rubber dust cover is cracked, split or perished, or if the movement of the balljoint is either sloppy or too stiff. Also check for other signs of damage such as worn threads.

17.2 Using a Torx socket to prevent the ball joint from turning

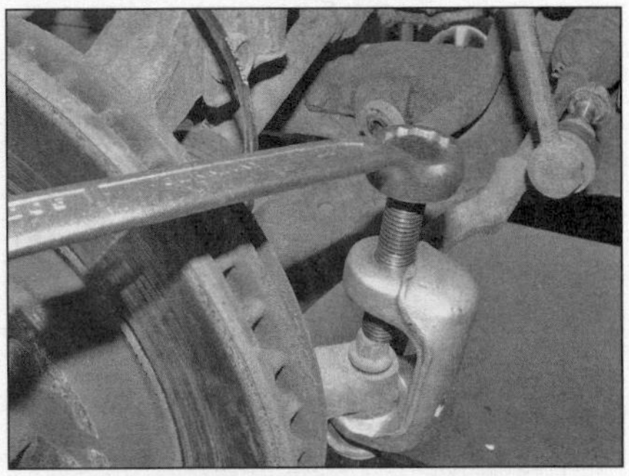

17.3a Use a balljoint separator...

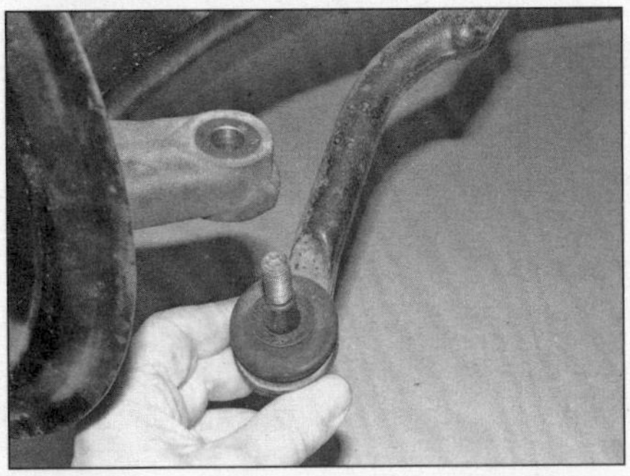

17.3b ...to release the tapered shank

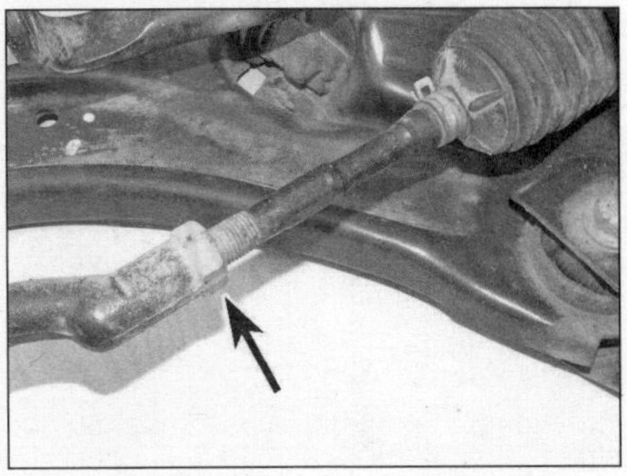

17.4 Slacken the track rod end locknut

8 Screw the track rod end onto the track rod by the number of turns noted before removal.

9 Counterhold the track rod arm using the flats provided, and then securely tighten the track rod lock nut.

10 Ensure that the balljoint taper is clean, and then engage the taper with the steering arm on the hub carrier.

11 Refit a new nut to the track rod end, and tighten to the specified torque.

12 Refit the roadwheel, and lower the vehicle to the ground.

13 Check the front wheel alignment with reference to Chapter 1A, Section 15 or Chapter 1B, Section 15.

Chapter 11
Bodywork and fittings

Contents

Degrees of difficulty

Easy, suitable for novice with little experience	**Fairly easy,** suitable for beginner with some experience	**Fairly difficult,** suitable for competent DIY mechanic	**Difficult,** suitable for experienced DIY mechanic	**Very difficult,** suitable for expert DIY or professional

Specifications

Torque wrench settings	**Nm**	**lbf ft**
Door hinge nuts/bolts	22	16
Door lock striker bolts	16	12
Front seat belt anchorage bolts	49	36
Front seat securing bolts	40	30
Inertia reel lower mounting bolt	49	36
Rear seat back-to-hinge retaining bolts	45	33
Rear seat belt mounting bolts (all bolts)	49	36

1 General Information

1 The bodyshell is made of pressed-steel sections, and is available in a 5-door Hatchback version. Most components are welded together, but some use is made of structural adhesives and some body components are bolted on.

2 Nissan vehicles have been designed with a rigid passenger safety compartment with reinforced pillars and sills, including safety 'waist' beams inside the doors. The use of high-strength steel in structural areas of the body enhances the rigidity of the structure.

3 Extensive use is made of plastic materials, mainly in the interior, but also in exterior components. The outer sections of the front and rear bumpers are injection-moulded from a synthetic material, which is very strong, and yet light. Plastic components such as wheel arch liners are fitted to the underside of the vehicle, to improve the body's resistance to corrosion.

2 Maintenance – bodywork and underframe

1 The general condition of a vehicle's bodywork is the one thing that significantly affects its value. Maintenance is easy, but needs to be regular. Neglect, particularly after minor damage, can lead quickly to further deterioration and costly repair bills. It is important also to keep watch on those parts of the vehicle not immediately visible, for instance the underside, inside all the wheel arches, and the lower part of the engine compartment.

2 The basic maintenance routine for the bodywork is washing – preferably with a lot of water, from a hose. This will remove all the loose solids, which may have stuck to the vehicle. It is important to flush these off in such a way as to prevent grit from scratching the finish. The wheel arches and underframe need washing in the same way, to remove any accumulated mud, which will retain moisture and tend to encourage rust. Paradoxically enough, the best time to clean the underframe and wheel arches is in wet weather, when the mud is thoroughly wet and soft. In very wet weather, the underframe is usually cleaned of large accumulations automatically, and this is a good time for inspection.

3 Periodically, except on vehicles with a wax-based underbody protective coating, it is a good idea to have the whole of the underframe of the vehicle steam-cleaned, engine compartment included, so that a thorough inspection can be carried out to see what minor repairs and renovations are necessary. Steam cleaning is available at many garages, and is necessary for the removal of the accumulation of oily grime, which sometimes is allowed to become thick in certain areas. If steam-cleaning facilities are not available, there are some excellent grease solvents available which can be brush-applied; the dirt can then be simply hosed off. Note that these methods should not be used on vehicles with wax-based underbody protective coating, or the coating will be removed. Such vehicles should be inspected annually, preferably just prior to winter, when the underbody should be washed down, and any damage to the wax coating repaired. Ideally, a completely fresh coat should be applied. It would also be worth considering the use of such wax-based protection for injection into door panels, sills, box sections, etc, as an additional safeguard against rust damage, where such protection is not provided by the vehicle manufacturer.

4 After washing paintwork, wipe off with a chamois leather to give an unspotted clear finish. A coat of clear protective wax polish will give added protection against chemical pollutants in the air. If the paintwork sheen has dulled or oxidised, use a cleaner/polisher combination to restore the brilliance of the shine. This requires a little effort, but such dulling is usually caused because regular washing has been neglected. Care needs to be taken with metallic paintwork, as special non-abrasive cleaner/polisher is required to avoid damage to the finish. Always check that the door and ventilator opening drain holes and pipes are completely clear, so that water can be drained out. Brightwork should be treated in the same way as paintwork. Windscreens and windows can be kept clear of the smeary film, which often appears, by the use of proprietary glass cleaner. Never use any form of wax or other body or chromium polish on glass.

3 Maintenance – upholstery and carpets

1 Mats and carpets should be brushed or vacuum-cleaned regularly, to keep them free of grit. If they are badly stained, remove them from the vehicle for scrubbing or sponging, and make quite sure they are dry before refitting. Seats and interior trim panels can be kept clean by wiping with a damp cloth. If they do become stained (which can be more apparent on light-coloured upholstery), use a little liquid detergent and a soft nail brush to scour the grime out of the grain of the material. Do not forget to keep the headlining clean in the same way as the upholstery. When using liquid cleaners inside the vehicle, do not over-wet the surfaces being cleaned. Excessive damp could get into the seams and padded interior, causing stains, offensive odours or even rot.

4 Minor body damage – repair

Minor scratches in bodywork

1 If the scratch is very superficial, and does not penetrate to the metal of the bodywork, repair is very simple. Lightly rub the area of the scratch with a paintwork renovator, or a very fine cutting paste, to remove loose paint from the scratch, and to clear the surrounding bodywork of wax polish. Rinse the area with clean water.

2 Apply touch-up paint to the scratch using a fine paintbrush; continue to apply fine layers of paint until the surface of the paint in the scratch is level with the surrounding paintwork. Allow the new paint at least two weeks to harden, and then blend it into the surrounding paintwork by rubbing the scratch area with a paintwork renovator or a very fine cutting paste. Finally, apply wax polish.

3 Where the scratch has penetrated right through to the metal of the bodywork, causing the metal to rust, a different repair technique is required. Remove any loose rust from the bottom of the scratch with a penknife, and then apply rust-inhibiting paint to prevent the formation of rust in the future. Using a rubber or nylon applicator, fill the scratch with body stopper paste. If required, this paste can be mixed with cellulose thinners to provide a very thin paste, which is ideal for filling narrow scratches. Before the stopper-paste in the scratch hardens, wrap a piece of smooth cotton rag around the top of a finger. Dip the finger in cellulose thinners, and quickly sweep it across the surface of the stopper-paste in the scratch; this will ensure that the surface of the stopper-paste is slightly hollowed. The scratch can now be painted over as described earlier in this Section.

Dents in bodywork

4 When deep denting of the vehicle's bodywork has taken place, the first task is to pull the dent out, until the affected bodywork almost attains its original shape. There is little point in trying to restore the original shape completely, as the metal in the damaged area will have stretched on impact, and cannot be reshaped fully to its original contour. It is better to bring the level of the dent up to a point, which is about 3 mm below the level of the surrounding bodywork. In cases where the dent is very shallow anyway, it is not worth trying to pull it out at all. If the underside of the dent is accessible, it can be hammered out gently from behind, using a mallet with a wooden or plastic head. Whilst doing this, hold a suitable block of wood firmly against the outside of the panel, to absorb the impact from the hammer blows and thus prevent a large area of the bodywork from being 'belled-out'.

5 Should the dent be in a section of the

bodywork, which has a double skin, or some other factor making it inaccessible from behind, a different technique is called for. Drill several small holes through the metal inside the area - particularly in the deeper section. Then screw long self-tapping screws into the holes, just sufficiently for them to gain a good purchase in the metal. Now the dent can be pulled out by pulling on the protruding heads of the screws with a pair of pliers.

6 The next stage of the repair is the removal of the paint from the damaged area, and from an inch or so of the surrounding 'sound' bodywork. This is accomplished most easily by using a wire brush or abrasive pad on a power drill, although it can be done just as effectively by hand, using sheets of abrasive paper. To complete the preparation for filling, score the surface of the bare metal with a screwdriver or the tang of a file, or alternatively, drill small holes in the affected area. This will provide a really good 'key' for the filler paste.

7 To complete the repair, see the Section on filling and re-spraying.

Rust holes/gashes in bodywork

8 Remove all paint from the affected area, and from an inch or so of the surrounding 'sound' bodywork, using an abrasive pad or a wire brush on a power drill. If these are not available, a few sheets of abrasive paper will do the job most effectively. With the paint removed, you will be able to judge the severity of the corrosion, and therefore decide whether to renew the whole panel (if this is possible) or to repair the affected area. New body panels are not as expensive as most people think, and it is often quicker and more satisfactory to fit a new panel than to attempt to repair large areas of corrosion.

9 Remove all fittings from the affected area, except those, which will act as a guide to the original shape of the damaged bodywork (e.g. headlight shells etc). Then, using tin snips or a hacksaw blade, remove all loose metal and any other metal badly affected by corrosion. Hammer the edges of the hole inwards, in order to create a slight depression for the filler paste.

10 Wire-brush the affected area to remove the powdery rust from the surface of the remaining metal. Paint the affected area with rust-inhibiting paint, if the back of the rusted area is accessible, treat this also.

11 Before filling can take place, it will be necessary to block the hole in some way. This can be achieved by the use of aluminium or plastic mesh, or aluminium tape.

12 Aluminium or plastic mesh, or glass-fibre matting, is probably the best material to use for a large hole. Cut a piece to the approximate size and shape of the hole to be filled, then position it in the hole so that its edges are below the level of the surrounding body-work. It can be retained in position by several blobs of filler paste around its periphery.

13 Aluminium tape should be used for small or very narrow holes. Pull a piece off the roll, trim it to the approximate size and shape required, then pull off the backing paper (if used) and stick the tape over the hole; it can be overlapped if the thickness of one piece is insufficient. Burnish down the edges of the tape with the handle of a screwdriver or similar, to ensure that the tape is securely attached to the metal underneath.

Filling and respraying

14 Before using this Section, see the Sections on dent, deep scratch, rust holes and gash repairs.

15 Many types of bodyfiller are available, but generally speaking, those proprietary kits, which contain a tin of filler paste and a tube of resin hardener, are best for this type of repair. A wide, flexible plastic or nylon applicator will be found invaluable for imparting a smooth and well-contoured finish to the surface of the filler.

16 Mix up a little filler on a clean piece of card or board – measure the hardener carefully (follow the maker's instructions on the pack), otherwise the filler will set too rapidly or too slowly. Using the applicator, apply the filler paste to the prepared area; draw the applicator across the surface of the filler to achieve the correct contour and to level the surface. As soon as a contour that approximates to the correct one is achieved, stop working the paste – if you carry on too long, the paste will become sticky and begin to 'pick-up' on the applicator. Continue to add thin layers of filler paste at 20-minute intervals, until the level of the filler is just proud of the surrounding bodywork.

17 Once the filler has hardened, the excess can be removed using a metal plane or file. From then on, progressively finer grades of abrasive paper should be used, starting with a 40-grade production paper, and finishing with a 400-grade wet-and-dry paper. Always wrap the abrasive paper around a flat rubber, cork, or wooden block – otherwise the surface of the filler will not be completely flat. During the smoothing of the filler surface, the wet-and-dry paper should be periodically rinsed in water. This will ensure that a very smooth finish is imparted to the filler at the final stage.

18 At this stage, the 'dent' should be surrounded by a ring of bare metal, which in turn should be encircled by the finely 'feathered' edge of the good paintwork. Rinse the repair area with clean water, until all of the dust produced by the rubbing-down operation has gone.

19 Spray the whole area with a light coat of primer – this will show up any imperfections in the surface of the filler. Repair these imperfections with fresh filler paste or bodystopper, and once more smooth the surface with abrasive paper. Repeat this spray-and-repair procedure until you are satisfied that the surface of the filler, and the feathered edge of the paintwork, are perfect. Clean the repair area with clean water, and allow to dry fully.

20 The repair area is now ready for final spraying. Paint spraying must be carried out in a warm, dry, windless and dust-free atmosphere. This condition can be created artificially if you have access to a large indoor working area, but if you are forced to work in the open, you will have to pick your day very carefully. If you are working indoors, dousing the floor in the work area with water will help to settle the dust, which would otherwise be in the atmosphere. If the repair area is confined to one body panel, mask off the surrounding panels; this will help to minimise the effects of a slight mis-match in paint colours. Bodywork fittings (e.g. chrome strips, door handles etc) will also need to be masked off. Use genuine masking tape, and several thicknesses of newspaper, for the masking operations.

21 Before commencing to spray, agitate the aerosol can thoroughly, and then spray a test area (an old tin, or similar) until the technique is mastered. Cover the repair area with a thick coat of primer; the thickness should be built up using several thin layers of paint, rather than one thick one. Using 400-grade wet-and-dry paper, rub down the surface of the primer until it is really smooth. While doing this, the work area should be thoroughly doused with water, and the wet-and-dry paper periodically rinsed in water. Allow to dry before spraying on more paint.

22 Spray on the top coat, again building up the thickness by using several thin layers of paint. Start spraying at one edge of the repair area, and then, using a side-to-side motion, work until the whole repair area and about 2 inches of the surrounding original paintwork is covered. Remove all masking material 10 to 15 minutes after spraying on the final coat of paint.

23 Allow the new paint at least two weeks to harden, then, using a paintwork renovator, or a very fine cutting paste, blend the edges of the paint into the existing paintwork. Finally, apply wax polish.

Plastic components

24 With the use of more and more plastic body components by the vehicle manufacturers (e.g. bumpers. spoilers, and in some cases major body panels), rectification of more serious damage to such items has become a matter of either entrusting repair work to a specialist in this field, or renewing complete components. Repair of such damage by the DIY owner is not really feasible, owing to the cost of the equipment and materials required for effecting such repairs. The basic technique involves making a groove along the line of the crack in the plastic, using a rotary burr in a power drill. The damaged part is then welded back together, using a hot-air gun to heat up and fuse a plastic filler rod into the groove. Any excess plastic is then removed, and the area rubbed down to a smooth finish. It is important that a filler rod of the correct plastic is used, as body components can be made of a variety of different types (e.g. polycarbonate, ABS, polypropylene).

25 Damage of a less serious nature (abrasions, minor cracks etc) can be repaired by the DIY owner using a two-part epoxy filler repair material. Once mixed in equal proportions, this is used in similar fashion to the bodywork filler used on metal panels. The filler is usually cured in twenty to thirty minutes, ready for sanding and painting.

26 If the owner is renewing a complete component himself, or if he has repaired it with epoxy filler, he will be left with the problem of finding a suitable paint for finishing which is compatible with the type of plastic used. At one time, the use of a universal paint was not possible, owing to the complex range of plastics encountered in body component applications. Standard paints, generally speaking, will not bond to plastic or rubber satisfactorily. However, it is now possible to obtain a plastic body parts finishing kit, which consists of a pre-primer treatment, a primer and coloured top coat. Full instructions are normally supplied with a kit, but basically, the method of use is to first apply the pre-primer to the component concerned, and allow it to dry for up to 30 minutes. Then the primer is applied, and left to dry for about an hour before finally applying the special-coloured top coat. The result is a correctly coloured component, where the paint will flex with the plastic or rubber, a property that standard paint does not normally possess.

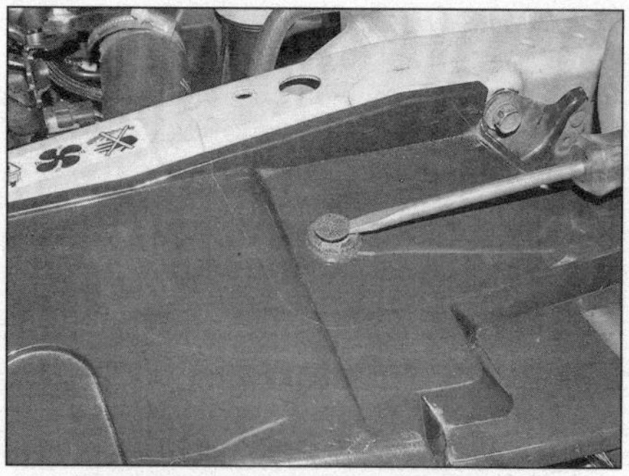

6.2a Prise out the centre pin...

6.2b ...and remove the four expanding rivets

5 Major body damage – repair

1 Where serious damage has occurred, or large areas need renewal due to neglect, it means that complete new panels will need welding-in, and this is best left to professionals. If the damage is due to impact, it will also be necessary to check completely the alignment of the bodyshell, and this can only be carried out accurately by a Nissan dealer or specialist, using special jigs. If the body is left misaligned, it is primarily dangerous, as the car will not handle properly, and secondly, uneven stresses will be imposed on the steering, suspension and possibly transmission, causing abnormal wear, or complete failure, particularly to such items as the tyres.

6 Front bumper – removal and refitting

Removal

1 Firmly apply the handbrake, and then jack up the front of the vehicle and support it securely on axle stands (see *Jacking and vehicle support*). To make access inside the wheel arch easier, remove the front roadwheels.

2 Prise out the centre pin and remove the four expanding plastic rivets from the top of the bumper and grille panel **(see illustrations)**.

3 Working under the front of the vehicle on each side, undo the screws and remove the two air guides **(see illustration)**.

4 Still working under the front of the vehicle, prise out the centre pin and remove the three expanding plastic rivets **(see illustration)**.

5 Remove the expanding rivet then carefully pull away the wheel arch trim on each side to release the retaining clips from the ends of the bumper **(see illustration)**.

Note: *The wheel arch trims do not have to be completely removed from the front wing panels, they just need to be released from the ends of the bumper to allow access to the bumper retaining bolt behind. Take care not to damage them as the bumper is removed.*

6 Undo the retaining bolt each side securing the side of the bumper to the front wing **(see illustration)**.

7 Reaching up behind the bumper, disconnect the foglight wiring connectors **(see illustration)**.

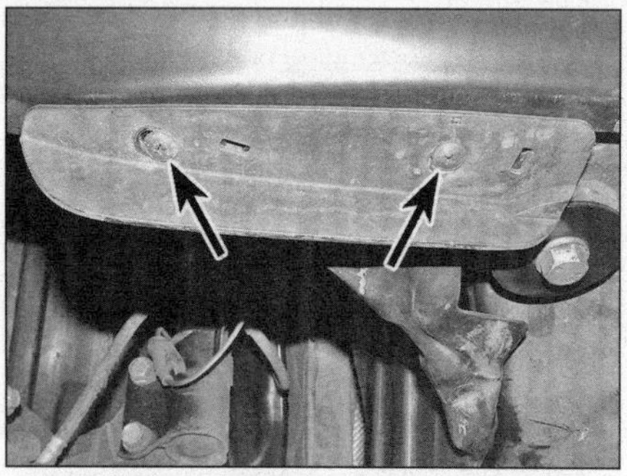

6.3 Undo the two screws and remove the air guide on each side

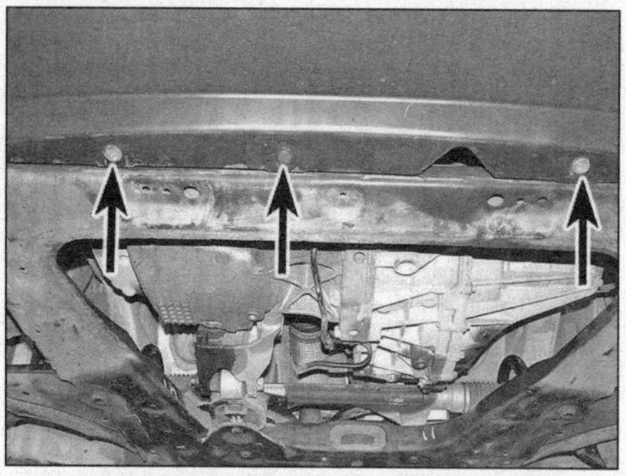

6.4 Remove the three expanding rivets on the lower edge of the bumper

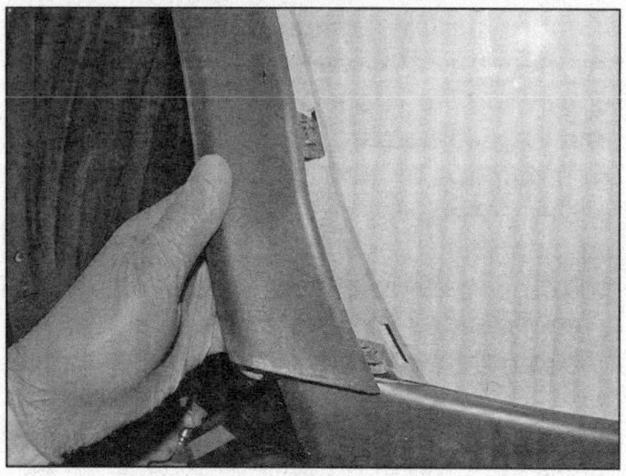

6.5 Unclip the wheel arch trim

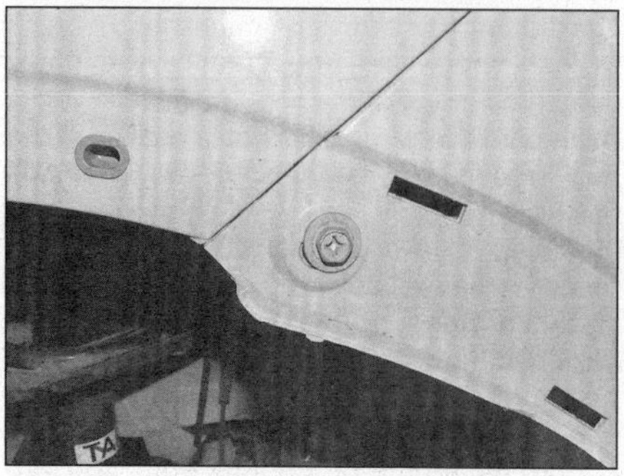

6.6 Undo the bolt each side securing the bumper to the wing

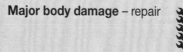

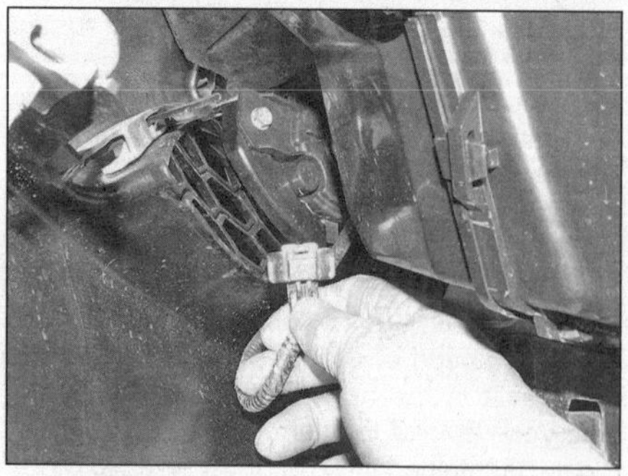

6.7 Disconnect the foglight wiring connectors

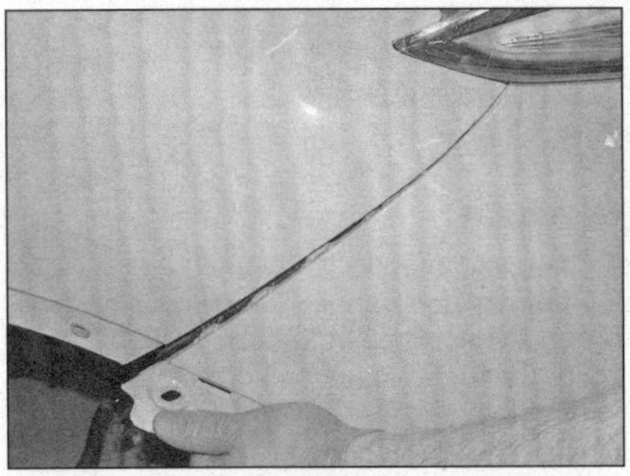

6.9 Release the bumper at each side, noting the locating slots

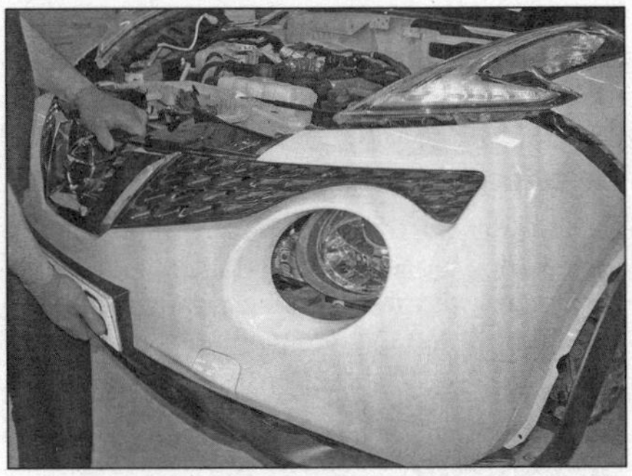

6.10 Draw the bumper forwards and remove it from the vehicle

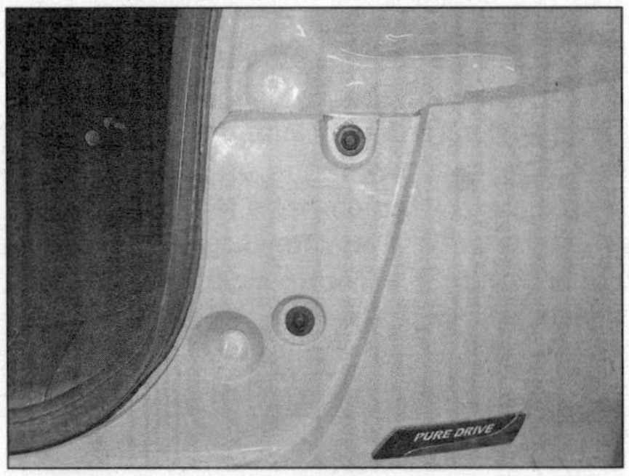

7.3 Undo the bolts below the rear light locations

8 Where fitted, disconnect the parking sensor wiring connector and headlight washer pipes.

9 Have an assistant support one end of the bumper, and then unclip the outer ends of the bumper from the front wing panels **(see illustration)**.

10 Check that there is nothing still connected to the bumper, and then with the aid of an assistant, draw the bumper forwards and remove it from the vehicle **(see illustration)**. If not completely removed, take care not to damage the wheel arch trims, as the bumper is removed.

Refitting

11 Refitting is a reversal of removal.

7 Rear bumper – removal and refitting

Removal

1 Firmly apply the handbrake, and then jack up the rear of the vehicle and support it securely on axle stands (see *Jacking and vehicle support*). To make access inside the wheel arch easier, remove the rear roadwheels.

2 Open the tailgate and remove the rear light units, as described in Chapter 12, Section 7.

3 Undo the two bolts each side located below the rear light locations **(see illustration)**.

4 Working under the rear of the vehicle, pull out the centre pins and release the expanding plastic rivets securing the lower edge of the bumper **(see illustration)**.

5 Remove the expanding rivet then carefully pull away the wheel arch trim on each side to release the retaining clips from the ends of the bumper **(see illustrations)**.

Note: *The wheel arch trims do not have to be completely removed from the front wing panels, they just need to be released from the ends of the bumper to allow access to the bumper retaining bolt behind. Take care not to damage them as the bumper is removed.*

6 Undo the retaining bolt each side securing the side of the bumper to the rear wing **(see illustration)**.

7 Have an assistant support one end of the bumper, and then unclip the outer ends of the bumper from the rear wing panels **(see illustration)**.

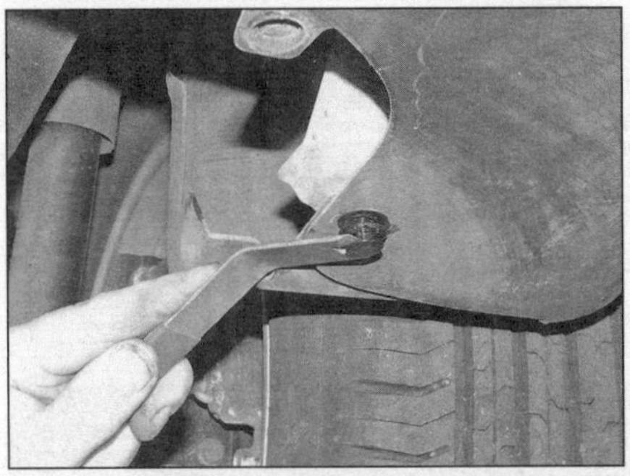

7.4 Pull out the centre pins and release the expanding plastic rivets

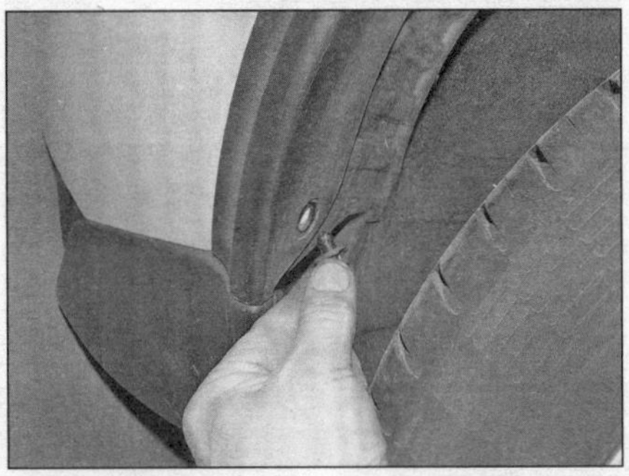

7.5a Extract the plastic rivet...

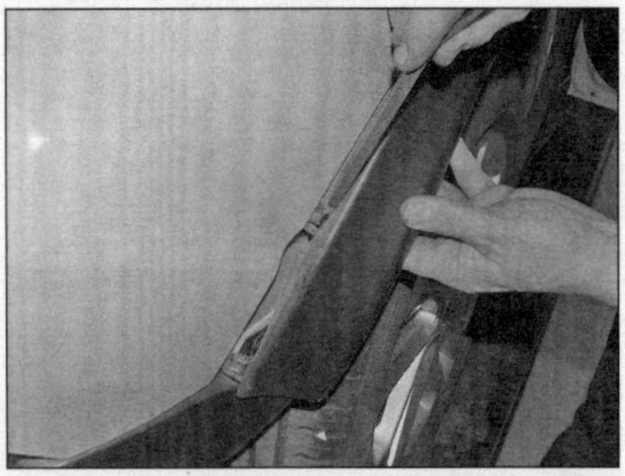

7.5b ...release the wheel arch trims with a plastic spatula...

7.5c ...then pull the trim away to gain access to the bumper retaining bolt

7.6 Undo the bolt each side securing the bumper to the wing

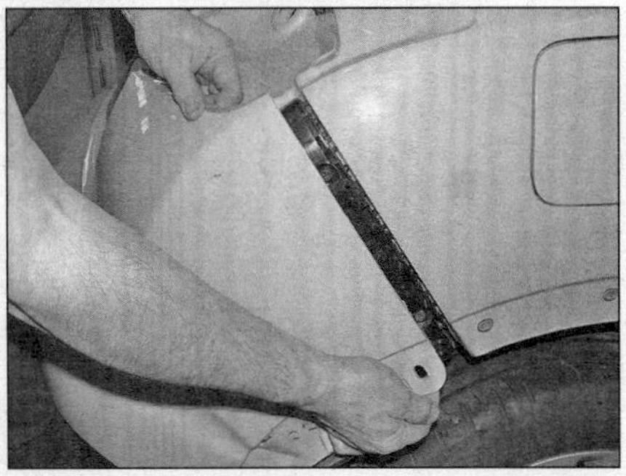

7.7 Release the bumper at each side of the wing panel

8 Check that there is nothing still connected to the bumper, and then with the aid of an assistant, draw the bumper rearwards and remove it from the vehicle. If not completely removed, take care not to damage the wheel arch trims, as the bumper is removed.

9 Disconnect the rear fog light wiring connector and, where applicable, the parking sensor wiring connectors, as the bumper is removed.

Refitting

10 Refitting is a reversal of removal.

8 Bonnet – removal, refitting and adjustment

Removal

1 Open the bonnet and have an assistant support it. Using a pencil or felt tip pen, mark the outline of each bonnet hinge relative to the bonnet, to use as a guide on refitting.

2 With the help of an assistant to support one side of the bonnet, unscrew the nuts securing the hinges to the bonnet. Carefully lift the bonnet clear of the vehicle and store it out of the way in a safe place.

3 Inspect the bonnet hinges for signs of wear and free play at the pivots, and if necessary renew. Each hinge is secured to the body by bolts.

Refitting

4 With the aid of an assistant, offer up the bonnet, and loosely fit the retaining nuts. Align the hinges with the marks made on removal, and then tighten the retaining nuts securely.

5 Adjust the alignment of the bonnet as follows.

Adjustment

6 Close the bonnet, and check for alignment with the adjacent panels. If necessary, slacken the hinge nuts/bolts and re-align the bonnet to suit. Once the bonnet is correctly aligned, tighten the relevant hinge bolts securely.

7 Once the bonnet is correctly aligned, check that the bonnet fastens and releases in a satisfactory manner. If adjustment is necessary, slacken the bonnet lock retaining bolts, and adjust the position of the lock to suit. Once the lock is operating correctly, securely tighten its retaining bolts.

8 If necessary, align the front edge of the bonnet with the wing panels by turning the rubbers screwed into the body front panel, to raise or lower the front edge as required.

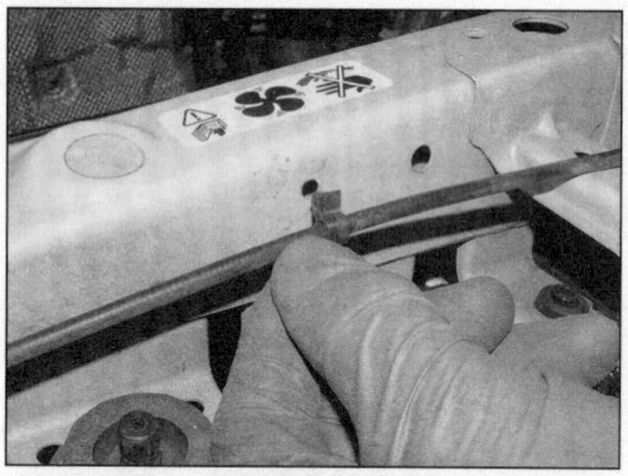

9.5 Release the cable from the retaining clips

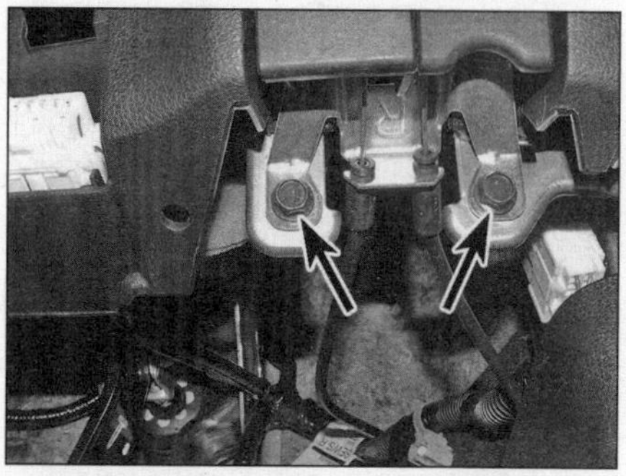

9.7a Undo the two retaining bolts...

9 Bonnet release cable – removal and refitting

Removal

1 Open and support the bonnet.

2 Remove the bonnet lock from the front panel, as described in Section 10.

3 The bonnet release cable travels from the bonnet lock, along the front panel, and then under the right-hand headlight unit.

4 Remove the front wheel arch liner on the right-hand side as described in Section 21.

5 Working along the length of the cable, release it from any securing clips to the vehicle body **(see illustration)**.

6 Remove the facia lower trim panel on the driver's side as described in Section 26.

7 Working in the driver's footwell, undo the two retaining bolts and withdraw the bonnet release lever mounting bracket from the facia **(see illustrations)**.

8 Unclip the outer cable from the bracket, and then unhook the end of the bonnet release cable from the bonnet release lever **(see illustration)**.

9 Note the routing of the cable, then feed the cable through the bulkhead grommet into the passenger compartment. It is advisable to tie a length of string to the end of the cable before removal, to aid refitting. Pull the cable through into the passenger compartment, then untie the string and leave it place until the new cable is to be refitted.

Refitting

10 Refitting is a reversal of removal, but use the string to pull the cable into position, and ensure that the bulkhead grommet is securely located. Make sure that the cable is routed as noted before removal, and reposition the cable in its securing clips in the engine compartment. Check the bonnet release mechanism for correct operation on completion.

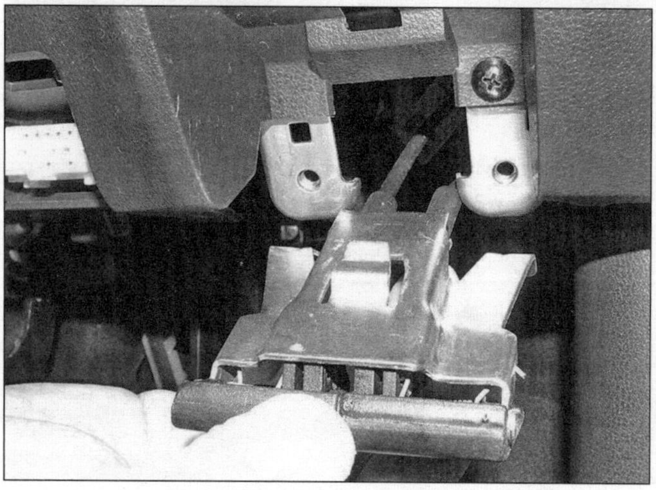

9.7b ...and unclip the release levers from the facia

9.8 Unhook the cable from the release lever

10.3a Undo the retaining nut and lift off the metal shield...

10.3b ...then remove the crash zone sensor from the bonnet lock stud

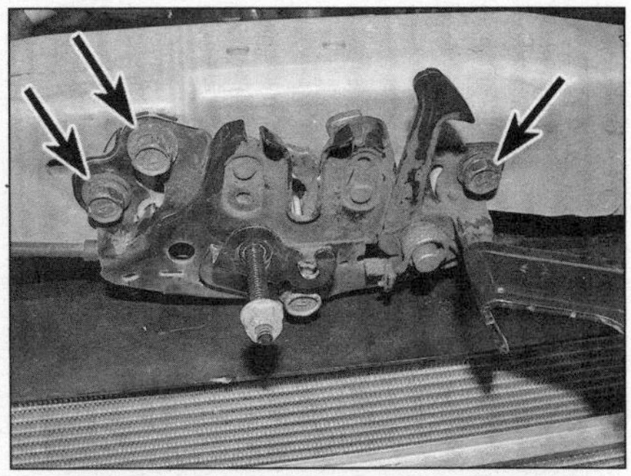

10.5a Undo the three retaining bolts...

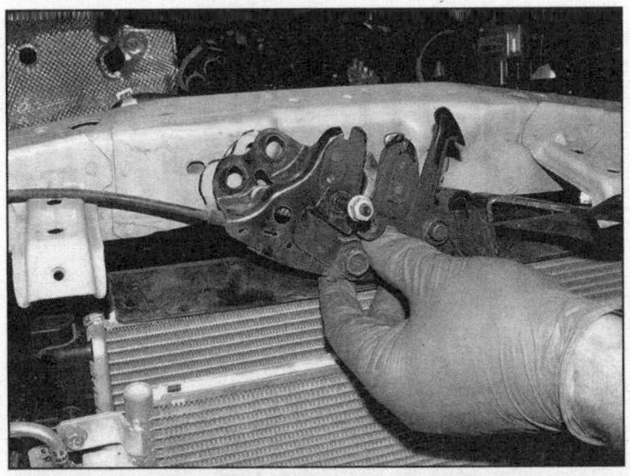

10.5b ...and withdraw the lock assembly

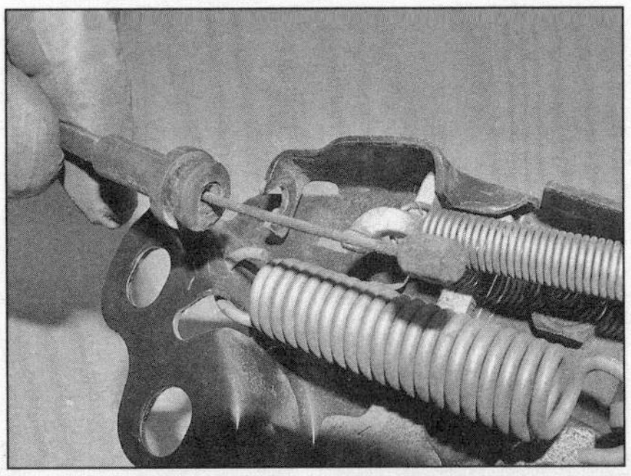

10.6 Unclip the outer cable, then unhook the end of the inner cable from the lock lever

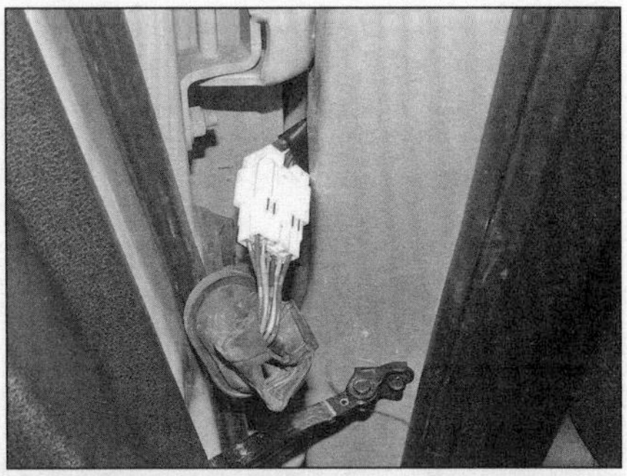

11.2 Unclip the gaiter from the door pillar and disconnect the wiring block connector

10 Bonnet lock – removal and refitting

Removal

1 Open and support the bonnet.

2 Remove the front bumper as described in Section 6.

3 Undo the retaining nut, lift off the metal shield, then remove the air bag crash zone sensor from the stud on the bonnet lock **(see illustrations)**.

4 Using a pencil or felt tip pen, mark the outline of the bonnet lock on the bonnet lock platform to use as a guide on refitting.

5 Undo the three securing bolts, and withdraw the lock assembly from the bonnet lock platform **(see illustrations)**.

6 Unclip the outer cable from the bracket, and then unhook the end of the bonnet release cable from the lock lever **(see illustration)**.

7 The bonnet lock assembly can then be removed from the vehicle.

Refitting

8 Refitting is a reversal of removal. If necessary see adjustment, as described in Section 8.

11 Door – removal, refitting and adjustment

Removal

1 Disconnect the battery negative terminal (refer to battery disconnection and reconnection in Chapter 5A, Section 3).

2 On the rear doors, open the door and unclip the rubber gaiter from the door pillar, withdraw the wiring block connector from within the door pillar and disconnect it **(see illustration)**.

3 On the front doors, open the door and push down the wiring connector locking bar, then disconnect the connector **(see illustrations)**.

4 Undo the bolt securing the door check strap to the body panel **(see illustration)**.

5 Mark the positions of the hinges on the door, to aid alignment of the door on refitting.

6 Suitably support the door under its lower edge on a jack or axle stands covered with pads of rag.

7 Have an assistant support the door, then unscrew the nuts securing the door hinges

11.3a Push down the locking bar...

11.3b ...and disconnect the wiring block connector

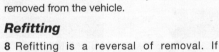

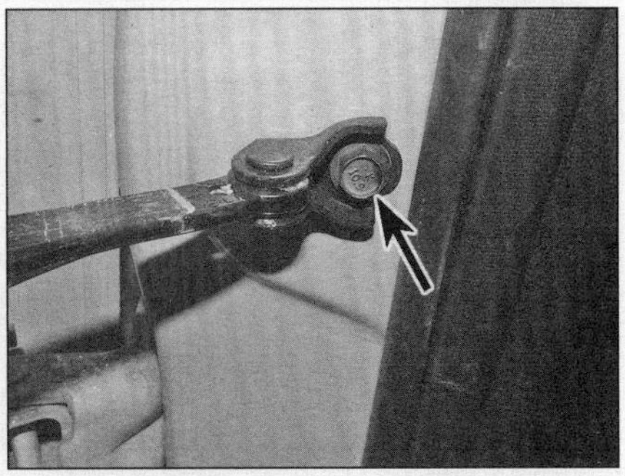

11.4 Undo the door check strap bolt

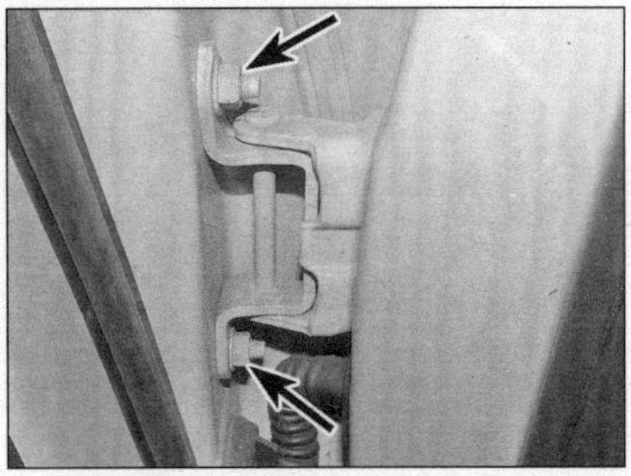

11.7 Upper door hinge retaining nuts

to the door, and lift the door from the vehicle **(see illustration)**.

8 Examine the hinges for wear and damage. If necessary, the hinges can be unbolted from the body and renewed.

Refitting

9 Refitting is a reversal of removal, but align the hinges with the marks made on the body before removal, and before finally tightening the hinge securing bolts, check the door

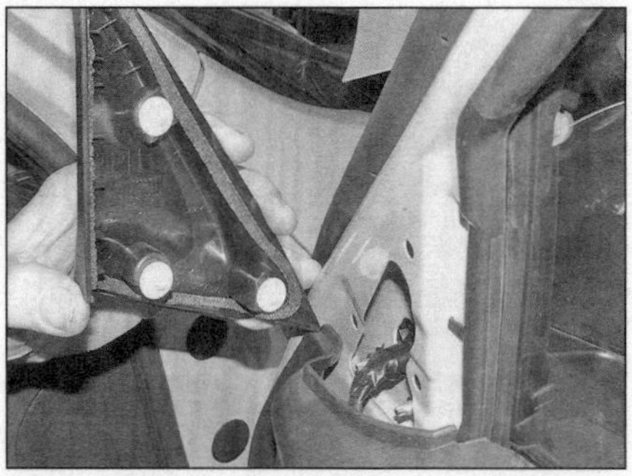

12.2 Carefully prise free the mirror inner trim panel

adjustment as described in the following paragraphs.

Adjustment

10 Close the door carefully, in case the alignment is incorrect, which may cause scratching on the door or the body as the door is closed, and check the fit of the door with the surrounding panels.

11 If adjustment is required, loosen the hinge securing nuts/bolts (the hinge-to-door and the hinge-to-body nut/bolt holes are elongated), and move the hinges as required to achieve satisfactory alignment. Tighten the securing nutsbolts to the specified torque when the alignment is satisfactory.

12 Check the operation of the door lock. If necessary, slacken the securing bolts, and adjust the position of the lock striker on the body pillar to achieve satisfactory alignment.

12 Door inner trim panel – removal and refitting

Front door trim panel

1 Disconnect the battery negative terminal (refer to battery disconnection and reconnection in Chapter 5A, Section 3).

2 Using a plastic spatula or similar tool, carefully prise off the door mirror inner trim panel **(see illustration)**.

3 Carefully unclip the switch panel from the top of the armrest and disconnect the wiring connectors **(see illustrations)**.

4 Using a small screwdriver, prise off the trim

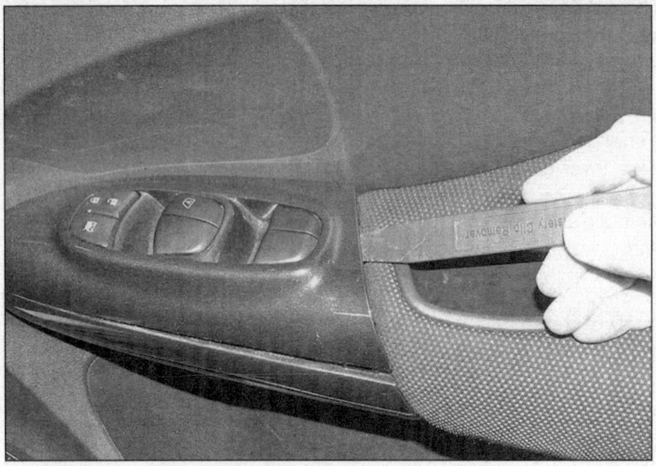

12.3a Unclip the switch panel...

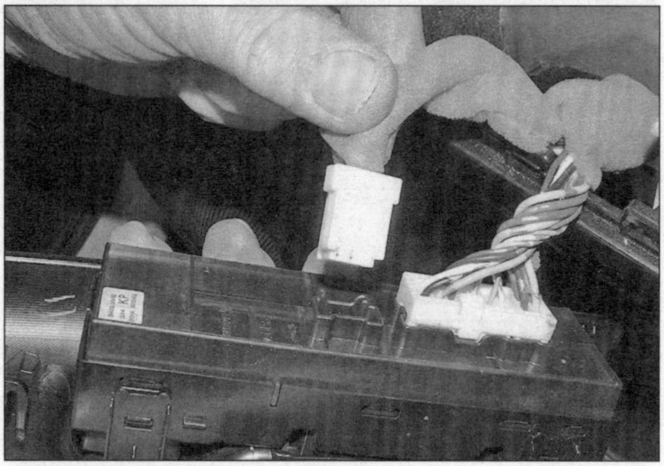

12.3b ...and disconnect the wiring connectors

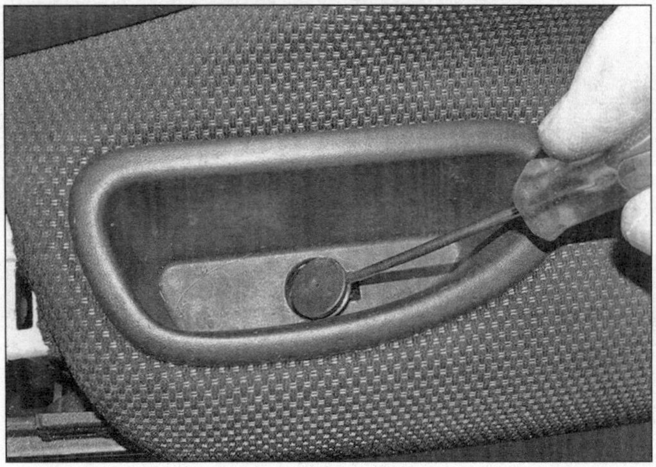

12.4a Prise off the trim cap...

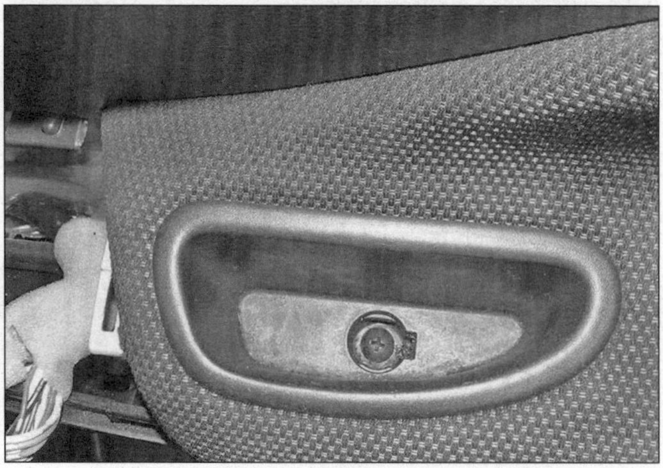

12.4b ...and undo the pull handle securing screw

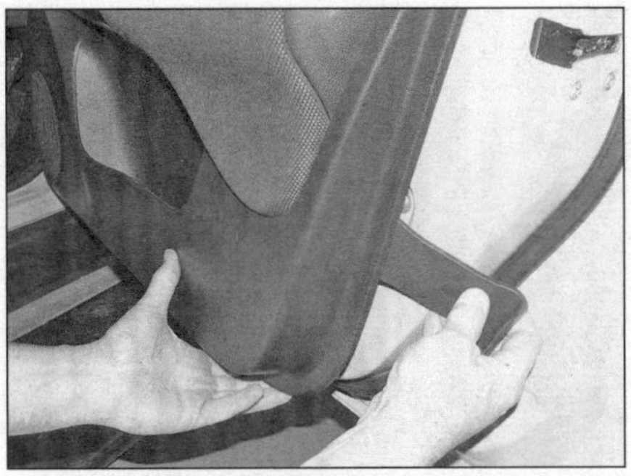

12.5a Using a suitable forked tool, release the retaining clips...

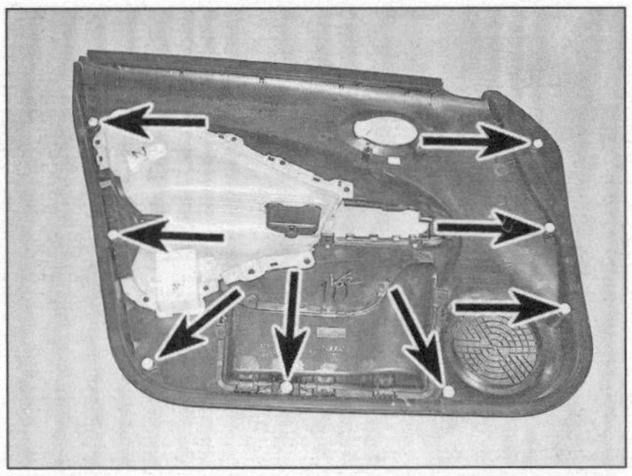

12.5b ...around the edge of the trim panel

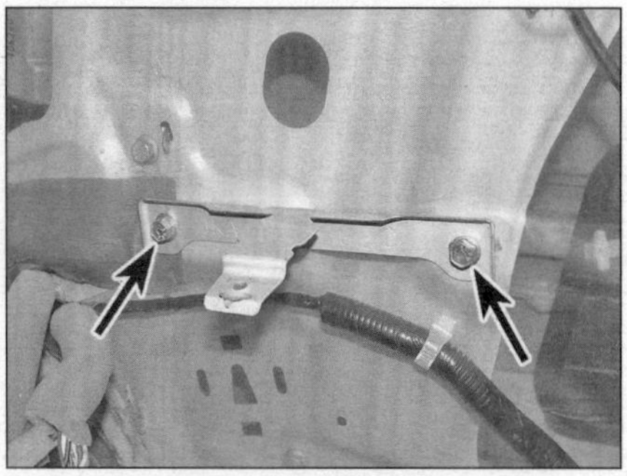

12.6a Undo the pull handle bracket retaining bolts...

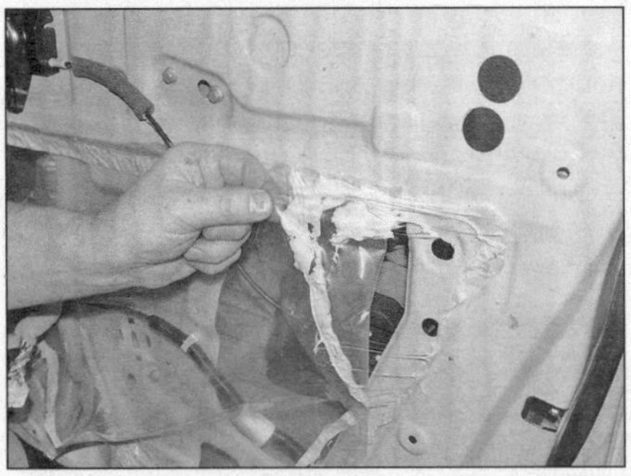

12.6b ...and carefully remove the sealing sheet

12.9a Prise off the trim cap...

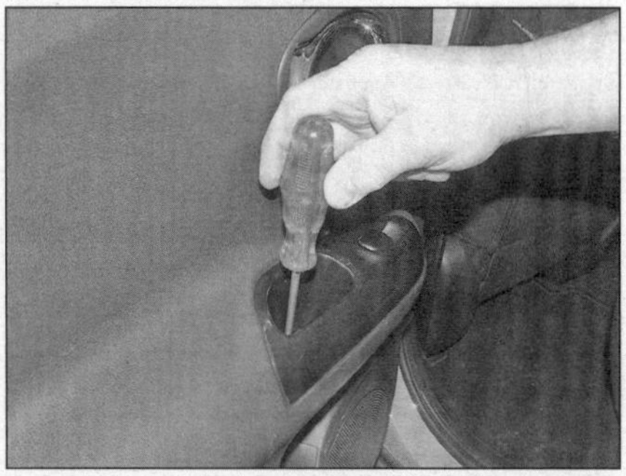

12.9b ...and undo the pull handle securing screw

cap and undo the door pull handle securing screw **(see illustrations)**.

5 Using a suitable forked tool, release the internal securing clips around the edge of the trim panel, then lift the panel upwards to release it from the door frame **(see illustrations)**.

6 If work is to be carried out on the door internal components, it will be necessary to remove the plastic sealing sheet. Undo the retaining bolts and remove the pull handle bracket from the door panel. Then using a sharp knife, carefully release the sealant bead and pull the plastic sealing sheet from the door **(see illustrations)**. Try to keep the sealant intact as far as possible, to ease refitting.

7 Refitting is a reversal of removal, bearing in mind the following points:

a) *Ensure that the sealing sheet is correctly refitted, and sealed around its edge. It should be possible to use the original mastic sealant, but if necessary, new sealant can be obtained from a Nissan dealer.*
b) *Make sure that the trim panel securing clips engage correctly with the door panel. Renew any broken clips.*
c) *Check the upper weatherstrip engages correctly with the door trim panel as the panel is refitted.*

Rear door trim panel

8 Disconnect the battery negative terminal (refer to battery disconnection and reconnection in Chapter 5A, Section 3).

9 Using a small screwdriver, prise off the trim cap and undo the door pull handle securing screw **(see illustrations)**.

10 Carefully unclip the switch panel from the top of the armrest and disconnect the wiring connectors **(see illustration)**.

11 Undo the panel retaining screw in the switch panel aperture **(see illustration)**.

12 Unclip and remove the trim panel from the upper rear corner of the door **(see illustration)**.

13 Using a suitable forked tool, release the internal securing clips around the edge of the trim panel, then lift the panel upwards

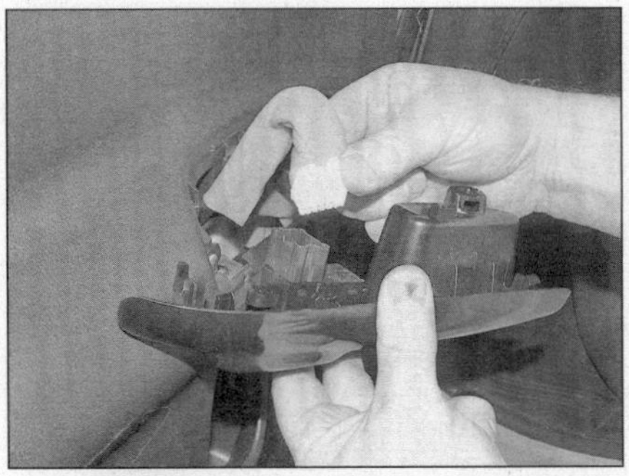

12.10 Unclip the switch panel and disconnect the wiring connector

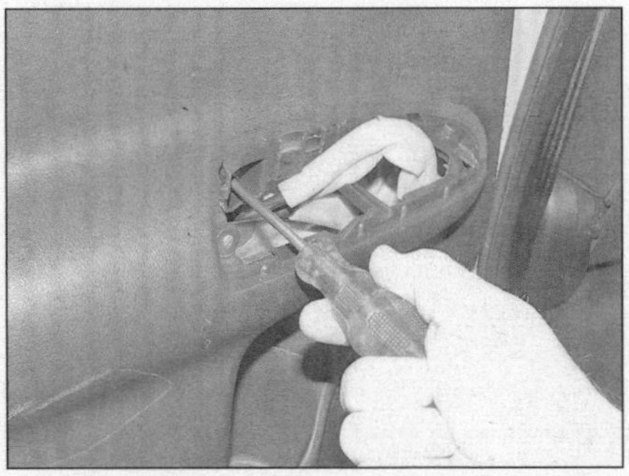

12.11 Undo the screw in the switch panel aperture

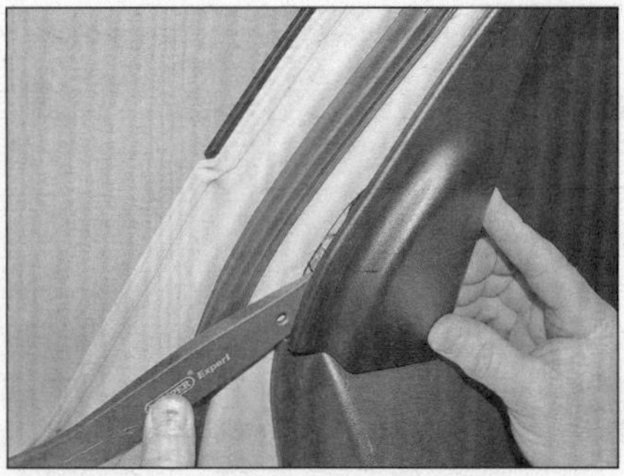

12.12 Unclip the upper corner trim panel

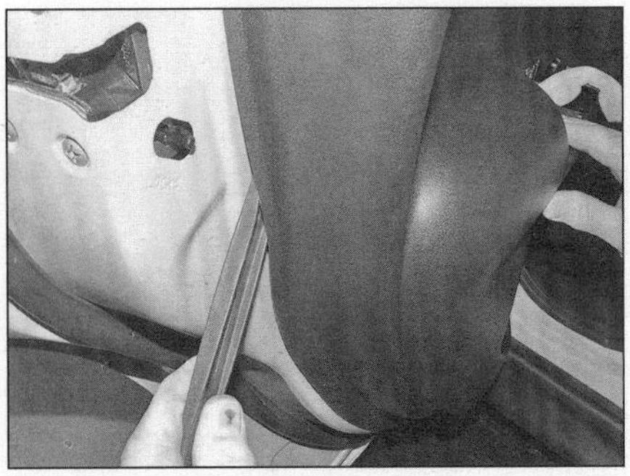
12.13a Using a suitable forked tool, release the retaining clips...

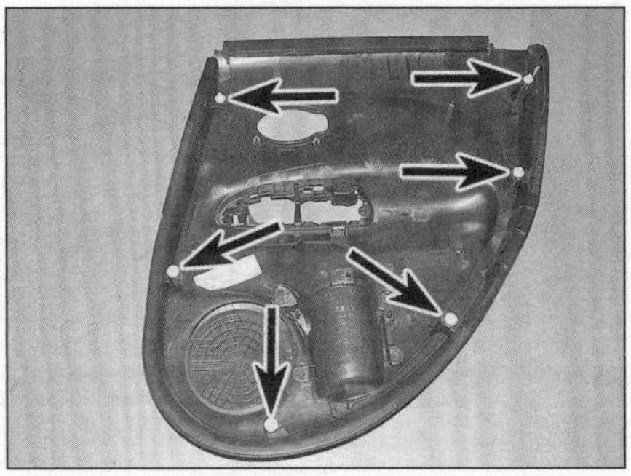
12.13b ...around the edge of the trim panel

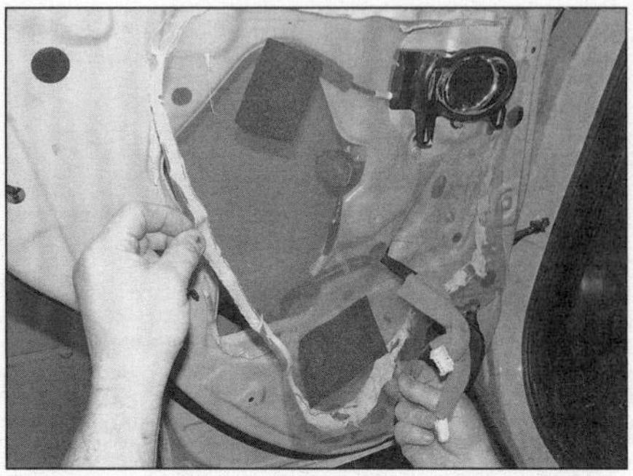
12.14 Carefully remove the plastic sealing sheet

to release it from the door frame **(see illustrations)**.

14 If work is to be carried out on the door internal components, it will be necessary to remove the plastic sealing sheet. Using a sharp knife, carefully release the sealant bead and pull the plastic sealing sheet from the door **(see illustration)**. Try to keep the sealant intact as far as possible, to ease refitting.

15 Refitting is a reversal of removal, bearing in mind the following points:

a) *Ensure that the sealing sheet is correctly refitted, and sealed around its edge. It should be possible to use the original mastic sealant, but if necessary, new sealant can be obtained from a Nissan dealer.*

b) *Make sure that the trim panel securing clips engage correctly with the door panel. Renew any broken clips.*

c) *Check the upper weatherstrip engages correctly with the door trim panel as the panel is refitted.*

13 Door handles and lock components – removal and refitting

Interior door release handle

1 Remove the door inner trim panel and plastic sealing sheet as described in Section 12.

2 Undo the securing bolt and slide the release handle to the rear of the door to withdraw it from the door panel **(see illustrations)**.

3 Unclip the operating cable outer sleeve from the release lever bracket, and then disengage the inner part of the operating cable from the lever **(see illustration)**.

4 Refitting is a reversal of removal, bearing in mind the following points:

a) *Check the operation of the release lever/ lock mechanism before refitting the door inner trim panel.*

b) *Refit the door inner trim panel with reference to Section 12.*

Exterior door handle (front doors)

5 Remove the front door window glass as described in Section 14.

6 Undo the retaining bolt, extract the retaining clip and remove the security cover over the handle and lock components **(see illustrations)**.

7 Open the door and remove the circular plastic disc from the rear end of the door, to

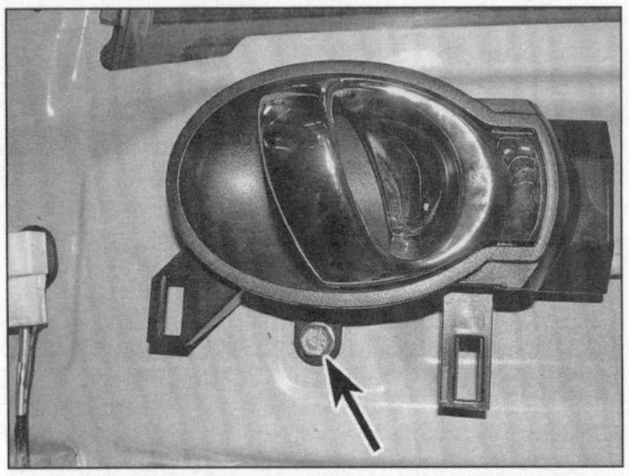
13.2a Undo the retaining bolt...

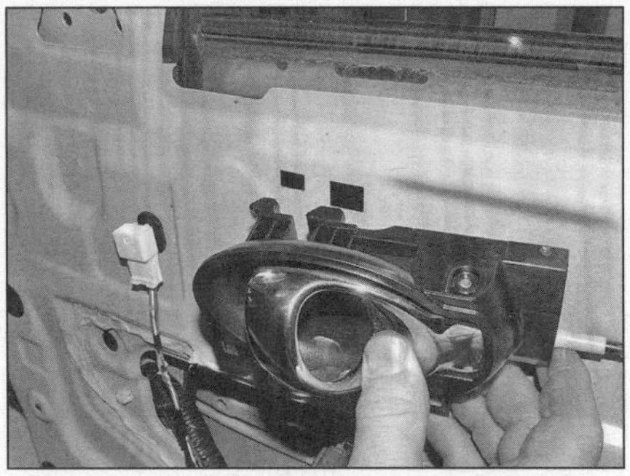
13.2b ...then slide the release handle from the door

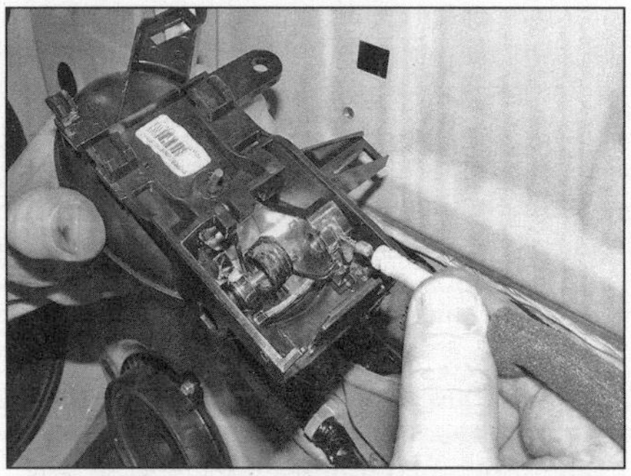
13.3 Disconnect the operating cable from the handle bracket and lever

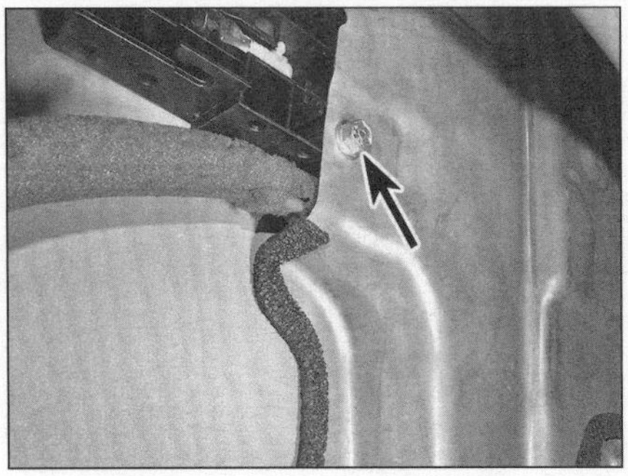
13.6a Undo the retaining bolt...

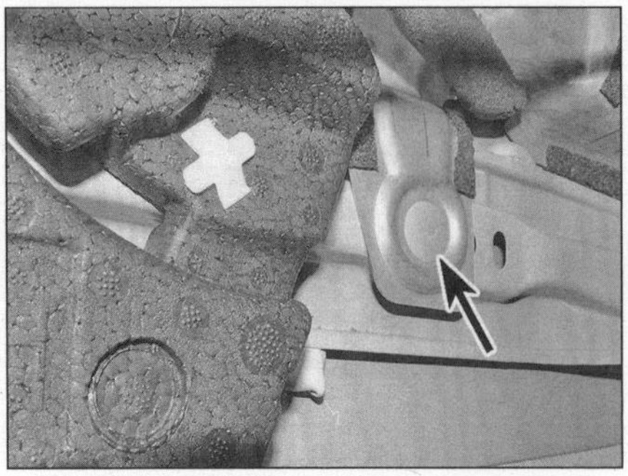
13.6b ...extract the retaining clip...

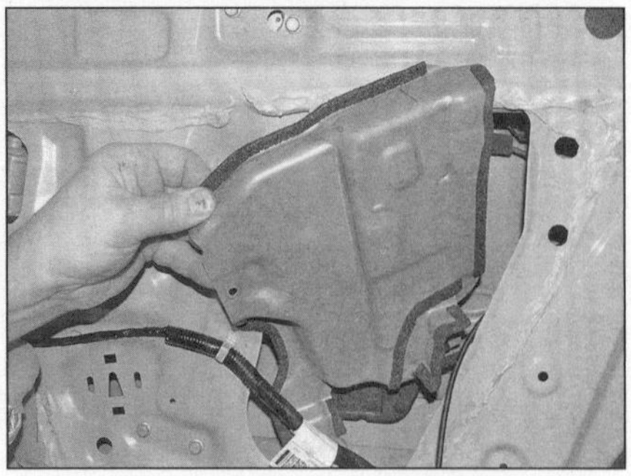
13.6c ...and remove the security cover

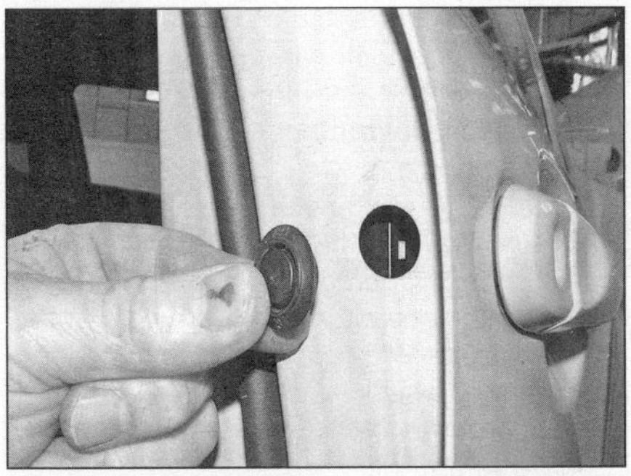
13.7 Remove the circular plastic disc covering the access hole

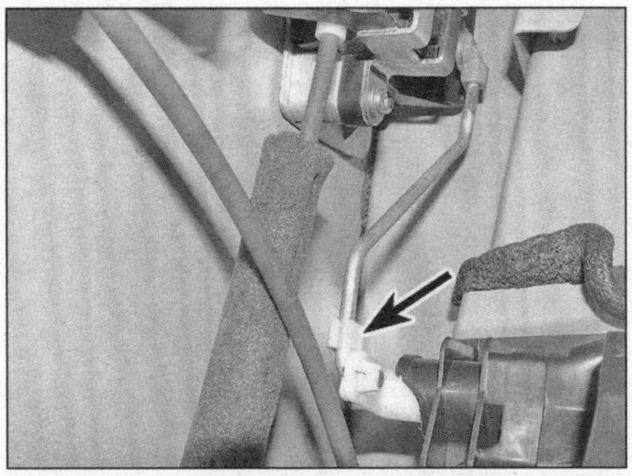
13.8 Release the retaining clip and disconnect the operating rod from the lock lever

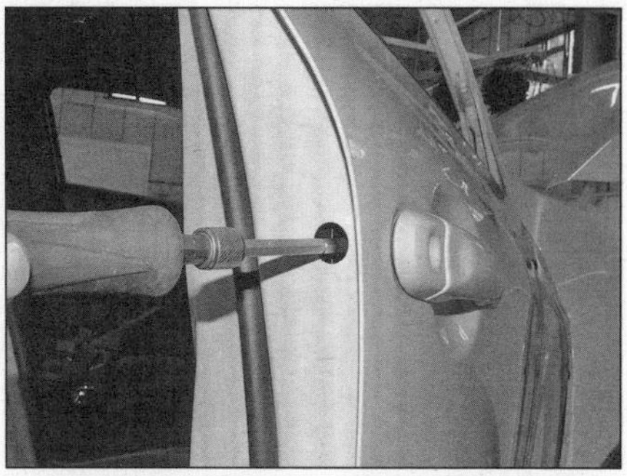
13.10a Slacken the retaining screw...

access the door handle retaining screw **(see illustration)**.

8 If working on the driver's door, release the retaining clip and disconnect the operating rod from the door lock lever **(see illustration)**.

9 On models with intelligent key system, disconnect the wiring connectors inside the door panel, to the door handle antenna and door switch.

10 Slacken the door handle retaining screw, until it cannot be turned any further and comes to a stop (DO NOT force the screw when it reaches the stop). The screw does not come completely out from the door panel. Pull open the outside handle and carefully withdraw the push button out from the door handle assembly **(see illustrations)**. Take care not to damage the paintwork as it is removed.

11 Detach the handle by sliding it to the rear of the door, and then pulling it out from the handle recess **(see illustration)**.

12 Unclip the rubber seals from around the handle recess in the door panel **(see illustrations)**.

13 Slide the outside handle frame towards the rear of the vehicle and withdraw it into the inside of the door **(see illustration)**.

14 Disengage the door lock operating cable from the outside handle frame and remove the frame **(see illustration)**.

15 Refitting is a reversal of removal, bearing in mind the following points:

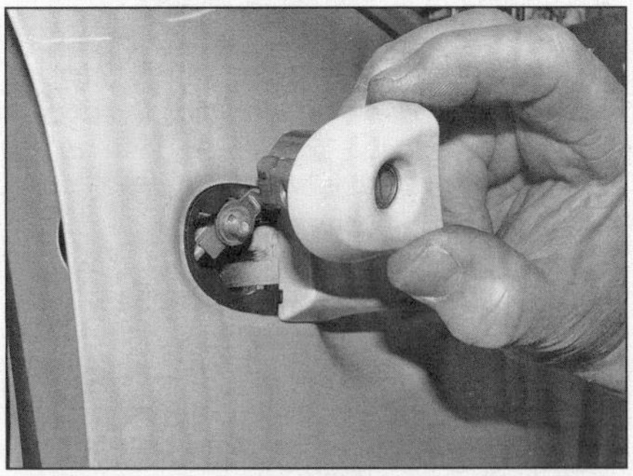
13.10b ...and withdraw the door push button...

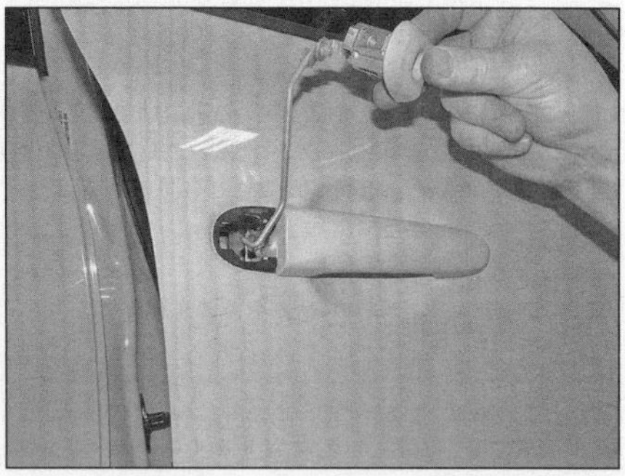
13.10c ...together with the operating rod, if working on the driver's door

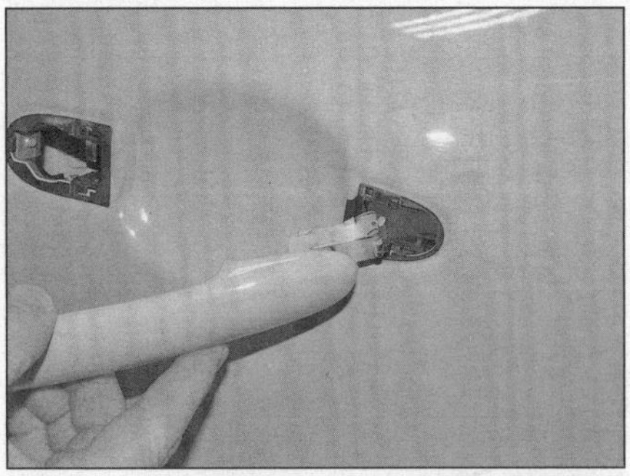
13.11 Slide the handle to the rear and pull it out to disengage it from the door

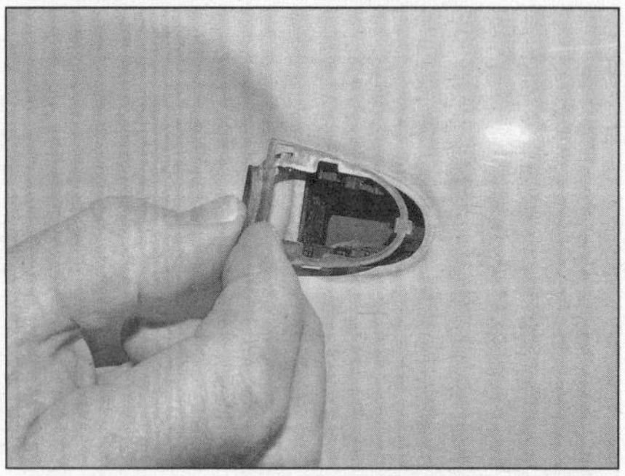
13.12a Remove the front rubber seal...

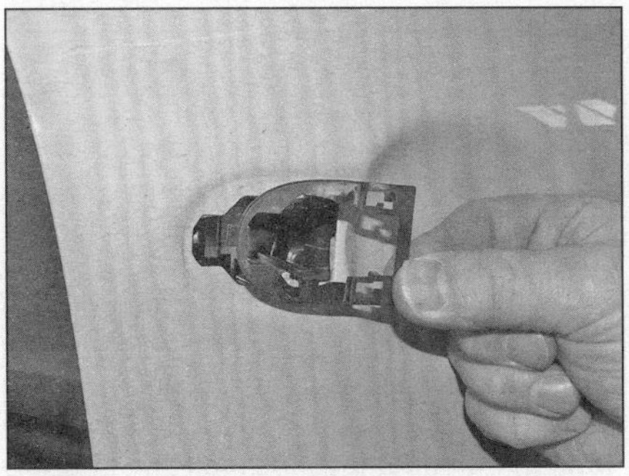
13.12b ...and rear rubber seal from around the handle recess

13.13 Withdraw the outside handle frame into the inside of the door

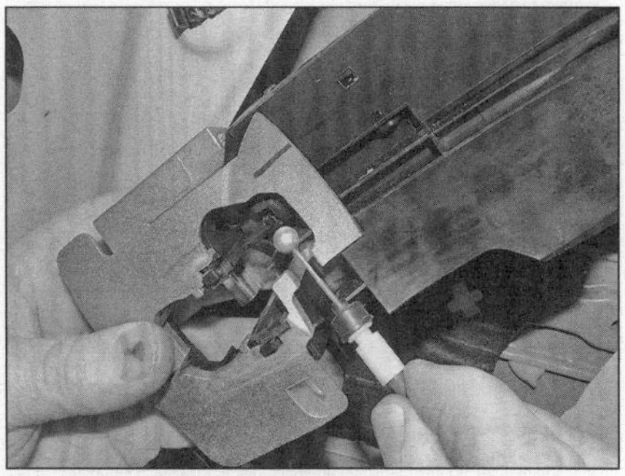
13.14 Disengage the lock operating cable from the outside handle frame

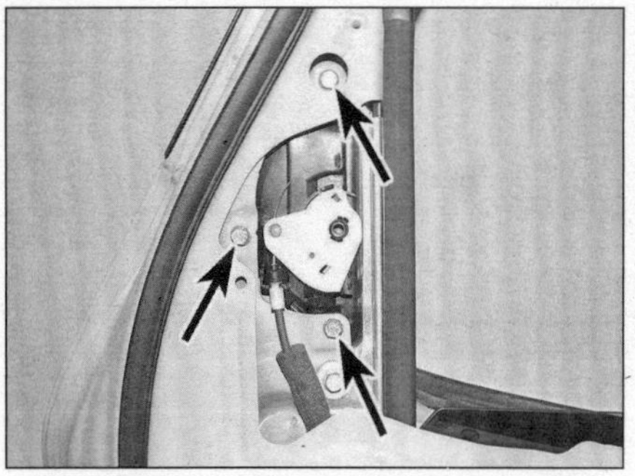

13.17 Undo the outside handle retaining bolts

13.18a Withdraw the outside handle from the door...

a) *Check the operation of the exterior handle/ lock mechanism before refitting the door inner trim panel.*
b) *Refit the front door window glass as described in Section 14.*
c) *Refit the door inner trim panel with reference to Section 12.*

Exterior door handle (rear doors)

16 Remove the door inner trim panel and plastic sealing sheet as described in Section 12.

17 Undo the three bolts securing the outside handle to the door frame **(see illustration)**.

18 Withdraw the outside handle from the door, disconnect the lock operating cable and remove the outside handle **(see illustrations)**.

19 Refitting is a reversal of removal, bearing in mind the following points:

a) *Check the operation of the exterior handle/ lock mechanism before refitting the door inner trim panel.*
b) *Refit the door inner trim panel with reference to Section 12.*

Front door lock

20 Remove the door inner trim panel and plastic sealing sheet as described in Section 12.

21 Remove the interior door release handle, as described previously in paragraphs 1 to 3.

22 Remove the exterior door handle, as described previously in paragraphs 5 to 14.

23 Working at the rear edge of the door, unscrew the three lock securing screws. Disconnect the lock wiring connector, then withdraw the lock assembly through the door aperture **(see illustrations)**.

24 Refitting is a reversal of removal, bearing in mind the following points:

a) *Ensure that the lock operating cable/rods are correctly routed.*
b) *Check the operation of the release handle/ lock mechanism before refitting the door inner trim panel.*
c) *Refit the exterior door handle as described in paragraph 15.*
d) *Refit the interior release handle as described in paragraph 4.*
e) *Refit the door inner trim panel with reference to Section 12.*

Rear door lock

25 Remove the door inner trim panel and plastic sealing sheet as described in Section 12.

26 Remove the front door window glass as described in Section 14.

27 Remove the exterior door handle as described previously in paragraphs 16 to 18.

28 Undo the bolt securing the interior release handle to the door **(see illustration 13.2a)**.

29 Working at the rear edge of the door, unscrew the three lock securing screws. Disconnect the lock wiring connector and withdraw the lock assembly through the door aperture. Slide the interior release handle to the rear, then remove the door lock, complete with interior release handle, from the door **(see illustrations)**.

30 Refitting is a reversal of removal, bearing in mind the following points:

a) *Ensure that the lock operating cables are correctly routed.*
b) *Refit the exterior door handle as described in paragraph 19.*
c) *Refit the front door window glass as described in Section 14.*
d) *Check the operation of the handle/lock mechanism before refitting the door inner trim panel.*
e) *Refit the door inner trim panel as described in Section 12.*

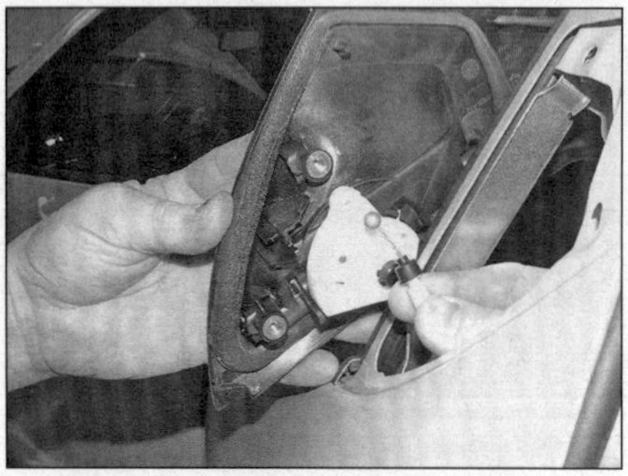

13.18b ...and disconnect the lock operating cable

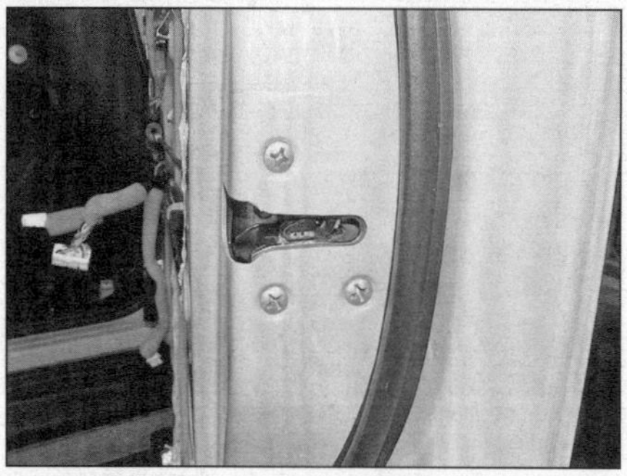

13.23a Undo the three screws securing the lock to the door...

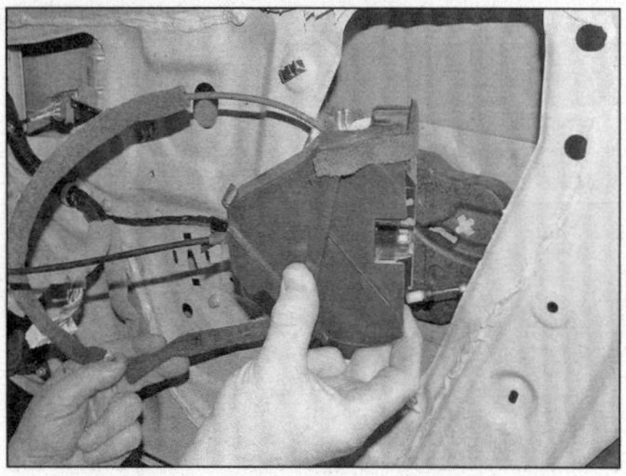

13.23b ...then disconnect the wiring connector and withdraw the lock from inside the door

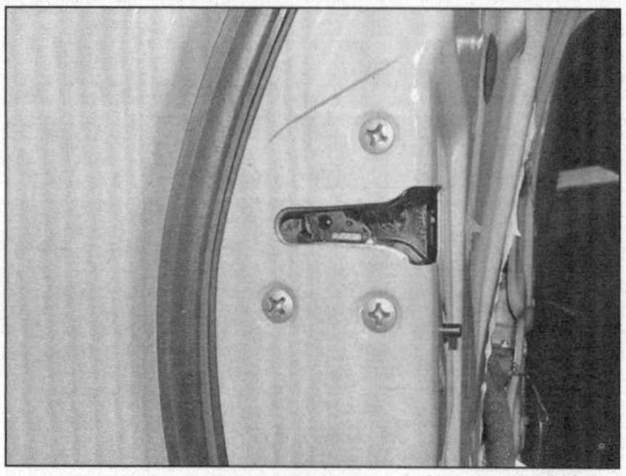

13.29a Undo the three lock securing screws...

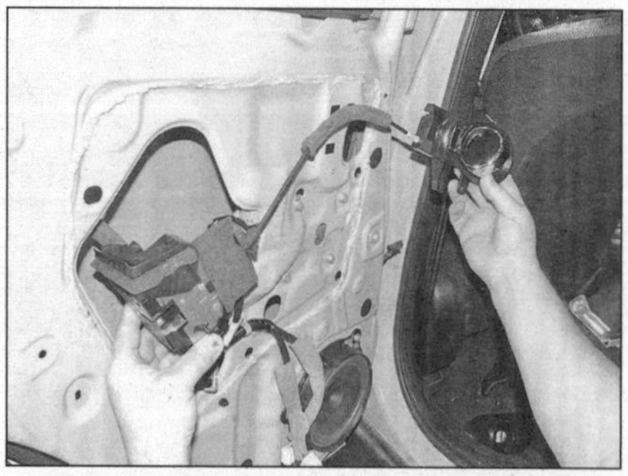

13.29b ...then remove the lock and interior release handle from the door

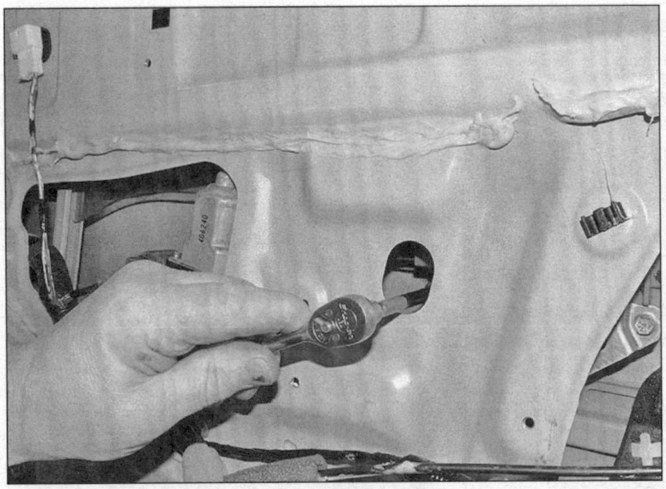

14.2a Undo the window glass front retaining bolt, working through the circular hole in the door...

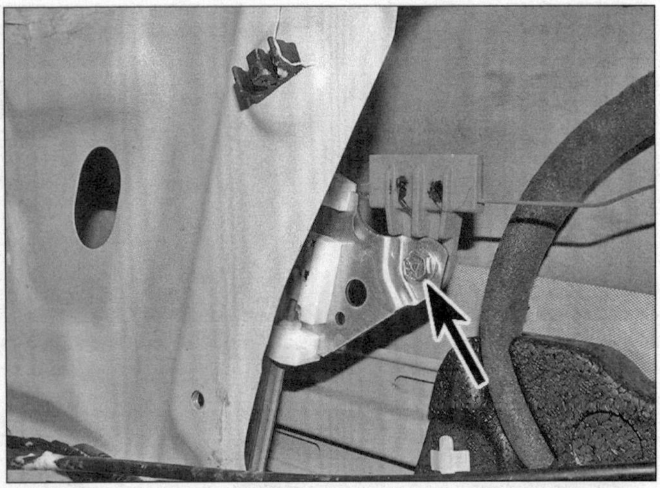

14.2b ...then undo the rear bolt, working through the large door aperture

14 Door window glass and regulator – removal and refitting

Front window glass

1 Remove the door inner trim panel and plastic sealing sheet as described in Section 12.

2 Temporarily reconnect the electric window switch (and the battery negative terminal, if removed), and lower or raise the window until the two bolts securing the lower edge of the window glass to the regulator mechanism are accessible through the holes in the door panel. Support the glass, and then undo the two bolts **(see illustrations)**.

3 Disengage the window glass from the regulator and carefully lower the glass to the bottom of the door.

4 Working your way around the upper door frame, carefully remove the inner window channel/seal **(see illustration)**. Note this is one piece that is inserted all around the upper window frame and into the front and rear guide channels; take care not to damage it, as it is removed.

5 Undo the bolt securing the window glass rear guide channel to the door. Disengage the top of the guide channel from the door, then remove the channel through the door aperture **(see illustrations)**.

6 Raise the glass at the rear, tip it forward at the top and withdraw it from the outside of the door frame **(see illustration)**.

7 Refitting is a reversal of removal, bearing in mind the following points:

a) *Check that the glass moves satisfactorily in the window channel/seal and guide channels, without excess side clearance or binding. If necessary, slacken the retaining bolts and reposition the window glass, guide channels and regulator as required. Fully tighten the retaining bolts on completion.*
b) *Check the operation of the window mechanism before refitting the door inner trim panel.*
c) *Refit the door inner trim panel with reference to Section 12.*

Front window regulator

8 Remove the front window glass as described in paragraphs 1 to 6 in this Section.

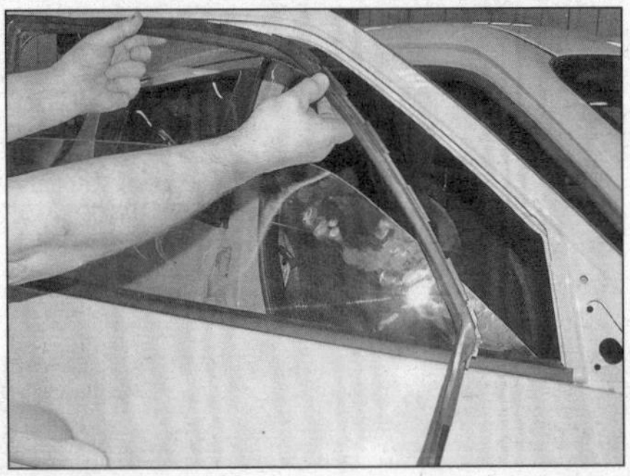

14.4 Carefully remove the rubber window channel/seal

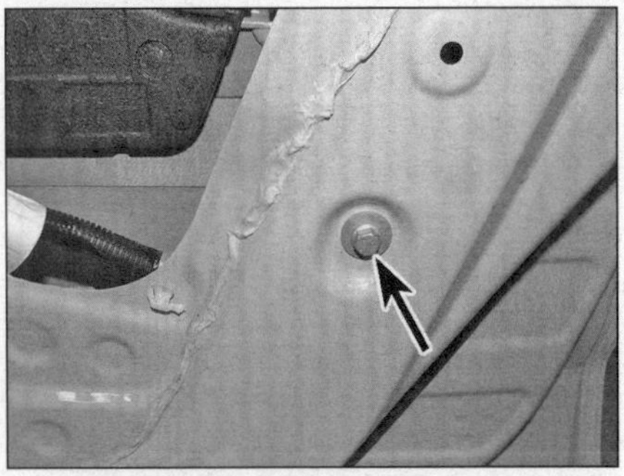

14.5a Undo the rear guide channel retaining bolt...

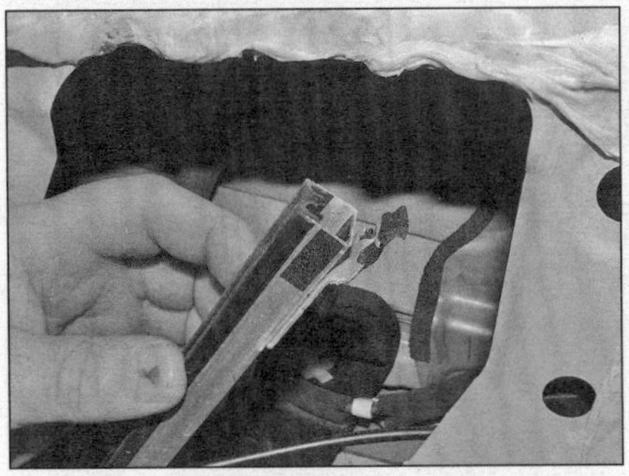

14.5b ...disengage the top of the guide channel from the door...

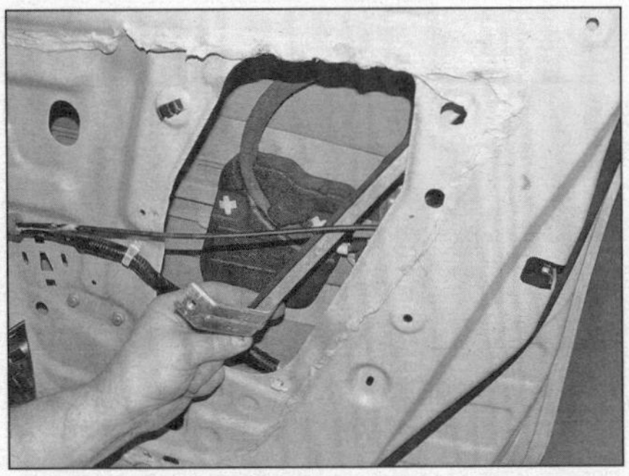

14.5c ...and remove the channel from the door

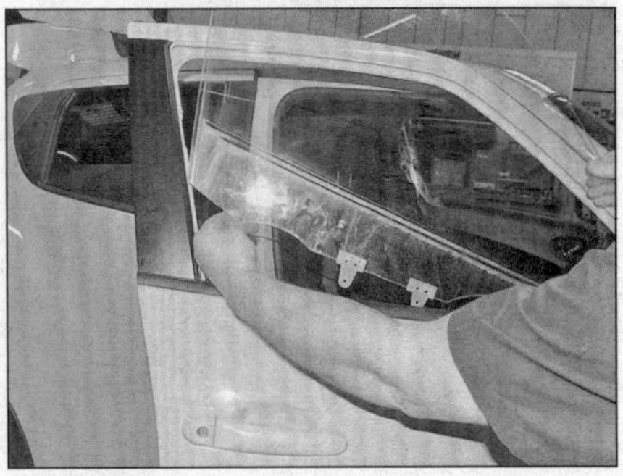

14.6 Withdraw the window glass from the door

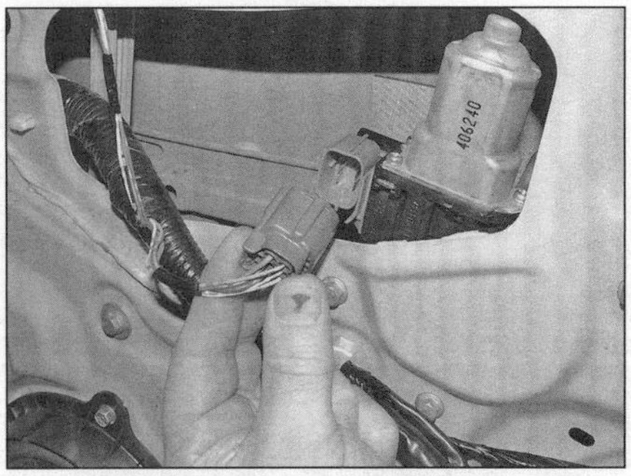

14.9 Disconnect the motor wiring connector

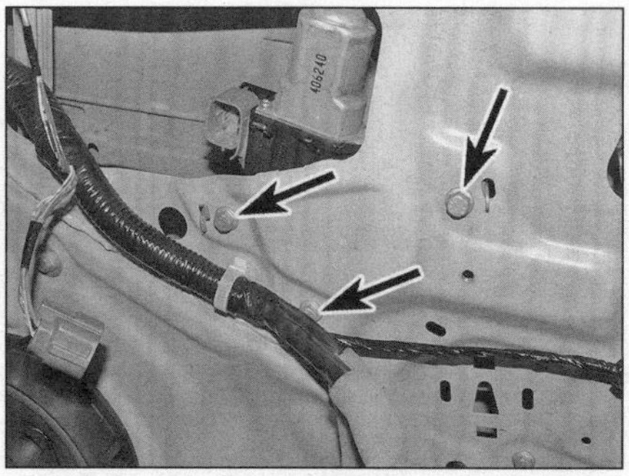

14.10a Undo the regulator assembly centre mounting bolts...

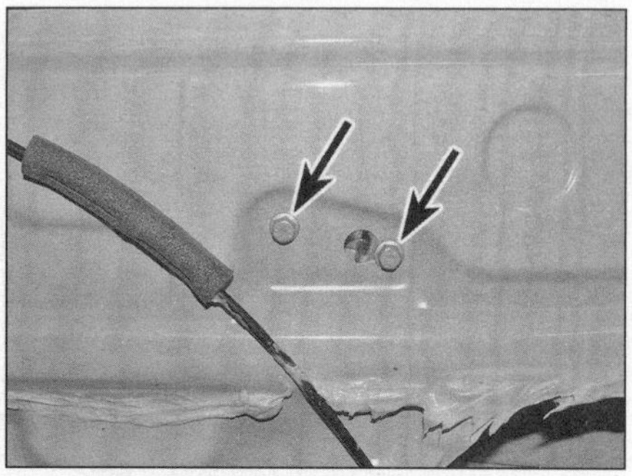

14.10b ...upper mounting bolts...

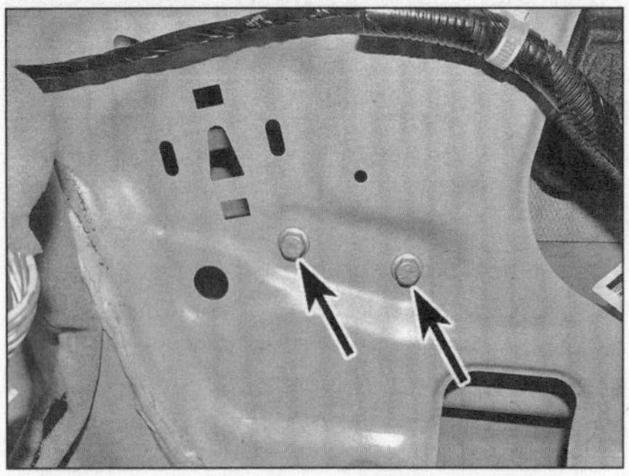

14.10c ...and lower mounting bolts...

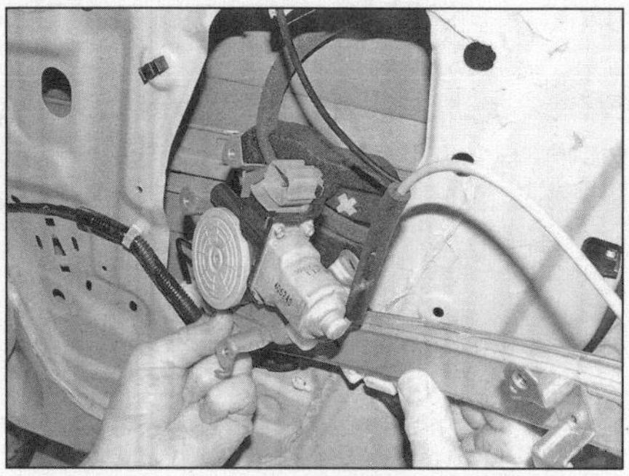

14.10d ...then manipulate the complete assembly out through the door aperture

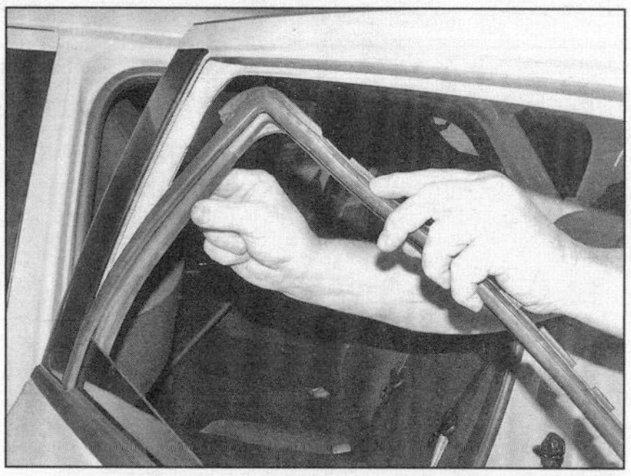

14.15 Carefully remove the rubber window channel/seal

9 Disconnect the wiring connector from the window regulator motor **(see illustration)**.

10 Undo the window regulator assembly securing bolts, then manipulate the complete motor/regulator assembly out through the aperture in the door **(see illustrations)**.

11 If necessary, undo the retaining bolts and separate the motor from the regulator.

12 Refitting is a reversal of removal, bearing in mind the following points:

a) Refit the front window glass with reference to paragraph 7.

b) Check the operation of the window mechanism before refitting the door inner trim panel.

c) Refit the door inner trim panel with reference to Section 12.

Rear window glass

13 Fully open the rear window glass.

14 Remove the door inner trim panel and plastic sealing sheet, as described in Section 12.

15 Working your way around the upper door frame, carefully remove the inner window channel/seal **(see illustration)**. Note this is one piece that is inserted all around the upper window frame and into the front and rear guide channels; take care not to damage it, as it is removed.

16 Temporarily reconnect the electric window switch (and the battery negative terminal, if removed), and raise the window until the two bolts securing the lower edge of the window glass to the regulator mechanism are accessible through the holes in the door panel. Support the glass, and then undo the two bolts **(see illustrations)**.

17 Undo the two lower bolts and the

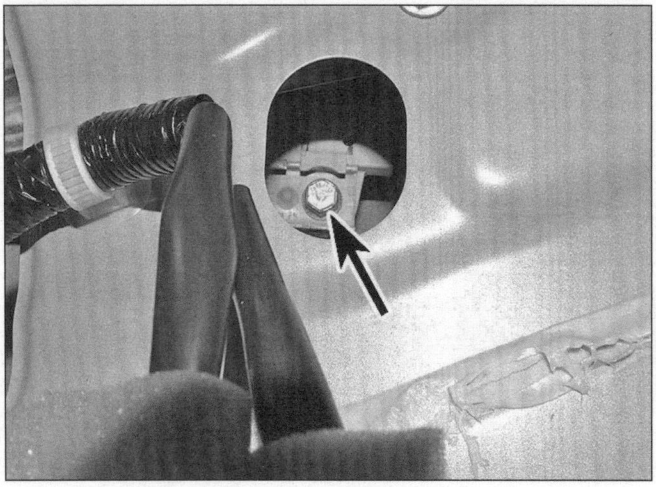

14.16a Undo the window glass front retaining bolt, working through the circular hole in the door...

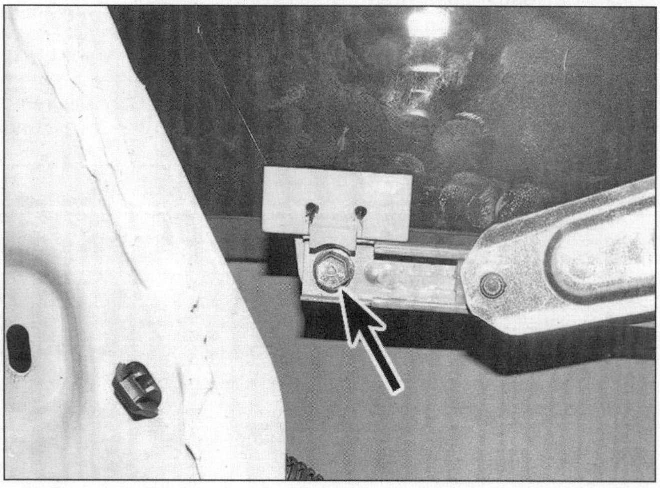

14.16b ...then undo the rear bolt, working through the large door aperture

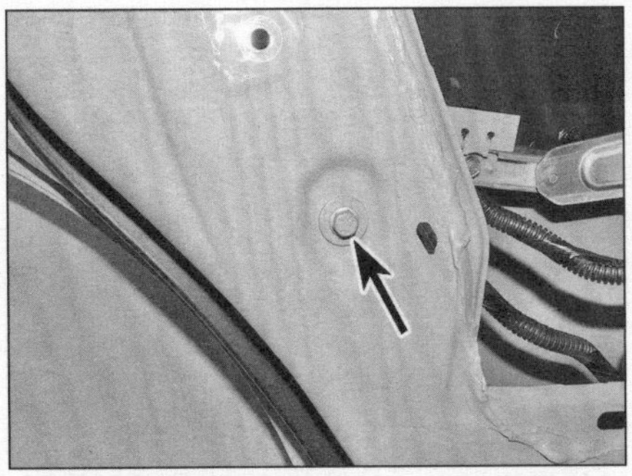

14.17a Undo the lower retaining bolt...

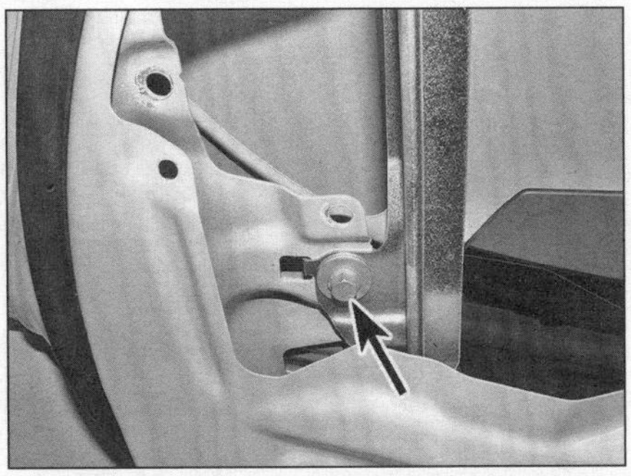

14.17b ...centre retaining bolt...

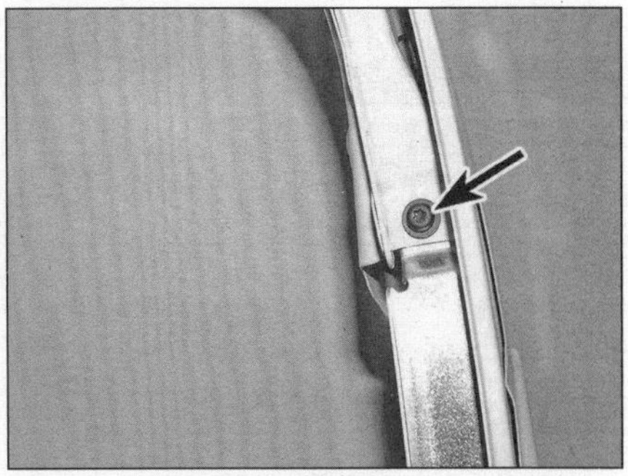

14.17c ...and upper retaining screw...

upper screw securing the rear guide channel to the door, then remove the guide channel **(see illustrations)**. It may be necessary to reposition the window glass to provide clearance for removal of the channel.

18 Disengage the window glass from the regulator, raise the glass at the rear, and then withdraw it from the inside of the door frame **(see illustration)**.

19 Refitting is a reversal of removal, bearing in mind the following points:

a) Check that the glass moves satisfactorily in the window channel/seal and guide channels, without excess side clearance or binding. If necessary, slacken the retaining bolts and reposition the window glass, guide channels and regulator as required. Fully tighten the retaining bolts on completion.

b) Check the operation of the window mechanism before refitting the door inner trim panel.

c) Refit the door inner trim panel with reference to Section 12.

Rear window regulator

20 Remove the door inner trim panel and plastic sealing sheet, as described in Section 12.

21 Temporarily reconnect the electric window switch (and the battery negative terminal, if removed), and lower or raise the window until the two bolts securing the lower edge of the window glass to the regulator mechanism are accessible through the holes in the door **(see illustrations 14.16a and 14.16b)**. Support the glass, and then undo the two bolts.

22 Disengage the window glass from the regulator and slide it to the top of the window frame and tape it in position.

23 Disconnect the wiring connector from the window regulator motor **(see illustration)**.

24 Note the rearmost upper regulator bolt does not have to be removed completely, as the mounting hole is elongated. Also the regulator has a locating lug that protrudes through a hole in the door frame, to prevent it falling down inside the door panel, when the bolts are removed.

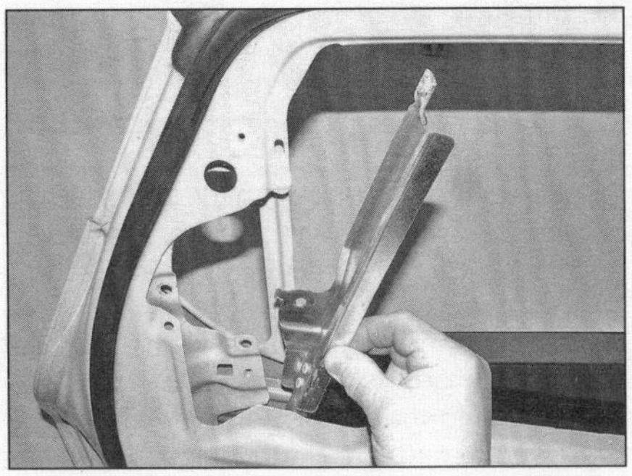

14.17d ...then remove the rear guide channel

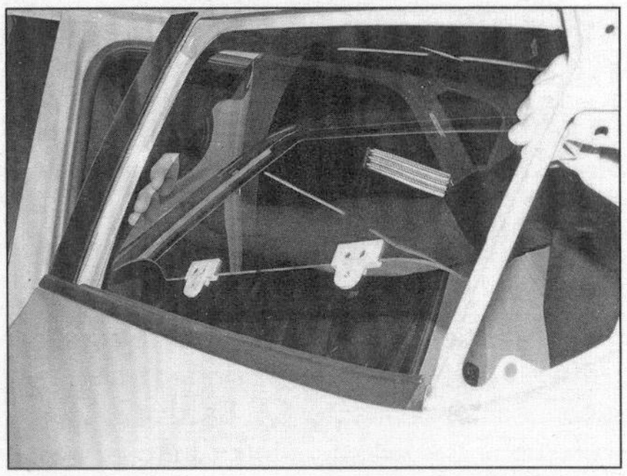

14.18 Withdraw the window glass out from the door

25 Undo the window regulator and motor securing bolts, and then manipulate the complete motor/regulator assembly out through the aperture in the door **(see illustrations)**.

26 If necessary, undo the retaining bolts and separate the motor from the regulator.

27 Refitting is a reversal of removal, bearing in mind the following points:

a) Refit the window glass and tighten the retaining bolts.

b) Check the operation of the window mechanism before refitting the door inner trim panel.

c) Refit the door inner trim panel with reference to Section 12.

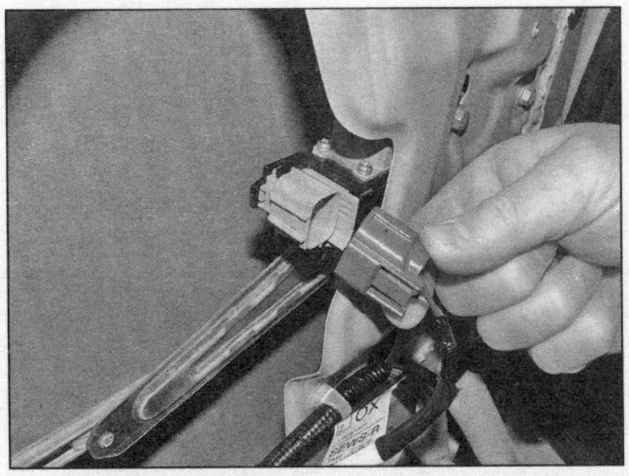

14.23 Disconnect the motor wiring connector

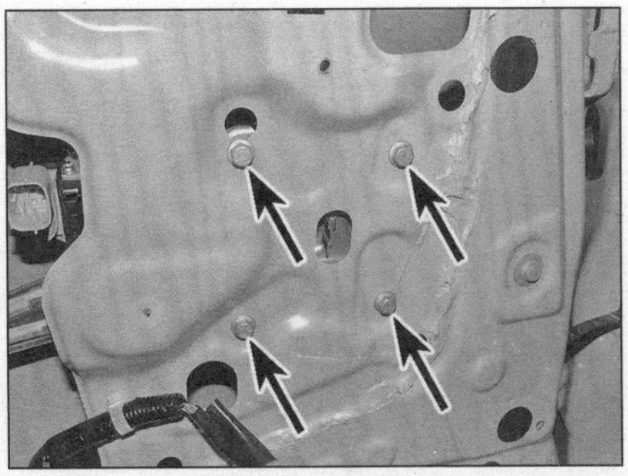

14.25a Undo the window motor/regulator retaining bolts...

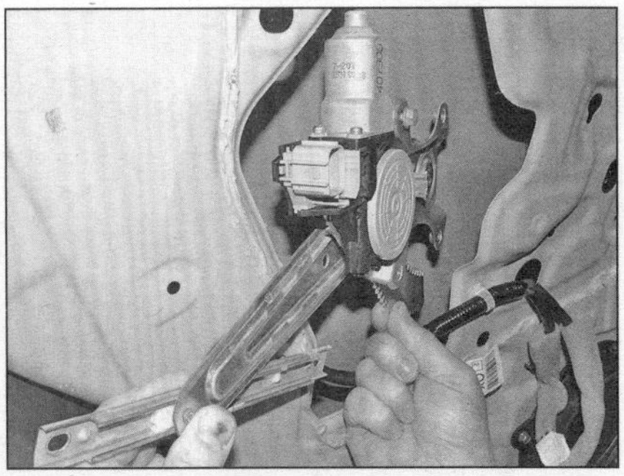

14.25b ...and remove the window motor/regulator from the door

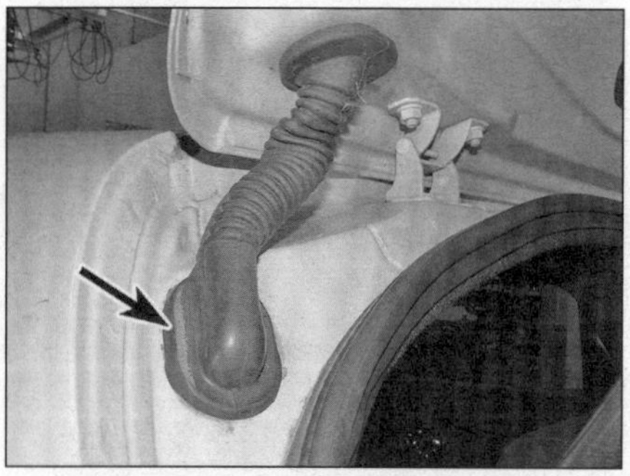

15.10 Prise out the wiring harness grommet from the body attachment

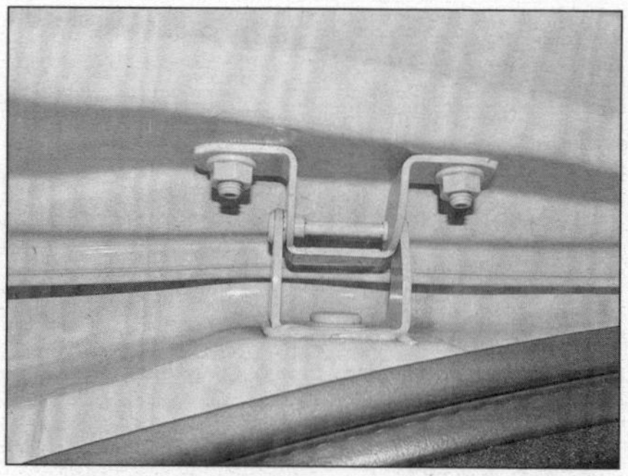

15.14 Undo the hinge retaining nuts

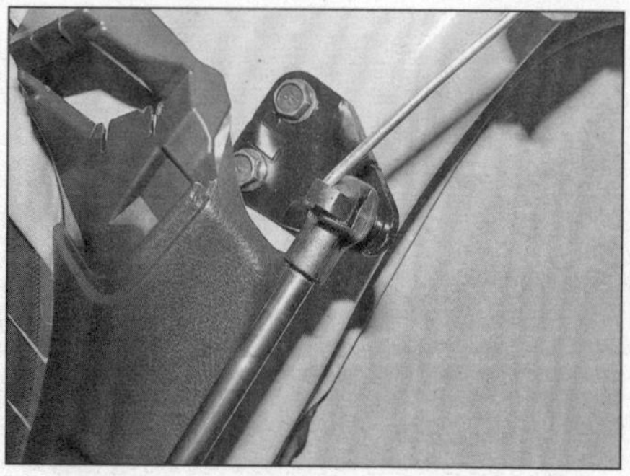

15.20 Prise out the securing clips and release the struts from their upper and lower mountings

15 Tailgate and support struts – removal, refitting and adjustment

Tailgate

Removal

1 Disconnect the battery negative terminal (refer to battery disconnection and reconnection in Chapter 5A, Section 3).

2 Remove the tailgate interior trim panels as described in Section 24.

3 Remove the luggage compartment trim panels on both sides and the B-pillar trim on both sides as described in Section 24.

4 Working on the left-hand side, disconnect the tailgate wiring harness connectors.

5 Working on the right-hand side, release the tailgate washer hose from the retaining clip, then disconnect the washer hose at the connector.

6 Locally remove the tailgate weatherstrip in the area of the headlining.

7 Remove the rear grab handles on both sides as described in Section 24.

8 Carefully release the rear portion of the headlining from the roof.

9 On the left-hand side, undo the earth cable retaining bolt and release the wiring harness retaining clip.

10 Prise out the wiring harness grommet from the body attachment on the left-hand side and pull out the disconnected wiring harness **(see illustration)**.

11 Similarly, prise out the wiring harness grommet from the body on the right-hand side and pull out the disconnected washer hose.

12 Have an assistant support the tailgate in the open position.

13 Remove the securing clips and release both support struts from their upper mounting point on the tailgate **(see illustration 15.20)**.

14 Using a pencil or felt tip pen, mark the outline of each hinge relative to the tailgate, to use as a guide on refitting. Unscrew the nuts securing the hinges to the tailgate **(see illustration)**, and then lift the tailgate from the vehicle.

Refitting

15 Refitting is a reversal of removal, but do not tighten the hinge securing nuts until the tailgate adjustment has been checked as described in the following sub-Section.

Adjustment

16 Close the tailgate carefully, in case the alignment is incorrect, which may cause scratching on the tailgate or the body as the tailgate is closed, and check for alignment with the adjacent panels.

17 If adjustment is required, it will be necessary to slacken the hinge retaining nuts and re-align the tailgate to suit. Once the tailgate is correctly aligned, tighten the hinge retaining nuts fully.

18 Once the tailgate is correctly aligned, check that the tailgate fastens and releases in a satisfactory manner. If adjustment is necessary, slacken the tailgate lock striker retaining screws, and adjust the position of the catch, as described in Section 16. Once the tailgate lock is operating correctly, securely tighten the retaining screws.

Support struts

Removal

19 To remove a strut, first ensure that the tailgate is adequately supported.

20 Remove the securing clips and release both support struts from their upper and lower mounting points **(see illustration)**.

Refitting

21 Refitting is a reversal of removal.

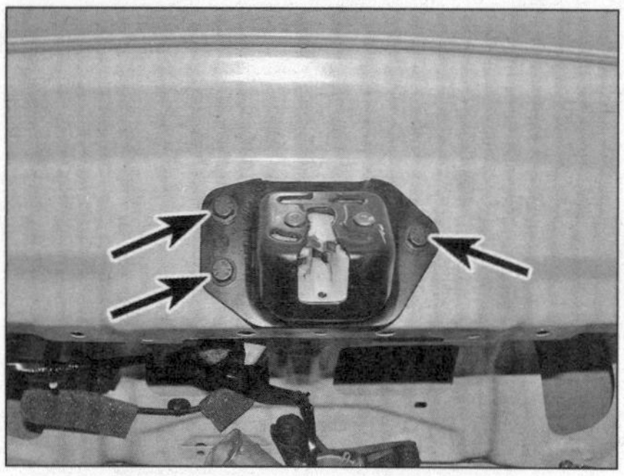

16.3a Undo the three bolts...

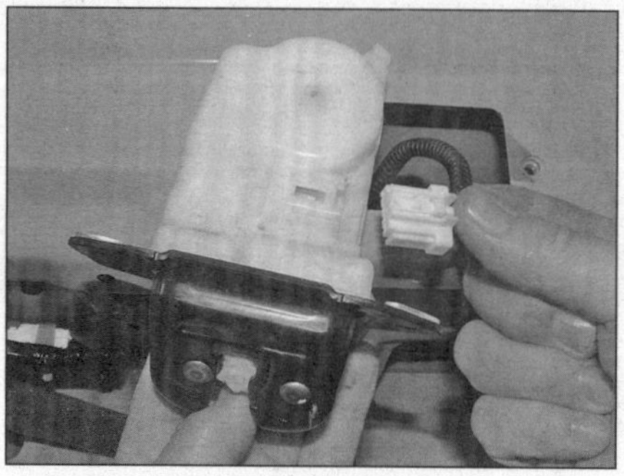

16.3b ...then withdraw the lock and disconnect the wiring connector

16 Tailgate lock components – removal and refitting

Tailgate lock

1 Disconnect the battery negative terminal (refer to battery disconnection and reconnection in Chapter 5A, Section 3).

2 Remove the tailgate interior trim panel as described in Section 24.

3 Unscrew the three lock securing bolts, withdraw the lock from the tailgate and disconnect the wiring connector as the lock is removed **(see illustrations)**.

4 Refitting is a reversal of removal, but before refitting the trim panel, check that the tailgate fastens and releases in a satisfactory manner. If adjustment is necessary, slacken the tailgate lock retaining bolts, and adjust the position of the lock to suit. Once the lock is operating correctly, securely tighten its retaining bolts.

Tailgate lock striker

5 Using a plastic spatula or similar, carefully prise free the tailgate aperture lower trim panel.

6 Note the position of the striker plate, then unscrew the two securing screws, and withdraw the lock striker from the rear panel.

7 Refitting is a reversal of removal, but check the operation of the tailgate release mechanism.

8 Check that the tailgate fastens and releases

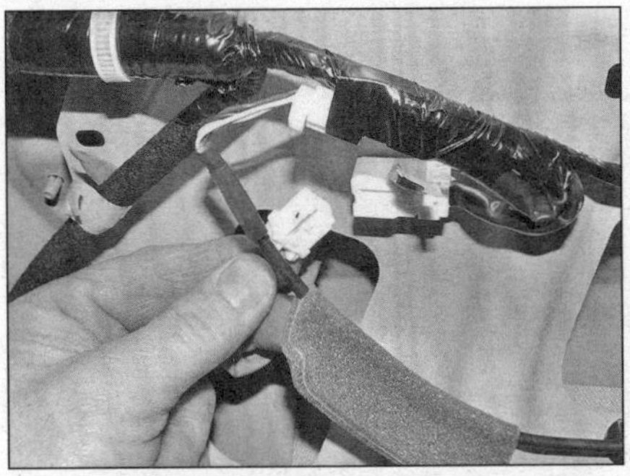

16.10 Disconnect the wiring plug connector

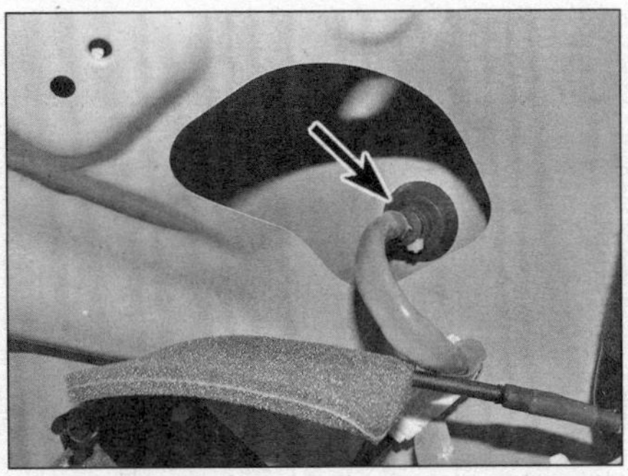

16.11 Release the wiring harness grommet

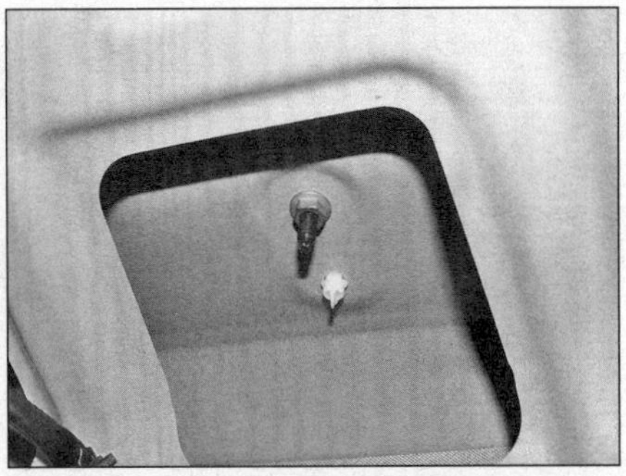

16.12a Undo the retaining nuts (one shown) and compress the legs of the retaining lugs...

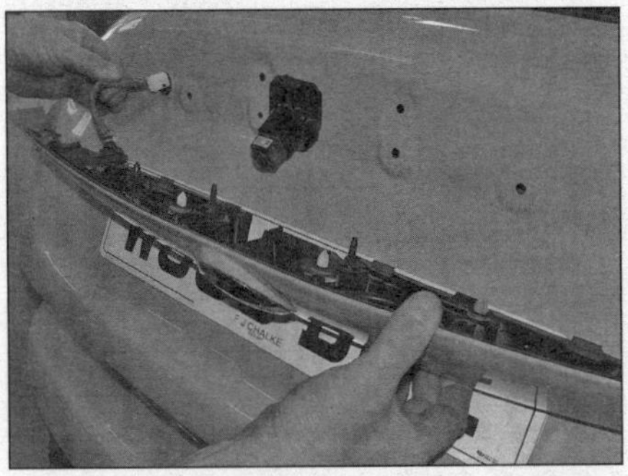

16.12b ...and remove the tailgate finisher

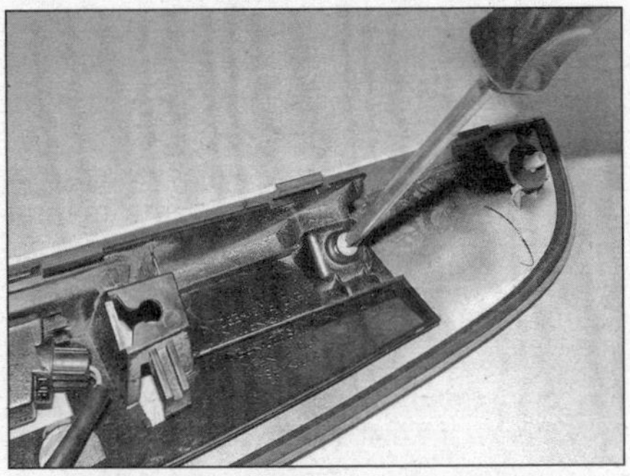

16.13a Undo the retaining screws...

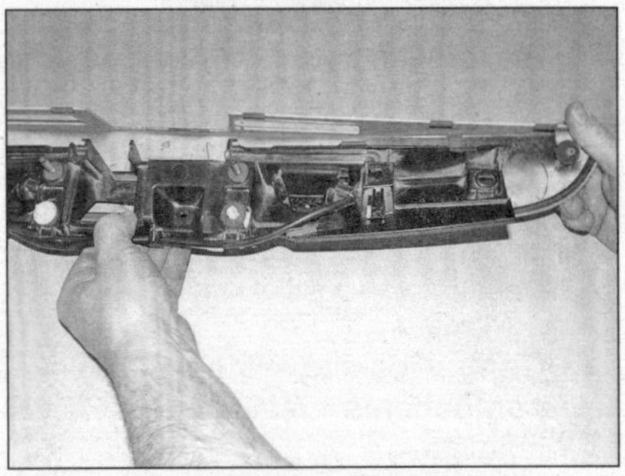

16.13b ...and separate the two parts of the finisher

in a satisfactory manner. If adjustment is necessary, slacken the striker retaining screws, and adjust the position of the striker to suit. Once the lock is operating correctly, securely tighten the striker retaining screws.

Tailgate exterior switch

9 Remove the tailgate interior trim panel as described in Section 24.

10 Reach inside the tailgate and disconnect the wiring connector for the tailgate switch and number plate lights **(see illustration)**.

11 Release the wiring harness grommet from the tailgate panel **(see illustration)**.

12 Undo the two nuts, securing the tailgate finisher to the tailgate. Compress the legs of the retaining lugs and remove the finisher from the tailgate **(see illustrations)**.

13 Undo the retaining screws and separate the two parts of the tailgate finisher **(see illustrations)**.

14 Carefully prise free the number plate light units from the tailgate finisher, then turn the bulbholders anti-clockwise and remove them from the light units **(see illustration)**.

15 Note the routing of the exterior switch and number plate wiring, then release the wiring from the tailgate finisher **(see illustration)**.

16 Withdraw the tailgate exterior switch from

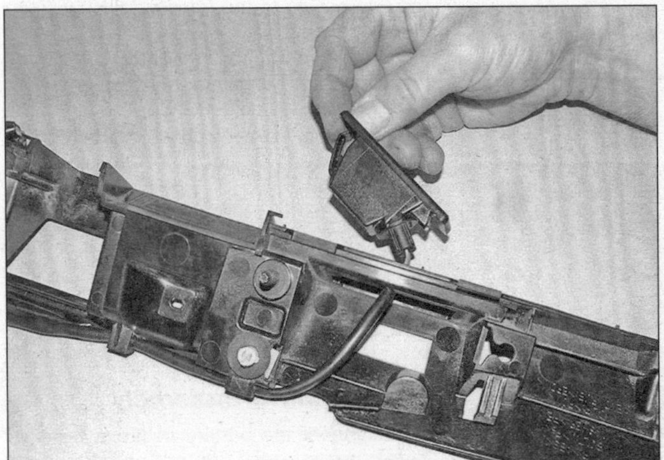

16.14 Release the number plate light units, then remove the bulbholders

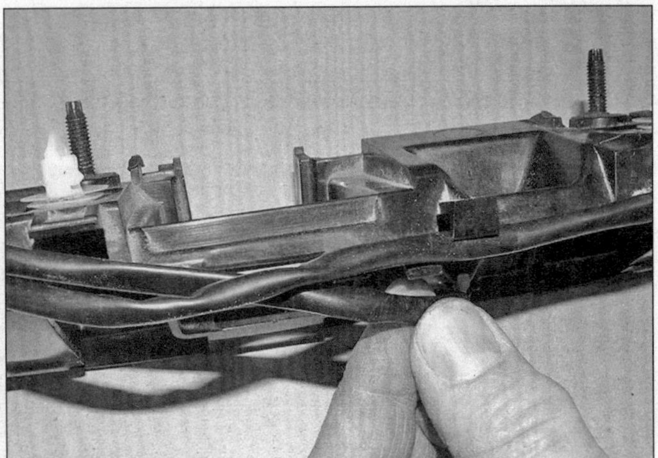

16.15 Note the routing and release the wiring harness from the tailgate finisher

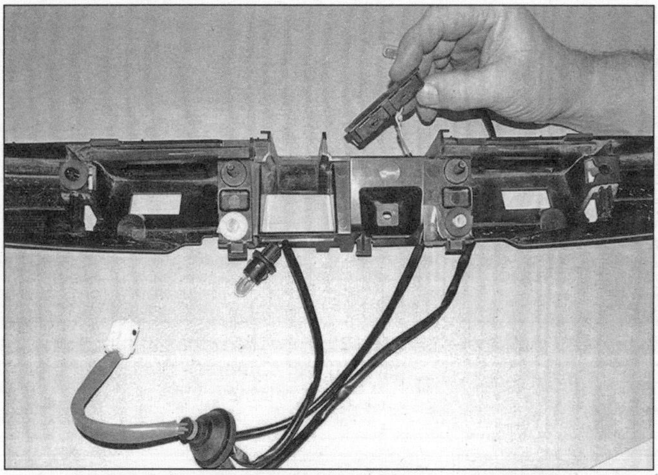

16.16a Withdraw the tailgate switch from the finisher...

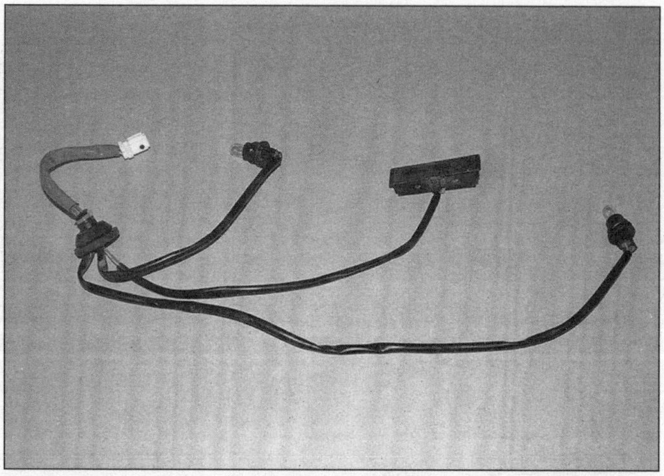

16.16b ...and remove the switch, bulbholders and wiring as an assembly

the finisher and remove the switch, number plate bulbholders and wiring from the finisher as an assembly **(see illustrations)**.
17 Refitting is a reversal of removal.

17 Central locking system components – removal and refitting

Body Control Module (BCM)

1 The electronic body control module it is located behind the glovebox, on the left-hand side of the facia.
2 Disconnect the battery negative terminal (refer to battery disconnection and reconnection in Chapter 5A, Section 3).
3 Remove the glovebox as described in Section 26.
4 Remove the wiring harness retaining clip, then undo the BCM mounting screws.
5 Withdraw the unit and disconnect the wiring connectors.
6 Refitting is a reversal of removal.

Door lock motor

7 The motor is integral with the door lock assembly. Removal and refitting of the lock assembly is described in Section 13.

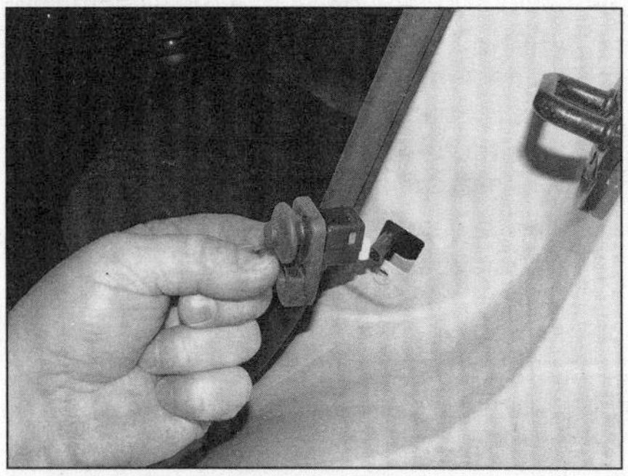

17.10 Remove the door switch from the pillar

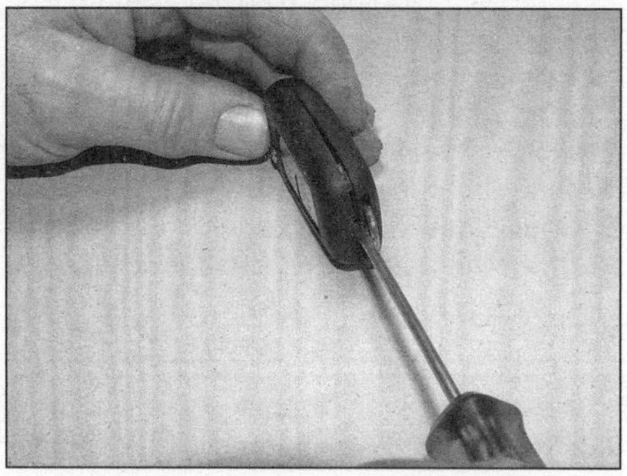

17.14a Twist a small screwdriver in the slot...

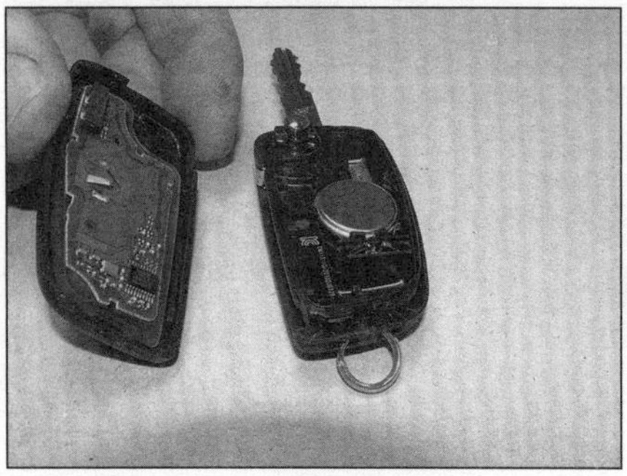

17.14b ...and unclip one side of the transmitter

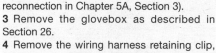

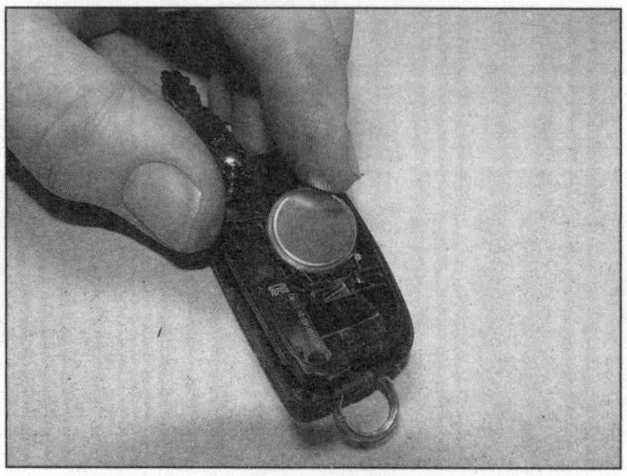

17.15 Lift the battery from its location in the remote

Tailgate lock motor

8 Removal of the tailgate lock motor is described as part of the tailgate lock removal and refitting procedure described in Section 16.

Door switches

9 Disconnect the battery negative terminal (refer to battery disconnection and reconnection in Chapter 5A, Section 3).
10 Undo the retaining screw and withdraw the relevant switch from the door pillar **(see illustration)**.
11 Disconnect the wiring connector and remove the switch.
12 Refitting is a reversal of removal.

Remote control battery renewal

13 Where fitted, undo the small screw securing the two halves of the transmitter together.
14 Using a small screwdriver, carefully prise the two halves of the transmitter apart **(see illustrations)**.
15 Carefully unclip the battery from its position in the transmitter housing, noting its fitted position **(see illustration)**.
16 Fit the new battery, observing the correct polarity, and clip the transmitter housing back together.

18 Exterior mirrors and associated components – removal and refitting

Exterior mirror assembly

1 Disconnect the battery negative terminal (refer to battery disconnection and reconnection in Chapter 5A, Section 3).
2 Remove the door inner trim panel, as described in Section 12.

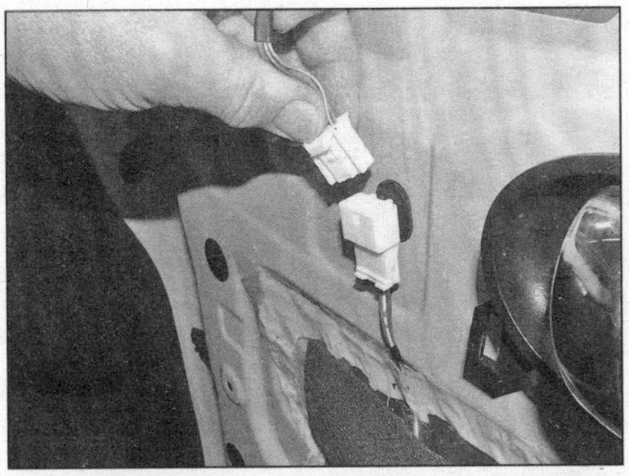

18.3 Disconnect the wiring connector

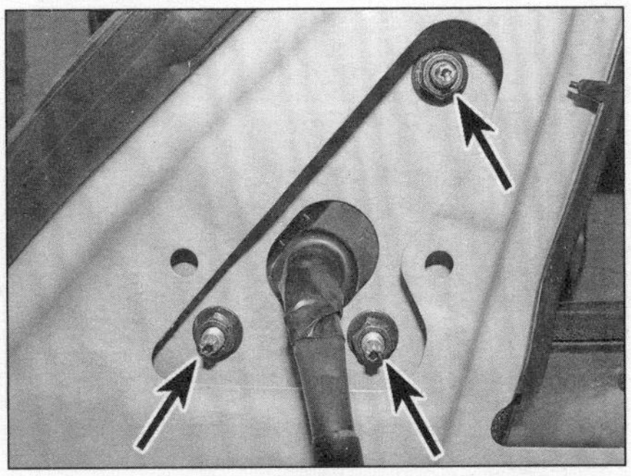

18.4a Undo the three securing nuts...

18.4b ...and remove the mirror assembly

3 Disconnect the mirror wiring connector **(see illustration)**.
4 Undo the three securing nuts, and withdraw the mirror from the outside of the door **(see illustrations)**.
5 Refitting is a reversal of removal.

Exterior mirror glass

6 Carefully press the mirror glass in at the top, and then working through the gap at the bottom edge of the mirror glass, use a lever to release the clips that secure the mirror glass to the mirror body **(see illustration)**.
7 Withdraw the glass, and (where applicable) disconnect the heating element wiring connectors **(see illustration)**.
8 To refit, carefully push the mirror glass evenly until the securing clips lock into position on the mirror adjuster base.

Warning: It is advisable to wear gloves to protect your hands, even if the glass is not broken, due to the risk of glass breakage.

Exterior mirror outer shell

9 Remove the mirror assembly from the door, then remove the mirror glass as described previously in this Section.
10 Working from inside the mirror housing, press the retaining pawls together and disengage them from the mirror body **(see illustration)**.
11 Insert two removal tools between the mirror shell and mirror body to disengage the retaining pawls, then remove the outer shell **(see illustration)**.
12 To refit, carefully push the mirror shell onto the mirror body until the securing pawls and clips lock into position.
13 Refit the mirror and mirror glass as described previously in this Section.

Exterior mirror electric motor

14 Remove the mirror glass as described previously in this Section.
15 Working from inside the mirror housing, undo the three retaining screws and withdraw the motor from the mirror body **(see illustration)**.
16 Disconnect the wiring connector as it is removed **(see illustration)**.
17 Refitting is a reversal of removal, ensuring that the mirror glass is fitted securely as described previously in this Section.

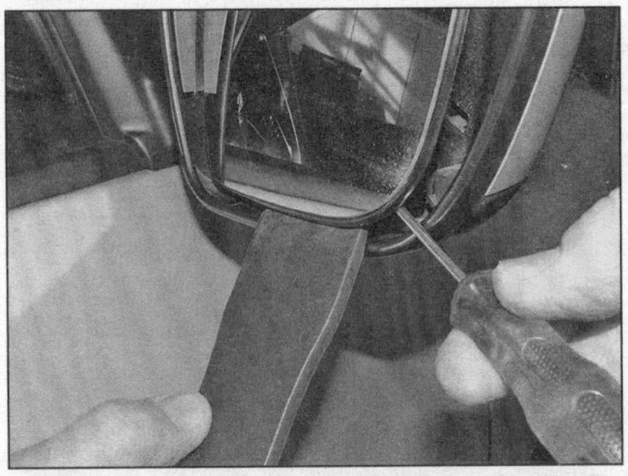

18.6 Carefully lever the lower edge of the mirror glass

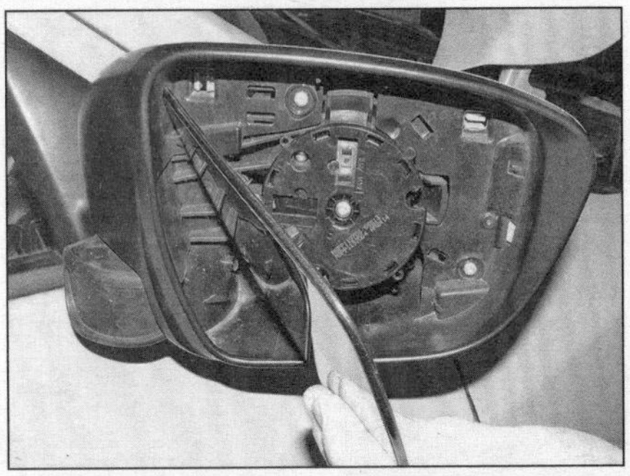

18.7 Unclip the mirror glass from the mirror base

18.10 Press the retaining pawls together and disengage them from the mirror body

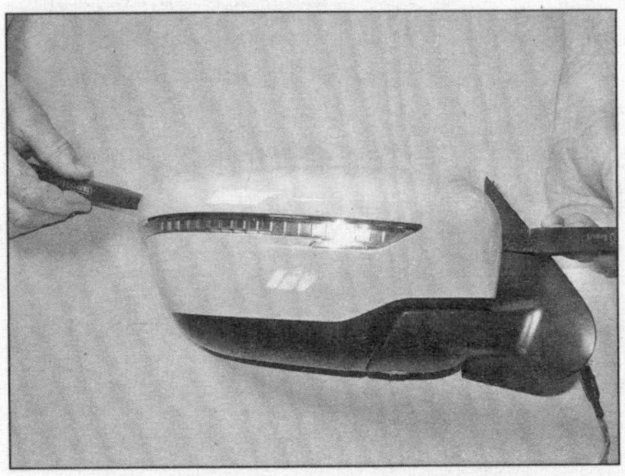

18.11 Use two removal tools to remove the mirror outer shell

18.15 Undo the three motor retaining screws...

18.16 ...and disconnect the wiring connector

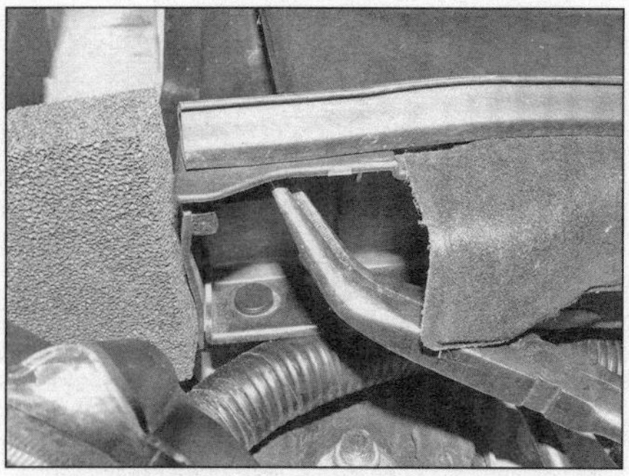
21.3a Squeeze together the legs of the outer blue clips...

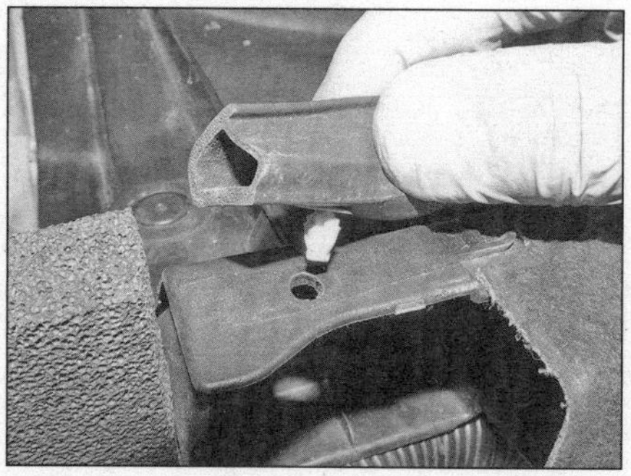
21.3b ...and lift the rubber seal upward

21.3c Release the centre white clips by prising them upward

19 Windscreen, tailgate glass and fixed windows - general information

1 The windscreen, tailgate and fixed window glasses are cemented in position with a special adhesive and require the use of specialist equipment for their removal and refitting. Renewal of such fixed glass is considered beyond the scope of the home mechanic. Owners are strongly advised to have the work carried out by one of the many specialist windscreen fitting specialists.

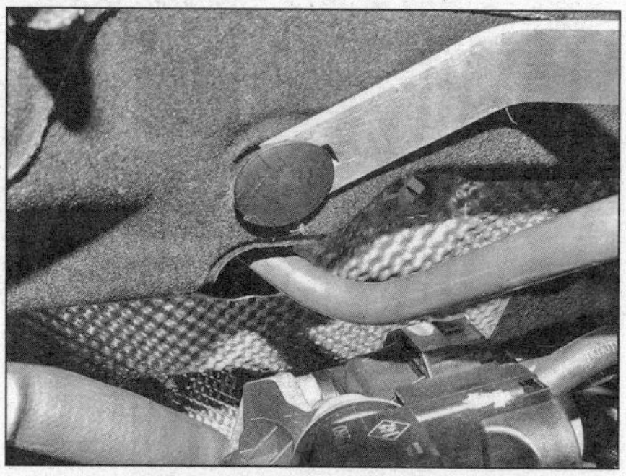
21.4a Extract the retaining clips...

21.4b ...and remove the cowl panel insulator

20 Sunroof - general information

1 Due to the complexity of the sunroof mechanism, considerable expertise is required to repair, renew or adjust the sunroof components successfully. Removal of the roof first requires the headlining to be removed, which is a tedious operation, and not a task to be undertaken lightly. Any problems with the sunroof should be referred to a Nissan dealer.

21 Body exterior fittings - removal and refitting

Windscreen cowl panel

1 Open and support the bonnet.

2 Remove the windscreen wiper arms as described in Chapter 12, Section 11.

3 Release the retaining clips and remove the rubber seal from the top of the cowl panel. The blue retaining clips at the outer ends of the seal can be released by squeezing together the clip legs using pliers and lifting the seal upward. The white clips in the centre of the seal can be released by prising them upwards **(see illustrations)**.

4 If fitted, extract the retaining clips and remove the cowl panel insulator **(see illustrations)**.

5 Disconnect the washer fluid hose at the connector on the right-hand side of the cowl panel **(see illustration)**.

6 Remove the cowl panel upper extensions on the left-hand and right-hand sides **(see illustration)**.

7 Working along the front edge of the cowl

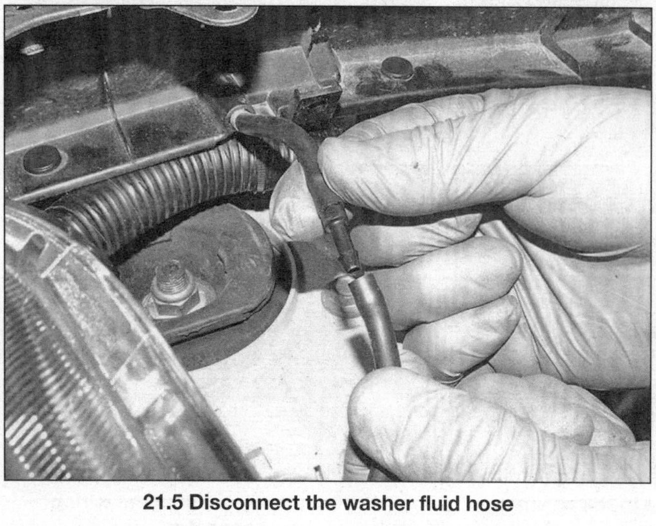
21.5 Disconnect the washer fluid hose

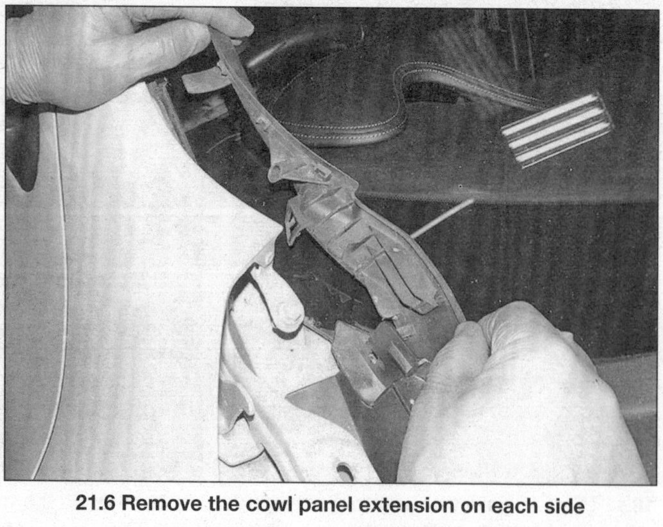
21.6 Remove the cowl panel extension on each side

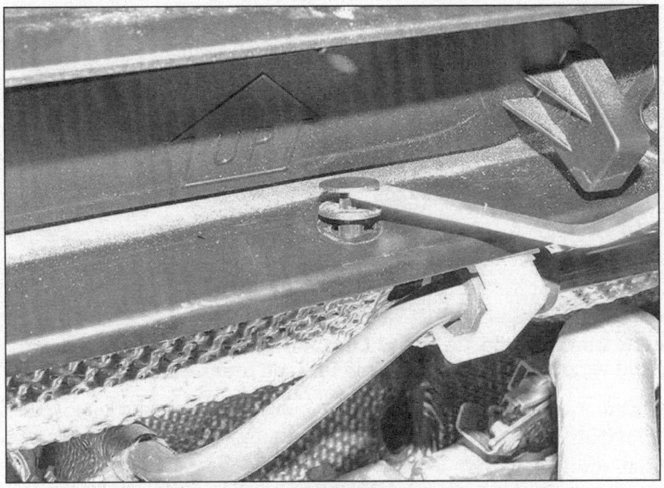

21.7 Release the retaining clips

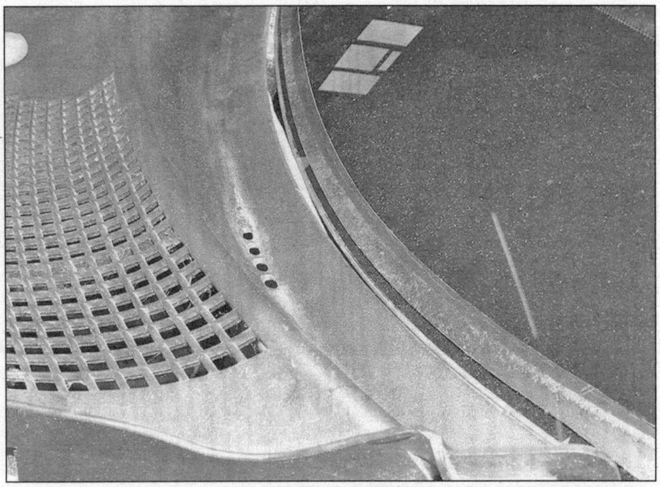

21.8a Pull the cowl panel forward to release it from the windscreen...

panel, pull out the centre pin and release the cowl panel retaining clips **(see illustration)**.

8 Pull the cowl panel forward to release it from the windscreen, then lift it up and remove it from the car **(see illustrations)**.

9 Refitting is a reversal of removal.

Cowl panel extension

10 Remove the windscreen cowl panel as described previously in this Section.

11 Remove the windscreen wiper motor and linkage as described in Chapter 12, Section 12.

12 Open the retaining clips and release the relevant hoses and/or wiring harness from the cowl panel extension.

13 Undo the four retaining bolts on each side and remove the cowl panel extension **(see illustrations)**.

14 Refitting is a reversal of removal.

Wheel arch trim

Front trim

Note: *The design of the retaining clips is such that three will break during removal. Ensure that new clips are obtained for refitting.*

15 Prise out the centre pin and remove the expanding rivet at the front centre and rear of the trim **(see illustrations)**.

16 Carefully prise away the wheel arch trim to release the retaining clips and remove the

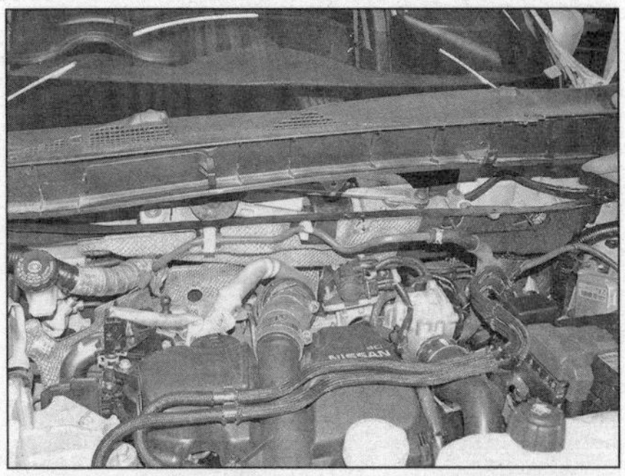

21.8b ...then lift it up and remove it from the car

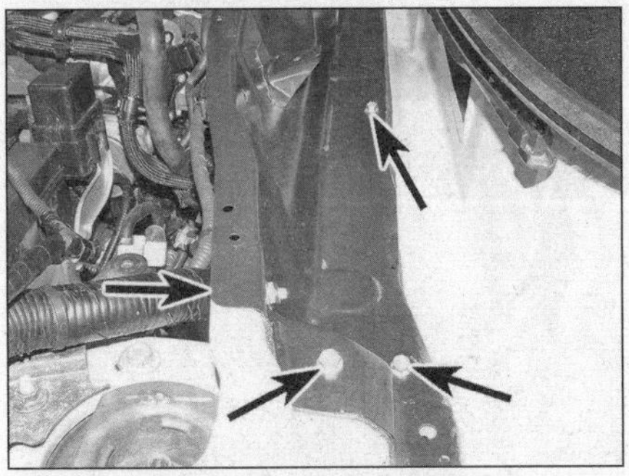

21.13a Undo the bolts on the left-hand side...

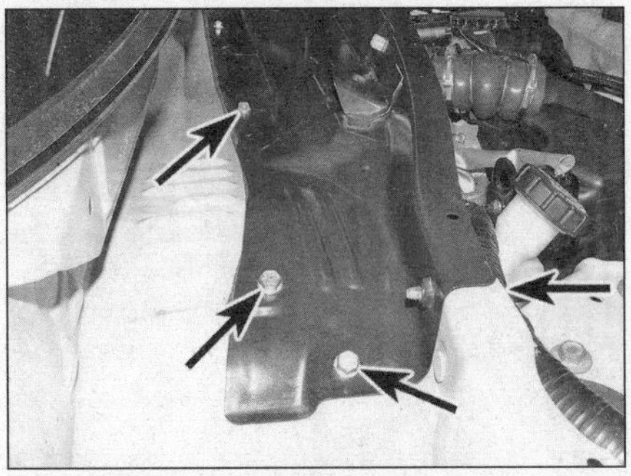

21.13b ...and right-hand side...

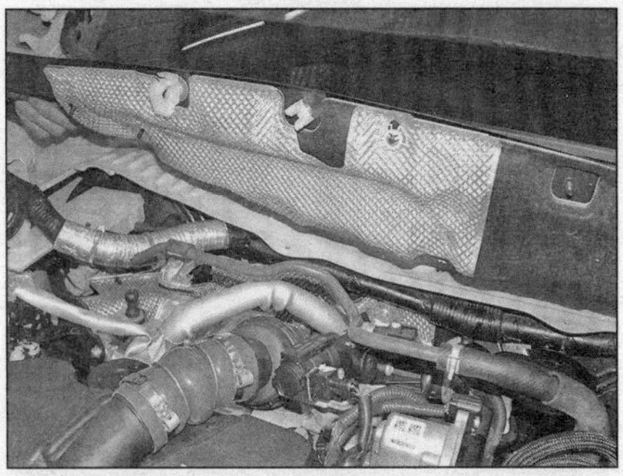

21.13c ...and remove the cowl panel extension

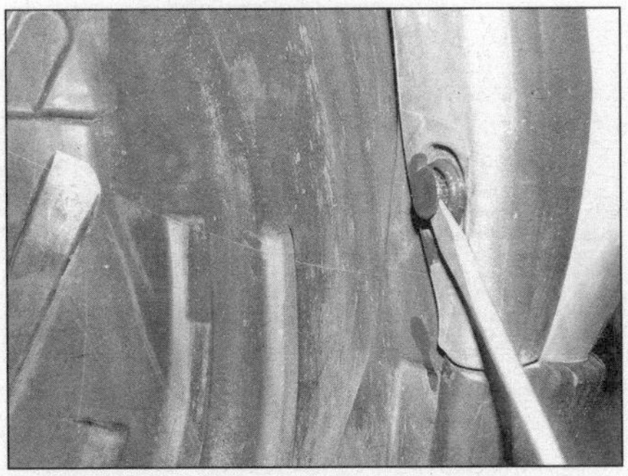

21.15a Prise out the centre pin and remove the expanding rivet at the front...

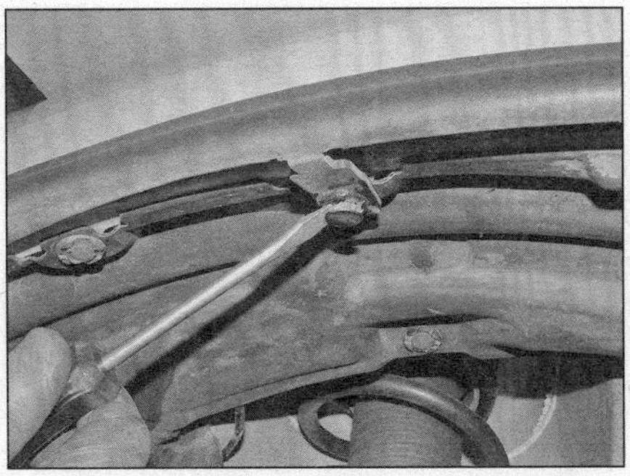

21.15b ...centre...

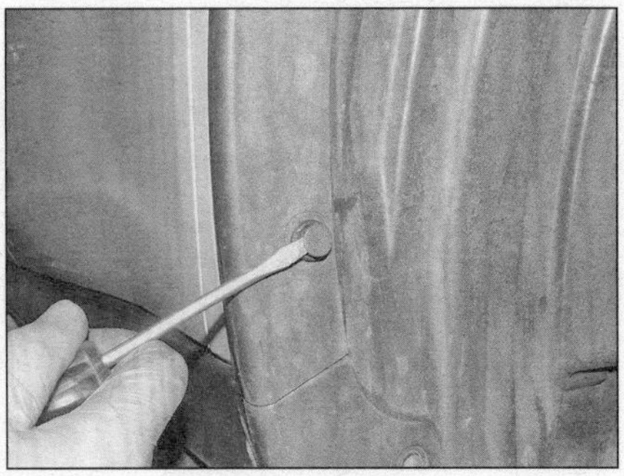

21.15c ...and rear

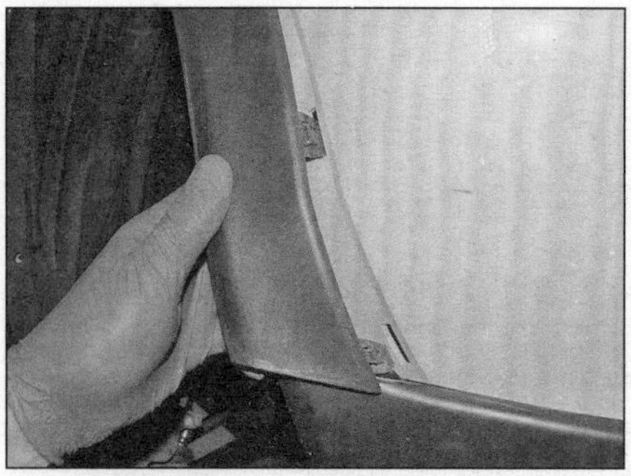

21.16a Prise free the wheel arch trim to release the retaining clips...

trim from the bumper and front wing **(see illustrations)**.

17 Refitting is a reversal of removal ensuring that all broken clips are renewed **(see illustration)**.

Rear trim

Note: *The design of the retaining clips is such that four will break during removal. Ensure that new clips are obtained for refitting.*

18 Prise out the centre pin and remove the expanding rivet at the rear of the trim **(see illustration)**.

19 Carefully prise away the wheel arch trim to release the retaining clips and remove the trim from the bumper and rear wing **(see illustrations)**.

20 Refitting is a reversal of removal ensuring that all broken clips are renewed **(see illustration)**.

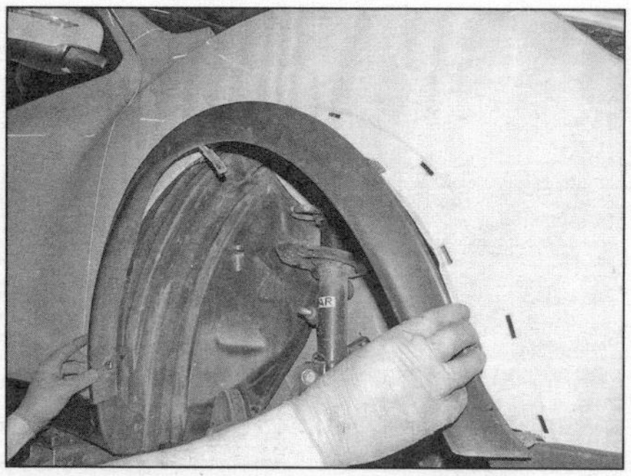

21.16b ...then remove the trim from the bumper and front wing

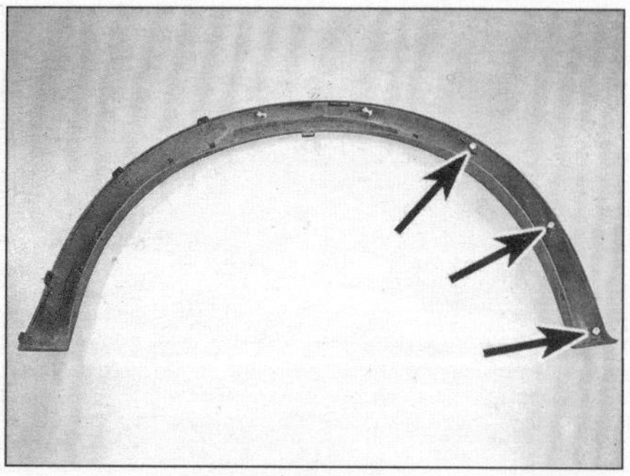

21.17 Location of wheel arch trim retaining clips that will break during removal

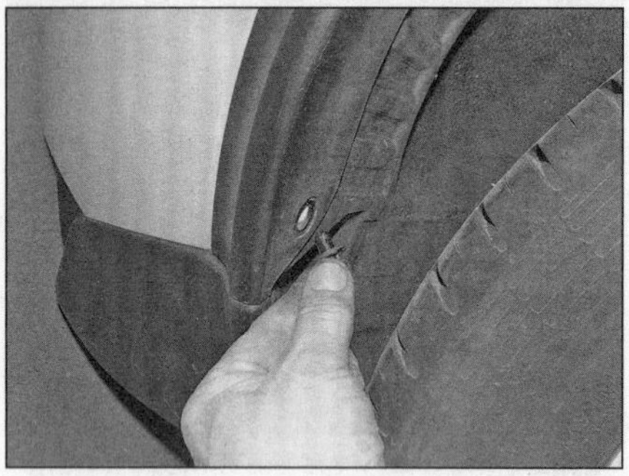

21.18 Prise out the centre pin and remove the expanding rivet

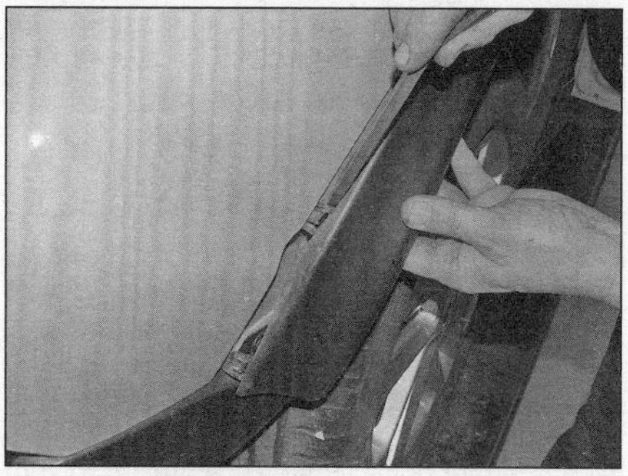

21.19a Carefully prise free the wheel arch trim...

Wheel arch liners

21 The wheel arch liners are secured by expanding plastic rivets, clips and screws.

22 Firmly apply the handbrake, and then jack up the vehicle and support it securely on axle stands (see *Jacking and vehicle support*). To improve access to the fasteners, remove the roadwheel(s).

23 Remove the relevant wheel arch trim as described previously in this Section.

24 To remove the liners, release the plastic rivet centre pins, and then prise the complete plastic rivet from place. Prise out the ordinary retaining clips and undo the retaining screws as applicable. With all the fasteners removed, manoeuvre the liner from the wheel arch **(see illustrations)**.

25 Refitting is a reversal of removal.

21.19b ...and remove the trim from the bumper and rear wing

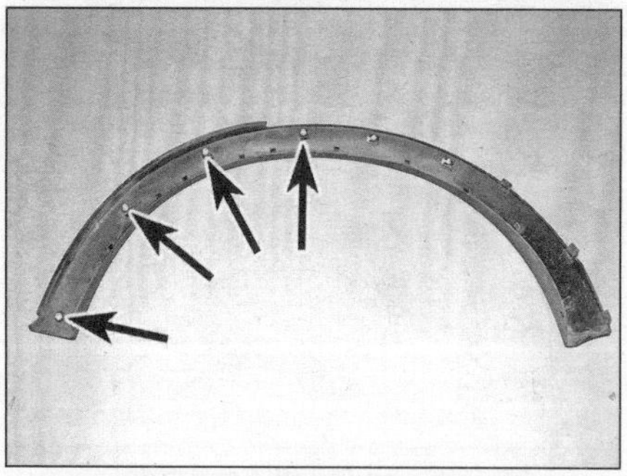

21.20 Location of wheel arch trim retaining clips that will break during removal

21.24a Release the centre pins and pull out the expanding plastic rivets...

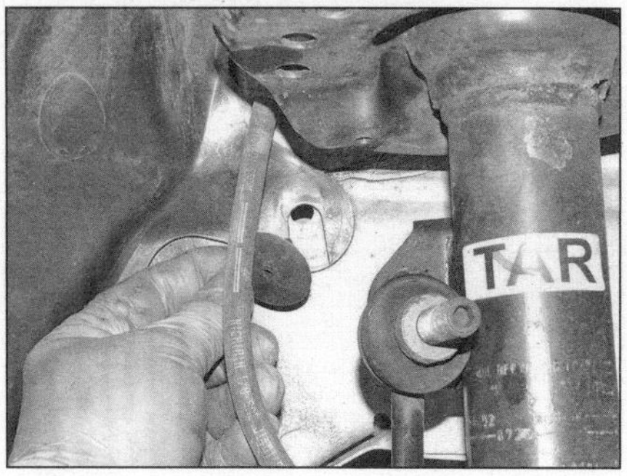

21.24b ...prise out the ordinary retaining clips...

21.24c ...undo the retaining screws...

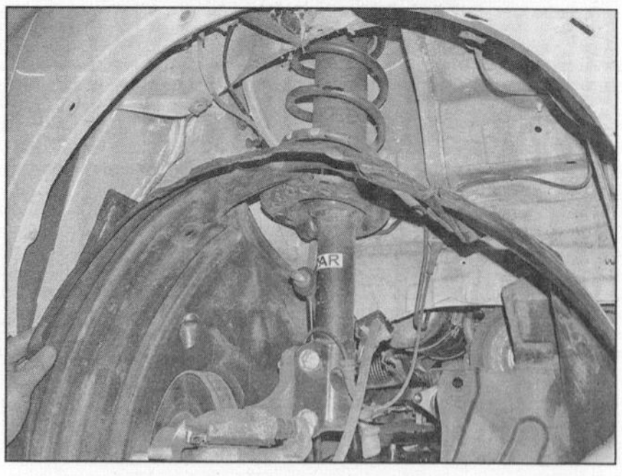

21.24d ...and remove the relevant wheel arch liner

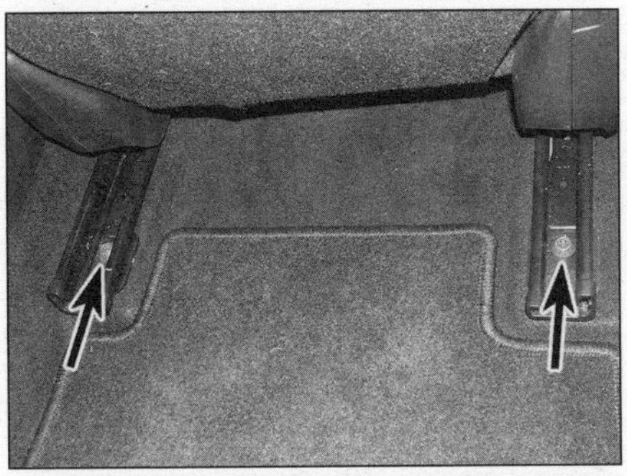

22.3 Undo the two bolts at the rear of the seat rails

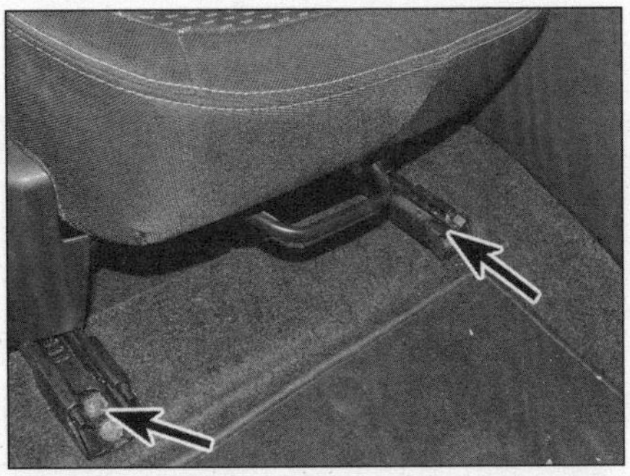

22.4 Undo the two bolts at the front of the seat rails

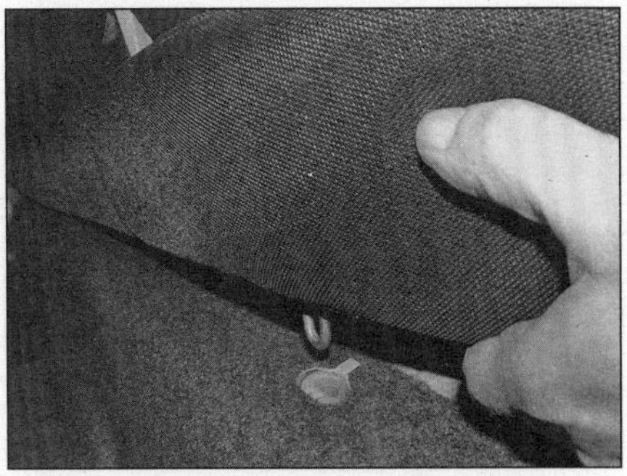

22.7 Release the front securing clip

Body trim strips and badges

26 The various body trim strips and badges are held in position with a special adhesive tape. Removal requires the trim/badge to be heated, to soften the adhesive, and then cut away from the surface. Due to the high risk of damage to the vehicle paintwork during this operation, it is recommended that this task should be entrusted to a Nissan dealer.

22 Seats – removal and refitting

Front seat

⚠ ***Warning: All models are equipped with side airbags built into the outer sides of the front seats. Refer to Chapter 12, Section 20, for the precautions, which should be observed when dealing with an airbag system. Do not tamper with the airbag unit in any way, and do not attempt to test any airbag system components. Note that the airbag is triggered if the mechanism is supplied with an electrical current (including via an ohmmeter), or if the assembly is subjected to a temperature of greater than 100°C.***

1 De-activate the airbag system as described in Chapter 12, Section 20, before attempting to remove the seat.

2 Release the retaining clips and withdraw the headrest out from the top of the seat backrest. This will give more room, when removing the seat out through the door aperture.

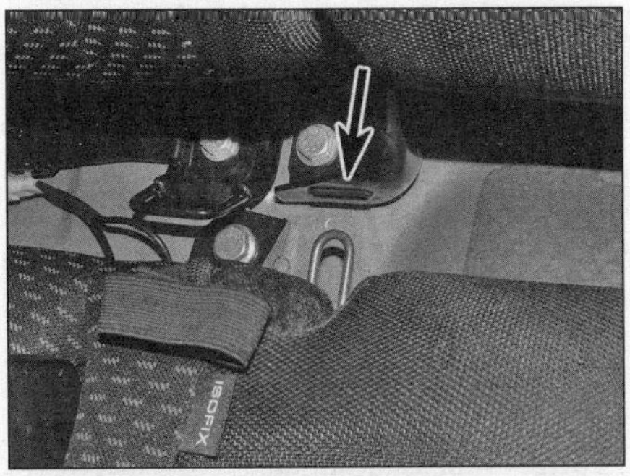

22.8 Slide the seat forwards from the locating bracket

3 Move the seat fully forwards and undo the two retaining bolts from the rear of the seat rails **(see illustration)**.

4 Slide the seat fully rearwards, and then unscrew the seat rail front securing bolts **(see illustration)**.

5 Tilt the seat backwards and disconnect the wiring connectors, then release the wiring loom from any retaining clips under the seat base. Lift the seat, complete with the rails out from the vehicle, taking care that the seat rails do not catch on the vehicle paintwork as it is being removed.

6 Refitting is a reversal of removal, but tighten the securing bolts to the specified torque.

Rear seat cushion

7 Lift the seat cushion at the front, and then give a sharp pull upwards, to release the securing clip from the vehicle floor panel **(see illustration)**.

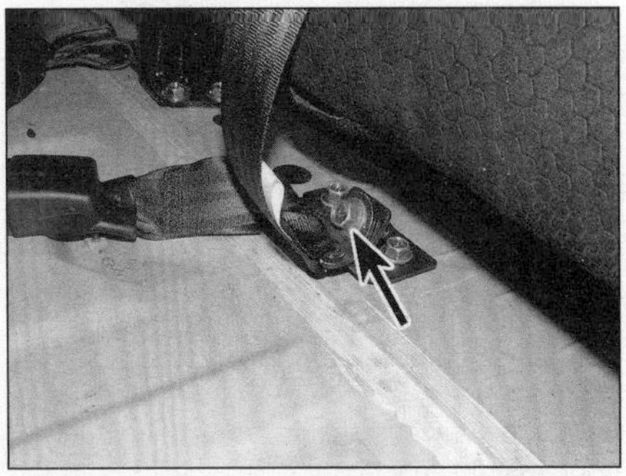

22.12 Centre seat belt centre anchor retaining bolt

8 Slide the seat cushion forward, releasing the rear locating clip **(see illustration)**.

9 Then lift the seat cushion upwards and withdraw the seat belt buckles from the seat cushion.

10 Refitting is a reversal of removal.

Rear seat backs

11 Remove the rear seat cushions as described previously in this Section.

12 If removing the left-hand seat back, undo the centre seat belt centre anchor retaining bolt **(see illustration)**.

13 Remove the headrests out from the top of the seat back, then release the catches and fold the seat backs forward.

14 Lift up the seat back carpet and undo the seat back hinge mounting bolts **(see illustrations)**. Remove the relevant seat back from the vehicle.

22.14a Centre hinge retaining bolts...

22.14b ...and outer hinge retaining bolts

15 Refitting is a reversal of removal, tightening the hinge bolts to the specified torque.

23 Seat belt components – removal and refitting

Note: *Record the positions of the washers and spacers on the seat belt anchors, and ensure they are refitted in their original positions.*

Front seat belt

1 The front seat belt inertia reels are equipped with a mechanical or pyrotechnic pretensioner

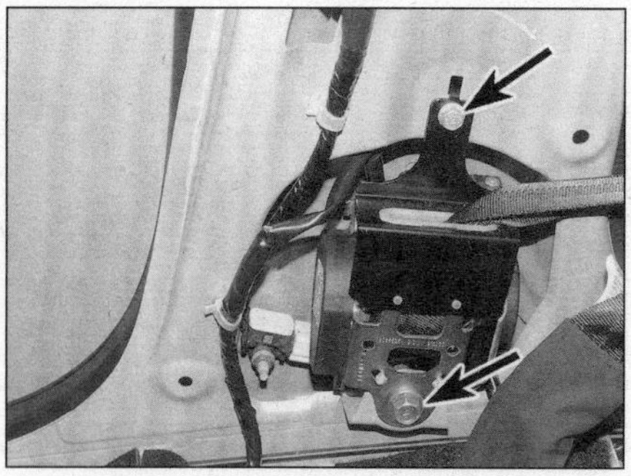
23.7 Inertia reel mounting bolts

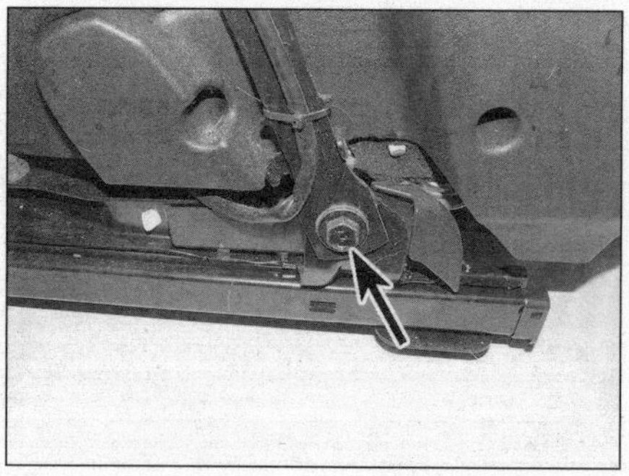
23.12 Undo the seat belt stalk anchor bolt

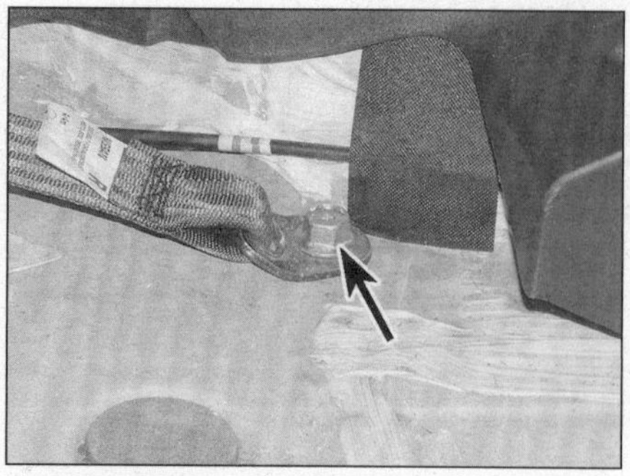
23.16 Undo the seat belt lower anchor bolt

mechanism. Refer to the airbag system precautions contained in Chapter 12, Section 20, which apply equally to the seat belt pretensioners. Do not tamper with the inertia reel pretensioner unit in any way, and do not attempt to test the unit.

2 De-activate the airbag system (which will also de-activate the pyrotechnic pretensioner mechanism) as described in Chapter 12, Section 20, before attempting to remove the seatbelt.

3 To make access easier, remove the relevant front seat as described in Section 22.

4 Remove the centre pillar trim panels as described in Section 24.

5 If working on the driver's side, unclip and remove the trim over the pretensioner on the seat belt lower anchorage. Lift up the locking catch and disconnect the pretensioner wiring connector, then undo the pretensioner mounting lower anchorage bolt.

6 If working on the passenger's side, undo the seat belt lower anchorage bolt.

7 Undo the inertia reel upper and lower mounting bolts and withdraw the reel from the centre pillar **(see illustration)**.

8 Release the locking clip and disconnect the wiring connector from the inertia reel, then remove the reel and seat belt from the car.

9 Refitting is a reversal of removal, ensuring that all mounting bolts are tightened to the specified torque.

Front seat belt stalk

10 Remove the relevant front seat as described in Section 22.

11 Trace the wiring back from the seat belt stalk and under the seat cushion, then unclip it from the wiring securing clips.

12 Unscrew the bolt and withdraw the stalk assembly from the side of the front seat **(see illustration)**.

13 Refitting is a reversal of removal, but tighten the stalk anchor bolt to the specified torque.

Rear side seat belt

14 Remove the rear seat cushion and the relevant rear seat back as described in Section 22.

15 Working as described in Section 24, remove the luggage compartment lower and upper trim panels for access to the inertia reel.

16 Unscrew the lower anchor bolt from the rear floor panel **(see illustration)**.

17 Unscrew the seat belt upper anchor bolt and the inertia reel mounting bolt, then remove the seat belt assembly from the vehicle **(see illustrations)**. Note the fitted position of the inertial reel on the mounting bracket before removal.

18 Refitting is a reversal of removal, ensuring that all mounting bolts are tightened to the specified torque.

Rear centre seat belt

19 The inertia reel for the rear centre seat belt is located internally within the rear seat back. To gain access, the seat back must be removed and completely dismantled. This is a complex operation and considerable expertise is needed to remove and refit the seat upholstery and internal components without damage. Therefore, any problems with the centre seat belt and reel should be referred to a Nissan dealer.

Rear seat belt buckle

20 Remove the rear seat cushion, as described in Section 22.

21 Unscrew the bolt and withdraw the relevant buckle assembly from the floor panel **(see illustration)**.

22 Refitting is a reversal of removal, but tighten the buckle anchor bolts to the specified torque.

24 Interior trim panels – removal and refitting

General

1 The interior trim panels are secured by a combination of metal and plastic clips and screws. When releasing certain types of securing clips, a suitable forked tool will prove invaluable to avoid damage to the panel and clips. A degree of force will be necessary to pull some of the panels from their locations, especially where numerous internal retaining clips are used. Be prepared for some of the plastic clips to break when their relevant panel is being removed.

Door inner trim panel

2 Refer to Section 12.

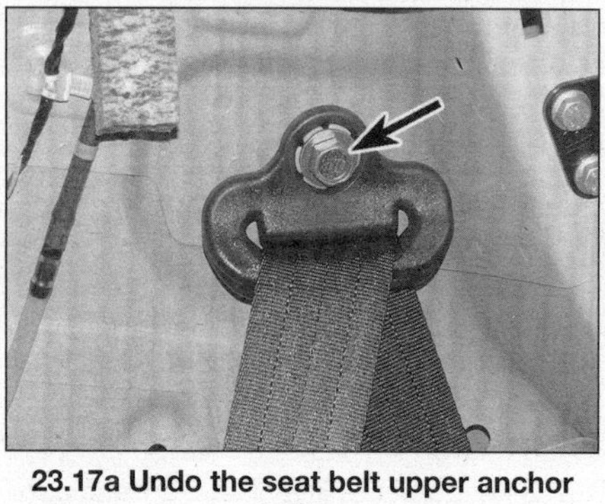
23.17a Undo the seat belt upper anchor bolt...

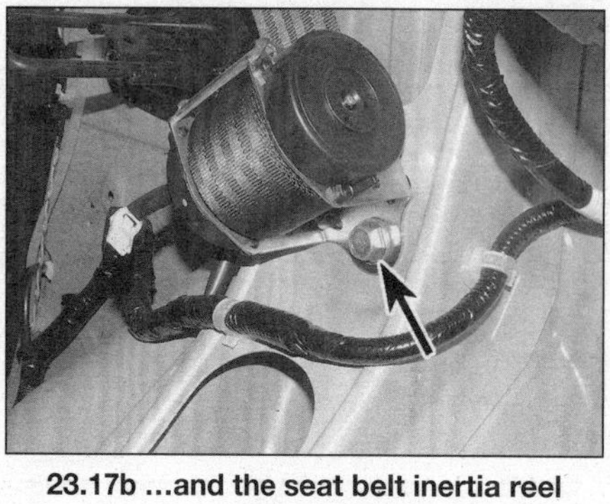
23.17b ...and the seat belt inertia reel mounting bolt

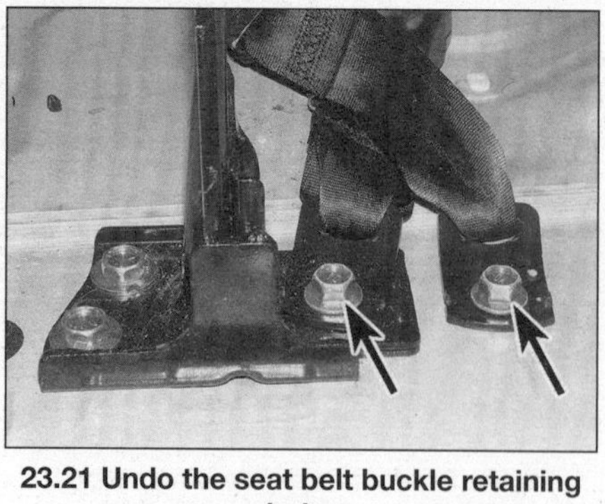
23.21 Undo the seat belt buckle retaining bolts

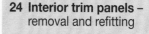

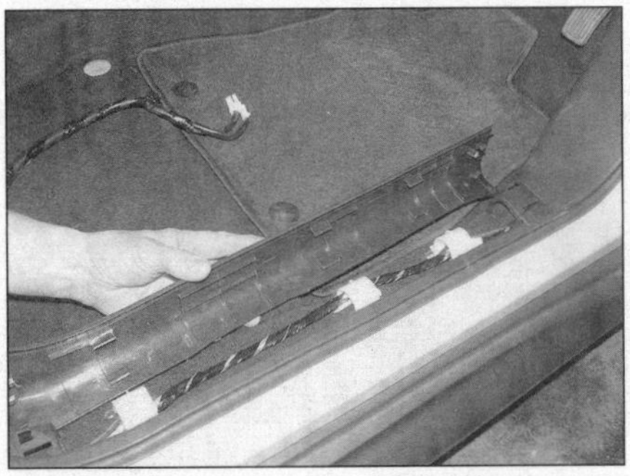

24.3 Unclip the front sill trim

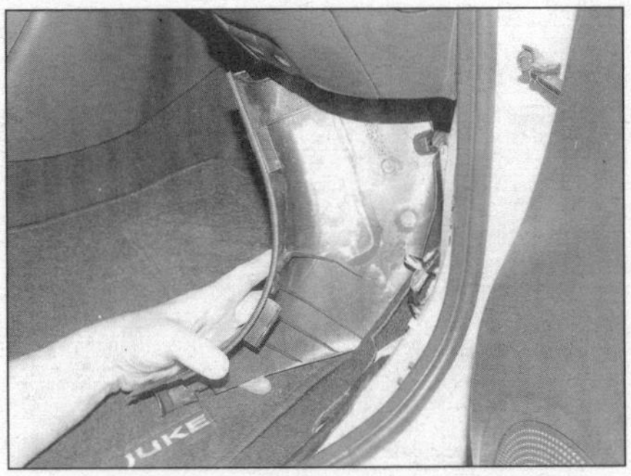

24.4 Unclip the front footwell side trim

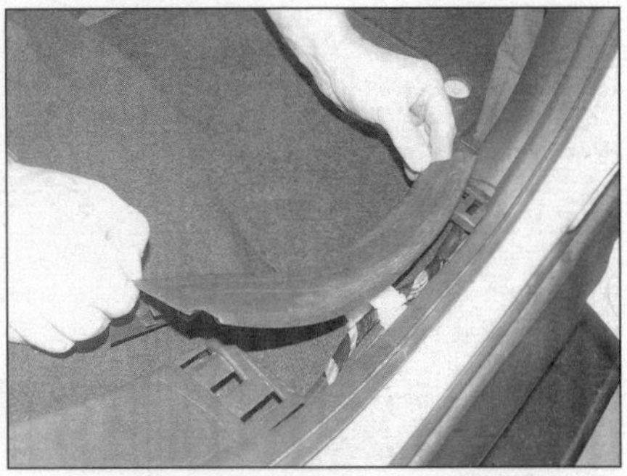

24.6 Unclip the rear sill trim panel

Footwell sill trim panels

3 Unclip the front sill trim panel from the bottom of the B-pillar trim, and then from the front footwell side trim panel **(see illustration)**.

4 Unclip the front footwell side trim panel from the bottom of the A-pillar **(see illustration)**.

5 Remove the rear seat cushion as described in Section 22.

6 Unclip the rear sill trim panel from the bottom of the B-pillar trim, and the luggage compartment lower trim panel **(see illustration)**.

7 Refitting is a reversal of removal.

Front A-pillar trim panels

Note: *Because the retaining clips are likely to become distorted during removal, Nissan stipulate that a new trim panel must be used when refitting.*

8 Carefully prise the front door weatherstrip from along the edge of the panel.

9 Pull the upper part of the panel from the pillar, then release the two retaining clips from the pillar using a suitable forked tool **(see illustrations)**. Lift the panel up to disengage the lower lugs from the facia and remove the trim panel.

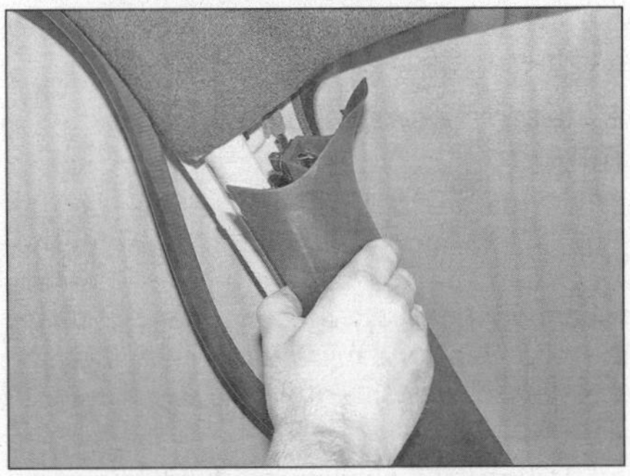

24.9a Pull away the upper part of the A-pillar trim panel...

10 Refitting is a reversal of removal, ensuring the weatherstrip is correctly seated.

Centre B-pillar trim panels

11 To make access easier, slide the front seat as far forward as possible.

12 Remove the sill trim panels from the front and rear door apertures, as described in paragraphs 3 to 5 in this Section.

13 Carefully prise the front and rear door weatherstrip from the edges of the centre B-pillar trim panels.

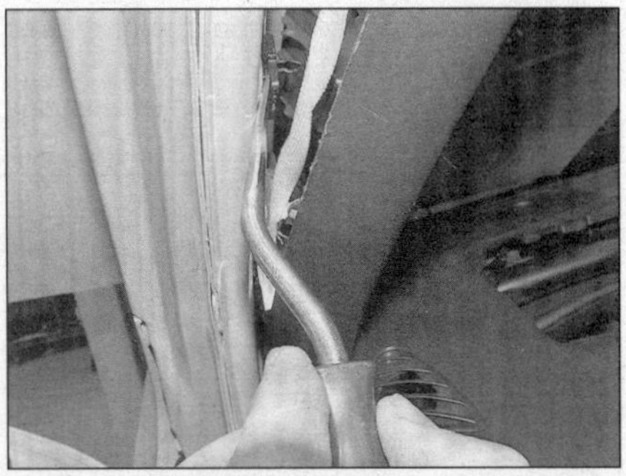

24.9b ...then use a forked tool to release the retaining clips from the A-pillar

14 Unclip the lower trim panel from the B-pillar, and then disengage the seat belt through the slot in the trim panel **(see illustration)**.

15 Carefully unclip the trim from around the seat belt height adjuster, then undo the seat belt upper anchorage bolt **(see illustration)**.

16 Unclip the lower part of the B-pillar upper trim panel.

17 Release the trim panel upper retaining clip by inserting a plastic spatula or similar tool behind the panel on each side. Push the tools

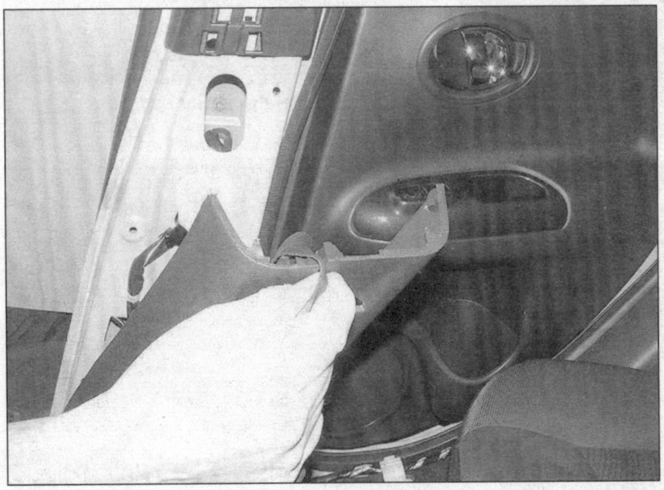

24.14 Unclip the B-pillar lower trim panel and pass the seat belt through the slot

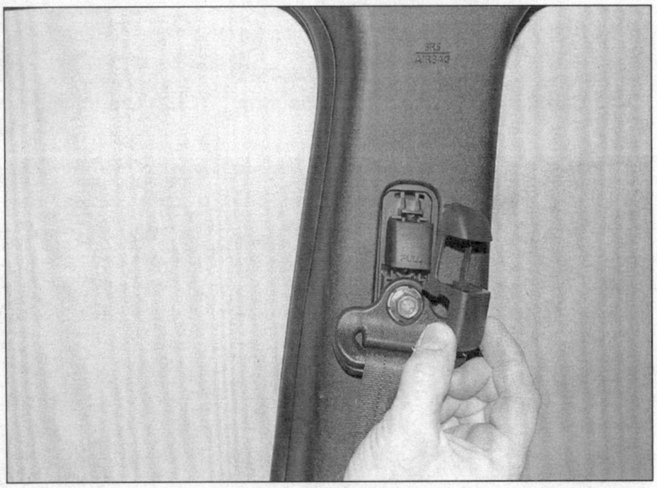

24.15 Unclip the trim from around the seat belt height adjuster

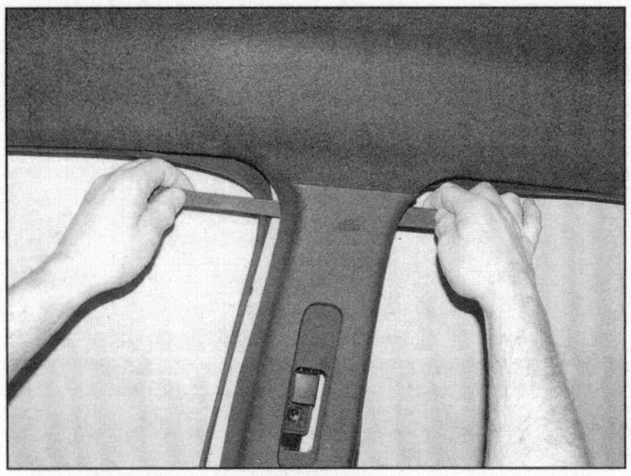

24.17a Insert a plastic spatula or similar tool behind the trim panel on each side...

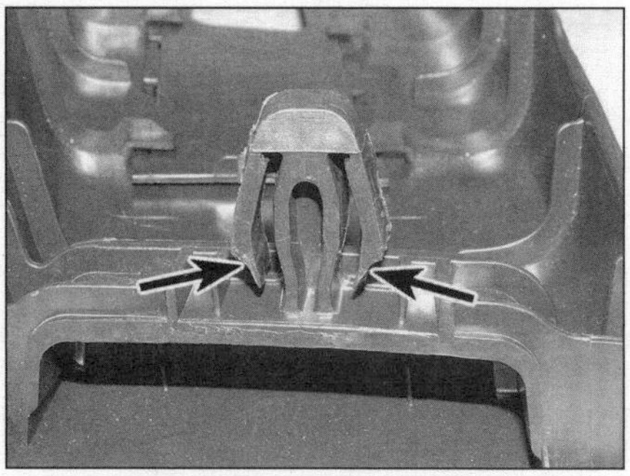

24.17b ...push the tools together to compress the legs of the clip...

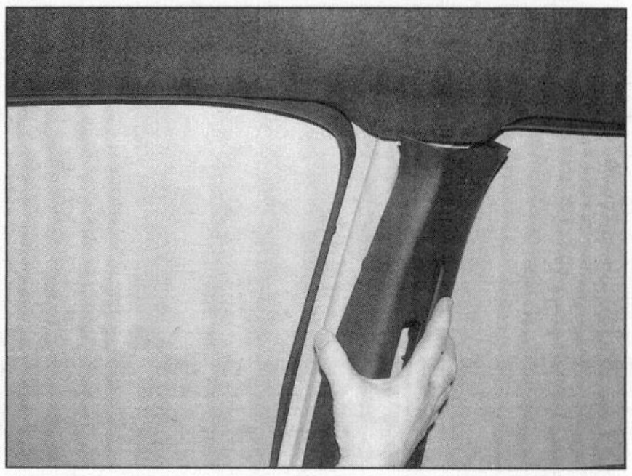

24.17c ...then pull the panel away from the pillar

together to compress the legs of the clip, then pull the panel away from the pillar **(see illustrations)**.

18 Refitting is a reversal of removal, ensuring that all retaining clips are fully engaged. Refit the seat belt upper anchorage bolt and tighten it to the specified torque.

24.21 Prise free the tailgate aperture lower trim

Luggage compartment trim panels

19 If removing the trim panels on the right-hand side, disconnect the battery negative terminal (refer to battery disconnection and reconnection in Chapter 5A, Section 3). Remove the luggage compartment light unit as described in Chapter 12, Section 6.

20 Remove the luggage compartment carpet and floor panel.

21 Using a plastic spatula or similar, carefully prise free the tailgate aperture lower trim panel **(see illustration)**.

22 Carefully prise the rear door weatherstrip from the edges of the rear pillar **(see illustration)**.

23 Remove the rear seat cushion and the relevant rear seat back as described in Section 22.

24 Undo the retaining bolt and remove the rear seat side hinge **(see illustration)**.

25 Undo the trim panel retaining bolt **(see illustration)**.

26 Carefully prise the lower trim panel to release the securing clips, and then disengage it from the rear inner wheel arch **(see illustration)**.

27 Unscrew the seat belt lower anchor bolt from the rear floor.

28 Prise free the upper trim panel to release the securing clips **(see illustration)**.

29 Feed the seat belt through the opening in the panel and remove the upper trim panel **(see illustration)**.

30 Refitting is a reversal of removal, ensuring that all retaining clips are fully engaged.

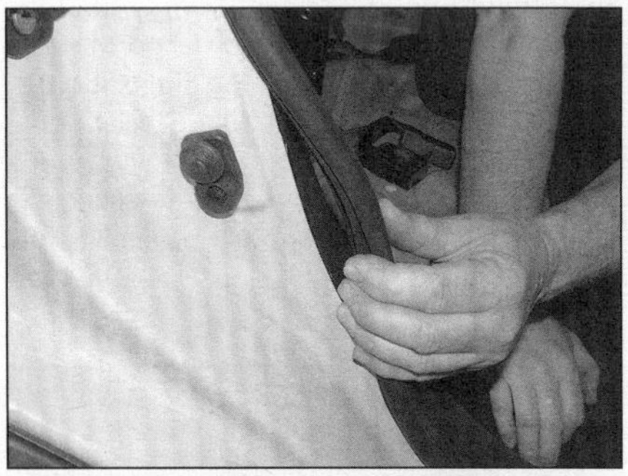

24.22 Carefully prise free the weatherstrip

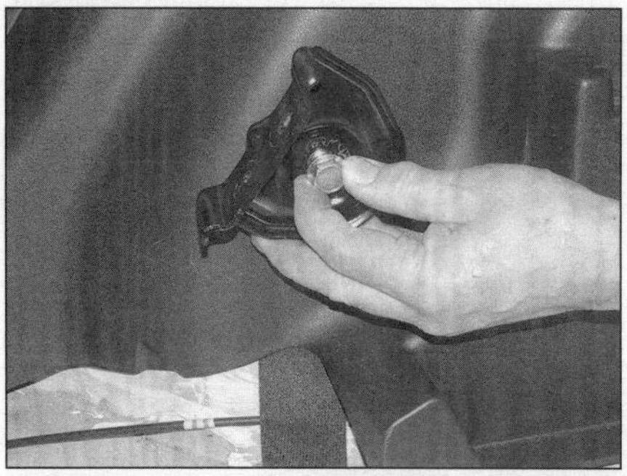

24.24 Unbolt and remove the rear seat side hinge

24.25 Undo the panel retaining bolt

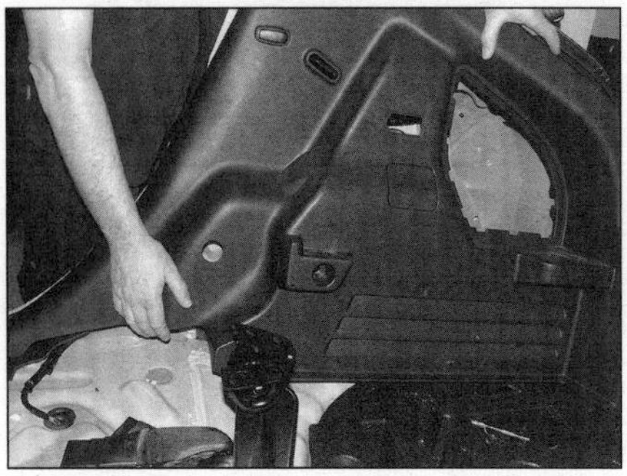

24.26 Prise free the lower trim panel

24.28 Prise free the upper trim panel

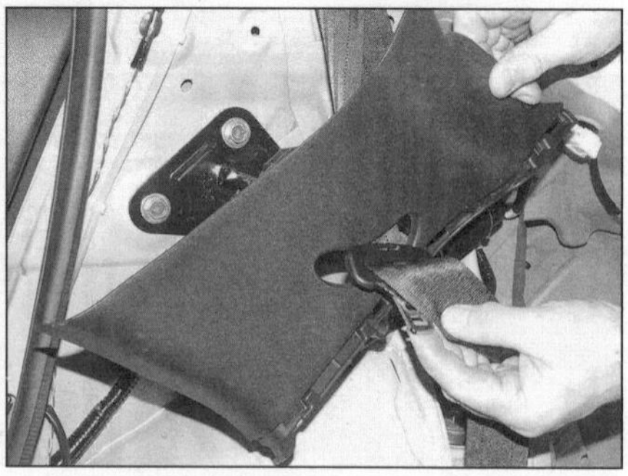

24.29 Feed the seat belt through the opening and remove the upper trim panel

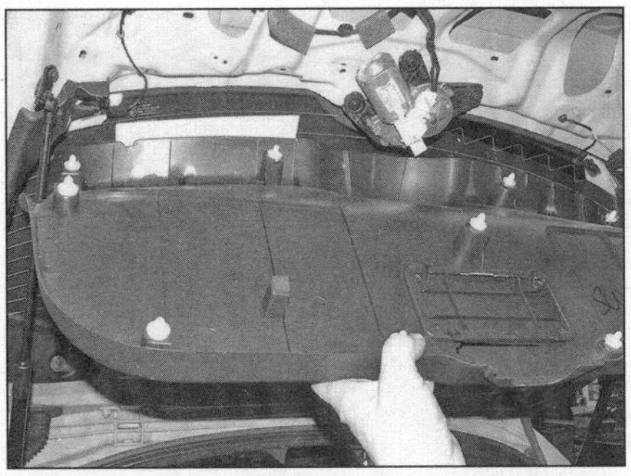

24.32 Unclip and remove the tailgate trim panel

Tailgate inner trim

31 Open the tailgate and remove the parcel shelf

32 Carefully working your way around the outer edge of the trim panel, release the retaining clips and remove the panel from the tailgate **(see illustration)**.

33 Pull out the centre pins, and release the two securing clips, from the tailgate side trim panels on each side. Withdraw the panels from the tailgate.

34 Refitting is a reversal of removal, but ensure that all clips are securely engaged.

25 Centre console – removal and refitting

Removal

1 Disconnect the battery negative terminal (refer to battery disconnection and reconnection in Chapter 5A, Section 3).

2 On models with a centre armrest, lift up the armrest, undo the retaining screw and lift off the trim panel. Undo the three bolts securing the armrest to the centre console and remove the armrest **(see illustrations)**.

3 Carefully prise free the gear lever gaiter surround and fold the gaiter up and over the gear lever knob **(see illustrations)**.

4 Starting at the rear, lift up the centre console upper finisher to release the retaining clips, then move it to the rear and remove it from the console **(see illustration)**.

5 Measure and record the length of exposed thread on the end of the handbrake cable, then slacken the adjustment nut until it nearly reaches the end of the thread. This will allow the handbrake lever to be pulled up further and allow easier removal of the centre console **(see illustration)**.

6 Move the front seats fully forward.

7 Pull the console rear finisher towards the rear to release the retaining pawls and retaining clips **(see illustration)**.

25.2a Undo the retaining screw...

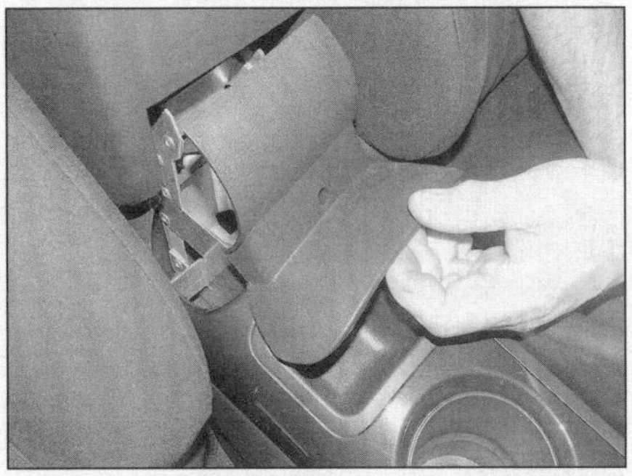

25.2b ...and lift off the trim panel

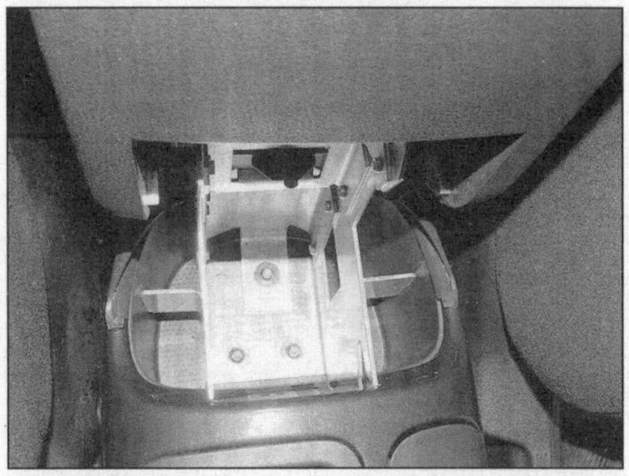

25.2c Undo the three bolts securing the armrest to the console...

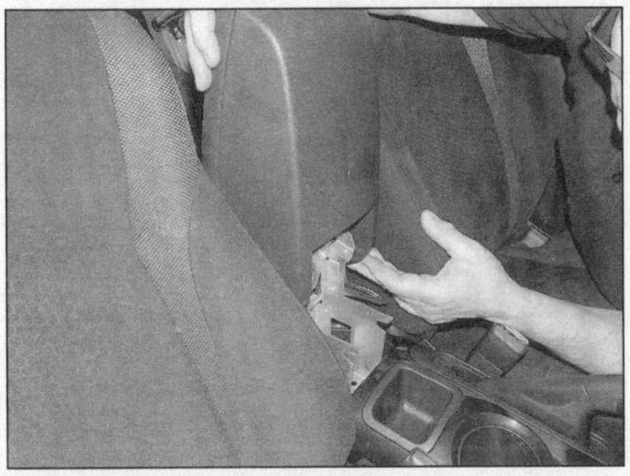

25.2d ...and remove the armrest

25.3a Prise free the gear lever gaiter surround...

25.3b ...and fold it up over the gear lever knob

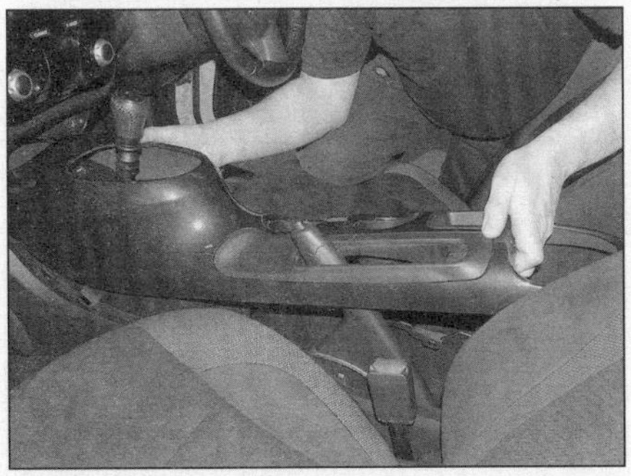

25.4 Lift up and remove the console upper finisher

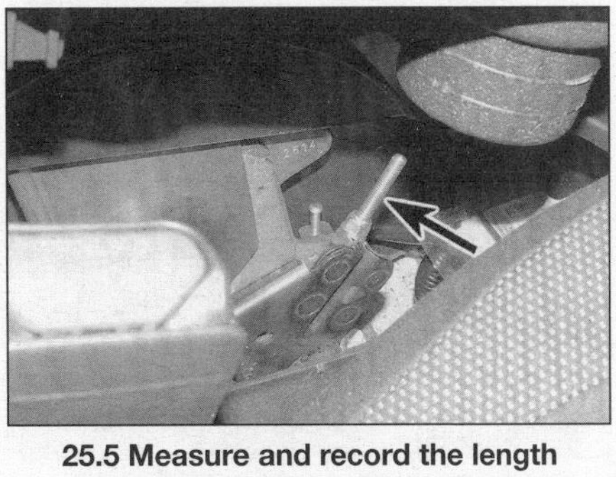

25.5 Measure and record the length of exposed thread on the end of the handbrake cable

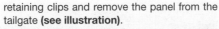

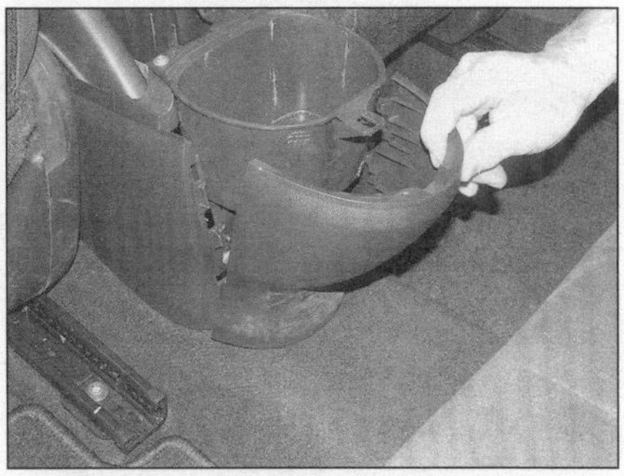

25.7 Remove the centre console rear finisher

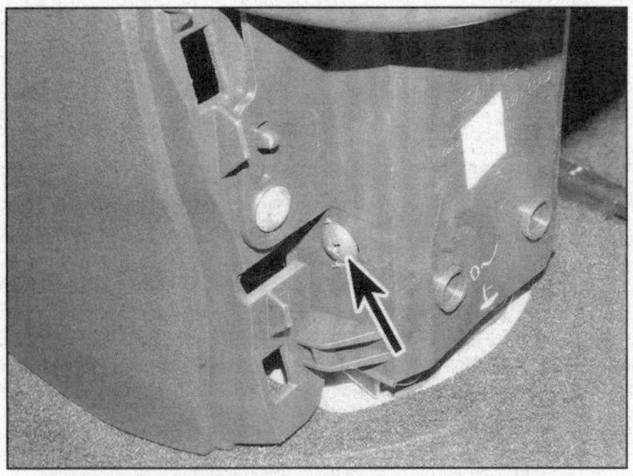
25.8 Undo the console rear retaining screws each side

25.10a Pull out the centre pin and remove the plastic rivet...

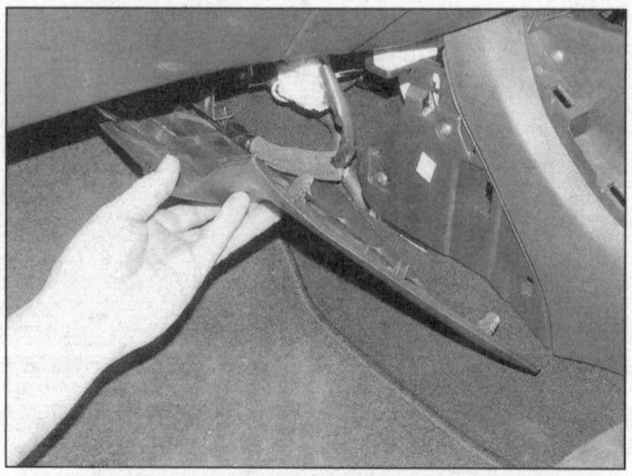
25.10b ...then pull away the rear of the panel to release the clips

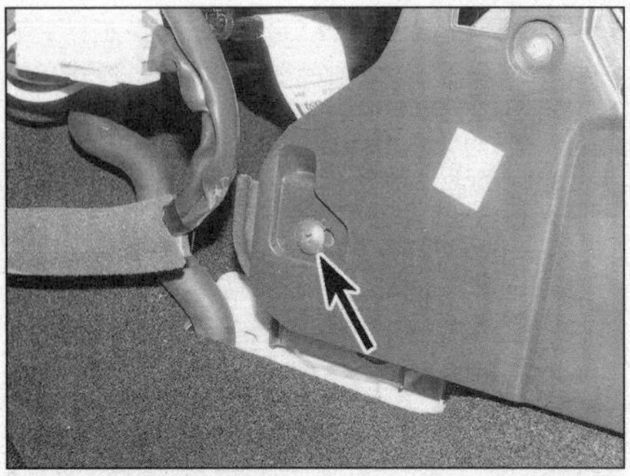
25.11 Undo the console front retaining screws

25.12 Undo the screws securing the console to the gear lever housing

25.13 Lift the console at the rear, slide it back and remove it from the car

8 Undo the centre console rear retaining screws on each side **(see illustration)**.

9 Move the front seats fully to the rear.

10 Working on one side at a time, remove the footwell trim panels on each side of the centre console. To do this, pull out the centre pin and remove the expanding plastic rivet, then pull away the rear of the panel to release the retaining clips, and remove the panel **(see illustrations)**.

11 Undo the centre console front retaining screws on each side **(see illustration)**.

12 Undo the two screws securing the centre console to the gear lever housing **(see illustration)**.

13 With the handbrake lever pulled up fully,lift the centre console up at the rear, slide it back and remove it from the car **(see illustration)**.

Refitting

14 Refitting is a reversal of removal. Making sure that the handbrake adjustment nut is screwed back down the threads to the measurement noted before removal. If necessary, adjust the handbrake as described in Chapter 1A, Section 8 or Chapter 1B, Section 9.

26 Facia panels – removal and refitting

Warning: All models are equipped with an airbag system. The driver's airbag is mounted in the steering wheel centre pad and the passenger's airbag is mounted in the passenger's side of the facia. Make sure that the safety recommendations given in Chapter 12, Section 20 are followed, to prevent personal injury.

Glovebox

1 Remove the lower trim panel under the glovebox by pulling it down to release the pawl and the retaining clips **(see illustration)**.

2 Open the glovebox lid, depress the retaining tab and slide the damper strut off the peg on the lid **(see illustration)**.

3 Carefully pull the glovebox lid rearward to disengage the hinges from the facia. Disengage the lid arms from the facia and remove the lid **(see illustration)**.

4 Undo the retaining screws from the

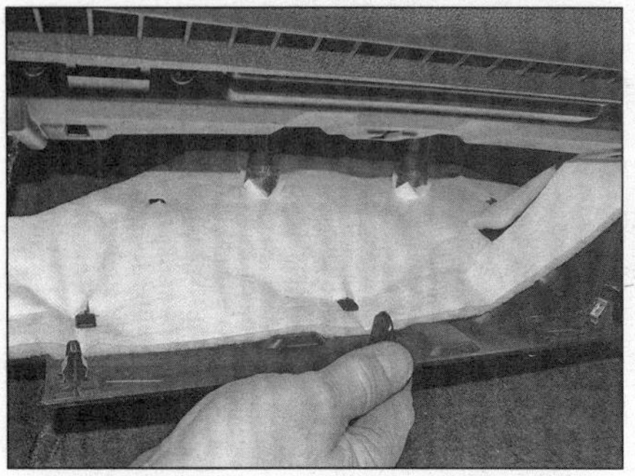
26.1 Release the pawl and clips and remove the lower trim panel

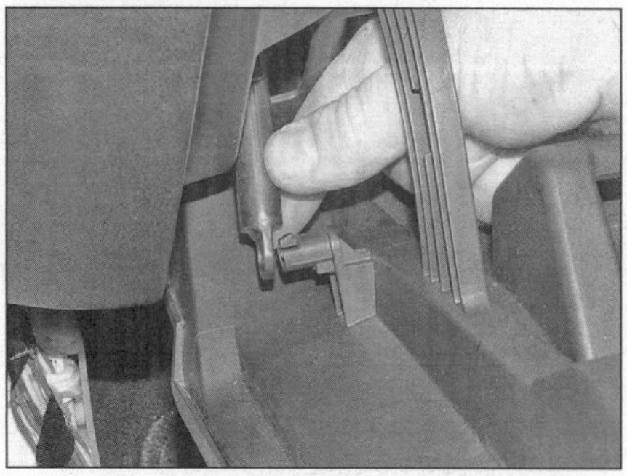
26.2 Remove the damper strut from the peg on the glovebox lid

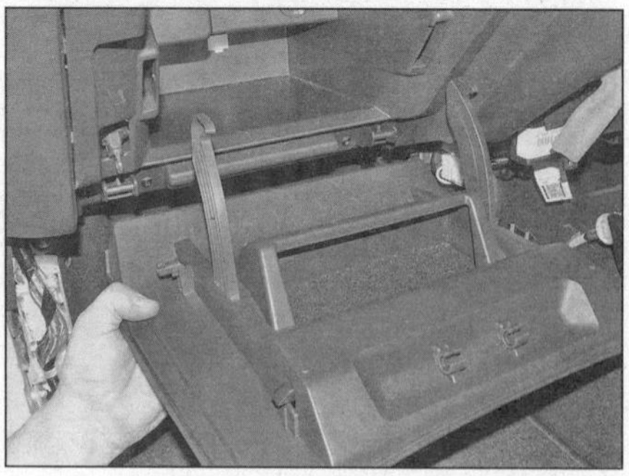
26.3 Disengage the hinges and arms and remove the glovebox lid

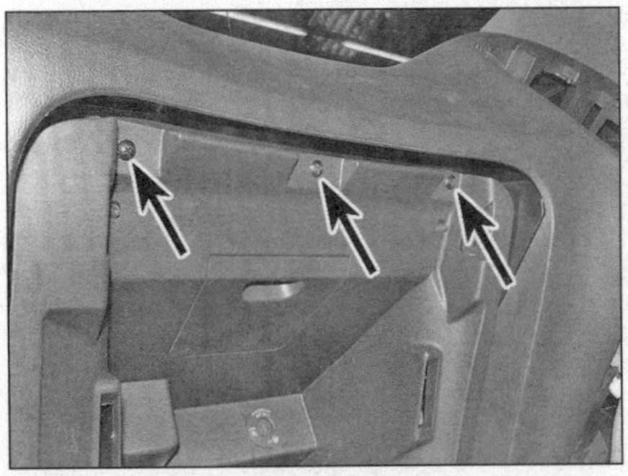
26.4a Undo the glovebox upper retaining screws...

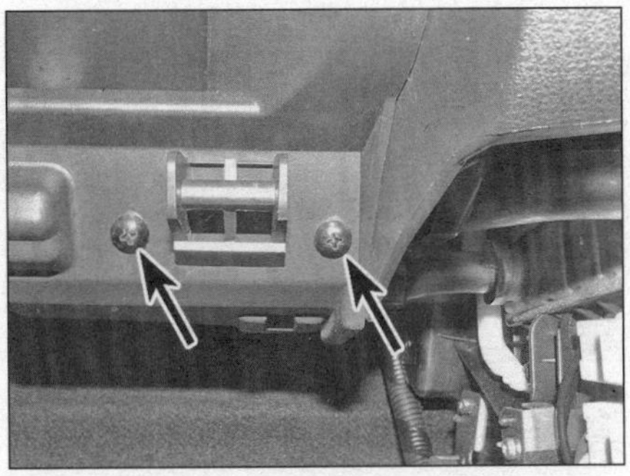
26.4b ...and the two lower retaining screws on each side

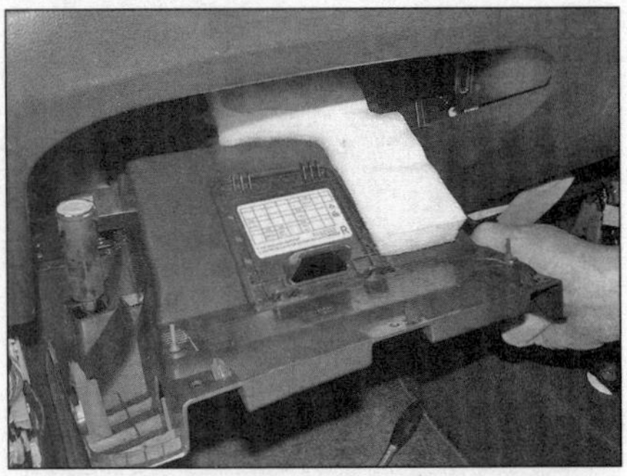
26.5a Withdraw the glovebox from the facia...

26.5b ...and disconnect the wiring connectors

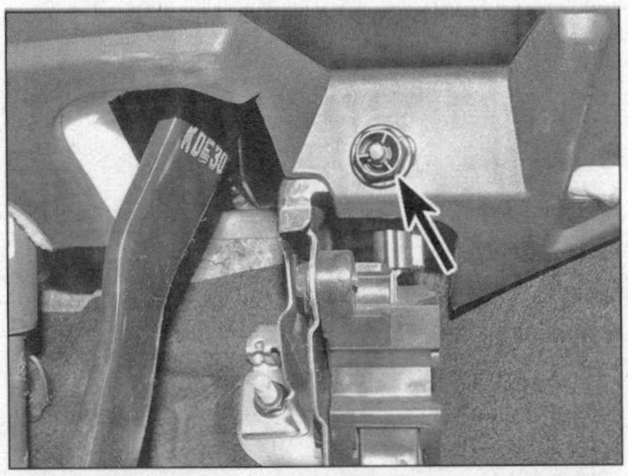
26.7a Undo the nut above the accelerator pedal...

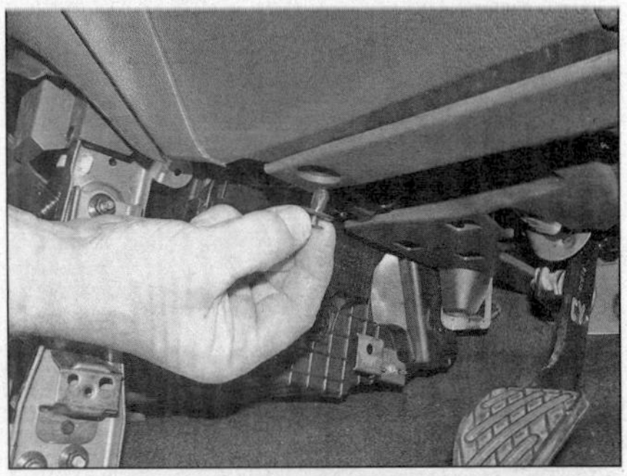
26.7b ...and the expanding rivet on the left-hand side...

26.7c ...and right-hand side

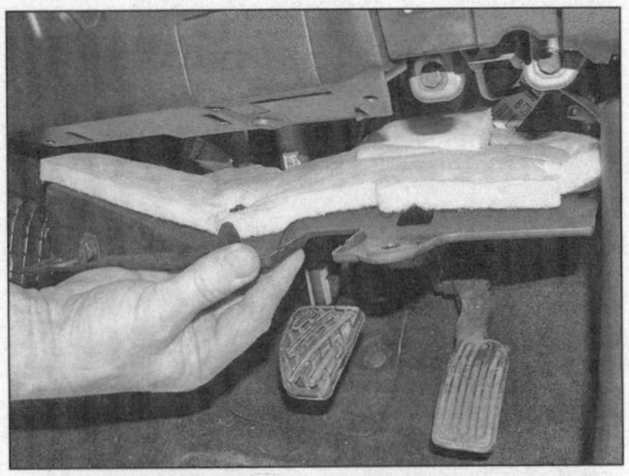
26.8 Pull the panel down and remove it from under the facia

upper and lower edge of the glovebox **(see illustrations)**.

5 Withdraw the glovebox from the facia and disconnect the wiring connectors **(see illustrations)**.

6 Refitting is a reversal of removal.

Driver's side lower trim panel

7 Unscrew the retaining nut above the accelerator pedal, then unscrew the centre pins and remove the two plastic expanding rivets along the top edge **(see illustrations)**.

8 Pull the panel down to release the retaining clips and remove it from under the facia **(see illustration)**.

9 Refitting is a reversal of removal.

Driver's side switch panel

10 Remove the driver's side lower trim panel as described previously.

11 Undo the two retaining bolts and unclip the bonnet and fuel flap release levers from the lower edge of the switch panel **(see illustrations)**.

12 Undo the switch panel lower retaining screw now exposed **(see illustration)**.

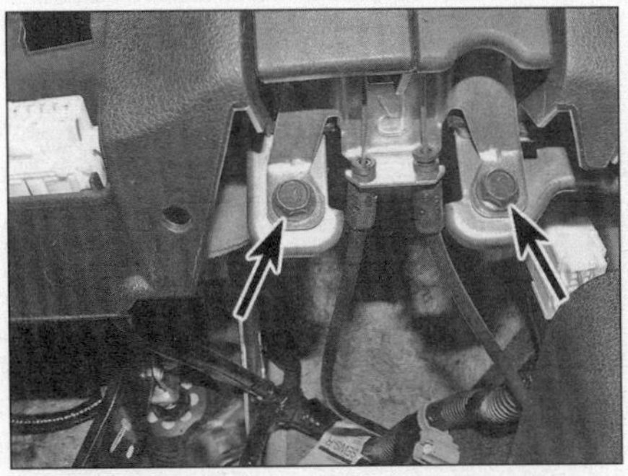
26.11a Undo the two retaining bolts...

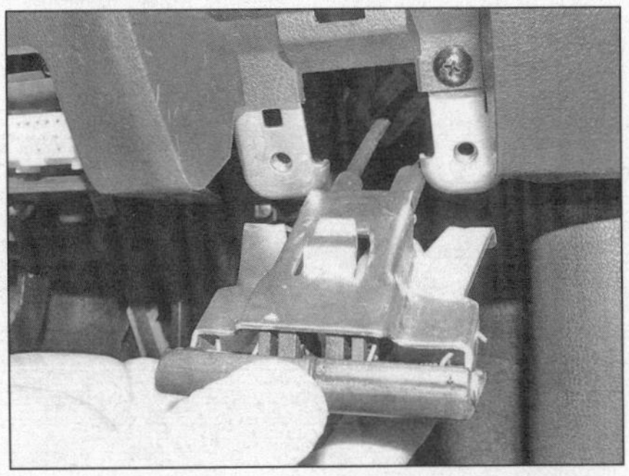
26.11b ...and unclip the release levers

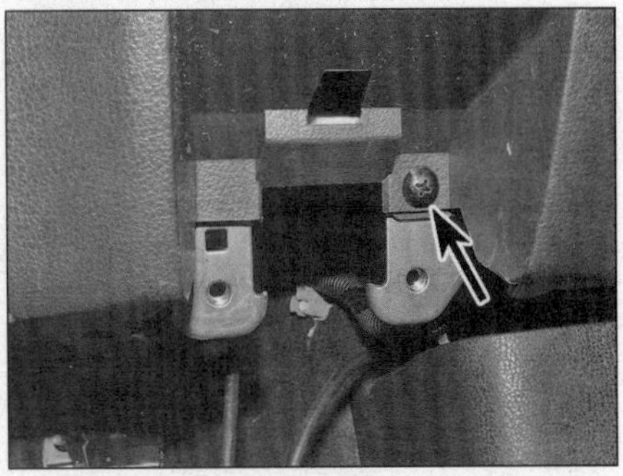
26.12 Undo the switch panel retaining screw

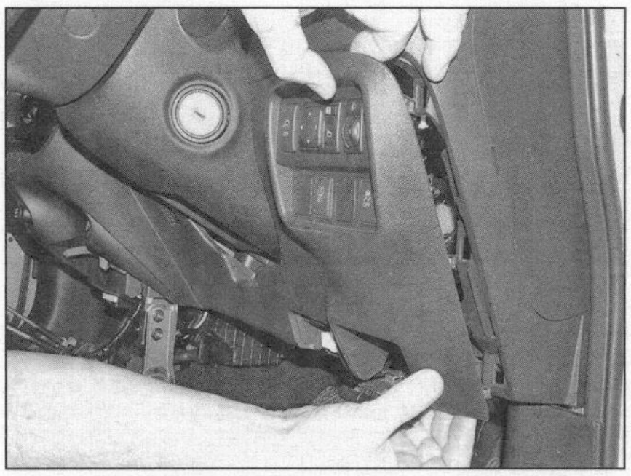

26.13 Carefully pull the panel from the facia

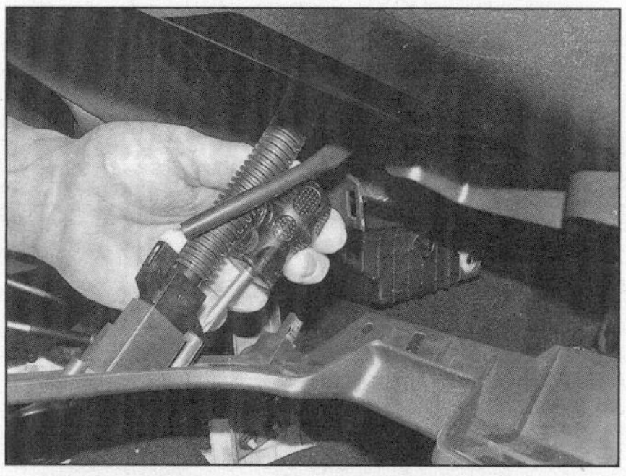

26.14a Undo the retaining screw...

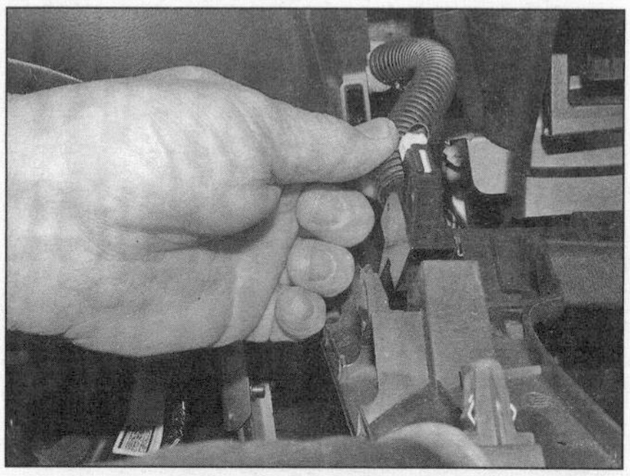

26.14b ...and release the air tubing

13 Carefully pull the panel from the facia to release the retaining clips **(see illustration)**.

14 As the panel is withdrawn, disconnect the wiring connectors, then undo the retaining screw and release the air tubing from the rear of the panel **(see illustrations)**.

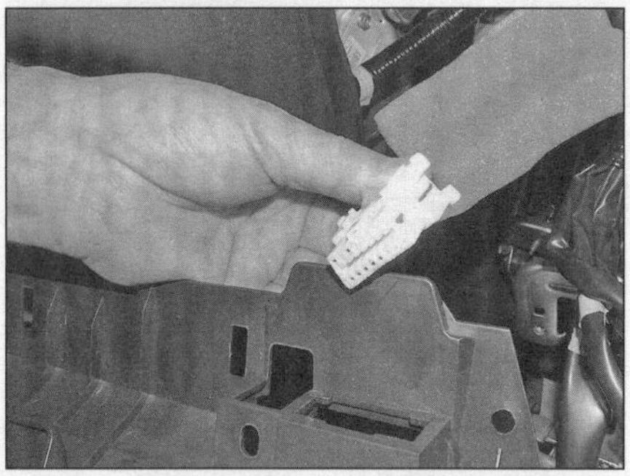

26.15 Unclip the diagnostic socket from the switch panel

15 Unclip the diagnostic socket from the switch panel and remove the panel **(see illustration)**.

16 Refitting is a reversal of removal.

Lower centre trim panel

17 Remove the centre console as described in Section 25.

18 Using a plastic spatula or similar tool, carefully prise the panel away from the facia **(see illustration)**.

19 Disconnect the wiring connectors at the rear of the panel and remove the panel **(see illustration)**.

20 Refitting is a reversal of removal.

Centre ventilation trim panel

21 Remove the heater control panel as described in Chapter 3, Section 9.

22 Undo the two screws securing the lower corners of the panel to the facia **(see illustration)**.

23 Starting at the lower corners, then the upper centre, release the panel retaining clips using a plastic spatula or similar tool **(see illustration)**.

24 As the trim panel is withdrawn disconnect the wiring connector from the rear of the panel **(see illustration)**.

25 Refitting is a reversal of removal.

Steering column shrouds

26 Remove the steering wheel as described in Chapter 10, Section 12.

27 Where applicable, unclip the plastic trim from around the ignition switch.

28 Release the height adjustment lever and move the steering column downwards to its fully lowered position.

29 Undo the two screws securing the shrouds to the steering column combination switch **(see illustration)**.

26.18 Prise the lower centre trim panel away from the facia

26.19 Disconnect the wiring connectors and remove the lower centre trim panel

26.22 Undo the centre ventilation trim panel retaining screws

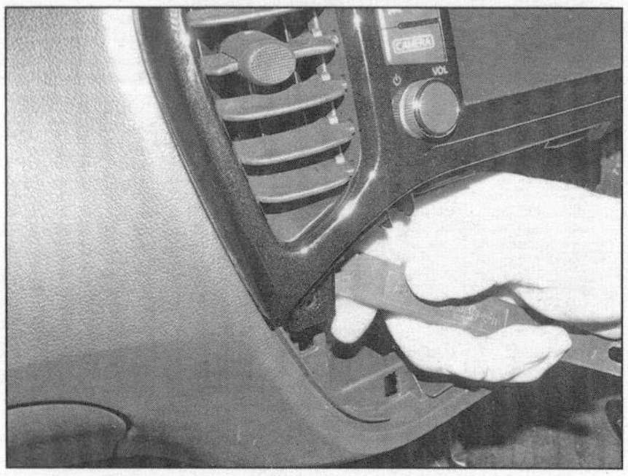

26.23 Release the panel retaining clips starting at the lower corners

26.24 Disconnect the wiring connector

26.29 Undo the steering column shroud retaining screws

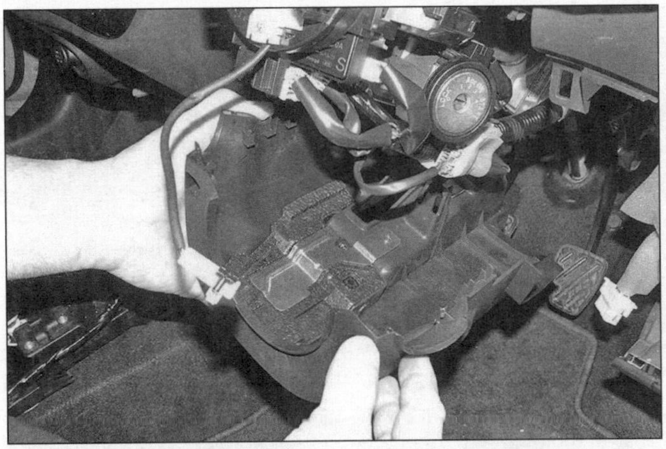

26.30 Disengage and remove the lower cover...

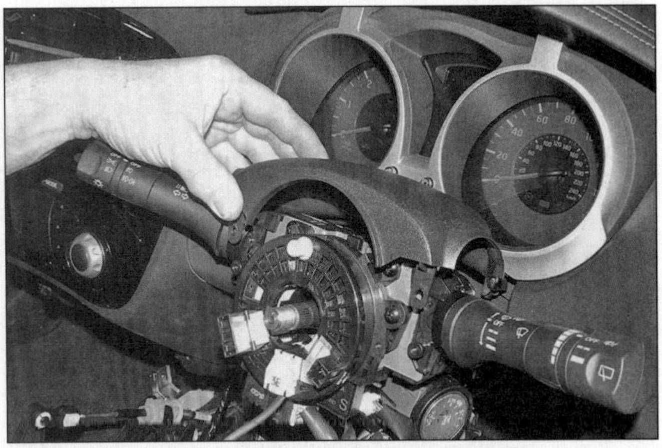

26.31 ...followed by the upper cover

30 Disengage the lower cover from the upper, pull the lower cover down to release the centre retaining pawl and remove the lower cover **(see illustration)**.

31 Release the retaining pawls at the front and lift off the upper cover **(see illustration)**.

32 Refitting is a reversal of removal, but ensure that the shroud halves engage correctly with each other.

Instrument panel surround

33 Remove the steering column shrouds as described previously.

34 Starting at the bottom, pull the surround away from the instrument panel and facia to release the retaining clips, then lift away the surround **(see illustrations)**.

35 Refitting is a reversal of removal.

Facia end trim panels

36 Insert a small screwdriver into the slot on the panel and carefully release the trim panel from the end of the facia **(see illustrations)**.

37 Refitting is a reversal of removal.

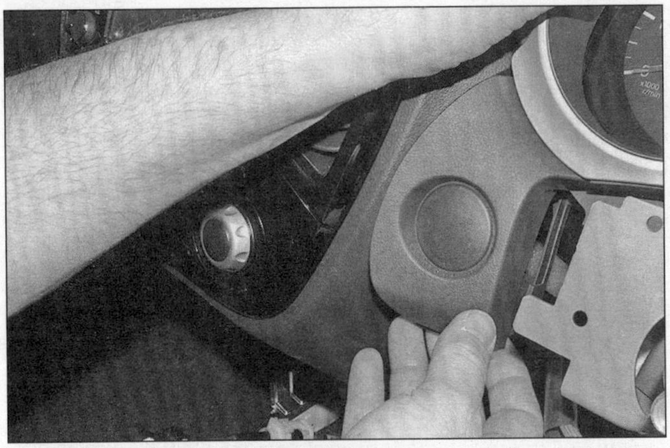

26.34a Starting at the bottom pull the surround away from the instrument panel...

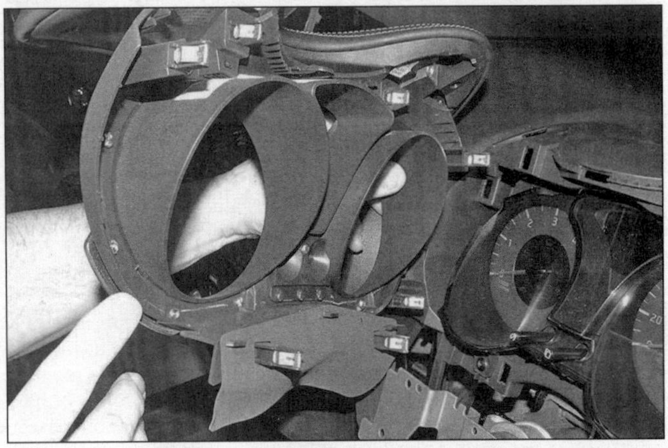

26.34b ...to release the retaining clips

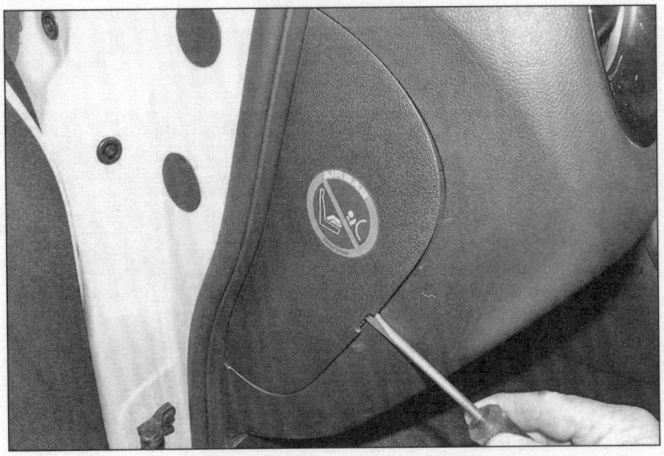

26.36a Insert a small screwdriver into the slot...

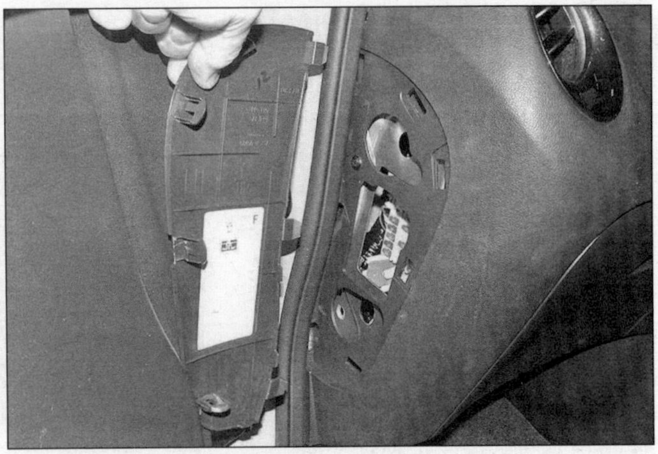

26.36b ...and carefully release the panel from the end of the facia

26.43 Unclip the sensor panel and disconnect the wiring connector

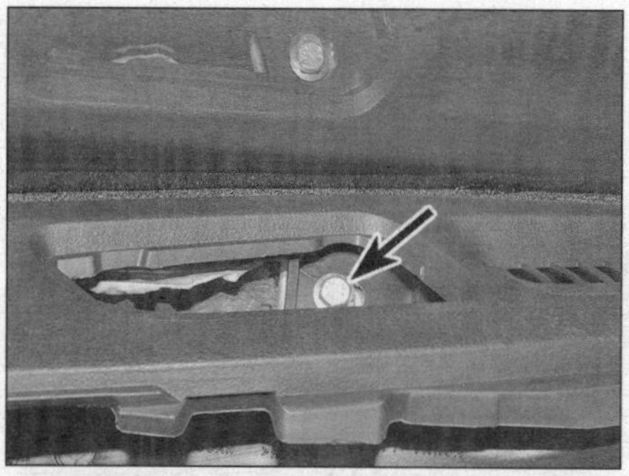

26.48a Undo the bolt in the sensor aperture...

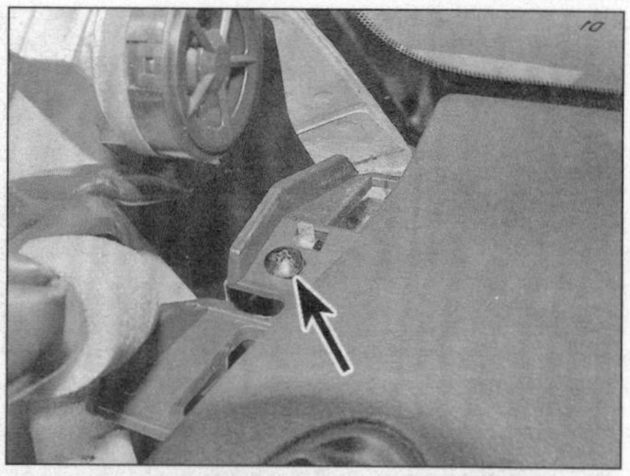

26.48b ...the screw at the top front of the facia on each side...

26.48c ...the screw behind the end panels on each side...

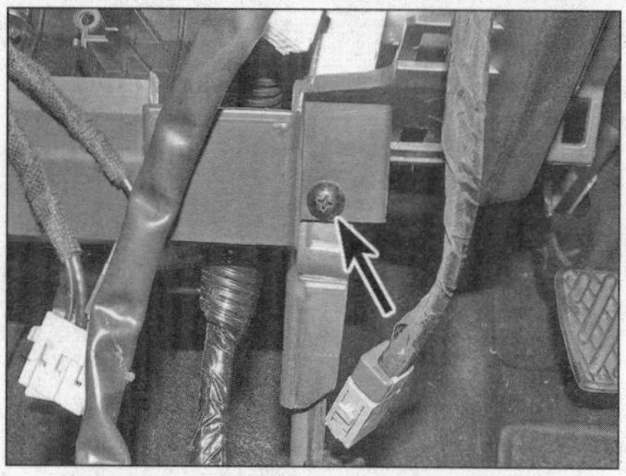

26.48d ...the lower centre screw...

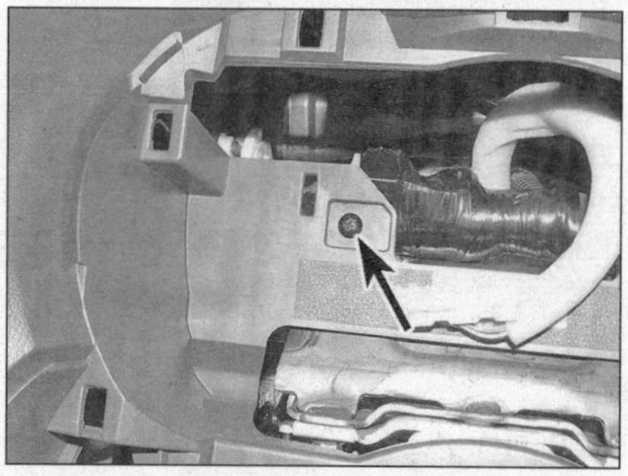

26.48e ...and the screw in the instrument panel aperture

Complete assembly

Note: *This is an involved procedure, and it is suggested that this complete Section is read through thoroughly before beginning the operation. It is advisable to make careful note of all wiring connections, and the routing of all wiring, to aid refitting.*

Removal

38 Disconnect the battery negative terminal (refer to battery disconnection and reconnection in Chapter 5A, Section 3).

39 Remove the front footwell trim panels as described in Section 24.

40 Remove the front A-pillar trim panels as described in Section 24.

41 Remove the centre console as described in Section 25.

42 Remove the following facia panels, as described previously in this Section. Note the routing of all wiring, and keep all securing screws and fixings with the relevant panels to avoid confusion on refitting.

a) Glovebox.
b) Driver's side lower trim panel
c) Driver's side switch panel
d) Lower centre trim panel
e) Centre ventilation trim panel
f) Steering column shrouds.
g) Instrument panel surround
h) Facia end trim panels

43 Carefully unclip the sensor panel from the top of the facia and disconnect the wiring connector **(see illustration)**.

44 Remove the radio/CD player, as described in Chapter 12, Section 15.

45 Remove the instrument panel, as described in Chapter 12, Section 9.

46 Remove the passenger's airbag as described in Chapter 12, Section 21.

47 Remove the steering column/motor as described in Chapter 10, Section 14.

48 Undo the facia mounting bolt/screws from the following locations:

a) One bolt in the sensor aperture at the top of the facia **(see illustration)**.
b) One screw at the top front of the facia on each side **(see illustration)**.
c) One screw behind the end panels on each side **(see illustration)**.
d) One lower centre screw **(see illustration)**.
e) One screw in the instrument panel aperture **(see illustration)**.

49 Disconnect the hazard warning light switch wiring connector, then make a final check to ensure that all relevant wiring has been disconnected, and any wiring loom retaining clips disconnected.

50 With the aid of an assistant, pull the upper part of the facia panel towards the rear of the car to disengage it from the bulkhead – some manipulation may be required. Once the facia panel has been released, withdraw it through the door aperture **(see illustration)**.

51 If required, the metal support crossmember can be removed from across the front of the vehicle. This will need to be removed to access the heating/ventilation housing.

52 Undo the retaining nuts and remove the metal bracket from the right-hand side of the heater housing **(see illustration)**.

53 Undo the bolts securing the heater/air conditioning housing to the crossmember.

54 Working along the length of the metal crossmember, trace the wiring loom and

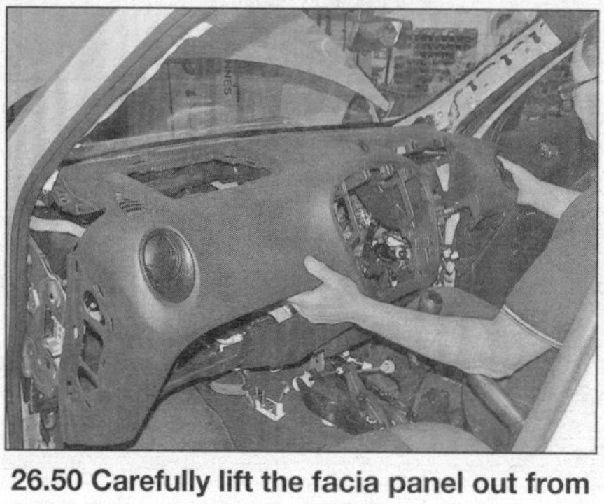

26.50 Carefully lift the facia panel out from the vehicle

26.52 Undo the nuts and remove the support bracket

26.56 Remove the plastic covers and undo the crossmember securing bolts

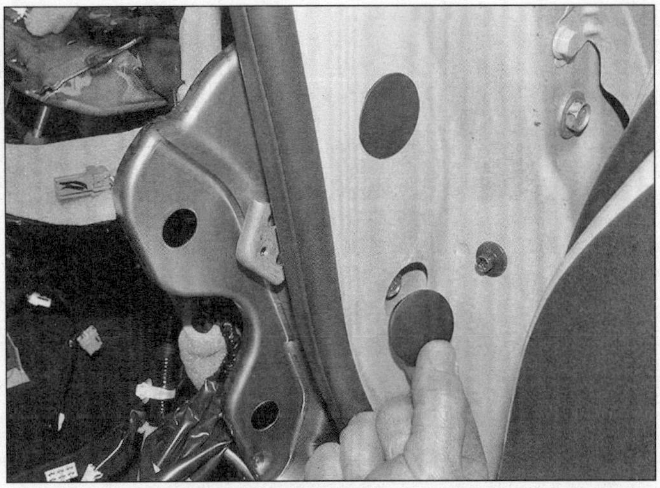

26.57a Remove the plastic covers...

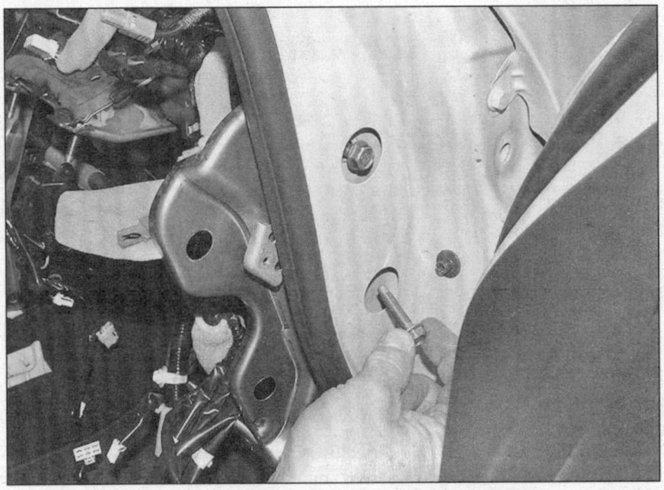

26.57b ...and remove the securing bolts

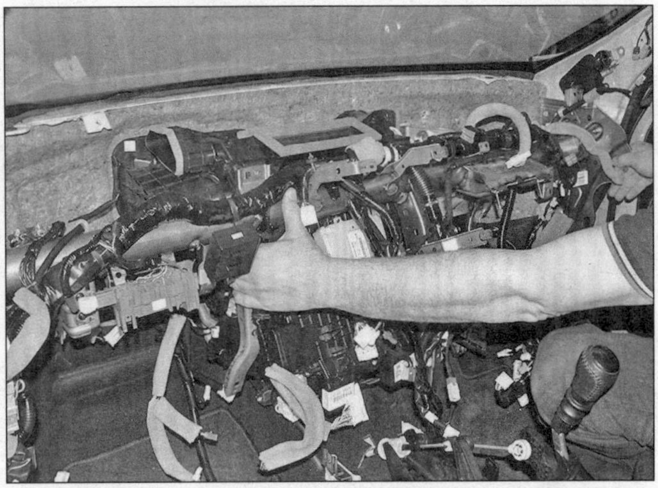

26.59 Carefully lift the crossmember complete with wiring loom out from the vehicle

disconnect/detach the wiring connectors and components as necessary to enable the wiring loom to be removed with the crossmember. Make a note, or take pictures of the connections to refer to on refitting.

55 Remove the air vents and ducting as necessary to enable removal of the crossmember.

56 Working at the left-hand side of the vehicle, remove the plastic covers and undo the crossmember securing bolts **(see illustration)**.

57 Working at the right-hand side of the vehicle, remove the plastic covers and undo the crossmember securing bolts **(see illustrations)**.

58 Remove the windscreen cowl panel as described in, Section 21. Undo the retaining bolt under the wiper linkage on the right-hand side of the bulkhead.

59 Make a final check along the length of the metal crossmember, to check that there is nothing still connected and lift the crossmember complete with wiring loom, out through the door aperture **(see illustration)**.

Refitting

60 Refitting is essentially a reversal of the removal procedure, bearing in mind the following points:

a) *Ensure that all wiring is correctly reconnected, and routed.*
b) *Refit all surrounding facia panels with reference to the relevant paragraphs of this Section.*

Notes

Chapter 12
Body electrical systems

Contents

Degrees of difficulty

Easy, suitable for novice with little experience	**Fairly easy,** suitable for beginner with some experience	**Fairly difficult,** suitable for competent DIY mechanic	**Difficult,** suitable for experienced DIY mechanic	**Very difficult,** suitable for expert DIY or professional

Specifications

Bulb ratings	**Watts**
Front direction indicator light	21
Front direction indicator repeater light (in front wing)	5
Front direction indicator repeater light (in door mirror)	LED
Front foglight (H8)	35
Front foglight (H11)	55
Front sidelight (early models)	5
Front sidelight/daytime running light (later models)	LED
Headlights (early models):	
Main/dipped beam (H4)	60/55
Headlights (later models):	
Main beam (HB3)	60
Dipped beam – Halogen (H11)	55
Dipped beam – Xenon (D2S)	35
High-level stop-light	LED
Luggage compartment light	5
Map reading lights	5
Interior reading lights	5
Glovebox light	1.4
Rear direction indicator light	21
Rear foglight	21
Rear number plate light	5
Reversing light	16
Stop/tail light	21/5

Torque wrench settings	**Nm**	**lbf ft**
Driver's airbag retaining bolts	10	7
Passenger's airbag retaining bolts	22	16

1 General information and precautions

General information

1 The electrical system is of 12-volt negative earth type. Power for the lights and all electrical accessories is supplied by a lead-acid type battery, which is charged by the alternator.

2 This Chapter covers repair and service procedures for the various electrical components not associated with the engine. Information on the battery, alternator and starter motor can be found in Chapter 5A.

3 It should be noted that, prior to working on any component in the electrical system, the battery negative terminal should first be disconnected, to prevent the possibility of electrical short-circuits and/or fires (refer to battery disconnection and reconnection in Chapter 5A, Section 3).

Precautions

Warning: Before carrying out any work on the electrical system, read through the precautions given in Safety first! and in Chapter 5A, Section 1.

Warning: All models are equipped with an airbag system and pyrotechnic seat belt pretensioners. When working on the electrical system, refer to the precautions given in Section 20 to avoid the possibility of personal injury.

2 Electrical fault finding – general information

1 Refer to the precautions given in *Safety first!* and in Chapter 5A, Section 1 before starting work. The following tests relate to testing of the main electrical circuits, and should not be used to test delicate electronic circuits (such as anti-lock braking systems), particularly where an electronic control unit is used.

General

2 A typical electrical circuit consists of an electrical component; any switches, relays, motors, fuses, fusible links or circuit breakers related to that component, and the wiring and connectors which link the component to both the battery and the chassis. To help to pinpoint a problem in an electrical circuit, wiring diagrams are included at the end of this chapter.

3 Before attempting to diagnose an electrical fault, first study the appropriate wiring diagram, to obtain a more complete understanding of the components included in the particular circuit concerned. The possible sources of a fault can be narrowed down by noting whether other components related to the circuit are operating properly. If several components or circuits fail at one time, the problem is likely to be related to a shared fuse or earth connection.

4 Electrical problems usually stem from simple causes, such as loose or corroded connections, a faulty earth connection, a blown fuse, a melted fusible link, or a faulty relay (refer to Section 3 for details of testing relays). Visually inspect the condition of all fuses, wires and connections in a problem circuit before testing the components. Use the wiring diagrams to determine which terminal connections will need to be checked, in order to pinpoint the trouble spot.

5 The basic tools required for electrical fault finding include a circuit tester or voltmeter (a 12 volt bulb with a set of test leads can also be used for certain tests); a self-powered test light (sometimes known as a continuity tester); an ohmmeter (to measure resistance); a battery and set of test leads; and a jumper wire, preferably with a circuit breaker or fuse incorporated, which can be used to bypass suspect wires or electrical components. Before attempting to locate a problem with test instruments, use the wiring diagram to determine where to make the connections.

6 To find the source of an intermittent wiring fault (usually due to a poor or dirty connection, or damaged wiring insulation), a 'wiggle' test can be performed on the wiring. This involves wiggling the wiring by hand, to see if the fault occurs as the wiring is moved. It should be possible to narrow down the source of the fault to a particular section of wiring. This method of testing can be used in conjunction with any of the tests described in the following sub-Sections.

7 Apart from problems due to poor connections, two basic types of fault can occur in an electrical circuit – open-circuit, or short-circuit.

8 Open-circuit faults are caused by a break somewhere in the circuit, which prevents current from flowing. An open-circuit fault will prevent a component from working, but will not cause the relevant circuit fuse to blow.

9 Short-circuit faults are normally caused by a breakdown in wiring insulation, which allows a feed wire to touch either another wire, or an earthed component such as the bodyshell. This allows the current flowing in the circuit to 'escape' along an alternative route, usually to earth. As the circuit does not now follow its original complete path, it is known as a 'short' circuit. A short-circuit fault will normally cause the relevant circuit fuse to blow.

Finding an open-circuit

10 To check for an open-circuit, connect one lead of a circuit tester or voltmeter to either the negative battery terminal or a known good earth.

11 Connect the other lead to a connector in the circuit being tested, preferably nearest to the battery or fuse.

12 Switch on the circuit, bearing in mind that some circuits are live only when the ignition switch is moved to a particular position.

13 If voltage is present (indicated either by the tester bulb lighting or a voltmeter reading, as applicable), this means that the section of the circuit between the relevant connector and the battery is problem-free.

14 Continue to check the remainder of the circuit in the same fashion.

15 When a point is reached at which no voltage is present, the problem must lie between that point and the previous test point with voltage. Most problems can be traced to a broken, corroded or loose connection.

Finding a short-circuit

16 To check for a short circuit; first disconnect the load(s) from the circuit (loads are the components which draw current from a circuit, such as bulbs, motors, heating elements, etc).

17 Remove the relevant fuse from the circuit, and connect a circuit tester or voltmeter to the fuse connections.

18 Switch on the circuit, bearing in mind that some circuits are live only when the ignition switch is moved to a particular position.

19 If voltage is present (indicated either by the tester bulb lighting or a voltmeter reading, as applicable), this means that there is a short circuit.

20 If no voltage is present, but the fuse still blows with the load(s) connected, this indicates an internal fault in the load(s).

Finding an earth fault

21 The battery negative terminal is connected to 'earth' – the metal of the engine/transmission and the car body – and most systems are wired so that they only receive a positive feed, the current returning via the metal of the car body. This means that the component mounting and the body form part of that circuit. Loose or corroded mountings can therefore cause a range of electrical faults, ranging from total failure of a circuit, to a puzzling partial fault. In particular, lights may shine dimly (especially when another circuit sharing the same earth point is in operation), motors (e.g. wiper motors or the radiator cooling fan motor) may run slowly, and the operation of one circuit may have an apparently unrelated effect on another. Note that on many vehicles, earth straps are used between certain components, such as the engine/transmission and the body, usually where there is no metal-to-metal contact between components, due to flexible rubber mountings, etc.

22 To check whether a component is properly earthed, disconnect the battery, and connect one lead of an ohmmeter to a known good earth point. Connect the other lead to the wire or earth connection being tested. The resistance reading should be zero; if not, check the connection as follows.

23 If an earth connection is thought to be faulty, dismantle the connection, and clean

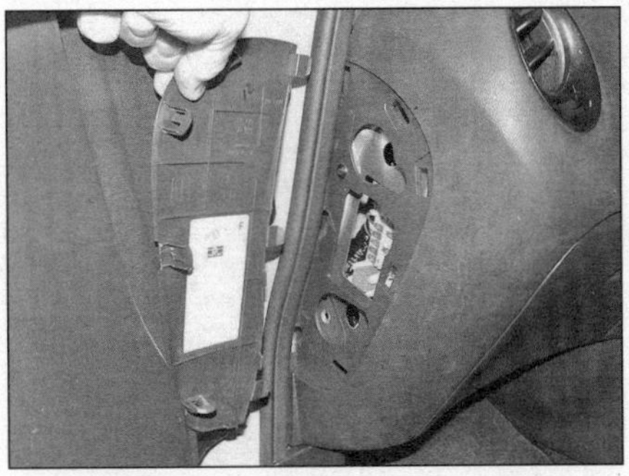
3.3 Vehicle passenger compartment fusebox

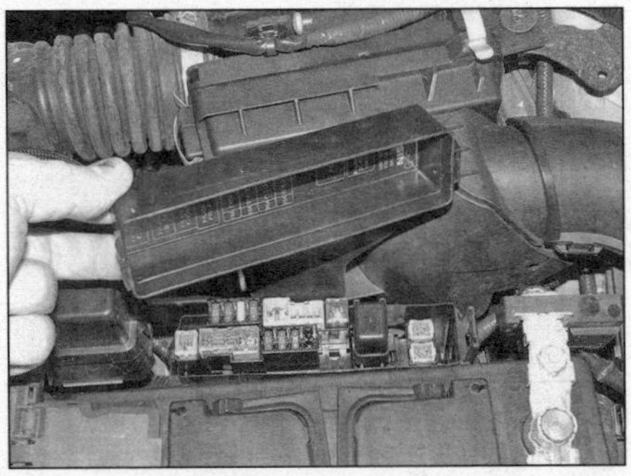
3.4a Vehicle engine compartment fusebox

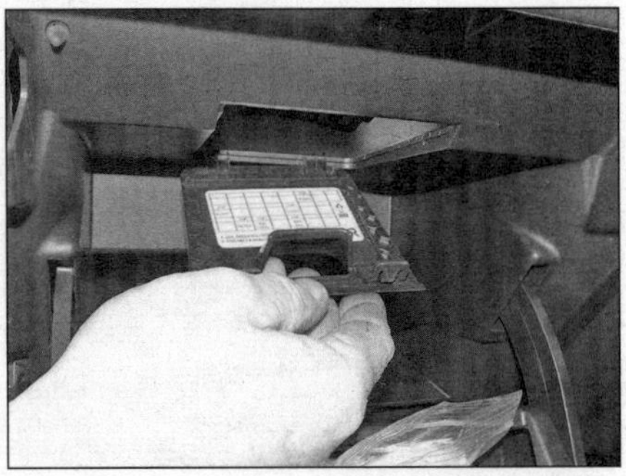
3.4b Open the cover for access to the fuses above the glovebox

back to bare metal both the bodyshell and the wire terminal or the component earth connection mating surface. Be careful to remove all traces of dirt and corrosion, and then use a knife to trim away any paint, so that a clean metal-to-metal joint is made. On reassembly, tighten the joint fasteners securely; if a wire terminal is being refitted, use serrated washers between the terminal and the bodyshell, to ensure a clean and secure connection. When the connection is remade, prevent the onset of corrosion in the future by applying a coat of petroleum jelly or silicone-based grease, or by spraying on (at regular intervals) a proprietary ignition sealer.

3 Fuses and relays – general information

Fuses

1 Fuses are designed to break a circuit when a predetermined current is reached, in order to protect the components and wiring, which could be damaged by excessive current flow. Any excessive current flow will be due to a fault in the circuit, usually a short-circuit (see Section 2).
2 The main fuses are located behind a cover at the left-hand end of the facia.
3 For access to the fuses, pull open the cover flap **(see illustration)**.
4 Additional fuses and circuit-breakers are located in an auxiliary fusebox in the engine compartment, either in front of, or behind the battery **(see illustrations)**. On some models, there may be further fuses located in a fusebox above the glovebox, accessible after opening a cover in the roof of the glovebox.
5 A blown fuse can be recognised from its melted or broken wire. Before removing a fuse, first ensure that the relevant circuit is switched off.
6 Using the plastic tool clipped inside the main fusebox, pull the fuse from its location **(see illustration)**.
7 Spare fuses are usually provided in the main fusebox.
8 Before renewing a blown fuse, trace and rectify the cause, and always use a fuse of the correct rating (fuse ratings are usually specified on the inside of the fusebox cover flap). Never substitute a fuse of a higher rating, or make temporary repairs using wire or metal foil; more serious damage, or even fire, could result.
9 Note that the fuses are colour-coded as follows.

Colour	Rating
Orange	5A
Red	10A
Blue	15A
Yellow	20A
Clear or White	25A
Green	30A

Relays

10 A relay is an electrically operated switch, which is used for the following reasons:
a) *A relay can switch a heavy current remotely from the circuit in which the current is flowing, therefore allowing the use of lighter-gauge wiring and switch contacts.*
b) *A relay can receive more than one control input, unlike a mechanical switch.*
c) *A relay can have a timer function – for example, the intermittent wiper relay.*

11 Various relays are located behind the facia, in the fuseboxes and in numerous other locations throughout the car.
12 If a circuit or system controlled by a relay develops a fault, and the relay is suspect, operate the system. If the relay is functioning, it should be possible to hear it 'click' as it is energised, If this is the case, the fault lies with the components or wiring of the system. If the relay is not being energised, then either the relay is not receiving a main supply or a switching voltage, or the relay itself is faulty. Testing is by the substitution of a known good unit, but be careful – while some relays are identical in appearance and in operation, others look similar but perform different functions.
13 To remove a relay, first ensure that the relevant circuit is switched off. The relay can then simply be pulled out from the socket, and pushed back into position.

3.6 Pull the fuse from its position in the fusebox

4 Switches – removal and refitting

Note: *Disconnect the battery negative terminal (refer to battery disconnection and reconnection in Chapter 5A, Section 3), before removing any switch, and reconnect the terminal after refitting the switch.*

Ignition switch/steering lock

1 Remove the ignition switch/steering lock, as described in Chapter 10, Section 13.

Steering column switches

2 Remove the airbag rotary connector as described in Section 21.
3 Disconnect the wiring connector from the base of the left-hand switch.
4 Lift the switch assembly up and remove it from the steering column **(see illustration)**.

4.4 Lift the switch assembly up and off the steering column

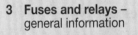

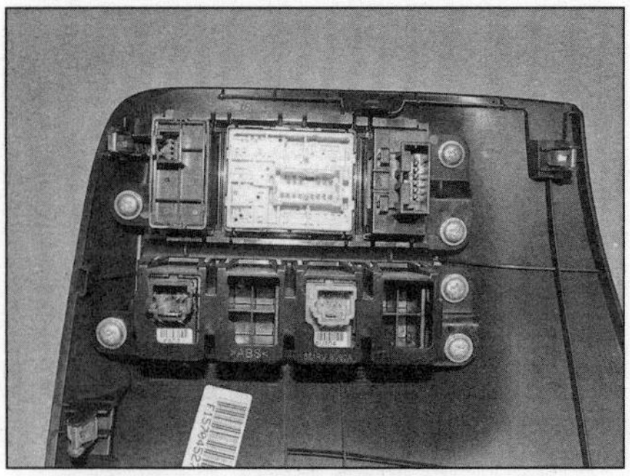

4.10 Undo the retaining screws and withdraw the relevant switch cluster

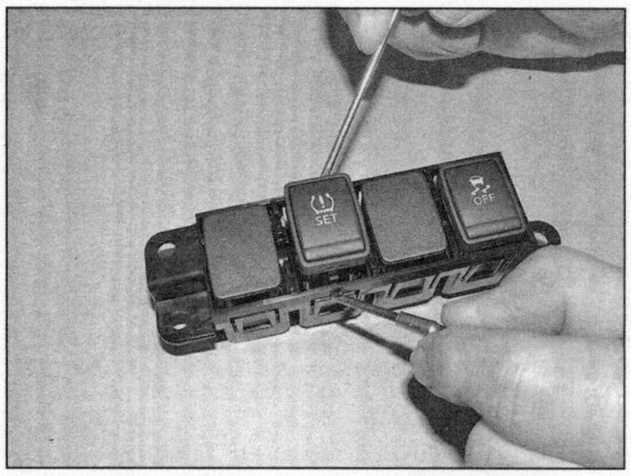

4.11 Depress the retaining lugs and withdraw the switch from the cluster

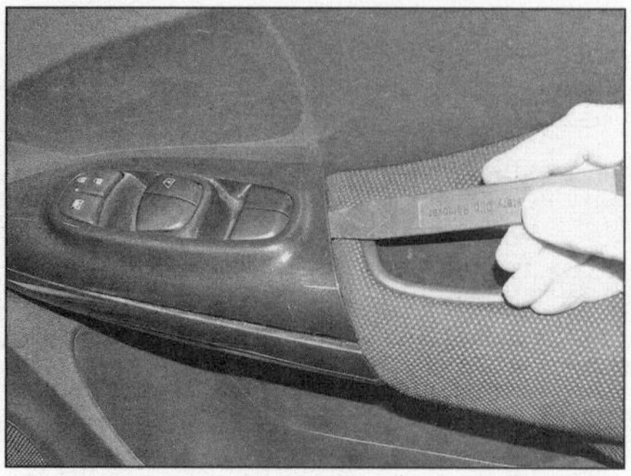

4.13 Unclip the trim panel from the door panel...

The two switched are a combined assembly and no further dismantling is possible.

5 Refitting is a reversal of removal.

Heater/ventilation switches

6 The heater/ventilation switches are integral with the heater control panel, remove the heater control panel, as described in Chapter 3, Section 9.

Heated rear window switch

7 The heated rear window switch is integral with the heater control panel, remove the heater control panel, as described in Chapter 3, Section 9.

Driver's side panel switches

8 These switches include the electric door mirror switch, the headlight height adjustment switch, electronic stability programme (ESP) switch and the stop/start on/off switch, according to model.

9 To gain access to the switches, remove the driver's side switch panel as described in Chapter 11, Section 26.

10 To remove the relevant switch, turn the trim panel over, undo the retaining screws and withdraw the relevant switch cluster from the trim panel **(see illustration)**.

11 Using two small screwdrivers, depress the retaining lugs and withdraw the switch from the cluster **(see illustration)**.

12 Refit the relevant switch and trim panel, using a reversal of the removal procedure.

Electric window switches

13 Unclip the door switch trim panel from the top of the armrest in the door trim panel **(see illustration)**.

14 Disconnect the wiring connectors from the switch panel as it is removed **(see illustration)**.

15 To remove the relevant switch, release the retaining tabs and withdraw the switch from the rear of the trim panel **(see illustration)**.

16 Refit the relevant switch and trim panel, using a reversal of the removal procedure.

Hazard warning light switch

17 The hazard warning switch is fitted to the top centre of the facia. To gain access, remove the radio/CD player as described in Section 15.

18 To remove the switch, disconnect the wiring connector, then reach in through the facia aperture and push the switch out of the facia **(see illustration)**.

19 Refit the switch using a reversal of the removal procedure.

Centre console switches

20 Carefully unclip the switch panel from the top of the centre console, and then disconnect the wiring connectors on removal.

21 Undo the three screws and remove the switch mounting bracket from the switch panel.

22 To remove the relevant switch, release the retaining clips and withdraw the switch from the mounting bracket.

23 Refit the relevant switch and switch panel, using a reversal of the removal procedure.

Courtesy light/door warning switches

24 The door warning switches are part of the central locking system components, remove the switches as described in Chapter 11, Section 17.

Luggage area light switch

25 The switch is integral with the boot lid/tailgate lock. Removal and refitting details for the boot lid/tailgate lock are provided in Chapter 11, Section 16.

Map reading/courtesy light switches

26 The switches are integral with the interior light assembly and cannot be renewed independently. See Section 6 for interior light bulb renewal.

Steering wheel switches

27 These switches include the audio control switches to the left-hand side of the steering wheel, and cruise control system operation to the right-hand side of the steering wheel, according to model.

Warning: When working on the airbag system, refer to the precautions given in Section 20 to avoid the possibility of personal injury.

4.14 ...and disconnect the wiring connectors

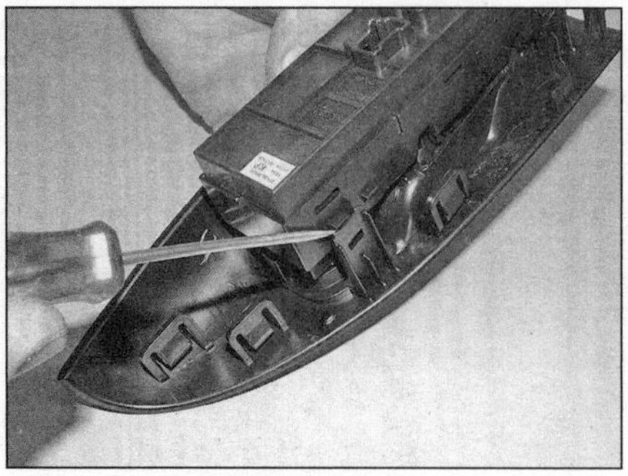

4.15 Release the retaining tabs and remove the switch

4.18 Reach in and push the hazard warning light switch out of the facia

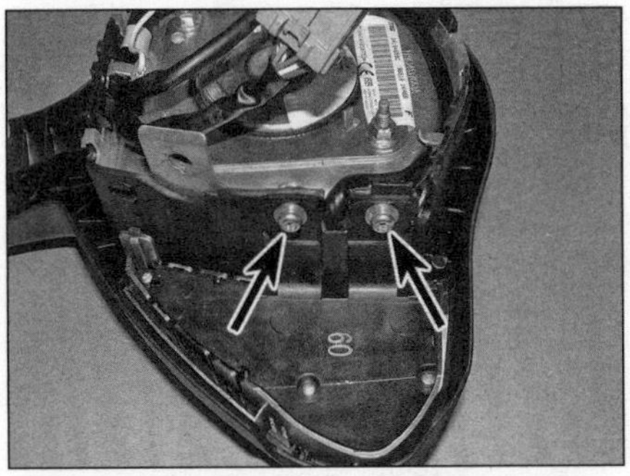

4.29a Undo the switch retaining screws...

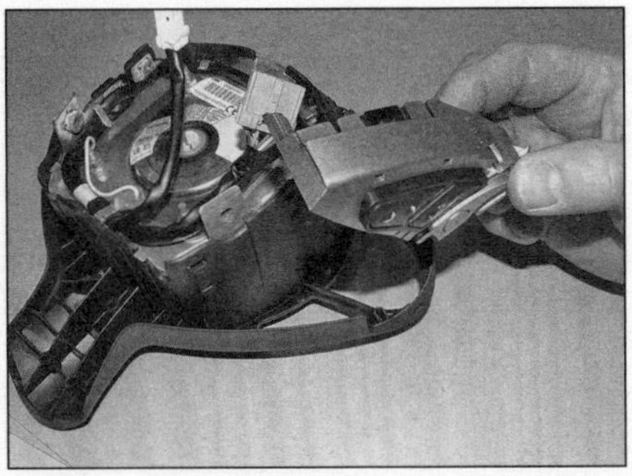

4.29b ...and remove the switch from the airbag

5.3 Remove the headlight protective cover

28 Remove the airbag from the centre of the steering wheel, as described in Section 21.
29 Undo the retaining screws, and disconnect the relevant switch panel from the side of the airbag **(see illustrations)**.
30 Refit the switch using a reversal of the removal procedure. Refer to Section 21, when refitting the airbag.

5 Bulbs (exterior lights) – renewal

5.4 Pivot the spring clip away from the bulb

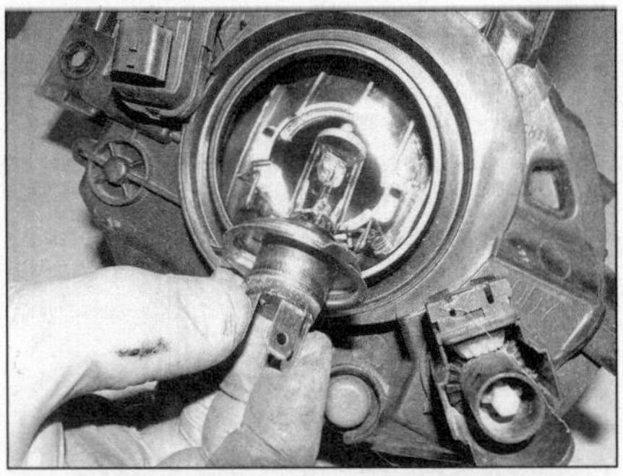

5.5 Remove the bulb from light unit

General

1 Whenever a bulb is renewed, note the following points:

a) *Disconnect the battery negative terminal (refer to battery disconnection and reconnection in Chapter 5A, Section 3).*
b) *Remember that, if the light has just been in use, the bulb may be extremely hot.*
c) *Always check the bulb contacts and holder, ensuring that there is clean metal-to-metal contact between the bulb and its live contact(s) and earth. Clean off any corrosion or dirt before fitting a new bulb.*
d) *Wherever bayonet-type bulbs are fitted, ensure that the live contact(s) bear firmly against the bulb contact.*
e) *Always ensure that the new bulb is of the correct rating (see Specifications), and that it is completely clean before fitting it; this applies particularly to headlight/foglight bulbs (see following paragraphs).*

Headlight (early models)

Dipped/main beam

2 Reach behind the headlamp, and disconnect the wiring connector from the headlight bulb.
3 Remove the protective cover from the rear of the headlight unit **(see illustration)**.
4 Squeeze together the legs of the retaining spring clip and pivot it away from the bulb **(see illustration)**.
5 Withdraw the bulb from the light unit **(see illustration)**.
6 Install the new bulb, ensuring that it is located correctly in the headlight unit, then locate the retaining spring clip over the bulb. When handling the new bulb, use a tissue or clean cloth to avoid touching the glass with the fingers; moisture and grease from the skin can cause blackening and rapid failure of this type of bulb. If the glass is accidentally touched, wipe it clean using methylated spirit.
7 Refit the protective cover.

Headlight (later models)

Note: *If working on the left-hand headlight, remove the air cleaner air ducts as necessary as described in Chapter 4A, Section 2 or Chapter 4B, Section 2. If working on the right-hand headlight, remove the washer fluid reservoir as described in Section 14.*

Dipped beam

8 Remove the protective cover from the rear of the headlight unit **(see illustration)**.
9 Rotate the bulbholder anti-clockwise and withdraw it from the light unit **(see illustration)**.
10 Disconnect the wiring connector and remove the bulbholder and bulb **(see illustration)**. Note that the bulbholder and bulb are a single assembly.

5.8 Remove the headlight dipped beam protective cover

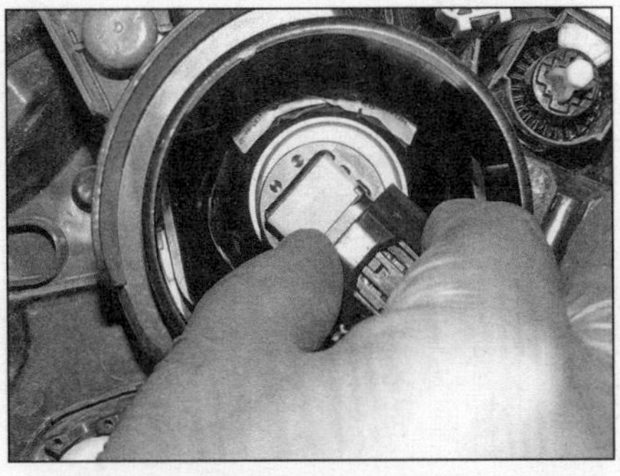

5.9 Rotate the bulbholder anti-clockwise and withdraw it

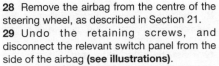

5.10 Disconnect the wiring connector

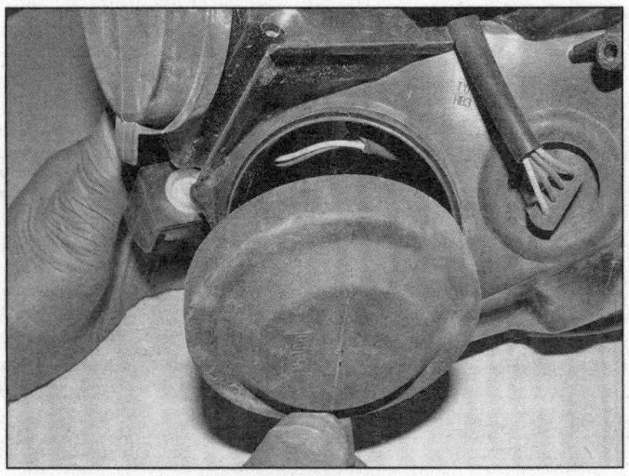

5.13 Remove the headlight main beam protective cover

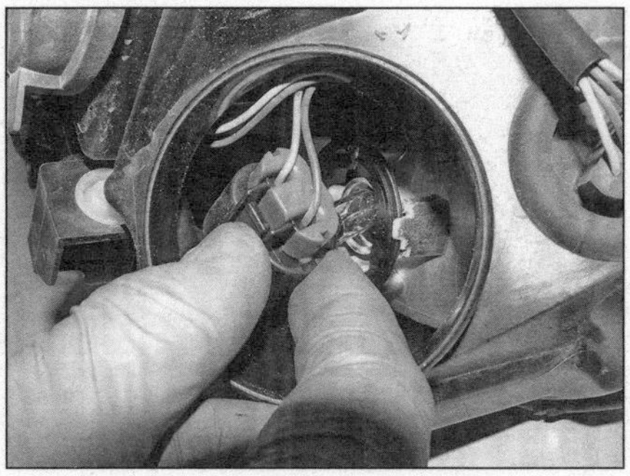

5.14 Rotate the bulbholder clockwise and withdraw it

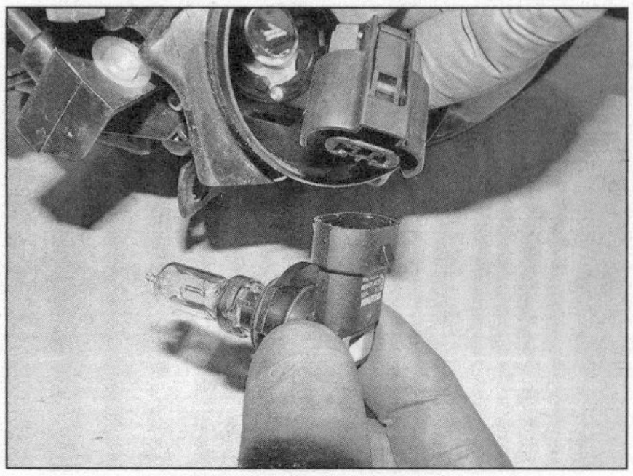

5.15 Disconnect the wiring connector

11 Install the new bulb, ensuring that it is located correctly in the headlight unit, then turn it clockwise to lock it in position. When handling the new bulb, use a tissue or clean cloth to avoid touching the glass with the fingers; moisture and grease from the skin can cause blackening and rapid failure of this type of bulb. If the glass is accidentally touched, wipe it clean using methylated spirit.

12 Refit the protective cover.

Main beam

13 Remove the protective cover from the rear of the headlight unit **(see illustration)**.

14 Rotate the bulbholder clockwise and withdraw it from the light unit **(see illustration)**.

15 Disconnect the wiring connector and remove the bulbholder and bulb **(see illustration)**. Note that the bulbholder and bulb are a single assembly.

16 Install the new bulb, ensuring that it is located correctly in the headlight unit, then turn it anti-clockwise to lock it in position. When handling the new bulb, use a tissue or clean cloth to avoid touching the glass with the fingers; moisture and grease from the skin can cause blackening and rapid failure of this type of bulb. If the glass is accidentally touched, wipe it clean using methylated spirit.

17 Refit the protective cover.

Sidelight/daytime running light

Note: *The following procedure is only applicable to early models. On later models, the sidelight/daytime running light is an LED and is integral with the light unit.*

18 Disconnect the wiring connector from the side light bulb holder in the combination light unit.

19 Twist the bulb holder and withdraw the sidelight bulb and holder from the combination light unit **(see illustration)**.

20 The bulb is a push-fit in the bulbholder, pull the sidelight bulb to remove it from the bulbholder **(see illustration)**.

21 Fit the new bulb using a reversal of the removal procedure.

Front indicator

22 Twist the bulbholder anti-clockwise and withdraw it from the combination light unit **(see illustration)**.

23 The bulb is a bayonet fit in the bulbholder, push lightly and turn anti-clockwise to remove the bulb **(see illustration)**.

24 Fit the new bulb using a reversal of the removal procedure.

Front indicator side repeater

Note: *The following procedure is only applicable to early models. On later models the side repeater is an LED and is incorporated in the door mirror assembly.*

25 Push the light unit toward the front of the car and carefully unclip the rear end of the light unit from the wing panel **(see illustration)**.

26 Withdraw the light unit, and then twist the

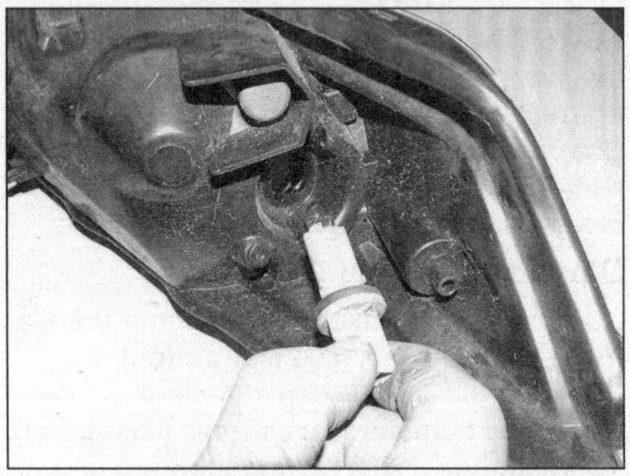

5.19 Rotate the bulbholder to remove...

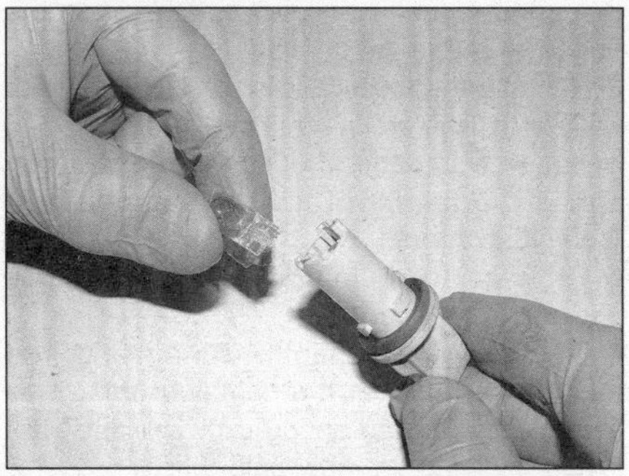

5.20 ...then pull the bulb from its holder

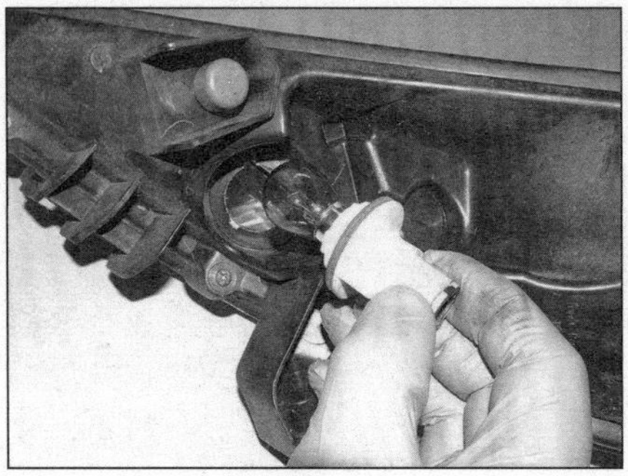

5.22 Rotate the bulbholder anti-clockwise to remove

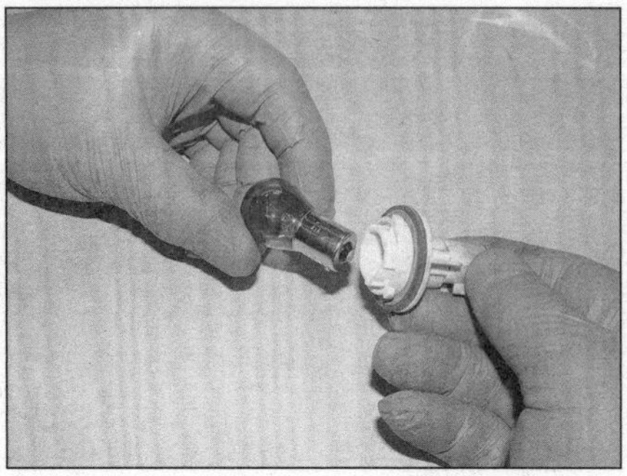

5.23 Press in the bulb and rotate it anti-clockwise to remove it

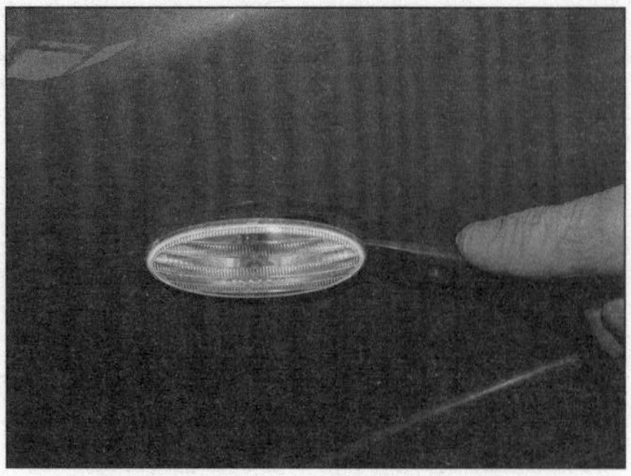

5.25 Carefully unclip the light unit

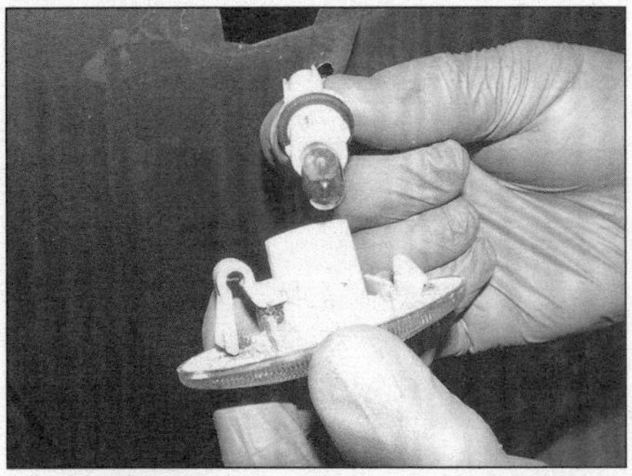

5.26 Remove the bulb holder...

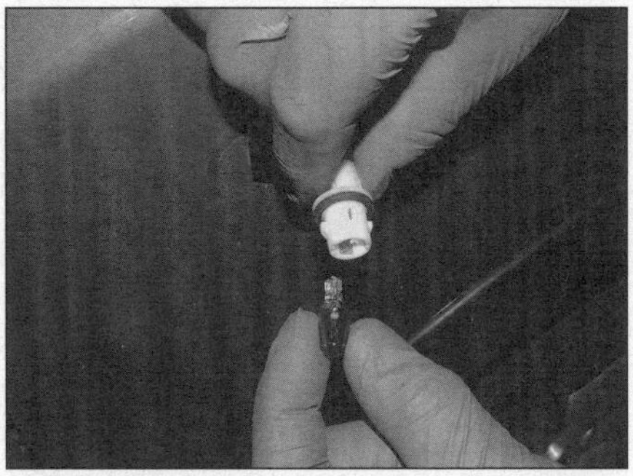

5.27 ...then pull the bulb from its holder

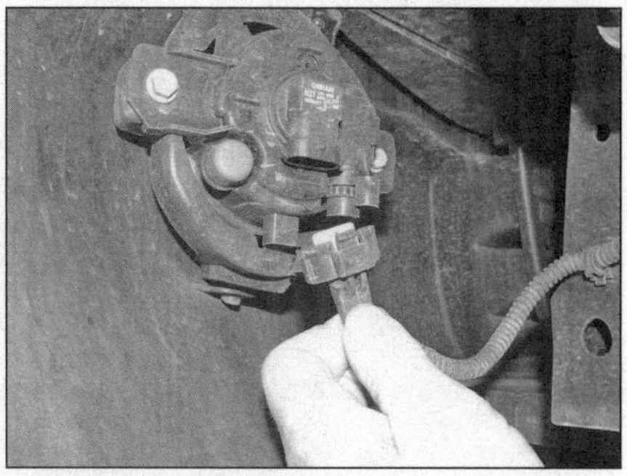

5.30 Disconnect the foglight wiring plug

5.31 Rotate the bulbholder anti-clockwise to remove

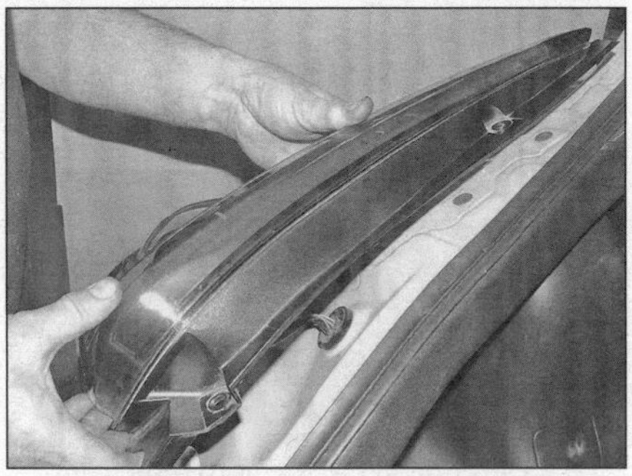

5.35a Withdraw the light unit...

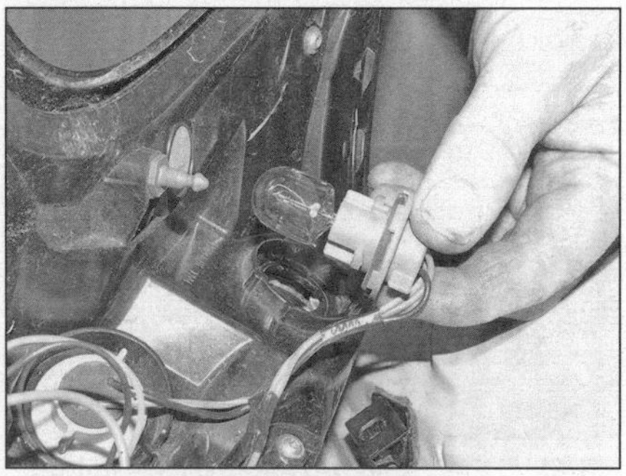

5.35b ...and turn the bulbholders anti-clockwise to remove

bulbholder anti-clockwise to release it from the light unit **(see illustration)**.

27 The bulb is a push-fit in the bulbholder **(see illustration)**.

28 Fit the new bulb using a reversal of the removal procedure.

Front foglight

29 Remove the inner wheel arch liner as described in Chapter 11, Section 21.

30 Reach behind the bumper and disconnect the wiring connector from the bulbholder **(see illustration)**.

31 Turn the bulbholder anti-clockwise and withdraw it from the rear of the foglight **(see illustration)**.

32 The bulb can then be removed from the bulbholder, check new bulb before removing the bulb from its holder, as some new bulbs come with the bulb holder as part of the bulb. When handling the new bulb, use a tissue or clean cloth to avoid touching the glass with the fingers; moisture and grease from the skin can cause blackening and rapid failure of this type of bulb. If the glass is accidentally touched, wipe it clean using methylated spirit.

33 Fit the new bulb using a reversal of the removal procedure.

Rear lights (indicator/stop/tail/ reversing lights)

34 Open the tailgate and undo the two rear light unit retaining bolts.

35 Withdraw the light unit, then turn the relevant bulbholder anti-clockwise and remove it from the light unit **(see illustrations)**.

36 Remove the push-fit bulbs from the bulbholders **(see illustration)**.

37 Fit the new bulb using a reversal of the removal procedure.

Rear fog light

38 Pull out the centre pin and extract the plastic expanding rivet from the lower edge of the bumper **(see illustration)**.

39 Pull the lower edge of the bumper down, then reach in and turn the bulbholder anti-clockwise to withdraw it from the rear of the foglight **(see illustration)**.

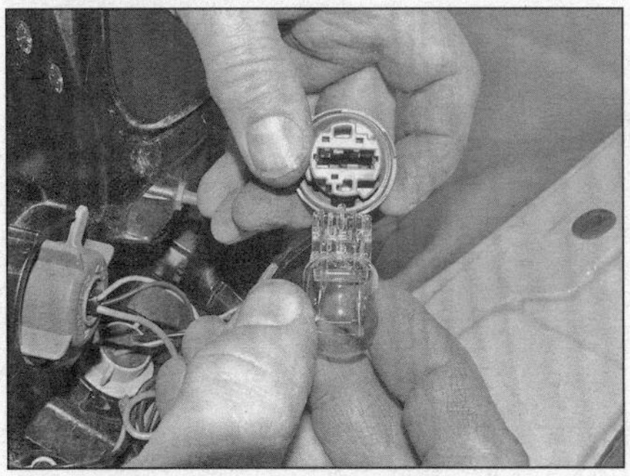

5.36 Remove the push-fit bulbs

5.38 Extract the plastic expanding rivet from the lower edge of the bumper

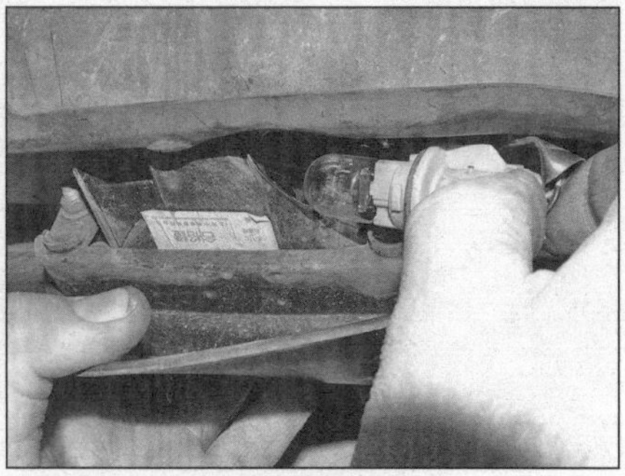

5.39 Rotate the bulbholder anti-clockwise to remove

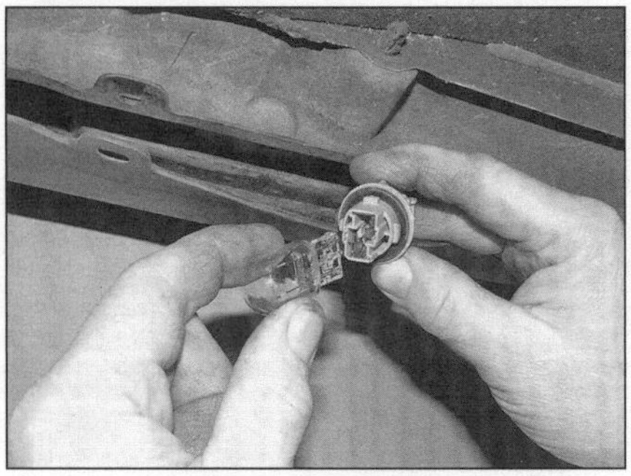
5.40 Remove the push fit bulb

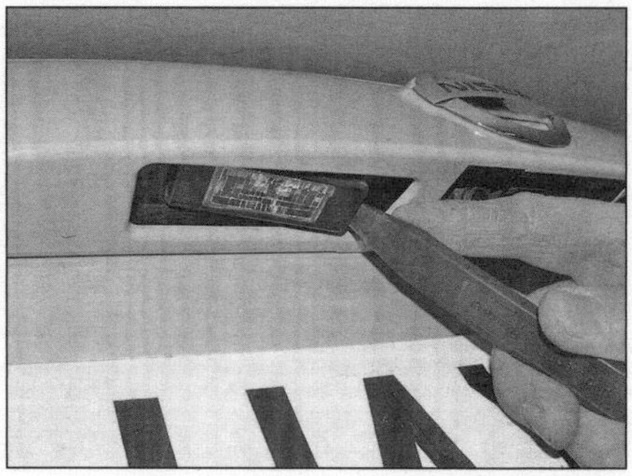
5.42 Carefully unclip the light unit

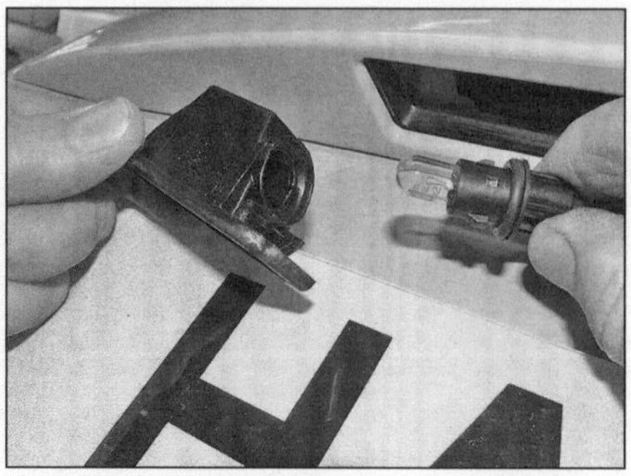
5.43 Twist the bulbholder to remove...

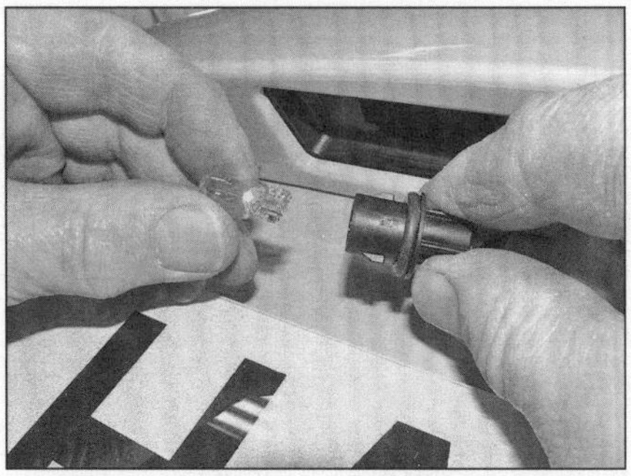
5.44 ... then pull the bulb from its holder

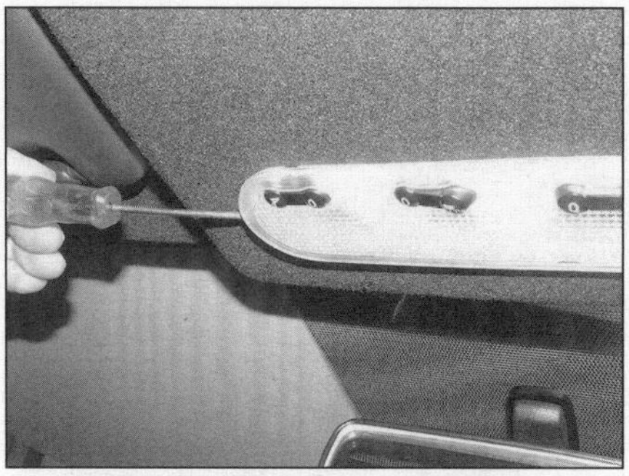
6.2 Carefully prise the light lens from place...

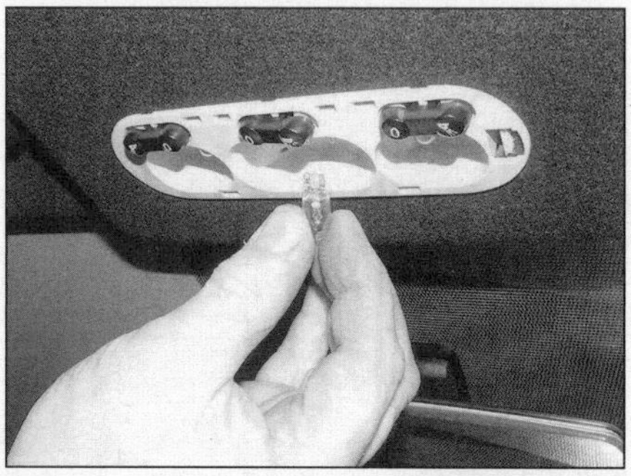
6.3 ...and pull the bulb(s) from the light unit

40 Remove the push-fit bulb from the bulbholder **(see illustration)**.

41 Fit the new bulb using a reversal of the removal procedure.

Number plate light

42 Unclip the light unit from the tailgate trim **(see illustration)**.

43 Turn the bulbholder anti-clockwise and withdraw it from the number plate light **(see illustration)**.

44 Pull the bulb to remove it from the bulbholder **(see illustration)**.

45 Fit the new bulb using a reversal of the removal procedure.

6 Bulbs (interior lights) – renewal

General

1 Refer to Section 5, paragraph 1.

Map reading/courtesy light (front)

2 Carefully prise the lens from the light unit (if necessary, carefully use a flat-bladed screwdriver) **(see illustration)**.

3 Pull the bulb from the light unit; note that the bulb is a capless type **(see illustration)**.

4 If required, release the securing clips to release the light unit from the headlining, then disconnect the wiring connector and remove the unit **(see illustrations)**.

5 Fit the new bulb using a reversal of the removal procedure.

Courtesy light (rear)

6 Carefully prise the lens from the light unit

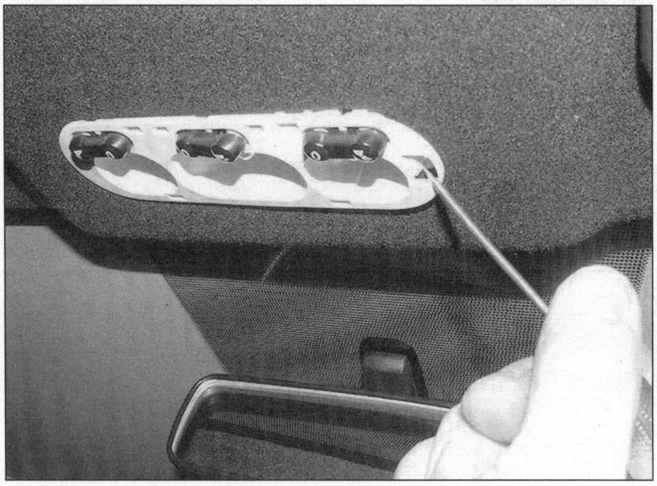
6.4a Release the light unit from the headlining...

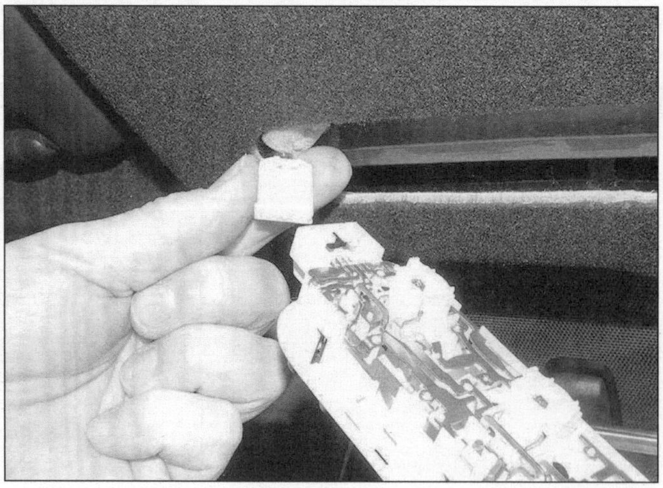
6.4b ...disconnect the wiring connector and remove the unit

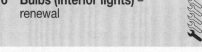

(if necessary, carefully use a flat-bladed screwdriver) **(see illustration)**.

7 Pull the bulb from the light unit; note that the bulb is a capless type **(see illustration 6.3)**.

8 If required, release the securing clips to release the light unit from the headlining **(see illustration)**.

9 Fit the new bulb using a reversal of the removal procedure.

Luggage area light

10 Open the tailgate.

11 Unclip the light unit from the trim panel, disconnect the wiring connector and remove the unit **(see illustrations)**.

12 Unclip the light unit lens and remove the push-fit bulb from the light unit **(see illustrations)**.

13 Fit the new bulb using a reversal of the removal procedure.

Glovebox light

14 Remove the glovebox as described in Chapter 11, Section 26.

15 Turn the bulbholder anti-clockwise and remove it from the rear of the glovebox **(see illustration)**. The bulb is integral with the bulbholder.

7 Exterior light units – removal and refitting

Note: *Disconnect the battery negative terminal (refer to Disconnecting the battery in Chapter 5A, Section 3), before removing any light unit, and reconnect the terminal after refitting the light.*

Headlight

1 Remove the front bumper, as described in Chapter 11, Section 6.

2 Unscrew the two headlight upper securing bolts **(see illustration)**.

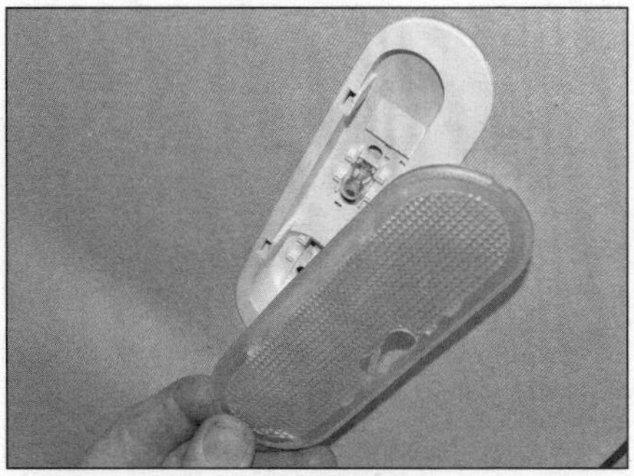

6.6 Carefully prise the light lens from the light unit

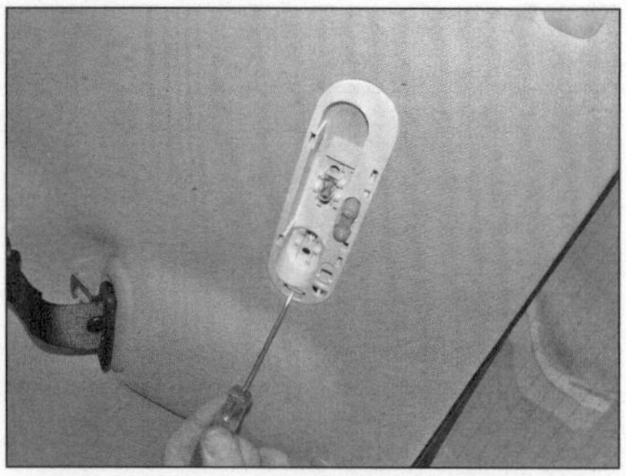

6.8 Release the light unit from the roof panel

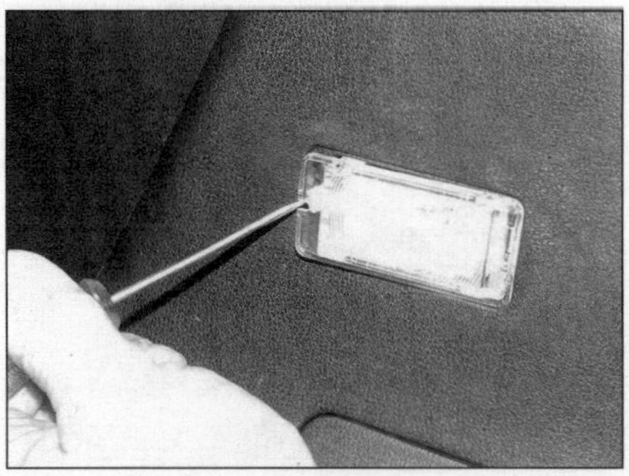

6.11a Unclip the light unit...

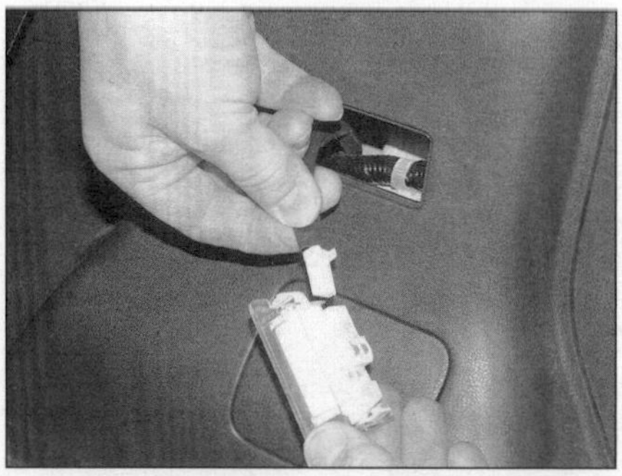

6.11b ...then disconnect the wiring connector and remove the light unit

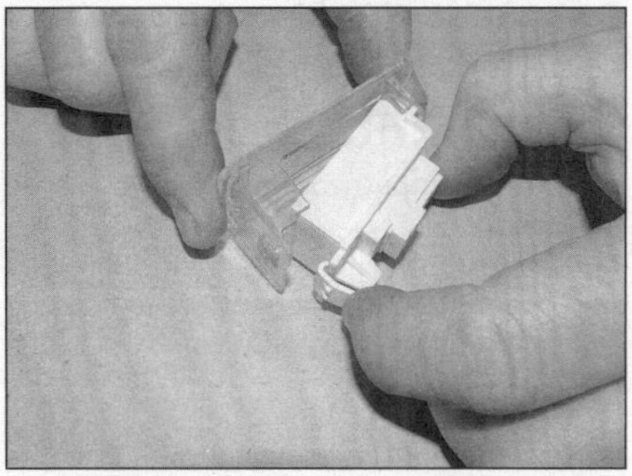

6.12a Unclip the light unit lens...

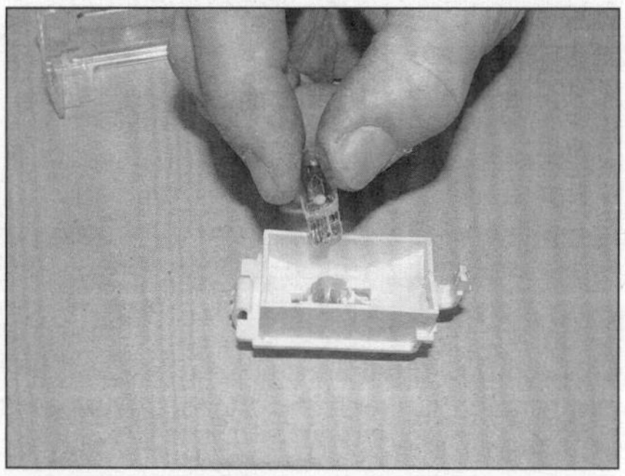

6.12b ...and remove the push-fit bulb

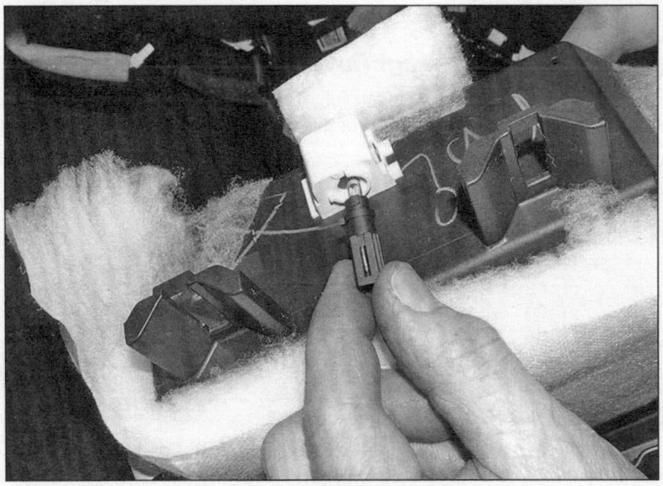

6.15 Remove the bulbholder from the glovebox

7.2 Headlight upper mounting bolts

7.3a Headlight lower inner mounting bolt...

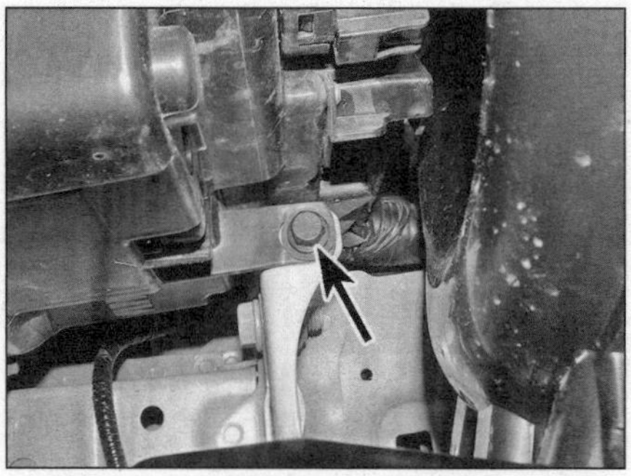

7.3b ...and lower outer mounting bolt

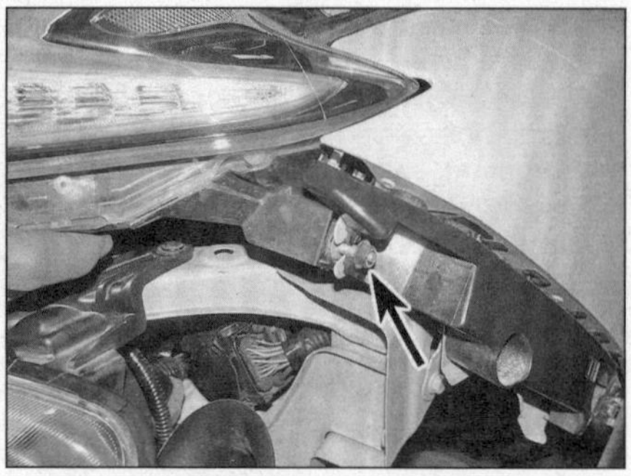

7.10a Slacken the nut...

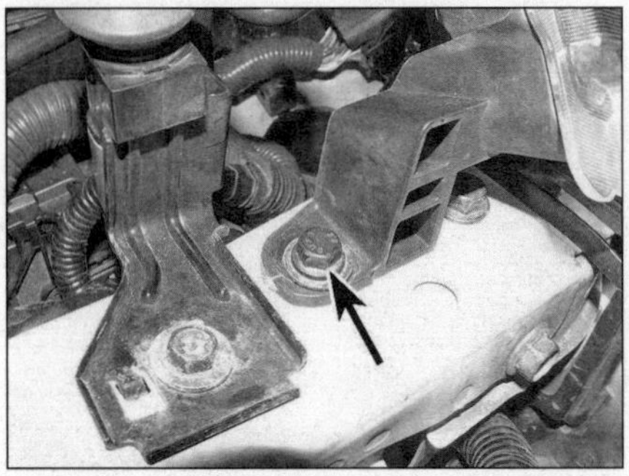

7.10b ...undo the lower mounting bolt...

7.10c ...and the upper mounting bolt

7.14a Undo the foglight retaining bolts...

3 Unscrew the two headlight lower mounting bolts **(see illustrations)**.

4 Remove the headlight unit, and disconnect the wiring connectors as the headlight is withdrawn from the vehicle.

5 Refitting is a reversal of removal. On completion, it is wise to have the headlight beam alignment checked (see Section 8).

Front sidelight

6 The front sidelight unit is part of the combination light unit and cannot be renewed separately.

Front indicator

7 The indicator unit is part of the headlight unit and cannot be renewed separately.

Front indicator side repeater

8 The procedure is described as part of the bulb renewal procedure in Section 5.

Combination light

9 Remove the front bumper, as described in Chapter 11, Section 6.

10 Slacken the combination light mounting nut and undo the two mounting bolts **(see illustrations)**.

11 Remove the combination light unit, and disconnect the wiring connectors as the unit is withdrawn from the vehicle.

Front foglight

12 Remove the inner wheel arch liner as described in Chapter 11, section 21.

13 Disconnect the wiring connector from the bulbholder.

14 Undo the two securing bolts and remove the light unit from the rear of the bumper **(see illustrations)**.

15 Refitting is a reversal of removal.

Rear light

16 The procedure is described as part of the bulb renewal procedure in Section 5.

Rear fog light

17 Remove the rear bumper as described in Chapter 11, Section 7.

18 Undo the two retaining nuts and remove the light unit from the bumper **(see illustration)**.

19 Refitting is a reversal of removal.

Number plate light

20 The procedure is described as part of the bulb renewal procedure in Section 5.

High-level stop-light

21 Carefully remove the blanking strip from the top of the tailgate **(see illustration)**.

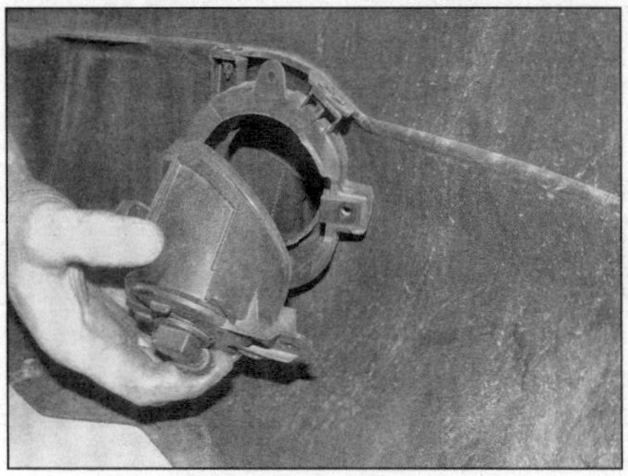

7.14b ...and remove the light unit

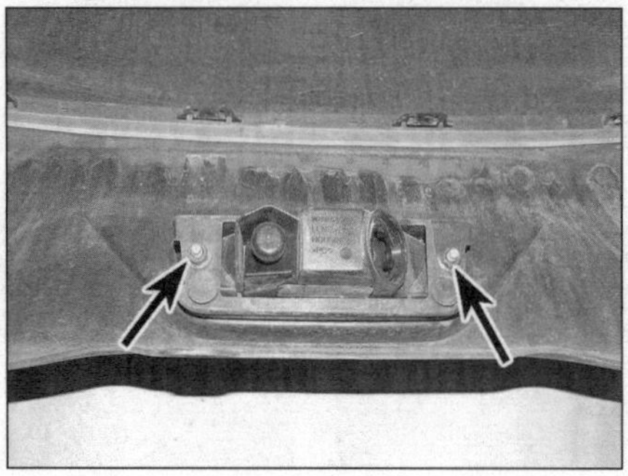

7.18 Rear fog light retaining nuts

7.21 Carefully remove the tailgate blanking strip

7.22 Undo the two mounting nuts

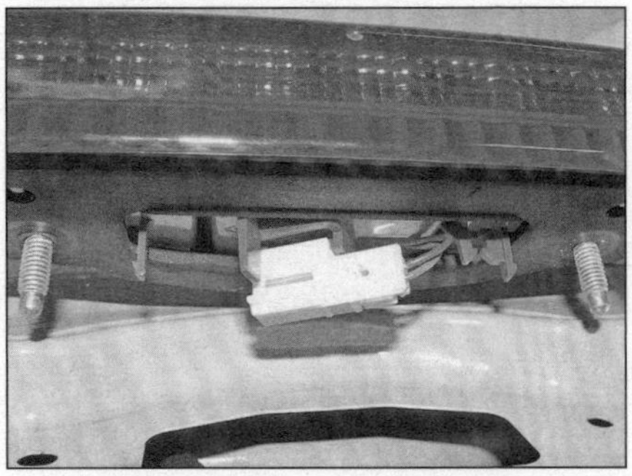

7.23 Withdraw the high-level stop-light and disconnect the wiring connector

9.3 Undo the two instrument panel retaining screws

22 Undo the two nuts securing the stop-light to the tailgate **(see illustration)**.

23 Withdraw the high-level stop-light from the tailgate, disconnect the wiring connector and remove the unit **(see illustration)**.

24 Refitting is a reversal of removal.

8 Headlight beam adjustment components – general information

1 Models with Halogen headlights are equipped with a headlight beam adjustment system, controlled by a switch located on the facia, which allows the aim of the headlights to be adjusted to compensate for the varying loads carried in the vehicle. The switch should be positioned according to the load being carried in the vehicle – e.g. position 0 for driver with no passengers or luggage, then increase the position to 1, 2, or 3 as the load is increased, or when towing.

2 Models with Xenon headlights are equipped with an automatic levelling system, which is controlled from a level sensor fitted to the rear suspension. If a fault occurs in the system, a warning light will show up on the instrument panel, and the headlights will be angled down to avoid dazzling on coming traffic. If it happens, the driving speed must be adjusted accordingly to allow for decreased visibility.

Warning: Before carrying out any operations on xenon headlight units, it is recommended that protective gloves and safety glasses be worn. It is essential that the wiring connectors are disconnected from the rear of the headlight unit, and then wait until the module and bulbs have cooled down before removal. DO NOT switch the headlights on with the bulb removed, as it is harmful to the eyes.

3 Accurate adjustment of the headlight beam is only possible using optical beam-setting equipment, and this work should therefore be carried out by a Nissan dealer or suitably-equipped workshop. To make temporary adjustment of the headlights, position the vehicle on a level surface, 10 metres from a wall. The tyres must be all at the correct pressures, the fuel tank half full, and a person be sitting in the drivers seat. Turn on the ignition, and check that the manual adjustment inside the vehicle is set at 0. Measure the distance from the ground to the centre of the headlight, and then deduct 5.0 cm for models with halogen headlights, and 7.5 cm for models with xenon headlights. Draw a mark on the wall at this height, and then adjust the headlight beam centre point onto this mark by turning the adjustment screws on the rear of the headlight unit.

9 Instrument panel – removal and refitting

Removal

1 Disconnect the battery negative terminal (refer to battery disconnection and reconnection in Chapter 5A, Section 3).

2 Remove the instrument panel surround as described in Chapter 11, Section 26.

3 Undo the two instrument panel lower securing screws **(see illustration)**.

4 Pull the instrument panel forwards, and disconnect the wiring connectors from the rear of the panel **(see illustrations)**. Withdraw the instrument panel from the facia.

Refitting

5 Refitting is a reversal of removal.

10 Horn – removal and refitting

Removal

1 Disconnect the battery negative terminal (refer to battery disconnection and reconnection in Chapter 5A, Section 3).

2 Remove the front bumper, as described in Chapter 11, Section 6.

3 Disconnect the wiring connectors from the horn **(see illustration)**.

4 Unscrew the securing bolt, and withdraw the horn complete with its mounting bracket.

Refitting

5 Refitting is a reversal of removal.

9.4a Withdraw the instrument panel...

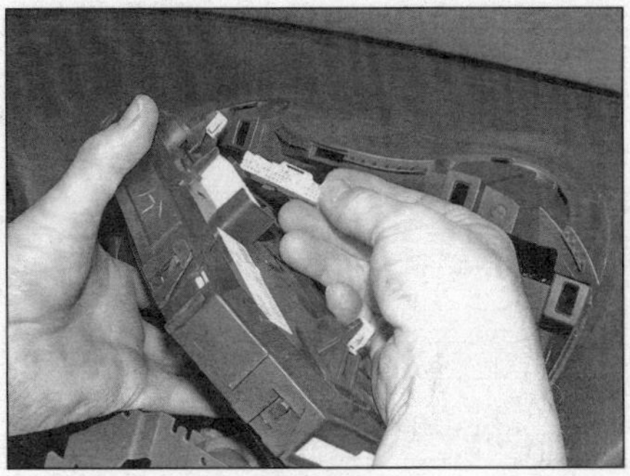

9.4b ...and disconnect the wiring connector

10.3 Disconnect the wiring connectors

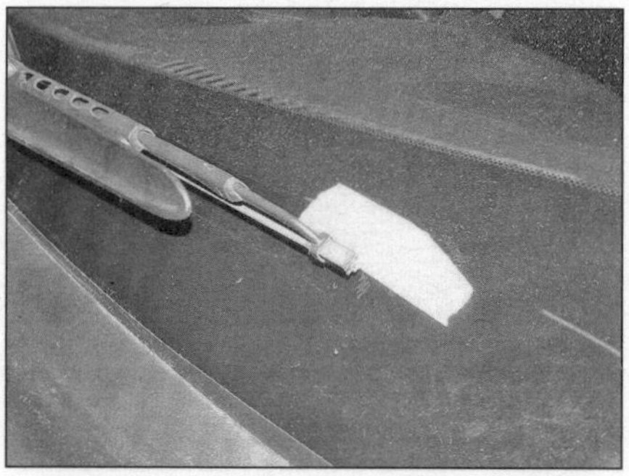

11.2 Stick a piece of tape alongside the edge of the wiper blade, to use as an alignment aid

11.3a Unclip the plastic cap...

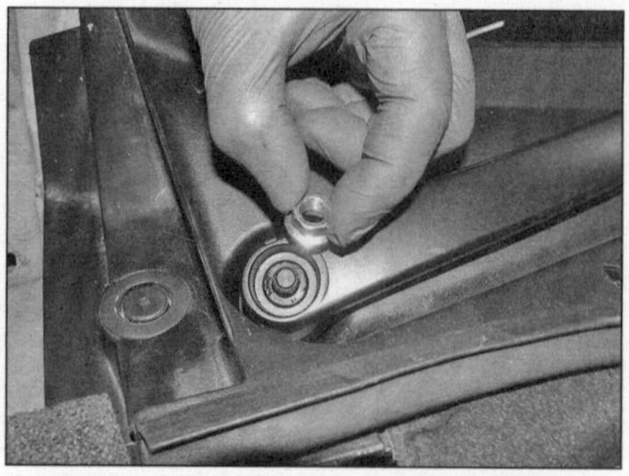

11.3b ...and undo the retaining nut

11 Wiper arm – removal and refitting

Removal

1 Operate the wiper motor, and then switch it off so that the wiper arm returns to the at-rest/parked position.

2 If a windscreen or tailgate wiper is being removed, stick a piece of tape alongside the edge of the wiper blade, to use as an alignment aid on refitting **(see illustration)**. On some models there are marks on the screen to aid refitting.

3 Unclip the plastic cover from the wiper arm spindle nut, then slacken and remove the nut **(see illustrations)**.

4 Lift the blade off the glass, and pull the wiper arm off its spindle.

5 If necessary, the arm can be removed from the spindle, by using a suitable puller. If both windscreen wiper arms are removed, note their locations, as different arms are fitted to the driver and passenger's sides.

Refitting

6 Ensure that the wiper arm and spindle splines are clean and dry.

7 When refitting a windscreen or tailgate wiper arm, refit the arm to the spindle, aligning the wiper blade with the mark on the screen or tape fitted before removal.

8 If both front windscreen wiper arms have been removed, ensure that the arms are refitted to their correct positions as noted before removal.

9 Refit the spindle nut, tighten it securely and, clip the plastic nut cover back into position.

12 Windscreen wiper motor and linkage – removal and refitting

Removal

1 Disconnect the battery negative terminal (refer to battery disconnection and reconnection in Chapter 5A, Section 3).

2 Remove the windscreen cowl panel as described in Chapter 11, Section 21.

3 Release the wiring harness from the linkage frame, then disconnect the wiring connector from the wiper motor **(see illustration)**.

4 Unscrew the motor and linkage securing bolts, and withdraw it from the scuttle panel **(see illustrations)**.

Refitting

5 Refitting is a reversal of removal.

11.3c Rear wiper arm retaining nut

12.3 Disconnect the wiper motor wiring connector

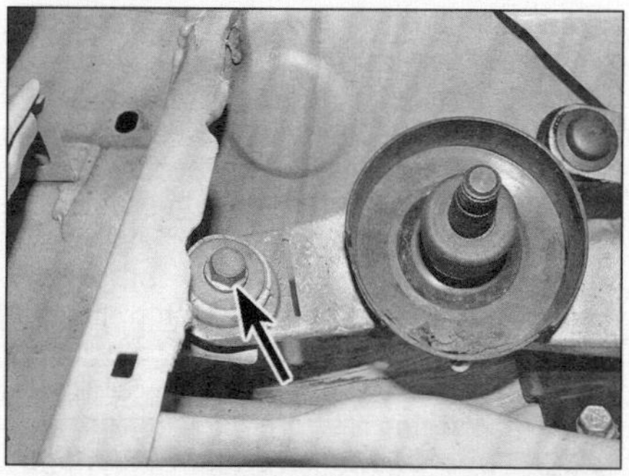

12.4a Undo the wiper linkage right-hand retaining bolt...

12.4b ...centre retaining bolt...

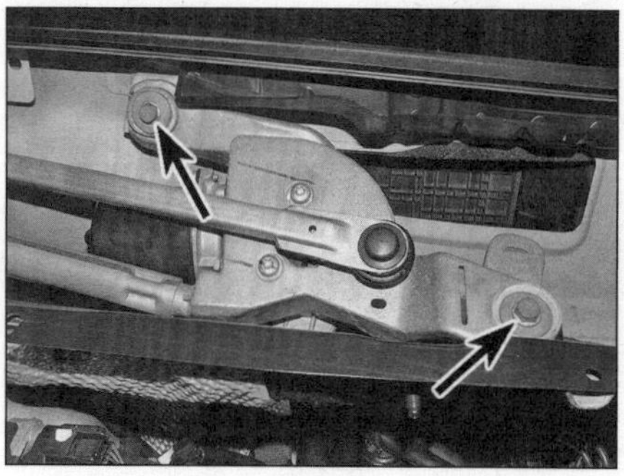

12.4c ...and left-hand retaining bolts...

12.4d ...then remove the motor and linkage assembly

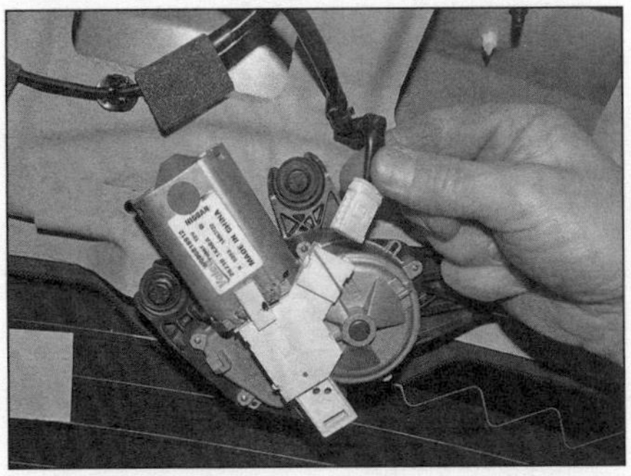

13.4 Disconnect the wiper motor wiring connector

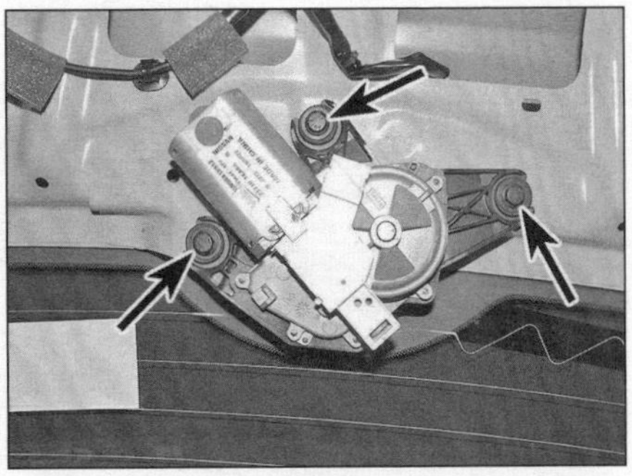

13.5 Undo the rear wiper motor mounting bolts

14.1 Release the retaining clip and remove the filler neck

13 Tailgate wiper motor – removal and refitting

Removal

1 Disconnect the battery negative terminal (refer to battery disconnection and reconnection in Chapter 5A, Section 3).

2 Open the tailgate and remove the inner tailgate trim, as described in Chapter 11, Section 24.

3 Remove the rear wiper arm with reference to Section 11.

4 Disconnect the tailgate wiper motor wiring connector **(see illustration)**.

5 Unscrew the three bolts securing the wiper motor assembly to the tailgate and withdraw it from the tailgate **(see illustration)**.

Refitting

6 Refitting is a reversal of removal.

14 Windscreen/tailgate washer system components – removal and refitting

Washer fluid reservoir

Removal

1 Working in the engine compartment, release the retaining clip and then pull the filler neck upwards to remove it from the top of the reservoir **(see illustration)**. Make sure the washer fluid level is low before removing the reservoir; be prepared for some spillage.

2 Disconnect the battery negative terminal (refer to battery disconnection and reconnection in Chapter 5A, Section 3).

3 Remove the front bumper, as described in Chapter 11, Section 6.

4 Remove the front left-hand wheel arch liner as described in Chapter 11, Section 21.

5 Release the wiring harness and fluid hoses from the retaining clips in the reservoir **(see illustration)**, and move the harness and hoses to one side to allow sufficient clearance to remove the reservoir.

6 Disconnect the fluid hose(s) from the washer pump **(see illustration)** – if the reservoir still contains fluid, be prepared for fluid spillage.

7 Disconnect the wiring connector(s) from the washer pump(s), and from the fluid level sensor, where applicable.

8 Remove the reservoir securing bolts, and then lower the reservoir from under the wheel arch **(see illustrations)**.

Refitting

9 Refitting is a reversal of removal.

Washer pump

Removal

10 Proceed as described in paragraphs 2 to 7.

11 Pull the washer pump from the reservoir and recover the grommet. If the reservoir still contains fluid, be prepared for fluid spillage.

Refitting

12 Refitting is a reversal of removal, making sure the grommet is fitted correctly in the reservoir before refitting the washer pump.

Windscreen washer nozzle

Removal

13 Remove the windscreen cowl panel as described in Chapter 11, Section 21.

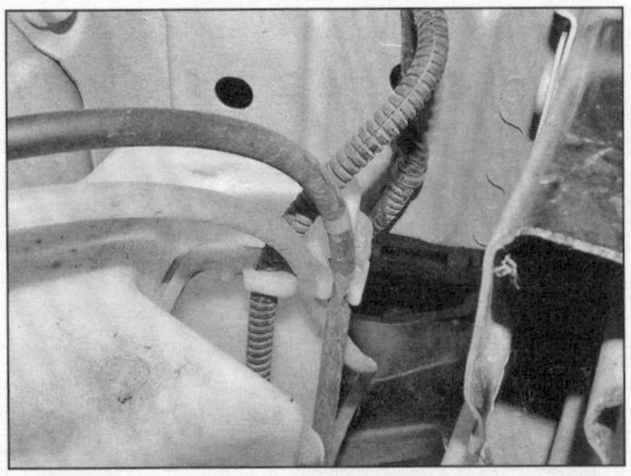

14.5 Unclip the wiring and the hoses from the reservoir

14.6 Disconnect the hoses from the washer pump

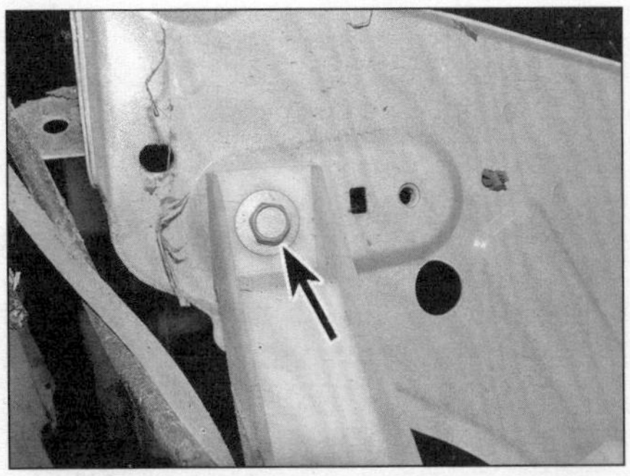

14.8a Undo the reservoir upper mounting bolt...

14.8b ...and lower mounting bolt

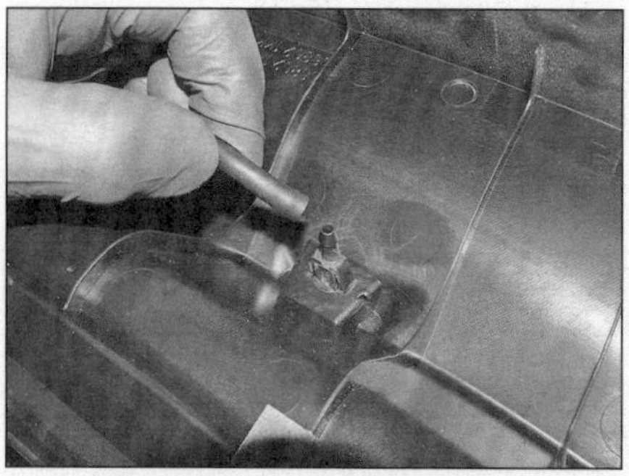

14.14 Disconnect the hose from the washer jet

14.15a Compress the legs of the washer jet...

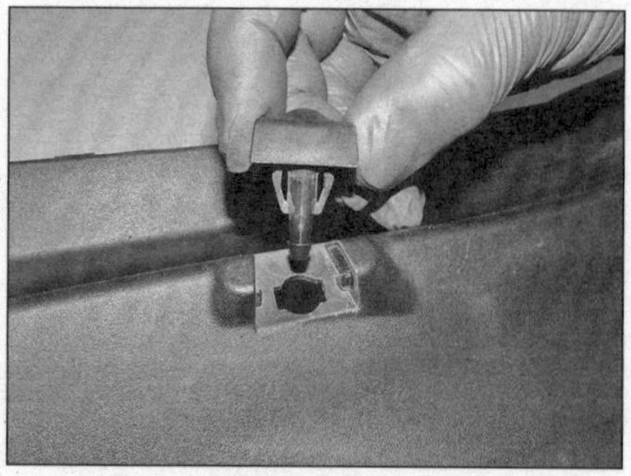

14.15b ...and remove it from the cowl panel

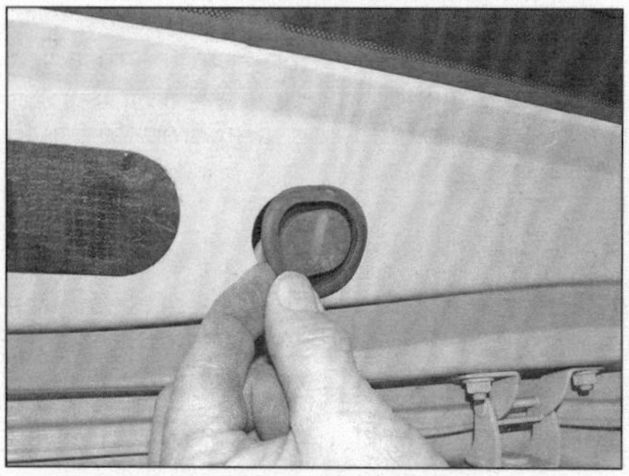

14.17 Remove the rubber grommet from the tailgate

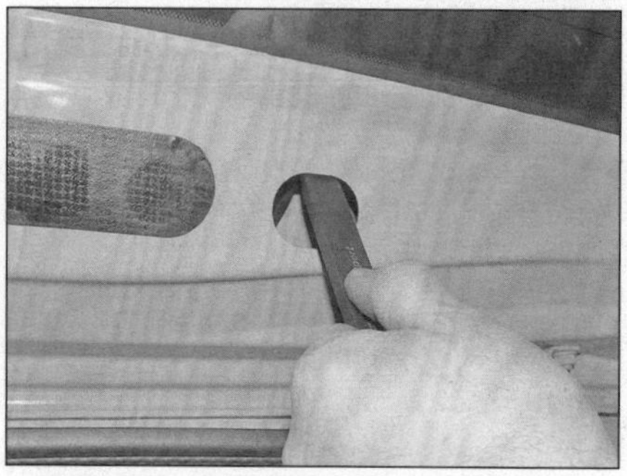

14.18a Insert a suitable tool into the tailgate...

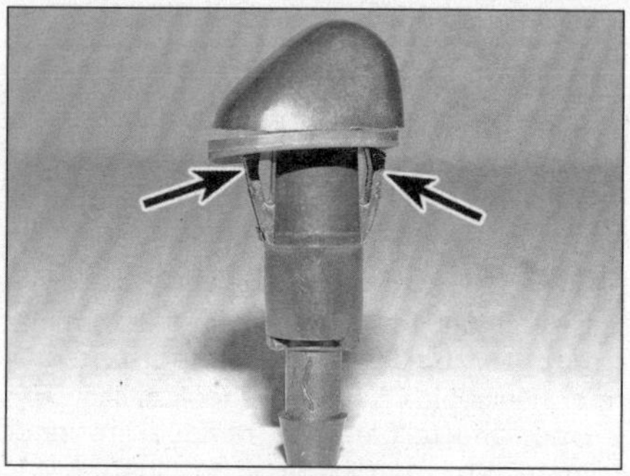

14.18b ...and compress the legs of the washer nozzle

14 Disconnect the washer hose from the relevant washer jet **(see illustration)**.

15 Using pliers, compress the legs of the washer jet and remove it from the cowl panel **(see illustrations)**.

Refitting

16 Refitting is a reversal of removal.

Tailgate washer nozzle

Removal

17 Open the tailgate and remove the rubber grommet below the washer nozzle location **(see illustration)**.

18 Insert a plastic spatula or similar into the tailgate aperture and compress the legs of the washer nozzle, while at the same time pulling it out of the tailgate **(see illustrations)**.

19 Disconnect the washer hose and remove the nozzle **(see illustration)**.

Refitting

20 Refitting is a reversal of removal.

Headlight washer nozzle

Removal

21 Remove the front bumper, as described in Chapter 11, Section 6.

22 If not already done, disconnect the washer fluid hose from the headlight washer nozzle.

23 Disengage the washer hose fixing clip from the bumper.

24 Remove the washer nozzle bracket and remove the washer nozzle from the bumper.

Refitting

25 Refitting is a reversal of removal.

15 Radio/CD player – removal and refitting

Removal

1 Disconnect the battery negative terminal (refer to battery disconnection and reconnection in Chapter 5A, Section 3).

2 Remove the facia centre ventilation trim panel, as described in Chapter 11, Section 26.

3 Remove the four now-exposed securing screws **(see illustration)**.

4 Pull the unit forwards from the facia, and then disconnect the wiring connectors and the aerial lead from the rear of the unit **(see illustration)**.

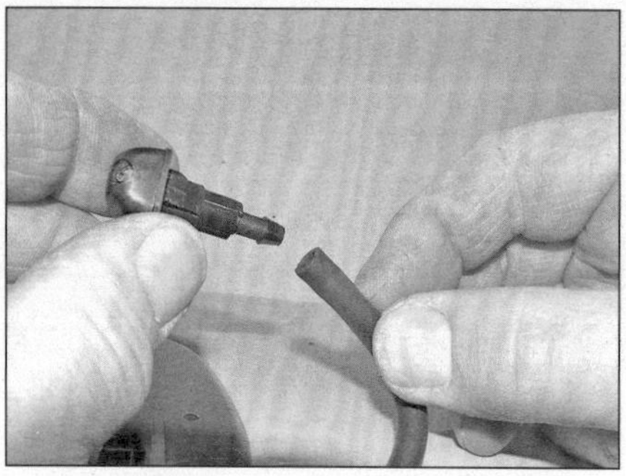

14.19 Disconnect the washer hose from the nozzle

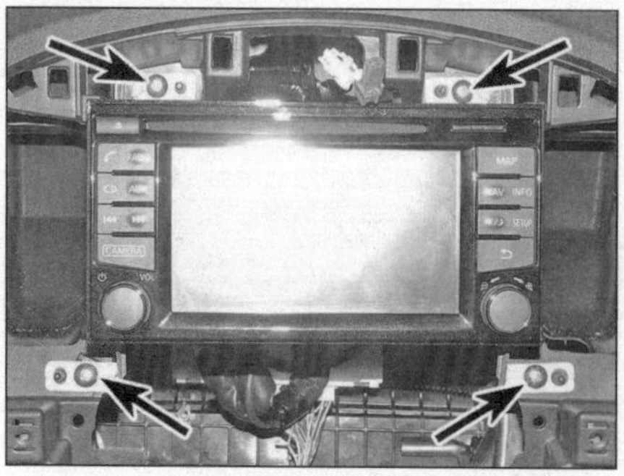

15.3 Undo the four retaining screws

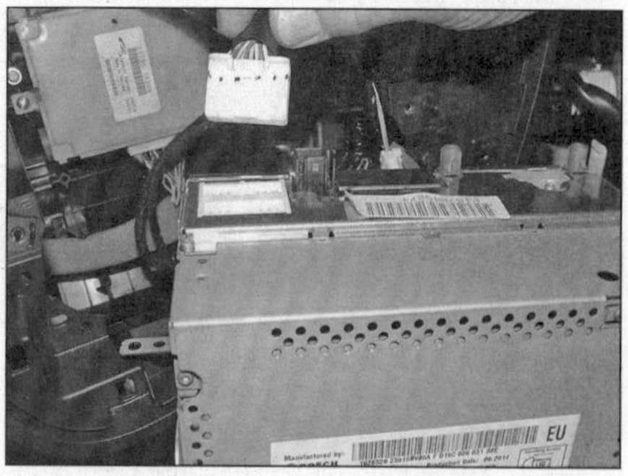

15.4 Withdraw audio unit from the facia and disconnect the wiring

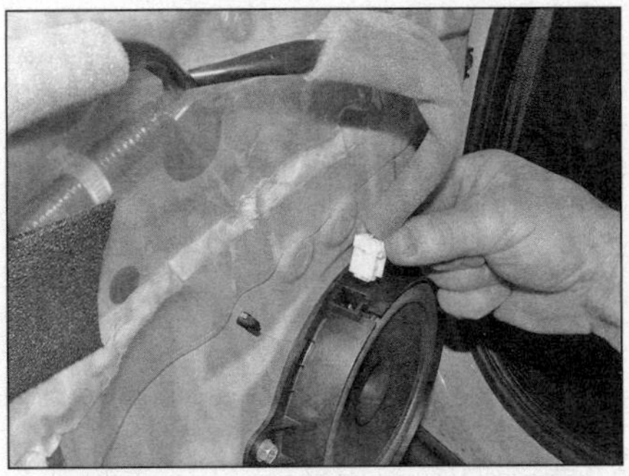

16.3 Disconnect the speaker wiring connector

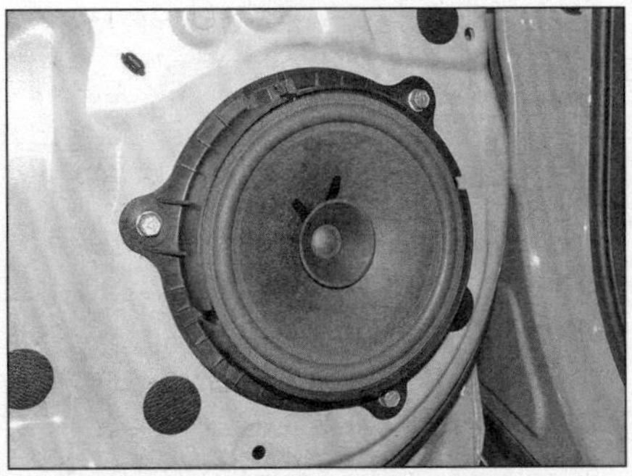

16.4 Undo the screws and remove the speaker

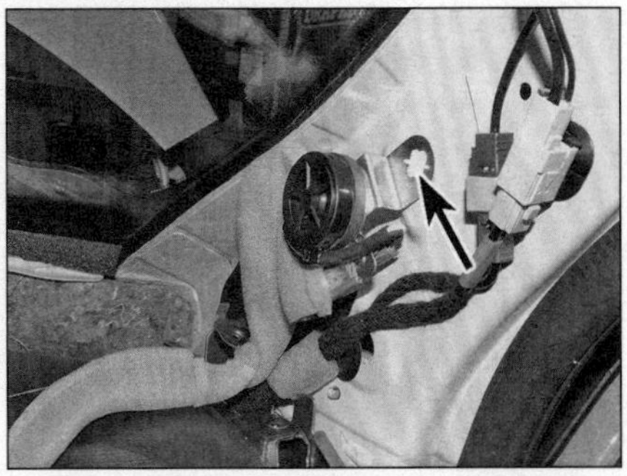

16.7 Release the clip and withdraw the speaker

Refitting

5 Refitting is a reversal of removal, ensuring that the wiring is freely routed behind the unit.

16 Loudspeakers – removal and refitting

1 Disconnect the battery negative terminal (refer to battery disconnection and reconnection in Chapter 5A, Section 3).

Door-mounted loudspeakers

2 Remove the door inner trim panel as described in Chapter 11, Section 12.

3 Disconnect the wiring connector from the door speaker **(see illustration)**.

4 Undo the three securing screws, and then withdraw the loudspeaker from the door panel **(see illustration)**.

5 Refitting is a reversal of removal, but refit the inner door trim panel with reference to Chapter 11, Section 12.

Pillar-mounted loudspeakers

6 Remove the relevant A-pillar trim panel as described in Chapter 11, Section 24.

7 Release the retaining clip and withdraw the speaker from the A-pillar **(see illustration)**.

8 Disconnect the wiring connector and remove the speaker.

9 Refitting is a reversal of removal.

17 Radio aerial – removal and refitting

Removal

1 Carefully release the rear portion of the headlining just sufficiently to gain access to the aerial.

2 Undo the retaining nut and disconnect the aerial lead, remove the aerial from the roof.

Refitting

3 Refitting is a reversal of removal, but ensure that the aerial lead is securely connected.

18 Anti-theft system and engine immobiliser – general information

1 All models in the range are equipped as standard with a central locking system incorporating an electronic engine immobiliser function.

2 The electronic engine immobiliser is operated by a transponder fitted to the ignition key, in conjunction with an analogue module fitted around the ignition switch.

3 When the ignition key is inserted in the switch and turned to the ignition 'on' position, the control module sends a preprogrammed recognition code signal to the analogue module on the ignition switch. If the recognition code signal matches that of the transponder on the ignition key, an unlocking request signal is sent to the engine management ECU allowing the engine to be started. If the ignition key signal is not recognised, the engine management system remains immobilised.

4 When the ignition is switched off, a locking signal is sent to the ECU and the engine is immobilised until the unlocking request signal is again received.

19 Intelligent key system components – general information

1 The intelligent key system is a keyless entry system, which allows you to operate your vehicle without using an actual key. This can only be used when the Intelligent Key remote is within a specified operating distance (80 cm with new battery) from the antennas or ignition switch. The antennas are located at various positions around the vehicle:

2 As the battery discharges over time, the operating distance becomes less, so a new battery will be required. Do not hold the Intelligent Key remote too close to the door, as this may also cause it to not function correctly. If a door is not closed securely, this will cause the Intelligent Key not to function properly. There is also a warning buzzer, which is positioned behind the front bumper.

20 Airbag system – general information, precautions and system de-activation

General information

1 A driver's and passenger's airbag are fitted as standard on all models. The driver's airbag is located in the steering wheel centre pad and the passenger's airbag is located above the glovebox in the facia. Side airbags are also available on certain models and are located in the front seats. Curtain airbags are also fitted to some models and are located behind the headlining around the outer edge.

2 The system is armed only when the ignition is switched on; however, a reserve power source maintains a power supply to the system in the event of a break in the main electrical supply. The steering wheel and facia airbags are activated by a sensor (deceleration sensor), and controlled by an electronic control unit located under the centre console. The side and curtain airbags are activated by severe side impact and operate in conjunction with the main system.

3 The airbags are inflated by a gas generator, which forces the bag out from its location in the steering wheel, facia or seat back frame.

Precautions

Warning: The following precautions must be observed when working on vehicles equipped with an airbag system, to prevent the possibility of personal injury.

General precautions

a) Do not disconnect the battery with the engine running.

b) Before carrying out any work in the vicinity of the airbag, removal of any of the airbag components, or any welding work on the vehicle, de-activate the system as described in the following sub-Section.

c) Do not attempt to test any of the airbag system circuits using test meters or any other test equipment.

d) If the airbag warning light comes on, or any fault in the system is suspected, consult a Nissan dealer without delay.

e) Do not attempt to carry out fault diagnosis, or any dismantling of the components.

Precautions when handling an airbag

a) Transport the airbag by itself, bag upward.
b) Do not put your arms around the airbag.
c) Carry the airbag close to the body, bag outward.
d) Do not drop the airbag or expose it to impacts.
e) Do not attempt to dismantle the airbag unit.
f) Do not connect any form of electrical equipment to any part of the airbag circuit.

Precautions when storing an airbag

a) Store the unit in a cupboard with the airbag upward.
b) Do not expose the airbag to temperatures above 80ºC.
c) Do not expose the airbag to flames.
d) Do not attempt to dispose of the airbag – consult a Nissan dealer.
e) Never refit an airbag that is known to be faulty or damaged.

De-activation of airbag system

4 The system must be de-activated before carrying out any work on the airbag components or surrounding area:

a) Switch on the ignition and check the operation of the airbag warning light on the instrument panel. The light should illuminate when the ignition is switched on, then extinguish.
b) Switch off the ignition.
c) Remove the ignition key.
d) Switch off all electrical equipment.
e) Disconnect the battery negative terminal (refer to battery disconnection and reconnection in Chapter 5A, Section 3).
f) Insulate the battery negative terminal and the end of the battery negative lead to prevent any possibility of contact.
g) Wait for at least ten minutes before carrying out any further work.

Activation of airbag system

5 To activate the system on completion of any work, proceed as follows:

a) Ensure that there are no occupants in the vehicle, and that there are no loose objects around the vicinity of the steering wheel. Close the vehicle doors and windows.
b) Ensure that the ignition is switched off then reconnect the battery negative terminal.
c) Open the driver's door and switch on the ignition, without reaching in front of the steering wheel. Check that the airbag warning light illuminates briefly then extinguishes.
d) Switch off the ignition.
e) If the airbag warning light does not operate as described in paragraph c), consult a Nissan dealer before driving the vehicle.

21 Airbag system components – removal and refitting

Warning: Refer to the precautions given in Section 20 before attempting to carry out work on any of the airbag components. Any suspected faults with the airbag system should be referred to a Nissan dealer – under no circumstances attempt to carry out any work other than removal and refitting of the front airbag unit(s) and/or the rotary connector, as described in the following paragraphs.

Note: *Disconnect the battery negative terminal (refer to battery disconnection and reconnection in Chapter 5A, Section 3), before the removal and refitting of components in the airbag system.*

Driver's airbag unit

Removal

1 De-activate the airbag system as described in Section 20.
2 Working at each side of the steering wheel, carefully extract the trim caps over the airbag retaining bolts **(see illustration)**.
3 Undo the two Torx bolts securing the airbag to the steering wheel **(see illustration)**.
4 Withdraw the airbag from the steering wheel and disconnect the two wiring connectors **(see illustration)**.
5 Using a thin screwdriver, release the centre locking catch and disconnect the airbag wiring connector from the rear of the airbag unit **(see illustrations)**.
6 Carefully remove the airbag from the steering wheel.
7 If the airbag unit is to be stored for any length of time, refer to the storage precautions given in Section 20.

Refitting

8 Refitting is a reversal of removal, bearing in mind the following points:

a) Do not strike the airbag unit, or expose it to impacts during refitting.
b) On completion of refitting, activate the airbag system as described in Section 20.

Airbag rotary connector assembly

Removal

9 Remove the driver's airbag unit, as described previously in this Section.
10 With the steering in the straight–ahead position, remove the steering wheel as described in Chapter 10, Section 12.

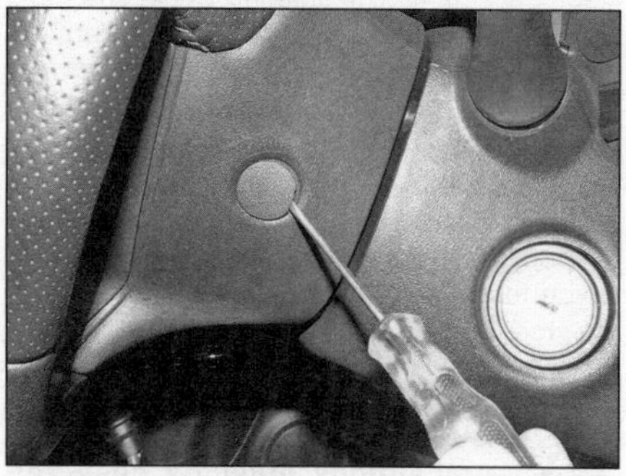

21.2 Extract the trim caps from each side of the steering wheel

21.3 Undo the airbag retaining bolt on each side of the steering wheel

21.4 Disconnect the wiring connectors from the steering wheel

21.5a Lift up the locking catch...

21.5b ...and disconnect the wiring connector from the airbag

21.12 Disconnect the unit wiring connectors

21.13 Undo the rotary connector retaining screws

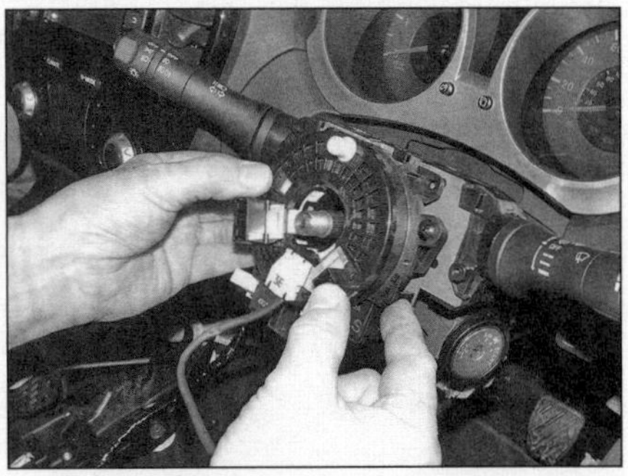

21.14 Release the clips and withdraw the rotary connector assembly

11 Remove the steering column upper and lower shrouds, as described in Chapter 11, Section 26.

12 Disconnect the wiring connectors, below the steering column, for the rotary connector and steering angle sensor **(see illustration)**.

13 Undo the two screws securing the rotary connector to the steering column **(see illustration)**.

14 Release the lower retaining clips and withdraw the rotary connector assembly from the steering column **(see illustration)**.

15 Use insulating tape to keep the rotary switch in position to prevent it from turning whilst it is removed **(see illustration)**.

Refitting

16 Refitting is a reversal of removal, bearing in mind the following points:

a) Make sure the rotary connector has not been turned and the insulating tape is still in position.

b) Ensure that the roadwheels are in the straight-ahead position before refitting the rotary connector and steering wheel.

c) If there is any doubt about the position of the rotary connector, turn it clockwise to the stop, then turn it anti-clockwise approximately two and a half turns. When the arrow appears in the window, the unit is centralised **(see illustration)**.

d) Before refitting the steering column shrouds, ensure that the rotary connector wiring harness is correctly routed as noted before removal.

e) Refit the steering wheel as described in Chapter 10, Section 12, and refit the airbag unit as described previously in this Section.

Passenger's airbag unit

Removal

17 The passenger's airbag is fitted to the upper part of the facia, above the glovebox.

18 De-activate the airbag system as described in Section 20.

19 Remove the glovebox as described in Chapter 11, Section 26.

20 Disconnect the airbag wiring connector **(see illustration)**.

21 Undo the two bolts securing the airbag assembly to the facia support rail, and then release the retaining clips and carefully withdraw the airbag from the facia **(see illustration)**.

22 If the airbag unit is to be stored for any length of time, refer to the storage precautions given in Section 20.

Refitting

23 Refitting is a reversal of removal, bearing in mind the following points:

a) Use new bolts to secure the airbag unit and tighten the bolts to the specified torque.

b) Do not strike the airbag unit, or expose it to impacts during refitting.

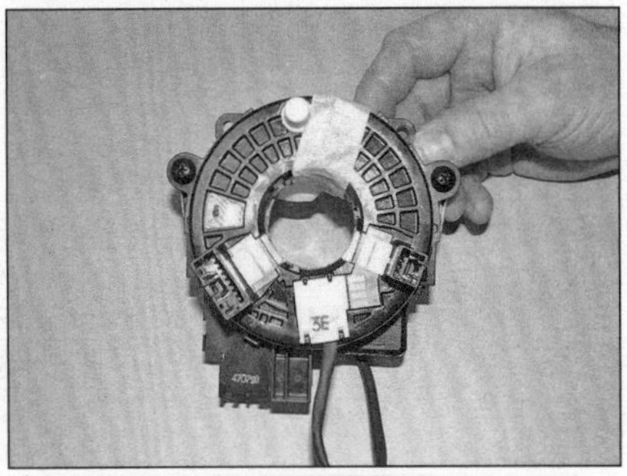

21.15 Secure the rotary switch in place using tape

c) On completion of refitting, activate the airbag system as described in Section 20.

Side airbag units

24 The side airbags are located internally within the front seat back and no attempt should be made to remove them. Any suspected problems with the side airbag system should be referred to a Nissan dealer.

Curtain airbag units

25 The curtain airbags are located internally behind the headlining and no attempt should be made to remove them. Any suspected problems with the curtain airbag system should be referred to a Nissan dealer.

21.16 When the arrow appears in the window, the rotary connector is centralised

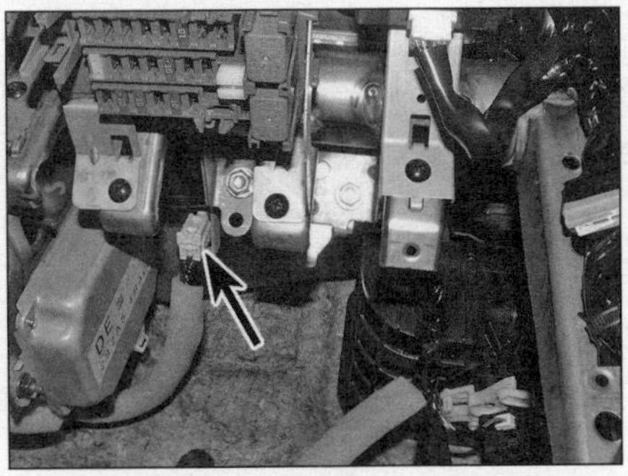

21.20 Disconnect the airbag wiring connector

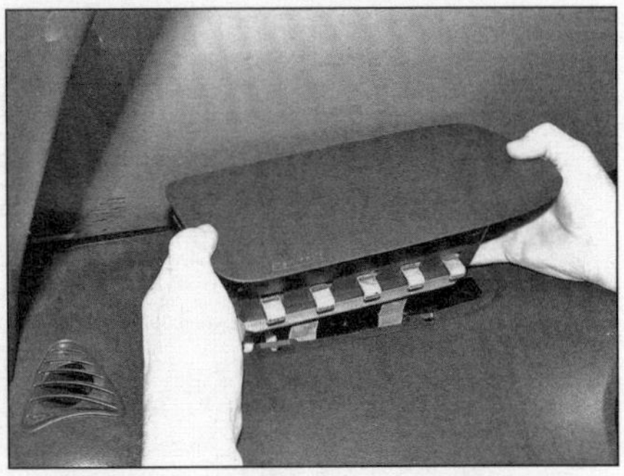

21.21 Release the retaining clips and withdraw the airbag from the facia

INTELLIGENT POWER DISTRIBUTION MODULE IN ENGINE COMPARTMENT

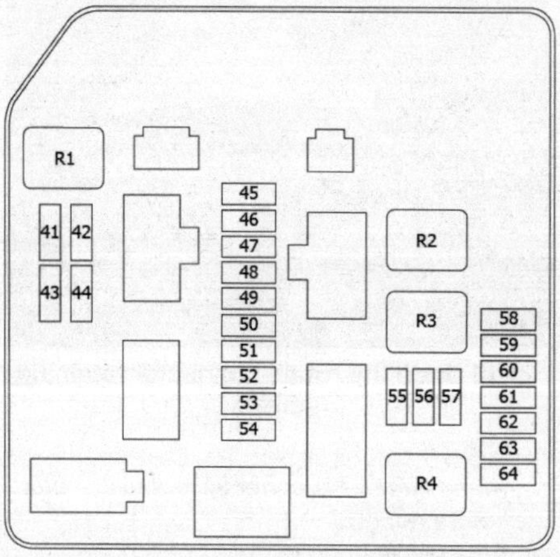

FUSE/RELAY	VALUE	DESCRIPTION
F41	20 A	Rear windscreen defroster relay
F42	-	Not used
F43	20 A	Engine control unit relay
F44	10 A	Steering column lock relay (power steering)
F45	30 A	Front wiper relay
F46	10 A	Rear left combination light, Illumination lights, Luggage compartment opening
F47	10 A	Rear right combination light, Illumination lights
F48	-	Not used
F49	10 A	Air-conditioning relay
F50	15 A	Front right fog lights, Fuel pump relay
F51	10 A	Right dipped beam
F52	10 A	Left dipped beam
F53	15 A	Left dipped beam
F54	15 A	Right dipped beam
F55	10 A	Transmission, Engine management
F56	10 A	Transmission, Intelligent power distribution module, Starter relay
F57	10 A	ABS control unit
F58	-	Not used
F59	-	Not used
F60	15 A	Fuel pump relay
F61	15 A	Condenser Ignition coils
F62	15 A	Injectors Engine control unit
F63	-	Not used
F64	15 A	Throttle control motor relay
R1	-	Rear window defogger relay
R2	-	Cooling fan relay 2
R3	-	Cooling fan relay 1
R4	-	Ignition relay

Fuses and relays

FUSE AND RELAY BOX IN PASSENGER COMPARTMENT 1

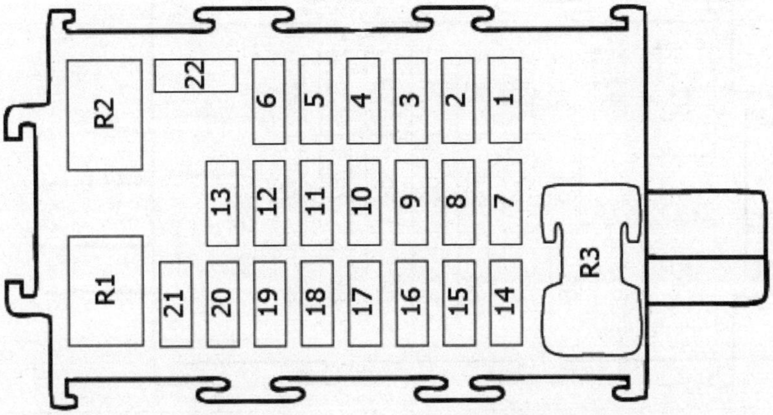

FUSE/RELAY	VALUE	DESCRIPTION
F1	10 A	Airbag diagnostic module
F2	10 A	Combination switch
F3	10 A	Data link connector, Brake pedal position sensor, Combination switch, Engine control unit, Brake light switch, EPS, Audio amplifier, Door-lock motors, PTC heater relay, Brake pedal switch, Heated seat relay, Steering angle sensor Headlight(s) Optional
F4	10 A	Body control unit
F5	10 A	Parkeutral position switch, Combination meter
F6	-	Not used
F7	10 A	Clutch switch, Ignition switch
F8	15 A	Heated seat relay
F9	10 A	Body control unit, Optional connector
F10	20 A	Optional connector
F11	10 A	Combination meter
F12	-	Not used
F13	10 A	Clutch interlock switch (manual transmission), Ignition switch Or Data link connector, Amplifier PTC heater control Key warning buzzer, Door mirrors Lights switch, Rain sensor Key switch, Optional connector, Multimedia display
F14	15 A	Air conditioning, Blower motor, Power transistor
F15	10 A	Amplifier, Air-conditioning thermostat Or Amplifier Air-conditioning thermostat, Engine restart control relay
F16	15 A	Air conditioning, Blower motor, Power transistor
F17	10 A	Daylight running system relay, Intelligent power distribution module
F18	10 A	Body control unit, Door mirrors, Audio unit, Combination meter, Navigation control unit, Optional connector
F19	10 A	Audio Combination meter, Navigation Handsfree control unit, Optional connector
F20	-	Not used
F21	20 A	Power socket
F22	10 A	Door mirrors
R1	-	Accessory relay
R2	-	Ignition relay
R3	-	Blower relay

Fuses and relays (continued)

FUSE AND RELAY BOX IN PASSENGER COMPARTMENT 2

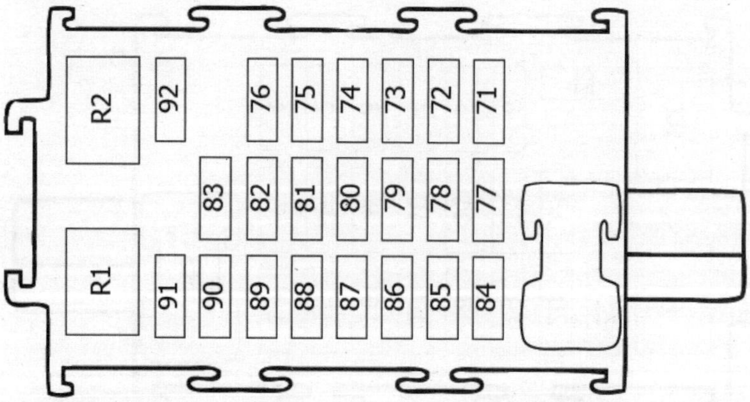

FUSE/RELAY	VALUE	DESCRIPTION
F71	-	Not used
F72	10 A	Combination meter
F73	10 A	Amplifier, Multimedia display
F74	-	Not used
F75	10 A	ABS actuator unit, Steering angle sensor
F76	-	Not used
F77	10 A	Audio Navigation
F78	-	Not used
F79	-	Not used
F80	-	Not used
F81	10 A	Multimedia display
F82	-	Not used
F83	-	Not used
F84	-	Not used
F85	-	Not used
F86	-	Not used
F87	-	Not used
F88	-	Not used
F89	10 A	No information is available
F90	-	Not used
F91	-	Not used
F92	-	Not used
R1	-	Accessory relay
R2	-	Ignition relay

Fuses and relays (continued)

FUSE AND RELAY IN BATTERY COMPARTMENT WITHOUT START / STOP SYSYEM

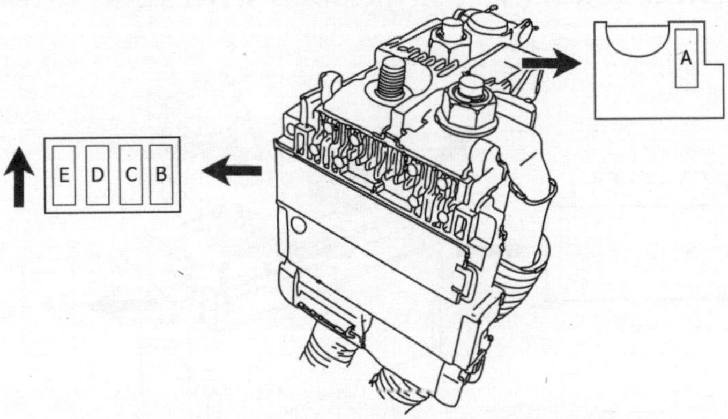

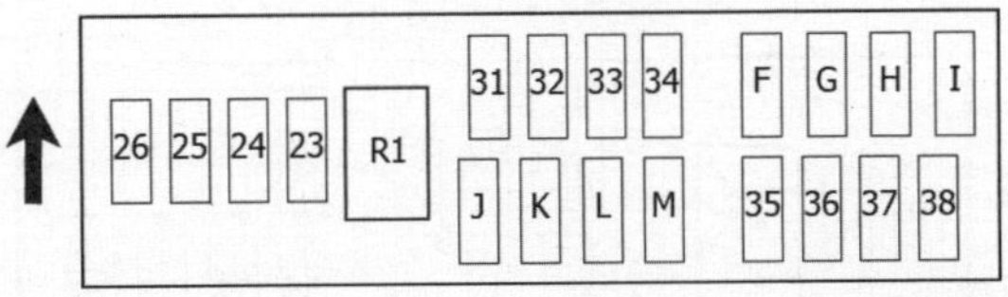

FUSE/RELAY	VALUE	DESCRIPTION
F A	225 A	Main fuse, Alternator, Starter motor
F B	100	ABS control unit, Headlight washer relay, Horn relay, Alternator, TCM, PTC, Fuel pump, EPS control unit, Security alarm, Brake light switch, BCM
F C	60 A	Front wipers
F D	100 A	Front wipers, Front fog light relay, Headlights, main beam and dipped beam, Tail lights, Air conditioning, Ignition supply or Ignition supply, Headlights, Tail lights, Front fog lights (80 A also used)
F E	80 A	No information is available
F F	40 A	ABS control unit
F G	40 A	Body control unit
F H	40 A	Starter relay, Engine restart relay, Ignition swich, IPDM
F I	50 A	ABS control unit (40 A also used)
F J	50 A	IPDM, Cooling fan relay (40 A also used)
F K	30 A	ABS control unit
F L	30 A	Headlight washer relay
F M	60 A	EPS control unit,
F 23	-	Not used
F 24	-	Not used
F 25	10 A	Daylight running system
F 26	10 A	Daylight running system
F31	20 A	Daylight running system, Fuel running system (10 A also used)
F32	15 A	PTC, Fuel injector relay
F33	10 A	TCM, Daytime running system
F34	10 A	Optional connector, Audio, Navigation
F35	10 A	Alternator, Horn relay
F36	10 A	TCM, PTC, Fuel pump relay
F37	10 A	Alarm horn relay
F38	10 A	Body control unit, Brake light switch
R1	-	Horn relay

Fuses and relays (continued)

FUSE AND RELAY IN BATTERY COMPARTMENT WITH START / STOP SYSYEM

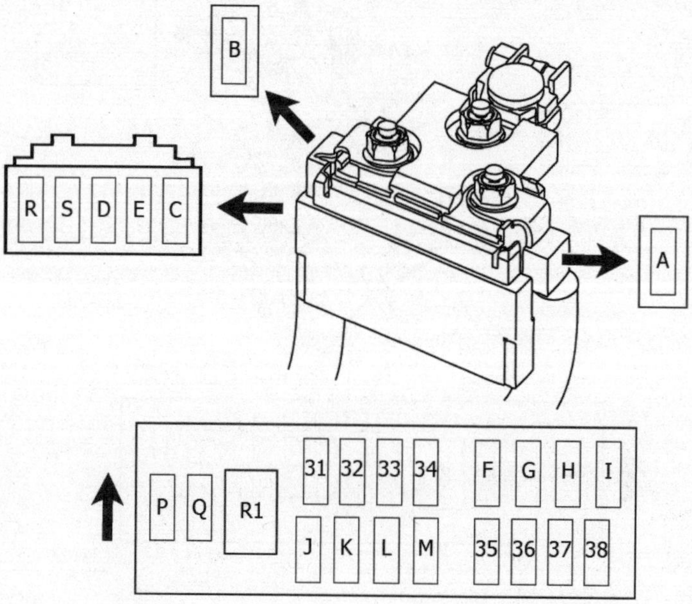

FUSE/RELAY	VALUE	DESCRIPTION
F A	450 A	Alternator
F B	450 A	Engine restart bypass relay
F C	100 A	ABS control unit, Headlight washer relay, Horn relay, Alternator, TCM, PTC, Fuel pump relay, EPS control unit, Brake lightswitch, BCM,
F D	100 A	Front wipers, Front fog light relay, Headlights, main beam and dipped beam, Tail lights, Air conditioning, Ignition supply or Ignition supply, Headlights, Tail lights, Front fog lights (80 A also used)
F E	100 A	No information is available
F F	40 A	PTC
F G	40 A	Body control module
F H	40 A	Starter relay, Engine restart relay, Ignition switch
F I	30 A	PTC
F J	50 A	IPDM
F K	30 A	ABS control unit
F L	30 A	Headlight washer relay
F M	60 A	EPS control unit
F P	30 A	DC-DC converter
F Q	30 A	DC-DC converter
F R	100 A	No information is available
F S	50 A	ABS control unit
F 31	20 A	Daytime running system, Fuel injector relay(10 A also used)
F 32	30 A	PTC, Fuel injector relay (10 A also used)
F 33	10 A	Daytime running system
F 34	10 A	Engine control relay
F 35	10 A	Alternator, Horn relay
F 36	20 A	Fuel preheater relay (10 A also used)
F 37	10 A	Alarm horn relay
F 38	10 A	BCM, Brake light switch
R1	-	Horn relay

Fuses and relays (continued)

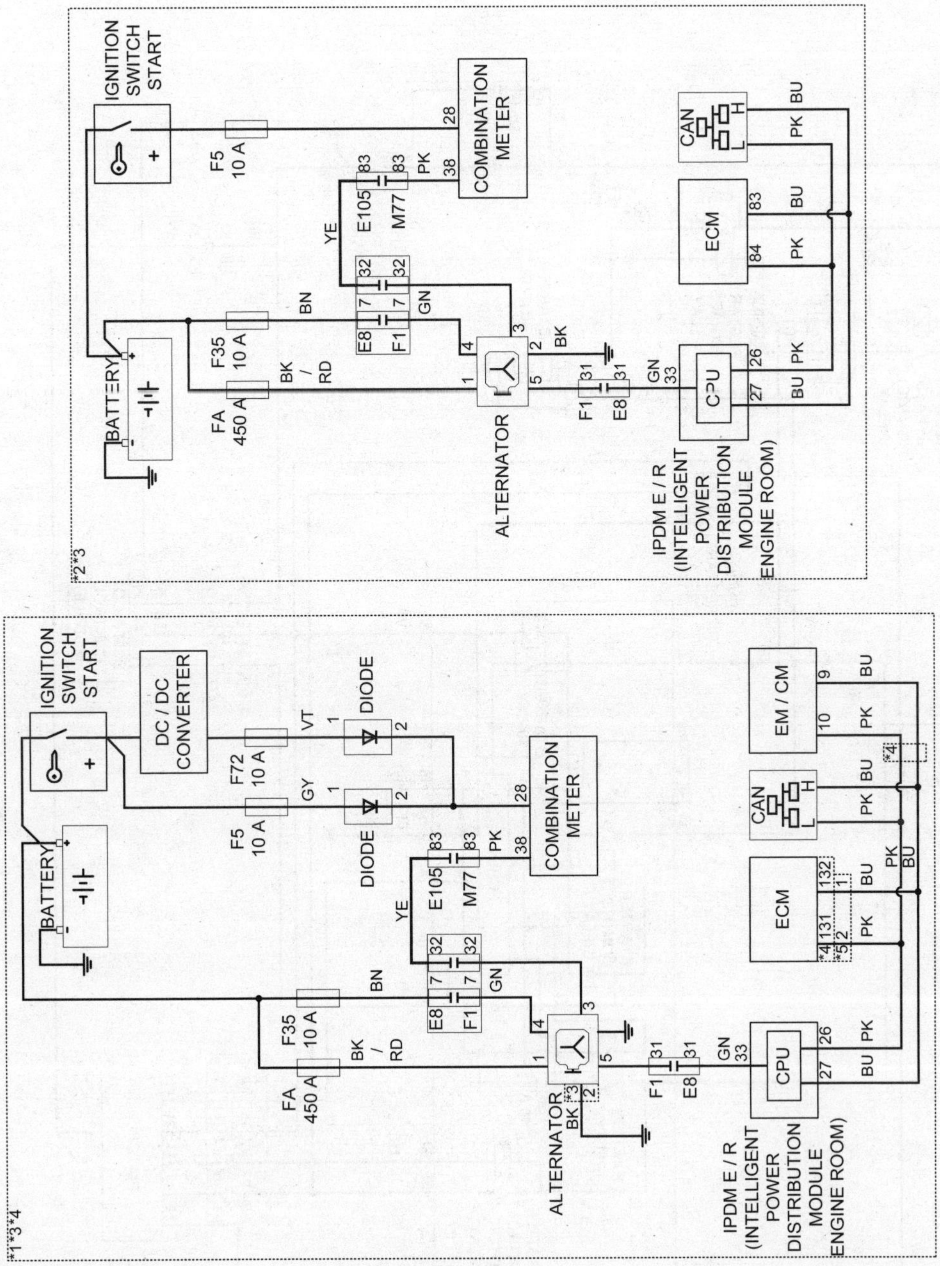

Charging system

*1 With start stop
*2 Without start stop
*3 Petrol
*4 Diesel

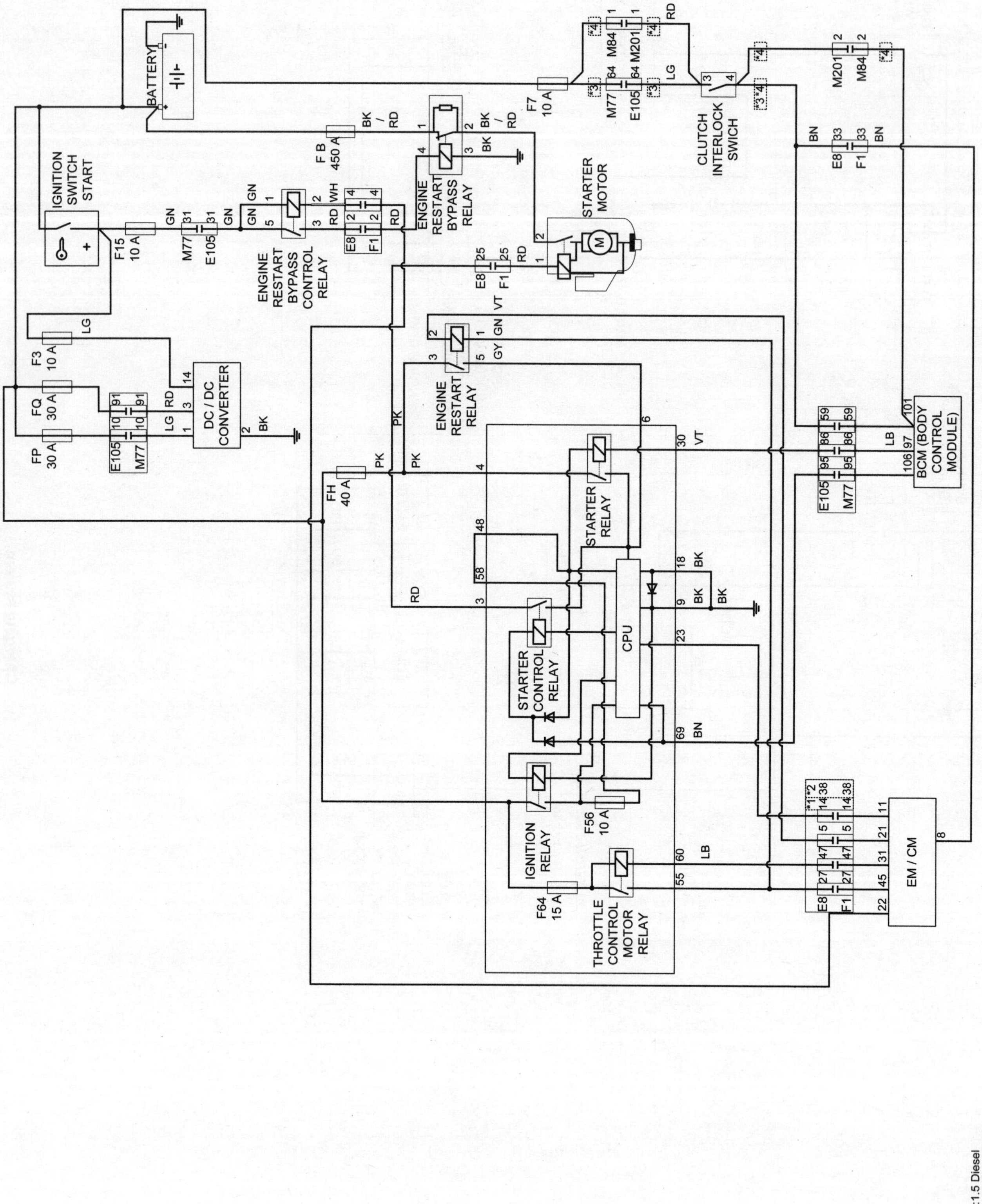

Starting – with keyless

*1 Engine:1.5 Diesel
*2 Engine:1.2 Petrol
*3 LHD models
*4 RHD models

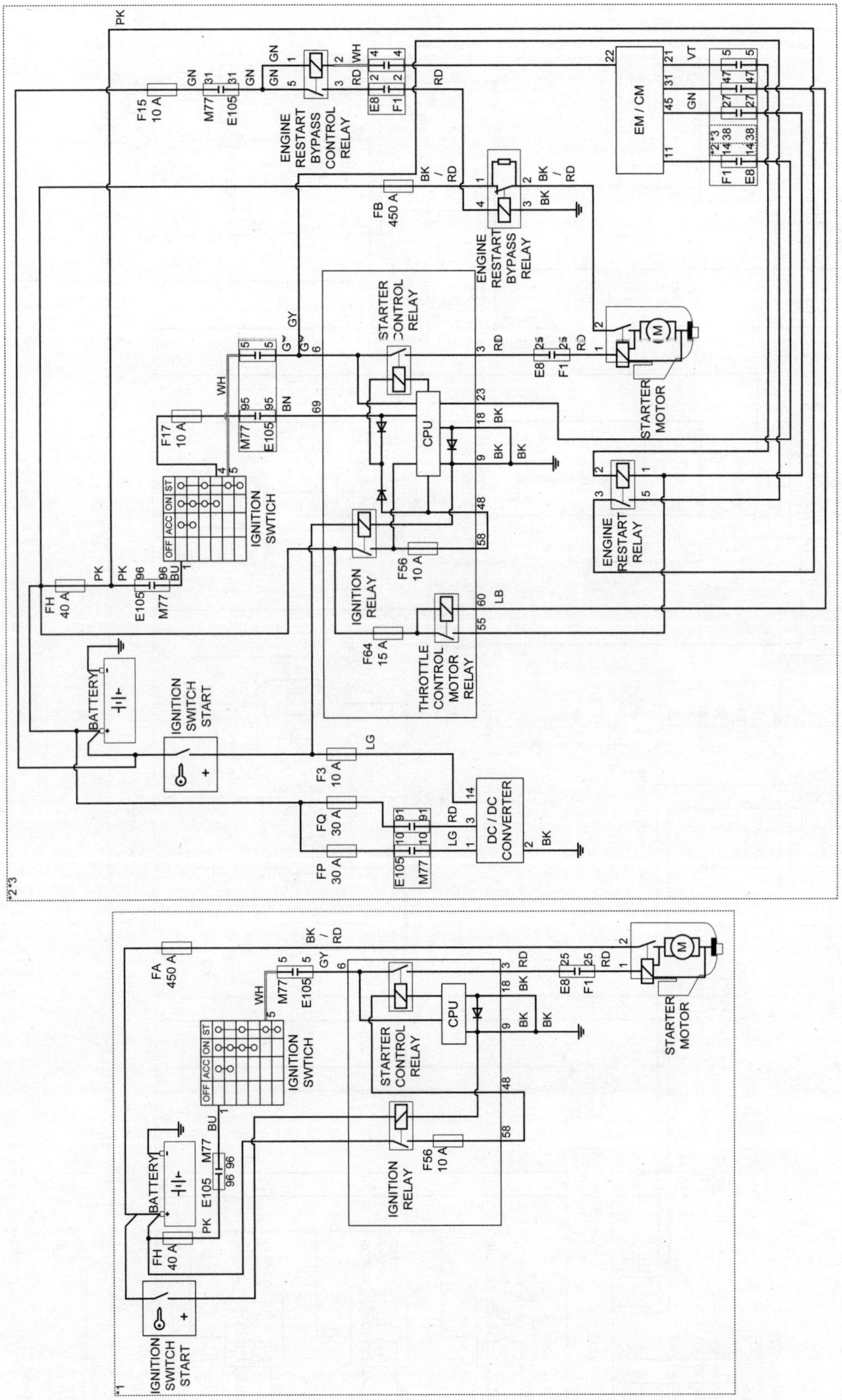

Sarting – without keyless

*1 Engine: 1.6 Petrol
*2 Engine: 1.2 Petrol
*3 Engine: 1.5 Diesel

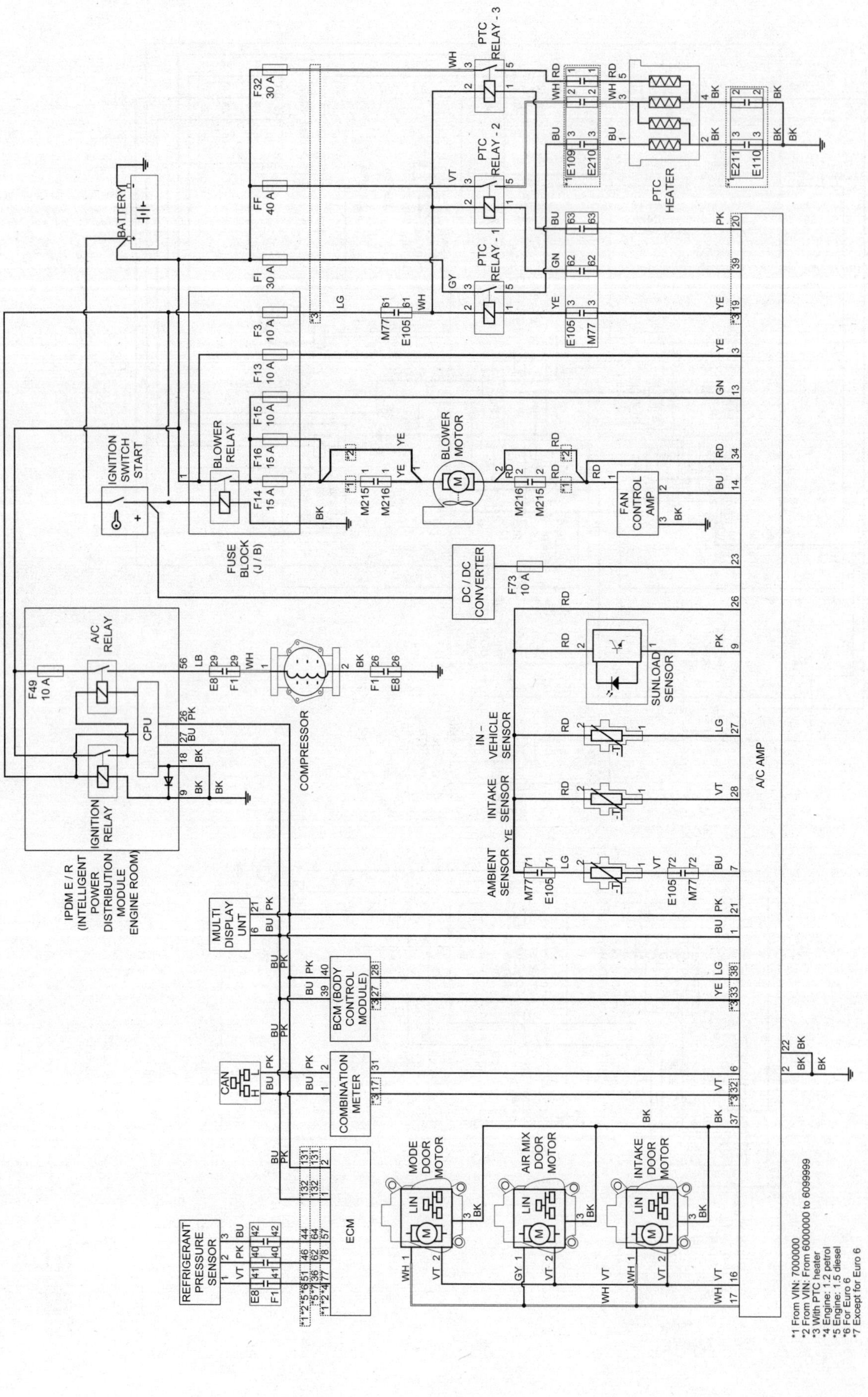

*1 From VIN: 7000000
*2 From VIN: From 6000000 to 6099999
*3 With PTC heater
*4 Engine: 1.2 petrol
*5 Engine: 1.5 diesel
*6 For Euro 6
*7 Except for Euro 6

AC Heating & Cooling – Auto air conditioning with Start stop

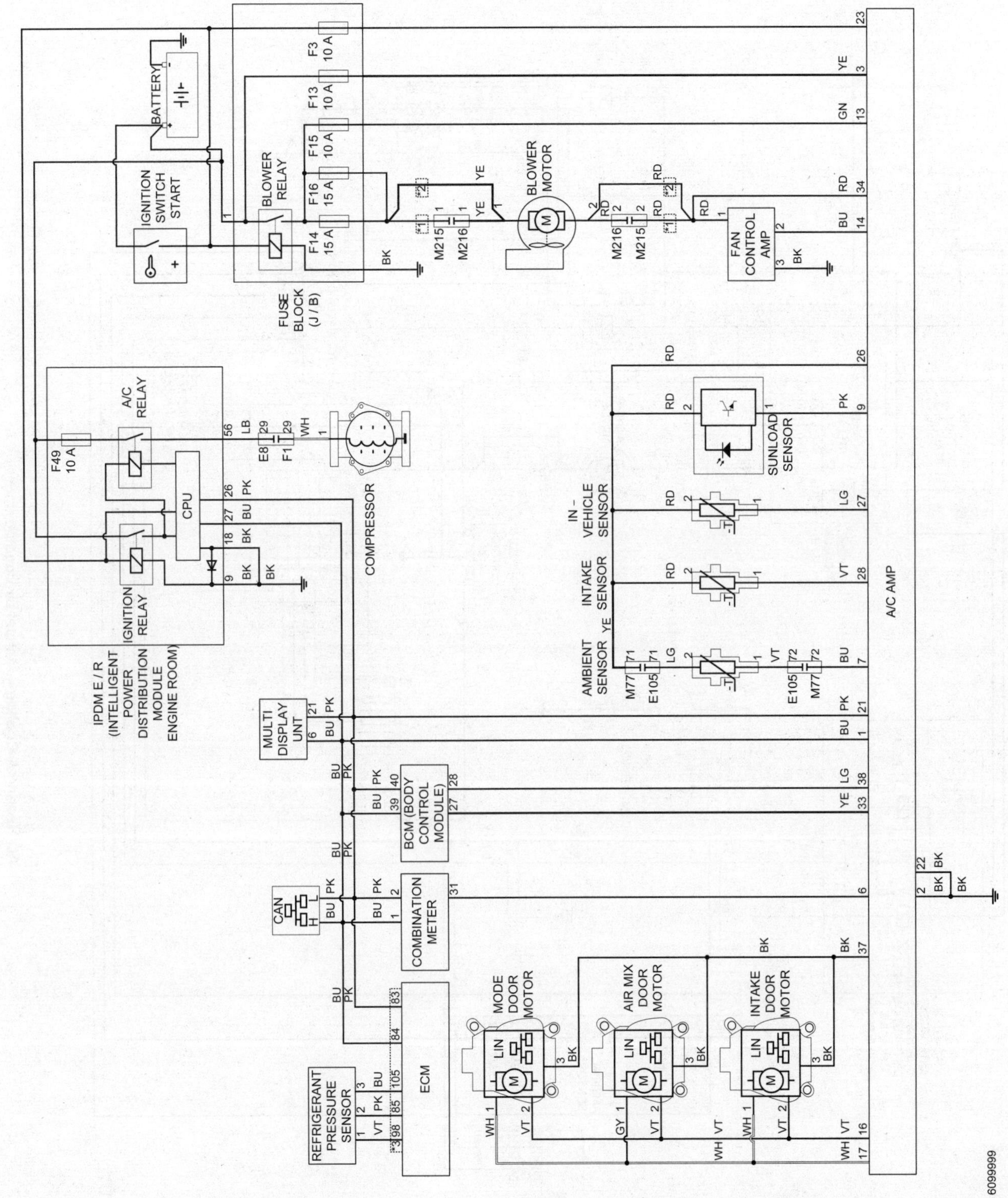

AC Heating & Cooling – Auto air conditioning without Start stop

*1 From VIN: 7000000
*2 From VIN: From 6000000 to 6099999
*3 Engine: 1.6 petrol

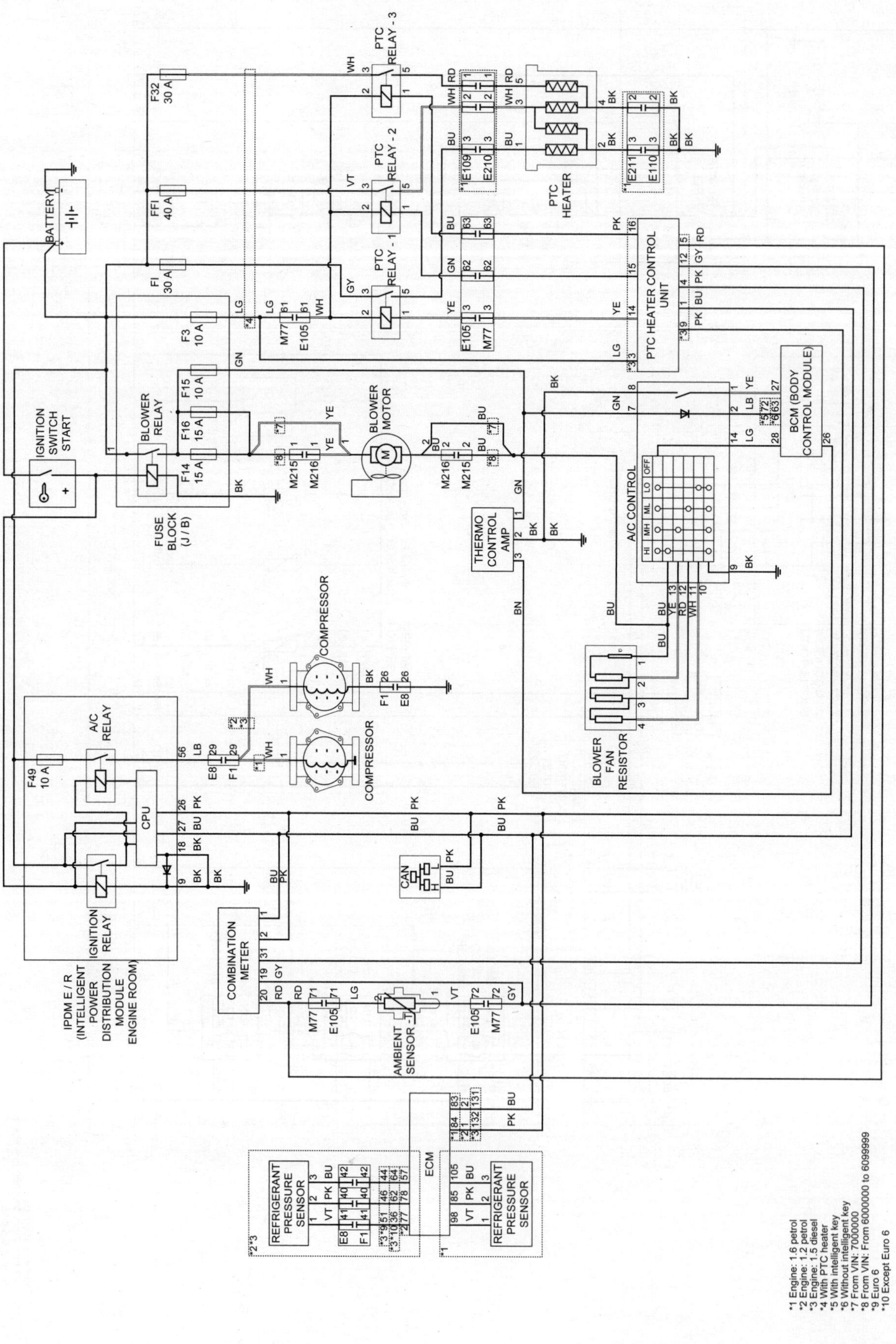

*1 Engine: 1.6 petrol
*2 Engine: 1.2 petrol
*3 Engine: 1.5 diesel
*4 With PTC heater
*5 With intelligent key
*6 Without intelligent key
*7 From VIN: 7000000
*8 From VIN: From 6000000 to 6099999
*9 Euro 6
*10 Except Euro 6

AC Heating & Cooling – Manual air conditioning

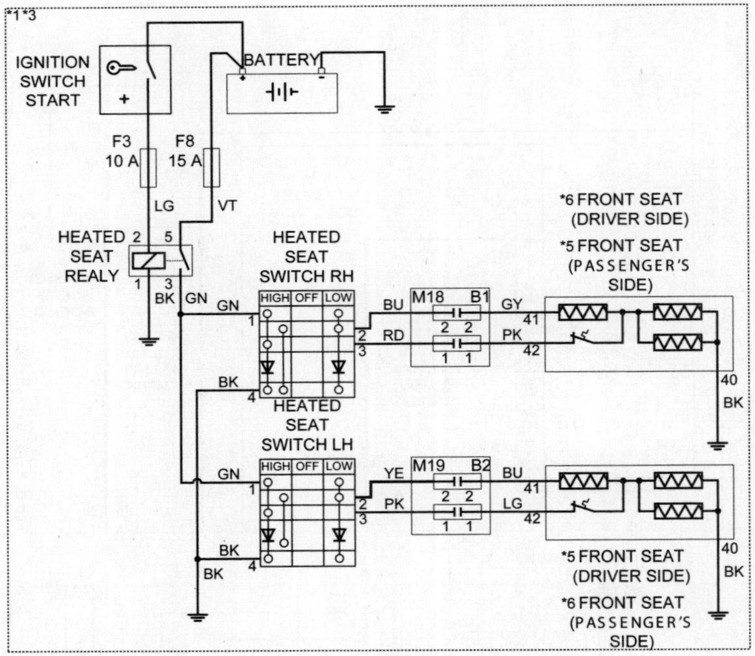

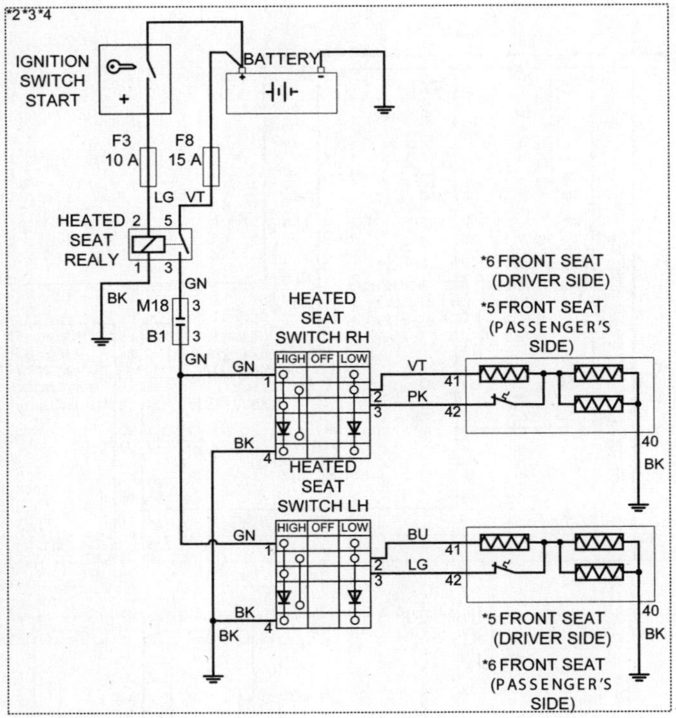

*1 From 07.2010 to 04.2014
*2 From 05.2014
*3 Type A
*4 Type B
*5 LHD models
*6 RHD models

AC Heating & Cooling - Seat heater

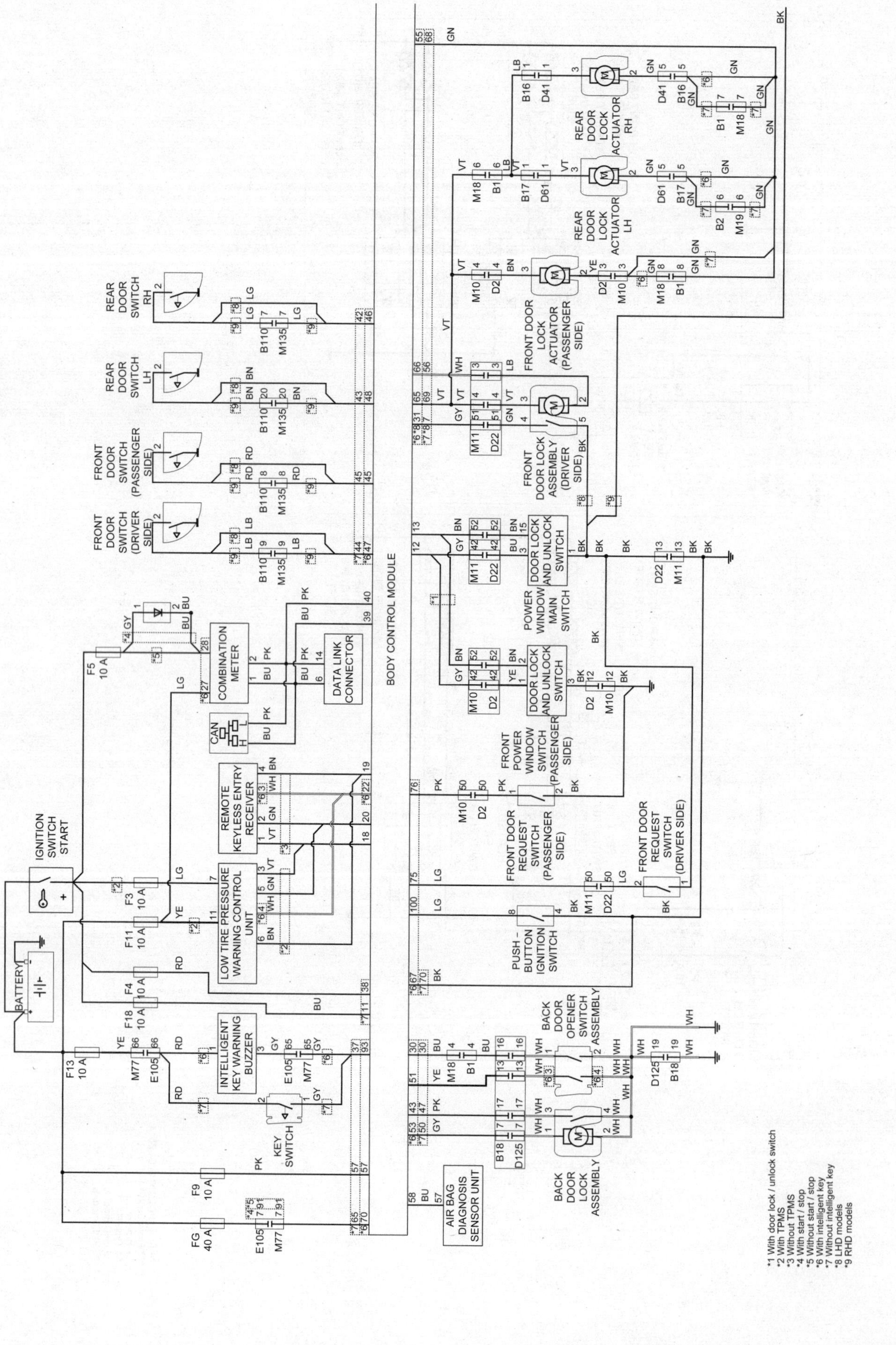

Power door locks (1 of 2)

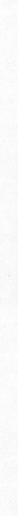

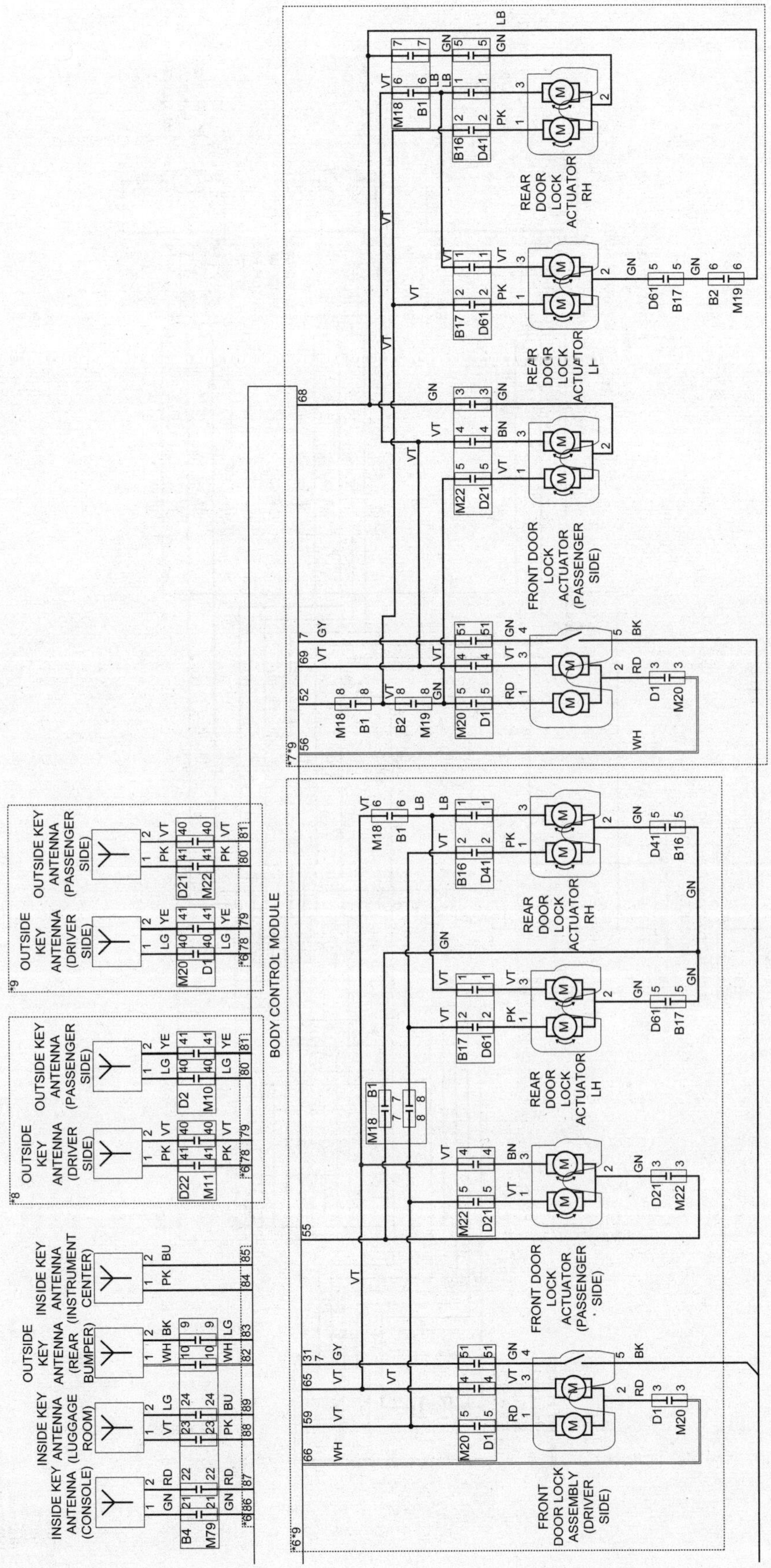

Power door locks (2 of 2)

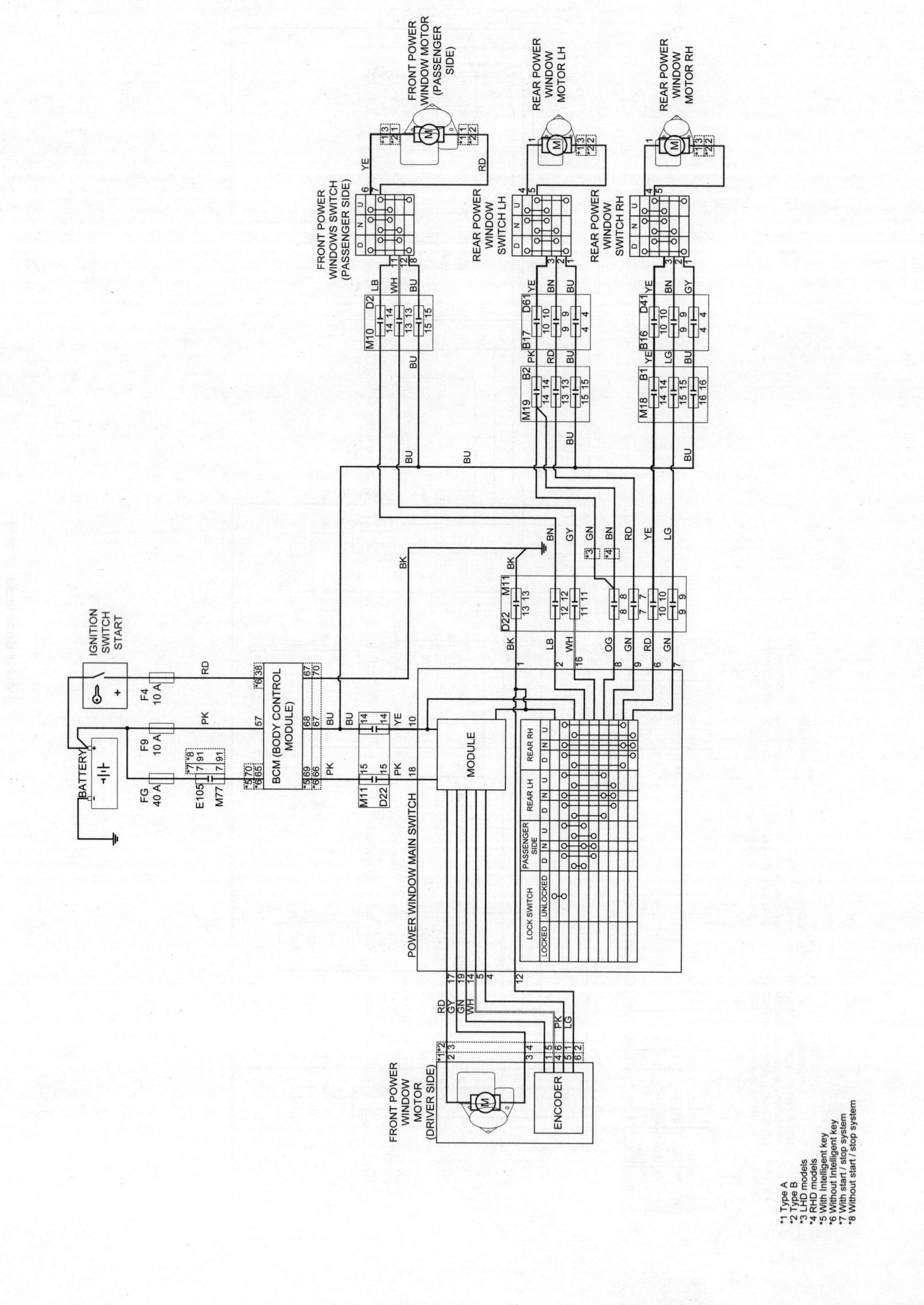

Power windows

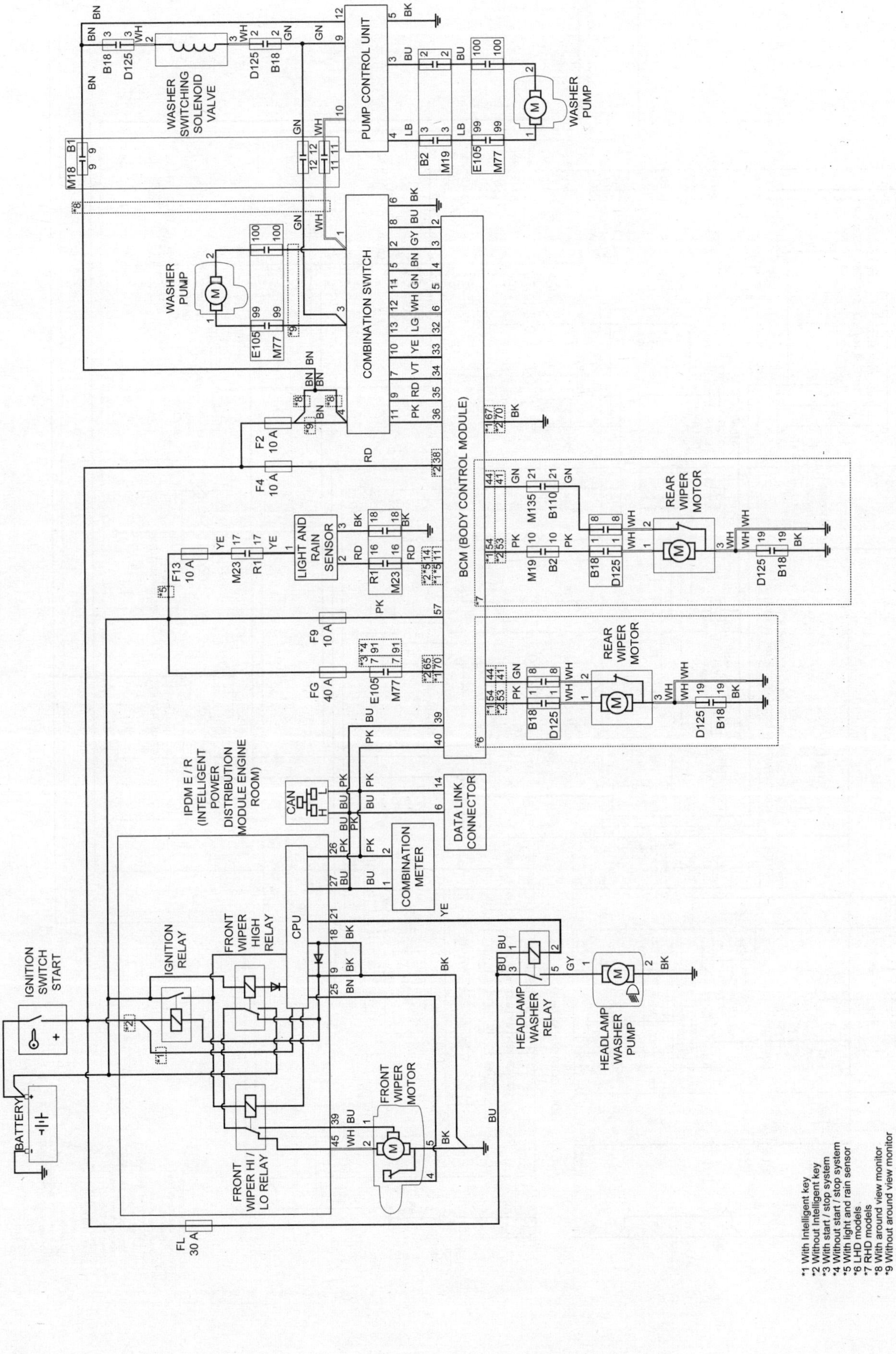

Wiper / washer

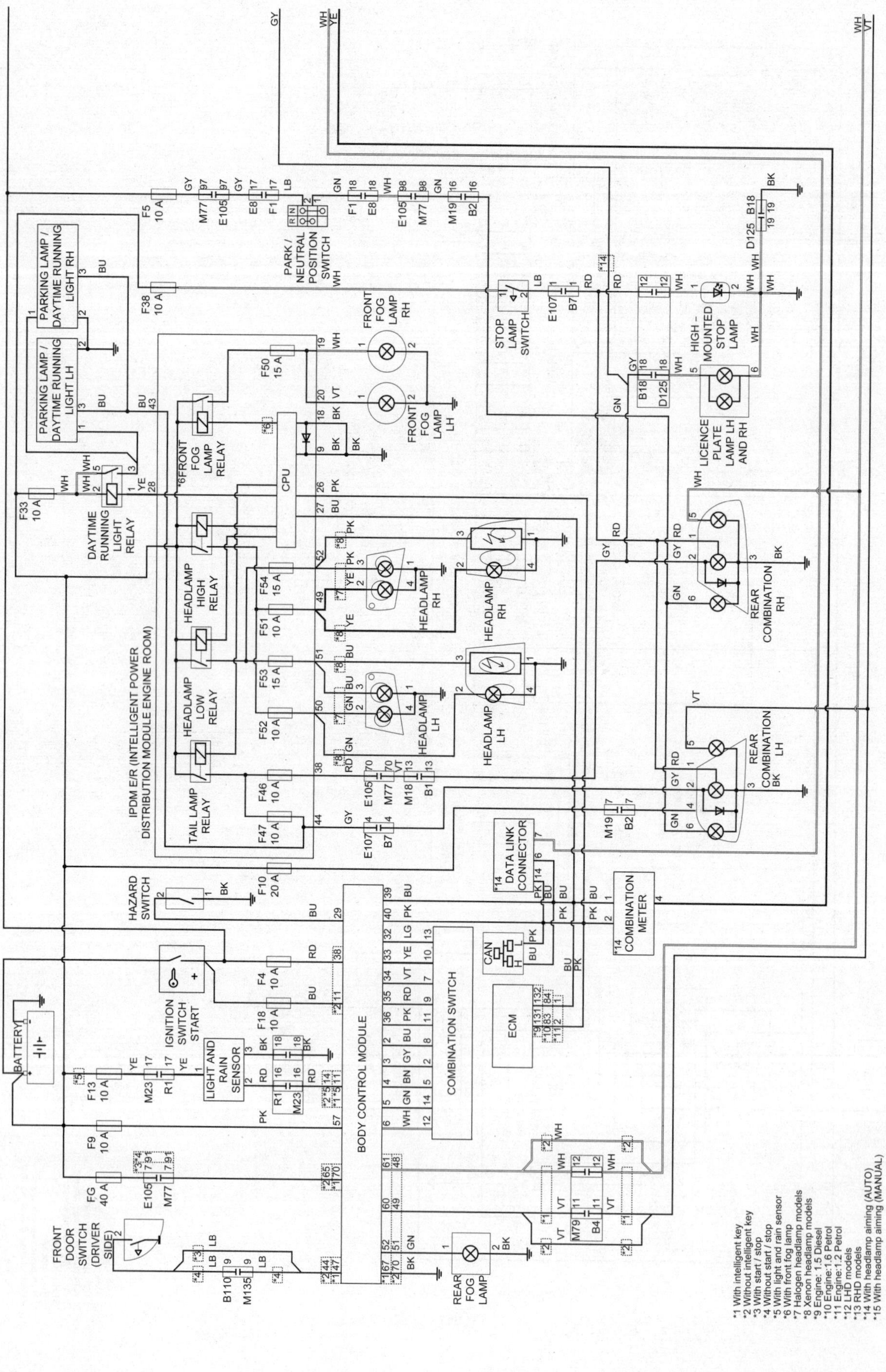

Exterior lights (1 od 2)

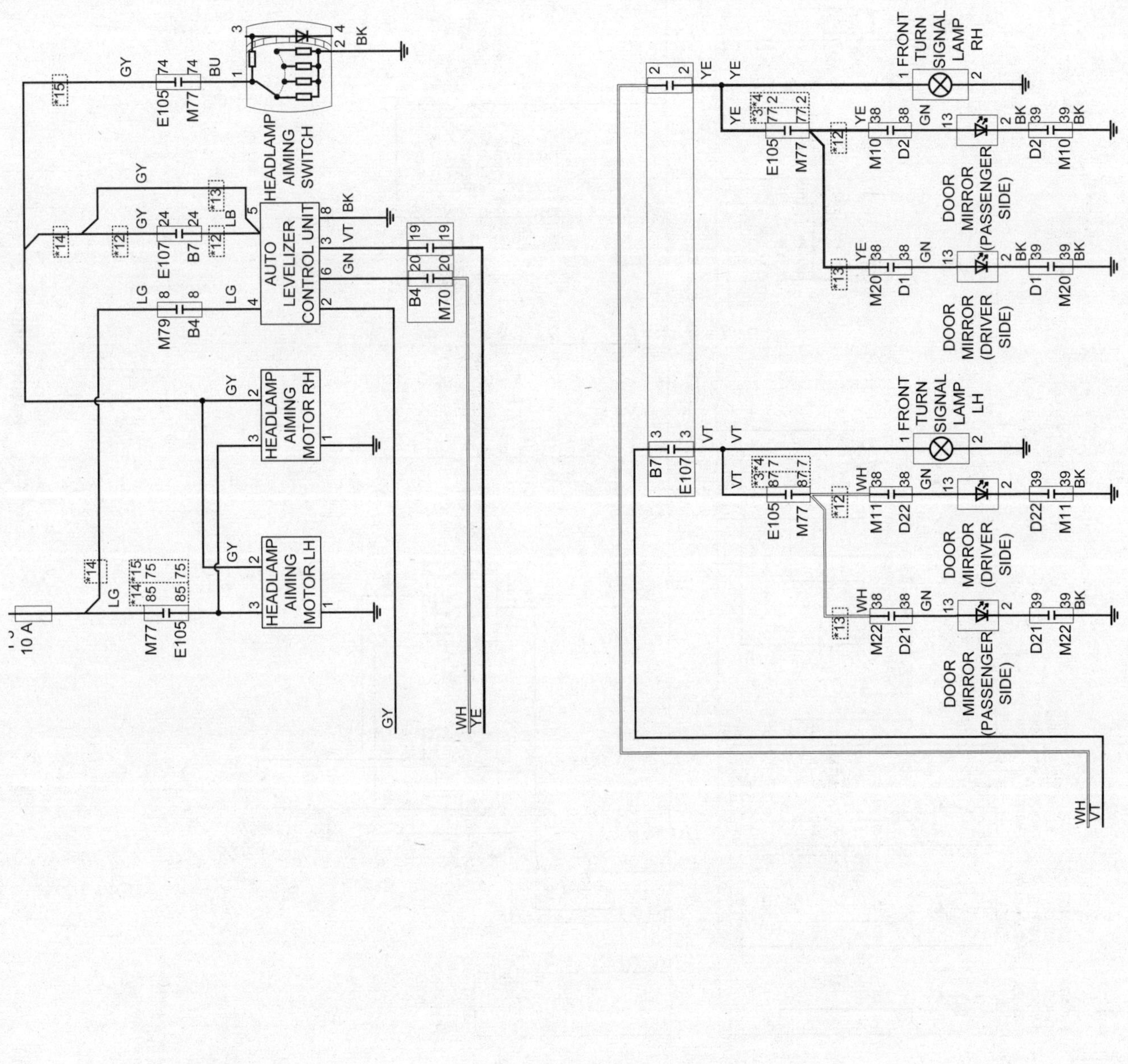

Exterior lights (2 of 2)

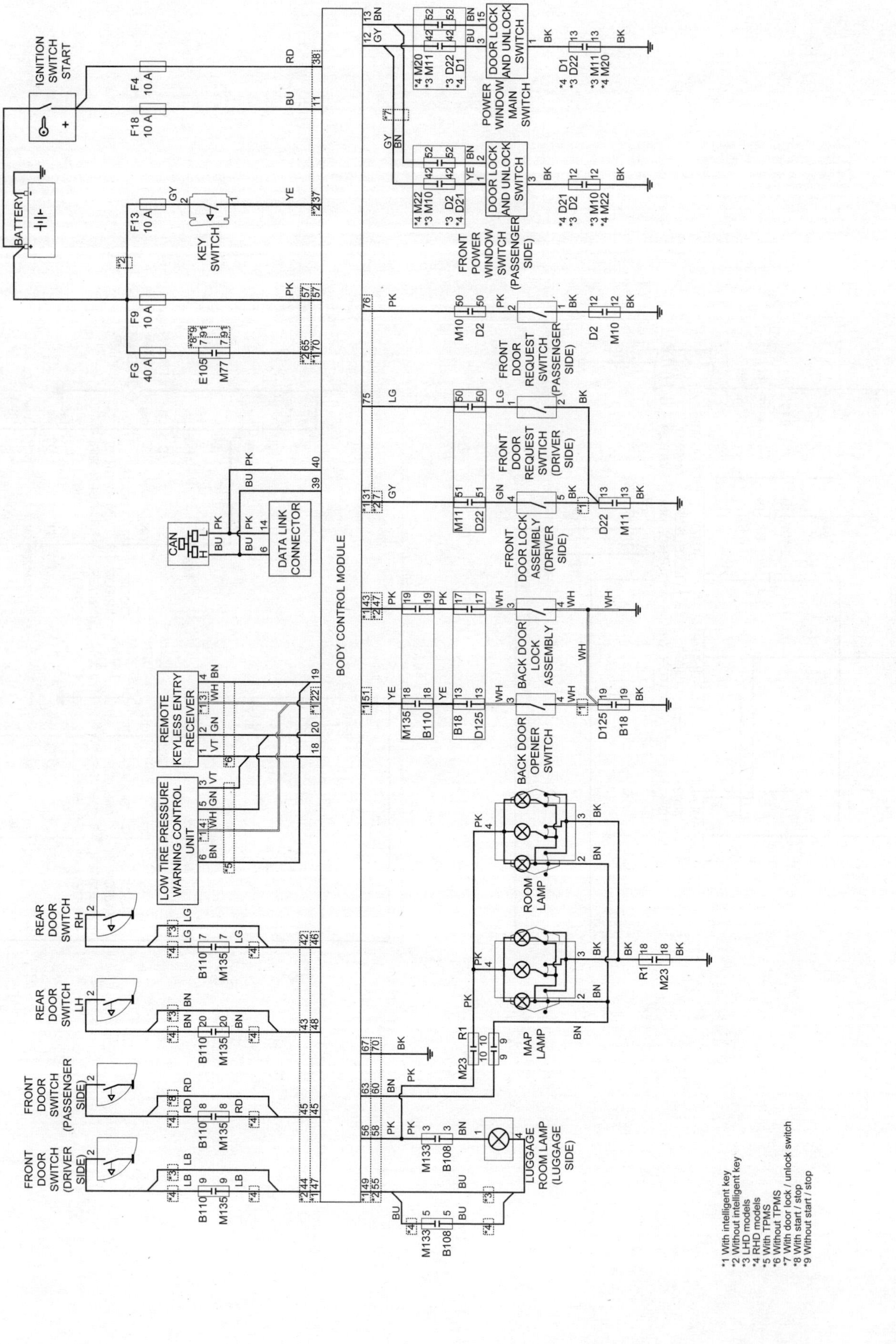

Interior lights

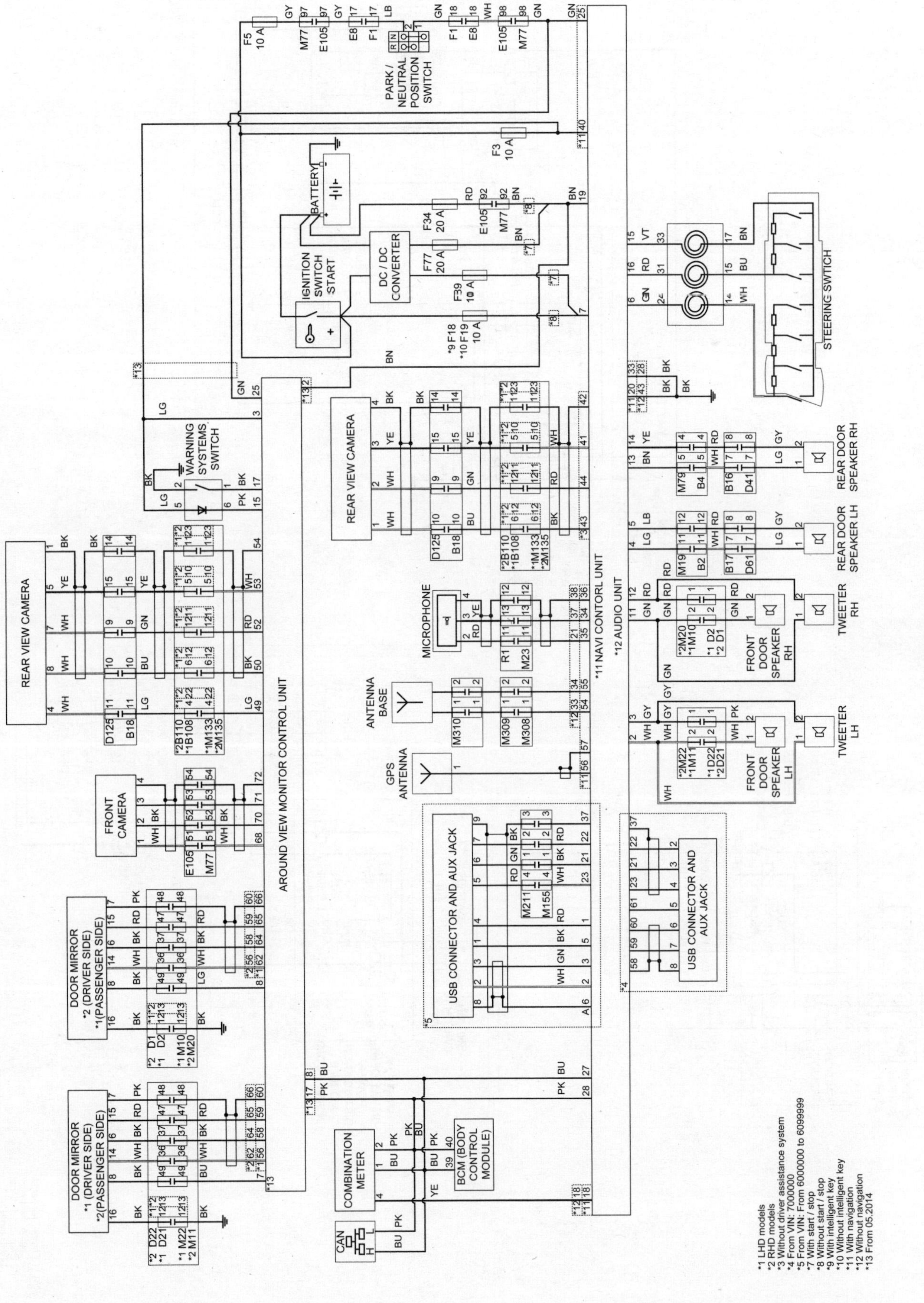

*1 LHD models
*2 RHD models
*3 Without driver assistance system
*4 From VIN: 7000000
*5 From VIN: From 6000000 to 6099999
*7 With start / stop
*8 Without start / stop
*9 With intelligent key
*10 Without intelligent key
*11 With navigation
*12 Without navigation
*13 From 05.2014

Sound system

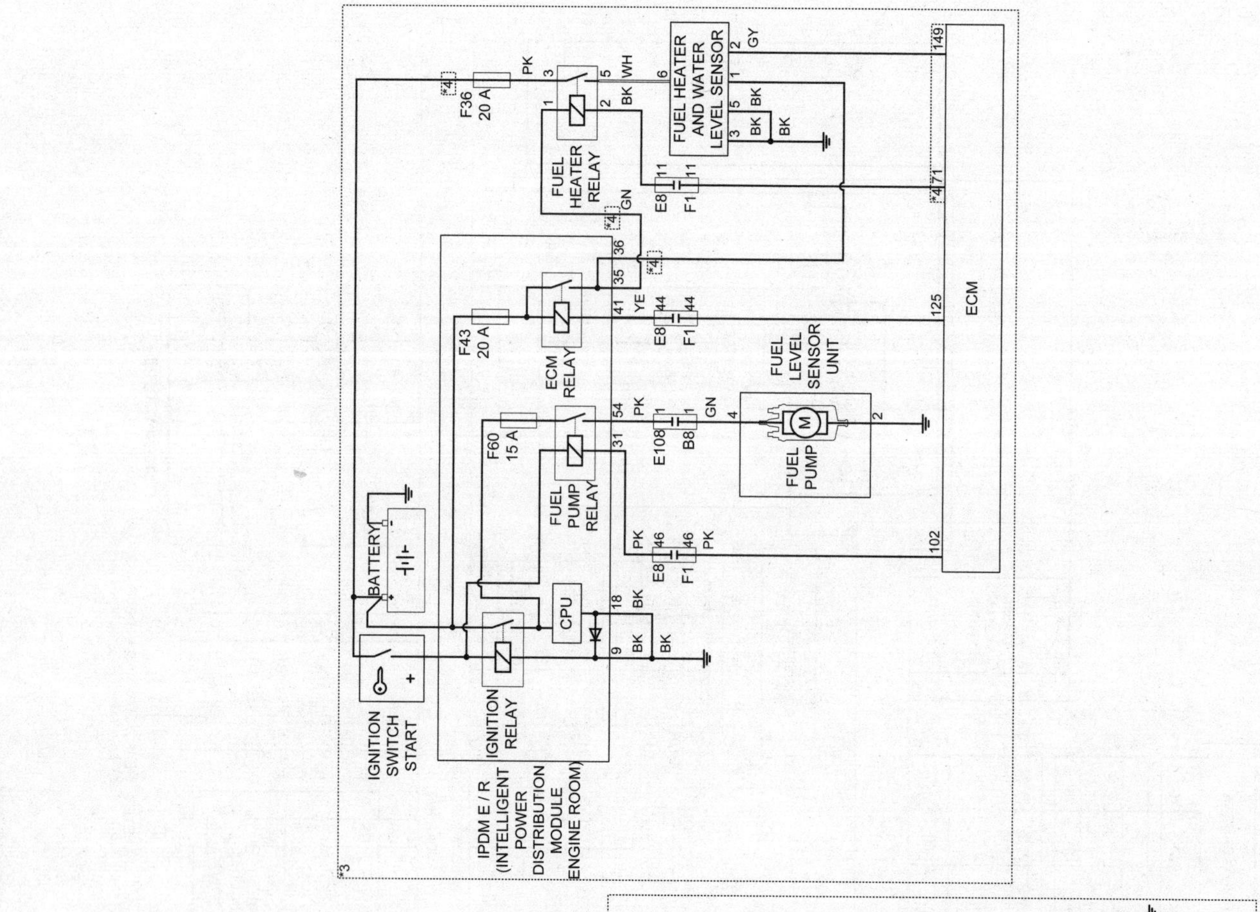

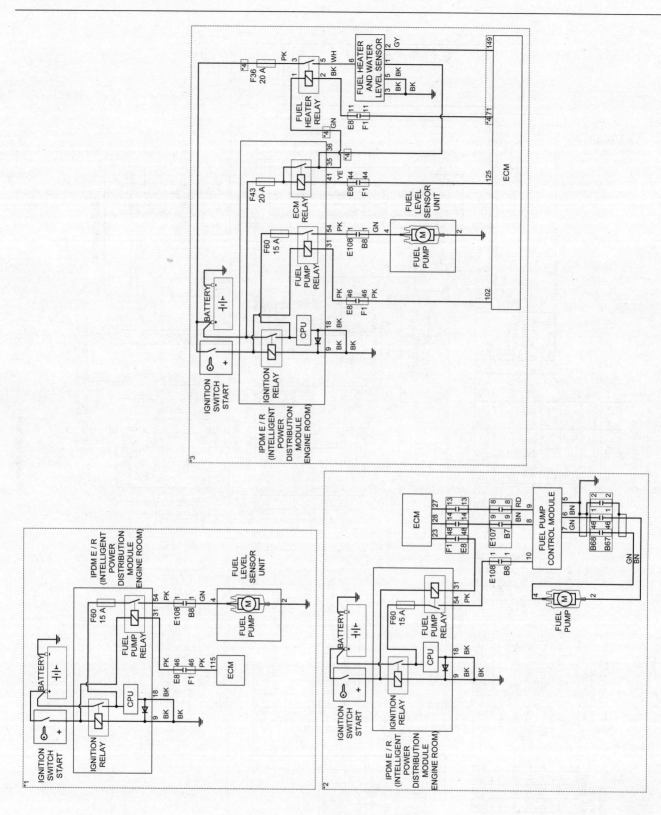

Fuel pump

*1 Engine: 1.2 petrol
*2 Engine: 1.6 petrol
*3 Engine: 1.5 diesel
*4 RHD models

Dimensions and weights

Note: *All figures are approximate, and may vary according to model. Refer to manufacturer's data for exact figures.*

Dimensions

Overall length	4135 mm
Overall width	1765 mm
Overall height (unladen)	1570 mm
Wheelbase	2530 mm
Front track:	
Models with 16 inch wheels	1540 mm
Models with 17 inch wheels	1525 mm
Rear track:	
Models with 16 inch wheels	1535 mm
Models with 17 inch wheels	1525 mm

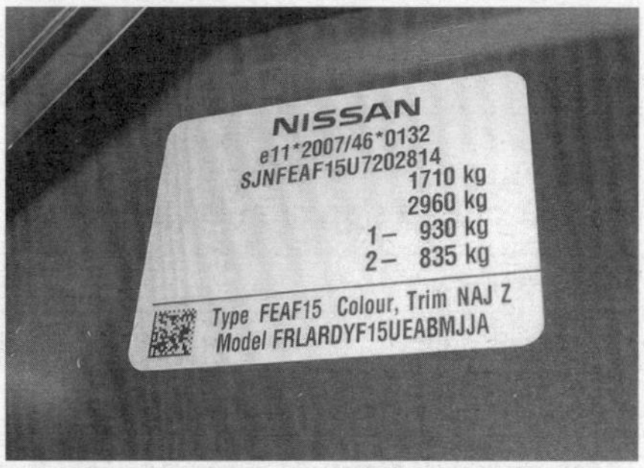

Weights

Vehicle weights are listed on the VIN label on the driver's side door pillar **(see illustration)**.

First (kg) figure is	Gross vehicle weight
Second (kg) figure is	Gross vehicle weight + Gross trailer weight
Third (kg) figure is	Gross axle weight (front)
Fourth (kg) figure is	Gross axle weight (rear)

Fuel economy

Although depreciation is still the biggest part of the cost of motoring for most car owners, the cost of fuel is more immediately noticeable. These pages give some tips on how to get the best fuel economy.

Working it out

Manufacturer's figures

Car manufacturers are required by law to provide fuel consumption information on all new vehicles sold. These 'official' figures are obtained by simulating various driving conditions on a rolling road or a test track. Real life conditions are different, so the fuel consumption actually achieved may not bear much resemblance to the quoted figures.

How to calculate it

Many cars now have trip computers which will display fuel consumption, both instantaneous and average. Refer to the owner's handbook for details of how to use these.

To calculate consumption yourself (and maybe to check that the trip computer is accurate), proceed as follows.

1. Fill up with fuel and note the mileage, or zero the trip recorder.
2. Drive as usual until you need to fill up again.
3. Note the amount of fuel required to refill the tank, and the mileage covered since the previous fill-up.
4. Divide the mileage by the amount of fuel used to obtain the consumption figure.

For example:

Mileage at first fill-up (a) = 27,903
Mileage at second fill-up (b) = 28,346
Mileage covered (b - a) = 443
Fuel required at second fill-up = 48.6 litres

The half-completed changeover to metric units in the UK means that we buy our fuel in litres, measure distances in miles and talk about fuel consumption in miles per gallon. There are two ways round this: the first is to convert the litres to gallons before doing the calculation (by dividing by 4.546, or see Table 1). So in the example:

48.6 litres ÷ 4.546 = 10.69 gallons
443 miles ÷ 10.69 gallons = 41.4 mpg

The second way is to calculate the consumption in miles per litre, then multiply that figure by 4.546 (or see Table 2).

So in the example, fuel consumption is:

443 miles ÷ 48.6 litres = 9.1 mpl
9.1 mpl x 4.546 = 41.4 mpg

The rest of Europe expresses fuel consumption in litres of fuel required to travel 100 km (l/100 km). For interest, the conversions are given in Table 3. In practice it doesn't matter what units you use, provided you know what your normal consumption is and can spot if it's getting better or worse.

Table 1: conversion of litres to Imperial gallons

litres	1	2	3	4	5	10	20	30	40	50	60	70
gallons	0.22	0.44	0.66	0.88	1.10	2.24	4.49	6.73	8.98	11.22	13.47	15.71

Table 2: conversion of miles per litre to miles per gallon

miles per litre	5	6	7	8	9	10	11	12	13	14
miles per gallon	23	27	32	36	41	46	50	55	59	64

Table 3: conversion of litres per 100 km to miles per gallon

litres per 100 km	4	4.5	5	5.5	6	6.5	7	8	9	10
miles per gallon	71	63	56	51	47	43	40	35	31	28

Maintenance

A well-maintained car uses less fuel and creates less pollution. In particular:

Filters

Change air and fuel filters at the specified intervals.

Oil

Use a good quality oil of the lowest viscosity specified by the vehicle manufacturer (see *Lubricants and fluids*). Check the level often and be careful not to overfill.

Spark plugs

When applicable, renew at the specified intervals.

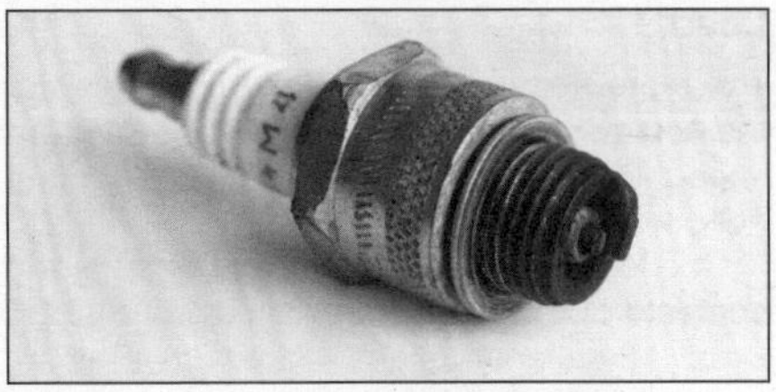

Tyres

Check tyre pressures regularly. Under-inflated tyres have an increased rolling resistance. It is generally safe to use the higher pressures specified for full load conditions even when not fully laden, but keep an eye on the centre band of tread for signs of wear due to over-inflation.

When buying new tyres, consider the 'fuel saving' models which most manufacturers include in their ranges.

Driving style

Acceleration

Acceleration uses more fuel than driving at a steady speed. The best technique with modern cars is to accelerate reasonably briskly to the desired speed, changing up through the gears as soon as possible without making the engine labour.

Air conditioning

Air conditioning absorbs quite a bit of energy from the engine – typically 3 kW (4 hp) or so. The effect on fuel consumption is at its worst in slow traffic. Switch it off when not required.

Anticipation

Drive smoothly and try to read the traffic flow so as to avoid unnecessary acceleration and braking.

Automatic transmission

When accelerating in an automatic, avoid depressing the throttle so far as to make the transmission hold onto lower gears at higher speeds. Don't use the 'Sport' setting, if applicable.

When stationary with the engine running, select 'N' or 'P'. When moving, keep your left foot away from the brake.

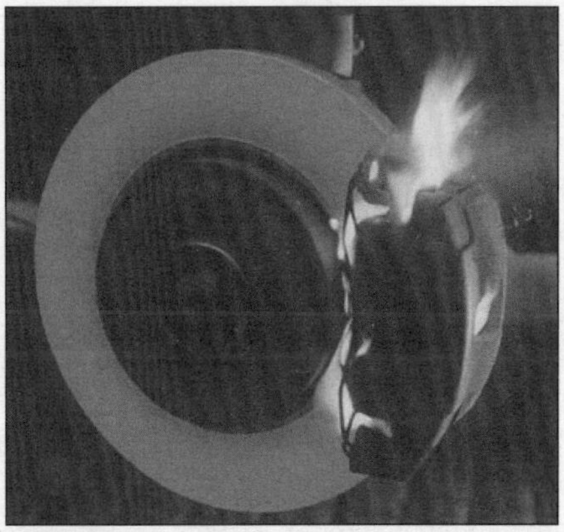

Braking

Braking converts the car's energy of motion into heat – essentially, it is wasted. Obviously some braking is always going to be necessary, but with good anticipation it is surprising how much can be avoided, especially on routes that you know well.

Carshare

Consider sharing lifts to work or to the shops. Even once a week will make a difference.

Electrical loads

Electricity is 'fuel' too; the alternator which charges the battery does so by converting some of the engine's energy of motion into electrical energy. The more electrical accessories are in use, the greater the load on the alternator. Switch off big consumers like the heated rear window when not required.

Freewheeling

Freewheeling (coasting) in neutral with the engine switched off is dangerous. The effort required to operate power-assisted brakes and steering increases when the engine is not running, with a potential lack of control in emergency situations.

In any case, modern fuel injection systems automatically cut off the engine's fuel supply on the overrun (moving and in gear, but with the accelerator pedal released).

Gadgets

Bolt-on devices claiming to save fuel have been around for nearly as long as the motor car itself. Those which worked were rapidly adopted as standard equipment by the vehicle manufacturers. Others worked only in certain situations, or saved fuel only at the expense of unacceptable effects on performance, driveability or the life of engine components.

The most effective fuel saving gadget is the driver's right foot.

Journey planning

Combine (eg) a trip to the supermarket with a visit to the recycling centre and the DIY store, rather than making separate journeys.

When possible choose a travelling time outside rush hours.

Load

The more heavily a car is laden, the greater the energy required to accelerate it to a given speed. Remove heavy items which you don't need to carry.

One load which is often overlooked is the contents of the fuel tank. A tankful of fuel (55 litres / 12 gallons) weighs 45 kg (100 lb) or so. Just half filling it may be worthwhile.

Lost?

At the risk of stating the obvious, if you're going somewhere new, have details of the route to hand. There's not much point in achieving record mpg if you also go miles out of your way.

Parking

If possible, carry out any reversing or turning manoeuvres when you arrive at a parking space so that you can drive straight out when you leave. Manoeuvering when the engine is cold uses a lot more fuel.

Driving around looking for free on-street parking may cost more in fuel than buying a car park ticket.

Premium fuel

Most major oil companies (and some supermarkets) have premium grades of fuel which are several pence a litre dearer than the standard grades. Reports vary, but the consensus seems to be that if these fuels improve economy at all, they do not do so by enough to justify their extra cost.

Roof rack

When loading a roof rack, try to produce a wedge shape with the narrow end at the front. Any cover should be securely fastened – if it flaps it's creating turbulence and absorbing energy.

Remove roof racks and boxes when not in use – they increase air resistance and can create a surprising amount of noise.

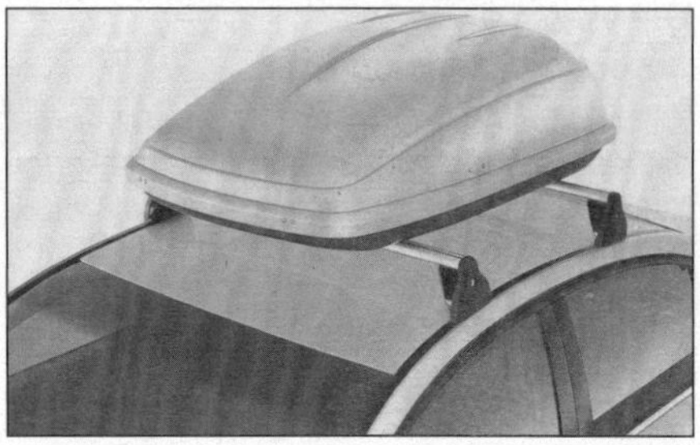

Short journeys

The engine is at its least efficient, and wear is highest, during the first few miles after a cold start. Consider walking, cycling or using public transport.

Speed

The engine is at its most efficient when running at a steady speed and load at the rpm where it develops maximum torque. (You can find this figure in the car's handbook.) For most cars this corresponds to between 55 and 65 mph in top gear.

Above the optimum cruising speed, fuel consumption starts to rise quite sharply. A car travelling at 80 mph will typically be using 30% more fuel than at 60 mph.

Supermarket fuel

It may be cheap but is it any good? In the UK all supermarket fuel must meet the relevant British Standard. The major oil companies will say that their branded fuels have better additive packages which may stop carbon and other deposits building up. A reasonable compromise might be to use one tank of branded fuel to three or four from the supermarket.

Switch off when stationary

Switch off the engine if you look like being stationary for more than 30 seconds or so. This is good for the environment as well as for your pocket. Be aware though that frequent restarts are hard on the battery and the starter motor.

Windows

Driving with the windows open increases air turbulence around the vehicle. Closing the windows promotes smooth airflow and reduced resistance. The faster you go, the more significant this is.

And finally . . .

Driving techniques associated with good fuel economy tend to involve moderate acceleration and low top speeds. Be considerate to the needs of other road users who may need to make brisker progress; even if you do not agree with them this is not an excuse to be obstructive.

Safety must always take precedence over economy, whether it is a question of accelerating hard to complete an overtaking manoeuvre, killing your speed when confronted with a potential hazard or switching the lights on when it starts to get dark.

Conversion factors

Length (distance)

Inches (in)	x 25.4	= Millimetres (mm)	x 0.0394	=	Inches (in)
Feet (ft)	x 0.305	= Metres (m)	x 3.281	=	Feet (ft)
Miles	x 1.609	= Kilometres (km)	x 0.621	=	Miles

Volume (capacity)

Cubic inches (cu in; in^3)	x 16.387	= Cubic centimetres (cc; cm^3)	x 0.061	=	Cubic inches (cu in; in^3)
Imperial pints (Imp pt)	x 0.568	= Litres (l)	x 1.76	=	Imperial pints (Imp pt)
Imperial quarts (Imp qt)	x 1.137	= Litres (l)	x 0.88	=	Imperial quarts (Imp qt)
Imperial quarts (Imp qt)	x 1.201	= US quarts (US qt)	x 0.833	=	Imperial quarts (Imp qt)
US quarts (US qt)	x 0.946	= Litres (l)	x 1.057	=	US quarts (US qt)
Imperial gallons (Imp gal)	x 4.546	= Litres (l)	x 0.22	=	Imperial gallons (Imp gal)
Imperial gallons (Imp gal)	x 1.201	= US gallons (US gal)	x 0.833	=	Imperial gallons (Imp gal)
US gallons (US gal)	x 3.785	= Litres (l)	x 0.264	=	US gallons (US gal)

Mass (weight)

Ounces (oz)	x 28.35	= Grams (g)	x 0.035	=	Ounces (oz)
Pounds (lb)	x 0.454	= Kilograms (kg)	x 2.205	=	Pounds (lb)

Force

Ounces-force (ozf; oz)	x 0.278	= Newtons (N)	x 3.6	=	Ounces-force (ozf; oz)
Pounds-force (lbf; lb)	x 4.448	= Newtons (N)	x 0.225	=	Pounds-force (lbf; lb)
Newtons (N)	x 0.1	= Kilograms-force (kgf; kg)	x 9.81	=	Newtons (N)

Pressure

Pounds-force per square inch (psi; lbf/in^2; lb/in^2)	x 0.070	= Kilograms-force per square centimetre (kgf/cm^2; kg/cm^2)	x 14.223	=	Pounds-force per square inch (psi; lbf/in^2; lb/in^2)
Pounds-force per square inch (psi; lbf/in^2; lb/in^2)	x 0.068	= Atmospheres (atm)	x 14.696	=	Pounds-force per square inch (psi; lbf/in^2; lb/in^2)
Pounds-force per square inch (psi; lbf/in^2; lb/in^2)	x 0.069	= Bars	x 14.5	=	Pounds-force per square inch (psi; lbf/in^2; lb/in^2)
Pounds-force per square inch (psi; lbf/in^2; lb/in^2)	x 6.895	= Kilopascals (kPa)	x 0.145	=	Pounds-force per square inch (psi; lbf/in^2; lb/in^2)
Kilopascals (kPa)	x 0.01	= Kilograms-force per square centimetre (kgf/cm^2; kg/cm^2)	x 98.1	=	Kilopascals (kPa)
Millibar (mbar)	x 100	= Pascals (Pa)	x 0.01	=	Millibar (mbar)
Millibar (mbar)	x 0.0145	= Pounds-force per square inch (psi; lbf/in^2; lb/in^2)	x 68.947	=	Millibar (mbar)
Millibar (mbar)	x 0.75	= Millimetres of mercury (mmHg)	x 1.333	=	Millibar (mbar)
Millibar (mbar)	x 0.401	= Inches of water (inH_2O)	x 2.491	=	Millibar (mbar)
Millimetres of mercury (mmHg)	x 0.535	= Inches of water (inH_2O)	x 1.868	=	Millimetres of mercury (mmHg)
Inches of water (inH_2O)	x 0.036	= Pounds-force per square inch (psi; lbf/in^2; lb/in^2)	x 27.68	=	Inches of water (inH_2O)

Torque (moment of force)

Pounds-force inches (lbf in; lb in)	x 1.152	= Kilograms-force centimetre (kgf cm; kg cm)	x 0.868	=	Pounds-force inches (lbf in; lb in)
Pounds-force inches (lbf in; lb in)	x 0.113	= Newton metres (Nm)	x 8.85	=	Pounds-force inches (lbf in; lb in)
Pounds-force inches (lbf in; lb in)	x 0.083	= Pounds-force feet (lbf ft; lb ft)	x 12	=	Pounds-force inches (lbf in; lb in)
Pounds-force feet (lbf ft; lb ft)	x 0.138	= Kilograms-force metres (kgf m; kg m)	x 7.233	=	Pounds-force feet (lbf ft; lb ft)
Pounds-force feet (lbf ft; lb ft)	x 1.356	= Newton metres (Nm)	x 0.738	=	Pounds-force feet (lbf ft; lb ft)
Newton metres (Nm)	x 0.102	= Kilograms-force metres (kgf m; kg m)	x 9.804	=	Newton metres (Nm)

Power

Horsepower (hp)	x 745.7	= Watts (W)	x 0.0013	=	Horsepower (hp)

Velocity (speed)

Miles per hour (miles/hr; mph)	x 1.609	= Kilometres per hour (km/hr; kph)	x 0.621	=	Miles per hour (miles/hr; mph)

Fuel consumption*

Miles per gallon, Imperial (mpg)	x 0.354	= Kilometres per litre (km/l)	x 2.825	=	Miles per gallon, Imperial (mpg)
Miles per gallon, US (mpg)	x 0.425	= Kilometres per litre (km/l)	x 2.352	=	Miles per gallon, US (mpg)

Temperature

Degrees Fahrenheit = (°C x 1.8) + 32

Degrees Celsius (Degrees Centigrade; °C) = (°F - 32) x 0.56

** It is common practice to convert from miles per gallon (mpg) to litres/100 kilometres (l/100km), where mpg x l/100 km = 282*

Spare parts are available from many sources, including maker's appointed garages, accessory shops, and motor factors. To be sure of obtaining the correct parts, it will sometimes be necessary to quote the vehicle identification number. If possible, it can also be useful to take the old parts along for positive identification. Items such as starter motors and alternators may be available under a service exchange scheme - any parts returned should be clean.

Our advice regarding spare parts is as follows.

Officially appointed garages

This is the best source of parts which are peculiar to your car, and which are not otherwise generally available (e.g. badges, interior trim, certain body panels, etc). It is also the only place at which you should buy parts if the vehicle is still under warranty.

Accessory shops

These are very good places to buy materials and components needed for the maintenance of your car (oil, air and fuel filters, light bulbs, drivebelts, greases, brake pads, touch-up paint, etc). Components of this nature sold by a reputable shop are usually of the same standard as those used by the car manufacturer.

Besides components, these shops also sell tools and general accessories, usually have convenient opening hours, charge lower prices, and can often be found close to home. Some accessory shops have parts counters where components needed for almost any repair job can be purchased or ordered.

Motor factors

Good factors will stock the more important components, which wear out comparatively quickly, and can sometimes supply individual components needed for the overhaul of a larger assembly (e.g. brake seals and hydraulic parts, bearing shells, pistons, valves). They may also handle work such as cylinder block reboring, crankshaft regrinding, etc.

Tyre and exhaust specialists

These outlets may be independent, or members of a local or national chain. They frequently offer competitive prices when compared with a main dealer or local garage, but it will pay to obtain several quotes before making a decision. When researching prices, also be sure to ask what "extras" may be added - for instance, fitting a new valve, balancing the wheel, and checking the tracking (front wheels) are all commonly charged on top of the price of a new tyre.

Other sources

Beware of parts or materials obtained from market stalls, car boot sales or similar outlets. Such items are not invariably sub-standard, but there is little chance of compensation if they do prove unsatisfactory. In the case of safety-critical components such as brake pads, there is the risk not only of financial loss, but also of an accident causing injury or death.

Second-hand components or assemblies obtained from a car breaker can be a good buy in some circumstances, but this sort of purchase is best made by the experienced DIY mechanic.

Modifications are a continuing and unpublicised process in vehicle manufacture, quite apart from major model changes. Spare parts manuals and lists are compiled upon a numerical basis, the individual vehicle identification numbers being essential to correct identification of the component concerned. When ordering spare parts, always give as much information as possible. Quote the car model; year of manufacture, body and engine numbers as appropriate.

Vehicle identification numbers

The vehicle identification number is stamped into the bulkhead behind the plastic scuttle panel and there is an additional sticker on the driver's side door pillar **(see illustration)**. The VIN is also visible through the windscreen, at the lower left hand corner.

The engine number is stamped on a machined surface on the front side of the cylinder block, at the flywheel end on petrol engines. On diesel engines, the number is stamped on a plate on the front of the cylinder block. The first part of the engine number gives the engine code – e.g. HR16DE.

The transmission number is on a label on top of the transmission housing.

VIN plate location on driver's side B-pillar

Whenever servicing, repair or overhaul work is carried out on the car or its components, observe the following procedures and instructions. This will assist in carrying out the operation efficiently and to a professional standard of workmanship.

Joint mating faces and gaskets

When separating components at their mating faces, never insert screwdrivers or similar implements into the joint between the faces in order to prise them apart. This can cause severe damage which results in oil leaks, coolant leaks, etc upon reassembly. Separation is usually achieved by tapping along the joint with a soft-faced hammer in order to break the seal. However, note that this method may not be suitable where dowels are used for component location.

Where a gasket is used between the mating faces of two components, a new one must be fitted on reassembly; fit it dry unless otherwise stated in the repair procedure. Make sure that the mating faces are clean and dry, with all traces of old gasket removed. When cleaning a joint face, use a tool which is unlikely to score or damage the face, and remove any burrs or nicks with an oilstone or fine file.

Make sure that tapped holes are cleaned with a pipe cleaner, and keep them free of jointing compound, if this is being used, unless specifically instructed otherwise.

Ensure that all orifices, channels or pipes are clear, and blow through them, preferably using compressed air.

Oil seals

Oil seals can be removed by levering them out with a wide flat-bladed screwdriver or similar implement. Alternatively, a number of self-tapping screws may be screwed into the seal, and these used as a purchase for pliers or some similar device in order to pull the seal free.

Whenever an oil seal is removed from its working location, either individually or as part of an assembly, it should be renewed.

The very fine sealing lip of the seal is easily damaged, and will not seal if the surface it contacts is not completely clean and free from scratches, nicks or grooves. If the original sealing surface of the component cannot be restored, and the manufacturer has not made provision for slight relocation of the seal relative to the sealing surface, the component should be renewed.

Protect the lips of the seal from any surface which may damage them in the course of fitting. Use tape or a conical sleeve where possible. Where indicated, lubricate the seal lips with oil before fitting and, on dual-lipped seals, fill the space between the lips with grease.

Unless otherwise stated, oil seals must be fitted with their sealing lips toward the lubricant to be sealed.

Use a tubular drift or block of wood of the appropriate size to install the seal and, if the seal housing is shouldered, drive the seal down to the shoulder. If the seal housing is unshouldered, the seal should be fitted with its face flush with the housing top face (unless otherwise instructed).

Screw threads and fastenings

Seized nuts, bolts and screws are quite a common occurrence where corrosion has set in, and the use of penetrating oil or releasing fluid will often overcome this problem if the offending item is soaked for a while before attempting to release it. The use of an impact driver may also provide a means of releasing such stubborn fastening devices, when used in conjunction with the appropriate screwdriver bit or socket. If none of these methods works, it may be necessary to resort to the careful application of heat, or the use of a hacksaw or nut splitter device. Before resorting to extreme methods, check that you are not dealing with a left-hand thread!

Studs are usually removed by locking two nuts together on the threaded part, and then using a spanner on the lower nut to unscrew the stud. Studs or bolts which have broken off below the surface of the component in which they are mounted can sometimes be removed using a stud extractor.

Always ensure that a blind tapped hole is completely free from oil, grease, water or other fluid before installing the bolt or stud. Failure to do this could cause the housing to crack due to the hydraulic action of the bolt or stud as it is screwed in.

For some screw fastenings, notably cylinder head bolts or nuts, torque wrench settings are no longer specified for the latter stages of tightening, "angle-tightening" being called up instead. Typically, a fairly low torque wrench setting will be applied to the bolts/nuts in the correct sequence, followed by one or more stages of tightening through specified angles.

When checking or retightening a nut or bolt to a specified torque setting, slacken the nut or bolt by a quarter of a turn, and then retighten to the specified setting. However, this should not be attempted where angular tightening has been used.

Locknuts, locktabs and washers

Any fastening which will rotate against a component or housing during tightening should always have a washer between it and the relevant component or housing.

Spring or split washers should always be renewed when they are used to lock a critical component such as a big-end bearing retaining bolt or nut. Locktabs which are folded over to retain a nut or bolt should always be renewed.

Self-locking nuts can be re-used in non-critical areas, providing resistance can be felt when the locking portion passes over the bolt or stud thread. However, it should be noted that self-locking stiffnuts tend to lose their effectiveness after long periods of use, and should then be renewed as a matter of course.

Split pins must always be replaced with new ones of the correct size for the hole.

When thread-locking compound is found on the threads of a fastener which is to be re-used, it should be cleaned off with a wire brush and solvent, and fresh compound applied on reassembly.

Special tools

Some repair procedures in this manual entail the use of special tools such as a press, two or three-legged pullers, spring compressors, etc. Wherever possible, suitable readily-available alternatives to the manufacturer's special tools are described, and are shown in use. In some instances, where no alternative is possible, it has been necessary to resort to the use of a manufacturer's tool, and this has been done for reasons of safety as well as the efficient completion of the repair operation. Unless you are highly-skilled and have a thorough understanding of the procedures described, never attempt to bypass the use of any special tool when the procedure described specifies its use. Not only is there a very great risk of personal injury, but expensive damage could be caused to the components involved.

Environmental considerations

When disposing of used engine oil, brake fluid, antifreeze, etc, give due consideration to any detrimental environmental effects. Do not, for instance, pour any of the above liquids down drains into the general sewage system, or onto the ground to soak away, as this is likely to pollute your local environment. Many local council refuse tips provide a facility for waste oil disposal, as do some garages. You can find your nearest disposal point by calling the Environment Agency on 03708 506 506 or by visiting www.oilbankline.org.uk.

OIL CARE®

Note: It is illegal and anti-social to dump oil down the drain. To find the location of your local oil recycling bank, call 03708 506 506 or visit www.oilbankline.org.uk.

The jack supplied with the vehicle tool kit should only be used for changing the roadwheels in an emergency – see *Wheel changing* in the prelims chapter. When carrying out any other kind of work, raise the vehicle using a hydraulic (or 'trolley') jack, and always supplement the jack with axle stands positioned under the vehicle jacking points.

When using a hydraulic jack or axle stands, always position the jack head or axle stand head under one of the relevant jacking points **(see illustration)**. Nissan recommend the use of adapters when supporting the vehicle with axle stands – the adapters should be grooved, and fit over the sill edge to prevent the vehicle weight damaging the sill. Do not jack the vehicle under the sump or any of the steering or suspension components other than those indicated.

Warning: Never work under, around, or near a raised vehicle, unless it is adequately supported in at least two places.

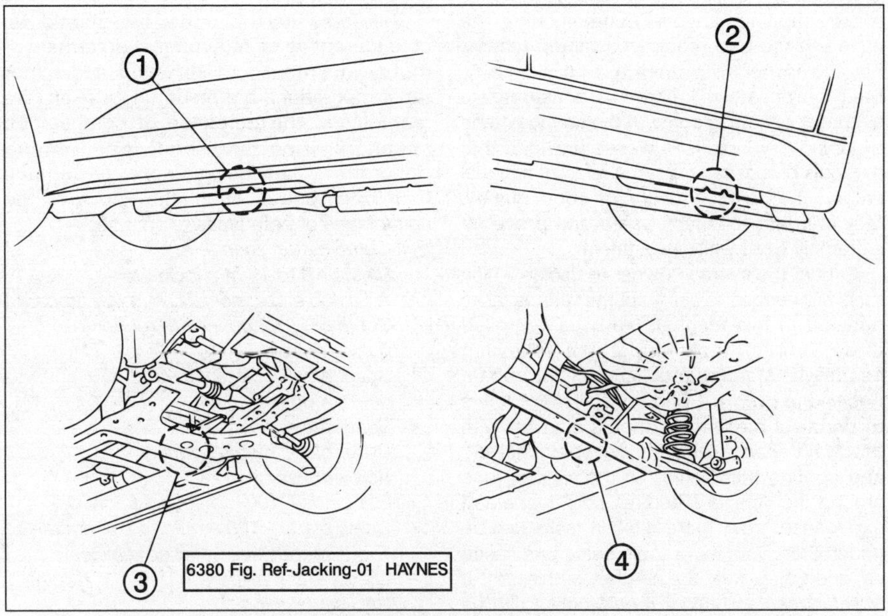

5.2 Vehicle jacking points

1 Front side jacking and supporting point
2 Rear side jacking and supporting point
3 Front centre jacking point
4 Rear centre jacking point

Introduction

A selection of good tools is a fundamental requirement for anyone contemplating the maintenance and repair of a motor vehicle. For the owner who does not possess any, their purchase will prove a considerable expense, offsetting some of the savings made by doing-it-yourself. However, provided that the tools purchased meet the relevant national safety standards and are of good quality, they will last for many years and prove an extremely worthwhile investment.

To help the average owner to decide which tools are needed to carry out the various tasks detailed in this manual, we have compiled three lists of tools under the following headings: *Maintenance and minor repair, Repair and overhaul*, and *Special*. Newcomers to practical mechanics should start off with the *Maintenance and minor repair* tool kit, and confine themselves to the simpler jobs around the vehicle. Then, as confidence and experience grow, more difficult tasks can be undertaken, with extra tools being purchased as, and when, they are needed. In this way, a *Maintenance and minor repair* tool kit can be built up into a *Repair and overhaul* tool kit over a considerable period of time, without any major cash outlays. The experienced do-it-yourselfer will have a tool kit good enough for most repair and overhaul procedures, and will add tools from the *Special* category when it is felt that the expense is justified by the amount of use to which these tools will be put.

Maintenance and minor repair tool kit

The tools given in this list should be considered as a minimum requirement if routine maintenance, servicing and minor repair operations are to be undertaken. We recommend the purchase of combination spanners (ring one end, open-ended the other); although more expensive than open-ended ones, they do give the advantages of both types of spanner.

- ☐ *Combination spanners:*
  Metric - 8 to 19 mm inclusive
- ☐ *Adjustable spanner - 35 mm jaw (approx.)*
- ☐ *Spark plug spanner (with rubber insert) - petrol models*
- ☐ *Spark plug gap adjustment tool - petrol models*
- ☐ *Set of feeler gauges*
- ☐ *Brake bleed nipple spanner*
- ☐ *Screwdrivers:*
  Flat blade - 100 mm long x 6 mm dia
  Cross blade - 100 mm long x 6 mm dia
  Torx - various sizes (not all vehicles)
- ☐ *Combination pliers*
- ☐ *Hacksaw (junior)*
- ☐ *Tyre pump*
- ☐ *Tyre pressure gauge*
- ☐ *Oil can*
- ☐ *Oil filter removal tool (if applicable)*
- ☐ *Fine emery cloth*
- ☐ *Wire brush (small)*
- ☐ *Funnel (medium size)*
- ☐ *Sump drain plug key (not all vehicles)*

Repair and overhaul tool kit

These tools are virtually essential for anyone undertaking any major repairs to a motor vehicle, and are additional to those given in the *Maintenance and minor repair* list. Included in this list is a comprehensive set of sockets. Although these are expensive, they will be found invaluable as they are so versatile - particularly if various drives are included in the set. We recommend the half-inch square-drive type, as this can be used with most proprietary torque wrenches.

The tools in this list will sometimes need to be supplemented by tools from the *Special* list:

- ☐ *Sockets to cover range in previous list (including Torx sockets)*
- ☐ *Reversible ratchet drive (for use with sockets)*
- ☐ *Extension piece, 250 mm (for use with sockets)*
- ☐ *Universal joint (for use with sockets)*
- ☐ *Flexible handle or sliding T "breaker bar" (for use with sockets)*
- ☐ *Torque wrench (for use with sockets)*
- ☐ *Self-locking grips*
- ☐ *Ball pein hammer*
- ☐ *Soft-faced mallet (plastic or rubber)*
- ☐ *Screwdrivers:*
  Flat blade - long & sturdy, short (chubby), and narrow (electrician's) types
  Cross blade – long & sturdy, and short (chubby) types
- ☐ *Pliers:*
  Long-nosed
  Side cutters (electrician's)
  Circlip (internal and external)
- ☐ *Cold chisel - 25 mm*
- ☐ *Scriber*
- ☐ *Scraper*
- ☐ *Centre-punch*
- ☐ *Pin punch*
- ☐ *Hacksaw*
- ☐ *Brake hose clamp*
- ☐ *Brake/clutch bleeding kit*
- ☐ *Selection of twist drills*
- ☐ *Steel rule/straight-edge*
- ☐ *Allen keys (inc. splined/Torx type)*
- ☐ *Selection of files*
- ☐ *Wire brush*
- ☐ *Axle stands*
- ☐ *Jack (strong trolley or hydraulic type)*
- ☐ *Light with extension lead*
- ☐ *Universal electrical multi-meter*

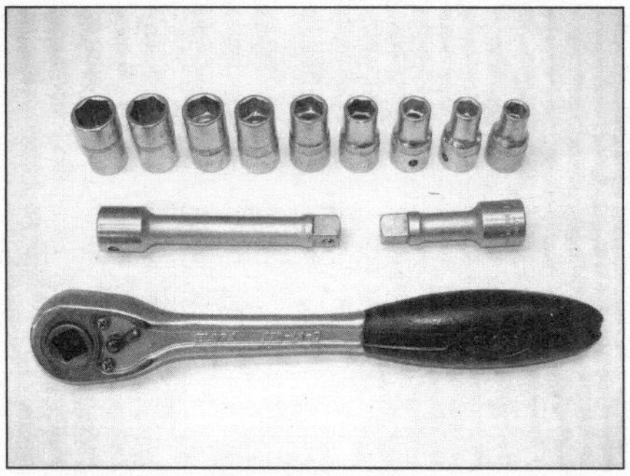

Sockets and reversible ratchet drive

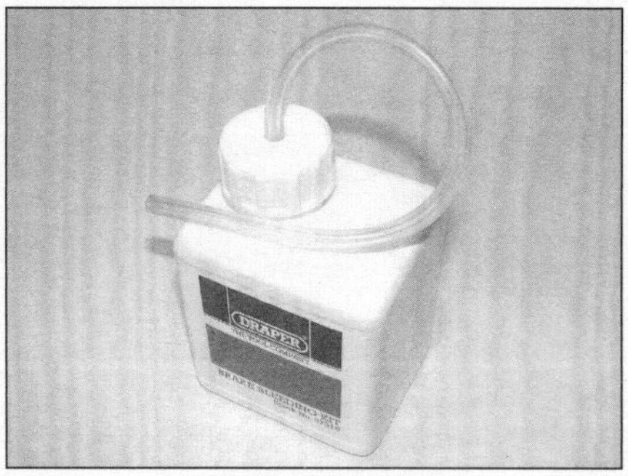

Brake bleeding kit

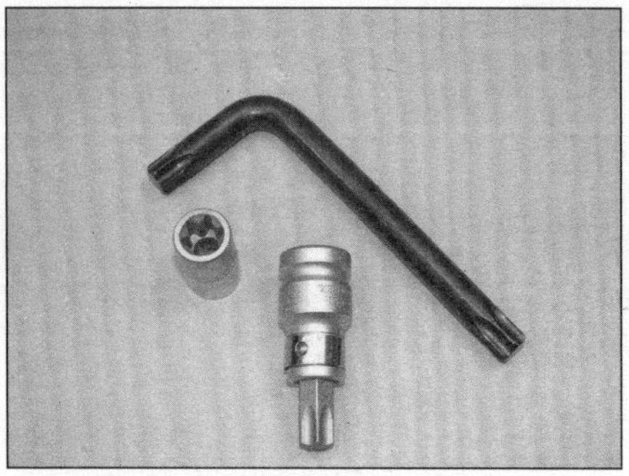

Torx key, socket and bit

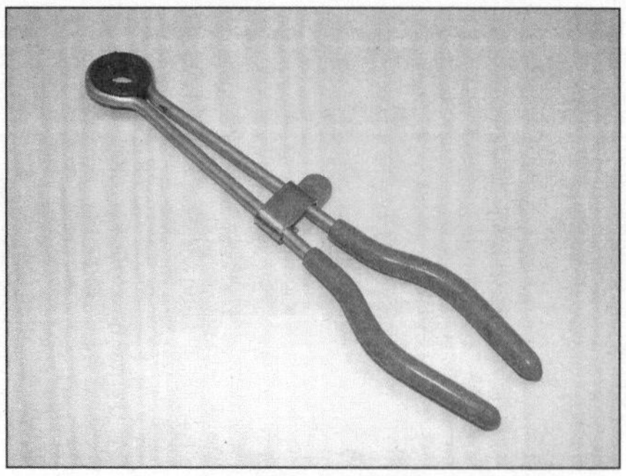

Hose clamp

Angular-tightening gauge

Special tools

The tools in this list are those which are not used regularly, are expensive to buy, or which need to be used in accordance with their manufacturers' instructions. Unless relatively difficult mechanical jobs are undertaken frequently, it will not be economic to buy many of these tools. Where this is the case, you could consider clubbing together with friends (or joining a motorists' club) to make a joint purchase, or borrowing the tools against a deposit from a local garage or tool hire specialist.

The following list contains only those tools and instruments freely available to the public, and not those special tools produced by the vehicle manufacturer specifically for its dealer network. You will find occasional references to these manufacturers' special tools in the text of this manual. Generally, an alternative method of doing the job without the vehicle manufacturers' special tool is given. However, sometimes there is no alternative to using them. Where this is the case and the relevant tool cannot be bought or borrowed, you will have to entrust the work to a dealer.

- ☐ *Angular-tightening gauge*
- ☐ *Valve spring compressor*
- ☐ *Valve grinding tool*
- ☐ *Piston ring compressor*
- ☐ *Piston ring removal/installation tool*
- ☐ *Cylinder bore hone*
- ☐ *Balljoint separator*
- ☐ *Coil spring compressors (where applicable)*
- ☐ *Two/three-legged hub and bearing puller*
- ☐ *Impact screwdriver*
- ☐ *Micrometer and/or vernier calipers*
- ☐ *Dial gauge*
- ☐ *Tachometer*
- ☐ *Fault code reader*
- ☐ *Cylinder compression gauge*
- ☐ *Hand-operated vacuum pump and gauge*
- ☐ *Clutch plate alignment set*
- ☐ *Brake shoe steady spring cup removal tool*
- ☐ *Bush and bearing removal/installation set*
- ☐ *Stud extractors*
- ☐ *Tap and die set*
- ☐ *Lifting tackle*

Buying tools

Reputable motor accessory shops and superstores often offer excellent quality tools at discount prices, so it pays to shop around.

Remember, you don't have to buy the most expensive items on the shelf, but it is always advisable to steer clear of the very cheap tools. Beware of 'bargains' offered on market stalls, on-line or at car boot sales. There are plenty of good tools around at reasonable prices, but always aim to purchase items which meet the relevant national safety standards. If in doubt, ask the proprietor or manager of the shop for advice before making a purchase.

Care and maintenance of tools

Having purchased a reasonable tool kit, it is necessary to keep the tools in a clean and serviceable condition. After use, always wipe off any dirt, grease and metal particles using a clean, dry cloth, before putting the tools away. Never leave them lying around after they have been used. A simple tool rack on the garage or workshop wall for items such as screwdrivers and pliers is a good idea. Store all normal spanners and sockets in a metal box. Any measuring instruments, gauges, meters, etc, must be carefully stored where they cannot be damaged or become rusty.

Take a little care when tools are used. Hammer heads inevitably become marked, and screwdrivers lose the keen edge on their blades from time to time. A little timely attention with emery cloth or a file will soon restore items like this to a good finish.

Working facilities

Not to be forgotten when discussing tools is the workshop itself. If anything more than routine maintenance is to be carried out, a suitable working area becomes essential.

It is appreciated that many an owner-mechanic is forced by circumstances to remove an engine or similar item without the benefit of a garage or workshop. Having done this, any repairs should always be done under the cover of a roof.

Wherever possible, any dismantling should be done on a clean, flat workbench or table at a suitable working height.

Any workbench needs a vice; one with a jaw opening of 100 mm is suitable for most jobs. As mentioned previously, some clean dry storage space is also required for tools, as well as for any lubricants, cleaning fluids, touch-up paints etc, which become necessary.

Another item which may be required, and which has a much more general usage, is an electric drill with a chuck capacity of at least 8 mm. This, together with a good range of twist drills, is virtually essential for fitting accessories.

Last, but not least, always keep a supply of old newspapers and clean, lint-free rags available, and try to keep any working area as clean as possible.

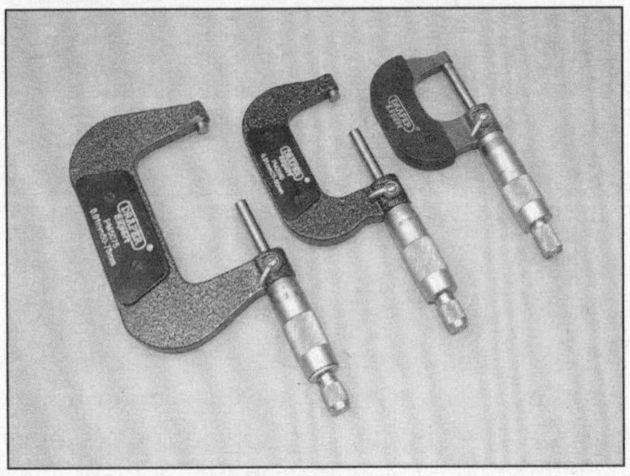

Micrometers

Dial test indicator ("dial gauge")

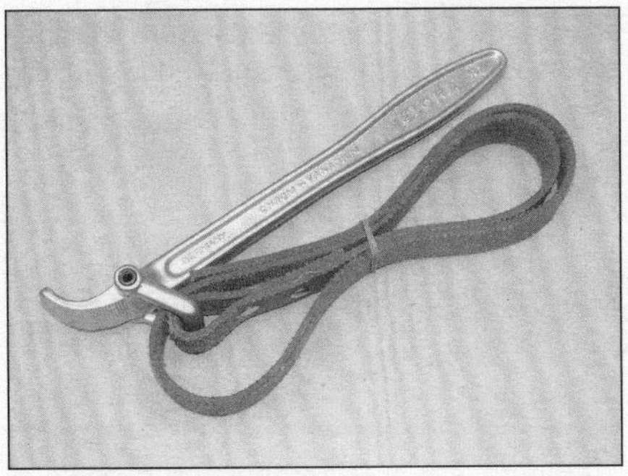

Oil filter removal tool (strap wrench type)

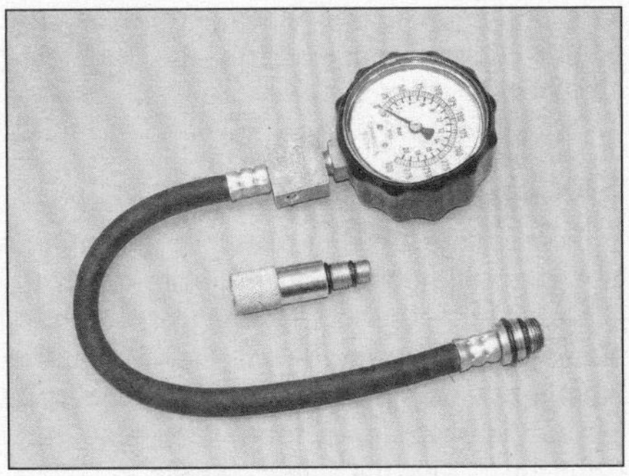

Compression tester

Bearing puller

This is a guide to getting your vehicle through the MOT test. Obviously it will not be possible to examine the vehicle to the same standard as the professional MOT tester. However, working through the following checks will enable you to identify any problem areas before submitting the vehicle for the test.

It has only been possible to summarise the test requirements here, based on the regulations in force at the time of printing. Test standards are becoming increasingly stringent, although there are some exemptions for older vehicles.

An assistant will be needed to help carry out some of these checks.

The checks have been sub-divided into four categories, as follows:

1 Checks carried out **FROM THE DRIVER'S SEAT**

2 Checks carried out **WITH THE VEHICLE ON THE GROUND**

3 Checks carried out **WITH THE VEHICLE RAISED AND THE WHEELS FREE TO TURN**

4 Checks carried out on **YOUR VEHICLE'S EXHAUST EMISSION SYSTEM**

1 Checks carried out FROM THE DRIVER'S SEAT

Handbrake (parking brake)

☐ Test the operation of the handbrake. Excessive travel (too many clicks) indicates incorrect brake or cable adjustment.

☐ Check that the handbrake cannot be released by tapping the lever sideways. Check the security of the lever mountings.

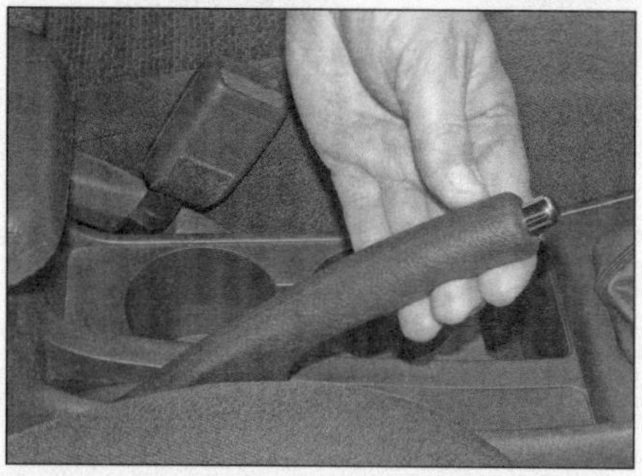

☐ If the parking brake is foot-operated, check that the pedal is secure and without excessive travel, and that the release mechanism operates correctly.

☐ Where applicable, test the operation of the electronic handbrake. The brake should engage and disengage without excessive delay. If the warning light does not extinguish when the brake is disengaged, this could indicate a fault which will need further investigation.

Footbrake

☐ Depress the brake pedal and check that it does not creep down to the floor, indicating a master cylinder fault. Release the pedal, wait a few seconds, then depress it again. If the pedal travels nearly to the floor before firm resistance is felt, brake adjustment or repair is necessary. If the pedal feels spongy, there is air in the hydraulic system which must be removed by bleeding.

☐ Check that the brake pedal is secure and in good condition. Check also for signs of fluid leaks on the pedal, floor or carpets, which would indicate failed seals in the brake master cylinder.

☐ Check the servo unit (when applicable) by operating the brake pedal several times, then keeping the pedal depressed and starting the engine. As the engine starts, the pedal will move down slightly. If not, the vacuum hose or the servo itself may be faulty.

Steering wheel and column

☐ Examine the steering wheel for fractures or looseness of the hub, spokes or rim.

☐ Move the steering wheel from side to side and then up and down. Check that the steering wheel is not loose on the column, indicating wear or a loose retaining nut. Continue moving the steering wheel as before, but also turn it slightly from left to right.

☐ Check that the steering wheel is not loose on the column, and that there is no abnormal movement of the steering wheel, indicating wear in the column support bearings or couplings.

☐ Check that the ignition lock (where fitted) engages and disengages correctly.

☐ Steering column adjustment mechanisms (where fitted) must be able to lock the column securely in place with no play evident.

Windscreen, mirrors and sunvisor

☐ The windscreen must be free of cracks or other significant damage within the driver's field of view. (Small stone chips are acceptable.) Rear view mirrors must be secure, intact, and capable of being adjusted.

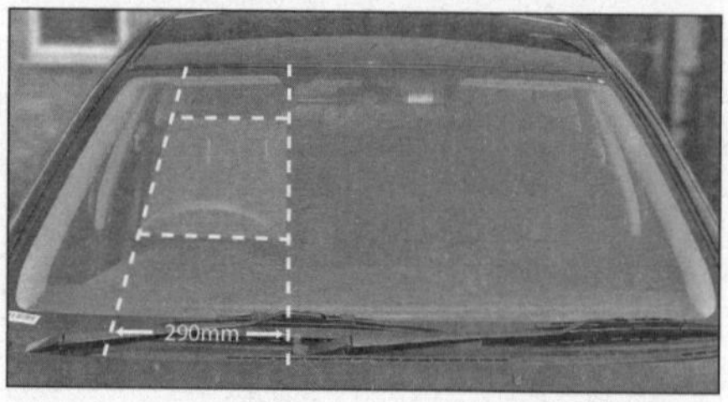

☐ The driver's sunvisor must be capable of being stored in the "up" position.

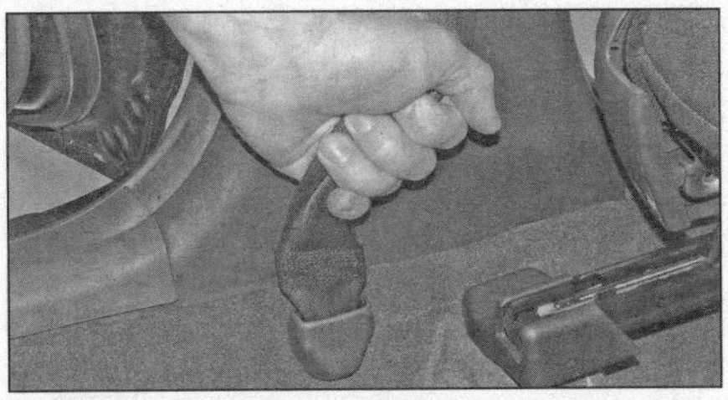

Seat belts and seats

Note: *The following checks are applicable to all seat belts, front and rear.*

□ Examine the webbing of all the belts (including rear belts if fitted) for cuts, serious fraying or deterioration. Fasten and unfasten each belt to check the buckles. If applicable, check the retracting mechanism. Check the security of all seat belt mountings accessible from inside the vehicle, ensuring any height adjustable mountings lock securely in place.

□ Seat belts with pre-tensioners, once activated, have a "flag" or similar showing on the seat belt stalk. This, in itself, is not a reason for test failure.

□ The front seats themselves must be securely attached and the backrests must lock in the upright position.

Doors

□ Both front doors must be able to be opened and closed from outside and inside, and must latch securely when closed.

Bonnet and boot/tailgate

□ The bonnet and boot/tailgate must latch securely when closed.

2 Checks carried out WITH THE VEHICLE ON THE GROUND

Vehicle identification

□ Number plates must be in good condition, secure and legible, with letters and numbers correctly spaced – spacing at (A) should be 33 mm and at (B) 11 mm. At the front, digits must be black on a white background and at the rear black on a yellow background. Other background designs (such as honeycomb) are not permitted.

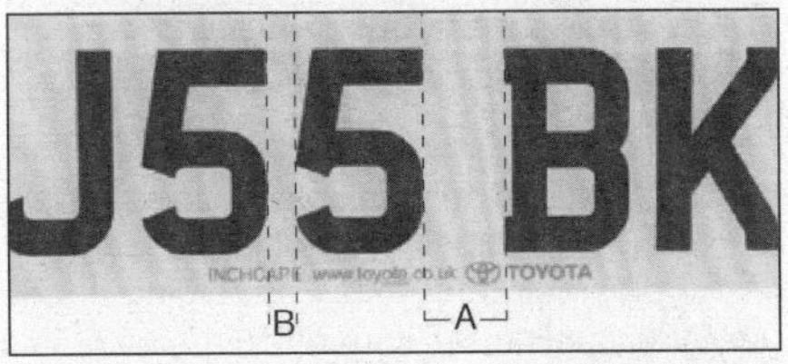

□ The VIN plate and/or homologation plate must be permanently displayed and legible.

Electrical equipment

□ Switch on the ignition and check the operation of the horn.

□ Check the windscreen washers and wipers, examining the wiper blades; renew damaged or perished blades. Also check the operation of the stop-lights.

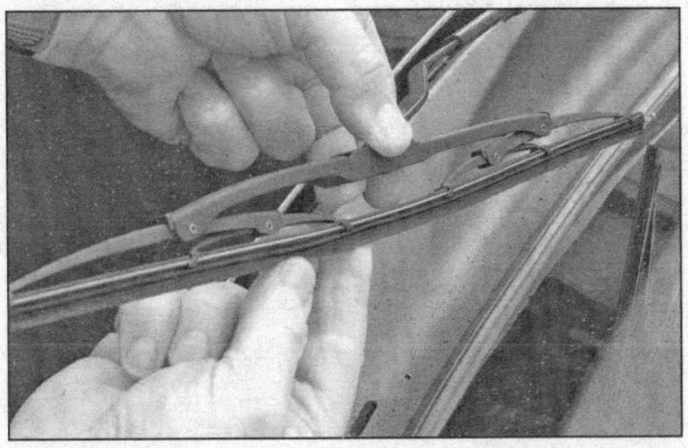

□ Check the operation of the sidelights and number plate lights. The lenses and reflectors must be secure, clean and undamaged.

□ Check the operation and alignment of the headlights. The headlight reflectors must not be tarnished and the lenses must be undamaged.

□ Switch on the ignition and check the operation of the direction indicators (including the instrument panel tell-tale) and the hazard warning lights. Operation of the sidelights and stop-lights must not affect the indicators - if it does, the cause is usually a bad earth at the rear light cluster. Indicators should flash at a rate of between 60 and 120 times per minute – faster or slower than this could indicate a fault with the flasher unit or a bad earth at one of the light units.

□ Check the operation of the rear foglight(s), including the warning light on the instrument panel or in the switch.

□ The warning lights must illuminate in accordance with the manufacturer's design. For most vehicles, the ABS and other warning lights should illuminate when the ignition is switched on, and (if the system is operating properly) extinguish after a few seconds. Refer to the owner's handbook.

Footbrake

□ Examine the master cylinder, brake pipes and servo unit for leaks, loose mountings, corrosion or other damage. If ABS is fitted, this unit should also be examined for signs of leaks or corrosion.

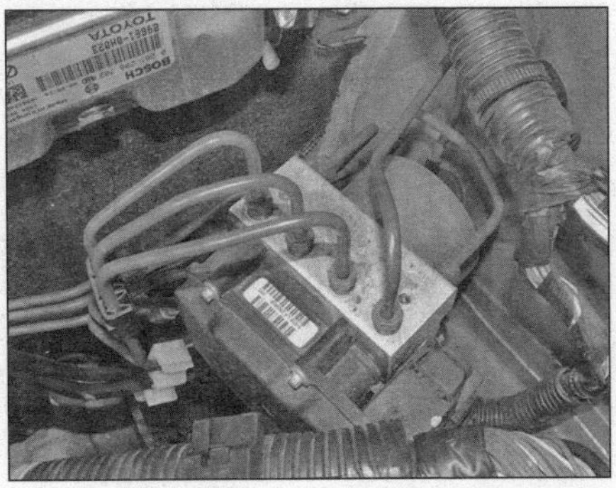

□ The fluid reservoir must be secure and the fluid level must be between the upper (**A**) and lower (**B**) markings.

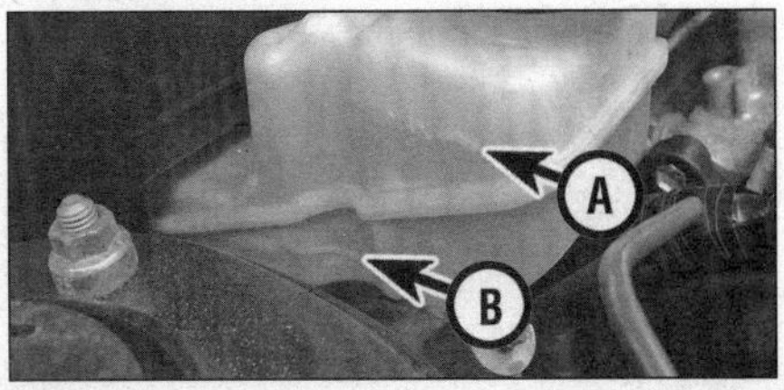

□ Inspect both front brake flexible hoses for cracks or deterioration of the rubber. Turn the steering from lock to lock, and ensure that the hoses do not contact the wheel, tyre, or any part of the steering or suspension mechanism. With the brake pedal firmly depressed, check the hoses for bulges or leaks under pressure.

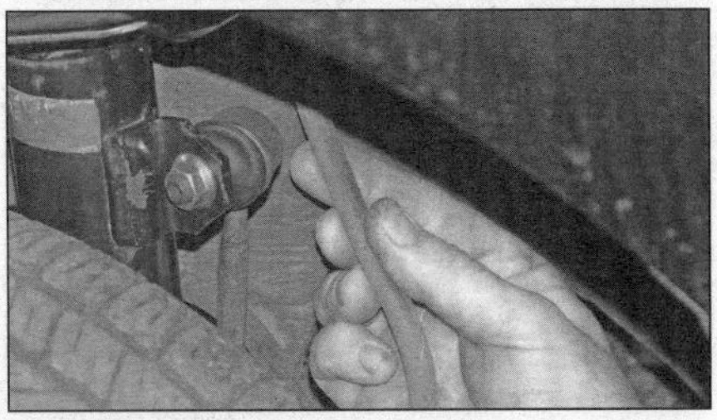

Steering and suspension

□ Have your assistant turn the steering wheel from side to side slightly, up to the point where the steering gear just begins to transmit this movement to the roadwheels. Check for excessive free play between the steering wheel and the steering gear, indicating wear or insecurity of the steering column joints, the column-to-steering gear coupling, or the steering gear itself.

□ Have your assistant turn the steering wheel more vigorously in each direction, so that the roadwheels just begin to turn. As this is done, examine all the steering joints, linkages, fittings and attachments. Renew any component that shows signs of wear or damage. On vehicles with power steering, check the security and condition of the steering pump, drivebelt and hoses.

□ Check that the vehicle is standing level, and at approximately the correct ride height.

Shock absorbers

□ Depress each corner of the vehicle in turn, then release it. The vehicle should rise and then settle in its normal position. If the vehicle continues to rise and fall, the shock absorber is defective. A shock absorber which has seized will also cause the vehicle to fail.

Exhaust system

☐ Start the engine. With your assistant holding a rag over the tailpipe, check the entire system for leaks. Repair or renew leaking sections.

3 Checks carried out
WITH THE VEHICLE RAISED AND THE WHEELS FREE TO TURN

Jack up the front and rear of the vehicle, and securely support it on axle stands. Position the stands clear of the suspension assemblies. Ensure that the wheels are clear of the ground and that the steering can be turned from lock to lock.

Steering mechanism

☐ Have your assistant turn the steering from lock to lock. Check that the steering turns smoothly, and that no part of the steering mechanism, including a wheel or tyre, fouls any brake hose or pipe or any part of the body structure.

☐ Examine the steering rack rubber gaiters for damage or insecurity of the retaining clips. If power steering is fitted, check for signs of damage or leakage of the fluid hoses, pipes or connections. Also check for excessive stiffness or binding of the steering, a missing split pin or locking device, or severe corrosion of the body structure within 30 cm of any steering component attachment point.

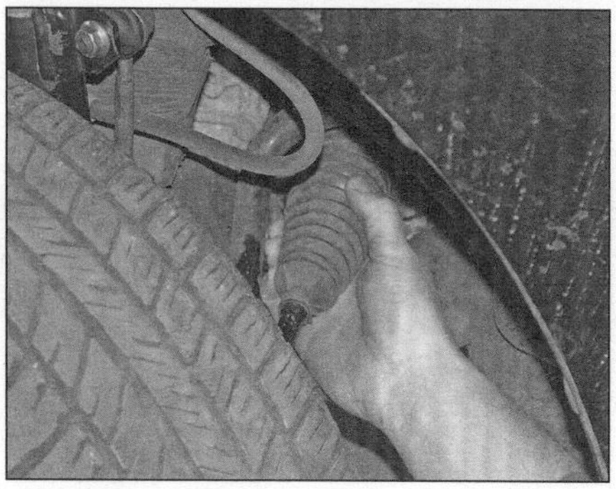

Front and rear suspension and wheel bearings

☐ Starting at the front right-hand side, grasp the roadwheel at the 3 o'clock and 9 o'clock positions and rock gently but firmly. Check for free play or insecurity at the wheel bearings, suspension balljoints, or suspension mount-ings, pivots and attachments.

☐ Now grasp the wheel at the 12 o'clock and 6 o'clock positions and repeat the previous inspection. Spin the wheel, and check for roughness or tightness of the front wheel bearing.

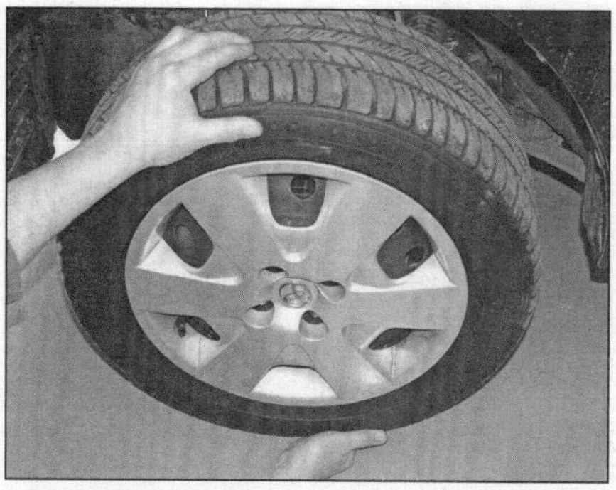

☐ If excess free play is suspected at a component pivot point, this can be confirmed by using a large screwdriver or similar tool and levering between the mounting and the component attachment. This will confirm whether the wear is in the pivot bush, its retaining bolt, or in the mounting itself (the bolt holes can often become elongated).

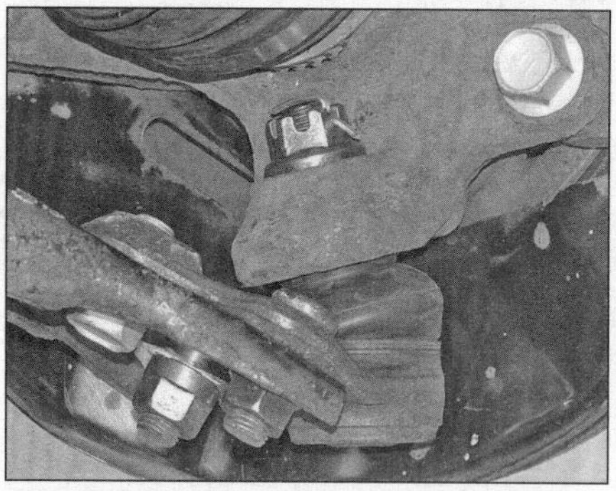

☐ Carry out all the above checks at the other front wheel, and then at both rear wheels.

Springs and shock absorbers

☐ Examine the suspension struts (when applicable) for serious fluid leakage, corrosion, or damage to the casing. Also check the security of the mounting points.

☐ If coil springs are fitted, check that the spring ends locate in their seats, and that the spring is not corroded, cracked or broken.

☐ If leaf springs are fitted, check that all leaves are intact, that the axle is securely attached to each spring, and that there is no deterioration of the spring eye mountings, bushes, and shackles.

☐ The same general checks apply to vehicles fitted with other suspension types, such as torsion bars, hydraulic displacer units, etc. Ensure that all mountings and attachments are secure, that there are no signs of excessive wear, corrosion or damage, and (on hydraulic types) that there are no fluid leaks or damaged pipes.

☐ Inspect the shock absorbers for signs of serious fluid leakage. Check for wear of the mounting bushes or attachments, or damage to the body of the unit.

Driveshafts (fwd vehicles only)

☐ Rotate each front wheel in turn and inspect the constant velocity joint gaiters for splits or damage. Also check that each driveshaft is straight and undamaged.

Braking system

☐ If possible without dismantling, check brake pad wear and disc condition. Ensure that the friction lining material has not worn excessively, (A) and that the discs are not fractured, pitted, scored or badly worn (B).

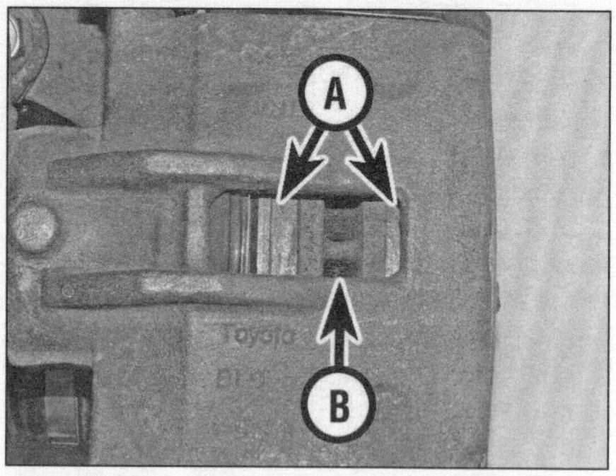

☐ Examine all the rigid brake pipes underneath the vehicle, and the flexible hose(s) at the rear. Look for corrosion, chafing or insecurity of the pipes, and for signs of bulging under pressure, chafing, splits or deterioration of the flexible hoses.

☐ Look for signs of fluid leaks at the brake calipers or on the brake backplates. Repair or renew leaking components.

☐ Slowly spin each wheel, while your assistant depresses and releases the footbrake. Ensure that each brake is operating and does not bind when the pedal is released.

☐Examine the handbrake mechanism, checking for frayed or broken cables, excessive corrosion, or wear or insecurity of the linkage. Check that the mechanism works on each relevant wheel, and releases fully, without binding.
☐It is not possible to test brake efficiency without special equipment, but a road test can be carried out later to check that the vehicle pulls up in a straight line.

Fuel and exhaust systems

☐Inspect the fuel tank (including the filler cap), fuel pipes, hoses and unions. All components must be secure and free from leaks. Locking fuel caps must lock securely and the key must be provided for the MOT test.
☐Examine the exhaust system over its entire length, checking for any damaged, broken or missing mountings, security of the retaining clamps and rust or corrosion.

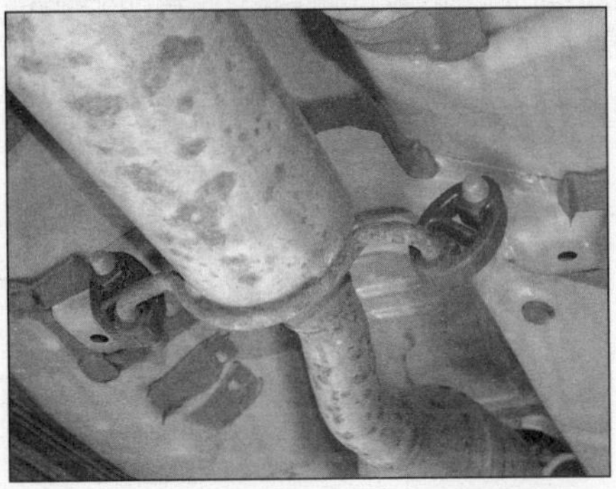

Wheels and tyres

☐Examine the sidewalls and tread area of each tyre in turn. Check for cuts, tears, lumps, bulges, separation of the tread, and exposure of the ply or cord due to wear or damage. Check that the tyre bead is correctly seated on the wheel rim, that the valve is sound and properly seated, and that the wheel is not distorted or damaged.

☐Check that the tyres are of the correct size for the vehicle, that they are of the same size and type on each axle, and that the pressures are correct.

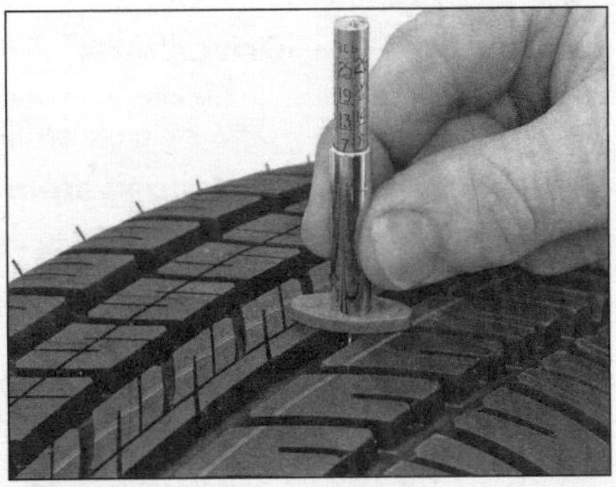

☐Check the tyre tread depth. The legal minimum at the time of writing is 1.6 mm over the central three-quarters of the tread width. Abnormal tread wear may indicate incorrect front wheel alignment or wear in steering or suspension components.
☐If the spare wheel is fitted externally or in a separate carrier beneath the vehicle, check that mountings are secure and free of excessive corrosion.

Body corrosion

☐Check the condition of the entire vehicle structure for signs of corrosion in load-bearing areas. (These include chassis box sections, side sills, cross-members, pillars, and all suspension, steering, braking system and seat belt mountings and anchorages.) Any corrosion which has seriously reduced the thickness of a load-bearing area (or is within 30 cm of safety-related components such as steering or suspension) is likely to cause the vehicle to fail. In this case professional repairs are likely to be needed.
☐Damage or corrosion which causes sharp or otherwise dangerous edges to be exposed will also cause the vehicle to fail.

Towbars

☐Check the condition of mounting points (both beneath the vehicle and within boot/hatchback areas) for signs of corrosion, ensuring that all fixings are secure and not worn or damaged. There must be no excessive play in detachable tow ball arms or quick-release mechanisms.

4 Checks carried out on **YOUR VEHICLE'S EXHAUST EMISSION SYSTEM**

Petrol models

☐The engine should be warmed up, and running well (ignition system in good order, air filter element clean, etc).
☐Before testing, run the engine at around 2500 rpm for 20 seconds. Let the engine drop to idle, and watch for smoke from the exhaust. If the idle speed is too high, or if dense blue or black smoke emerges for more than 5 seconds, the vehicle will fail. Typically, blue smoke signifies oil burning (engine wear); black smoke means unburnt fuel (dirty air cleaner element, or other fuel system fault).
☐An exhaust gas analyser for measuring carbon monoxide (CO) and hydrocarbons (HC) is now needed. If one cannot be hired or borrowed, have a local garage perform the check.

CO emissions (mixture)

☐The MOT tester has access to the CO limits for all vehicles. The CO level is measured at idle speed, and at 'fast idle' (2500 to 3000 rpm). The following limits are given as a general guide:

At idle speed – Less than 0.5% CO
At 'fast idle' – Less than 0.3% CO
Lambda reading – 0.97 to 1.03

☐If the CO level is too high, this may point to poor maintenance, a fuel injection system problem, faulty lambda (oxygen) sensor or catalytic converter. Try an injector cleaning treatment, and check the vehicle's ECU for fault codes.

HC emissions

☐The MOT tester has access to HC limits for all vehicles. The HC level is measured at 'fast idle' (2500 to 3000 rpm). The following limits are given as a general guide:

At 'fast idle' – Less then 200 ppm

☐Excessive HC emissions are typically caused by oil being burnt (worn engine), or by a blocked crankcase ventilation system ('breather'). If the engine oil is old and thin, an oil change may help. If the engine is running badly, check the vehicle's ECU for fault codes.

Diesel models

☐The only emission test for diesel engines is measuring exhaust smoke density, using a calibrated smoke meter. The test involves accelerating the engine at least 3 times to its maximum unloaded speed.

Note: *On engines with a timing belt, it is VITAL that the belt is in good condition before the test is carried out.*

☐With the engine warmed up, it is first purged by running at around 2500 rpm for 20 seconds. A governor check is then carried out, by slowly accelerating the engine to its maximum speed. After this, the smoke meter is connected, and the engine is accelerated quickly to maximum speed three times. If the smoke density is less than the limits given below, the vehicle will pass:

Non-turbo vehicles: 2.5m-1
Turbocharged vehicles: 3.0m-1

☐If excess smoke is produced, try fitting a new air cleaner element, or using an injector cleaning treatment. If the engine is running badly, where applicable, check the vehicle's ECU for fault codes. Also check the vehicle's EGR system, where applicable. At high mileages, the injectors may require professional attention.

Engine

- ☐ Engine fails to rotate when attempting to start
- ☐ Engine rotates, but will not start
- ☐ Engine difficult to start when cold
- ☐ Engine difficult to start when hot
- ☐ Starter motor noisy or excessively rough in engagement
- ☐ Engine starts, but stops immediately
- ☐ Engine idles erratically
- ☐ Engine misfires at idle speed
- ☐ Engine misfires throughout the driving speed range
- ☐ Engine hesitates on acceleration
- ☐ Engine stalls
- ☐ Engine lacks power
- ☐ Engine backfires
- ☐ Oil pressure warning light illuminated with engine running
- ☐ Engine runs-on after switching off
- ☐ Engine noises

Cooling system

- ☐ Overheating
- ☐ Overcooling
- ☐ External coolant leakage
- ☐ Internal coolant leakage
- ☐ Corrosion

Fuel and exhaust systems

- ☐ Excessive fuel consumption
- ☐ Fuel leakage and/or fuel odour
- ☐ Excessive noise or fumes from exhaust system

Clutch

- ☐ Pedal travels to floor – no pressure or very little resistance
- ☐ Clutch fails to disengage (unable to select gears)
- ☐ Clutch slips (engine speed increases, with no increase in vehicle speed)
- ☐ Judder as clutch is engaged
- ☐ Noise when depressing or releasing clutch pedal

Manual transmission

- ☐ Noisy in neutral with engine running
- ☐ Noisy in one particular gear
- ☐ Difficulty engaging gears
- ☐ Jumps out of gear
- ☐ Vibration
- ☐ Lubricant leaks

Driveshafts

- ☐ Clicking or knocking noise on turns (at slow speed on full-lock)
- ☐ Vibration when accelerating or decelerating

Braking system

- ☐ Vehicle pulls to one side under braking
- ☐ Noise (grinding or high-pitched squeal) when brakes applied
- ☐ Excessive brake pedal travel
- ☐ Brake pedal feels spongy when depressed
- ☐ Excessive brake pedal effort required to stop vehicle
- ☐ Judder felt through brake pedal or steering wheel when braking
- ☐ Brakes binding
- ☐ Rear wheels locking under normal braking

Suspension and steering

- ☐ Vehicle pulls to one side
- ☐ Wheel wobble and vibration
- ☐ Excessive pitching and/or rolling around corners, or during braking
- ☐ Wandering or general instability
- ☐ Excessively-stiff steering
- ☐ Excessive play in steering
- ☐ Tyre wear excessive

Electrical system

- ☐ Battery will not hold a charge for more than a few days
- ☐ Ignition/no-charge warning light remains illuminated with engine running
- ☐ Lights inoperative
- ☐ Instrument readings inaccurate or erratic
- ☐ Horn inoperative, or unsatisfactory in operation
- ☐ Windscreen/tailgate wipers inoperative, or unsatisfactory in operation
- ☐ Windscreen/tailgate washers inoperative, or unsatisfactory in operation
- ☐ Electric windows inoperative, or unsatisfactory in operation
- ☐ Window glass fails to move
- ☐ Central locking system inoperative, or unsatisfactory in operation

Introduction

The vehicle owner who does his or her own maintenance according to the recommended service schedules should not have to use this section of the manual very often. Modern component reliability is such that, provided those items subject to wear or deterioration are inspected or renewed at the specified intervals, sudden failure is comparatively rare. Faults do not usually just happen as a result of sudden failure, but develop over a period of time. Major mechanical failures in particular are usually preceded by characteristic symptoms over hundreds or even thousands of miles. Those components, which do occasionally fail without warning, are often small and easily carried in the vehicle.

With any fault-finding, the first step is to decide where to begin investigations. Sometimes this is obvious, but on other occasions, a little detective work will be necessary. The owner who makes half a dozen haphazard adjustments or replacements may be successful in curing a fault (or its symptoms), but will be none the wiser if the fault recurs, and ultimately may have spent more time and money than was necessary. A calm and logical approach will be found to be more satisfactory in the long run. Always take into account any warning signs or abnormalities that may have been noticed in the period preceding the fault – power loss, high or low gauge readings, unusual smells, etc – and remember that failure of components such as fuses or spark plugs may only be pointers to some underlying fault.

The pages that follow provide an easy-reference guide to the more common problems, which may occur during the operation of the vehicle. These problems and their possible causes are grouped under headings denoting various components or systems, such as Engine, Cooling system, etc. The general Chapter that deals with the problem is also shown in brackets; refer to the relevant part of that Chapter for system-specific information. Whatever the fault, certain basic principles apply. These are as follows:

Verify the fault. This is simply a matter of being sure that you know what the symptoms are before starting work. This is particularly important if you are investigating a fault for someone else, who may not have described it very accurately.

Don't overlook the obvious. For example, if the vehicle won't start, is there petrol in the tank? (Don't take anyone else's word on this particular point, and don't trust the fuel gauge either!) If an electrical fault is indicated, look for loose or broken wires before digging out the test gear.

Cure the disease, not the symptom. Substituting a flat battery with a fully charged one will get you off the hard shoulder, but if the underlying cause is not attended to, the new battery will go the same way. Similarly, changing oil-fouled spark plugs for a new set will get you moving again, but remember that the reason for the fouling (if it wasn't simply an incorrect grade of plug) will have to be established and corrected.

Don't take anything for granted. Particularly, don't forget that a 'new' component may itself be defective (especially if it's been rattling around in the boot for months), and don't leave components out of a fault diagnosis sequence just because they are new or recently fitted. When you do finally diagnose a difficult fault, you'll probably realise that all the evidence was there from the start.

Engine

Engine fails to rotate when attempting to start

- ☐ Battery terminal connections loose or corroded (*Weekly checks*).
- ☐ Battery discharged or faulty (Chapter 5A, Section 2).
- ☐ Broken, loose or disconnected wiring in the starting circuit (Chapter 5A, Section 7).
- ☐ Defective starter solenoid or switch (Chapter 5A, Section 9).
- ☐ Defective starter motor (Chapter 5A, Section 9).
- ☐ Starter pinion or flywheel ring gear teeth loose or broken (Chapter 2A, Section 8, 2B, Section 14 or 2C Section 14).
- ☐ Engine earth strap broken or disconnected (Chapter 12, Section 2).

Engine rotates, but will not start

- ☐ Fuel tank empty.Battery discharged (engine rotates slowly) (Chapter 5A, Section 2).
- ☐ Battery terminal connections loose or corroded (*Weekly checks*).
- ☐ Ignition components damp or damaged (*Roadside Repairs* or Chapter 5B, Section 2).
- ☐ Broken, loose or disconnected wiring in the ignition circuit (Chapter 12, Section 2).
- ☐ Worn, faulty or incorrectly-gapped spark plugs (Chapter 1A, Section 26).
- ☐ Fuel injection/engine management system fault (Chapter 4A, Section 5 or 4B, Section 1).
- ☐ Major mechanical failure (e.g. camshaft drive) (Chapter 2A, 2B or 2C).

Engine difficult to start when cold

- ☐ Battery discharged (Chapter 5A, Section 2).
- ☐ Battery terminal connections loose or corroded (*Weekly checks*).
- ☐ Worn, faulty or incorrectly-gapped spark plugs (Chapter 1A, Section 26).
- ☐ Fuel injection/engine management system fault (Chapter 4A, Section 5 or 4B, Section 1).
- ☐ Other ignition system fault (Chapter 1A or 5B).
- ☐ Low cylinder compressions (Chapter 2A, Section 2, 2B, Section 2 or 2C, Section 2).

Engine difficult to start when hot

- ☐ Air filter element dirty or clogged (Chapter 1A, Section 24 or 1B, Section 25).
- ☐ Fuel injection/engine management system fault (Chapter 4A, Section 5 or 4B, Section 1).
- ☐ Other ignition system fault (Chapter 1A or 5B).
- ☐ Low cylinder compressions (Chapter 2A, Section 2, 2B, Section 2 or 2C, Section 2).

Starter motor noisy or excessively rough in engagement

- ☐ Starter pinion or flywheel ring gear teeth loose or broken (Chapter 2A, Section 8, 2B, Section 14 or 2C, Section 14).
- ☐ Starter motor mounting bolts loose or missing (Chapter 5A, Section 8).
- ☐ Starter motor internal components worn or damaged (Chapter 5A, Section 9).

Engine starts, but stops immediately

- ☐ Loose or faulty electrical connections in the ignition circuit (Chapter 12, Section 2).
- ☐ Vacuum leak at the throttle housing or inlet manifold (Chapter 4A or 4B).
- ☐ Fuel injection/engine management system fault (Chapter 4A, Section 5 or 4B, Section 1).

Engine (continued)

Engine idles erratically

- ☐ Air filter element clogged (Chapter 1A, Section 24 or 1B, Section 25).
- ☐ Vacuum leak at the throttle housing, inlet manifold or associated hoses (Chapter 4A or 4B).
- ☐ Worn, faulty or incorrectly-gapped spark plugs (Chapter 1A, Section 26).
- ☐ Uneven or low cylinder compressions (Chapter 2A, Section 2, 2B, Section 2 or 2C, Section 2).
- ☐ Camshaft lobes worn (Chapter 2C, Section 9, 2B, Section 9 or 2C, Section 9).
- ☐ Timing chain incorrectly fitted (Chapter 2D, Section 6 or 2B, Section 7).
- ☐ Fuel injection/engine management system fault (Chapter 4A, Section 5 or 4B, Section 1).

Engine misfires at idle speed

- ☐ Worn, faulty or incorrectly-gapped spark plugs (Chapter 1A, Section 26).
- ☐ Vacuum leak at the throttle housing, inlet manifold or associated hoses (Chapter 4A or 4B).
- ☐ Fuel injection/engine management system fault (Chapter 4A, Section 5 or 4B, Section 1).
- ☐ Uneven or low cylinder compressions (Chapter 2A, Section 2, 2B, Section 2 or 2C, Section 2).
- ☐ Disconnected, leaking, or perished crankcase ventilation hoses (Chapter 4C, Section 2 or 4C, Section 3).

Engine misfires throughout the driving speed range

- ☐ Fuel filter choked (Chapter 1B, Section 24).
- ☐ Fuel pump faulty, or delivery pressure low (Chapter 4Aor 4B).
- ☐ Fuel tank vent blocked, or fuel pipes restricted (Chapter 4A, Section 8 or 4B, Section 4).
- ☐ Vacuum leak at the throttle housing, inlet manifold or associated hoses (Chapter 4A or 4B).
- ☐ Worn, faulty or incorrectly-gapped spark plugs (Chapter 1A, Section 26).
- ☐ Faulty ignition coil (Chapter 5B, Section 3).
- ☐ Uneven or low cylinder compressions (Chapter 2A, Section 2, 2B, Section 2 or 2C, Section 2).
- ☐ Fuel injection/engine management system fault (Chapter 4A, Section 5 or 4B, Section 1).

Engine hesitates on acceleration

- ☐ Worn, faulty or incorrectly-gapped spark plugs (Chapter 1A, Section 26).
- ☐ Vacuum leak at the throttle housing, inlet manifold or associated hoses (Chapter 4A or 4B).
- ☐ Fuel injection/engine management system fault (Chapter 4A, Section 5 or 4B, Section 1).

Engine stalls

- ☐ Vacuum leak at the throttle housing, inlet manifold or associated hoses (Chapter 4A or 4B).
- ☐ Fuel filter choked (Chapter 1B, Section 24).
- ☐ Fuel pump faulty, or delivery pressure low (Chapter 4A or 4B).
- ☐ Fuel tank vent blocked, or fuel pipes restricted (Chapter 4A, Section 8 or 4B, Section 4).
- ☐ Fuel injection/engine management system fault (Chapter 4A, Section 5 or 4Bor 4B, Section 1).

Engine lacks power

- ☐ Timing chain incorrectly fitted (Chapter 2D, Section 6 or 2B, Section 7).
- ☐ Timing belt incorrectly fitted (Chapter 2C, Section 6).
- ☐ Fuel filter choked (Chapter 1B, Section 24).
- ☐ Fuel pump faulty, or delivery pressure low (Chapter 4Aor 4B).
- ☐ Uneven or low cylinder compressions (Chapter 2A, Section 2, 2B, Section 2 or 2C Section 2).
- ☐ Worn, faulty or incorrectly-gapped spark plugs (Chapter 1A, Section 26).
- ☐ Vacuum leak at the throttle housing, inlet manifold or associated hoses (Chapter 4A or 4B).
- ☐ Fuel injection/engine management system fault (Chapter 4A, Section 5 or 4B, Section 1).
- ☐ Brakes binding (Chapter 1A, 1B and 9).
- ☐ Clutch slipping (Chapter 1A, Section 21 or 1B, Section 21).

Engine backfires

- ☐ Timing chain incorrectly fitted (Chapter 2D, Section 6 or 2B, Section 7).
- ☐ Timing belt incorrectly fitted (Chapter 2C, Section 6).
- ☐ Vacuum leak at the throttle housing, inlet manifold or associated hoses (Chapter 4A or 4B).
- ☐ Fuel injection/engine management system fault (Chapter 4A, Section 5 or 4B, Section 1).

Oil pressure warning light illuminated with engine running

- ☐ Low oil level, or incorrect oil grade (*Weekly checks*).
- ☐ Faulty oil pressure warning light switch (Chapter 5A, Section 11).
- ☐ Worn engine bearings and/or oil pump (Chapter 2D, 2B or 2C).
- ☐ High engine operating temperature (Chapter 3).
- ☐ Oil pressure relief valve defective (Chapter 2D, Section 10, 2B, Section 12 or 2C, Section 12).

Engine runs-on after switching off

- ☐ Excessive carbon build-up in engine (Chapter 2D, Section 12).
- ☐ High engine operating temperature (Chapter 3).
- ☐ Fuel injection/engine management system fault (Chapter 4A, Section 5 or 4B, Section 1).

Engine noises

Pre-ignition (pinking) or knocking during acceleration or under load

- ☐ Ignition timing incorrect/ignition system fault (Chapter 4A and 5B).
- ☐ Incorrect grade of spark plug (Chapter 1A, Section 26).
- ☐ Incorrect grade of fuel (Chapter 4A, Section 4).
- ☐ Vacuum leak at the throttle housing, inlet manifold or associated hoses (Chapter 4A or 4B).
- ☐ Excessive carbon build-up in engine (Chapter 2D, Section 12).
- ☐ Fuel injection/engine management system fault (Chapter 4A or 4B).

Whistling or wheezing noises

- ☐ Leaking inlet manifold or throttle housing gasket (Chapter 4Aor 4B).
- ☐ Leaking exhaust manifold gasket or pipe-to-manifold joint (Chapter 4Aor 4B).
- ☐ Leaking vacuum hose (Chapter 4A, 4B, 4C or 9).
- ☐ Blowing cylinder head gasket (Chapter 2D, 2B or 2C).

Tapping or rattling noises

- ☐ Worn valve gear or camshaft (Chapter 2A, 2B, 2C or 2D).
- ☐ Ancillary component fault (coolant pump, alternator, etc) (Chapter 3, 5A, etc).

Knocking or thumping noises

- ☐ Worn big-end bearings (regular heavy knocking, perhaps less under load) (Chapter 2D).
- ☐ Worn main bearings (rumbling and knocking, perhaps worsening under load) (Chapter 2D).
- ☐ Piston slap (most noticeable when cold) (Chapter 2D).
- ☐ Ancillary component fault (coolant pump, alternator, etc) (Chapter 3, 5A, etc).

Cooling system

Overheating

- ☐ Insufficient coolant in system (*Weekly checks*).
- ☐ Thermostat faulty (Chapter 3, Section 4).
- ☐ Radiator core blocked, or grille restricted (Chapter 1A, Section 25 or Chapter 1B, Section 26).
- ☐ Electric cooling fan faulty (Chapter 3, Section 5).
- ☐ Pressure cap faulty (Chapter 1A, Section 25 or 1B, Section 26).
- ☐ Inaccurate coolant temperature sensor (Chapter 3, Section 6).
- ☐ Airlock in cooling system (Chapter 1A, Section 25 or 1B, Section 26).

Overcooling

- ☐ Thermostat faulty (Chapter 3, Section 4).
- ☐ Inaccurate coolant temperature sensor (Chapter 3, Section 6).

External coolant leakage

- ☐ Deteriorated or damaged hoses or hose clips (Chapter 3, Section 2).
- ☐ Radiator core or heater matrix leaking (Chapter 3, Section 3 or Chapter 3, Section 9).
- ☐ Pressure cap faulty (Chapter 1A, Section 25 or 1B, Section 26).
- ☐ Coolant pump seal leaking (Chapter 3, Section 7).
- ☐ Boiling due to overheating (Chapter 3).
- ☐ Cylinder block core plug leaking (Chapter 2D).

Internal coolant leakage

- ☐ Leaking cylinder head gasket (Chapter 2D, Section 8, 2B, Section 10 or 2D, Section 9).
- ☐ Cracked cylinder head or cylinder bore (Chapter 2D).

Corrosion

- ☐ Infrequent draining and flushing (Chapter 1A, Section 25 or 1B, Section 26).
- ☐ Incorrect coolant mixture or inappropriate coolant type (Chapter 1A, Section 25 or 1B, Section 26).

Fuel and exhaust systems

Excessive fuel consumption

- ☐ Air filter element dirty or clogged (Chapter 1A, Section 24 or 1B, Section 25).
- ☐ Fuel injection/engine management system fault (Chapter 4A, Section 5 or 4B, Section 1).
- ☐ Tyres under-inflated (*Weekly checks*).

Fuel leakage and/or fuel odour

- ☐ Damaged or corroded fuel tank, pipes or connections (Chapter 1A, Section 6 or 1B, Section 7).

Excessive noise or fumes from exhaust system

- ☐ Leaking exhaust system or manifold joints (Chapter 4A or 4B).
- ☐ Leaking, corroded or damaged silencers or pipe (Chapter 4A or 4B).
- ☐ Broken mountings causing body or suspension contact (Chapter 4A or 4B).

Clutch

Pedal travels to floor – no pressure or very little resistance

- ☐ Leaking hydraulic fluid (Chapter 6).
- ☐ Faulty slave or master cylinder (Chapter 6, Section 8 or Chapter 6, Section 5).
- ☐ Broken diaphragm spring in clutch pressure plate (Chapter 6, Section 7).

Clutch fails to disengage (unable to select gears)

- ☐ Leaking hydraulic fluid (Chapter 6).
- ☐ Clutch friction plate sticking on gearbox input shaft splines (Chapter 6, Section 7).
- ☐ Clutch friction plate sticking to flywheel or pressure plate (Chapter 6, Section 7).
- ☐ Faulty pressure plate assembly (Chapter 6, Section 7).
- ☐ Clutch release mechanism worn or incorrectly assembled (Chapter 6, Section 8).

Clutch slips (engine speed increases, with no increase in vehicle speed)

- ☐ Leaking hydraulic fluid (Chapter 6).
- ☐ Clutch friction plate linings excessively worn (Chapter 6, Section 7).
- ☐ Clutch friction plate linings contaminated with oil or grease (Chapter 6, Section 7).
- ☐ Faulty pressure plate or weak diaphragm spring (Chapter 6, Section 7).

Judder as clutch is engaged

- ☐ Clutch friction plate linings contaminated with oil or grease (Chapter 6, Section 7).
- ☐ Clutch friction plate linings excessively worn (Chapter 6, Section 7).
- ☐ Leaking hydraulic fluid (Chapter 6).
- ☐ Faulty or distorted pressure plate or diaphragm spring (Chapter 6, Section 7).
- ☐ Worn or loose engine or gearbox mountings (Chapter 2A, Section 9, 2B, Section 15 or 2C, Section 15).
- ☐ Clutch friction plate hub or gearbox input shaft splines worn (Chapter 6, Section 7).

Noise when depressing or releasing clutch pedal

- ☐ Worn clutch release bearing (Chapter 6, Section 8).
- ☐ Worn or dry clutch pedal bushes (Chapter 6, Section 3).
- ☐ Faulty pressure plate assembly (Chapter 6, Section 7).
- ☐ Pressure plate diaphragm spring broken (Chapter 6, Section 7).
- ☐ Broken clutch friction plate cushioning springs (Chapter 6, Section 7).

Manual transmission

Noisy in neutral with engine running

- ☐ Input shaft bearings worn (noise apparent with clutch pedal released, but not when depressed) (Chapter 7).*
- ☐ Clutch release bearing worn (noise apparent with clutch pedal depressed, possibly less when released) (Chapter 6, Section 8).

Noisy in one particular gear

- ☐ Worn, damaged or chipped gear teeth (Chapter 7).*

Difficulty engaging gears

- ☐ Clutch fault (Chapter 6).
- ☐ Oil level low (Chapter 1A, Section 20 or Chapter 1B, Section 20).
- ☐ Worn or damaged gearchange linkage (Chapter 7, Section 3).
- ☐ Worn synchroniser units (Chapter 7).*

Jumps out of gear

- ☐ Worn or damaged gearchange linkage (Chapter 7, Section 3).
- ☐ Worn synchroniser units (Chapter 7).*
- ☐ Worn selector forks (Chapter 7).*

Vibration

- ☐ Lack of oil (Chapter 1A, Section 20 or Chapter 1B, Section 20).
- ☐ Worn bearings (Chapter 7).*

Lubricant leaks

- ☐ Leaking driveshaft oil seal (Chapter 7, Section 4).
- ☐ Leaking housing joint (Chapter 7).*
- ☐ Leaking input shaft oil seal (Chapter 7, Section 4).

Note: **Although the corrective action necessary to remedy the symptoms described is beyond the scope of the home mechanic, the above information should be helpful in isolating the cause of the condition, so that the owner can communicate clearly with a professional mechanic.*

Driveshafts

Clicking or knocking noise on turns (at slow speed on full-lock)

- ☐ Lack of constant velocity joint lubricant, possibly due to damaged gaiter (Chapter 8, Section 3).
- ☐ Worn outer constant velocity joint (Chapter 8, Section 4).

Vibration when accelerating or decelerating

- ☐ Worn inner constant velocity joint (Chapter 8, Section 4).
- ☐ Bent or distorted driveshaft (Chapter 8, Section 4).

Braking system

Vehicle pulls to one side under braking

Note: *Before assuming that a brake problem exists, make sure that the tyres are in good condition and correctly inflated, that the front wheel alignment is correct, and that the vehicle is not loaded with weight in an unequal manner. Apart from checking the condition of all pipe and hose connections, any faults occurring on the anti-lock braking system should be referred to a Nissan dealer for diagnosis.*

- ☐ Worn, defective, damaged or contaminated brake pads on one side (Chapter 9, Section 4 or Chapter 9, Section 5).
- ☐ Seized or partially-seized front brake caliper piston (Chapter 9, Section 9).
- ☐ A mixture of brake pad lining materials fitted between sides (Chapter 9, Section 4 or Chapter 9, Section 5).
- ☐ Brake caliper or backplate mounting bolts loose (Chapter 9, Section 9 or 9, Section 10).
- ☐ Worn or damaged steering or suspension components (Chapter 1A, 1B or 10).

Noise (grinding or high-pitched squeal) when brakes applied

- ☐ Brake pad friction lining material worn down to metal backing (Chapter 9, Section 4 or 9, Section 5).
- ☐ Excessive corrosion of brake disc. (May be apparent after the vehicle has been standing for some time (Chapter 9, Section 7 or 9, Section 8).
- ☐ Foreign object (stone chipping, etc) trapped between brake disc and shield (Chapter 1A, 1B or 9).

Excessive brake pedal travel

- ☐ Faulty master cylinder (Chapter 9, Section 11).
- ☐ Air in hydraulic system (Chapter 9, Section 2).
- ☐ Faulty vacuum servo unit (Chapter 1A, Section 21 or 1B, Section 21).

Brake pedal feels spongy when depressed

- ☐ Air in hydraulic system (Chapter 9, Section 2).
- ☐ Deteriorated flexible rubber brake hoses (Chapter 9, Section 3).
- ☐ Master cylinder mounting nuts loose (Chapter 9, Section 11).
- ☐ Faulty master cylinder (Chapter 9, Section 11).

Excessive brake pedal effort required to stop vehicle

- ☐ Faulty vacuum servo unit (Chapter 9, Section 14).
- ☐ Disconnected, damaged or insecure brake servo vacuum hose (Chapter 9, Section 15).
- ☐ Primary or secondary hydraulic circuit failure (Chapter 9).
- ☐ Seized brake caliper piston(s) (Chapter 9, Section 9 or 9, Section 10).
- ☐ Brake pads incorrectly fitted (Chapter 9, Section 4 or 9, Section 5).
- ☐ Incorrect grade of brake pads fitted (Chapter 9, Section 4 or 9, Section 5).
- ☐ Brake pads contaminated (Chapter 9, Section 4 or 9, Section 5).

Judder felt through brake pedal or steering wheel when braking

- ☐ Excessive run-out or distortion of discs (Chapter 9, Section 7 or 9, Section 8).
- ☐ Brake pad linings worn (Chapter 9, Section 4 or 9, Section 5).
- ☐ Brake caliper or brake backplate mounting bolts loose (Chapter 9, Section 9 or 9, Section 10).
- ☐ Wear in suspension or steering components or mountings (Chapter 1A, 1B or 10).

Brakes binding

- ☐ Seized brake caliper piston(s) (Chapter 9, Section 9 or 9, Section 10).
- ☐ Incorrectly-adjusted handbrake mechanism (Chapter 1A, Section 8 or 1B, Section 9).
- ☐ Faulty master cylinder (Chapter 9, Section 11).

Rear wheels locking under normal braking

- ☐ Rear brake pad linings contaminated (Chapter 9, Section 5).

Suspension and steering

Vehicle pulls to one side

Note: *Before diagnosing suspension or steering faults, be sure that the trouble is not due to incorrect tyre pressures, mixtures of tyre types, or binding brakes.*

- ☐ Defective tyre (*Weekly checks*).
- ☐ Excessive wear in suspension or steering components (Chapter 1A, Section 13, 1B, Section 13 or 10).
- ☐ Incorrect front wheel alignment (Chapter 1A, Section 15 or 1B, Section 15).
- ☐ Accident damage to steering or suspension components.

Wheel wobble and vibration

- ☐ Front roadwheels out of balance (vibration felt mainly through the steering wheel).
- ☐ Rear roadwheels out of balance (vibration felt throughout the vehicle).
- ☐ Roadwheels damaged or distorted (*Weekly checks*).
- ☐ Faulty or damaged tyre (*Weekly checks*).
- ☐ Worn steering or suspension joints, bushes or components (Chapter 1A, 1B or 10).
- ☐ Wheel bolts loose.

Excessive pitching and/or rolling around corners, or during braking

- ☐ Defective shock absorbers (Chapter 1A, Section 13, 1B, Section 13 or 10).
- ☐ Broken or weak spring and/or suspension component (Chapter 1A, Section 13, 1B, Section 13 or 10).
- ☐ Worn or damaged anti-roll bar or mountings (Chapter 10, Section 6).

Wandering or general instability

- ☐ Incorrect front wheel alignment (Chapter 1A, Section 15 or 1B, Section 15).
- ☐ Worn steering or suspension joints, bushes or components (Chapter 1A, Section 13 or 1B, Section 13).
- ☐ Roadwheels out of balance.Faulty or damaged tyre (*Weekly checks*).
- ☐ Wheel bolts loose.Defective shock absorbers (Chapter 1A, Section 13, 1B, Section 13 or 10).

Excessively-stiff steering

- ☐ Lack of steering gear lubricant (Chapter 10, Section 16).
- ☐ Seized track rod end balljoint or suspension balljoint (Chapter 1A, 1B or 10).
- ☐ Incorrect front wheel alignment (Chapter 1A, Section 15 or 1B, Section 15).
- ☐ Steering rack or column bent or damaged (Chapter 10).

Excessive play in steering

- ☐ Worn steering track rod end balljoints (Chapter 1A, 1B or 10).
- ☐ Worn rack-and-pinion steering gear (Chapter 1A, 1B or 10).
- ☐ Worn steering or suspension joints, bushes or components (Chapter 1A, 1B or 10).

Tyre wear excessive

Tyres worn on inside or outside edges

- ☐ Tyres under-inflated (wear on both edges) (*Weekly checks*).
- ☐ Incorrect camber or castor angles (wear on one edge only).
- ☐ Worn steering or suspension joints, bushes or components (Chapter 1A, 1B or 10).
- ☐ Excessively-hard cornering.Accident damage.

Tyre treads exhibit feathered edges

- ☐ Incorrect toe setting (Chapter 1A, Section 15 or 1B, Section 15).

Tyres worn in centre of tread

- ☐ Tyres over-inflated (*Weekly checks*).

Tyres worn on inside and outside edges

- ☐ Tyres under-inflated (*Weekly checks*).

Tyres worn unevenly

- ☐ Tyres/wheels out of balance.Excessive wheel or tyre run-out.
- ☐ Worn shock absorbers (Chapter 1A, Section 13 or Chapter 1B, Section 13).
- ☐ Faulty tyre (*Weekly checks*).

Electrical system

Battery will not hold a charge for more than a few days

Note: *For problems associated with the starting system, refer to the faults listed under 'Engine' earlier in this Section.*

- ☐ Battery defective internally (Chapter 5A, Section 2).
- ☐ Battery terminal connections loose or corroded (*Weekly checks*).
- ☐ Auxiliary drivebelt worn or incorrectly adjusted (Chapter 1A, Section 12 or 1B, Section 12).
- ☐ Alternator not charging at correct output (Chapter 5A, Section 4).
- ☐ Alternator or voltage regulator faulty (Chapter 5A, Section 6).
- ☐ Short-circuit causing continual battery drain (Chapter 12, Section 2).

Ignition/no-charge warning light remains illuminated with engine running

- ☐ Auxiliary drivebelt broken, worn, or incorrectly adjusted (Chapter 1A, Section 12 or 1B, Section 12).
- ☐ Alternator brushes worn, sticking, or dirty (Chapter 5A, Section 6).
- ☐ Alternator brush springs weak or broken (Chapter 5A, Section 6).
- ☐ Internal fault in alternator or voltage regulator (Chapter 5A, Section 6).
- ☐ Broken, disconnected, or loose wiring in charging circuit (Chapter 5A, Section 4).

Lights inoperative

- ☐ Bulb blown (Chapter 12, Section 5).
- ☐ Corrosion of bulb or bulbholder contacts (Chapter 12 Section 6).
- ☐ Blown fuse (Chapter 12, Section 3).
- ☐ Faulty relay (Chapter 12, Section 3).
- ☐ Broken, loose, or disconnected wiring (Chapter 12, Section 2).
- ☐ Faulty switch (Chapter 12, Section 4).

Instrument readings inaccurate or erratic

Fuel or temperature gauges give no reading

- ☐ Faulty gauge sender unit or temperature sensor (Chapter 4A, Section 7, 4B, Section 3 or 3, Section 6).
- ☐ Wiring open-circuit (Chapter 12, Section 2).
- ☐ Faulty instrument panel (Chapter 12, Section 9).

Fuel or temperature gauges give continuous maximum reading

- ☐ Faulty gauge sender unit or temperature sensor (Chapter 4A, Section 7, 4B, Section 3 or 3, Section 6).
- ☐ Wiring short-circuit (Chapter 12, Section 2).
- ☐ Faulty instrument panel (Chapter 12, Section 9).

Horn inoperative, or unsatisfactory in operation

Horn operates all the time

- ☐ Horn switch contacts faulty.

Horn fails to operate

- ☐ Blown fuse (Chapter 12, Section 3).
- ☐ Cable or cable connections loose, broken or disconnected (Chapter 12, Section 2).
- ☐ Faulty horn (Chapter 12, Section 10).

Horn emits intermittent or unsatisfactory sound

- ☐ Cable connections loose (Chapter 12, Section 2).
- ☐ Horn mountings loose (Chapter 12, Section 10).
- ☐ Faulty horn (Chapter 12, Section 10).

Windscreen/tailgate wipers inoperative, or unsatisfactory in operation

Wipers fail to operate, or operate very slowly

- ☐ Wiper blades stuck to screen, or linkage seized or binding (Chapter 12, Section 12).
- ☐ Blown fuse (Chapter 12, Section 3).
- ☐ Cable or cable connections loose, broken or disconnected (Chapter 12, Section 2).
- ☐ Faulty relay (Chapter 12, Section 3).
- ☐ Faulty wiper motor (Chapter 12, Section 12).

Wiper blades sweep over too large or too small an area of the glass

- ☐ Wiper arms incorrectly positioned on spindles (Chapter 12, Section 11).
- ☐ Excessive wear of wiper linkage (Chapter 12, Section 12).
- ☐ Wiper motor or linkage mountings loose or insecure (Chapter 12, Section 12).

Wiper blades fail to clean the glass effectively

- ☐ Wiper blade rubbers worn or perished (*Weekly checks*).
- ☐ Wiper arm tension springs broken, or arm pivots seized (Chapter 12, Section 11).
- ☐ Insufficient windscreen washer additive to adequately remove road film (*Weekly checks*).

Windscreen/tailgate washers inoperative, or unsatisfactory in operation

One or more washer jets inoperative

- ☐ Blocked washer jet (Chapter 12, Section 14).
- ☐ Disconnected, kinked or restricted fluid hose (Chapter 12, Section 14).
- ☐ Insufficient fluid in washer reservoir (*Weekly checks*).

Washer pump fails to operate

- ☐ Broken or disconnected wiring or connections (Chapter 12, Section 2).
- ☐ Blown fuse (Chapter 12, Section 3).
- ☐ Faulty washer switch (Chapter 12, Section 4).
- ☐ Faulty washer pump (Chapter 12, Section 14).

Washer pump runs for some time before fluid is emitted from jets

- ☐ Faulty one-way valve in fluid supply hose (Chapter 12, Section 14).

Electric windows inoperative, or unsatisfactory in operation

Window glass will only move in one direction

- ☐ Faulty switch (Chapter 12, Section 4).

Window glass slow to move

- ☐ Incorrectly-adjusted door glass guide channels (Chapter 11, Section 14).
- ☐ Regulator seized or damaged, or in need of lubrication (Chapter 11, Section 14).
- ☐ Door internal components or trim fouling regulator.Faulty motor (Chapter 11, Section 14).

Electrical system (continued)

Window glass fails to move

- ☐ Incorrectly-adjusted door glass guide channels (Chapter 11, Section 14).
- ☐ Blown fuse (Chapter 12, Section 3).
- ☐ Faulty relay (Chapter 12, Section 3).
- ☐ Broken or disconnected wiring or connections (Chapter 12, Section 2).
- ☐ Faulty motor (Chapter 11, Section 14).

Central locking system inoperative, or unsatisfactory in operation

Complete system failure

- ☐ Blown fuse (Chapter 12, Section 3).
- ☐ Faulty relay (Chapter 12, Section 3).
- ☐ Broken or disconnected wiring or connections (Chapter 12, Section 2).
- ☐ Faulty control unit (Chapter 11, Section 17).

Latch locks but will not unlock, or unlocks but will not lock

- ☐ Faulty master switch (Chapter 11, Section 17).
- ☐ Broken or disconnected latch operating rods or levers (Chapter 11, Section 17).
- ☐ Faulty relay (Chapter 12, Section 3).
- ☐ Faulty control unit (Chapter 11).
- ☐

One solenoid/motor fails to operate

- ☐ Broken or disconnected wiring or connections (Chapter 12, Section 2).
- ☐ Faulty solenoid/motor (Chapter 11, Section 17).
- ☐ Broken, binding or disconnected latch operating rods or levers (Chapter 11, Section 17).
- ☐ Fault in door latch (Chapter 11, Section 13).

A

ABS (Anti-lock brake system) A system, usually electronically controlled, that senses incipient wheel lockup during braking and relieves hydraulic pressure at wheels that are about to skid.
Air bag An inflatable bag hidden in the steering wheel (driver's side) or the dash or glovebox (passenger side). In a head-on collision, the bags inflate, preventing the driver and front passenger from being thrown forward into the steering wheel or windscreen.
Air cleaner A metal or plastic housing, containing a filter element, which removes dust and dirt from the air being drawn into the engine.
Air filter element The actual filter in an air cleaner system, usually manufactured from pleated paper and requiring renewal at regular intervals.

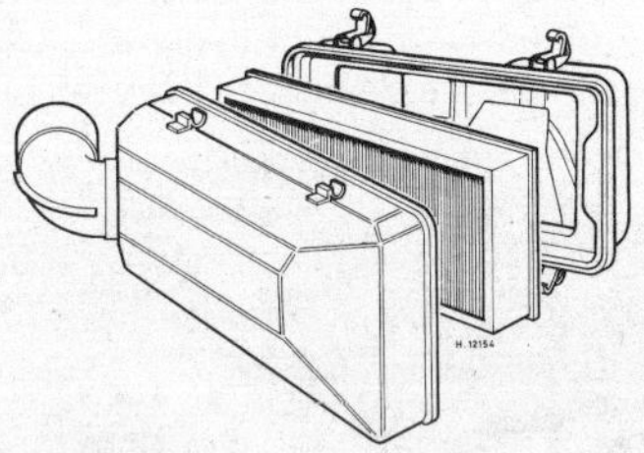

Air filter

Allen key A hexagonal wrench which fits into a recessed hexagonal hole.
Alligator clip A long-nosed spring-loaded metal clip with meshing teeth. Used to make temporary electrical connections.
Alternator A component in the electrical system which converts mechanical energy from a drivebelt into electrical energy to charge the battery and to operate the starting system, ignition system and electrical accessories.
Ampere (amp) A unit of measurement for the flow of electric current. One amp is the amount of current produced by one volt acting through a resistance of one ohm.
Anaerobic sealer A substance used to prevent bolts and screws from loosening. Anaerobic means that it does not require oxygen for activation. The Loctite brand is widely used.
Antifreeze A substance (usually ethylene glycol) mixed with water, and added to a vehicle's cooling system, to prevent freezing of the coolant in winter. Antifreeze also contains chemicals to inhibit corrosion and the formation of rust and other deposits that would tend to clog the radiator and coolant passages and reduce cooling efficiency.
Anti-seize compound A coating that reduces the risk of seizing on fasteners that are subjected to high temperatures, such as exhaust manifold bolts and nuts.
Asbestos A natural fibrous mineral with great heat resistance, commonly used in the composition of brake friction materials. Asbestos is a health hazard and the dust created by brake systems should never be inhaled or ingested.
Axle A shaft on which a wheel revolves, or which revolves with a wheel. Also, a solid beam that connects the two wheels at one end of the vehicle. An axle which also transmits power to the wheels is known as a live axle.
Axleshaft A single rotating shaft, on either side of the differential, which delivers power from the final drive assembly to the drive wheels. Also called a driveshaft or a halfshaft.

B

Ball bearing An anti-friction bearing consisting of a hardened inner and outer race with hardened steel balls between two races.
Bearing The curved surface on a shaft or in a bore, or the part assembled into either, that permits relative motion between them with minimum wear and friction.

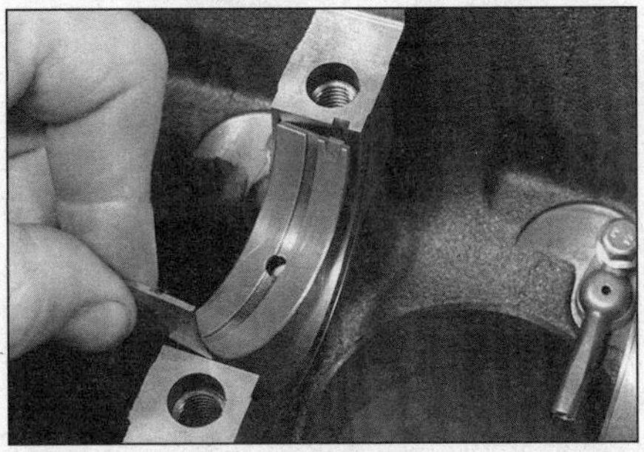

Bearing

Big-end bearing The bearing in the end of the connecting rod that's attached to the crankshaft.
Bleed nipple A valve on a brake wheel cylinder, caliper or other hydraulic component that is opened to purge the hydraulic system of air. Also called a bleed screw.
Brake bleeding Procedure for removing air from lines of a hydraulic brake system.

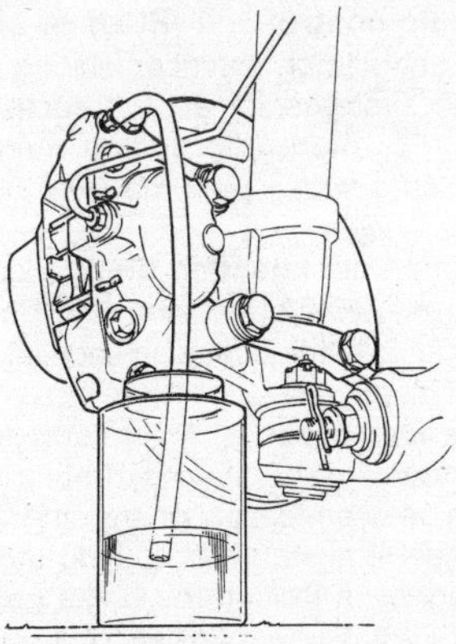

Brake bleeding

Brake disc The component of a disc brake that rotates with the wheels.
Brake drum The component of a drum brake that rotates with the wheels.
Brake linings The friction material which contacts the brake disc or drum to retard the vehicle's speed. The linings are bonded or riveted to the brake pads or shoes.
Brake pads The replaceable friction pads that pinch the brake disc when the brakes are applied. Brake pads consist of a friction material bonded or riveted to a rigid backing plate.
Brake shoe The crescent-shaped carrier to which the brake linings are mounted and which forces the lining against the rotating drum during braking.
Braking systems For more information on braking systems, consult the *Haynes Automotive Brake Manual*.
Breaker bar A long socket wrench handle providing greater leverage.
Bulkhead The insulated partition between the engine and the passenger compartment.

C

Caliper The non-rotating part of a disc-brake assembly that straddles the disc and carries the brake pads. The caliper also contains the hydraulic components that cause the pads to pinch the disc when the brakes are applied. A caliper is also a measuring tool that can be set to measure inside or outside dimensions of an object.
Camshaft A rotating shaft on which a series of cam lobes operate the valve mechanisms. The camshaft may be driven by gears, by sprockets and chain or by sprockets and a belt.
Canister A container in an evaporative emission control system; contains activated charcoal granules to trap vapours from the fuel system.

Canister

Carburettor A device which mixes fuel with air in the proper proportions to provide a desired power output from a spark ignition internal combustion engine.
Castellated Resembling the parapets along the top of a castle wall. For example, a castellated balljoint stud nut.
Castor In wheel alignment, the backward or forward tilt of the steering axis. Castor is positive when the steering axis is inclined rearward at the top.

Catalytic converter A silencer-like device in the exhaust system which converts certain pollutants in the exhaust gases into less harmful substances.

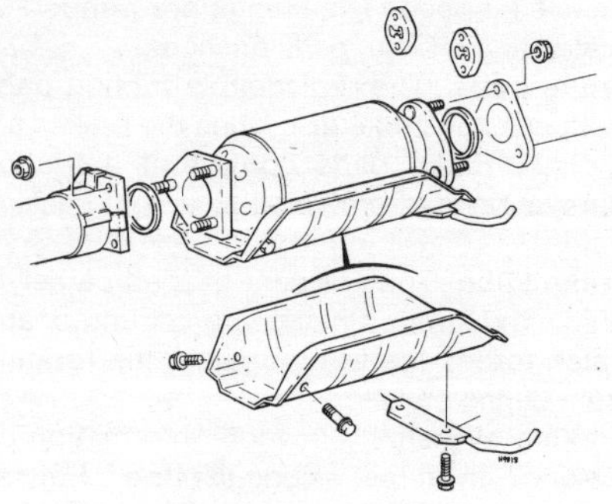

Catalytic converter

Circlip A ring-shaped clip used to prevent endwise movement of cylindrical parts and shafts. An internal circlip is installed in a groove in a housing; an external circlip fits into a groove on the outside of a cylindrical piece such as a shaft.

Clearance The amount of space between two parts. For example, between a piston and a cylinder, between a bearing and a journal, etc.

Coil spring A spiral of elastic steel found in various sizes throughout a vehicle, for example as a springing medium in the suspension and in the valve train.

Compression Reduction in volume, and increase in pressure and temperature, of a gas, caused by squeezing it into a smaller space.

Compression ratio The relationship between cylinder volume when the piston is at top dead centre and cylinder volume when the piston is at bottom dead centre.

Constant velocity (CV) joint A type of universal joint that cancels out vibrations caused by driving power being transmitted through an angle.

Core plug A disc or cup-shaped metal device inserted in a hole in a casting through which core was removed when the casting was formed. Also known as a freeze plug or expansion plug.

Crankcase The lower part of the engine block in which the crankshaft rotates.

Crankshaft The main rotating member, or shaft, running the length of the crankcase, with offset "throws" to which the connecting rods are attached.

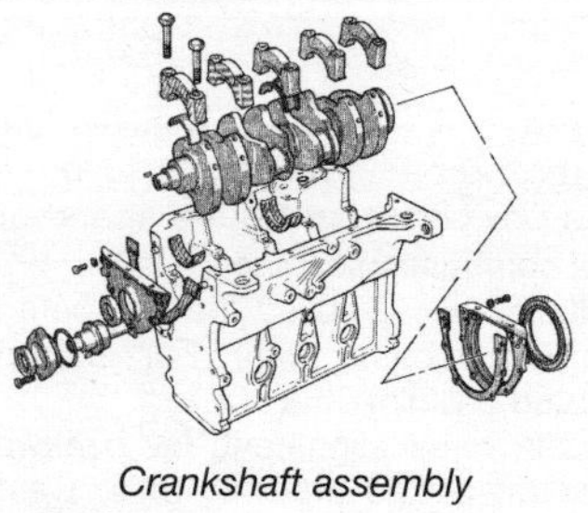

Crankshaft assembly

Crocodile clip See Alligator clip

D

Diagnostic code Code numbers obtained by accessing the diagnostic mode of an engine management computer. This code can be used to determine the area in the system where a malfunction may be located.

Disc brake A brake design incorporating a rotating disc onto which brake pads are squeezed. The resulting friction converts the energy of a moving vehicle into heat.

Double-overhead cam (DOHC) An engine that uses two overhead camshafts, usually one for the intake valves and one for the exhaust valves.

Drivebelt(s) The belt(s) used to drive accessories such as the alternator, water pump, power steering pump, air conditioning compressor, etc. off the crankshaft pulley.

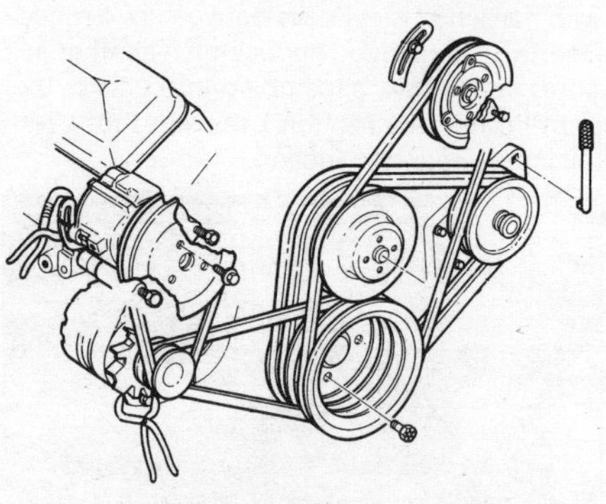

Accessory drivebelts

Driveshaft Any shaft used to transmit motion. Commonly used when referring to the axleshafts on a front wheel drive vehicle.

Drum brake A type of brake using a drum-shaped metal cylinder attached to the inner surface of the wheel. When the brake pedal is pressed, curved brake shoes with friction linings press against the inside of the drum to slow or stop the vehicle.

E

EGR valve A valve used to introduce exhaust gases into the intake air stream.

Electronic control unit (ECU) A computer which controls (for instance) ignition and fuel injection systems, or an anti-lock braking system. For more information refer to the *Haynes Automotive Electrical and Electronic Systems Manual.*

Electronic Fuel Injection (EFI) A computer controlled fuel system that distributes fuel through an injector located in each intake port of the engine.

Emergency brake A braking system, independent of the main hydraulic system, that can be used to slow or stop the vehicle if the primary brakes fail, or to hold the vehicle stationary even though the brake pedal isn't depressed. It usually consists of a hand lever that actuates either front or rear brakes mechanically through a series of cables and linkages. Also known as a handbrake or parking brake.

Endfloat The amount of lengthwise movement between two parts. As applied to a crankshaft, the distance that the crankshaft can move forward and back in the cylinder block.

Engine management system (EMS) A computer controlled system which manages the fuel injection and the ignition systems in an integrated fashion.

Exhaust manifold A part with several passages through which exhaust gases leave the engine combustion chambers and enter the exhaust pipe.

F

Fan clutch A viscous (fluid) drive coupling device which permits variable engine fan speeds in relation to engine speeds.

Feeler blade A thin strip or blade of hardened steel, ground to an exact thickness, used to check or measure clearances between parts.

Feeler blade

Firing order The order in which the engine cylinders fire, or deliver their power strokes, beginning with the number one cylinder.

Flywheel A heavy spinning wheel in which energy is absorbed and stored by means of momentum. On cars, the flywheel is attached to the crankshaft to smooth out firing impulses.

Free play The amount of travel before any action takes place. The "looseness" in a linkage, or an assembly of parts, between the initial application of force and actual movement. For example, the distance the brake pedal moves before the pistons in the master cylinder are actuated.

Fuse An electrical device which protects a circuit against accidental overload. The typical fuse contains a soft piece of metal which is calibrated to melt at a predetermined current flow (expressed as amps) and break the circuit.

Fusible link A circuit protection device consisting of a conductor surrounded by heat-resistant insulation. The conductor is smaller than the wire it protects, so it acts as the weakest link in the circuit. Unlike a blown fuse, a failed fusible link must frequently be cut from the wire for replacement.

G

Gap The distance the spark must travel in jumping from the centre electrode to the side electrode in a spark plug. Also refers to the spacing between the points in a contact breaker assembly in a conventional points-type ignition, or to the distance between the reluctor or rotor and the pickup coil in an electronic ignition.

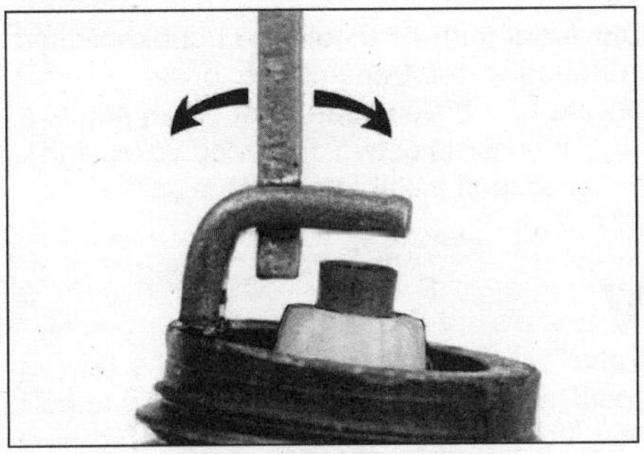

Adjusting spark plug gap

Gasket Any thin, soft material - usually cork, cardboard, asbestos or soft metal - installed between two metal surfaces to ensure a good seal. For instance, the cylinder head gasket seals the joint between the block and the cylinder head.

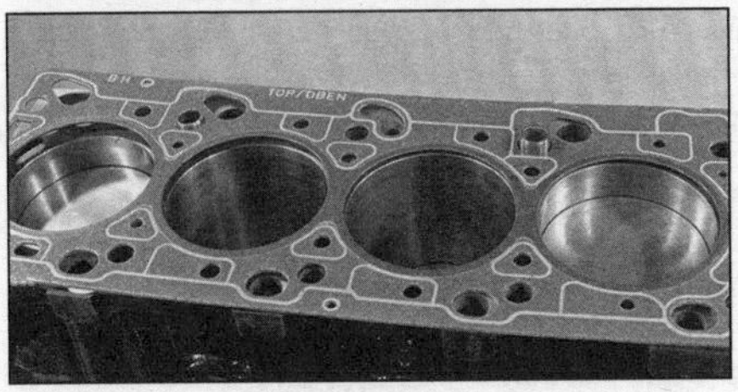

Gasket

Gauge An instrument panel display used to monitor engine conditions. A gauge with a movable pointer on a dial or a fixed scale is an analogue gauge. A gauge with a numerical readout is called a digital gauge.

H

Halfshaft A rotating shaft that transmits power from the final drive unit to a drive wheel, usually when referring to a live rear axle.

Harmonic balancer A device designed to reduce torsion or twisting vibration in the crankshaft. May be incorporated in the crankshaft pulley. Also known as a vibration damper.

Hone An abrasive tool for correcting small irregularities or differences in diameter in an engine cylinder, brake cylinder, etc.

Hydraulic tappet A tappet that utilises hydraulic pressure from the engine's lubrication system to maintain zero clearance (constant contact with both camshaft and valve stem). Automatically adjusts to variation in valve stem length. Hydraulic tappets also reduce valve noise.

I

Ignition timing The moment at which the spark plug fires, usually expressed in the number of crankshaft degrees before the piston reaches the top of its stroke.

Inlet manifold A tube or housing with passages through which flows the air-fuel mixture (carburettor vehicles and vehicles with throttle body injection) or air only (port fuel-injected vehicles) to the port openings in the cylinder head.

J

Jump start Starting the engine of a vehicle with a discharged or weak battery by attaching jump leads from the weak battery to a charged or helper battery.

L

Load Sensing Proportioning Valve (LSPV) A brake hydraulic system control valve that works like a proportioning valve, but also takes into consideration the amount of weight carried by the rear axle.

Locknut A nut used to lock an adjustment nut, or other threaded component, in place. For example, a locknut is employed to keep the adjusting nut on the rocker arm in position.

Lockwasher A form of washer designed to prevent an attaching nut from working loose.

M

MacPherson strut A type of front suspension system devised by Earle MacPherson at Ford of England. In its original form, a simple lateral link with the anti-roll bar creates the lower control arm. A long strut - an integral coil spring and shock absorber - is mounted between the body and the steering knuckle. Many modern so-called MacPherson strut systems use a conventional lower A-arm and don't rely on the anti-roll bar for location.

Multimeter An electrical test instrument with the capability to measure voltage, current and resistance.

N

NOx Oxides of Nitrogen. A common toxic pollutant emitted by petrol and diesel engines at higher temperatures.

O

Ohm The unit of electrical resistance. One volt applied to a resistance of one ohm will produce a current of one amp.

Ohmmeter An instrument for measuring electrical resistance.

O-ring A type of sealing ring made of a special rubber-like material; in use, the O-ring is compressed into a groove to provide the sealing action.

Overhead cam (ohc) engine An engine with the camshaft(s) located on top of the cylinder head(s).

Overhead valve (ohv) engine An engine with the valves located in the cylinder head, but with the camshaft located in the engine block.

Oxygen sensor A device installed in the engine exhaust manifold, which senses the oxygen content in the exhaust and converts this information into an electric current. Also called a Lambda sensor.

P

Phillips screw A type of screw head having a cross instead of a slot for a corresponding type of screwdriver.

Plastigage A thin strip of plastic thread, available in different sizes, used for measuring clearances. For example, a strip of Plastigage is laid across a bearing journal. The parts are assembled and dismantled; the width of the crushed strip indicates the clearance between journal and bearing.

Plastigage

Propeller shaft The long hollow tube with universal joints at both ends that carries power from the transmission to the differential on front-engined rear wheel drive vehicles.

Proportioning valve A hydraulic control valve which limits the amount of pressure to the rear brakes during panic stops to prevent wheel lock-up.

R

Rack-and-pinion steering A steering system with a pinion gear on the end of the steering shaft that mates with a rack (think of a geared wheel opened up and laid flat). When the steering wheel is turned, the pinion turns, moving the rack to the left or right. This movement is transmitted through the track rods to the steering arms at the wheels.

Radiator A liquid-to-air heat transfer device designed to reduce the temperature of the coolant in an internal combustion engine cooling system.

Refrigerant Any substance used as a heat transfer agent in an air-conditioning system. R-12 has been the principle refrigerant for many years; recently, however, manufacturers have begun using R-134a, a non-CFC substance that is considered less harmful to the ozone in the upper atmosphere.

Rocker arm A lever arm that rocks on a shaft or pivots on a stud. In an overhead valve engine, the rocker arm converts the upward movement of the pushrod into a downward movement to open a valve.

Rotor In a distributor, the rotating device inside the cap that connects the centre electrode and the outer terminals as it turns, distributing the high voltage from the coil secondary winding to the proper spark plug. Also, that part of an alternator which rotates inside the stator. Also, the rotating assembly of a turbocharger, including the compressor wheel, shaft and turbine wheel.

Runout The amount of wobble (in-and-out movement) of a gear or wheel as it's rotated. The amount a shaft rotates "out-of-true." The out-of-round condition of a rotating part.

S

Sealant A liquid or paste used to prevent leakage at a joint. Sometimes used in conjunction with a gasket.

Sealed beam lamp An older headlight design which integrates the reflector, lens and filaments into a hermetically-sealed one-piece unit. When a filament burns out or the lens cracks, the entire unit is simply replaced.

Serpentine drivebelt A single, long, wide accessory drivebelt that's used on some newer vehicles to drive all the accessories, instead of a series of smaller, shorter belts. Serpentine drivebelts are usually tensioned by an automatic tensioner.

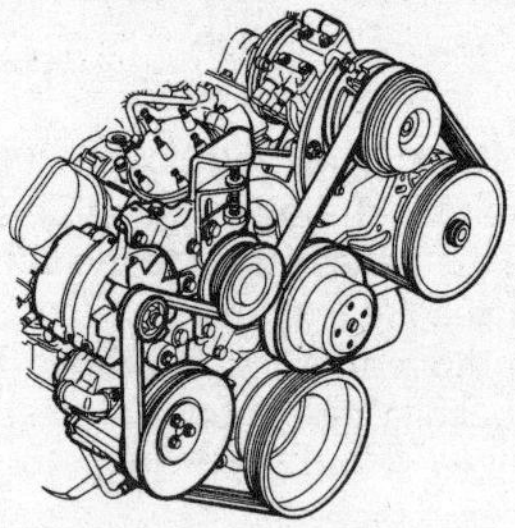

Serpentine drivebelt

Shim Thin spacer, commonly used to adjust the clearance or relative positions between two parts. For example, shims inserted into or under bucket tappets control valve clearances. Clearance is adjusted by changing the thickness of the shim.

Slide hammer A special puller that screws into or hooks onto a component such as a shaft or bearing; a heavy sliding handle on the shaft bottoms against the end of the shaft to knock the component free.

Sprocket A tooth or projection on the periphery of a wheel, shaped to engage with a chain or drivebelt. Commonly used to refer to the sprocket wheel itself.

Starter inhibitor switch On vehicles with an automatic transmission, a switch that prevents starting if the vehicle is not in Neutral or Park.

Strut See MacPherson strut.

T

Tappet A cylindrical component which transmits motion from the cam to the valve stem, either directly or via a pushrod and rocker arm. Also called a cam follower.

Thermostat A heat-controlled valve that regulates the flow of coolant between the cylinder block and the radiator, so maintaining optimum engine operating temperature. A thermostat is also used in some air cleaners in which the temperature is regulated.

Thrust bearing The bearing in the clutch assembly that is moved in to the release levers by clutch pedal action to disengage the clutch. Also referred to as a release bearing.

Timing belt A toothed belt which drives the camshaft. Serious engine damage may result if it breaks in service.

Timing chain A chain which drives the camshaft.

Toe-in The amount the front wheels are closer together at the front than at the rear. On rear wheel drive vehicles, a slight amount of toe-in is usually specified to keep the front wheels running parallel on the road by offsetting other forces that tend to spread the wheels apart.

Toe-out The amount the front wheels are closer together at the rear than at the front. On front wheel drive vehicles, a slight amount of toe-out is usually specified.

Tools For full information on choosing and using tools, refer to the *Haynes Automotive Tools Manual.*

Tracer A stripe of a second colour applied to a wire insulator to distinguish that wire from another one with the same colour insulator.

Tune-up A process of accurate and careful adjustments and parts replacement to obtain the best possible engine performance.

Turbocharger A centrifugal device, driven by exhaust gases, that pressurises the intake air. Normally used to increase the power output from a given engine displacement, but can also be used primarily to reduce exhaust emissions (as on VW's "Umwelt" Diesel engine).

U

Universal joint or U-joint A double-pivoted connection for transmitting power from a driving to a driven shaft through an angle. A U-joint consists of two Y-shaped yokes and a cross-shaped member called the spider.

V

Valve A device through which the flow of liquid, gas, vacuum, or loose material in bulk may be started, stopped, or regulated by a movable part that opens, shuts, or partially obstructs one or more ports or passageways. A valve is also the movable part of such a device.

Valve clearance The clearance between the valve tip (the end of the valve stem) and the rocker arm or tappet. The valve clearance is measured when the valve is closed.

Vernier caliper A precision measuring instrument that measures inside and outside dimensions. Not quite as accurate as a micrometer, but more convenient.

Viscosity The thickness of a liquid or its resistance to flow.

Volt A unit for expressing electrical "pressure" in a circuit. One volt that will produce a current of one ampere through a resistance of one ohm.

W

Welding Various processes used to join metal items by heating the areas to be joined to a molten state and fusing them together. For more information refer to the *Haynes Automotive Welding Manual.*

Wiring diagram A drawing portraying the components and wires in a vehicle's electrical system, using standardised symbols. For more information refer to the *Haynes Automotive Electrical and Electronic Systems Manual.*

Note: *References throughout this index are in the form* "**Chapter number**" • "**Page number**". *So, for example, 2C•15 refers to page 15 of Chapter 2C.*

A

B

C

D

Note: *References throughout this index are in the form* **"Chapter number" • "Page number"**. *So, for example, 2C•15 refers to page 15 of Chapter 2C.*

Note: *References throughout this index are in the form* **"Chapter number" • "Page number"**. *So, for example, 2C•15 refers to page 15 of Chapter 2C.*